CONTEMPORARY BRITISH POLITICS

AUTHOR	CLASS
COXALL & ROBINS	320.941

TITLE	
Contemporary British politics	

THIS BOOK MUST BE RETURNED ON OR BEFORE THE LATEST DATE SHOWN	048725

Also by Bill Coxall

Politics, Compromise and Conflict in Liberal Democracy
Parties and Pressure Groups

Also edited by Lynton Robins

Introductory Political Science
The American Way
Political Institutions in Britain
Politics and Policy-Making in Britain
Two Decades in Bristish Politics (with Bill Jones)
Public Policy under the Conservatives (with S. Savage and R. Atkinson)
Governing Britain in the 1990s (with R. Pyper)
Britain's Changing Party System (with H. Blackmore and R. Pyper)

CONTEMPORARY BRITISH POLITICS

Second Edition

Bill Coxall and Lynton Robins

MACMILLAN

First edition 1989
Reprinted with corrections 1989
Reprinted with new postscript 1991
Reprinted with revised postscript 1991
Reprinted with new postscript 1992
Reprinted 1993
Second edition 1994

Published by
MACMILLAN PRESS LTD
Houndmills, Basingstoke, Hampshire RG21 6XS
and London
Companies and representatives
throughout the world

ISBN 0–333–59324–3 hardcover
ISBN 0–333–59325–1 paperback

A catalogue record for this book is available
from the British Library.

11 10 9 8 7 6 5 4 3
04 03 02 01 00 99 98 97 96

Printed in Malaysia

This book is dedicated to Hazel and Vivien

Contents

PART I *THE CONTEXT OF BRITISH POLITICS*

PART II *INSTITUTIONS AND THE POLITICAL PROCESS*

PART III *DECISION-MAKING, ISSUES AND POLICIES*

PART IV *ANALYSING BRITISH POLITICS*

List of Figures

List of Tables

List of Exhibits

Abbreviations and Acronyms

ALRA	=	Abortion Law Reform Association
ANC	=	African National Congress
ANL	=	Anti-Nazi League
ARA	=	Anti-Racist Alliance
ARM	=	Activity and Resource Management
BBA	=	British Bankers' Association
BBC	=	British Broadcasting Corporation
BCCI	=	Bank of Credit and Commerce International
BMA	=	British Medical Association
BNP	=	British National Party
BPPS	=	British Political Participation Study
BR	=	British Rail
BUF	=	British Union of Fascists
CAA	=	Civil Aviation Authority
CAG	=	Comptroller and Auditor-General
CAP	=	Common Agricultural Policy (of the EU)
CBI	=	Confederation of British Industry
CCT	=	Compulsory competitive tendering
CCO	=	Conservative Central Office
CET	=	Common External Tariff
CID	=	Criminal Investigation Department
CIS	=	Commonwealth of Independent States
CLCB	=	Committee of London Clearing Banks
CLP	=	Constituency Labour Party
CLPD	=	Campaign for Labour Party Democracy
CND	=	Campaign for Nuclear Disarmament
COREPER	=	Committee of Permanent Representatives (of the EU)
COPA	=	Committee of Professional Agricultural Organisations of the European Union
CPAG	=	Child Poverty Action Group
CPGB	=	Communist Party of Great Britain
CPS	=	Centre for Policy Studies
CSCE	=	Conference on Security and Co-operation in Europe
CSSB	=	Civil Service Selection Board
DEA	=	Department of Economic Affairs
DES	=	Department of Education and Science
DHA	=	District Health Authority
DIS	=	Defence Intelligence Staff
DMU	=	Directly Managed Unit
DOE	=	Department of the Environment
DPP	=	Director of Public Prosecutions
DSC	=	Departmental Select Committee
DSO	=	Direct Service Organisations
DSS	=	Department of Social Services

DTI	=	Department of Trade and Industry
EC	=	European Community
ECU	=	European Currency Unit
ECSC	=	European Coal and Steel Community
EEA	=	European Economic Area
EEC	=	European Economic Community (1957)
EFTA	=	European Free Trade Association
EMS	=	European Monetary System
EMU	=	Economic and Monetary Union
EP	=	European Parliament
ERM	=	Exchange Rate Mechanism
ESC	=	Economic and Social Committee (of the EC)
ETUC	=	European Trade Union Confederation
EU	=	European Union
Euratom	=	European Atomic Community
FCO	=	Foreign and Commonwealth Office
FHSA	=	Family Health Services Authority
FMI	=	Financial Management Initiative

FO	=	Foreign Office
GATT	=	General Agreement on Tariffs and Trade
GCHQ	=	Government Communications Headquarters
GDP	=	Gross Domestic Product
GLC	=	Greater London Council
GNP	=	Gross National Product
GPs	=	general (medical) practitioners
GREA	=	Grant-Related Expenditure Assessment
HAT	=	Housing Action Trusts
ICI	=	Imperial Chemical Industries
ICM	=	International Communications and Marketing Research
IEA	=	Institute for Economic Affairs
ILEA	=	Inner London Education Authority
ILP	=	Independent Labour Party
IMF	=	International Monetary Fund
IMG	=	International Marxist Group
IPPR	=	Institute for Public Policy Research
IRA	=	Irish Republican Army

IRC	=	Industrial Reorganisation Corporation
IS	=	Intelligence Services
JIC	=	Joint Intelligence Committee
LCC	=	Labour Coordinating Committee
LDDC	=	London Docklands Development Corporation
LEA	=	local education authority
LMS	=	local management of schools
LSE	=	London School of Economics
LSVT	=	large-scale voluntary transfers
MAFF	=	Ministry for Agriculture, Food and Fisheries
MEP	=	Member of the European Parliament
MINIS	=	Management Information Systems for Ministers
MLR	=	Minimum lending rate
MMS	=	Mixed Member System
MP.	=	Member of Parliament
MTFS	=	Medium Term Financial Strategy

NAFTA = North African Free Trade Area

NATO = North Atlantic Treaty Organisation

NCCL = National Council for Civil Liberties

NEB = National Enterprise Board

NEC = National Executive Committee

NEDC = National Economic Development Council

NF = National Front

NFU = National Farmers' Union

NHS = National Health Service

NUM = National Union of Mineworkers

NUPE = National Association of Public Employees

OAP = Old age pensioner

OECD = Organisation for Economic Cooperation and Development

OEEC = Organisation for European Economic Co-operation

OFGAS = Office of Gas Supply

OFFER = Office of Electricity

OFWAT = Office of Water

OMOV = one member, one vote

OPD = Cabinet Overseas and Defence Committee

OPEC = Organisation of Petroleum Exporting Countries

PAC = Public Accounts Committee

PCA = Parliamentary Commissioner for Administration

PCA = Police Complaints Authority

PESC = Public Expenditure Survey Committee

PLP = Parliamentary Labour Party

PM = Prime Minister

PNC = Police National Computer

PROP = Preservation of the Rights of Prisoners

PSBR = Public Sector Borrowing Requirement

PSIS = Permanent Secretaries Committee on Intelligence Services

Quango = quasi-autonomous non-government organisation

RAP = Radical Alternatives to Prison

RHA = Regional Health Authority

RSPB = Royal Society for the Protection of Birds

RSPCA = Royal Society for the Prevention of Cruelty to Animals

RUC = Royal Ulster Constabulary

SAS = Special Air Service

SDP = Social Democratic Party

SHA = Special Health Authority

SL = Socialist League

SMMT = Society of Motor Manufacturers and Traders

SNP = Scottish National Party

SPUC = Society for the Protection of the Unborn Child

SSA = Standard Spending Assessment

SV = Supplementary vote

SWP = Socialist Workers' Party

TEC = Training and Enterprise Council

TGWU = Transport and General Workers' Union

TUC = Trades Union Congress

UDC = Urban Development Corporation

UK	=	United Kingdom	USSR	=	Union of Soviet Socialist Republics	WRP	=	Workers' Revolutionary Party
UN	=	United Nations						
UNICE	=	Union of Industries in the European Community	UVF	=	Ulster Volunter Force			
USA	=	United States of America	VAT	=	Value-Added Tax			

Preface to the Second Edition

The first edition of this book was based on two organising principles: first, that political institutions and issues are inseparable and need to be discussed together; and second, that to be fully comprehensible, such a discussion requires context. Whilst retaining the structure and aims of its predecessor, this second edition of *Contemporary British Politics* has been substantially rewritten and expanded in order to take account of a fast-moving political situation. Much new material on the historical and socio-economic context of British politics has been added to Part I (Chapters 2 and 3) and Part II gains a new chapter reflecting the increased prominence of Britain's relations with the European Union (Chapter 7). Part III begins with a new chapter on the policy process (Chapter 19) and also contains new chapters on Northern Ireland and foreign and defence policy (Chapters 29 and 30) as well as separate treatments of education, health and housing (Chapters 21, 22 and 23). The issue of law and order – formerly dealt with in Part II in the context of the courts and redress – now receives consideration on its own in Part III. The book concludes in Part IV with an examination of the Thatcher record and the continuing impact of her legacy on present-day British politics.

It is hoped that this new edition – now in larger format with much-enhanced illustrative material – will continue to be of use to BTEC, A-level and first-year University students and also to the general reader. We would like to record our thanks to our publisher Steven Kennedy for much encouragement and practical advice, to Jane Powell (also of Macmillan), to our anonymous readers for their comments on the final draft, and finally to all those teachers who made suggestions for the improvement of the first edition.

BILL COXALL
LYNTON ROBINS

Acknowledgements

The authors and publishers wish to thank the following who have kindly given permission for the use of copyright material.

Philip Allan, for material from Stephen Hunt, 'State Secrecy in the UK', *Politics Review*, 1(4) (April 1992).

Blackwell, for table from L. Pliatzky, *Getting and Spending*, (1982, Table 5.2).

The Economist, for figures from *The Economist* (17.8.91). Copyright © The Economist 1991.

The Guardian, for tables and graphs sourced to issues, 24.10.85, 13.3.87, 20.6.91, 15.10.91, 24.9.91, 12.3.92, 15.5.92, 19.5.92, 13.7.92, 19.3.93 Copyright 19.10.93 and 17.9.93. © *The Guardian*.

Harvester Wheatsheaf, for figure from, Wyn Grant, *The Politics of Economic Policy* (19— Figure 3.1).

The Controller of Her Majesty's Stationery Office, for tables, data and graphs from *Social Trends*, CSO.

Longman; for adapted tables from Philip Norton, *The Commons in Perspective*, and Philip Norton, *The British Polity*.

Macmillan Publishers, for material from G. Stoker, *The Politics of Local Government* (1991, Tables 2.1, 2.3); D. Saunders, *Losing an Empire*: *Finding a Role* (1990); J. Gyford, Citizens, *Consumers and Councils* (1991, Table 1); and M. Moran, *Politics and Society in Britain* (1989).

Ewan MacNaughton Associates, on behalf of *The Telegraph* plc, for tables from issue, 13.4.92, The *Daily Telegraph*, Copyright © The Telegraph plc (London 1992).

Manchester University Press, for A. Adonis, *Parliament Today* (1993, Figure 5.1), and Colin Thain, *Two Decades of British Politics* (1992, Table 14.3).

National Commission on Education, for material from, A. H. Halsey 'Opening Wide The Doors of Higher Education', Briefing No. 6 (August 1992).

Newspaper Publishing PLC, for graph from issue of 12.4.92, *The Independent*.

Open University Press, for table from D. Marsh and R. A. W. Rhodes (eds), *Implementing Thatcherite Policies* (1992, Table 3.1).

Oxford University Press, for material from Maureen Mancuso, 'The Ethical Attitudes of British MP's: A Typology', *Parliamentary Affairs*, 46 (2) (April 1993), and William L. Miller *et al*. *How Voters Change* (1990, Figure 4.2).

The Politics Association, for material sourced to various issues of *Talking Politics*.

Routledge, for material from A. H. Hanson (ed.), *Nationalization*: *A Book of Readings* (Urwin Hyman, 1963); M. Smith, S. Smith and B. White (eds), *British Foreign Policy* (Unwin Hyman, 1988); and Kathleen Jones, 'Mythology and Social Policy', in J. Hutton *et al*, (eds)., *Dependency to Enterprise*, (Routledge, 1991).

Solo Syndication, for front page of Daily Mail.

The Sun, for front pages of *The Sun*.

Syndication International, for front page of *The People*.

Times Newspapers Ltd, for material sourced to issues, 12.4.92, 26.4.92, 19.2.92, 19.7.92, *The Sunday Times*.

Every effort has been made to trace all the copyright-holders but if any have been inadvertently overlooked the publishers will be pleased to make the necessary arrangement at the first opportunity.

PART 1
THE CONTEXT OF BRITISH POLITICS

■ *Chapter 1* ■

What is Politics?

Interests, Viewpoints and Conflicts	What Makes a Disagreement Political?
Do All Social Groups Possess Politics?	Politics, Persuasion and Force
Authority, Power and Influence	The Politics of Liberal Democracy
The State	

In seeking an understanding of the nature of politics we begin by considering those features of human society out of which the need for politics arises. We next consider whether, as some people allege, certain areas of life are inherently non-political, seeking to answer the question 'What makes a disagreement political?'. We move from this to an analysis of the role of violence in politics. Is politics a particularly non-violent way of resolving disagreements or does it comprehend all methods including force? Finally, we examine the main features of liberal democracy as a political regime, noting in particular its provision for institutionalised disagreement and the peaceful transfer of power.

■ Interests, Viewpoints and Conflicts

Politics arises out of a basic feature of human social life: the fact of differing interests and viewpoints. Differences of material interest develop because we live in a world of scarcity, and not abundance. In a utopia, where objects of need and desire are as freely available as the air we breathe, there would be no problems because we could all have everything we wanted. The real world, however, is one of limited resources, which are always more or less unevenly divided. And this is true wherever we look, equally true of states within the world community (Table 1.1

and Exhibit 1.1) and of individuals and social groups within each national community.

Of course, logically, no disagreement, let alone conflict, *need* flow from this situation if, for example, each individual, social group and state were perfectly satisfied with the distribution of international and national resources and were prepared to put up with shortage and inequality. But such a situation is a figment of the imagination. In reality, few *are* content and the world we actually inhabit is one of competition, often severe, for scarce resources. Each individual or group can only get a larger share at the expense of everyone else. And it is this that creates the political problem – that of settling competing claims upon a limited economic product. Politics, it has been said, crudely but not inaccurately, is concerned with 'who gets what, when and how'. It is the arena where conflicts arising from such disagreements are fought out. Its role is to

Table 1.1   *World inequality*

	1991 GNP per capita (US$)
Low-income countries	350
Middle-income countries	2 500
High-income countries	20 570
OECD members	21 020
United States	22 240
Japan	26 930

Source: World Tables 1993 (published for World Bank by Johns Hopkins, Baltimore and London), p. 5.

Exhibit 1.1   *The North–South divide*

Just under a third of the world's population lives in the North, with over four-fifths of the world's income at its disposal ... The number of people suffering from malnutrition is still 500 million and the number of those living in 'absolute poverty' is around 800 million ... enough food is being produced worldwide... but famine disasters such as the African catastrophes still occur. Every minute, thirty children die for lack of food and clean water ... The export to the Third World of the East–West conflict, and the increasing militarisation of the Third World severely encumber the development process ... In Africa as a whole (south of the Sahara) we may say that: 150–450 million are suffering from inadequate nutrition; 30–35 million face the threat of famine. Expectation of life has indeed risen, even in the Third World, but is still not much above 40 in a number of countries. In 1984 the USA had one doctor to 520 people, the Federal Republic of Germany had one to 450, but in Indonesia the ratio was one to 11 500, in Mali one to 32 00, and in Ethiopia one doctor to 58 000 people ... In 1983/4 as many as 29 per cent of the population of the world were unable to read and write. In 24 countries, over 70 per cent of adults could not read and write. In the developing countries, 300 million children between the ages of six and eleven do not go to school at all. And half of those who do go to school leave before the end of their second year.

Source: Brandt (1986, pp. 86, 49–50, 62, 72, 160).

---

aggregate, adjust and settle (although it can never finally resolve) these conflicts. It has been an important aspect of the life of all societies that have existed in history and is likely to be an important part of all societies that will or might exist. It is as ineliminable a characteristic of human existence as food, sex or play.

The disagreements that lead to the need for politics arise from differences of viewpoint as well as economic conflicts. There are disagreements because customs, moralities and ultimate goals differ. These differences, in turn, may reflect divisions of class, religion and race. They are expressed in membership of a variety of social institutions – such as clubs, trade unions, business and professional associations, political parties and churches. For modern societies are not monolithic structures, but present, on the contrary, a very considerable diversity. Pluralism – of beliefs and social groupings – is a fact, and it is by means of politics that the disagreements which flow from this fact are either reconciled or fail to be reconciled. Many of these differences stem from those systems of opposed beliefs which we call *ideologies* – for example nationalism, liberalism, anarchism, communism and fascism. These belief systems – or ideologies – shape a great deal of political action in the modern world. However, differences which call for political solution may, and often do, arise on less exalted grounds than ideology. Opinions may differ about the *truth* of a proposition (statement, theory, hypothesis) depending on its degree of elaboration and complexity, and about the *merits* of a thing (person, institution, decision, action). Controversy occurs because of the frequent need to make judgements of fact without conclusive

Table 1.2   *Causes of political conflict and disagreement*

Political actors	Cause of conflict/disagreement
Individuals	Ambition, desire for power
Groups e.g. ethnic, gender-based	Ideology Religion
Classes	Material interests
Nations	Disagreements over:
States	1. Policy 2. Interpretation of fact 3. Ultimate goals

evidence and judgements of value without conclusive reasons. Disagreements and conflicts which may call for political resolution are expressed schematically in Table 1.2.

None of this is meant to imply that disagreement is more common or intrinsic a feature of human communities than is agreement. In fact, we do have many things in common with other members of the community we inhabit. A shared nationality is perhaps the most significant factor, overriding differences of class and religion to bind members of the same territorial state together. Often, also, as we shall see, a considerable degree of consensus exists on the decision-making procedure, or constitution, even if this is rarely complete. Again, material interdependence is another source of identity of interest: we may not be able to agree on the relative worth in terms of financial reward of various occupations – of doctors, nurses, teachers, solicitors, miners and dustmen – only that these jobs are essential and that the community as a whole is poorer if one or the other fails to carry out its tasks properly.

To summarise, agreement or consensus may derive from the following factors:

- Shared national identity (i.e. membership of same 'tribe');
- Agreement on decision-making procedure, or constitution (i.e. on method for resolving differences);
- Sense of common interest and material interdependence (i.e. of being in the same 'boat' and needing to 'row together').

But this takes us only part of the way towards an understanding of the nature of politics. We now need to be more precise in specifying what is meant by such terms as 'groups', 'disagreement' and the 'expression' and 'settlement' of disagreements in this context. In particular, we need to ask three important questions. First, do all human social groupings have a political aspect and even if so do we nonetheless accord some groups a special status when we think about politics? Second, assuming that not all disagreements are political, by what criteria do we place a dispute in this category? What makes a controversy 'political'? Third, does politics involve a particular way of seeking to settle controversies – for example, by non-violent verbal persuasion – or can it include all methods of articulating and resolving conflicts?

Do All Social Groups Possess Politics?

In one sense, the answer to this question must be 'yes'. It is common practice to refer to subordinate groups in society as having a political element. We speak, for example, of the 'politics' of a school, of a company, of a civil service department, even of the 'politics' of the family. Clearly, the well-established usage involved here goes beyond a mere manner of speaking. In fact, it has a twofold justification:

- Social subgroups contain structured patterns of relationships culminating in **decision-procedures.**
- These structures involve relationships of **authority, power** and **influence,** terms which are themselves pre-eminently political.

All social groups – from a trade union to the United Nations – possess a **decision-procedure** of some kind. Decision-procedure means a method of reaching collective decisions about what rules to have, how to change them once in existence, and how to apply them. This basic or fundamental rule which prescribes the form by which policy and executive decisions shall be taken is usually called the **constitution**. In a club, society or association, a constitution normally lays down such matters as the purposes of the organisation, the conditions of membership and, above all, the way in which its officials are to be selected. In other words, it will make provision for the government of the association. The need for **government** springs from the fact that in life decisions have constantly to be made and made now, not at some indefinite point in the future. Considerations of time and practicality have to be taken into account. Some matters are postponable; others, such as what action to take with regard to an unruly member, must be made quickly. Nor is it generally practicable to consult the entire membership on matters of urgency and routine. The constitution therefore designates who in an association may take such decisions and the procedures to be followed in reaching them. The 'politics' of the organisation may be said to consist in the attempts to influence the procedures and outcomes of its decision-making process.

All but the most random of social groupings are also political in another sense. There is **competition** to influence collective decisions. The phrase most commonly invoked to describe this feature of their existence is 'struggle for power'. The English political philosopher, Thomas Hobbes, writing in the seventeenth century, found the motive springs of this struggle in man's restlessness and ambition, in 'a general inclination of all mankind, a perpetual and restless desire of power after power, that ceaseth only in death'. There is competition both to achieve the positions of authority within a group or organisation and also among the ordinary members, employees and so on, to influence the possessors of authority. Indeed, the concept of power is so fundamental in the study of politics that it requires careful consideration at the outset. In particular, we need to distinguish three related terms which are often confused – 'authority', 'power' and 'influence'.

■ Authority, Power and Influence

☐ *Authority*

The term 'authority' is generally employed to designate the rightful use of power. It refers to power that is conferred by a rule and exercised in accordance with rules. This is pre-eminently the modern way of legitimating power. In contemporary advanced societies, the authority or **legitimacy** of governments derives from their being elected by a legal process and exercising their rule according to law. Max Weber (1864–1920), the German sociologist, saw this kind of authority – '**legal-rational**' authority – as characterising the modern bureaucrat exercising power according to norms and laws, and contrasted it with '**traditional**' and '**charismatic**' forms of authority (Exhibit 1.2). A party secretary, a judge or a teacher, indeed anyone with an 'official' position within an organisation or society, may be said to be 'in authority' because a rule in a system of rules authorises each to give orders. So long as the authority continues to act within his legally defined sphere, those to whom he or she issues commands (however crudely or subtly) are required to obey. They may not, in fact, do so, but we should not regard their refusal to obey orders as justified unless the authority himself had abused or exceeded his jurisdiction. The word 'authority' in its legal sense refers not to any personal characteristics of its possessor but to the

Exhibit 1.2 *Max Weber's types of authority*	
Traditional:	is legitimated by appealing to the ways and customs of the past and the respect due to ancestors
Charismatic:	derives from the compelling personal qualities of a single individual, whose capacity to command a following also may stem from invocation of religion or sense of 'mission' or 'destiny'. Seen as an important source of social change, including breaks with the traditional order.
Legal-rational:	rests on a belief in rules and laws, i.e. in an impersonal system of authorisation. The kind of authority exercised by governments in modern societies (based on properly conducted elections) and by bureaucrats (sanctioned by democratic governments).

qualities of an **office.** When the term of office ends, the authority disappears. Of course, as already implied, a considerably part of the meaning of 'authority' is normative rather than descriptive. It refers to what should be, rather than what is, the case. A policeman who is overpowered by a criminal does not cease to be an authority. He simply lacks control over events. But it is at this point that we need a word other than 'authority' if we are to describe the realities of the situation adequately.

☐ *Power*

The term 'power', to a much greater extent than 'authority', has an empirical and descriptive connotation. Power, in the words of Michael Oakeshott, is 'the ability to procure … a wished-for response in the conduct of another' although he adds that this effect can never be achieved with certainty because power as a social relationship must always contain an element of uncertainty and unpredictability. Indeed, against much in our common usage and ways of thought which suggests that power is a **possession** – as, for example, when we speak of the Chairman of ICI (Imperial Chemical Industries) as a powerful individual – it is worth emphasising the extent to which power is a **relationship.** Thus, whereas the concept of authority focuses upon the **entitlement** of an agent to issue commands, the word 'power' points to the way in which orders are received. It draws attention to whether they are actually obeyed. It constantly brings us back to the **consequences** of the competition for control which is always taking place.

Power and authority come together where commands can be described as not only rightful in the sense that the issuer is authorised to make them but also effective in the sense that they are carried out by those who receive them. But they move apart in cases where we say that although a group undoubtedly has **power** in the sense it can impose its will on others even against opposition – as the Mafia, for example, can maim, kill and generally terrorise its enemies into submission – it has no **authority** to do so. This does not mean,

of course, that the exercise of power necessarily involves force, although not infrequently it does. Equally, however, money, status, intelligence, education, knowledge, time, social connections and organisation can all influence group decisions and consequently may be identified as important political resources. Typically, in modern industrial societies, governments combine **authority** – the right to decide and act – and **power** – the capacity to compel obedience by means of physical force.

☐ *Influence*

To a very considerable extent in modern industrialised societies the exercise of power depends upon the ability to persuade people to behave in one way rather than another. The word 'influence' is useful here because it directs attention to the **process** by which opinions are changed and behaviour altered. It points beyond a purely formal analysis of a structure of authority in terms of institutions and offices to the complex interplay between people within institutions and between institutions and groups outside. The politics of any institution appears rather like an iceberg even to those who try to follow it closely: nine-tenths of it lies beneath the surface, hidden from view. The term 'influence' directs attention to the ways in which collective decisions are moulded by a whole range of individuals and organisations other than – but of course not excluding – the formal authorities.

The concept of **pressure** entails the deliberate pursuit of influence by an individual or group. Attempts to influence the political process are often made by means of **pressure groups.** Pressure groups are discussed in detail later in the book (Chapter 15) and so it is sufficient at this stage to note that these include a very wide range of organisations in Britain, including economic groups such as the City, the CBI (Confederation of British Industry) and TUC (Trades Union Congress); cultural, such as the press and broadcasting media; and environmental, such as Greenpeace and Friends of the Earth. In its broadest sense, **pressure** upon governments may

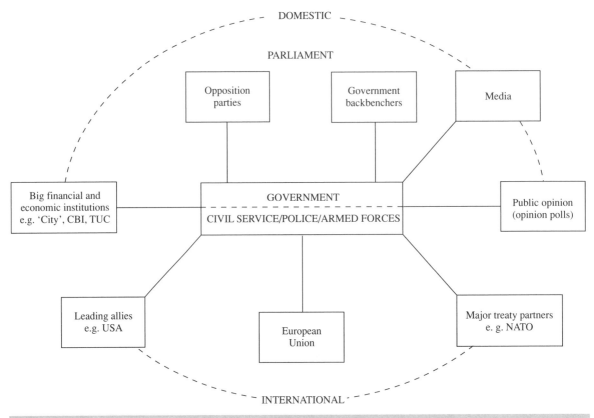

Figure 1.1 *Important influences upon a British government*

come not only from pressure groups themselves but also from backbenchers in the government party, the opposition parties, the upper house, and outside the country from old-established allies or partners within a treaty (Figure 1.1).

It is now convenient to summarise these three terms. In the neat formulations of J.R. Lucas:

'Someone or some group has *authority* if it follows from his saying "Let *X* happen" that *X* ought to happen.'
'Someone or some group has *power* if it follows from his saying "Let *X* happen" that *X* does happen.'
'Someone or group has *influence* if the result of his saying "Let *X* happen" is that others say "Let *X* happen".' (Lucas, 1985 – italics ours).

Politics, then, is about collective decision-making by groups, the political relationships of

whose members are appropriately characterised by the terms 'authority', 'power' and 'influence'. But although this takes us some of the way towards an understanding of the subject, it does not take us far enough. Etymology enables us to complete the definition. 'Politics' derives from the Greek word *polis* meaning 'city-state'. This term had a broader significance than the modern word 'state': it meant state and church rolled into one. But the word has the merit in this context of directing attention to a dimension of meaning which has remained absolutely central to the word 'politics'. In its most fundamental sense, it relates to matters of state or the government of the state. Its concern, then, is not primarily with individuals in their private lives – as members of voluntary groups or in the family circle (although, as we have seen, these relationships do have a political aspect). Its major reference is to individuals in their *public* relationships, as holding office in and seeking to influence affairs of *state*.

■ The State

The term 'state' refers to the supreme law-making authority within a particular geographical area. The concept first emerged in the sixteenth century to denote a novel form of association claiming sovereignty and exercising power within a given territory. Three characteristics of this new entity are of special importance here:

- The state is a **compulsory** form of association. Membership of a state, although not of a particular one, is obligatory. Indeed, although change of citizenship is normally possible, it is also difficult, and most remain as citizens of the state in which they are born.
- It is **comprehensive**. It stands above and includes all partial associations and groups within its territory, giving or denying them rights of legal existence, regulating their powers over their members and helping to settle their disputes.
- The state is a **sovereign body** possessing extreme powers of coercion over its members. Alone among associations, the state may imprison us and, in the ultimate analysis, it may have the right to take our lives. Modern states conscript, punish and even put to death their citizens. Of course, the possession by the state of supreme sanctions over its members does not mean that it is the sole wielder of force in a particular community. It merely means that the state has the ultimate responsibility for deciding by whom force may be used (parents, schools, sportsmen) and to what degree, and for controlling and punishing the illegitimate users of violence (criminals, terrorists).

Quite clearly, these characteristics place the state in *a completely different category* from the other forms of association considered so far. Moreover, its possession of these characteristics transforms the significance of *those features which it shares* with voluntary and subordinate social groups and associations. To non-members, the decision-making procedures no less than the actual processes of the competition for authority, power and influence of a particular family, club, society, association, union or company are of no direct significance. But the constitution of the state and the struggle for power within it between individuals, groups and classes *must concern us all because we are all citizens.* Like it or not and whether we interest ourselves in public affairs or not, the nature of the regime and the outcome of the competition for power must affect us because of the non-voluntary, inclusive and sovereign nature of the state. We may choose whether or not to join a club; we cannot choose whether or not to be citizens of a state. In the modern world, there is no escaping it.

The comprehensive concept of 'the state' needs to be distinguished from the more limited concept of 'government'. The term 'government' refers to a specific set of individuals – ministry, administration or junta – which on a day-to-day basis directs the affairs of the state and exercises its authority. Whereas the term 'state' is comprehensive and embraces all law-making and law-enforcing agencies (government, legislature, judiciary, police, army), 'government' refers simply to the ruling body, whose power may be circumscribed by the legislature, judiciary, and so on.

The answer to our first question is now clear. Whereas partial associations have political aspects, such secondary, limited groupings are not our major concern when we think of 'politics'. Rather, the term 'politics' inevitably centres upon decision-making within the only 'society' which touches us all – the community of communities – the state.

■ What Makes a Disagreement Political?

The analysis to date – which has concentrated upon isolating a specifically 'political' element in the activities of social groups – also takes us far towards answering our second and third questions. Perhaps the best approach to the second problem – what makes a controversy political – is via a number of commonly expressed opinions. It is often said, for example, that religion, art, education or sport should either never become matters of political controversy or, in so far as they already are so, should be taken out of political debate. The suggestion implicit in such remarks is that these spheres of human activity are inherently non-political. There is the further, pejorative, implication that they are sullied by being made 'political' since they naturally inhabit a finer, purer air.

What should we make of this contention? Our principal comment must be that it appears to misunderstand the nature of politics. This, as we have seen, involves a competitive struggle between individuals and groups who disagree about ultimate goals and collective priorities, material and non-material. Potentially, any matter at all may become a subject of public debate. Nothing exists in a watertight compartment sealed off from the political arena. Many people criticise sporting boycotts – for example, preventing cricketers from playing in South Africa before the recent dramatic changes there or athletes from competing in the Moscow Olympics in 1980 – for (wrongly, in their view) bringing politics into sport. But politics is already in sport: athletes train with facilities provided by governments. Above all, sporting achievement is one facet of international rivalry between states. The gesture of withdrawing from sporting contacts as a sign of disapproval of a country's foreign policy (the Soviet invasion of Afghanistan) or domestic affairs (apartheid in South Africa) may be criticised for being unfair to athletes but not for politicising the unpolitical.

This does not mean that it is not to be regretted when activities like athletics or cricket become the means of making political gestures, weapons in the international rivalry of states (although as instruments of persuasion not sending athletes or cricketers is infinitely preferably to sending gunboats). What it does contend is twofold:

First, the conditions under which a whole range of human social activities considered as 'unpolitical' by nature (art, sport, religion, educa-

tion) are practised depend ultimately upon political decision. The main reason for this is that the decision to establish and maintain a voluntary sphere of life for the free and unimpeded practice of these activities is itself a political decision and depends for its existence upon a continuing public commitment. In other words, it rests upon the particular system of moral values embodied in the liberal state, which has developed in Western societies over the past 200 years. This point that the rights of individuals and groups to practise these activities are inherently a matter for political decision can be simply illustrated. In the sixteenth century, the state imposed religious uniformity on its citizens, a practice which in succeeding centuries gradually gave way to toleration of a variety of religious denominations, which now possess the right to worship as they please. But the decision to tolerate – as formerly to prosecute and even persecute, for non-observance of a state-ordained creed – is a political one. It now becomes clear that those who maintain that politics should be kept out of a particular activity are expressing a (liberal) political preference, which itself reflects the conventional division between state – an area of compulsory activity – and society – the sphere of voluntary activity – that has grown up in the West since the eighteenth century. Equally, it is clear that the division itself depends upon a prior political guarantee (by the state) and that the boundaries of this division may from time to time shift.

Secondly, sometimes the desire to keep politics out of a particular activity arises out of a simple distaste for controversy and disagreement and a wish that it would stop (e.g. the resentment of businessmen, educationalists and the medical profession at political interference). But these demands are in themselves political. What they require by implication is that public discussion of these affairs in terms of preferences and priorities should cease in favour of administration by their practitioners. But there is no such thing as 'pure' administration unsullied by ideas and values. In practice, the 'experts' would have to make 'political' decisions – allocate scarce resources between the various parts of their enterprises – and engage in political activities – lobby governments for a greater share of the public funds to be devoted to their concerns. A matter becomes political not because of the malign intent of politicians but because disagreement exists about it – e.g. how much 'private' medical practice to allow, and on what terms; or about a claim to a particular share of public expenditure. The differences of opinion and the clashes of interest which demand and generally receive public resolution in free societies do not cease if they are ignored or driven underground. The public saw little of it, but controversy over collective goals still took place in 'closed' societies like the former USSR (Union of Soviet Socialist Republics) (over the relative importance to be attached to defence, investment and current consumption, for example).

Because agreement in society can never be complete, politics will remain a permanent feature of human life. Agreement will never be complete for three fundamental reasons: first, because material resources are likely to remain scarce and their distribution at any given moment will be unacceptable to some; second, because our images of the 'good society', our 'Utopias', will almost certainly continue to diverge; and, finally, because, however much we eliminate irrelevant factors like wealth and status of birth from the struggle for positions of authority, these remain in their nature limited and, therefore, subject to competition. (The office of prime minister is a *positional* good – if I get it, you cannot have it, and vice versa.) For these reasons, disagreement, competition and the need for politics are likely to be with us for a long time yet. The idea that the world can be rid of politics and its practitioners reflects a secret desire for a kind of conflict-free, unchanging society that has never existed nor is ever likely to.

■ Politics, Persuasion and Force

'What words mean few can say, but with words we govern men', said Disraeli. Language is fundamental to politics. How could it be otherwise in a sphere of activity wholly concerned with persuasion? How else could the expression of varying viewpoints and the search for common ground be conducted except through talk and writing, verbal and written communications?

Some writers have been so impressed with the centrality of words to politics that they have sought to define politics in terms of verbal communication. In other words, they have equated politics with *a particular (peaceful) method* of expressing and settling disagreements. Thus, Bernard Crick writes:

> If the argument is, then, that politics is simply the activity by which government is made possible when differing interests in an area to be governed grow powerful enough to need to be conciliated, the obvious objection will be: 'why do certain interests have to be conciliated?' And the answer is, of course, that they do not have to be. Other paths are always open. *Politics is simply when they are conciliated – that solution to the problem of order which chooses conciliation rather than violence and coercion*, and chooses it as an effective way by which varying interests can discover that level of compromise best suited to their common interest in survival (Crick, 1993, p. 30, italics ours).

This contention gains support, first from much in the European tradition of theorising about politics. **Political rule**, to Aristotle, was that method of ordering the affairs of a community which sought to draw all interests into government rather than a system in which one group overwhelmed all the others and ruled in its own interest alone. Indeed, the word 'politician', although increasingly signifying simply a person who engages in politics as a profession or career, does retain something of its earlier meaning as a kind of broker of interests, someone whose developed skills of articulacy were put to the service of expressing and mediating between the differing interests in a community.

Second, this understanding of politics gets some endorsement from contemporary usage. For example, on occasions when countries become bogged down in wars or in struggles against terrorists, like the British government with the Irish Republican Army (IRA) in Northern

Ireland, it is often said that ultimately there will have to be a *political* solution. In the long run, the various parties to the dispute will have to sit down round a table and seek to resolve their differences by bandying words rather than by firing bullets. In both these well-established usages of the terms 'politics' and 'political', the contrast is with *force*. A political *solution* or *method* (discussion) is opposed to the use of violence (terrorism, war) in the settlement of conflicts.

However, this value-loaded understanding of politics is clearly at variance with the more neutral definition offered so far and, equally clearly, incompatible with it. Politics is here defined as the arena where social disagreements are expressed, and conflicts are reconciled or fail to be reconciled. This process may be peaceful or violent. In the real world, as is only too obvious, violence is everywhere. Just consider. The states which had experienced no political killing in the postwar period up to 1975 can be numbered on fewer than the fingers of one hand: New Zealand, Fiji and Iceland. At that date (1975) perhaps as many as half of the world's regimes owed their existence to a violent stroke within the previous generation. The collapse of communism in Eastern Europe and the USSR after 1989 was largely bloodless (except in Romania) but it was followed by an atrocious civil war in the former Yugoslavia and by nationalist armed struggles in parts of the former Soviet Union. Terrorism and counter-terrorism accounted for thousands of deaths throughout the 1970s and 1980s in Western Europe, the Middle East, South America, India and Sri Lanka. Between 1969 and 1992, political violence caused over 3000 fatalities in Northern Ireland and between 1980 and 1988 over 11 000 deaths in Peru, where the 'Shining Path' (*Sendero Luminoso*) guerillas were active.

However, it is unnecessary to invoke such extreme – in some cases pathological – examples in order to realise the close relationship that exists between power and violence. Will rather than force may be the basis of the state in the sense that ultimately it rests on public opinion. But since survival is the primary requirement of any state and since its enemies, internal and external, may at any time deploy violence against it, clearly force – its possession of and readiness to deploy weapons – always backs up the state. This is not, of course, to equate violence with power. Indeed, all states, if they are wise, will seek to minimise the violence they use. Excessive violence by the authorities may reduce their power by undermining public respect.

But this is by the way. The point is that to exclude violence from our definition of politics would be to rule out from consideration a very high proportion of actual behaviour in the real world. It would eliminate from our vocabulary a number of concepts – revolution, rebellion, *coup d'état*, terrorism, repression – vital to any understanding of recurrent social phenomena. Violent means may be, and frequently are, used both in the maintenance and the overthrow of states and regimes. We need to adopt a conception of 'politics' which recognises this fact. None of this is in any way to justify violence, of course. It is simply to say that no conception of politics which ignored it as a major means of social change would be realistic. And it is also to suggest that to equate politics in general with the non-violent resolution of conflicts is to identify it (narrowly, as well as somewhat misleadingly, since these states ultimately depend upon force, too) with a particular type of political system, the liberal democratic state.

■ The Politics of Liberal Democracy

In the modern world, virtually all governments claim to be democratic including those described as autocratic. The reason for this apparently strange fact is not far to seek. The etymological origin of the word 'democracy' is the Greek word '*demos*' (people) and the modern meaning of the term reflects its Greek origin – 'rule by the people'. Since 1918 'democracy' has been the primary principle by which governments and governmental systems have sought to justify their existence. It is *the* contemporary method of legitimating power. Few political systems in the modern world do not claim to be operated by, with the consent or in the interests of the people. Thus, not only do the USA (United States of America), France and the UK (United Kingdom) call themselves 'democracies', so also do China, North Vietnam and many other countries.

There are three possible responses to this situation. One is to argue that the fact that the word can be employed to describe such widely differing systems suggests that it has now lost all usefulness as a term of political classification; at best, it denotes a precondition of *all* modern government – that it needs to carry the mass of the population along with it if it is to accomplish its purposes. Accordingly, rather than continue to employ such a meaningless term, it may be preferable to abandon it completely and turn to a word such as 'republic' when a contrast with autocratic systems is sought (Crick, 1973, pp. 22–7). This seems a mistaken approach, if only, but not only, because historically and conceptually 'republicanism' has very specific associations with *non-monarchical government*.

A second response is to maintain, as C.B. MacPherson does in *The Real World of Democracy* (1966), that a wide variety of states may legitimately call themselves 'democratic': for example, not only do China and Egypt describe themselves as democracies, they are right to do so. The weakness of this approach is that it seems to blur important distinctions between political systems.

The third response – the one adopted here – is to continue to employ the word 'democracy' as a useful term of political classification, but prefaced by the adjective 'liberal'; thus, **liberal democracy**. We decide to employ this expression as a way of characterising a form of government which institutionalises both political *choice*, even if limited, and universal *participation*, even if falling short of this ideal.

Joining the two terms enables us to express two basic features of this political system. It is **liberal** in two senses: first, because it is a **pluralist regime** in which there is open competition for power between individuals, groups and parties; and second, because it is a **limited system of government** in which the powers of rulers are curtailed by laws enforceable in the courts and

the scope of government is restricted by a combination of convention, ideology and public opinion. It is **democratic** because government is both derived from and accountable to public opinion; derived from it in the sense that government owes its existence to regularly held elections based on universal franchise, and accountable to it in the sense that a legally guaranteed political opposition keeps government responsive to public opinion in the intervals between elections.

The term 'liberal democracy', then, expresses both a number of political values and a set of constitutional mechanisms for putting them into practice. This section explores further the values and institutions of liberal democratic systems of government.

Since 'democracy' must in a genuine way mean 'rule by the people', we begin by asking how popular government can be achieved in geographically extensive territories with large populations. Clearly, 'rule by the people' in its most fundamental meaning of direct democracy – that is, participation in decision-making by all citizens – is out of the question in any but the smallest and most primitive face-to-face communities. In large, populous modern states, democracy must be of the **representative** kind, in which popular participation in politics is largely indirect, through representatives whom 'the people', defined in terms of the universal franchise, elect to some kind of representative institutions, i.e. an assembly or parliament. However, the fact that the only practicable system in the modern world is **representative democracy** does not mean that the idea of direct democracy is without influence. On the contrary, this concept has continued to infuse both the values and the institutions of representative democracies.

It is clear that the degree of popular influence upon governmental decision-making in this political system may vary greatly. The minimal conditions of democracy may reasonably be said to include regular uncoerced elections – from which corruption and intimidation have been removed – universal voting rights, a party system based on two or more competing parties and free communications media.

States exceed these criteria to differing degrees. In the spectrum of democracy, the USA appears in many ways to be a more democratic country than the United Kingdom. It goes to the polls more often, at local, State and Federal (i.e. national) levels, has an elective Upper House and a more egalitarian culture. As well as being a major element in a liberal democratic political system, then, democracy is also an ideology. At the centre of democratic ideology is the doctrine that the more strongly the political system manages to incorporate popular influence, the better it is. This radical conception derives from the eighteenth-century European and American revolutions in general and from the theory of Jean Jacques Rousseau in particular. It is the doctrine of the sovereignty of the people.

To a very considerable extent, representative democracy as a whole rests on this political principle. What legitimates the activities of governments in this type of political system is **popular consent**. This does not mean that individuals, groups and parties may be taken to endorse every single decision a government may make. It simply means that because citizens possess the means to effect peaceful and genuine changes of government, their **support for the system in general** can be assumed.

Radical democrats, however, propound a strong version of the theory of popular sovereignty. They seek to make the promise of democracy into a reality. To close the gap between the public and its representatives, they favour a combination of constitutional devices, theories and institutions. In particular, they advocate frequent use of referendums, the delegate rather than the Burkean theory of the representative and the mandate theory of elections.

It is enough to notice here that the model of direct democracy underlies radical theory. One example points up the contrast between what may be called the minimalist and maximalist versions of representative democracy. For the radical, the representative is an agent of the people, a mere instructed delegate; to the conservative, whilst the representative must at all times listen carefully to what his constituents say, his ultimate responsibility is to his own judgement.

In any case, it is clear that democracy in the modern world must be **representative**. But whom or what do the representatives represent? One obvious answer, implicit in the above discussion, is: their constituents or more simply, their constituencies. The basis of representation in this sense is a particular unit of territory. Historically, both in the UK and the USA, this was the primary meaning of political representation, and, even after the right to vote became universal, it has remained of great importance. But territorial representation alone could not provide the basis of democratic government without the existence of another factor: that of **party**.

Party systems developed in the age of the universal franchise as the sole practicable method of enabling voters **to choose their rulers**. To understand the significance of party, it is enough simply to imagine a representative system without them. Voters could certainly decide which individual they wished to represent them in parliament, congress or assembly, but, without party, that is all that they would decide. And the assembly would be an unstructured grouping of individuals. The only way a government could emerge in such circumstances would be by the actions of the representatives themselves. Again, in the absence of party, this too would be a difficult task, even though informal groupings might well exist. So far as the electorate were concerned, government would be both indirect, operating at one remove from popular influence, and also irresponsible. Modern representative democracy depends upon the existence of competing political parties.

In terms of the system as a whole, parties have two main functions:

1. They enable voters to elect **governments**. This is because, in seeking election in particular constituencies, candidates stand as party men or women, not just as individuals; and are voted for (and against) as such, that is, as the representatives of party. Parties, therefore, group candidates coherently so that votes in one constituency can be related to votes in another. They narrow down the alternatives at elections in such a way as to enable the

verdicts of constituencies to be aggregated into the selection of a government. Democratic government is, above all, **party** government. By deciding the party composition of parliament, voters in the United Kingdom also determine the party complexion of the government; in the United States, they elect the president directly.

2. Party provides the primary source of political **opposition** to the government of the day. The role of the opposition parties is twofold: to criticise and to win concessions from the executive; and to provide an alternative government. Sometimes, the practice of institutionalising opposition by means of party causes irritation, even in well-established democracies: half the cleverest people in the country uniting to prevent the other half governing, was how one nineteenth-century

writer, Sir Henry Maine, put it. In fact, however, effective party opposition is essential in liberal democratic theory because it makes governments accountable and provides genuine electoral choice as well as strengthening the system as a whole by enabling dissent to be openly expressed.

Indeed, it is possible to go even further and to argue that it is their legitimisation of the open expression of political dissent that constitutes the fundamental distinguishing mark between liberal democracies, on the one hand, and autocratic regimes, on the other. It reflects a particular conception of the basic nature of political activity. Because disagreement is a basic feature of social life, it is considered wiser to make institutional provision for it – through free mass media and voluntary groups as well as through competing

Exhibit 1.3	*The liberal democratic political system*	
Major features	Open regime
	High level of competition for power
	Two-or-more party system
	Variety of voluntary groups
	Universal suffrage
	Widespread popular political participation although for most people largely confined to elections
	Free mass media
	Legal and constitutional limitations on powers of office-holders
	Political opposition is both permitted and legally provided for
	System legitimated in terms of doctrine of popular sovereignty
	Adherence to liberal ideas and norms of behaviour is widely diffused
Social and economic structure	Mainly advanced industrialised capitalist societies
	Some poor market economies, such as India
	Most market economies are now 'mixed economies' in that they contain – as a result of political decision – significant public enterprise sectors
	Large and expanding middle classes
Geographical distribution	e.g. USA, UK, Australia, New Zealand, Canada, France, West Germany, Italy, The Netherlands, Belgium, Scandinavian countries, Israel, Japan, India, Sri Lanka

parties – than to attempt to suppress it. By these means, a minority may seek to transform itself into a majority and, above all, power may change hands peacefully. That liberal democracy as a political system rests on rule by the ballot-box rather than by the bullet is undeniably a cliché yet one worth reiteration since it embodies an important truth. It does not mean, of course, that minorities *will* always 'play the political game' according to constitutional rules but it does put a high premium upon such behaviour. Nor is it intended to deny that force as an ultimate sanction lies behind the liberal democratic state as it does other types of regime. What it does suggest is that liberal democracies, in permitting a high degree of legitimate dissent, are also far more reluctant than other political systems to coerce recalcitrant minorities. Above all, it indicates that pluralist regimes regard compromise, conciliation and the willingness to negotiate as major political virtues and, in principle, consider political differences to be reconcilable.

Liberal democracy is by far the most difficult political system to operate successfully. This is because its complex pattern of institutions – which include a system of competing parties, free mass media, a diverse range of voluntary groups and an independent judiciary – are not only inherently hard to achieve but also themselves depend for their effective working upon favourable social and cultural conditions. These include a politically mature electorate and a political culture which is both tolerant of social diversity and respectful of legality. These circumstances have been virtually non-existent throughout the bulk of recorded history and remain comparatively uncommon at the present day. Only about forty countries – constituting less than one-third of the states of the world – can be described as liberal democracies. They include the USA, Canada, Israel, the UK, France, Germany, Italy, Belgium, The Netherlands, Switzerland, Iceland, India, Sri Lanka, and the Irish Republic in the northern hemisphere, and, in the southern part of the globe, Australia and New Zealand. It is no accident that this list contains most of the world's

wealthy countries and is, in fact, largely composed of rich countries, the exceptions being India and Sri Lanka.

Considered in social and economic terms, these liberal democratic states have three major characteristics. They are by world standards – with the exceptions we have noted – all rich or very rich; in most of them wealth tends to be – again by world criteria – relatively evenly distributed; and they are all market economies. This argument does not imply economic determinism. Libya has a high level of income *per capita* but is a military political system.

The strongest correlation seems to be not between levels of wealth as such nor even between relatively even distribution of wealth and liberal democracy but between the market economy and a pluralist political regime. This is understandable since historically liberalism, as a political system, and capitalism have developed together over the past three hundred years, largely in the north-west corner of Europe and in North America. Indeed, in the present-day world, it is the liberalism rather than the 'democracy' of the liberal democracies that stands out. The features which most distinguish them from other types of regime are their constitutionalism, their social and political freedom and the fact that they permit political opposition, rather than the degree of participation they achieve.

Summary

Disagreement is an inevitable feature of human groups and politics is the area of life in which such disagreements are expressed, modified and settled. Disagreements may arise out of differences of material interest and as a consequence of conflicts of belief and opinion. The existence of controversy and conflict in human groups does not preclude the existence of cooperation, solidarity and interdependence.

Politics is concerned with the machinery, processes and outcomes of collective decision-making

by social creatures whose common life is characterised as much by disagreement over the allocation of resources and values as by interdependence, cooperation and mutual need. People
in societies therefore require an authoritative
centre of resource allocation, which in turn is
provided by a compulsory, comprehensive, territorial association possessing ultimate powers of
coercion known as a 'state'. States themselves
contain a pattern of offices (constitution), a set of
decision-makers (government) and an apparatus
of power (army, police).

The intrinsically non-political society does not
exist. All social activities are potential sources of
disagreement and welfare, and also potential con-
tributors to the resolution of disagreements; hence,
all possess a political aspect. Even the decision to
create a private–public division of spheres, with a
predisposition towards non-intervention in the
'private' sphere (art, religion, family life), is a
political decision, as would be any decision to by-
pass it.

Politics as a concept cannot be identified with a
non-violent competition for authority, power and
influence over the allocation of goods and the
determination of collective goals. In the world as
it is, violence is constantly used to maintain and
overthrow states, regimes and governments, and
we need a concept of politics broad enough to
recognise this fact. We may say, therefore, that
'politics' includes all methods (violent and non-
violent) of influencing the machinery, processes
and outcomes of collective decision-making.

Liberal democracy is a form of state which
institutionalises disagreement and the peaceful
transfer of power. Liberal democratic regimes are
open systems of government with competing
parties, a variety of voluntary groups, widespread
unforced participation and an official opposition
both permitted and formally provided for.

Questions

1. What is politics?
2. Analyse the main characteristics of liberal
   democracy. Is liberal democracy based on a
   more realistic understanding than other
   political systems of the nature of politics?
   How far does it depend for its success on a
   society having reached a certain level of
   economic development?

Assignment

Examine the 'news' as presented in a daily
newspaper (the newspaper can be either 'quality'
or 'tabloid'). List the items which may be
described as 'political' and state the criteria by
which you have formed your conclusions.

Further reading

Crick, B. (1993) *In Defence of Politics*, 4th edn
(London: Penguin).

Dunn, J. (ed.) (1992) *Democracy: The Unfinished
Journey 508 BC to AD 1993* (Oxford: Oxford
University Press).

Gearty, C. (1991) *Terror* (London, Faber & Faber).

Leftwich, A. (ed.) (1984) *What is Politics?* (Oxford:
Blackwell).

Lucas, J.R. (1985) *The Principles of Politics* (Oxford:
Oxford University Press) paperback edition.

Renwick, A. and Swinburn, I. (1990) *Basic Political
Concepts*, 3rd edn (London: Stanley Thornes).

Ridley, F.F. and Doig, A. (1992) 'It's not all Politics',
Politics Review, 2: 2 November.

Wilkinson, P. (1986) *Terrorism and the Liberal State*,
2nd edn (London: Macmillan).

Chapter 2

British Politics Since the War

1940–55: The Making of the Post-War Consensus
1955–79: The Consensus Under Strain
1979–90s: The Ending of the Consensus

This chapter rests squarely on the assumption that British politics today cannot be properly grasped without an understanding of the country's postwar history. In the years between 1940–1955, a broad policy consensus emerged between the two major parties. It was a product primarily of the work of the Labour Government of 1945–51, which laid the foundations of postwar policies, but also of initiatives taken by the wartime Coalition led by Churchill and of the Conservative Government of 1951–5 which in broad terms accepted Labour's key legislation and policies. The dominant consensus, which lasted from the early 1950s to the mid-1970s, is variously described as 'Butskellite' (after successive Labour and Conservative Chancellors of the Exchequer, Hugh Gaitskell and R.A. Butler) and 'Keynesian' (after the economist, John Maynard Keynes). It covered all aspects of policy – foreign, social and economic. This chapter tells the story of its rise, decline and fall.

Exhibit 2.1 ***The postwar consensus***

- **Britain's 'World Role':** Foreign policy was based on the view that Britain's 'special relationship' with the United States, leadership of a large multiracial Commonwealth, possession of nuclear weapons and large conventional military capability gave the country a continuing leading status as a world power.

- **A Welfare State:** The accepted basis of social policy was that a wide range of publicly provided benefits and 'universal' services should be available to all on demonstration of need and, in the case of the services, 'free' at the point of receipt. The keystones of the welfare state were a National Health Service providing health care to all regardless of income, a comprehensive system of social security and pensions based on national insurance contributions, and a state educational service compulsory to the age of 15 from which all fee-paying had been abolished.

- **A Mixed Economy:** The main elements of economic policy were: largely private enterprise economy with a significant public sector of recently nationalised industries; governments' acceptance of the responsibility to manage the economy at a level of demand sufficient to maintain 'a high and stable' rate of employment; their adoption of Keynesian methods (i.e. the manipulation of fiscal and monetary mechanisms) in order to do so; and the operation of a 'corporatist' style partnership with the 'peak' organisation of business and labour in order to curb inflationary pressures and contain industrial conflict.

| Exhibit 2.2 | *British history since 1945: main phases and themes* |

Phase 1: 1940–55 The Making of the Post-War Consensus
World Role and Welfare: The Years of Attlee and Churchill
Governments: Coalition 1940–5 (Churchill); Conservative 1945 (Churchill);
        Labour 1945–50, 1950–1 (Attlee); Conservative 1951–5 (Churchill):
Framework of Britain's foreign, social and economic policy to 1970s established.

The consensus involved
- A major world role for Britain – still the world's third economic and military power in 1945;
- A welfare state based on 'cradle to grave' provision of benefits and services for all citizens;
- A mixed economy – four-fifths private sector, one-fifth public sector – run by governments in such a way as to maintain full employment.

But Britain's claim to an independent world role suffered a severe setback at Suez (1956).
The resignation of Churchill as Conservative premier in April 1955 and of Attlee as Labour leader in December 1955 removed the two main architects of the postwar world in Britain from the political scene.

Phase 2: 1955–79 The Consensus Under Strain
External Reorientation and Economic Difficulties
Governments: Conservative 1955–64 (Eden, 1955–7; Macmillan, 1957–63; Douglas-Home, 1963–4);
        Labour 1964–70 (Wilson); Conservative 1970–4 (Heath); Labour 1974–9 (Wilson, 1974–6; Callaghan, 1976–9).
Decline in comparative position of the British economy and in Britain's international status.

Main changes in Britain's external affairs:
- Rapid decolonisation (virtually complete by 1974);
- Erosion of Commonwealth as political entity and trading bloc;
- Weakening of 'special relationship' with USA (although Britain became totally dependent upon US for supply of nuclear weapons (1962));
- Reorientation of external policy towards Europe with a successful application to join the European Community (1972) following two unsuccessful ones (1961 and 1967).

In domestic affairs, governments faced unforeseen problems:
- Slow growth, mounting inflation and persistent balance of payments crises;
- Rising public expectations regarding welfare combined with increasing public disenchantment at the levels of taxation required to sustain the welfare state.

Incomes policies used to control inflation but usually ended in disarray despite some temporary successes.
1979 collapse of Government pay norm in public sector strikes ('Winter of Discontent') preceded Conservative election victory.
Consensus already under attack: in practice, by the Heath Government's non-interventionist experiment (1970–2) and the Labour Government's setting of monetary targets after 1976; and intellectually, in the emergence of alternatives to Keynesianism on the Right (monetarism) and Left (Alternative Economic Strategy – import controls) in the 1970s.

Phase 3: 1979–90s: The Ending of the Consensus
Prestige Abroad and Economic Liberalism at Home: The Premierships of Margaret Thatcher
Governments: Conservative 1979 to the present (Thatcher, 1979–83; 1983–7; 1987–90; Major 1990–2; 1992–)
Thatcher years marked by pursuit of New Right policies. *cont. p. 20*

Exhibit 2.2—*continued*

In foreign affairs, Conservatives sought restoration of national prestige based on vigorous policy involving:

- Aggressive pursuit of British interests in EC;
- Revival of 'special relationship' with US;
- Robust anti-Soviet stance (in early 1980s);
- Emphasis on strong defence based on nuclear weapons;
- Willingness to use armed force in pursuit of national objectives (Falklands).

In domestic policy, Thatcher Governments departed from consensus by:

- Monetarist policies giving priority to reduction of inflation over maintenance of high rate of employment;
- Tax cuts to encourage individual enterprise;
- Privatisation of public sector industries and services; legislative curbs on trade unions;
- Emphasis on 'selective' rather than 'universal' welfare and encouragement of private pensions, education and health;
- Constant search for reductions in public spending.

☐ *The Post-War Consensus*

The consensus theory (Exhibit 2.1) contains a large amount of truth but it should be remembered that broad consensus on fundamentals is compatible with significant differences in emphasis – as well as fierce rhetorical warfare – between the parties. Thus differences continued over nationalisation (Labour for modest increases, Conservatives in favour of denationalising to a small extent) and over welfare, where Labour's collectivist bias and enthusiasm for public spending, municipal housing and comprehensive schools contrasted with the Conservative Party's individualist bias and greater sympathy with private landlordism, private house-building, private schooling and the grammar school/ secondary modern system in state education.

Postwar British history may be conveniently divided into three distinct but overlapping phases: (1) 1940–55: The making of the consensus; (2) 1955–79: The consensus under strain; and (3) 1979–90s: The ending of the consensus. Exhibit 2.2 summarises the main features of these phases.

■ 1940–55: The Making of the Postwar Consensus

☐ *Britain's World Role after 1945*

Britain in 1945 saw itself and was perceived by others as a great world power. Although far outmatched in population, industrial production and military capacity by the new super powers, the USA and USSR, it was far in advance of other potentially second-rank but heavily defeated countries such as Germany, Italy, France and Japan. The distinctive features of Britain's international position in 1945 were as follows:

- **One of the three major victorious powers in the Second World War:** Britain was one of the three major powers at the two conferences (Yalta and Potsdam) which, in default of a treaty, constituted the postwar settlement. Moreover, in Churchill, the country had a towering leader who, by a combination of personal magnetism and bluff, seemed able to

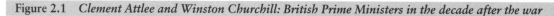

Figure 2.1 *Clement Attlee and Winston Churchill: British Prime Ministers in the decade after the war*

Source: Popperfoto

treat on equal terms with the American and Soviet leaders, Roosevelt and Stalin.

- **Possessor of a huge empire:** At its peak in 1933, the British Empire covered nearly one-quarter of the world's land surface and contained almost one quarter of its population. Although to some extent destabilised by the growth of nationalist movements in the non-white territories, the empire remained of considerable economic and military significance.

- **Having a 'special relationship' with the United States:** Strong historical, cultural and linguistic links between the two Anglo-Saxon powers underpinned their cooperation in both world wars. From 1942, Britain was a military ally of the United States in the war against Germany and Japan, but earlier the Lend-Lease Agreement (1941) provided a system of credits enabling Britain to obtain a continuous supply of American goods and materials in order to sustain its war effort.

Britain's postwar role in the world was powerfully shaped by Labour's Foreign Secretary, Ernest Bevin. A fervent patriot, Bevin based his policies on two principles – first, that a vigorous British foreign policy was vital to world peace; and second, that Britain was still a great power with important global interests to protect. To

these ends, he presided over the development of a system of treaties for the global containment of communism (in alliance with the United States); the emergence of a complex imperial policy combining the development of the empire, the creation of the Commonwealth, and a system of global bases and strong points; and powerful defence forces backed by a British atomic bomb. The Conservative Government (1951–55) led by Winston Churchill with Anthony Eden as Foreign Secretary continued these policies.

The Containment of Communism

Bevin aimed at the close involvement of the United States in the defence of Western Europe against possible Soviet aggression. Hence he played a leading role in negotiating the formation of the **North Atlantic Treaty Organisation** (NATO) in 1949, which obliged the United States, Canada, Britain, France, the Netherlands, Belgium, Luxemburg and six other European countries to assist each other if attacked.

The Attlee Government also allowed American strategic bombers (with atomic capability from 1949) to be stationed in Britain (1946) and, when the Soviets blockaded Berlin (1948–9) participated with the US in an airlift of supplies to keep the city open.

Empire and Commonwealth

Britain saw its empire as an important asset in the postwar period and sought to maximise its value in a number of ways:

- Strategic withdrawal from untenable positions: e.g. the granting of independence to India and Pakistan (1947) and Burma and Ceylon (1948).
- Fostering the emergence of the Commonwealth as a method enabling it to continue to exercise informal influence as formal empire receded – a Commonwealth Premiers' Conference was held in 1949.
- Providing financial assistance for colonial and Commonwealth development, e.g. by participating in the Colombo Plan (1951) to help India and its neighbours.
- Using force to defend its interests e.g. the long war fought against communist terrorism in Malaysia, suppression of revolts in Kenya and Cyprus and imprisonment of nationalist leaders such as Kwame Nkrumah (Gold Coast) and Dr Hastings Banda (Nyasaland).
- Preserving a worldwide system of naval and military bases, e.g. the Suez Canal Zone, Mombasa, Aden, Bahrein, Singapore and Hong Kong.

Defence and the British A-Bomb

When the US brought atomic collaboration with Britain to an end (1946), a Cabinet Committee took the decision to develop a British A-Bomb (successfully tested in 1952). The Churchill Cabinet later decided – in the wake of US and Soviet development of the more powerful H-Bomb – that Britain should have this weapon too (1954).

Britain's extensive international security obligations and overseas commitments necessitated a large defence budget which rose to almost 8 per cent of GDP (Gross Domestic Product) in 1954, when Britain had a higher per capita burden of defence spending even than the United States.

European Integration

Britain held back from taking part in talks about closer economic union with France (1948); the Schumann Plan for a European Coal and Steel Community (1952); and the Messina Conference (1955) which led to the creation of the European Economic Community (EEC) by the Treaty of Rome (1957). Several factors lay behind Britain's decision to hold aloof from membership of the Common Market at its foundation.

- Britain's conception of itself as a great power with a world role;
- Its unwillingness to compromise its national sovereignty and suspicion of the supranational, 'federalist' aspirations of the founders of the EEC.
- Its belief that its most important international relationships were with the United States and the Commonwealth and that closer economic ties with continental Europe were not in its long-term interest.

☐ *The Welfare State*

Wartime changes prepared the way for the development of the postwar welfare state.

- **The prominent role assumed by Labour** – the party of radical change – in the wartime Coalition Government: Labour held two posts in Churchill's War Cabinet and also key posts in home front Ministries.

- **A massive expansion in the role of government:** The Government took on large-scale powers over the production and distribution of resources and over the labour force – e.g. its allocation of raw materials to priority purposes, manpower planning, price controls and rationing.

- **The development of blueprints for vast new government responsibilites in the provision of welfare and the maintenance of full employment:** The two main developments were the **Beveridge Report** (1942) and the **White Paper** on **Employment Policy** (1944). The Beveridge Report called for a new social security system based on compulsory social insurance and fixed subsistence-level benefits in return for flat-rate contributions. In the White Paper, the Government accepted the maintenance of 'a high and stable level of employment' as one of the 'primary aims and responsibilities' of government after the war. The architects of these new policies were respectively W.H. Beveridge (1879–1963) and J.M. Keynes (1883–1946), both Liberals, both academics (Beveridge was a former Director of the London School of Economics (LSE) and Keynes a Cambridge don) and both temporary civil servants during the war. Beveridge assumed that in order to function properly his scheme would need to be accompanied by other sweeping changes – family allowances, a comprehensive national health service and full employment. Keynes allocated government a central role in maintaining consumer demand for goods and services at a level sufficient to achieve and preserve full employment.

- **Government commitment to postwar social reconstruction:** This was signalled by actual legislation (e.g. the 1944 Education Act and the introduction of family allowances (1945)) and by the 1944 White Papers entitled **A National Health Service** (which envisaged a comprehensive health service with 'free' treatment financed by taxation) and **Social Insurance** (which accepted virtually the whole of the Beveridge Report and was quickly followed by the establishment of a new Ministry of National Insurance (1944)).

- **A leftward ideological shift in both elite opinion and public opinion:** Postwar social reconstruction enjoyed widespread support from reformist intellectuals, civil servants, the political parties, leading figures in the Churches, universities and media, and from public opinion, as indicated by the enthusiastic reception of the Beveridge Report, and the anti-Conservative trends in by-elections,

the Mass Observation Survey, and opinion polls during the war.

The main welfare state measures introduced by the Labour Governments (1945–51) – and by the wartime Coalition – and broadly continued by the Conservative Governments in the 1950s are shown in Exhibit 2.3.

□ *The Mixed Economy*

The major theme of postwar economic policy in Britain was closer government involvement in running the economy than at any previous period. This greater state involvement had three main aspects.

- **The creation of a mixed economy:** This was done by a series of important nationalisation measures introduced by the Attlee Government which, with the exceptions only of steel and road haulage, were retained by the Conservative Governments of 1951–64. Major industries moving into public ownership included coal, the railways, iron and steel, gas, electricity and civil aviation (see further Table 10.1).

- **Government responsibility for economic management:** Chancellors of the Exchequer – both Labour and Conservative – used a combination of fiscal techniques (i.e. manipulation of tax rates) and monetary methods (i.e. interest rate changes) to manage the economy in order to ensure full employment, stable prices, economic growth, protection of the value of sterling, and avoidance of balance-of-payments crises.

- **'Corporate bias':** This is a phrase coined by the historian Keith Middlemas to describe the close relationship between government and the 'peak' organisations of industry and the trade unions which was already embryonic in 1940, cemented during the war and continued after it. The rationale of corporate bias for government was the need to avoid the damaging industrial conflict that had occurred in the

---

Exhibit 2.3   *The welfare state: the main measures*

- **Family Allowances Act** (1945): 5 shillings (25p) per week to every family for the second and every subsequent child. Indicated state adoption of the principle of contributing financially to the upkeep of children regardless of parental means.

- **National Insurance (Industrial Injuries) Act** (1946): established four types of benefit – injury benefit (payable for six months); disablement benefit (payable after that according to the degree of disability); supplementary benefit (e.g. hardship allowances); and death benefits for dependants.

- **National Insurance Act** (1946): in return for flat-rate contributions, the state provided seven types of benefit – sickness; unemployment; retirement pension; maternity; widow's; guardian's allowance for orphans; and a death grant for funeral expenses. The new pension, 26 shillings (130p), represented an increase of 16 shillings (80p) on existing pensions and was more generous than Beveridge had recommended. This Act began the extensive state responsibility for citizen welfare often referred to at the time and later as 'cradle to grave' provision.

- **National Assistance Act** (1948): supplementary allowances payable on a means-tested basis to bring National Insurance benefits up to subsistence level or to provide for people not entitled to those benefits.

- **National Health Service Act** (1946): provided a comprehensive service available free to all at the point of receipt and financed mainly by taxation. The NHS was managed by three agencies: Regional Hospital Boards appointed by the Minister of Health to run the former local authority and voluntary hospitals; local executive councils (half lay members, half professional) to administer the general practitioner and dental, opthalmic and pharmaceutical services; and the local authorities whose health and welfare services included maternity and child care, vaccination and immunisation, domestic help, home nursing and home visiting.

- **Education Act** (1944): introduced tripartite system of secondary education based on grammar, modern and technical schools, with selection by the 11+ examination; each type of school was intended to have 'parity of esteem'. Fee-paying in secondary schools was abolished and the school leaving age was to be raised to 15 in 1945, and to 16 as soon as possible after that (in fact, these intentions were not achieved until 1947 (15) and 1973 (16)). The Act created the office of Minister of Education to whom it gave the duty of providing a national education service. It gave more state aid to the voluntary (i.e. church) schools but subjected them to stronger public control.

- **Employment policy:** Government commitment to the maintenance after the war of 'a high and stable level of employment' (1944 White Paper) was seen by leading contemporaries such as Beveridge and Attlee to be as important as the measures described above in the attack on poverty and deprivation.

1920s; the rationale of informal incorporation for business and the unions was that it gave them a permanent voice in policy-making, thereby increasing their capacity to serve the interests of their members.

The tasks facing British governments immediately after the war were: to achieve the smoothest possible transition from a wartime to a peacetime economy; to negotiate foreign loans on the best terms available in order to cover the huge

Exhibit 2.4 *The postwar settlement under attack*

This exhibit summarises some important criticisms of the postwar settlement which appeared in the 1980s.

- **Failure to modernise the economy.** Corelli Barnett has argued in *The Audit of War* (1986) that major sectors of the British economy were in desperate need of modernisation after 1945. General weaknesses – to be found in significant degrees in coal, steel, shipbuilding, textiles and the motor industry – included antiquated machinery, poor design, inadequate standards of training and education at all levels, deficient organisation and antagonistic industrial relations. These weaknesses were well known to the Government during the war and appear frequently in Cabinet Reconstruction Committee minutes and Board of Trade reports. For example, an internal government report in 1945 identified the following major failings in the car industry: too many companies, too many models, insufficient standardisation of production and parts to ensure low costs, failure to design vehicles that could compete in overseas markets, limp marketing, and poor service and spares organisation. A report on shipbuilding in 1942 recommended large-scale modernisation of plant and machinery, and the Cabinet Reconstruction Committee was aware that this needed to be carried out within 8–10 years, before the industry was outmatched by foreign competition. However, in the postwar period, governments failed to act, with the consequence that, despite a good export performance when facing little foreign competition in the late 1940s, British industries were increasingly at a disadvantage in the 1950s when confronting European competitors which *had* modernised their industries in the postwar period.

- **Failure to modernise the educational system.** Barnett has further maintained that, far from being a triumph, the Butler Education Act (1944) was a great missed opportunity. It gave far too much attention to traditional liberal educational ideas (which favoured the arts against scientific and technical education and the grammar school élite against the rest) and to the requirements of the Church of England and far too little attention to scientific, technical, vocational and further education. R.A. Butler began in 1941 with the realisation that the first question was the need for industrial and technical training and the linking up of schools closely with employment, but ended by spending the bulk of his time in negotiations with the Church over the future of church schools and religious education. The consequence was a complete failure to evolve coherent medium- or long-term educational strategies capable of transforming Britain's obsolete industrial culture. Instead of raising the school leaving age to 15 in 1947, the Labour Government should have brought in compulsory part-time education for one day per week for all 14–18-years-olds. Educational planners in the 1940s should have devoted more effort to consideration of the content of education rather than focusing almost exclusively on questions of organisation. Between 1945 and 1965, technical schools, the third leg of the secondary education tripod, educated a mere 2 per cent of the school population and secondary modern schools, which educated the vast majority, received barely one-third of the resources per child allocated to grammar schools.

- **Mistaken priorities, excessive commitments and delusions of grandeur.** 'We persist in regarding ourselves as a Great Power, capable of everything and only temporarily handicapped by economic difficulties. We are not a Great Power and never will be again. We are a great nation, but if we continue to behave like a Great Power we shall soon cease to be a great nation' (Sir Henry Tizard, Chief Scientific Adviser to the Ministry of Defence, 1949). According to Margaret Gowing who cites this advice of Tizard to a superior in the postwar period in her book *Independence and Deterrence* (1974, vol. 1, p. 230), the words were greeted with 'the kind of horror one would expect if one made a disrespectful remark about the king'. But according to some critics, they encapsulate much that went wrong immediately after the war when, instead of 'cutting Britain's suit to match its

cont. p. 26

Exhibit 2.4—*continued*

cloth', governments assumed Britain's economic problems were only temporary, and committed the country to attempting more than its economic resources would bear. On this argument, maintaining a large colonial empire and global system of military bases *plus* a welfare state *plus* a large house-building programme *plus* the development of nuclear weapons *plus* large conventional military forces were too much for the country.

But opinions differ on what the priorities should have been (and should *not* have been). Barnett criticises the emphasis on the welfare state (the 'New Jerusalem') and housing mainly, but also too high defence expenditure, the latter flowing from the refusal to admit that the era of imperial greatness was over, as the main mistakes. On the other hand, Paul Addison (1987) argues that Britain's welfare commitments were broadly in line with those of other Western European countries in the postwar period and that Britain's high burden of defence spending was what distinguished it from all other West European countries except France, which did not, however, have such a large house-building commitment as Britain. Addison finds 'kernels of truth' in Barnett's criticisms of the Coalition's failure to attach sufficient priority to industrial and educational modernisation, but believes that Barnett greatly underestimates both the long-term nature of Britain's economic problems and the way in which social reconstruction after the war was politically imperative as the price of working-class participation during the war.

- **Failure to create a 'developmental state'.** For David Marquand (1987) Britain's main failing post-1945 was not to evolve an adequate theory and practice of the modern state. There was a failure to develop a theory of public power in the mixed economy, a theory which Marquand calls the 'developmental state'. Resources would continue to be allocated by market forces but such a state would intervene 'on a significant scale to supplement, constrain, manipulate, or direct market forces to public ends'.

  Whilst the British state mobilised resources for war very efficiently, fairly and with respect for individual liberties, it failed to evolve machinery which would have enabled successful economic intervention in time of peace. For Peter Hennessy (1990) the failure to maintain the wartime reforms forced upon the civil service was 'probably the greatest lost opportunity in the history of British public administration'. The main failures in his view were *(1)* to see the need to recruit more scientific and economic expertise; and *(2)* to develop a more managerial approach, with greater emphasis on effective action and tackling problems directly rather than the more negative 'looking all round a problem to see the snags' and 'failure avoidance'.

---

balance of payments deficits predicted for 1946 and 1947 (themselves the result of Britain's massive loss of foreign assets and exports during the war); and to encourage the recovery of Britain's export trade. By the mid-1950s, under Labour Chancellors Hugh Dalton, Stafford Cripps and Hugh Gaitskell, and Conservative Chancellor R.A. Butler, these goals had been largely achieved. But they were not achieved without crises, the worst year being 1947, when Britain faced both a severe fuel crisis (coal having failed to regain its prewar levels of output)

and even more damaging massive balance-of-payments and sterling convertibility crises.

However, assisted by the recovery in world trade, by a financial injection through the US Marshall Aid programme for European Recovery (1948) and by a large fall in the cost of imports (1953), Britain's current account balance of payments came back into surplus in 1948 and more decisively in 1952–4. Moreover, by the mid-1950s, the removal of the wartime regime of physical controls over the economy was virtually complete and Keynesian methods of economic management effectively in place. The new fiscal and monetary methods of economic management had even acquired a name, – 'Butskellism'. Moreover, after a sharp increase in 1947 to over 1 million, unemployment fell to around 300 000 (1.5 per cent) for the next ten years.

▮ 1955–79: The Consensus Under Strain:

☐ *External Relations*

The main themes of Britain's external relationships in this period were the collapse of the world role, the displacement of the Commonwealth by Europe, and the increasing reliance upon the United States. The major strand in Britain's domestic history was the continued reluctance to sacrifice its pursuit of national 'greatness' in order to dedicate itself to the goal of developing an efficient modern economy.

Decolonisation, which had slowed to a mere trickle in the 1950s, became a flood after 1960, with 17 colonial territories achieving their independence between 1960 and 1964. By 1979 the process was virtually complete, and little remained of the British Empire. Its dissolution was inevitable; only the factors underlying the timing of the process are in some dispute. Some historians attribute the post-1960 acceleration to the Suez affair (1956), when – in response to the nationalisation of the Suez Canal by the Egyptian leader, Gamal Abdel Nasser – Britain colluded with France and Israel to launch a joint military expedition against Egypt. However, the combination of a run on sterling and pressure from the USA and international opinion forced Britain to withdraw before its object had been achieved, thereby dealing a shattering and long-lasting blow to the country's self-image as a great power.

But Suez may well have been a less decisive influence on Prime Minister Macmillan's decision to speed up decolonisation in Africa after 1960 than President de Gaulle's decision to liquidate French colonial entanglements in North and West Africa after 1958 and the sudden decision of Belgium to withdraw from the Congo in mid-1960. Also, Britain was anxious to avoid further acute embarrassments such as the 1959 revelations of the Hola Camp 'massacres' in Kenya and of 'police state' conditions in Nyasaland (Holland (1991) p. 298; Reynolds (1991) p. 223; also, see Exhibit 9.5 below).

Many historians argue that by the mid-1950s, Britain's over-stretched global commitments and the huge burden of defence expenditure they necessitated were already damaging the country's economy. British Governments were well aware of the problem. In 1956 Harold Macmillan as Chancellor of the Exchequer observed that

> for every rifle our comrades in Europe carried we were carrying two. If we were to follow the European example, we could save £700 million a year. If only half of these resources were shifted into exports the picture of our foreign balances would be transformed. If the other half were available for investment, there would be less critical comment about our low rate of investment compared to many other countries (Chalmers (1985) p. 65).

However, Macmillan as Prime Minister, even in the aftermath of Suez, remained committed to a world role for Britain, as signalled by the search for a genuinely independent British nuclear deterrent, the attempt to broker peace between the superpowers at Summit meetings and the adoption of a costly policing commitment 'East of Suez'.

By the end of the 1960s all these policies had collapsed. The British attempt at real nuclear independence ended in the cancellation of the surface-to-surface missile 'Blue Streak' in 1960 and the negotiation of an agreement to purchase a new generation of nuclear weapons launched from Polaris submarines from the United States (Nassau Agreement, 1962). Summitry collapsed spectacularly at Paris in the same year whilst Denis Healey as Defence Secretary finally managed to wind down military commitments 'East of Suez' with the 1967 promise to withdraw British forces from Singapore and Malaysia in the mid-1970s. Figure 2.2 compares British defence spending 1950–80 with that of other advanced industrial countries.

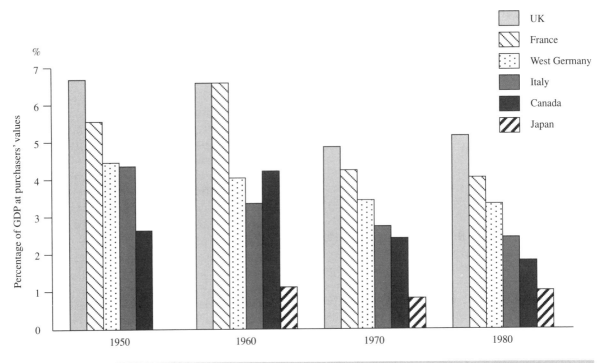

Figure 2.2   *Comparative defence spending 1950–80*

By the mid-1960s, the notion of the Commonwealth as a world force was at an end, although the concept had succeeded in disguising the British retreat from empire. Britain's trade with the Commonwealth was also in decline, gradually in the 1950s, more quickly in the 1960s when exports to the EEC grew more rapidly than exports to the Commonwealth. Britain had responded to the formation of the EEC in 1957 by first attempting to block it and then by forming EFTA (the European Free Trade Association), the so-called 'Outer Seven'. It had banked on French political instability wrecking the EEC from within, but the emergence of de Gaulle as President (1958) turned this into a vain hope.

In 1960 Macmillan began a swift reorientation of Britain's external policy as it became evident that the EEC was succeeding. His motives were predominantly political – since the USA wanted Britain inside the Community as a counterpoise to Germany and France, membership was an important way to continuing the Atlantic partnership. But they were also economic. By the late 1950s it

was already apparent that Britain's postwar rate of economic growth, although good by historical standards, was lagging well behind other European (and world) competitors (see below).

However, Britain's applications to join the EEC in 1962 and 1967 were both humiliatingly rejected by de Gaulle on the grounds that Britain was not truly European. The General's vetoes also owed much to wartime antagonisms and to French unwillingness to share European leadership with Britain. But he undoubtedly had a point about Britain's pro-American sympathies: Britain's 1962 application was made in the immediate aftermath of Macmillan's negotiation of the Polaris deal with President Kennedy, whilst the 1967 application came in the wake of a secret deal by which the Americans agreed to support sterling, thus enabling the Wilson Government to stave off devaluation, in return for Britain's retaining its East of Suez commitment (Reynolds, 1991, p. 227).

When the Conservative Government led by the Europhile Edward Heath finally managed to secure entry to the EEC in 1973, it was on rather disadvantageous terms to Britain. By the end of the transitional period in 1978, Britain provided about one-fifth of Community income, which was reasonable, but in return, because the EEC's payments were skewed towards farm support in the Common Agricultural Policy, received back under one-tenth of EEC spending. However, a major change had occurred in the orientation of Britain's external politics which, from the early 1970s, became increasingly more European.

☐ *Welfare and the Economy*

The bi-partisan consensus on the welfare state continued in this period, with government social spending rising ever more rapidly as a proportion of GNP. But broad overall consensus was compatible with differing policy priorities and emphases, especially in education and housing. Thus in education Labour began a rapid movement towards comprehensive schools which was continued by the Conservatives after 1970, even though their preference for selectivity (and the preservation of the grammar schools) would have made them unlikely initiators of such a policy.

In housing Labour stressed increasing the stock of council houses whilst the Conservatives prioritised encouraging owner occupation. Both parties moved increasingly towards means testing in their social security policies but for Labour this was a regrettable departure from the principle of universality, whereas the Conservatives approved it as preserving work incentives and containing the growth of state welfare. (Digby, 1989, pp. 65, 69).

There was little change in the sectoral balance of the 'mixed economy' before 1970 but rather more after that date. Road haulage and steel were both denationalised in the 1950s by the Conservatives, but Labour returned steel to public ownership in 1967. After 1970 Labour nationalised aerospace and shipbuilding (1977) and formed the British National Oil Corporation in order to influence the exploitation of North Sea oil. The nationalisation of Rolls-Royce (1971) by the Conservatives and the acquisition of a

majority shareholding in British Leyland (1975) by Labour were prompted by the desires of governments to ensure the survival of major ailing companies.

However, the consensus on economic management came under increasing strain during the 1970s, with new directions in economic policy being proposed by the Conservative New Right and the Labour Left (Alternative Economic Strategy). The challenge to the consensus emerged against a background of accelerating economic decline, with Britain slipping ever more rapidly down the international 'league table' (see Chapter 3).

In addition, hitherto favourable economic indicators took a sharp downward turn. The inflation rate, which had been running at 2–3 per cent in the 1950s and 4–5 per cent in the late 1960s, rose to over 9 per cent in the early 1970s and thence, after the quadrupling of OPEC (Organisation of Petroleum Exporting Countries) oil prices in 1973–74, to over 24 per cent in 1975. Unemployment, which had averaged an annual 335 000 in the 1950s and 447 000 in the 1960s, also increased sharply after 1970, rising to an annual average of 1.25 million (1974–79). Economic growth, which had averaged 2.8 per cent per annum between 1948–1973 plummeted to a mere 1.4 per cent between 1973–1979. A new term – 'stagflation' – was coined to describe this unprecedented situation of slow growth combined with both rising unemployment and accelerating inflation.

The years 1972–9 were the heyday of 'corporatist' economic management between government, employers and unions, with interventionist governments using incomes policies including wage freezes in order to contain inflationary pressures. This approach was symbolised by Labour's 'social contract' with the unions (1974–5), in which the unions agreed to voluntary restraint on wages in return for favourable government social and industrial policies. Whatever the final judgement of historians on incomes policies (whether statutory, 1972–4, or compulsory non-statutory, 1976–9), they had the undoubted disadvantage of politicising industrial relations. The Heath Government's clash with the miners (1972–4) and the Callaghan

Government's battle with the public sector unions (1978–9) helped to bring about their downfall (see Chapters 2, 20 and 25).

The welfare state was also under severe strain by the mid-1970s. In the 1950s, it had been expected that the rapid growth of the economy would enable welfare spending to rise without adding to the tax burden on households. But by the 1970s this expectation had been eroded. National income had failed to grow as rapidly as expected but government welfare commitments had increased dramatically. The result was a steady rise in public expenditure which reached a postwar peak as a proportion of GDP of just under 46 per cent in 1975–6 (Table 2.1). The gap between public expenditure and revenue – which has to be filled by state borrowing (the Public Sector Borrowing Requirement) – increased dramatically even though the tax burden was at record levels. By 1975 even people officially classified as amongst the poorest in the community paid tax and the average wage-earner with two children paid one-quarter of his income in direct taxes compared with 3.3 per cent in 1955. By the mid-1970s public expectations of the welfare state were running well ahead of public willingness and national capacity to finance it.

Rapidly rising inflation and unemployment, slowing economic growth, and high and increasing levels of public expenditure and taxation led the Labour Government to move away to a certain extent from Keynesian methods and priorities of economic management in the late 1970s. First, Chancellor Denis Healey in his 1975 Budget refused to increase demand in the face of rising unemployment, thereby initiating a new emphasis on control of inflation as the major goal of government policy rather than the maintenance of a 'high and stable' level of employment. Dennis Kavanagh has called this policy shift 'a historic breach with one of the main planks of the postwar consensus' (Kavanagh 1990, p. 127).

Second, during the sterling crisis of 1976, the Government adopted formal targets for the growth of the money supply (notes and coins in circulation plus sterling current accounts in the private sector and sterling deposit accounts held by British residents) as a way of reducing the rate of inflation. Finally, Labour also began the change from the Public Expenditure Survey Committee (PESC) method of controlling public spending to the use of cash limits. Under PESC, public spending plans were not adjusted when growth turned out be lower or inflation higher than expected when the expenditure plans were drawn up. Under the cash limits methods, which began in 1976, each spending programme received a cash limit for the year and was expected to keep within its budget. However, although Labour initiated new priorities and methods in economic management, it was far from launching a new philosophy of government based on these new directions. That was the task the Thatcher Government, coming to power in 1979, set itself to carry out.

1979–90s: The Ending of the Consensus

The erosion of the consensus in the 1970s paved the way for its overthrow by Margaret Thatcher. During this time, consensus ideas lost intellectual credibility and consensus governments lost political authority. The decline in the ideological persuasiveness of the post-1945 consensus was evident in the growing influence within the two major parties of anti-consensual ideas: the neo-liberal New Right (Conservative) and the left-wing Alternative Economic Strategy (Labour) (see Chapter 5).

In both parties, the political centre was in retreat – in the Conservative Party because of the failure of Heathite Statism between 1972 and 1974; in the Labour Party because of dissatisfaction with Labour's record on welfare and the economy, and the rise of radical single-issue

Table 2.1 *Public expenditure as a proportion of GDP, 1955–76 (current prices)*

	OECD average	United Kingdom
1955–7	28.5	32.5
1967–9	34.5	38.5
1974–6	41.4	44.5

Source: Pliatzky (1982, p. 166).

Exhibit 2.5 Margaret Thatcher

When Margaret Thatcher was forced to resign from the premiership by her party on 21 November 1990, her record contained an amazing number of 'firsts'. She was the first British leader in modern democratic times to win three consecutive general elections, she had been prime minister for a longer period than any of her twentieth-century predecessors, and above all, perhaps, she was the first woman to lead a major Western country. It was an astonishing achievement but – because of her sex (only relatively few women even get to Westminster) – more precariously based and fortuitous than it may appear in retrospect. How did such a career happen? And what sort of a politician was Margaret Thatcher?

She owed more directly and indirectly to Edward Heath than she might have liked later to admit (the two became bitter enemies). It was Heath who in 1970 appointed her to her first major government post (Education Secretary) and it was Heath who, in stubbornly clinging to the Conservative leadership after his third general election defeat in October 1974 and refusing to withdraw in favour of his own supporters in the first ballot, gave Margaret Thatcher her chance. She challenged him and – to most people's surprise – not only beat him (130–119) on the first ballot but also developed an unstoppable momentum which enabled her easily to defeat her new opponents in the second ballot.

Up to this point she had had a good but by no means exceptional political career. Education (at Kesteven and Grantham Girls' School – a grant-aided grammar school – and Oxford University, where she gained a Chemistry degree) was followed by three years' work as a research chemist and success in the Bar exams (1953). Marriage – in 1951 to a North Kent businessman, Denis Thatcher – gave her financial security.

But her political ambition – born in her University days and evident in her unsuccessful attempts to win Dartford for the Conservatives in the General Elections of 1950 and 1951 – did not gain its first reward until 1959, when she finally entered Parliament as MP for Finchley. Soon afterwards she became a junior Minister in the Macmillan Government. It was during her time at the Ministry of Pensions (1961–4) that she confided to the Departmental Permanent Secretary that her highest ambition was to be Chancellor of the Exchequer. Now, as Conservative Leader, she could exceed that goal. Would she do so?

Just over four years later, the answer was known, when Margaret Thatcher led the Conservatives to a 43-seat majority in the 1979 General Election. Once more, her chances had been improved by her opponent's misjudgement. Had Prime Minister Callaghan called an election in autumn 1978, as widely expected, she might have lost. Would she then have been allowed to contest another election as leader? She herself certainly thought not. In the event, however, the industrial strife of the 'Winter of Discontent' produced more favourable circumstances for the Conservatives and she rode the tides of political and ideological change to victory.

How far could the country have expected the tempestuous times that would follow? Certainly, Margaret Thatcher was already committed to reverse the 'weak-kneed' consensual politics that she blamed for British decline. In the process, she aimed to destroy socialism both at home and abroad and to transform Britain into a middle-class nation. Her values and goals then were known. What might have been less apparent from her generally cautious four years as Leader of the Opposition was the uncompromising zeal and determination with which she would pursue them. Several previous prime ministers had been blown off course by events. Although already dubbed the 'Iron Lady' she was as yet untested in action. She herself provided some clues to her character on the day she became Prime Minister. She owed everything, she said, to her father, Alderman Alfred Roberts of Grantham. Six years later she spelled out what he had taught her – 'that you first sort out what you believe in. You then apply it. You don't compromise on the things that matter'. The country in 1979 was soon to discover how Margaret Thatcher dealt with the things that mattered to her.

Figure 2.3   *Margaret Thatcher*

Source: *Guardian*.

groups representing feminists, blacks, gays and CND. Governments had lost political authority because of their apparent incapacity to reverse national decline. In particular, they were increasingly perceived by the public as at the mercy of over-mighty interest groups and as unable to deal with Britain's long-term problems of low productivity, backward industry and strife-torn management–union relations. Wilson's attempt at trade union reform had been blocked by his own party (1969) while Heath's industrial relations legislation had collapsed in a wave of industrial militancy (1971–2). The breakdown of Government union reforms and wage restraint policies in the decade before 1979 engendered a sense of ungovernability, chaos and mounting public frustration. When first the Ford workers, then the lorry drivers, then the public sector unions in a series of well-publicised strikes, broke through the Callaghan Government's 5 per cent pay norm in 1978–9, their actions seemed to symbolise the failure of consensus government.

The full range of policies known as Thatcherism were not present in their entirety in 1979 but emerged during the course of Thatcher's three Administrations. Put simply, the economic project of 'rolling back the frontiers' of the state

was there (although little in the way of privatisation was promised) but, despite projected increases in defence spending, a more vigorously assertive and nationalist foreign policy did not emerge until the early 1980s. Similarly, although the 1979 manifesto promised the sale of council houses, the application of the philosophy of 'internal markets' to the health and education services had to wait until the late 1980s. These policies, especially in relation to the economy, industrial relations and welfare, represented a deliberate reversal of the postwar consensus, a change of political tack aimed at turning the country round and halting decline. We now summarise these changes.

☐ *Foreign and Defence Policy*

Arguably, the main elements of postwar foreign policy remained in place: what changed was that British interests (e.g. within the EEC) were asserted more aggressively, defence received greater emphasis and political rhetoric became more stridently nationalist. It is unlikely that any of Thatcher's immediate predecessors would have fought the Falklands War.

The European Community

In 1980 Britain's payments to the EEC exceeded its receipts by over £1 billion, and Thatcher, aiming at 'a broad balance' between contributions and receipts, fought a vigorous and largely successful campaign against the other eight countries to get 'our money' back (she eventually got about two-thirds of it). Later in the 1980s, having already signed the Single European Act (1986), she fiercely resisted 'Euro-federalism' (the idea of a United States of Europe) and significantly delayed Britain's entry into the European Exchange Rate Mechanism (ERM) until October 1990.

The 'Special Relationship' with the United States

Margaret Thatcher's fierce anti-communism drew her into close support of US policy in the new Cold War of the early 1980s. In this revived 'special relationship' (seen as in decline from the late 1960s) she strongly backed the deployment of a new generation of American Cruise and Pershing missiles in Europe together with the 'dual track' NATO strategy of arms modernisation combined with negotiations for arms control. Thatcher's close personal relations (from 1981) with President Reagan cemented Britain's ties with the US and she repaid her debt for American intelligence and other support in the Falklands War by permitting the US to carry out retaliatory air strikes against Libya from its British bases (1986).

In the mid-1980s, she used her ability to 'do business' with Soviet leader Gorbachev to flexibly broker détente between the US and the USSR, gaining her a (brief) high profile world role and a (more effective) resumption of the 'summitry' of earlier prime ministers.

Defence

Thatcher gave an increased commitment to defence, involving increased expenditure (the defence budget was one-fifth higher in the later 1980s than a decade earlier) and the commissioning from the United States of a new generation of more powerful nuclear weapons (Trident).

The Falklands War (1982)

When the Argentinian President General Galtieri invaded the Falkland Islands, the Thatcher Government despatched a Task Force which successfully recaptured the islands at a cost of 255 British dead and 777 wounded. In addition, six British ships were sunk. A 'Fortress Falklands' policy was then put in place for the defence of the islands at a cost of £5 billion. The result of the war – brought on to a significant extent by the Government's own diplomatic failings – enabled the Prime Minister to claim: 'Great Britain is great again'.

Decolonisation

The Conservative Government negotiated the independence of Southern Rhodesia as Zimbabwe (1980) and a special status for Hong Kong from 1997 within the People's Republic of China, but resisted Commonwealth pressure for wide-ranging sanctions against South Africa (1985–6).

'Rolling Back the Frontiers of the State'

Public Expenditure

The Conservative Government believed that *public expenditure was 'at the heart of Britain's present difficulties'* and came to power promising substantial cuts in all areas except the National Health Service (NHS), defence and law and order; the overall purpose was to reduce the claims of the public sector on savings and to cut taxes in order to promote an 'enterprise culture'. Accordingly, the Government sought to reduce the Public Sector Borrowing Requirement (PSBR), apply cash limits to all public sector spending programmes and shift the emphasis from direct to indirect taxation.

Privatisation

The 1979 manifesto promised only modest de-nationalisation (of aerospace and shipbuilding) but *privatisation emerged* during the early 1980s *as a central plank of the Government's pro-gramme*. Between 1979 and 1992 it carried out a massive transfer of assets from the public to the private sector, thereby virtually extinguishing the 'mixed economy' as it had existed since 1951. The goal was increased efficiency, the New Right believing as an article of faith that private enterprise was more efficient than public enterprise.

Industry and Labour

The Government *abandoned the corporatist, tripartite approach to industrial and incomes policy*, replacing it with an arm's length attitude to the employers and trade unions. The Conservatives also *sharply reduced the powers of the unions*. The goal of these policies was to shift responsibility for economic decisions away from the state on to 'the market' and within industry to move the balance of power towards management.

Social Policy

Government social policy was less directly anti-consensual: housing represents the purest application of New Right principles, with large-scale sales of council houses to sitting tenants, reductions in public sector house-building, the scaling down of council rent subsidies and the encouragement of house purchase (with mortgage interest relief trebling down to 1987–8); in *social security* benefits, there was a pronounced move away from universality of provision towards the targeting of help on the most needy.

However, major changes in health and education were not made until the late 1980s, the aim being to break the dominant rule of the regional health authorities and local councils as providers by encouraging 'opting-out' in both services.

☐ *From Keynesianism to Monetarism*

The Government rejected demand management as a mechanism and full employment as an objective of economic policy in favour of the control of the money supply (and public expenditure cuts) as a means of curbing inflation, which

became the main objective of macroeconomic policy. By the mid-1980s, however, the setting of monetary targets was discredited and Chancellor Nigel Lawson adopted the financial discipline of a stable exchange rate in order to control inflation. Ultimately, under John Major as Chancellor, this policy led to the Government entering the European Exchange Rate Mechanism (ERM) in October 1990.

Margaret Thatcher was deposed in November 1990 because in the opinion of a large number (but not a majority) of Conservative MPs she had become an electoral liability. Her last term had been marred by seemingly intractable divisions within her Cabinet over economic policy and the European Community and by the adoption of the politically disastrous poll tax. We provide an overall assessment of her legacy in Chapter 33. In the meantime, it is sufficient to say that, although she had changed less than she would have liked, she had certainly shaken the country up and shifted the basis of public debate on social and economic policy.

Summary

The main theme of this chapter has been the forging of the postwar policy consensus, its persistence in the face of both domestic and external pressures down to 1979 and the demise of large parts of it after 1979 under the Conservative Government of Margaret Thatcher. Because this consensus emerged during the war, it was necessary to begin this survey of recent British history in 1940 and, because it was never complete, it was important to indicate where the parties' differences of emphasis lay.

An interlinked theme has been the decline of Britain as a front-ranking world power (the Conservative Right from the late 1970s argued that there was a causal link between consensual politics and decline), the adjustments and changes of orientation this has required (from an imperial role to a predominantly European one) and the extent to which Britain made these changes in timely and adequate fashion or persisted too long in what one historian has called 'the pursuit of greatness'.

Questions

1. Discuss the contention that the postwar consensus was a 'myth'.
2. Analyse the view that Britain failed to adjust sufficiently quickly in the postwar period to changes in its international status.

Assignment

The following table contains the judgements of fifty leading historians in points out of 10 on British prime ministers since the war. Study the table and then state how far you agree with these judgements, and for what reasons.

Table 2.2   *Greatest postwar premier?*

Personal effectiveness:		Impact on British prestige abroad:	
1. Thatcher	7.6	1. Thatcher	7.5
2. Attlee	7.5	2. Churchill	7.0
3. Macmillan	6.7	3. Macmillan	6.5
4. Wilson	5.5	4. Attlee	5.8
5. Callaghan	5.1	5. Heath	5.0
6. Heath	4.9	6. Callaghan	4.3
7. Churchill	4.4	7. Wilson	3.8
8. Home	3.4	8. Home	3.1
9. Eden	3.0	9. Eden	3.0
Impact on British society:		Overall greatest prime minister since the second world war (average of above ratings):	
1. Attlee	8.1	1. Thatcher	7.5
2. Thatcher	7.5	2. Attlee	7.1
3. Wilson	5.1	3. Macmillan	6.1
4. Macmillan	5.0	4. Churchill	5.3
5. Heath	4.6	5. Heath	4.8
6. Churchill	4.4	6. Wilson	4.8
7. Callaghan	4.4	7. Callaghan	4.6
8. Eden	2.6	8. Home	3.0
9. Home	2.4	9. Eden	2.8

Source: Guardian, 20 June 1991.

Further Reading

Cairncross, A. (1981) 'The Post-War Years, 1945–77' in R. Floud and D. McCloskey, *The Economic History of Britain Since 1700*, vol. 2 (Cambridge: Cambridge University Press).

Clarke, P. (1992) *A Question of Leadership*, (Harmondsworth: Penguin).

Digby, A. (1989) *British Welfare Policy* (London: Faber and Faber).

Holland, R. (1991) *The Pursuit of Greatness* (London: Fontana).

Kavanagh, D. (1990) *Thatcherism and British Politics*, 2nd edn (Oxford: Oxford University Press).

Marquand, D. (1987) *The Unprincipled Society* (London: Fontana).

Morgan, K. (1990) *The People's Peace: British History 1945–1989* (Oxford: Oxford University Press).

Reynolds, D. (1991) *Britannia Overruled* (London: Longman).

Riddell, P. (1991) *The Thatcher Era* (Oxford: Blackwell).

Young, H. (1990) *One of Us* (London: Pan in association with Macmillan – Expanded edition with new epilogue).

■ *Chapter 3* ■

The Social and Economic Context

Population
Social Class in Britain
Gender

Race
Nation and Region
The Changing British Economy

The links between politics and society and politics and the economy are both close. Political issues such as the optimum organisation of the health service, how to tackle racial discrimination and how to encourage more women to enter politics are themselves thrown up by developments in society. Political scientists study voting behaviour in terms of the links between class and party, and institutions such as parties, Parliament, the civil service and the Cabinet are analysed in relationship to the social background of their members. Since 1945, when government assumed new responsibilities for management of the economy and even more since the 1960s when arresting British economic decline became a central concern of Cabinets, the disciplines of politics and economics have seemed ever more closely intertwined. Today's politics to a considerable extent is economic politics, with a high proportion of each day's news being economic news, concerned with inflation and unemployment rates, the trade figures, balance of payments and so on.

This chapter examines the social and economic background to British politics. It focuses first on divisions in British society in terms of class, gender, race, nation and region; and second, on recent trends in the British economy.

■ Population

In terms of population, the United Kingdom (UK) is one of the larger states in the European Union (EU), smaller than the unified Germany but similar to France and Italy. In world terms, Britain ranks about seventeenth. UK population growth has slowed dramatically in the twentieth century in common with other industrialised nations, increasing from 41.46 million in 1901 to 49.2 million in 1945 and to 57.2 million in 1989.

Compared with slowing growth in the economically advanced countries, however, world population is growing at an ever faster rate. For example, in the 1920s it was 2 billion; 1960, 3 billion; 1974, 4 billion; 1987, 5 billion; and it is projected to reach 6 billion in 1999 and 7 billion in 2010. The UK is also one of the most densely populated nations in Europe and the population density of its most densely populated country, England (at 366 people per square kilometre), is slightly higher than that of The Netherlands (363). Since the war there has been a redistribution of the population from Scotland and the North of England to the English South-East, East Anglia, the East Midlands and the South-West.

	Population (millions) 1971	1989	Population density (per sq. km) 1989
United Kingdom	55.9	57.2	234.1
European Community	322.4	342.7	144.3
China	787.2	1 104.0	115.0
India	550.4	796.6	242.0
USA	207.0	246.3	26.0
Japan	104.7	122.6	325.0

Source: Data extracted from *Social Trends* (1992).

Table 3.1 *Population: some international comparisons*

■ Social Class in Britain

Class remains of great importance as the major source of social stratification in Britain. It is of central significance when considering individual life-chances, work experiences, political behaviour and popular perceptions of social division.

But there is no agreed method of allocating people into distinct classes. For example, Karl Marx (1818–83) stressed the schism between capital and labour, owners and workers, propertied and propertyless, as the fundamental class division. Max Weber, the German sociologist (1864–1920), variously emphasised the importance of status distinctions based on social recognition, differential life-chances grounded on different 'market' situations, and authority relations at work as determinants of social position. Both thinkers have latter-day followers who have developed more complex schema of stratification based respectively on relationships to the means of production and on status and 'life-chances'.

Some contemporary social commentators continue to use the 'language of class' first developed in the nineteenth century, referring to the upper, middle and working classes and to internal subdivisions (e.g. upper and lower) within the latter two categories. This classification has the merit of being easily comprehensible since it is the one

Figure 3.1 *Self-rated social class in Britain*

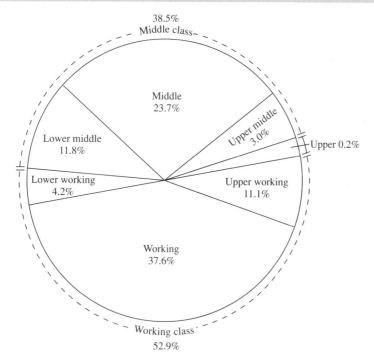

Source: Data from Marshall *et al.* (1988, p. 144).

people employ in everyday life. For example, respondents to a large survey (of 1 770) in 1984 had little difficulty in assigning themselves to a specific segment of a social class (Figure 3.1). But critics of this categorisation say that it lacks precision because it is not immediately apparent where particular occupational groups should be located.

Government, market researchers and sociologists agree in defining class in relation to work and in producing classificatory schemes based on *occupation*. The Registrar-General's categorisation is often seen as definitive. It forms the basis for social analysis of the ten-yearly census and is used in government publications. Market researchers divide people into six socio-economic categories, but usually in practice reduce these to four: AB, C1, C2 and DE. This method of classification is employed in opinion polls.

Other systems of social classification have been proposed by social scientists Anthony Heath, Roger Jowell and John Curtice (Table 3.2) and by the historian, Guy Routh (Figure 3.2).

All of these classifications avoid the terms 'upper class' and 'middle class' and only one employs the term 'working class'. Unlike traditional descriptions of social class, categorisation by occupation avoids built-in value judgements. It is more specific and apparently more objective.

However, as reflections of social reality, occupational classifications face problems too. For example, only one of the listed schemes finds a place for the unemployed and other state dependents and none includes the wives of salaried or manual workers, or great landowners like the Duke of Devonshire. Clearly, despite possessing the advantage of a more 'neutral' language, occupational class cannot be equated with social class.

We conclude that both the traditional classification and the one based on occupations have value and that for political scientists their usefulness will depend to a large extent on the purpose for which they are required. Thus it may be feasible in discussions of voting behaviour to employ basically occupational categories (AB, C1, C2, DE) but it makes less sense to rely solely on these categories when analysing the social background of the Cabinet or the reasons for the decline of the Labour Party. The traditional classification, based on a division of British society into a small upper class, a middle class and a working class, with important sub-divisions within the two last-named classes, is of continued relevance.

The use of this classification is quite compatible with a recognition that the boundaries between classes are fluid and shifting and that this may lead on occasion to problems of definition. For example, in the 1960s it was often wondered whether the skilled worker as a result of greater affluence had become essentially middle class in lifestyle and attitude – the 'embourgeoisement' thesis. More recently, in the 1980s, it became more customary to ask whether, with the advance

Table 3.2   *Occupational class in Britain*

Registrar-General		Market Research Categories		Heath, Jowell and Curtice
I	Professional	A	Professional/senior managerial	Salariat: (Managers, administrators, professionals, semi-professionals, supervisors of non-manual workers)
II	Intermediate	B	Middle managers/executives	Petty bourgeoisie: (Farmers, self-employed manual workers, small proprietors)
III	Skilled non-manual	C1	Junior managers/non-manual	Routine non-manual: (Clerks, salesworkers, secretaries)
IV	Partly-skilled manual	C2	Skilled manual	Foremen and technicians: (Blue-collar workers with supervisory functions)
V	Unskilled manual	D	Semi-skilled/unskilled manual	Working class: (Rank-and-file manual)
		E	Unemployed/state dependents	

Sources: Office of Population and Censuses; Heath *et al.* (1985).

'New' working class	'Traditional' working class
Works in private sector	Works in public sector
Not a member of a trade union	Member of a trade union
Buying house on a mortgage	Council house tenant
Lives in the South-East	Lives in North, Scotland or Wales

Table 3.3   *Typical attributes of the new and traditional working class*

of white collar trade unionism, clerical workers had in effect become working class.

Nor is the traditional classification undermined by the recognition of new sectoral and regional divisions – between public and private sector workers, council house tenants and home owners, trade unionists and non-trade unionists, and workers living in the North and in the South-East, for example. Such new divisions enable the contrast to be drawn at its most extreme between a traditional and a 'new' working class, between e.g. a trade unionist, public sector worker living in a council house in the North and a non-unionist, private sector worker buying his house on a mortgage in the South-East (Table 3.3).

With the increase in unemployment and part-time (and temporary) working, other internal divisions within the classes have become important too – between the employed and the un-employed and between those in full-time and those in part-time work. But these complicate rather than erode the class structure. Factors of birth, education, social expectation, and professional training or trade skill which form the bases of class identity continue to operate whether a person has part-time or temporary work or is unemployed.

☐ *Social Change Since the War*

The main change in the structure of British society since the war has been the growth of the middle class and the shrinkage of the working class. This has led to a considerable shift in the

Figure 3.2   *Occupational class in Britain, 1951–81 (percentages)*

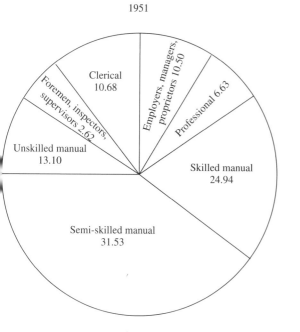

1951

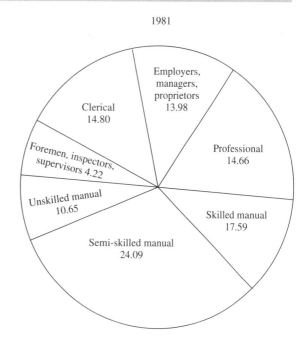

1981

Source: Data from Routh (1987, p. 38).

size and balance of classes. Broadly speaking, in 1951 the middle class constituted about one-third, the working class approximately two-thirds, of the working population. By 1980s the situation had been transformed, with the middle class close to being a majority of the occupied population for the first time. Underlying this change has been the sharp increase in non-manual employment and a contraction of manual occupations (Figure 3.2). During the late 1980s manual groups probably became a minority of the occupied population.

Some commentators – impressed by the growth of the professional, managerial administrative and clerical strata – have suggested that Britain has become a 'middle class' society and is even in sight of becoming a 'classless' society. It is certainly the case that white collar now outnumber blue collar jobs and that, with the spread of affluence, standards of living and lifestyles formerly associated with the middle class are now enjoyed by the majority.

However, there are several arguments which tell against the thesis that Britain has become a 'middle class' or 'classless' society: first, all recent research points to the continuing sense of class identity among the working class; second, very large inequalities in wealth, income, housing, education and health – themselves related to class – remain, and may even have increased in recent years; finally, as already seen, people do perceive themselves not only as belonging to a particular class but as occupying a certain position within it. Even if increasing general prosperity, improvements in diet and dress and the spread of consumerism have reduced the visible differences between classes, class differences persist.

Figure 3.3   *The British Class System on display at Ascot*

Source: Guardian.

■ Gender

Social divisions based on gender, race, nation and region have increased in significance in recent decades. In the case of women, the reasons for this are, first, their growing prominence in the labour force and, second, the social and political impact of feminism since the later 1960s. (This latter change is discussed further in Chapter 5.) In the immediate postwar period – before these developments took place – the role of women rarely achieved separate treatment in books like this, but was most often dealt with – if at all – under a theme such as 'the family'.

Women's participation in the workforce began to increase significantly after 1951 and accelerated after 1971. In 1951 men made up over two-thirds of the workforce and still constituted over three-fifths of it in 1971. By 1992, the situation was very different, with women composing nearly half of all employees (Table 3.4). A range of demographic economic, social and cultural factors underlie women's increasing participation in waged work. These include comparatively low birth rates in the 1970s, the need of households for a second wage-earner in order to maintain living standards, improvements in women's health and educational qualifications, and changing attitudes to the employment of women by managements.

The rise in part-time working is closely connected with women's increasing participation in the labour force. In 1990 over one-fifth of all jobs were part-time, and four-fifths of part-time workers were women.

Women's activity in the labour workforce differs from men's in several ways. First, because of their role in raising young children, women spend a lower proportion – about two-thirds – of their potential working lives in the labour market. Second, the majority of employed women – two-thirds in 1990 – are in non-manual occupations, whereas under half of employed men are. About half of full-time women workers are employed in clerical and related occupations, another fifth in education, health and welfare services; women working part-time tend to be employed in catering, cleaning and other service jobs. Third, women's pay lags significantly behind men's. In April 1991, the average weekly wages of full-time women workers were only 70 per cent of the average weekly earnings of full-time male workers. Gender segregation in the labour market, with women relegated to badly paid, low-status jobs, is an important factor underlying this differential. However, this situation may be expected to change considerably in coming decades as a result of women's educational progress and of employer initiatives aimed at making better use of women's abilities (see Chapter 27 for further discussion).

■ Race

A further source of social division and inequality in Britain is race. A 1992 survey suggested that the ethnic minority population of Great Britain numbers 2.62 million, which represents 4.8 per cent of the total population. The largest single ethnic grouping (about 52 per cent) is Indian, Pakistani and Bangladeshi; approximately 23 per cent are of Afro-Caribbean origin whilst a further 17 per cent are of mixed, Arab and Chinese origin.

This important change in the British population was brought about largely by immigration from the former colonial Caribbean and the South Asian subcontinent in the post-1945 period. Earlier labour migrations into Britain in the twentieth century – by the Irish and by the Jews and other displaced European nationals in the 1930s and 1940s – resulted in primarily *cultural* differences between the immigrants and the native population. The postwar immigration from the New Commonwealth and Pakistan, however, introduced ethnic differences of race as

Table 3.4 *Employees in employment by gender*

	1971 Total number (000s)	%	1992 Total number (000s)	%
Men	13 726	62	11 253	52
Women	8 413	38	10 504	48

Source: Extracted from *Social Trends* (1993), p. 56.

well as culture to the country for the first time, thereby challenging the traditional meanings attached to 'Britishness'.

Coloured immigration is not unique to Britain but common throughout the industrialised West. Between 1945 and 1985 other West European countries and the United States experienced a considerable amount of immigration, much of it from the third world. The large proportion of immigrant families who took up permanent residence, however, distinguished Britain from many other migrant labour-importing countries in Western Europe in the postwar era. (Miles, 1982 in McDowell *et al.* (eds) 1989, pp. 93–110). In 1987–9, according to a sample survey, 46 per cent of the ethnic minority population had been born in Britain. The consequence of New Commonwealth immigration has been to make Britain into a multiracial, multicultural society.

The presence of a sizeable ethnic minority population, especially in the inner cities, has intensified social tensions in Britain, with racial discrimination, widespread although often hard to prove, overlapping and compounding inequalities based on class and gender. The House of Commons Home Affairs Committee commented in 1981 that ethnic communities suffered disadvantages of unemployment, bad housing, educational under-achievement and social tensions 'more than the rest of the community and more than they would if they were white'. The ethnic minorities have presented British governments with the formidable challenge of achieving a racially non-discriminatory society. Their political impact in Britain is further discussed in Chapters 5 and 26.

■ Nation and Region

Another source of differentiation within the UK is between the constituent nations. Quite simply, in population and wealth, England is hugely predominant. The Union is an asymmetrical one, with 83 per cent of the UK population living in England. In terms of population, England outnumbers Scotland by a ratio of 9 to 1, Wales by over 16 to 1 and Northern Ireland by 29 to 1. This degree of domination was not always the case: in 1801, when the United Kingdom was formed, England contained 53 per cent of the UK population, Ireland, 33 per cent. Mass Irish emigration in the nineteenth century and the secession of Southern Ireland in 1922 produced the present imbalance. There is an equally marked economic disparity, with England in 1989 containing 85 per cent of total UK household income (Table 3.5).

Cultural differences persist between the nations of the UK. These go beyond superficial differences such as accent to include patterns of religious observance, the speaking of Gaelic languages, educational systems and the mass media. Thus in England a majority identify with the Church of England, in Scotland with the Church of Scotland (Presbyterian), in Wales, where the Church of England was disestablished in 1920, with one of the Nonconformist sects, and in Northern Ireland with either the Protestant Episcopalian or Presbyterian Church. Only in Northern Ireland, where there is a sizeable minority of Roman Catholics, do religious divisions possess political salience.

Table 3.5   *The nations of the United Kingdom*

	1991		1989	
	Population (000s)	% UK total	Household income (£ million)	% UK total
England	46 170	83	357 469	85.1
Wales	2 798	5	17 812	4.2
Scotland	4 957	8.9	35 075	8.3
Northern Ireland	1 583	2.8	9 654	2.3
United Kingdom	55 508		420 011	

Source: Data extracted from *Social Trends* (1992).

Linguistic differences have also greatly diminished from the early nineteenth century when about nine-tenths of Welsh people, half of the Irish and just under one-quarter of Scots spoke a variety of Gaelic as their first or only language. Today only a small minority (21 per cent) speak Welsh and a very much smaller proportion of Scots (under 2 per cent) speak Gaelic. Welsh schools were fully integrated with the English system after 1944, but education in Scotland and Northern Ireland is run on different lines, and in Northern Ireland is subject to strong sectarian influences. Finally newspapers produced in Northern Ireland and Scotland have large readerships in those countries (Birch, 1979, pp. 37–8).

During the 1980s a growing economic division between the relatively prosperous South and less well-off North attracted considerable attention. Included for the purposes of this analysis in 'the North' were the regions of Yorkshire and Humberside, the North-West, the North of England, Wales, Scotland and Northern Ireland; included in 'the South' were the South-East, East Anglia, the South-West, and the East and West Midlands. It was frequently observed that on a number of criteria, including income per head and unemployment rate, the gap between the North and the South increased during the 1980s (Table 3.6). To take one example only, the gap between the richest region – the South-East – and the poorest region – Northern Ireland – widened considerably both in terms of GDP (Gross Domestic Product) per head and unemployment during the 1980s. The regional division, broadly into areas north and south of the Severn–Humber line, is by no means clear-cut: although in some ways sharing in the prosperity of the South-East, both Midlands regions may be more appropriately seen as a kind of intermediate zone, generally better placed economically than regions to the west and north, but less well-off than regions to the South. There are also striking regional disparities in health. The Black Report (1982) observed that 'death rates were highest in Scotland, followed by the north and north west regions of England, and were lowest in the south east of England and East Anglia, confirming the long established North–South gradient' (Townsend, Davidson and Whitehead, 1990, p. 352).

Table 3.6 *Regional incomes and unemployment in the UK*

	Incomes (GDP per head) (percentages of UK figure)		Unemployment (%)	
	1978	1988	1979	Oct. 1989
North	91.8	88.3	6.5	9.1
Yorkshire and Humberside	94.0	91.1	4.1	7.1
North West	97.8	93.3	5.0	8.0
West Midlands	95.1	91.1	4.0	6.0
East Midlands	95.1	94.6	3.3	5.1
East Anglia	95.4	97.1	3.1	3.5
South-West	90.5	93.8	4.0	4.2
South-East	114.8	119.4	2.6	3.7
England	102.2	102.3	4.0	5.8
Wales	85.0	84.0	5.3	7.0
Scotland	94.7	93.9	5.7	8.9
Northern Ireland	77.7	78.0	7.9	14.5
United Kingdom	100.0	100.0	4.0	5.9

Source: Data from Central Statistical Office and Department of Employment, *The Guardian*, 10 January 1990.

The North–South divide in health, wealth and employment is a significant one, but should not be exaggerated. The gap in economic welfare – although not in health – is to some extent offset by a standard of living index, which evaluates regional living standards in terms of the relationship between average incomes and the cost of living, including house prices. On such a 'quality of life' calculation, the North of England region came top, with Yorkshire and Humberside second, whereas Greater London was at the bottom, with the South-East next to bottom (Reward Group Regional Cost of Living Report, 1988). Moreover, the early 1990s recession hit the South-East far harder than the rest of the UK: in the year to June 1991, the region lost 89 000 jobs whilst job losses in the North, Yorkshire and Humberside (11 000), Wales (15 000), Scotland (7000) and Northern Ireland (2000) were much lower. The overall effect was to slightly narrow the North–South gap in average GDP per head and unemployment rates.

■ The Changing British Economy

Major developments in recent decades have been:

- A continuing decline in manufacturing industry and growth in the services sector;
- A large-scale shift of ownership from the public to the private sector and a significant increase in inward and outward investment;
- The discovery and development of offshore oil and gas resources;
- Important labour market changes, including declining employment in manufacturing and a rise in self-employment and part-time working;
- Changing long-term patterns of trade and changes in the 1980s in Britain's trade accounts and balance of payments;
- An economic performance which since 1945 has combined growing prosperity for the whole community with national economic decline.

The Decline of Manufacturing and the Growth of Services

The major trends in the British economy since the war have been a further decline in the already (by European standards) small agricultural sector, a reduction in the industrial sector and a sizeable expansion of the services sector (retailing, banking, tourism, public services). Thus agriculture generated 6 per cent of Gross Domestic Product (GDP) 1951 but only 2 per cent in 1980; manufacturing – at its peak in 1951 – contributed 36 per cent of national income then, but had declined to 26.8 per cent in 1980; and services constituted 51 per cent of GDP in 1951 but had risen to 55.3 per cent in 1980. These trends continued during the 1980s. Table 3.7 shows sectoral changes, 1969–90.

Economists and politicians disagree about the significance of the process of 'de-industrialisation' – another term for the decline of manufacturing industry – as it affects Britain. On the one hand, the overall trend is common to most advanced economies. On the other hand, the decline in British manufacturing has been sharper than elsewhere, with the result that by 1990 Britain had a smaller industrial base and a larger services sector than other advanced industrial nations. One opinion of this trend is that it need not be taken too seriously since improvements in the service sector can offset losses in employment and

Table 3.7   *GDP, percentage by sector, 1969–90*

	1969	1980	1985	1990
Agriculture	3.1	2.1	1.9	1.5
Energy	4.9	9.7	10.6	5.1
Construction	7.0	6.1	5.8	7.6
Manufacturing	34.1	26.8	23.9	22.4
Private services	38.5	39.0	42.1	47.4
Public services	12.4	16.3	15.7	16.0
	100.0	100.0	100.0	100.0

Source: UK National Accounts 'Blue Book', (1991, Table 16.4).

foreign earnings in manufacturing industry. Another view is that the decline of manufacturing matters a lot because services cannot be expanded at a sufficient rate to compensate for the decline in the capacity of manufacturing to earn foreign currency for Britain through exports.

The Privatisation of Nationalised Industries

During the 1980s the British economy became more capitalist, with a massive transfer of assets taking place from the public to the private sector. Between 1979 and 1992, the Conservative Government privatised 46 major businesses with net proceeds to 1992–3 of about £50 billion. By 1992, of the major public corporations formed by the 1945–51 Labour Government, only British Rail (BR) and British Coal remained. However, the Government announced plans for the partial sale of BR in July 1992 and also aim to sell off British Coal and Royal Mail Parcel Force.

As a result of privatisation, the proportion of GDP accounted for by the nationalised industries declined from 9 per cent to 3.5 per cent (1979–89) and the number of their employees dropped from 1.8 million to 700,000 over the same period. Individual share-ownership jumped from 3 million (about 7 per cent of the adult population) in 1979 to 11 million (26 per cent) in 1991. However, over half of the shareholders in privatised companies owned shares in one company only. Moreover, as a proportion of total shareholding, individual share-ownership continued to decline, with the value of individual shares as a proportion of the value of all shares falling from 54 per cent in 1963 to under 20 per cent in 1990. (see Chapter 10).

The 1980s were also marked by large-scale inward and outward investment. In 1982 foreign enterprises were already responsible for almost 15 per cent of total employment in Britain and just under 20 per cent of UK industrial output. In the late 1980s, however, inward investment rose dramatically and the UK received nearly 44 per cent of all EC foreign investment in 1990. In that year 40 per cent of Japanese EC investment – and 60 per cent of US investment in the Community – went to the UK. At the same time, British overseas investment also leaped to exceptional levels in the late 1980s (Curwen, 1992, pp. 176–7).

The Discovery and Exploitation of North Sea oil

North Sea oil made a huge impact on the British economy in the 1980s. Before the mid-1970s, Britain was almost entirely dependent for its oil supplies upon imports. As a consequence, like most other advanced industrial countries, it was extremely vulnerable to sudden upward movements in the price of oil, as happened in 1973–4 when the Organisation of Petroleum Exporting Countries (OPEC) suddenly quadrupled its oil prices, immediately plunging Britain along with the rest of the industrialised world into recession. The first significant discovery of offshore oil was made in 1969 and the first oil came ashore in from the North Sea in 1975. Within five years Britain became a major exporter of oil, with large current account surpluses. A trade deficit in oil of nearly £4 billion in 1976 was transformed into a surplus of £273 million in 1980.

Oil production peaked in the mid-1980s – when Britain became the world's sixth largest producer – but declined steadily thereafter. However, Britain was still a net oil exporter in 1990 (Table 3.8) and it is officially predicted that the country will remain self-sufficient in oil well into the 1990s and a significant producer into the twenty-first century. In 1990, the UK was also the world's seventh largest producer of natural gas, with production mainly centred on fields in the North Sea.

North Sea oil and gas had a considerable impact on government revenues in the 1980s. Over the whole decade they brought £65 billion into the Exchequer and helped keep government income buoyant in a period which saw a large increase in spending on unemployment benefits.

(a) North Sea oil production, 1980–90 (million tonnes)				
1981	*1986*	*1989*	*1990*	*1991*
89.3	126.5	91.1	89.8	87.6

(b) UK trade balance in oil, 1978–90 (constant 1980 prices, £m)					
1978	*1980*	*1982*	*1984*	*1986*	*1990*
–2 212	315	3 987	5 318	3 420	1 500

Sources: (a) *Britain 1993: An Official Handbook* (1993, p. 281).
(b) *UK Balance of Payments 1987; Britain 1992: An Official Handbook* (1992, p. 367).

Table 3.8   *Britain's oil*

However, with falling production and a sharp decline in oil prices after 1986, government North Sea revenues dropped to £2.8 billion in 1990–1, compared with over £12 billion in 1984–5. North Sea oil also made a signficant contribution to GDP and the balance of payments. In the mid-1980s, offshore oil production amounted to over 5 per cent of UK GDP and after Britain in 1983 went into deficit on its trade balance in manufactures for the first time, the trade surplus in oil helped for a few years to compensate for this shortfall.

□ *Changes in the Labour Market*

The main recent trends in the workforce have been increased employment in services and declining employment in manufacturing, and a rise in self-employment and part-time working. Table 3.9 shows the trends in the main sectors of the labour market in the last two decades, together with the percentage employed in each sector in 1992. The trend out of manufacturing into services is a long-term one. Between 1955 and 1990 employment in services rose from 36 per cent to 69 per cent whilst manufacturing employment declined from 43 per cent of all employment to under 23 per cent. Services now account for almost three-quarters of all jobs, manufacturing for just over one-fifth. Underpinning the shift from manufacturing to service are changing patterns of consumption as a consequence of greater prosperity and the impact of new – especially computer-based – technology.

Both self-employment and part-time working rose during the 1980s. In part as a result of government policy, the number of self-employed people increased by 75 per cent between 1979 and 1990, when there were 3.2 million self-employed. Part-time work also increased, but more gradually; over one-fifth of all jobs were part-time in 1992.

Table 3.9   *Employment trends, 1971–92*

Sector of employment (Standard Industrial Classification)	*1971*	*Thousands* *1981*	*1992*	*Percent* *1992*
Primary sector	1 248	1 073	686	3.1
Agriculture, forestry and fishing	450	363	283	1.3
Energy and water supply	798	710	403	1.8
Manufacturing	8 065	6 222	4 589	21.1
Construction	1 198	1 130	839	3.9
Services	11 627	13 468	15 644	71.9
Total	22 139	21 893	21 758	100.0

Source: Social Trends (1993, p. 56).

Trade and the Balance of Payments

Overseas trade is of vital importance to the British economy. Britain is currently the fifth largest trading nation in the world and, as a member of the EU, part of a trading bloc which accounts for about a third of world trade. From the late nineteenth century down to the 1960s, British trade with the rest of the world conformed to a particular pattern. Britain imported a large proportion of its food and raw materials and paid for these imports by exports of manufactured goods ('visibles') and services ('invisibles' – banking, insurance and the like). Over the last thirty years, however, this pattern has changed significantly. Imports of food and raw materials have declined – from 60 per cent of the total value of imports in 1956–63 to 15 per cent in 1990. Over the same period the value of manufactured (and semi-manufactured) goods as a proportion of the total value of UK imports increased from 28 per cent to 78 per cent. The long-term position with regard to exports has changed little, with manufactures constituting over four-fifths of the total value of exports in 1955 and in 1990.

The disappearance of Britain's trade surplus in manufactures and the continuing trade deficit in manufactures from that year have been the subject of much comment. The reason for this occurrence was that, despite strong growth in British manufacturing exports, imports of manufactures grew even faster. Import penetration (i.e. imported manufactures as a proportion of all manufactures sold in the UK) rose dramatically during the 1980s from 25 per cent (1980) to 37 per cent (1990).

The geographical distribution of Britain's trade has also changed considerably in recent decades. The main trends in British exports between the early 1960s and the late 1980s may be summarised as follows (proportions shown are of total exports).

- Exports to North America held steady at about one-sixth;
- Exports to former sterling-area countries (mainly Empire and Commonwealth) fell from about two-fifths to one-twentieth;
- Exports to Western Europe rose from about one-third to three-fifths.

By the early 1990s Western Europe – especially the EC – had replaced the Commonwealth as the major focus of British trade, supplying nearly two-thirds of UK imports. In 1990 EC countries provided seven of the UK's top ten export markets and six of the ten main exporters to Britain. For most of the 1980s the US was Britain's largest single market but it was overtaken in this respect in 1990 by Germany, which now accounts for about one-seventh of Britain's total trade. During the 1980s Britain's trade gap (excess of imports over exports) with the European Community grew steadily to a deficit of £9.8 billion in 1990.

Another significant trend has been a decline in Britain's trade with non-oil developing countries (since 1970) and with oil-exporting countries (since the early 1980s). By 1990 Britain's trade was mainly with other developed countries, which supplied 85 per cent of Britain's imports and provided the destinations for 81 per cent of Britain's exports.

International Comparisons

The British economic record since 1945 exhibits something of a paradox. On the one hand, the economy grew faster over the period 1948–73 than during any previous period of similar length in British history – at an annual average rate of 2.8 per cent. This compares with an annual average growth rate of 2 per cent between 1874 and 1914, and with just over 2 per cent between 1923 and 1937 (Cairncross, 1981, p. 376). The growth rate slowed to a little over 1 per cent per annum between 1974 and 1984 but increased to an

	Growth rates in per cent per annum (GDP)						
	1950–55	*1955–60*	*1960–64*	*1964–69*	*1969–73*	*1973–9*	*1979–87*
UK	2.9	2.5	3.4	2.5	2.8	1.4	1.7
USA	4.2	2.4	4.4	4.3	3.4	2.6	2.3
West Germany[1]	9.1	6.4	5.1	4.6	4.5	2.3	1.5
France	4.4	4.8	6.0	5.9	6.1	2.8	1.7
Italy	6.3	5.4	5.5	5.6	4.1	2.6	2.3
Japan	7.1[2]	9.0	11.7	10.9	9.3[3]	3.6	3.9

Notes:
[1] Germany from 1990
[2] 1952–5
[3] GNP

Source: Cairncross (1981) updated with OECD figures for 1973–87.

Table 3.10 *Rates of growth of the UK economy and some international comparisons*

annual average of 3.6 per cent between 1984 and 1988 (Thain, in Jones and Robins 1992, p. 237). These rates of growth meant that income per head in the UK more than doubled between 1951 and 1985. Put another way, the average Briton – man, woman and child –was rather over twice as well off economically in 1985 than in 1951.

However, although the British economy grew at a historically rapid rate for much of the post-war period, it was outstripped by most other advanced industrial countries (Table 3.10). Britain's relative economic decline – which many historians date back to the late nineteenth century – therefore continued. This is the postwar paradox for Britain: faster growth (for much of the period) and greatly increased per capita wealth has been combined with continuing relative economic decline.

Another index of Britain's decline has been its falling share of world trade, which declined from a 10.7 per cent of total world exports (by value) in 1950 to 6.7 per cent in 1970 and 5.3 per cent in 1989. With the exception of the USA, other major advanced nations have either held their own or increased their share. (Table 3.11)

Measuring the wealth of nations is of course a complex matter. Some evaluations are based on more than narrowly economic criteria. According to a United Nations report (1991), Britain ranked

11th out of 160 countries on a human development index which combines expectation of life, levels of education and basic purchasing power. In terms of income per head, Britain ranked rather lower in the early 1990s, having slipped from 9th in 1961 (Gamble, 1990, p. 16). (See Table 3.12.)

The main political consequence of Britain's comparative economic decline has been that from the early 1960s improving the country's economic performance has been a major issue between the parties and a leading goal of governments. Britain's lack of international competitiveness has stemmed in the long term from comparatively

Table 3.11 *Percentage share of world exports (by value), 1970–89*

	1970	*1980*	*1989 (percent)*
UK	6.7	5.8	5.3
USA	14.9	11.8	12.5
West Germany	11.8	10.1	11.7
France	6.2	6.1	6.2
Italy	4.6	4.1	4.9
Japan	6.7	6.8	9.5

Source: Extracted from Thain (1992, p. 238).

Switzerland	35 810
Japan	30 007
Sweden	29 770
Finland	29 700
Norway	28 200
Denmark	26 150
Germany	25 500
Canada	23 870
US	23 720
France	22 900
Austria	22 270
Belgium	21 280
Italy	20 300
Netherlands	19 400
Australia	18 080
UK	17 710
Spain	12 850
Republic of Ireland	12 800
Greece	7 300
Hungary	4 186

Source: Data extracted from *The World in 1992.*

Table 3.12   *GDP per head, 1991 (US dollars)*

low productivity, and the country has also suffered from high rates of inflation and over-valued exchange rates. Although productivity improved during the 1980s, Britain still lags behind other major competitors. Explanations of it have focused on weaknesses in investment, innovation and training, on incompetent economic management by governments, on the excessive influence of the City, and on poor industrial relations.

Summary

Class remains of considerable importance in British society but disagreements over its definition continue. Both occupational and traditional systems of social classification are useful, as is the quite recent distinction between the 'new' working class and the 'traditional' working class.

The main structural change in British society since 1945 has been the expansion of the middle class and the contraction of the working class as a result of the growth in professional and white collar and the decrease in manual occupations. Social mobility has occurred largely through this process rather than through the operation of greater equality of opportunity. In the period since 1960, as visible class differences have diminished, social divisions based on gender, race, nation and region have become increasingly significant.

Important structural changes have occurred in Britain's economy, involving the continuing decline of manufacturing industry, large-scale transfers of ownership from the public to the private sector (in the 1980s) and a redirection of UK trade away from the Commonwealth and former empire towards Western Europe, especially the EC. Increasing prosperity (the result of historically rapid growth rates over much of the postwar period) helped to soften – and to some extent masked – the fact of continuing and accelerating economic decline. Differences of analysis and policy over de-industrialisation and decline lie at the heart of the party debate which is explored later in the book.

Questions

1. 'Class is the most important division in British society.' Discuss.
2. Why is the state of economy so important in politics?

Assignment

Study the following extract from *Social Trends* (1992, p. 27), and then:
(i)   Work out the percentages of the numbers of people in the 65–79, the 80 and over, and the 65 and over age-groups, 1951–86.
(ii) Briefly state the trends you find.
(iii) After examining the projections for 1991–2011, write a short report on the possible consequences of these trends and projections for social policy.

	Under 16	16–39	40–64	65–79	80 and over	All ages
Mid-year estimates						
1951			15.9	4.8	0.7	50.3
1961	13.1	16.6	16.9	5.2	1.0	52.8
1971	14.3	17.5	16.7	6.1	1.3	55.9
1981	12.5	19.7	15.7	6.9	1.6	56.4
1986	11.7	20.6	15.8	6.8	1.8	56.8
1990	11.6	20.3	16.5	6.9	2.1	57.4
Males	6.0	10.3	8.2	3.0	0.6	28.0
Females	5.7	10.0	8.3	3.9	1.5	29.4
Mid-year projections[1]						
1991	11.7	20.3	16.5	6.9	2.2	57.6
1996	12.3	19.9	17.1	6.8	2.4	58.4
2001	12.6	19.3	18.1	6.7	2.5	59.2
2006	12.5	18.4	19.5	6.7	2.6	59.7
2011	12.1	18.0	20.2	7.0	2.7	60.0
2025	12.0	18.5	19.0	8.6	2.9	61.0
Males	6.1	9.5	9.5	4.0	1.1	30.2
Females	5.8	9.1	9.5	4.6	1.8	30.8

Source: *Social Trends* (1992).
[1] 1989-based projections

Table 3.13   *Age and sex structure of the population of the UK in millions*

Further Reading

Abercrombie, N. and Warde, A. (1988) *Contemporary British Society* (Cambridge: Polity).

Ball, M., Gray, F. and McDowell, L. (1989) *The Transformation of Britain* (London: Fontana).

Cairncross, A. (1981) 'The Post-War Years, 1945–1977' in R. Floud and D. McCloskey (eds) (1981) *The Economic History of Britain Since 1700*, vol. 2 (Cambridge: Cambridge University Press).

Curwen, P. (ed.) (1992) *Understanding the UK Economy*, 2nd edn (London: Macmillan).

Donaldson, P. and Farquhar, J. (1988) *Understanding the British Economy* (Harmondsworth: Penguin).

Gamble, A. (1990) *Britain in Decline*, 3rd edn (London: Macmillan).

Halsey, A.H. (ed.) (1988) *Trends in British Society Since 1900* (London: Macmillan).

McDowell, L., Sarre, P. and Hamnett, C. (1989) *Divided Nation: Social and Cultural Change in Britain* (London: Hodder & Stoughton).

Rose, R. (1982) *Understanding the United Kingdom: The Territorial Dimension in Government* (London: Longman).

Routh, G. (1987) *Occupations of the People of Great Britain 1901–1981* (London: Macmillan).

Smith, D. (1989) *North and South: Britain's Economic, Social and Political Divide* (Harmondsworth: Penguin).

Smith, K. (1989) *The British Economic Crisis* (Harmondsworth: Penguin).

Annual Abstract of Statistics (HMSO).

Britain 1992: An Official Handbook (HMSO).

Britain 1993: An Official Handbook (HMSO).

Social Trends (HMSO).

■ *Chapter 4* ■

Political Culture

Political Culture: A Definition
National Identity and Symbols of
 Nationhood

Political Competence and Participation
Political Socialisation

In the last two chapters, we have considered the major themes in postwar British history and outlined the main social and economic characteristics of contemporary society. These provide an essential context for an understanding of contemporary British politics. We now turn to another important dimension. What feelings do people hold towards the political unit in which they live? What are people's attitudes towards government itself – its scope, competence and trustworthiness? How capable of influencing its decisions do they consider themselves? Finding an answer to such questions involves us in a consideration of political culture.

■ Political Culture: A Definition

A political culture may be defined as the pattern of understandings, feelings and attitudes which dispose people towards behaving in a particular way politically. It consists of the opinions and beliefs that shape political behaviour. A political culture is the collective expression of the political outlooks and values of the individuals who make up society. It has been well described as 'the totality of the citizenry's collective feelings about the political system and each individual's place in it'. (Parry *et al.*, 1992, p. 172). All societies possess a political culture.

In the immediate post-1945 period, it was customary to describe British political culture in terms of three main characteristics: homogeneity;

consensus; and deference. These concepts may be summarised as follows:

- **Homogeneity:** the view that shared political values and a sense of community over and above cultural, national and political differences are prevalent in Britain. These facilitated political cooperation and fostered a widespread feeling of common purpose.

- **Consensus:** a reference to the way in which political divisions are held in check by common adherence to certain procedures for settling differences, to 'the rules of the democratic game', i.e. peaceful parliamentary methods.

- **Deference:** this term in its most common meaning denotes the willing submission of the majority to a political élite often seen as 'born to rule'. Such an attitude is underpinned by a broader popular acceptance of social inequality and hierarchy. A study of Britain researched in the 1950s found that the balance between active, participatory "citizen" attitudes and more passive, deferential "subject" inclinations was weighted 'too heavily' in the direction of the latter (Almond and Verba, 1965, p. 361).

This general model of British political culture has been subjected since 1970 to important criticisms. The general point is that, far from bringing out its timeless characteristics, the model simply describes the political culture at a particular time – the 1950s. Specific criticisms are:

Homogeneity: the 'homogeneity' thesis under-estimated the impact of differences of national culture upon the United Kingdom. Historically, diversity and plurality rather than homogeneity have been the rule. Since the 1960s, the effects of New Commonwealth immigration, the rise of Scottish and Welsh nationalism, and the recurrence of the Irish question have combined to undermine social homogeneity and fragment political values within the UK.

Consensus: the consensus theory ignored the role played by military force and economic power in the making of the UK. In other words, it gave too little consideration to the historical dimension – and to the extent to which conflicts were settled by force rather than consensus. Procedural consensus remains important although since the 1970s it has been challenged 'on the streets' by groups using direct action such as striking miners, city rioters – in Toxteth, Brixton, Handsworth and North Tyneside – and poll tax protestors, and by groups using extreme violence such as the IRA (Irish Republican Army).

Deference: traditionally, deferential attitudes depended upon the social isolation of the political élite supported by a powerful norm of secrecy. Increasingly, in recent decades, these attitudes have been eroded by the emergence of a populist culture characterised and shaped by media disrespect for authority figures. Pragmatic evaluations of governments' competence together with calculations of self-interest have displaced deference to a political élite as the main influence on voting behaviour. (Kavanagh, 1971 and 1980; Moran, 1989).

National Identity and Symbols of Nationhood

The political culture of the United Kingdom is no longer – if it ever was – 'homogeneous', but rather multinational. Most people in the UK see themselves as primarily English, Welsh, Scottish, Northern Irish or Irish (Tables 4.1 and 4.2). But these national identities are not exclusive and for

Thinks of self as	*England* %	*Scotland* %	*Wales* %
British	38	35	33
Scottish	2	52	–
Welsh	1	–	57
English	57	2	8
Irish	1	1	–
Other; mixed; don't know	1	10	2

Sources: Extracted from Rose (1982, p. 14).

Table 4.1   *National identity in Mainland Britain*

the great majority of inhabitants of the UK they coexist with a fundamental sense of 'Britishness'. Britain, as Hugh Kearney has aptly said, is both 'four nations and one' (Crick (ed.) 1991, p. 4) and Britons possess a dual loyalty – to a particular segment of the UK and to Britain as a whole. A sizeable minority of people in each part of the UK see themselves as primarily 'British'.

Each of the mainland UK nations has a different sense of 'Britishness'. The English identify more closely with 'Britishness' than the other two; traditionally, they have tended to equate the two and even now often confuse them. However, many Scots and Welsh have become cooler towards the 'British' identity in recent decades. The disappearance of the British Empire, a unifying force which bound the nations of the UK in a common enterprise, provided the psychological space for the growth of nationalism in the countries on the periphery of the UK. This movement has been strongest in Scotland where a substantial minority would like to shed the British connection altogether.

In Northern Ireland, the situation is different again. A larger proportion than on the mainland define themselves as 'British', although using the term in its legal and political rather than its cultural meaning; on the other hand, a sizeable minority think of themselves as 'Irish', thereby identifying themselves with a nation outside the United Kingdom, the Republic of Ireland.

Percentage thinking of themselves as	Total	Protestant	Roman Catholic
British	44	66	10
Irish	25	4	60
Ulster	7	10	2
Northern Irish	20	16	25
Sometimes British/ sometimes Irish	3	3	4

Source: R. Jowell *et al.* (eds) (1990, p. 198).

Table 4.2 *Religious affiliation and cultural identity in Northern Ireland*

Religious differences underlie the divisions in the political culture (Table 4.2).

The strong correlation between religious affiliation and cultural/political identity in Northern Ireland is evident from this table. Two-thirds of Protestants think of themselves as British whilst three-fifths of Catholics consider themselves to be Irish. (For further discussion of the multinational nature of the United Kingdom and its political consequences, see Chapters 5,13 and 29.)

In various ways, then, the concept of 'Britishness' has become more problematic since 1945, more obviously a political and legal concept, less of a cultural one. It is threatened from below by peripheral nationalisms, but also from above by the development of the European Union. Large numbers of Britons continue to resist the EU as a source of loyalty. An ICM 'State of the Nation' poll (1992) found that 45 per cent supported closer British links with the EC even if this meant some loss of sovereignty. A Gallup poll of 15 000 Europeans (1991) found that of the ten countries surveyed Britain was the most fearful of losing national identity and sacrificing national economic interests. As many as 68 per cent of Britons expressed their willingness 'to fight for their country', compared with the European average of 45 per cent, whilst 51.6 per cent of Britons were very proud of their nationality against a European average of just over 36 per cent. But the EU is more popular with the 18–24 age group than the rest of society so a sense of 'European-ness' is likely to increase. In another very important

sense, however, 'Britishness' has been an integrative force since the 1950s – in providing a focus for the allegiance of New Commonwealth immigrants and their descendants, who have become 'Black Britons' rather than 'Black English', 'Black Scots' or 'Black Welsh'.

□ *The British Monarchy*

The UK has many national and ethnic subcultures but a sense of unity does exist. The major symbols of this national cohesion are the Union Jack – the United Kingdom flag – and the monarchy. Whereas the main focus of people's attachment in a republic such as the United States is the President, who combines the ceremonial role of head of state with that of effective head of government, in Britain it is the monarch, now almost reduced to a purely ceremonial function, who symbolises the nation. A comparative survey of social attitudes in Britain and Germany confirmed the central significance of the monarchy as a source of national pride in Britain whilst suggesting that the Basic Law (Constitution) performed a similar role for West Germans (Table 4.3).

There are interesting social differences in the disposition of people to place the monarchy first as a source of national pride. Thus, women had a greater propensity to do so than men; those aged over 60 than younger groups; people professing allegiance to the Church of England than Roman Catholics; those without qualifications more than those with intermediate qualifications; manual and routine non-manual workers more than salaried workers, and far more than graduates; and finally inhabitants of the English North, Midlands, East Anglia, South-East and South-West rather more than people living in Greater London, Wales and Scotland. Unsurprisingly, then, attachment to the major national symbol is influenced by social and subcultural differences of gender, age, religion, occupational class and region. How far the well-published marital difficulties of the younger Royals in the early 1990s will affect long-term public support for the monarchy remains to be seen, but a Gallup poll

Percentage expressing pride in	Britain		West Germany	
	1st choice (%)	In top three (%)	1st choice (%)	In top three (%)
Monarchy	37	65	–	–
Basic law	–	–	30	51
Scientific achievements	22	61	8	38
Welfare state	16	52	11	40
Parliament	8	33	1	10
Sporting achievements	5	29	7	21
Artistic achievements	3	21	6	21
Economic achievements	2	16	17	51
Nothing	7	n/a	20	n/a

Source: R. Jowell *et al.* (eds) (1989, p. 125).

Table 4.3   *Sources of national pride in Britain and West Germany*

in 1993 – in which a mere 26 per cent expressed pride in the monarchy – suggested that in the short term at least public confidence in the institution had declined.

□ *Support for the Political System*

There is widespread endorsement by Britons of the system of liberal democracy and how it is currently functioning. Only a tiny minority consider that the political system does not work well and needs to be completely changed. However, support for the system is not uncritical, and three-quarters of those who consider it is working well believe it requires some changes (Table 4.4). The British political culture is profoundly unrevolutionary and revolution is literally inconceivable to most of the population. In 1984, a

mere 7 per cent said that they thought it likely that the Government would be overthrown in the next decade (Jowell and Airey (eds.) 1984, p. 31). It has been aptly stated that the British remain 'improbable revolutionaries' (Jowell and Topf, 1988). Support for the democratic system – and procedural consensus – remains widespread.

□ *Support for Government*

However, a basic public confidence in the political *system*, even if for the majority this is linked with the feeling that it could be improved, is accompanied by fairly widespread cynicism about governments and politicians. Thus, two researchers in the late 1980s concluded that:

> For all Britain's political and social stability over the years, and despite the obvious pride its people have in their system of government, the British reveal an uncompromisingly irreverent and critical streak which runs too deep to be dismissed as a mannerism. The public trust in the pillars of the British Establishment is at best highly qualified. (Jowell and Topf, 1988, p. 120)

Under two-fifths of respondents to a survey trusted governments to place national needs above the interests of their own party (Figure 4.1). Large majorities of respondents to *British Social Attitudes* (BSA) surveys agreed with the

Table 4.4   *Support for liberal democracy in Britain*

System of democracy	(%)
.....works well and needs no changes	15
.....works well and needs some changes	66
.....does not work well and needs a lot of changes	15
.....does not work well and needs to be completely changed	4

Extracted from R. Jowell *et al.* (eds) (1989, p. 133).

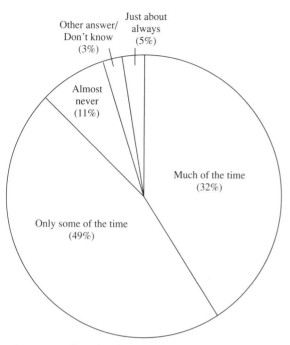

Other answer/
Don't know
(3%)

Just about
always
(5%)

Almost
never
(11%)

Much of the time
(32%)

Only some of the time
(49%)

Source: Based on data from R. Jowell *et al.* (eds) (1988, p. 123).

Figure 4.1   *Trust in government in Britain*

(Percentages trusting British Governments of any party to place the needs of the nation above the interests of their own party)

propositions that 'Generally speaking... MPs lose touch with people pretty quickly' (70 per cent) and that 'parties are only interested in people's votes, not in their opinions' (66 per cent) (Jowell *et al.* (eds) 1987).

Whilst extremely cynical, disaffected attitudes are confined to a tiny minority (Parry *et al.*, 1992 pp. 180–1), a degree of political cynicism is widespread.

In fact, however, political cynicism in British political culture is nothing new and has been found by virtually all political investigators going back to the 1940s. It was present but unstressed in the Civic Culture study in 1950s and it was also evident in a 1944 study which revealed that only 36 per cent of those questioned trusted politicians to do what was best for the country whereas 35 per cent saw them as out for themselves and 22 per cent as out for their party (Almond and Verba, 1965; Topf, 1989; Kavanagh 1980).

Comparative studies within and outside the UK shed further light on this aspect of the British political culture. Unsurprisingly, perhaps, trust in government is lower in Northern Ireland than in the UK as a whole: only a quarter of respondents to a survey of opinion in the Province trusted British government to act in the interests of Northern Ireland 'just about always' (4 per cent) and 'most of the time' (21 per cent) (Jowell *et al.* (eds) 1990, p. 205.) But a study comparing Britain with other advanced industrial democracies found Britain occupying a slightly below median position with regard to trust in government and politicians: less trusting and more cynical than West Germany, Austria and Switzerland but more trusting and less cynical than the USA and Italy (Parry *et al.*, 1992, p. 181).

☐ *Support for Public Officials*

A certain amount of cynicism about governments and politicians in Britain is combined with a much higher degree of trust in public officials such as civil servants and the police (Table 4.5). Public confidence varies to some extent according to party sympathies. For example, confidence in the police is significantly higher among Conservative than Labour supporters. Of Conservative identifiers, 62 per cent trusted the British police not to bend the rules in trying to get a conviction 'just about always' (14 per cent) and 'most of the time' (48 per cent) whereas only 41 per cent of Labour identifiers expressed this degree of trust (6 per cent 'just about always' and 35 per cent 'most of the time'). Unsurprisingly, in view of the

Table 4.5   *Confidence in public officials*

	Can be trusted to serve the public interest 'just about always' or 'most of the time' (%)
The police	51
Civil servants	46
Governments of any party	37
Local councillors of any party	31

Source: taken from R. Jowell *et al.* (eds) (1988, p. 112).

well-publicised cases of police malpractice, public confidence in the police seems to have declined in the early 1990s, although an ICM poll reported 60 per cent had retained their faith in police honesty (*The Guardian*, 12 December 1991).

The evidence therefore suggests that the public has greater confidence in public officials than in politicians but also that its trust is far from complete.

For the majority of Britons, therefore, trust in political authority – government, MPs and public officials – is generally qualified. Complete trust in political authority and total alienation from it are almost equally unusual. The majority express a greater or lesser degree of scepticism. A survey of political trust in the late 1980s concluded: 'the British do not, and perhaps never did, hold their leaders in any awe. Public figures and the institutions they run are regarded realistically as fallible and flawed' (Jowell and Topf, 1988, p. 120).

Political Competence and Participation

Traditionally, citizen efficacy or competence – the belief by individuals that they are able to influence government decisions – has been seen as a vital element in an effective democratic society. How able to wield political influence do British citizens feel today, by what means would they seek to do so and how many of them have actually tried to act on their beliefs?

There are several measures of citizen competence or, put another way, individual political efficacy. The main ones are: people's perceptions of the efficacy of their votes in general, local and other elections; their perceptions of their ability acting both as individuals and in groups to influence Members of Parliament (MPs); and their notions of their capacity through individual and collective action to change an unjust law. A major study has addressed the first two questions. It found that about three-quarters of the sample believed that their individual votes could make a difference in elections. However, only about one-third believed that people like themselves *as individuals* could have any influence over MPs.

But when asked what influence over MPs they might possess when acting *in a group*, people gave more optimistic responses, approximately two-thirds considering that in those circumstances they would be able to exercise some influence. This study concluded that 'feelings of political efficacy are fairly widely held in the population at large' (Parry *et al.* (1992), p. 174). A recent survey addressed the third theme. Over two-fifths of its respondents (44 per cent) stated that they had taken some action to change an unjust law (Jowell *et al.* (eds) 1987, p. 57).

How do British citizens seek to exercise political influence? Table 4.6 gives the responses to a survey in which those questioned were asked to imagine that a law which they considered to be unjust or harmful was under consideration by parliament and then to choose which if any of a series of listed actions they would take and which they believed to be effective. They were also asked to state whether they had ever actually carried out any of these actions. The most popular form of action was signing a petition; nearly two-thirds stated that this is what they *would* do, and over one-third had actually done so. Next most popular was contacting an MP: about half the sample testified both that this is the action they

Table 4.6 *Citizen competence and participation in Britain*

	I Would do	II Had ever done	III Believed 'very' or 'quite effective'
Sign petition	65	34	45
Contact your MP	52	11	50
Contact radio, TV or newspaper	15	3	58
Contact government department	12	3	26
Go on protest or demonstration	11	6	21

Raise issue in organ-
  isation you
  belong to
	10	5	32

Form group of like- minded people	8	2	26

Source: R. Jowell *et al.* (eds) (1987, p. 56).

would take *and* believed it to be effective, but only a little over one-tenth had actually done so.

These figures suggest several conclusions. First, the least strenuous mode of political expression (petition-signing) was easily the most common and, when this is set aside, attempts to influence legislators are confined to a small, albeit significant, minority. According to the *BSA* survey, excluding signers of petitions, 20 per cent of respondents had done something in an effort to influence parliament (R. Jowell *et al.* (eds) 1987, p. 57). Parry and his colleagues also found that 'substantial minorities' had contacted political institutions and political figures of various sorts, with as many as one-fifth having got in touch with local representatives. Second, potential for action was higher than actual involvement, judging from responses to the question about what respondents *would do* if they deemed it necessary. Even accepting that this is an area where it is necessary to proceed with caution, responses to columns I and III of the *BSA* survey suggest that an even larger proportion of people than actually participate feel confident in their ability to influence the political process if necessary and also believe that effective mechanisms exist for them to do so. Parry *et al.* also found a larger proportion would 'certainly' or 'probably' consider certain key forms of action than had actually done so: for example, nearly one-quarter (24.2 per cent) would consider contacting an MP, nearly one-fifth (18.8 per cent) a civil servant and over one-tenth (11.0 per cent) the media (Parry *et al.*, p. 423). All this suggests that despite the political passivity of the majority, participation potential and a sense of political efficacy are relatively widespread.

□ A 'Moderate' Political Culture

Has the often-remarked increasing resort to violence in British society in the 1980s and early 1990s with regard to rising levels of recorded crime, IRA terrorism and urban rioting at Brixton, Toxteth, Handsworth and elsewhere spilled over into the political culture? At least since the eighteenth century, Britain has been widely regarded as possessing a 'moderate' political culture, in which the norms of the rule of law and parliamentary government enjoy wide public endorsement. Even under the severe social strains and ideological pressures of the 1930s, there was no descent by more than a tiny minority into illegal or violent forms of protest. How far has this relatively mild political culture survived the impact of rapid and far-reaching postwar social change?

The evidence points to continuing high levels of public support for orderly, peaceful methods of political protest, but only minority support for direct action such as political strikes and very little support for methods involving violence against property such as damaging government buildings. The 1987 *BSA* survey which asked people to state what forms of protest should 'definitely' or 'probably' be allowed provides a useful indication of the public legitimacy accorded to various means of protest (Table 4.7).

The British Political Participation Study (BPPS) focused on what protest action people themselves 'would', 'might' and 'would never' consider. It might be expected that forms of orderly protest which require a certain amount of effort would

Table 4.7 *Opinions on the legitimacy of types of public protest*

Percentage saying that different forms of protest should 'definitely' or 'probably' be allowed	
Organising public meetings to protest against the government	83
Publishing pamphlets to protest against the government	78
Organising protest marches and demonstrations	58
Organising a nationwide strike of all workers against the government	28
Occupying a government office and stopping work there for several days	10
Seriously damaging government buildings	2

Source: R. Jowell *et al.* (eds) (1987, p. 58).

	Would 'certainly' or 'probably' consider (%)	'Might' consider (%)	Would 'never' consider (%)
Attending protest meeting	23.8	39.8	36.4
Circulating petition	14.0	36.4	49.6
Blocking traffic	2.4	9.2	88.4
Protest march	7.3	20.3	72.4
Political strike	8.0	15.8	76.2
Political boycott	9.5	25.8	64.7

Source: Extracted from Parry *et al.* (1992, p. 423).

Table 4.8   *Personal attitudes to types of public protest*

receive less support than in the *BSA* survey simply because people might consider that a particular type of protest should be lawful, e.g. a protest march or demonstration, but never themselves consider going on one. Thus, nearly three-fifths in the BSA survey consider that organising protest marches and demonstrations ought to be permitted but only just over one-quarter of respondents to the BPPS would or might consider going on a protest march. But for the other main categories of protest there is a considerable and quite predictable overlap between the findings of the two studies. Thus the study by Parry and his colleagues shows that whilst a majority are prepared to engage in the milder forms of protest such as attending a protest meeting, far larger majorities would 'never' consider more vigorous – including illegal – protest actions. (Table 4.8)

The conclusion reached by the BPPS – that the only form of protest to have increased down to the mid-1980s was the signing of petitions (p. 420) – may require modification in the early 1990s in the light of the widespread discontent and protest generated by the 'poll tax' between 1989 and 1992. The Anti-Poll Tax Movement employed a wide range of methods of protest, including lobbying of MPs and councillors, petitions and demonstrations; on occasion, it was involved in violent disturbances such as the riot in March 1990 at Trafalgar Square which ended with over 140 being injured. More significant still, its massive campaign of non-payment

'tapped into' a long tradition of civil disobedience in Britain. In the first six months of 1992 alone, nearly 4 million people were summonsed for failing to pay the tax. This popular non-cooperation – fuelled by an admittedly rare combination of moral outrage and material self-interest – forced the Government to back down and withdraw the tax (Barr, 1992).

Participation and Political Culture

We now examine political participation in its broadest sense, including voting, party and group activity, alongside the contacting and protesting forms of behaviour already considered.

Figure 4.2 provides a breakdown of the incidence of types of participation on a simple scale ranging from virtual inactivity through simply casting a vote in elections to various kinds of greater political activity. It is based on the British Political Participation Survey, which contains an

Figure 4.2   *Political participation in Britain*

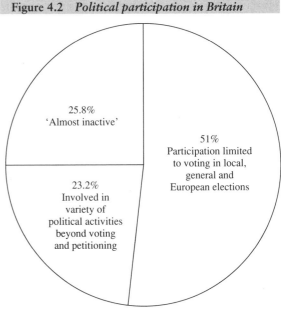

Source: Adapted from Parry and Moyser (1990, p. 150).

informative sub-division of the most politically active category of citizens. This category included – 'collective activists' (8.7 per cent), who tended to be members of groups and to be involved in such activities as organising or signing a petition and attending a protest meeting; 'contacting activists' (7.7 per cent), who were mainly contact officials and representatives; 'direct activists' (3.1 per cent), characterised mainly by the frequency of their direct action; and party campaigners (2.2 per cent), who were principally engaged in fund-raising, canvassing and clerical work and attending rallies. Only a tiny minority – 1.5 per cent of the BPPS sample – were involved in a wide variety of political activity across the range, which encompassed voting, party campaigning, group activity, contacting and numerous kinds of protest. On this basis, it was estimated that real activists number about 625 000 in an adult population of about 41.6 million (Parry and Moyser, 1990, p. 150). However, demanding activity over such a wide field may be regarded as too 'heroic' a requirement for the active citizen. Perhaps it would be more reasonable to consider involvement on a fairly regular basis in any of the activities beyond voting and petition signing as an indicator of a politically active individual. On such rather less stringent criteria, a significant minority of Britons (between one-fifth and one-quarter) may be regarded as active citizens.

There are strong links between education and participation. The BPPS found that graduates were among the top 12 per cent on the overall participation scale whereas those without formal qualifications had on average performed little in the way of political activity beyond voting and petitioning. The *BSA* investigation found that graduates were more likely to have contacted an MP, signed a petition and gone on a demonstration than those with intermediate qualifications, and the last-named group were more likely to have engaged in these three activities than those with no qualifications (Parry and Moyser, 1990 p. 155; R. Jowell *et al.* (eds) 1987, p. 65). Education builds self-confidence, increases political knowledge and provides literary skills, all of which are necessary for significant political participation.

There is an even stronger connection between group membership, especially trade unions and parties, and vigorous political participation. According to the BPPS, about two-thirds of the population belong to at least one formal voluntary group but only about one-seventh belong to four groups or more. This latter minority, however, is disproportionately represented among all types of political activist, especially collective (over one-third), party campaigners (nearly three-quarters) and the tiny proportion of 'complete activists' whose activities span the whole range of political involvement (nearly half). Group resources are cumulative, with members of trade unions and political parties tending to be associated also with other voluntary groups, and this degree of social integration in turn frequently generates a higher than average level of political activism, especially among party members (Parry *et al.*, 1992, pp. 91, 234).

Finally, higher than average political participation is related to political values. Those holding strong or extreme political views tend to participate well above average, with overall participation highest on the extreme left. By contrast, the moderate centre tends to under-participate. Parry and Moyser conclude: 'The 1980s may have been an era of Conservative electoral hegemony but the voice of activism was generally from left of stage' (Parry and Moyser, 1990, p. 162). Secondly, in this sphere, political values associated with the 'new' or 'post-materialist' politics of environmentalism, peace and feminism are also linked to higher than average participation. But whereas holders of strong/extreme views on the traditional left–right spectrum were very active in all fields of political activity, strong adherents of the 'new' politics express their ideological commitments through collective and direct action far more than through more conventional forms of participation (Parry *et al.*, 1992, p. 216). Much of the new concern for the environment was expressed at the local level by people who have been described as 'sporadic interventionists' – individuals protesting about a threat to their own backyards who withdraw from the public arena once their purpose has been achieved. To the extent that 'green', internationalist, lifestyles and feminist issues continue to rise in political significance, it may be expected that political activism too will increase.

Public Opinion and Participation

The ideal for radical democrats such as John Stuart Mill is the active citizen, the person who is not only politically well informed but who also plays a vigorous part in the affairs of the community. To what extent, however, do people today themselves wish for a greater political role? How widespread are participatory values?

The BPPS tested the desire for more participation by asking respondents whether they thought (1) that ordinary citizens should have more say in the decisions made by government or whether those decisions were best left to elected representatives such as MPs or local councillors; (2) whether the public should be given more access to government documents even if it made the government's job more difficult; and (3) whether workers and employees should have more say in how the places where they work are run. These questions probed public opinion not only on political participation but also upon more open government, which may be seen as a prerequisite of a more participatory society, and on workplace democracy.

Only in the sphere of work did an overwhelming majority (four-fifths) express a wish for greater participation. This seems to be an issue which has steadily gained in public favour since the 1970s. According to the British Election Studies, the proportion of respondents agreeing that 'workers should be given more say in running the places where they work' rose from 56 per cent in 1974 to 80 per cent in 1986. (*British Social Attitudes*, 1987, p. 58). With regard to political participation, however, the majority – although a small one – favoured leaving decision-making to elected representatives. On the other hand, there was a majority (nearly three-fifths, 58.3 per cent) in support of more open government. These findings suggest a widespread desire for greater involvement and autonomy at work

combined with rather less widespread but still majority support for reforms that would bring about a more politically informed society. A sizeable minority (47.6 per cent) would like to play a greater role in government decision-making at local and/or national level.

To what extent do those who believe strongly in a more participatory society act on their principles by themselves participating politically more than the average? It has already been noticed that people who are strongly committed to a particular ideology tend to participate above the norm. The BPPS also found that a firm belief in the value of participation provided an impetus to greater activism, although a 'relatively modest' one. However, this generalisation requires careful analysis. A belief in greater participation did not increase participation in such matters as voting, contacting and party campaigning. Only with regard to collective action and, especially, direct action was there a strong link between holding participatory beliefs and greater political activism. Committed participationists were involved in direct action (e.g. strikes, demonstrations, road blocks) to a degree second only to the far left and higher than the most fervent supporters of feminism, environmentalism and the peace movement (Parry *et al.*, 1992, pp. 218, 221–3).

■ Political Socialisation

The process by which people come to understand and mentally absorb the culture of their society is referred to as socialisation, and the process by which they acquire knowledge of their political culture is known as political socialisation. The notion of **political socialisation** holds that people's political knowledge, values, attitudes and beliefs are *learned* in a process which begins in childhood and continues throughout their adult lives. Although political socialisation is best seen as continuous, certain phases seem to be particularly important. Because of the malleability of the young and their greater exposure and susceptibility to influences, it is generally held that the pre-adult years are of critical significance to political socialisation, even though political orientations learned when young may be modified or changed as a result of later experiences and pressures.

The sources which influence the political learning of an individual are called **the agencies of political socialisation**. These agencies supply a range of political information, values and attitudes which individuals may absorb both consciously and subconsciously. The most influential agencies are the family, education, peer groups and the media. Inevitably, they reflect a changing political context. The manner in which these agencies combine and which of them is the major influence varies, of course, for each individual. Often, because of the depth and intensity of the emotional relationships it involves, the family is the predominating influence. It passes on an ethnic, religious and class identity, which normally is associated with a particular set of political orientations, and it powerfully shapes a child's attitude to authority, to gender roles, and to values (individualistic/cooperative, authoritarian/ democratic, tough-minded/tender-minded) which have clear implications for political behaviour. But no influence, however powerful, is totally determinative of political outlooks. Even in the case of the family, people may rebel as teenagers or gradually grow away from its values as adults. Often the political 'messages' emitted by the various agencies of political socialisation overlap and mutually reinforce each other. They may be all the more influential as a result. But sometimes – from books, films or television, from friends or at work – an individual receives and has to accommodate a 'message' which conflicts with the overall view of the world derived from the other agencies. If it cannot be reconciled with the existing cultural perspective, it may bring about change in it.

The main agencies of political socialisation are themselves continually evolving. The considerable increase in recent decades of divorce and birth outside marriage may be weakening the family, thereby undermining its effectiveness as a mechanism for transmitting the political culture. In recent decades, also, the proportion of the population with qualifications at all levels has risen steadily and in the longer term an educated population may be expected to be a more participatory one. To date, however, the educational developments of the last twenty years do not seem to have produced any significant changes in political knowledge among young people, whilst in the 1987 General Election voting turn-out amongst the 18–24 age group was almost 20 per cent below that for 25–64-year-olds (Denver and Hands, 1992, pp. 101–2).

Changes in the media may also be expected to have had an impact on the political socialisation process. The period since the 1970s has been characterised by the growing predominance of television as the major source of public information about politics and an increasing pro-Conservative bias in the press (see Chapter 16).

Finally, the political outlook of each generation is powerfully shaped by the dominant ideas and institutions of the age into which it is born. Table 4.9 illustrates the changes – and the continuities – in the political contexts of people growing up over the last four decades. In seeking to understand political attitudes and behaviour, it makes sense to consider the often sharply contrasting experiences of political 'generations', whether these are moulded by the carnage of the First World War, the 1930s Depression, the post-1945 welfare state, the 'permissive society' of the 1960s, or the Thatcherite era of free markets and the 'enterprise culture'.

A political culture then is dynamic rather than static and itself subject to constant modification as a consequence of social, economic and political change. There are always, of course, important continuities. For example, despite the Thatcherite attack on statism, support for state welfare provision remained undiminished among the general public and among the young in the late 1980s. A survey of 6 250 sixth-formers between 1986 and 1988 found strong approval of the core principles of the welfare state among both sexes. (Denver and Hands, 1990, p. 111). Amongst young first-time voters (aged 18–24), Labour had a small lead over the Conservatives, of respectively 3 per cent and 4 per cent in the 1987 and 1992 General Elections (Butler and Kavanagh 1988, p. 275, and 1992, p. 277).

Table 4.9   *Political 'generations' and the political culture*

Political generation	Political context
1960s	Consensus over interventionist role of the state. Two-party domination and prevalence of traditional left-right issues. 'Permissive society' reforms: liberalisation of laws on abortion, divorce, homosexuality and capital punishment. Abroad: Cold War, USA in Vietnam.
1970s	Erosion of consensus. Two-party politics but rapid growth of third parties – Nationalists, Liberals. Emergence of new issues: Europe, feminism, environmentalism, peace, nationalism. Union militancy leading to 'ungovernability' debate. Northern Ireland issue again; IRA terrorism. Abroad: Cold War, USA pulls out of Vietnam.
1980s	Thatcherite conviction politics; rejection of consensus. Sharply polarised politics as major parties move left and right; formation of Liberal–Social Democratic Alliance and strong electoral performance by centre. Continuing IRA terrorism. Falklands War. Abroad: intensification of nuclear rivalry between two major powers followed by disintegration of USSR, break-up of its East European empire and end of Cold War.
1990s	Conservative political domination continues; Labour's fourth consecutive general election defeat (1992); collapse of Alliance. IRA terrorism. Abroad: only one major power remaining (USA). Gulf War (1991) and further attacks on Iraq (1992); civil war in former Yugoslavia.

However, to return to the theme of discontinuity between the political experience of generations with which we began, support for Labour among the young was far stronger twenty years previously. In 1970, coming of age at a time when Labour was in power and the class-based labourist ethos still vigorous, young people aged 18–24 divided nearly 2–1 in favour of Labour (Butler and Stokes, 1974), p. 241). Again, although majorities or substantial pluralities of the sixth-formers surveyed between 1986 and 1988 favoured left-wing positions on the redistribution of wealth, the health service and the welfare state, majorities or substantial pluralities took right-wing positions on unilateralism and the renationalisation of privatised industries (Denver and Hands, 1992, p. 106). Political and ideological change mould the political culture transmitted by the main agencies of political socialisation.

Summary

Political culture consists of the pattern of feelings, attitudes and understandings disposing people to behave in particular ways politically; it embodies people's collective perceptions of the political system and their place in it. Key attitudes are those relating to the political unit, the nation, the regime, the government, parties, politicians and public officials, political competence (or efficacy) and political participation.

In the UK more people think of themselves as primarily English, Scots, Welsh or 'Irish' than as British, although the monarchy is an important source of cohesion within the political unit, as is pride in certain British achievements and institutions. There is strong support for the liberal democratic regime within a moderate political culture profoundly addicted to parliamentary methods.

There is little public support for direct action and, in a deeply non-revolutionary country, absolutely negligible sympathy for violent methods of political protest. These attitudes are combined with a significant degree of cynicism about governments, parties and politicians, although confidence in public officials remains at a higher level. Although political activism (i.e. activity beyond voting and petitioning) is limited to a minority (just under one-quarter), feelings of political competence are more widespread. Political participation beyond the average is linked to levels of education, group membership and the holding of specific political values, especially those on the far left, those concerned with the 'new politics' and those favouring a more participatory society. Surveys suggest that a majority of Britons favour more participation.

The political culture is transmitted through the process of political socialisation, the main agencies of which are the family, education, peer groups and the media. These agencies themselves are subject to continual change and are especially responsive to developments in the political context itself.

Questions

1. Define political culture and discuss its significance for political behaviour.
2. Examine your own political attitudes to the political unit, nation, regime, government, party allegiance, public officials and participation, and attempt an analysis of the main influences on their formation.

Assignments

1. Political scientists have conducted a number of surveys to investigate the political opinions, attitudes and knowledge of young people. Construct a brief questionnaire which could be used to discover such matters as party allegiance, opinions on a range of important issues, and attitudes towards local and national politicians, public officials and reform of the political system among Britain's 16-year-olds. Check that each question is clearly worded and cannot be interpreted in different ways.
2. The Monarchy

Does the monarchy still have a useful constitutional role to play? Has the monarchy been eclipsed by a publicity-seeking Hollywood-type Royal Family? Are the Royals the same as they ever were; is it tabloid newspapers and their readers which have changed? What are the arguments for and against the monarchy? Supporters of the monarchy maintain that

- the monarchy has an important constitutional role in the formation and dissolution of governments. This role would be crucial if a general election resulted in a hung parliament. The monarch is above party politics and can act without being suspected of favouring any individual or political grouping.
- the monarch symbolises the nation and its continuity. In times of national crisis, the monarch can draw people together and raise morale.
- the monarch sets an example to the nation in terms of behaviour and values. Without question, the Queen is devoted to her duty. She has provided a model of family life.

Others argue that the monarchy is in a crisis because of a change in public attitudes. The public outcry at the idea of taxpayers' money being used to restore Windsor Castle after the fire was a turning point in Britain's political culture. The antics of the Young Royals have ensured that the monarchy will not survive long in the next century. Critics maintain that:

- other arrangements can be set up to perform the monarch's constitutional tasks, as exist in other countries.
- nationalism is a backward-looking value, and has no place in Britain's future in the European Union. The growth of nationalism in Scotland, Wales and Northern Ireland suggests that the monarch is failing to unite the country.
- the marriages of the Queen's children have all failed. Princess Diana is a 'single parent'. The behaviour of the Young Royals has included a number of scandals. None of the Queen's children has sufficient credibility with the public to become a respected figurehead.

(i) Evaluate and elaborate the arguments made above. Attempt to identify bias, selectivity and exaggeration in the points raised above.
(ii) 'The monarchy and Empire were tied together. The problem for the monarchy is that the Empire has gone.' Discuss.

Further Reading

Almond, G. and Verba, S. (1965) *The Civic Culture* (Boston and Toronto: Little, Brown).

Crick, B. (ed.) (1991) *National Identities* (Oxford: Blackwell).

Curtice, J. and Gallagher, T. (1990) 'The Northern Irish Dimension' in R. Jowell *et al.* (eds) *British Social Attitudes: The 7th Report* (Aldershot: Gower).

Denver, D. and Hands, G. (1992) 'The Political Socialisation of Young People', in B. Jones and L. Robins *Two Decades in British Politics* (Manchester and New York: Manchester University Press).

Denver, D. and Hands, G. (1990) 'A New Gender Gap: Sex and Party Choice among Young People', *Talking Politics*, 2: 3 (spring).

Gibbins, J.R. (ed.) (1989) *Contemporary Political Culture* (London California and New Delhi: Sage).

Heath, A. and Topf, R. (1987) 'Political Culture' in R. Jowell *et al.* (eds) *British Social Attitudes: The 5th Report* (Aldershot: Gower).

Jowell, R. and Topf, R. (1988) 'Trust in the Establishment' in R. Jowell *et al.* (eds) *British Social Attitudes: The 6th Report* (Aldershot: Gower).

Kavanagh, D. (1971) 'The Deferential English: A Comparative Critique' in Kavanagh (1990) *see below*.

Kavanagh, D. (1980) 'Political Culture in Great Britain: The Decline of the Civic Culture' in G. Almond and S. Verba *The Civic Culture Revisited* (Boston: Little Brown).

Kavanagh, D. (1990) *Politics and Personalities* (London: Macmillan) for 'The Deferential English: A Comparative Critique, (1971) and 'The Monarchy in Contemporary Political Culture' (1976, with R. Rose).

Kavanagh, D. and Rose, R. (1976) 'The Monarchy in Contemporary Political Culture' in Kavanagh (1990) *see above*.

Parry, G. and Moyser, G. (1990) 'A Map of Political Participation in Britain', *Government and Opposition*, 25: 2.

Parry, G. and Moyser, G. and Day, N. (1992) *Political Participation and Democracy in Britain* (Cambridge: Cambridge University Press.)

Topf, R., Mohler, P. and Heath, A. (1989) 'Pride in One's Country: Britain and West Germany' in R. Jowell *et al.* (eds) *British Social Attitudes: Special International Report*.

■ *Chapter 5* ■

Ideology and Politics

We noticed in Chapter 1 that politics not only involves conflict over the distribution of scarce resources but also public competition between differing beliefs. These beliefs, when expressed as or forming part of systems of ideas, are called **ideologies**. This chapter aims to look more closely at ideology. After offering a brief definition of the concept, it focuses on the leading ideologies of the modern world and the form they take in the British context.

■ The Meaning and Political Significance of Ideology

The term 'ideology' has often been used – and is still sometimes employed – in a pejorative sense. For example, Marx saw 'ideological' ideas as presenting false pictures of society compared with his own 'scientific' approach, whilst liberals have often used 'ideology' in a hostile sense to denote totalitarian systems of thought such as Soviet Communism pre-1989. In everyday parlance in Britain, the term 'ideology' is often equated with rigid adherence to dogma in defiance of the facts, as for instance in attacks upon Thatcherism by the political centre or upon the 'loony left' by the tabloid press. These usages all deploy 'ideology' in a negative way, as offering (respectively) a fallacious, an intolerantly absolutist or an excessively dogmatic set of beliefs about society. Contemporary political scientists, however, prefer a *neutral* definition of the term which can include

all systems and closely related sets of ideas. In this non-pejorative, comprehensive usage, an ideology is *any connected set* of beliefs. On this definition, conservatism, liberalism, socialism, fascism, nationalism and feminism are all ideologies. What general characteristics do they have in common? What are the defining features of ideology?

Political ideologies are **action-orientated**. They shape political behaviour in particular directions, e.g. to bring about national independence or resurgence (nationalism) or sexual equality (feminism). In serving as guides to political action, ideologies provide pictures of contemporary society which show how it has come to be as it is, what it ought to be like (and what it ought not to be like) and how it can achieve desirable changes and avoid undesirable ones. In other words, ideologies normally contain three elements: **description and interpretation** of the past and present; **prescription of an ideal** to be attained in the future; and **strategic advice** on how to reach this social destination. Ideologies appeal to people as members of particular social groups – governing, business, ethnic, national, religious – as classes and as sexes. They aim to extend such groupings (which includes adding to them sympathisers who are not actually 'members') and to build up their morale.

An ideology may be distinguished from an academic discipline, a political idea and a party policy. In comparison with academic subjects such as history, philosophy or physics, which aim

---

Exhibit 5.1   *Ideology: a definition*

Ideology is any system of interrelated ideas offering a comprehensive world-view and able to mobilise large numbers of people for or against political change. Ideologies contain interpretations of how societies have come to be as they are, prescriptions of goals to strive for in the future, and recommendations of strategies and policies by which these goals can be achieved. Typically, they combine conceptions of human nature, views on the roles of the key social groupings such as class, race, gender and nation, and theories of the state.

---

at *understanding*, the intention of ideology is to *persuade*. Unlike a political idea or ideas, an ideology provides a more or less systematic interrelated **set of ideas** or even **system of thought**. Finally, although an ideology may influence policy, it generally operates at a more abstract level. Ideologies characteristically offer wide-ranging conceptions of human nature, society and the state.

Although its name may be the same, the form taken by an ideology varies from country to country. For example, socialism in Britain in its mainstream sense has meant social democracy. By contrast, in the pre-1989 USSR, it denoted Marxism-Leninism, social democracy having been extinguished by the Bolshevik Revolution of 1917.

Ideologies also change their function over time, the same ideology appearing as revolutionary in one age but as conservative in succeeding eras. Thus, liberalism was a revolutionary ideology in the late eighteenth century when pitted against the European *ancien regime*, but by the mid-nineteenth century it had become the dominant ideology and was itself under attack from the new revolutionary ideology of socialism.

We are now in a position to define ideology (Exhibit 5.1) after which we examine the major modern ideologies in turn.

■ Liberalism

Liberalism has a strong claim to be regarded as the dominant ideology of modern times. Liberal capitalism and liberal democracy are the prevalent economic and political systems in the industrially advanced West and, in the wake of the collapse of communism, free market economies and pluralist political systems have been seen as emergent in Eastern Europe and the former USSR. Key liberal ideas such as freedom of conscience, freedom of expression, freedom of contract and the right to own property have entered the political culture in Western democracies and enjoy a 'taken for granted' status.

In Britain, liberal thinkers from the modern – i.e. post-1880 – tradition played a prominent role in shaping the postwar consensus, and intellectuals from the pre-1880 tradition of classical liberalism which emphasised the free market were important influences on the overthrow of that consensus in the 1970s. This liberal influence has occurred despite the fact that the Liberal Party has not been a major political force since 1918.

Liberalism is a complex ideology which has undergone considerable changes since the seventeenth century, but certain concepts remain fundamental to it.

□ *Individualism*

Whereas pre-modern societies took the community as the starting point of their social analysis and defined the individual in terms of his/her social role, liberalism takes the individual as its starting point and envisages society primarily as a collection of separate individuals. Thus, in contrast to feudal society which saw people as possessed of social duties and obligations as, for example, peasants, priests or lords, liberalism focused on the integrity of the individual personality – its distinctive needs, interests, rights, capacities, dignity and potential. Because possessed of unique personalities, individuals, for the liberal, are not only worthy of respect in their own right, they are – or should be – autonomous, or self-directing: hence the evil of all social practices which destroy or threaten the supreme and intrinsic worth and autonomy of each individual, such as slavery, torture, violence, arranged marriages, and manipulation of other persons.

☐ *Rationalism*

In forming their purposes, pursuing their interests, conducting their relationships and deciding by what principles to live their lives, individuals make use of their reason. They can calculate, adapt means to ends, deploy logic, analyse and compare – in short, they possess rationality. In addition to enabling individuals to live their private lives according to clear principles, this reasoning capacity can be directed at the analysis of social arrangements based on prejudice, custom or tradition.

☐ *Freedom*

For many, freedom is the central liberal concept. In the liberal tradition, it has appeared in two guises: **negative freedom** and **positive freedom**. Because individuals are the best judges of their interests, it follows that they should be free to pursue them uncoerced by external pressures. Negative freedom is thus the absence of constraints upon individual activity in all spheres. It gives rise to the demand for specific 'freedoms' – of conscience, of worship, of association, of speech, of meeting, of trade, of contract, from arbitrary arrest, and so on. This aspect of liberalism is concerned with controlling the power of governments: it is a doctrine of constitutional limitations and safeguards. In the late nineteenth century another doctrine of freedom emphasising individual development or self-realisation emerged: positive freedom. By then, the practice of economic liberalism had led to considerable social deprivation, inequality and poverty: clearly un-

regulated capitalism benefited the few but not the many, who led stunted lives. In these circumstances, 'New Liberals' advocated a more interventionist state in order to create the conditions for individual self-fulfilment – or positive liberty – by providing a decent education and some security against the contingencies of life, such as unemployment and old age.

Exhibit 5.2 explains how specific political doctrines flow from the central liberal ideological concepts of individualism, rationality and freedom.

☐ *Liberalism in Britain Since 1945*

With the Liberal Party remaining politically weak in this period, despite a revival in its electoral fortunes from the 1960s, the influence of liberal ideology has been necessarily through other parties. The shaping of the postwar welfare state and managed economy by Beveridge and Keynes and the reaction against this consensus embodied in the resurgence of neo-liberal free market ideas under the aegis of the New Right in the 1970s have been already examined in Chapter 2.

But liberal ideas were also the guiding influence in three further instances. These were the so-called 'permissive society' reforms carried out during Labour rule in the 1960s, most notably the reform of the laws on divorce, abortion and homosexuality, the abolition of capital punishment and the relaxation of censorship; the equal pay for women and anti-racial-discrimination legislation implemented by Labour in the 1970s; and more recently, the campaign for constitutional reform including freedom of information and a Bill of Rights in the late 1980s.

■ Conservatism

There were conservatives before the late eighteenth century but modern conservatism began in the 1790s as a reaction against the French Revolution. It originated in opposition to political radicalism – that is, to a particular set of doctrines about human nature, society and political

> **Exhibit 5.2   *The ideology of liberalism***

- **Government by consent:** Because, in the liberal view, human beings are autonomous creatures, no one can have authority over them except by their explicit consent: hence popular self-government, government of the people by elected representatives, is the only legitimate form of government. Representation, moreover, is of individuals, and not of estates, classes or other sectional groups.

- **Limited government:** A central concern of liberal thought is with 'the taming of Leviathan' – i.e. with guaranteeing the liberty of individuals against their rulers. This concern has led to the evolution of a number of constitutional concepts and mechanisms aimed at constraining government, such as the rule of law, the separation of powers, bicameralism, the legalisation of political opposition, Bills of Rights, and the Ombudsman. In the twentieth century, liberalism has increasingly emphasised pluralism – the legitimacy of a variety of competing groups in society and their role as a constraint on governmental power.

- **Freedom under the law:** The classic goal of liberals is a government of laws, not men. This is impossible since judges will always be necessary to interpret the law. But the phrase catches liberalism's fear of the individual becoming subject to the arbitrary power of another, and its consequent desire to establish a set of objective external limits over everyone – the law. Where the law, conceived in these impersonal terms as a body of rules applicable to everyone, is sovereign, no one need fear the power of another. As John Locke (1632–1704), one of the founders of liberalism, wrote: 'where there is no law, there is no freedom. For liberty is to be free of restraint and violence by others, which cannot be where there is no law'.

- **Rights:** Simply by virtue of their humanity, individuals possess rights, which it is the task of government to protect. Some states express these in lengthy Bills of Rights, e.g. the first ten amendments of the US Constitution. In the eighteenth and nineteenth centuries, these rights were civil, legal, economic, political and religious; in the twentieth century, social rights – to health, education and a decent standard of living – have been added. Some commentators have seen these as socialist rather than liberal but others maintain that the welfare capitalism of New Liberals such as L.T. Hobhouse (1864–1929), J.M. Keynes and W.H. Beveridge remains well within the liberal tradition.

- **Equality of opportunity:** Liberals advocate equality of opportunity, not absolute equality or equality of outcome: in other words, they are meritocrats not egalitarians. They favour a society in which what counts is individual ability, not inherited wealth or social position, and historically have fought against social privilege to secure 'a level playing field'.

- **Equality before the law:** For liberals, social justice implies not only equality of opportunity but also legal equality. This principle entails no discrimination on the grounds of race, colour, creed, gender, or religion.

- **Toleration:** Liberals believe in a plural society in which all individuals and groups have a right to express their views. In practice, this means toleration of the expression of views with which one may not agree. Traditionally, liberals have fought censorship of opinion, and still do – short of favouring freedom for the views of parties which would destroy the freedom of others. Liberal-minded people from all the mainstream British parties have been outraged at the *fatwa* (death sentence) declared by the Ayatollah Khomeini against Salman Rushdie, author of the *Satanic Verses*.

Exhibit 5.2—*continued*

- **Devolution**: Liberals believe in national self-government: in the nineteenth century British Liberals supported movements for national independence abroad and Home Rule within the British Isles. In the twentieth century, they have argued for devolution of power within Britain both on the grounds of fairness to the smaller British nations and of more effective government.

- **Internationalism**: Liberals believe that as a matter of fact the nation-state is being superseded and as a matter of principle ought to be superseded by supra-national and international organisations. British Liberals were the first to advocate joining the European Economic Community (EEC) and have been consistent supporters of the League of Nations and then the United Nations. Liberal internationalism, with its idealistic vision of an international community in which national identities are transcended, rests upon a typical liberal perception of the individual, shorn of subordinate loyalties, as 'a citizen of the world'.

---

change. These were respectively – the inherent goodness and rationality of humanity; the idea of society as a mere collection of isolated individuals; and the feasibility and desirability of root and branch change, accomplished if necessary by revolution. Modern conservatism continued in the nineteenth century in opposition to political and economic liberalism, and in the twentieth century has seen its main enemy as statist and totalitarian socialism.

Nineteenth-century conservatives opposed political liberalism – the idea that the only legitimate form of government is self-government, or democracy – on several grounds. Among other things, they believed that democracy would destroy the internal checks and balances of the traditional 'mixed constitution' (monarch, Lords and Commons) and that it would lead to the plunder of the rich by the poor majority. By the late nineteenth century, however, conservatives had accepted democratic government not only as inevitable but also as reconcilable with a privileged class, the constitution and the empire. Nineteenth-century conservatives opposed economic liberalism (the doctrine of *laissez-faire*) because they considered that an unrestricted market economy led to excessive and unnecessary suffering, especially of groups like women and children who could not defend themselves. In doing so, they drew upon a tradition of *paternalism*, which embodied the concern of the propertied for those worse off than themselves.

The 1920s and 1930s brought a major reorientation of conservatism – in domestic politics, to face the assertion of class interest by organised labour together with the socialist threat to use the state as an instrument of social levelling, and, internationally, to counter the menace of left totalitarianism following the Bolshevik Revolution. It became clear then that modern conservatism contained two strands – a libertarian, individualist and free market tradition, and a collectivist, paternalist and state interventionist one (Greenleaf, 1983).

The first strand, muted in the nineteenth century because of the need to oppose economic liberalism, goes back to Edmund Burke (1727–97), the founder of modern conservatism. Burke saw the free market as sacrosanct and any intervention in it by government as likely to undermine wealth-creation and harm the poor. After the First World War, as institutional liberalism (in the form of the Liberal Party) collapsed, conservatism drew upon the libertarian side of its inheritance, emphasising capitalist values and individual liberty against socialism in all its varieties.

After 1945, its paternalist, 'one nation' tradition, deriving from Disraeli, enabled conservatism to adapt to the interventionist welfare state and managed economy. This collectivist, interventionist vein became the dominant strand in the Conservative Party for the next thirty years. However, Enoch Powell kept alive the free market tradition of thought within conservatism until this was vigorously reasserted by Margaret Thatcher in the 1970s.

To sum up: Conservatism over two centuries has changed in various ways – most notably in the character of the élite it has defended (from territorial-aristocratic to business-professional-managerial) and in the nature of the state it has been required to endorse (from non-democratic to democratic). On the role of government, it contains two strands – libertarian and collectivist – one of which at any given time has been dominant. However, as an ideology, certain themes have been and remain of significance to conservatism and these are set out in Exhibit 5.3.

Exhibit 5.3   *The ideology of Conservatism*

- **Human nature:** Generally pessimistic: human beings seen as morally imperfect and as intellectually fallible.

- **Society:** Seen in hierarchical terms as a command structure held together by people exercising their allotted duties as parents, teachers, captains of industry, etc. Emphasis in social thought on inequality and variety and the 'naturalness' of certain groups, e.g. family, nation. Traditional conservatives see society as organic, i.e. as growing like a plant rather than being built like a machine.

- **Economy:** Capitalism endorsed as optimum economic system, both because of its capacity to generate wealth for societies and individuals and because of its close connection with political freedom: but note different approaches of libertarians and collectivists.

- **Change:** Generally pro-gradual against radical change, but note exceptions – e.g. Joseph Chamberlain, Margaret Thatcher. Anti-revolutionary

- **Nation:** Intensely patriotic and nationalistic, regarding the nation as the primary historical and political unit, the product of shared customs, traditions and values. The preservation of its integrity against internal and external threats is the first task of political leadership.

- **Property:** Unqualified regard for property as giving people independence, security, satisfaction and a means of expressing their personalities; consequent desire to extend property ownership. Unworried by unequal distribution because it is seen as result of differences in energy and ability. Private property is regarded as the main bulwark of political freedom and its security is in everyone's interest.

- **Leadership and authority:** Authority seen as social necessity at all levels – in the family, at work, in the nation. National leadership should be by an élite of the capable and experienced, formerly found largely in the aristocracy, now in the middle class. Élite rule not only desirable but also inevitable, and rest of society expected to respond to its initiatives.

- **Public order:** Strong emphasis on need to respect rule of law and on powerful law-enforcing agencies in order to preserve public order.

- **The Constitution:** Reverence for British Constitution as product of gradually evolving historical process which has proved its value over time. Sees authority as always flowing downwards from the top, never emanating from the people. Traditionally believe in authoritative but limited government, restrained by rule of law, institutional checks, conventions, and tacit understandings.

□ *The New Right*

The 'New Right' is the term used to describe the combination of neo-liberal economic ideas with certain more traditional conservative themes which surfaced in Britain and the United States in the 1970s and became dominant in the two countries under the Thatcher and Reagan Governments in the 1980s. Economic neo-liberals are anti-statist: for them the free market is sacrosanct as the mechanism for the allocation of resources to their most profitable use. Governments therefore should not seek to manage the economy in order to secure full employment, to run industries themselves or in any other way try to 'second guess' the market. Rather they should limit themselves to ensuring 'sound money' (i.e. controlling inflation), security of property and the enforceability of contracts. In practice, 'rolling back the frontiers of the state' under Margaret Thatcher's Governments meant cutting direct taxes, seeking to reduce public expenditure, privatising publicly owned assets, ending 'corporatist' relationships with producer groups, and curbing the powers of the trade unions.

The New Right are anti-statist in social policy too: they see welfarism as undermining individual initiative and leading ultimately to a 'dependency' culture. The emphasis of their social policy is therefore on building up a country of more self-reliant individuals whose first question is not to ask what the state can do for them but what they can do for themselves. If New Right Conservatives reacted in social and economic policy against any 'over-blown' welfare state and Keynesian economics, they reacted in matters of personal morality against the liberal 'permissiveness' of the 1960s, especially with regard to abortion, homosexuality and pornography. Anti-liberal pluralism in morality, the New Right in the US called for an end to legalised abortion and a restoration of 'family values', by which they meant the traditional two-parent family based on deference to adult authority, especially that of the father. Finally, New Right Conservatives support a 'strong state' with regard to internal order and external defence. For example, Thatcherism in Britain involved strengthening the police, administering a tougher penal policy, and investing more heavily in defence; in the US, it meant a hard-line anti-communist stance.

Was Thatcher – who looked for intellectual inspiration to famous neo-liberals such as Milton Friedman, the American propounder of monetarism, and Friedrich von Hayek, whose *Road to Serfdom* (1944) saw the free market economy as the precondition of political liberty – truly a conservative? Friedman himself described her as 'a nineteenth century liberal' and, for other critics, her radical rather than gradualist approach to change, her rejection of pragmatism and moderation in favour of doctrinaire, 'conviction' politics, her dismissal of even the concept of 'society', and her contempt for constitutional checks and balances (as in her assault upon local government, civil service neutrality and other traditional institutions) place her outside the conservative tradition. However, as we have already seen, modern conservatism contains both libertarian and collectivist strands of thought and, in fact, even in the post-1945 period when the collectivist vein predominated, libertarianism was present in Conservative rhetoric (which promised economic decontrol in the 1950s), in Conservative policies such as modest denationalisation and the launching of commercial television, and in the ideas of Enoch Powell and of Edward Heath before 1972. Arguably, Thatcher's vigorous assertion of the merits of the free market economy, private property, a powerful state (national defence and policing) and of primary institutions like the family place her squarely in the tradition of libertarian conservatism.

■ Socialism

Like the other major ideologies, socialism emerged *in opposition* to a particular type of society and its ideological justification: nineteenth-century capitalism and *laissez-faire* liberalism. Like the other ideologies too, socialism has changed greatly through time, adapting to altered circumstances and different areas of the world.

But its concern with how the market society can be modified, reformed or transcended to bring about greater social justice has remained.

□ *Socialism as a World Force*

In the nineteenth century, Marx's socialism had many rivals. These included the cooperative model proposed by the British mill-owner, Robert Owen, the utopian visions of ideal communities pictured by the early French socialists, and the various strains of anarchism developed by Proudhon, Bakunin and Kropotkin. But as a systematic theory of the new class society generated by industrial capitalism, Marx's socialism had no equal. The heart of his analysis is the notion of capitalism as exploitative of the working class. For Marx, capitalism as a system of production structured into society a fundamental and irreconcileable conflict of interest between the bourgeoisie, the owners of capital, and the property-less workers.

Because it was *systemic* – i.e. built into the system – this division of interest could lead only to class conflict: it could not be resolved by any change of heart by the capitalist, or trade union action to gain workers their fair rewards, or government intervention to palliate or remove the resultant social injustice and inequality. Eventually, as increasing competition between capitalists increased the misery of the workforce, the system would be overthrown by a workers' uprising. Proletarian revolution would end class rule and destroy the oppressive bourgeois state; after an interlude of worker dictatorship during which the last vestiges of bourgeois rule would be rooted out, a communist society characterised by democracy and social equality would follow.

By the early 1900s a fierce controversy had broken out among European socialists over whether Marx's aims would inevitably have to be accomplished by violent revolution or whether, in circumstances of rising working-class living standards, a revolutionary transformation could be attained by peaceful parliamentary methods. Events during the 1914–18 war soon provided an answer to this speculation.

The year 1917 was a major watershed in the history of socialism. The triumph of the Bolshevik Party during the Russian Revolution led to its division into two major strands, democratic socialism (Western) and communism (Eastern). With the victory of an anti-liberal, revolutionary party, the USSR became a one-party state with Marxism-Leninism as its official ideology.

World socialism thenceforth had a national base from which after 1945 it established itself in Eastern Europe and achieved considerable influence in the Third World. The success of the Chinese Communists under Mao after 1949 provided not only a further variant of socialist ideology but also another – and for the Soviets, a rival – source of communist support in the underdeveloped countries. The revival of Marxist theory which gathered strength from the 1960s in the West looked for inspiration to the libertarian writings of the early Marx, to the Italian socialist of the 1920s, Antonio Gramsci, and to the exiled Bolshevik leader, Leon Trotsky, whose reputation survived the moral discredit into which Soviet communism fell under Stalin.

In the late 1980s, communism in the Soviet Union and Eastern Europe suddenly collapsed. The catalyst for the disintegration was the policy of political and economic liberalisation promoted by Mikhail Gorbachev, the General Secretary, after 1985. Within a tumultuous few years, communist governments in Eastern Europe and the USSR were swept away and replaced by multi-party political systems and embryonic free market economies. The Soviet Union itself fell apart and was succeeded by a looser confederation, the Commonwealth of Independent States (CIS). Confined to China, Cuba, North Korea and a few other countries mainly in the Far East, communism had been much diminished as a world force.

□ *Socialism in Britain, 1900–90*

The central tenet of mainstream British socialism has been the idea of winning control of the State by democratic methods in order to eradicate poverty and create a more equal society. In other words, British socialism has been gradualist, parliamentary and reformist rather than revolutionary, and statist rather than decentralist. Its major vehicle has been the Labour Party. There have been three major influences upon Labour Party socialism: the ethical socialism of the Independent Labour Party (ILP) (1893) which preached a new morality based on altruism and cooperation; the collectivism of the Fabian Society (1884), which believed in 'the inevitability of gradualness' and equated socialism with state intervention; and the trade unions, which have provided a 'labourist' ethos, tying the party to the pursuit of working-class interests.

Labour socialism shares with new liberalism a willingness to use the state to modify the operation of the market in favour of the poorer sections of society and has drawn upon it (Beveridge and Keynes). But it has gone beyond new liberalism in its preparedness to eliminate market forces altogether by nationalisation. Formed in 1900 by the trade unions and middle-class socialists (the ILP, Fabians and the Marxist Social Democratic Federation, which soon left), the party did not adopt a socialist constitution until 1918. This included the famous commitment to nationalisation – the public ownership of the means of production, distribution and exchange (clause 4).

The new party combined a moral critique of capitalism with labourism and statism. By the late 1920s, it had definitively excluded certain other variants of socialism including syndicalism – the belief in the use of industrial power to achieve political ends, guild socialism, which argued for the decentralisation of power to self-governing industrial guilds, and Marxism, with its emphasis on class struggle. The failure of the General Strike (1926) finally undermined syndicalism, guild socialism withered away, whilst Marxism, always relatively weak in Britain, became separated from mainstream socialism after the formation of the Communist Party of Great Britain (1920), whose members were debarred from belonging to the Labour Party.

Meanwhile, Labour in the interwar period, imbued with a utopian vision of the ultimate disappearance of capitalism at some point in the future, totally lacked policies to reform capitalism in the present, and, in office (1924 and 1929–31), could resort only to conventional panaceas. In the 1930s it gradually moved towards a reformist strategy which combined the public corporation form of nationalisation, improvements in social welfare and neo-Keynesian ideas on economic recovery.

There has always been tension within the Labour Party between its left and right wings. In the 1950s, with the party in opposition, having implemented its welfarist and nationalisation programme between 1945 and 1951, left–right conflict broke out again, this time over whether public ownership remained a central socialist objective or should be relegated to one means among many for the attainment of a socialist society.

The revisionists, supported by the party leader, Hugh Gaitskell (1955–63), argued that clause 4 should be abandoned; the fundamentalists, who looked for leadership to Aneurin Bevan, saw it as essential that the party should retain its unequivocal support for nationalisation. The revisionist case was expressed most notably by Anthony Crosland in *The Future of Socialism* (1956): he argued that a blend of economic growth, progressive taxation and welfare policies had produced a reformed capitalism in which Governments through Keynesian policies and control of a significant public sector could manage the economy in the public interest. Ownership of the means of production was no longer crucial since power in industry had passed to a new stratum of salaried managers.

The left countered that, despite the social progress made by the Attlee Governments, Britain remained largely a capitalist society and in order to complete its transformation into a socialist one, public ownership retained a key role. The revisionists failed in their attempt (1960) to remove clause 4 from the party constitution but Labour Governments in the 1960s and 1970s pursued revisionist policies based on high public spending, prices and incomes policies to counter inflation, industrial interventionism, the introduction of comprehensive schools and improvements in the rights of workers.

During the 1970s, fuelled by disappointment with Labour's performance in government, the left emerged as a much more formidable force within the party. Fed from a variety of sources, including a resurgent Marxism, ethical socialism, neo-syndicalism, militant trade unionism, the new feminism, black activism, and a reborn peace movement, the left produced a wide range of reform proposals. These included more nationalisation and state-directed investment, import and exchange controls, withdrawal from the European Community (EC), unilateral nuclear disarmament, workers' control in industry and more intra-party democracy. Leading figures were Tony Benn, an ethical socialist deriving inspiration from Christianity, and Ken Livingstone, a key member of the 'new urban left'.

Left influence in the party increased dramatically between Labour's election defeat in 1979 and 1983. A left-winger, Michael Foot, became leader (1980), Benn failed by only the narrowest of margins to become deputy-leader (1981), the party adopted mandatory reselection of Members of Parliament (MPs) and a new electoral college method for electing the leader (1979–81), and a very left-wing manifesto – promising unilateralism, withdrawal from the EC and renationalisation of public assets privatised by the Conservatives – was put forward at the 1983 General Election.

Labour's lurch to the left provoked a party split which ended with the formation of the Social Democratic Party (SDP) (1981) by four former Labour Cabinet Ministers, David Owen, Shirley Williams, Bill Rodgers and Roy Jenkins. The SDP saw itself as in the revisionist tradition: it stood for a mixed economy, incomes policy, continued membership of the EC, and retention of nuclear weapons. After 1983, led by David Owen, it stressed both the role of the private sector (the social market economy) *and* generous welfare provision and redistributive taxation. But it failed to achieve an electoral breakthrough and, after the 1987 General Election, the party split, a majority voting for merger with the Liberals.

Meanwhile, the Labour Party under the leadership of Neil Kinnock and Roy Hattersley moved to the right after 1983, abandoning the commitments to withdrawal from the EC, renunciation of nuclear weapons and substantial extensions of public ownership. Tacitly acknowledging that Thatcherism had redrawn the political agenda, the 1989 Labour Policy Review, 'Meet the Challenge Make the Change', stressed the role of the market economy in wealth creation and distribution but, in keeping with a more traditional left-wing emphasis, favoured a regulatory and interventionist economic role of the state and higher welfare benefits (see Exhibit 5.4 for a summary of the main concepts and doctrines of socialism).

■ Feminism

Modern feminism has gone through two phases. The main objective of 'first wave' feminism was the attainment of political and legal equality for women. This movement developed during the nineteenth century, drawing inspiration from such texts as Mary Wollstonecraft's *Vindication of the Rights of Woman* (1792) and John Stuart Mill's *The Subjection of Women* (1869). Wollstonecraft argued that women should possess the same civil rights as men on the basis of their fundamental equality as human beings, whilst Mill put the case for the legal equality of women and for women's right to vote on the same terms as men. This individualist or liberal variant of feminism was the dominant strand down to the late 1960s, when it included among its achievements the right to vote for women (1918/28 in the UK), the liberalisation of the laws on divorce and abortion (1967–9), equal pay legislation, the right to education and the right to pursue a career on the same terms as men. However, at that time, liberal feminism came under vociferous attack from 'second wave' feminists who argued that it had failed to address the root causes of women's exploitation and oppression.

Although 'second wave' feminism did continue to express the liberal demand for equal career opportunities for women, its main thrust was provided by socialist and radical feminists who felt that women's liberation required more far-reaching social change than civil equality. A resurgent **socialist feminism** focused on the continuing exploitation of women in the family

---

Exhibit 5.4 *The ideology of Socialism*

- **Human nature:** In socialist theory, human nature is inherently and potentially good but in capitalist economies human relationships are distorted and human goodness thwarted by an economic system which is geared to produce profits for the few rather than to satisfy the basic needs of the many. Capitalism makes people greedy, selfish and competitive rather than generous, altruistic and cooperative. It divides rather than unites people and dehumanises them by treating them as mere 'units' of production or 'consumers' rather than as individual human beings.

- **Society:** To socialists, individuals are inconceivable apart from their social relationships. They see language, knowledge, technology and capital as social products and human behaviour as fundamentally conditioned by the social environment.

- **Community:** People's sense of identity is defined by membership of groups and communities: this sense of belonging is of the highest value to their lives and the communities they have built by their collective effort and sacrifices should be defended and not undermined.

- **Social class:** Although they have defined it in different ways, socialists focus on social class as the most important source of social division and social inequality.

- **Equality:** This is the central socialist value. Socialists advocate the creation of a more equal society in which class differences in wealth, income, education, health and power are sharply reduced. Only greater equality, they believe, can produce genuine freedom for everyone.

- **Fraternity:** Another important socialist value. Socialists aspire to a society in which differentials of reward are justified in terms of social function and differentials are allocated by a collective decision about the relative social worth of each job. They think such a society is likely to be a fraternal one, characterised by cooperativeness not individualism.

- **Social change:** Socialists call for a fundamental transformation of society whether by reform or revolution. A large-scale redistribution of income, wealth and power is required but socialists have disagreed over how far this can be achieved by progressive taxation and welfare measures or whether public ownership is also required.

- **Representation:** Socialists see representation primarily in class terms, with power as a delegation from below and the function of the 'Labour' or 'Socialist' party as being to serve the interests of the working class. Politics has tended to be seen in collectivist terms as a matter of class loyalty or 'solidarity'. In practice, in Britain, Labour has always appealed to significant sections of the middle class, whilst over one-third of the working class has voted for non-socialist parties.

- **The state:** Although tainted by class interest, the state can be captured by democratic means and used as an instrument to improve the lives of the majority.

---

and in the labour market: at home, women provided unwaged labour in the form of housework and childcare; at work, they are still to be found disproportionately in the lowest-paid, most insecure jobs.

For socialist feminists, women's inequality derives from capitalist property relations. Friedrich Engels stated the argument in his *The Origins of the Family, Private Property and the State* (1884): in history, as societies based on private property displaced communist societies in which property and social position could be inherited through the female line, women were relegated to subordinate positions in the patriarchal family. The transition from communism to capitalism thereby brought about what Engels called 'the world historical defeat of the female sex'. For traditional Marxist feminists, since the primary oppression is by class, women's liberation can come about only through the overthrow of capitalism, and the consequent liquidation of the bourgeois family.

A modern Socialist feminist, Juliet Mitchell, in *Women's Estate* (1971) – although writing in the Marxist tradition – gave sexual oppression as much emphasis as class exploitation. She analysed the role of women in terms of the part they played in four 'key structures': production (as members of the workforce), and, within the family, reproduction, sex and the socialisation of children. Women's liberation required the transformation of all four structures and should include the diversification of the family into a variety of differing forms, but not its abolition.

The most original and powerful element in the women's liberation movement, however, has been radical feminism. For **radical feminists**, the reason why women are exploited and oppressed is, quite simply, men. They see patriarchy – literally, the rule of the fathers – as the socially dominant concept, and patriarchal attitudes as culturally all-pervasive. For them, gender – not class, race or nation – is the most important social cleavage but, rather than being a 'natural' division, based on immutable biological differences between men and women, they regard it as a politically created and therefore removable one.

But gender differences – meaning superior male and subordinate female roles – are the consequence of a lengthy and deep-rooted process of social conditioning and as such cannot be eliminated either by liberal reformism or the socialist abolition of capitalism. Unless attacked directly, patriarchal attitudes can and would survive such changes; this is because so much of women's oppression takes place in the private sphere – in the family and in personal and sexual relationships. Hence radical feminists have sought to break down the traditional division in political

thought between the public and private realms, arguing that 'the personal is the political'. For them, the two spheres cannot be separated since women are at the receiving end of male-dominated power relationships throughout all areas of life.

Key texts in the development of radical feminism have been Eva Figes's *Patriarchal Attitudes* (1970), Germaine Greer's *The Female Eunuch* (1970), Shulamith Firestone's *The Dialectic of Sex* (1970) and Kate Millett's *Sexual Politics* (1970). Radical feminists differ over the remedies they prescribe. Some, believing human nature to be essentially androgynous, argue for women's liberation through the abolition of the family (Millett and Firestone). Others, rejecting sexual equality as a goal, adopt a 'pro-woman' position, stressing rather than minimising the biological and behavioural differences between the sexes and maintaining that traditional roles and caring virtues should be celebrated rather than abandoned.

■ Fascism

Fascism is an extreme right-wing ideology which rose to prominence in inter-war Europe, declined with the defeat and death in war of Hitler and Mussolini, and has resurfaced in recent decades. Basically a doctrine of ultra-nationalism, fascism is a twentieth-century phenomenon (although with roots in the the nineteenth century) whose precise form has varied according to different national histories and cultures. It has tended to emerge in countries which are suffering from severe social dislocation owing to some combination of defeat in war, rapid industrialisation, the collapse of authoritarian leadership, frustrated nationalist ambitions, intense economic problems and the need to absorb large numbers of foreigners (Exhibit 5.5).

□ *Fascism in Britain*

A version of fascism appeared in Britain in the 1930s associated with Oswald Mosley and the

British Union of Fascists (BUF). Mosley's book *The Greater Britain* (1932) put forward a plan for British economic regeneration – 'Britain First' – which combined the idea of the corporate state with protectionism to guarantee industry a secure home market.

Mosley was thoroughly Fascist in his attacks first on the politicians and parties of the parliamentary system (the 'Old Gang') for failing to measure up to the contemporary 'crisis', and second on the communists, seen as the major enemies of the state. Anti-semitism is not a theme of the book but there is little doubt that Mosley was prepared to inveigh against the Jews opportunistically in his speeches or that his supporters in the BUF were virulently anti-semitic.

Mosley himself stressed the significance of the Second World War in bringing British fascism to a halt, but the reality is that it never got going,

held back by the strong support for the parliamentary system, by the respect for constitutionalism and moderation in the political culture, by the resilience of the class system, and most important of all perhaps, by the modesty of the economic problem, grave as it was, compared with the situation in Germany after 1918, and by the fact that Britain did not experience defeat in war.

In 1967 another racialist party of the extreme right emerged: the **National Front** (NF). Its central ideological idea was a redefinition of the 'real' or 'authentic' British community in terms of colour, with whites conceived as true Britons, and blacks denied this identity, and blamed for social problems with regard to jobs, services and housing in the tradition of fascist 'scapegoating'. The party stood for the repatriation of New Commonwealth immigrants and its leader for most of

---

Exhibit 5.5 *Fascism: the main features*

- **The 'new man':** Fascists stress the malleability of human nature and seek to reshape it in a new mould. Fascist 'new man' is a Superman able to transcend materialist drives in pursuit of an ideal and subordinate selfish motives in the service of the Leader.

- **Ultra-nationalism and racialism:** Fascism exalts the consciousness of belonging to the nation, thriving on the contrast between its present state – perceived as corrupted by communists, traitors and Jews (or blacks) – and the true or authentic nation of its imagining, rid of these alien elements.

- **The leadership principle:** A charismatic leader is accorded absolute, dictatorial power as the embodiment of the will of the nation.

- **Dynamism and violence:** Fascism appeals overtly to brutality and violence and glorifies physical force and strength. Fascist 'new man' is a dynamic individual constantly prepared to test his beliefs in action against the national enemies.

- **Irrationalism:** Fascism appeals to the irrational side of human nature – to instinct and to ties of blood and race.

- **Anti-liberal and anti-communist:** Fascism is contemptuous both of liberal parliamentary regimes – because they are based on majority rule and pluralism rather than elitism and the leadership principle – and of communist states – because they exalt class interests and class conflict above national unity.

- **Statism:** The fascist goal is to create a totally unified 'organic' community to which the individual owes complete, unquestioning obedience.

the 1970s, John Tyndall, advocated resistance to racial integration and the maintenance of racial 'separateness' on apartheid lines.

The **British National Party** (1983), currently the leading party on the extreme right, emerged after the NF faded in the late 1970s (see Chapter 13).

■ Nationalism

The core of nationalism as an ideology is reducible to four propositions (Exhibit 5.6). As is immediately apparent, the central concept of nationalist ideology is the idea of the 'nation'. Its basic political doctrine flows from this idea: that each nation should possess its own state. It has proved to be a doctrine of striking potency in the modern world.

For the emergence of nationalism as an ideology, the era of the French Revolution (*c.* 1789–1815) was decisive. During these years, three ideas fused to create the modern doctrine:

- The concept of the state as a particular form of territorially based civil association;
- The idea of the sovereignty of the people, popular government or democracy;
- The definition of a 'people' or 'nation' in terms of its culture, including, especially, its language.

The Revolution brought about a combination of the first two of these ideas by extending the basis of a previously monarchical state to include the whole people; and the German writer, J.G. Herder (1744–1803) suggested that the distinguishing marks of a 'people' or 'nation' was its possession of a unique culture – a distinctive blend of habits, customs, manners, literature, art, religion and notably language, which had grown up over the centuries.

The concept of the 'nation' is – in Benedict Anderson's phrase – an 'imagined community'. It is *imagined* because it is quite impossible for members of even the smallest nation to know any but a tiny proportion of their fellow nationals, yet each feels a sense of kinship with the rest – 'in the minds of each lives the image of their communion'. It is imagined as a *community* because, despite the social inequalities that may exist, the nation is always conceived as 'a deep, horizontal comradeship' – a sense of fraternity which ultimately makes it possible for people to sacrifice their lives for it (Anderson, 1985, pp. 15–16).

Superficially, the idea of nationalism is similar to an older concept like **patriotism**, but is distinguishable from it by its sharply political frame of reference. Whereas nationalism is a political doctrine which holds that all nations should govern themselves, patriotism is a sentiment, a feeling of love for one's country. As Orwell wrote, patriotism means 'devotion to a particular place, a particular way of life'. It may be a precondition of nationalism, but not the thing itself. Nor is nationalism to be identified with *national self-consciousness*, an awareness of separate identity by a nation, which predates it by hundreds of years – although nationalism may develop and use such a feeling.

Nationalism as a specific political doctrine almost invariably asserts the claims of a particular nationality against an external force, an alien, an outsider. In so doing, it normally relies on – and stimulates – the discovery, revival,

---

Exhibit 5.6   *Nationalism: core ideas*

- The world is naturally divided into nations.
- Each nation has its own unique character resulting from its history and culture.
- Each nation should be independent or possess a large degree of autonomy; only in running its own affairs can it achieve self-realisation.
- The primary allegiance of the individual is to the nation or, if it exists, to the nation-state.

systematisation and propagandist expounding of historic national cultures. This process then often culminates in the demand for political recognition of the national community by independence (separation), federalism or devolution.

Anthony D. Smith in *Nationalism in the Twentieth Century* (1979) has suggested a valuable typology of the main forms taken by nationalism in the modern world.

- **Liberation struggles against empires:** These aim at independence and the creation of a new state – e.g. Latin America against Spain and Portugal in the nineteenth century, Afro-Asian countries against the European empires post-1945, Eastern European nations against the Soviet empire in the 1980s.
- **State 'renewal':** The regeneration of an old-established state by an appeal to national pride, often associating this with a quest for economic revitalisation – e.g. de Gaulle in France in the 1950s and 1960s, Thatcher in Britain after 1979.
- **Nation-building in post-colonial societies:** The mobilisation of support for the new 'nation' (e.g. Kenya, Nigeria, Zimbabwe) is aimed at weakening tribalism and, often in combination with socialist principles and methods, achieving modernisation.
- **Ethnic separatism in old multinational states:** Separatist movements base themselves on traditional national identities and demand independence from or greater autonomy within the multinational state – e.g. the Bretons, Basques, Welsh and Scots.

Nationalities and Nationalism Within the United Kingdom

The United Kingdom of Great Britain and Northern Ireland originated in various acts of absorption by the Westminster government. These expansionist measures – undertaken for motives of national security and economic advantage – successively brought Wales (1536), Scotland (1707) and Ireland (1801) under the rule of the British Crown. In this process both

Scotland and Ireland lost the separate parliaments which had met in Edinburgh and Dublin respectively; in Wales, no parliament existed at the time it was absorbed into the British state. Essentially, then, the United Kingdom dates from 1801, but it fragmented in 1922 when 26 of the 32 Irish counties split away to form the Republic of Ireland. The other six northern counties remained part of the UK.

The circumstances of the formation of the British state profoundly shaped the character of the various nationalisms which emerged within it. Of particular significance were the facts that the UK was created by the assertion of English domination (against which peripheral nationalisms would later define themselves) and that the British Empire which emerged in the eighteenth and nineteenth centuries was for a lengthy period a unifying force within the new state (although not in Ireland). Other unifying factors were: the use of the English language; a party system found everywhere but in Northern Ireland; the Protestant religion; a shared experience of the economic benefits of industrialisation; the modern media and mass entertainments; and, above all, the British Crown and Parliament. These forces are still at work but the upsurge of support for Scottish and Welsh nationalism in the 1970s and the resurgence of Irish republicanism in Northern Ireland brought British nationalisms into unprecedented prominence. The remainder of this section discusses English, Welsh and Scottish nationalism; Northern Ireland receives separate consideration in Chapter 29.

English Nationalism

The dominant strand in English nationalism is traditionalism. The slow, gradual and above all successful nature of English imperial expansion; the absence from English history since the seventeenth century of major popular uprisings, and since the eleventh century of invasion, despite the frequent threats of it; and the massive wealth generated by early industrialisation: all these factors contributed to the conservative, traditional character of English nationalism. It is insular – witness the arm's length attitude to

'Europe' – and non-popular, which is not to be confused with 'unpopular', but simply means that English nationalism lacks any symbolic association of the common people with the nation such as exists in the French celebration of the Fall of the Bastille (14 July) or the American celebration of Independence Day (4 July). What it celebrates are institutions and constitutional achievements (parliament, monarchy, common law) predominantly associated with élites, together with moments of national deliverance from invasion – the defeat of the Spanish Armada, of Napoleon, and of Hitler. The English national myth is – not unusually – 'freedom' ('Britons never, never shall be slaves').

Since the 1960s, English nationalism has been characterised by a traditionalist defence of the Union against peripheral nationalisms and of parliamentary sovereignty against the European Community; a call for economic modernisation and regeneration; and an assertion of the ethnic and cultural homogeneity of 'the English'.

Welsh Nationalism

Welsh nationalism is at root cultural, a response to the threat to Welsh civilisation posed by industrialisation, centralisation and 'anglicisation'. Plaid Cymru, the 'Party of Wales' (1925), adopted the promotion of the Welsh language as its primary goal and favoured self-government (but not independence) as a means of enhancing the status of the language. The party founded by J. Saunders Lewis (1893–1985) was socially conservative; anti-materialist; and imbued with a romantic idealisation of the mediaeval European Order which permitted diverse local cultures to flourish. In the 1960s, the party moved to the left and adopted bilingualism as its ultimate goal.

Welsh nationalism has been profoundly shaped by the Welsh historical experience – by the fact that the national sense of identity never found political expression in a state; by the overwhelming predominance of religious Nonconformity; and by the survival of the language (one-fifth were Welsh speakers in 1971).

Scottish Nationalism

In contrast to Welsh nationalism, Scottish nationalism is predominantly economic. Scottish nationalists blame neglect by remote Westminster governments for Scottish economic difficulties and argue that Scottish interests would be better served by the dissolution of the Act of Union (1707) with England and the establishment of an independent Scotland.

The **Scottish National Party** (SNP) (1934) was the creation mainly of John MacCormick, who believed complete independence was unattainable and favoured greater autonomy for Scotland through an all-party approach. He and his followers seceded from the SNP in 1942 and went on to form the Convention movement for a Scottish Parliament. Meanwhile, the SNP had decided in favour of the goal of independence through an electoral strategy which equipped it to profit from more favourable circumstances for nationalism following the discovery of offshore oil in the 1960s.

Whereas the appeal of Plaid Cymru is limited by its divisive emphasis on the language issue, the SNP has invoked the traditional pride of the entire nation in its distinctive identity. Unlike Wales, Scotland was once a state and, after 1707, retained its own systems of law, education and local government and its own established (Presbyterian) Church. Nationalism in Scotland, therefore, has a strong foundation to build upon and has been a threat to the Union since the 1970s.

Summary

Ideologies are belief-systems which function as guides to action. Targeted at people as members of particular groups, they are of immense importance in shaping political behaviour and producing political change. They normally describe society from a particular perspective in the past and present, prescribe specific goals to be attained in the future and offer strategic advice on how to reach this destination. Although retaining identifiable features, ideologies themselves alter through time, assuming revolutionary form in one epoch, a conservative guise in the next, being dominant in one century, displaced and under attack in the following one. They also contain within themselves different traditions and emphases.

The key concept of **liberalism** is individual freedom. Its thrust is individualist – towards the demarcation and protection of a sphere of activity in society against the claims of the state in which individuals may enjoy their rights and express their interests. The expanded state recommended by twentieth-century liberals is carefully defined in terms of the minimum functions compatible with a decent life for all.

Conservatism combines pessimism about human nature, a preference for gradual change, support for leadership by an experienced, able èlite, assertive nationalism, and a strong commitment to the preservation of order.

Socialism, like liberalism, is optimistic about human nature. Its leading tenets are that societies which are based on a more equal distribution of wealth, income and power and upon cooperation will be more humane, civilised and productive than societies founded upon hierarchy, inequality and competition. Gradual reform and modification of the free play of market forces has typified British socialism.

For contemporary **feminists**, gender is the primary source of social division and for most of them the attainment of complete equality between the sexes is the overriding objective.

Fascism is an ideology of the extreme right: it is racist, elitist, authoritarian, and fiercely hostile both to liberalism and socialism.

The core doctrine of **nationalism** is that nations defined in cultural-linguistic terms should form states or possess considerable autonomy within multinational states. Contemporary nationalism takes four main forms: colonial liberation, state renewal and regeneration, nation-building in post-independence regimes and ethnic separatism.

Questions

1. What do you understand by the concept of ideology? Explain its political significance.
2. Analyse the main tenets of Thatcherism in the context of the conservative tradition.
3. What are the theoretical fundamentals of fascism?
4. Is the contemporary British Labour Party socialist?

Assignments

1. Choose a particular political ideology (e.g. conservatism, socialism) and try to show the relationship between its doctrines of human nature, society and government and its policies on, for example, taxation, property ownership, education, welfare and crime.
2. Scottish Nationalism
   Scottish politics have become open to different interpretations in the light of the 1992 General Election result. On the one hand, there is a long-term trend with Conservatives losing support. For example, their level of support has fallen dramatically from 50% in 1955 to 25% in 1992. But on the other hand, predictions that Scotland would become 'Tory free' after the election were wildly inaccurate. In fact, the Conservatives enjoyed a small swing which won them an extra MP compared with the 1987 result. There was a 7.5% swing to the SNP, which won the party three seats, the same number as 1987. Political commentators are putting different interpretations on these results. They are summarised below:

- 'Scotland is a nation but not a state'
  This fact is the cause of political tension in Scotland, and the tension will disappear only when Scotland reclaims its statehood. It is argued that the Scots gave up their independence in 1707 in order to gain access to the

markets of the then expanding British empire. But today the reason for being part of the United Kingdom has long disappeared. The time has come for Scotland to become a separate state once again. Scotland has always retained its own distinctive culture–with its own legal system, educational system and separate church. The Conservatives have no mandate to govern Scotland – which votes Labour but is governed by a Westminster Parliament dominated by Tories from the South of England. It is a fact that in 1992 all Scottish voters who supported Labour, the Liberal Democrats and the SNP – 74.3% in total–were voting for constitutional change. The only disagreement is about the nature of that change; some want Scotland to have full independence within the European Union, whilst others want devolution for Scotland within in UK.

- 'The importance of nationalism has been exaggerated'
This argument claims that political commentators have been fooled by SNP propaganda; if they had examined political reality they would have seen a very different picture. The General Election in Scotland was fought around the same issues as in England – unemployment, the NHS and education–with the constitutional issue playing a very minor role. In fact, it was generally recorded as the tenth most important issue in voters' minds, and was mentioned in polls by around 12% of respondents. This hardly suggests that a vote for the Labour party or the Liberal Democrats represents a vote for Scottish devolution. The hard fact which is difficult for the SNP to accept is that the constitutional issue was, and remains, of low political significance in Scotland. The best way of describing Scotland is to say that it is part of the UK with an above-average Labour vote and a below-average Conservative vote.

Discuss the importance of nationalism in Scottish politics. Which of the above accounts best describes the situation in contemporary Scotland?

Further reading

Charvet, J. (1982) *Feminism* (London: Dent).

Eccleshall, R. (1986) *British Liberalism* (London: Longman).

Eccleshall, R., Geoghegan, V., Jay, R., and Wilford, R. (1984) *Political Ideologies* (London: Hutchinson).

Foote, G. (1986) *The Labour Party's Political Thought* (London: Croom Helm).

Gamble, A. (1994) *The Free Economy and the Strong State: The Politics of Thatcherism*, 2nd edn (London: Macmillan).

Greenleaf, W.H. (1983) *The British Political Tradition: Vol. 2 The Ideological Heritage* (London: Methuen).

Heywood, A. (1992) *Political Ideologies: An Introduction* (London: Macmillan).

Leach, R. (1991) *British Political Ideologies* (London: Philip Allan).

McLellan, D. (1980) *The Thought of Karl Marx* (London: Macmillan).

Millett, K. (1977) *Sexual Politics* (London: Virago).

Nisbet, R. (1986) *Conservatism* (Milton Keynes: Open University Press).

O'Gorman, F. (1986) *British Conservatism* (London: Longman).

O'Sullivan, N. (1983) *Fascism* (London: Dent).

Skidelsky, R. (1975) *Oswald Mosley* (London: Macmillan).

Smith, A.D. (1991) *National Identity* (London: Penguin).

Thurlow, K.C. (1986) *Fascism in Britain: A History 1918–1985* (Oxford: Blackwell).

Tivey, L. and Wright, A. (eds) (1989) *Party Ideology in Britain* (London: Routledge).

Wright, A. (1983) *British Socialism* (London: Longman).

PART II

INSTITUTIONS AND THE POLITICAL PROCESS

■ *Chapter 6* ■

The British Constitution

This chapter discusses the distribution of power and authority within Britain. We begin by examining constitutions in general, including the meaning of the term 'constitution', how a constitution may be distinguished from a 'political system', differing types of constitution, and the reasons why constitutional issues are inherently political. We then consider the major sources, leading principles and actual working of the British Constitution before looking at how it is perceived by the main political ideologies. Finally, we give an account of recent constitutional developments, concluding with the debate about whether Britain needs a written constitution.

■ What is a Constitution?

Political science has sometimes neglected the study of constitutions. This is for two main reasons. First, formal constitutions are imperfect guides to political reality – to the *actual* as compared with the *supposed* distribution of power within a state. For example, many constitutions either omit or scarcely mention the roles in the political process of such important institutions as parties, pressure groups and civil services. In fact, the structure and number of parties are so influential upon the way political systems work that some leading political scientists see these factors as the major determinants of the whole nature of political regimes. None the less, the formal constitutions of at least two of the major liberal democracies, the United States of America (USA)

and the United Kingdom (UK), omit or virtually ignore their role. Clearly, much important political behaviour occurs outside the formal legal framework. Second, formal constitutions have been frequently and easily flouted and overthrown. The constant demolition of allegedly binding constitutions since 1918 appears to mock the nineteenth-century belief in the capacity of written codes of rules to mould political actions. The tearing up of written constitutions by dictators are merely dramatic examples of this process.

Yet, powerful though these considerations undoubtedly are, they represent arguments for not expecting too much from the study of formal constitutions rather than for abandoning the exercise altogether. Even though formal constitutions are *incomplete* as guides to political practice, this lack of comprehensiveness is not a sound reason to neglect their study altogether. For one thing, no document or limited set of documents could ever incorporate the whole of a country's political system in its vastly complex entirety. For another, constitutions' lack of correspondence with political realities can be – and has been – exaggerated. As S.E. Finer has commented, few formal constitutions bear 'no relationship whatsoever to what goes on' in a political system and in some countries – the USA, France and Germany, for example – 'the practice of politics does not widely diverge from the guidelines in the constitutional texts' (Finer, 1979, pp. 13–14, 16).

Formal constitutions, then, do matter for a number of reasons. They contain the most important – if not all – of the procedural rules of

---

Exhibit 6.1   *Definition of a constitution*

A constitution allocates political authority within a state: it states where power is legally located, how it is to be exercised and what limits there are upon it. It defines the composition and powers of the main offices and institutions of state, and regulates their relations with each other and with the ordinary citizen.

---

a political system. They serve as revelations – and reminders – of the political principles a particular people considers important, and wishes to live up to. Alongside moral codes and cultural norms, they provide a means of restraint on politicians and civil servants. And finally, they are the major way of giving legitimacy to a particular system of government, to a particular way of organising the distribution of power within a state.

'Realistic' students of politics, it seems clear, need to distinguish between the formal and informal elements in a political system, between the 'public' constitution, normally contained in a specific document or a number of documents, and the 'private' constitution, the unspecified activities of individuals, groups, parties and other institutions. Both elements are necessary to a comprehensive description of the structure and operations of power and authority in a political community.

But what is a formal constitution? Exhibit 6.1 provides a definition.

It is customary to classify constitutions according to whether they are 'unitary' or 'federal', 'written' or 'unwritten', and 'flexible' or 'inflexible'.

□ *Unitary and Federal Systems*

Constitutions seek to create a viable order out of the diversity which confronts them – a diversity of classes, regions and ethnic groups. All these various subgroups demand from the framers of constitutions inclusion in the state in a manner which accords with their self-respect. The claims of ethnic and regional groupings are normally the hardest to accommodate constitutionally. Where the differing cultures and races in a state are not physically separate from the rest of the community – e.g. blacks in the United States, West Indians, Indians and Pakistanis in the United Kingdom – they may seek protection of their civil rights by special constitutional guarantees and legislation. Where ethnic, cultural and national groups are located in geographically distinct areas – e.g. the Bretons, Basques, Walloons, Welsh and Scots – a classic problem of state-making exists: that of providing a single government for several territorial regions each with its own culture.

The two major forms of political union are unitary and federal systems (Exhibit 6.2). Each recognises the territorial aspect of government –

Exhibit 6.2   *Unitary and federal constitutions*

In a **unitary state**, supreme authority remains in the hands of a single source; devolved power is always subject to supervision by the sovereign body and can be revoked by it.

In a **federal state**, authority is constitutionally divided between several coordinate agencies. The central government may have the more important responsibilities but the provincial governments are all-powerful within their constitutionally allocated spheres of responsibility. Clashes between coordinate governments are resolved by means such as a supreme court or similar institution.

the need to provide for regional cultural diversity – in a different way. In the contemporary world, the United Kingdom, France and Japan are unitary states; the USA, Australia and Germany have federal constitutions.

Written and Unwritten Constitutions

All formal constitutions are selections of the most important legal and political rules and practices. Countries with 'written' constitutions encapsulate the main body of their constitutional law in a single document. Britain, which does not do so, has on this conception an 'unwritten' constitution. However, it has been suggested that this is an incorrect description of the UK constitution, much of which is 'written' although not 'codified' in a single document. In popular, everyday parlance, the British Constitution will probably continue to be referred to as 'unwritten'. But a more precise form of classification would be to use terms such as 'codified' and 'uncodified' to distinguish between those countries which incorporate their major constitutional rules into a single document and those like Britain which, apart from a few Middle Eastern kingdoms, is the only country in the world which does not do so.

Flexible and Inflexible Constitutions

It is a major characteristic of 'written' or 'codified' constitutions that the constitutional law they embody has the status of a higher form of law. For example, Article VI, Clause 2 of the US Constitution states: 'This Constitution ... shall be the supreme law of the land'. Whereas written constitutions are normally only alterable by special procedures, uncodified constitutions can be amended by the same process as the ordinary law. In the matter of ease of amendment, therefore, codified constitutions are generally described as inflexible, uncodified constitutions as flexible.

What Makes Constitutions Political?

Sometimes textbooks on this subject have given the impression that constitutions are somehow 'above politics'. But, in fact, this is not the case. Constitutions are both *about* politics and *in* politics. Constitutions are *about* politics because they provide the framework of rules which shape political behaviour – the main 'rules of the game'. No more than in football or cricket do you have to learn long lists of such rules in order to be able to play the political 'game'. But a grasp of their main features is essential for an understanding of the 'play'. Second, constitutions are *in* politics because as bodies of the most important rules in a country they are subject to pressure from the competing individuals, groups and classes whose activities they constrain. Constitutions at any given moment are always more or less advantageous to some and disadvantageous to others. For example, the single member, simple majority electoral system benefits the British Conservative Party but operates against the Liberal Democrats. A constitution, therefore, is something which politicians and political activists are always seeking to change, radically modify, keep the same or, if they are revolutionaries, overthrow.

Because constitutions are inherently political, they have to be seen in a dynamic rather than a static way. The British Constitution, like other constitutions to a lesser extent, is a *historical* formation. Its provisions reflect a continually changing balance of power between classes, groups and interests. This balance and those constitutional provisions have been changed as a result of *political* action by 'new' groups using such means as demonstrating, lobbying and marching in order to bring about concessions from the established order. Thus the aristocratic 'balanced' constitution of the eighteenth century became the middle-class liberal constitution of the nineteenth century which in turn – as a consequence particularly of the franchise extensions of 1918 and 1928 – became the liberal democratic constitution of the twentieth century.

These changes have involved major shifts of power between the leading national institutions. By the mid-nineteenth century the monarchy and the House of Lords had been supplanted as dominative bodies by the House of Commons which – one hundred years later – had itself been in part displaced from the centre of the constitutional scene by a large bureaucracy and by a vast web of outside interests. Clearly rules which have changed so often and so dramatically over the past two centuries will change again, and change considerably.

One point is worth stressing about the *process* of constitutional change and about the *nature* of the constitutional 'settlement' which results from any period of intense constitutional activity. The process itself always consists of a kind of dialogue between (crudely) the forces of conservation and the forces of transformation and the upshot – *the* constitution at any particular moment – represents in essentials a compromise between them. In that sense, the constitution represents the terms, the arrangements, on which a country can be ruled.

In this quite abstract but very important sense, constitution-making is about engineering consent to government. Thus, in Britain agitation by the middle and working classes and by women broke the constitutional settlements prevailing respectively in the early nineteenth, late nineteenth and early twentieth centuries. At each point in time,

public consent to the constitution was no longer possible on the old terms; change was a condition of political stability. In essence, the nature of constitutions is to express the conditions under which people will consent to be governed.

▌ The main sources of the British Constitution

It is clear from the discussion so far that Britain neither lacks a constitution – as sometimes used to be said – nor that its constitution is unwritten – as also used to be said. In fact, the British constitution can best be described as partly written, but uncodified, i.e. not set down in a single document. It is not codified because, although often compelled to alter course, the country's political authorities have never in modern times faced the kind of crisis which forced them to think the constitution through to first principles, and to set these down. The major sources of the British Constitution are: legislation; common law; conventions; European Union law; the law and custom of Parliament; and works of authority. These are defined and described in more detail – with examples – in Exhibit 6.3.

Exhibit 6.3   *The British Constitution: the major sources*

Legislation: Easily the most significant source of British constitutional law. It consists both of Acts of Parliament and of subordinate legislation such as Orders in Council (made by the Queen in her Privy Council) and rules and regulations made by Ministers under statutory authority. Key constitutional matters regulated by legislation include:
● The composition of the electorate (Representation of the People Acts, 1832–1928);
● Relations between the Crown and Parliament (Bill of Rights, 1689); between the two Houses of Parliament (Parliament Acts, 1911 and 1949); between the component parts of the UK (Act of Union with Scotland, 1707); between the UK and the EEC (European Communities Act, 1972) and between the individual and the state (Habeas Corpus Act, 1679, and the Administration of Justice Act, 1960).

Common Law: Common law means case law and custom, the law made by the decisions of courts or which has grown up as accepted practice over the years. Having declined over the centuries, it is now less important than legislation but remains significant in three main ways:
● The fundamental constitutional principle of parliamentary sovereignty derives from a small number of customary rules (now in part qualified by legislation).

Exhibit 6.3—*continued*

- The remaining prerogative powers exercised by or in the name of the Crown derive from common law, e.g. the appointment of Ministers, the dissolution of Parliament, the power of pardon and the award of honours. By convention, these powers are now predominantly exercised on the advice of ministers.
- Decisions made by the courts under the principle of judicial review of administrative action.

Conventions: Conventions have been persuasively defined as 'certain rules of constitutional behaviour which are considered to be binding by and upon those who operate the Constitution, but which are not enforced by the law courts (although the courts may recognise their existence), nor by the presiding officers in the Houses of Parliament' (Marshall and Moodie, 1967, p. 26).

Conventions are a major means by which the constitution adapts to changing circumstances and are absolutely essential to its working. Many relate to the powers of the monarch, including those that the Queen must appoint as prime minister a person who has the confidence of the House of Commons (this will normally be the leader of the majority party), must assent to measures passed by both Houses of Parliament, and must exercise her powers on Ministerial advice. Other conventions regulate the relations between the executive and legislature (e.g. Ministerial responsibility), and the operation of the two Houses of Parliament, the civil service and the judiciary.

Conventions are observed largely because of the political difficulties which would follow if they were not: for example, for the monarchy if it refused a request for a dissolution, for a prime minister if he or she came from the Lords. Conventions are vaguer than laws and sometimes – when challenged – are superseded by legislation: for example, in 1910, a convention that the upper House should defer to the lower House on matters of finance was threatened by the Lords' rejection of a budget, which led to this aspect of relations between the two Houses being settled by legislation (Parliament Act, 1911) Normally, a rule becomes a convention once it has been accepted and operated by governments of differing political persuasions.

European Union Law: From 1973, when Britain joined the European Economic Community, Community law (now Union law) has been a source of British constitutional law. (The European Economic Community became the European Community in 1987 and the European Union in 1993). Some EU rules – mainly regulations made by the Council of Ministers and the Commission – are 'directly applicable' in the UK: this means that they are applied by British courts without re-enactment as though they are Acts of Parliament. Membership of the EU has general constitutional implications with regard to the doctrine of parliamentary sovereignty (discussed in text). More specifically, the EU can levy certain customs duties directly in the United Kingdom (UK) and the UK may not restrict the employment or occupation of any EU national given leave to enter the country.

The law and custom of Parliament: The rules relating to the functions, procedure, privileges and immunities of each House of Parliament: sources of these are the resolutions of each House, conventions (e.g. the duty of impartiality required of the Speaker of the House of Commons) and other informal understandings (e.g. relating to the allocation of time to the Opposition), and to a lesser extent statute law and judicial interpretation.

Works of authority: Its partly written and uncodified character means that constitutional experts and works of authority have occasionally to be consulted for guidance on the British Constitution. Post-1945, for example, constitutional authorities have been turned to on such matters as peerage law, aspects of the royal prerogative, the law of treason and constitutional conventions (de Smith, 1983, p. 38). On the law and custom of Parliament, Sir Thomas Erskine May's treatise on the *Law, Privileges, Proceedings and Usage of Parliament* is regarded as definitive.

▌ The Main Characteristics of the British Constitution

As well as being flexible and partly written but uncodified, the British Constitution is unitary rather than federal, based on the principle of parliamentary sovereignty, and generally considered to enshrine the rule of law.

□ *A Unitary Constitution*

The United Kingdom of Great Britain and Northern Ireland is a political union of several countries, each with a different constitutional status. Legally, it consists of the Kingdoms of England and Scotland, the Principality of Wales and two-thirds of the province of Ulster (Northern Ireland) which remained loyal to the British Crown in 1922 when the rest of Ireland split away to form what eventually became the Republic of Ireland (1949).

However, although the national sub-divisions of the British Isles lend themselves in theory to a federal constitution, the United Kingdom has become – and remains – a **unitary state**. The major reason for this is the strength of political will displayed by mediaeval and early modern English ruling groups in successively incorporating Wales (1536), Scotland (1707) and Ireland (1801) into a political union on terms dictated by its most powerful member.

The argument that the UK is not a true unitary state is unconvincing. This claim rests in particular upon Scotland's retention of its own legal system and upon the degree of devolution to Northern Ireland between 1921 and 1972 which allegedly made it more like a provincial unit in a federal system than a constitutionally subordinate part of a unitary state. However, the constitutionally subordinate status of Scotland and Wales was revealed over the issue of devolution in 1978 when, having legislated devolved powers upon Scottish and Welsh assemblies, the Westminster Parliament repealed them in the following year. The fundamentally subordinate position of Stormont, the Northern Ireland parliament, within the UK was shown in 1972 when the Westminster government revoked its powers and reasserted direct rule over the province from Westminster. The Westminster Parliament (in strict legal terms, the Crown-in-Parliament) remains the supreme constitutional authority in the United Kingdom.

□ *Parliamentary Sovereignty*

A unitary state and **parliamentary sovereignty** go together. If there were not a single source of sovereignty, the state would not be a unitary one. In formal terms, parliamentary authority is unlimited: it can make or unmake law on any subject whatsoever; and it can do so retrospectively. The classic statement of its omnicompetence derives from William Blackstone, the eighteenth-century jurist, who declared that parliament 'can do everything that is not naturally impossible'. No person may question its legislative competence and the courts must give effect to its legislation.

However, it should be remembered, first, that Parliament has liquidated its own authority as a result of political pressures over large areas of the world this century and could do so again, e.g. by introducing a federal structure within the UK itself. Such a fundamental structural change may seem improbable but as long as it had the support of public opinion as well as a parliamentary majority, it is likely that it would be recognised by the courts. And from that moment, supreme authority in the British state would be divided between several coordinate governing institutions – i.e. the Westminster Parliament and assemblies in Scotland, Wales and Northern Ireland – rather than, as now, residing wholly in one.

Second, we need to consider how far the sovereignty of the UK Parliament has already been impaired by membership of the European Union (EU). The European Communities Act (1972) gave the force of law in the United Kingdom to obligations arising under the EC treaties; it gave EC law general and binding authority within the United Kingdom; it provided that Community law should take precedence over all inconsistent

UK law; and it precluded the UK Parliament from legislating on matters within EC competence where the Community had formulated rules to 'occupy the field'.

On the face of it, parliamentary sovereignty is seriously impaired, if not dead. However, the position is less clear-cut than it appears. First, membership of the EU has not, it seems, broken the principle that Parliament cannot bind its future action. Thus, the European Communities Act was overturnable and indeed had the 1975 Referendum on continuing membership of the EC gone the other way, the United Kingdom would probably have withdrawn from the Community. Second, what happens should a member state refuse to pass amending legislation where its law is inconsistent with EU law? It seems clear that the European Court of Justice cannot hold national legislation void because it is inconsistent with European law. In fact, this is an 'extreme' case which normally would not arise because the amending legislation would be passed (de Smith and Brazier, 1990, p. 82).

Despite these qualifications, however, a reasonable summary of the present constitutional position would be that Britain's membership of the European Union has impaired the doctrine of parliamentary sovereignty which can only be restored to its pre-1973 state by Britain's withdrawal from the Union. Britain's legal subordination to Brussels was underlined by an important legal case in 1991, *R.v. Secretary of State for Transport ex parte Factortame Ltd* no 2. (The Factortame case). The European Court of Justice in effect quashed sections of a British Act of Parliament (the Merchant Shipping Act 1988) which provided that UK-registered boats must be 75 per cent British-owned and have 75 per cent of crew resident in the UK. The Act had been designed to prevent boats from Spain and other EC countries 'quota-hopping' by registering under the British flag and using the UK's EC fishing quotas. British legislation had been overturned before by the Court but no earlier case had provoked such an outcry. This was mainly because *Factortame* concerned a matter traditionally associated with national sovereignty

– the registration of vessels. (See further Peele (1993) pp. 25–6).

Also, the UK Parliament is subject to *political* constraints on what it can actually – as opposed to what it may theoretically – do. In addition to needing to take into account a wide variety of day-to-day pressures, the government is inhibited by obligations assumed under treaties, for example as a member of the North Atlantic Treaty Organisation (NATO), or even by the terms of foreign loans. In 1976 the Labour Government had to promise to introduce deflationary legislation as a condition of a loan from the International Monetary Fund (IMF).

Although it may occasionally pass legislation which is genuinely unpopular, such as suspending capital punishment, the government must also govern in broad accordance with public opinion. This is largely what is meant by saying that whereas Parliament is the legal sovereign (or possesses constitutional supremacy), the electorate is the *political* sovereign. Governments must therefore pay some regard to pressure-group views and to the opinion polls. Trade union resistance wrecked the 1971 Trade Union Act and widespread popular revolt destroyed the poll tax. The prohibition of alcoholic liquor would be as unpopular in Britain as it was for a brief spell in the USA, and no government has yet tried it.

☐ *The Rule of Law*

The British Constitution is commonly said to be based on the principle of *the rule of law* but this principle has proved hard to define precisely. It broadly comprises the following meanings:

- The powers exercised by politicians and public servants must have a legitimate foundation, i.e. they must be exercised in accordance with authorised procedures.
- Redress – i.e. legal remedy for wrongs – is available to all citizens both against any other citizen, no matter how powerful, and against officers of the state.

The leading jurist A.V. Dicey (1835–1922) saw the rule of law as a fundamental characteristic of the British Constitution, viewing it as of equal importance to the doctrine of parliamentary sovereignty. In reality however, although of key significance, it is subsidiary to it since in strict constitutional terms parliamentary sovereignty could be used to remove the rights entailed by the rule of law.

Certain twentieth-century developments have led to concern about the contemporary validity of the principle of the rule of law. Anxieties have been expressed in these areas:

● The wide range of discretionary powers assumed and exercised by public authorities;
● The powers and accountability of the police and security services;
● The ability of the state to guarantee equality of rights to blacks and other minority groups;
● The impartiality of the courts especially in trade union and race relations cases.

At the same time, from the 1970s the rule of law came under threat increasingly from terrorists and other groups prepared to resort to illegal methods to change the law. In response, the state was propelled into detention without trial and other abuses of legal procedure. Concern about the threat to individual liberties has led to calls for a Bill of Rights to protect basic freedoms such as freedom of expression, association and movement (see Chapter 17).

The general characteristics of the British Constitution as discussed so far are summarised in Exhibit 6.4.

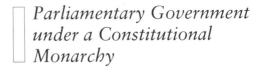

The Working of the Constitution

Parliamentary Government under a Constitutional Monarchy

This phrase is the most apt description of the British liberal democratic state. Its leading features are as follows. At least once every five years, everyone over 18 votes either for the party in government or one of the opposition parties in a general election, the main purpose of which is to elect a government. The party which gains the majority of seats in the House of Commons wins the election. By convention, the monarch then asks the leader of the majority party to form a government. If the leader lacks an overall majority, he or she may consult with other party leaders about the possibility of a coalition, but need not do so.

The victorious party leader normally becomes the prime minister and forms a Cabinet and then a government from party colleagues. Names are submitted to the monarch who, by convention, assents to the prime minister's choice. The Cabinet is the committee which governs the country. Its major tasks are to make decisions on policy and legislation and submit these decisions to Parliament for its assent. It also controls and coordinates the major Departments of State. The Cabinet is collectively responsible to the House of Commons for its decisions and, if defeated on a vote of confidence, must either request a dissolution of Parliament – i.e. call a general election –

Exhibit 6.4 *Main features of the British Constitution*
● Unitary ● Flexible ● Partly written but uncodified ● Parliamentary sovereignty ● Rule of law

or resign. Although this did occur in March 1979, in normal circumstances it happens only rarely because party discipline ensures that the party in government, which normally commands a majority in the House of Commons, is secure against parliamentary defeat. All government Ministers are formally responsible to the monarch and, by convention, through the doctrine of Ministerial responsibility, to Parliament.

The Cabinet is assisted in the policy-making process by the civil service. At all stages of this process, there is consultation between government and outside interests (pressure groups). The House of Commons is the major legislative chamber but the House of Lords retains a significant largely amending role in the parliamentary process. Once it has been passed by both Houses of Parliament, a bill goes to the monarch for assent which, by convention, is never refused. The bill is now an Act of Parliament (statute), has binding authority (it cannot be challenged in the courts) and is enforced by the agencies of state.

So far we have been dealing with the major institutions of central decision-making – Cabinet Ministers, other Ministers, Civil Service, Parliament. This emphasis is a fair reflection of a highly centralised political system: Britain is a unitary state with the power of policy-making for the entire UK located in a Cabinet responsible to the Westminster Parliament. Parliamentary sovereignty means that parliament can both give and remove powers from subordinate units of government. In recent years, it has undoubtedly removed more powers from than it has given to such institutions. Nevertheless, subordinate units of government operating at national, regional and local levels remain of constitutional significance.

Nationally, the main subordinate institutions are the nationalised industries and the non-departmental bodies known as 'quangos' (quasi-autonomous non-governmental organisations). Although the boards which run them are appointed by the appropriate Ministers, the **nationalised industries** are able to function in considerable independence from detailed day-to-day political control. By the early 1990s, however, their number had been severely reduced by large-scale Conservative privatisations.

'**Quangos**' are public bodies established by government to advise on or administer matters of public concern which carry out their work at arm's length from government. Good examples are the New Town Development Corporations, the UK Atomic Energy Authority, the British Broadcasting Corporation (BBC), the Arts Council of Great Britain and the Higher Education Funding Council. The Conservative Government came to office in 1979 pledged to reduce their numbers, but although there were about one-fifth fewer 'quangos' by 1990–1 (1846) these unelected organisations spent about three times as much as in 1978–9.

Regionally, the highest subordinate institutions are the government departments responsible for the administration of a wide range of functions in Northern Ireland, Scotland and Wales. In each country, the respective Department or Office is given the responsibility for such matters as health, housing, education and environmental services within the territorial area. At an intermediate level, non-elected quasi-governmental bodies administer certain services throughout England, Scotland and Wales. The best examples are the 14 regional health authorities (eight from 1994) created under the 1973 Health Service Reorganisation Act. In addition, government departments such as the Department of the Environment and the Department of Trade and Industry devolve authority to regional offices.

Finally, the only elected form of government below national level on the British mainland (but not in Northern Ireland) exists in local government. The powers of local authorities are strictly curtailed: they can exercise only those functions authorised by law; they have to operate within the framework set by national government; and a high proportion of their expenditure is provided by central government. During the 1980s the large-scale transformation of the responsibilities of local government by the Conservative Administrations did not require any special procedures. However, some argued that an important constitutional 'understanding', if not convention, had been breached: that fundamental changes in the balance of central–local power and in local democracy should not be made in haste but only after the considered reflection generated by a public inquiry.

This deliberately brief summary of the main features of the British system of parliamentary government is intended to provide a succinct framework for the fuller discussions in the rest of the book. It has brought out the close inter-dependence between institutions like Parliament, the monarchy and the electorate with a formal constitutional role and those informal institutions like parties, without which the formal constitution could not work, and pressure groups, without which no realistic description of the contemporary system would be possible. Exhibit 6.5 both summarises and completes this brief survey by relating key concepts employed in the analysis of liberal democratic systems to the British Constitution.

Exhibit 6.5   *The British Constitution: the main concepts*

These items are often used to describe the British Constitution; this table contains a guide to their meanings.

- **Constitutional government**

(a) Government according to recognised rules, including rules about how the rules can be changed, these rules being both regular and well known. To be legitimate, authority has to be exercised according to certain procedures so that where misuse or abuse of authority takes place, it is readily apparent; the citizen suffering misuse or abuse of authority may seek redress through the ordinary courts; and there are legal procedural restraints on rulers, such as hear the other side, the rule against bias.

(b) Constitutionalism is linked in liberal theory with the desire to avoid concentrations of power, for which purpose the doctrine of *the separation of powers* was developed in the eighteenth century: the idea that the institutions that make, carry out and adjudicate the laws should be both separate and in the hands of different persons. The only way in which the British system embodies this theory is in the independence of the judiciary; executive and legislature overlap in that the government (executive) is elected through the House of Commons (lower house of legislature) not separately as in the USA, and Ministers are drawn from and remain within parliament. A related concept with the similar purpose of preventing the growth of absolute power is *checks and balances*, the idea of the division of authority between numerous governing institutions so that they provide curbs upon each other; such devices include judicial review and a bicameral legislature. Britain has a bicameral legislature (two houses of parliament), but not, as we have seen, judicial review or, except for an independent judiciary, separation of powers.

(c) Two concepts which are negatively related to constitutionalism need examining here: unconstitutional and anti-constitutional. *Unconstitutional* means behaviour which breaks or threatens to break the constitution, or, more usually, a part of it; *anti-constitutional* refers to the effort to undermine the whole constitution out of a disbelief in the desirability of any constitutional restraints or a wish to produce a superior one more representative of the will of the people.

- **Parliamentary government**

The British form of constitutional and representative government in which executive and legislative power is fused in and exercised through a single two-chamber assembly, cf. their separation in the USA into two distinct institutions, the Presidency and Congress. Legislation and taxation originated by government are validated by the consent of Parliament whose acceptance signifies and symbolises the consent of the nation. Parliament does not itself govern but the policies and activities of governments are criticised in Parliament and, most importantly, all legislation emanates from Parliament.

Exhibit 6.5—*Continued*

- **Representative government**

A form of democratic rule in which government is by representatives (e.g. MPs or Congressmen) elected by popular votes; the exercise of authority is legitimated ultimately (although not solely, since it must be exercised also according to constitutional rules) by the popular election of power-holders. The idea of a representative in this system varies between two meanings:

(a) the Burkean view, in which the representative, whilst having the duty to consult and take into account constituents' opinions, owes the primary duty to the national interest and to conscience. Parliament in this view is 'a deliberative assembly of one nation rather than a congress of ambassadors'; i.e. it should lead public opinion rather than simply reflect it. This idea of the representative has prevailed in the UK.

(b) the delegate theory, in which the elected representatives are considered to be the agent of and directly accountable to their constituents; the national assembly on this view is or should be a direct register or mirror of public opinion, rather than a director of it (always suspected as manipulation); this theory is part of the ideology of radical democracy and became increasingly influential in the late 1970s on the Labour Party (p. 74, above; p. 247, below)

- **Responsible government**

This is the idea that government should be both strong – and therefore able when necessary to take unpopular decisions – *and* accountable for its actions to the elected representatives of the people. In the UK, the *collective* responsibility to Parliament of Ministers for the policy of the Cabinet, and the *individual* responsibility to Parliament of Ministers for the work of their Departments are the devices intended to achieve responsible government. It is often claimed that responsible government is more easily achieved by the UK parliamentary system than by the US system where President and Congress are separately elected and to a large extent function independently of each other.

- **Party government**

Within liberal democratic systems, competition between two or more cohesive parties for votes and their alternation in power is the method by which popular wishes are translated into public policy. So essential are parties to the successful working of democratic systems that some political commentators now prefer to describe them in terms of 'party government' rather than of 'representative' or 'parliamentary government'. They claim this not only because government and opposition are both by party but also because much of the behaviour of representatives suggests they owe their first loyalty to party rather than to their consciences, their constituents or the national interest.

Ideological Perceptions of the British Constitution

The political parties have differing perceptions of the British Constitution, both of how it works and of how – if at all – it should be changed.

☐ *Conservative Party*

Conservatives see authority as flowing from above: they emphasise strong government and accord popular participation a minimal role. So government, backed by a loyal party, governs; and the electorate, through Parliament, consents to this firm leadership. Conservatives regard loyalty to the party leader as a primary political virtue and party as a socially integrative force, enabling people of ability to bind the nation together by drawing support for their policies from all classes and groups. By tradition and instinct, Conservatives are committed to the preservation of the Union and, in office, reluctant to disturb the historical constitution. In the late

1970s, some Conservatives (Lord Hailsham, Sir Ian Gilmour, Rhodes Boyson, Sir Keith Joseph) did call for reforms to strengthen limited government by checking an over-mighty executive. But the Thatcher Governments in the 1980s combined traditional concerns to uphold the Union and preserve the existing electoral system with measures leading to even greater centralisation of power.

☐ *The Labour Party*

The mainstream Labour tradition also endorses the strong executive embodied in British constitutional arrangements, but for a different reason. It perceives the Labour Party as a vehicle for the parliamentary representation of the working class and argues that, once having gained an electoral majority for its programme, the party has a mandate to enact it without check or hindrance.

The loyalty owed by the individual Labour MP to the party springs from solidarity with the cause it serves. Group representation (the trade unions, cooperative societies) is entrenched in its own constitution, which gives party members a role in shaping the party programme. Reforms of Labour's constitution proposed by the left in the late 1970s were aimed at enforcing leadership accountability to the rank and file, whilst reforms of the national constitution advocated by a leading left-winger (Tony Benn) entailed its replacement by a republican democracy.

A decade later, as left influence waned, the mainstream Labour Party took up the cause of constitutional reform but stopped short of advocating either electoral reform or a 'written' constitution. However, in early 1993, the Labour leader, John Smith, committed himself to support for a Bill of Rights through incorporation of the European Convention of Human Rights into British law, arguing that common law rights are incomplete, ill-defined and inaccessible to the ordinary citizen. His statement marked a growing individualism in Labour's constitutional thought, a concern to protect the rights of the individual against institutions of government at all levels.

☐ *The Liberal Democrats*

The Liberal Democrats put radical constitutional reform at the centre of their programme, seeing it as the major precondition of social and economic progress. Strong supporters of parliamentary government, they consider that the role of Parliament has been downgraded in the twentieth century by the growth of executive power, the main contributory factors being the emergence of programmatic parties each with a collectivist ethos together with a massive bureaucracy. In addition, the electoral system is unfair, making for minority government and penalising the smaller parties.

Adherents of individual liberties and the rights of minorities, Liberal Democrats believe that political over-centralisation combined with the emergence of a multicultural society have eroded individual liberties and produced problems in the protection of national, regional and black minorities. They therefore advocate far-reaching constitutional reforms, including proportional representation, a Bill of Rights, the strengthening of Parliament, and large-scale devolution and de-centralisation of power away from Westminster and Whitehall (see Table 6.1).

☐ *The Nationalist Parties*

In their 1992 manifesto, the Scottish Nationalists (SNP) called for an immediate move to independence after the election, bypassing devolution which would lead to endless feuds with Westminster. An independent Scotland would remain a member of the EC.

The Welsh Nationalists called for an elected Welsh parliament as an interim step towards the achievement of full independence by the end of the century. Their vision was of 'a self-governing Wales within a democratic European confederation'.

In Northern Ireland, the Protestant Unionist parties support the maintenance of the Union with Britain. But the Catholic Social Democratic and Labour Party (SDLP) wants the ending of

Table 6.1 *The parties and the Constitution: the main manifesto proposals in 1992*

	Conservative	Labour	Liberal Democrat
Parliament		Fixed parliamentary term	Fixed term of 4 years
House of Commons	'Appropriate' reforms to ensure parliament conducts its business 'more efficiently and effectively'.	Improve procedures and facilities, strengthen scrutiny of EC legislation, and end ministerial misuse of the Royal Prerogative. Public register for political donations, party accounts to be published, aid for political parties. Shareholders to have right to vote on companies' political donations.	Strengthen against executive by boosting powers of select committees, improving staff support for backbenchers and increasing financial and civil service assistance for opposition parties. Improve quality of legislation by pre-legislative committees and better scrutiny of delegated legislation. Improve debates by fairer allocation of time for Commons business, timetabling committee sessions of bills and ending all-night sittings.
House of Lords		New elected second chamber with power to delay Bills reducing individual or constitutional rights over lifetime of a parliament.	Reform as senate mainly elected by citizens of regions and nations and with power to delay non-money Bills for up to two years.
Devolution	UK 'far greater than the sum of its parts'. Nationalist independence plans 'a recipe for weakness and isolation'; plans for devolution 'run risk' of separation.	Scottish assembly elected by PR. Welsh assembly and Regional government in England.	Elected Scottish parliament and Welsh senedd. Regional government in England. Decentralise power to new regional and national governments.
Local government	No demand for regional government in England. Commission to examine appropriate local government arrangements. Plan to recreate wasteful and bureacratic GLC rejected. New council tax.	Simplify with 'most purpose' single tier authorities based usually on district councils. New elected Greater London Council. Fair rates tax. Annual elections for one-third councillors.	Reform as new unitary system based on natural communities and local wishes. Strengthen with new powers, fairer voting system and local income tax.
Individual rights	Citizen's Charter to improve quality of public services.	Charter of rights to establish rights of every citizen in law. Stronger laws against racial and sexual discrimination	Bill of Rights by incorporation of European Convention on human rights into British law. British Bill of Rights to include also rights not currently in the convention.
Electoral system		Continued debate. Working party to report.	Reform by introducing proportional representation (PR) system at local, national and European elections; single transferable vote (STV) in multi-member constituencies.
Freedom of information	More openness. Will reduce restrictions on disclosure of information, provide greater access to personal files held by government and publish Cabinet committees and guidance for Ministers on procedure.	Freedom of Information Act with 'tightly-drawn' exceptions.	Freedom of Information Act

partition (the settlement in 1922 which created the present division between Northern Ireland and the Irish Republic): it seeks the reunification of Ireland by political means whereas the Provisional IRA (Irish Republican Army), whose goal is also reunification, sees itself as involved in a war against an occupying power.

■ The Changing Constitution

In the last two decades, constitutional change and pressures for further change have mounted steadily. From being considered a settled matter, the Constitution is now firmly on the political agenda. One vital development was the change which occurred in parliamentary sovereignty.

□ *Parliamentary Sovereignty*

As already noticed, Britain's membership of the European Community (1973) has had a fundamental impact on this central doctrine of the Constitution. Legislation by the British Parliament must be compatible with Community law and, if not, it can be challenged in the European Court of Justice and its provisions overridden by Community legislation. The Single European Act (1986) and the Treaty of Maastricht (1992) together with the ensuing parliamentary debate on the Maastricht Bill further underlined this change.

In addition, doubts and uncertainties arose in the following areas.

□ *Centralisation of Government*

The concern expressed here has three main aspects.

Relations between the Westminster Government and the Periphery

This question became an issue in the 1970s with the upsurge of nationalism in Wales and Scotland and the resumption of direct rule over Northern

Ireland by the British Government in 1972. Devolution proposals for Wales and Scotland (1979) were rejected in referendums but the issue of devolution has remained prominent especially in Scotland where four successive elections between 1979 and 1992 left the Scots being governed by a party for which only about one-quarter of them had voted.

Central–Local Relations

The existence of a vigorous local government as a counterweight to the power of the centre has no firm embodiment in the Constitution but was for a long time considered to be a pluralist check. During the 1980s, however, the Government introduced sweeping changes which included the abolition of the Greater London Council and the metropolitan counties, the reallocation of some responsibilities and functions of local government to other institutions, and the introduction of a new local tax – the 'poll tax'.

Intermediary Institutions

Organisations as diverse as trade unions, the BBC, the universities and the nationalised industries were the subject of restrictive government intervention in the 1980s, having their influence pruned or, in the latter case, being largely eliminated. Some commentators believed that these developments cumulatively eroded political pluralism – the idea of the value of a range of vital intermediate institutions standing as buffers between the state and the citizen.

□ *Executive Power*

There were two major sources of constitutional attention.

Relations Between Parliament and the Executive

Despite certain changes aimed at increasing the capacity of Parliament to hold the executive to account, such as the establishment of Commons

Select Committees, the concern persisted that Parliament remained a rather ineffective critic of and check upon government. The House of Lords at times showed surprising vigour, but its hereditary basis continued to be widely criticised as an anachronism in a democratic society.

The 'Politicisation' of Government

This phrase became increasingly used in the 1980s and early 1990s to denote anxiety at what was felt to be improper use of governmental powers in the interests of party rather the nation. Fears expressed under this umbrella term include the alleged 'politicisation' of the higher ranks of the civil service, the use of patronage to 'pack' quangos with politically sympathetic people and the employment of the honours system to reward MPs for political services and company chairmen for donations to party funds.

☐ *Parliamentary Government*

On two occasions during the 1970s – in 1975 to vote on the re-negotiated terms of British membership of the EC and in 1979 for the Scots and Welsh to vote on devolution legislation – British governments have used referendums, hitherto considered an alien constitutional mechanism quite out of keeping with a parliamentary system. Since then, calls for a referendum have been heard from time to time, e.g. on the ratification of the Maastricht Treaty. But it is hard to maintain that referendums have become 'part of the Constitution' since there remains considerable controversy about their value and no certainty at all over the circumstances in which they will be used, if at all.

☐ *The Electoral System*

Electoral reform mattered to few outside the Liberal Party before the 1970s but became of increasing interest after 1974 as the major parties began to receive diminishing shares of the total vote. From 1979, government was by a party

which gained only just over two-fifths of the popular vote whilst the very sizeable proportion of the vote gained by smaller parties was not reflected in parliamentary seats. Hence, criticism of the 'first past the post' simple majority system grew and support for proportional representation extended well beyond the Liberals.

☐ *Civil Liberties*

Civil liberties as a political issue became increasingly prominent from the early 1970s as a consequence of a series of cases involving individual rights against the state. Controversy arose over such matters as the use of police powers, the banning of trade unions at the government communications headquarters (GCHQ), the prosecution of civil servants for 'leaking' information classified under the Official Secrets Acts, restrictions on freedom of movement during the Miners' Strike (1984–5) and Government pressure on the broadcasting authorities (BBC and ITV) over programmes involving state security.

☐ *A 'Hung' Parliament*

Uncertainty arose over what the monarch would do in a situation in which no party had an overall majority after a general election. There seemed to be three alternatives for the Queen:

- To permit the leader of the previously largest party to continue;
- To invite the leader of the largest party to attempt to form a government (assuming, of course, this were not the existing governing party);
- To invite any individual from the House of Commons to try to constitute a government with a Commons majority.

What happened in this situation in February 1974 may be taken as a precedent. On that occasion, when the Conservative Government failed to gain an overall majority at the General Election, Edward Heath, the existing Prime

Minister, did remain in office for four days whilst he sought support from the Liberals to enable him to form a government. He failed and Harold Wilson, the leader of the largest party, formed a minority Labour Government which he led as Prime Minister for eight months until seeking a dissolution in order to obtain an overall majority.

On the other hand, the Labour Party believes that the largest party in such a situation is entitled to form a minority government whilst the Liberal Democrats and the Nationalists consider that one or other of the major parties should try to form a Coalition Government. These beliefs were not put to the test in the 1992 General Election – as pre-election polls suggested they might be; hence, this remains one of the 'grey' areas of the Constitution where no widely accepted understanding has emerged to make up a convention.

Opinions also differ about how soon and in what circumstances the Queen would grant a dissolution. Would she invite more than one party leader to attempt to form a government or would she grant a dissolution to the first person to fail? Labour believes that a prime minister leading a minority government is automatically entitled to a dissolution whilst the Liberal Democrats consider that the Queen might grant a dissolution only if she was convinced that another government could not be formed from the existing House of Commons.

Much depends upon the view her advisers take about the degree of independent authority remaining to the monarch. Some constitutional experts argue that very little remains of the royal prerogative; others maintain that in such circumstances sufficient residual power exists to justify the monarch playing a decisive role. A further consideration is the extent to which the monarch might be willing to be seen to be acting politically. One prominent view is that she would not wish her influence to be a crucial factor in resolving a crisis since this would impair her neutral stance 'above politics' and that consequently she would be likely to grant an immediate dissolution to whoever requested it in order that the electorate should decide.

Constitutional Reform – Arguments and Proposals

Constitutional reform moved to the centre of the political stage in the late 1980s in a way not seen since before 1914. Compared with the earlier period of constitutional concern in the 1960s and 1970s, this new phase was about fundamentals, and produced radical proposals for reform. An important step was the formation of **Charter 88**, which brought together leading individuals from all walks of life under the aegis of the *New Statesman and Society* and the Constitutional Reform Centre in a movement consciously modelled on the Czech Charter 77 (Exhibit 6.6).

Although deriving mainly from individuals, groups and parties of the centre and left and from the Nationalist parties, constitutional reform proposals also came from the political right, e.g. *The Economist* weekly newspaper, the Institute of Economic Affairs (IEA) and a former head of Margaret Thatcher's Political Unit, Ferdinand Mount.

The reforming mood also gained some endorsement by public opinion. In March 1991, a MORI 'State of the Nation' poll revealed that over 70 per cent of the sample questioned were in favour of a Freedom of Information Act, a Bill of Rights and more use of referendums; over three-quarters supported the limitation of national and local campaign spending by political parties.

The most important difference between reformers is between those who advocate piecemeal reform and those who favour a written constitution. But there is a considerable amount of common ground between the two groups in the specific reforms they advocate. Exhibit 6.7 indicates the large area of agreement existing between constitutional reformers (excluding the Conservative Party, which of course does not favour constitutional reform).

There was less agreement on for example the remaining Royal Prerogative powers, including such matters as the sovereign's role in the choice of a prime minister and in dealing with a request for a dissolution. Tony Benn would abolish the

---

Exhibit 6.6 *Charter 88*

The time has come to demand political, civil and human rights in the United Kingdom. The first step is to establish them in constitutional form, so that they are no longer subject to the arbitrary dictat of Westminster and Whitehall.

We call, therefore, for a new constitutional settlement which would: Enshrine, by means of a Bill of Rights, such civil liberties as the right to peaceful assembly, to freedom of association, to freedom from discrimination, to freedom from detention without trial by jury, to privacy and to freedom of expression.

Subject executive powers and prerogatives, by whomsoever exercised, to the rule of law.

Establish freedom of information and open government.

Create a fair electoral system of proportional representation.

Reform the upper house to establish a democratic, non-hereditary second chamber.

Place the executive under the power of a democratically renewed parliament and all agencies of the state under the rule of law.

Ensure the independence of a reformed judiciary.

Provide legal remedies for all abuses of power by the state and the officials of central, regional and local government.

Guarantee an equitable distribution of power between local, regional and national government.

Draw up a written constitution, anchored in the idea of universal citizenship, that incorporates these reforms.

Our central concern is the law. No country can be considered free in which the government is above the law. No democracy can be considered safe whose freedoms are not encoded in a basic constitution.

We, the undersigned, have called this document Charter 88. First, to mark our rejection of the complacency with which the tercentenary of the Revolution of 1688 has been celebrated. Second, to reassert a tradition of demands for constitutional rights in Britain, which stretches from the barons who forced the Magna Carta on King John, to the working men who drew up the People's Charter in 1838, to the women at the beginning of this century who demanded universal suffrage. Third, to salute the courage of those in Eastern Europe who still fight for their fundamental freedoms.

Exhibit 6.7 *Constitutional reform: the common ground*

- Fixed four-year term for Parliament.
- Strengthen parliament against executive (not Labour).
- Reform House of Lords on elective principle.
- Decentralise power by devolution to regions (not IEA).
- Bill of Rights by incorporation of European Convention of Human Rights into UK law (not Tony Benn).
- Electoral reform by some variant of proportional representation (not Labour, IEA).
- Freedom of information.

---

monarchy entirely, other reformers would transform it into a merely dignified institution by removing the remaining prerogative powers, whilst most reformers fail to tackle the issue at all.

If enacted piecemeal, the reform proposals would make a very great difference to the working of the British Constitution but they would not transform it completely. Even if eroded by EC membership, parliamentary sovereignty would remain its cardinal principle. However, the proposal that constitutional reforms should be codified in a single document would make an enormous difference, if accomplished. Parliamentary sovereignty would no longer be the basic principle of the British Constitution: rather, the Constitution itself would be supreme.

Two further consequences are worthy of note. First, constitutional change itself would require a special procedure and would therefore be more difficult to achieve than under the present system. Second, judges – their authority institutionalised is in a supreme or a high court – would play a decisive role in the interpretation of the Constitution. By 1991, when a Charter 88 convention met to consider how to fuse a consensus out of them, draft constitutions had been proposed by the Labour left-winger, Tony Benn, the left of centre Institute for Public Policy Research, the Liberal Democrat, John MacDonald, and the Conservative-leaning think-tank, the Institute of Economic Affairs.

We end this chapter by considering the arguments for and against a codified constitution for Britain. Constitutional radicals argue that a codified constitution would:

- Replace the uncertainty of the existing Constitution with constitutional rules which have far greater clarity thereby *(a)* providing a fixed point of reference for constitutional debate; *(b)* encouraging a citizen rather than subject-based political culture in which people know and feel able to assert their rights; and *(c)* bringing the UK into line with other advanced democracies.
- Eliminate the doctrine of parliamentary sovereignty which, however liberating in the seventeenth century, has been the means not only of the development of an insufficiently accountable and over-powerful executive but also of difficulties in the acceptance of the binding force of supra-national treaties such as those with the EC.
- Provide secure legal limitations upon the powers of governments; greater protection for the rights of individuals and groups; and firm obstacles against further centralisation of

power in Westminster. The constitution would form a kind of higher law only changeable by special procedures and therefore removed from easy modification by the government of the day.

Constitutional conservatives argue that a codified constitution is:

- **Unnecessary** because the present Constitution is still serving the country well, with both Parliament and pressure groups more capable than they were earlier in the century of checking government and individual rights as secure as in regimes which specify and entrench them.
- **Undesirable** because *(a)* the existing 'flexible' constitution is well able to respond to new demands. That new demands have so far not been accommodated reveals only that they are insufficiently urgent and deeply felt to gain constitutional recognition; therefore, to replace a constitution which is simple to modify in accordance with popular wishes with one that is not is a retrograde step: *(b)* written constitutions tend to place too much power in the hands of an unelected, unaccountable judiciary; and *(c)* piecemeal reform is preferable to sweeping change.
- **Impractical** because *(a)* there is no agreement even among its advocates over what it should contain; and *(b)* both major parties are opposed to the idea even though Labour now supports some constitutional reforms. In no readily foreseeable circumstances could a 'written constitution' be achievable.

Summary

Constitutions deserve close attention even though they form imperfect guides to political reality and are often overthrown. They need to be complemented by the study of the actual working of key political institutions such as parties, pressure groups and civil services and their roles in the political process, and by the study of political cultures. Constitutions are valuable as guides both to countries' political aspirations and, to varying degrees, to their political practices. They are always important as sources of legitimacy for a particular distribution of power.

The main broad classification of constitutions is as unitary or federal; codified or uncodified (generally preferable terms to 'written' and 'unwritten'); and flexible and inflexible.

Constitutions are part of rather than above politics and are constantly subject to political pressures for change.

The British Constitution may be categorised as unitary, partly written but uncodified, and flexible. Its main sources are: legislation, common law, conventions, European Community law, the law and customs of Parliament, and works of authority. It is based on the principle of parliamentary sovereignty although this is modified by EC membership.

The rule of law is also commonly said to be an underlying principle of the Constitution. It means, first, that the powers of the authorities must be conferred by law and exercised according to authorised procedures; and, second, that redress of wrongs is available to all citizens against other citizens and against officers of the state. But as a constitutional principle the rule of law is inferior to parliamentary sovereignty because parliamentary sovereignty could be used to undermine it.

Parliamentary government under a constitutional monarch is the most appropriate description of the particular form taken by the British liberal democratic state. The main concepts required for its analysis include constitutional, parliamentary, representative, responsible and party government. Perceptions of the Constitution and proposals for its reform are shaped by ideological influences. Constitutional innovations and pressures for reform which emerged in the 1960s and 1970s intensified in the 1980s and early 1990s and included proposals for a 'written constitution'.

Questions

1. What is a 'constitution'? How far are constitutions influenced by politics?

2. What are the main distinguishing features of liberal democracy as a form of government?
3. How democratic is the British Constitution?
4. List the main characteristics of the rule of law and discuss the extent to which the British Constitution is based on this principle. (It would be helpful to read Chapters 17 and 18 before attempting this question.)
5. Distinguish between parliamentary, representative, responsible, party and constitutional government and relate each concept to the British Constitution.
6. Discuss the arguments for and against a written constitution for the UK.

Assignments

1. Study the statement by Charter 88 on p. 101 above and then discuss how far you agree with it and for what reasons.
2. Procedure as constitution

'Procedure is all the constitution the poor Briton has'–so said Sir Kenneth Pickthorn, the distinguished constitutional historian and Member of Parliament in a Commons debate in 1960. The Cabinet Minister's guide to 'procedure', *Questions of Procedure for Ministers*, has since 1945 laid down some of the procedures of high government. The content of *Questions* has been known more or less since the 1980s, when some part of the 1976 version was published in the *New Statesman and Nation*. The document was then classified as 'Confidential'; disclosure would be 'prejudicial to the interests of the nation'.

About the same time Peter Hennessy printed a significant section of the 1952 version which was then available in the Public Record Office. Until these revelations, the citizen's freedom to know about such matters was rather less than his freedom to take tea at the Ritz. Hence the recent publication of *Questions* in a full and up-to-date version by the Cabinet Office (May 1992) is something of an achievement, at least by British standards, in open government and constitutional understanding.

Questions of Procedure has grown over the years, from 37 paragraphs in 1945 to 134 in the 1992 version; but bulk has not added excitement. We are not dealing here with Magna Carta, or a Bill of Rights. Questions of Procedure is no more than 'tips for beginners', 'a book of etiquette' in the words of a former Cabinet Secretary, Lord Trend. Peter Hennessy calls it a 'kind of highway code'. It is a prosaic compendium of advice to ministers on how to keep out of trouble and very far from being a constitution or a proto-constitution. Yet leaving aside rules about pensions or membership of Lloyds, close study does indicate some of the assumptions and undertones of high British government.

The objectives of the document are stated in the opening paragraph.

- The integrity of public life
  Questions lists 'the rules and the pre-cedents which may apply ... in the context of protecting the integrity of public life'-and to do with 'uphold[ing] the highest standards', and avoiding conflict between 'private interests and public duties'. These matters take up altogether about one third of the document.
- Openness
  'Ministers will wish to be as open as possible with Parliament and the public'.

The objective of openness appears to relate to the public-private conflict and the general question of integrity-but, for what it is worth, there is no need to interpret so narrowly the commitment to openness.

In addition to these avowed objectives *Questions* is concerned with the machinery of central government and in particular

- the collectivity of government, specific-ally the structure, procedures and politics of cabinet government;
- the disposition of authority between prime minister, ministers and the higher civil service.

On these matters the document approaches constitutional significance. [See further Exhibit 8.6, p. 138 below.]

Adapted from Peter Madgwick and Diana Woodhouse, 'The British Constitution: ISBN 0 7115 0233 T', *Talking Politics*, 6(1) (Autumn 1993)

- To what extent is the guide to ministers on questions of procedure also a guide to the British constitution?

Further reading

Brazier, R. (1988) *Constitutional Practice* (Oxford: Clarendon).

Brazier, R. (1991) *Constitutional Reform* (Oxford: Clarendon).

Finer, S.E. (1979), *Five Constitutions* (Harmondsworth: Penguin).

Harden, I. and Lewis, N. (1987) *The Noble Life: The British Constitution and the Rule of Law* (London: Hutchinson).

Holme, R. and Elliott, M. (1988) *1688–1988 Time for a New Constitution* (London: Macmillan).

Jowell, J. and Oliver, D. (1989) *The Changing Consti-tution*, 2nd edn (Oxford: Clarendon).

McAuslan, P. and McEldowney, J. (1985) *Law, Legitimacy and the Constitution* (London: Sweet & Maxwell).

Marshall, G. (1984) *Constitutional Conventions* (Oxford: Clarendon).

Ridley, F.F. (1988) 'There is no British Constitution: A Dangerous Case of the Emperor's Clothes', *Parlia-mentary Affairs*, 41: 3, July.

Ridley, F.F. (1991) 'Using Power to Keep Power: The Need for Constitutional Checks', *Parliamentary Affairs*, 44: 4, October.

Ridley, F.F. (1992) 'What Happened to the Constitution under Mrs. Thatcher?', in B. Jones and L. Robins (eds) *Two Decades in British Politics* (Manchester: University Press).

de Smith, S. and Brazier, R. (1990) *Constitutional and Administrative Law*, 6th edn (Harmondsworth: Penguin).

Parliamentary Affairs, 44: 4, October. Special issue on constitutional reform.

Chapter 7

Britain and the European Union

Europe has experienced dramatic developments during the last decade which have reshaped the political map. There has been a series of democratic revolutions in Eastern Europe which have ended years of dictatorial government but created many new problems. At the same time as the old Soviet empire fragmented there have been attempts in Western Europe to forge greater political and economic union. The creation of a single market within the European Union (EU), together with other goals including the creation of a single currency, has caused serious divisions within British opinion. What is it about the way in which the EU operates which frequently results in Britain being the most reluctant member? In which directions might the EU develop in order to solve both the old pressures which have been present since its formation and the new challenges it now faces?

■ Building the Peace in Europe

By the time the Second World War ended in 1945 European politicians were searching for ideas to solve the problems now experienced by this troubled continent. Massive economic, political and social change had already taken place during the first half of the century, with the postwar world demanding yet more change to deal with both the opportunities and threats posed by the new European order. Like Britain, many other European countries had colonies overseas but, again like Britain, they no longer had the re-

sources necessary to retain these possessions as the basis of their economic and military position in the world. In other words, countries which before the war led great empires were being forced through circumstances to rethink and find new international roles during the early years of peace.

By 1945 Europe had been ripped apart by two world wars, resulting in the loss of millions and millions of lives at the front in battle, at home through bombing or invasion, and through the horror of the Holocaust death camps. Rightly or wrongly, many believed that the blame for this havoc lay with Germany. Some believed that Prussian militarism was deeply engrained in German society: others blamed contemporary Germans for inventing fascism and following Hitler.

The methods by which Germany might be contained was not the only problem facing European politicians. A policy of containment was also required for the hostile regimes in Eastern Europe, particularly the Soviet Union. The common purpose which had brought the Soviets into alliance with the Western powers during the Second World War did not last through to times of peace. The new Attlee Government had hoped that 'left could talk with left' and that friendly relations would be possible between Labour Britain and the Soviet Union. However this was not to be and an 'iron curtain' was drawn across Europe which divided Western capitalist democracies from communist workers' democracies of the East.

The economic and political reconstruction of postwar Europe provided politicians with opportunities to solve, at least in part, the German problem, the dangers posed by the Soviet Union as well as the international problems resulting from imperial decline. The solution proffered – that Europe should unite – was far from being novel, and the early postwar years saw a number of new organisations come into being to promote this particular goal such as the North Atlantic Treaty Organisation (NATO), the Council of Europe and the Organisation for European Economic Co-operation (OEEC). In 1946 Winston Churchill, Britain's wartime Prime Minister, called for the creation of a United States of Europe with Franco-German reconciliation and cooperation providing the first crucial step. Although Churchill did not believe that Britain should play a major role in such a Europe, he can be counted amongst the 'Founding Fathers' of the EC who shared the vision of a politically united, economically integrated Europe.

The Development of the European Community

In 1950 two French politicians, Jean Monnet and Robert Schuman, proposed that France and Germany should pool their coal and steel industries by placing them under the control of a supra-national 'High Authority'. Putting detailed substance to Churchill's proposal, the French plan envisaged taking two of the main industries which supported war from the control of national governments with the consequence of Germany being tied economically to its old rival France. Other countries were invited to join this scheme and in 1951 Belgium, Germany, France, Italy, Luxembourg and the Netherlands signed the Treaty of Paris which set up the European Coal and Steel Community (ECSC). This organisation – the ECSC – was the foundation on which the European Community and later European Union was to be constructed. In theory at least it had solved the German problem by making another war between Germany and France impossible.

A committee chaired by the Belgian Foreign Minister, Paul-Henri Spaak, proposed the creation of two new 'communities'. The first, and most important, was the creation of the European Economic Community (EEC) which would establish a customs union and increase economic integration. The EEC Treaty committed its signatories to 'lay the foundations of an ever closer union among the people of Europe'. It was clear, then, that although the EEC was primarily concerned with economic integration that this, in turn, was seen as a prerequisite for the ultimate goal of political unity. The EEC would develop common policies on trade, agriculture and transport, as well as coordinate economic and monetary policies of the six. A common market would be created by liberalising trade within the EEC with a Common External Tariff (CET) between the six and the rest of the world. The second community, the European Atomic Community (Euratom) was concerned with the development of nuclear industries. The two Treaties of Rome setting up the EEC and Euratom were signed in 1957.

The national economies of the EC's member states were hard hit by recession during the 1970s and 1980s, and some resorted to protectionist measures in order to promote recovery. The protection of national markets was, of course, a barrier to European economic integration as spelled out in the EEC Treaty. By 1985 the Commission, chaired by Jacques Delors, decided it was timely to relaunch the original ideal of a truly common market. The Single European Act of 1986 amended the founding treaties by extending the principle of majority voting, strengthening the power of the European Parliament in the legislative process, but most importantly by creating 'an area without frontiers in which the free movement of goods, persons, services and capital is ensured' as from 31 December 1992. The Single European Act also included a general commitment to improve cooperation over matters of economic and monetary policy. An EC report written by Paolo Cecchini predicted that the effects of creating a single market would help solve the problems being experienced by national economies by raising output, creating more jobs, reducing prices and increasing European competitiveness abroad.

The Single European Act represented a huge stride forward in the cause of Europeanism. As before, major reforms towards economic integration inside the EC took the Community closer to the threshold of political unity. For a single European market would never be totally achieved without a single European currency, and a single currency would mean that much freedom in economic policy-making would be lost by the governments of the member states. It was argued that this sacrifice of sovereignty by the twelve national governments would be replaced by increasing federal decision-making powers inside Community institutions.

The Delors Plan for economic and monetary union (EMU) was presented to the Council by Ministers in 1989, and was based on a three-stage progression. Stage One included the establishment of the single European market by the end of 1992, with closer co-ordination of different countries' economic and monetary policies. This was to be achieved by all member states joining the Exchange Rate Mechanism (ERM) of the European Monetary System (EMS). The effect of the ERM is that each country's currency becomes fixed more tightly to the values of other currencies in the EC. Implementing the EMS also involves making greater use of the European Currency Unit (ECU) which is best thought of as a theoretical unit of currency the value of which is calculated from the values of members' currencies in agreed proportions.

Stage Two of the Delors Plan involves setting up a new European central bank to coordinate the monetary policies of individual member states. This would mean that a number of important functions performed by national central banks, such as the Bank of England, would from this stage onwards be performed by a European central bank. This development would also have implications for taxation policy and the setting of interest rates, which would also move towards being decided at the European rather than member state level. Stage Three will be a crucial one in the history of the EU for the exchange rates of member countries will be firmly locked together with a view to their being replaced by a single European currency. Responsibility for monetary policy will be with the European central bank. The target date for movement to Stage Three will not be set until the EU is three years into Stage Two.

Britain and the European Union

Britain remained rather aloof from developments in Europe during the early postwar years. Regarding the ECSC in particular, the Labour Government led by Clement Attlee welcomed the Schuman Plan but felt unable to join in and kept only tenuous associational links with this new venture. Britain was in the throes of nationalising its own coal and steel industries and it was therefore not an appropriate time to consider further radical experiments of the type Monnet and Schuman were proposing.

The success of Britain's European neighbours, particularly in the area of economic growth and trade, made it clear that Britain had to come to terms with the European integration of the six. The idea of the EEC forming a customs union with an ever-rising Common External Tariff alarmed the Government, and British relations with Europe assumed an air of urgency.

In particular there were two features about the way in which European unity was being achieved that concerned British politicians. The first was the concept of supra-nationalism. The idea that national governments should sacrifice sovereignty to European institutions in a process that might lead to a federal 'United States of Europe' was not attractive in Britain. Secondly, Britain preferred international free trade to the idea of a customs union. This, it was argued, reflected a fundamental difference between the globally outward-looking British and the narrow inward-looking internationalism of the six members of the EEC. And, of course, those who feared a revanchist Germany saw in the EEC a repetition of the Zollverein customs union which strengthened Germany in the last century.

Britain's solution to the new economic threats posed by the successful EEC was to propose a different route to economic integration which involved neither a loss of national sovereignty nor a customs union. In 1956 the Paymaster-General, Reginald Maudling, attempted to negotiate a free-trade area which would include the six members of the ECSC, the UK, and any other OEEC country which wished to join. Britain wanted tariffs between members of such a free trade area to be dismantled, but there would not be a Common External Tariff and each country would retain its freedom of action regarding trade with non-members. Maudling's proposals were rejected by the French and so, in 1958, efforts to 'bridge-build' between Britain and the six collapsed. Britain's response was to establish a free-trade area without the participation of the EEC members. In 1959 the European Free Trade Association (EFTA) was set up to include Britain, Norway, Sweden, Denmark, Austria, Portugal and Switzerland. Europe, it was said at the time, was at sixes and sevens with the inner-six of the EEC being rivalled by the outer-seven of EFTA. But only a year later, Britain was to begin a reassessment of its position regarding the EEC. In 1960 an interdepartmental committee, chaired by Sir Frank Lee, considered all the options available and concluded that Britain's future lay in Europe and that it would be to Britain's advantage to be a member of the EEC.

The Conservative Government, led by Harold Macmillan, announced in 1961 that Britain intended to apply for membership of the EEC.

Figure 7.1 *British Prime Minister Edward Heath signs the Treaty of Accession to the EEC in Brussels on 22 January 1972. Ireland, Denmark and Norway also signed for what was to be the first enlargement of the European Community, on 1 January 1973. Norway, however, did not ratify the treaty, so the six only became the nine in 1973, and not the ten*

Source: Popperfoto.

This decision represented a major change in the direction of foreign policy and recognised that Britain was now a regional rather than a global power. Macmillan faced considerable opposition inside the Conservative Party, and the mood of the Labour Party was firmly against British membership of the EEC. The Government was to be humiliated in 1962, when the French President, General de Gaulle, vetoed the British application.

The Labour Government of 1964 largely ignored the European Community (or 'Common Market', as it was then known) issue and pursued a foreign policy which stressed Atlantic and Commonwealth ties. But the problem with this policy was that the US Administration was becoming increasingly involved in Asia rather than Europe, and the Commonwealth was experiencing numerous political difficulties. By 1965 Harold Wilson decided to 'build bridges' between EFTA and the EEC, but the six made it clear that they were not interested in closing the EFTA–EEC gap. In 1966, having followed the same path as Harold Macmillan, Harold Wilson announced that the British Government was to start investigations to discover whether Britain could open negotiations to join the EEC. In 1967 General de Gaulle again vetoed Britain's application.

De Gaulle's retirement from public office removed the major obstacle to British membership of the EEC. In 1969 European governments informed Britain that a third veto was unlikely. A new Conservative Government led by an enthusiastic pro-European prime minister, Edward Heath, was elected in 1970 and negotiations led to the successful entry of Britain into the EEC on 1 January 1973.

The Labour Party had once again changed its policy on British membership of the EEC and opposed Edward Heath's negotiations. When a Labour Government was formed in 1974, Harold Wilson inherited a Government that was 'in Europe' but led a party which was 'against Europe'. Labour solved this dilemma by deciding the issue of Britain's continued membership of the EEC through holding a referendum. The Foreign Secretary, James Callaghan, 'renegotiated' the terms of Britain's entry. The Commons voted to endorse continued membership of the EEC by

396 votes to 170, although a majority of Labour MPs voted against. Labour held a special conference which also voted against continued membership. However, in the referendum held on 5 June 1975, in a turn-out of 63.2 per cent. 17 378 581 voted for continued membership and 8 470 073 voted for withdrawal.

During the 1980s the Labour Opposition became increasingly committed to the European cause. To a large extent this was because the only hope of defeating the Thatcher Government's policies on issues such as trade union rights or welfare rights was in the context of European Community laws. Margaret Thatcher did not disagree with Labour on this, for in her eyes the EC seemed to be developing into a semi-socialist, highly bureaucratic, federal Euro-state which increasingly threatened to curtail her government's freedom of action. The Social Charter – or 'Socialist Charter' as Thatcher insisted in calling it – together with proposals to harmonise social policies, were both interventionist and egalitarian in purpose and clearly at odds with the free-market philosophy of Thatcherism. The EMS was also opposed by Thatcher, who preferred exchange rates to move freely. Her personal economic adviser, Sir Alan Walters, described the EMS as a 'half-baked' idea, and Thatcher agreed with him, arguing that the pound sterling was 'the most powerful expression of sovereignty you can have'. Thatcher's hostility to Britain's closer involvement with the EC, particularly Britain's full membership of the EMS in 1990, led to the resignation of her Chancellor, and later her Deputy Prime Minister, which then contributed to her own downfall.

Although Margaret Thatcher was frequently portrayed as a 'little Englander' in the media and by her opponents, this was in some ways unfair. She had her own vision of Europe, which was 'broader' in geographical terms but 'shallower' in terms of institutional development than the plans unveiled by Jacques Delors. She argued that

the Community should declare unequivocally that it is ready to accept all countries of Eastern Europe as members if they want to join. ... I want the larger wider Europe in which Moscow is also a European power... We must create ... a European Community which is fair, which is open, which preserves the diversity and nationhood of each of its members. (Jones and Robins, 1992, p. 253).

John Major's Government was more positive generally towards the EC although there were aspects of federalism and centralisation in the proposed development of the Community which have been opposed. When Chancellor of the Exchequer, John Major challenged Delors' concept of Europe having a *single* currency with an alternative of Europe having a *common* currency. Major's rival plan centred around what was known as the 'hard ECU' which would be legal tender in each country alongside national currencies. As Prime Minister, Major 'opted out' of specific aspects the Maastricht deal (see later) which reassured the Euro-sceptics in the Bruges Group. In the Treaty on European Union, all references to 'federalism' were removed; Britain alone won the right to opt out of joining a single currency if the other EC members decided to go ahead as planned in 1999; and the Social Chapter, which was akin to the Social Charter, was dropped from the Maastricht Treaty. In debating the European Communities (Amendment) Bill which ratified the Maastricht Treaty, Major stressed his victory in getting the principle of 'subsidiarity' enshrined in the Treaty: by which is meant that 'the Community only tackles tasks which it is able to deal with more effectively than the Member States acting alone' (Commission of the European Communities, 1991, p. 32).

With these points in mind, it appeared that Conservative Prime Minister John Major shared Margaret Thatcher's enthusiasm to widen the membership of the EC and shared many of her reservations about a federal Europe, whilst not displaying her seeming inflexibility towards European unity nor her bombastic style in negotiating with other EC heads of state. In this sense he was more positive towards the EC and was aware that Britain had no role other than as a member of the EC, being more akin to Conservative Prime Minister, Edward Heath, who took Britain into the EC, than to Margaret Thatcher.

▌The Institutions of the European Union

☐ *The Commission*

The image of the Commission with the general public is that of the 'Brussels bureaucrats'. Indeed, the Commission is the biggest of the European Union's institutions and employs around 16 000 people. But considering the scope of the Commission's role in the Union, this is a relatively small number of employees. At the apex of the Commission are 17 Commissioners, with larger EU countries appointing two Commissioners and small members one. They are appointed to serve for a four-year term of office, which is renewable. Commissioners generally come from the ranks of senior politicians, but as members of the Commission they are guardians of the EU treaties rather than representatives of their own country's national interest. This can cause tensions, as in 1989 when Prime Minister Margaret Thatcher did not reappoint Lord Cockfield to serve as a Commissioner because she felt that he had become too European in outlook. Individual Commissioners are in charge of specific policy areas, and they meet once a week in a forum known as the College of Commissioners.

At the head of the Commission is its President, a post which is currently filled by Jacques Delors. The President's duties include coordinating the work of the Commission, but the position also provides an opportunity to inject political direction into the way the Community develops. Delors has been a controversial President in terms of the ways in which he has performed his duties, but his energy and personal commitment to the EU have resulted in helping to create a new impetus in developing the Community into the Union, which has not always been welcomed by the British Government.

The Commission is often described as being the 'civil service of the European Union'. There is some truth in this, although at the higher levels it has wider responsibilities than many national civil services, but at lower levels it delivers many

---

Exhibit 7.1 *The six professions of an EC official*

President Delors has said that a Commission official has six professions:
- to innovate, as the needs of the Community change;
- to be a law-maker, preparing the legal texts needed for Community decisions;
- to manage the growing number of Community policies;
- to control respect for Community decisions at all levels;
- to negotiate constantly with all the different actors in the Community process;
- to be a diplomat in order to be successful in the five other professions.

---

fewer services. Rather like national civil services, the work of the Commission is divided up into a number of 'ministries' called Directorates General. Most of the work of the Commission is completed by 23 Directorates General, the biggest of which has responsibility for agriculture, but others cover areas such as transport, environment, fisheries, energy, regional policies, as well as by some specialised agencies such as a statistical office, translation service, and Office for Official Publications (which supplied some of the illustrations in this chapter). As might be expected, the work of the Commission is serviced by a complex committee structure, which no doubt contributes to its bureaucratic image. Each Commissioner is assisted by a small *cabinet* or team of officials, usually civil servants seconded to work in Brussels. There is also a large and complex web of committees set up to provide advice, consultation and expert opinion as a form of input into the EC's legislative process.

What, then, is the nature of the Commission's contribution to the running of the Union? Firstly, the Commission acts as the Union's watchdog by ensuring that EU Treaties are respected by all the member states. The Commission can, if necessary, refer cases where states contravene Union law to the Court of Justice. There have been newspaper reports in recent years that 'Britain will be taken to court by the Commission' over failing to implement Union law on the purity of drinking water and the safety of coastal bathing water. Rather than flagrantly breaking these laws Britain, like other countries in a similar position, will play for time and act very slowly in conform-

ing to EU standards since British Ministers know that it will be many years before either the Commission or the Court of Justice will act and bring matters to a head. The Commission does, however, have much sharper claws when it comes to regulating competition policy since it can fine individuals or firms which break EU rules. In 1986 a number of large European companies, including ICI (Imperial Chemical Industries) and Shell, were fined for fixing the market so that consumers were paying too much for one of their products.

Secondly, the Commission initiates EU policy. It does this principally by formulating proposals which are put to the Council of Ministers. As Nugent has commented,

> What this means, in practice, is that the Council's legislative capacity is heavily dependent on the willingness and ability of the Commission to put proposals before it. The Council cannot initiate and draft legislation itself. Furthermore, if the Council wishes to amend a Commission proposal, Article 149 of the EEC Treaty states that it can only do so either with the Commission's agreement or by acting unanimously if the Commission disagrees. If either of these two routes are open, the Council must accept the Commission's proposal as it stands, reject it, or refer it back to the Commission for reconsideration and resubmission at a later date. (Nugent, 1991, p. 73)

Thirdly, the Commission has a broad executive role in terms of supervising and implementing EU policies. It is called upon to make rules for situations where no rules yet exist. Recently, for

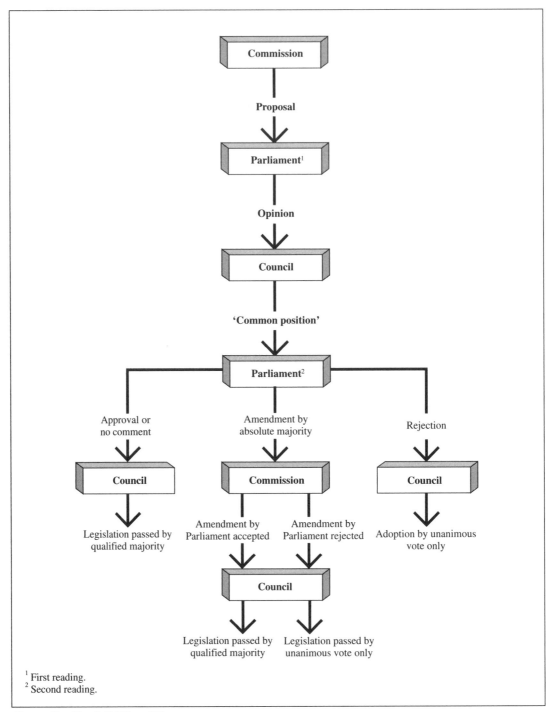

Source: Borchhardt (1990, p. 32).

Figure 7.2   *Decision-making in the European Union*

example, it was necessary to decide whether Jaffa Cakes were in fact cakes or biscuits. Although there is a humorous side to this matter, since the definition depended upon the location of the jam in the confectionery, the decision had serious commercial implications for the product. Fourthly, the Commission has the task of managing the Community's budget. Finally, the Commission negotiates with other international organisations, such as the UN and GATT, and with other countries, such as with developing countries through the Lome Agreement.

The Commission is responsible for relatively little public administration, since as long as the domestic law of member states is parallel with European law that will be performed by the twelve public sectors of members. However, there is more politics involved in the work of the Commission than implied by the treaties. Much of its work in preparing, liaising and consulting requires the Commission to be aware of what is possible in political terms. Added to this is the increasing cultural diversity of EU members, which necessarily means that values or practices which are traditional and accepted by one member are unacceptable to others. The Commission has to be constantly mindful of this and conduct its business in a diplomatically sensitive manner. Developing the EU, through harmonisation, involves the Commission creating a general consensus in those areas where there is scope for the Union to move forwards whilst at the same time tolerating diversity in other areas where nationalistic attitudes and values are deeply ingrained.

☐ *The Council of Ministers*

If the work of the Commission reflects the federal process of the EC, then the Council of Ministers reflects the intergovernmental process. For in the

---

Exhibit 7.2 *Community legal instruments*

(Article 189 of the EEC Treaty)
The Council and the Commission issue regulations, directives and decisions, make recommendations and deliver opinions.

Regulations are directly applicable in every Member State. They are comparable to national laws.

Directives are addressed to Member States. They are binding as to the result to be achieved but leave the choice of form and methods for incorporating them into national legislation to the national authorities.

Decisions are binding on those to whom they are addressed (e.g. a government or a company).

Recommendations and opinions are not binding.

Community legislation is published in the *Official Journal of the European Communities*. The *Bulletin of the European Communities* gives a monthly review of current developments. The Commission publishes an annual *General Report on the Activities of the European Communities*. All three publications appear in the nine official Community languages: Danish, Dutch, English, French, German, Greek, Italian, Portuguese and Spanish.

Source: Commission of the European Communities (1991).

Council of Ministers national governments are able to exert greatest influence and thereby protect their respective national interests. Because national sovereignty is a sensitive matter and because the Council of Ministers is a crucial decision-making body within the EU, the voting method by which the Council of Ministers reaches its decisions has sometimes been a contested issue. The Council can make decisions by (*i*) **unanimity**, particularly appropriate when a new policy is being considered, (*ii*) a **qualified majority**, where an already established policy is being modified. Britain, along with Germany, France and Italy, has 10 'weighted' votes out of a total of 76; and the minimum requirement for a qualified majority is 54 votes which must be cast by at least 8 members, and (*iii*) a **simple majority**, which is usually used only where procedural issues are being decided upon.

The Luxembourg Compromise, which focused on agriculture but extended to wider issues, enshrined the principle that any member had the right to exercise a veto on Council decisions if it affected a vital national interest. This seemed to be challenged in 1982 when the Council of Ministers used a majority vote to force through farm price increases despite Britain's protests. Britain argued that its national interests were being damaged by the Common Agricultural Policy, but other members argued that this was not the case and Britain was simply holding up agricultural policy as a means of exerting influence to get its way on other issues. The Single European Act envisaged that the Commission should make an increasing number of decisions through majority voting.

The central function of the Council of Ministers is to decide European Union law on the basis of proposals it receives from the Commission. It is important to note that although the Council converts proposals into legislation, normally it does not have the constitutional right to initiate those proposals. In reality, however, the Council can guide and influence the shape of the proposals made to it by the Commission despite not having the right to draft those proposals itself. The work of the Council is divided up into policy areas – such as agriculture, transport or foreign

affairs – with the appropriate Ministers attending meetings depending upon the nature of the business in hand. As might be imagined, the meetings of the Council of Agricultural Ministers have included some of the most acrimonious sessions.

The business of the Council of Ministers is organised in large part by its President, a position which rotates between member states on a six-monthly basis. It is an influential role in terms of shaping the agenda of the Council, conducting negotiations with the Commission and Parliament, and thereby steering the direction and deciding the speed at which the Union develops.

Each member country has a permanent delegation of diplomats to assist in the work of the Council. These delegations meet together as the 'Committee of Permanent Representatives' (referred to by the French abbreviation of COREPER). Much of the work of COREPER involves completing tasks unfinished by the Council and preparing the political and technical ground for future Council meetings.

☐ *The European Council*

The heads of government of member states have met on a regular basis since 1975 to discuss specific matters affecting the EC. These EC 'summits' are not part of the original Community structure, but have come to play an important political role in EC affairs. Heads of State meet on a personal basis and can attempt to solve any pressing problems or provide a forum in which agreement is forged on the next phase of policies that should be implemented. Examples of initiatives coming from the European Council include moving to direct elections to the European Parliament; agreeing the expansion of the EC to include Greece, Spain and Portugal; creation of the EMS; and reform of the Common Agricultural Policy.

It was at one such summit meeting held in Madrid that the then British Foreign Secretary, Sir Geoffrey Home and Chancellor Nigel Lawson persuaded the Prime Minister, Margaret Thatcher, to agree, reluctantly, that the pound sterling should enter the ERM 'when the time is right'. Thatcher did not think that in fact the time would be right until well into the next century, but this was not the case and Britain joined the ill-fated ERM in the following year.

☐ *The European Parliament*

The European Parliament has 518 directly elected MEPs of which 81 are elected to represent British constituencies. In the 1989 elections, British turnout was at its highest level to date at 36.2 per cent; but when compared with other national electorates Britain was firmly at the bottom of the turnout league table. In some ways the apathy of British voters towards the elections to the European Parliament was a healthy reaction since it is not really a Parliament with a legislative role. It is as if the British electorate realised that whether it returned Labour or Conservative MEPs made no impact on the European order. At the same time it is the case that since MEPs have been directly elected rather than appointed, they have behaved in a more assertive manner yet found that they can still be overruled or ignored whenever it suits the convenience of the Union's executive. Why is this?

Firstly, there are areas of Union action where the European Parliament still has no right to be consulted. Where it does have the right to be consulted, its approval is not required. In the rare cases where it does have power, it is the 'all or nothing' power of the veto or dismissal which can deter from its usage. Finally, if the European Parliament was an authentic legislative body it would have supra-national implications unacceptable to many national governments. Thus it remains a democratically elected bogus institution with its MEPs (Members of the European Parliament) walking, as one journalist put it, the corridors of weakness. Basically, then, the European Parliament (EP) plays a consultative role in the legislative process. Such influence as it has is won not only through formal channels but also informally in behind-the-scene negotiations:

It is very difficult to estimate the precise effect of EP deliberations on the final form of legislative acts. One reason for this is that a great deal of EP per-

suading and lobbying is impossible to monitor because it is carried out via informal contacts with the Commission and Council representatives. Another reason is that the Commission and the Council often go halfway in agreeing to the sense of EP amendments, but object to the way in which they are phrased or to specific parts of them. In general, however, it is clear that the Commission is more sympathetic than is the Council: so, whereas the Commission, on average, accepts between about 65–80 per cent of EP amendments at the first or the single reading stage, with much of the remaining 20–30 per cent being rejected for technical rather than political reasons, the Council's acceptance rate is considerably lower, especially where there is only a single reading. Sometimes less than 20 per cent of EP amendments appear in the final legislative text (Nugent, (1991), p. 133).

The exceptional circumstances in which the MEPs wield power concern the EU budget and dismissal of the Commission. The European Parliament can play a creative role in the budget process as well as having the power to reject draft budgets, a power that has been used on a number of occasions. However, when the Parliament does confront the Council of Ministers over budget proposals, MEPs find that they are more restricted by Treaty obligations than are the Council of Ministers. Also the European Parliament has the power, which it has not yet used, to dismiss the Commission. The European Parliament has no formal powers over the Council of Ministers, whose members see themselves as generally responsible to their national governments. Even the access of MEPs to the Council can prove difficult, depending on the membership of the Council at any particular time.

The European Parliament offers opinions on legislative proposals put before it, with MEPs doing much of their work in one of the 18 standing committees or one of the *ad hoc* committees. Their deliberations result in having some influence on European Union affairs, but the absence of democratic accountability inside the EU – the 'democratic deficit' – is a source of embarrassment to the Community. The powers of the European Parliament are increased marginally from time to time. For example, the Maastricht

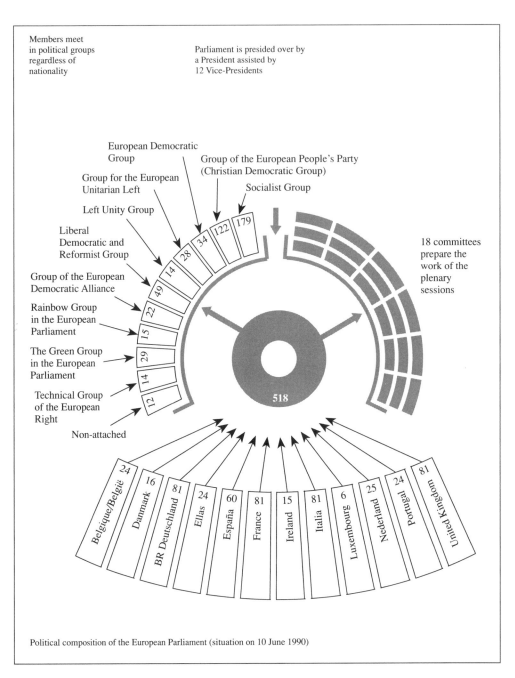

Members meet in political groups regardless of nationality

Parliament is presided over by a President assisted by 12 Vice-Presidents

European Democratic Group

Group of the European People's Party (Christian Democratic Group)

Group for the European Unitarian Left

Socialist Group

Left Unity Group

Liberal Democratic and Reformist Group

Group of the European Democratic Alliance

Rainbow Group in the European Parliament

The Green Group in the European Parliament

Technical Group of the European Right

Non-attached

34   122   179

28

14

49

22

15

29

14

12

518

18 committees prepare the work of the plenary sessions

24   16   81   24   60   81   15   81   6   25   24   81

Belgique/België   Danmark   BR Deutschland   Ellas   España   France   Ireland   Italia   Luxembourg   Nederland   Portugal   United Kingdom

Political composition of the European Parliament (situation on 10 June 1990)

Source: Noël (1992).

Figure 7.3   *European Parliament: 518 Members*

Treaty provided the European Parliament with greater powers of scrutiny as well as a new 'negative assent' procedure whereby certain legislation can be blocked should it be found unacceptable. It seems likely that the influence of the European Parliament will increase incrementally in this manner, unless the EU moves in a federalist direction, in which case reforms giving an increase in real power can be anticipated.

Party Organisation within the European Parliament

Party organisation is complex in so far as parties or political groups come in all ideological shapes as well as different sizes. Some groups, such as the European right, are relatively small and ideologically unified. Others, such as the socialists, are large and contain a number of distinct ideological factions. All but one of Britain's MEPs are found in two such political groups. Labour MEPs have joined the largest group, the socialists, which has members from every member country. In contrast, Conservative MEPs sit alongside two Danish MEPs to form the most nationalist European Democratic grouping. A problem endured by this group is the split between 'those who might broadly be described as Euro-sceptic Thatcherites, and those who are sympathetic to further integration' (Nugent, 1991, p. 149).

Labour's recently found enthusiasm for the EU can be explained in part by the changing balance of power within the European Parliament. In the past the centre-right held sway, but over a period of years influence slipped to the left, putting the socialist group, including Labour, into the ascendancy.

The Economic and Social Committee

This advisory body was established within the EU to ensure the representation of important sectional interests and the general public. The

Economic and Social Committee (ESC) has 189 members, of which the UK supplies 24. Around half the members are drawn from industry, commerce or other business organisations. Trade unions are represented also along with other interests such as the professions, local authorities and consumer groups. Trade unionists have long complained that they are outnumbered on the ESC by employers of one sort or another.

The ESC has been described as the 'other Parliament' of the Union, but this comparison flatters the significance of the ESC in European affairs. For if the European Parliament is weak, then the ESC is occasionally heard but rarely listened to. It is consulted, but often at such an advanced stage in the decision-making process that it is too late to amend or modify. It is possible, however, that the role of the ESC will become a little more influential after the creation of the single market, should that lead, in turn to greater union in general.

The Court of Justice

Thirteen judges, assisted by six Advocates-General, provide the judicial authority of the Union and ensure that European law is uniformly enacted. The Court of Justice's task is to

ensure uniformity in the interpretation and application of Community law, to review the legality of acts adopted by the Council and the Commission, and to rule on questions of Community law referred to it by national courts. Any Member State may, if it considers that another Member State has failed to comply with an obligation under the Treaties, bring the matter before the Court, as may the Commission. The Court of Justice also rules on complaints by natural and legal persons who wish to challenge decisions affecting them taken by the Community (*The European Community 1992 and Beyond*, 1991, p. 25).

The Court of Justice has dealt with cases which cover a wide range of areas, such as social welfare and agriculture, but the main thrust of its activities are concerned with business law. As the Community has developed, so the workload of the Court has increased in both the number and complexity of the cases brought before it.

Where the domestic law of a member state clashes with Community law, the latter takes precedence over the former. The primacy of Community law was once challenged by the Italian constitutional court which argued that since the Treaty of Rome had been ratified by an ordinary law, any later laws which conflicted with the Rome Treaty would take precedence. European judges disagreed and argued the formal case which exists today, namely, 'By creating a Community of unlimited duration ... the Members States have limited their sovereign rights, albeit within limited fields, and have thus created a body of laws which binds both their nationals and themselves' (OPEC, 1986 p. 37).

▮ Britain, the Community Process and European Prospects

The terms in which the Community has been discussed in domestic politics have differed very widely. On the one hand, there has been a debate concerning the future of European union which has involved aspirations about whether or not the EC and later EU should develop into a federal superstate. On the other hand, there have been arguments over the 'nuts and bolts' of the Common Agricultural Policy (CAP) and the EC budget. With what seemed equal degrees of commitment concerning the EC, politicians may have been discussing either the destiny of our continent or the price of sugarbeet.

This puzzling situation can be explained in part because (*i*) from the outset agriculture was one of the 'foundations of the Community' and has accounted for the largest proportion of Community legislation and spending (65.3 per cent of the EC's total budget in 1990) and (*ii*) agriculture is not just 'domestic policy' but is caught up in world politics in terms of GATT world trade regulations and Third World development. The

American agricultural lobby, in particular, has argued that the protectionist CAP blocks US imports into the EU whilst at the same time European surpluses are dumped at artificially cheap prices on world markets, again making it difficult for American farmers to compete.

Before Britain joined the EC it had a 'cheap food' policy, in sharp contrast to the CAP which is based on artificially high food prices to encourage production. Whereas Britain's system of agricultural support generally provided a balance in the demand and supply of food, the CAP results in a surplus of food production which has to be either destroyed, stored or sold off cheaply to consumers outside the EU. Not surprisingly, the CAP was popular with Britain's farmers but had many enemies on the political left and right. Labour politicians pointed out that because of the effects of the CAP, British families were paying by 1992 an extra £17 a week for food through higher prices and extra tax. Margaret Thatcher and the Tory right, with their preference for free markets and low public spending detested the highly interventionist and wasteful CAP.

There were also divisions on the CAP within Whitehall. The Ministry of Agriculture, reflecting farmers' interests rather more than consumers', generally supported the CAP; the Treasury, concerned at the CAP's rapidly increasing costs, were anxious that it should be reformed. This split was reflected within the Council of Ministers, with Finance Ministers generally sharing the Treasury's view on the need for reform, whilst Agriculture Ministers, having greater responsibility in the making of agricultural policy, were much more inclined to leave the CAP intact. However, by the mid-1980s the cost of the CAP was rising rapidly, with Britain paying into the EC far more than it got out. Attitudes hardened inside the Ministry of Agriculture with the Minister telling the Conservative Conference that 'The CAP has grown obese and needs slimming ... we cannot go on producing more and more food which we cannot either eat or sell.'

At the same time public attitudes towards the farming community were changing. In the past the public held farmers in high regard and appeared willing to subsidise the family farm. Pressure groups have helped to inform the public that most farming is now done by large mechanised undertakings controlled by 'farm managers' rather than 'yeoman farmers'. The intensive methods used in both the stock and arable sectors have increased efficiency but at a cost to the environment. Over the last fifty years England has lost 80 per cent of its woodland and 95 per cent of its meadows through 'prairification', which has ripped out enough hedgerow to encircle the earth six times. At the same time greater reliance on agrochemicals has resulted in the pollution of waterways as well as increased levels of mineral residues in meat, cereals and other products. Given these changes, it is not surprising that public sympathy for the farming community has weakened together with support for high levels of subsidy.

The Commission and Council of Ministers agreed that the CAP was in fact a bankrupt policy and that its reform was essential. The agriculture Commissioner, Ray McSharry, led the negotiations which resulted in the reform of the CAP in 1992. The reform involved a new mix of subsidies together with reduced farm incomes. Much more land was to be taken out of agricultural production, with the subsidies being switched from agricultural output to farm incomes. Quotas for dairy farmers were to be cut still further, with a 29 per cent reduction in the prices paid for cereals. Thus the new method for subsidising agriculture no longer encouraged farmers to produce ever larger surpluses of meat, cereals, milk, etc.

The CAP was the most federalist, most integrated, and most completely community-wide of all EC policies. It was also the most absurd. This was a great political convenience for Mrs Thatcher during the 1980s: 'The right and Mrs Thatcher used the issue of agricultural policy as a means of attacking the EC and its profligacy.' (Martin J. Smith, 1992, p 141.) Thatcher tended to see the EC as a socialist bureaucracy wanting to reintroduce to Britain many features of economic intervention, trade union privileges and socialist policies which her Governments had banished. Jacques Delors, the President of the Commission,

alarmed many Thatcherites still further when he predicted that by the end of the century 80 per cent of economic and social legislation in member states would be decided by the EC. In this way, fears about British sovereignty in the future, the development of the EC, and the reform of the CAP were interwoven strands in right-wing thinking. Finally, of course, Thatcher's distrust of the EC lay at the heart of the events which were to lead to her resignation from prime ministerial office.

■ The Maastricht Summit

The summit meeting held in Maastricht in 1991 was proclaimed by some commentators as being the latter-day equivalent of the Congress of Vienna (1815) or Yalta (1945) in terms of its influence over the shaping of Europe. The Danish referendum, which subsequently rejected the Maastricht Treaty, dented this sort of media-hype and proved useful in providing time for governments to have further thoughts about European development whilst reminding themselves of the political dangers which existed when the integration process became detached from the democratic process.

The Maastricht summit was held when important developments were taking place both inside and outside the EC. Within the EC there had been efforts, pursued by Jacques Delors, to *deepen* the institutions of the EC. This involved the EC developing along federal lines, with a single European market being followed by a single European currency, leading eventually to common economic, social, foreign and defence policies. The deepening process had accelerated since the creation of the single market, with economic and monetary union seeming feasible by the end of the century.

Outside the EC were two sets of potential members, the admission of which would *widen* the Community. Firstly, the members of EFTA (Switzerland, Austria, Norway, Sweden, Finland, Iceland and Liechtenstein) had made an agreement with the EC to form the world's largest trade zone, the European Economic Area (EEA).

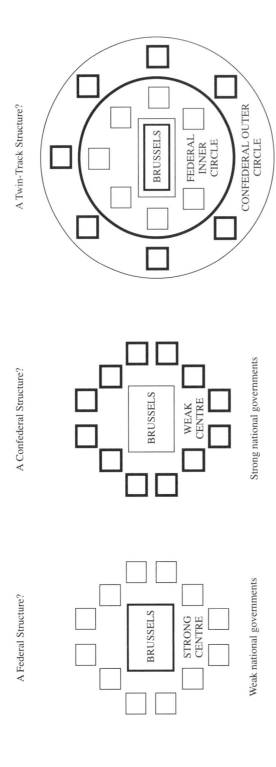

Euro-sceptics fear the gradual loss of national sovereignty if the EU develops into a 'United States of Europe'. If the UK had signed the Treaty of Maastricht like the other 11 members, it would have led to one market, single currency, and common defence and foreign policies. But their critics point to the principle of 'subsidiarity' which, like devolution, means that decisions are made at levels as close to the people as appropriate. Sceptics reply that employment law is best made at Westminster, so why did federalists want it included in the Social Chapter?

Rather than 'supra-nationalism' or 'federalism', sceptics such as Thatcher prefer 'intergovernmental' policy-making and decision-taking. This could take place in a confederal structure, with a relatively weak centre and national governments which are strong and play the dominant roles. Some EU enthusiasts feel that the Union institutions would stagnate, or even disintegrate, if future developments were to follow this pattern. They argue that the chance of making the EU a world power would then be lost.

John Major stated that he wanted Britain at the heart of the EU. Yet critics say that opting out of the single currency and Social Chapter will sideline the UK. Whilst others move towards a federal future, Britain and some other, mostly poorer countries, will be left in the slow lane. But others argue that this is unthinkable – should the time come when other leading EU countries move to have a single currency, Britain simply could not afford to say no and stay in the slow lane. If Britain hopes to wield influence in a 'variable geometry' EU Euro enthusiasts argue that it is crucial that Britain stays in the fast track.

Figure 7.4 *Which future for the European Union?*

The EEA will be made up of 380 million people from 19 countries and account for 40 per cent of the world's trade. By 1995 it is planned that Austria, Finland, Norway, Sweden and Switzerland will have become full members of the EU. Secondly, the democratic revolution in Eastern Europe has also produced a dozen or so candidates for EC membership, with East Germany having already entered through German unification and with Poland and Hungary expecting to follow by the end of the decade.

The crucial question regarding the EU's future is whether the widening process and the deepening process are politically compatible. In other words, can both these processes work within the Union or only one of them? Some argue that some institutional reforms inside the EU will facilitate both processes. The original EC, it is argued, was designed for six members and could not operate with around thirty members. A new streamlined supra-national executive body, balanced by a more powerful European Parliament, would be needed to integrate the economics and policies of an expanded Union. Others argue that any significant widening of the EU automatically means that it will become a looser, less federal and more intergovernmental type of organisation. This is primarily because new member states, particularly those from Eastern Europe, could not share a single currency with the more powerful economies to the West for the foreseeable future. And a single currency, it is argued, is a minimum prerequisite for federal deepening.

Margaret Thatcher, and later John Major, emphasised the importance of the Community expanding to include new members. At the same time, Major negotiated the right of Britain to opt out of joining a single currency arrangement when the other members proceeded to Stage Three of the Delors Plan which will be by no later than January 1999 (see Chapter 33). Because of British opposition to the Social Charter, the 'Social Chapter' of the Maastricht Treaty was dropped, leaving the other eleven members to move ahead of new members. There is no longer any argument about Britain's role being in Europe, but there is a conflict of views about what the nature and shape of the European Union should be.

Summary

The institutions of the EU are based on supra-national principles, whereas the British Government has always preferred intergovernmental cooperation as the basis for greater European unity. Although Britain supported the creation of a single market, it was one of the least enthusiastic EC members about a federal political union. In the past, Labour was the party most deeply divided over the EC issue, but under Margaret Thatcher's leadership the Conservatives became increasingly split over the direction in which the EC was developing. Inevitably membership of the EC involves a loss of national sovereignty and John Major has to pacify Tory Euro-sceptics by promising the possibility of 'opting out' of future federal developments and by stressing non-federal aspects of the EU such as 'subsidiarity'. The Maastricht Treaty took effect on 1 November 1993.

Questions

1. To what extent has Britain been a 'bad European' inside the EC?

2. 'The EU is no more than an undemocratic and highly interventionist bureaucracy'. How valid is this criticism? What sort of reforms might improve the reputation of the Union?

3. Why has the EU issue divided opinion in Britain's main political parties?

Assignment

Table 7.1 *Attitudes to membership of the European Community*

Country	1985 Good Thing %	1985 Bad Thing %	1990 Good Thing %	1990 Bad Thing %
Belgium	64	6	69	5
FRG	54	7	62	7
NL	77	3	82	3
Luxemburg	84	2	72	8
France	68	6	63	7
Italy	72	4	75	3
EC SIX	65	6	68	6
UK	32	40	52	19
Ireland	53	20	74	8
Denmark	29	31	49	25
Greece	45	17	70	5
Spain	62	6	65	8
Portugal	28	10	62	4
EC 10/12	60	11	65	8

Respondents were asked, 'Generally speaking, do you think that your country's membership of the common market is a good thing, a bad thing, or neither good nor bad?' Answers to the first two categories are included in this table. Eurobarometer Trends 1974–90, no. 33, June 1990 as published in Brigid Laffan, *Integration and Cooperation in Europe* (London: Routledge, 1992).

(i)   Identify the two countries whose populations appear least enthusiastic about the EC in 1990.

(ii) In your view, what sort of developments need to take place which would increase the number of people thinking that EC membership was a 'good thing'?

(iii) Use your library to obtain voting statistics on the most recent British election to the European Parliament. What was the level of turn-out? How many seats were obtained by parties other than Labour and Conservative? What reforms (institutional and electoral) might increase the level of public interest in these elections?

Further Reading

Crouch, C. and Marquand, D. (eds) (1992) *Towards greater Europe? A continent Without an Iron Curtain* (Oxford: Blackwell).

Jones, B. and Robins, L. (eds) (1992) *Two Decades in British Politics* (Manchester University Press).

Laffan, B. (1992) *Integration and Cooperation in Europe* (London: Routledge).

Marsh, D. and Rhodes, R.A.W. (eds) (1992) *Implementing Thatcherite Policies* (Milton Keynes: Open University Press).

Nugent, N. (1991) *The Government and Politics of the European Community*, 2nd edn (Basingstoke: Macmillan).

■ *Chapter 8* ■

Prime Minister and Cabinet

In this chapter and the next one we consider the institutions which make up what has been aptly termed 'the core executive'. This complex of offices and institutions at the pinnacle of the central decision-making process goes beyond the prime minister and Cabinet to include both their support institutions (the Prime Minister's Office and the Cabinet Office) and, in addition, the Departments themselves, headed by Ministers assisted by a small number of senior civil servants. Our focus in this chapter is on the prime minister and Cabinet system. We first describe its principal features before concluding with an examination of its strengths and weaknesses, and of proposals for reform.

■ The Prime Minister

The modern office of prime minister (PM) embodies a formidable concentration of power. In summary, the prime minister is responsible for forming a government; for directing and co-ordinating its work; and for general supervision of the civil service. The prime minister takes particular interest in – and exercises strong influence over – decisions on the economy (as first lord of the Treasury) and on defence and foreign affairs; the prime minister also has special responsibilities in the sphere of national security. The prime minister decides upon the date for a general election (normally after consultation with

senior colleagues) and, subject to the formality of royal assent, dissolves Parliament. Finally, the prime minister is the national leader, as evidenced by his or her role in representing the country at international conferences and meetings, signing treaties and playing host to leaders of other states.

□ *The Role of the Prime Minister*

Patronage

The most important element of prime ministerial patronage is the power to select the one hundred or so politicians – drawn mainly from the House of Commons but also from the House of Lords – who at any given moment form the government. As Table 8.1 shows, the prime minister appoints not just the Cabinet of normally 20–22 members but also ministers of state, under-secretaries of state, whips and law officers such as the attorney-general and solicitor-general.

Three points are worthy of note here. First, there is the sheer extent of the patronage. Between one-third and one-quarter (depending on the number of seats won) of the victorious party at a general election can realistically expect office. By no means all politicians seek office but a large number, probably the majority, do. The fact that so many share this goal is a formidable source of control for the prime minister. Second, this particular responsibility is not a once-for-all affair but

	House of Commons	House of Lords	Total
Cabinet ministers (excluding PM)	19	2	21
Ministers of state	23	5	28
Law officers	4	0	4
Under-secretaries of state	25	8	33
Whips	14	5	19
Total	85	20	105

Table 8.1 *The Conservative Government after the 1992 General Election*

a continuing one, with ministerial changes – by forced or deliberate reshuffle – occurring quite frequently. By April 1986, for example, only half the ministers appointed to Margaret Thatcher's Cabinet in June 1983 occupied the same ministerial positions and, as a result of demotion and resignation, one-third of them were no longer in the Cabinet at all. The frequency of government changes keeps this aspect of prime ministerial power firmly in the forefront of public attention. Third, despite the constraints on the prime minister's power of appointment (see below, pp.142–3), it is a real power. Swift promotion – such as John Major's rapid advance to Foreign Secretary and then Chancellor of the Exchequer by Margaret Thatcher, and David Owen's elevation to the Foreign Secretaryship by James Callaghan – is in the PM's hands, as is equally rapid demotion. By the end of 1981, only two and a half years after taking office, Margaret Thatcher had moved five 'wets' out of the Cabinet whilst Callaghan sacked Barbara Castle, the Health and Social Security Secretary, immediately upon taking over from Harold Wilson as premier.

The prime minister also plays a key role in the selection of individuals to fill a wide variety of other leading posts in national life. This influence extends over the creation of peers as well as over the appointment of top civil servants at the permanent secretary and deputy secretary levels, the chairmen of (the few remaining) nationalised industries, the heads of the security services and the chairmen of royal commissions. In addition, the prime minister has ultimate responsibility for

recommendations of baronetcies, knighthoods, CBEs (Commander of the British Empire), MBEs (Member of the Order of the British Empire) and the like in the various New Year, Queen's Birthday and special honours lists.

Direction and Organisation of the Government

The prime minister is responsible for directing and organising the work of the government at the highest level. The PM must steer the government: colleagues expect such leadership and governments tend to drift without it. This involves setting broad policy objectives (within the framework of party ideology and the party manifesto) and devising short-term and long-term strategies for attaining these goals. The leadership, of course, is always in a collective context: the PM is not a single executive like the US President. Within that framework, there are clearly differences in style. Margaret Thatcher is well known for having led from the front. Harold Wilson, on the other hand, although a good short-term tactician, was generally more concerned to conjure consensus from his colleagues than to lead them in a particular direction (Madgwick, 1991, pp. 140–1). Unless he or she specifically exempts them, the PM expects ministerial colleagues to support government policy according to the convention of collective responsibility.

This steering role means that the prime minister with his or her top advisers must decide upon the allocation of work between the Cabinet, its committees, ministerial groups, and bilateral meetings and consultations. Structuring the framework of decision-making involves the PM in drawing up the Cabinet agenda, and in deciding the composition, terms of reference and chairmanship of Cabinet committees. The special status of the prime minister is also evident in his or her special responsibility for and strong personal involvement in certain key policy areas: thus, the PM plays a decisive role in the determination of economic policy in consultation with the chancellor of the exchequer, the treasury and the governor of the Bank of England, and of important foreign policy and defence matters in concert

Exhibit 8.1	*Prime ministerial decision-making*	
The economy	Harold Wilson	Decision not to devalue (1964–7).
	James Callaghan	Prioritisation of fight against inflation (1976).
	Margaret Thatcher	Monetarist policy (1979–80).
Foreign policy	Anthony Eden	Decision to make airborne attack on Port Said went to full Cabinet but Suez was undeniably a prime ministerial venture and Eden hid from Cabinet the full extent of Anglo–French collusion with Israel (1956).
	Harold Wilson	Decision to maintain British military presence East of Suez (post-1964).
	Margaret Thatcher	Decision to permit US to use British bases to attack Libya (1986).
Defence	Clement Attlee	Decision to manufacture British A-Bomb (1947).
	Harold Macmillan	Negotiation of Polaris deal with US (1962).
	Harold Wilson	Chevaline project (late 1960s).
	Margaret Thatcher	Negotiation of new generation of Trident (post-1979).

with the foreign secretary and defence secretary respectively. Recent history contains many examples of major strategic commitments in these areas occurring as a consequence of the prime minister's personal intervention without full Cabinet participation. (Exhibit 8.1)

The prime minister alone is ultimately responsible for matters of national security which never go before Cabinet. Finally, issues may arise over the whole field of governmental concern in which the prime minister either has to get involved or chooses to take a particular interest. Thus, prime ministers in the 1960s and 1970s were unavoidably involved in industrial, trade union and pay policies; they have consistently taken leading roles in the development of initiatives in Northern Ireland; and, more recently, John Major had to take a close interest in the abolition of the 'poll tax'. They may choose to become involved in any area which attracts their interest, although they risk upsetting the departmental minister concerned: thus, James Callaghan intervened in the fields of education, hospitals, personal tax reform, nuclear policy and aircraft purchasing policy whilst Margaret Thatcher on her own initiative cancelled a research programme on the transmission of Aids, pushed for more British history in

the National Curriculum, insisted on the introduction of market principles into the NHS (National Health Service), and put her weight behind a national identity card scheme to curb football hooliganism (Donoughue, 1987, pp. 5–6; Young, 1990, pp. 548–9).

As well as playing a key part in deciding the nature, timing and ordering of issues reaching the Cabinet agenda, the prime minister chairs Cabinet meetings. Prime Ministerial 'styles' of chairmanship have included the clipped and businesslike (Attlee), the dominant but discursive (Churchill), the relaxed yet efficient (Macmillan), the non-directive consensual (Wilson), the aloof (Heath), the managerial (Callaghan) and the directive non-consensual (Thatcher) (James, 1992, pp. 128–9). Whatever their particular style, the chairmanship gives prime ministers the capacity to shape the direction and result of policy discussions, for example, by making their views known beforehand and during the meeting, by their handling of Cabinet (who is called to speak and in what order) and by their summing up of 'the sense of the meeting' at the end. In the process, they may deploy various manipulative 'arts' of chairmanship including delay, obfuscation of the issue, verbosity, deliberate ambiguity, adjournment (followed by 'arm-twisting'), briskness (some-times Cabinets have complained of being 'bounced' into decisions), sheer persistence, and authoritativeness. For all these wiles, they may not always succeed and examples abound of pre-miers failing to get their way (see below, pp. 143–4). Votes are almost never taken in Cabinet: they encourage division, dilute collective responsib-ility, and are vulnerable to 'leaks' and misleading reports in the media. But it is the task of the prime minister to summarise the decisions reached, taking into account the weight of opinion for or against a course of action as well as the numerical balance of opinion, and sometimes concluding against what appears to be the majority view. After the meeting, Cabinet conclusions are recorded by the Cabinet secretary in consultation with the prime minister.

The prime minister also makes decisions about the *structure* of the government, involving in particular the allocation of duties between the departments of state. The fluctuations in the number of departments – 30 in 1951, 21 in 1983, 19 in 1993 – and the changes in their functions are evidence of considerable prime ministerial activity in this sphere. The recent history of the departments concerned with trade, industry and power provides a good example. Edward Heath brought the Board of Trade and the Ministries of Technology and Power together in 1970 to form a new 'super-ministry', the Department of Trade and Industry (DTI), only to hive off Power to form the Department of Energy after the oil crisis in 1973. On gaining office in 1974, Harold Wilson broke up the DTI into separate Depart-ments of Trade and Industry again and, in add-ition, created a new Ministry of Prices and Con-sumer Affairs. Margaret Thatcher, after 1979, merged Trade and Industry again, gave Prices and Consumer Affairs back to Trade, and kept Energy separate. John Major after his 1992 elec-tion victory abolished Energy, handing over its functions to Trade and Industry (whose depart-mental head, Michael Heseltine, reverted to the title of President of the Board of Trade). He also created a new National Heritage department.

Finally in this regard, the prime minister has overall responsibility for the work of the civil service (the Cabinet secretary is head of the civil service). This power has three main aspects – appointments, organisation, and practices. Thatcher's premiership provides examples in all three areas. Prime ministers are frequently willing simply to endorse the recommendations of the Senior Appointments Selection Committee on top appointments at permanent secretary and deputy secretary levels, but it was widely suggested that Thatcher's close involvement in such appointments led to a 'politicisation' of the top civil service. One recent commentator has doubted this, whilst con-ceding, however, that her views were on at least one occasion decisive in securing the promotion of a particular official (Hennessy, 1990, pp. 634–40). Second, Thatcher in 1981 abolished the Civil Service Department, handing over its functions to the Treasury and Cabinet Office. Finally, she tried very hard to make the civil service more efficient by such methods as establishing an efficiency unit to recommend economies, reducing its overall size, and holding down civil service pay in relation to the private sector.

The Power of Dissolution

The prime minister has the exclusive right to recommend to the monarch the timing of the dissolution of Parliament within a five-year period. Whilst not an important power in relation to Cabinet and the prime minister's own party, the ability to call for a dissolution undoubtedly strengthens a prime minister's hand against the opposition parties. However, it is a weapon that may backfire since misjudgements like those of Edward Heath in calling a General Election in February 1974 and of James Callaghan in failing to call one in autumn 1978 can contribute to a party's electoral defeat and, in doing so, lose many MPs their seats. Normally, the PM consults with senior ministers, including the chief whip, before making a decision about an election date and then informing Cabinet of the final choice.

National Leadership

The prime minister occupies a special role in the life of the country which quite distinguishes the

Figure 8.1 *John Major*

Source: *Guardian*.

occupant of the office from other Cabinet members – as national leader. This is always the case but becomes especially apparent at times of national crisis such as war – for example, Churchill's role in 1940–5, Thatcher's in the Falklands War (1982) and Major's during the Gulf War (1991). But the public spotlight focuses upon the PM at other times, also – during general elections, when key decisions affecting the nation's future are being made (e.g. the Maastricht negotiations in December 1991) and at times of political difficulty.

During autumn 1992, for instance, John Major was constantly at the centre of public attention because of the many-sided political crisis, involving Britain's forced withdrawal from the ERM (Exchange Rate Mechanism), the continuing recession, the mishandling of the issue of pit closures and the simmering discontent within his own party over the ratification of the Maastricht Treaty. The sharp drop in his popularity rating – a MORI poll published on 1 November 1992 in the *Sunday Times* revealed that a mere 21 per cent were satisfied with his performance as prime minister – was a serious matter for Major. This is because prime ministers must please more than their close associates and their parties if they are to succeed. Ultimately they are judged by their success in providing effective national leadership

among opponents and neutrals as well as friends. Failure in key areas of policy destroyed the premierships of Heath, Callaghan and Thatcher and severely weakened Wilson.

The prime minister's relations with party, Parliament and the media are often closely linked to the authority with which prime ministers are able to carry out their executive and national leadership roles. It is as the leader of the party which has gained a parliamentary majority in a general election that a prime minister gains office in the first place; it is as a consequence of the regular support of that party in Parliament that the Prime Minister can expect to govern and in particular to translate the party programme into legislation. Relationships with the party, therefore, are of the greatest significance and these are two-way. The prime minister seeks to maximise control of the party while the party strives for influence over the prime minister. This process is clearly illustrated by events before the vote on the Government's so-called 'paving' motion on ratification of the Maastricht Treaty on 4 November 1992. Major – together with senior ministers and Conservative Whips – made personal appeals to Conservative Euro-dissidents whilst the Tory rebels tried to win concessions in return for supporting the Government on a motion which

Labour were treating as a vote of confidence in the Government.

Faced by recalcitrant backbenchers, the PM can appeal to personal ambition (his power of patronage is a potent weapon) and party loyalty (a general desire to do nothing to assist the 'other side'). In general, prime ministers are strongest in their relations with their parties in the months following victory in a general election or leadership election. Such 'honeymoon' periods may be very brief indeed, as John Major's experience in 1992 showed. In April, the fact that he enjoyed much greater popularity than Neil Kinnock made an important contribution to the Conservatives' election victory but by early November, he had become the most unpopular prime minister since records began.

PMs are at their weakest when Government policies seem not to be working and provoke popular hostility and opposition. It was Thatcher's mounting unpopularity as a result of high interest rates, a stagnant economy and the 'poll tax', that led the party to revolt against her in November 1990.

The prime minister's performance in Parliament is always the subject of close scrutiny. Twice a week – for fifteen minutes – the premier appears in the House of Commons to answer 'Prime Minister's Questions'. 'Question Time' is by far the most common prime ministerial activity in Parliament. Prime ministers can expect to answer about 1000 questions per session, a large proportion of them on economic and foreign affairs. Many of the questions appear as supplementaries which are more difficult to prepare for. Question Time is a testing ordeal, therefore, at which much is at stake, including personal reputation, command of party, and the authority of the government. Between 1974 and 1979 Labour premiers Harold Wilson and James Callaghan faced 400 Question Times whilst Margaret Thatcher answered 7500 oral questions in her eleven years as PM (Madgwick, 1991, p. 174).

Whilst Parliament is sitting, premiers may expect to be constantly preoccupied with it in other ways, too. Their concerns include the progress of government legislation, set-piece speeches in full-dress parliamentary debates and, more generally, the state of party morale. 'Parliamentary business' is always an item on Cabinet agenda. A recent study has suggested that, whereas before 1940 prime ministers were often 'multi-faceted parliamentary performers who would, for example, both make a speech in a debate and then intervene subsequently', in the period after 1940 they have tended to attend the Commons 'only for a set and specific purpose, especially the effectively mandatory Prime Minister's question time' (Exhibit 8.2).

Contemporary prime ministers need to pay particular attention to the way they and their governments are presented in the media. They inevitably spend much of their lives in public – being interviewed on television, briefing lobby correspondents, making speeches at this or that public function, responding impromptu in the street or airport lounge or on the doorstep to queries about the latest crisis, scandal or leak. If they succeed in presenting a decisive image, they will be given credit for their handling – or, more pejoratively, for their 'manipulation' – of the media; if they are tripped up, or fluff their lines, or in any way give a less than positive impression, not only their own reputation but also that of the Government will suffer. In other words, self-presentation through newspapers, radio and television has become another vital prime ministerial concern. John Major was rarely out of the headlines during 1992.

Thus, in the usual personalised election campaign characterised by 'photo opportunities' and 'sound bites', he edged ahead of his party rivals, making 175 broadcasting appearances to Neil Kinnock's 162 and Paddy Ashdown's 152, the degree of the leaders' domination of the campaign being evident in the respective total appearances of leading party figures (425 Conservative, 346 Labour, 270 Liberal Democrat) (Loughborough University Communications Research Centre, *The Guardian*, 11 April 1992). Necessarily prominent in the news media during September owing to the speculators' attack on sterling, Major took the opportunity provided by the annual party conference in order to try to rally party opinion ('Major toughs out Euro-mutiny', 'Major plays the patriot card', *The Guardian*, 7, 10 October 1992). By the middle of the following month, he was maintaining his high

---

Exhibit 8.2 *Prime ministers and Parliament*

Patrick Dunleavy, G.W. Jones and Brendan O'Leary have shown that:

- **Answering questions** at Question Time was over four times as common as any other kind of prime ministerial parliamentary activity;

- **Statements** to the House by prime ministers have become more frequent in the post-1940 period but prime ministerial *speeches* have become much rarer, with postwar PMs on average making speeches about half as often as PMs before 1940;

- **Interventions** in debates – in a spontaneous, unscripted way – is the second most common type of parliamentary activity by PMs; and finally,

- Taking all these kinds of parliamentary activity together (namely, answering questions, statements, speeches and interventions), Margaret Thatcher was 'far and away the least active Prime Minister in the Commons for the last one hundred and twenty years': she made very few debating interventions (none at all in the three sessions between 1985 and 1988), very infrequent speeches, and even on statements was 'a sporadic performer' by postwar standards.

Source: Dunleavy, Jones and O'Leary (1990).

---

media profile, conducting a damage-limitation exercise by denying knowledge of arms sales to Iraq as Foreign Secretary before the Gulf War ('Major: Nobody told me', *Observer*, 15 November 1992) and using the occasion of a speech at the Lord Mayor's Banquet in the City to underline the Government's new-found commitment to industry ('PM talks up confidence', *The Guardian*, 17 November 1992.).

Prime ministers need also to be concerned about their personal standing in the opinion polls. The polling organisations – Mori, Gallup, Marplan and the like – repeatedly sound public opinion on such matters as the moral qualities (toughness, integrity, truthfulness and compassion), leadership style (dictatorial/consensual) and policy achievements of the prime minister. They compare the premier's political standing with that of his or her main rivals (Table 8.2) and then often compare these ratings with party support.

These relative positions – prime ministers compared with other leaders; party leaders compared with their parties – fluctuate continually during the lifetime of a Parliament.

We are now in a position to summarise the role of the prime minister in the British political system (Exhibit 8.3).

Table 8.2 *The political popularity of the party leaders during the 1992 General Election*

Question: Who do you think would make the most capable Prime Minister?

	March 11–12	March 16	March 30	April 7–8
	(per cent)			
John Major	40	42	38	38
Neil Kinnock	27	28	29	27
Paddy Ashdown	22	20	21	20

Note: Figures do not add up to 100%: missing responses are 'None/Don't know'.

Source: Data from MORI/*The Times*, 11 April 1992.

Exhibit 8.3   *The role of the prime minister*

- **Elected by the people**: authority of PM derives from being leader of the party which gains a parliamentary majority in a general election. Leader of party with overall majority gains constitutional status of the monarch's first minister.

- **Appoints government** (and many more people to positions of national eminence): PM hires, reshuffles and dismisses ministers; decides order of rank – 'pecking order' – of Cabinet, signified by seating arrangements in Cabinet room.

- **Steers Government**: PM directs and coordinates government policy and strategy; provides motive force of Cabinet system, exerting significant influence over Cabinet agenda, meetings and conclusions, and also determining pattern of decision-making at top (i.e. specific use of Cabinet committees, *ad hoc* ministerial groups, bilateral meetings). PM has special interest in economic, defence and foreign policy and may intervene in particular Departments. PM has special responsibilities in the field of national security.

- **Organises Government**: this may involve abolition of old and creation of new Departments of State. As head of civil service, PM oversees appointments, organisation and practices.

- **Requests dissolution of Parliament from the monarch**, normally after consultation with senior ministers. This is an important power, enabling PM (within certain time limits) to call a general election at a moment of maximum advantage to his or her party.

- **Controls House of Commons** through leadership of majority party combined with (in most circumstances) its disciplined voting behaviour.

- **Gives leadership to the nation**: this is most obvious during national crises (e.g. wars) and key international negotiations (e.g. EC treaty-making and budget discussions) but in fact is continuous, as shown by the PM's constant activity in hosting receptions of foreign leaders and in making official visits abroad. PM has continuous high political profile because of frequent appearances on TV and radio and in press.

■ The Prime Minister's Office

The prime minister has a personal staff of around 100 people, about one-third of whom are senior officials and advisers. The prime minister's office includes the following: the Private Office; the Press Office; the Political Office; the Policy Unit; Special Advisers; the Efficiency Unit; and the 'Kitchen Cabinet' (Figure 8.2).

□ *The Private Office*

The task of the Private Office is to support the PM in any way required. This involves it in en-suring that the PM's relationships as head of government with Whitehall, Parliament and public function as smoothly and efficiently as possible. The Private Office acts as a 'gate-keeper' for all incoming communications to the PM, forwarding them with appropriate comments; shadows the PM in his or her dealings with the outside world, including ministers; and, finally, provides any other support services needed, including advice, information, and the drafting of letters and speeches. The Private Office is headed by the prime minister's principal private secretary and has five other officials – all senior civil servants on secondment from their departments – backed up by a number of secretaries, executive officers and duty clerks.

131

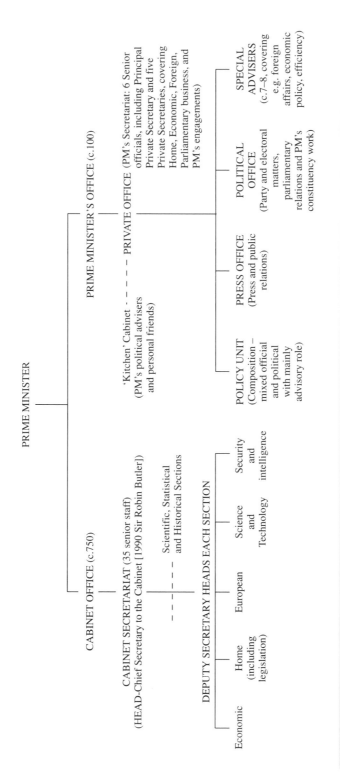

Figure 8.2 *The executive centre of British Government*

☐ *The Press Office*

As already seen, media management is now considered an essential task of government and the role of the Press Office (the first Press Officer was appointed in 1931) is to handle the prime minister's relations with the media and the flow of government information. It briefs lobby correspondents 'off the record' on a daily basis and plans the PM's media appearances. Because of the central role of the press officer in presenting government policy to the media, recent holders of the job have been close confidantes of the prime minister. Bernard Ingham, Margaret Thatcher's Press Officer, gained a controversial reputation for pugnacious defences of the Prime Minister and occasional scathing denigrations of ministers.

☐ *The Political Office*

The task of the political office, which is staffed not by civil servants but by temporary outsiders, is to deal with all matters concerning the prime minister as a party politician. It keeps in constant contact with party headquarters, with constituency parties – including the PM's own constituency – and generally with party developments at Westminster and in the country.

☐ *The Policy Unit*

The Policy Unit provides policy and analysis and advice for the prime minister. The first policy unit was set up in 1974. Specifically, its main purposes are:

- commenting critically upon Departmental proposals;
- bringing forward new ideas and identifying new areas requiring attention;
- following up policy proposals.

In order to be effective the Unit needs and generally gets privileged access to Departmental officials and to ministers, including the right to attend top-level Cabinet and official committees. Its members, – except for the two civil servants the Unit borrowed from the Departments on a short-term basis in the 1980s – are politically partisan outsiders, usually recruited from business and academic life. The Policy Unit has been an undoubted success in providing prime ministers with an alternative source of policy advice to that emanating from the Departments on all areas except foreign policy. Its head in 1993 was Sarah Hogg.

☐ *Special Advisers*

Modern prime ministers also appoint specialist advisers. Among those appointed by Margaret Thatcher were Sir Anthony Parsons, a former diplomat, to advise on foreign policy, and Sir Alan Walters, to advise on economic affairs. The continuing influence of Walters with the prime minister in the late 1980s created difficulties in the relationship between No. 10 and the Chancellor of the Exchequer, Nigel Lawson, ultimately leading to Lawson's resignation in October 1989. At the heart of the differences between the two men was the desirability of joining the ERM, which Lawson favoured and Walters opposed. Lawson's resignation letter stated:

> The successful conduct of economic policy is possible only if there is, and is seen to be, full agreement between the Prime Minister and the Chancellor of the Exchequer. Recent events have confirmed that this essential requirement cannot be met so long as Sir Alan Walters remains your personal economic adviser.

The recent events referred to included the publication of an article by Walters in which he described the European Monetary system as half-baked. Thatcher's response to a query about Walter's position by the Leader of the Opposition earlier in the week of the resignation had drawn attention to the constitutional position: 'Advisers advise, ministers decide.' Whilst true, this was also evasive about the particular significance of the role of *this* adviser. Lawson's relationship with Thatcher had been deteriorating for 18 months when he resigned and would probably have ended in resignation at some later point anyway. But there is little doubt either that Walter's advice had not only strengthened Thatcher's resistance to her Chancellor, thereby widening the division between them, but also contributed signally to her habit of covertly distancing herself from the policy of her own Government. In this particular case, she had gone along with British membership of the EMS but, by failing to repudiate Walter's attacks on it, encouraged the view among Conservative anti-Europeans and the public at large that she really opposed it. This tactic led first to policy confusion and then to political disaster, with Walters vacating his part-time £31 000-a-year job immediately after Lawson's resignation.

The Efficiency Unit

The Efficiency Unit was established in 1979 when, in the quest for greater efficiency and value for money in the civil service, Thatcher appointed Sir Derek Rayner, then joint Managing Director of Marks and Spencer, to head a small unit of about six civil servants in her Private Office. Rayner was succeeded in 1983 by Sir Robin Ibbs, an executive director of ICI (Imperial Chemical Industries), who also did the job part-time. By 1985, the Unit had conducted 266 scrutinies, leading to savings of about £750 million.

The 'Kitchen Cabinet'

Finally, most prime ministers have had a 'kitchen Cabinet' of close confidants, a circle of 'friends' to whom they can look for personal support. Margaret Thatcher's most trusted aides came from the PM's Office, in fact, and included Charles Powell, a foreign affairs adviser in her Private Office, Bernard Ingham, her Chief Press Secretary, and – over a much shorter period of time – her Parliamentary Private Secretary, Ian Gow.

■ The Cabinet

The Cabinet is the country's top executive committee. It usually consists of between 20 and 22 members. In April 1994 the Conservative Cabinet contained 22 members (Table 8.3). Status within the Cabinet is not equal and most Cabinets divide into a small circle of ministers who may expect to be frequently consulted by the prime minister and an outer circle who count for less. The 'plum' jobs are the chancellorship of the Exchequer and the foreign and home secretaryships, which a victorious party's leading few politicians may expect to occupy. On occasion, and notably in times of war, a small 'inner Cabinet' of 5–6 ministers has been formed, as in the Falklands and Gulf wars, for example. Thus, although the decision to commit the Task Force in 1981 was taken by full Cabinet, Margaret

Table 8.3 *The Conservative Cabinet in April 1994*

Prime Minister	John Major
Lord Chancellor	Lord Mackay of Clashfern
Foreign Secretary	Douglas Hurd
Home Secretary	Michael Howard
Chancellor of the Exchequer	Kenneth Clarke
Lord Privy Seal and Leader of the House of Lords	Lord Wakeham
Chancellor of the Duchy of Lancaster	William Waldegrave
Environment	John Gummer
Defence	Malcolm Rifkind
Education	John Patten
Lord President of the Council and Leader of the House of Commons	Tony Newton
Transport	John MacGregor
Employment	David Hunt
Trade and Industry	Michael Heseltine
Social Security	Peter Lilley
Health	Virginia Bottomley
Agriculture	Gillian Shephard
Northern Ireland	Sir Patrick Mayhew
Wales	John Redwood
Scotland	Ian Lang
National Heritage	Peter Brooke
Chief Secretary to the Treasury	Michael Portillo

Period/prime minister	Meetings: total per year/ average number per week
Pre-1914	40 per year: under one per week
1918–1939	60 per year: just over one per week
1946–54	90 per year: two per week.
Harold Wilson (1964–70, 74–6)	59 per year: just over one per week. 472 meetings in approx. 8 years.
Margaret Thatcher (1979–90)	35 per year: under one per week. 394 meetings in over 11 years.

Sources: Data from Hennessy (1986, p. 100); Madgwick (1991, p. 53).

Table 8.4   *Frequency of Cabinet meetings*

Thatcher formed a War Cabinet consisting of herself, her deputy, William Whitelaw, Foreign Secretary, Francis Pym, Defence Secretary, John Nott, and Paymaster-General and Party Chairman, Cecil Parkinson, to run the war on a day-to-day basis.

The full Cabinet meets at least once a week – under Thatcher, on Thursdays between 10 a.m. and 1 p.m. – and sometimes also on Tuesdays. In times of crisis, it tends to meet more frequently and on other days of the week. Cabinet meetings became more numerous throughout the century down to the 1960s but declined thereafter, slowly at first but then dramatically under Thatcher (Table 8.4).

□ Cabinet Business

Very few decisions in the modern Cabinet system are actually *made* by Cabinet although virtually all the major policy issues come before it in some form. Its agenda over a period of time consists predominantly of three kinds of matter: *routine items* such as forthcoming parliamentary business, reports on foreign affairs and major economic decisions, e.g. the budget, interest rate changes; in the 1980s regular slots were found for opinions to be aired on EC and home affairs; *disagreements referred upwards for Cabinet arbitration*, e.g. from Cabinet committees or from a departmental minister in dispute; and *important contemporary concerns* – a broad range, including national crises such as a war, issues of major controversy such as a large-scale strike and matters of considerable political sensitivity, such as the public furore over the Government's proposed closure of 31 pits in October 1992. Not only does the Cabinet itself not make many of the major policy decisions (even the key decision on the abolition of the 'poll tax' and the form of its replacement in 1991 was made by Cabinet committee before going to Cabinet for approval) it does not itself *initiate* policy either. Exhibit 8.4 summarises the role of the modern Cabinet.

Exhibit 8.4   *The role of the Cabinet*

Formal approval: Formal approval of decisions taken elsewhere.

Final court of appeal: Final court of appeal for disagreements referred from below.

Crisis management: Management of crises and issues of major political controversy.

Brake: Blocking, slowing down, amending and qualifying policies and legislation.

Debating forum: Sounding board for general debate by leading ministers.

Legitimiser: Conferment of authority upon government decisions.

Symbol of collective executive: Ultimate symbol of collective rather than single executive in Britain.

☐ *Cabinet Committees*

Because of the sheer volume and complexity of modern governmental business, the bulk of decisions within the Cabinet system are taken by **Cabinet committees**. Important matters largely dealt with by Cabinet committees in the 1980s include not only the ending of the 'poll tax' but also the abolition of the metropolitan counties, privatisation, and reform of the NHS. Cabinet committee decisions have the status of Cabinet decisions and only when they are unable to reach agreement is a matter referred to full Cabinet. The committee chairman must agree any request to take a dispute to full Cabinet, but in general such appeals are strongly discouraged. Treasury ministers however, in 1975, gained the right of automatic appeal to Cabinet if defeated on public spending in committee (James, 1992, p. 69).

The establishment, composition, terms of reference and chairmanship of Cabinet committees are the responsibility of the prime minister. Before 1992, their structure was supposedly a secret but gradually came to light from the 1970s as a result of ministerial memoirs and partial statements by the prime minister. After the 1992 General Election, however, John Major decided to make public the entire system of Cabinet standing committees and the subjects they deal with (Figure 8.3).

In addition to the 25 or so standing committees at a given moment, there are also a much larger number of *ad hoc* committees set up by the prime minister to deal with particular issues as they arise. Table 8.5 gives some examples of *ad hoc* committees in the 1980s. Standing committees are normally classified under a set of code letters, *ad hoc* committees under the term 'GEN' for 'General' (in the 1980s under 'MISC' for 'Miscellaneous').

The prime minister and senior members of the Cabinet chair the most important Cabinet committees. Figure 8.3, for example, shows the PM presiding over nine standing committees and non-Departmental ministers – the Lord Privy Seal and Lord President of the Council – each responsible for five. Key standing committees are Economic and Domestic Policy (EDP), Overseas Policy and Defence (OPD), Nuclear Defence Policy (OPDN) and Security and Intelligence Services (IS) – all chaired by the PM (see Exhibit 8.5 for membership of EDP and OPD).

A very important *ad hoc* committee is the so-called 'Star Chamber' (MISC 62 in Margaret Thatcher's time as PM) whose task is to arbitrate between the claims of the spending Departments, especially Defence, Social Services and the Environment, and the Treasury's demands for economy. There is also a network of 'shadow' committees chaired by leading civil servants whose function is to clear away inter-departmental disputes before the ministerial committees meet.

Cabinet committees have become central to decision-making in the postwar period. During the 1980s, Thatcher certainly attempted to reduce the number of such committees, establishing a mere 30–35 standing committees and 120 *ad hoc* committees in six and a half years between 1979 and 1987. These figures may be compared with the 148 standing and 313 *ad hoc* committees established by Attlee in six and a quarter years between 1945 and 1951 and the 137 standing committees and 109 *ad hoc* committees set up by Churchill in three and a half years between 1951 and 1954. By late 1992, John Major had appointed 27 standing (or ministerial) committees: the standing committee on Public Expenditure (EDX) was added during summer 1992 to the list published in May. It was stated in May that the total number of *ad hoc* committees would be disclosed annually.

☐ *The Cabinet Office*

The Cabinet Office is another institution at the heart of the core executive which has developed in response to the large growth in the volume of government business. Dating from 1916, its most important component so far as central government is concerned is the **Cabinet Secretariat**, a group of about 35 senior civil servants on secondment from other Departments working under the direction of the Cabinet secretary. Its main tasks are threefold:

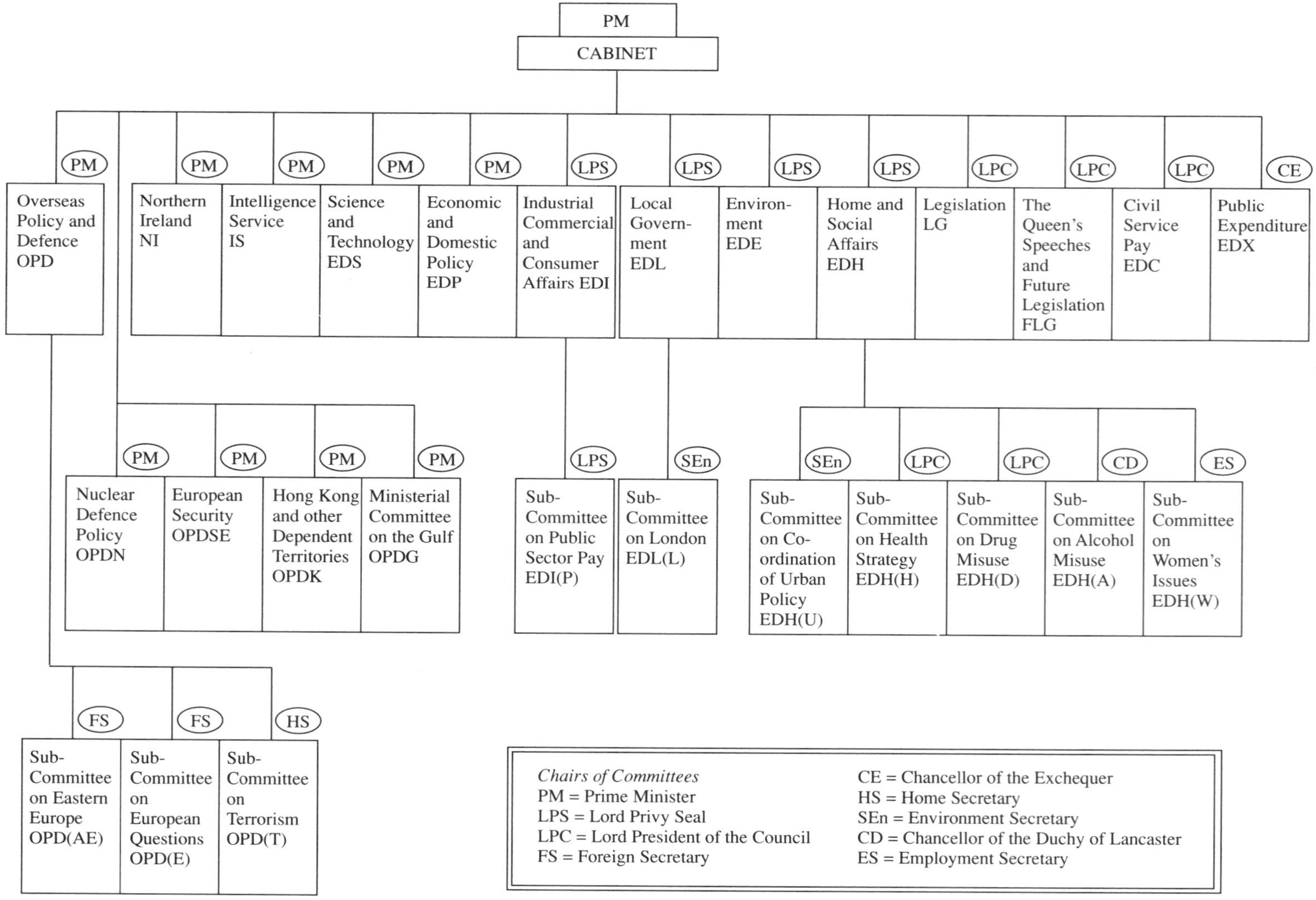

Source: Dunleavy et al. (1993)

Figure 8.3 Cabinet standing committees in 1992

Committee	Functions
MISC 62 ('Star Chamber')	Adjudication of public expenditure disputes between 'spending' departments and the Treasury and enforcement of spending cuts.
MISC 7	Replacement of the Polaris force with Trident.
MISC 57	Contingency planning for a miners' strike.
MISC 95	Abolition of the GLC and the metropolitan counties.
MISC 101	Day-to-day planning of the 1984–5 miners' strike.
MISC 107	Youth training.
MISC 111	Future of the Welfare State.
MISC 122	Handling of the teachers' dispute 1985–6.

Table 8.5 *Some key* ad hoc *Cabinet committees in the 1980s*

- to service Cabinet and its committees, preparing agendas, briefing Chairmen, taking minutes, circulating conclusions & chairing official committees which 'shadow' Cabinet committees
- to coordinate and plan Cabinet business: Robert Armstrong (Cabinet Secretary 1979–87) held weekly meetings to plan business over forthcoming weekly, three-weekly and six-monthly spans of time;
- to supervise the implementation of decisions emanating from the Cabinet system. The Cabinet Secretariat is organised in six secretariats, each corresponding to a main area of Cabinet (Cabinet Committee) business. These are: Economics; Home; Overseas and Defence; European; Science and Technology; and, operating rather differently from the other Secretariats, Security and Intelligence.

Exhibit 8.5 *Membership of some leading Cabinet standing committees in 1992*

Economic and Domestic Policy (EDP)
Prime Minister (chair), Chancellor of the Exchequer, Home Secretary, President of the Board of Trade, Lord Privy Seal, Lord President of the Council, Environment Secretary, Welsh Secretary, Chancellor of the Duchy of Lancaster, Scottish Secretary, Northern Ireland Secretary, Employment Secretary, Chief Secretary to the Treasury.

Overseas Policy and Defence (OPD)
Prime Minister (Chair), Foreign Secretary, Chancellor of the Exchequer, President of the Board of Trade, Defence Secretary, Attorney-General. Chief of Defence Staff attends as required.

Ministerial Committee on Home and Social Affairs (EDH)
Lord Privy Seal (Chair), Lord Chancellor, Home Secretary, President of the Board of Trade, Transport Secretary, Lord President of the Council, Chancellor of the Duchy of Lancaster, Scottish Secretary, National Heritage Secretary, Northern Ireland Secretary, Education Secretary, Health Secretary, Employment Secretary, Chief Secretary to the Treasury, Chief Whip. Agriculture Minister, the Attorney-General and the Lord Advocate receive papers and attend as necessary.

Ministerial Committee on the Queen's Speeches and Future Legislation (FLG)
Lord President of the Council (Chair), Lord Chancellor, Lord Privy Seal, Chancellor of the Duchy of Lancaster, Attorney-General, Lord Advocate, Chief Whip, Financial Secretary to the Treasury, Captain of the Gentlemen-at-Arms. Foreign Secretary or a representative is invited to attend discussion of Queen's Speeches

☐ *Collective responsibility*

Like the office of prime minister, the Cabinet lacks formal constitutional existence. Both institutions are creations of convention. The document *Questions of Procedure for Ministers* – which is the first Cabinet paper a new minister is handed – has been described as the nearest thing to a written constitution for Cabinet government in Britain. (Exhibit 8.6) This document was also published in May 1992 along with the details about Cabinet ministerial committees; prior to that, knowledge of it had been available only through leaked editions.

An important concern of *Questions of Procedure for Ministers* is the collective responsibility of Cabinet ministers. The doctrine of **collective responsibility**, which holds that ministers accept responsibility collectively for the decisions made in Cabinet, is the main convention influencing the operation of the Cabinet. The practical implications of the doctrine are as follows:

- **Cabinet solidarity.** However much they disagree with a decision, ministers are expected to support it publicly or, at least, not express their lack of support for it. If they feel they

---

Exhibit 8.6 *Cabinet practice: 'Questions of Procedure for Ministers'*

This paper lays down guidelines to ministers and civil servants in the operation of Cabinet government. It requires ministers

- To ensure that no conflict arises or appears to arise between their private interests and their public duties;
- To be as open as possible with Parliament and the public;
- Not to disclose either the internal process through which a decision has been made or the level of committee by which it was taken;
- To maintain complete secrecy about opinions expressed in Cabinet and ministerial committees and to protect the privacy of Cabinet business and the security of government documents;
  if Privy Councillors, to give precedence to meetings with the Queen over all other matters;
- To make important announcements in the first instance in Parliament, to avoid leaving significant announcements to the last day before the recess and to channel all announcements through the Downing Street Press Office;
- To pay particular attention in making appointments to securing on merit proper representation of women and members of ethnic minorities on public bodies;
- Not to ask civil servants to attend party conferences although they may ask civil servants to attend party meetings in order to enable the minister to attend to urgent departmental business;
- If in receipt of gifts over £125 from a foreign government to hand them over to their department (gifts under £125 may be retained so long as reported to the permanent secretary);

The document also informs ministers about Cabinet procedure:
- That minutes of Cabinet and Cabinet committees are restricted to summaries and that the Cabinet Office is instructed to avoid as far as practicable recording the opinions expressed by individual ministers;
- That *ad hoc* Committees may take important decisions which never reach the Cabinet but which the Government as a whole must accept responsibility for;
- That only Treasury ministers have an automatic right of appeal to full Cabinet from lower committees over spending decisions with which they disagree;
- That a minister wishing to raise a matter in Cabinet or in Cabinet committee must give the Cabinet Secretary at least seven days notice of it.

must dissent publicly, they are expected to resign; if they fail to resign, it falls to the prime minister to require them to do so. The underlying purpose of this is to create and maintain the authority of the government which public squabbling between ministers could be expected to damage.

- **Cabinet secrecy.** A precondition of Cabinet solidarity is that Cabinet discussion is secret. Ministers need to feel free to speak their minds secure in the knowledge that their views will not be divulged to the media. Ministers who are known to disagree with a policy may be expected to have little commitment to it: well-publicised disagreements, therefore, have potentially damaging consequences for public confidence in government.
- **Cabinet resignation if defeated on a Commons vote of confidence.** The convention requires that the Cabinet – and therefore the entire Government – should resign if defeated on a vote of confidence in the House of Commons. This aspect of the convention still operates unambiguously: when the Labour Government elected in October 1974 was defeated on a vote of confidence on 28 March 1979, the Prime Minister James Callaghan immediately requested a dissolution.

The doctrine of collective responsibility is clearly of value to the prime minister in the control of Cabinet colleagues. On the other hand, it does lay reciprocal obligations on the PM first, not to leak decisions and second, to run the government in a collegial way, making sure that ministers have reasonable opportunities to discuss issues. This latter point has implications not only for the conduct of Cabinet itself but also for the composition of Cabinet committees which - if they are to take authoritative decisions in the name of the Cabinet - must be representative of the Cabinet as a whole (James, 1992, p. 9).

In recent times, the convention of collective responsibility has been repeatedly broken in several ways. These are:

- **Suspension by the PM:** Labour Prime Minister Harold Wilson in 1975 suspended the con-

vention on the issue of Britain's continued membership of the European Community rather than risk public squabbling between members of the Government and resignations by ministerial opponents of the Community. James Callaghan also did so in 1977 on the question of the most suitable electoral system for the European Parliament.

- **Leaks and memoirs:** unattributable leaks of confidential information by ministers, including the prime minister, and the publication of diaries by former Cabinet ministers such as Richard Crossman, Barbara Castle and Tony Benn which reveal details of Cabinet discussions.
- **Non-resignation despite serious disagreement with Cabinet policy over major issues:** in theory, dissent on an important aspect of government policy should be a resigning matter but there are fewer resignations than serious divisions within the Cabinet. Thus, James Callaghan campaigned openly against trade union reform in 1969 and Sir Geoffrey Howe openly argued in favour of joining the ERM after his demotion from the Foreign Office in summer 1989 but whilst still a member of a Cabinet which officially did not support joining it. In late 1974 Tony Benn announced his opposition to EC membership in open defiance of a Cabinet agreement to observe collective responsibility until the process of re-negotiation of entry terms had been completed. (Callaghan,1987, p. 318).

Nonetheless, the habitual practice of Cabinet government is still best described in terms of 'the unanimity rule and the confidentiality rule' (Marshall, 1984, p. 55), respectively solidarity and secrecy. Between 1964 and 1990, 21 ministers left governments on the grounds of collective responsibility, including six (one dismissed, five resigned) from governments led by Thatcher. (Pyper, 1991, pp. 243–4). Table 8.6 shows collective responsibility resignations between 1985 and 1990.

	Position	Reason for resignation
Ian Gow	Minister of State, Treasury, November 1985	Opposed to Anglo-Irish Agreement
Michael Heseltine	Secretary of State for Defence, January 1986	Opposed to PM's management of Westland affair
Nigel Lawson	Chancellor of the Exchequer, October 1989	Opposed to PM's conduct of economic policy and to role of special adviser Sir Alan Walters
Nicholas Ridley	Secretary of State Trade and Industry, July 1990	Resigned after pressure from PM following controversy over his comments on Germany
Sir Geoffrey Howe	Lord President of the Council and Leader of the House of Commons ('Deputy Prime Minister') November 1990	Opposed to PM's conduct of policy on Europe

Table 8.6   *Resignations on grounds of collective responsibility, 1985–90*

☐ *Cabinet Minutes*

Cabinet minutes – which are the responsibility of the Cabinet Secretariat – aim not to record every shift and turn of Cabinet debate but simply to reflect, in the words of a former Cabinet Secretary, Sir John Hunt, 'as much agreement as is there'. Controversy has occurred over the extent of prime ministerial involvement in the process, with certain members of Labour Cabinets suggesting that this could be considerable (Castle, 1980 p. 252; Crossman, 1979, p. 702). But the then Prime Minister, Harold Wilson, denied it, maintaining at the time (1970) that only 'very, very occasionally' was he consulted about the minutes before issue. He later stated that 'the writing of the conclusions is the unique responsibility of the Secretary of the Cabinet.... The conclusions are circulated very promptly after Cabinet, and up to that that time no minister, certainly not the Prime Minister, sees them, asks

to see them or conditions them in any way' (cited in King, 1985, p. 40). This later statement is widely accepted now as a correct account of routine procedure.

A recent detailed account of practice in the 1980s states:

> On most items before Cabinet, the Cabinet Secretary and at least one member...of the secretariat most directly responsible...would record a full record of the discussion in their notebooks. From their notes, the officials would compile a draft minute to send to Armstrong's office later on the day of the meeting... Armstrong then collated and edited the drafts sent in by the secretariats, and produced a final copy of the Cabinet's minutes...*His final record was never cleared with the PM or with the individual ministers concerned, contrary to the views of some.* (Seldon, 1990, our italics)

Figure 8.4 provides a summary overview of the personnel and role of the main institutions in the central executive territory.

▮ The impact of Margaret Thatcher's Premiership on the Prime Ministerial Power Thesis

Margaret Thatcher's premiership has been seen by some commentators as validating the prime ministerial power thesis advanced by Richard Crossman (1964) and Tony Benn (1985). Briefly, these writers argued that a considerable concentration of power in the premiership has occurred, resulting – according to Benn – in 'a system of personal rule in the very heart of our parliamentary democracy'. The prime minister's powers of patronage, control over government business, special responsibilities in the spheres of defence, foreign policy and security, command over government information and publicity, and constitutional capacity to request a dissolution of Parliament have elevated the premiership at the expense of the Cabinet. As a consequence, the prime minister can 'use the government to bring forward the policies which s/he favours and to stop those to which s/he is opposed' (Benn) and the Cabinet has become 'a dignified part of the Constitution' (Crossman). Symptomatic of prime ministerial power are those decisions in the

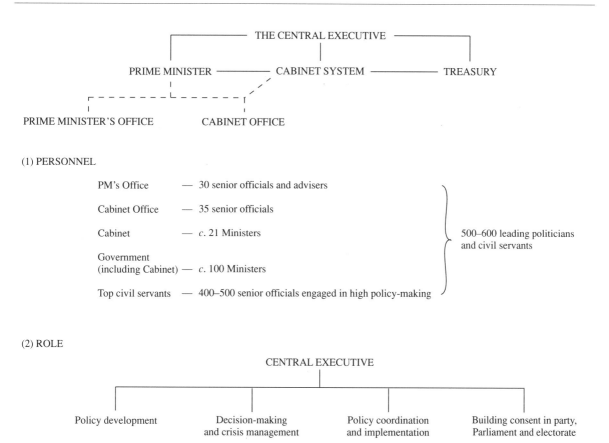

Figure 8.4 *The central executive: personnel and role*

postwar period taken by premiers without full consultation of Cabinet.

According to this argument, the way in which power in modern Britain has flowed remorselessly away from Cabinet towards the prime minister is perfectly exemplified in Thatcher's exercise of the office. The main features of Thatcher's 'style' of government have been described as:

- Systematic by-passing of Cabinet by use of Cabinet committees, especially *ad hoc* committees, informal ministerial groups and bilateral meetings with a minister and officials;
- The holding of fewer Cabinet meetings – down to one per week, possibly fewer than her predecessors in the 1970s and half the number in the immediate postwar period; also fewer Cabinet papers–about 60–70 in 1984, cf. 402, 1954 (Hennessy, 1986, pp. 99–100);

- Personal involvement over a wide range of government policy-making, including e.g. GCHQ, (Government Communications Headquarters), the 'poll tax', opting-out schools, industrial relations legislation, the environment, football hooliganism;
- Use of PM's Policy Unit to promote policies and follow up initiatives; also, extensive reliance on special advisers, outside advice from right-wing think-tanks such as the Adam Smith Institute, the Centre for Policy Studies and the Institute of Economic Affairs, and outside experts convened in special seminars, e.g. on German unification, the future of the film industry;
- Tendency to make policy 'on the hoof' in a conference speech or TV interview without consultation with ministerial colleagues (e.g. 'poll tax');

- Brusque treatment of ministers regarded as weak, 'wet', 'not one of us' – e.g. especially the sacking of Foreign Secretary Francis Pym (1983), and Leader of the House John Biffen (1987), and the demotion from the Foreign Secretaryship and subsequent humiliation of Sir Geoffrey Howe (1989–90);
- Use of PM's Press Office to undermine ministers, sometimes as a prelude to sacking them (e.g. Pym, Biffen, Peter Rees(1985), Patrick Jenkin (1985)).

Thatcher's high-handedness as PM and failure to run the Cabinet in a collegial way culminated in the resignations of three Cabinet 'heavy weights', Michael Heseltine, Nigel Lawson and Sir Geoffrey Howe, in her last four years of office.

Heseltine resigned in 1986, maintaining that 'the basis of trust' necessary in the relationship between the Prime Minister and Defence Secretary had broken down. Thatcher had summoned two *ad hoc* ministerial meetings followed by a meeting of the Cabinet's Economic Affairs (EA) Committee in order to resolve the widely-publicised dispute about the best solution for the problems of an ailing helicopter company, Westland. Later Heseltine claimed that his case for a 'European' – against the case for an American – solution had not been given a fair hearing within the Cabinet system, alleging in particular (*a*) that a further meeting of the Economic Affairs Committee promised at the 9 December meeting for 13 December 1985 had not been held (the PM denied that such a meeting was ever fixed) and (*b*) that his request to discuss Westland at a Cabinet meeting on 12 December was refused by the PM and that his protest about this was not recorded in the Cabinet minutes as he asked and nor was it recorded after he had complained to the Cabinet Secretary about the matter. He then felt justified in arguing his case about Westland helicopters publicly – in breach of Cabinet confidentiality – and when, after a further controversy involving the leaking of a vital letter by the DTI (see Chapter 9), the PM sought to restrain him by the requirement that all future statements on Westland would have to be cleared with the Cabinet Office, he resigned (9 January 1986).

Like Heseltine, **Nigel Lawson** in resigning (see above pp. 132–3) argued that there had been a breakdown in the constitutional principle of collective Cabinet government. Shortly after resigning he stated in the House of Commons: 'For our system of Cabinet government to work effectively, the prime minister of the day must appoint ministers that he or she trusts and then leave them to carry out the policy. When differences of view emerge, as they are bound to do from time to time, they should be resolved privately and, wherever appropriate, collectively'. The political reality, however, was that in this case there was no agreed policy (on whether to join the ERM) and the PM – probably fearing that her own preference for remaining outside the ERM was the minority view – was unwilling to put the matter to the test of collegial discussion.

Sir Geoffrey Howe's resignation one year later (1 November 1990) occurred after Britain had joined the ERM but also immediately in the wake of vigorous prime ministerial attacks on European federal ideals and monetary integration. Sir Geoffrey avowed his belief that Cabinet government was 'all about trying to persuade one another from within'. He resigned because he believed that the PM's negative attitudes on Europe prevented him from any longer being able to resolve the conflict between his loyalty to the PM and his loyalty to what he perceived as the true interests of the nation from within the Government.

Despite Thatcher's comprehensive assertion of the powers of the PM's office, it remains inappropriate to describe the British system as 'prime ministerial government'. In practice, political, administrative and personal constraints prevent the prime minister from achieving the degree of predominance suggested by this thesis.

Political Constraints on the Power of the PM

Appointment and Dismissals

Constitutionally the PM has a free hand in the making of government appointments but *politically* selection is constrained by the pool of talent within a particular party, by party standing and by the need to please sections of the party (left and right, 'wets' and 'dries', Euro-enthusiasts and Euro-sceptics) by ensuring that these have sufficient representation, especially at Cabinet level. This means in practice that Cabinets contain individuals whom the PM would rather be without.

It also means that many Cabinets contain one or two politicians of the highest calibre and with a following in the party who may rivals be for the party leadership: 'these are people whom the Prime Minister needs as much, or maybe more sometimes, than they need the Prime Minister' (Roy Jenkins, cit. James, 1992, p. 133). Attlee faced an attempt by colleagues to replace him – in 1947 when Cripps and Dalton sought to make Bevin premier – and Harold Wilson sometimes thought there were plots against him. Political considerations also constrain the PM's power of dismissal and demotion:Macmillan in dismissing seven Cabinet ministers and nine ministers outside the Cabinet in July 1962 (the so-called 'Night of the Long Knives') damaged his own standing as the brutality of the sackings caused resentment in the party and gave the appearance of panic to the country. Thatcher's big Cabinet reshuffle of July 1989 which included the demotion of the reluctant Sir Geoffrey Howe from the post of Foreign Secretary also had very damaging consequences (Young, 1990, pp. 555–7).

☐ *Policy*

Party also serves as a constraint in matters of *policy*. A dramatic illustration of this is policy towards Europe which has caused a series of PMs from Macmillan to Major often acute problems of party management. Wilson suspended collective responsibility and held a referendum to avoid splitting Labour and, with the Conservative Government facing rebellion over the ratification of the Maastricht Treaty in November 1992, Douglas Hurd warned of the dangers of a party split rivalling the split over the Corn Laws (1846).

☐ *Removability*

Ultimately the party may remove a sitting PM, but this is a rare event, having been the fate of just four of the seventeen PMs in the twentieth century: in addition to Thatcher (November 1990), Asquith (1916), Lloyd George (1922) and Chamberlain (1940) resigned after losing the support of senior colleagues and a sizeable section of the majority parliamentary party.

The very unusual combination of circumstances which led to the downfall of Thatcher included the availability of a strong prime ministerial candidate outside the Cabinet (Heseltine), the recent resignations of two Cabinet 'heavyweights' (Lawson and Howe), with Howe giving a particularly wounding resignation speech, a by-election disaster at a normally safe Conservative seat (Eastbourne), adverse economic indicators, public anger at the 'poll tax' for which Thatcher was generally blamed, and the considerable unpopularity of the Prime Minister and the party she led in the polls.

☐ *Administrative Constraints*

The major institutional constraint upon a PM is **the Cabinet**: however great their powers of manipulation, PMs have often suffered defeats in Cabinet, e.g. Wilson on trade union reform (1969), Callaghan on his wish to declare a state of emergency during the 'Winter of Discontent' (1979) and even Margaret Thatcher on a number of issues including radical anti-union and privatisation measures (early 1980s), a Northern Ireland assembly, and the sale of Ford Motors to Austin-Motors (1986): major settlements such as those relating to Rhodesia/Zimbabwe (1981) and Hong Kong (1984) and the decision to enter the ERM (1990) were pushed through against her resistance. On crucial issues, PMs are careful to bind the whole Cabinet to a decision: on the sending of the Task Force to the Falklands, Thatcher asked every member of the Cabinet individually to indicate a view. This has been even more the case with John Major, a weaker PM running the Cabinet in a more collegiate way.

The PM can also be restrained in a number of ways by the **civil service**: much policy is developed in the Departments and may arrive at the PM at such a late stage that effective challenge becomes difficult; or a prime ministerial request may be frustrated by officials – as Harold Wilson said, 'I'm tired of asking for this or that suggestion to be followed up only to have Michael (Stewart's) or Jim's (Callaghan) officials report back three weeks later that nothing could be done' (cited James, 1992, p. 220).

□ *Personal Constraints*

Finally, there are **personal limits** upon the power of the prime minister – the limits of any single individual's ability, energy, resources and time, together with the (very considerable) extent to which decisions are shaped by circumstances beyond any individual's ability to control. A survey of the prime minister's 'diary' during the 1970s has shown how stretched a single individual is to fulfil such a punishing schedule of consultations, meetings, appointments, conferences, receptions, and visits: according to this estimate – assuming a 13-hour day, a five-day Whitehall week and a Cabinet year of 44 weeks – only about one day per week is available to the PM for 'the Cabinet role', rising to over one and a half days when time spent with civil servants is taken into account; the rest of the time is spent on party matters, Parliament, and hosting and visiting (Donoughue, 1988). Even Thatcher, who intervened influentially over a large number of policy areas, ultimately failed to assert prime ministerial dominance over European policy (Dunleavy 1990, pp. 108–9). Moreover, the PM's special concerns (foreign affairs, the economy and security) are particularly vulnerable to setbacks which rebound swiftly on the popularity and even credibility of the premier: thus, security services disasters undermined Macmillan, pay policy problems leading to industrial conflict helped to destroy Callaghan, whilst difficulties over Europe ultimately eroded the authority of Thatcher.

To summarise: the British prime minister has very considerable powers – and these were stretched to the limit by a dynamic PM such as Thatcher. But the constraints upon the premier make 'prime ministerial government' an inappropriate description. Is 'Cabinet government' a more apt one? Our earlier discussion suggested that the Cabinet itself neither originates policy nor takes more than a small proportion of major decisions. However, the institution retains what may be described as 'a residual and irreducible' authority; it has not sunk into merely 'dignified' status (Madgwick, 1991, p. 259).

Its partial resurgence after November 1990 perfectly illustrates this. Its role in the downfall of Thatcher followed by the reassertion of collegiality – a Cabinet of 'chums' – under John Major and its high, crisis-generated profile in autumn 1992 revealed some vitality in the Cabinet itself. Strong enough to help depose a dominant PM, it then provided a collective shield to protect a weaker PM and his leading ministers (Lamont, Heseltine) when they got into political difficulties. In November 1992, instead of being negotiated privately between the Departments and the Treasury, major spending decisions for the Autumn Statement were thrashed out by the full Cabinet. The British system of decision-making at the top has grown more complex, diffuse, and extensive but it is still a collective executive in which the prime minister provides leadership within a Cabinet system. However, many commentators have drawn attention to weaknesses such as fragmentation and lack of coordination and accountability within this system. How may these be remedied?

■ Proposals for reform

Ministers in Cabinet rarely look at the totality of their responsibilities, at the balance of policy, at the progress of government towards its objectives as a whole...The form and structure of a modern Cabinet and the diet it consumes almost oblige it to function like a group of individuals, and not as a unity. (Sir Douglas Wass, 1983)

One of the most frequent criticisms of the operation of modern Cabinet government is the weakness of coordination and strategic direction at the top. Recent examples of confusion and lack of direction include the unresolved tension between PM and Chancellor of the Exchequer over European policy in the late 1980s, the failure of government to reconcile its free market ideology with the pursuit of 'green' objectives in the same period, and the two-month gap which appeared in government economic policy when Britain was forced out of the ERM in mid-September 1992. Many reform proposals therefore have focused on strengthening the capacity of prime minister and/or Cabinet to provide improved policy-making coordination and better long-term strategic direction (Table 8.7). Reformers argue that there is a crying need to overcome the 'short-termism' seemingly endemic in postwar British government, which has had especially damaging consequences in the fields of foreign and economic policy.

A second line of criticism maintains that too much power has become concentrated in the prime minister, who has developed into an 'elected monarch'. Reforms proposed by this school of thought focus on limiting the premier's political and other patronage, circumscribing his/her power to recommend a dissolution and making the premiership more accountable to Parliament.

Table 8.7   *Proposals for reform: Prime Minister and Cabinet*

Reform proposal	Aims	Comments
• Revive Central Policy Review Staff (CPRS)		Founded by Edward Heath (1971); abolished (1983) by Thatcher.
• Strengthen Cabinet Office by adding analysis and strategy units		Had some success.
• Ministerial 'Cabinets'	To improve policy coordination and long-term strategic direction at the top of central government by increasing the time and resources available to Cabinet Ministers to consider general policy.	To brief ministers for Cabinet on general policy.
• Cabinet Review Committees		To relate policy areas to overall Government strategy.
• Reduce Ministerial workloads and increase length of time spent in posts		
• Prime Minister's Department	To increase the capacity of the PM to provide well-informed leadership of the Cabinet system.	Proposed by Lord Hunt (1984). Critics say might strengthen PM *against* Cabinet.
• Strengthen Prime Minister's Office		
• Fixed-term Parliament/PM to take dissolution request to full Cabinet	To curtail the PM's dissolution power.	
• Curb PM's patronage by party elections to Cabinet and making most public appointments subject to parliamentary confirmation	To reduce PM's patronage powers and make PM more accountable to party and parliament.	PM would retain power to allocate Ministerial portfolios.
• More open government including Freedom of Information Act	Increase governmental accountability and improve quality of policies by requiring leading politicians to argue their cases publicly.	Small start made by Major but in conflict with long tradition of secrecy in British government.

Finally, many critics argue that government would be both stronger – in the sense of better able to deliver its objectives – and more publicly accountable if it were less secretive and more open. Noting the start made by the Major Government in this direction in May 1992, they argue that this process needs to be taken much further, culminating in a Freedom of Information Act.

Summary

The modern premiership is a powerful office, its formidable array of powers and responsibilities making the prime minister very much more than 'first among equals' in relation to the rest of the Cabinet. Nonetheless, Britain does not have 'prime ministerial government'; rather, it has a Cabinet system of government driven and organised by the prime minister.

The Cabinet itself, although neither initiating policy nor making more than a small number of important decisions, retains a vital core of authority. Although not always observed, the principle of collective responsibility – Cabinet solidarity and confidentiality – still applies.

In the twentieth century, with the growth in the scope of complexity of government, the Prime Minister's Office, the Cabinet Secretariat (Cabinet Office) and an extensive Cabinet committee system have developed to enable the core executive to deal with its vastly increased volume of business.

Proposals for reform focus on strengthening strategic direction and policy coordination within the Cabinet system and making British government more open and more accountable.

Questions

1. How appropriate is it to describe the modern British prime minister as 'an elective dictator'?

2. How far do you agree with the proposition that the Cabinet has been reduced to a merely 'dignified' institution in British government?

Assignment

Imagine you occupy a Cabinet post as head of a 'spending department'. Make a case for your Department to be allocated additional money or to avoid the cuts imposed on other Departments in the annual spending round.

Further reading

Burch, Martin (1990) 'Cabinet Government', *Contemporary Record*, 4: 1, September.
Burch, Martin (1990) 'Power in the cabinet system', *Talking Politics*, 2: 3, spring.
Dorey, Peter (1991) 'The Cabinet Committee System in British Government' *Talking Politics*, 4: 1, autumn.
Dunleavy, Patrick (1990) 'Government at the Centre' in P. Dunleavy, A. Gamble and G. Peele, (eds) *Developments in British Politics*, Vol. 3 (London: Macmillan).
Hennessy, Peter (1987) *Cabinet* (Oxford: Blackwell).
Jones, G. W. (1990) 'Mrs Thatcher and the power of the Prime Minister', *Contemporary Record*, 3: 4.
James, Simon (1992) *British Cabinet Government* (London: Routledge).
Kavanagh, D. (1991) 'Prime Ministerial Power Revisited', *Social Studies Review*, 6: 4, March.
King, Anthony (1985) *The British Prime Minister* (London: Macmillan).
Madgwick, Peter (1991) *British Government:the Central Executive Territory*, (London: Philip Allan).
Plowden, W. (1987) (ed.) *Advising the Rulers* (Oxford: Blackwell).
Seldon, Anthony (1990) 'The Cabinet Office and Co-ordination 1979–87', *Public Administration*, 68: 1, spring.
Willetts, David (1987) 'The Role of the Prime Minister's Policy Unit', *Public Administration*, 65.
Young, Hugo (1990) *One of Us* (London: Pan/Macmillan).

■ *Chapter 9* ■

Ministers, Departments and the Civil Service

This chapter continues our examination of the 'core executive' by considering the major Departments of State. We begin by characterising them in terms of structure, size and recruitment.

We then turn to the two leading themes of this chapter – first, to a consideration of the roles of ministers and civil servants, with special emphasis upon the nature of the relationship between them; and second, to an analysis of the convention of ministerial responsibility, which in traditional accounts is held to describe the accountability of ministerial heads of Departments to Parliament. We examine the precise meanings that are attached to this convention today. Our dual focus, therefore, is upon how decisions are made throughout the bulk of British government and how those decisions are made constitutionally accountable. Finally, the Governments of Margaret Thatcher during the 1980s introduced radical changes in the civil service; these changes are explored in the course of the chapter.

■ The Main Departments of State

In forming an administration, as we have already seen (Chapter 8, above), a prime minister makes scores of appointments. These include, in addition to government whips, ministers who head Departments – most of whom are of Cabinet rank –, non-Departmental ministers such as the lord president of the council and the chancellor of the Duchy of Lancaster, and a large number of junior ministers, i.e. ministers of state and parliamentary under-secretaries of state. As well as a Departmental head (secretary of state), each ministry frequently contains at least one minister of state and two or more parliamentary under-secretaries of state: these junior ministerial appointments are the route by which aspiring politicians gain experience of government and often but not invariably lead in time to promotion to full ministerial rank. The Department of the Environment – a very large ministry – has a Cabinet minister at its head assisted by three Ministers of state and three parliamentary under-secretaries of state. By contrast, a very small ministry like the Welsh Office has one Cabinet minister, one minister of state and one parliamentary under secretary of state. Junior ministers normally assume responsibility for specific tasks: in the Department of Transport, for example, they cover public transport, aviation and shipping, roads and traffic, and transport in London.

Ministers are the political and constitutional heads of Departments. Departments, however, are largely composed of permanent officials. Below the ministerial 'team' there is a body of civil servants headed by the permanent secretary, the most senior official in the departmental hierarchy. In addition to acting as the minister's top policy adviser, the permanent secretary is in

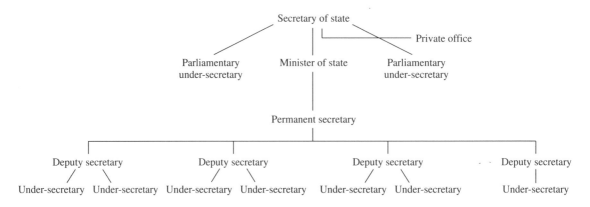

Figure 9.1   *Structure of a typical department of state*

charge of the daily work of the Department, is responsible for its staffing and organisation, and is also its accounting officer. Below the permanent secretary, in order of rank, are the deputy secretaries, under-secretaries and three other grades down to principal. Broadly speaking, each Department is normally divided up, first into several areas of policy, with each the responsibility of a deputy secretary, and then into a number of functional units (or branches), each with an under-secretary in charge. Figure 9.1 brings together the points made so far about departmental structure in diagrammatic form.

There are nineteen major Whitehall departments, including the three legal ones. Table 9.1 sets out their main responsibilities together with the size of their staff (1992) and projected budgets for 1992–3. For top politicians, the most coveted Departments are the three mentioned first – the Treasury, the Foreign Office and the Home Office. But of these 'plum' jobs only the Home Office confronts its head with a major task of management. In terms of size, the Home Office is a middle-ranking Department along with Employment, but well behind large Departments such as Social Security and even more behind giant Departments like Defence. Table 9.1 well brings out the disparities not only in size but also in

budgets between these Departmental giants and Departmental 'minnows' such as the Northern Ireland Office.

The Tomlin Commission (1931) suggested a definition of 'civil servant' which has become widely used: civil servants are 'Servants of the Crown, other than holders of political or judicial

Figure 9.2   *Whitehall*

Photo: Lynton Robins.

Table 9.1 *The main government departments: responsibilities, size, budgets (1992)*

Department (headed by)	Responsibilities	Size (number of personnel)	Budget (£bn) November 1992 forecasts for 1992–3
The Treasury (Chancellor of the Exchequer)	Economic policy	2 846	
Foreign and Commonwealth Office (Foreign Secretary)	Foreign policy	9 975	1.36
Home Office (Home Secretary)	Administration of justice, police, prisons, immigration, public safety, public morals	49 739	5.97
Trade and Industry (President of the Board of Trade)	Trade policy, industrial policy, technology and civil research and development, monopolies	11 389	1.65
Health (Secretary of State)	National Health Service	4 772	28.28
Environment (Secretary of State)	Housing, local government and inner cities, environment and countryside	8 172	41.14
Defence (Secretary of State)	Defence policy, armed services	139 454	23.80
Agriculture (Secretary of State)	Agriculture, fisheries, food	9 782	2.28
Employment (Secretary of State)	Employment policy; industrial relations, job training	52 383	3.64
Education and Science (Secretary of State)	Primary, secondary, further and higher education, science policy	2 689	6.98
Social Security (Secretary of State)	Social security benefits of all kinds.	78 277	61.20
Transport (Secretary of State)	Transport policy	14 960	6.75
Scottish Office (Secretary of State)	Social and economic policies with regard to Scotland	6 172	12.67
Welsh Office (Secretary of State)	Wide range of policies and services relating to Wales	2 411	6.02
Northern Ireland Office (Secretary of State)	Economic and social policies, law and order, and security policy, constitutional developments relating to Northern Ireland.	206	6.58

cont. p. 150

Department (headed by)	Responsibilities	Size (number of personnel)	Budget (£bn) November 1992 forecasts for 1992–3
National Heritage (Secretary of State)	Arts, media, heritage, sport		1.02
Lord Chancellor's Department	Administration of the law and the courts	11 598	3.56
Law Officers' Department (Attorney-General)	Enforcement of criminal law; advice to government on legal matters; represents Crown in major court cases.	24 }	
			2.40
Lord Advocate's Department	Has same functions in Scotland as Law Officer's Department in England	20 }	

Sources: Civil Service Statistics (1992, pp. 23–5); *The Guardian*, 13 November 1992.

Table 9.1—continued

offices, who are employed in a civil capacity and whose remuneration is paid wholly and directly out of moneys voted by Parliament'. This definition covered 565 319 individuals on 1 April 1992 who collectively constituted about 10 per cent of all public sector employees and about 2 per cent of the working population. Their numbers had declined from 732 000 in 1979 as a result of a deliberate policy designed to prune the bureaucracy carried out by Margaret Thatcher's governments during the 1980s.

Within the civil service as a whole it is useful to distinguish between the non-industrial and the industrial civil servants – i.e those employed in factories and workshops. As a proportion of the whole, industrial civil servants – who numbered a mere 61 000 in 1992 – have declined from 53 per cent in 1939 to just under 11 per cent in 1992; a sharp decrease in their numbers accounts for nearly two-thirds of the reduction in the civil service between 1979 and 1992. Of the non-industrial civil servants, only a relatively small proportion – about 15 per cent – work in Inner London; the rest work outside – 8 per cent in Outer London, and virtually all of the remainder, amounting to nearly three-quarters of the non-industrial civil service, in the provinces.

This chapter is primarily concerned with a tiny fraction of the non-industrial civil service – the top policy-making grades of the open structure who mostly work in London. There were just under 3500 in the first five grades in 1992, constituting a mere 0.7 per cent of the entire non-industrial civil service (504 237) (Table 9.2). Members of this group form the administrative élite who, in cooperation with their ministerial superiors, 'run the country'.

Recruitment to the ranks of the leading administrators is mainly at graduate level by a qualifying literacy and numeracy test followed by an extremely rigorous series of written appreciations, drafting tests and simulated committee work over two days at the Civil Service Selection Board (CSSB). Successful candidates at this stage then go before a Final Selection Board (FSB). The Fulton Report (1968) called for changes in civil service recruitment, promotion and training, recommending preference to be given to graduates with more relevant degrees, a considerable expansion of late entry in order to enable people from many walks of life to bring in their experience, and the widening of the social and educational base from which top civil servants were recruited. The idea of demanding 'relevance' was rejected

Grades		Number of staff at April 1 1992	Percentage of staff in London
Grade 1	Permanent Secretary	36	93
Grade 2	Deputy Secretary	130	86
Grade 3	Under Secretary	487	77
Grade 4	Executive directing bands and corresponding scientific and professional grades	280	56
Grade 5	Assistant Secretary	2 557	66
Grade 6	Senior Principal	4 569	39
Grade 7	Principal	13 321	47

Source: Data extracted from *Civil Service Statistics* (1992, p. 36).

Table 9.2   *The top civil servants: the open structure 1992*

but, although expansion of late entry had disappointing results, by the mid-1980s there was a significant programme of two-way temporary secondments between Whitehall and industry, commerce and other institutions (Hennessy, 1990, pp. 523–4). Broadening the base of recruitment away from Oxbridge-educated arts graduates has proved difficult: in 1985, for example, 85 per cent of Administrative Trainee candidates were non-Oxbridge, but this group provided only 36 per cent of successful applicants whereas a mere 15 per cent of candidates but 64 per cent of successful entrants were from Oxbridge: 56 per cent of successful candidates had Arts degrees. A further attempt to counter the prevailing bias of recruitment began in 1991 with top civil servants at permanent secretary and chief executive level 'adopting' a 'redbrick' institution at which to canvass for recruits.

The British Civil Service – Three Major Features

British constitutional theory makes a clear distinction between the *political* role of ministers and the *administrative* role of civil servants. Ministers are in charge of Departments and responsible to Parliament for running them, whilst civil servants advise ministers on policy and implement government decisions. Three major features of civil servants are linked to this distinction:

- **Permanence**: unlike the position in the United States, where large numbers of administrative posts change hands when the political complexion of the government changes, in Britain civil servants are career officials prepared to serve Governments of any party;
- **Political neutrality**: British civil servants are required to be politically impartial, not allowing their own political opinions to influence their actions and loyally carrying out decisions whether they agree with them or not; they must not engage in any partisan political activity;
- **Anonymity**: it is the function of ministers to be politically answerable for their Departments to Parliament and public, whereas it is the role of civil servants to offer confidential advice in secret. If civil servants became public figures, this might compromise their neutrality since they would become associated in the public mind with a particular policy; it also might undermine the frankness of the advice offered to ministers.

These general points are valuable as guidelines but also need to be handled with care. For example, civil servants, although not allowed to play a formal (party) political role, are much more involved in the political process than the description of their work in terms of 'administration' suggests. They are obviously heavily involved in the politics of bargaining for influence *within* Departments, *between* Departments, *with* outside interests and *in their relations with* ministers. This inherently political (and problematic) aspect of the role of civil servants will become amply evident in the discussion of decision making within Departments in the next section. Moreover, in the postwar period, and with increasing rapidity in the 1980s, traditional features of the civil service have been to a significant degree eroded, especially its neutrality and anonymity, and this is examined in the final section.

Decision-Making Within Departments

The vast majority of governmental decisions nowadays are made in Departments. As we have seen in the previous chapter, the proportion of Departmental decisions which are either sufficiently important or controversial to be taken to Cabinet has become very small indeed. An examination of decision-making in Departments, therefore, takes us to the centre of contemporary British government. Not only do Departments take the bulk of decisions – from the relatively minor to the undeniably major, it is no accident that they do so. For whenever new responsibilities are created by legislation, Parliament confers them squarely upon Departments. New powers developed by statute are given to ministers, not to the Cabinet or the prime minister. The political and administrative importance of Departments stems directly from the legal-constitutional pre-eminence.

How decisions are taken within Departments is consequently of vital significance in British government. To what extent are ministers the real decision-makers or, to put the question in another way, how far does the real power lie with civil servants? There are five models of the minister–civil servant relationship (Exhibit 9.1).

The **traditional public administration model** expresses the perception of minister–civil servant relations which is embedded in formal constitutional theory. It is the orthodox account according to which ministers take policy decisions and defend them publicly whilst civil servants brief ministers, processing information so that their political superiors can choose between options in an informed way and then unquestioningly implementing ministerial decisions. In this view, ministers always have the final say whilst civil servants are neutral advisers who are permanently 'on tap but never on top'.

This model assumes a clear dividing-line between political decision-making, which is what ministers do, and administration, which is the job of civil servants in tendering advice and carrying out decisions. This is not only the traditional textbook view but also predominates within the civil service itself and among ministers. It is the model re-affirmed by the Cabinet Secretary, Sir Robert Armstrong in his *Note of Guidance on the Duties and Responsibilities of Civil Servants in Relation to Ministers* (1985) in the wake of the Ponting case (see below, p. 344). The Armstrong Memorandum asserted that the civil service has '*no constitutional personality or responsibility separate from the duly elected government of the day*' and stressed that the duty of the civil servant was first and foremost to the ministerial head of Department. A new version of the memorandum issued after the Westland affair in 1987 also stated the traditional view that ministers are responsible to Parliament for the conduct of their Departments whilst civil servants are answerable to ministers.

Exhibit 9.1   *Models of minister – civil servant relations*

- The traditional public administration or liberal-democratic.
- The new public administration or liberal-bureaucratic.
- The 'Whitehall village'.
- The power bloc or socialist.
- The bureaucratic over-supply or New Right.

Many observers believe that the traditional model simply describes the norm to which participants in government aspire but ignores the political realities of a situation in which the 'Departmental view' often prevails. The **liberal-bureaucratic model** best expresses the fact of civil service power in a context in which lip-service is still paid to the textbook theory of ministerial–civil servant relations. This approach does not exclude the possibility that a minister can dominate a Department. But it does suggest that a variety of factors often tilt the balance of power in a Department away from the minister and towards the permanent officials.

The **'Whitehall Village' model** draws attention to aspects of the minister–civil servant relationship largely ignored by the other models. It posits that the relationship is much more complex than can be expressed by a theory suggesting simple domination by either elected politician or official. In practice, in the enclosed world of Whitehall, relationships between ministers and mandarins are cooperative as well as conflictual and in addition operate *across* Departments as well as within them. The central focus of this model is on the way in which civil servants sharing a common language and culture 'prepare the ground' for ministerial decisions through their own networks of informal contacts and official committees. This theory was first developed by two American academics, Hugh Heclo and Aaron Wildavsky in their book, *The Private Government of Public Money* (1974). Applied by them to public expenditure decision-making, the relevance of the model to virtually all areas of Whitehall was soon realised.

According to the **power-bloc model,** the civil service functions as an Establishment veto group. On this view, the civil service comprises an administrative cadre whose conservative bias reflects the interests of the privileged sections of society from which it is largely recruited. It deploys its administrative expertise and exploits its permanency of tenure to thwart radical policy moves by socialist governments. Important advocates of this far-left view of the civil service are Ralph Miliband in *The State in Capitalist Society* (1973), Brian Sedgemore in *The Secret Constitution* (1980) and Tony Benn.

The **bureaucratic over-supply model** came to the fore in the 1970s and is mainly but not exclusively linked with the New Right critique of civil service expansionism in previous decades. The views of this school of thought do not bear directly on the minister–civil servant relationship but focus rather on the disastrous *consequences* of a situation in which a self-interested civil service holds the upper hand. The result of its single-minded pursuit of its own interests with regard to pay, pensions, conditions of service and its own size and status was a bloated, inefficient and wasteful bureaucracy. This analysis produced its own programme: the bureaucracy, according to the Thatcherite right, needed 'cutting down to size'.

The Resurgence of the Traditional Model?

In 1979 the liberal-bureaucratic, power-bloc and bureaucratic over-supply theories held the field, the traditional liberal-democratic model of the civil service was in eclipse. By the early 1990s, as a result of the changes in Whitehall launched by the Thatcher governments in the 1980s, this situation had been largely reversed: little was heard of the far left critique, and the reassertion of political control over the civil service by Conservative governments inspired by New Right Theory had brought about a resurgence of the traditional, liberal-democratic theory. Indeed some commentators went further, arguing that its traditional detachment and impartiality had been eroded and that the civil service had been politicised. This section briefly traces the history of these evolving interpretations.

By the late 1970s, in large part in order to explain Labour's failures in office, theories stressing the obstructiveness and the potential for obstruction of the British bureaucracy had become commonplace. The liberal-bureaucratic model, and its more extreme variant the power-bloc theory, were often invoked in academic discussion. Such factors as the numbers, permanence, expertise, coordinating role, and control over information and policy implementation of

Exhibit 9.2 *Models of civil service power: factors tilting the balance away from ministers towards civil servants*

- **Numbers:** Ministers are heavily outnumbered in their contacts with leading mandarins: in 1992, the ratio of Ministers to leading civil servants of the rank of under-secretary and above was 1: 6.5

- **Permanence:** Civil servants are permanent and, moreover, often spend their entire careers in the same Department; by contrast, ministers are 'birds of passage' who change jobs frequently. The average tenure of ministerial office since 1945 is about two years: between April 1944 and April 1992, when John Patten became Education Secretary, there were 24 Ministers of Education. It takes ministers a lengthy period to master the business of their Departments (according to Crossman about 18 months) and during this time they are largely dependent on briefing by their officials.

- **Expertise:** Few ministers, on taking office, have specialised knowledge of their Departments, a situation which increases civil service influence. Some ministers have 'shadowed' their Departments in Opposition, but this became of even less significance after 1979 during the Conservative hegemony: Kenneth Clarke for example, held no less than five Cabinet posts between 1987 and 1994, being successively Chancellor of the Duchy of Lancaster, Health Secretary, Education Secretary, Home Secretary and, from May 1993, Chancellor of the Exchequer.

- **Coordinating role:** both formally through official committees and through informal contacts with their opposite numbers in other Departments, top civil servants prepare and to a varying extent predetermine the work of ministers. As Crossman wrote in his *Diaries*, 'very often the whole job is pre-cooked in the official committees to a point from which it is difficult to reach any other conclusion than that already determined by officials in advance' (p. 92). Civil servants can also use their contacts with other officials to delay and obstruct ministerial wishes if that is what they decide to do: they can do so by contacting colleagues in other Departments (say B, C and D) to brief ministers in those Departments to resist policies emanating from their own minister (Department A) in Cabinet and elsewhere.

- **Control of information:** top civil servants control the *content* of the information going before ministers, the *way* in which it is presented and its *timing*, all of which gives them a formidable capacity to shape decisions. Thus officials decide what ministers learn and also what they do not learn, can manipulate the presentation of policy options in order to suggest one policy rather than another, and can 'bounce' ministers into a particular decision by submitting papers at the last minute. They can also influence public opinion by the secret briefing of known opponents of their minister's policy or by 'leaking' to the media.

- **Implementation:** civil servants can employ a variety of tactics to thwart implementation of policy including delay, finding practical difficulties and even 'losing things'. The permanent secretary at the DES successfully opposed Labour's pledge to withdraw tax concessions from private schools after 1974.

- **Ministerial workload:** another factor weighting the scales of influence towards civil servants is ministers' massive workloads. Ministers face multiple demands upon their time – from Cabinet, Parliament, constituency, media and increasingly from the EU in addition to their Departments: indeed an analysis of the working week of fifty ministers between 1964 and 1974 by Bruce Headey suggested that ministers spent three-quarters of their 60-hour week on work outside their Departments (cited Kellner and Crowther-Hunt, 1980, p. 216).

Exhibit 9.2—*continued*

- **Weak preparation for office**: in the postwar period, few ministers have come to office with clearly defined policies, priorities or objectives and even those who did possess broad goals were dependent upon civil servants to translate these into practical proposals. In addition, ministers invariably confront unexpected situations during their terms of office which further increases their dependence upon officials: these include policies which become more significant than originally envisaged (e.g. privatisation), pressure group-promoted initiatives (e.g. anti-smoking and lead-free petrol legislation) and the emergence of new problems (e.g. AIDS, child abuse and cable and satellite television) (James, 1992, p. 39).

- **Lack of alternative policy advice**: the practice of importing special political advisers into Departments to provide an alternative source of policy advice for ministers and to strengthen their hand against permanent officials effectively began in the mid-1960s; Labour brought in 38 such advisers between 1974 and 1979 and the Conservatives continued the practice, the PM stating that there were 42 special advisers in June 1993. But estimates of their effectiveness vary – on occasion, it seems, outside experts have worked harmoniusly with officials but it is also true that the civil service has numerous ways of neutralising them; overall, it is unlikely that 'outsiders' are deployed in sufficient numbers or systematically enough to make serious dents in civil service dominance.

the civil service in conjunction with the heavy workload, weak preparation for office and lack of alternative policy advice of ministers were frequently assumed to have shifted the balance of power away from ministers and towards the top civil servants. Exhibit 9.2 provides an up-to-date version of the bureaucratic power thesis.

The plausibility of the far-left **power-bloc model** declined rapidly in the 1980s. It remains broadly true that the higher civil service is largely recruited from socially privileged groups. But it clearly does not follow (*i*) that it will refuse to carry out the radical policies of left and right governments; (*ii*) that it invariably curbs the reformist impulses of radical politicians; or (*iii*) that it constitutes a monolithic bloc in terms of views and perceptions.

With regard to (*i*): arguably, the two most radical Governments since 1945 have been the Labour Administrations of 1945–51 and the Conservative Administrations of 1979–92, yet the civil service can scarcely be said to have blocked either the Keynesian, welfare and nationalisation policies of the one or the monetarist, anti-welfare and privatisation policies of the other. (*ii*) Tony

Benn as Secretary of State for Industry in the Labour Government of February 1974 is often cited as an example of a radical minister whose schemes for sweeping nationalisation of shipbuilding, aircraft and pharmaceuticals and for planning agreements with industry were thwarted largely by civil service resistance. In fact, however, it is much more likely that Benn failed (he was eventually transferred to Energy in June 1975) because of the opposition he encountered from the prime minister and other Labour ministers, i.e. from his own colleagues in government.

The radical reforms of education, health and local government effected by Conservative ministers in the 1980s provide further evidence against this argument. Finally, if argument (*iii*) were the case, the sharp inter-Departmental struggles which are a frequent occurrence in Whitehall could hardly be expected to take place. In the words of a recent study, 'Whitehall is a seething mass of discrete departmental interests', in which Departments – each with its own distinctive 'view' and 'ethos' – continually bargain and compete with each other for, amongst other things, larger shares of public expenditure and a place in the parliamentary legislative timetable. (Drewry and Butcher, 1991, pp. 84–5).

The **liberal-bureaucratic theory** retains some validity as an approach to the relationship between ministers and civil servants. It remains relevant in situations in which weak ministers are 'captured' by their officials and also to describe occasions when the scales of departmental power tilt towards the officials. The value of the model consists in bringing out that minister–civil service relations are a matter of balance rather than automatically accepted authority (as the traditional theory holds) and also in pointing out the factors which *may* operate in various combinations to give the advantage to the bureaucrat. In the apt conclusion of one study: 'The exact balance between ministerial and civil service power will very much depend on what is being decided, the political circumstances surrounding it, and the relative abilities of civil servants and Ministers' (Kellner and Crowther-Hunt, 1980, p. 234).

However, the reassertion of political control over the civil service by the Thatcher governments in the 1980s meant that the theory was applicable in far fewer instances by the early 1990s. The combined effect of the Thatcherite assault on the size and privileges of the civil service, of intervention in its workings on a broad scale by a strong-willed Prime Minister and of the pervasive influence of the radical New Right ideology (see below) was the re-establishment of the traditional public administration model. In the words of Hugo Young: 'The constitutional textbooks are truer now than they have been for some time' (cited Theakston, 1991–2, p. 94).

The **Whitehall village model** usefully draws attention to the inner life of the political administrative community at the centre of British government. Its emphases – on cooperation between ministers and mandarins within Departments and on the role of inter-departmental collaboration between civil servants in the preparation of decisions – captures much of the reality of top-level policy-making. But it has been justly criticised as inherently too limited in focus to capture that reality in its entirety. For example, in focusing on life in the Whitehall village, it largely ignores that 'community's' external relationships, both in terms of policy inputs from pressure groups, ideological 'think-tanks', party manifestos and so on, and in terms of the manner in which ministers' need to defend policies before Parliament and public actually helps to shape the policies themselves. (Pliatzky, 1982, pp. 35, 37; Theakston, 1991–2, pp. 93–4).

Finally, as will be shown in detail in the next section, the **bureaucratic over-supply model** was the inspiration for a sustained, successful attack on the power, prestige and privileges of the civil service in the 1980s and remains of relevance in the 1990s.

■ The Thatcher Reforms: A Revolution in Government?

Margaret Thatcher came to power in 1979 convinced that the civil service was too big, too expensive, too negative and too consensual. It had become an over-blown bureaucracy, wasteful and inefficient, more adapted to finding problems in new initiatives that to solving them, and compromised by the failures of postwar British governments. The reforms she launched in 1979 – which were still in the process of implementation in the early 1990s – were aimed at curtailing the privileges, increasing the efficiency and transforming the culture of the civil service. The overriding goal was to make the bureaucracy into an obedient servant of the government of the day rather than a source of disinterested policy advice.

□ *Size*

The Conservatives achieved a very large reduction in civil service numbers (732 000 to 565 000) between April 1979 and April 1992, a drop of nearly 23 per cent. The lower manpower targets were attained by a combination of natural wastage, early retirement, the non-filling of vacant posts, the transfer of civil service functions to appointed public sector boards, and privatisation.

☐ *Curtailment of privileges*

The Thatcher Government 'de-privileged' the civil service by setting aside the settlement of pay based on the system of 'fair comparison' and then offering relatively low increases related to 'market forces' and introducing performance-related pay; holding out successfully against the 21-week strike by civil service unions in support of their pay claim (1981); banning trade union membership at the Government Communications Headquarters (GCHQ), which had been shut down for a short period in 1981 as a result of the strike action; and abolishing the Civil Service Department (1981), which Thatcher regarded as too much the champion of the civil service and as insufficiently supportive of the Government's efforts to defeat the civil service strike. Its responsibility for civil service pay, conditions of service and manpower was transferred to the Treasury and the Cabinet Secretary became the official head of the Civil Service. The relative isolation of the civil service was reduced by a rapid increase in inward and outward secondments, which trebled between 1977 and 1985.

☐ *The Efficiency Strategy*

In a series of managerial reforms, the Rayner Scrutinies (1979) were followed by the Financial Management Initiative (1982) and then by the hiving off of large numbers of civil servants into executive agencies under the 'Next Steps' programme (1988), the most radical reform of the civil service since the mid-nineteenth century.

The Rayner Scrutinies

The quest for greater efficiency and the elimination of 'waste' in government began in 1979 with the establishment in the Cabinet Office of a small Efficiency Unit headed by Sir Derek Rayner, who was then the joint Managing Director of Marks and Spencer. Rayner initiated a series of Scrutinies of Departments with the aim of increasing efficiency and eliminating waste: each inquiry was headed by a member of the Department and guided by the Efficiency Unit. Rayner wrote a Cabinet paper, 'The Conventions of Government' (1980), recommending more precise costings, more stress on managerial skills and incentives for civil servants who showed initiative in reducing waste; he also launched an attack on unnecessary paperwork which led to the scrapping of 27 000 forms. Huge savings resulted from the Scrutinies, amounting to £1.3 billion by 1988 and averaging an annual £325 million in 1989.

The Financial Management Initiative (FMI)

Begun in 1982, the FMI sought to improve financial management in all Departments by laying down three principles. Managers at all levels were to have: (*i*) a clear view of their objectives and the means to assess and, wherever possible, measure outputs of performance in relation to those objectives; (*ii*) well-defined responsibility for making the best use of their resources, including a critical scrutiny of output and value for money; and (*iii*) the information (particularly about costs), the training and the access to expert advice that they need to exercise their responsibilities effectively.

A variety of management information systems designed to enable ministers to discover 'who does what, why and at what cost?' in their Departments developed under the Rayner and FMI approaches, e.g. MINIS (Management Information System for Ministers) at the Department of Environment (DOE) and Activity and Resource Management (ARM) at the Department of Trade and Industry (DTI). The overall aim was to transform civil service culture along business lines, to enhance the role of civil servants as managers of people and resources and to downgrade their role as policy advisers. The reforms reflected the Thatcherite ethos that the task of the civil service was to manage resources with maximum effectiveness in pursuit of policy goals set by ministers.

The 'Next Steps' Programme (1988)

This programme originated in a certain disappointment at the slow progress of the FMI and other 'managerial' reforms, as a result of which the Efficiency Unit – now headed by Sir Robin Ibbs, a former Imperial Chemical Industries (ICI) executive – produced a report focusing on the obstacles to further improvement in civil service management. Entitled 'Improving Management in Government: The Next Steps', it argued that there had been insufficient focus on the delivery of services, even though the vast majority of civil servants (95 per cent) were in service delivery or executive rather than policy advice roles. Believing that the civil service was too large and diverse to be run as a single entity, the report advocated its division into *(i)* a small 'core' engaged in supporting ministers with policy advice within the traditional Departments; and *(ii)* a wide range of executive agencies responsible for the delivery of services, each headed by a chief executive. Departments would set the policies and budgets and monitor the work of the agencies but within that framework, agencies would have considerable managerial independence.

Peter Kemp, a Deputy Secretary at the Treasury, was made Project Manager to oversee the implementation of the Next Steps programme. By early November 1992, huge progress had been made: 75 agencies had been established, employing over 200 000 civil servants, and another 27 were under consideration. Altogether, over half the Civil Service (nearly 300 000) was working in Next Steps Agencies or along Next Steps lines. Some – such as the massive Benefits Agency (63 000) and the Employment Service Agency (43 000) – had considerably reduced the size of their 'parent' Departments, the Department of Social Services (DSS) and the Department of Employment. The majority of Next Steps Agencies, however, are small or medium-sized: they include the Vehicle Inspectorate (1816 on April 1 1992), the Central Statistical Office (1159), the Royal Mint (1014), the Public Record Office (430) and the Teachers' Pensions Agency (287).

Supporters of the 'Next Steps' programme argue that the reforms will improve delivery of service, increase cost-effectiveness and produce significant savings. The Driver and Vehicle Licensing Agency – an agency since 1990 – may be cited as an example: it sets itself clear targets, e.g. to reduce average waiting time for a driving test from 8–9 weeks (1991) to 6 weeks and to issue 90 per cent of driving licenses within 13 days (1992) instead of 16 days (1991); has shown considerable enthusiasm for marketing, e.g. customised number-plates; and cut costs by putting provision of security and cleaning services out to private tender.

Critics point to the potential dangers of the programme. These are fourfold:

- **Blurred accountability**
  Ibbs called for chief executives to be directly accountable to Parliament but the Government rejected this proposal in favour of retaining the parliamentary accountability of ministers. But this can lead to confusion and the worry that proper accountability no longer exists: this is because MPs expect ministers to answer their questions directly but in practice ministers often refer their queries to chief executives, incorporating the replies of the Chief Executives into their own replies to the House of Commons. Direct ministerial responsibility, say critics, is diminished.

  A further potential source of confusion arises from the fact that *financial* accountability is divided between permanent secretaries (for Departments) and chief executives (for Agencies).

- **The break-up of a national civil service** – there is a concern that the civil service is in the process of 'Balkanisation' i.e. fragmentation into a large number of separate Agencies, each with its own structure, as a result of which career progression and cooperation between hived-off agencies and sponsoring Departments both suffer.

- **A 'stalking-horse' for privatisation?** – critics' fears that 'hiving off' might lead to privatisation were given additional impetus by the

Major Government's 'Competing for Quality' scheme (November 1991) by which Departments were required to make plans for competitive tendering of 130 000 civil service posts; by October 1992, William Waldegrave announced that over £1 billion of work would be tendered for, a proportion of which would go to the private sector. In November 1992 a Government report revealed that a further 44 000 civil service posts were to be 'market-tested' for privatisation by September 1993 and three more Agencies (Companies House, the Driver and Vehicle Licensing Agency and the Vehicle Inspectorate) were earmarked for privatisation; plans to privatise the National Engineering Laboratory had already been announced. It was the view of Sir Peter Levene, the head of the Efficiency Unit in 1992, that hiving off functions to agencies had not gone far enough and that full privatisation was the optimum solution.

- **Erosion of the public service ethic** – by 1992 the concern was being expressed that managerialism, performance-related pay, competitive tendering and hiving off were de-motivating and demoralising the civil service and in the process undermining its traditional ethic of disinterested public service.

Change in the Political Culture of the Civil Service

If the Efficiency Strategy was designed to inject entrepreneurial values into the civil service, a second prong of Conservative strategy was to replace the traditional negative, detached, sceptical attitudes of senior civil servants with a vigorous commitment to overcoming difficulties in the service of the government of the day. The Conservatives had a clear sense of ideological direction and could draw on a combination of special advisers, external 'think-tanks' and the prime minister's Policy Unit for policy advice; as a consequence, the policy advice of top civil servants was downgraded. Margaret Thatcher told her civil servants that she did not want 'whingeing, analysis and integrity' from them but rather obedience combined with a 'can do' approach to government. Unlike previous prime ministers who normally rubber-stamped the recommendations for top posts of the Senior Appointments Selection Committee, Thatcher took a close personal interest in senior appointments. Her influential interventionism together with the retirement in the 1980s of large numbers of permanent secretaries and deputy secretaries enabled her to shape the top echelons of the service according to her preferences. Those she did not favour did not prosper (the Head of the Civil Service, Sir Ian Bancroft, was pushed into early retirement in 1981), 'leakers' such as Clive Ponting and Sarah Tisdall (see below, p. 344) were ruthlessly pursued in the courts, and officials affected by a crisis of conscience when actually commanded by their superiors to 'leak', e.g. Colette Bowe in the Westland affair, were simply told by the Armstrong Memorandum (1985) to consult their personnel officer, the permanent secretary of their Department, or resign.

'Iraq-gate', 1992

Two incidents coming to light in late 1992 raised questions about ministerial and civil service ethics. The first controversy blew up in November 1992 over sales of British arms to Iraq in the late 1980s. The Opposition parties alleged that the Government secretly relaxed its own guidelines on the sale of arms to Iraq in 1988, that numerous Government ministers over the following years told Parliament that this was not the case, and that leading officials in the Foreign Office and DTI assisted ministers in the misleading of Parliament. The incident had come to light accidentally during the prosecution by Customs and Excise of three businessmen of the Matrix Churchill Company for illegally exporting arms for Iraq. Denying charges of deception, the Prime Minister, John Major, set up an inquiry into the affair under Lord Justice Scott, whose report is due in late 1994.

Payment of the private legal fees of the Chancellor of the Exchequer

In November 1992 it was revealed that the Treasury had sanctioned a payment of £4 700 to Norman Lamont, the Chancellor of the Exchequer, in part settlement of his legal fees for the eviction of a sex therapist from his Notting Hill Gate flat in 1991. The Government argued that the payment – which was sanctioned by the then Permanent Secretary to the Treasury, Sir Peter Middleton – was within guidelines laid down by the 'Guidance to Permanent Secretaries' and 'Questions of Procedure for Ministers'. The former states that ministers can be indemnified by the Treasury Solicitor with the approval of the law officers so long as the action 'relates to the conduct of Ministers and bears upon the conduct of...official duties', whilst the latter document states that 'Ministers occasionally become engaged in legal proceedings primarily in their personal capacities, but in circumstances which also involve their official responsibilities'. Lamont's contention was that it was in the public interest to defend the reputation of a senior minister against embarrassing publicity. The Opposition, however, insisted that Lamont's action was unethical and its justification so wide that it 'could permit public funds being used to legally resist almost any attack on any government minister'. More specifically, Labour argued that the Chancellor had ignored a rule in 'Questions of Procedure for Ministers' that ministers should consult the Law Officers before engaging their own solicitors.

■ Ministerial Responsibility

The convention of individual ministerial responsibility governs relations between ministers, civil servants and Parliament. It means that ministers – and ministers alone – are responsible to Parliament for the actions of their Departments (Exhibit 9.3).

This section examines the contemporary validity of this convention.

Individual ministers certainly remain responsible to Parliament in the first sense. They constantly explain and defend departmental policy – at Question Time, during the committee stage of legislation, before select committees and privately to MPs. Of course, ministerial answers to political questions are not always entirely full or satisfactory and sometimes they are downright evasive. Nonetheless, individual ministerial responsibility in its first meaning of 'answerability' or 'explanatory accountability' still applies. But how accountable are ministers, in the second sense of the term, for the policy failures, mistaken judgements, maladministration and improper conduct of themselves and their officials?

Exhibit 9.3   *The convention of individual ministerial responsibility*

The convention denotes:
- **Answerability**: Ministers have an obligation to explain and defend the work of their Departments in Parliament.
- **Accountability**: Ministers are responsible for their own and their officials' conduct and for departmental policy and should resign if serious faults are revealed in any of these matters.

The convention implies and assumes that civil servants are anonymous, responsible to their ministers alone and without any wider accountability to Parliament or general public, and that their advice to ministers is secret.

☐ *Personal Misconduct*

Ministers still sometimes resign for personal misconduct, which has been the largest single category of resignations between 1962 and 1992. The misconduct has usually involved mixing with unsavoury or shady associates or sexual impropriety. Between 1962 and 1979, six resignations (Galbraith, Profumo, Maudling, Lambton, Jellicoe and Brayley) and since 1979 three further resignations (Parkinson, Nicholls and Mellor) fall under this heading, although that of Nicholls did not involve keeping shady company or sexual misconduct. In addition, the resignation of Nicholas Fairburn had an element of personal misconduct to it.

Cecil Parkinson resigned after the revelation that he had had an affair with his secretary, Sarah

Table 9.3   *Individual ministerial responsibility: resignations, 1962–92*

Minister	Post	Date	Reason
Thomas Galbraith	Under-Secretary Scottish Office	1962	Security: consorting with the spy, Vassall
John Profumo	Minister for War	1963	Sexual misconduct followed by lying to the House of Commons about it.
James Callaghan	Chancellor of the Exchequer	1967	Devaluation of sterling (Re-shuffled to Home Office).
Reginald Maudling	Home Secretary	1972	Involvement with corrupt architect, Poulson.
Lord Lambton	Under-Secretary of State, Defence	1973	Call-girl scandal.
Earl Jellicoe	Lord Privy Seal	1973	Call-girl scandal.
Lord Brayley	Under-Secretary of State, Defence	1974	Irregularities in business life.
Nicholas Fairburn	Solicitor-General, Scotland	1982	Mixture of personal misconduct and political failings arising out of Glasgow rape case.
Lord Carrington	Foreign Secretary	1982	Misjudgements over Argentine intentions in Falklands.
Humphrey Atkins	Lord Privy Seal	1982	Misjudgements over Argentine intentions in Falklands.
Richard Luce	Minister of State, Foreign Affairs	1982	Misjudgements over Argentine intentions in Falklands.
Cecil Parkinson	Secretary of State, Trade and Industry	1983	Sexual misconduct: Sarah Keays affair.
Leon Brittan	Secretary of State, Trade and Industry	1986	Political misjudgement over leak of letter in Westland affair.
Edwina Currie	Under-Secretary of State, Health	1988	Misleading statement with regard to salmonella in eggs.
Patrick Nicholls	Under-Secretary of State, Environment	1990	Arrest for driving with excess alcohol.
David Mellor	Secretary of State, National Heritage	1992	Errors of judgement in personal conduct.

Keays, who had become pregnant by him. David Mellor resigned following allegations first about his extra-marital affair with an actress, Antonia de Sancha, and then about a Spanish holiday taken by his family which had been paid for by Mona Bauwens, the daughter of a senior official of the Palestine Liberation Front. Both Parkinson and Mellor enjoyed the support of the Prime Minister and both clung to office. But both were brought down eventually, Parkinson by a letter from Keays to *The Times* indicating her unwillingness to allow the matter to be swept aside, and Mellor when it became clear he had lost the support of Conservative backbenchers.

Patrick Nicholls resigned when arrested for 'drink driving' a few hours after he had expressed enthusiastic support for his Secretary of State's promise of a tough campaign against 'drink drivers'.

☐ *Political Misjudgements and* ☐ *Mistakes*

Most ministerial resignations in the 1980s (Fairburn, Carrington, Atkins, Luce, Brittan and Currie) fall into this category. Nicholas Fairburn resigned after committing the error of informing the Scottish press about his reasons not to prosecute the suspects in a rape case before answering questions about it in the House of Commons, where his explanations proved unconvincing. He had also suffered from bad publicity about his private life.

The **Falklands crisis** brought the resignations of the Foreign Office team. The reason Lord Carrington gave for his resignation was his failure to foresee and to take steps to prevent the Argentinian invasion, which he later called 'a humiliating affront to this country'. However, John Nott, the Defence Secretary, who was criticised for the weakness of the Falkland Islands' defences and, more realistically, for signalling an apparently diminished British commitment to the retention of the Islands by a proposal to withdraw *HMS Endurance*, remained in office.

On this occasion, because of the seriousness of the situation and the intensity of parliamentary

and public disquiet, collective responsibility could not save the Foreign Office ministers. In order to minimise damage to the credibility of a Government in which blame for misreading the situation and for military unpreparedness spread as far as the Prime Minister, a considerable sacrifice was called for but not so great a one that it rocked the Government. So Carrington and his subordinates went, but Nott stayed.

In the **Westland affair** (1986), Leon Brittan, the Trade and Industry Secretary, resigned after severe pressure from Conservative backbenchers over the role of his Department in 'leaking' to the press a select passage in a letter from the Solicitor-General to the Defence Secretary, Michael Heseltine. The letter requested the correction of the 'material inaccuracies' contained in a letter Heseltine had written to the European consortium who were the rivals of the American Sikorsky Company for the take-over of the ailing Westland Helicopters. The leaking of the letter – 'an improper act' in the words of the Commons Select Committee on Defence which investigated the affair – was one episode in the semi-public struggle between the Ministry of Defence and the Department of Trade and Industry over the destiny of the British helicopter firm. The leak was wrong, first because the letter was marked 'Confidential' and second, because, according to convention, advice from the Government's Law Officers is never revealed. Brittan apparently authorised the leak but only 'subject to the agreement of No. 10' (Young, 1990, p. 442).

At the time, Bernard Ingham, the PM's Press Officer, and Charles Powell, her Private Secretary, sought to distance themselves from the leak but Brittan later (1989) claimed that they both 'approved' it. It was the contention of Colette Bowe, the information officer at the DTI who actually leaked the letter, that she would not have done so without both the authorisation of her minister and the consent of top officials at No. 10. This resignation is similar to the Foreign Office resignations in 1982 in that responsibility for improper behaviour extended even as far as the Prime Minister, the political outcry from the Conservative backbenches demanded a ministerial sacrifice, and the protective cloak of collective responsibility could not be extended. Therefore, Brittan resigned: it was his misfortune to become imbroiled in the political struggle between Thatcher and Heseltine but his political misjudgement to authorise the leak of the letter *in any circumstances*.

Edwina Currie, the Parliamentary Under-Secretary of State for Health, resigned after making the statement that 'most of the egg production of this country, sadly, is now infected with salmonella'. As well as causing considerable public alarm, this 'gaffe' led to several egg producers issuing writs against the Government, the need to offer financial support to the egg production industry, and strong criticism of the minister by backbenchers of her own party.

☐ *Policy Errors*

Ministers do not normally resign if associated with a **failed policy**. In such circumstances, the Prime Minister and Cabinet usually come to the aid of a beleaguered colleague, expressing support in public, whatever may be said privately. In other words, individual ministers in political difficulties are shielded by the convention of **collective responsibility**. There are numerous examples of non-resignation after serious failures of policy, in several of which – Suez, the spy scandals of the early 1960s, *Concorde*, and Britain's departure from the ERM – the close involvement of the prime minister was probably conclusive in 'saving' the minister concerned (Exhibit 9.4).

In 1967, **James Callaghan**, a Chancellor who, like Norman Lamont in 1992, presided over a devaluation of sterling, did resign. But the political circumstances were rather different in that unlike Lamont, Callaghan had long wanted to move from the Treasury, and Prime Minister Wilson, unlike John Major, had been anxious to have a new Chancellor. But Callaghan was careful not to resign from the Cabinet and his resignation was followed immediately by a discreet

---

Exhibit 9.4 *Ministerial non-resignation: policy failure*

- The East African groundnuts scheme (1949), a spectacular fiasco which cost the taxpayer £36.5 million and which failed to provide either margarine for Britain or jobs for Africans. The Minister for Food, John Strachey, was closely associated with the scheme, having described it as 'one of the most courageous, imaginative and well-judged acts of this government for the sake of the world'.

- The Suez affair (1956), a discreditable failure which brought major international humiliation upon Britain.

- Various spy scandals (early 1960s). The then Prime Minister, Harold Macmillan, rejected the need for resignations on the grounds that it was the reputation of the government as a whole that was in question and this was best left to the judgement of voters at a general election.

- Large-scale miscalculations of the cost of the Concorde programme (early 1960s).

- The evasion of sanctions against Rhodesia by the major oil companies with covert Government acquiescence (late 1960s).

- The collapse of the central plank of the Government's economic policy when Britain was forced out of the Exchange Rate Mechanism (ERM) (mid-September 1992). The Chancellor of the Exchequer, Norman Lamont, whose reputation was already dented by a series of economic misjudgements, was saved from resignation by the close identification of the Prime Minister, John Major, with the failed policy and the consequent extension of the protective shield of collective responsibility.

reshuffle in which he moved to the Home Office and Roy Jenkins took over as Chancellor. A similar manoeuvre occurred in 1948 when **Emanuel Shinwell** was moved from Fuel and Power to the War Office eight months after the Fuel Crisis of 1947.

These cases suggest that, while parliamentary criticism over failed policies can certainly damage a minister and can sometimes prompt policy changes, it cannot force resignation if the minister wishes to remain in office and has the support of prime minister and party.

☐ *Official Errors*

It is even more unusual for ministers to accept vicarious responsibility for their officials and resign after mistakes within their Departments have been brought to light. The assumption by ministers of personal accountability for all that happens in their Departments has been undermined, it is often said, by the sheer size and complexity of modern Whitehall Departments and the consequent impossibility of one person being able to keep informed of all that goes on in them. Numerous cases in the postwar period suggest the reluctance of ministers to shoulder the blame for civil servants when things go wrong (Exhibit 9.5).

Today, it seems, ministers are not normally held responsible for decisions made in their name but of which they could have had no knowledge. As Reginald Maudling stated after the Vehicle and General debate: 'One must look at this classic doctrine in the light of modern circumstances. In

---

Exhibit 9.5   *Ministerial non-resignation: official errors*

- Alan Lennox-Boyd, the Colonial Secretary, after eleven prisoners died and others received injuries from beatings meted out by colonial wardens at the Hola Camp in Kenya (1959).

- Sir Julian Amery, the Minister for Aviation, after it had been revealed that the Ferranti Company had made excess profits from Defence Ministry contracts to make the Bloodhound missile (1964).

- John Davies, President of the Board of Trade, after a Tribunal of Inquiry had revealed the failure of his Department to deal with the risk of the imminent insolvency of the Vehicle and General Insurance Company (1971).

- Tony Benn, Secretary of State for Industry, after being blamed by the Ombudsman for giving misleading public assurances about the holiday operations of the Court Line travel company (1975).

- William Whitelaw, Home Secretary, after security arrangements at Buckingham Palace were revealed to be deficient and the Queen was confronted by an intruder in her bedroom (1982).

- James Prior and Nicholas Scott, respectively Secretary of State and Parliamentary Under-Secretary of State for Northern Ireland, after 38 Republican prisoners escaped from the Maze Prison in Belfast, killing a prison officer (1983).

- Kenneth Baker, Home Secretary, after two Republican prisoners escaped from Brixton Prison (1991).

- Peter Lilley, Secretary of State for Trade and Industry, after it was revealed that his Department had sanctioned sales of nuclear and chemical material to Iraq until three days after Iraq's invasion of Kuwait (1991).

Exhibit 9.6   *The politics of individual and collective responsibility*

In cases involving governmental failure and criticism:
- A matter of **collective responsibility** may be treated as a matter of **individual responsibility** in order to minimise loss of public confidence in the government; however
- A matter of individual responsibility is sometimes transformed into a case of collective responsibility in order to shield a particular minister.

---

my own department we get one and a half million letters a year, any one of which may lead to disaster. No Home Secretary could be expected to supervise all those one and a half million letters'. Sir John Hunt, then Cabinet Secretary, giving evidence to the Commons Expenditure Committee in 1977, commented that the idea of ministers resigning over the mistakes of someone they had never heard of was 'out of date and rightly so'. Normally, the support of the prime minister is sufficient to shield a minister under parliamentary attack for administrative errors from resignation. No postwar case, Geoffrey Marshall has observed, has involved the assumption that 'a ministerial head must roll for civil service error' (Marshall, 1989, p. 130).

The resignation of Sir Thomas Dugdale in the Crichel Down affair (1954) used to be regarded as an example of a minister resigning for the mistakes of his officials. Dugdale, it was said, accepted full responsibility for the negligence of his civil servants in dealings with a landowner who was anxious to buy back land which had been compulsorily acquired by the Government for use as a bombing range in 1938. In fact, the issue was less clear-cut. Dugdale, it seems, was personally involved in the maladministration which led to his downfall. Moreover, hounding by his own backbenchers played a key part in the resignation (Hennessy, 1990, p. 503; Brazier, 1988, p. 139).

☐ *Conclusions*

Table 9.3 shows that 16 ministers resigned under the convention of individual ministerial responsibility between 1962 and 1992. At face value,

these figures suggest that the convention is far from being a myth and neither is it in decline, since resignations over these three decades occurred at a rate of about one every two years and there were nine in the thirteen years after 1979. However, nine resignations were for personal misconduct of one sort or another, four were for political misjudgements, one (Currie) was for a misleading political statement, one (Fairburn) was for a mixture of political failings and personal misconduct, and only one (Callaghan) was for a failure of policy (and even that did not involve leaving the Government). There were no ministerial resignations for mistakes by officials.

Ministers rarely resign immediately upon the outbreak of some scandal or crisis – the Foreign Office resignations in 1982 are an exception – which means that in the following days and weeks the attitudes of the prime minister, the Cabinet, the backbenchers of the governing party, the press and public opinion will all play a part in whether a minister stays or goes. The inter-relatedness of individual and collective responsibility, in particular, should be noticed together with the political considerations underlying their invocation (Exhibit 9.6).

▮ The Anonymity of Civil Servants

The anonymity of civil servants – an important corollary of ministerial responsibility – has been seriously eroded since the war. As ministerial willingness to assume responsibility for the mistakes of officials has declined, so the practice has grown of naming and blaming individual

---

Exhibit 9.7   *Naming and blaming civil servants: some examples*

- **Bloodhound missile contract** (1964): officials in the Ministry of Aviation blamed for excessive profits made by Ferranti Ltd on this contract.

- **Sachsenhausen case** (1968): faults in the conduct of Foreign Office (FO) officials (and the Minister, George Brown) revealed by the Parliamentary Commissioner's investigation into the FO's refusal to pay compensation to British victims of Nazi persecution. During its consideration by the Commons Select Committee, Airey Neave MP named the official whom he considered to have the greatest responsibility for the day-to-day administration of the case.

- **Vehicle and General Insurance Company collapse** (1971): officials in the Board of Trade criticised by the Tribunal of Inquiry for negligent conduct.

- **Westland affair** (1986): leading civil servants in the Prime Minister's Office and the DTI who were involved in the leaking of the Solicitor-General's letter were all identified in Parliament and the press: in addition to Bernard Ingham, Charles Powell and Colette Bowe, these included John Mogg, Private Secretary to Leon Brittan, and John Mitchell, an Under-Secretary at the DTI.

---

bureaucrats (Exhibit 9.7). In the Westland case, in addition to its criticisms of the minister and the other civil servants involved, the House of Commons Select Committee on Defence censured Sir Robert Armstrong, the Cabinet Secretary and Head of the Home Civil Service, for failing 'to give a clear lead'. The Government's defence of its behaviour on this occasion in terms of the traditional doctrine of ministerial responsibility was not entirely satisfactory: *(i)* because – as the Defence Select Committee noted – ministers did not make themselves fully accountable to Parliament during the affair, and *(ii)* because the Committee was not allowed to question any of the officials. Exhibit 9.8 sets out the contrasting positions taken on the affair by the Government and the House of Commons through its select committees.

Exhibit 9.8   *The Westland affair: the role of ministers and civil servants*

The House of Commons View
- 'a mechanism must be provided to make officials in cases in which Ministers deny responsibility for their actions accountable to Parliament' (Treasury and Civil Service Select Committee, 1985–6).
- 'When the conduct of individual officials is a matter of general comment and controversy, ministers discharge their obligations to officials by satisfying the House that those officials have behaved properly. Officials who do their duty have a right to expect that support from ministers. If ministers cannot demonstrate that officials have behaved properly, the question of disciplinary proceedings arises' (Defence Select Committee 1986).

The Government View
- 'Constitutionally ministers are responsible and accountable for all actions carried out by civil servants of their departments in pursuit of government policies or in discharge of responsibilities laid upon them by Parliament' (Civil servants and Ministers: duties and responsibilities. Government Response, 1986).

Another important reason for the increasing tendency to name and criticise civil servants for misconduct and maladministration is the emergence of procedures for investigating the shortcomings of the administration outside the floor of the House of Commons. These are formal inquiries and tribunals of inquiry; the Parliamentary Commissioners (Ombudsmen), and Parliamentary Select Committees. Such procedures can give a sharper quasi-judicial edge to inquiry into the executive, although few would argue that they yet provide a wholly satisfactory answer to the problem of accountability, if only (but not only) because governments continue to adhere so firmly to the doctrine of ministerial responsibility.

Summary

The bulk of governmental decisions are made in the Departments – hence, the importance of establishing *(i)* an appropriate model to understand how departmental decisions are made; and *(ii)* of analysing the contemporary validity of the convention which purports to describe ministerial accountability.

Under *(i)* it was suggested that the reassertion of political control over the Civil Service has led to the reinstatement of the traditional **liberal democratic** or **public administration** model of minister–civil servant relations; although limited in scope, the **Whitehall village** model is also relevant. However, the far-left **power-bloc** and New Right **bureaucratic over-supply** theories have been undermined (the latter because of the 'correctives' applied by Conservative Governments since 1979) and the **liberal bureaucratic** model, although containing valuable insights, is – perhaps temporarily – of reduced significance in practice.

The sweeping managerial reforms of the 1980s including the radical 'Next Steps' programme have led to fears about the future of a cohesive, properly accountable civil service whilst other political developments and incidents have raised questions about its impartiality.

With regard to *(ii)*, although still normally invoked, the traditional doctrine of ministerial responsibility does not mean that ministers automatically resign after public criticism of their own or their officials' errors and misconduct. They resign mainly for personal misconduct – but even then, seldom immediately, more rarely for political misjudgements, more rarely still for policy failures and, in recent times, are not expected to resign at all for the errors of their officials.

As a consequence, officials' anonymity is in the process of erosion by the growing practice of naming and blaming civil servants. But, although its working is far from satisfactory, it is difficult to maintain that the principle of ministerial responsibility has been dislodged, so central is it to understanding British constitutional practice. Ministers remain (at least) *answerable* for the conduct of their Departments, and the maximum sanction (resignation) still exists, even if its practice at any given moment is more a function of the political circumstances of the government, of relationships within it, and of relations between the erring politician and his own party, than of the automatic play of ministerial consciences or of enforcement by Parliament.

Questions

1. 'Civil Servants owe their primary duty to the state, not to the government which happens to be in office'. Discuss this statement in the light of developments and cases in the 1980s.
2. 'Anonymous, permanent and politically neutral'. How far is this still an apt description of top civil servants in Britain?
3 . 'Apart from personal misconduct, ministerial responsibility is now an outmoded convention'. Discuss.

Assignments

1. Write a brief account of the managerial reforms of the civil service in the 1980s and early 1990s and examine the benefits and disadvantages occurring as a result of them.

2. MPs and lobby groups have complained that civil servants often form a barrier to change and resist amendments which would improve legislation. A small team of civil servants – the "bill team" – will accompany the Minister when he attends the Standing Committee. They see their job as keeping the bill "on course", and admit that once a measure reaches a Standing Committee their duty is to support it. Their loyalty is to their Minister and not to the MPs on Standing Committees who are scrutinising legislation. In the case of the Child Support bill, the team of civil servants refused to meet representatives from pressure groups, refused to consider their proposed amendments, and advised the Minister not to consider any of the Opposition's proposed amendments.

From the civil servants' point of view, they are justified in ignoring outside experts and rejecting all proposed amendments at the Standing Committee stage because all such difficulties will have been ironed out beforehand. To put it another way, the Committee Stage is not the time to seriously reconsider legislation. Basically, Standing Committees are concerned with picking up on small technical difficulties contained in the legislation. If by chance the bill did contain a serious flaw, then this would be taken into account and a new amendment would be introduced by the Government at report stage.

   Are civil servants more interested in getting legislation through Parliament than in the contents of the legislation? Civil servants argue that they provide impartial advice to Ministers at an early stage when legislation is being considered. A confidential report circulated at the Home Office stated that:

> The officials' relationship with Ministers is emphatically not one of passive obedience. It is not the officials' job to give Ministers the advice they want to hear, but to make sure

the financial, practical and other consequences of a course of action have been properly worked out and are firmly in the Ministers' minds before a decision is taken.

Some have argued that this may have summed up the relationship between civil servants and their Ministers in the past, but it no longer applies because the Conservatives have been in power for so long. Civil Servants temper their advice and are now reluctant to challenge Ministers.

> 'The greater the ideology in any legislation before Parliament, the less the consultation that takes place in its preparation.' Discuss.

Further reading

Brazier, R. (1988) *Constitutional Practice*, Oxford: Clarendon.

Dunleavy, P. (1990) 'Government at the Centre' in P. Dunleavy, A. Gamble and G. Peele (eds) *Developments in British Politics* (London: Macmillan).

Drewry G. and Butcher, T. (1991) *The Civil Service Today*, 2nd edn (Oxford: Blackwell).

Greenaway, J.R. (1992) 'The civil service: twenty years of reform,' in Jones, B. and L. Robins, (eds.), *Two Decades in British Politics*, Manchester, Manchester University Press

Greenwood, J. and Wilson, D. (1989) *Public Administration in Britain Today*, 2nd edn (London: Unwin Hyman).

Hennessy, P. (1990) *Whitehall*, rev. edn (London: Fontana).

Jones, G.W. (1989) 'A Revolution in Whitehall? Changes in British Central Government since 1979', *West European Politics*, 12.

Marshall, G. (ed.) (1989) *Ministerial Responsibility*, (Oxford: Oxford University Press).

Pyper, R. (1991) 'Governments, 1964–90: A Survey', *Contemporary Record*, 5: 2, autumn.

Pyper, R. (1992) 'A New Model Civil Service?', *Politics Review*, 2: 2, November.

Theakston, K. (1991–2) 'Ministers and Mandarins', *Talking Politics*, 4: 2, Winter.

■ *Chapter 10* ■

Quasi-Government

This chapter examines the politics and organisation of quasi-government in Britain. The scope of government activity in society has increased considerably since 1954 and a great variety of bodies have been established to administer the expanded public sector. Such bodies, notably quangos and the nationalised industries, have been viewed with hostility by the political right. There have been many practical reasons for nationalising specific industries or establishing certain quangos, but such measures have provoked ideologically-based opposition. Margaret Thatcher's Government attempted to reduce the number of quangos in existence and to reduce the scope of the nationalised industries through pursuing a policy of privatisation. But did such policies bring the advantages that she and her colleagues envisaged? We will examine the cases for and against nationalisation and privatisation. At the local level too the functions performed in the past by the public sector are now being performed by the private sector. We will conclude with an examination of the Training and Enterprise Councils (TECs) and Urban Development Corporations (UDCs).

■ The World of the Quango

By the 1980s around 8 million of Britain's 25-million-strong labour force were employed in the public sector. This growth led to anxiety in some circles about the power that the government now had over the individual. It was argued that the political liberty of the individual was increasingly threatened by 'red tape', 'Big Government' or the 'mega-bureaucracy'.

Organisations in the public sector have been established as the need has arisen at different times to perform a variety of tasks. The result is a hotchpotch of bodies that frequently differ very much from one another and make it difficult to generalise about them or even to classify them into distinctive categories.

□ *Indirect Government*

The world of quasi-government is inhabited by organisations referred to by political scientists as 'fringe bodies', 'non-departmental organisations', 'governmental bodies', 'semi-autonomous authorities' and 'quangos'. Even the latter name has been modified so that it may now refer to organisations which are 'quasi-non-governmental', 'quasi-autonomous-non-governmental' or 'quasi-autonomous-national-government'.

Quasi-government has been described as 'arm's length' or 'indirect' government. It is made up of organisations involved in government which is not done by central government departments such as the Inland Revenue or local authorities. It consists of state-related organisations which may or may not have been created by government but which are influential in making or applying government policy.

The *Pliatzky Report on Non-Departmental Public Bodies* (1980) examined the world of quasi-government. It was reported that there were 489 non-departmental bodies which were 'executive' in nature and had a regulatory function; these employed 217 000 staff. Examples of executive-type quangos are the Arts Council,

169

Agricultural Wages Board, Eggs Authority, United Kingdom Atomic Energy Authority, Countryside Commission, British Council, General Nursing Council and Commission for Racial Equality. In addition, there were 1561 'advisory' bodies which directly employed relatively few staff. Examples include the Food Hygiene Advisory Council, the Advisory Committee on the Supply and Education of Teachers, the Advisory Committee on the Safety of Nuclear Installations, the China Clay Council, the Police Advisory Board and the Parliamentary Boundary Commission for England. Finally, there were 67 systems of tribunals which were often staffed by the department concerned. Examples include the Supplementary Benefits Appeal Tribunals, Pneumoconiosis Medical Panels, Vaccine Damage Tribunals, Rent Tribunals and Rent Assessment Committees, Agricultural Land Tribunals and the Independent Schools Tribunal. Sir Leo Pliatzky's report did not include the nationalised industries, public corporations or local government 'quangos'. Fifty-six of the latter were identified by Paul Cousins in his study of the London Borough of Bromley. Examples at the local level include the Bromley Library and Theatre Panel, Home Safety Committee, Bromley Savings Committee and the Kent Land Drainage Committee.

What are the reasons behind the growth of quasi-government? The answer frequently lies in the wishes of the government to have a function performed, and in not wanting this function to be the direct responsibility of a minister. There are advantages for a minister in establishing a quango to do a particular task rather than having that task done by civil servants in his department. It may be that the particular task is done more effectively by a single-purpose quango than by a department which is involved in a wide and complex area of administration. Establishing a quango also enables people from outside government to be involved in administration; this is particularly the case with advisory bodies which may enlist outsiders with expertise which is not available amongst civil servants.

There may also be political advantages for a minister in establishing a quango rather than in having his own civil servants perform certain tasks.

Ministers may wish to distance themselves from sensitive or controversial issues such as race relations or arms sales. Quangos can monitor these issues without involving the minister to any great extent in their day-to-day operations. This remoteness from certain sensitive issues can also be very useful to a minister because it insulates him from parliamentary attacks. He is seen as 'not responsible' for certain quango activities and therefore escapes criticism from both his own and opposition backbenches. Finally, having set up a quango which enables the participation of outside interests, the minister is likely to find that the policy recommendations made by that quango will be publicly acceptable.

Is Quasi-Government Democratic?

A considerable number of individuals remain unpersuaded by these administrative arguments which favour the growth of quasi-government. The main thrust of their case has been stated forcefully by Sir Norman Chester in his article 'Fringe Bodies, Quangos and All That', *Public Administration* (1979). He argued that:

> The growth of fringe bodies is a retreat from the simple democratic principle evolved in the nineteenth century that those who perform a public duty should be fully responsible to an electorate – by way either of a minister responsible to Parliament or of a locally elected council. The essence of a fringe body is that it is not so responsible for some or all of its actions (Chester, 1979, p. 54).

In examining the issues raised by Sir Norman, Nevil Johnson comments that 'accountability and control are closely related terms. Accountability provides some assurance of control, whilst effective control is required if public office-holders are to be held accountable' (N. Johnson, 1982, p. 210). Political scientists have tended to make finely-balanced judgements about accountability and control in the light of their research into quasi-government. There is general agreement that little is known yet about the control of quasi-governmental bodies. Although quangos produce annual reports, these do not always provide much useful information on how the bodies actually operate. Reports can be written in very bland terms which reveal little or nothing of the policy disagreements, tactics or personality clashes which emerged during the year in question. Also the control of one quango may differ very much from that of another. For example, in some quangos the only full-time salaried member is the chairman and there is a tendency to see him as the most important influence. In others, there is a large full-time staff and it becomes far less easy to locate those who wield control.

Consequently there is a feeling that quangos should be monitored more closely by Parliament. Since quangos receive public money, it is argued that in principle they should be made more accountable. Some believe that the system of select committees provides the best machinery for Parliament to scrutinise the work of quasi-government. Others doubt the practicability of this. Although select committees have scrutinised the nationalised industries and other bodies they lack the resources needed for the mammoth task of reviewing quangos.

Indirect Government: 'Quangoland'

There is an increasing interest in the growth of government by quango. As prime minister,

Margaret Thatcher waged a campaign against quangos because they appeared to her as part-and-parcel of the corporate state. Quangos were non-elected, secretive and largely unaccountable bodies which provided 'jobs for the boys', by which she meant the appointment of trade unionists by Labour governments. As a result of her attack on quangos, some were wound up, some merged, and some disappeared only to reappear with a new title. But in overall terms she was successful; there were 2167 public body quangos in 1979 and only 1412 of them in 1992.

Having said that there are fewer quangos today than in the past, it is also true to say that today there are more quangos than ever. Why is there no contradiction in saying this? The answer is that the narrowly defined type of quango which annoyed Mrs Thatcher has declined, but today there are new types of quango which did not exist in 1979, and these have exploded in number. The more broadly defined quangos have resulted in particular from the opting-out process in health (e.g. NHS trusts), education (e.g. funding councils, opted-out schools) as well as the loss of other local government functions (Training and Enterprise Councils, Urban Development Corporations, Housing Actions Trusts). Figure 10.1 shows the growth in thousands from the old corporate state style quango (Apple and Pear Research Council, Eggs Authority) to the new-

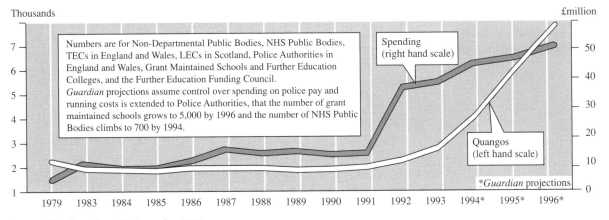

Numbers are for Non-Departmental Public Bodies, NHS Public Bodies, TECs in England and Wales, LECs in Scotland, Police Authorities in England and Wales, Grant Maintained Schools and Further Education Colleges, and the Further Education Funding Council.
Guardian projections assume control over spending on police pay and running costs is extended to Police Authorities, that the number of grant maintained schools grows to 5,000 by 1996 and the number of NHS Public Bodies climbs to 700 by 1994.

Source: *The Guardian*, 19 November 1993.

Figure 10.1   *Growing quangos*

Exhibit 10.1   *The New Magistracy*

The recent and rapid growth in quangos has led to concern about the *democratic control* and *accountability* of these bodies. Sometimes political commentators refer to these problems as the *democratic deficit*. Since members are not elected on to quangos, but appointed by government, the term *the new magistracy* is being used to describe this new elite which is becoming responsible for so many areas of government.

- Since it is the Government which appoints members of the new magistracy, some are worried that there will be a Conservative bias among those who serve on quangos. Ministers are responsible for making nearly 40,000 quango appointments. There have already been accusations that the Government is biased in appointing Conservative sympathisers and managers of businesses which make donations to the Conservative Party.

- Conservative support is relatively low in Wales and Scotland; for example, only 6 of the 38 Welsh seats have Conservative MPs, and only 11 of the 72 Scottish seats have Conservative MPs. There are fears amongst the opposition parties that quangos are being used to compensate for this by providing Conservative influence. Many Scottish and Welsh affairs are now dealt with by quangos (Welsh affairs alone come under 100 quangos, twice as many as in 1979). Opposition parties are worried that the same process might happen in England, with the Government appointing Conservative-biased quangos to compensate for their losses in local government.

- The large number of quangos in existence leads to problems concerning control and scrutiny. At the same time, the greater involvement of businessmen may lead to differing ethics and ways of making decisions than existed previously in public service. Some are concerned about the number of scandals which have already come to light – the House of Commons' Public Accounts Committee slammed into the Welsh Development Agency and found it guilty of a long list of misdemeanours. These included making unauthorised payments, running up extravagant expenses and appointing a convicted con-man to a top post.

- Critics argue that corruption and policy failure will occur more in quangos than in local government. This is because in a democratically elected council there will normally be one or more opposition parties which will work hard to expose all the faults of those wielding power. Quangos lack the vital ingredient of critical opposition. Also, councils can ensure that there is a public debate about issues which concern local people, whereas quangos decide vital issues in private. Because of the democratic process, decisions made by councillors are generally seen as legitimate – even if they are unpopular – whereas decisions made by quangos have little legitimacy.

- The Citizen's Charter Minister, William Waldegrave, has argued that many of these fears are unfounded. For example, accountability is maintained because the relevant Minister remains answerable to Parliament for what quangos do. But perhaps more important than this, he argued, is that the power of citizens as consumers over public services means that there is no democratic deficit.

---

style quangos of indirect government. Along with the rise in numbers has gone a remarkable increase in spending. Many political commentators were astonished to learn that quangos are responsible for a fifth of all public spending, which amounts to £47.1 billion a year. And it is important to note that these calculations do *not* include spending by the Next Steps agencies. For comparison, the total of all spending by local government is £61.3 billion a year. What surprised so many was the massive shift in spending power from elected to non-elected bodies which has taken place in the 1990s. In 1992-93 for example, a total of £25 billion was spent by quangos which during the 1980s would have been spent by local authorities.

■ The Era of Public Ownership

The nationalised industries form part of the public sector and represent another example of arm's length government. In the same way as it proved difficult to define and classify non-departmental organisations, it is difficult to generalise about organisations concerned with public ownership. Even what is understood as existing under the umbrella term 'public ownership' varies from one political scientist to the next. For example, some argue that in the strictest sense schools, colleges, universities, roads, libraries, and recreation grounds are 'publicly owned'. Others accept that in practice 'public ownership' is a term used to cover business or commercial undertakings in which the state plays a major role.

Not far below the surface of arguments about public ownership or the role that government should play in the economy are the ideological outlooks of the people concerned. The labels 'left-wing' and 'right-wing' really describe an individual's attitude towards property. Left-wing indicates sympathy towards the idea of public ownership: right-wing favours private ownership.

At its most simple, there are those who believe in the doctrine of *laissez-faire* and who believe that government involvement in the economy is undesirable. They believe that the market left to itself will solve economic or industrial problems. For example, they oppose attempts by the government to modernise industry, because, if the market mechanism is not disturbed, it will restructure industry with inefficient firms going out of business and efficient ones prospering. In other words, competition and the working of the free market always produce the best solutions.

In disagreement with this economic philosophy are those who wish to see an economy which is controlled by the government. They believe that the free market creates problems (such as poverty) that it cannot solve and that 'market-displacing' policies would provide a better economic climate. Such policies might include import controls, planning agreements with private firms, and nationalisation.

▯ *Arguments For and Against Public Ownership*

When he was a leader of the Transport and General Workers' Union (TGWU), Frank Cousins commented that it was possible to have public ownership without having socialism but it was not possible to have socialism without having public ownership. His friends on the left wing of the Labour Party agreed with him and opposed those in the party who argued that 'modern' socialism did not require massive nationalisation. It was feared that if right-wing revisionists got their way, Labour would be turned into another capitalist party such as the Liberals or Conservatives. The left pointed out that in 1918 Labour added Clause IV to its constitution and became a 'socialist' party, which committed it to securing:

> for the workers by hand or by brain the full fruits of their industry and the most equitable distribution thereof that may be possible upon the basis of the common ownership of the means of production, distribution and exchange, and the best obtainable system of popular administration and control of each industry or service.

Capitalism was seen as an evil system which produced extremes of wealth – that is, it led to 'poverty in the midst of plenty'. Capitalism also brought mankind's worst motives to the forefront of economic activity – greed and competitiveness. In capitalist language, 'profit' was a polite word for 'greed' and 'competition' stood for 'conflict'. Socialists wanted to build a new society to replace capitalism in which people would enjoy greater equality. Socialism would, therefore, be based on public ownership, not private ownership, and would promote cooperation between people rather than competition.

The first Labour Government with a majority in Parliament was elected in 1945. In a series of nine Acts of Parliament, major areas of the economy were brought into public ownership. The return of the Conservatives to power in 1951 did not lead to large-scale denationalisation of industries that Labour brought into public ownership. Only the road haulage and steel industries were returned to private ownership. Why did the Conservative Government retain so much of a socialist nationalisation programme? Frank Cousins's comment provides a clue to answering this question because many non-socialist, and even anti-socialist, governments have nationalised industries.

In Britain many concerns were 'publicly owned' long before socialist ideas had become fully developed. For example, the General Post Office has been in public hands for over 300 years, Trinity House received its charter in 1514, and some municipal authorities were supplying domestic gas at the end of the eighteenth century. In 1908, a Liberal Government set up the Port of London Authority. Indeed, there were a considerable number of publicly owned enterprises in Britain before the election of the Attlee Government in 1945.

These publicly-owned enterprises were established because they provided practical solutions to the problems faced at the time. The Conservative Government accepted most of Labour's nationalisation programme because it solved many economic problems. For example, after two world wars the coal mines were in a run-down state and in need of massive investment to help Britain's post war recovery. Who else but the government would have been willing to provide the massive resources necessary for this vital but otherwise unattractive investment? Much the same could be said regarding the railways, which were also in a poor condition. Thus, for pragmatic reasons, the Conservative Government headed by Winston Churchill was content to see these and most of the other nationalised industries remain publicly owned.

Although Conservative instinct is to oppose nationalisation in principle, many Tories have accepted that it has a limited role to play in a modern economy. Edward Heath used the nationalisation of Rolls-Royce in 1971 as a way of rescuing the company from financial collapse. In 1975, Labour mounted a similar rescue operation to save British Leyland. On the right wing of the Labour party since the late 1950s have been MPs who feel that future nationalisation should be limited to such rescue operations as are needed from time to time, and that it should no longer have a central place in economic policy. Labour revisionists argue that modern socialism was more concerned with the distribution of wealth than with whether that wealth happens to be produced in the private or the public sector. Labour's policy review resulted in public owner-

Table 10.1 *The nationalised industries*

	Royal Assent	Vesting Date
1. Bank of England	14 February 1946	1 March 1946
2. Civil Aviation	1 August 1946	1 August 1946
3. Coal	12 July 1946	1 January 1947
4. Cable and Wireless (entrusted to Post Office)	6 November 1946	1 January 1947
5. Transport	6 August 1946	1 January 1948
6. Land Development Rights (Town & Country Planning Act)	6 August 1947	1 July 1948
7. Electricity	13 August 1947	1 April 1948
8. Gas	30 July 1948	1 May 1949
9. Iron and Steel	24 November 1949	15 February 1951

Source: Hanson (ed.) (1963, p. 36).

ship playing only a minor role in the party's manifesto for the 1990s. Even with the newly privatised industries, Labour was more concerned over control of the enterprises than with their ownership by the state.

Opponents of public ownership have argued that nationalisation created monopolies, which could work against the interests of consumers. For example, all homes require energy for cooking, heating and lighting. The supply of electricity, gas and coal is each in the hands of a monopoly. Consumers cannot realistically escape being the customer of one or other of these monopolies. Others have argued that monopolies also exist in the private sector, and at least nationalised monopolies are subject to public control. In addition, it is often the Government which insists on measures which are not in the consumers' interest, and not the boards of nationalised industries. For example, before privatisation Thatcher's Government – not the Board of the British Gas Corporation – set the levels of successive increases in the price of gas to the domestic user. Too often the nationalised industries have been blamed for decisions or policies made by the government.

A common argument is that nationalised industries tend to be inefficient because they are not spurred on by the need for profits. Both management and workforce adopt a leisurely attitude towards their business, knowing that they will be bailed out by public money if they turn in losses. This view is disputed by those who point out that many nationalised industries were making huge losses before they were nationalised. Nationalisation provided the opportunity for rationalisation and modernisation. Many firms, such as Ferranti, were rescued and put on the road to recovery by the National Enterprise Board. Also, publicly owned concerns provide a social service as well as making a profit. A good example of this is the Post Office, which offers the same service at the same price to people no matter whether they live in John O'Groats or London. The Post Office could maximise profits by charging an 'economic' rate for people living in remote areas or by cutting out services to such areas altogether.

■ "Rolling Back the State"

During the 1970s the Labour Government experienced 'stagflation' in the economy together with a severe balance-of-payments crisis. The Labour Prime Minister, James Callaghan, told his party conference in 1976 that:

> we used to think you could spend your way out of recession and increase employment by cutting taxes and boosting government spending. I tell you in all candour that that option no longer exists and that in so far as it ever did exist, it only worked by injecting a bigger dose of inflation into the economy, followed by a higher level of unemployment as the next step.

In other words the era of Keynesian economics, which involved massive state intervention in managing the economy, was over. In order to help finance government spending in this difficult situation his Chancellor, Denis Healey, sold part of the state's shareholding in British Petroleum.

What a Labour Government had done reluctantly as a short-term solution to its financial problems, the new Conservative Government was to adopt enthusiastically as a long-term strategy. Although the term 'privatisation' did not appear in their 1979 manifesto, Conservatives were committed to denationalising the aerospace and shipbuilding industries, selling council houses to tenants, selling shares in the National Freight Corporation, deregulating bus services and limiting the activities of the Labour-created National Enterprise Board. From the outset, then, the privatisation policy included a variety of ways in which the public sector was to be 'rolled back'.

□ *What is Privatisation?*

Privatisation covers a variety of techniques which reduce or eliminate the role of the state in owning, managing and providing services in favour of the private sector. Privatisation policy includes:

● Denationalisation – of public enterprises, such as the Government's plan to dispose of British Coal, and of public assets, such as Labour's sale of BP shares.

- Liberalisation and deregulation – in order to encourage greater competition in the provision of services, such as past policy with bus transport and future policy with rail transport.
- Contracting out of public sector services – health authorities and local authorities put many of their services out to tender. A private company may provide the best value for money and replace the service previously provided by public sector employees.
- Reduction of the public sector control – in areas such as urban redevelopment and youth training – through increasing the responsibility of the private sector.
- Introduction of market forces into public sector welfare areas such as health care and education. 'Realistic' charges or 'competing for customers' result in welfare departments being run more like commercial businesses than traditional public services. Also tax relief may be given to encourage the use of private sector services, such as private health care.

Privatisation under the first Thatcher Government began as a piecemeal process but quickened in pace after the 1983 general election. Table 10.2 indicates a selection of the biggest privatisation sales, with the exception of council house sales which accounted for 43 per cent of the entire proceeds from privatisation up to 1988–9. Some sales of state assets, as in the case of council houses, were to the public. Other examples include the sale of shares in public utilities such as water, gas and electricity. The latter were publicised with 'Tell Sid' and 'Frank N Stein' television advertising campaigns which were seen by 96 per cent of the adult population. Other state assets, such as Sealink, Fairey Engineering and the National Bus Company, were sold to private concerns or to the existing management.

The flotation of half the state's holding in British Telecom raised nearly £4 billion in 1984. In 1986 over £5 billion was raised by the sale of British Gas and in 1990 nearly 13 million investors applied for shares in the electricity supply companies, the sale of which raised £5.2 billion.

British Petroleum	1979/1981/1983/1987
British Aerospace	1981/1985
Cable & Wireless	1981/1983/1985
Amersham International	1982
National Freight Consortium	1982
Britoil	1982/1985
Associated British Ports	1983/1984
Enterprise Oil	1984
Jaguar	1984
British Telecom	1984
British Gas	1986
British Airways	1987
Royal Ordnance	1987
Rolls Royce	1987
British Airports Authority	1987
Rover Group	1988
British Steel	1988
Water Companies (10)	1989
Electricity Companies (12)	1990
National Power/Powergen	1991
Scottish Electricity Companies	1991
British Telecom	1993

Based on Butcher, T. (1991/2) 'Rolling Back the State', *Talking Politics* 4, 2, Winter.

Table 10.2   *Privatisation: major sales 1979–93*

□ *Privatisation – The Case For and Against*

Those in favour of privatisation argued that civil servants and local government officers are poorly qualified to run commercial organisations. Traditionally, they were cautious and did not have the entrepreneurial flair of businessmen. And because the government was there to subsidise any losses the nationalised industries made, there was no incentive either to be efficient or to provide the sort of services the public wanted. Without the profit motive, it was argued, nationalised industries became wasteful, overmanned, bureaucratic and inefficient. Any company in the private sector which fitted this description would soon be out of business.

Radicals on the New Right thought that privatisation was important for philosophical as well as practical reasons. They argued that less government coupled with lower taxes resulted in there being greater freedom for the individual. Others argued that privatisation would help create an 'enterprise culture' which would help bring about Britain's economic revival. Too many people, it was argued, had their initiative sapped by a 'dependency culture' in which they looked towards the welfare state to provide everything rather than take control of their own lives. Through privatisation people, and not just the middle class, would get into the habit of buying shares and come to see the advantages and benefits of the free market system. The radical 'No Turning Back' group, influential in the later Thatcher years, argued that the growth of an enterprise culture would result in the 'welfare state' being privatised away into the 'enabling state'. The welfare state would wither away as more and more citizens purchased their own health care, education and pensions, rather than relying upon the state for provision.

Another advantage of privatisation was that it took the government out of the troublesome area of industrial relations. The Labour Government, led by James Callaghan, had been electorally damaged by the 'Winter of Discontent' comprising a series of unpopular strikes by public sector unions. Once, however, the services concerned are privatised then such disputes are between the unions and private sector employees, not the government. Also, transferring union members from the public to the private sector brings them into contact with the discipline of the marketplace. They can no longer make unreasonable wage demands, as they did when they were public sector employees, without putting their jobs at risk.

Critics of privatisation policies have argued that frequently they fail to improve the quality of services provided or offer the public greater choice – since in many cases all that happened on privatisation was that a public sector monopoly became a private sector monopoly. As with other monopolies, the consumer has no choice but to accept whatever is provided. For example, in 1992 complaints about water companies more than doubled with most grievances being about high water charges, the excessive salaries paid to top executives, and the poor quality of service provided.

The argument that privatisation helps to foster popular capitalism and an enterprise culture has also been challenged. The record shows that,

firstly, state assets have been sold off too cheaply. The National Audit Office criticised the Government over the sale of British Steel which was underpriced by between £100 and £250 million. Criticisms was also made over the sale of the Rover Group to British Aerospace where a £44 million hidden subsidy was provided by the Government as a 'sweetener' for the sale. Given these examples, the popularity of share-ownership in the privatised industries was not evidence of popular capitalism. It was argued that selling of state assets at below their true value is just like selling £10 notes for £5; of course people will buy them. In addition, share-buying in the privatised industries did not develop into a long-term habit for most, but simply provided opportunities to make 'a quick buck':

> although the number of shareholders trebled between 1979 and 1989, due in large part to privatisation, there is evidence that a large proportion of new shareholders in privatised industries turn out to be short term investors. The number of shareholders in British Gas fell from 4.5 million to 2.8 million in two years after flotation. (Butcher, 1991–2, p. 104)

Secondly, an enterprise culture cannot be universal in its influence since an increasing number of Britain's population live in or close to poverty. For them, the option of buying privatisation shares, sending their children to private schools and buying their own homes simply does not exist.

Finally, critics of privatisation have argued that the Conservative governments' motive in pursuing the policies were no different from that of Denis Healey, Chancellor in the beleaguered Labour Government of 1974–9. In other words, Thatcher's governments were not interested primarily in rolling back the state for ideological reasons, nor in increasing consumer choice, nor in raising efficiency – what the Chancellor was most interested in was using proceeds from privatisation sell-offs to reduce government borrowing. The main points in this argument are that from the outset it was realised that privatisation would not roll back the state very far. Since the market does not offer adequate protection to the consumer a number of regulatory agencies were necessary from the outset to act as watchdogs to

---

Exhibit 10.2   *TECs: what will they do?*

- Promote more effective training by employers and individuals in their area, using public programmes and private funds.
- Provide practical help to employers wishing to improve their training efforts, using Business Growth Training, delivered flexibly to meet local requirements.
- Deliver and develop youth training, including YTS, under contract with the Government according to local needs.
- Develop Employment Training under contract with the Government so that unemployed people are trained for local jobs.
- Stimulate enterprise and economic growth in the locality through the Enterprise Allowance Scheme; enterprise training and counselling programmes for small firms; and by developing their own initiatives.
- Improve the local enterprise and training system so that individuals and firms have easy access to the information and help they need.
- Stimulate business education partnerships.

Source: Training Agency (1990, p. 7).

---

monitor prices and quality – such as the Office of Telecommunications (OFTEL), the Office of Gas Supply (OFGAS), the Office of Water (OFWAT) and the Office of Electricity (OFFER). In addition, EU directives and provisions in the Citizen's Charter may regulate privatised enterprises. As we have seen, such regulation is required since, compared with pre-privatisation, prices have risen and quality has fallen in some instances.

Having stripped away the radical rhetoric, critics return to the 'true rationale' for privatisation as 'the need to finance the PSBR [Public Sector Borrowing Requirement]'. The evidence is in the nature of the industries which were privatised first. These were not the inefficient nationalised industries which would have benefited from privatisation, but 'anything that could be sold quickly and for a clear profit. This indicates the desire to finance the PSBR ...' (Cox, 1987, p. 156). The most memorable criticism of this policy came from the former Conservative Prime Minister, Harold Macmillan, who, as Lord Stockton, compared the Thatcher Government's privatisation policy to 'selling off the family silver'. It brings financial benefits in the short run, but represents a loss of assets and income in the long run.

■ Rolling Back the Local State

The hostility of recent Conservative governments to local government will be explored further in Chapters 11, 21 and 23. At this point, two examples of privatisation by central government of functions carried out in the past by local government will be examined.

Training and Enterprise Councils

Employers have for some time expressed concern over the relatively low level of skills found in Britain's workforce. It is feared that this deficiency could result in international uncompetitiveness, particularly with Britain facing the challenge of the single European market from 1993 onwards. In order to build up the level of vocational skills, particularly amongst young people, 80 Training and Enterprise Councils (TECs) have been set up.

TECs were launched in 1989 in the form of independent companies, directed by local businessmen, with a budget redirected from the

Training Agency. In the past the curriculum for vocational skills training would have been the responsibility of technical colleges run by local education authorities. In contrast, TECs involved local businessmen in vocational education, a move intended to shift 'the planning and management of training and enterprise from the public to the private sector' (Training Agency, 1989). Since TECs would be locally based and run by local businessmen, it was argued that education would respond to the needs of the local market in a way a public sector college curriculum could not. In addition, TECs would do a better job in educating the young since they could draw in 'private enterprise drive, flair, energy and commitment', qualities absent by implication in the public sector colleges acting in a sole capacity.

The Government's experiences in moving assets and services from the public to the private sector have often been disappointing. The question is whether the Government was prejudiced against the public sector, which was never as inefficient as the Thatcherites claimed. Or, as with the TECs, the Government puts too great a burden on the private sector since it works with an unrealistic image of what the private sector is capable of delivering.

Urban Development Corporations

The ideological belief that 'the private sector can do it better than the public sector' formed part of the thinking behind the establishment of UDCs to regenerate inner cities rather than providing local authorities with the necessary resources. It is true that during the 1970s plans to regenerate local economies were held back by numerous planning restrictions, and the need to remove 'red tape' was becoming increasingly obvious. Enterprise zones were set up which swept away planning restrictions and offered inducements such as grants, tax concessions, and the abolition of rates in order to attract private investors. These enterprise zones were administered by UDCs.

Amongst the first UDCs to be set up in 1981 was the London Docklands Development Corporation (LDDC) which was to oversee the economic rejuvenation of the riverside enterprise zone in East London. In other words, London's old docklands were to be redeveloped by the private sector and not by local government agencies. Partly as a result of this political message from the Government, one of LDDCs projects became something of a symbol of Thatcherite free enterprise – Canary Wharf. 'Canary Wharf was intended to be Britain's proof that the private sector could do such a huge project on its own' commented William Keegan in the *Observer* on the financial collapse of Olympia and York, the firm of private developers responsible for Canary Wharf.

The collapse of the Canary Wharf project provided a lesson in the relationship between the public and the private sectors. Despite the Thatcher Government's enthusiasm for the private sector, UDCs and developments such as Canary Wharf need the public sector to provide infrastructure. The central problem for Canary Wharf was its inaccessibility – without new roads and a tube line, in addition to a light railway and riverbus, transporting people to and from it was complicated and took a long time. At the same time, critics attacked the LDDC for the very concept of Canary Wharf – a development which would bring few benefits to London's East Enders. The emphasis of redevelopment had been on office blocks and prestigious shops, which provided little in the way of facilities or jobs for the local population. Had local government been responsible rather than a UDC, it was argued, the docklands would have been redeveloped with the main purpose of providing local jobs. In other words, factories rather than offices would have been located in the East End.

The same critics of the UDCs are now anxious that the Government does not bail out Canary Wharf with public money. But perhaps this attitude is unwise since it keeps the wasteful ideological conflicts of the 1980s alive. Rather than 'privatise' or 'municipalise', many local authorities believe that a partnership between both sectors marks the way ahead.

Summary

Indirect government is a useful, if undemocratic, way of making decisions and providing services. Although there have been attempts to reduce the size of quasi-government and the number of quangos in existence, some government policies have led to a proliferation of quango-like bodies.

Nationalised industries also represent a form of 'government at arm's length', and, as with other forms of quasi-government, problems of accountability and control have never been satisfactorily resolved.

In Britain, nationalisation and privatisation are highly political issues. The Thatcher Governments reduced the scope of public-sector activity through selling off assets and contracting-out, but the advantages promised have not always materialised once a concern has been privatised. The Thatcher Governments believed that privatisation would help to create 'popular capitalism', but there is little evidence that this has occurred.

Questions

1. Quasi-government is undemocratic. If so, can it be justified?

2. Two views on privatisation:

> Individual share ownership in Britain has been reborn. The number of individual holders of stocks and shares has grown sharply over the past six years. The idea has captured the imagination of the public. It is a sea-change of fundamental importance.
>
> Nigel Lawson

> Privatisation has represented an unrepeatable sale of state assets at knock-down prices. It has transferred rights to profits from state enterprises for present and future generations to private shareholders. It has elevated the pursuit of private profit above the imperatives of public service in our once public utilities. It has created private sector monopolies and thereby exposed the whole nation to the danger of monopolistic exploitation.
>
> John Smith

(a) Evaluate the merits of the two view points on privatisation.

(b) What is the case for and against the public ownership of the major utilities (gas, electricity and water) and the telecommunications industry?

(c) Why, generally speaking, is Labour sympathetic towards public ownership whilst Conservatives support privatisation?

Assignment: BR privatisation case-study

Task: Using the data provided, plus material which you may gather yourself, assess the economic and political case for privatising BR. Evaluate the political risks of introducing stronger market forces into rail transport services.

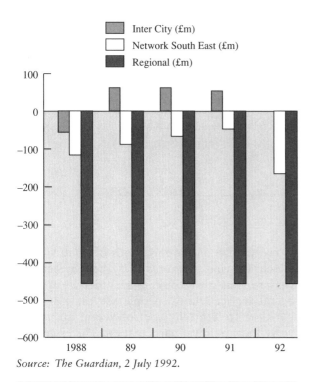

Source: *The Guardian, 2 July 1992.*

Figure 10.2   *Profit/loss before grant*

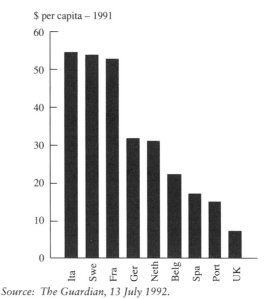

Source: *The Guardian, 13 July 1992.*

Figure 10.3   *New rail investment*

Further reading

Cox. Andrew (1987) 'The Politics of Privatisation', in L. Robins (ed.) *Politics and Policy-Making in Britain* (London: Longman).

Butcher, T. (1991–2) 'Rolling Back the State: The Conservative Governments and Privatisation 1979–91', *Talking Politics*, 4: 2, pp. 101–5.

Dunn, M. and Smith, S. (1990) 'Economic Policy and Privatisation' in S. Savage, and L. Robins (eds) *Public Policy Under Thatcher* (London: Macmillan) pp. 23–44.

Hood, C. (1981) 'Axeperson, Spare that Quango ...', in C. Hood and M. Wright, *Big Government in Hard Times* (Oxford: Martin Robertson).

■ Chapter 11 ■

Local Government

The world of local government is in turmoil. During the 1980s no fewer than 124 Acts of Parliament had a direct or indirect bearing on the work of local authorities. Having to absorb this constant stream of legislation, much of which has heaped problems on to councils, has produced a 'policy mess' in the area of local government. Some of the turmoil has ideological origins. No longer are arguments about topics such as structure 'politically neutral' or 'technical' in nature. Now the debate is essentially ideological, and argued by individuals who hold contrasting visions of what local government should be about. To some, local government means local democracy, with voters deciding priorities; to others, local government concerns responding to customers' needs efficiently and economically through greater reliance on market forces.

At the same time, ideological differences have plagued the central–local government relationship, with central government anxious to control public spending whilst some authorities have been just as concerned to spend in order to supply vitally needed local services.

■ Local Government in Crisis?

Services can be delivered at a local level for people without providing them through local government. For example, there are post offices in every town and in thousands of small villages which provide not only for the payment of welfare, but also banking facilities as well as postal services. Local people use these services but they are centrally controlled and do not involve local political participation. The essence of local government is that those who provide services are accountable to the local electorate for their actions. Local government is based on the idea of representation. Advocates of local government argue that local people best understand the needs of their particular community and therefore decisions affecting their community should be made by representatives who can reflect those views. Centralised bodies, whether in Whitehall or the boardrooms of large corporations, cannot understand or meet local needs as effectively as local government.

The Thatcher ambition of curbing the finance and activities of the public sector identified local government as a major target. At the same time many Labour-controlled councils, disappointed by Labour's ineffective opposition in the Commons, took up the banner to defend what became seen as the last bastions of socialism in Britain. Academic interest focused on this troublesome relationship between central and local government as well as the sort of functions a reformed local government system might perform, the structure that would be needed to support it, and the financial arrangements which would make it accountable to its electorate.

What is the Purpose of Local Government?

Under the last Labour Government Tony Crosland cut local government finance telling councillors that 'the party is over'. Under the Conservative governments which followed, cutting local government spending was seen as part and parcel of monetarism and the goal of reducing public expenditure generally. In basic terms local government was to be trimmed back by a variety of controls which would restrict the activities of councils, get councils to carry out their functions in a more efficient and less costly way, and mobilise electoral opposition to excessive council spending. What sort of local authorities were seen as capable of delivering these changes?

New Right Municipalism

Many on the political right felt that councils were out of touch with local communities – by the mid-1980s some had got involved in 'silly politics' such as the setting up of 'nuclear-free zones'; they were wasting too much public money through inefficiency, and too often they were challenging the authority of democratically elected central government. It had argued that this sorry situation should be remedied by stripping local government of some responsibilities and getting them run in ways which would offer greater consumer choice, and by the introduction of more competition generally. The biggest 'overspenders', in the eyes of the right, were the Metropolitan Counties (the 'mets') and the Greater London Council (GLC), and these were abolished in 1986. New bodies which had local responsibilities, such as the Urban Development Corporations (UDCs), Training and Enterprise Councils (TECs) and City Technology Colleges, were set up beyond the remit of local government. Even the 'core services' of local government, education and housing, were eroded as the public were given in appropriate ways the right to opt out from local government control.

Radical right-wing think-tanks, such as the Adam Smith Institute, prepared blueprints setting out their vision of councils in the future. It was argued that councils should not be run *like* businesses, but *as* businesses. It was proposed that councils should be replaced by private companies run by elected directors. Local people would have the responsibility of shareholders rather than that of voters. A company like Marks & Spencer would provide the model for radically reformed councils. None of the goods on sale in Marks & Spencer are manufactured by the company, but are made by private contractors and sold as 'St. Michael' products. Marks & Spencer keep a very careful eye on the quality of the products supplied to them, and if a company fails to meet the standards set by Marks & Spencer then it will either have to improve or be replaced by another firm. In the same way, it was argued, a council would be responsible for getting the best quality services at the best price through competitive tendering. The council's principal role would be to monitor the quality of services provided by private firms and renew or cancel contracts accordingly.

This radical vision of local government influenced the thinking of the Conservative minister, Nicholas Ridley, who argued the case that councils should provide an enabling framework for the provision of services without necessarily providing those services themselves. The 'enabling council' was seen

> as only one of a number of suppliers, contracting out to other agencies and the private sector to produce and deliver services. It will be customer centred, seeking to understand its 'customers and client', responding to the electorate and identifying and serving the community needs. The image underlying the Ridley model is that of a marketing agency identifying markets and devising strategies to meet consumer demands. (Horton, 1990, p. 185).

Part of the reforms also included the replacement of the domestic rates by the community charge, or 'poll tax', which was intended to make the entire local electorate more cost-conscious. It was thought that when the whole electorate, and not just ratepayers, were responsible for providing local government revenue they would vote for 'prudent' candidates for the council who promised 'value for money' rather than for 'profligate' candidates who would be 'high-spenders'. But as we shall see, this unpopular tax was replaced with the council tax early in John Major's first term. But in other respects, John Major's Government has not strayed from the Thatcher path on local government reforms.

□ *Municipal Socialism*

Labour's response to the right's 'enabling authority' concept was based on the argument that councils should respond to the local community's needs and not the demands of local markets. Councils should remain the principal providers of services and employers of the people who provide those services. Labour argued that this is the only way in which a council can provide what local people want. Councils which rely on the private sector alone to provide services cannot offer what people want. This is because private firms are motivated by profit and thus will only provide profit-making services; but many of the things which people want cannot be run on profit-making basis and only the council can provide these. For example, making a profit out of running a day centre for old people would certainly be impossible – it is hard to envisage many old age pensioners (OAPs) paying an economic entrance charge of £5 or so a day. Yet there is a clear local need for such centres. Municipal socialists argue that only councils can provide all the services to meet local needs. In this sense, local authorities as multi-service, monopoly providers 'enable' all community needs to be satisfied regardless of individuals' ability to pay for those services.

▮ Central–Local Government Relations

The relationship between central and local government is an extremely complex one which political scientists have devoted considerable re-

sources to analysing. There is agreement on the general trends but it is often the case that the complex detail uncovered in one particular case-study cannot be applied to all other cases. The relationship between central and local government is diverse, subject to changes in circumstance between one authority and another, and within one authority over time.

There has been a general trend in which central government has assumed more and more control over local government. Of course, in a democracy such as Britain where Parliament is sovereign, local government has never been autonomous. If an authority acts beyond the powers granted to it by Parliament, the doctrine of *ultra vires* will be invoked; the action of a local authority may be declared unlawful by the courts. Sometimes Acts of Parliament give ministers great powers over local authorities. Indeed, many Acts give ministers strong reserve powers over local authorities that fail to carry out their duties.

Recent years have seen a gathering momentum in the centralisation process which weakens the position of local government. As we have seen, many Labour-controlled authorities which challenged the government's policies on ideological lines were simply abolished. Many services once provided by local authorities, such as education, are now run increasingly by central government or, like rubbish collection, street cleaning and office-cleaning, contracted out to private bodies. And, as we shall see, the financing and spending of local authorities has come under great government control.

It has been argued that increased centralised powers over local authorities had become necessary because local democracy was not working. Local mandates were often extremely weak because of the low turn-outs in local government elections. And surveys suggested that local issues did not feature in influencing the way people voted in local elections since they voted on national considerations. Counter-arguments to these points have been made with some vehemence. For example, although local government elections attract a lower turn-out than general elections, the former are held far more frequently.

To this extent, it is argued, local authorities are much more subject to electoral pressure than is Parliament. Also, the fact that in some areas people tend to vote the same way in both local and general elections should not be surprising. The argument does not invalidate the local mandate; it just means that the local mandate favours one party because that party is strongest locally.

Some political scientists have explored ways in which central–local relationships might be understood in more theoretical terms. Basically, three models have been fashioned, each based upon a different type of relationship.

● The first portrays local government as an *agency* for central government. In this model, local government is simply the servant of central government, implementing the policies which central government lays down. In terms of power, local government is subordinate to central power.

● The second model portrays the central–local relationship in terms of a *partnership* with both sides working together for common ends. The two partners might not be equal in terms of power, but local government is not totally subordinate to central government.

● The third and most recently developed model sees central–local links in terms of a *power-dependence* relationship. It is argued that both central government Departments and local authorities have a number of resources which each can use against the other. According to this model, central and local government are both independent of each other with neither having total control; their relationship is one of bargaining, exchange and negotiation. How might the 'power-dependence' relationship work in practice? Central government might supply (or refuse) financial resources to get a local authority to do (or not to do) something over which central government has no authority. R.A.W. Rhodes, who first applied this model to central–local relations, states that for both parties concerned 'their

relative power potential is a product of their resources, the rules of the game and the process of exchange ... the process of exchange is influenced by the resources of the participants, strategies, personalities' (Rhodes, 1981, pp. 97–108).

In a 20-year review of the central–local relationship, Rhodes identifies five distinct phases:

● **Partnership, 1970–4**: 'Consultation was the "normal" style of central–local relations throughout the post-war period until the mid-1970s. For most of this time, local service spending was buoyant, and the numbers of local-government employees grew fairly regularly'. (Rhodes 1992a, p. 206). In terms of policy implementation, central government adopted a consensual approach through fostering local government cooperation rather than forcing councils to comply with central policy through legislation. For example, a Labour minister achieved near universal comprehensive schooling by means of 'a strong letter of advice (backed up with Department of Education and Science controls over new school building), rather than by new legislation to compel councils to change their ways' (ibid., p. 206)

● **Corporatism, 1974–9**: 'Corporatism means that a few powerful organisations are extensively co-opted into closed relations with central government, taking on a dual role of representing their members to government and of controlling their members on behalf of government' (ibid., p. 207). The Labour Government, having incorporated the unions into a 'social contract' on wages and welfare, attempted to incorporate the local authority associations into policy-making on local government spending through a consultative body, the Consultative Council on Local Government Finance, 'remarkable because it brought the Treasury and local-authority representatives into face-to-face contact for the first time' (ibid., p. 207).

- **Direction, 1979–83:** The Thatcher Government was, as we have noted, committed to cutting local government spending as part of its policy to reduce public expenditure generally. The means of getting cuts in local government spending were provided by the Local Government, Planning and Land Act 1980, which introduced financial penalties for 'overspending' authorities. As Rhodes observed: 'Consultation was abandoned. Michael Heseltine used the Consultative Council to announce what he was going to do .... This shift epitomised the government's style: it knew best and consequently saw no need to consult and negotiate. Direction was the order of the day.' (Ibid., p. 209).

- **Abolition, 1983–7:** Some authorities chose to confront the government and exceeded their spending targets, such as the GLC and the Inner London Education Authority (ILEA). These authorities, along with the 'mets', were abolished. Their functions were devolved to district and borough councils, to a variety of public and private bodies, as well as upwards to central government. 'In effect' concluded Rhodes 'if local government would not do as it was told, it would be replaced or ignored.' (Ibid., p. 210)

- **Revolution, 1987–90:** Government policy changed direction from simply attempting to control local authority spending to introducing market forces into local government, best exemplified by the radical 'enabling' authority discussed on pp. 183–4. As Rhodes stated, 'The emphasis fell on accountability to the local electorate, responsiveness to clients, competition and contracting-out to the private sector, greater efficiency and better management.' (Ibid., p. 213) The government argued that the new community charge would make 'local authorities more accountable to their electors' by ensuring that 'the local electors know what the costs of their local services are, so that armed with this knowledge they can influence the spending decisions of their councils through the ballot box.' In the event

the community charge, or 'poll tax', proved to be a disastrous error of judgement by the Government, provoking widespread public disorder as well as considerable opposition within the Conservative Party.

To this can be added:

- **Further reforms, 1990 onwards:** Aspects of 'enablement' pursued with a Council Tax to replace the 'poll tax' together with discussions on the future structure and management of local government.

■ Local Government Finance

As we have seen, the Conservative Government's economic policy, aimed at controlling public expenditure, became increasingly involved in controlling local government finance. This situation became particularly acute in the eyes of Treasury ministers since they provided local authorities with the majority of their income. Table 11.1 shows, for example, that for 1991–2 central government grants accounted for 57.4 per cent of all council spending. According to the Treasury 'red book' estimates, only one pound in every ten of current and capital spending came from the 'poll tax'. The remaining nine pounds came from central government grants and the business rate. The percentage of revenue coming from central government had been even higher in the past, and to compensate for receiving less, some authorities began raising much more locally.

Since the government was in direct control of the block grant (formerly the rate support grant) it provided, it would appear to be an easy step for central government to take to extend its control

Table 11.1 *Local Authority Revenues, 1991–2*

	£bn	% of total
Poll tax	7.3	11.0
Business rates	14.1	21.2
Grants from central government	38.3	57.4
Other sources	6.9	10.4

over the element of revenue which councils raised locally. In reality, this became a bitter political struggle between increasingly dogmatic ministers and some alarmingly irresponsible councils.

From the government's point of view, local government had been guilty of 'overspending', with a relatively small number of 'high-spending' authorities contributing disproportionately to the problem. Throughout the 1980s the government had set up ever more stringent controls to limit local government spending.

Since most of the 'overspending' was in 'high-spending' Labour-controlled authorities, there was a demand for specific controls to contain their spending and not general controls which sometimes penalised 'low-spending' Conservative authorities. Overspending was calculated by how much an authority spent over and above what the government assessed it needed to spend, the Grant-Related Expenditure Assessment (GREA). Some low-spending Tory shires had been penalised for spending less than their GREA but more than their target. In 1986, spending targets for local authorities were scrapped, with the new system of central government control known as 'rate-capping' replacing them. Rate-capping enabled central government to control the budgets of overspending councils through setting upper limits on the amounts they could spend and the amounts they could raise in rates. An authority which ran into financial difficulties would no longer be able to get the money it needed to fund its spending from demanding higher rates because asking the public to pay 'excess' rates would be illegal.

Local government finance had become a 'policy mess' by the mid-1980s. On the one hand, 11 significant changes in local government finance had been introduced during the first two Thatcher Governments which had the effect of increasing uncertainty and making it very difficult for town halls to plan their budgets for the year ahead. Although councils lost £713 million in penalties by 1984, the penalty system was not preventing large rate increases. Local government spending continued to rise faster than government had planned. On the other hand, some local authorities had got themselves into a mess in trying to dodge central controls on spending. In

1985, for example, Liverpool City Council was left with enough resources to run its services for nine months but not for a full year. Councillors from the 'hard left' wanted to 'shut up shop' for three months and make council employees redundant. The Council avoided bankruptcy on this occasion by borrowing from Swiss banks. Other authorities, particularly in London, escaped government controls through 'Deferred Purchase Agreements' which were basically a form of borrowing. This loophole was closed by central government, leaving councils with the 'spend now, pay later' problem that debts have to be paid back one day.

The nuts and bolts of local government financing stayed in place after the introduction of the 'poll tax', even though the terminology changed. In 1990, for example, 21 authorities were [community] 'charge capped' because they planned to spend 12.5 per cent more on average than the Standard Spending Assessments (SSAs). The ideological hostility between the Conservative government and Labour authorities was still in evidence – as Wilson observed,

No Conservative controlled authorities were charge capped although many levied high charges. Conservative controlled Berkshire which had increased spending by 20.6% escaped capping while Labour-controlled Brent, whose spending had risen by 1.4% did not .... Invariably these [charge capped] councils were Labour controlled, thereby guaranteeing that 'party politics' was widely seen as a major motivating factor behind the specific capping formula utilised by the Minister, a formula which, it was held by some commentators, militated against Labour controlled inner-city councils. (Wilson 1990, pp. 3–4).

☐ Rate Reform

Since the time when Margaret Thatcher was a shadow Environment Minister in the mid-1970s, she championed the idea of abolishing the rating system and replacing it with a new method of raising local revenue. Rates were an ancient tax on property and were unpopular for a variety of reasons. They were a highly visible form of taxation unlike, for example, value-added tax

(VAT) which is 'hidden' within the price of goods. Rates are not directly related to the use made of local authority services: individuals in the 18–30 age group, for example, who made great use of services, paid disproportionately little in rates; improvements made to a property led to an increase in rates on that property; rates tended to hit poorer households hardest in the sense that they paid a higher proportion of their incomes in rates than more affluent households; and finally, rates were often based on the assumption that urban areas were wealthier than they actually were.

The advantages of rates tended to be procedural – they were easy to collect; they were cheap to administer; they were a form of tax which people understood and which it was difficult to avoid paying; and finally, there was great certainty about the amount of money rates would produce and they could be easily adjusted.

After intense deliberations during 1985–6, the Government came down in favour of a 'community charge' to replace the rates. It was very similar to a poll tax, although it was based on residence rather than on the electoral register. Critics, including many Tories, argued that the community charge was regressive. In other words, individuals would pay the same despite differences in income. The community charge would be a 'bureaucratic nightmare' according to some Tories, who pointed out that it would cost £400 million a year to collect – twice as much as the old rating system.

The Thatcher Government's rejoinder to these criticisms included the point that no taxation system was popular or perfect. The regressive nature of the community charge was no different from VAT where individuals pay the same rate regardless of whether they are rich or poor. The Government believed that a flat rate was appropriate for the consumption of local authority services. It admitted that the community charge would be more costly to administer but pointed out that many more people would be paying it. A total of 35 million individuals would pay the new community charge including 17 million who had never previously paid rates. This was seen as the great advantage of the community charge, since it is likely to make all people who use local authority services take an interest in the affairs of local government. Under the old rating system, many people who used local authority services voted in the local elections yet did not pay rates. The community charge, argued the Government, would restore the link between taxation and representation which had been absent in local government.

Poll Tax Reform

It had been argued that whatever system replaced the rates, it should have the following characteristics:

- It should be seen as a fair system of raising revenue from citizens.
- It should be easy to collect from those who paid it.
- It should be hard for dishonest citizens to evade payment.

The 'poll tax', it was argued, failed on all three counts, and the Government was thrown into a crisis entirely of its own making. When things began to go wrong at a very early stage in implementation, Margaret Thatcher acknowledged that 'adjustments' had to be made in the way the community charge worked. A six-month review took place which resulted in some amendments being made to 'transitional relief' and to some of the issues raised by worried Tory backbenchers, such as second home ownership and the plight of businessmen who 'lived above the shop'. Critics argued that this review changed little – the community charge remained a deeply flawed tax. What were the problems associated with the poll tax?

It was seen by many as even more unfair than the rates because people living under the same council would be paying the same amount, no matter how wealthy they were. Many of the poorest in the community receiving income support, and who had not previously paid rates, now found that they had to pay at least 20 per cent of the 'poll tax '.

As critics had predicted, collecting the 'poll tax' proved to be a bureaucratic nightmare for many councils. Generally speaking, it was twice as costly to collect as the rates. Often the cost of

---

Exhibit 11.1	*Rate reform: the alternatives*

- **Local Sales Tax:** This method of raising local revenue was opposed by many Conservatives because it was not consistent with the notion of the Tories being a tax-cutting party. The Treasury also disliked the idea of a local sales tax since it might limit the chancellor's freedom to raise VAT. Also, concern was expressed about the distorting effects this form of local tax would have if neighbouring authorities levied it at differing rates.
- **Local Income Tax:** This option was recommended by the Layfield Committee, 1976, and a decade later was supported strongly by the Alliance parties. But, as with local sales tax, it is contrary to the Tory party's tax-cutting image. Again the Treasury is opposed to this alternative because it would weaken the Department's control over income tax in general.
- **Poll Tax:** This alternative was opposed by a former Environment Secretary, Michael Heseltine, as well as by many others who did not want a tax based on the electoral register.
- **A combination of two or more of these alternatives or a hybrid fashioned from a compromise between two or more:** An example of the former would be a combination of a local sales tax together with a modified rating system; an example of the latter would be a 'variable poll tax' graduated according to income or the rateable value of the area lived in.

---

collection from the poorest in the community was greater than the amounts collected. Whereas the 'poll tax' proved easy to collect from rural and suburban areas, non-payment was a major problem with the mobile and shifting populations of the big inner cities.

Finally, the unfairness of the 'poll tax' provided a moral justification for some people who were seeking any excuse not to pay. For them, 'Can't Pay, Won't Pay' broke the habit of paying taxes. The 'poll tax' may have had the unintended effect of producing a 'culture of non-payment' which could result in greater evasion of any new tax introduced in the future.

The Council Tax

A government consultation document on local finance argued that the poll tax's replacement should be fashioned by five principles. Firstly, there should be clear lines of accountability in terms of local people seeing a link between their level of payments and council spending. People should agree generally that the new tax is fair. It should be easy to collect. There should be a fair sharing of the tax burden with more people, rather than fewer, contributing towards paying for council services. Finally, central government

should be able to control local authority spending through means of 'strong and effective capping powers'. With these principles in mind, government policy retained the uniform business rate but replaced the community charge with a new 'council tax', of which the main features are:

- **A single bill for each household.**

- **There will be no register of adults.** The bill falls on the occupier of the house – normally the 'head of the household'.

- **It will reflect the value of property.** Each domestic property – house, flat, bungalow etc. – will be allocated to a **valuation band**. The scheme first suggested by the Government included seven bands:

Band	*Property value band*	*Ratio of tax bill*
A	Up to £40 000	0.67
B	£40–52 000	0.78
C	£52–68 000	0.89
D	£68–88 000	1.00
E	£88–120 000	1.22
F	£120–160 000	1.44
G	Over £160 000	1.67

Later a new value band 'H' was added at the top end, for properties over £320 000. The ratio of tax bill shown in the final column refers to the proportion of the council tax paid; for example, a household living in a Band A home would pay two-thirds of the council tax; a Band D household would pay all of it; and a Band G household would pay one and two-thirds. A different scale of property band values will be used in Scotland and Wales.

- **It will allow rebates to 'the poorest section of the community'.** Even the poorest people in society had to pay 20 per cent of their 'poll tax'. People on very low incomes will receive full rebates of their council tax bill. Where only one person lives in a house, he or she will get a 25 per cent discount on the council tax bill.

- **It will relate the size of the council tax bills to the spending of each local authority.** As at present, the government grant to each council is based on a Standard Spending Assessment of what is needed for each council to provide a standard level of services. In future this will be adjusted for each council according to the spread of properties within each band. So, in theory, all households in the same value band across the country will pay the same council tax for the same level of service. If a council decides to spend more in order to provide a higher standard of service then, subject to capping, the council tax would go up accordingly. In other words, there will still be a strong link between what an authority spends and the level of the council tax locally.

In many ways the council tax is a hybrid tax (see Exhibit 11.1) which is based on principles found in a variety of other taxes. For example, it contains elements of a **property tax**, since it reflects the value of property, a **poll tax**, since there is a personal element with two or more adults paying the full tax, and a **tax based on income**, since the least well-off will receive rebates. Whether in practice the council tax represents a happy blend of elements or 'the

worst of all worlds' remains to be seen. Some critics of the council tax predict that it will not prove as 'efficient' as the rates since it still involves 'counting heads', and that councils will receive many appeals from people about their property having been put into the wrong band.

■ Responding to Customers and Voters

Political scientists have noted that the democratic link between local authorities and the populace can range from 'authentic participation', where the electorate shares power in making decisions, to 'bogus participation', where the public may be given the feeling that they are participating whilst not actually being allowed to influence any decisions. In a recent study, John Gyford has redefined these links in terms of three broad relationships. Firstly, there is the **participative** relationship in which the electorate take a real part in local government through sharing in decision-making and service provision. Non-elected individuals may be co-opted on to council committees, tenants may participate in running their estates, and parents may participate in the local management of schools.

The link between a local authority and its public may be **consultative** in nature with the electorate having the right to be heard even if no direct part is taken in decision-making. For example:

> Some councils have established consultative and liaison committees with social service user groups and voluntary organisations in line with the recommendations of the Seebohm Report in 1968. Housing departments have set up consultative committees and councillor-tenant meetings. Leisure and recreation departments have devised ways of consulting users of their facilities in the sporting and artistic fields. Planning departments have employed a variety of means to consult public opinion on planning proposals since the publication of the Skeffington Report in 1969 (Gyford, 1991, p. 82).

Finally, there is the **informative** relationship. It has to be acknowledged that most people do not

1 Traditional passive roles	2 New active roles	3 Character of active roles	4 Mode of provision	5 Nature of related initiatives
Ratepayer	Shareholder	Protective	Market-based and privatised	Municipal pluralism with a private sector leading edge
Client	Consumer	Instrumental	Individual consumer responsive	Informative and consultative
Voter	Citizen	Developmental	Democratic and collectivist	Participative and consultative

Source: Gyford, 1991, p. 181.

Table 11.2   *Three models of change*

wish to become actively involved in the local decision-making process and are happy to leave it to others in local government to supply them with the services they want. But even those not wishing to participate in local government require information from local government about the services provided. Some councils have made it easier for the public to gain such information through setting up 'one-stop information shops' in the town hall or library. Rather than members of the public having to traipse from one department to another in search of information, some councils provide 'a contact point for all council services, together with information on local organisations and their activities, free "hot-lines" to all council departments, space for displays and promotions by both the council and outside bodies and a tourist information centre' (ibid., p. 109).

How far have the radical changes which have taken place in local government affected the relationship between citizens and their elected representatives? Possible ways in which the relationship may be redefined are set out in Table 11.2. The debate then focuses on which set of roles and relationships brings councils 'closer to the public'. Would the enabling authority, responding to market forces, provide exactly the right services at the right quality which local consumers demand? Or would it provide too narrow a range of services, ignoring those demands not backed by cash from the less well-off amongst the public? Or, finally, would the citizen role draw the public and councils closer through giving influence to all members of the public in decisions about what services should be provided? The development of

local government in the years ahead will be influenced by the outcome of this debate.

□ *The Political Dimension*

In what ways might party politics influence the links between councils and the public? One researcher, Gerry Stoker, concluded that the willingness of councils to respond to various types of pressure groups depended closely on their prevailing politics. In broad terms, in urban left-wing authorities

> Voluntary sector, cause and community groups are highly active and the local authorities have responded to and supported this development ... tenants', women's, ethnic minority and single-issue cause groups will be amongst those that are active. Good relations with local authority trade unions and other trade unions are also prized by councillors. Relationships with other producer interests notably business organisations may, however, be antagonistic and even hostile. (Stoker, 1991, p. 133).

Soft-left Labour councils 'are less likely to support radical cause groups and more willing to work with business interests.' (Ibid.) In centre-right Labour authorities, and those where Liberal Democrats have influence, pressure-group activity appears actively encouraged. There is, however, preferential treatment of groups representing the voluntary sector and professional groups over and above the treatment of some community groups. For example, councils may be cool towards tenants' associations because they are seen as being led by extremists and hostile towards residents' associations which are viewed as selfish or simply a front for the Conservative Party.

Suburban and rural authorities dominated by Conservative and Liberal Democrat councils have produced a different pattern of pressure-group activity. What might be described as 'respectable' voluntary sector groups, along with farming, landowning and environmental interests play an active role. But in such areas 'some interests may never find a voice, for example, agricultural workers or those who require housing for rent' as well as other politically unacceptable cause groups (ibid., p. 134). In authorities led by radical New Right Conservatives 'there is likely to be a willingness to work closely with a select group of middle-class residents' associations, amenity groups and business interests' but a hostility towards any groups considered to be left-wing, such as CND, Shelter and feminist organisations.

□ *The Electoral Dimension*

Margaret Thatcher was said to use the May local government election results as a guide for timing when to call general elections. In the early postwar years the equivalent local elections results would not have been considered as a reliable predictor of general elections held in the following month. This is because local government was then far less 'political' in nature. But this is not to say that contemporary local government is no more than a reflection of national politics at the local level. For example, hung parliaments, producing coalition or minority government, have been rare in postwar national politics. Yet in local government, hung councils and coalition politics are relatively common: in 1985, 25 of the 46 counties had hung councils.

Where local elections produced a hung council with no one party having overall control, local parties had to bargain with each other in order to produce a working arrangement. In some cases, the largest of the parties governed with the support of another party in a coalition; in other cases, the smallest party was left holding the balance of power and able to exert the most influence on policy-making.

Some political commentators argued that hung councils were more democratic than councils ruled by one party. This was because in many hung councils the chairpersons of both the council and its committees rotated between two or even three parties, and council officers were now responsive to all parties and not just the ruling party. Local government appeared far more open under hung councils, since meetings were no longer 'rubber stamps' of policy previously decided in private. Councils were reflecting all the opinions within the local electorate, since no policy options were ruled out because they were politically unacceptable to the ruling party.

In contrast, councils firmly under the control of one party seemed undemocratic by comparison, with the ruling party meeting in secret to decide policy prior to the council meeting.

Local government elections have been described by some as 'limited exercises in democracy' because they attract far lower turn-outs than do general elections. Average turn-out in contested elections in Metropolitan Counties was 39% between 1973–8 compared with 75% in the four General Elections in the 1970s. Others have challenged this view, saying that lower turn-out is more than offset by the greater frequency of local elections. Also, they add, the lower levels of turn-out distort the pattern of political opinion held by the electorate as a whole. The problem of local democracy, it is argued, should be viewed from another perspective. The problem of low turn-out might be a reflection of local authorities which are still too large and remote, and of local electorates which are still under-represented. On an international scale, Britain has one councillor for every 1 800 people compared with one member for between 250 and 450 people in Europe. George Jones and John Stewart argue that the reason for this sharp contrast is because Britain has fewer councils, with the result that Britain's councillors have to represent a much bigger electorate. This results in local government being 'less deeply embedded in local communities' (G.W. Jones and J. Stewart, 1989). They point out that in countries where the ratio is around one councillor to 300 people, councillors are actually known and recognised by their electorate to a far greater extent than in Britain. In this sense, therefore, the state of local government democracy in Britain should not be judged in terms of low turn-out but by the poor quality of representation which exists.

How strong is the link between local government elections and national politics? Political journalists have encouraged the view that local government elections results can be converted, through calculation of the 'equivalent popular vote' (see page 272), into predicting which party would have won a general election had one been called. The assumption underlying this approach is that local factors play little or no role in local government elections. As Patrick Dunleavy has argued, 'local election results overwhelmingly reflect national swings of opinion for or against the incumbent government, as they are modified by the different social bases in different areas.' (Dunleavy, 1980, p. 136)

This view, however, has been modified by researchers for the Widdicombe Committee (1986) on local government. They found that local events can, 'in a small but not insignificant number of cases, ... have a decisive impact on individual ward-level elections, and occasionally, as a consequence, on the overall election outcome within an authority.' (Research Volume 1, 1986, p. 44) Others giving evidence to Widdicombe

thought that '80 per cent of local voters vote exactly in accordance with their national party choice. The remainder it could be claimed are making a local choice.' (Stoker, 1991, p. 53) If this estimate is accurate, then for at least a fifth of the electorate voting under typical circumstances, local factors are important. Whilst defenders of local government might wish that the proportion voting this way was greater, it represents for them a welcome departure from the pessimistic view that council elections are no more than a local reflection of national politics.

■ Local Government Personnel

□ *Councillors*

Councillors are not typical of the population at large in terms of social class. For example, only a quarter of councillors have working-class jobs. Councillors tend to be better educated and to earn more than the average person in Britain. Councillors also come from the older sections of the population: only 8.5 per cent of councillors are aged between 21 and 34 years, yet 28.5 per cent of the total population is in this age group. In contrast, people between the ages of 55 and 74 years form 29.5 per cent of the total population, yet 47.5 per cent of councillors are in this age group. A significant difference of another kind is found in the 17 per cent of councillors that are female. Although this is far below the percentage of women in the general population, it is far ahead of the 9 per cent of women MPs in the new Parliament of 1992. Clearly, participation in local politics is easier for women than is participation in national politics, since the former political role is easier to combine with the domestic roles of many women.

It has been argued that paying a salary to councillors would attract more women to come forward as candidates, as well as more working-class and young candidates. This was considered by the Robinson Committee (1977) which recommended an annual payment of £1000 a year for councillors, in addition to travelling and subsistence expenses. But Robinson fell well short of proposing that councillors should be paid a full-

Table 11.3   *Average population size of local authorities*

England and Wales	122 740
Sweden	29 527
Denmark	17 963
Australia	14 125
USA	12 000
Norway	8 891
New Zealand	7 980
Italy	6 717
Canada	5 011
West Germany	2 694
France	1 320

Source: Widdicombe Report (1986, p. 140, Table 5.4).

time salary. Some felt that paying councillors would attract the 'wrong sort of person' who would be encouraged to stand for office by thoughts of the salary rather than the idea of public service.

A survey of councillors carried out by Tony Wood and Gerald Crawley reported some interesting findings regarding gender and party differences in the attitudes and conduct of councillors. They found that on average councillors spent more than 30 hours a week on council business, but also that this average was made up from widely varying amounts of time. Firstly, women councillors work longer each week on council work than their male colleagues. In general women spend 22 per cent more time each week on council matters.

Women appeared to be more committed towards their council work than men since they 'expressed a more community centred view of their duties and were much readier to define their

Table 11.4   *Councillors by political party membership, age, gender, activity status, socio-economic group and income*

	Con. %	Lab. %	Lib. %	Ind. %	Other %	All councillors %
Age: 60+	37	32	22	52	30	36
45–49	42	33	30	36	33	37
18–44	19	33	49	11	33	26
Gender: Male	78	83	79	81	81	81
Female	21	17	21	19	19	19
Activity status:						
Employed (full or part-time)	64	59	74	47	67	60
Unemployed	2	8	3	1	2	4
Retired	24	22	13	40	30	25
Permanently sick/disabled	–	2	–	1	–	1
Looking after a home	9	6	9	9	7	8
Other	–	1	–	–	–	1
Socio-economic group:						
Professional	11	6	15	8	5	9
Employer/manager	42	20	28	37	26	32
Intermediate non-manual	14	22	23	11	30	18
Junior non-manual	8	11	15	6	2	10
Skilled manual/own						
account non-professional	10	25	8	14	14	16
Semi-skilled manual	1	8	4	5	–	4
Unskilled manual	–	2	–	1	–	1
Armed Forces/NA	12	8	8	16	5	11
Income						
15 000+	25	7	18	14	33	16
£10 000–£14 999	22	23	29	17	2	22
£6000–£9000	23	28	23	27	25	26
Up to £5999	22	38	23	29	23	28
None	1	1	2	2	–	1
Refused/NA	8	4	3	10	12	7
Base	(595)	(496)	(133)	(224)	(43)	(1557)

Note: As the numbers of Scottish National Party, Social Democratic Party, Plaid Cymru and 'other' party members are too small for separate analysis, all have been grouped into one category of 'other' political party.
Source: Widdicombe (39 1986c), Table 4.5, p. 39.
Source: Stoker (1991, p. 36).

council work as a full time job than were male councillors.' (T. Wood and G. Crawley, 1987). Younger women councillors with children could only manage if they lived in what the researchers called a 'political household'. Typically in such a household 'both adult members have strong ideologically based beliefs which makes their exceptional efforts worthwhile. In such cases, the husband's support for his wife in terms of housework and childcare is not only given for personal reasons, but because he believes equally strongly in the political work she is doing.'

The researchers also found that there was a difference in the time spent on council work between Labour and Liberal councillors on the one hand, and Conservative councillors on the other. Labour councillors spent 30 per cent more time on council work than Tories, Liberals 20 per cent more. In contrast to Labour and Liberal councillors, most Conservative councillors 'defined their role in more limited terms. It was seen as one of a number of leisure interests, but certainly nothing more than a voluntary activity requiring only limited commitment.'

☐ Councillors at Work

Where does power lie in local government policy-making? What influence do elected members have in making the decisions which affect their local communities? There are no simple answers to these questions, because different patterns of power exist in different authorities. Generally speaking, however, the prevailing situation is that there is a 'joint élite' comprising 'committee chairs and vice-chairs together with chief officers and their deputies' (Stoker, 1991, p. 92). But it has been stressed that this is not the situation to be found in every authority, and even where it does exist, the joint élite is not necessarily a unified and cohesive group. What might appear to be a joint élite is, in fact, made up of two or more élites competing with each other for influence. In many cases, the new management structures introduced into local government have opened up the policy-making process, enabling less senior officers and councillors to take policy initiatives.

Thus the picture of leading councillors, together with senior officers, dominating the policy-making process is an exaggeration. There are cases where the ruling party group exerts as much, or more, influence than the leading councillors. The case-study at the end of this chapter illustrates how internal party splits can undermine the position of senior members and officers. Although it is not commonplace, it is possible for inexperienced yet assertive councillors to initiate policy and play a 'crucial role in developing a whole range of new planning and industrial policies. They persuaded party leaders and the party group to adopt the intiatives and subsequently took an important role in the process of implementation.' (Stoker, 1991, p. 96) It is also possible, as we shall see below, for unelected local party members to pressurise a reluctant party group into adopting policies it would have otherwise decided against.

The roles of the 'party caucus' and non-elected constituency party members became a matter of political controversy during the 1980s. Some argued that the role of the party caucus distorted the working of the council system. In authorities where one political party had a ruling majority, the party caucus may have become the dominant decision-making body. Although there may have been nothing intrinsically wrong in this since it represented the reality of power, some voices became alarmed by irregularities which had increased in custom and practice. In a number of authorities, including some London boroughs, those permitted at group meetings included not only the elected councillors but also members of constituency committees. Decisions arrived at by both elected and non-elected members of the party caucus would then be rubber-stamped in council meetings.

The Widdicombe Committee examined practices and procedures in local government and made a number of important recommendations. One proposal was that committees which take decisions for the council as a whole should reflect the political make-up of the whole council. It was felt that such committees take decisions on behalf of the whole council, not just part of it. Where a party group existed, this should be made clear to the public. Widdicombe recommended that decisions should be taken only by elected members.

□ *Local Government Officers*

Local authorities employ administrators to assist them in carrying out their duties and in implementing their policies. The relationship between officers and councillors is frequently the focus of academic attention because it contains a number of inherent tensions. In the crudest sense, these tensions spring from the differences between professional administrators and amateur politicians. The former are selected for their qualities of expert knowledge, experience and professionalism. The latter are elected as candidates of political parties, often in elections with low turnouts. Frequently, the electorate will have little personal knowledge of the candidates and vote for them solely on party political lines.

There may be occasions when officers recommend a policy which is rejected by members. Typically, the officers will feel that the policy formed on the basis of their professional expertise is superior. It will develop out of their specialised knowledge of the problems concerned and, in this sense, is politically neutral. Councillors may not perceive professional values as being politically neutral and will prefer policies which are consistent with their own party's political philosophy. Also, councillors will be concerned with the political impact of policies on the electorate and may reject the 'best' policy if it is unattractive to local voters.

Some commentators have been concerned that officers wield too much influence in local government. This situation arises in part from the fact that the officers are permanent whereas councillors are essentially temporary, coming and going on the tides of electoral fortune. They feel that the contest between the permanent full-time professionals and the temporary part-time councillors is not evenly matched. This is why some support the case for full-time salaried councillors in the belief that this reform would allow councillors to build up their expertise and thereby become a match for the professionals.

In most authorities the senior officer is known as the chief executive, and the most important officer–member relationship is that between the chief executive and the leader of the council. It was sometimes alleged that this officer–member link could develop into a powerful, cosy but essentially private relationship in which deals were 'sewn up', sometimes with scant regard for the wishes of other elected members. But as we have seen, recent changes in the world of local government, including greater politicisation, more assertive councillors and even the election of hung councils, have challenged this 'behind closed doors' view of decision-making.

■ Local Government Structure

Providing a system of local government that matches the demographic structure is a complex affair. Most of the population live in one of the great conurbations, but some live in small market towns, and others in remote rural areas such as Dartmoor or East Anglia. Some areas are much more prosperous than others: unemployment is relatively low in the South and higher in the North. Some populations have a different age-structure from others: for example the 'dependency ratio' – calculated as the number of young children under 15 and people of pensionable age per 100 people of working age – is 0.99 in Worthing, 0.87 in Eastbourne but only 0.45 in Oxford and 0.20 in the City of London. Finally, some areas have relatively large ethnic communities which may have special needs. Thus, in terms of the diversity found amongst the population alone, organising one single pattern of local government that can be applied across the country seems an impossibility.

□ *The Heseltine Review*

It came as no surprise when, during his second term at the Department of the Environment (DOE), Michael Heseltine set up a review of *(i)* local government finance, which resulted in the replacement of the poll tax by the council tax *(ii)* the internal management of local government, and *(iii)* the structure of local authorities. In terms of the latter, it was argued that a new structure would be required as councils moved from a providing to an enabling role. The Local

Table 11.5 *The organisation of elected local government, 1990*	
	Main functions
Wales	
8 county councils	Strategic planning, transport, police, fire services, education and social services
37 district councils	Housing, local planning, environmental health and leisure services
About 800 community and town councils	Consultation
Scotland	
9 regions	Strategic planning, transport, police, fire services, education, social services and water
53 districts	Housing, local planning, environmental health and leisure services
Over 1200 community councils	Consultation
3 island areas	All regional and district powers
England Non-metropolitan areas	
39 counties	Much the same split of respons-
296 districts	ibilities as authorities in Wales
About 900 local (parish & town) councils	Consultation and local amenities
Metropolitan areas (West Midlands, South Yorkshire, West Yorkshire, Tyne & Wear, Greater Manchester & Merseyside) 36 districts	Education, social services, housing, local planning, environmental health, leisure services; and (via joint boards) transport, police, fire services and civil defence; and (via other joint arrangements) strategic planning, waste disposal, grants to voluntary organisations, trading standards, etc.
London 32 London boroughs City of London Corporation	Housing, social services, local planning leisure, environmental health, education; and (via joint boards) fire services and civil defence; and (via other joint arrangements) strategic planning, waste disposal, grants to voluntary organisations, etc.

Source: Stoker (1991, p. 30).

Government Act 1988 required authorities to put specified services out to Compulsory Competitive Tendering, and the Education Reform Act 1988 and the Housing Act 1988 provided for 'opting out' from authority control. In short, local authorities were being 'reduced', which brought with it the opportunity to simplify the structure that would be needed in the 1990s.

The two-tier system which applied to most of Britain was seen by some as too complicated, because local citizens were never sure which tier was responsible for what (see Table 11.5). At the same time, there were political tensions between the two tiers which resulted in more confusion and inefficiency. Not everyone agreed that these weaknesses amounted to reasons serious enough to warrant abolishing one tier, Indeed, it was argued, two tiers in local government bring certain advantages. Above all, two-tier structures combine economy with maximum local responsiveness. For example, the top tier can obtain economies of scale in providing appropriate services to large populations (such as policing), whilst the lower tier can provide services which require closer contact with the public (such as housing). A Local Government Commission will advise the government on what shape the reforms should take, but it is clear that many English counties will disappear as new unitary authorities are recommended.

From the outset of the Heseltine review, it was clear that the unitary (single-tier) authorities which existed after the abolition of the GLC and the mets was the ministerially preferred model of local government for the future. Exhibit 11.2 sets out the principal contents of the structure review for England, Scotland and Wales.

Internal Structure

The third of the Heseltine consultation papers was concerned with the internal management of local authorities. It was recognised that different structures would suit the needs of different authorities, and that no single management structure should be recommended universally. Where changes took place, they should *(i)* promote more effective and business-like decision making *(ii)* enhance the scrutiny of decisions *(iii)* increase the interest

---

Exhibit 11.2   *Synopsis of main local government structure proposals*

Local Government Structure (in England)
- Establishment of an independent Local Government Commission to consult locally and advise the Secretary of State on structural reforms.
- A move towards unitary authorities where these do not already exist (i.e. outside Greater London and the Metropolitan areas).
- A flexible approach. In some cases existing large district councils may become the new unitary authority. Elsewhere existing authorities may be merged or new authorities created. In some cases two tiers could be retained.
- An enhanced role for parish councils to be considered.
- The Commission to have powers to make recommendations about how any local government functions which would need arrangements across a wider area than that covered by unitary authorities should be handled.
- The first new unitary authorities to be in place by 1st April 1994.

Local Government Structure Proposals
(Scotland and Wales)
The **Welsh** Secretary (David Hunt) announced on 17 June 1991 proposals to move to single tier local authorities, although no timetable for implementation has been set. Unlike the proposals for England and Scotland, the Welsh re-structuring is likely to see an exclusively one-tier arrangement in future. Each of the new one-tier authorities will carry out all local government functions. Boundary changes have been suggested, which would see the removal of all the Welsh County Councils created in 1974, along with the 37 districts beneath them. In their place would be 12, 20 or 24 unitary authorities. Under the 20-authority option, several of the old pre-1974 counties – such as Pembrokeshire, Anglesey and Cardiganshire – could re-appear in roughly their old boundaries, though as single all-purpose authorities. The most recent proposal (1994) is for 21 unitary authorities.

In **Scotland** a similar move to (28) single all-purpose authorities is envisaged although as in England two-tier arrangements might remain in some places. The Consultation Paper hints that the four cities – Edinburgh, Glasgow, Aberdeen and Dundee – will become unitary authorities, but makes no other boundary suggestions. It is envisaged that it will take 'a few years' to implement these proposals.

Both the Scottish and Welsh proposals effectively rule out the creation of national assemblies with devolved legislative powers.

Source: Greenwood (1991–2, pp. 68–9).

---

taken by the public in local government, and *(iv)* provide scope for councillors to devote more time to their constituency role. The paper includes various options 'as an aid to the consultation process', which are summarised by John Greenwood in Exhibit 11.3.

The Future of Local Government

The state of local government has been described as a 'policy mess'. A large part of that mess was caused by the Thatcher flagship policy of introducing the community charge or 'poll tax'. The new council tax, despite its problems, represents an improvement in this important area of local government finance. But there are still many other fundamental issues concerning local government which have yet to be resolved. The review inaugurated by Michael Heseltine questions the very purpose of local government. Is there really any need for local government? If so, what functions should it perform and how should its services be delivered to the public?

There are those who defend local government's existence as part of the democratic process in Britain, and who see local democracy as an im-

---

Exhibit 11.3   *The internal management of local authorities*

Options for the future: While stressing that the government wishes not to emphasise uniform changes, but to encourage individual solutions appropriate to local circumstances, several options are presented 'as an aid to the consultation process'. The following models are described in the Consultation Paper.

- **Retention of the present system**
  It is acknowledged that in some local authorities the present system works satisfactorily, and where this happens the government do not wish to impose changes. Elsewhere, however, as the government points out, councils have sought to streamline arrangements: for example, by establishing joint member/officer working parties to deal with specific projects, or by delegating urgent decision-taking to small representative sub-committees or to officers. The government expresses the view that, because of the existing legislative framework, there are limits to the new systems and streamlining that can be adopted. If the present system is retained consideration, it suggests, might be given to allowing councils to delegate decision-making to committee chairmen (at present prohibited by law). More controversially, consideration might be given to removing the requirement, given legislative force only as recently as 1989, for minority representation on committees. A theme running through the consultation paper is that the present arrangements – which vest decision-taking in the full council – blur the executive and constituency roles of councillors, and involve minority party members in time consuming activity out of all proportion to their influence. In future, it is suggested, committees *might* consist primarily or exclusively of those members of the majority party with executive responsibilities, although as a safeguard minorities could be given more opportunity to demand debates in council on specific issues and to question 'the executive'.

- **Cabinet system**
  This option, essentially, envisages the introduction of the existing central government model into local government. An executive of elected councillors (or 'ministers') would be chosen from the council as a whole, possibly on the nomination of the leader of the majority party. The majority of council members, whether in the party forming the executive or in opposition parties, would not take part in day-to-day decision making. They would scrutinise the work of the executive, and concentrate on constituency cases. The whole council, however, would be responsible for approving the budget.

- **Council managers**
  In this option the council would appoint an officer to run authorities on a day-to-day basis. The council would retain *overall* policy responsibilities, and could scrutinise the managers' work but would have little involvement in day-to-day decision-making.

- **Directly elected executives**
  Under this arrangement the executive (or Cabinet) would be directly elected by the local electorate. This would involve separate elections to the council and to the executive, but in other respects the executive would operate in the same way as the cabinet model.

- **Directly elected mayor**
  A variation of the previous option which Mr Heseltine was widely known to have supported whilst on the back benches. A directly elected single individual would take over the council's executive responsibilities. In an arrangement similar to that found in many cities in the USA, the 'mayor' would be elected separately from the council. The Consultation Paper leaves open the question of whether the directly elected mayor should be able to make political appointments ('ministers') to support him.

Source: Greenwood (1991–2).

portant complement to parliamentary democracy. Whilst general elections measure the electorate's preferences at national level, local government responds to what its electorates want locally. In other words, the ballot box ensures that local government provides the services which are most demanded by voters.

This view has been challenged by those who argue that a greater reliance on market forces is the most efficient way of responding to what people want locally. In other words, more competition, greater consumer choice and an increased use of the private sector is the most efficient way of providing what local government customers want. Under these new circumstances, the most important role of local government is to provide the structure within which greater competition and choice will take place.

How is local government going to solve the problems of decaying urban areas, associated with social unrest, poor housing, inadequate schooling, ill health and high crime rates? Will the Citizen's Charter reduce the alienation felt by people living in the deprived inner cities? Or is the Citizen's Charter a sick joke when confronted with the multiple problems of poverty experienced by an increasing number of people living in desperate circumstances? Will the future involve local government assuming additional managerial responsibilities, such as community care, or entering new 'empowerment' partnerships with local people? Will urban unemployment, poverty and other social ills be tackled indirectly by local government through encouraging local people to participate in regenerating their communities from within?

Summary

Commentators have observed that since the 1950s local government has become increasingly political in nature. During the 1980s ideas from the New Right began to redefine the very purpose of local government, from being a direct provider of services to an indirect enabling role in service provision. Along with this radical shift are more subtle changes in the roles and rela-tionships between voters and elected members. Reforms are called for in local government structure in order to facilitate the new working relationships underpinned by greater reliance on market forces.

Questions

1. Is there a case for local government in Britain?

2. To what extent can it be said that local government is 'alive and kicking' in Britain?

3. 'Recent developments have upset the balance between central and local government.' Explain the nature of this balance and the ways in which it may have been 'upset'.

4. 'The community charge was a moral tax, despite its unpopularity with the public.' Examine the case for and against the introduction of the community charge (or 'poll tax'). In what ways is the council tax an improvement on the community charge?

5. Explain the philosophy behind the case for 'enabling' local authorities.

6. High levels of poverty are now found in Liverpool. A recent city council survey found that 40 per cent of the city's population live in 'poverty' with 15 per cent living in 'intense poverty'. Around a third of the population is either unemployed, sick or retired. Despite attempts to 'regenerate' Liverpool's economy, unemployment is running close to the 20 per cent level. Around three-quarters of Liverpool's 50 000 council tenants receive housing benefit, and in the poorest areas, two-thirds of school pupils receive free school dinners. Not surprisingly, the 'poll tax' has added to the town's problems: around 40 per cent have not yet paid, with poll tax arrears amounting to £37 million.

A central controversy in the town's politics is the role played by Militant. Although the days when Derek Hatton and Tony Mulhearn wielded power are over, the hard left still remain. Writing in the *Sunday Times* (6.1.91) David Selbourne states:

> On the 99-seat city council there are, in effect, now two Labour parties .. 'Harry Rimmer's mob' is composed of 33 more-or-less steady 'Kinnockites' or 'moderates'. Closely advised by Walworth Road minders, and hard-pressed by a district auditor armed with new statutory powers, they are struggling – in growing recession and with Militant trade unionists breathing down their necks – to avoid illegality in the financial management of the city. Their policy is to increase revenue (as by raising council rents) and to cut costs, including by sacking council workers .... The other Labour party (or gang) consists of a 30 strong 'Broad Left' .... The Broad Left is flatly opposed to cuts in jobs and services, rent increases, competitive tendering for public services – now being made compulsory – and cooperation with Harry Rimmer .... The Broad Left is accused by the Kinnockites of being 'out of touch with reality'; the Broad Left heavies – claiming to be pursuing 'principled socialist policies' – denounce the Kinnockites as 'crypto-Tories' [like hidden or concealed Tories].

Answer the following questions using the text above as well as your own knowledge:

- What are the main policy differences concerning finance and services between moderate Labour councillors and those from the Broad Left? What are the attitudes of these two factions towards each other? Which faction, if any, does David Selbourne appear least sympathetic towards?
- Why did Liverpool's relations with central government involve so much political conflict during the 1980s?

Assignment

☐ *Why do they do it?*

The following extract is based on Barron *et al.* (1991 pp. 42–3).

> We decided to ask political activists (councillors, candidates and non-candidates) a series of deliberately open-ended questions regarding their decision to stand – or not – for their local council. We received a wide variety of responses, of which the following are examples:

> I'm not the sort of person to be able to sit back if I don't agree with what's going on. I can't just sit back and do nothing, I have to become involved. (Daphne Herriott, Conservative candidate and town councillor)

> Mrs Carlisle asked me if I would stand for selection. I didn't think I was ready. There may come a time .... But I didn't feel I was ready then. I hadn't thought about it enough. (Audrey Lightfoot, Conservative Party member and non-candidate)

Table 11.6   *Pressures on councillors*

Externally imposed ←————————————————————→ *Self-generated*

Structural changes to local government
    e.g. larger authorities and larger wards.
        Electoral pressures
            e.g. increasing electoral volatility, more hung councils.
                Socio-demographic changes
                    e.g. increasing number of old people.
                        Economic pressures
                            e.g. scarcer resources, unemployment.
                                Central government pressures
                                    e.g. more complicated legislation, more central intervention
                                        Community pressures
                                            e.g. from local parties and interest groups
                                                Councillors' own interests
                                                    e.g. implementing the manifesto, distrust of senior officers.

Adapted from Widdicombe Report (1986, p. 63) by Barron, Crawley and Wood (1991, p. 74).

At the time, my branch was rather small and it took me three months to decide whether I'd do it or not – with very little confidence, I might add .... I know what I wanted to do, and what I wanted to change, but I didn't really know that [the council] was the avenue I wanted to do it through. (Pauline Smith, Labour backbencher)

How can we make sense of these various reactions? In our view, these responses suggest a subtle interplay between the resources available to them, the opportunities open to them and personal motivations and intentions. Our general conclusion was that candidature was not necessarily a deliberate or consciously worked-for objective, as the classic model would lead us to expect, but nor was it strictly an 'accidental' outcome.

... we see this as a process of drift, 'a gradual process of movement, largely unperceived by the actor', the outcome of which may at any stage be accidental or unpredictable

Some individuals who eventually become councillors engage initially in sporadic community activity, may become party members, hold party office and stand for an unwinnable seat before successfully contesting a local election. For these people, the final decision to stand for election may be seen as the culmination of an extended process which commences long before the formal selection stage.

... Some candidates – having been persuaded merely to fly the flag for their party – had no real intention of becoming councillors and felt it would be personally disastrous if they were elected.

(i)   'People stand for election as councillors for a variety of reasons.' Explain at least two different sets of reasons and motives behind individuals' willingness to stand for office.

(ii)   Explain the sort of pressures that councillors may have to cope with in office. Which councillors are likely to be subject to the greatest pressures? How might the pressures experienced by many councillors have been greater in the 1980s and 1990s than in the 1960s and 1970s?

(iii) Evaluate the case for councillors being full-time paid representatives.

(iv)   The extract mentions some individuals who might be described as 'reluctant councillors'. Explain how these people ended up in this role.

Further reading

Greenwood, J. (1991–2) 'Local Government in the 1990s: The Consultation Papers on Structure, Finance and Internal Management', *Talking Politics*, 4: 2, pp. 62–9.

Gyford, J. (1991) *Citizens, Consumers and Councils: Local Government and the Public* (London: Macmillan).

Horton, S. (1990) 'Local Government 1979–89: A Decade of Change' in S. Savage and L. Robins (eds) *Public Policy Under Thatcher* (London: Macmillan) pp. 172–86.

Rhodes, R.A.W. (1992) 'Local Government Finance' in D. Marsh and R.A.W. Rhodes (eds) *Implementing Thatcherite Policies* (Buckingham: Open University Press) 1992, pp. 50–64.

Rhodes, R.A.W. (1992) 'Local Government' in B. Jones and L. Robins (eds) *Two Decades in British Politics* (Manchester University Press) pp. 205–18.

Stoker, G. (1991) *The Politics of Local Government* (London: Macmillan).

Wilson, D. (1990) 'More Power to the Centre? The Changing Nature of Central Government/Local Authority Relationships', *Talking Politics*, 3: 1, pp. 2–7.

■ *Chapter 12* ■

Parliament

The central concern of this chapter is the role of Parliament in national politics. We examine the importance of party to the working of the House of Commons, the nature of the representativeness of the lower House of Parliament, the functions of Parliament in the political system, party organisation, recent changes in parliamentary behaviour and organisation, the role of the House of Lords and prospects for the future. The theme of party is the connecting link between these topics. It is argued that the role of Parliament in the political system has to be understood primarily in terms of the working of the party system within the context of a democratic electorate channelled in a particular way by the electoral system (Chapter 14). We begin by exploring this key statement.

■ The Importance of Party in the House of Commons

The House of Commons is the country's premier assembly. It consists of 651 MPs returned by that number of single-member constituencies, each elected on a simple majority by about 67 000 electors on average. MPs are elected as representatives of party, and party underpins their activities once in the House.

Table 12.1 shows how party determines the composition of the House of Commons, structuring it decisively into a party of government (Conservative) and a party of official opposition

Conservative	336	Governing party
Labour	271	Official Opposition party
Liberal Democrat	20	
Ulster Unionist	13	
Scottish National Party	3	Combined opposition parties
Plaid Cymru	4	
Social Democratic and Labour Party	4	
Overall Conservative majority	21	

Table 12.1 *Party allegiance in the House of Commons after the 1992 General Election*

(Labour) flanked by several much smaller opposition parties. Party underlies the activities of government in the House of Commons in four ways – by providing it with a programme based on its election manifesto, which forms the basis of the legislation it puts before the Commons; by supplying a team of leading politicians to fill ministerial posts (Chapter 9); by influencing backbenchers by its ethos, ideology and organisation to vote cohesively in support of the Government; and by providing a mass organisation to select parliamentary candidates, campaign on their behalf, and, once they are elected, assist in keeping them up to the mark. Its overall majority taken together with the normally loyal support of its backbenchers ensures that the governing party can govern – that is, gain overall support for its executive activity and legislation from the House of Commons.

Party also underpins the activities of the official opposition, sustaining its two main constitutional functions of providing an alternative programme and team of leaders with which to replace the government and regular criticism of the Government of the day. Equally, the minor political groupings are swayed by the imperatives of party to behave and vote cohesively behind a united policy.

Party, then, dominates Parliament, but the reverse is also true. Parliament equally clearly dominates party. Thus virtually all UK parties accept the legitimacy of Parliament, have as their major aim the winning of seats in the House of Commons, and choose their leaders from their MPs, who also have a major influence on their policies. (Adonis, 1993, pp. 40–1) In addition, Parliament provides the main arena for the party battle between elections. Although not well reported in many sections of the press, the consequences of the struggle in the House of Commons between competing teams of party leaders to establish the authority of their respective cases and of backbenchers to make their mark gradually filters down to the electorate via television, radio and the quality press.

■ Functions of the Lower House

The House of Commons has five main functions. (Exhibit 12.1)

The middle three functions are shared with the House of Lords, although the Commons is easily the predominant partner.

The essence of Parliament, its primary role in the political system, is **legitimation**. It serves as the fundamental agency whereby the actions of the rulers gain acceptance by the ruled. And it can fulfil this purpose because of its historic status, constantly renewed, as a unique forum for national representation, law-making, political criticism, debate and leadership recruitment.

□ *Representation*

The representative character of the House of Commons underpins its other roles. It is 'representative' in three senses: party, pressure group and constituency. These three kinds of representation combine in the member of Parliament, who is a representative of party (almost always), of interest (frequently) and of constituency (invariably).

In the case of *party*, representativeness does not mean that the party composition of the Commons exactly reflects the distribution of party support in the country. The difference between the actual representation of parties in the Commons after the 1992 General Election and the distribution of party support if an alternative system had been in operation is shown in Chapter 13. What 'representativeness' in this context does mean is that MPs are elected to the House and speak and vote there as representatives of party.

Second, an MP may represent an **interest**. Representation of interests in the Commons can occur in many ways: sponsorship of election candidates through a particular party; payment of fees to MPs to serve as advisers, consultants or directors; direct lobbying by establishing privileged access to the Commons as MPs' 'research assistants'; the provision of specialised assistance to MPs involved in specific legislation, e.g. the promotion of private members' bills; lobbying of MPs by professional consultancy firms; direct or 'amateur' contacting of

---

Exhibit 12.1   *House of Commons: main functions*
● Representation
● Legislation
● Scrutiny
● Forum for national debate
● Recruitment of a government

MPs by pressure groups; and the actual pursuit of outside occupations by MPs.

The most clear-cut example of the first category is the activity of the trade unions which in the 1992 General Election sponsored 173 Labour candidates, of whom 143 (over half the Parliamentary Labour Party) were elected. Unions cannot of course instruct their MPs how to speak or vote in Parliament – to do so would put them in breach of parliamentary privilege – but none the less they expect those whom they sponsor to keep a close watch over their interests. Many union-sponsored MPs were among Labour opponents of the Industrial Relations Bill in 1969 and some unions have lobbied for particular causes through the MPs they help to fund (Table 12.2).

Second, groups pay MPs to represent their causes on a permanent basis as advisers, consultants and directors. Mainly Conservative MPs are involved: in 1993, for example, *Labour Research* reported that 146 (58 per cent) of Conservative backbenchers were advisers or consultants to 322 organisations. Such outside consultancy work enables many MPs to increase their salaries substantially. Drug, tobacco and alcohol interests are particularly well represented in the Commons.

Third, professional lobbyists for commercial groups gain privileged access to the House of Commons as MPs' aides and research assistants. It was reported in 1991 that over 200 MPs from all parties were giving research passes to individuals employed by outside organisations, many of them public relations firms.

Fourth, groups provide specialised assistance to MPs such as briefings by constituency action groups and help with the details of private members' bills.

Fifth, professional lobbyists make frequent contacts with MPs on behalf of commercial clients. During the 1980s commercial lobbying expanded rapidly into a multi-million-pound industry; the total fee income earned by 50 consultancy firms was reported to be over £10 million a year in 1991.

Sixth, another scene of rapid expansion in the 1980s was 'amateur' lobbying by pressure groups of all kinds.

Finally, MPs also represent particular interests by themselves pursuing outside occupations. As James Callaghan remarked in 1965: 'When I look at some Members discussing the Finance Bill I do not think of them as the Hon. Member for X, Y or Z. I look at them and say "investment trusts" "capital speculators" or "that is the fellow who is a Stock Exchange man who makes a profit on gilt-edged"'. *Labour Research* in 1993 found that out of 253 Conservative backbenchers 135 (53 per cent) held 287 directorships in private companies; 27 Labour MPs (10 per cent) declared 58 directorships. Whilst some directorships are unpaid, many are paid and provide significant numbers of MPs with lucrative outside employment. Exhibit 12.2 gives specific examples of the various types of contact between outside interests and parliament.

Since 1975, Parliament has kept an annual register of interests to strengthen the custom that MPs declare their interests at the beginning of any debate to which they contribute. However, although it remains difficult to state precisely what benefits economic interests derive from these contacts, concern grew about the adequacy of existing public information about MPs' financial interests. Also in the light of the huge growth of the commercial lobbying industry and the spate of privatisation legislation, opportunities

Table 12.2   *Trade Union sponsored MPs, 1945–92*

	1945	1950	1951	1955	1959	1964	1966	1970	1974	1974	1979	1983	1987	1992
Total TU MPs	120	111	108	95	92	120	127	112	127	126	134	115	129	143
Total Labour MPs	393	315	295	277	258	317	363	287	301	319	269	209	229	271

Exhibit 12.2   *Some examples of MPs' interests*

Alton, David (Dem. (now Lib. Dem.), Liverpool Mossley Hill): Research Assistant for Abortion Bill paid for by Christian Action Research and Education (CARE) and Society for the Protection of the Unborn Child (SPUC).

Dalyell, Tam (Lab., Linlithgow): Columnist, *New Scientist*. Sponsored by National Union of Railwaymen (NUR), £750 paid to constituency party.

Johnson-Smith, Sir Geoffrey (Con., Wealden): Director, Taylor Siden Ltd, Industrial Public Relations and Marketing; Glengate Holdings, commercial and industrial property; London Weekend Television (Holdings) Ltd, MDA (Benelux) construction consultants and quantity surveyors, Brands Hatch Leisure plc (all non-executive). Consultant, Eagle Star Group, MEL, division of Philips Electronic and Associated Industries; AT & T, Philips Telecommunications Ltd. Hosted private lunch for Railex, a filings company; dinner for Taylor Alden Ltd.

Pendry, Tom (Lab., Stalybridge and Hyde): Financially sponsored by National Association of Public Employees (NUPE), £800 per annum. Assistant provided by Tottenham Hotspur plc.

Wardle, Charles (Con., Bexhill and Battle): Director, Political Advisory Services Ltd. Chairman of Governors, Charters-Ancaster School, Bexhill-on-Sea. Adviser, Peat Marwick McLintock, Unichem. Shareholder, Political Advisory Services Ltd.

---

for real conflicts of interest among elected representatives appeared to increase.

In three well-publicised cases in the early 1990s, John Browne MP was suspended from the Commons for a month for failing to declare an £88,000 payment from the Saudis; Michael Grylls MP was criticised for having submitted an 'insufficiently detailed' entry which failed to show that he had received commission payments from a lobbying company; and Michael Mates MP was admonished for failing to inform his Defence Select Committee colleagues of his interest in companies whose business was relevant to issues discussed by that committee, of which he was chairman. Accordingly, successive reports of the Select Committee on Members' Interests in 1991–2 recommended tighter rules both for commercial lobbyists and MPs' self-regulation (Exhibit 12.3).

Third and finally, the House of Commons is representative of the United Kingdom in a geographical sense – that is, as divided up into territorial units called **constituencies**. Candidates for Parliament may stand as representatives of party but, once elected, each MP is expected to

represent the interests of the constituency as a whole and to be at the service of all constituents. In this way, as Members for particular constituencies, MPs collectively may be said to represent the entire country, which would not be true of their roles as party and group representatives. This is the oldest meaning of 'representation' and formed the basis of the individualist liberal concept of parliamentary representation, which prevailed in the nineteenth century but now coexists with the collectivist concept of party representation which came to prominence in the twentieth century.

The idea of the MP as constituency representative and of Parliament as an assembly of constituency representatives is a resilient one. It has undergone a resurgence since the 1960s, primarily because people facing the complexities of local and national welfare bureacracies have turned to MPs to assist them in understanding and asserting their rights. The burden of constituency work upon MPs is now very considerable, with most MPs receiving large postbags from their constituents and setting aside 2–3 days each

---

Exhibit 12.3 *Tightening the rules on declaration of interests*

- **A compulsory register of professional lobbyists working in Parliament.** Lobbying companies would be required to name clients and MPs acting on their behalf and the new code of practice would also outlaw bribes to MPs (and civil servants) and ban 'success' fees i.e. bonus payments to MPs if they succeed in changing the law to a client's benefit (1991).

- **The banning of chairmen and members of parliamentary Select Committees from holding any direct financial interest in companies benefiting from Government contracts.** Chairmen would be banned from holding both directorships and consultancies with such firms whilst members would be permitted to retain consultancies but banned from holding directorships (1991).

- **Increased disclosure of interests by MPs.** MPs should list clients with whom they have personal connections; declare the receipt of gifts, hospitality and material benefits over £125; disclose whether their staffs receive visits, gifts or other benefits from lobbying companies and if they are engaged in any other relevant occupation; state the nature of their own business; disclose membership of Lloyds; and declare shareholdings where these are worth over £25 000 or constitute more than 1 per cent of the share capital of the company. Sponsors of Early Day Motions (see below) should declare their relevant interests. The Committee did not recommend statutory powers of enforcement of the declaration of Members' interests (1992).

---

week as well as a sizeable part of the weekend to the task. MPs' constituency work falls into two main categories.

First, there is the local welfare officer/social worker role, dealing with a wide variety of problems on behalf of individual constituents. Problems and grievances connected with the National Health Service (NHS), housing and social security predominate but other concerns include education, pensions, local taxation, conservation, animal testing, law and order and Sunday trading. MPs tackle the problems at the appropriate level, conducting a voluminous correspondence with ministers, Departments, local authorities, 'quangos', local Department of Social Security (DSS) offices and so on: when Parliament is sitting, ministers receive about 15 000 letters from MPs per month, up 50 per cent even on the early 1980s. Also MPs can raise constituents' grievances through the medium of parliamentary questions and debate and, if all these means fail, they can refer cases of alleged public maladministration to the Ombudsman.

Second, MPs act as promoters of local interests, working to further the interests of the constituency as a whole by, for example, working to

get orders for local industries, to attract new commercial and industrial investment, to get roads built, to find solutions for local industrial disputes, and to prevent local factories, schools and hospitals closing. In a democratic society, this MP–constituency relationship is of profound practical and theoretical importance, serving as a barometer of public opinion for representatives and as both safety-valve and potential mechanism of grievance resolution for citizens.

The House of Commons, then, can be seen as representative in these three distinct but overlapping ways. It is not, however, a *social* microcosm of the nation, MPs being predominantly white, male, middle-aged and middle class. Thus, there were only six black/Asian MPs in 1992 (five Labour, one Conservative), constituting under 1 per cent of the House of Commons. Whilst a record number of women were elected (60, cf. 41 in 1987), women still constitute a mere 9.2 per cent of the House. The main reason for the larger total was the significant increase in Labour Party women MPs (up 16 cf. 1987), the party breakdown being: Labour 37, Conservative 20, Liberal Democrat 2, SNP 1. A majority (72 per cent) of MPs in 1992 were aged between 40 and 59.

Finally, parliament is socially untypical in that over two-thirds of MPs have received higher education and over four-fifths have professional or business backgrounds.

☐ *Legislation*

Parliament no longer makes policy either in the sense of initiating legislation or strongly influencing it (Figure 12.1). Most legislation originates with government and emerges from its passage through Parliament more or less in the form intended by the government. The government's majority backed by generally cohesive party voting normally ensures that this is so. Nevertheless, in order to become law, Government measures must pass through both Houses of Parliament in a series of stages with amendment

and, very occasionally, even defeat of a bill a possibility. Table 12.3 details these stages, commenting on the points (column 3) at which amendment is possible. Not only is the parliamentary legislative process a constitutional necessity, politically, owing to the possibility of amendment or even defeat of the Government's legislation, it is more than a formality or foregone conclusion. Even if Parliament no longer makes policy, its assent is vital to the establishment of the legitimacy of that legislation.

☐ *Scrutiny and Influence of the Executive*

Serving as an arena for constitutional opposition is another major function of Parliament. It is in Parliament (primarily in the House of Commons)

Table 12.3   *Legislative stages in Parliament*

Stage	Where taken	Comments
First Reading	Floor of the House of Commons	Formal introduction only, no debate.
Second Reading	Floor of the House of Commons (non-contentious bills may be referred to a second reading committee).	Debate on the general principles of a measure; if these are contested, a bill may be voted on, and even defeated.
Committee	Standing committee (Constitutionally important and certain other measures e.g. finance bills may be taken in committee of the whole House).	Considered in detail, clause by clause; amendments can be made, but normally most successful ones are by ministers since standing committee composition reflects party representation in the House.
Report	Floor of the House of Commons (there is no report stage if the bill reported is unamended from Committee of the whole House).	Reported to the House by the standing committee; amendments can be made.
Third Reading	Floor of the House of Commons (there is no debate unless six members submit a motion beforehand).	Final approval of the bill – generally a formality for all but controversial bills. Debate limited to final text of bill.
House of Lords	Bill passes through similar stages to House of Commons (committee stage of public bills is normally taken on the floor of the Lords not in standing committee).	Lords can propose amendments, which Commons accepts, rejects or substitutes amendments of its own, returning bill to Lords with 'reasons' for its actions. Lords then agrees not to insist on its rejected amendments or accepts Commons amendments; if Lords insists or proposes another amendment, search for agreement between two Houses continues. If no agreement is reached, bill lapses (this happens very rarely). Bill can then be reintroduced in the next session and passed without the Lords' consent.

Source: Adapted from Norton (1981, p. 86).

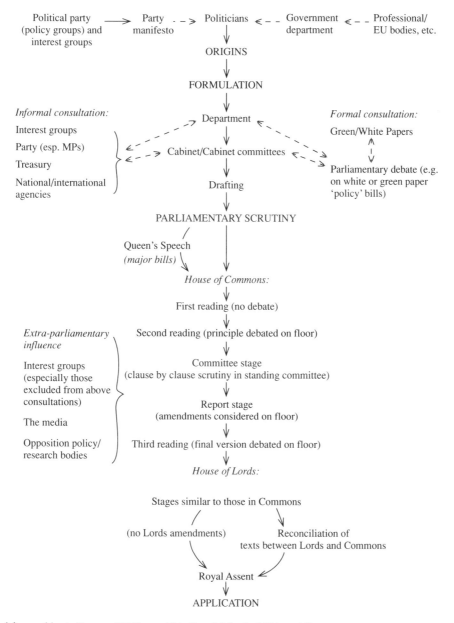

Political party (policy groups) and interest groups → Party manifesto --> Politicians <-- Government department <-- Professional/ EU bodies, etc.

↓

ORIGINS

↓

FORMULATION

↓

Informal consultation:

Interest groups

Party (esp. MPs)

Treasury

National/international agencies

}

--> Department <--

↓

Cabinet/Cabinet committees <--

↓

Drafting

Formal consultation:

Green/White Papers

↕

Parliamentary debate (e.g. on white or green paper 'policy' bills)

↓

PARLIAMENTARY SCRUTINY

Queen's Speech *(major bills)*

↓

House of Commons:

↓

First reading (no debate)

↓

Extra-parliamentary influence

Interest groups (especially those excluded from above consultations)

The media

Opposition policy/ research bodies

}

Second reading (principle debated on floor)

↓

Committee stage (clause by clause scrutiny in standing committee)

↓

Report stage (amendments considered on floor)

↓

Third reading (final version debated on floor)

↓

House of Lords:

Stages similar to those in Commons

(no Lords amendments)

Reconciliation of texts between Lords and Commons

↓

Royal Assent

↓

APPLICATION

Source: Adapted from tables in Drewry (1988, pp. 124–5) and Adonis (1993, p. 93).

Figure 12.1 *Principal stages in the legislative process for government bills*

that the government must explain and defend its actions.

Nowadays, the backbenchers of the governing party have more to do with setting the limits of government action than do the opposition parties. Faced by a government with a working majority, there is normally little the opposition can do except resort to delaying tactics. This perhaps is as it should be since the primary function of Parliament is to sustain a government. Nonetheless, the constitutional requirement embodied in specific parliamentary procedures that government must publicly subject its activities to appraisal is of paramount importance. Major scrutinising procedures and agencies of the House of Commons are Questions, general, adjournment and emergency debates, early day motions, select committees, and correspondence with ministers (Table 12.4).

□ *Forum for National Debate*

Parliament commands attention as the focus of national debate on all kinds of occasion in a manner no other institution can match. Such occasions include – Prime Minister's Question Time and at the beginning and end of major

debates in normal circumstances; more heated moments such as the Westland affair (1986) when a government's, a prime minister's or a leading Cabinet minister's reputations are at stake with even a whiff of resignation in the air; and, lastly, the great historic occasion such as the fall of the Chamberlain Government in May 1940, Suez in 1956 and the Falklands crisis in 1982. On these occasions, the *theatrical* element in Parliament is to the fore as a tense but almost ritualistic rhetorical combat takes place between rival teams of political gladiators urged on by compact stage armies of supporters. The House of Commons, it has been said, provides a forum in which a continuing general election is fought (Brazier, 1988, p. 169).

Table 12.4 *Main methods of Commons scrutiny of the executive*

Procedure	Function
Questions	Backbenchers may submit both oral and written questions. Ministers reply to oral questions daily (Mon–Thurs, usually for about 40–50 minutes from 2.35 p.m.). MPs are allowed one further unscripted question (a 'supplementary') after which other MPs may continue the interrogation. On Tuesdays and Thursdays for 15 minutes from 3.15 p.m. the Leader of the Opposition can tackle the PM directly at Prime Minister's Question Time. Most questions to ministers (about three-fifths) are written and are recorded – together with the replies – in *Hansard*.
Debates	*General* – Debate on the government's programme (Queen's Speech) at outset of each parliamentary session; also on 'no confidence' motions (rare except when government majority is very small) and, mainly, on motions tabled by the government to discuss government policy (about 20 days per session) or motions tabled by the opposition (20 days per session, with three allocated to the second largest opposition party). **Adjournment debates** and **private members' motions**: adjournment motions enable backbenchers to raise issues relating to government policy or items of constituency interest and get a reply from a junior minister; 11 days per session are allocated for private members' motions and backbenchers may also initiate short debates immediately before each recess, providing about another 7 days. **Emergency** – way for MPs to raise urgent matters for debate which lie within responsibility of the government and cannot be raised rapidly in another way; very rarely granted (one or two per session) but popular with backbenchers because of the media attention even when not granted.
Early day motions	Much-used method of enabling MPs to express their views, although no debate follows on points raised; increasingly popular, with numbers tabled rising from well under 200 per session before 1960 to over 1400 in 1988–9.
Select committees	Able to scrutinise executive away from the floor of the Commons; have powers to send for 'persons, papers and records' and can interrogate civil servants and on occasion ministers; 16 departmental select committees now exist together with the Public Accounts (examining government expenditure) and Parliamentary Commissioner for Administration ('Ombudsman') Committees. The party balance on select committees reflects that of the House as a whole.
Correspondence with ministers	Main way in which MPs pursue case-work on behalf of constituents.

Recruitment and Training of the Personnel of Government

Parliament no longer selects ministers but it remains 'a school of statesmanship' in the sense that ministers are invariably drawn from Parliament, predominantly from the House of Commons. Thus, whilst the electorate effectively elects the government directly, it is in the Commons that politicians serve as members of 'shadow' teams before receiving office or, as ministers, defend government policy. The skills of parliamentary debate are widely acknowledged to be no real preparation for running a Department nor are the two kinds of ability invariably present in the same person. Nevertheless, it is in the House of Commons that ambitious politicians first attempt to make, and then as ministers try to sustain, their reputations.

Party organisation in the House of Commons

There are three main elements in party organisation in the House of Commons: whips, party meetings and party committees.

Whips

Since government and opposition are by party, it is vital for parties to remain united, especially in their formal activities such as voting in Parliament. It is essential to avoid overt expressions of disagreement by significant numbers, and to minimise and counteract those which do occur. Failure to do so may, at the least, give encouragement to the rival party and at worst, for a government, may jeopardise the passing of legislation and, for an opposition, destroy any chance to embarrass or defeat a government. The worst eventuality is that a party will split and, and as may happen as a result, suffer electoral defeat – as Labour did in 1983 and 1987 after splitting in 1981.

MPs are subject to three influences conducive to party loyalty before any formal mechanisms might begin to operate. These are, first, their natural sympathy for the causes and purposes their party represents; second, their desire (especially if they are ambitious) not to alienate the leadership; and, third, their concern to keep on good terms with their local parties which tend to dislike rebellions against party policy. MPs, then, vote with their parties for many reasons, other than the formal power of the whips.

Whips nonetheless play a key part in the management of their parties in parliament. The whips' main task is administrative: to keep their own MPs informed by producing and sending to them the documentary whip. This is a weekly outline of parliamentary business which indicates the degree of importance attached by the party to the various items by the number of underlinings. Thus, for items of minor importance, an MP's attendance is merely requested (a one-line whip); for items of greater importance on which a division will take place, an MP's presence is expected (a two-line whip); and for very important items, an MP's attendance is regarded as essential (a three-line whip). Defiance of a three-line whip constitutes a serious breach of political conduct.

An MP wishing to be absent for a vote must find a member of the opposing party who also wishes to stay away. This practice is known as 'pairing' and is arranged through the whips; routinely used on two-line whips, it may even on occasion be permitted on three-line whips.

The written whip also informs members of the forthcoming business of standing, select, party and other committees.

Whips play a central role in linking the party leaderships with the backbenchers. It is the whips who advise leaders on what the party will or will not stand; who offer ideas to leaders on how to head off backbench rebellion; and who indicate to disaffected backbenchers the likely consequences of their actions. Whips are personnel managers rather than disciplinarians. The ultimate sanction against a party rebel – withdrawal of the party whip (i.e. expulsion from the parliamentary party) – almost never happens: it is hardly a realistic threat against 20 or 30 backbenchers. More realistically, the whips employ cajolery, bribes and threats against potential rebels: the bribes may include recommendations for improved office accommodation, a party-sponsored overseas trip or a place on a particular select committee, even a favourable mention for junior ministerial office; the threats, non-preferment in any of these ways. After a 'rebellion', recalcitrant MPs may suffer at least personal abuse and sharp rebukes, at worst long periods on the backbenches without hope of office. Most of the time, the whips just seek to persuade, often by invoking party loyalty and the desirability of not 'rocking the boat' or giving aid and comfort to the 'other lot', and, if they fail, just resign themselves to failure. There is always a certain number of MPs in both major parties who are beyond the reach of blandishments and threats. But the way in which many threatened rebellions peter out suggests that – whilst the model of their role as disciplinarians is inappropriate – the whips possess an armoury of 'persuasion' which is far from negligible.

□ *Party Meetings*

The Conservative Party meets weekly in the 1922 Committee when Parliament is sitting. When the party is in government, only backbenchers attend but not ministers; when it is in opposition, the Committee includes all Conservative MPs except the leader. Its chairman, who enjoys direct access to the leader, is an important figure and the '1922' plays a key role in the party especially in times of controversy and crisis.

When in opposition, the Labour Party meets as the PLP (Parliamentary Labour Party) i.e. it is attended by members of the shadow Cabinet. When the party is in government, Labour ministers attend meetings of the PLP when the work of their Departments is under discussion; communication between the Government and its backbenchers is maintained by the Parliamentary Committee whose members include the leader and deputy leader, the chief whip, four min-

isters (three from the Commons) and six backbenchers.

The minor parties also meet weekly and appoint whips.

□ *Party Committees*

Each major party in opposition forms a Shadow Cabinet. In the Conservative Party, it is chosen by the leader and known formally as the Consultative Committee. In the Labour Party, the Shadow Cabinet or Parliamentary Committee consists of the leader and deputy leader, the chief whip in the Commons, the chairman of the PLP, 15 backbenchers (who like the chief whip and the chairman are elected by the PLP), the leader and chief whip in the House of Lords and an elected Labour peer. The leader allocates Shadow Cabinet portfolios and appoints additional members of 'Shadow' teams.

Each major party also forms a large number of specialist committees. In 1988, the Conservatives had 24 specialist committees, 7 regional groups, a committee on party organisation and one on unpaired members. When the party is in office, the committees elect their own chairpersons; when it is in opposition, the committees are chaired by the appropriate shadow minister who is appointed by the Leader. In 1988, the PLP had 14 subject and 8 regional committees, each appointing its own chair. In opposition, frontbenchers as well as select committee members are expected to attend their appropriate committees; in office, ministers are expected to attend when requested. (Griffith and Ryle, 1989, pp. 107–13).

Consideration of party organisation in the House of Commons suggests first, the extent to which already existing party loyalties are reinforced by party activities within the House, especially those of the Whips but also those of party meetings and committees as parties strive to govern or prepare themselves for government; and second, the considerable amount of important political activity which takes place away from the floor of the House in backstage party gatherings.

Recent Changes in House of Commons Behaviour and Structure

The government controls Parliament but cannot always rely on getting its way. In the following sections, this point is explained first with reference to the behaviour and structure of the House of Commons and then with reference to the House of Lords. We start with the mechanisms of government control before considering the ways in which the will of governments can be flouted.

Government control of the House of Commons rests on four main factors: its possession in normal circumstances of a majority, allied with the habit of loyal voting by its own supporters (in the next chapter, Table 13.1 shows the size of government majorities since 1945); its power to determine the parliamentary timetable; its ability to curtail debate; and its control over the drafting of legislation.

Thus, first, over two-thirds of elections since the war have produced governments with majorities ranging from the adequate (17) to the massive (over 100) and we have already looked at the forces constraining those majorities to vote cohesively.

Second, although a significant proportion of Commons business is initiated by the opposition and backbenchers, government business has priority on the majority (75 per cent) of the sitting days of the House. (*Note*: The actual breakdown of Commons time in a particular session will look rather different: more like 55 per cent–45 per cent in favour of the government; this is because much debate on government business is inspired by the opposition or backbenchers – e.g. by moving amendments to government bills).

Third, two devices mainly enable the government to restrict debate: the closure and the guillotine. The closure – the request 'that the question be now put', stopping debate if successful – is rarely used now to restrict debate on government business (a mere three times in 1987–8, cf. eleven times, 1961–2). The guillotine – an 'allocation of time' motion regulating the

amount of time to be spent on a bill – is normally used when the government considers that progress on a major piece of legislation is unsatisfactory at committee stage. In recent years, guillotine motions have been used more frequently – six times in 1987–8, and ten in 1988–9, a record number. But it is also true that the length of time elapsing before an allocation of time order is moved at standing committee stage is now much greater – over 80 hours for the 19 bills guillotined in standing committee between 1979 and 1988, compared with under 30 hours which was common between 1946 and 1961.

Finally, despite often extensive consultations by government at the pre-legislative stage (Figure 12.1), policy-making – including legislation down to the final drafting – is dominated, as we have seen in Chapters 8 and 9, by the Cabinet, Cabinet committees and the Departments.

The result of these factors is that it is virtually impossible in normal circumstances (i.e. government possession of a working majority) to bring a government down and, in practice, very difficult to engineer any defeat in the House of Commons. Of course, an opposition can make life awkward for a government in a number of ways, which include harassment of ministers in debates and at Question Time, motions of censure and the frequent use of delaying tactics. Censure motions ('That this House has no confidence in Her Majesty's Government') are normally rare in periods of sizeable government majorities, but more frequent when the opposite situation prevails: there were three between 1976 and 1979, the final one – in March 1979 – resulting in defeat for the Labour Government. Oppositions can delay the passage of government measures by stalling ploys at the committee stage of bills and by calls for frequent divisions at the second and third reading stages.

In fact, notwithstanding its adversarial context, much government business is conducted by mutual agreement between government and opposition and the question of opposition obstructiveness does not arise. Indeed, for much of the time, a consensual model is more appropriate to the House of Commons than an adversarial model: it has been calculated that between 1945 and 1983, 79 per cent of government bills were not divided against on second reading; the Opposition forced divisions against a mere 18 per cent of bills, and backbenchers of the other opposition parties forced divisions on the other 3 per cent (Van Mechelen and Rose, 1986, p. 57).

This consensual aspect of the House arises for several reasons. First, much government legislation – notably that of a technical or administrative kind – is uncontroversial. Second, the Opposition may have its own motives for not pressing resistance too far: in addition to recognising the difficulties of governing, it wants to avoid being stigmatised as merely factious, provoking similar treatment when the roles of government and opposition are reversed, and to avoid opposing legislation which is popular or for which there is a mandate.

□ *Increasing Backbench Dissent*

In practice, governments may be defeated by a combination of their own backbenchers with MPs from the Official Opposition and the smaller parties. Between 1945 and 1970, no government was defeated in the House of Commons as a result of the dissenting votes of its own backbenchers. After 1970, however, the situation changed and cross-voting increased. The Conservative Government of Edward Heath (1970–4, majority 30) was defeated six times, three of these defeats being on three-line whips.

Combinations of opposition parties – rather than cross-voting – were all that was required to bring about the defeat of the minority Labour Government of 1974 on 17 occasions. The Labour Government of 1974–9 suffered 42 defeats; 23 occurred as a result of its own backbenchers voting with the Opposition whilst the other 19 defeats were brought about by combinations of opposition parties.

Backbench dissent continued in the 1979–83 Parliament with 10 or more Conservative backbenchers voting against the Government or abstaining on 16 occasions and over 40 doing so on four occasions. Even though this cross-voting

brought about the defeat of the Government only once (in 1982 on the immigration rules), the *threat* of cross-voting by its own backbenchers persuaded the Government to retreat on several occasions, including student grants, charges for eye tests, reductions in the external services of the BBC, 'hotel' charges for patients in NHS hospitals, and the sale of parts of British Leyland to Americans.

The large majority (144) enjoyed by Margaret Thatcher's second administration initially immunised it against defeat, although again the threat of rebellion by its own backbenchers forced it to make concessions on various matters including housing benefits, the Police and Criminal Evidence Bill and the rate support grant. In 1986, however, a combination of large numbers of dissident Conservatives with backbenchers from the opposition parties together with large-scale abstentions brought about the defeat of the Conservative Government on the second reading of its bill to liberalise the rules of Sunday trading. On that occasion, over one-quarter of Conservative backbenchers (72) voted against the Government. In January 1990, although it turned out to be smaller than expected, another Conservative revolt took place, with 38 backbenchers, including Michael Heseltine, voting against the flat-rate poll tax.

Backbench Conservative rebellion erupted again in the 1992–3 parliamentary session over pit closures and over the ratification of the Maastricht Bill. Rebellion was a very serious matter for the Major Government which unlike its predecessor possessed only a small majority (21). In October 1992 the threat that over two dozen of its backbenchers would support a Labour motion calling for a freeze on all pit closures forced a Government retreat and a promise to undertake a fresh review of 21 of the threatened pits.

Throughout the Maastricht ratification process (May 1992–July 1993), the 22 Conservative diehard opponents of the Bill took advantage of the Major Government's narrow majority to keep the Bill's progress through its parliamentary stages on a knife-edge of uncertainty.

On occasion, even more widespread rebellions occurred. Thus, 22 Conservative backbenchers voted against the Government on the Bill's

Table 12.5 *Conservative rebels on the Maastricht Treaty in the 1992 Parliament*

Tory 'Euro-sceptics' fall into several groups: 'Anti-marketeers' such as Sir Teddy Taylor, John Biffen and Sir Richard Body; 'Constitutionalists', who include Bill Cash and Richard Shepherd; 'Free marketeers' or 'Thatcherites', the largest subgroup, prominent among whom are Michael Spicer, Nicholas Budgen and Teresa Gorman; and 'Patriots' or 'British is best' nationalists like Ann and Nicholas Winterton, Tony Marlow and Rhodes Boyson (Baker, Gamble and Ludlam, 1993). The following table shows the extent of Conservative rebellions on Maastricht from second reading to the end of the committee stage. It is presented in the form of a league, with two points awarded for every vote against the Government (because it reduces its majority by two) and one for every abstention. The abstentions figure includes those for matters like illness as well as principled ones.

R = Rebellion: a vote against the Government. A = No vote. G = voted with the Government. * shows a member of the 1992 intake.

		R	A	G	Pts
Cash, W	Stafford	47	13	2	107
Winterton, N	Macclesfield	46	15	1	107
Taylor, Sir T	Southend E	48	10	4	106
Winterton, Mrs A	Congleton	44	17	1	105
*Knapman, R	Stroud	44	16	2	104
Gill, C	Ludlow	43	17	2	103
Skeet, Sir T	Beds N	41	19	2	101
Jessel, T	Twickenham	42	16	4	100
Gorman, Mrs T	Billericay	40	19	3	99
Walker, B	Tayside N	39	19	4	97
Lawrence, Sir I	Burton	38	21	3	97
Spicer, M	Worcs S	37	23	2	97
Marlow, T	Northampton N	36	25	1	97
Budgen, N	Wolverhampton SE	36	24	2	96
Shepherd, R	Aldridge	34	26	2	94
Lord, M	Suffolk Central	35	23	4	93
Cran, J	Beverley	30	31	1	91
Wilkinson, J	Ruislip	31	28	3	90
Body, Sir R	Holland	30	28	4	88
Biffen, J	Shropshire N	26	35	1	87
Tapsell, Sir P	Lindsey E	24	34	4	82
Carlisle J	Luton N	21	40	1	82
Butcher, J	Coventry SW	19	43	0	81
Gardiner, Sir G	Reigate	23	34	5	80
Hawksley, W	Stourbridge	18	44	0	80
*Sweeney, W	Vale of Glam	21	36	5	78
*Legg, B	Milton Keynes SW	18	41	3	77
Carttiss, M	Yarmouth	17	41	4	75
Porter, D	Waveney	15	44	3	74
Allison, R	Torbay	12	46	4	70
Duncan-Smith, I	Chingford	11	47	4	69
Bendall, V	Ilford N	4	56	2	64
Boyson, Sir R	Brent N	12	39	11	63
Pawsey, J	Rugby	14	34	14	62
Townend, J	Bridlington	6	50	6	62
Moate, Sir R	Faversham	4	53	5	61
Bonsor, Sir N	Upminster	3	55	4	61
*Jenkin, B	Colchester N	1	58	3	60
Baker, K	Mole Valley	1	56	5	58
Fry, P	Wellingborough	5	47	10	57
Clark, Dr M	Rochford	2	51	9	55
*Whittingdale, J	Colchester S	1	41	20	43

cont. p. 216

R = Rebellions a vote against the Government. A = No vote. G = voted with the Government. * shows a member of the 1992 intake.

		R	A	G	Pts
Hunter, A	Basingstoke	5	24	33	34
Vaughan, Sir G	Reading E	1	27	34	29
Walden, G	Buckingham	0	24	38	24
Grylls, Sir M	Surrey NW	0	17	45	17
Greenway, H	Ealing N	4	8	50	16

The figures were compiled by Mark Leonard.
Source: The Guardian, 5 May 1993.

Table 12.5—*continued*

second reading (May 1992), 84 signed an anti-Maastricht 'Fresh Start' Early Day Motion (June 1992), 26 voted against a 'paving' motion (November 1992) preparing for the return of the Bill later in the month, and 26 voted in favour of a Labour amendment to the Bill (March 1993), ensuring that the Commons would have to debate the Report stage, thereby delaying ratification. Finally, 23 Conservative 'Eurosceptics' voted against the Government after a debate on the Social Chapter (July 1993) (Table 12.5).

This meant the Report stage of the Bill would have to be debated by the Commons, thereby delaying ratification.

Contemporary trends in Commons voting behaviour can now be summarised. The Government controls parliament and the bulk of its legislation still goes through without dissent even in the more volatile parliamentary circumstances prevailing after 1970. On the other hand, especially when it has – as after April 1992 – a small majority, it certainly needs to exercise more vigilance to get its way than it did 30 years ago and has become susceptible to occasional embarrassing defeats.

□ *Private Members' Legislation*

Only a small proportion of private members' legislation reaches the statute book but it has become an important method for making laws on controversial social matters with a strong moral dimension. In the 1960s, private members' legislation liberalised the law on capital punishment, homosexuality, divorce and abortion and in the 1980s, private members' bills outlawed video 'nasties', compelled front-seat passengers to wear seat belts and restricted advertising on cigarettes. Normally such legislation requires Government support, including Government Commons time, if it is to succeed.

□ *Commons Workload*

The legislative burden upon parliament has increased massively in recent decades primarily because of the length rather than the number of Bills and Statutory Instruments. The Water Bill (1989) – only one of several very extensive bills – was nearly 350 pages. Much of the increased workload necessarily has fallen on Standing Committees, sittings of which increased from under 200 to over 300 per session on legislation and from nothing to between 45 and 95 per session on Statutory Instruments between the 1960s and the late 1980s (Norton, 1992, p. 141).

□ *Select Committees*

Parliamentary reformers from the 1960s advocated the greater use of **Departmental Select Committees** (DSCs) to improve scrutiny of the executive and their case was reaffirmed by the

Select Committee on Procedure (1978) which recommended the establishment of a new system of select committees to provide regular scrutiny of the work of every Government Department. These proposals were implemented by Norman St John Stevas as Leader of the House in 1979. Some existing Select Committees were abolished; those retained included Public Accounts, which scrutinises the Government's use of public funds, the Parliamentary Commissioner (to oversee the work of the Ombudsman), Statutory Instruments and European legislation. The new departure was the introduction of fourteen new Departmental Select Committee (DSCs) to scrutinise the work of Government departments (although not the Lord Chancellor's Office). Subsequently, one DSC (Energy) has been disbanded with the Department it shadowed and three (Science and Technology, Health and National Heritage) have been added. (Table 12.6) With each DSC composed of eleven members allocated according to the party balance of the House as a whole, the DSCs gave employment to 176 back-benchers in the 1992 parliament, the total party composition being 96 Conservative (54%) 70 Labour (40%), 5 Liberal Democrat (3%) and 5 minor parties (3%). Their task is to investigate Government Departments and to make reports with recommendations.

Although levels of activity vary between committees, as a whole DSCs have been extremely industrious, issuing 193 reports in the 1979–83 parliament, 306 reports in the 1983–87 parliament, and a total of 591 reports by June 1990. The DSCs possess the power to send for 'persons, papers and records', spend much of their time interviewing witnesses including civil servants and ministers, employ specialist advisers including normally one full-time researcher, and generally seek consensus (although they do not always achieve it). In assessing their role it is necessary to remember that the select committees 'are, and can realistically only aspire to be, in the business of scrutiny and exposure, not of government'. (Drewry (ed) 1989, p. 426). How effective are they?

Positive Influence on Policy

The DSCs have had some influence on policy both in the short term and the longer term: in the short term, one academic study investigating the early 1980s has claimed twelve successes for the DSCs, including changes in the 'sus' law and,

Table 12.6 *The Departmental Select Committees as at 14 April 1993*

Committee	Chairman	Party
Agriculture	Sir Jerry Wiggin	Conservative
Defence	Sir Nicholas Bonsor	Conservative
Education	Sir Malcolm Thornton	Conservative
Employment	Greville Janner	Labour
Environment	Robert Jones	Conservative
Foreign Affairs	David Howell	Conservative
Health	Mrs Marion Coe	Conservative
Home Affairs	Sir Ivan Lawrence	Conservative
National Heritage	Gerald Kaufman	Labour
Science and Technology	Sir Giles Shaw	Conservative
Scottish Affairs	William McKelvey	Labour
Social Security	Frank Field	Labour
Trade and Industry	Richard Caborn	Labour
Transport	Robert Adley	Conservative
Treasury and Civil Service	John Watts	Conservative
Welsh Affairs	Gareth Wardell	Labour

more unequivocally, the transfer of Heavy Goods Vehicle testing to the private sector, the building of a new British Library, North Sea oil taxation and energy conservation (Griffith and Ryle, 1989, pp. 431–2). Another study suggests that 26.5% of recommendations by the Education, Science and Arts Select Committee and 35.1% of the Social Services Select Committee were accepted by Government between 1979–83 (Rush, 1989, pp. 100 and 249). Finally, taking the DSCs as a whole, answers to written parliamentary questions have revealed that 324 of their 'main recommendations' were accepted by the government between 1983–6 (Rush, 1991, p. 107). Over the longer term, Griffith and Ryle consider that there is 'much evidence that Ministers and civil servants are influenced in policy-making by the knowledge that what they propose may well come under the scrutiny of these committees and by the very process of committee inquiries' (p. 520)

Negative Influence on Policy

Four points need to be stressed. First, Ministers habitually ignore the bulk of 'main recommendations' by the DSCs. Second, DSCs pay too little attention to questions of expenditure and financial management within the Departments. Third, reports of the Select Committees are rarely debated on the floor of the House of Commons – only a quarter were debated between 1979–1988. The publicity they receive is therefore more limited than it need be. Fourth, although they often try to 'get round' the restriction by considering subjects about to lead to government legislation, the DSCs are not permitted to consider legislation.

Positive Scrutiny of the Executive

The DSCs constitute a great advance on Commons machinery to scrutinise the executive available before 1979. The system of DSCs is comprehensive (covering every Government Department) and popular with MPs who are given an opportunity to increase their professional expertise in a given specialist area. The

system has slowly gained in authority after the early years in which the DSCs' choice of subjects which would not be too divisive led to criticisms of them for 'blandness and marginality' (Drewry 1985). Subsequently, however, they tackled such subjects as the ban on trade unions at GCHQ, Westland, and the future of the NHS (1984–8); in 1992–3, DSCs demanded a large-scale reversal of the run-down of the British army, criticised delays in the asylum rules applicable to Bosnian refugees, and condemned Whitehall guidance to local authorities over the Community Care legislation. Moreover, although its final report seemed at best likely only to put a brake on the run-down of the industry, the Trade and Industry Select Committee achieved wide-spread publicity during 1992–3 during the public campaign against pit closures. Squabbles over chairmanships of the DSCs in July 1992 highlighted the DSCs' growing influence and their potential to embarrass the government.

Negative Scrutiny of the Executive

The DSCs still suffer from several constraints upon their effectiveness. First, although ministers normally attend when requested, some have been extremely unforthcoming e.g. Edwina Currie when questioned by the Agriculture SC about the salmonella in eggs scare and Leon Brittan who stonewalled before the Defence Committee investigating the Westland affair (1986). Ministers are not obliged to answer questions. Second, the Government can on occasion prevent civil servants from attending the DSCs – as, for example, over Westland, when the Defence Committee was not allowed to interview five named civil servants (three from the DTI and two from the PM's Office) and was given the Cabinet Secretary and the Permanent Under-Secretary at the DTI to interrogate instead. Also, under the 1980 Memorandum of Guidance (Osmotherly Rules) to civil servants appearing before the DSCs, civil servants are told that they may withhold information in the interests of 'good government' or national security, and that they should not disclose advice given to Ministers, inter-departmental exchanges on policy issues, the level at which decisions were taken, the manner in which a Minister has consulted his colleagues, or information about Cabinet committees and their discussions. Third, in addition to these restrictions upon the DSCs, their independence of the Executive came into question in July 1992 when a furious row erupted over allegations of interference by the Government Whips in the selection of members. Apparently their pressure led to the removal of Nicholas Winterton, the independent-minded chairman of the Health Select Committee, from that committee, nominally as a consequence of a newly devised rule by which no MP can serve for more than three terms on a select committee. This rule also led to the exclusion of another DSC chairman, Sir John Wheeler, from the Home Affairs Select Committee. Fourth, the DSCs detract attention from scrutiny on the floor of the House and make MPs too pro-Minister.

The Public Accounts Committee (PAC). Established in 1860, the PAC has a central role in the Commons' scrutiny of government expenditure. A committee of fifteen members, chaired by a senior member of the Opposition, it is particularly concerned to ensure the taxpayer gets value for money from public spending. It has been powerfully assisted in its work since 1983 by the *National Audit Office*, an independent body directed by the *Comptroller and Auditor-General* (CAG) with a staff of 900. Reports of both the PAC and the CAG are often extremely critical of Government Departments. In 1993, for example, PAC reports revealed considerable deficiencies in the standard of services delivered to the disabled by the Benefits Agency and the DSS (27th. Report) and called for senior civil servants who authorised the expenditure on Ministry of Defence 'junketing' to be disciplined (28th. Report). CAG reports exposed massive losses to the taxpayer in the chaotic disposal of Girobank by the Government, widespread public dissatisfaction at BT's handling of customer complaints, a fraud ring operating inside the Ministry of Defence during the Gulf War, and a huge multi-million pound overspend on the British Antarctic Survey by the Thatcher Governments. The 'economy, efficiency and

effectiveness' audits of the PAC and the CAG have thus produced some hard-hitting reports. However, PAC reports are rarely debated by the House and, when they are, are poorly-attended and receive little public attention. Moreover, certain aspects of public expenditure are excluded from the CAG's remit – the latest to come to light (in July 1992) being the Sovereign's expenditure under the Civil List. Nonetheless, the scrutiny of government expenditure by parliamentary officers has improved considerably in the last decade; what remains inadequate is parliament's own ability to deploy to maximum effect the information they provide.

■ The House of Lords

The powers of the House of Lords have been considerably reduced in the twentieth century so much so that by the 1950s – according to one commentator – the institution was 'dying in its sleep' (Hennessy, 1987). However, since the failure of the 1968 attempt to reform its composition, the Lords has undergone a resurgence and currently enjoys more public respect than at any time in its modern history. This section examines the overall significance of this recent revival. Has the Upper House become 'the only constitutional counterweight to elective dictatorship' (Brazier, 1991, p. 73) or has the constitutional impact of its new-found vigour been exaggerated (Adonis, 1993, p. 247)?

□ *Powers and Functions*

By convention, the House of Lords is part of the legislative sovereign – 'the Queen-in-Parliament'. Constitutionally, therefore, despite its reduced powers, the Upper House remains an essential part of the legislative process. By the Parliament Act of 1911, the Lords completely lost its power to delay or amend money bills: these go for the Royal Assent one month after leaving the House of Commons, whether approved by the Lords or not. But it retained other powers which included the power to delay non-money bills for up to two successive sessions (reduced to one session only by the Parliament Act of 1949). The present powers of the House of Lords – as defined by the Parliament Acts of 1911 and 1949 – are as follows:

1. To delay non-money bills for up to one year;
2. To veto (a) bills to prolong the life of parliament beyond the statutory five-year period; (b) private bills (not to be confused with private members' bills); and (c) delegated legislation.

The bulk of the work of the House of Lords may be conveniently summarised in terms of the following functions:

- **Deliberation**: the provision of a forum for debates on matters of current interest;
- **Legislation**: revision of House of Commons bills, giving Ministers the opportunity for second thoughts; initiation of non-controversial legislation, including Government bills, private bills (promoted by bodies outside parliament e.g. local authorities) and bills by individual peers; and consideration of delegated legislation;
- **Scrutiny**: the Lords subjects Government policy and administration to scrutiny through questions and through the work of its select committees (e.g. European Communities, Science and Technology);
- **Supreme court of appeal**: the Lords is the ultimate court of appeal in the United Kingdom.

☐ *Composition*

Membership of the Upper House is determined by birth, creation (by the Crown on the advice of the prime minister) and position. Nearly two-thirds (776) of its approximately 1200 members are hereditary peers, just under one-third (385) are life peers and there are twenty-six Church of England bishops (including two archbishops) who hold their seats until they retire and nineteen Law Lords (including the Lord Chancellor).

Seventy-six of its members (6.3%) are women. Its composition has been significantly affected by the Life Peerages Act 1958, which empowered the Crown to create life peers and peeresses, and the Peerages Act 1963, which allowed hereditary peers to disclaim their titles and admitted hereditary peeresses into the House of Lords in their own right. Nominally very large for an Upper House, the Lords is much reduced in practice by non-attendance: only about 400 of its members attend on a regular basis (i.e. more than a third of sittings per session). Life peers – outnumbered roughly 2:1 by hereditary peers in the House as a whole – figure disproportionately in the 'working House' (defined as peers attending at least 33% of sittings), constituting 56% to the hereditary peers' 44% in the 1987–8 session.

☐ *Political Allegiances*

Party functions rather differently in the Upper House compared with the Commons but is still very important. One marked difference is the large number of peers who choose to remain independent of political ties – the crossbenchers. However, over two-thirds of peers holding firm political views support one of the major parties, with the Conservatives in an overall majority and the Liberal Democrats better represented and Labour worse represented than in the Commons (Table 12.7).

Conservative strength in the 'working House' is less pronounced owing to the conscientiousness of Labour and Liberal Democrat peers. In the 1991–2 session, for example, 75% of Labour

Table 12.7 *Party strengths in the House of Lords*

	as at 15 February 1993
Conservative	478 (51.7%)
Labour	116 (12.5%)
Liberal Democrat	59 (6.4%)
Crossbenchers	272 (29.4%)
	925 (100%)

(Peers attending at least 33% of sittings, 1991–2)	
Conservative	203 (50%)
Labour	87 (22%)
Liberal Democrat	39 (10%)
Crossbenchers	66 (17%)
Other	5 (1%)
	400 100%

Source: House of Lords Information Office.

Table 12.8 *Party strengths in the 'working House'*

peers, 66% of Liberal Democrats but only 42% of Conservatives attended over one-third of sittings. However, even when only regular attendance is taken into consideration, the Conservatives still possess a narrow overall majority. (Table 12.8).

□ *Recent Behaviour*

House of Lords activity has increased steadily over recent decades. (Table 12.9). On average in the four sessions 1988–1992, it devoted 56.85% of its time to legislation (55.8% public bills, 1.05% private bills), 17.8% to general debates, 6.3% to starred questions (i.e. questions taken as first business and not leading to debate because

Table 12.9 *Growth in activity of the House of Lords, 1950–92*

	1950–1	1960–1	1970–1	1991–2
Average daily attendance	86	142	265	337
Total hours sat	292	599	966	518*
Average length of sittings (hrs./mins.)	3.03	4.48	6.19	7.01

Sources: Griffith and Ryle (1989, p. 472); House of Lords Information Office.

*This figure is distorted because the 1991–2 session only had 74 sitting days because of the General Election.

Figures for previous years are more typical: 885 (1990–1), 1072 (1989–90), 1076 (1988–9).

intended for information only), 5.25% to unstarred questions (which can lead to debate and are comparable to adjournment debates in the Commons) and 3.37% on Statutory Instruments (delegated legislation). In short, the Upper House spends rather over half its time on legislation (an increasing proportion in recent years), about one-fifth on general debates and about one-tenth on Questions (starred and unstarred), its main mechanism for scrutiny of the executive. How effective in its major tasks is the contemporary House of Lords?

Legislation

The Lords accepts certain limitations on its own power of delay. The main guiding rule – firmly established by Conservative Opposition peers in the immediate post-war period – is that the Upper House does not oppose measures included in the governing party's manifesto at the previous election. In addition, the Lords rarely presses an amendment or delays a measure to the point where the Parliament Acts (Parliament Act 1911, S.2, as amended by Parliament Act 1949, S.1) have to be invoked: i.e. the requirement that if the Commons passes a public Bill in two successive sessions and the Lords rejects it in both of them, the Bill receives the Royal Assent after the second rejection. On only four occasions since 1911 has this clause of the Parliament Act been employed – the Government of Ireland Act (1914), the Welsh Church Act (1914), the Parliament Act (1949) and the War Crimes Act (1991). This last Bill – which allowed former Nazi war criminals living in Britain to be tried in British courts – was twice rejected by the Lords but forced through by the Conservative Government using Parliament Act procedures. Of more importance, however, are those cases where the Lords has passed adverse amendments on Government legislation, thereby causing delay. A Conservative-dominated Lords often subjected Labour Governments in the 1960s and 1970s to legislative defeats. What surprised many commentators was the continuation of this Upper House rebelliousness against Conservative Governments after 1979. (Table 12.10)

		1964–1992
Years	*Government*	*Number of defeats*
1964–70	Labour	116
1970–4	Conservative	25
1974	Labour	15
1974–9	Labour	347
1979–83	Conservative	45
1983–7	Conservative	62
1987–92	Conservative	72

Table 12.10　*Government defeats in the House of Lords*

The constitutional and political significance of the Lords' so-called 'independence' is controversial. One recent commentator regards the Lords as the only constitutional bulwark against dictatorship, having proved its capacity to treat the legislation of both parties 'with something approaching impartial rigour' whilst, by contrast, another academic maintains that, although it may no longer be a rubber stamp, it still has not provided anything more than 'minor obstructions' to the government's legislative programme. (Brazier, 1991, p. 73; Adonis, 1993, p. 247). Where does the truth lie? These observations help place the debate in perspective.

First, Government defeats in the Lords still do not occur very often. Between 1979–92, Conservative Administrations suffered 179 adverse votes in 2,275 divisions (7.9%) However, this rate of defeat is greater than that of their Conservative predecessors: 3.7%, 1959–64 and 5.7%, 1970–74. Second, defeats on major legislation are even more rare. Moreover, governments do not invariably react to hostile amendments by 'thinking again': on the contrary, they frequently use their Commons majority to reverse the Lords' vote and then force the Upper House to give way by threatening to use the Parliament Act or since 1979 to call upon their 'reserve army' of peers in the Lords. A notorious example of an actual deployment of this 'hidden' vote in the Lords occurred in 1988 when Conservative Whips mobilised large numbers of 'backwoodsmen' peers to vote down an amendment to its poll tax legislation which would have required the Government to relate the charge to ability to pay within a year of its introduction. The amendment was defeated 317–183: on only one another occasion since 1931 had 500 or more peers turned out to vote (1971). This episode symbolised the determination of the third Thatcher Administration to reverse hostile Lords' amendments by using its Commons majority e.g. on charges for eye tests, increases in dental charges and the preservation of local authority contracts compliance protecting job opportunities for disabled people (1988). In contrast, the first two Thatcher Administrations gave way more often when defeated in the Lords, accepting quite important changes over school transport in rural areas, the sale of council houses built for the elderly, and interim councils for its abolished authorities (1984). Third, Lords' rebelliousness has a relatively narrow focus – issues affecting the Constitution, local government, the old, the disabled, the countryside, and the voluntary services and their users. (Adonis, 1993, p. 238; Welfare, 1992).

The truth, therefore, appears to lie in between the two propositions: whilst far from being a severe constitutional obstacle to the Government of the day, the Upper House has on numerous occasions impeded its legislation and forced concessions. Its greater 'independence' dates from the failure of the Parliament (no.2) Bill (1969) which would have reduced its delaying power to six months and eliminated the voting rights of hereditary peers. The failure of this reform attempt boosted its morale by prompting the realisation that it had a valuable role to fulfil after all. The advent of life peers after 1958 enhanced the quality of debates and the televising of the Lords from 1983 increased its prestige. Finally, the political situation after 1979 when large Government majorities and weak Oppositions prevailed encouraged the Lords to take an oppositional role upon itself.

Another significant trend in recent decades has been the greater use made of the Lords by

Governments to revise and generally tidy up their legislation. The extent of this change may be gauged from the fact that between 1987–90 the Upper House made 7868 amendments to Government bills compared with 2854 amendments to Government legislation between 1970–3. Most of these changes are introduced by Ministers. Because much of this tidying-up process has to be done hurriedly at the end of sessions, one peer has described the Upper Chamber as 'a gilded dustpan and brush'. Suggested causes for this development include inadequate consultation, Government indecisiveness and poor drafting in the early stages of legislation, but whatever the reasons, it has made the House of Lords an increasingly attractive target for pressure groups (Shell, 1992a, pp. 165–6).

Deliberation and Scrutiny

The House of Lords – which devotes approximately one day per week to general debate – is often praised for the overall quality of its debates but, whilst their overall impact is not easy to assess, it is probably not large. Its exercise of its scrutiny functions (through Questions and Select Committees) is of greater consequence. Thus, Conservative Governments since 1979 were embarrassed by ad hoc Select Committee Reports on Unemployment (1979–82) and Trade and Industry (1984–5) and by the Science and Industry Select Committee's criticisms of cuts in the Government's budget for scientific research (1991). In addition, the House of Lords Select Committee on the European Communities, which considers initiatives proposed by the EC Commission, is well-staffed, able to consider EC proposals on their merits, and expert; it produces over 20 reports a year which, like other Lords Select Committee reports but unlike their equivalents in the Commons, are all debated. Overall, however, the House of Lords has made no attempt to establish through its Select Committees a mechanism for consistent, comprehensive scrutiny of Government but has rather used them to fill gaps left by the Commons Select Committee system.

□ *Reform of the House of Lords*

The value of the work done by the Lords in the initiation and revision of legislation and the occasional frustration of Government by delaying its measures is to some extent offset by persisting concern about its anomalous, unrepresentative and Conservative-dominated composition. What should be done? Two main attitudes may be discerned towards it.

1. Retain it with its present composition and powers; or
2. Reform its composition while according it increased, broadly similar or reduced powers.

For a long period over the late 1970s and 1980s Labour favoured a third option – abolition – but moved away from this stance in 1989 towards reform, an attitude it shares with the Liberal Democrats. The early 1990s saw a variety of other reform schemes produced by individuals and groups also seeking to 'mend' the institution rather than end it. The Conservatives, however, who hold the whip hand, currently offer no plans to change the Upper House. The Party's last major proposals on the matter appeared in the Report of the Home Committee (1978), which recommended phasing out hereditary peers and introducing elected peers (with a view to the House becoming one-third appointed and two-thirds elected) and restoring the House's delaying power to two years.

The main stumbling block to reform – apart from Conservative political domination – is lack of agreement among reformers (Table 12.11). Some commentators have discerned a 'Second Chamber paradox' regarding reform: that, whilst election provides the only appropriate basis for a second chamber in a democracy, reform along such lines – by increasing the legitimacy of the Upper House – might transform it into a dangerous rival of the Commons, thereby precipitating more bitter and more frequent clashes between the two bodies. This fear, however, may be exaggerated: most modern States have elected second

Source	Proposed reforms
Labour	Replace with elected Second Chamber with power to delay legislation reducing individual and constitutional rights for the lifetime of a parliament
Liberal Democrat	Replace with a Senate primarily elected by proportional representation by citizens of the nations and regions with powers to delay all legislation other than money bills for up to two years.
The Economist 6–12 July, 1991	Replace with Senate, four-fifths elected by proportional representation, one fifth appointed with right to speak but not vote; similar powers as at present, except for reduction in delaying power to six months and stronger role on EC.
Institute for Public Policy Research (1991)	Replace with Second Chamber elected by proportional representation (Single Transferable Vote) for fixed four-year term; subordinate as now to Commons in relation to financial and general legislation but equal powers concerning constitutional legislation and amendments
Tony Benn Commonwealth of Britain Bill (1991)	Replace with elected Second Chamber drawn from England, Scotland and Wales in proportion to their populations with powers to delay legislation for one year and Statutory Instruments for one month.

Table 12.11 *Proposals for reforming the House of Lords*

chambers without facing this situation. On the last occasion (1968) when broad agreement on reform existed between the parties, Labour left and Conservative right combined to defeat the proposals in the Commons. The Labour legislation then would have phased out hereditary peers and provided for a chamber of appointed members with voting rights dependent upon attending at least 30% of sittings, and with the Government guaranteed a 10% majority over the Opposition and the delaying power reduced to six

months. For the present, evolution rather than drastic reform seems the most likely way for the Lords to change.

■ Retrospect and Prospect

Parliament as an institution has changed considerably over recent decades. The increased propensity of MPs to defy the Whips by voting against the party line, the activities of a wide range of Select Committees, the growth in importance of Private Members' legislation especially on 'conscience' but also on other issues, the rising significance of the 'welfare officer' role of MPs, and a modest revival in the position of the House of Lords have all boosted the capacity of parliament to scrutinise Government policy, influence legislation and reflect public opinion. MPs are better paid, better equipped, harder-working and more professional than ever before. However, the *Westminster model* of the role of parliament – as outlined in the opening sections of this chapter – retains its validity. Parliament is dominated by party and party discipline ensures that even in a time of narrow majorities the bulk of government legislation goes through as intended. Reformers' increasing recognition of the unlikelihood of parliament evolving into a policy-making body in its own right (the *revived independent powerhouse* or *transformative* model) prompted them to focus in the early 1990s on strengthening Parliament's functions of representation, scrutiny (of both Government legislation and decisions) and public debate. Two concerns came to loom particularly large in the early 1990s. The Conservatives' fourth consecutive election victory (1992) with its further consolidation of one-party rule (see Chapter 13) brought the House of Commons' role as a representative of national opinion into even sharper focus. Second, the spate of EC legislation and initiatives in the late 1980s and early 1990s concentrated attention on the inadequacy of the Commons' ability to scrutinise and debate them. Table 12.12 outlines some major proposals for reform of the House of Commons.

Table 12.12 *The House of Commons: proposals for reform*

Reform	Aim
Representation	
Proportional representation	To ensure fairer representation of national opinion
Fixed-term parliaments	To abolish advantage to Governments of control over election date
Legislation	
Reform all Standing Committees on lines of Special Standing Committees (introduced 1980 but little used) or Select Committees	To improve scrutiny of Government legislation
Introduce ability to amend Statutory Instruments which at present must be accepted or rejected as a whole	To encourage more careful and more serious scrutiny of delegated legislation
Scrutiny	
More debate of Select Committee reports on the floor of the House.	To foster greater Executive accountability.
Require Departmental Select Committees to investigate Departments' expenditure, extend remit of Public Accounts Committee to include all public spending, improve staffing levels of PAC and NAC, and increase number of Estimates days from present four or so per session.	To strengthen Commons' ability to act as a financial watchdog on the raising and spending of public funds.
Extend scrutiny and debate of EU documents and policies beyond present Select Committee on European Legislation and two special (European) Standing Committees (established in 1991)	To improve scrutiny and debate of European legislation and policies.
Forum for debate	
Reform hours of sitting, improve resources, research facilities and working conditions of MPs. Improve capability of Opposition by secondment of civil servants to Shadow Front Bench. Accord minor parties greater role in planning Commons business and greater status by salaries for their leaders. Clarify Commons documents, language and procedure.	To modernise the House, improve its sources of information and make the imbalance of facilities between Government and opposition parties less pronounced, thereby rendering it a more effective forum for debate.

Summary

The government of the day controls Parliament through the exercise of its party majority but parliament remains important as a representative, legislative and scrutinising body, as a focus for political Opposition, as a forum for debate and as a training-ground for aspiring politicians. Over the last quarter century, for a variety of reasons, backbench independence has increased in the House of Commons and Government defeats have occurred more frequently although remaining relatively rare. The capacity of the House of

Commons to scrutinise the activities of government has improved but important weaknesses still exist especially in relation to oversight of public expenditure. The House of Lords retains its constitutional importance as primarily, but by no means exclusively, a checking and revising chamber. Gaining strength from modest reforms of its composition (1958), from the failure of more drastic reform (especially 1969), and from various other developments, and adopting a calculatedly self-imposed limitation on its own powers of amendment and delay, the Upper House has inflicted some significant defeats on governments since 1970. However, its power to obstruct government remains strictly limited and its predominantly hereditary composition makes it the subject of continuing political controversy. In general, the 'power of parliament' continues to fall short of the hopes of parliamentary reformers, and schemes for reform of both Houses abound.

Questions

1. Discuss the view that Parliament is no longer of central importance in the contemporary British political system.

2. Analyse the effectiveness of the Commons select committees as a system of scrutiny of the executive.

Assignments

1. Lobbying of MPs by pressure groups intensified during the 1980s and with this trend came increased potential for conflicts of interest between MPs' personal financial advantage and their public duty. A study of MPs' own ethical attitudes used the following hypothetical scenarios to test them, asking the 100 MPs surveyed to rank the activities on a seven-point scale with 1 as 'very corrupt' and 7 as 'not corrupt at all'.

(a) An MP uses his position to get a friend or relative admitted to Oxford or Cambridge or some other prestigious institution.

(b) A Cabinet minister uses his influence to obtain a contract for a firm in his constituency.

(c) An MP is retained by a major company to arrange meetings and dinners at which its executive can meet parliamentarians.

(d) An MP hires his wife or other family member to serve as his secretary.

(e) At Christmas, an MP accepts a crate of wine from an influential constituent.

(f) An MP is issued a first-class airline ticket as part of a parliamentary delegation. He exchanges the ticket for an economy fare and pockets the difference.

(g) An all-party group on the aged secures a full-time research assistant at the expense of Age Concern.

(h) An MP on retainer to a PR company representing a foreign government submits several written questions for the Order Paper on British industrial development in that country.

Source: Mancuso (1993).

Evaluate these activities yourself on the scale suggested, making sure to identify the precise conflicts of interest in each case; conduct a survey of the opinions on MPs' interests of your friends and colleagues; then write a short report.

2. In an ideal world, Government would take great care in preparing legislation, basing it on the considered response to proposals contained in White Papers. Bills would be examined in detail by both the Commons and the Lords; they would debate bills in principle, then examine them in great detail clause by clause, making amendments to improve the legislation whenever necessary; and there would always be the chance for re-examination of proposals by either House.

But what really happens? The Education Bill is a good example. The White Paper outlining this bill was published in July, so that the consultation period took place during the school summer holidays. Consequently, relatively little real consultation took place with those who would be most affected by the legislation (despite the fact that the poll tax was still fresh enough in mind as a warning to Ministers over what can happen when there is little consultation.) In addition to this, the sheer complexity of legislation is becoming an issue. The Education Bill began with 225 clauses and 17 schedules, which makes it twice the size of the Act which has become a milestone in educational history – the (Butler) Education Act of 1944. The Government then made 278 amendments in the Commons committee stage, 78 more at report stage, 258 more in the Lords committee stage, 296 more on report, and 71 at third reading. Some amendments appeared only hours before they were debated, leaving members very little time in which to consider them.

The position has been reached where Parliament enacts more legislation than it can handle efficiently. Commonsense suggests that this must affect the quality of legislation.

The Child Support Act provides another example of how the legislative process can fail. Labour and Conservative MPs supported the Act but, only months after its introduction, they are receiving a massive number of complaints and demands for radical alterations to be made in the legislation. Many of them are wondering how they managed to pass it in the first place without picking up all the problems the Act now contains. The Government rushed the bill through Parliament, and Labour failed to operate as an effective opposition.

The Child Support Act has its origins in the last days of the Thatcher era. Mrs Thatcher wanted quick action on the problem of absent fathers who refused to pay maintenance to help bring up their children. A White Paper was published and sent to over 90 pressure groups which had six weeks in which to respond. As with the Education bill, this is not long enough for proper consultation. Many pressure groups supported the ideas and principles in the White Paper, but felt that there were many practical faults which needed sorting out. But groups like the National Council for One Parent Families felt that the Government was not really interested in what they had to say, since the contents of the bill was almost identical to the White Paper. The lobby felt that the consultation process had failed.

(1) Discuss the advantages and disadvantages of 'outside experts' playing a bigger role in drafting legislation.
(2) Is it true that Parliament 'enacts more legislation than it can handle efficiently'? If so, how has this situation come about?

Further reading

Adonis, A. (1993) *Parliament Today*, 2nd edn (Manchester: Manchester University Press).

Berry, S. (1993) 'Lobbying: A Need to Regulate?', *Politics Review*, 2: 3, February.

Dorey, P. (1992) 'Much Maligned: Much Misunderstood: The Role of the Party Whips', *Talking Politics*, 5, 1, Autumn.

Drewry, G. (ed.) (1989) *The New Select Committees*, 2nd edn (Oxford: Clarendon).

Garrett, J. (1992) *Westminster. Does Parliament Work?* (London: Gollancz).

Griffith, J.A.G. and Ryle, M. (1989) *Parliament* (London: Sweet and Maxwell).

Jones, B. and Robins, L. (eds) (1992) *Two Decades in British Politics*, (Manchester: Manchester University Press).

Judge, D. (1992) 'Disorder in the "Frustration" Parliaments of Thatcherite Britain', *Political Studies*, 40: 3, September.

Norton, P. (1991) 'Reforming the House of Commons', *Talking Politics*, 4: 1, autumn.

Radice, L., Vallance, E. and Willis, V. (1987) *Member of Parliament* (London: Macmillan).

Rush, M. (ed.) (1990) *Parliament and Pressure Politics* (Oxford: Clarendon).

Rush, M. (1991) 'The Departmental Select Committees: Into the 1990s', *Talking Politics*, 3: 3, summer.

Ryle, M. and Richards, P. (eds) (1988) *The Commons under Scrutiny* (London: Routledge).

Shell, D. (1992a) 'The House of Lords: the best second chamber we have got?' in B. Jones and L. Robins (eds) *Two Decades in British Politics* (Manchester: Manchester University Press).

Shell, D. (1992b) *The House of Lords*, 2nd edn (London: Harvester Wheatsheaf).

■ *Chapter 13* ■

Political Parties

Parties have been encountered at several points already. In Chapter 1 we saw that democratic government was basically party government and in Chapter 6 we noted that, although unknown to the British Constitution, voluntary organisations such as parties were in fact essential to its working. In Chapter 8, we examined the role of party in government and in Chapter 12, the functions and organisation of the parties in parliament with special reference to their tasks in opposition. Chapter 14 will consider voting behaviour and the role of parties in the electoral system. This chapter focuses on the parties themselves, explaining both the overall working of the British party system and the internal organisation, financing and membership of the parties together with recent trends in their popular support. We begin, however, by briefly summarising the major functions of party. These are: first, to provide government and opposition; second, to serve as agencies of representation; and third, alongside other means such as pressure groups, to enable popular participation in politics to take place.

■ The Functions of Party in Britain

□ *Government and Opposition*

Parties form governments – not all parties have an equal chance of forming a government, but government is always by *some* party. Parties recruit the politicians by their selection of party candidates, develop the programmes expressed in manifestos on which government policy is (largely) based and run the major offices of State.

Opposition, as we have seen, is also by party. The party with the second highest number of seats forms both the official Opposition and the alternative government. All the non-governing parties in parliament are collectively said to be in opposition.

□ *Representation*

Parties are the single most important agency of political representation. They organise a mass electorate by enabling it to make meaningful choices. Parties in the UK enable voters to elect governments by grouping parliamentary candidates together in a coherent way (i.e. under a limited range of 'labels') so that votes in one constituency can be related to votes in another: voters in other words vote for a party first and foremost, and for a particular candidate only to an extremely small extent. The elector has probably never heard of most if not all of the candidates on the ballot paper, but s/he *has* heard of the Conservative and Labour parties, the Liberal Democrats, and the various nationalist parties. In voting, electors are (largely) expressing an opinion on which party would form the most effective government and which party leader would make the most capable Prime Minister. Parties are important instruments of communication between governments and governed. Parties shape the ideas of groups and individuals to their purposes and bring them into the public arena and into government. Conversely, through their conferences, their canvassing of voters at election time and in the meetings of MPs with party 'activists' and with constituents, parties take the concerns of government to their supporters and the electorate at large.

□ *Participation*

Parties are the main agencies of political participation. Participation can range from the fairly minimal – voting in elections – to the maximal – joining a party and working for it by canvassing, attending meetings and conferences and even – for a few – representing it in parliament and government. Parties enable individuals to assert their distinctive political identities; to register a commitment to what can be an important cause in their lives; ultimately, at the deepest level, to express a preference for one kind of society rather than another. Parties can represent classes, ethnic groups, regions, economic interests and ideologies. Because they offer the opportunity to participate in politics from the highest level to the most moderate and because they are the sole agencies of comprehensive choice at elections, parties deserve to be considered the leading agencies of political participation.

■ The Party System in the UK

Is UK politics best described as a two-party system, a dominant party system, a two-and-a-half party system, a three-party system, or a multi-party system? Answers to this question depend to a considerable extent on the criteria, perspective and time period adopted.

□ *A Two-Party System?*

Britain has been traditionally regarded as a two-party system. The academic orthodoxy has held that Britain has a system in which two major parties – each of them willing to govern alone – have regularly competed for all seats in the country and alternated in power with working majorities. The period between 1945–79 – when the political pendulum did swing at fairly regular intervals between Labour and the Conservatives – seems to confirm this notion (Table 13.1). However, even though occupying government after six general elections in this period, Labour was elected only twice with working majorities (defined as an overall advantage of 20 or more seats). Moreover, if we extend our historical perspective to cover the period after 1979 – and before 1945 – the situation is even less clear-cut. Labour lost four consecutive general elections after 1979 and by 1993 had been out of office for fourteen years. Moreover, Labour held power for only the briefest periods inter-war (1924 and 1929–31), and did not begin to contest over 80% of constituencies until 1924 or all constituencies until 1945.

Finally, sometimes neither major party has achieved an overall majority and the minority party taking office has become dependent for its continuation in power upon the support of a third party. Periods of minority government (each time involving Labour) occurred in 1924, 1929–31, 1974 (February–October) and again in 1977. In 1977, Labour lost its overall majority and, in

Table 13.1 *The major parties, 1945–92: parliamentary majorities*

Election	Party returned to office	Size of overall majority
1945	Labour	146
1950	Labour	5
1951	Conservative	17
1955	Conservative	58
1959	Conservative	100
1964	Labour	4
1966	Labour	96
1970	Conservative	30
1974 (Feb.)	Labour	−33
1974 (Oct.)	Labour	3
1979	Conservative	43
1983	Conservative	144
1987	Conservative	101
1992	Conservative	21

order to prevent continual defeats in the House of Commons, made a pact with the Liberal Party. This arrangement fell short of being a formal coalition as the Liberals did not enter the Government. But it constitutes another exception to a purported 'normal' situation in which one or other major party rules alone without the tolerance or assistance of a third party. In short, if Britain has a two-way party system, it is not a particularly well-balanced one: often, the electoral pendulum has failed to swing sufficiently either to give the main opposition power at all or to provide it with a working majority.

☐ *A Dominant Party System?*

Some commentators consider that the most appropriate term to describe the British polity is 'dominant party system'. Between 1918–1993, the Conservatives were in government for fifty-four years – 72% of the time – ruling either alone or as the dominant partner in national coalitions and enjoying several lengthy uninterrupted spells in power – 1931–45; 1951–64; and after 1979. Assuming the party continues in office until 1997, it will have held power continuously for eighteen years, – the longest period of unbroken rule by a single party since 1832. (Table 13.2). Put in these terms, the dominant party thesis appears persuasive. But critics argue that Conservative dominance in government is the consequence of specific factors, namely a divided opposition and the employment of a majoritarian electoral system which routinely translates a minority of votes into a majority of seats. Only twice since 1918 – in 1931 and 1935 – have the Conservatives gained over 50% of the vote and in their four election victories since 1979 they have failed to achieve over 44% total share. Moreover, the lowest percentage by which the Conservative share of the vote was exceeded by the combined share of the main national opposition parties (Labour/ Liberal/ Alliance/Liberal Democrat) between 1974–1992 was 6.8% in 1979; in other years the difference in percentage share of the vote between the Conservatives and the combined share of its two major rivals was: 18.5% (1974 Feb.), 21.7%

(1974 Oct.), 10.6% (1983), 11.1% (1987) and 10.3% (1992). In 1992, nearly 58% of voters cast their votes for parties other than the Conservatives. In terms of electoral votes, Britain is far from possessing a 'dominant party' system.

☐ *A Two-and-a-Half or Three-Party System?*

The case for saying that Britain has a $2\frac{1}{2}$ or three party system rests on the proposition that the Liberal Democrats (pre-1989 Liberals) are virtually or in reality a major party. The main arguments for this proposition are that since the General Election of February 1974, either alone or together with the Social Democrats as 'the Alliance', the party has contested all or nearly all constituencies nation-wide and regularly polled very highly, 4.3m. in 1979 being its lowest in this period and 7.8m. (with the SDP) in 1983 its highest vote. Under any alternative electoral system but AV (Alternative Vote), its 6m. votes in 1992 would have gained it about 100 seats and given it decisive influence in a 'hung parliament'. The party is very strong at the political grassroots, as indicated by its successes in by-elections and local elections, and is the main opposition party to the Conservatives in 145 constituencies. However, despite a willingness to serve in government, the Liberals have not held power alone as a party since 1915. In parliamentary terms – with an apparent 'ceiling' of about 20 seats – they are

Table 13.2   *One-party dominance after 1979*

	1979	1983	1987	1992
Conservative MPs elected	339	397	376	336
Labour MPs elected	269	209	229	271
Conservative majority over Labour	70	188	147	65
Conservative percentage share of the UK vote	43.9	42.4	42.3	41.9
Labour percentage share of the UK vote	36.9	27.6	30.8	34.4
Conservative percentage majority over Labour	7	14.8	11.5	7.5

a minor party, victims of the remorseless 'squeeze' exercised by the British 'first past the post' electoral system on third parties. However, the possibility that a third party might gain rough parity in seats as well as votes with the two other parties remains. This happened during the first half of the century as Labour rose to the position of alternative governing party while the Liberal party declined. For a time during this process – in the early 1920s – the Liberals were 'neck and neck' with Labour, gaining seats (159 in 1923, for example) roughly commensurate with their total vote, and people spoke and wrote of the 'naturalness' of the three-party system.

☐ *A Multi-Party System?*

Like the argument that Britain has a $2\frac{1}{2}$ or three party system, the case that it possesses a multi-party system focuses on *electoral choice*. Thus, at the constituency level, the system is to a considerable extent regionalised, with differing patterns of parties confronting electors in each geographical area of the UK. Indeed, the Ulster parties, the Scottish National Party (SNP) and the Welsh Nationalists (Plaid Cymru) exist only in their particular regions. Alongside the other UK parties, the Nationalists increase the range of electoral choice in Scotland and Wales. In Northern Ireland, where down to 1992 the mainland parties had no presence, the regional (Ulster) parties constitute almost the entire choice. But although a vote for the nationalist parties or for other small parties like the Green Party, expresses a political preference, it does not help to choose a government since none of these puts forward enough candidates to have any chance of gaining a UK majority. Nor would contesting more constituencies necessarily bring any electoral rewards: for example, the SNP would be unlikely to pick up many votes in SE England.

The answer to the question with which we began this section may be expressed as follows. Britain is still best described as a two-party system (Table 13.3). But two qualifications need to be borne in mind. First, and most important, is the post-1979 period of one-party domination which has led to the suggestion that the system consists of 'a natural party of government and a natural party of opposition' (Crewe, 1992, p. 254). Second, at the constituency level, voters are offered a range of electoral choice extending well beyond the two main parties to encompass, particularly, one minor party of importance throughout the mainland and nationalist parties

Table 13.3 *The major parties, 1945–92: seats, votes and share of the total vote*

General Election	Seats		Votes (in millions)		Percentage share of total vote	
	Lab.	Con.	Lab.	Con.	Lab.	Con.
1945	393	213	11.9	9.9	47.8	39.8
1950	315	298	13.2	12.5	46.1	43.5
1951	295	321	13.9	13.7	48.8	48.0
1955	277	344	12.4	13.2	46.4	49.7
1959	258	365	12.2	13.7	43.8	49.4
1964	317	304	12.2	12.0	44.1	43.4
1966	363	253	13.0	11.4	47.9	41.9
1970	287	330	12.1	13.1	43.0	46.4
1974 (Feb.)	301	297	11.6	11.8	37.1	37.9
1974 (Oct.)	319	277	11.4	10.4	39.2	35.8
1979	268	339	11.5	13.6	36.9	43.9
1983	209	397	8.4	13.0	27.6	42.4
1987	229	375	10.0	13.7	30.8	42.3
1992	271	336	11.5	14.1	34.4	41.9

of purely regional significance. The term 'two-party system', therefore, needs to be used with caution, especially in the light of the important changes which have taken place in recent decades.

The two major trends since 1970 have been a decline in support for the two major parties and an increase in the followings of the minor parties. In 1951, at the 'peak' of two-party electoral dominance, the Conservative and Labour parties together received 96.8 per cent of the total vote and minor parties a negligible 3.2 per cent. By 1987, the combined vote of the two major parties had dropped to 73 per cent of the total vote and that of the minor parties had risen dramatically

Table 13.4 *The minor parties, 1945–92: seats, votes and share of the total vote*

General Election	Seats	Votes (in millions)	Percentage of total vote
1945	34	3.1	11.8
1950	12	3.0	10.4
1951	9	0.9	5.8
1955	9	1.0	3.9
1959	7	1.7	6.8
1964	9	3.4	12.5
1966	14	2.7	9.7
1970	13	3.0	10.7
1974 (Feb.)			
GB	25	7.1	22.7
NI	12	0.7	2.3
1974 (Oct.)			
GB	27	6.5	22.6
NI	12	0.7	2.4
1979			
GB	15	5.2	16.9
NI	12	0.6	2.2
1983			
GB	27	8.4	27.5
NI	17	0.7	2.5
1987			
GB	28	8.0	24.8
NI	17	0.7	2.3
1992			
GB	27	6.8	20.1
NI	17	0.7	2.2

Note: Before 1974 Ulster Unionists were affiliated to the Conservative Party but they broke this link in that year. From 1974, their results (together with those of smaller Ulster groupings) appear separately from the other British minor parties.

to 26.9 per cent (Tables 13.3 and 13.4) In 1992, the vote of the major parties recovered to 76.3 per cent. Nonetheless, in forty years they had lost the support of over one-fifth of voters. Overall, Labour has suffered a much greater loss of support than the Conservatives. Whereas the Conservative share of the vote has fallen by about 6 per cent since 1951 and has remained steady at just over two-fifths of voters since 1979, Labour's share of the vote has dropped by over 14 per cent in the same period. Its electoral weakness in the 1980s and early 1990s raised questions about its capacity to win and exercise power single-handedly ever again.

The main landmark in the break-up of major party domination was the General Election of February 1974 when the mainland minor parties almost doubled their parliamentary representation and more than doubled their share of the vote (Table 13.4). The leading elements in this change were the very large increase in electoral support for the Liberals and the more modest increase in the following of the SNP. By 1983, the vote share of the Liberal-SDP Alliance rose to 25.4%, a mere 2.2 per cent below Labour's, but in 1992 the Liberal vote slipped back to 17.8%. All told, however, just under one-quarter of voters (23.6 per cent) supported minor parties in 1992.

☐ Choice at Elections

In the hey-day of political consensus thirty years ago, it was often said that parties at elections merely offered electors the choice between Tweedledum and Tweedledee. Hardly true then, this observation is even further from reality today, as is revealed by Table 13.6, comparing the manifestos of the nation-wide parties on the main issues in 1992. Table 13.5 identifies the five issues of most concern to voters. On all these issue-areas, there were broad contrasts of policy and/or emphasis between the parties. A possible exception is prices, where both the Conservatives and Labour made continued membership of the ERM a key element – for the Conservatives 'central' – in their counter-inflation strategy.

	All voters	Party advantage
NHS/Hospitals	41	Labour + 34
Unemployment	36	Labour + 26
Education	23	Labour + 23
Prices	11	Conservative + 59
Taxation	10	Conservative + 72

Proportion of respondents mentioning an issue as one of the two most important in influencing their vote

Question: 'Think of all the urgent problems facing the country at the present time. When you decided which way to vote, which two issues did you personally consider most important?'
The party advantage shows the lead of the party chosen as the best on that issue over the next party, among respondents for whom the issue was important.

Source: Adapted from Crewe (1992, p. 7).

Table 13.5 *The key issues in the 1992 General Election*

However, whatever the policy similarities, voters certainly *perceived* a difference between the two major parties' respective competence on this issue, with 50 per cent of respondents to an NOP exit poll stating their belief that prices would rise faster under a Labour than a Conservative Government, and only 28 per cent who did not consider that this would be the case. (NOP/BBC exit poll, 9 April 1992). Overall, the Conservatives enjoyed a considerable advantage over Labour with regard to perceptions of general economic competence: 53 per cent of respondents in the NOP/BBC exit poll felt that the Conservatives and only 35 per cent considered that Labour would take the right decisions on the economy. Table 13.7 summarises public perceptions of the three parties with regard to policies and competence in the 1992 General Election.

Table 13.7 *Perceptions of parties' policies and competence, 1992 General Election (%)*

	Conservative	Labour	Liberal Democrat
Best policies	46	37	14
Most competence	45	40	13

Source: Data from Gallup post-election survey, 10–11 April 1992.

Thus, British electors in April 1992 were offered genuine choices by the political groupings which aspired to government. When the presence in many constituencies of candidates from parties seeking to influence but not to form a government is taken into account, that choice was wider still. Both party policies and public perceptions of parties, of course, are shaped by a broad complex of factors, including ideology, ethos, institutional interests, party groups, organisation and personalities. We now examine more closely the character of the parties which make up the British party system.

■ The Conservative Party

The Conservative Party is the most successful modern party. Since the Third Reform Act (1884), it has dominated its rivals, being in power, either singly, in coalition or in some looser form of alliance, for just over two-thirds of the time. On the face of it, this fact requires some explanation. How has a party drawn predominantly from the upper and upper middle classes and whose political reason for existence is the defence of property and the Constitution consistently gained the support of one-third of the working class? The answer lies in a combination of its own merits, political circumstances and the misfortunes of its rivals.

□ Conservative Strengths

- **Cohesiveness:** The party puts a high premium on party loyalty and overall has been less subject to damaging faction fights than its rivals, or to splits, although it did split over tariff reform in the first quarter of the twentieth century.
- **Adaptability:** Traditionally, Conservatives have valued pragmatism, a non-doctrinaire approach to politics combined with an ability to adapt to changing circumstances, and this quality served the party well in helping it adjust to the post-1945 transition to a 'managed economy' and 'Welfare State', the loss of empire and British entry into Europe.

Table 13.6   *The 1992 General Election manifestos on the main issues*

Conservative	Labour	Liberal Democrat
The economy		
Fight inflation by continued membership of ERM ('central to our counter-inflation discipline')	Fight inflation by ERM membership, 'sensible' credit management and halting 'excessive' price rises in water, electricity, telephones, transport, and NHS prescriptions	Independent Bank of England to form 'the rock' of counter inflation strategy
Move to 'narrow band' of ERM in due course.	Influence collective bargaining by annual national economic assessment	Move to 'narrow band' of ERM 'as soon as possible'.
Reduce share of National Income taken by public spending, return to a balanced budget as the economy recovers	Recovery programme to regenerate country's economy	£6b. recovery programme aimed at reducing unemployment by 600,000 over two years
Continue income tax reductions to 20p in the pound	Reform national insurance and tax system: abolish NI on lowest incomes, introduce new 50% tax rate on incomes over £40,000 and end exemption of incomes over £22,000 from NI payments	Unify income tax and employees' National Insurance contributions. New combined tax and NI rates of 35p in the pound (paid by about 80%), 42p in the pound on incomes over £33,000 and 50p in the pound on over £50,000
Industry		
More privatisation – British Coal, local authority bus services, Northern Ireland water, parts of British Rail (parcels, freight, stations)	Restore water and electricity to public control, halt bus deregulation, and secure future of coal by reducing coal imports and stopping 'dash for gas'	No privatisation of British Rail but allow private operators access to rail network. Increase economic competition by tough anti-monopolies and merger policy involving new Restrictive Practices Act to penalise anti-competitive behaviour and end price-fixing by cartels; end BT and British Gas monopolies. Licenses to operate
Regulator to advise on introduction of competition in the Post Office	No privatisation of British Rail; allow BR to raise private capital	
More contracting out, market testing and competitive tendering of government services		
More curbs on trade union powers	Retain strike ballots and union elections, but restore union rights at GCHQ and give employees new rights to be consulted and informed about decisions affecting them	pits to other groups as well as British Coal.
No statutory minimum wage	Statutory minimum wage of £3.40 per hour to benefit 4m. low-paid	
Citizen's Charter to improve choice and standards in all public services	Employee share ownership scheme	All private sector employees in a substantial company to have access to shares or profit-sharing scheme.
Employment and training		
Vouchers for 'skill checks' Training credits for 16 and 17 year olds	Programme for unemployed with three days' work per week ('paid at the proper rate') and three days' training	£6b. programme includes £75m. for training and £320m for cutting business rates
New system of national vocational qualifications to cover virtually every occupation by end of next parliament	New £300m. skill training fund to upgrade skills of those in work	

Table 13.6—*continued*

Conservative	Labour	Liberal Democrat
Europe		
Pro-Maastricht with social chapter 'opt-out' and freedom to make 'own unfettered decision' in due course on whether to join monetary union with a single currency	Will 'opt in' to social chapter of the Treaty of Maastricht Play 'active part' in negotiations on economic and monetary union.	Will 'opt in' to social chapter of Treaty of Maastricht; also, pro-monetary union, including independent European Bankand a single currency, and therefore renounce 'opt-out' on monetary union and accept timetable for EMU
Pro-widening the EC	Pro-widening the EC	Pro-widening the EC Reform EC institutions in direction of greater democracy and accountability
Welfare		
Social Security		
Extra £2 per week for single pensioners, £3 for married couple Child benefit to increase with prices Equal treatment for men and women in pensions Encourage occupational and personal pension schemes	Extra £5 per week for single pensioners, £8 per week for married couples Increase child benefit to £9.95 per week for all children. Restore benefit rights to 16 and 17 year olds 'as soon as possible' Equal treatment to men and women in pensions. Flexible retirement between 60 and 70. New national pensions plan building on SERPS; guarantee minimum pension in occupational and personal pension schemes	Extra £5 per week for single pensioners, £8 per week for married couples Increase child benefit by £1 per week for each child Restore right to claim income support to 16 and 17 year olds Annual pension increases in line with average earnings paid for by abolishing SERPS which has not helped poorer pensioners. Protection for members of occupational pension schemes Work towards creation of 'citizen's income' for all
New disability benefits	Reform disability benefits Improve and extend invalid care allowance 'as resources allow'.	New comprehensive disability income scheme and new carer's benefit
Health		
Year by year increase of real resources for NHS More hospital trusts. GPs encouraged to apply for fund-holding Reduce in-patient waiting times by binding guarantees locally. From March 1993, none to wait over 18 months for a hip or knee replacement or a cataract operation Goals for employment of women in professional and managerial posts in the NHS	Additional resources of at least £1 billion for NHS within 22 months Return opted-out hospitals to local NHS. Halt commercial market which is creating 'two-tier' NHS. Performance Agreements with each Health Authority. New Health Quality Commission to monitor care and raise standards Restore free eye tests Ban tobacco advertising End compulsory competitive tendering for hospital support services	Annual real increase rising to £1.1 billion over 5 years End ability of NHS trusts to dispose of capital assets, set staff terms and conditions and withdraw from local health planning. Replace 'internal market' with service agreements between health authorities and hospitals and other health units. Replace GP fund-holding with new system. Restore free eye-tests and dental check-ups and free prescription charges Ban tobacco promotion

cont. p. 236

Table 13.6—*continued*

Conservative	Labour	Liberal Democrat
Education		
Complete introduction of National Curriculum with regular testing of all 7, 11 and 14 year olds by 1994	Additional £600m for investment in education over 22 months New national reading standards programme with £20m. for 'reading recovery' in first year	Additional £2 billion for investment in education in first year (funded by increasing basic income tax rate by one penny)
More opt-out schools Expand technology schools initiative Annual school performance lists Continue assisted places scheme	Bring opted-out schools and City Technology Colleges (CTCs) back into local education system End selection at 11 Scrap assisted places scheme	End two-tier system by returning grant-maintained schools and CTCs to local authority control
	Give all 3 and 4 year olds the chance of a nursery school place by 2000 AD. General Teaching Council to help teachers improve their standards Education Standards Commission together with HMIs to monitor standards in schools Voluntary aided schools available for all religions	Phase out assisted places scheme and review independent schools' charitable status Guarantee all children access to two years nursery education General Teaching Council to improve professional standards Fully independent inspectorate to report on entire educational system public and private at all levels National qualifications council to
Free further education and sixth form colleges from local authority control		coordinate single system of academic and vocational courses at 14–19.
	New advanced certificate including a five subject 'A' level	Increase numbers in higher education to 2m.
Reform teacher training Expand higher education together with student loans commitment	Double numbers in higher education within twenty years and replace student loans with fairer system	by 2000 AD. Abolish student loans and replace with student income entitlement and student allowances.
Housing		
New 'rents-to-mortgages' scheme to encourage council house purchase; 'right-to-buy' discounts to continue	Keep right to buy council houses but increase number of rented houses by release of capital receipts from earlier sales Mortgage rescue schemes	Relax controls on local authority capital receipts especially to build more council houses
Maintain mortgage tax relief New rent-a-room scheme to encourage homeowners to take in lodgers without being taxed	Continue mortgage tax relief	Replace mortgage tax relief with housing cost relief weighted to those most in need and available to buyers and renters
Help first-time buyers Increase private renting Spend £6,000m through Housing Corporation over three years to provide 153,000 homes	Help for first-time buyers Restore housing benefit to under-18s Council rents to reflect local incomes Leasehold reforms	Urgent action on homelessness

- **Ethos:** The party's ethos blends nationalism ('Putting Britain first'), individualism ('making the best of your talents and circumstances') and the claim to good government (the country's 'natural' and most competent rulers) and consistently translates these elements into policies which sound like common sense in a political culture in which symbols and values of nation, individual striving and leadership retain a firm hold.

- **Leadership:** Conservatives have continually produced leaders able to dominate their political generations, in part by coining, or latching on to, phrases expressive of the popular mood – thus, Baldwin ('Safety First') in a period of economic insecurity (the 1930s); Macmillan ('You've never had it so good') in an age of dawning affluence (the 1950s); and Mrs.Thatcher ('Roll back the Frontiers of the State') at a time of growing public anxiety about high levels of government spending and taxation (the 1970s).

Favouring Political Circumstances

Also, the party has benefited from political circumstances which favoured its appeal to nationalism. These have occurred quite frequently and include threats to the integrity of the British state from within (Home Rule in the late nineteenth and early twentieth centuries) or from outside (the Kaiser's Germany in 1914–18, Hitler's Germany, 1939–45) or to its economy (the World Economic Depression of the 1930s).

☐ Rivals' Misfortunes

The Conservatives have derived indirect assistance from the misfortunes of their main rivals and from a divided opposition. The Liberals (the Conservatives' main opposition until the 1920s) split in 1886 (over Home Rule for Ireland), in 1916–18 (over Lloyd-George's replacement of Asquith as war-time Prime Minister) and again in

1932 (over the abandonment of Free Trade). In the 1980s, turmoil in the Labour Party after its electoral defeat in 1979 produced the secession of the SDP. Both in the 1920s and 1930s and again since the 1970s the Conservatives have profited from the drawn-out struggle between Labour and the Liberals to be the major force on the political left.

☐ Conservative Groups

The Conservative Party consists of three main elements – the parliamentary party; the National Union together with the Constituency Associations (the members, the 'party in the country'); and Central Office (the professional side, the party bureaucracy). Of these, the parliamentary party is undoubtedly the pre-eminent entity with the other two parts of the party having been brought into existence historically as its 'servants'. Conservative Party organisation in parliament was described in Chapter 12 and we focus here on the main political divisions. Research in the late 1980s identified the following groupings amongst Conservative MPs: Thatcherites (Neo-liberals, Tory Right) – 72 (19%); Party Faithful (Party Loyalists plus 20 – 30 Thatcher Loyalists) – 217 (58%); Populists (right-wing on law and order, left-wing on social issues) – 17 (under 5%); and Critics (Wets and Damps) – 67 (18%). (Norton (1990a)). The main focus of the struggle between the party's right and left in parliament (Dries versus Wets, Thatcherites against One Nation Tories) is the annual elections for officers of the backbench committees. The two groups predominantly involved are the **92 Group**, a neo-liberal, right-wing Thatcherite grouping named after the address (92 Cheyne Walk) of its meetings, and **The Lollards**, a grouping which represents the 'One Nation', 'wet' side of the party: each grouping puts forward a slate of candidates for these elections.

Traditionally seen pre-Thatcher as a party of 'tendencies' rather than factions, the Conservatives became increasingly ideological and factionalised from the mid-1970s. In the late 1980s and early 1990s, faction-fighting intensified over the two main issues dividing the party: preservation or movement away from the neo-liberal Thatcherite social and economic legacy; and support for Britain's growing integration within the EC or 'Euro-scepticism'. Many current groupings reflect these internal divisions.

Conservative groups fall into two main categories: those existing to provide forums for discussion; and those promoting a particular strand of thought. Also, there are a number of formally-independent 'think-tanks' sympathetic to the party. Few groups are exclusively parliamentary and there is considerable overlapping of memberships.

The **Bow Group** (1951) is a research group adopting a freely-critical viewpoint which aims to foster discussion through its pamphlets and quarterly magazine, *Crossbow*. The **Monday Club** (1961) is a bastion of right-wing Conservatism formed to organise grass-roots support against what was perceived as the alarming left-ward drift of the party under Macmillan on matters of empire and race. The Club combines 'free market' opinions on economic and welfare matters with a tough stance on foreign affairs, defence, law and order and immigration. Membership was 2000 in 1984 but declined to about 1000 (1991) as the Club suffered losses first to groups on the libertarian right and then through resignations following fears of infiltration by extreme right-wingers.

The **Selsdon Group** (1973) was founded to support free market economic principles in the aftermath of the Heath Government's desertion of such ideas in the economic policy U-turn of 1972. It has a relatively small membership, including a handful of MPs, and in the 1970s and 1980s cooperated with 'free market' think-tanks outside the party. These include the **Centre for Policy Studies** (CPS, 1974) which was established by Mrs. Thatcher and Sir Keith Joseph and, although formally independent, played a key role in influencing the policy of Conservative Governments in the 1980s; the **Institute of Economic Affairs**, (IEA, 1957); and the **Adam Smith Institute** (1981). The **Social Affairs Unit** has been mainly concerned with dismantling the welfare state and attacking the 'dependency culture'. The **Salisbury Group** (1979), founded in honour of the Third Marquess of Salisbury, is an exclusive group of right-wing intellectuals which propounds New Right social and economic ideas and produces a journal, the **Salisbury Review**, and the **Tory Philosophy Group** is a private right-wing supper club hosted by the Conservative MP, Jonathan Aitken.

The Thatcher and immediately post-Thatcher years saw the foundation of more groups to promote her ideas and protect her legacy. The **No Turning Back** group (1985), which was founded by the veteran right-wing economist, Lord Ralph Harris of High Cross, is a monthly dining club of Ministers and backbenchers pledged to support Thatcherite ideas in social and economic policy whilst the **Bruges Group** (1988) is a predominantly Conservative organisation formed in the wake of Mrs Thatcher's Bruges speech to fight for the Thatcherite anti-'federalist' view of Europe. **Conservative Way Forward** (1991), whose chairman is Cecil Parkinson and whose governing council includes former party chairman Norman Tebbit, was founded to press John Major to keep up the momentum of radical reform in the Thatcher tradition and to counter 'leftish' influence within the party. It publishes a magazine, **Forward**. Right-wing neo-liberal groups looked to Michael Portillo and Peter Lilley for influence at Cabinet level.

The **Tory Reform Group** (1975) provides a counterweight to the neo-liberal groups, advocating 'moderate' Conservatism in the Disraelian 'one nation' tradition. It adopts a more consensual approach supportive of cooperation between State and individual and between capital and labour and sympathetic to government intervention. The Group publishes a journal, *The Reformer*, and numbers among its patrons Cabinet members Michael Heseltine, Douglas Hurd and Kenneth Clarke.

The ferment of ideas following the downfall of Mrs. Thatcher saw the revival of the consensual **One Nation Group** amongst Conservative MPs (chairman, David Howell); its pamphlet 'One Nation 2000' (1992) advocated 'supportive' social, industrial and planning policies, 'substantial extra support' for those dependent on the state pension, and a large expansion of the rented sector in housing. Finally, a group of former Owenites became increasingly influential within the party through the **Social Market Foundation** which has links with the Conservatives and has argued for the application of Keynesian techniques, and called for improved investment in the infrastructure.

☐ *Conservative Organisation*

The Conservative Party is an autocracy tempered by consent. Thus, authority is concentrated in the leader who appoints the Party Chairman, the party's Shadow Cabinet when it is in opposition, and, after consultation only with the close colleagues, decides party policy. The party has no deputy leader and, unlike the situation in the other nationwide parties, the leader is elected by a relatively restricted constituency: Conservative MPs. Firm leadership is expected by the party and this involves establishing definite priorities of policy and strategy and communicating them clearly downwards through the party organisation. On the other hand, since the modern Conservative Party expects to be in government, leaders need to deliver success. Electoral defeat or even the threat of it places the position of the leader in immediate jeopardy. Defeat in October 1974 – his third in four elections – led to the swift deposition of Edward Heath and in 1990, in unprecedented fashion, the party even ousted its leader, Margaret Thatcher, when Prime Minister. Mrs Thatcher had in fact been extremely successful in General Elections, winning three in a row, but this was more than offset by her unwillingness to reverse the policies, especially with regard to the poll tax and the economy, which had helped bring about the Government's unpopularity at the time, and the consequent likelihood of defeat in the next General Election.

☐ *The Election of the Conservative Leader*

The system of election of Conservative leaders by Conservative Members of Parliament dates from 1965; before that the leader 'emerged' after a process of secret soundings of party opinion by senior Conservatives. The rules adopted in 1965 were amended in 1975 and further revised in 1989 and 1991 to take account of various problems as they arose. Exhibit 13.1 sets out the current procedure.

Exhibit 13.1 *How the Conservative Party elects its leader*

Unless the Party leadership is already vacant, an election can be launched by 10% of Conservative MPs who notify the Chairman of the 1922 Committee that they consider a contest is desirable. The notification has to be made within three months of the opening of a new parliament or fourteen days of the start of a new session. Names of the 10% of MPs backing a challenger are kept secret. Before the first ballot, constituency associations inform MPs of their views and the opinions of Conservative peers are also canvassed by the Conservative leader and Chief Whip in the Lords.

- *First ballot*   Winner needs an overall majority of those eligible to vote (i.e. all Conservative MPs) plus a 15% lead over nearest rival. If not achieved by any candidate, contest goes to a second ballot.
- *Second ballot* New candidates may now stand. Original candidates may continue or withdraw. Winner needs overall majority; if not achieved, candidates are allowed 24 hours to withdraw and, if a third ballot *is* required, only the top two candidates go forward.
- *Third ballot*   In the event of a tie, a fourth ballot is held unless candidates 'can resolve the matter between themselves'.

The winner (after whichever ballot) is confirmed at a party meeting attended by MPs, MEPs, Peers, and members of the National Union executive.

A third ballot has never been necessary in any of the four contests held under the elective system. In 1965, when Edward Heath gained an overall majority but only a 5.7% lead over his nearest rival, his opponents withdrew and no new candidates were forthcoming. In 1975, Mrs Thatcher – who, on the first ballot, lacked both an overall majority and a sufficient lead over her nearest rival – decisively defeated her opponents in the second ballot. In 1989, she easily beat off the challenge from a 'stalking-horse' candidate, although a surprisingly large number of her parliamentary party (60) opposed her. Finally, in 1990, although Mrs. Thatcher obtained an overall majority on the first ballot, she was four votes short of gaining the required 15% lead and, with her authority already damaged and her support reportedly ebbing, was persuaded to stand down

---

Exhibit 13.2   *Conservative leadership elections, 1965–90*

1965   Sir Alec Douglas–Home resigned and the leadership became vacant

	First ballot	Edward Heath	150	(49.3%)
		Reginald Maudling	133	(43.8%)
		Enoch Powell	15	(4.9%)
		Abstentions/spoiled papers	6	(2%)

Maudling and Powell retired after first ballot; Heath became leader.

1975   Heath's leadership was challenged

	First ballot	Margaret Thatcher	130	(47.1%)
		Edward Heath	119	(43.6%)
		Hugh Fraser	16	(5.8%)
		Abstentions	11	(4%)

Fraser withdrew; Whitelaw, Prior, Howe and Peyton came forward

	Second ballot	Margaret Thatcher	146	(52.9%)
		William Whitelaw	76	(28.6%)
		Geoffrey Howe	19	(6.9%)
		James Prior	19	(6.9%)
		John Peyton	11	(4%)
		Abstentions/spoiled papers	2	(0.7%)

Thatcher had overall majority and became leader.

1989   Sir Anthony Meyer challenged for the leadership

	First ballot	Margaret Thatcher	314	(84%)
		Sir Anthony Meyer	33	(8.8%)
		Spoilt ballots	24	(6%)
		Absent	3	(1%)

Thatcher won an overwhelming majority and remained leader.

1990   Michael Heseltine challenged for the leadership

	First ballot	Margaret Thatcher	204	(54.8%)
		Michael Heseltine	152	(40.9%)
		Spoilt ballots	16	(4.3%)

Thatcher withdrew; Major and Hurd entered the contest

	Second ballot	John Major	185	(49.7%)
		Michael Heseltine	131	(35.2%)
		Douglas Hurd	56	(15.1%)

Heseltine and Hurd conceded defeat; Major became leader.

by the Cabinet (whose members she consulted individually). In the second ballot, John Major lacked an overall majority but a third ballot was declared to be unnecessary as his two rivals conceded defeat (Exhibit 13.2).

☐ *The National Union*

The National Union of Conservative Associations is the second (voluntary) side of the Conservative Party's three main components, representing and supervising the party membership. It was formed in 1867 after the Second Reform Act by the parliamentary leadership. Their aims were to create a nationwide Conservative organisation which would coordinate the work of existing Associations, encourage the formation of new ones and disseminate Conservative publicity to the new working-class electors.

Established in order to assist but definitely not to control the party leaders, in formal terms the National Union exercises a purely 'advisory' role (Maxwell-Fyfe Report, 1949). Its main task is to convene an annual conference, whose proceedings are often dismissed as bland, uncritical affairs where votes are rarely taken and which are carefully stage-managed to avoid any appearance of disunity. However, this negative view undoubtedly underestimates the role of the National Union and its annual conference as *a two-way channel of communication* between party members and the leadership. Although provision for intra-party democracy is conspicuously absent from its formal arrangements, the actual practice of the party is more complex. The influence of the 'feedback' from party members upon the leadership is hard to measure because conference is always more a matter of 'mood' than specific resolutions, but, historically, conference debates have played an important part in preparing the way in the 1880s and 1890s for the party's later adoption of protectionism, in bringing about the downfall of the Coalition Government (and of Austen Chamberlain) in 1922 and in the passing of the Trades Disputes Act in 1927.

The increase in the importance of Conference in the 1980s and 1990s, which has been the result first of a populist then of a less decisive style of leadership, social levelling between the platform and the conference hall, and the decline of 'deference', may constitute a permanent trend. Recent research suggests that far from being a 'one-off' event, the annual conference is more appropriately depicted as the culmination of a series of less publicised area and sectional conferences at which senior party figures invite and receive frank and critical advice from representative 'experts' in, for example, regional Conservatism or trade unionism. According to this thesis, applause at annual conference, rather than registering unthinking loyalty, records grass-roots Conservatives' perceptions that ministers have listened to the advice offered at these earlier meetings; expressions of dissent occur when a minister has failed to make concessions on a matter of importance. Since 1983, the influence of this largely-hidden 'system' of grass-roots representation may be discerned in government policies on trade union reform, married women's taxation, disability pensions and the revival of interest in rates reform (Kelly, 1989, 1992).

To summarise: Conservative Party conferences have more than one 'face'. They are certainly exercises in public relations but this is only one aspect. They are demonstrations of enthusiasm and solidarity with the leadership, inspirers of the party 'activists' and occasions for their letting off steam on such matters as law and order and immigration, but also vehicles for the expression of serious dissent (e.g. over Europe in 1992) and occasionally for policy influence.

☐ *Constituency Associations*

The major roles of Conservative constituency associations are threefold: campaigning for the party in local and national elections; fund-raising; and the selection of parliamentary candidates.

Local Conservative associations possess considerable freedom from outside interference in choosing a parliamentary candidate. Candidates must either be on the party's approved list of candidates or, if not, gain acceptance by the party's Standing Advisory Committee on candidates. A Vice-Chairman at Central Office is in charge of the 700-strong candidates' list. Applications are considered by a sub-committee of the local Association's Executive Council: it draws up a short-list of candidates who then go before a final selection meeting which usually consists of the full Executive Council. The Council then either recommends one name for approval by a general meeting of the Association or submits more than one name leaving it to make the final selection. Local associations have largely resisted Central Office pressure to select more working class and women candidates – even in 1992 the Conservatives fielded only 63 women candidates, less than half the number nominated by Labour (137) and the Liberal Democrats (143).

Readoption struggles have been relatively rare – there were 23 between 1945–1975 – and largely remain so. Eight Conservative MPs failed to gain selection in 1983 but that was the inevitable result of extensive boundary revisions. Sir Anthony Meyer was deselected by Clwyd NW following persistent problems with his constituency party and ultimately his leadership challenge to Mrs. Thatcher and also in 1991, in the wake of Michael Heseltine's leadership challenge and the ousting of Margaret Thatcher, nine more MPs survived deselection struggles. John Browne survived a deselection attempt by his local association in Winchester in 1987 but was forced out before the 1992 General Election after being censured in the Commons for non-disclosure of interests. A bitter dispute occurred in Cheltenham following the selection of a black barrister, John Taylor and, after a racist remark and a claim that the candidate had been 'foisted' on the constituency by Central Office, a local member was expelled.

☐ *Central Office*

Conservative Central Office (CCO), founded in 1870, is the party's third main component: it constitutes the professional element, the party bureaucracy, and is staffed by officials many of whom make their work a full-time career. Its

Chairman (normally a leading politician) is appointed by and responsible to the party leader, a fact which has led to the description of Central Office as 'the personal machine of the Leader'. Its main tasks are money-raising, the organisation of election campaigns, assistance with the selection of candidates, research and political education and, in carrying out these functions, it must liaise both with the parliamentary party and with the party outside Westminster. A particularly vital role performed by CCO is the training, certification and promotion of agents. Agents are the key professionals in politics and another aspect in which the Conservatives enjoy an advantage over their rivals; they employed about 300 full-time agents in the 1992 General Election compared with Labour's 100 and the Liberal Democrats' 30. Normally employed by the constituency associations, agents play an important part in liaising between the party's central headquarters and its regional, area and local bodies; in fund-raising; and in election campaigns, especially in marginal seats.

Central Office was subjected to drastic changes after both the 1987 and 1992 elections as a result of leadership dissatisfaction. After 1987, it was substantially restructured and now consists of three Departments (Communications, Campaigning and Research), and a Board of Finance, whose Heads are responsible to the Party Chairman. After 1992, Sir Norman Fowler became Chairman, and devised a new Party Board of Management (13), to which he is accountable (the Board includes three representatives from the National Union), together with a new post of director general, charged specifically with the task of pulling together the elected, voluntary and professional sides of the party. A stringent economy drive was launched involving large numbers of redundancies among the party's 140 workers at CCO and 400 in the country. Central Office also faced severe criticisms from the **Charter Movement**, which was set up in 1981 by activists in Kent to campaign for greater democracy and accountability within the party. The Movement, through its journal **Charter News**, regards Central Office 'waste, carelessness and profligacy' as largely to blame for the party's huge deficit, considers large donations from foreign backers 'a degredation' and calls for an elected Chairman.

☐ *Party Finances*

The Conservative Party is the wealthiest party, its money being provided by business, the constituency membership and gifts from individuals. Its formidable capacity to raise funds enables the party to outspend its opponents by significant amounts at general elections. At the 1992 General Election, for example, the party spent more (£10.1 million) than Labour (£7.1m.) and the Liberal Democrats (£2.1m.) combined.

However, huge increases in expenditure during the 1980s and early 1990s led to persistent deficits and an accumulated deficit reportedly in the region of £19m. in 1993. In recent years, contributions from the constituencies and from companies have both declined and private donations increased as a proportion of central party income (Table 13.8).

Local contributions have suffered because of the decline in membership (down from 2.75m (1953) to 1.5m. (1976) and 1/2m. (1993)) and gifts from industry as a result of the recession. There is political controversy both over business contributions (Table 13.9) and over the scale, secrecy and source of individual donations (concealed in the 'unspecified' category). Labour argues that the Conservatives are over-dependent on business, the Conservatives say Labour is 'in hock' to the unions. Labour maintains that company contributions to the Conservatives are not published and companies are not legally required to seek shareholders approval of such gifts (as trade unions, since 1984, have been legally required to ballot members before making political donations). The Conservatives reply that companies may seek shareholders' authority for political gifts if they wish. Labour admits this but ripostes that very few do so: only the National Freight Corporation – out of 38 large companies making gifts to the Conservatives – gave its shareholders a vote on its political donation in 1991, and the result was an 87% majority against such gifts.

Finally, large individual donations aroused a furore in 1993, with critics expressing concern about the total sum involved – £17m. (paid just before the General Election); their secrecy and the determination of the party leadership to maintain this secrecy; the dubious origins of at least some of them – the discredited Polly Peck chairman, Asil Nadir, and foreign business tycoons like the Greek shipping magnate John Latsis; and the non-domicile tax exempt status which enables very wealthy foreigners to bring capital into the country and make large donations direct to the Conservatives. Early in 1993 it was disclosed that the Commons Home Affairs Select Committee would undertake an inquiry into the funding of political parties and would consider in particular the question of secret donations and whether parties should receive State subsidies.

Table 13.8 *Conservative Party finances, 1988–1992*

| (in £million sterling) | | | | |
Income	Constituencies	Industry	Unspecified	Deficit
1988 £15	£1.2	£4.5	£9	£6
1989 £8.6	£1.2	£3.5	£3.2	(£0.3)
1990 £9.1	£1.2	£2.9	£4.2	£4.1
1991 £13	£1.2	£2.8	£7.7	£5
1992 £22	£1.3	£2.93	£17	£5.5

Source: adapted from *The Guardian*, 13 March 1993.

Table 13.9 *Top Business donations to the Conservative Party, 1991*

Allied Lyons	£100 000
P & O Shipping	£100 000
Glaxo	£60 000
Tarmac Construction	£55 000
Scottish and Newcastle Breweries	£50 000
Trafalgar House	£40 000
Kleinwort Benson	£40 000
Tate and Lyle	£25 000
Lucas Aerospace	£25 000
Hammerson Properties	£25 000
GKN Engineering	£25 000
Racal Electronics	£25 000

■ The Labour Party

The Labour Party originated in a decision of representatives of socialist societies and trade unions in 1900 to press for independent working-class representation in Parliament. A Labour Representation Committee with five representatives from the socialist societies and seven from the trade unions was established to guide this enterprise and gained its first major success in 1906, when 29 Labour MPs were elected. After the large-scale franchise extensions of 1918 and 1928, Labour gained ground steadily, displacing the Liberals in the 1920s as the second largest party and forming minority governments in 1924 and 1929–31. Labour did not achieve an absolute majority over the other parties until 1945, however, and, although alternating in power with the Conservatives down to 1979 by ruling for seventeen out of the thirty-four years, the party gained a working majority only once more (1966) in this entire period (Table 13.1). Nonetheless, from the vantage-point of the 1990s, the pre-1979 era came to seem like the 'good times' for Labour: while special factors could be invoked to explain its defeats in 1979 ('Winter of Discontent'), 1983 (Falklands War) and 1987 (eco-nomic boom), none such was available for the 1992 defeat. On the contrary its leader Neil Kinnock (1983–1992) seemed to have done much to make the party once more electable, reasserting central control over the party organisation, purging the extreme left, dropping unilateralism and accepting much Thatcherite change as permanent, especially privatisation and council house sales. Yet Labour achieved little more than 34% of the vote, once again failing to gain as much as half the vote of the working class – its 'natural' constituency. 1970 was the last occasion on which the party gained over 40% of the total vote in a general election.

Debate within the party since the 1992 General Election continued to address the question of the strategy and policies necessary to avoid being condemned to perpetual opposition. There were four main areas of controversy: internal reform of the party constitution, with special reference to the role of the trade unions; the development of policy, with particular regard to the economy; electoral reform; and relations with the Liberal Democrats. By late 1993, some points had become a little clearer. The party leader, John Smith, whose allegiance before becoming leader was with the centre-right of the party, had

Figure 13.1 *John Smith, the Labour leader from 1992 to his sudden death in 1994. He was widely considered the man who once more made the party electable.*

Source: *Guardian*/Don McPhee.

adopted a modernising stance like his predecessor. He had succeeded in persuading Conference to introduce an important change to one member, one vote (OMOV) in the selection of parliamentary candidates. He had given the party three years to rethink its entire policy and had established a Commission on Social Justice to examine such themes as the scale of poverty and the advantages of integrating the tax and benefit systems. In the wake of the report of the party's own internal working group on electoral reform (the Plant Committee), which recommended in favour of the supplementary vote, the Labour leader proposed to hold a referendum on the issue. On relations with the Liberal Democrats, there would be no pact, only practical cooperation between local activists and councillors of the two parties where this was feasible. Unsurprisingly, the internal debate within the party between factional groupings traditionally on the right/centre right, 'soft left' and 'hard left' of the party took place around these issues. Allegiances of Labour MPs in the 1992 parliament are estimated as – 140 right/centre right; 100 – including 33 of the 69 new Labour MPs – soft left; 31 hard left.

□ *The Labour Leader*

Because of Labour's federalistic constitution – which enshrines the position of particular sections like the trade unions – and its egalitarian ethos, leadership of the party has traditionally been a more complex task than that of the Conservative Party. The leader must balance the claims of parliamentarians, trade unionists and constituency activists; in addition, the voices of the Cooperative party (which sponsors 14 MPs), the Socialist societies, Young Socialists, women's groups and black activists demand a hearing. Even this grossly oversimplifies, for each element within the party contains its own divisions between left and right with shades of opinion within each sub-division, which have to be taken into account. In conducting this balancing act and defusing actual and potential conflicts, Labour leaders command certain resources: personal prestige, the authority inherent in the position,

the power to appoint the Cabinet (in government) and allocate shadow Cabinet portfolios and form shadow teams (77-strong in July 1992) in opposition, and ex officio membership of the NEC; above all, perhaps, the leader can exploit the desire of the party for office, which has often provided a motive for compromise.

□ *Party Groups*

In recent decades, the right wing of the party have organised in the **Manifesto Group** (1974) and **Solidarity** (1981). Right-wingers in the 1970s and 1980s supported continuing membership of the EC, the retention of nuclear weapons, and a mixed economy and opposed further nationalisation. By 1987, Neil Kinnock had become converted to Solidarity's main ideological positions and with key Solidarity figures (Roy Hattersley, John Smith and Gerald Kaufman) occupying the three main shadow Cabinet portfolios, the rationale for the group had disappeared and, in 1988, Solidarity voted to dissolve itself.

The **Fabian Society** (1884), one of Labour's founding groups, has a local as well as parliamentary membership. Its main function is to float ideas through the publication of pamphlets and through providing a forum for discussion. It publishes a journal, *Fabian News*. It favours the election of the leader by the PLP, reducing the trade union vote at conference to 50% and abolishing the block vote, a new post of party president to be elected by conference, and the replacement of clause 4 with a new clause 2 simply stating the party's aims and objects as a social democratic party.

The **Tribune Group**, the leading 'soft left' faction which had allied with the Labour right after 1987, regained its oppositionist vigour in the 1992 parliament. It takes its name from the weekly newspaper, *Tribune*, which it still publishes and which dates back to 1937. The remoulded group has attacked the 'modernising' leadership. Its leading members reaffirm the party's traditional socialist commitment to collectivist values, strong links with the unions, and the defence of the poor. In 1993 two leading members criticised the supply side economics of the

---

Exhibit 13.3   *The trade unions: Labour's dilemma*

The trade unions provide about three-quarters of Labour's funds; sponsor over half of its MPs; wield seven-tenths of the votes at its conference; play a major role in the election of its executive committee; and have a one-third share in the election of its leader.

But Labour's relationship with the unions is now in crisis: Labour's leaders want to reduce the party's union links drastically; however, according to a MORI poll on May 17 1993, 65% of members of the big six unions want to retain links with the party.

The following developments form the background to the present crisis within the party:

- Labour's link with the unions is an electoral liability: with whatever justice, the party is widely perceived by voters as 'in hock' to the unions ('no say, no pay') – that is, as being prevented from carrying out or even contemplating certain policies because of union opposition.
- Trade unionists' support for Labour is weakening: 55% of trade unionists voted Labour in October 1974, but only 46% in 1992; and trade unionists form a smaller proportion of the electorate – 29% in 1974 but under one-fifth (19%) in 1992.

---

shadow Chancellor, Gordon Brown and called for a greater emphasis on Keynesian demand management. The Group, which contains some prominent anti-Europeans, also advocated voting against the Treaty of Maastricht.

The **Campaign Group** is a far left group, whose leading members are Tony Benn and Dennis Skinner. It was set up in 1982 by Bennites opposed to the expulsion of Militant. Its chair in the 1992 parliament is Dawn Primarolo. It believes in maintaining the party's 'umbilical link' with the trade unions and Clause 4, and dislikes any cooperation with the Liberal Democrats. Alarmed at the rightward movement of the party under Kinnock, the Group challenged for the leadership in 1988 but was prevented from running a candidate in the 1992 leadership election by the new rule 20% (see below). In 1993, Tony Benn saw the choice facing the party as being between 'the so-called revisionists, who want, in effect, to dismantle the party as it now stands, and build a new SDP, ... others who are happy to leave well alone and wait for victory by default,' and the traditional democratic socialist alternative offered by the far left.

The **Labour Coordinating Committee** (LCC) (1978), a constituency grouping, began on the far left but adopted a 'soft left' position in 1983, supporting Kinnock for the leadership, and after 1985 backed the realignment of the party to the

right. After the 1992 election defeat, it argued that Labour should reorientate itself fundamentally by adopting compulsory competitive tendering (as long as it is backed by a minimum wage and employment rights); electoral reform; an integrated tax and benefit system; and a more critical approach to the existing European settlement. It contended that the manifesto commitments to raise pensions and child benefit substantially were 'old-fashioned doses of welfarism' and Labour's tax plans were 'a cap on people's aspirations, the single biggest vote loser and a substitute for an economic policy'. In its view, the party needed to develop a new welfare strategy which would be less dependent on automatic assumption of the superiority of universal benefits; its new welfare policies should not throw generalised child benefit increases at high income families and pensions increases at those with large occupational schemes. The LCC launched a new journal, *Renewal*, in 1993.

The **Institute for Public Policy Research** is a left-of-centre think-tank, of which Patricia Hewitt, a former policy coordinator for Neil Kinnock, is a founder-member and Deputy Director. The IPPR is acting as the secretariat for Labour's Commission on Social Justice.

Labour's divisions on electoral reform are reflected in the existence of the **First Past the Post Campaign**, formed in 1993 with the support of

86 MPs, and the **Labour Campaign for Electoral Reform,** which claims the sponsorship of 62 MPs and 1900 party members. Jeff Rooker, the chairman of the electoral reform group, put proposals for a variant – the Mixed Member System (MMS) – of the German Additional Member System to the Plant Commission in late 1992 and then, when Plant came out in favour of the supplementary vote (SV), switched to supporting a hybrid of MMS and SV.

Other new groups to emerge in 1993 were the **New Agenda Forum** which was formed by a group of new Labour MPs to formulate ideas for Labour and the **Full Employment Forum,** which was launched by Bryan Gould to provide the party with a radical economic policy. The latter group supports a highly interventionist economic policy and rejects the Maastricht terms for economic union.

☐ *Organisation*

In *formal* terms, the distribution of power within the Labour Party reflects its origins in a mass movement, with the party outside Westminster accorded a significant role in key party institutions such as conference and the National Executive Committee (NEC). However, the **Campaign for Labour Party Democracy** (CLPD) (1973) broadly adopted the view – already expressed by a leading political scientist some years previously (McKenzie, 1964) – that in practice power was wielded by the parliamentary leadership, and the wishes of constituency activists and conferences were routinely ignored. Accordingly, the CLPD set out to make the parliamentary leadership more accountable to the rank-and-file by (*i*) extending the right to elect the leader and deputy leader to a wider constituency than the parliamentary Labour Party (PLP); (*ii*) introducing mandatory re-selection of MPs; and (*iii*) according final control over the party manifesto to the NEC rather than the party leader. By 1981, the first two of these objectives had been achieved, and developments since then revolve around the attempt of the leadership to regain the ground lost to the Bennite left at that time.

The Election of the Labour Leader

Before 1981, the party leader and deputy leader were elected by Labour MPs, but a special constitutional conference in that year introduced a new system. The right advocated election by 'one member, one vote' (by individual, not trade union affiliated, members). But the method adopted was the one favoured by the left: an **electoral college,** with a system of weighting which allocated a greater role to the trade unions (40 per cent) than to the PLP (30 per cent) and the Constituency Labour Parties (CLPs) (30 per cent) and more influence to the party outside parliament (70 per cent) than to the parliamentary party (30 per cent). Voting is open, not secret, and since 1988 MEPs have been able to vote in the parliamentary section. Leaders may be challenged both in government and opposition although, since Benn's leadership challenge in 1988, challengers have been required to get 20 per cent in the ⁕PLP (rather than 5 per cent as before) in order for their challenge to proceed. The system was first used in the deputy-leadership election of 1981 when Denis Healey narrowly defeated Tony Benn and it has been used in all subsequent leadership and deputy leadership elections, including the 1992 election for deputy-leader when Margaret Beckett (57.3 per cent) defeated John Prescott (28.1 per cent) and Bryan Gould (14.6 per cent) (Table 13.10).

The 1993 Conference adopted a small modification of this procedure whereby the union share of the electoral college was reduced to one-third and the shares of the PLP and CLPs were increased slightly to one-third each. In order to stand for the leadership in Labour's electrol college, candidates need the support of 12.5% of PLP. Voting takes place in three equal sections: MPs and MEPs; party members; and affiliated trade unions and socialist societies. Only political levy-paying Labour supporters may vote in the trade union section. MPs, MEPs and odinary members vote by postal ballot; trade unions are not required to use postal ballots but may do so if they wish. Candidates are allocated their proportional share of the vote in each section and these shares are then added together to provide a

Table 13.10 *Labour leadership elections, 1983, 1988 and 1992*

	PLP section (30%) (%)	Constituency section (30%) (%)	Trade union section (40%) (%)	Total (%)
1983				
Neil Kinnock	14.8	27.5	29.0	71.3
Roy Hattersley	7.8	0.6	10.9	19.3
Eric Heffer	4.3	2.0	0.1	6.3
Peter Shore	3.1	0.0	0.1	3.1
1988				
Neil Kinnock	24.8	24.3	39.7	88.6
Tony Benn	5.2	5.9	0.3	11.4
1992				
John Smith	23.2	29.3	38.5	91.0
Bryan Gould	6.8	0.7	1.5	9.0

winner. This system was in place in 1994, when the sudden death of John Smith on 12 May left the leadership vacant.

Annual Conference

According to the Constitution of 1918, Conference is the ruling body of the party. It decides the policies which compose the party programme and elects the National Executive Committee (NEC) to manage the party on a day-to-day basis. In practice, the influence of Conference on Labour policy in government has normally been considerably less than this suggests. Policies agreed at Conference can be ignored or toned down by the parliamentary leaders when drawing up the manifesto or, even if they do appear in the manifesto, jettisoned by a Labour Government. Alternatively, Labour's leaders can form tacit or explicit agreements with the major power-blocs at Conference, thereby pre-empting hostile resolutions. Traditionally, this alliance between the PLP leaders and the union 'bosses' has run the party and given it stability. The period between 1968 and 1979, when the unions resisted the party leadership over industrial relations reform and incomes policy, is a relatively unusual break with this pattern, which was restored in the 1980s. However, although not the ultimate arbiter of party policy, Conference as the major forum of grass-roots opinion certainly shapes and constrains the initiatives of the leadership.

Despite recent changes aimed at reducing their influence, the trade unions remain dominant at Conference. They now cast 70 per cent of the Conference vote (reduced from 90 per cent by a rule change accepted in 1991) and, in 1993, accepted a further reform of the block vote system. Beginning in 1994, the votes of affiliated unions will no longer be cast as a block but divided up among the members of union delegations. CLPs cast the remaining 30 per cent of Conference votes. The composition of the NEC (30) also reflects the strong influence of the unions, who, in addition to electing twelve members to its trade union section, possess – through their domination of Conference – a major role in the election of five women's representatives and the party treasurer, who are elected by the conference as a whole. In addition, the NEC contains seven members elected by the constituency parties (CLPs), one representative elected by the Socialist societies, and a youth representative elected by the Young Socialists; the leader and deputy-leader are *ex-officio* members and the party secretary is also secretary of the NEC. Constitutionally, any proposal receiving a two-thirds majority at conference goes into the party programme. But the programme is not the manifesto, which is the joint responsibility of the Parliamentary Committee of the PLP and the NEC, or–when the party is in government – of the Cabinet and the NEC. In practice, whether in government or opposition, the leader plays a decisive role in drawing up the manifesto.

Along with its procedures for electing its leadership and selecting its parliamentary candidates, Labour's **policy-making process** is in flux in the early 1990s.

Proposed changes include:

- A further cut in **union voting power** at annual conference to 50 per cent. This could happen when party membership exceeds 300 000, when the NEC and Conference will review the situation. A further possibility is the creation of a 'third force' (of MPs and MEPs) to take 20% of the vote.
- **A new National Policy Forum** (81) consisting of representatives from all sections of the party (MPs, unions, local government, the constituencies and regional parties) will meet four times a year to agree a rolling programme. A new **joint policy committee** (16) drawn mainly from the Shadow cabinet and NEC, will coordinate policy-making and act as a steering committee for the Forum.
- **An increasing role for women**: at its 1990 Conference, the party set itself to achieve a quota of 40% women on the NEC, National Policy Forum and other policy-making bodies, and a target of 50% women in the PLP and as constituency party officials within ten years. The party leader in 1993 expressed the wish that the figure for the NEC and the National Policy Forum would be achieved by 1995. The party agreed that half of CLP officers have to be women in 1993.
- **Black representation**: the eight-year campaign for fully-recognised, constitutional black sections ended in compromise (1990) by which a group open only to black and Asian members would be established at constituency level. It will be entitled to vote in elections to the Socialist Society's seat on the NEC and, if it gains enough members, it is likely to be entitled to its own NEC seat.
- **CLP ballots for the NEC**: The CLPs were merely requested in 1989 to ballot their mem-

bers before casting their votes in their section of the NEC but mandatory balloting of memberships began in 1993. One seat on the constituency section of the NEC was reserved for a woman in 1993 and two seats will be allocated to women from 1994.

Constituency Labour Parties (CLPs)

- **Selection of parliamentary candidates**: Selection of Labour parliamentary candidates is done by the constituency parties (CLPs). CLPs consist of delegates from a wide variety of labour organisations and societies and are run by General Committees (GCs).

  Selection of parliamentary candidates cannot begin without permission from the NEC which automatically forwards its lists of approved candidates (List A – trade union sponsored, List B – CLP recommended, List C – Cooperative party recommended and, since 1988, List W – candidates recommended by the Women's Section) to the constituency party concerned. Sub-committees of the CLPs shortlist candidates (which must include at least one woman). Between 1989– 1992, shortlists were then voted upon by an electoral college consisting of a mix of individual members (at least 60%) and affiliated trade unions (up to 40%) – who were not, however, required to ballot their members before casting their votes. But the 1993 Conference accepted a new procedure. From that date, selection of Labour parliamentary candidates will be by one member one vote (OMOV) in the CLPs. Trade unionists who agree to pay an additional levy of £3 on top of the political levy will be entitled to vote. The 1993 Conference also agreed that in future there would be women-only parliamentary candidate shortlists in half of its winnable seats (i.e. marginals and those where a sitting member retires).

- **Union sponsorship**: The trade unions sponsored 173 candidates in the 1992 election; the Cooperative Party sponsored 26. Union sponsorship typically involves a grant of £2000–

£3000 towards a candidate's election expenses plus £150 per quarter paid to his or her constituency. Virtually all of the Labour Shadow Cabinet in 1993 was union-sponsored, with the TGWU and GMB each sponsoring five members. Reform of the sponsorship rules is also likely in the future with unions giving £1000 a year to a sponsored constituency, less than at present to campaigns, and sponsoring MEPs.

- **The ending of mandatory re-selection:** The party operated the system of mandatory re-selection of MPs from 1980–1992. This meant that all sitting Labour MPs had to face a re-selection process no less than three years after the previous General Election. Fourteen Labour MPs were de-selected under this procedure between 1981 and 1986 (some also retired early or left the party) and another two MPs – Syd Bidwell (Southall) and John Hughes (Coventry NE) – were deselected between 1987–92. In addition, two deselections – those of Frank Field (Birkenhead) and Gerry Bermingham (St Helens South) – were contested and overturned, and one MP (Ron Brown (Leith)) was barred from contesting a second selection process after winning the first one. Two MPs who belonged to the Militant Tendency – Terry Fields (Liverpool Broadgreen) and Dave Nellist (Coventry SE) – were expelled from the party, after having been reselected. The 1990 Conference ended mandatory reselection; in future, reselection would take place only if requested in a ballot of CLP members.

Labour Party Central Headquarters

The leading official of the Party (General Secretary) – Larry Whitty in 1993 – works from Walworth Road, the Labour Party headquarters. Following the 1992 General Election, sweeping changes and economies were planned. The main thrust of a paper prepared by the General Secretary involved shifting major responsibility for policy-making away from the NEC and the Walworth Road professionals to front-bench spokesmen, the leader's office, and a new joint policy commission agreed at the 1992 Conference. In May 1993, three new directors were appointed to head the party's campaigning, research and organisation departments.

Facing a £2.5 million deficit in 1992, and with a sharply reduced income owing to declining membership, the party planned cuts in both its Head Office and regional spending, involving a reduction in its headquarters staff from 120 to 90 and in its regional offices from nine to six.

A key position is that of National Agent but although the party had more agents in the field during the 1992 General Election (100), than in 1987, the Conservatives had three times this number.

Finance and Membership

During most of the period since 1945, the trade unions contributed over three-quarters of both Labour's central income and its General Election funds. However, trade union affiliated membership is in decline: it fell from 6 million in 1980 to an estimated 4.6 million in 1992 and is projected to fall further – to well under 4 million during the 1990s. The unions – faced with falling membership themselves and wishing to diversify their efforts into other avenues such as the EU – currently contribute only a little over half to Labour headquarters funds; the remainder comes from individual members (about 16%) and fund-raising and other sources (about 30%). Individual membership – estimated at about 1 million in 1953 – has fallen steadily since then to 261 000 in 1991, a record low, and even this figure almost certainly exaggerates the number of fully-paid up members. This decline, which the national membership campaign launched in 1989 apparently failed to reverse, is serious as recent academic research suggests that local campaigns by party members play an important role in mobilising the vote for Labour at constituency level. Its authors argue that 'the decline in party membership ... is ... a powerful causal factor in explaining electoral decline' and postulate that if Labour had had double its membership in 1987, it would probably have won the General Election (Seyd and Whiteley, 1992, pp. 220, 198).

■ The Liberal Democrats

The Liberal Democrats emerged in 1988, the product of a merger between the Liberal Party and its former partner in the Alliance, the Social Democratic Party (SDP). The merger imposed severe strains on both former parties: although 88% of Liberals and 65% of SDP members who voted supported it, nearly half of each party did not vote. Disgruntled minorities refused to accept the new party, Michael Meadowcroft leading a small group of 'old Liberals' and David Owen, the 'continuing SDP'. However, neither grouping proved to be viable. The 'old Liberals' performed very badly in the 1992 General Election, with only Meadowcroft of its 73 candidates saving his deposit, whilst the Owenite SDP decided to disband in 1990, Owen himself shortly afterwards announcing his retirement from politics and the two remaining SDP MPs being defeated in 1992.

Meanwhile, the new merged party, which began with 19 MPs (17 of them former Liberals) and a claimed 3500 councillors and 100 000 members, moved quickly to appoint a new leader to replace the interim joint leadership of David Steel and Robert Maclennan. In a ballot of the whole membership in July 1988, Paddy Ashdown was elected leader, gaining 71.9% of the vote to Alan Beith's 28.1%. By November 1990, the Liberal Democrats had recovered from their inauspicious start: good local election results in May had been followed in November with a classic by-election victory at Eastbourne. Yet another phase in the turbulent twentieth-century history of the Liberal Party was under way.

The experience of the Liberals since 1900 encompassed major party status (down to the First World War), decline to a sizeable third party (inter-war), near-extinction (immediate post-1945 period), revival (the 1960s and 1970s) and Alliance politics (1981–1988). We focus here on its post-1945 fortunes.

□ Post-War, 1945–59

The party came close to extinction (Table 13.11) but somehow survived partly through the persistence of a traditional Liberal vote (now found largely in rural areas and the Celtic fringe), partly through the enthusiasm of its small but dedicated membership and partly, rather paradoxically, because its very weakness prompted its major rivals to consider its absorption hardly worthwhile (Stevenson, 1993).

□ Revival – the 1960s and 1970s

Prominent among the reasons for the Liberal improvement were effective leadership (by Jo Grimond (1956–67) Jeremy Thorpe (1967–76) and David Steel (1976–88), vigorous local campaigning by the Young Liberals (who pioneered 'community politics') and the Association of Liberal Councillors, and increasing electoral disillusion with the two major parties which occasionally brought about sensational Liberal by-election victories such as Torrington (1958) and Orpington (1962) and underlay the massive surge of support in 1974.

Figure 13.2   *David Steel presents the desk used by himself and every Liberal Leader since Herbert Asquith to Paddy Ashdown*

Source: *Guardian*.

Table 13.11   *The Liberal Party: votes, candidates, seats and share of the vote, 1945–1992*

	Votes (m.)	Candidates	Seats	Share of the vote (%)
1945	2.25	306	12	9.0
1950	2.62	475	9	9.1
1951	0.74	109	6	2.6
1955	0.72	110	6	2.7
1959	1.64	216	6	5.9
1964	3.10	365	9	11.2
1966	2.33	311	12	8.5
1970	2.12	332	6	7.5
1974 (Feb)	6.06	517	14	19.3
1974 (Oct)	5.35	619	13	18.3
1979	4.31	577	11	13.8
1983*	7.78	633	23	25.4
1987*	7.34	633	22	22.6
1992+	5.99	632	20	17.8

*The Liberal–Social Democrat Alliance
+The Liberal Democrats

The Liberal–SDP Alliance (1981–88)

The formation of the Social Democratic Party (1981) by the 'gang of four' (Roy Jenkins, Shirley Williams, Bill Rodgers and David Owen), a group of former Labour right-wingers disillusioned with the leftward drift of Labour, paved the way for the attempt of the Liberal–SDP Alliance to 'break the mould' of British politics by creating a viable force in the political centre. However, despite achieving in 1983 the best performance by a third party since the 1920s, the Alliance failed for a number of reasons: first, the working of the electoral system favoured the major parties with their regionally concentrated support and disadvantaged the Alliance, whose vote was evenly spread; second, both major parties bounced back from their low points in the early 1980s; and third, there were strains and divisions between the Liberal and SDP leaderships within the Alliance over strategy and policy (especially defence)

The 1992 General Election result was a disappointment to the Liberal Democrat Party. Its overall vote and vote share were lower than it had achieved in alliance with the SDP in 1987

and the number of seats in which it occupied second place had fallen from 261 to 154. Its by-election gains (Eastbourne, Ribble Valley and Kincardine and Deeside) were all lost. Most important, a 'hung parliament', in which it would have been able to trade its support for the largest party in return for proportional representation, had not happened. Once again, the party was the victim of the lack of proportionality between votes and seats: whereas the Conservatives won 52% of the seats on 42% of the vote and Labour won 42% of the seats on 34% of the vote, the Liberal Democrats won a mere 3% of the seats on nearly 18% of the vote. Its $1\frac{1}{2}$ million votes in the South-East (23.3%) did not gain the party a single seat.

The Liberal Democrats are a non-socialist reforming party of the centre, enthusiastically European, environmentalist (they propose a pollution added tax), in favour of constitutional reform, and supportive both of a free enterprise culture and a massive governmental programme for economic recovery.

By mid-1993, the party's strengths were well in evidence. Opinion polls showed its leader to be more popular than either John Major or John Smith. In May it won a classic by-election victory at Newbury on a 28.4% swing from the Conservatives and accompanied this performance with sweeping gains in the county council elections. Although the Liberal Democrats controlled only three of the 47 counties, 28 were under no overall control and in a large number of these, the party had soon come to a 'working accord' with Labour. Practical cooperation at grass-roots level while avoiding formal alliance or pacts which would alienate groups of their own supporters seemed to be the preferred option for both opposition parties.

The Scottish and Welsh Nationalist Parties

The 1992 manifestos of both nationalist parties called for 'independence in Europe' for their countries. **Plaid Cymru** wrote of Wales having 'a government of its own' by the end of the century but, buoyed by pre-election opinion polls showing rising support for independence and devolution, the **Scottish National Party** (SNP) suggested that winning a majority of Scottish seats would give it a mandate to negotiate the details of separation with Westminster. In the event, the 1992 General Election turned out to be a pleasant surprise for Plaid Cymru, which gained a seat and increased its share of the vote, but a bitter disappointment for the SNP, which, despite a considerable increase in its share of the vote, failed to gain a single seat. Labour, with 49 of the 72 seats in Scotland and 27 of the 38 seats in Wales, remained the dominant party in both countries.

To a certain extent, Plaid Cymru and the SNP have experienced similar electoral fortunes since 1945 (Table 13.12).

However, SNP support has remained at a much higher level than that for Plaid Cymru, reflecting the greater potential of Scottish nationalism. Plaid Cymru's close links with the language issue effectively confines its appeal to the regions containing a high percentage of Welsh-language speakers in the North-West and West of the country. By contrast, the SNP can legitimately aim to become the main challenger to Labour in most Scottish (including working class) seats: in 1992, the SNP in total vote (just under 630 000) and share of the vote (21.5%) was only just

behind the Conservatives (just over 750 000 and 25.7%) and was second in far more seats (36, cf.25).

Both parties were deflated by the failure of the devolution referendum in March 1979: legislation which would have established assemblies in both countries received the support of only 32.5% of the electorate (51.6% of voters) in Scotland and a mere 11.8% of electors (20.26% of voters) in Wales. The referendum result underlined the difficulty faced by the nationalist parties – namely, that only a minority of Scots and an even smaller minority of Welsh endorse their major aim of self-government. But the 1992 election result suggests that support for both Plaid Cymru and the SNP is starting to increase again.

■ The Extreme Right

Support for the extreme right – never great – peaked in the 1970s, declined in the 1980s and revived slightly in the early 1990s. The main far right party in the 1970s, the **National Front** (NF) (1967), rose by exploiting the immigration issue but, although displacing the Communist Party as Britain's fourth party in 1974, it failed to win a parliamentary seat. Its highest poll – 191 000 votes (0.6% of the total vote) – was achieved in

Table 13.12 *The Scottish National Party and Plaid Cymru: candidates, seats and share of the vote, 1945–92*

	SNP			Plaid Cymru		
	Candidates	Seats	Share of Scottish vote	Candidates	Seats	Share of Welsh vote
1945	8	0	1.2	7	0	1.2
1950	3	0	0.4	7	0	1.2
1951	2	0	0.3	4	0	0.7
1955	2	0	0.5	11	0	3.1
1959	5	0	0.8	20	0	5.2
1964	15	0	2.4	23	0	4.8
1966	23	0	5.0	20	0	4.3
1970	65	1	11.4	36	0	11.5
1974 (1)	70	7	21.9	36	2	10.7
1974 (ii)	71	11	30.4	36	3	10.8
1979	71	2	17.3	36	2	8.1
1983	71	2	11.8	38	2	7.8
1987	71	3	14.0	38	3	7.3
1992	72	3	21.5	38	4	8.8

1979 but was divided between over 300 candidates and the party enjoyed more success at local level, winning two seats on Blackburn Council (1976) and polling over 18% in local elections in Leicester (1976) and over 10% in some east London boroughs (1977).

In the late 1970s and 1980s, the NF faded: its electoral appeal was undermined by the tough stance on immigration taken by the Conservatives under Thatcher, it encountered increasing resistance at street level from the Anti-Nazi League, and it was weakened by internal faction fights and then by the formation of a rival group – at first the New National Front and subsequently the **British National Party** (BNP) (1983) – by its former leader, John Tyndall. The NF and BNP received a mere 41 000 votes between them in 1983; deterred by the rising cost of deposits, neither party put forward any candidates in 1987. Its street challenge continued with violent anti-black and anti-Jewish propaganda, but electorally it seemed to be finished.

British fascism stirred again in the early 1990s, encouraged by resurgent racism in Europe and the re-emergence of a political space to the right of the Conservative Party after the demise of the authoritarian populism of Margaret Thatcher. Both the BNP – now the leading party on the extreme right – and the NF ran candidates in the 1992 General Election (26 in all, average vote 532 and 343 respectively), and the BNP gained 20% of the vote in a by-election in Tower Hamlets in late 1992 and won a seat on Tower Hamlets Council in 1993. Against a background of rising racial violence (reported racial attacks doubled between 1988–1991), the Anti-Nazi League was re-launched in 1992 to destroy the British National Party and stop the spread into Britain of European neo-fascist groups with which the BNP has links.

■ Leftist Groups

The Communist Party of Great Britain (CPGB) (1920) finally abandoned its name, constitution and commitment to Marxism-Leninism at its 43rd Congress in 1991. Since its peak in the 1940s, when it had a membership of 56 000 (1942), 200 councillors and two MPs (1945), it had been in steady decline, losing members at the rate of about 1000 a year (membership stood at about 6 000 in late 1990) and with the circulation of its newspaper falling from 122 000 in 1947 (*Daily Worker*) to 28 250 in 1985 (*Morning Star*). The collapse of Communism in the USSR was the final blow to the CPGB; accepting that the Bolshevik political experiment of 1917 had 'ended in disaster', the party – now led by Nina Temple – changed its name to **Democratic Left** and replaced its authoritarian system of democratic centralism with a looser, federal structure. In the same year (1991) came the revelation – hitherto always denied – that the CPGB had received up to £100 000 a year from Moscow between 1958–79. The journal *Marxism Today*, which had provided a forum for informed left debate in the 1980s under its Eurocommunist editor Martin Jaques, also closed down in 1991.

The **Militant Tendency** is a far-left Trotskyist grouping which down to 1993 practised entryist tactics and gained a foothold in the Labour Party after 1973 when Labour abolished its list of proscribed organisations. By the mid-1980s, with a membership of about 4500, an annual income of over £1m., a staff of over 140 and a weekly newspaper selling thousands of copies, Militant was well-entrenched within the party. Aware of the electoral damaged caused by its link with the Tendency, Labour launched a policy of expelling members of Militant, its task complicated by Militant's denial of its own existence and counterclaim that it was merely a collection of like-minded newspaper readers. By 1991, large numbers of expulsions had taken place; in particular, sections of the party where Militant was extremely influential such as the Liverpool Labour Party had been purged and two Militant Labour MPs had been de-selected. Militant was thus forced into the decision to work outside the Labour Party, a move which led to bitter in-fighting culminating in a split and the expulsion of its founder, Ted Grant, in 1992. Militant stood its own candidate in the Liverpool Walton by-election in July 1991 and Scottish Militant won a seat on the Glasgow City Council and one on the

Strathclyde regional council in 1992 after campaigning against the poll tax. The launch of **Militant Labour** as an open independent grouping, with Peter Taaffee as its General Secretary, came formally in 1993.

Other far left groups include the **Socialist Workers' Party** (SWP) and the Trotskyist **Workers' Revolutionary Party** (WRP) and **Socialist League** (SL), which was formerly the International Marxist Group (IMG). In the late 1980s and early 1990s, the SWP, rejecting Labour Party 'electoralism', sought to build support for Socialism around opposition to the poll tax, the Gulf War and the destruction of the NHS. Both Trotskyist groups suffered severely from the factionalism endemic on the extreme left in the 1980s: the WRP fragmented into as many as nine groupings after the expulsion of its founder, Gerry Healy, in 1985 whilst the SL split three ways after 1985. By the time the collapse of Communism in the USSR had made such labels as 'Stalinism', 'Trotskyism' and 'Eurocommunism' virtually redundant, neither entryism nor independent party-building had brought the far left much reward.

■ The Green Party

The **Green Party**, which began as the Ecology Party in 1973, rejects the industrial and agricultural practices which pollute and destroy the environment. Its 1992 manifesto called for unilateral disarmament and the scrapping of all nuclear weapons; a shift from income tax and VAT to taxes on energy, pollution and raw materials; the cancellation of all but the most essential road-building schemes in favour of an expanded system of public transport, including more cycle paths, canals and railways; and aimed to cut carbon dioxide emissions (the gas causing the greenhouse effect) by 80% by the year 2005 and to ban ozone-depleting gases. In terms of public education in environmentalism, the Green Party is part of a wider 'green' movement which has had considerable success. However, since 1989 when the Greens gained 2.3 million votes (15% of the total vote) in the Euro elections and their

membership soared to 20 000 (1990) in the wake of this success, their political support and membership have plummeted. In the 1992 General Election, the party put forward nearly double the number of candidates (254 cf.133) than in 1987 but – at 1.3% – gained a slightly lower average share of the vote in the seats it contested. Membership slumped to under 8000 (1992). Although the party did slightly better in the May local elections, its share of the vote (4%) was only half of the 8% achieved in 1990. Explanations for the electoral decline of the Greens include asset-stripping of its ideas and policies by the main parties; lack of resources (it spent a mere £50 000 on the 1992 General Election campaign); and internal squabbling between pragmatists and fundamentalists which led in September 1992 to the resignation of its chairman, Sara Parkin, declaring that 'the Green Party has become a liability to green politics', and the decision by its other leading light, Jonathan Porritt, to take 'no active role in the party' in future.

Summary

Britain still has a two-party system in the sense that only two parties stand a realistic chance of exercising government, alone or (possibly) in some form of agreement with a third party. But the run of Conservative victories – and Labour failures – have led some commentators to argue that Britain now has 'a natural party of government' and 'a natural party of opposition' operating in 'a dominant party system'.

There are important differences of ideology, policy, ethos and organisation between the two major parties: internally, each is a broad coalition, with groups representing differing strands of opinion competing for influence.

Electorally, the rise of minor parties in the 1970s produced multi-partyism at constituency level. However, the Liberal-SDP Alliance became a 'third force' only in votes – not in seats – in the 1980s and the Liberal Democrats – the party which emerged when it collapsed – failed in 1992 to recapture the levels of support enjoyed by the Liberals in 1974. The challenge of the mainland nationalist parties faded without disappearing after 1979, reviving only slightly in 1992. The political activity of the extreme right and far left was largely confined to the streets: both were prominent in the early 1990s, the extreme right against a background of growing racism in Europe and the far left in the Anti-Poll Tax Movement. The CPGB transformed itself into the Democratic Left and Militant Tendency, with many of its members drummed out of the Labour Party, decided upon an independent strategy as Militant Labour. The Greens helped raise environmental consciousness but, short of funds and internally divided, proved unable in the early 1990s to capitalise on their remarkable success in the 1989 Euro elections.

Questions

1. Has Britain got 'a dominant party system'?

2. Compare the two major parties in leadership (style and method of election), organisation, ideology, policy and ethos.

3. Critically examine the relationship between the Conservative Party and business interests and between the Labour Party and the trade unions. Why have these relationships become such an important political issue?

Assignment

Conduct a study of the ways in which the two major parties organised for the General Election campaign of 1992. Be sure to include in your coverage a consideration of the following features: party manifestos (both contents and how the contents were selected); campaign teams; strategies; candidate selection; role of the media (TV, radio and newspapers); finances; attention to marginals; use of advertising agencies; and role of opinion polls.

Analyse the result at national and regional levels; attempt to identify the factors mainly responsible for the particular outcome, and place them in order of importance.

Useful reading for this assignment includes D. Butler and D. Kavanagh (1992) *The British General Election of 1992* (London: Macmillan); A. King (ed.) (1992) *Britain at the Polls* (Oxford: Oxford University Press); *The Times Guide to the House of Commons April 1992* (1992) (London: Times Newspapers); and *The Guide to the House of Commons New Parliament: A Guardian Book* (1992) (London: Fourth Estate).

Further reading

Alderman, G. (1989) *Britain A One-Party State?* (London: Croom Helm).

Butler, D. and Kavanagh, D. (1992) *The British General Election of 1992* (London: Macmillan).

Cook, C. (1993) *A Short History of the Liberal Party 1900–1992*, 4th edn (London: Macmillan).

Garner, R. and Kelly, R. (1993) *British Political Parties Today* (Manchester University Press).

Heffernan, R. and Marqusee, M. (1992) *Defeat from the Jaws of Victory: Inside Kinnock's Labour Party* (London: Verso).

Heywood, A. (1993) 'The Dominant Party System: A Threat to Democracy?' *Talking Politics*, 5: 2, winter.

Hunt, S. (1992) 'Fascism and the "Race Issue" in Britain', *Talking Politics*, 5: 1 autumn

Ingle, S. (1989) *The British Party System*, 2nd edn (Oxford: Blackwell).

Kelly, R. (1989). 'Party Conferences: Do They Matter?' *Talking Politics*, 2: 1, autumn.

Kelly R. and Foster, S. (1991) 'Power in the Labour Party' *Politics Review*, 1: 1, September.

Norton, P. and Aughey, A. (1981) *Conservatives and Conservatism* (London: Temple Smith).

Punnett, R.M. (1992) *Selecting the Party Leader: Britain in Comparative Perspective* (London: Harvester Wheatsheaf).

Seldon, A. (ed.) (1990) *UK Political Parties since 1945* (London: Philip Allan).

Seyd, P. and Whiteley, P. (1992) *Labour's Grass Roots: The Politics of Party Membership* (Oxford: Clarendon).

Stevenson, J. (1993) *Third Party Politics since 1945* (Oxford: Blackwell).

■ *Chapter 14* ■

Voting Behaviour and Elections

In the late 1960s a political scientist could observe with considerable justification that in Britain 'class is the basis of party politics; all else is embellishment and detail'. Twenty years later social class appears to explain much less about variations in political behaviour and today political scientists talk of 'class dealignment' as having taken place. But, as we shall see, there is much disagreement about the extent to which dealignment has occurred. Political scientists have developed various models to help explain the changes which have taken place in voting behaviour. Each model is useful in that it explains some aspect or other of voting, but none explains voting patterns entirely. How reliable are the opinion poll data which political scientists use in their research? Political scientists can also be frustrated by trends such as tactical voting, which change the meaning of the voting act and which can distort the significance of correlations between party allegiance and social characteristics. Would the patterns of voting change if a different, and some would say fairer, electoral system were introduced? The chapter concludes with an examination of alternative situations in terms of systems and behaviours.

■ The Decline of the Two-Party System

The electorate is not an unchanging entity, nor is it stable. Some changes will occur because its composition is changing as young people attain voting age and become included, whilst others die. Other changes will occur because of movements in attitudes, values and behaviour from one election to the next.

Thus there may be long term and short term changes which help explain voting trends. Although it is a basic point, it has to be remembered that when comparing the electorate of the 1950s with that of the 1990s very different groups of voters are involved. Many voters in the 1950s would have remembered the Boer War as well as two World Wars; they might have experienced great economic hardship during the 1930s or been involved in the suffragette movement; they would certainly have witnessed the election of the Attlee government. None of these voters will have lived long enough to vote in the 1990s. In contrast, many first time young voters in 1992 will have no real memories of the last Labour government which left office in 1979. But these young voters may well be aware of short term changes in the political agenda on which elections have been fought; they may have noticed, for example, that the defence issue seemed to play a smaller role in the 1992 campaign than it did in 1987. The impact of these processes on voting behaviour has contributed to the decline of two-party voting. This can be seen in three closely related developments which have occurred during the last forty years.

Firstly, there has been a more or less steady decline in the percentage of the total vote won in general elections by the Conservative and Labour parties. For example, in 1951 nearly 97% of voters supported either Labour or Conservative. After touching a low point of 72% in 1983, the percentage rose to 78% in 1992, which nevertheless remains far below the 1951 level.

Secondly, one of the major causes for this decline has been the weakening of *partisan attachment*. In other words, the links between voters and parties have grown weaker and weaker as fewer and fewer voters identified with particular political parties (see question 4 on page 276). As party loyalties have weakened so electoral *volatility* has increased. Because an increasing number of voters do not have such strong emotional ties to particular parties, they find it easier to switch their vote to another party or decide not to vote at all.

A Gallup survey (*Daily Telegraph* 13.4.92) asked voters 'How long ago did you decide which way you would finally vote?' The poll findings in Table 14.1 showed that last-minute vote-switching decisions were made by nearly one in seven in the 1992 general election, which was almost double the figure for the 1987 election.

Thirdly, there has been a decline in class-based voting during the post-war years. In the 1950s approximately two-thirds of the working class voted Labour, and four-fifths of the middle-class voted Conservative.

Since those early post-war years the links between class and party have weakened. Political scientists refer to this process as *dealignment*. What processes have been at work to cause the weakening of class and party links, voter and party links, resulting in greater volatility with a quarter of voters switching their support away from the two major parties? As might be expected of such a complex question, no single theory can explain adequately all the changes that have occurred in recent decades. Various

explanations, however, can be grouped into two main types – those sharing the primacy approach and those sharing the recency approach.

▮ The Primacy Approach: The Social Basis of Voting Behaviour

Much human behaviour reflects social divisions. For example, in terms of leisure and cultural behaviour patterns, almost all those attending a rave will be young people: far more elderly than young will spend a night at bingo. Only the more affluent in society will be found picnicking at Glyndebourne. Many more men than women go fishing. Can voting behaviour be explained in this way by social divisions – such as age, gender, ethnicity, and class? How far are the very different experiences of individuals living in society reflected in their voting behaviour?

If the way in which individuals vote is an expression of their position in the social structure, then voting would tend to be stable. This is because an individual's sex, ethnicity etc. is fixed. Of course an individual's voting habits might well change from time to time but such changes that occur do so within an overall pattern of stability. It might be argued, for example, that four consecutive Tory election victories, each won with around 42% of the vote, is a reflection of great stability in voting behaviour.

In order to analyse the loyalties of voters, Richard Rose and Ian McAllister devised a theoretical framework for exploring how a lifetime of learning steadily shapes how an individual might vote (*The Loyalties of Voters* (1990) Sage). A modified version of their framework is shown in Figure 14.1. The process begins with childhood political socialisation, since young children develop attitudes towards authority based on their own experience within the family. Some children will learn about authority in a strict authoritarian family where they are punished if they disobey the rules, whereas others will learn in a more open or democratic family where they may even be involved in making family decisions. Each individual's family is located in the class structure, and so provides a social class identity and

Table 14.1 *When the voting decision was made*			
	1983	*1987*	*1992*
Decided a long time ago (%)	78	81	73
Two or three weeks ago	14	12	13
During the last few days	8	7	14

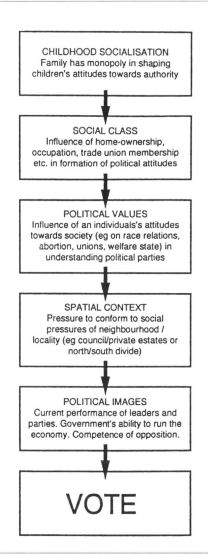

Figure 14.1   *A Framework for analysis of voting behaviour (adapted from Rose and McAllister, 1990)*

value system. All the learning experiences shown in the framework may influence a particular voter, whilst another voter might only be influenced by one or two of the experiences. The framework does not attempt to analyse voting loyalty in terms of one explanation only, but is flexible enough for new findings to be 'hung' on the framework in order to build up a fuller understanding of voting behaviour. A well-known American book, *The American Voter*, influenced

political scientists into believing that long term factors in an individual's life were the most important in influencing his or her vote. The authors, Angus Campbell, Philip E. Converse, Warren E. Miller and Donald E. Stokes, set out a framework similar in principle to Rose and McAllister's but referred to theirs as the 'funnel of causality'.

Social Class and Voting Behaviour

Of all the social divisions – such as age, gender, ethnicity, and the urban-rural split – it is social class that has preoccupied political scientists. As Table 14.2 indicates, in the early post-war years there was a fairly positive relationship between social class membership and voting behaviour. Political scientists of the time were more interested in the 'class defectors' – the middle-class socialists and the working-class Tories – than they were in the majorities of voters who supported their 'natural' class party. Most research focused on the working-class Tories since this was the most extensive of the deviant behaviour. Did a third of the working class vote Tory because they were deferential and preferred being governed by their social superiors? Was society – in the form of the mass media and education – undermining working-class consciousness and thereby confusing a minority of working people as to which political party they ought to support? Had other social processes, such as slum clearance, the decline of occupational communities and the decline in workplace contacts brought about by increasing automation, resulted in weakening the ties for some between class and

Table 14.2   *Class percentages voting Labour and Conservative 1945–58*

	AB	*C1*	*C2*	*DE*
Conservative	85	70	35	30
Labour	10	25	60	65

Source: Tapper and Bowles (1982, p. 175).

party? Or, finally, were some workers motivated more than others by affluence and voting Tory on pragmatic or instrumental grounds because they believed they would be better off in material terms under a Conservative government? These were the sort of questions that political scientists posed and set about answering.

During the 1960s and particularly during the 1970s the relationship between class and party weakened. This process of class *dealignment* was reflected in a reduction in Conservative support from the professional and managerial classes and a reduction in Labour support from the working classes. Table 14.3 indicates the voting behaviour of social classes in the 1992 General Election.

In exploring causes of class dealignment some researchers focused on changes that had taken place within the social structure: how far were changes in voting behaviour influenced by changes in the class structure? Some social scientists such as Erik Olin Wright had argued that since the Second World War a 'new' middle class had come into existence alongside the 'old' middle class. This new middle class was one which was largely based on people employed in the public sector – such as health authority staff, social workers, teachers and civil servants. It was argued that, unlike the old middle class, the new one was in what is termed 'a contradictory class location' insofar as there was a divergence between the security of class members in the social structure and their ideological orientation. The contradictory class location of this group can be illustrated with the example of college lecturers. They work in the public sector and the overwhelming majority are middle class or bourgeois in outlook. Yet, as recent cutbacks in

some authorities have shown, lecturers are not much safer from the threat of redundancy than factory workers. At its simplest, a contradiction exists between the political views of lecturers (which are middle class) and their job security (which is similar to working-class conditions). For this new middle class, then, their contradictory location would appear to present a barrier to their support for the traditional party of the middle class, the Conservatives.

Changes have also occurred amongst the working classes. According to one theory, an increased number of individuals whom social scientists would describe as being working class actually see themselves as being middle class. This subjective form of class membership frees them from any loyalties that in the past would have resulted in their support of Labour. This misidentification of class is an extreme example of how the working class has fragmented during the post-war years. The work of K. Roberts *et al.* has revealed the nature of these changes. It is possible to split the working class into union and non-union, affluent and poor, public sector employed/private sector employed, and so on, with each division having distinct political implications.

Ivor Crewe has drawn some of these divisions together in compiling what he terms the 'new' and 'traditional' working classes. His data from previous election studies led him to conclude that whilst Labour remained largely working class, the working class was no longer largely Labour. The 1992 General Election analysis, updated by Anthony King, revealed that whilst Labour had improved its working class support, the position described by Crewe remained essentially the same. Although Labour had a big lead in support from the traditional working class, it was running neck-and-neck with the Conservatives amongst the new working class. In other words, Labour had come to represent the declining fragment of the traditional working class whilst failing to attract the more affluent and expanding working class of the high-tech and service economy (Table 14.4).

Three political scientists, Anthony Heath, Roger Jowell and John Curtice (1985), conducted a survey which led them to conclude that class

Table 14.3   *Class voting in the 1992 General Election (%)*

	AB	C1	C2	DE
Conservative	57	49	35	29
Labour	17	28	40	48
Liberal Democrat	20	19	17	14

Source: Gallup poll published in the *Daily Telegraph* (14 April 1992).

Table 14.4 *The fragmentation of the working-class vote (%)*

The new working class

	Lives in South	Owner-occupier	Non-union
Conservative	38	38	34
Labour	36	39	43
Liberal Democrat	22	18	16

The traditional working class

	Lives in Scotland/North	Council tenant	Union member
Conservative	23	20	23
Labour	52	57	45
Liberal Democrat	13	12	16

Source: Gallup poll published in the *Daily Telegraph* (14 April 1992).

dealignment had not taken place on such a large scale as previously thought. They argued that social class is still an important factor in determining the way people vote; hence Labour's electoral problems sprang mainly from the shrinking size of the working class, not just from weakening class loyalties. Their research received a critical reception from fellow political scientists since they used a number of new and controversial techniques in their analysis. They rejected the class categories that are generally used by social scientists (AB:C1:C2:DE) in favour of five categories (salariat; routine non-manual; petty bourgeoisie; foreman and technicians; the working class). At the same time they used a different statistical technique – the odds ratio – to calculate class voting which led to them concluding that rather than a process of class dealignment having taken place, the changing statistics simply represented a 'trendless fluctuation'.

Source: Guardian.

Figure 14.2 *Kenneth Clarke in open mouthed retreat after a doorstep confrontation with a retired police sergeant in the 1992 General Election Campaign*

Finally, the 1992 General Election results dispelled the myth that C2 voters were uniquely important amongst the electorate. Some political commentators had argued that C2 voters – skilled manual and supervisory workers – had put Margaret Thatcher into Number Ten in 1979, for they swung 9% to the Conservatives whilst the rest of the electorate swung by only 3.5%. For this reason alone, C2s won a reputation for being 'the shock troops of Thatcherism'. Writing in the *Guardian* (23 April 1990) Martin Linton and David McKie emphasised their importance: 'There is no more powerful group in politics than the C2s. They are the largest of the six socio-economic classes ... and it is their support that makes or breaks every government' which is why 'voters in class C2 are a target group for all parties in every election'. Writing in *New Statesman and Society* (13 July 1990) Robert Waller took a different view on the significance of C2 support in determining which party won elections. He agreed that the C2s were an *influential* group, but not an *all-important* one. For Labour to make inroads on the Conservative vote, a swing in the DE group was equally important as one amongst the C2s.

In the 1987 General Election the Conservatives won 42% of the C2 vote and Labour won 35%. In 1992 Labour received 40% of C2 support and the Conservatives 35%. Despite a Labour lead of 5 points, giving Labour the largest swing it received from any social class, the Conservatives won the election. It seems that Robert Waller is correct and that other political commentators over-emphasised in the past the importance of the C2 vote in deciding the occupant of Number Ten.

☐ Sectoral Cleavages in Employment and Consumption

Some political scientists were unhappy with attempting to explain voting behaviour in terms of a crude socialisation model based on class or occupation. Not only were the different occupational classes becoming more difficult to define in a more technologically-based society, but other changes such as more women going out to work meant that an increasing number of families were now of 'mixed' class. Patrick Dunleavy attempted to explain voting behaviour in terms of *sectoral cleavages* rather than class divisions. He argued that there were two important sectors – in employment and consumption – which were crucial to voting behaviour. Firstly, it was significant whether voters were employed in the public or private sector. Secondly, it was significant whether voters consumed important items such as housing, education, health care and transport from the public sector or the private sector. Of course there is a dimension of social class in this explanation since voters who are council tenants, use state schools, the NHS and public transport are likely to be in a different class than others who are owner-occupiers, send their children to private schools, have private health insurance and use private cars rather than buses. These differences it was argued, are likely to be reflected in voting behaviour with those who rely on private provision giving their support to the Conservatives whilst those relying on state provision supporting other parties, particularly Labour.

There is some evidence that supports sectoral cleavage as an explanation of voting choice, but in a rather patchy way. The decline in support for the Conservatives amongst middle class professions may well be a result of the growth in white collar public sector employment (compare Tables 14.2 and 14.3). Although there may be other factors at work, Gallup found that only 17% of secondary teachers – a middle class public sector profession – intended to support the Conservatives in 1992 whilst 48% intended to vote Labour and 22% Liberal. In terms of a consumption cleavage, Table 14.4 indicated that even within the working class, council tenants and owner occupiers vote in different ways.

☐ Gender and Voting

The pattern of gender and voting has changed considerably over recent years. Writing in 1967 it was possible to argue that 'there is overwhelming evidence that women are more Conservatively inclined than men ...' (Pulzer, 1967, p. 107). There appeared to be sound reasons why this situation existed. Some argued that since women stayed at home more than men, it was natural that their attitudes should be shaped by the traditional values of the family. It was likely that women were more religious and more deferential than men. Also, not having a job meant that such women never experienced industrial conflict at the workplace and so did not value the role of trade unions. All these factors were believed to produce a political outlook amongst women that was more inclined towards supporting Conservatives than men. Others argued that women voting Conservative more was a reflection of the fact the people generally became more Conservative as they grow older, and women live longer than men. Female political conservatism, then, was more likely to be related to demographic factors than it was to attitudes towards politics.

Table 14.5 shows that in the 1960s women voted Conservative by a margin of 6% or 7% over men, but from 1979 the gender gap narrowed until it disappeared in 1987. The great mystery is why it returned in such a marked way in 1992. For Labour campaigned hard in order to win female support, and many of the issues at the top of its political agenda were 'women's issues'. Part of the answer may lie in the different ways different age groups of women voted. In a survey conducted between 1986–88 David Denver and Gordon Hands revealed that a gender gap existed amongst young people, but it represented a reversal of the traditional picture. Boys gave more support (50%) to the Conservatives than girls (35%). It appeared that young males were attracted by Margaret Thatcher's 'macho' image whereas young females were attracted more by Labour's 'caring' image on health and education (surprisingly attitudes on 'women's issues', such as abortion and divorce accounted for little difference). Table 14.6 reveals that a gender gap continued to influence voting patterns in different ways at different ages.

It can be seen that men in each generation shown voted Conservative more than Labour, and as they grow older Conservative support increased. The same pattern is true for older women, but from the youngest generation of female voters Labour received the most support.

Table 14.5 *Sex and party choice in general elections, 1964–92*

		Conservative (%)	Labour (%)	Liberal/ All/L-D (%)
1964	Men	40	48	11
	Women	46	42	12
1966	Men	38	53	8
	Women	45	46	9
1970	Men	44	49	8
	Women	51	41	8
Feb. 1974	Men	40	41	19
	Women	40	38	22
Oct. 1974	Men	34	46	19
	Women	40	39	21
1979	Men	47	39	13
	Women	46	39	14
1983	Men	46	30	24
	Women	43	28	28
1987	Men	44	33	22
	Women	44	31	25
1992	Men	38	36	19
	Women	44	34	16

Sources: 1964–Oct. 1974, Nuffield Studies; 1979–1987, I. Crewe, *The Guardian*, 13 June 1983, 15 June 1987; Anthony King, *Daily Telegraph*, 14 April 1992.

Table 14.6 *The gender gap in party support: 1992 General Election*

		Con.	Lab.	Lib Dem.
18–24 years old	men	39	35	18
	women	30	43	19
35–54 years old	men	40	37	19
	women	46	32	19
65 years and older	men	44	38	16
	women	51	31	17

Source: Sunday Times, 12 April 1993.

☐ *Age and Voting*

There has been a long recognised association between increasing age and Conservative support. This was evident in the data on sex and voting as well as in Table 14.7 below.

Why should age be an influence on voting behaviour? It has been argued that for most people property and wealth increase as they grow older, and as their families grow up so aspects of the welfare state become less important to them, resulting in a more Conservative outlook. Others have suggested that age is an influence on voting in terms of 'political generations' passing through the electorate. Each generation forms its views and votes for the first time in a distinct political climate. Table 14.7 shows that with 37% support of young people in the 'Thatcher generation' the Conservatives were the most popular party. But in 1966 just over half (51.2%) of under twenty-four year olds in the 'sixties generation' supported Labour. By 1992 this 'cohort' of voters has reached middle age and would be within the 45–64 age group in Table 14.7. It is difficult to be precise, but the figures suggest that the generational influence (voting Labour) is outweighed by the age factor (increasing Conservative support).

☐ *Ethnicity and Voting*

In his book, *Immigration and 'Race' Politics in Post-War Britain*, (1992) Zig Layton-Henry made the point that participation by the ethnic minorities in elections can be used as a measure of political integration and support for democratic politics. As the same time, discrimination against ethnic minorities could result in political responses such as apathy, alienation or even rebellion. He argued that the support of black voters (the word 'black' is used here as a political term to refer to both Afro-Caribbean and Asian voters) can be crucial in close run elections, such as those in 1974. A study of the October 1974 General Election drew four conclusions about ethnic minority voting: (1) the minorities swung more to Labour than the electorate as a whole; (2) members of minority groups were five times more likely not to be registered to vote than whites in the same area; (3) although ethnic minorities tended to conform with their social class in voting Labour, other parties could attract their support if an effort was made, and (4) the ethnic minorities played a significant part in determining the outcome of the election. (Community Relations Commission: *Participation of Ethnic Minorities in the General Election, October 1974*, 1975). Although this report was criticised for its methodology, it ensured that black voters were now to be taken as a matter of academic and political interest.

A later study of the 1987 General Election revealed that Labour had held on to its support from the ethnic minorities. Table 14.8 analyses the black vote according to social class. It can be seen that black working class support for Labour is at very high levels. It is remarkable that the professional and managerial class AB supported Labour *more* than the national working class.

Summing up ethnic minority voting behaviour, Layton-Henry stated 'survey data for the three general elections [1979, 1983, 1987] suggest that there has been remarkable stability in black

Table 14.7   *The 1992 General Election: party support (%) by age*

Age	Con.	Lab.	Lib Dem.
18–24	37	34	21
25–34	36	39	17
35–44	37	37	20
45–64	42	34	17
65+	49	31	13

Source: Gallup Poll in the *Daily Telegraph*, 14 April 1992.

Table 14.8   *Party support by class among black voters (%)*

	AB	C1	C2	DE
Conservative	33	30	14	10
Labour	54	52	78	84
Liberal-SDP Alliance	13	17	9	5

Source: Harris Poll, May 1987, published in *Talking Politics*.

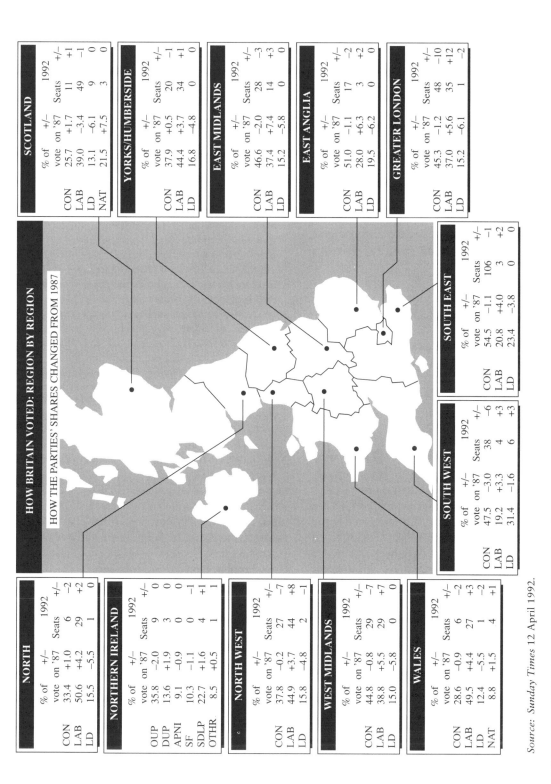

HOW BRITAIN VOTED: REGION BY REGION

HOW THE PARTIES' SHARES CHANGED FROM 1987

SCOTLAND

	% of vote	+/- on '87	Seats 1992	+/-
CON	25.7	+1.7	11	+1
LAB	39.0	-3.4	49	-1
LD	13.1	-6.1	9	0
NAT	21.5	+7.5	3	0

YORKS/HUMBERSIDE

	% of vote	+/- on '87	Seats 1992	+/-
CON	37.9	+0.5	20	-1
LAB	44.4	+3.7	34	+1
LD	16.8	-4.8	0	0

EAST MIDLANDS

	% of vote	+/- on '87	Seats 1992	+/-
CON	46.6	-2.0	28	-3
LAB	37.4	+7.4	14	+3
LD	15.2	-5.8	0	0

EAST ANGLIA

	% of vote	+/- on '87	Seats 1992	+/-
CON	51.0	-1.1	17	-2
LAB	28.0	+6.3	3	+2
LD	19.5	-6.2	0	0

GREATER LONDON

	% of vote	+/- on '87	Seats 1992	+/-
CON	45.3	-1.2	48	-10
LAB	37.0	+5.6	35	+12
LD	15.2	-6.1	1	-2

SOUTH EAST

	% of vote	+/- on '87	Seats 1992	+/-
CON	54.5	-1.1	106	-1
LAB	20.8	+4.0	3	+2
LD	23.4	-3.8	0	0

SOUTH WEST

	% of vote	+/- on '87	Seats 1992	+/-
CON	47.5	-3.0	38	-6
LAB	19.2	+3.3	4	+3
LD	31.4	-1.6	6	+3

NORTH

	% of vote	+/- on '87	Seats 1992	+/-
CON	33.4	+1.0	6	-2
LAB	50.6	+4.2	29	+2
LD	15.5	-5.5	1	0

NORTHERN IRELAND

	% of vote	+/- on '87	Seats 1992	+/-
OUP	35.8	-2.0	9	0
DUP	13.6	+1.9	3	0
APNI	9.1	-0.9	0	0
SF	10.3	-1.1	0	-1
SDLP	22.7	+1.6	4	+1
OTHR.	8.5	+0.5	1	1

NORTH WEST

	% of vote	+/- on '87	Seats 1992	+/-
CON	37.8	-0.2	27	-7
LAB	44.9	+3.7	44	+8
LD	15.8	-4.8	2	-1

WEST MIDLANDS

	% of vote	+/- on '87	Seats 1992	+/-
CON	44.8	-0.8	29	-7
LAB	38.8	+5.5	29	+7
LD	15.0	-5.8	0	0

WALES

	% of vote	+/- on '87	Seats 1992	+/-
CON	28.6	-0.9	6	-2
LAB	49.5	+4.4	27	+3
LD	12.4	-5.5	1	-2
NAT	8.8	+1.5	4	+1

Source: Sunday Times 12 April 1992.

Figure 14.3 *How Britain Voted: Region By Region*

support for the Labour party .... Although the Harris Poll did discover significant support for the Conservatives in areas of low ethnic concentration, which has probably always existed, even in these areas more Asians supported Labour than the Conservatives. Support for the Labour party is partly because the black electorate is more working-class than the electorate as a whole ... In addition, black voters give a higher priority to issues where the Labour party is seen as more trustworthy than the Conservatives, such as on unemployment, housing and racial discrimination. Issues where the Conservatives might be trusted more, such as defence and foreign affairs, are given a low priority' (Layton-Henry, 1988, pp. 20–4).

□ *The Geography of Voting*

Some of the social factors examined above are reflected in the geography of voting at the macro and micro level. At the macro level there is a regional pattern to voting behaviour, with Labour support stronger in the North, Scotland and Wales, and Conservative support stronger in the Midlands and South. Figure 14.3 shows the North-South divide in political geography with the Conservatives managing to secure only 25.7% of the 1992 Scottish vote and only 33.4% of the vote in the North compared with 54.5% in the South East. In contrast, Labour won only 20.8% of the vote in the South East, trailing third behind the Liberal Democrats, whereas support in the North was at 50.6%, and at 39% in Scotland making Labour the most popular party.

There is also an East-West divide in the Midlands and South. Although the Conservatives are the most popular party, their support is always stronger to the East. For example, Tory support in 1992 was at 54.5% in the South East, but 47.5% in the South West.

Is there an explanation for this North-South and, to a lesser extent, East-West pattern? A 'core-periphery' theory has been developed by Michael Steed as the basis of explaining much of Britain's history as well as contemporary British politics. It can be thought of as based on the idea

of Britain as a 'multi-national state', with its 'core' in South East Britain, and 'outer core' comprising East Anglia, the Midlands and Wessex, its 'inner periphery' made up of the North of England, Wales and the South west, and its 'outer periphery' being Scotland. These areas correspond with arcs drawn around London at 80, 200 and 300 miles. Steed argued

> The 17th-century civil war can be seen as a victory of the inner core over the inner periphery; most of the battles were fought in the outer core. From the mid-18th century onwards there came the fundamental shift from lowland Britain to upland Britain. The repeal of the Corn Laws in 1846, a turning point in British politics, reflected that shift; not only did the Anti-Corn Law League start in the periphery, in Manchester, and capture the core; it represented the interests of those parts of Britain trading westwards and wishing to import cheap food as opposed to those parts of Britain more able to produce food. By the end of the 19th-century peripheral Britain had been mobilized solidly (except Western Lancashire) for Gladstonian Liberalism, and core Britain for Unionism. In the 20th-century Labour and Conservative have reflected the same dichotomy ... Even the split in 1985 in the miners' strike could be seen as reflecting 'the division between north and south with its roots deep in the nation's history'. (Steed, 1986, pp. 591–5)

Steed's interpretation of British politics is fascinating since much of the data shown in the map, with the major exception of London, conforms to the pattern of a core and periphery.

At the micro-level of political geography, there is an influence on voting behaviour which political scientists refer to as the 'neighbourhood effect'. This effect is far too detailed to appear on the map since it occurs within local communities. Essentially it is argued that the dominant characteristic of a community will influence all voters. Denver has stated that 'The more middle-class an area was, then the more Conservative were both middle-class and working-class voters; the more working-class an area the more strongly Labour were both groups of voters ... Voters, then, tend to conform to the locally dominant political norm'. (Denver 1989, p. 39) This neighbourhood effect can be detected in Table 14.8 with the different voting patterns of Afro-Caribbeans and Asians who live side by side in ethnic communities and those who lived more isolated existences in the suburbs.

∎ The Recency Approach

This approach challenges the ideas behind the explanations of voting behaviour that fall within the primacy approach. In other words the argument that long term factors influence voting is largely dismissed, and much greater stress is put on the importance of recent events as explanations of voting behaviour. In terms of Figure 4.1 the recency approach would focus on perceptions of parties, leaders, issues, the campaign, and the government's ability to run the economy. These perceptions can, of course, change quite quickly. A new party leader, a fall in the interest rate or a period of poor industrial relations can result in large swings of support from one party to another. Unlike the primacy approach which embraces lifelong characteristics, such as gender, class, ethnicity and region, and so focuses on the relative stability of voting behaviour, the recency approach emphasises the volatility of voting behaviour which can result from relatively minor events which occur in politics.

Critics of the recency approach might argue that the last four general elections have resulted in Conservative governments elected on around 42% of the popular vote. Surely this points to an electorate which is very stable in its voting habits? The answer is that four consecutive Tory election victories with roughly the same level of electoral support is an account of events which obscures great upheavals in political behaviour. Firstly, the similar levels of support won by the Conservatives does not mean that it is the same people voting for them. Figure 14.4 shows that a great deal of 'churn' took place in 1992 which was not revealed in simple statistics. Although in 1992 the Conservatives won 43% of the popular vote, as they have since 1979, during the campaign period alone they won 3.20m. votes and lost 1.81m. Sixteen per cent of those who voted

Conservative did not decide to do so until the final week of the campaign.

The argument that four consecutive Conservative victories reflects a stable electorate is also misleading. The balance of support between the major parties is highly unstable, with support swinging from one party to another in response to economic events, personalities etc. Given this volatile public opinion, 'recent Conservative victories appear the results more of good timing and luck than of any fundamental, long-term dynamic in British politics.' (Mishler *et al.*, 1989). In other words, Labour Prime Minister James Callaghan 'lost' the 1979 general election through delaying going to the country for six months and so suffered the electoral consequences of the 'winter of discontent'. Thatcher 'won' in 1983 due in large part to the Falklands victory, and she 'won' again in 1987 in the middle of an economic boom. But between these Tory victories were periods of great unpopularity, such as when the SDP was formed in 1981, during the Westland affair in 1986, or prior to Thatcher's resignation in 1990, when calling an election would have led to inevitable defeat. Many believed that had John Major timed the election soon after the victory against Saddam Hussein in the Gulf War he would have won more convincingly than he did a year later in April 1992. Given a volatile electorate, it has been good timing by Prime Ministers in the decisions to call general elections which has resulted in Conservative successes rather than any fundamental shifts or realignments of support amongst the electorate in favour of the Conservative party.

□ *The Image of the Party Leader*

With the growth in the importance of television in political communication, and the emphasis of TV coverage on party leaders, are voters now influenced principally by their judgements on party leaders? In 1992, did a vote for the Conservatives really mean a vote for John Major as Prime Minister? The answers to these questions are far from straightforward.

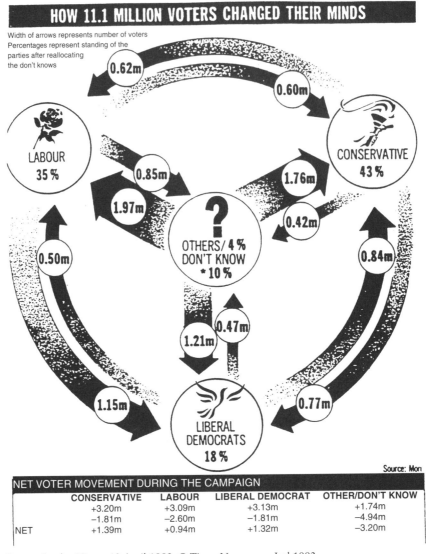

Figure 14.4 gives the following data.

HOW 11.1 MILLION VOTERS CHANGED THEIR MINDS

Width of arrows represents number of voters
Percentages represent standing of the parties after reallocating the don't knows

- LABOUR 35%
- CONSERVATIVE 43%
- OTHERS/ 4% DON'T KNOW +10%
- LIBERAL DEMOCRATS 18%

Arrow values: 0.62m, 0.60m, 0.85m, 1.76m, 1.97m, 0.42m, 0.50m, 0.84m, 1.21m, 0.47m, 1.15m, 0.77m

Source: Mori

NET VOTER MOVEMENT DURING THE CAMPAIGN	CONSERVATIVE	LABOUR	LIBERAL DEMOCRAT	OTHER/DON'T KNOW
	+3.20m	+3.09m	+3.13m	+1.74m
	−1.81m	−2.60m	−1.81m	−4.94m
NET	+1.39m	+0.94m	+1.32m	−3.20m

Source: Sunday Times, 12 April 1992. © Times Newspaper Ltd 1992.

Figure 14.4   *How 11.1 million voters changed their minds*

There is no doubt that the results of many polls found that, despite his strengths, Neil Kinnock was viewed as an electoral liability for the Labour party. Gallup findings suggested that had John Smith led Labour in the 1992 campaign the party would have gained an extra $5\frac{1}{2}$% support, mainly from those who decided not to vote with Kinnock leading Labour and from Liberal Democrats. Anti-Kinnock feelings amongst the electorate were fed and sustained by a press blitz against him in the tabloids. The *Sun*, for example, employed a psychic who revealed that Stalin, Mao and Lenin were all supporting Kinnock. Stories such as these may be ludicrous, but this does not mean that they have no impact. In the last week of the campaign, in which the *Sun* ran an intense anti-Kinnock campaign, Mori found there was a 4% swing to the Conservatives amongst the paper's readers.

Others do not believe that the image of the party leader is so crucial in influencing voters. Polls have shown that where voters prefer the policies of one party but the leader of the other party, they choose the policies by a ratio of six to one. Only if there is not much to choose between the parties in terms of policies will the qualities of their respective leaders become more important to voters. Also, the experience of past elections shows that unpopular leaders can win. For example, in 1970 Labour Prime Minister Harold Wilson with a 51% approval rating was far more popular than Conservative leader Edward Heath with only 28% approval. Yet Heath won the 1970 general election.

Can Issue Preferences Explain Voting Behaviour?

New issues can arise on the political agenda which do not fit into the traditional class interests of the parties, and can therefore blur the lines linking party and voter. For example, advocates and opponents of nuclear power development cross party lines causing divisions amongst trade unionists in particular. The miners have an interest in actually closing existing nuclear power stations, whilst workers in the nuclear power industry support its expansion. The issue of Britain's role inside the European Union has caused deep divisions within and between the major parties as well as within public opinion at large. Moral issues, such as the abortion issue or health education, can become salient issues which have little relation to party positions and are better understood in terms of authoritarian or liberal orientations. For example, there are Conservatives and Socialists who support an education campaign advising the public about precautions which will reduce the risks of catching and spreading AIDS. But within each party are those who take a stricter line arguing that chastity before marriage and fidelity afterwards are the only lessons that need to be taught.

With the weakening of class influences on voting and the emergence of new issues which did not fit traditional partisan splits, some political scientists argued that an increasing number of the electorate were voting on the basis of issue preferences. Mark Franklin found, for example, that the effect of voters deciding which party to vote for according to issue preferences more than doubled between 1964 and 1983 (Franklin, 1985). Some political scientists argued that Labour's electoral defeats since 1979 were accounted for in part because its policies were no longer popular, even with its long-standing supporters. For example, Ivor Crewe considers that trends in public opinion reveal a quite exceptional movement of opinion away from Labour's traditional positions amongst Labour supporters over the past twenty or thirty years. There has been a spectacular decline in support for the 'collectivist trinity' of public ownership, trade union power and social welfare. By contrast, the policy positions of the Conservative party and its supporters have remained strong and stable.

A 'consumer model' of voting behaviour has been constructed by H. Himmelweit and colleagues which is derived from an issue-based theory of voting (Himmelweit *et al.*, 1984). Voters 'shop around' to find the party with a programme of policies which offers the closest fit to their own policy preferences. Of course, voters may not have perfect information about various parties' policies and, even when they do have the relevant information, they may suspect that a party, if elected to office, would not implement its manifesto proposals. Although past studies showed that party support could be predicted with 80 per cent accuracy from consumer preferences, the 1987 General Election raised some doubts about seeing voters as analogous to shoppers in the political market-place. As Ivor Crewe commented in *The Guardian*,

> Labour's poor performance remains a puzzle because its campaign did succeed in placing its favourable issues much further up the agenda than in 1983 ... Had electors voted solely on the main issues Labour would have won. It was considered the more capable party on three of the four leading issues – jobs, health and education – among those for whom the issue was important ... On all three social issues there was widespread agreement even among Conservatives, that matters had deteriorated (*The Guardian*, 16 June 1987).

However, the 1992 General Election once again raised the possibility that issue-voting was an important factor which explained aspects of voting behaviour such as party choice and volatility. Although Labour succeeded in pushing some of its campaign issues – such as health, pensions and transport – well up amongst those the electorate saw as important, the top issues were inflation and taxation which lay at the heart of the Conservative's 'double whammy' propaganda drive. Along with these issues the Conservatives either increased their lead over Labour or reduced Labour's lead (Figure 14.5). Furthermore, Gallup's

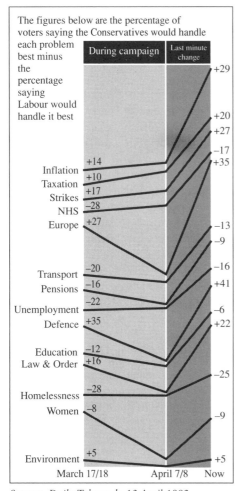

Figure 14.5 *How Tories Improved On The Issues*

The figures below are the percentage of voters saying the Conservatives would handle each problem best minus the percentage saying Labour would handle it best

	During campaign	Last minute change
		+29
		+20
		+27
		−17
Inflation	+14	+35
Taxation	+10	
Strikes	+17	
NHS	−28	
Europe	+27	−13
		−9
Transport	−20	−16
Pensions	−16	+41
Unemployment	−22	
Defence	+35	−6
		+22
Education	−12	
Law & Order	+16	
		−25
Homelessness	−28	
Women	−8	−9
Environment	+5	+5

March 17/18   April 7/8   Now

Source: Daily Telegraph, 13 April 1992.

monitoring revealed many of these switches to the Conservatives were made in the last week or even last hours of the campaign. It was to a great extent this high level of volatility which gave the Conservatives their unexpected success.

An Econometric Explanation of Voting Preference

Relatively minor events, such as a public sector strike or movements in inflation and interest rates, will have an undue influence on a volatile electorate. In the language of journalists, such events will cause the electorate to either 'feel good' or 'feel bad'. It was widely accepted that the 'feel good factor' contributed towards the Conservative victory in 1987 when the 'economic miracle' of falling inflation, falling unemployment, falling interest rates and a consumer boom formed the backcloth to the election.

A recent study has shown that the two most important economic measures which influenced the electorate's sense of well-being were movements in the interest and inflation rates. Surprisingly, perhaps, movements in the rate of unemployment and economic growth seemed to have little effect on the popularity of the government. David Sanders analysed the relationship between public support for the government and changes in the key 'feel good' economic factors. He found that there was a time lag of three to four months between voters experiencing improved economic conditions and a decision to change the party they were supporting. Using past patterns of the 'feel good' factor and government support as well as economic forecasts, Sanders predicted in August 1991 an outcome which was very close to the actual result in April 1992 (see Figure 14.6). His econometric model also forecast the correct level of Liberal Democrat support but underestimated how this would be translated into Commons seats. The question that Sanders' model does not answer is why, for example, inflation and interest rates influenced voting but the level of unemployment did not. For in many ways the 1992 General Election could not have been

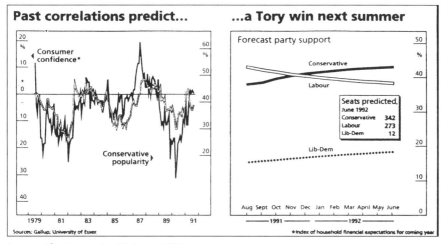

Source: *The Economist*, 17 August 1991.

Figure 14.6   *Voting behaviour and the state of the economy*

waged under worse economic conditions for the Conservatives, with the economy in the middle of a deep recession and record business failures creating a rapid rise in unemployment towards the 3 million mark. Although inflation and interest rates were falling, why did not the electorate punish the Conservatives for rising unemployment?

A possible explanation has been provided by the American liberal, J.K. Galbraith, who has argued that the Conservatives have been supported by 'a constituency of contentment'. These are people who may in the past have benefited from the welfare state but who are now well off and relatively secure. They form the majority of those amongst the electorate who vote. What is now in their interests are lower taxes and less government activity. Those people not in the constituency of contentment – the poor, the unemployed, the severely disadvantaged who make up the underclass – would benefit from a larger welfare state financed by higher taxation. They are, however, frequently found amongst the quarter of the electorate who do not bother to vote (Galbraith, 1992).

Multi-party politics: tactical voting and by-elections

It is difficult to argue whether the increase in voting for third parties is a cause or effect of the traditional links between the electorate and the two main parties becoming weaker. Nationalist parties – Plaid Cymru and the Scottish Nationalist Party – have enjoyed periodic surges of support as did the Liberals in the 1970s and the Liberal/Social Democratic Party Alliance in the 1980s. The Alliance parties 'bridged' the left-right divide that separated the two main parties whilst others such as the Nationalists and the Green Party fell outside the traditional left-right spectrum. This proliferation of parties together with declining levels of party attachment has resulted in increased electoral volatility. The increased presence of credible third parties makes it psychologically easier for voters to switch from one party to another, to support one party in local elections and another in general elections, or to vote tactically in order to keep out their 'most disliked' party.

A study of tactical voting found that it occurred principally under three circumstances: *(i)* where voters are strongly committed to unseating the MP, who is more likely to be a member of the government party than opposition party; *(ii)* where the chances of success in doing this are high, which is likely to be the case in the most marginal constituencies; and *(iii)* where the advantage of voting for one opposition party over voting for others is clear. It was found that 'about 4% of the British electorate voted tactically in 1983, as did nearly 6% in 1987' (R.J. Johnston and C.J. Pattie, 1990, pp. 95–108).

The growing volatility of the British electorate, caused in part by increased tactical voting, began in the by-elections of the late 1950s. The Liberals enjoyed huge surges of support, particularly, as it turned out, when Conservatives were in government. Incidentally, the share of the popular vote won by the Liberals also increased during the 1970s and 1980s reaching a peak of 26% in partnership with the SDP in the 1983 General Election. But it was frequently the case that by-election seats won by Liberals were lost in the following general election. In October 1990, for example, one of the events which led to Margaret Thatcher's resignation in November was the Conservative defeat in the Eastbourne by-election. It was a spectacular victory for the Liberal Democrats in what was seen as a safe seat in the Tory heartland. The Conservatives, however, regained the seat in the 1992 General Election.

By-elections receive considerable national attention, but psephologists have pointed out that by-elections are not necessarily a good guide to the forthcoming general election. Often the level of turnout varies from by-election to general election and in most by-elections voters know that their votes will not result in a change of government. Voters are not only volatile in switching support from one party to another but also fluctuate in terms of voting and abstaining.

■ Measuring Public Opinion

Many politicians believe that they can measure public opinion informally by reading newspapers, talking to party workers or listening to the views of their constituents. There are also more 'scientific' methods that are used by party managers who measure the response of the public to numerous aspects of their party's image. In terms of measuring the level of public support a party has, local election (and local by-election) results can provide a guide. Margaret Thatcher was said to have paid great attention to local election results when making her mind up as to when the next general election should be called. In crude terms, the number of council seats each party has won and lost and the number of councils where control has changed hands can provide a guide. More accurate use of local election results involves calculation of the *equivalent popular vote*, which enables the local results to be translated into 'general election' results.

Opinion polls provide greater flexibility in measuring public attitudes since they can be conducted any time. Newspapers and TV sponsor pollsters such as Mori, Gallup, NOP, ICM and Harris to carry out research. The most frequently published findings report on the general level of support for each of the main parties based on answers from a representative sample of around a thousand people. The sample, balanced in terms of social class, sex, age and region to represent the electorate as a whole, is asked which party it would vote for it there was an election.

In some countries, opinion polls have been banned in the last days of the election campaign on the grounds that they interfere with the way people vote. The effects of polls can vary according to particular circumstances, but a 'bandwagon effect' can result from more and more people supporting a party because they want to see its support increase still further. Or if one party has a large lead in the polls there can be a 'boomerang effect' on election day as over-confident voters stay at home because the polls have convinced them their party is going to win.

Predicting how the whole electorate will vote from the responses of a small sample of electors is bound to include a margin of error. This is usually estimated at 3% plus or minus the published finding. Occasionally a 'rogue' poll may be published which is based on faulty fieldwork and it will be far out of line with the results from other polls. In any election the most accurate poll is likely to be an 'exit' poll on election day which asks voters which way they *actually* voted rather than which way they *intend* to vote.

During the 1992 General Election campaign pollsters consistently predicted that the outcome would be a hung parliament, with most predicting that Labour would be the largest party. The fact that the Conservatives won with a respectable majority was the cause of considerable embarrassment for the polling organisations. Inquests into 'why did the pollsters get it wrong?' revealed a number of possible problems in both the fieldwork stage of collecting people's opinions and later in interpreting the results. It became clear that interviewing people in the street tended to exaggerate Labour support because it over represented those without jobs as well as poll tax protestors who had left the electoral register. Also it seemed as if there was a last minute swing to the Conservatives on the tax issue, but this occurred too late in the campaign for the pollsters to identify. To those who switched because of the tax issue can be added other individuals who were still undecided even as the campaign drew to a close. ICM, for example, had to exclude from its calculations 4% who remained undecided on which party to support but were certain that they would vote, and another 5% who were unwilling to say which party they intended voting for. A disproportionately high number of these 'secret voters' appeared to be Conservative supporters unwilling to admit their preference for tax cuts over improved public services. Some even wondered if those people who refused outright advances from pollsters in the streets were overwhelmingly Conservative. The final problem encountered by pollsters is in the interpretation of public support into parliamentary seats. Table 14.9 shows that the exit polls were fairly accurate.

But despite their accuracy, both put inaccurate interpretations on what these results would mean in terms of parties winning seats, and like other polls they predicted a hung parliament. Interpreting polls results is becoming increasingly difficult because a national swing may not have

	Harris Exit ITN	NOP Exit BBC	Result
Conservative	41	42	42.8
Labour	37	36	35.2
Liberal Democrat	18	18	18.3

Table 14.9   *Exit polls and 1992 General Election result (%)*

much meaning in individual constituencies. In the past swing was uniform: 'To know the swing in Cornwall was to know, within a percentage point or two, the swing in the highlands; to know the results of the first three constituencies to declare on election night was to know not only which party had won – but by how many seats'. (Crewe, 1985, pp. 101–3). But this is no longer the case. In 1992 neighbouring constituencies produced very different swings as well as the regional variations shown in Figure 14.3. Even when allowances are made for the differing social composition of individual constituencies, demographic changes and changes in the local economy can soon render polling information out of date.

■ The Electoral System Effect

Britain's first-past-the-post, or plurality, electoral system is not neutral in converting the share of votes received by a party into the share of seats won. It causes a distortion in the relation between the share of votes and the share of seats and, in many ways, can be thought of as a system of 'disproportional representation'. It has been argued that 'Electoral systems are not mere details but key causal factors in determining outcomes... Almost certainly, for example, if the British general election of 1979, 1983 and 1987 [and 1992] had been held under the West German type of party list electoral system, the votes cast would have resulted in minority government or the need for coalition government'. (Reeve and Ware, 1992) Britain's electoral system rewards parties which can concentrate their political support in specific areas and punishes parties, such as the Liberal Democrats, which have their support more evenly spread. This effect can be seen in the 1992 General Election where for each 42 356 votes cast for it, the Conservative party won an MP, and for every 42 875 votes cast for it, Labour won an MP. But it took the Liberal Democrats a massive 304,183 votes for every MP elected.

The Liberal Democrats, and more recently the Labour Party, have shown considerable interest in electoral reform. Many have come to believe that Britain's current system over-represents the Conservatives in Parliament, which in turn leads to an over-representation of the home counties and the South in the Cabinet. In terms of parliamentary representation, this has resulted in Labour becoming a party of permanent opposition based on the North and Scotland. A Labour working party set out criteria for evaluating different voting systems:

- It was agreed that proportionality, or the fairness between parties in terms of the share of votes won was an important criterion, but there were others.
- There should be fair representation for women, ethnic minorities and the regions.
- Any new electoral system should be easily understood so that effective voter participation is encouraged.
- The power to make and unmake governments should be in the hands of the people in the actual election, and not in the hands of parties making deals and building coalitions after an election.

- Election results should produce effective government.
- Finally, any proposal for electoral reform should be supported by a majority of MPs.

After the 1992 General Election the Conservatives were returned to govern with a reduced majority of 21. It has been calculated that this majority could have slipped away if just 3 899 voters in critical constituencies had voted differently. Under Britain's first-past-the-post system the winner takes all, and that now includes 17 seats where Conservatives were returned by majorities of less than a thousand over second-place Labour. What would have been the likely outcome of this pattern of support had another electoral system been in place?

It is, of course, a hypothetical question and it cannot be assumed that voters would act the same way under a different system. Nevertheless political commentators have made calculations about voting preferences, based on opinion poll data and found that under any of the major alternative systems a hung parliament would have been the outcome. With these reservations in mind, David Utting and Peter Wilby found that the Alternative Vote system still under-represented the Liberal Democrats, whereas STV would bring them large gains in the Commons. On the assumption that the Additional Member System would be based on the current 651 constituencies plus 100 additional members, the Liberal Democrats were seen as likely to gain 69 of the extra MPs, raising the possibility of government by 'Lib-Lab' pact (Table 14.10).

Table 14.10   *The 1992 General Election: actual and alternative outcomes*

	Percentage of total votes	First-past-the post		Alternative vote		Single transferable vote		Additional member system	
		Seats	(%)	Seats	(%)	Seats	(%)	Seats	(%)
Conservative	42	336	(51.6)	323	(49.6)	275	(42.2)	346	(45.9)
Labour	35.4	271	(41.6)	261	(40.1)	237	(36.4)	283	(37.7)
Liberal Democrats	17.9	20	(3.1)	39	(6.0)	102	(15.7)	89	(11.9)
SNP	2.1	3	(0.5)	6	(0.9)	17	(2.6)	10	(1.3)
Plaid Cymru	0.4	4	(0.6)	5	(0.8)	3	(0.5)	4	(0.5)
Ulster Parties	2.2	17	(2.6)	17	(2.6)	17	(2.6)	19	(2.5)

Source: The *Independent*, 12 April 1992.

Exhibit 14.1 *Electoral Systems*

- **First past the post**

  The current voting system is simple: voters mark one candidate with a cross, and the candidate with most votes wins in each constituency. However, MPs may be elected after gaining a minority of votes in their constituencies. The majority of votes which went to the other unsuccessful candidates are 'wasted'. Where an MP has a massive majority there will also be wasted votes, since all those above the minimum needed to win are 'wasted'. It has been calculated that around 70% of all votes in Britain are 'wasted' in one of these ways. FPTP has resulted in the election of only 5 black and 59 women MPs to the current parliament; in terms of strict proportionality the respective figures should be 32 and 328. Although there is an effective choice between alternative 'governments', the result can be hung parliaments and hung councils. Elections are decided by what happens in marginal constituencies, risking disillusionment of voters in safe seats who know that their votes will make no difference.

- **STV**

  The single transferable vote involves up to 5 MPs being elected in a constituency, with electors using their vote to mark the candidates in order of preference. In a 5 member constituency, each party would need around 20% of the vote to win a seat, 40% to win 2 seats, and so on. The formula for calculating the exact quota is

$$\left[\frac{\text{total number of votes}}{(\text{total number of seats} + 1)} \right] + 1 \; .$$

  In this case STV would exclude smaller parties with less than 20% support. But it is more proportional between parties which win support above this level. However at the national level STV cannot guarantee a proportional result. It has the advantage of offering voters the choice between candidates from the same party. This means candidates try to appeal to other parties' voters to win fourth and fifth preferences which they might need to beat their party colleagues. STV retains the link between MP and constituency. It is the system favoured by the Liberal Democrats. It is often described as a 'PR' system, but strictly speaking it is not although it offers greater proportionality than first-past-the-post. STV is used in many Northern Ireland elections.

- **List system**

  This system is based on the principle of pure proportionality with a party's proportion of seats the same as its proportion of voters. Britain would be treated as one constituency with the electorate voting for lists of candidates submitted by the parties. If the Liberal Democrat list won 25% of the votes, 25% of its candidates would be elected. Since the whole country is a single constituency, there is no link between MP and local constituency. However, it is relatively easy for women and ethnic minority MPs to get elected through the national list. A disadvantage is that it can lead to many small parties in parliament, making it difficult for the large parties to win an overall majority and provide effective government.

- **Alternative vote**

  This system involves voters ranking the candidates in order of preference, '1, 2, 3'. If a candidate gets 50% of first preferences, then he/she is elected. But if no candidate reaches this level, the bottom candidates are eliminated and their second preferences redistributed until one candidate reaches the 50% mark. The alternative vote ensures that an MP has the support of at least half of his constituency even if some of the support comes in second or even third preferences. Although not much more proportional than first-past-the-post, votes for minority candidates are not necessarily wasted because the second or third preferences may help elect the winner. Links between MP and local constituency are maintained. *cont. p. 276*

Exhibit 14.1—*Continued*

- **AMS**

  The additional member system is a combination of two other systems in order to get the advantages of local constituency links together with greater proportionality. Each voter has two votes – one for a constituency MP and the other for a party list. The constituency MP would be voted in under the alternative vote or first-past-the-post system, with the other MPs getting elected from a regional or national list. The list seats are allocated so as to help compensate for the disproportionality of the constituency vote. For example, the low number of Liberal Democrats directly elected to the Commons would be 'topped up' to some extent by the number who won on the party list. The creation of two classes of MPs is one of its disadvantages. The constituency link is maintained although new, larger constituencies would be required.

Summary

During the postwar years, there has been a declining attachment of voters to parties, and a subsequent increase in the volatility of voting behaviour. There has been a decline in the class basis of voting, but the extent to which that decline has taken place is not agreed upon by political scientists.

Models of class socialisation, sectoral cleavage and issue-based consumerism add to our understanding of voting behaviour although each explanation has weaknesses which limit its explanatory power.

The reputation of the opinion polls was damaged by their poor performance in the 1992 General Election, with questions raised about their validity which may reflect badly on the social scientific study of voting behaviour generally.

The geography of voting suggests that a simple split between the north and south of Britain is modified by an east-west split. However, the basic situation of Labour being strong in the north, the Conservatives strong in the south with Liberal Democrats under-represented generally has revived interest in electoral reform. It is almost certain that any of the principal alternative systems would produce a different parliamentary outcome from that of Britain's current system.

Questions

1. Evaluate the usefulness of the primacy and recency approaches in explaining voting behaviour.

2. Describe and account for the changing relationship between class and voting.

3. How accurately does it describe the dilemma of third parties in Britain to say that they need proportional government to enter government, but need to be in government to get proportional representation? Assess the likely impact of any two alternative electoral systems on third party voting.

4. Study Table 14.11 and then answer the question which follows:

Table 14.11   *Labour: Weakening Partisan attachment*

	% of voters with Labour identification	% of voters with 'very strong' Labour identification
1966	50	24
1970	47	21
1974	45	16
1979	42	11
1983	37	11
1987	36	13
1992	37	11

'The fact that in 1992 only 37% of voters think of themselves as Labour supporters but on Thursday [election day] only 35% actually voted Labour indicates that the party was scarcely able to poll its 'core' strength' (Anthony King).

Describe the pattern of Labour party identification from 1966 to 1992. What factors may account for this? Explain why these statistics have led to an interest in electoral reform inside the Labour Party.

5. To what extent can voting behaviour be explained by geographical factors? Describe the extent to which Scottish voting differs from the rest of Great Britain, and explain why this is the case (see Chapters 4, 5 and 13).

Assignments

The Referendum Debate

1. In contrast to the constitutional sovereignty with which citizens in the USA are familiar, constitutional purists in the UK often urge that even when a referendum is held there, it must be of a purely advisory character, so that the final judgement can be seen to be that of Parliament – thereby ensuring that the doctrine of Parliamentary sovereignty is not infringed. This was certainly the situation so far as the 1975 European Community Referendum was concerned. But the situation in the 1979 Referenda on Devolution was quite different. Here the term 'referendum' was being used in an American way. The legislation had already been passed by Parliament but it was not to take effect unless it was acceptable to a sufficiently high proportion of the electorate. Then, there is the interesting situation in Wales where once every seven years, on the issue of Sunday Opening, the UK gets nearest to the US practice of holding initiatives. Here too there is nothing 'advisory' about the referendum; the voters actually make the final decision. In any case, the reality is that no referendum – no matter how 'advisory' in theory – could be ignored by a Parliament if the result was decisive. Indeed the question needs to be asked whether we in Britain place an unrealistically heavy reliance on the sovereignty doctrine. The truth is that for years governments have been using their party majority to do in the name of Parliament anything and everything that was or was not in their party manifestoes. Accountability of ministers individually or governments collectively to Parliament is a largely theoretical proposition as long as the party's nerve holds and its majority is sustained.

Recent years have revealed many instances in UK general elections where a party has been elected with far less than majority support among the electorate (Mrs. Thatcher's massive Parliamentary majorities have been sustained by only slightly over 30% of the electorate) and it has been shown time and again that even those voting for the government rarely agree with **all** the policies in the party's manifesto. Thus it is certainly reasonable to argue that the concept of a mandate being given to government to carry out a **specific** set of policies is, at the very least, flawed – and it may, in future, be better to regard the mandate as constituting a general permission to govern rather than an obligation to enact specific proposals.

If such a view were to be accepted, it would then be open to Parliament to pass a Referendum Act which gave the UK voters the right to challenge Acts of Parliament which were felt to lack popular consent. Perhaps two million signatures would be required to put the offending legislation into question on the ballot paper. That number of signatures would be difficult to obtain and therefore such referenda would not be likely to occur very often.

Many of those who usually oppose the more regular use of referenda argue that 'Parliament knows best'. I'm not sure whether I believe that – but even if it is true, wouldn't it do a power of good if the government was forced to explain to us and win our consent before imposing unpalatable Poll Taxes or other unwelcome legislation upon us in circumstances where we have little effective power to resist? Far from being out-of-date, the experience in the US shows that the referendum can be a very useful instrument of government and, as long as we had some written constitutional guarantees to protect minorities from abuse, couldn't it be just as useful here?

Source: Anthony Batchelor, Talking Politics, 3:1, 1990.

(i)   What are the views of the author on the use of the referendum?
(ii) In what way did the referendum on the European Community differ from the referendum on Devolution?
(iii) In 1973 the Northern Ireland referendum attracted a turnout of 58.1% when the electorate was asked whether or not the Province should remain part of the UK. Minority groups organised a boycott campaign, which was reflected in only 6,463 voting NO whilst a massive 591 820 voted YES. In 1975 the entire UK electorate was asked whether Britain should remain a member of the EC on renegotiated terms – see page 109 for the results. In the Devolution referenda of 1979 it was decided that at least 40 per cent of the electorate had to support devolved government if it was to be imple-

mented. A turnout of 62.9% in Scotland voted 51.5% in favour, which represented 32.8% of the whole electorate – a figure well below the 40% threshold. In Wales turnout was 58.8%, with only 20.3% of the voters (representing 11.9% of the electorate) supporting devolution. What information did these results provide, if any, which was not available from general election voting patterns? Would opinion polls have provided information which was more, or less, reliable about the way the public thinks than the referenda results above?

2. Poll accuracy

(i)   Give reasons why exit polls appear more accurate than other polls (see Table 14.12).
(ii) Explain possible reasons for the pre-election opinion polls seeming to be inaccurate.
(iii) 'Even if the opinion polls are absolutely correct, it is not possible to predict the number of seats each party will win.' How justified is this view? Explain the difficulties involved in translating poll data into parliamentary seats.

3. Labour's PR Debate

Basically, the Plant Commission argued that voters should have two choices and be able to express a first and second preference if they wanted to. Any candidate who wins more than 50% of first

Table 14.12 *Poll accuracy in 1992*

| | \multicolumn{7}{c}{Final Polls (%)} | | | | | | |
	NOP	Gallup	MORI	ICM	Harris[*]	NOP[*]	Result
Con.	39	38.5	38	38	41	42	42
Lab.	42	38	39	38	37	36	35
LDem.	17	20	20	20	18	18	18

[*]Exit polls
The two exit polls were thus well within the range of error claimed for such polls. The other polls had fieldwork conducted between Monday and Wednesday before the election.

Source: Talking Politics, 5: 2, 1993.

preferences is elected automatically on the first count. But if none of the candidates reaches 50%, then second preferences are added to the votes of the top two candidates (other candidates having been eliminated). Whichever candidate ends up with the biggest total wins the seat.

This is one of the least radical alternatives to the present system. The Supplementary Vote system would retain existing constituencies, with each one electing one MP. The vital MP-constituency link would not be broken. The Supplementary Vote is simple and easily understood. It is not PR, yet it offers greater proportionality since any MP elected is almost certain to have the support of a majority of voters.

- Some Labour MPs opposed all proposals for electoral reform, and argued that there was no easy way for Labour to win power except by converting people over from voting Lib-Dem or Conservative. They argued that Labour is fooling itself into believing that there is an 'anti-Tory' majority amongst the electorate and that PR will unlock it. This is because the second choice of most Lib-Dems is the Conservative Party and not Labour.
- Other Labour MPs attacked Plant for being too cautious and not backing true PR. Austin Mitchell said 'the Supplementary Vote system would help the Liberals. As everyone's second choice and the universal soft option, they would win more seats in run-offs where Labour comes third ... With PR, our supporters everywhere could get a return on their vote and elect Labour MPs ...'

(i) Discuss the advantages and disadvantages of the Supplementary Vote system.
(ii) 'The main reason why Labour has edged towards electoral reform is not idealism but because it now believes that it will never win again under the present system.' How valid is this view?

Further reading

Connelly, James (1993) 'The Single Transferable Vote: Some Questions and Answers', *Talking Politics*, 5: 2, winter.

Denver, David (1989) *Elections and Voting Behaviour in Britain*, London, Philip Allan.

Denver, David (1992) 'The 1992 General Election: In Defence of Psephology', *Talking Politics*, 5: 1 autumn.

Mishler, William, Hoskin, Marilyn and Fitzgerald, Roy (1989) 'British parties in the Balance: A Time-Series Analysis of Long-Term Trends in Labour and Conservative Support', *British Journal of Political Science*, 19: 2, pp. 211–36.

Reeve, Andrew and Ware, Alan (1992) *Electoral Systems – A Comparative and Theoretical Introduction* (London: Routledge).

■ *Chapter 15* ■

Pressure Groups

What are Pressure Groups?	Pressure Group Targets
Leading Sectional and Cause Groups	Pressure Group Influence
History and Recent Trends	Pressure Groups and Democracy

An article in *The Economist* in its 30 May 1992 issue offered 'a cheeky comparison' between Greenpeace, the international environmental lobby, and the Labour Party. Not only, it suggested, did Greenpeace possess more supporters than the Labour Party had members, and a larger income, it influences Government thinking whereas Labour has 'next to no influence on government'. Of course, the comparison can be pushed too far, as the author realised: Greenpeace has no MPs or local councillors; nor does it seek to rule. But the basic point is valid: politics away from Westminster matter as much as politics at Westminster, and for an understanding of how the British political system works, pressure groups are virtually as significant as parties. This chapter focuses on the role of these important institutions. Starting with a definition of pressure groups, it explores some leading examples and examines their targets for influence and the factors upon which actual influence may depend before concluding with a brief examination of the debate on 'pressure groups and democracy'.

■ What are Pressure Groups?

Pressure groups, like parties, are informal political institutions which seek to influence the making and implementation of public policy. An important difference, however, is that whereas pressure groups may occasionally contest elections, they do not normally do so. Nor, when they do stand for election, do they do so with the aim of forming a government or part of a government (like the nation-wide parties) or even of changing the constitution (like the Nationalists) but for publicity, to make a political point, like the Anti-Maastricht, Anti-Federalist League in the 1993 Newbury by-election. Pressure groups may play an important role within political parties, they may overlap with parties by providing funds and sponsoring candidates, as the trade unions do in the Labour Party, but the distinction remains: pressure groups do not seek to hold office in their own right. Pressure groups also differ from parties in being 'partial' organisations which as a rule contribute only selectively to the political debate from a particular standpoint or within a specific field of concern; they do not adopt – nor are they expected to take – a comprehensive, 'total' view of politics of the kind adopted by parties.

Although not aiming to exercise power directly or adopting an all-embracing perspective, however, pressure groups do share some characteristics with parties. In particular, they are agencies of **representation** and **participation**: they are mechanisms for the expression of interest and opinion, and for popular involvement in politics. They may also – even though they are not elected to it – play a significant role *in* government, wielding influence through hundreds of regulatory and supervisory bodies which depend on their cooperation to function at all. Exhibit 15.1 sums up this preliminary discussion by offering a definition of 'pressure group'.

> **Exhibit 15.1** *Pressure group: a definition*
>
> A pressure group is any organisation which – normally working through lobbying rather than standing for office – seeks to influence public policy and decisions at local, national and European Union levels usually within a particular, quite limited sphere.

☐ *Types of Pressure Group*

There are two main types of pressure group: – *(i)* sectional (or interest) groups; and *(ii)* cause (or promotional) groups.

Sectional groups arise out of the performance of an economic function: they exist to further the interests of people as engaged in certain professions, trades and occupations – as, for example, teachers, shopkeepers, miners and company directors. Trade unions and business groups fall into this category.

In contrast, **cause groups** come into existence to promote some belief, attitude or principle. They are also referred to as attitude, ideological and preference groups. Examples are Amnesty International, Shelter and Charter 88. The main difference between the two types of group is in the nature of their membership. Whereas membership of a sectional group is largely involuntary – one 'belongs' merely by virtue of engaging in a particular occupation or being part of a distinct section of society – the main feature of cause groups is their voluntary nature, the fact that membership of them is a matter of individual choice.

Although containing a large amount of truth, even this distinction does not hold completely. Whilst a group such as OXFAM is a cause or preference group in terms of its membership, it also possesses property and hence has material interests to defend. More importantly, sectional groups can act on occasion as cause groups too. In the early 1990s, for instance, the British Medical Association acted both as a sectional professional body when campaigning against the Government's restructuring of the NHS *and* as a cause group when demanding an independent inquiry into the safety of boxing.

Large numbers of pressure groups are not 'purely' political. For example, the main purposes of the churches, the universities, trade unions, the motoring organisations and charities are respectively religious, educational, economic, motoring and charitable. All, however, make political representations from time to time on behalf of their interests and those of their members. Such institutions may be described as **secondary groups** in that their main purpose is not political lobbying. **Primary groups** are those whose sole reason for existence is political lobbying. Examples include many national cause groups such as Charter 88, specific issue groups such as Doctors for Tobacco Law (against TV tobacco advertising), 'one-off' national campaigns such as the Maastricht Referendum Campaign and the Campaign to Save Radio 4 Longwave, local amenity groups, and local 'nimby' (Not in my backyard) campaigns.

☐ *Pressure Politics*

The term 'pressure' can describe a type of *activity* as well as a kind of organisation. All institutions whatever their purpose are subject to attempts at influencing their policies by individuals and groups. Pressure groups themselves are not immune: examples are the division of opinion within trade unions on unions' links with the Labour Party, and divisions within the National Trust on the attempt by radicals to get the institution to ban stag-hunting on Trust land. All this activity may be accurately termed 'pressure politics', even if these intra-organisational groups are impermanent, fluctuating in membership and relatively transient. This chapter focuses on pressure groups as organisations, but pressure as a form of activity in all institutions is of great importance and recurs frequently throughout this book

■ History and Recent Trends

There is nothing new about pressure groups. They have existed for a very long time. In the nineteenth century, for example, pressure groups campaigned successfully against the slave trade and the Corn Laws and in favour of extending the franchise to the working class and women. Politics was also continually swayed by the great economic interests – landowning, commercial, manufacturing, professional, ecclesiastical. However, the twentieth century has seen a transformation of the role of groups in the political system. There have been three major phases: *(i)* 1920s–1960s; *(ii)* 1960s–1970s; *(iii)* 1980s to date.

1920s–1960s

In the first period two significant developments occurred. First, a large number of permanent, well-organised *sectional* groups emerged, making demands on government. Second, it became *recognised practice for governments to consult the groups before making decisions affecting their interests and also a widely-accepted norm that they should do so.* Much of this change occurred after 1945 as governments took on the task of management of the economy and of maintaining large welfare and defence establishments. The system of functional (i.e. sectional) representation developed against this background first as a result of the mutual needs of government and groups. Government needed to consult interest groups in order to be able to carry out its policies effectively, especially with regard to economic management; producer groups had to lobby government to ensure that their members' interests were taken into account when decisions affecting them were made.

Second, functional representation developed on such a scale alongside the more traditional system of parliamentary representation because it fitted

in with the ethos of each major party during this period. Both the Labour and the Conservative Parties had collectivist rather than individualist theories of representation: both regarded it as legitimate for important social and economic interests (e.g. business and the trade unions) to seek influence not only within the parties themselves but also directly at the level of government.

1960s–1970s

This phase saw both the high point of the close relationship (often called 'neo-corporatist' or 'liberal corporatist') between producer groups and government and also a very considerable expansion in the numbers and memberships of cause groups.

(a) The pinnacle of 'neo-corporatism': in theory 'neo-corporatism' entails the involvement of the main sectional groups in both the formulation and implementation of policy. Having helped to 'make' deals with government on such matters as prices and incomes policy, producer groups such as the Confederation of British Industry (CBI) and Trades Union Congress (TUC) were then required to 'sell' these deals to their members i.e. ensure their compliance. In practice, in this fully-fledged form, 'neo-corporatism' never existed in Britain, a main reason for this being the weakness of the representative business and union organisations and their inadequate control over their members. Nonetheless, a tripartite – Government-CBI-TUC – relationship undoubtedly existed, as indicated by:

- The frequent appearance of the main producer groups in top-level consultations at 'No. 10' e.g. to avert strikes or get them called off;
- The representation of the CBI and TUC on a key institution of economic cooperation such as the National Economic Development Council (NEDC);
- The making of arrangements with business or the unions which went beyond mere prior consultation such as the 1976 Budget which made income tax cuts dependent on the

success of pay talks with the TUC on Stage 2 of the Government's wage restraint policy.

The closeness of the Government–industry relationship was further shown by:

- **Sponsorship divisions** within Government Departments, especially the Department of Trade and Industry (DTI), whose role was to represent the interests of industries, sections of industries and products within government, and to explain government policy to industries.
- The particularly strong links between the National Farmers' Union (NFU) and the Ministry for Agriculture, Food and Fisheries (MAFF) after the 1947 Agriculture Act which both created a legal obligation for MAFF to consult with (effectively) the NFU as the main representative of producer interests and established an annual price review by which guaranteed prices were set by MAFF in consultation with the NFU.

(b) The expansion of cause groups: in this period, joining a cause group became for large numbers of people a more effective way of achieving a desired political end than joining a political party. As membership of the two major parties declined, membership of pressure groups (and of the smaller parties) increased. People were attracted to a wide range of causes: feminism, anti-nuclear protest, the relief of poverty and deprivation, international aid and rights, and environmentalism. Much of this upsurge of activity took place at local level. Some groups such as tenants' associations, neighbourhood councils and 'nimbies' have a naturally local context. But, in addition, some 'national' movements such as the Campaign for Nuclear Disarmament (CND) and women's liberation have a participant ethos and decentralised structure which encourages local membership.

Why did cause group activity increase so dramatically in this period? Explanations include the spread of affluence; increases in educational standards; the emergence of individualist and libertarian philosophies; the intensified build-up of nuclear arms; the failure to eliminate poverty; the development of a multi-cultural society; and the decline of class. None of these explanations is more than partial; together they shed some light. A relatively wealthy society in which the majority are well-off can afford to take non-materialist issues such as the environment seriously. A more diverse and better-educated society with an increasing percentage of the age-group in higher education is likely to be more sensitive to issues involving the rights of minorities. As superpower strategies moved towards the 'winnability' of a nuclear war, peace and disarmament movements spread. Because poverty had not been eliminated, pressure groups were formed to represent the deprived – children of poor families, the mentally and physically handicapped, the homeless, the old. Because society is still disfigured by racism, ethnic minorities have to organise for self-protection. Finally, the weakening of social class in structuring political attitudes and loyalties means that people are more open than before to the influence of other factors – such as gender, race, intellectual conviction, personal tastes and morality – as guides to political action.

1980s to the present

This recent phase has been marked by three main characteristics:

- the ending of 'tripartism'
- a continuing rise in the political profile of cause groups
- the growing importance of Parliament, public campaigns and Europe as foci of pressure group effort.

(a) The ending of 'tripartism': perceiving 'tripartite' or 'neo-corporatist' arrangements as a major cause of Britain's economic decline, the Conservative Government after 1979 broke away from this system. It moved to an 'arm's length' relationship with business and the unions in the making of policy, especially economic policy; downgraded and then abolished (1992) the National Economic Development Council; severely curtailed trade union powers by legislation, facing down strikes e.g. the 1984–5 Miners' Strike, and policies giving higher priority to curbing inflation than unemployment; and selectively sought advice

from groups where needed e.g. merchant banks (privatisation), management consultants (NHS reforms)

(b) The continuing rise of cause groups: not all groups prospered – both the poverty lobby (adversely affected in the 1980s by the climate of opinion fostered by Thatcherism) and the Campaign for Nuclear Disarmament (undermined by the ending of the Cold War) declined. But overall promotional group membership continued to expand, often dramatically as in the case of the environmental and animal welfare lobbies.

(c) Changes in the direction of pressure group activity: Parliament – notably the new Select Committees and the House of Lords – became a more important target for pressure groups; publicity campaigns relying upon skilful use of the media became more prominent; and groups directed an increasing proportion of their energies into influencing the institutions of the European Community.

Leading Sectional and Cause Groups

The leading sectional groups may be divided into groups representing capital and groups representing labour. Capital is far from a homogeneous, united interest but in fact internally divided into sectors – finance, manufacturing industry, and commerce and retailing, with each sector itself internally sub-divided further (Table 15.1).

☐ *Groups Representing Capital*

Finance

Down to the 1970s, representation of the interests of the financial sector – often referred to as 'The City of London' – took place largely through the Bank of England. Since then, however, this has changed with the Bank of England moving away from its former role of expressing the 'City view' to government and this function being taken by trade associations representative of the various parts of the financial

Table 15.1   *The main business groups: industrial, financial and commercial*

Industry	Finance	Commerce
Confederation of British Industry	The Bank of England	Retail Consortium
Federation of Small Businesses	Committee of London Clearing	Association of British
British Institute of Management	Banks	Chambers of Commerce
Institute of Directors	British Bankers' Association	National Chamber of Trade
Aims of Industry	Accepting Houses Committee	Motor Agents' Association
Economic League	(Merchant Banks)	Road Haulage Association
Engineering Employers Federation	Investment Protection	National Food and Drink
National Federation of Building	Committee (Pension Funds)	Federation
Trades Employers	City Liaison Committee	National Grocers' Federation
United Kingdom Textile	Institution Shareholders	National Federation of
Manufacturers	Committee	Wholesale Grocers and
National Association of	Council for the Securities	Provision Merchants
Master Bakers, Confectioners	Industry (Stock Exchange)	
and Caterers	The British Insurance	
British Footwear Manufacturers	Association (Joint Stock	
Federation	Insurance Companies)	
Society of Motor	Building Societies Association	
Manufacturers and Traders		
National Farmers Union		

sector. Thus, the **Committee of London Clearing Banks** (CLCB, 1971) and the **British Bankers' Association** (BBA, 1972) emerged in banking, and the **Council for the Securities Industry** (1977) for the Stock Exchange. Both the insurance and building society interests have their own separate associations. The City lacks a 'peak' organisation, probably because its interests are so various. But this lack of a 'peak'organisation still matters less than in other sectors because of the formidable informal power of financial interests as evidenced by Government's habitual nervousness of 'City reaction' to deviations in economic policies.

Industry

The interests of industry may be represented by large companies, employers' associations, trade associations, and 'peak' organisations.

Employers' organisations originally developed in order to handle negotiations with trade unions over conditions and wages but subsequently established links with Whitehall in order to influence industrial and economic policy. The **Engineering Employers' Federation** which represents 5000 manufacturing companies is one of the most powerful. A particularly strong trade association is the **Society of Motor Manufacturers and Traders** (SMMT), which in 1992 lobbied successfully for a reduction in car tax.

The **Confederation of British Industry** (CBI), formed in 1965 by a merger of three earlier employers' groups, is the 'peak' employers' organisation. Shut out from consultation by government during the Thatcher years, the CBI edged its way back into favour in the wake of Britain's departure from the Exchange Rate Mechanism, which left the Government more willing to listen to advice from industry. Despite winning occasional concessions, however, the CBI lacks political 'clout' in its dealings with government. The main reason for this is the difficulty the organisation has found in reconciling the interests of a diverse membership.

The CBI has also found it impossible to date to recruit the whole of industry. Many large companies stand aloof, preferring to lobby government directly or through their trade association.

At the same time, small firms resent the domination of the CBI by the large firms, and many small firms withdrew in 1971 to form their own association.

Retailing

The **Retail Consortium** (1967), which organises 90 per cent of Britain's retail trade, speaks for retailing interests. It gained importance in the 1970s as a consequence of its usefulness to governmental price restraint policy but along with other major sectional groups lost influence in the 1980s.

☐ *Professional Associations*

The influence of professional groupings as a lobby can derive from several factors, including self-regulation, their expertise (which makes their advice valued by governments) and their capacity to withdraw their consent – in the manner of a trade union – to Government policies. Their potential for influence is also shaped by the ideological climate. Self-regulation, which means the profession controls such matters as the content of training, standards, intake, and often remuneration, increases its standing by simply removing the need to bargain about these key issues. The legal profession, whose professional body is the Law Society, is a classic example. The British Medical Association (BMA) is another powerful pressure group, long-established, well-organised and, although unable itself to determine doctors' pay, able to bargain forcefully about it

Table 15.2 *The leading professional associations*

British Medical Association
The Law Society
Institute of Chartered Accountants
Royal Institute of British Architects
Royal Institution of Chartered Surveyors
Institution of Mechanical Engineers
Institution of Electrical Engineers
Royal Town Planning Association
British Dental Association
Association of University Teachers

with governments. Both organisations found themselves at loggerheads with the Conservative Government in the early 1990s, the Law Society over the proposed cuts in legal aid, the BMA over the restructuring of the National Health Service (NHS).

☐ Groups Representing Labour

The Trades Union Congress (TUC) is the 'peak' organisation of labour. In 1993, it represented 71 affiliated unions with a combined membership of 7.7m., a sharp reduction on the over 100 unions with a membership of over 11.5m. with which it had begun the previous decade. The 1980s in fact saw a drastic curtailment in its influence.

Like any large 'umbrella' organisation, the TUC is a difficult organisation to manage. Unions retain their powers of independent action when they affiliate to the TUC. Compared with the top unions, moreover, the TUC is not well resourced and, in the wake of the creation of the new 'super-unions', the disparity in staff and income has grown wider. Expulsion of an 'out of step' union is relatively rare. Finally, not only has the TUC a somewhat unwieldy General Council of 50 members, it is hampered by internal divisions.

For example, differences over policy occurred over backing for the National Union of Mineworkers (NUM) in the miners' strike and over the re-admittance of the expelled electricians' union in the early 1990s.

☐ Cause Groups

Cause groups were active over the whole range of policy in the 1980s and early 1990s. We focus on five prominent areas of their activity.

International Lobbyists

In this sphere, three leading causes are expressed by the Campaign for Nuclear Disarmament (CND), Amnesty International and the Aid Lobby.

With the ending of the Cold War, **CND** declined: by 1991 it had lost 40 000 members from its mid-1980s peak (100 000) and was forced to cut 30 headquarters staff. Faced with the need to reorientate its strategy, its new leader Marjorie Thompson (1990) believed that CND should focus on lobbying for the peace dividend and campaigning against the arms trade.

Amnesty International (1961) campaigns to free prisoners of conscience throughout the world; to get fair and prompt trials for political prisoners; and against torture and the death penalty. By 1991 – the thirtieth anniversary of its launch with an article in *The Observer* by the lawyer Peter Benenson – it had adopted or investigated over 42 000 cases worldwide and had a membership of 700 000.

The purpose of the **Aid Lobby** is to raise and distribute aid to the underdeveloped countries in general and, increasingly from the mid-1980s, to the famine-torn countries of Africa. Leading aid agencies include Oxfam, Save the Children, Christian Aid, the Catholic Fund for Overseas Development (Cafod), and Action Aid.

☐ Campaigners for the Environment

By the early 1990s, when it had over 5 million supporters, the environmental movement had doubled every decade since the 1960s. Table 15.3 shows the range of groups – from old-established institutions such as the National Trust and the Royal Society for the Protection of Birds (RSPB) to the newer campaigning groups such as Friends of the Earth (1971).

It is the strong campaigning groups, with their concerns about pollution, the destruction of the natural environment and the depletion of the planet's resources, which are most typical of the contemporary environmentalist movement. **Greenpeace UK** (1977), with a membership of 410 000 in 1991 spread through 210 local groups, developed a particularly high profile in the late 1980s through its campaigns on the dumping of toxic waste and the extermination of the whale by

Great Britain	1971	1991
	thousands	
Council for the Protection of Rural England	21	45
Friends of the Earth (England and Wales)	1	111
National Trust	278	2 152
Ramblers Association	22	87
Royal Society for Nature Conservation	64	250
Royal Society for the Protection of Birds	98	852
Woodland Trust		150
World Wide Fund for Nature	12	227

Source: Extracted from *Social Trends* (1993), p. 126.

Table 15.3 *The growth of environmental organisations, 1971–91*

Age Concern England
Child Poverty Action Group (CPAG)
National Council for One-Parent Families
Disablement Income Group (DIG)
National Association for Mental Health
Shelter
Low Pay Unit
National Society for the Prevention of Cruelty to Children (NSPCC)
Abortion Law Reform Association (ALRA)
Society for the Protection of the Unborn Child (SPUC)
Action on Smoking and Health (ASH)
Voluntary Euthanasia Society

Table 15.4 *The main welfare groups*

excessive hunting. The early 1990s saw the emergence of a new type of radical environmentalist group, **Earth First!**, reliant on direct action by cell members using its 'monkey-wrenching' (ecological sabotage) methods rather than hard research and well-publicised campaigns.

Much environmental protest takes place at the local level and draws upon local sentiment of the 'Nimby' (Not in my backyard) kind. Groups such as Friends of the Earth and the Royal Society for Nature Conservation have strong local organisations. In addition, there are Alarm UK (1991), a network of local anti-road groups, which grew out of successful opposition to London road plans of the late 1980s, and another network of local direct action campaigners made up of groups such as Reclaim the Streets and Friends of Twyford Down. In the early 1990s, environmental protest focused especially on Kent (the route of the Chunnel Link) and Twyford Down near Winchester, which was part of an Area of Outstanding Natural Beauty destroyed by the completion of the 'missing link' of the M3 motorway. Protest over the destruction of wildlife sites by new roads and over a large number of projected superstores on greenfield sites may be expected to intensify throughout the 1990s.

☐ *Welfare Groups*

Welfare groups, often referred to as the 'poverty lobby', have emerged since the 1950s to represent and mobilise the clientele of the welfare state: pensioners, parents with dependent children, one-parent families, the mentally and physically handicapped, the homeless and the poor. The welfare field also contains more traditional organisations such as the NSPCC and campaigning groups on such issues as abortion, smoking and voluntary euthanasia (Table 15.4). The poverty lobby proved resilient in the face of a less sympathetic ideological climate in the 1980s: for example, the Child Poverty Action Group doubled its membership in the six years to 1988.

☐ *Civil Liberties Campaigners*

Liberty, formerly the National Council for Civil Liberties (1934), is the main civil liberties group. The NCCL fell upon hard times in the 1980s, ignored by government and the police, and torn by bitter internal divisions between left and right over the Miners' Strike and between feminists over pornography; hence, the re-launch as Liberty in 1989. Lacking a clear-cut public image such as that of Greenpeace, Amnesty International or Shelter, it has also suffered to some extent from the emergence of single-issue campaigns within its field of concern e.g. the Campaign for Freedom of Information and Charter 88. Central to its work in the early 1990s is a campaign for a Bill of Rights.

□ *Animal Rights Groups*

During the 1970s and 1980s, direct action and extremist groups emerged alongside moderate traditional associations such as the **RSPCA** and the **League against Cruel Sports** (1926). Some older organisations like the **British Union for the Abolition of Vivisection** (1894) were radicalised for a time in the early 1980s by a new generation prepared to resort to illegal methods and the new militancy led to divisions between radicals and traditionalists within the RSPCA and, in the early 1990s, in the National Trust (over deer-hunting on Trust land). In the 1990s, the struggle between opponents and supporters of vivisection and animal experiments and between pro-and anti-field sports groups became more intense. After the narrow failure of a Private Member's Bill aimed at banning hunting in 1992, the struggle between saboteurs and huntsmen grew more violent, with fierce physical confrontations taking place at the scene of many hunts. Leading militant groups are the **Animal Liberation Front** and the **Hunt Saboteurs Association**.

■ Pressure Group Targets

At which points in the political system do pressure groups seek to exert influence? British pressure groups have four main target areas: the 'core executive' – Government ministers (including the prime minister) and civil servants (Whitehall); Parliament (both Houses); public opinion (mainly through the media); and increasingly during the 1980s and 1990s – the European Community/Union.

A relevant distinction is between 'insider' and 'outsider' groups. As Wyn Grant has suggested:

Insider groups are regarded as legitimate by government and are consulted on a regular basis. Outsider groups either do not wish to become enmeshed in a consultative relationship with officials, or are unable to gain recognition. (Grant, 1989, pp. 14–15).

The insider/outsider distinction can refer both to *status* – insiders acceptable to government, outsiders not so – and to *strategy* – whether or not a group actually seeks acceptance by Whitehall, or – through necessity or choice – runs public campaigns. Most insiders are sectional groups, but many cause groups do gain insider status e.g. MENCAP, the Howard League for Penal Reform. Moreover, classic insider groups such as the British Medical Association and National Farmers' Union do not shrink from campaigning publicly when occasion demands.

Research suggests indeed that many groups – sectional and promotional – pursue multiple strategies, seeking to exercise influence – as resources permit – at a variety of points in the system. Thus, Baggott's study of a cross-section of pressure groups at national level (both sectional and cause) found that insider groups had more frequent contacts with the political system *at all points* than had outsider groups. A second significant finding, however, was that a relatively large number of outsider groups were *in quite frequent contact with the executive to junior civil servant level* (Table 15.5).

Table 15.5 *Pressure groups and the political system*

| | % of groups in contact on a weekly/monthly basis | | | |
| | Weekly | | Monthly | |
	Outsider	Insider	Outsider	Insider
Prime Minister	–	2	10	14
Cabinet Ministers	5	12	37	45
Junior Ministers	10	14	38	67
Senior Civil Servants	12	25	45	49
Junior Civil Servants	12	55	62	76
House of Commons	20	39	51	72
House of Lords	8	23	36	63
Political Parties	13	27	34	51
Media	74	86	84	94

Source: Baggott (1992b, p. 20).

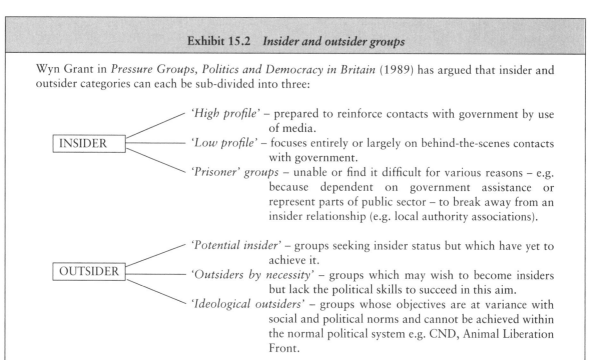

Exhibit 15.2   *Insider and outsider groups*

Wyn Grant in *Pressure Groups, Politics and Democracy in Britain* (1989) has argued that insider and outsider categories can each be sub-divided into three:

INSIDER
- *'High profile'* – prepared to reinforce contacts with government by use of media.
- *'Low profile'* – focuses entirely or largely on behind-the-scenes contacts with government.
- *'Prisoner' groups* – unable or find it difficult for various reasons – e.g. because dependent on government assistance or represent parts of public sector – to break away from an insider relationship (e.g. local authority associations).

OUTSIDER
- *'Potential insider'* – groups seeking insider status but which have yet to achieve it.
- *'Outsiders by necessity'* – groups which may wish to become insiders but lack the political skills to succeed in this aim.
- *'Ideological outsiders'* – groups whose objectives are at variance with social and political norms and cannot be achieved within the normal political system e.g. CND, Animal Liberation Front.

This finding fits in well with Grant's further sub-division of insider and outsider groups in which only two of the six sub-categories (insider 'prisoner' groups and 'ideological' outsiders) never cross the insider/outsider boundary line (Exhibit 15.2). In fact, the line is often crossed – first, because, as we have seen, groups adopt more than one *strategy*; second, because insider *status* can be lost or gained.

Pressure Groups and Government

A well-established system of formal and informal contacts links insider groups with government. Increasingly, formal contacts have become institutionalised through pressure group membership of a wide variety of government-established committees. These include advisory committees (over 1060 in 1985), executive committees (able to make regulations and dispense money; nearly 400 in 1985), tribunals (164 in 1985), Committees of Inquiry (over 1000 this century) and Royal Commissions (34 between 1944 and 1985). The great majority of contacts, however, are informal, and typically occur at quite a low level of government (see Table 15.5). Indeed, much business is done informally by telephone and face-to-face discussions between civil servants and representatives of the groups.

Two major features of the insider groups' relationship of regular consultation and negotiation with government Departments invite comment. First, the acceptability of a group to government – its recognition as an insider – depends upon its **credibility**. This rests upon such factors as

- **A group's representativeness** – its genuine capacity to speak for as large a number as possible of those it purports to represent.
- **The reasonableness of its demands and their compatibility with the aims of government** – realism, responsibility and negotiability are the watchwords.
- **The reliability and quality of its advice** – past 'track record' and the extent of government need can both be important.

- Its ability to 'talk the same language' as government – i.e. its familiarity with Whitehall procedures.
- Economic leverage and veto power – still can be a factor but diminished for some groups in 1980s e.g. CBI, Medical Associations.

Conversely, characteristics which make for a group's unacceptability to government (thereby ensuring that it remains an outsider) include

- Incompatibility – possessing aims incompatible with those of government e.g. the Marxist-inspired Radical Alternatives to Prison (RAP), which calls for the abolition of prison, and
- Contentiousness – the likelihood that a group will be opposed by other groups e.g. the Abortion Law Reform Association (ALRA) by the Society for the Protection of the Unborn Child (SPUC).

Second, there is the extent to which insider groups in their linkages with specific government Departments form policy communities. In other words, policy-making in British government is done in a series of semi-autonomous segmented areas – agriculture, education, transport, health and so on. In each area, policy emerges out of a continuous process of consultation between civil servants and group spokesmen, and this constitutes a 'policy community'. In transport, for example, the policy community is made up of the full-time officials of the Department of Transport together with representatives of such groups as the British Road Federation, the Society of Motor Manufacturers and Traders, the Freight Transport Association, Transport 2000 and the motoring organisations. As Wyn Grant comments, the real divisions in this system are between – rather than within – the different policy communities (1989, p. 30).

The relationship between groups and departments in policy communities has been called clientelism. This term describes a situation in which Ministers, permanent officials and groups share an interest in increasing the resources devoted to a given policy area. Departments and client groups inter-mesh. Groups can act or be used as allies of a Department in its battle for resources within Whitehall: for example, it helps civil servants when arguing with colleagues and ministers in other Departments to be able to point to outside pressure for a policy.

Often, civil servants will identify closely with group viewpoints: the Department of Transport, for example, has often been cited as being both pro-road and pro-lorry; the former Department of Energy tended to side with energy-producers against energy users. Sponsor departments (such as Transport, MAFF, the DHSS, Energy (before its abolition) and (down to 1988) the DTI) are expected to put the case within government for the interests they 'look after'.

In return for regular consultation by government, for being taken into the confidence of officials and ministers and being given the opportunity to state their case and conceivably gain concessions, groups are expected to conform to certain patterns of behaviour. They are expected at all times to be discreet about discussions in Whitehall and to refrain, even where they feel aggrieved, from 'going public' and, especially, from criticizing ministers. They may even be expected to sell the policy to their members. Occasionally, this cosy, symbiotic relationship will break down, and a group will attack its governmental 'patron': this happened in late 1992 when the Engineering Employers' Federation publicly called for 'a more effective and committed champion' (than Michael Heseltine) at the Department of Trade and Industry.

The benefits to government of this system of group representation include:

- up-to-date, often technical and highly specialised advice;
- 'market' information in the various sectors;
- compliance with their policies by the main interests in each specific field;
- assistance in the administration of schemes (where required).

In return, groups get

- a hearing for their case (at the least);

- the chance to influence policy (including legislation) and decisions in their formative, early stages;
- the possibility of gaining an executive role alongside government in the implementation of policy;
- funds from government: studies have shown that government is an important source of funds for large numbers of groups in the environmental and poverty lobbies.

Civil Servants/Government Departments	1
Ministers	2
The media	3
Parliament	4
Particular sections of public opinion	5
Public opinion generally	6
Other pressure groups	7
Political parties generally	8
One political party in particular	9

Source: Rush (ed.) (1990, p. 272).

Table 15.6   *Groups' ranking of influences upon public policy*

☐ Pressure Groups and ☐ Parliament

Survey evidence suggests the increased importance of parliament as a target for pressure group lobbying in the 1980s. In the Study of Parliament Group survey, 75 per cent of groups claimed to be in regular or frequent contact with MPs and 59 per cent of groups claimed regular or frequent dealings with peers (Rush (ed.) 1990, p. 14). In Baggott's smaller survey, 45 per cent of groups considered that their contact with the Commons – and 37 per cent that their contact with the Lords – had increased in the 1980s (Baggott, 1992b, p. 21).

The distancing of goverment from pressure groups by the Thatcher Administration; the large majorities enjoyed by Conservative Governments of the 1980s which focused attention on Conservative backbenchers and the House of Lords as the main obstacles to legislation; the discernible increase in backbench independence; the establishment of the new select committees which provided another channel of potential influence; the growth of specialist political influence; the growth of specialist political consultancy firms: all these factors facilitated the growing use of Parliament by groups. Groups remain realistic in their perceptions of where power lies in the political system, ranking Parliament below Government Departments, ministers and the media in influencing public policy (Table 15.6).

Nonetheless, Parliament is perceived as a policy-influencer, and because this is so, groups cannot ignore it. An important conclusion of the Study of Parliament Group survey is that 'contrary to what might be expected' more of the attention received by Parliament 'comes from insider than outsider, and more from sectional than promotional groups' (Rush (ed.), p. 277).

Contacts with Parliament are of value to groups in three main ways:

- To amend legislation or change policy in often slight but – for the affected interest or cause – significant ways;
- To sponsor legislation;
- To influence the climate of public opinion by gaining additional publicity and support for an issue first raised or raised concurrently outside Parliament.

Characteristic activities of groups concerned about legislation include – circularising MPs, asking an MP to arrange a meeting with the minister responsible for the bill, asking MPs to speak in a second reading debate, asking MPs to propose an amendment during the committee or report stages of a bill, and contacting a member or member of the House of Lords.

Because of its increased activity rate, greater impact on legislation and looser party discipline, the House of Lords became a more important focus for lobbying in the 1980s. Peers regularly put down Questions, speak in debates and table legislative amendments on behalf of groups. By prompting MPs or peers to act along such lines, groups can hope to persuade ministers to adopt a favourable amendment, back down on a controversial detail, clarify an ambiguous point, or gain a ministerial assurance on the interpretation of a particular clause.

The time allocated to private members' legislation (although small – under 5 per cent) gives groups an opportunity to promote change rather than simply react to it. In the 1960s, sympathetic MPs sponsored legislation liberalising the law on divorce, abortion and capital punishment. More recently, between 1979 and 1986, pressure groups promoted 25 bills – just under a quarter (23 per cent) of private members' bills introduced in this period (Rush (ed.), pp. 202–3). One such item of backbench legislation was the House Buyers Bill (1983–4): promoted by the Consumers' Association and sponsored by the Labour MP, Austin Mitchell, it aimed to remove the solicitors' monopoly over conveyancing, and eventually became government policy.

Finally, groups can use Parliament in a broader way – often in combination with other strategies – to publicise their cause and shape public policy in their interest over a longer time-span. Such mechanisms include working through party committees, all-party groups and select committees, prompting parliamentary questions and gaining the maximum number of signatures to an Early Day Motion. For example, the Wing Airport Resistance Association (formed to resist an inland site for the third London airport in 1970) used parliamentary contacts skilfully – first, through the good offices of sympathetic local MPs to set up an all-party committee of backbenchers and then to launch an Early Day Motion with an eventual 219 signatures. In 1988, organised interests provided secretarial assistance for 25 of the 103 all-party subject groups, e.g. the RSPCA services the Animal Welfare Parliamentary Group.

The various ways in which outside interests can be financially linked with MPs have been explored already in Chapter 12. It is sufficient merely to underline here the growth of professional lobbying companies in the 1980s. By 1990, such political consultancy firms had an estimated annual turnover of over £10m. A campaign organised by the consultants, Political Communications, on behalf of Lincolnshire County Council was successful in persuading the Government not to dump nuclear waste in Lincolnshire in 1986.

The benefits derived by groups from their contacts with parliament range over a spectrum from the very considerable to the quite modest to the minimal and negligible. At the former end was the successful campaign waged against the Shops Bill (1986) by the shopworkers' union, the churches and various voluntary organisations. In the middle of the range are the amendments to legislation which groups quite frequently obtain, such as the amendment secured by a lobby of the leading football clubs to the Public Order Bill (1986) which allowed alcohol to be served in the executive boxes at football grounds. Many groups, however, derive much less from their lobbying activities. When questioned by the Study of Parliament Group, just under 39 per cent of groups saw themselves as 'not very successful' at influencing legislation, and just under 6 per cent as 'unsuccessful'. By contrast, over 55 per cent claimed to be 'very' (7.2 per cent) or 'quite' (48.3 per cent) successful. In return, the input by groups to the legislative process gives MPs, especially opposition MPs, a 'critical capacity' they would otherwise lack and, in addition, it increases the legitimacy of measures by securing wider consent to them than would otherwise be achieved (Norton, 1990b, pp. 193, 196–7).

☐ *Public Campaigns*

Basically, pressure groups run two types of public campaign. These are **long-term educational and propaganda campaigns** designed to produce significant shifts in public opinion and **short-term 'fire brigade' campaigns** warning about – and seeking to avert – a specific threat. It used to be thought that only outsider groups employed public campaigning strategy – and it is true that such a strategy remains their leading resort. Increasingly, however, insiders – and sectional groups – have come to employ public campaigns in combination with parliamentary and Whitehall strategies.

Classic long-term educational and propaganda campaigns have been waged in recent decades by the Campaign for Nuclear Disarmament, Shelter and the Child Poverty Action Group. Wide publicity through the mass media can be used to get – and keep – an issue on the political agenda, to accelerate action where government is uninterested or complacent, to delay or prevent undesired change, and to achieve recognition and even inclusion on government's list of groups to be consulted. Typical fire-brigade campaigns in recent years have been waged by environmental groups protesting against road links through Twyford Down and Oxleas Wood and by the NUM against pit closures. There have also been a large number of local campaigns against e.g. hospital and school closures and to oppose the construction of greenfield superstores (this campaign coordinated by the National Sensitive Site Alliance).

Finally, much more a popular resistance movement than either of these two types, was the highly successful left-organised All-Britain Anti-Poll Tax Federation whose mass campaign of non-payment in the early 1990s destroyed the 'poll tax' (Barr, 1992).

☐ *Pressure Groups and Europe*

Three-fifths of the groups surveyed by Baggott reported an increase in contacts with Europe, (Baggott, 1992b, p. 21). Business and farming interests, the trade unions (increasingly), professional associations such as the Law Society and the BMA, and environmental groups such as Friends of the Earth and Greenpeace all lobby at European Union (EU) level. Although only a small minority have European offices, three-quarters of groups in Baggott's survey were members of a European-wide pressure group e.g. UNICE (Union of Industries in the European Community), ETUC (European Trade Union Confederation) and COPA (Committee of Professional Agricultural Organisations of the EC).

British pressure groups can seek to influence EU decisions in three main ways – by looking to the British Government to win concessions for them at the Council of Ministers; working through Euro-groups e.g. UNICE, which can pressurise other EU governments or influence counterparts in other EU countries; and lobbying the EU Community institutions directly by establishing offices in Brussels (Watts, 1993, pp. 115–20).

■ Pressure Group Influence

Figure 15.1 sums up in diagrammatic form the stages at which groups may seek to influence policy and legislation. Summarised schematically these are:

- **Agenda-setting:** getting an item on to the political agenda;
- **Policy-Formation:** helping to shape policy/ legislation at the consultation and (for Acts of Parliament) drafting stages;
- **Passage through Parliament (Commons and Lords) including Statutory Instruments;**
- **Implementation:** groups help identify flaws in the policy/legislation and suggest remedies.

Whether and how far pressure groups succeed in influencing political decision-making depends upon several factors including their resources, strategies and social and economic leverage.

Resources

Resources include finances, organisation, staffing, membership, expertise and leadership. It is commonly believed that sectional groups possess an advantage over cause groups in terms of financial backing, possession of coherent national organisations, staffing, and size of membership. Often this is so, but not invariably. Well-resourced campaigns by major sectional groups have been known to fail: the very considerable resources of the mineworkers' union(NUM) were insufficient to stave off defeat in 1984–5, undermined as they were by poor leadership and inadequate strategy, and the very expensive anti-nationalisation campaigns run by business between 1945 and 1979 were failures. By contrast, the much more modest sums available to cause or protest groups if backed by expertise can enable them to prevail: the Wing Airport Resistance Association, for example, deployed its relatively small amounts of money skilfully to put its case against Cublington as the site for London's third airport (1968–71) first before the Roskill Commission and then to backbench MPs. Again, some environmental

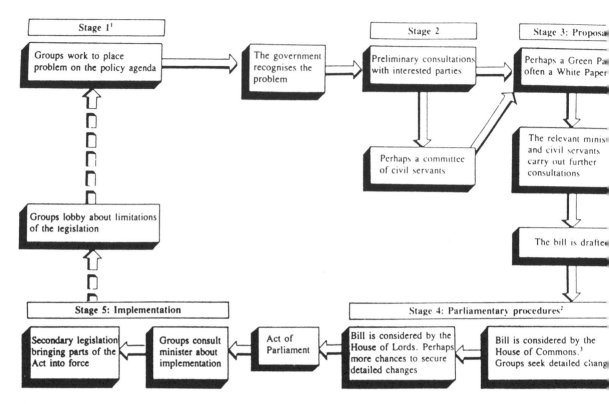

¹Not all the stages will necessarily occur in any particular policy initiative.
²Many policy changes do not require new legislation; they may, for example, depend upon
ministerial action.
³Bills may of course be introduced in the House of Lords.

Source: Grant (1989, p. 49).

Figure 15.1 *Pressure group influence: the main stages*

groups are now as well-resourced as the larger
sectional groups. But lack of resources undoubtedly handicapped the anti-nuclear lobby in
its protest against the extensive nuclear energy
programme of the Conservative Government,
which had the backing of the major forces in the
energy industry, including the Central Electricity
Generating Board, the Atomic Energy Authority,
large national firms such as the General Electric
Company (GEC) and big multinationals like
Westinghouse and Rio Tinto Zinc.

Resources – whether slender or considerable –
need to be expertly deployed if a group is to
achieve its aims. Thus, in order to stand the
maximum chance of influencing legislation at the
standing committee stage, group briefings of MPs
need to be succinct, clear, personalised and,

above all, timely: in practice, however, much
briefing material is the opposite, being over-long,
generalised (to all MPs rather than the specific
ones involved on the Committee) and too late to
affect proceedings. Consumer, local government
groups and certain trade unions apparently
possess the parliamentary 'know-how' to be
effective. By contrast, many – often wealthy –
groups lack such expertise: for example, many
City institutions demonstrated ignorance of such
procedure over the Financial Services Bill (1986)
(Norton, 1990b, pp. 194–6). A major reason for
the effectiveness of the pro-abortion lobby in first
liberalising the abortion law and then resisting
the campaign by anti-abortion groups such as the
Society for the Protection of the Unborn Child
(SPUC) and **LIFE** between 1967 and 1975 was its

ability at decisive moments to call upon knowledge of parliamentary procedure. Pro-abortionists attribute the failure of the pro-life lobby to reduce the abortion limit in 1990 to the counter-productive tactics adopted by SPUC, which sent a plastic foetus to every MP.

With regard to a pressure group's membership, size, density, solidarity, and quality have be considered. Sometimes, as in the case of demonstrations, absolute numbers can be important, to show that a cause is as well-supported as its proponents – or as poorly-supported as its opponents – respectively claim. Just as often, it is important to a group to show that it represents a high proportion of potential members. Thus, trade associations are strengthened by being able to claim – as they often can – that they represent over 90 per cent of an industry whereas the CBI's authority is undermined by its inability to speak for the whole of industry and trade unionism is weakened by the fact that well under half the workforce are members of trade unions. The solidarity of its membership can reinforce a group's case, especially if it can be demonstrated by ballot or opinion poll. Failure by the NUM to hold a strike ballot in 1984 enabled the government to speculate about divisions within the union. Similarly cause groups such as the anti-hunting and disablement lobbies have suffered from internal rivalries and differences over tactics. Finally, quality of membership matters, especially for small cause groups such as the Abortion Law Reform Association which relies on the dedication, knowledge and enthusiasm of a small membership.

Leadership can offset the difference in size and financial support between large sectional and often relatively small promotional groups. Thus, the CBI and TUC have often struggled to find effective national spokesmen whereas cause groups such as Shelter and the Child Poverty Action Group (CPAG) have benefited from being led by skilful lobbyists like Des Wilson and Frank Field.

Strategy

Adoption of an appropriate strategy can be a vital ingredient in pressure group success. The way in which a group allocates its efforts between government departments, parliament, and public (including media) campaigns depends upon the nature of the group, its cause and the congruence of its goals (or lack of congruence) with public opinion. The degree of choice is often more limited than this suggests: thus, trade associations have generally little option but to adopt an 'insider' strategy whereas 'ideological' groups like CND or oppositional movements like the Anti-Poll Tax Federation are forced necessarily into 'outsider' strategies. Within the field of law reform, a respectable group such as the Howard League for Penal Reform, which directs its efforts for liberal reforms within an acceptance of the legitimacy of the criminal law, has achieved 'insider' status with the Home Office to which the left-inspired Radical Alternatives to Prison (RAP) and Preservation of the Rights of Prisoners (PROP), the prisoners' pressure group, can never aspire. Some sectional groups pursue 'insider' and 'outsider' strategies simultaneously: thus, the TUC continued its institutionalised relationship with Whitehall while running effective national campaigns, involving parliamentary, legal and mass action, against industrial relations legislation in the late 1960s and early 1970s. Congruence with public opinion also affects a group's choice of strategy: workers enjoying widespread public sympathy such as firemen and nurses were still able to run public campaigns over pay in the 1980s but other industrial groups and the TUC generally had to take into account the likelihood of lukewarm, indifferent or even hostile public reactions when considering public campaigns.

Social and Economic Leverage

Economic leverage with government is a function of a group's general importance in the national economy and, more specifically, its capacity to disrupt government plans by resistance and/or non-compliance. With regard to sanctions and veto power, sectional groups are generally considered more powerful than promotional groups because they possess stronger weapons. This remains generally true but needs to be treated with caution. The power of sectional interests can

Table 15.7 *Pressure groups and democracy: for and against*

For	Against
• **Participation and political access** PGs increase participation and access to political system, thereby enhancing the quality of democracy. They enable the *intensity* of feeling on issues to be considered, opinions to be weighed as well as counted.	• **Sectionalism and selfishness** PGs improve participation, but *unequally*, benefiting the well-organised but disadvantaging the weakly organised. They benefit 'those who shout loudest' against the rest.
• **Improvement of government** Consultation with affected groups is the rational way to make decisions in a free society: the information and advice provided by groups helps to improve the quality of government policy and legislation.	• **Anti-parliamentary democracy** Secret, behind-the-scenes consultations between government and groups enables covert 'deals' to be made thereby detracting both from open government and the legitimate influence of elected legislators in Parliament.
• **Social progress** PGs enable new concerns and issues to reach the political agenda, thereby facilitating social progress and preventing social stagnation.	• **Pluralistic stagnation** Group opposition can slow down or even block desirable changes, thereby contributing to social immobilism.
• **Pluralism** PGs are a product of freedom of association, which is a fundamental principle of liberal democracy: its obverse is autocratic or tyrannical suppression of interests. Freely operating pressure groups are essential to the effective functioning of liberal democracy: they serve as vital intermediary institutions between government and society, assist in the dispersal of political power and provide important counterweights to undue concentration of power.	• **Elitism** Group system only *apparently* functions on 'level playing field'; in practice reinforces existing class and power structure – 'in the pluralist heaven the heavenly choir sings with a strong upper class accent' (Schnattschneider, 1960, cited Grant, 1989, p. 26).
• **Social cohesion** PGs increase social cohesion and political stability by providing 'safety-valve' outlet for individual and collective grievances.	• **Social disharmony and dislocation** Inegalitarian operation of groups increases social discontent and political instability by intensifying sense of social frustration and injustice felt by disadvantaged and excluded sections of the population.
• **Opposition** PGs assist surveillance of government by exposing information it would rather keep secret, thereby reinforcing and complementing work of official opposition through political parties.	• **Failure of opposition** True in theory but only to limited extent in practice: in contemporary Britain, groups and parties combined are unable to mount effective opposition to government policies because often lack adequate information.

fluctuate, in large part because of government needs and political will. For example, certain business groups became influential during the 1980s whereas the trade unions and professional groups saw their influence reduced.

Influential groups in the 1980s included:
   Right-wing 'think-tanks' such as the Centre for Policy studies and the Adam Smith Institute
   Merchant bankers
   Insurance companies
   Large retailers
   Oil companies
   Advertising agencies
   Estate agents
   Brewery companies
   Institute of Directors
   Business groups close to the Conservative Party
   Groups representing the police

Groups losing influence in the 1980s were:
   The TUC, the NUM and trade unions generally
   BMA
   The Law Society
   Teachers' unions
   The Poverty lobby
   Local government associations

It is worthy of note that the business groups which gained influence favoured finance and commerce rather than manufacturing and did not include the CBI. The impotence of the professional groups representing doctors and teachers was revealed in the restructuring of health and education at the end of the decade. In broader terms, the list of groups whose influence declined reveals the importance of **compatibility** of group aims with government policy if groups are to exercise influence. Groups losing influence were all perceived as 'vested interests' hampering the efficient performance of the 'enterprise economy'. In mid-1993, some professional groups were locked in well-publicised disputes with government: the teachers over educational testing and – together with the police – performance–related pay. The Law Society was suing the Lord

Chancellor over large-scale cuts in the legal aid scheme whilst the BMA at its annual conference informed the government that its health changes were not working.

Pressure Groups and Democracy

There is a serious debate about whether pressure groups (PGs) enhance or distort democracy. The main arguments on each side are summarised in Table 15.7.

Summary

The two major types of pressure group are sectional groups which seek to further the interests of people as engaged in particular occupations, and cause groups which arise to promote some attitude, belief or principle. The main developments with regard to pressure groups in the twentieth century have been the institutionalisation of consultation between sectional groups and government, an arrangement seen as advantageous by both sides; a rapid upsurge since the 1960s of cause group activity; and, in the 1980s, the systematic dismantling by government of corporatist-style consultation with the 'peak' producer groups together with some re-orientation of group efforts towards Europe.

In recent decades, participation in cause groups has become as important as joining a political party as a means for people to express their political commitments and preferences. The major channels of influence for groups are the executive (ministers and civil servants), Parliament, public opinion, and the European Union. The political parties, the courts and local government can also be targets for influence.

The distinction between 'insider' groups, which are regarded as legitimate by government and consulted on a regular basis, and 'outsider' groups, which are unable or unwilling to gain such recognition, is a useful one. A group's decisions about strategies and methods of influence are dependent on the nature and aims of the group and its perceptions of the location of power in the political system.

The debate continues about how far and in what ways pressure groups improve or detract from democracy.

Questions

1. Justify and criticise the role of pressure groups in democractic politics today.

2. To what extent and in what ways did the political influence of business and the trade unions change in the 1980s?

Assignment

Select a cause group and compile a dossier on its activities. Concentrate expecially on establishing its membership, staffing, financing, leadership, public support and strategy. Examine its influence (or lack of it) and suggest reasons.

Further reading

Baggott, R. (1992a) 'Pressure Groups and the British political System: Change and Decline?' in B. Jones and L. Robins (eds) *Two Decades in British Politics* (Manchester University Press).

Baggott, R. (1992b) 'The Measurement of Change in Pressure Group Politics', *Talking Politics*, Autumn, 5: 1.

Barr, G. (1992) 'The Anti-Poll Tax Movement: An Insider's View of an Outsider Group', *Talking Politics*, 4: 3, Summer.

Grant, W. (1989) *Pressure Groups, Politics and Democracy in Britain* (London: Philip Allan).

Holliday, I. (1993) 'Organised Interests after Thatcher', in P. Dunleavy, A. Gamble, I. Holliday and G. Peele (eds) *Developments in British Politics*, 4 (London: Macmillan).

Jordan, A.G. and Richardson, J.J. (1987) *Government and Pressure Groups in Britain* (Oxford: Clarendon).

Jordan, A.G. (ed.) (1991) *The Commercial Lobbyists* (Aberdeen University Press).

Marsh, D. (1992) *The New Politics of British Trade Unionism* (London: Macmillan).

Norton, P. (1991) 'The Changing Face of Parliament: Lobbying and its Consequences' in P. Norton. (ed.) *New Directions in British Politics?* (Aldershot: Edward Elgar).

Rush, M. (ed) (1990) *Parliament and Pressure Politics* (Oxford: Clarendon).

Watts, D. (1993) 'Lobbying Europe', *Talking Politics*, 5: 2, Winter.

■ *Chapter 16* ■

The Mass Media

The communication of political information is an important process in the political system, and the mass media play a central role in this activity. Some political scientists believe that the mass media in Britain help democracy work through allowing a wide variety of views to be expressed. Others believe that the media are anti-democratic because of their power to manipulate the way people think about politics at home and abroad. The media, in other words, are politically biased.

Other critics have accused the mass media of trivialising politics. Because different television channels and newspapers find that they are competing for a limited number of viewers and readers, there is the tendency to make the news more attractive by treating it as entertainment rather than as a serious business.

The chapter concludes by considering the impact of election television and newspaper reporting.

■ The Mass Media and Society

Only a small proportion of Britain's population is actively engaged in politics and therefore learns about political affairs from first-hand experience. What the majority 'know' about politics is made up principally from what they learn from the mass media. In other words, for those individuals who do not participate directly in politics the mass media define their 'real world' of politics. Peter Golding has argued that 'The media are central in the provision of ideas and images which people use to interpret and understand a great deal of their everyday experience' (Golding,

1974, p. 178). This, of course, gives the mass media enormous power since they can either set people's minds against the political system or help to generate popular support for it.

▢ The 'Media as part of Democracy' Viewpoint

There are two basic viewpoints concerning the relationship between the mass media and society. First, there is the view that *the media are part of democracy* since they are themselves a 'free' institution. The media assist the working of a democratic system through facilitating free speech and unrestricted public debate. In Britain, there is no state control of either the press or broadcasting, although the latter is regulated so that it always serves the interests of the community as a whole. This results in a great variety of political opinions being given an airing, and many of them are hostile to the government of the day.

Broadcasting is bound by law to be 'impartial'. For example the Independent Broadcasting Authority is legally required to ensure that all news is presented with due accuracy and impartiality and that 'due impartiality is preserved on the part of persons providing the programmes as respects matters of political or industrial controversy or relating to current public policy'. During times of national emergency the government may extend greater control over broadcasting as part of its strategy for coping. John Whale has pointed out that the laws relating to both the BBC and ITA make it clear that ministers could instruct them to broadcast or withhold whatever government wanted. He added 'That particular cannon has seldom been fired. It is not much use to party politicians: it was meant to guard the interests of the state (especially in wartime), not of any one political party' (Whale, 1977 p. 12). Direct intervention in broadcasting by the government is rare but we shall see that governments can be extremely sensitive about what is broadcast.

The government has no substantial role in the newspaper business. There is no censorship apart from D (Defence) Notices. Thus, unlike broadcasting, there is no obligation for newspapers to be politically impartial. The press provide what can be seen as a 'market place for ideas' in which a wide spectrum of political opinion is made available to the public. As might be expected, some newspapers will be bought more than others, with the popular papers providing the public with what they want to read. These papers will thrive, whilst unpopular and unread papers will struggle and eventually cease being published. The fact that the majority of British newspapers support the Conservative Party does not undermine this democratic view of the press; indeed, it provides crucial evidence that Britain does have a politically representative press.

John Whale argued that 'the media do more towards corroborating opinion than creating it' and with reference to newspapers, he used the *Morning Star* (a communist paper originally published as the *Daily Worker*) with its low circulation as an example: 'if any substantial number of people seriously wanted the structure of society rebuilt from the bottom, the *Morning Star* would sell more copies than it does' (ibid., p. 85). The same argument can be applied to a long list of pro-Labour newspapers, the *Daily Herald*, *Reynolds News* (which became the *Sunday Citizen*), and *News on Sunday* – all of which closed because they did not sell enough copies. Even the tabloid *Star* dropped its support for Labour in order to improve its circulation. The marketplace will support only one pro-Labour paper, the *Daily Mirror*, and the non-aligned *Guardian* and *Independent*. In other words, the British press is predominantly conservative in tone because its readers are.

The bias in the press towards the Conservative Party is inevitable for another reason in the current political culture: this is because the newspaper industry remains almost exclusively in private hands, and for as long as the tussle between public and private ownership is one of the central disputes in politics, and the private side is espoused mainly by the Conservatives, then there is a case for supposing that the press must be predominantly Conservative in its sympathies (ibid. p. 75). Having said this, the press plays an important 'watchdog' role for democracy, and has never shied away from criticising the Conservative Party or a Conservative Government.

The media's 'watchdog' role can, as might be expected, be the source of tension between journalists and the government. This is because government in Britain has grown accustomed to operating in a climate of greater secrecy than some other Western governments, notably the US administration. As a consequence there can be much greater political embarrassment when investigative journalism unearths information which might threaten the government's standing. Governments in the past have frequently tried to suppress such information. For example, Labour and Conservative governments alike have been very sensitive about documentary television programmes which probe beyond the 'bombs and bullets' level of news reporting on Northern Ireland. Edward Heath opposed screening of the BBC's 'A Question of Ulster'; Leon Brittan attempted to ban the programme 'Real Lives'; and the biggest uproar came in response to Thames Television's 'Death on the Rock'. This programme explored the circumstances surrounding the killing of three IRA (Irish Republican Army) terrorists in Gibraltar by the SAS (Special Air Service). On the one hand, Margaret Thatcher had suffered the assassination of her close colleague, Airey Neave MP, by an IRA bomb and she could not understand why journalists did not battle against the IRA as she did. She felt that the media provided terrorists with the 'oxygen of publicity' and attempted to counteract this by imposing a ban on broadcast interviews with individuals connected with terrorist groups. Roger Bolton, Series Director for 'Death on the Rock', defined the media's watchdog role:

> We, on the other hand, did not see ourselves as agents of the State. Our job was to ask what, why and how, to give the public in a democracy the information to which it is entitled. Put another way our job was not to further government policy but to report the facts, to get the truth. (Bolton, 1990, p. 41)

In 1992 Channel 4 was fined for a contempt of a court order requiring journalists to reveal their sources for a programme, 'The Committee', which alleged that a secret group of loyalist paramilitaries, RUC (Royal Ulster Constabulary) police officers and businessmen had been planning the assassination of republican sympathisers in Northern Ireland. Channel 4 representatives argued that individuals would not reveal to journalists examples of wrongdoing if their identities had to be disclosed – since this might be a risk to their own lives – and hence the Prevention of Terrorism Act was actually threatening the public's democratic 'right to know'. The watchdog role is played successfully even in cases where counter-evidence is produced, accusations are disproved, and suspicions of wrong-doing are removed.

Newspapers, particularly the tabloids, confronted the Government in 1992 over new legislation which also threatened the public's 'right to know'. But in this case, the 'right to know' concerned details of people's private lives rather than details of directly political issues which the Government would prefer kept confidential. This conflict was important, however, because it concerned both the power and the freedom of tabloid editors who felt that the Government, which owed them a favour for their loyal support during the election campaign, should now not be threatening them with restrictive laws. The Secretary of State for National Heritage, David Mellor, would be responsible for the new privacy legislation, and he had already warned the tabloids that they had broken too many promises about self-regulation and were now 'drinking in the Last Chance Saloon'. Mellor had projected a

strong family image during the election campaign, and it was a great embarrassment to him when the *People* alleged that he was having an affair with an actress (Exhibit 16.1).

Finally, the mass media play an important role in the democratic process by helping to set the political agenda. The agenda-setting function – defined as the correspondence between 'the order of importance in the media given to issues and the order of significance attached to the same issues by the public and politicians' (McQuail, 1987, p. 275) – is complex. Sometimes the agenda set in the media is for the media and far removed from the concerns of the electorate, other times not. Along with politicians, the public, parties and other organisations, the media play a crucial role in structuring and widening political debate in Britain so that issues such as the environment, industrial relations or the 'poll tax' receive attention until the problems are addressed by the government.

Through these functions the media, it can be argued, enhance and strengthen the quality of democracy in Britain. Despite concern expressed by politicians from the left and right that there is political bias in television, TV and radio maintain a careful balance between the parties. The BBC defines this balance in practice as coverage which should reflect the support obtained by the parties in the preceeding election. It is true that newspapers are partisan, mostly supporting the Conservatives, but this has not prevented the election of Labour governments. Despite the uncritical support the tabloids gave the Government in 1992, the Labour Opposition came very close to dislodging the Conservatives from power.

The 'Media as a Tool of the Ruling Class' Viewpoint

An alternative view of the mass media in relation to society sees *the media playing a much more creative role in shaping people's ideas, attitudes, beliefs and actions*. In other words, the mass media do not simply reflect public opinion so much as help to mould it in the first place.

Exhibit 16.1   *The Watchdog Role of the Press*

What is a 'free press'? How 'free' should the press be? One of the strongest arguments for a free press is that its existence will strengthen democracy and promote good government by guarding the political system like a watchdog. Others are more sceptical about this, and point out that newspapers are more interested in making profits than defending democracy. And what sells more copies is scandal – hence the watchdogs of the press are much more likely to bark about the private lives of politicians than about their public record. Two brief case-studies are provided below for you to research and discuss.

The tabloid message is clear during the Westland helicopter affair which took place during the winter of 1986/7. One minister had resigned from the Cabinet over what he considered to be bad government and the Press blamed another cabinet minister, Leon Brittan, for many of the mistakes which had been made. He resigned within hours of these headlines appearing on the news stands. But had journalists played the 'watchdog' role effectively? Subsequent disclosures suggested that the blame for the Westland affair lay with the Prime Minister, and that Leon Brittan had been sacrificed to save her political reputation.

The tabloid watchdogs alleged that the 'Minister for Fun' was having an extramarital affair. Should a politician's private life have any bearing on his or her public life? Would Britain have lost the services of some of its greatest leaders if scandal was allowed to bring them down? Or has the public got a right to know when a legislator, who may be setting the rules which govern their lives, is acting dishonourably outside Parliament?

The mass media structure the complexities of the social world and make it understandable to readers, viewers and listeners. For example, journalists invariably use a consensus view of society as a framework which is imposed on their reporting in order to explain or make sense out of events. In doing this, the media tend to give authority to certain institutions – such as Parliament – whilst making those who advocate non-parliamentary or direct political action appear as extremists or irresponsible fanatics. Journalists frequently consult or interview 'experts' for their opinions on issues; and these experts are invariably powerful people in society and naturally support the system which gives them power. Although experts may be seen to disagree with each other on specific issues, they are unlikely ever to challenge the consensus view of society in a fundamental way.

The mass media in Britain, even television and radio, cannot be neutral or impartial. This is because the media are a product of Britain's culture, a culture which is biased like any other culture, with assumptions and prejudices of its own. The imposition of this cultural framework is seen in what is referred to as the 'social manufacture' or 'social production' of the news. News does not 'just happen', rather 'it is made'. News programmes and newspapers have a number of predefined categories to be filled by 'the news' – e.g. sport, human interest, politics, economics, and so on. Visually interesting material is more likely to become 'news' than are abstract developments. The selection process of what will become news is known as 'agenda setting'.

Agenda-setting is important politically because of the consequences of an issue being placed on the agenda. If industrial strikes are put on the agenda rather than industrial accidents, it will lead to demands for tighter trade union legislation rather than stricter factory regulations. News about 'social security scroungers' or 'New Age' travellers will stir up different feelings about society than news about 'tax evaders'. Sometimes there is an over-reaction to what is seen as a threat to society and this is referred to as a 'moral panic'. During the 1970s there was a feeling that mugging was a new, violent and increasingly common street crime. The reaction was out of all proportion to the threat, which was not new, but nevertheless demands for more policing and tougher penalties were fed into the political system.

The leading stories in national newspapers influence the choice of issues covered by television and radio later in the day. In other words, the agenda set by television, which people see as being 'objective', takes its lead from stories in the national press. Invariably, since they come from a pro-Conservative press, there is a marked tendency for these stories to be anti-Labour and anti-union. At the same time, newspapers followed by television will be relatively uncritical of the Conservative Party or a Conservative Government. For example, the media in general failed to question the logic of Thatcherite monetarism in the early 1980s, accepted the 1981–2 recession as inevitable, repeated the Government's mid-1980s view of Britain being an 'economic miracle' and failed to scrutinise policies which resulted by the early 1990s in the longest and deepest recession since the war.

The media values of professional journalists together with the pro-Conservative bias found most explicitly in the press mean that the mass media fail to reflect the values found in society at large. In particular, working-class views do not find expression in the media. From time to time, Labour and the unions have considered launching their own papers in order to remedy this situation. But there are problems in publishing 'working-class' papers, already experienced by the defunct *Daily Herald*, *Daily Sketch* and *Sunday Graphic*: 'They all had a predominantly working-class readership and, in terms of marketing, relatively "small" circulations. They thus fell between two stools: they had neither the quantity nor the social "quality" of readership needed to attract sufficient advertising for them to survive' (Curran and Seaton, 1990, p. 97).

Newspapers and much of television and radio are commercial enterprises concerned with making a profit for their shareholders. Put simply, they form part of the capitalist system and this shapes the values which they promote. Indeed, the mass media are very big business. Six leading newspaper publishers – Reed International, News International, Beaverbrook, Associated Newspapers, Thomson, and S. Pearson and Son – account for some 80 per cent of all daily, Sunday and local newspaper sales. Most of these concerns are conglomerations which have financial interests in other sectors of the communication industry. For example, S. Pearson and Son publish *The Financial Times* but also have interests in Longman, Ladybird Books and Penguin Books. Some concerns, such as Thomson, have considerable interests in independent television and commercial radio. Other conglomerations have an even wider base in industry and commerce.

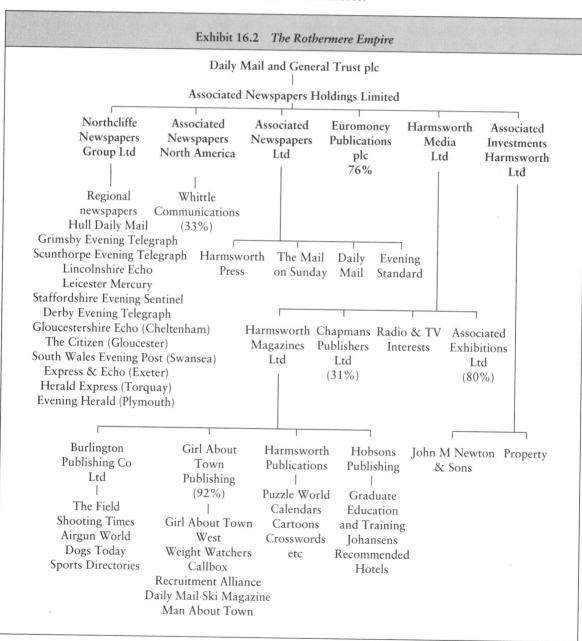

Exhibit 16.2   *The Rothermere Empire*

This pattern of ownership can represent a threat to democracy:

> First, concentration limits the range and diversity of views and opinions which are able to find public expression. More significantly, it is those views and opinions representing the least powerful social groups which are systematically excluded by the process of concentration . . . Second, concentration of control over the media into the hands of large conglomerates emphasises production for maximum profit at the necessary expense of other social goals that should be a vital aspect of communication media. Third, such concentration is undemocratic in two senses. It removes the media from public surveillance and accountability, that is, it renders them externally undemocratic. (Murdoch and Golding, 1977, pp. 105–6)

John Whale was considerably less worried about the effects of ownership on communication. For, at the time he was writing, the 'press baron' who owned papers and who personally dictated editorial policy had disappeared. There were no proprietors like Lord Beaverbrook or Lord Northcliffe, who used to instruct their editors what to put in the *Daily Express* and *Daily Mail* respectively. Contents and policy were determined by professional staff journalists who decided what items to cover, and what items to comment about. However, events were to overtake this argument with the emergence of a new generation of press barons such as Rupert Murdoch and the late Robert Maxwell. There was concern that not only were these new proprietors so powerful that they could intervene in the same ways as the old press barons but also that they did not usually have to intervene since editorial staff anticipated and wrote what they knew would find the approval of their respective proprietors. In addition John Whale saw the pattern of ownership as something which was inevitable in the modern communications newspapers.

However, issues of ownership and control have made a dramatic impact upon the press. The case of the *Sun* shows how a newspaper can be redirected away from the political views of its established readership. Rupert Murdoch purchased the broadsheet *Sun*, which developed from the pro-Labour *Daily Herald*. Murdoch had a reputation for moving his newspapers to the right, and in 1974 this was to happen to the *Sun* 'in opposition to the opinion of its readers', the majority of whom supported Labour. (Curran and Seaton, 1990 p. 81). Thus in a little over a decade, Labour had lost the support of a mass circulation daily paper and the Conservatives gained yet another supporter in Fleet Street which a further decade later was to be the most ardent champion of Thatcherism. The values of groups such as the ethnic minorities, unions, feminists and others beyond the Conservative domain are marginalised by the media and remain unrepresented. Even the major opposition party, Labour, is portrayed as a dangerous and unpatriotic enemy within. There is no comparison between the sycophantic British press at national and local level and the US Press which scrutines Republican and Democrat with equal rigour on behalf of American citizens. In this sense, therefore, the British media fails miserably in performing its 'watchdog' role. Indeed, the 'lobby system' is an expression of the cosy relationship between the media and the government, with the former depending on the latter for the supply of 'news' items. This dependency relationship between journalists and politicians is in sharp contrast to the American tradition of investigative journalism.

Differing Interpretations of News about Trade Unions

These two basic viewpoints – the media as part of democracy or tool of the ruling class – can be detected in the basic assumptions of media researchers who have studied the activity of news gathering and reporting. Some researchers are clearly more influenced by Marxist ideas than others. One case-study in particular, concerning a dispute in the car industry nearly twenty years ago, remains a landmark in media research and still the topic of academic controversy. Firstly, the findings of the Glasgow University Media Group will be examined then, secondly, a critique of the Group's methods and conclusions.

The Glasgow Group perceived television news as 'a manufactured product based on a coherent set of professional and ideological beliefs and expressed in a rigid formula of presentation' which 'conveys many of the culturally dominant assumptions of our society' (Glasgow Media Group 1976, p. 31). They concluded that the reporting of strikes was 'clearly skewed against the interests of the working class and organised labour' and 'in favour of the managers of industry' (Glasgow Media Group, 1980, p. 400).

Although television news usually appears to be 'neutral' in its approach to current events, radical critics have argued that a subtle ideology is possibly at its most visible in the reporting of trade unions. This is because society is divided into fundamentally antagonistic groups, and those who control the mass media sympathise with the management side of industry and are hostile to trade unions. The systematic management bias and routine news practices inevitably lead to the production of 'bad news' about trade unions.

In what has become an important piece of media research, the Glasgow University Media Group monitored all television reports of a month-long strike at the Cowley plant of British Leyland. Coverage began with the reporting of a speech delivered in Huyton by the then Prime Minister, Harold Wilson. The researchers observed that:

> This speech covered many areas notably government policy on industry and investment, but the section of it which received most attention from the television news was a reference made by Mr Wilson to 'manifestly avoidable stoppages of production' in the car industry. This reference was interpreted by all three channels in such a way that they presented strikes as the main problem facing the car industry in general and British Leyland Motor Corporation in particular (Glasgow University Media Group, 1976, pp. 256–7).

Initially the BBC reported that 'The Prime Minister, in a major speech tonight on the economy, appealed to *Management and Unions* in the car industry to cut down on what he called "manifestly avoidable stoppages"'. However,

within the space of two hours the BBC had changed the report to say that 'The Prime Minister has appealed to *workers* in the car industry to cut down on avoidable stoppages.' From the outset, ITN reports presented Harold Wilson's speech as applying only to the workforce: 'The Prime Minister tonight defended the government policy of stepping in to help companies where jobs were threatened but he also gave *workers* a blunt warning' (ibid., pp. 257–9).

Professor Martin Harrison has been foremost amongst the critics of both the Glasgow Group's scholarship and conclusions. Harrison found great professionalism displayed in television journalism whilst at the same time believing that there was still scope for improvement. He argued that the Glasgow Group members were unfair to television news in so far as whenever a number of different interpretations of news output was available, they always selected and emphasised the interpretation which put the unions in a bad light. He attacked the Group's use of sociolinguistics to illustrate this point, since it had been argued that certain code words used in reporting, such as 'claim', 'demand' and 'idle', all have ideological overtones which make trade unionists appear to be unreasonable and acting wrongly. Harrison takes the use of the latter word, 'idle' as an example of how the Glasgow Group's research drew unjustified conclusions:

> Far from being an everyday word in ITN's industrial relations vocabulary 'idle' appeared as an occasional synonym for 'laid off' about as often as 'put out of work' and 'workers will have to stay off work'. In four months' coverage of the car industry it was employed twice compared with 22 instances of 'laid off' – a slender base on which to identify it as yet another illustration of the media's role in hegemonic signification! It is perhaps no coincidence that *More Bad News* does not cite this other occasion when 'idle' was used in a car industry context:
>> 'Already the 3 week old strike has led to more than 13,000 other British Leyland workers being laid off, and another 1,200 will now be made idle'.
> It is clear both that 'idle' was used simply to avoid repeating ' laid off' and being *made* idle carries no overtone of prejudice to the workforce. (Harrison, 1985, p. 123)

■ Television Politics

Most people rely on television as their main source of information. As long ago as 1962 a BBC survey showed that 58 per cent of the sample learned the news primarily from TV whereas only 33 per cent learned it mainly from newspapers. Another study ten years later revealed that 85 per cent named television as their main source of information. There is a tendency for people to believe what they 'see' on TV but to be sceptical about what they read in the press. Nearly 70 per cent think that television is the 'most trustworthy' news source whilst only 6 per cent are prepared to rank newspapers so highly.

Since television is perceived by so many as providing a source of objective political information, it is not surprising that there are tensions between politicians and personnel in the media. Examples have been provided above of programmes in which the government of the day did not feel it was being treated fairly. In the long campaign leading up to the 1992 General Election the Government accused the BBC of biased coverage of the National Health Service (NHS) issue. Some years earlier grassroot Conservatives complained about what they saw as an anti-Tory bias in BBC radio and television and their party chairman, Norman Tebbit, set up a 'bias monitoring unit'. The BBC has a very difficult path to tread since it does not want to fall out with the Government at a time when the future of broadcasting is being discussed and its royal charter comes up for renewal in 1996. At the same time, the BBC does not want to let itself become a tool or agent of government, since it would lose all political integrity.

Government ministers sometimes come to see policy failure in terms of poor presentation in the media. In other words, rather than recognising that the policies in question are ill-thought-out, inappropriate or not working, it is argued that for some reason 'the message is not getting across'. This logic places the blame with the media for communicating poorly rather than with ministers for governing poorly. In order to receive favourable treatment, politicians and their parties will attempt to manipulate the media in a number of ways. Firstly, accusing television journalists of being biased, as did Norman Tebbit, may produce positive results:

> A party can try to bias television in its favour by alleging that the broadcasters are biased against them. If that produces any response at all it may encourage the broadcasters to alter the balance in its favour. Even if the *broadcasters do nothing it may* encourage the *viewers* to regard television as biased against the party and to make allowances for that when they watch. The political effectiveness of the press is much reduced because its readers often see it as 'the Tory press' and adjust their reactions to press stories accordingly. If they can be persuaded that television is not impartial but is dominated by trendy lefties, then the credibility of television reporting will go down and the credibility of press reporting will increase – to the advantage of the Conservatives. (Miller *et al.*, 1990, p. 72)

Secondly, parties will attempt to manipulate the media, particularly television, by what is known as 'spin control'. This involves dealing with events, particularly potentially damaging ones, in order to get them interpreted in a favourable way by journalists. A good example of a Conservative 'spin doctor' at work was the way in which the local government elections of May 1991, in which the party did badly, were presented as a considerable victory. In a political climate still influenced by the unpopular 'poll tax', Labour gained 490 seats and won 39 per cent of the popular vote compared with the Conservative losses of 890 seats and 37 per cent of the vote. Prior to the local elections being held, Tory spin doctors persuaded journalists that the London results, particularly Wandsworth and Westminster, where councils had set the poll tax at low levels, were the crucial ones to watch. In the event, the Conservatives did better in London than nationally with some results showing significant swings away from Labour. Thus through spin control, the Conservatives successfully imposed a meaning of 'victory' on a set of local election results which could have been portrayed as defeat on a national scale.

■ Newspaper Readership

The rack of papers seen outside any newsagents symbolises the British class system. The quality press is read overwhelmingly by the higher socio-economic groups whilst the mass circulation *Sun*, *Mirror* and *Star* have predominantly working-class readers. Between the 'haughties' and the 'naughties' are the *Mail*, *Today* and *Express* which, reflecting their lower middle class pitch, are read across the social spectrum (see Table 16.1)

Treatment of the news varies enormously between papers. The quality papers contain much more of what might be described as 'news' in addition to comment and editorial. The mass circulation papers more closely resemble adult comics and are designed for 'looking at' rather than 'reading'. Much space is taken up with photographs and large-print headlines. Where the quality press focuses on international events and city news, the mass circulation papers rarely fail to devote considerable space to 'scandal' of one sort or another.

Table 16.1   *Reading of national newspapers in Britain, by sex and social class, 1987*

	Percentage of adults reading each paper in 1987		Percentage of adults in each social class reading each paper in 1987						Readership[1] (millions)		Readers per copy (numbers)
	Males	Females	A	B	C1	C2	D	E	1971	1987	1987
Daily newspapers											
The Sun	28	23	5	10	20	32	37	27	8.5	11.3	2.8
Daily Mirror	23	18	4	8	16	27	29	19	13.8	9.1	2.9
Daily Mail	11	10	14	14	14	9	6	5	4.8	4.5	2.5
Daily Express	10	9	9	12	13	10	6	6	9.7	4.3	2.5
The Star	11	7	2	2	6	12	15	9	–	3.9	3.2
The Daily Telegraph	7	5	28	16	8	3	1	2	3.6	2.8	2.4
The Guardian	4	3	9	10	4	1	1	1	1.1	1.5	3.1
The Times	4	2	16	8	3	1	1	1	1.1	1.2	2.7
Today	3	2	1	2	3	3	3	1	–	1.1	3.3
The Independent	3	1	6	6	3	1	1	–	–	0.9	2.8
Financial Times	3	1	8	5	2	1	–	–	0.7	0.8	3.5
Any daily newspaper[2]	73	63	74	67	67	70	72	59		68.0	
Sunday newspapers											
News of the World	30	27	9	12	23	36	40	30	15.8	12.8	2.6
Sunday Mirror	22	19	5	10	17	27	27	18	13.5	9.1	3.1
The People	20	17	3	8	16	23	25	17	14.4	8.1	2.8
Sunday Express	14	13	24	22	18	12	8	7	10.4	6.1	2.7
The Mail on Sunday	12	11	16	16	16	11	7	4	–	5.1	2.9
The Sunday Times	9	7	35	22	10	3	3	2	3.7	3.6	2.9
The Observer	6	5	14	14	7	3	2	2	2.4	2.3	3.0
Sunday Telegraph	5	4	19	11	7	3	2	1	2.1	2.2	3.0
Any Sunday newspaper[3]	76	71	78	75	74	76	76	64		74.0	

[1] Defined as the average issue readership and represents the number of people who claim to have read or looked at one or more copies of a given publication during a period equal to the interval at which the publication appears.
[2] Includes the above newspapers plus the *Daily Record*.
[3] Includes the above newspapers plus *The Sunday Post* and *Sunday Mail*.

Source: Social Trends, 19, 1989, p. 166.

Only 21 per cent of the adult male population reads a quality broadsheet newspaper, and only 12 per cent adult females do so. Anxiety has been expressed about the declining quality of the tabloid press. Frequently the tabloids pander to basic prejudices – the 'Gotcha!' headline which reported the sinking of the *Belgrano* during the Falklands war and the 'Up Yours, Delors' headline on EC policy are examples likely to kindle jingoistic feelings. The issues, Britain's role in the South Atlantic or the future of the EC, are generally ignored by the tabloids. Some argue that this situation is particularly significant in so far as most tabloid readers are working class. Put another way, rather than inform their readers about the facts of political life, the tabloids maintain their working-class readership in a state of relative political ignorance. The class with the greatest interest in political change is fed a biased, anti-left and trivialised account of politics in Britain and the wider world.

Not only has the tabloid press become more tabloid in nature over recent years, but the press has generally undergone political change: 'national newspapers became markedly more partisan from 1974 onwards. This was partly due in response to the growing polarization of British politics. But it also reflected the cumulative impact of a new generation of partisan, interventionist proprietors.' (Curran and Seaton, 1990, p. 80) It was once assumed that such changes would have little impact upon the political behaviour of the electorate. But, as we shall see, this view has been challenged by the findings of recent research.

The Political Impact of the Mass Media

There is a view that the mass media can actually create news by 'setting up' newsworthy events that otherwise could not have taken place. Some think that the mere presence of TV cameras at a demonstration increases the risks that it will develop into a riot. If such a riot is shown on the TV news some people think that this creates 'copycat' riots in other areas. There is another view that the mass media may enhance or reduce the importance of events, but those events cannot be created by the media. For example, Colin Seymour-Ure argues that the media were influential in making Enoch Powell into a major political figure in 1968 'as the result of intense, sustained publicity for his views on immigration' (Seymour-Ure, 1974, p. 21). Yet 'that status depended also on the distinctive character of his views and the existence of a political crisis that gave them point' (ibid., p. 21). He continues by arguing that the political impact of any communication will be influenced by its timing, frequency and intensity.

☐ *Timing*

One of the most interesting examples of political impact resulting from the timing of news took place during the General Election campaign of 1924 with the publication of the Zinoviev letter. The letter, commonly believed to be a fake, was marked 'Very Secret' and was sent from the Third Communist International in Moscow to the Central Committee of the British Communist Party. It urged the need to stir the British working class into revolutionary action and form them into a British Red Army. The letter was published in the Press on 25 October and dominated the campaign until polling day on 29 October. The *Daily Mail* gave the letter the most sensational treatment and amongst the remaining papers only the *Herald* declared it to be a forgery. Some argue that the 'Red Scare' resulting from the Zinoviev letter lost Labour the election. In other words, had the news of this letter which had been known for some considerable period been released at a different time, then Labour would have won the General Election.

☐ *Frequency*

The constant repetition of messages over a period of time may make an impact on the political climate. Colin Seymour-Ure argues that the habit of the mass media in presenting a 'Westminster' view of British politics can mislead the public:

> The construction regularly put upon the nature of British politics by the mass media stresses heavily the 'Westminster' as opposed to the 'Whitehall' elements. The power of Parliament, and the extent to which it figures in political processes at all, are arguably emphasised more than they should be if an accurate impression of events is to be given. If that is so, the frequency of media coverage has much to do with it (Seymour-Ure, 1974, p. 36).

☐ *Intensity*

When one story dominates all others, it is said to be communicated more intensely.

An unexpected or urgent event can be turned into a crisis by the intensity of media coverage. The Falklands War of 1982 is an interesting example of a high-intensity media event. But because lives were at risk, there was a conflict of interests between the Government and the mass media. The essence of successful warfare is secrecy whereas the essence of successful journalism is publicity and disclosure. Despite the intensity of communication, there was relatively little raw information to transmit. It seems likely, also, that the British Government were bearing in mind that TV coverage of the war in Vietnam had undermined public support amongst Americans for the conflict to be pursued. Thus, whilst there was the technical capacity to send Falklands War pictures back to Britain from the South Atlantic, these facilities were denied to journalists. In the absence of 'live' coverage, news and current affairs programmes relied on military 'experts' to speculate on events with the aid of cartoons and models. The Gulf War, in which Saddam Hussein's Iraqi invasion of Kuwait was reversed by an alliance of American, British and Arab forces dominated the world's news media in January 1991. The intensity of reporting in Britain was reflected in a round-the-clock BBC radio channel being devoted to reporting the conflict.

☐ *Election Television and Press Coverage*

Research into the political impact of the mass media on both politicians and the electorate during general election campaigns is relatively recent. The Television Research Unit monitored the impact of the 1959 General Election programmes on voting intentions. In their study *Television and the Political Image* (1961), the researchers, J. Trenaman and Denis McQuail, reported that television had an educational function insofar as the more individuals watched campaign programmes the more accurately they became informed on issues. But television exposure did not appear to affect the voting or attitudes of electors to the Labour or Conservative parties. Although attitudes towards the Conservatives improved during the campaign, there was no evidence that the mass media played any role in this change of attitude.

Party political programmes are possibly the least popular element of election television. As long ago as 1964 a survey revealed that 55 per cent thought that there were 'too many' party political programmes and only 1 per cent thought that there were 'too few'. A survey conducted in 1983 revealed that over 50 per cent of those questioned thought television coverage of politics was excessive whilst 40 per cent thought it was about right.

Research into the 1987 General Election Campaign concluded that 'television failed to set the public agenda and the public failed to set the television agenda. Each influenced the other to 'a very modest extent' which was 'in the best interest of democracy since there was a massive partisan bias in British television news coverage' (Miller *et al.*, 1990, p. 232). Political parties did not receive equal treatment since 'the Conservative government got two bites at the television cherry – once as the Conservative party, once as the government. Coverage in non-controversial news items was very heavily biased towards the Conservatives and especially so towards the end of the campaign.' (ibid., p. 231). On controversial issues, a bias works against the Liberal Democrats' third voice since there is a television focus 'on the two-party Conservative-versus-Labour battle and again, this emphasis increased sharply towards the end of the campaign'. (Ibid., p. 231).

In terms of the political impact of newspapers during an election campaign, the position is complex and difficult to measure. This is because people are free to select their own papers – a surprising third of the pro-Tory *Sun* readers vote Labour – and because it is difficult to isolate the influence of newspapers from other political influences. Nevertheless, recent research has challenged the orthodox view that newspapers reinforce an individual's political views rather than change them. In addition, different papers appeared to have different impacts upon their readers:

Electors who read relatively heavyweight, intellectual papers such as the *Daily Telegraph* or the *Guardian* were remarkably stable in their political preferences between 1986 and 1987: amongst them the Conservative lead increased by about 7 per cent. Those who read no paper at all, or one of the middle-brow tabloids – the *Daily Express*, *Daily Mail*, or *Daily Mirror* – were moderately stable: amongst them the Conservative lead increased by about 12 per cent. But amongst those who read those quintessential low-brow tabloids, the *Sun* and the *Star*, the Conservative lead increased by about 34 per cent.

The prior partisanship of the papers and of their readers made no difference to the swing: *Daily Telegraph* readers were pro-Conservative, *Guardian* readers pro-Labour; *Daily Express* and *Daily Mail* readers were pro-Conservative, *Daily Mirror* readers pro-Labour; *Sun* readers were pro-Labour in 1986 but pro-Conservative in 1987, while *Star* readers were much more strongly pro-Labour than *Sun* readers in 1986, and so remained Labour in 1987 despite a huge shift to the Conservatives. But irrespective of the readers' initial party preference, the more 'tabloid' the paper, the more its readers swung to the Conservatives between 1986 and 1987 (Miller *et al.*, 1990, p. 88–9, see Figure 16.1).

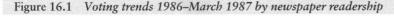

Figure 16.1 *Voting trends 1986–March 1987 by newspaper readership*

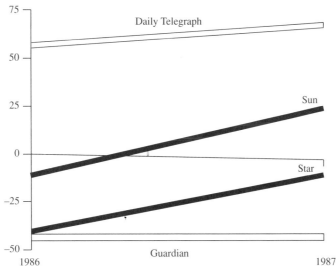

Source: Miller (1990, p. 90).

Bristol NW (Con maj 45)			Bury South (Con maj 788)		
Electorate 72,726	turnout 82.35%		Electorate 65,793	turnout 82.1%	
	Sun	Mirror		Sun	Mirror
Household penetration	34.5%	28.6%	Household penetration	16.6%	32.3%
Readers who voted	20,662	17,128	Readers who voted	8,967	17,444
Paper 'bonus'	2%	0.5%	Paper 'bonus'	2%	0.5%
Extra Tory votes	**413**	**86**	**Extra Tory votes**	**179**	**87**
Corby (Con maj 342)			Southampton Test (Con maj 585)		
Electorate 68,333	turnout 82.89%		Electorate 72,932	turnout 77.40%	
	Sun	Mirror		Sun	Mirror
Household penetration	41.1%	31.8%	Household penetration	40.1%	23.7%
Readers who voted	23,280	18,012	Readers who voted	22,636	13,378
Paper 'bonus'	2%	0.5%	Paper 'bonus'	2%	0.5%
Extra Tory votes	**466**	**90**	**Extra Tory votes**	**453**	**67**

The *Sun*'s 'bonus' was a swing to the Tories 2% greater than the national average; but there was a 0.5% 'bonus' even among *Mirror* readers

Sources: Mori, CCN Marketing

Source: *The SundayTimes*, 26 April 1992.

Table 16.2   *The tabloid effect*

The influence of newspapers, tabloids in particular, on voting behaviour in the 1992 General election was examined by Mori. The day following the election the *Sun* headline told readers 'It's the Sun Wot Won It' and some journalists agreed that the claim was largely justified. Poll data indicated that during the last week of the campaign the anti-Kinnock blitz in the Tory tabloids had produced swings to the Conservatives of 4 per cent amongst *Sun* readers, 3 per cent amongst *Daily Express* readers and 2 per cent amongst *Daily Mail* readers. Oddly enough, there had also been a 2.5 per cent swing to the Conservatives amongst readers of the pro-Labour *Mirror* although there had been no last-minute Conservative swing amongst readers of the relatively apolitical *Star*. Although the evidence is far from being conclusive, there is a case that the tabloids determined which candidate was to win,

particularly in the South, on 'bonus' votes produced in the main by the '*Sun* effect'. Table 16.2 speculates on how critical the *Sun* effect may have been in four marginals – if the data are valid, then the tabloid tipped the result to the Conservatives in three of the four constituencies shown.

Summary

The mass media are amongst the most powerful political institutions in society although it is difficult to be precise about the extent of their influence. Some academics see the mass media as free institutions which are part of democracy, whilst others see them as manipulators of public opinion in the interests of the ruling class.

The general population seem to be sceptical about the political content in newspapers but to trust what they see on television. Despite this, recent research suggests that newspapers, particularly the tabloid press, have a greater influence on political behaviour than was previously believed to be the case.

Questions

1. 'The mass media are persistently biased against the working class.' Evaluate this statement.

2. How far and in what ways can the media be used by politicians to project a favourable image?

3. Why do the majority of British newspapers support the Conservative Party? Can this situation be justified?

4. Conduct a 'content analysis' of a tabloid and a broadsheet newspaper, and calculate the percentage of each paper devoted to reporting politics. Devise your own categories (such as the economy, overseas news) and show your results as pie charts or bar graphs together with a brief commentary on your findings.

5. Consider whether 'balanced' political reporting on television undermines or strengthens the influence of a partisan tabloid press.

6. Televising the Commons has had no impact upon British politics. Discuss.

Assignments

1. (i) Which daily tabloid had the greatest percentage of readers supporting the Conservative party in the 1992 General Election? Why do political scientists focus so much attention on the *Sun*, where less than half voted Conservative?

   (ii) Identify the 'Labour' broadsheets from the daily or Sunday press. Comment on the sort of difficulties the trade union

Table 16.3 *How the voters read the election*

					DAILY READERSHIP %					
	Sun	*Mirror*	*Star*	*Mail*	*Express*	*Today*	*Telegraph*	*Guardian*	*Times*	*Independent*	*FT*
Con	45	20	31	65	67	43	72	15	64	25	65
Lab	36	64	54	15	15	32	11	55	16	37	17
LibDem	14	14	12	18	14	23	16	24	19	34	16
Con lead	9	−44	−23	51	52	11	61	-40	48	−12	48

				SUNDAY READERSHIP %					
	News of the World	*Sunday Mirror*	*The People*	*Mail on Sunday*	*Sunday Express*	*Sunday Times*	*Sunday Telegraph*	*Observer*	*Independent on Sunday*
Con	40	22	30	60	66	57	71	19	25
Lab	41	59	52	19	15	18	11	51	40
LibDem	15	16	15	19	15	22	16	26	31
Con lead	−1	−37	−22	41	51	39	60	−32	−15

Source: *The Sunday Times*, 12 April 1992. © Times Newspapers Ltd 1992.

movement might experience if the TUC attempted to publish its own newspaper.

(iii) What evidence does the above table provide for the idea that readers select newspapers which reinforce their own political beliefs?

2. A study conducted by Labour MP, Jack Straw, revealed a sharp decline in the reporting of Parliamentary debates in the quality broadsheet newspapers. He stated that "Until the late 1980s, the broadsheet press devoted substantial space to the straightforward reporting of Parliament ... In the past five years, systematic reporting of debate has all but been abandoned. Between 1933 and 1988, debates took between 400 and 800 lines each day in the **Times,** and between 300 and 700 lines in the **Guardian**. By 1992 coverage was fewer than 100 lines in both papers." Although the **Times** and **Guardian** were singled out for special criticism, he also noted that the **Daily Telegraph** had halved its coverage; he thought Parliament was best reported in the **Independent**.

Jack Straw argued that the decline in reporting Parliament reduces the public's understanding of politics, because political argument is a vital ingredient in democracy. He went as far as saying that "argument lies at the heart of the democratic system." He pointed out how the speeches in the Maastricht debate had changed attitudes on Labour and Conservative backbenches. The more Maastricht was debated, the greater the opposition to economic and monetary union on both sides.

But is Jack Straw right to be so concerned about this development? Others have argued that his point about speeches being at the heart of democracy is a myth. Martin Kettle asked "How many political speeches a year actually matter? I doubt the number exceeds two dozen, and most of them are made at party conferences ... In Parliament, only the Budget speech, and the occasional set piece from the parliamentary party leaders retain any civic interest or importance."

What factors have led to the recent decline in reporting Parliament in newspapers? There are probably two basic causes; firstly, the impact of televising the Commons despite the fact that only snippets of speeches are ever televised; secondly, MPs making greater use of press releases to publicise their arguments rather than relying on speeches made in the Commons.

Discuss the implications of Jack Straw's research in class.

Further reading

Curran, J. and Seaton, J. (1990) *Power Without Responsibility: The Press and Broadcasting in Britain* (London: Routledge).

Glasgow Media Group (1980) *More Bad News* (London: Routledge & Kegan Paul).

Harrison, M. (1985) *TV News: Whose Bias?* Hermitage, Policy Journals.

Miller, W. *et al.* (1990) *How Voters Change* (Oxford: Clarendon).

Whale, J. (1977) *The Politics of the Media* (London: Fontana).

■ *Chapter 17* ■

Politics, the Courts and Redress

This chapter is concerned with the broad question of the relationship between law and politics. It deals in turn with the general functions of law in our society, including types of law and the courts system; and the issue of citizens' rights and redress, with special reference to the procedures and institutions which exist to protect these rights.

■ The Law and Politics

Law and politics are closely related. Three key connections exist:

- at the level of *principle*, the 'language of the law' and its accompanying norms and practices inform political discourse in virtually all its guises;
- at the level of *personnel*, lawyers are to be found occupying important positions in politics and government;
- at the level of *practice*, the courts system provides an orderly method of settling disputes between individuals and between citizens and government.

We examine each of these links in turn.

□ *Principle*

First politics is consistently discussed in terms of law, notably in terms of *rights, obligations and remedies* – for example, of the right of the citizen

to a fair trial, of the obligation of the government to provide an education service under a particular Act of Parliament and of the remedies available to citizens in cases where their rights are infringed. Above all, politics is constantly discussed in terms of the *principle* of the rule of law. We last encountered this concept in Chapter 6 and will return to it shortly (below pp. 322–3).

□ *Personnel*

Legal personnel are strongly represented in politics. Lawyers formed one-eighth of the House of Commons in the 1992 Parliament and five of the twenty members of the 1992 Cabinet had legal qualifications. The **Lord Chancellor** is a Cabinet minister; heads an important office of state; presides over the House of Lords in its legislative and deliberative capacities; can sit as a judge; and appoints other judges. In other words, he is a practising politician as well as being the nation's senior judge and head of the legal profession. His Department has a £500 million budget. The **Attorney-General** and the **Solicitor-General** as well as the Scottish law officers are also members of the government. There are other important instances of overlap between political and legal personnel. Judges – generally considered to be politically impartial – are often used to head inquiries into politically sensitive events, e.g. the inquiries headed by Lord Justice Taylor into the Hillsborough football stadium disaster in 1989 and Lord Justice Woolf into the prison system in 1991. Finally, politics and the law mingle in the institution of the House of Lords, which draws a number of its members from the law (the Law lords) and which combines the major constitutional roles of upper House of Parliament and supreme court of appeal.

□ *Practice*

The role of the legal system is to provide an orderly method of settling disputes between citizens and between citizens and the state. Broadly speaking, the **criminal law** provides standards of conduct as well as machinery (police, courts system) for dealing with those who commit crimes. Crimes are normally classified as *(i)* against the state (treason, public order), *(ii)* against the person (murder, assault, rape) and *(iii)* against property (robbery, malicious damage). **Civil law** is concerned with the legal relations between persons. Normally, proceedings in a civil court depend upon a plaintiff pursuing an action against a defendant and they generally result in some 'remedy', such as damages, specific performance (where the defendant has to keep his side of the bargain), or a 'declaration' of the plaintiff's legal rights. Cases in criminal law have to be proved 'beyond reasonable doubt'; actions in civil law are decided on the 'balance of probabilities'. In general, and for the most part, a clear-cut distinction exists between civil and criminal law, but they may on occasion overlap, as, for example, where a private person initiates criminal proceedings, or the state takes action in the civil courts, or where someone is sued privately for damages and also prosecuted in the criminal courts, or, where a court has jurisdiction (as magistrates' courts have) in both civil and criminal matters.

    Administrative law, as H.W.R. Wade has stated, is 'the body of general principles which govern the exercise of powers and duties by public authorities' (Wade, 1988). This is the sphere of law which has undergone prodigious expansion in the twentieth century as the state through legislation has intervened in aspects of social life hitherto untouched. Administrative law is concerned with the legal restraints which surround the activities of those who apply policy decisions. It is a key example of the interconnectedness of politics and law, with a variety of judicial and quasi-judicial institutions (the ordinary courts, tribunals, the ombudsman) supplying and applying a framework of rules within which public authorities act. It is centrally involved in the question of citizen rights and redress of grievances.

▎ Civil Rights and the Redress of Grievances

The hallmark of a liberal democratic state, it is often said, is the effectiveness with which a range of basic citizen rights or civil liberties are guaranteed. These rights or liberties have long been enthusiastically extolled by British people and it is vital, therefore, to examine to what extent this confidence in the security of such rights is justified. Three points provide a context for this discussion:

- Virtually all British civil liberties stem from a fundamental principle: that people may do what they like so long as no law prevents them.
- Legal protections against infringements of this fundamental freedom in specific instances (e.g. freedom of expression, meeting, association and so on) have been established gradually throughout history and are not enshrined in any particular statute (whether they *should be* is considered later in the chapter).
- The question of citizen rights or liberties has both a positive and negative aspect: the right to do certain things *and* the right *not* to have certain things done to you.

Exhibit 17.1 is concerned with the civil rights enshrined in the principle of classical liberal theory, rights which have achieved gradual realisation, largely over the past two centuries.

Exhibit 17.1	***Civil liberties in the United Kingdom***

Freedoms/Rights	*Comments*
● **Political rights** Include right to vote in periodic elections, at local and national level (peers, prisoners, aliens and mental patients excluded).	Guaranteed by *Representation of the People Acts* (1918, 1928, 1948 and, the most recent, 1969, which lowered the franchise to 18).
● *Freedom of movement* Includes right to move freely within one's own country, to leave it; and not to be deprived of one's nationality.	Home Secretary has power to detain suspected terrorists under *Prevention of Terrorism Act* (1984) and confine them to British mainland or Northern Ireland.
● **Personal freedom** Includes freedom from police detention without charge, i.e. right to be brought promptly before a judge or court; freedom from police searches of home without warrant; right to a fair trial including assumption of innocence until proved guilty; freedom from torture or coercion by the state.	Protection against wrongful detention first enshrined in Magna Carta (thirteenth century) and Habeas Corpus legislation (seventeenth century). No person may be detained for more than 24 hours without charge or, if a 'serious arrestable offence', for more than 36 hours without charge (*Police and Criminal Evidence Act*, 1984). Exceptions in Northern Ireland, where police abuse of emergency powers has led to unlawful detention and local security forces have committed abuses against detained terrorists; also, in wartime when Defence Secretary (under Defence Regulation 18B) could detain any person he believed hostile to the state. Freedom from police searches of house without a warrant *not* applicable if arrested at one's premises or arrested elsewhere for an arrestable offence.
● **Freedom of conscience** Includes right to practise any religion (freedom of worship); to marry a person of another religion; to withdraw one's children from an Established religion in school; and not to be compelled to undergo military service.	Religious assemblies enjoy legal protection from disturbance.
● **Freedom of expression** Includes individual freedom to seek information and communicate ideas; freedom of the press, publishing houses and the broadcasting media from political censorship; and the absence of State policy and machinery to direct artistic work (theatre, cinema, literature) in accordance with a particular ideology.	Free expression limited by law on treason, sedition, blasphemy, obscenity, libel, insulting words or behaviour, incitement to racial hatred, defamation, contempt of court and parliament and Official Secrets Act; 'D Notice' system imposes constraints on press. No censorship of theatre (since 1968) but some of TV, cinema and videos. *cont. p. 318*

Exhibit 17.1—*continued*	

Freedoms/Rights

Comments

● **Freedom of association and meeting**
Includes the right to meet, process and protest freely; and to associate for political and other purposes.

Again no absolute freedom exists; public meetings are limited by laws on trespass, nuisance, obstruction, and local authority bye-laws; also, by discretion of police (who can re-route or ban a march they consider likely to provoke disorder) and of home secretary (who imposed a temporary ban on all marches in 1980). Whilst there are few restrictions on setting up or joining a trade union, picketing in furtherance of a trade dispute is that of 'first customers' /'first suppliers' (*Employment Act*, 1980).

● **Right to property**
Includes right to hold property, to use it as one will and not to be deprived of it without due process.

Frequently invaded by Parliament in twentieth century in name of nationalisation, compulsory purchase for slum clearance and safeguarding of public health. Right to use as one will also qualified by, e.g., legislation preventing certain forms of transfer or imposing taxation.

● **Right to privacy**
This 'right' not recognised in British law although as a moral norm it is invoked with increasing frequency against what are taken to be state intrusions on the individual by political surveillance, 'bugging', telephone tapping, and so on; also, on behalf of public figures (e.g. royalty) against harassment by the media.

Since no general right exists, privacy has to be protected in practice by specific laws, e.g. against trespass, nuisance, and breach of trust and confidence. Privacy legislation was under consideration by the Conservative Government in 1993.

● **Rights at work**
These include protection from unfair dismissal, the right to a satisfactory environment at work and freedom from racial and sexual discrimination in employment.

These rights have been the subject of recent legislation e.g. the *Employment Protection Act* (1978), which lays down the criteria for fair dismissal; workers may appeal to tribunals against unfair dismissal. The *Race Relations Act* (1976), the *Equal Pay Act* (1970) and the *Sex Discrimination Act* (1975) legislate against various kinds of racial and sexual discrimination, including at work.

● **Social freedoms**
These include the rights to marry and divorce (for men and women equally), to use contraceptive methods, to early abortion and to practise homosexual relations between consenting adults.

Divorce (1969), early abortion on broad social and medical grounds (1967) and homosexuality (1967) have all been the subject of post-war legislation

How are the rights and freedoms set out in Exhibit 17.1 protected? Six distinct areas of judicial and political support may be identified:

- An independent judiciary allied with the principle of judicial review of executive actions;
- A political culture and a public opinion in which the principle of the rule of law is widely understood and zealously guarded;
- The vigilance of members of Parliament in defence of civil liberties;
- The effectiveness of administrative law, and, in particular, the system of administrative tribunals and inquiries;
- The capacity of the ombudsman to investigate and provide remedies for cases of administrative injustice;
- The role of the European Court of Human Rights in assisting British citizens to obtain their rights.

We deal with each in turn, concluding with a consideration of the arguments for and against a British Bill of Rights.

The Independence of the Judiciary and Judicial Review

The independence of the judiciary from political control or influence is a fundamental safeguard of civil freedoms. It is achieved in the UK by a combination of statute, common law, parliamentary rules and the self-restraint of governments – that is, their acceptance of the rule-of-law principle that they should not interfere with the conduct of the courts. The practice of senior judges holding office 'during good behaviour', in fact, dates back to the Act of Settlement, 1701. Since then their conduct has been the subject of complaint in Parliament on less than a score of occasions and only one judge has been dismissed (in 1830). Their salaries are fixed by statute so that annual parliamentary debate is avoided; since 1971 their salaries have been kept under review by the Top Salaries Review Body.

The highest judges are appointed by the Queen on the advice of the prime minister (normally after consultation with the lord chancellor); judges at High Court level and below are appointed by the lord chancellor. Although they are appointed and promoted by or on the advice of politicians, professional rather than political grounds are paramount in their appointment. Judges have a statutory retiring age of 75. They enjoy immunity from civil proceedings for anything said or done while acting in a judicial capacity. It is sometimes said that because judicial independence in the UK is in large part secured by statute, it is illusory. What Parliament has given, Parliament can with equal ease take away. But this is almost certainly to go too far. Whilst the independence – from political pressures – of politically appointed judges sounds paradoxical and is not enshrined in a single written constitutional settlement, it nonetheless possesses a certain validity. Considerable political difficulties would follow any attempt to tamper with judicial independence.

Pressure for a more open, accountable system of appointing judges increased in the early 1990s. The Chairman of the Bar Council, Lord Williams of Mostyn, described the appointments system as 'hidebound by an obsessive secrecy and a degree of amateurism which are simply unacceptable'. Public anxiety had arisen for a number of reasons: the rather perfunctory training received by judges on appointment; their social unrepresentativeness; the comments made by certain judges in cases involving sexual morals; and, in particular, a series of grave miscarriages of justice and the legal system's extreme slowness in correcting these injustices. The handling of the appeal of the Birmingham Six by the Lord Chief Justice, Lord Lane, in 1988 led to a Commons motion for his dismissal signed by 102 MPs from all parties. Lord Williams called for a number of reforms, including the setting up of a Judicial Studies Board, with representatives from the public, solicitors and barristers, to make appointments to the judiciary; the creation of a watchdog body composed of lawyers, judges and laymen, to monitor judges' performance; earlier retirement ages; and a more intensive and structured training for judges.

In the last 30 years, the political role of the courts in scrutinising the actions of government and public officials has become steadily more important. Judges work, of course, within the framework of parliamentary sovereignty. Because Parliament is sovereign, judges cannot strike down legislation as unconstitutional. Nor can they pronounce on its *merits* – that is, they are not justified in substituting what they would have done for what parliament enacted on a given occasion. Nonetheless, a range of remedies exists in the courts for individuals who feel aggrieved by the behaviour of a public authority and a remedy may be sought by means of an application to the High Court for **judicial review**. Certain conditions must be fulfilled for an application to be allowed to proceed: for example, the applicant must begin proceedings without delay (within three months of the grounds for the application arising) and must have sufficient interest ('standing') in the matter to which the application relates. Specific legal remedies are available. Thus, it is possible for a court to quash (*certiorari*) or prevent (*prohibition*) an order or decision; to compel the performance of a public duty (*mandamus*); to restrain the commission or continuance of unlawful conduct (an *injunction*); and simply to clarify the legal position (a *declaration*).

The basic principle followed by the courts in reviewing administrative action is to ensure that public authorities have not exceeded the powers vested in them (normally) by Act of Parliament. The higher courts may also review decisions taken in inferior tribunals – which include lower courts, special tribunals, professional disciplinary bodies and ordinary clubs, unions and associations – to prevent them from exceeding their jurisdiction. The fundamental doctrine invoked by the courts is *ultra vires*, which prevents public servants taking actions for which they have no statutory authority i.e. from acting illegally. When courts consider an administrative action under an enabling statute, they have a regard to whether the power in question was directly authorised by the statute or whether it may be construed as reasonably incidental to it. The action of the Secretary of State for Trade in

the case of Laker Airways was struck down as *ultra vires* because he had exceeded his authority as laid down in the 1971 Civil Aviation Act.

Much legislation confers *discretionary* powers upon public authorities, licensing action on such conditions as if the authority 'thinks fit' or has 'reasonable cause' to believe (a certain situation exists). When reviewing alleged abuse of a discretion, courts will take into consideration the *reasonableness* of the action, restraining actions taken from improper motives or without regard to legal relevance or which are so devoid of logic or accepted moral standards that no reasonable person could have arrived at them. In a case involving the Minister of Agriculture, the Minister was held to have misused his discretion by having regard to irrelevant considerations.

Finally, in reviewing administrative actions, the courts invoke the common law principles of *natural justice*. These are twofold – first, the rule against bias (noone to be a judge in his own cause); and second, the right to a fair hearing (hear the other side). Under the first rule, administrators must not have any direct (including financial) interest in the outcome of proceedings; nor must they be reasonably suspected of being biased or of being likely to be biased. Justice must not only be done but manifestly must be seen to be done.

The right to a fair hearing requires that no one should be penalised in any way without receiving notice of the case to be met and being given a fair chance to answer that case and put one's own case. The action of a Watch Committee in dismissing a Chief Constable without notifying him of the charge or giving him an opportunity to put his case was struck down. Exhibit 17.2 provides examples of the three most important grounds on which judicial review is available, summarised in 1985 by Lord Diplock as 'illegality', 'irrationality' (or 'unreasonableness') and 'procedural impropriety' (de Smith and Brazier, 1990, p. 579).

Judicial review has undergone considerable expansion in recent years. In 1980, there were 525 applications for review of administrative decisions by the courts; in 1984 there were 918; and in 1991 there were 2089. There has also been

Exhibit 17.2   *Review of administrative action by the courts*

Laker Airways Ltd v. Department of Trade (1977)

At issue Freddie Laker obtained a licence from the Civil Aviation Authority (CAA) in 1972 to operate his Skytrain on the transatlantic route. However, in 1975 the Secretary of State for Trade directed the CAA that British Airways were to retain a monopoly on scheduled transatlantic routes and Skytrain's licence was withdrawn. Laker appealed.

The decision The High Court found that the Secretary of State's action was *ultra vires (a)* because he was statutorily authorised (by the Civil Aviation Act, 1971) only to guide and not to direct the Civil Aviation Authority; and *(b)* because his advice was contrary to the criteria laid down in the Act for the licensing of air services by the CAA, which included the principle that British Airways should not have a monopoly on any route.

Result The court held that the Secretary of State had acted unlawfully. Laker Airways accordingly won their action and hence their right to compete on the transatlantic route.

Padfield v. Minister of Agriculture (1968)

At issue South-east milk producers complained to the Minister of Agriculture that the prices paid by the Milk Marketing Board were too low and requested him to refer the question to a committee of investigation. The Minister refused to do so, giving his reasons, which included the political difficulties which would ensue if the committee found against him and he were forced to implement its report.

The decision The House of Lords held that the Minister had allowed irrelevant considerations to weigh with him and had failed to promote the purposes of the Act establishing the milk marketing scheme. An order of *mandamus* was issued directing the Minister to consider the complainants' case. The Minister was held to have *misused his discretion*.

Result The Minister appointed a committee, whose report in favour of the south-east milk producers was subsequently rejected by the Minister.
However, the important principle established was the subjection of executive discretion to review by the courts and their identification and remedy of misuse of administrative power.

Ridge v. Baldwin (1964)

At issue The Chief Constable of Brighton, who by statute could only be removed on the grounds of neglect of duty or inability, was dismissed by the Watch Committee without a hearing.

The decision The House of Lords held that the Watch Committee's act was invalid. In dismissing the Chief Constable (a) without prior notification of the charge and (b) without giving him the opportunity to put his case, it had failed to observe *natural justice* (hear the other side). It had not given the Chief Constable a fair hearing.

Results A very important decision: hitherto, the courts had limited the application of the rules of natural justice to authorities acting in a *judicial* or *quasi-judicial* capacity; thereafter, the courts were prepared to extend the application of the rules of natural justice to any *administrative* authority whose decisions affected people's rights or legitimate expectations.

an extension of the legal criteria judges are prepared to consider in helping them decide the legality of a particular decision. Before *Pepper v. Hart* (1992), the courts – for whatever reason – had observed a self-limiting rule not to refer to the records of parliamentary debates in *Hansard* in order to clarify the meaning of an ambiguous statute, but in this case reference was made to a parliamentary debate to establish the meaning of legislation (Loveland, 1993).

In certain respects, however, judicial review can be restricted. First, it can be subject to statutory exclusion by some such wordings as 'The decision of X shall not be called into question in any court of law'. This type of exclusion is less common today, however, than the restriction of judicial review to *a limited period of time*. Second, the courts themselves in particular types of case – for example, those touching on national security – have imposed strict limitations on their own power to scrutinise executive action.

Support for the Rule of Law in Political Culture and Public Opinion

A second main support for civil liberties is well-established public support for the rule of law. It is important as a norm constraining the behaviour of authorities and guiding the expectations of citizens. To a considerable extent, it is institutionalised in the procedures and practices of the legal, political and constitutional systems.

The modern principle of the rule of law owes much to the nineteenth century lawyer, A.V. Dicey, who remains important because he stated well two of its cardinal principles (indicated below). A modern definition, however, needs to go further than Dicey for a number of reasons. First, Dicey saw the judge-made common law as the foundation of individual liberties: the twentieth century has revealed the extent to which these can be undermined by a sovereign Parliament which has conferred arbitrary powers on governments in war-time and in emergencies. Second, Dicey distrusted what he called

'administrative law' as savouring of Continental systems of law which gave a privileged position to state officials; however, under the aegis of the welfare state, vast new empires of administrative power have been established. The modern problem is neither to dismiss, ignore nor keep administrative law at arm's length but rather, to infuse into 'the administrative powers of the state . . . the legal ideals of fair procedure and just decision' (Wade, 1977). Even though the rule of law guidelines need to be more extensive than in Dicey's day, however, and their coverage wider, the *point* of producing such a list remains the same: to provide a constant witness of legal ideals for both public and practitioners.

These are the main principles, then (Dicey's formulations indicated):

- **All persons are equal before the law:** in more detail, people of any class, race or gender are universally subject to one law administered in the ordinary courts and there is no distinction in law between ordinary citizens and servants of the state (Dicey).
- **No one is punishable except for a breach of the law:** the laws are published and publicly accessible – that is, they are known or can be discovered (Dicey); and they are enforced through independent courts.
- **The powers held by the authorities must be conferred by law (i.e. by Parliament) and exercised according to authorised procedures:** in particular, powers conferred by Parliament must be defined and exercised within strict limits – by a combination of administrators' self-restraint and the vigilance of the courts.
- **Certain basic standards of justice should permeate the law:** natural justice (the right to a fair hearing, the rule against bias) should inform procedures wherever people's rights and legitimate expectations are under consideration; since rights depend upon remedies, remedies should be available against those who exceed and abuse discretionary authority.
- **Redress – i.e. legal remedies for wrongs – should be available to all citizens against any other citizen no matter how powerful and against officers of the State.**

As the *British Social Attitudes* survey has shown, there is widespread support in Britain both for the rule of law and for individual rights. Society, it has been argued, is becoming more 'rights-conscious' in the two senses of increasing awareness of rights and greater willingness to protect them through the political system (Norton, 1993, p. 150). Having noted strong support for freedom of speech and assembly in British political culture, Anthony Heath and Richard Topf conclude: 'Protecting freedom of speech and assembly can be seen as part of that "sturdy independence"... which makes up the "active" component of the civic culture. Such evidence as we have suggests that this sturdy independence is increasing'. (Jowell *et al.* (eds) 1987, p. 58).

Members of Parliament as Defenders of Civil Liberties

According to traditional constitutional theory, MPs occupy a prominent role in the defence of civil liberties. The rights of citizens, so the theory goes, are protected in two ways: first, by means of ministerial accountability to Parliament; second, through the case-work of members on behalf of their constituents. Few now consider this theory to be valid. For whilst Parliament remains the central forum for scrutiny of the actions of the executive (see Chapter 12), it is equally clearly no longer the mechanism (if indeed it ever was) through which aggrieved individuals can pursue remedies for perceived injustices. Basically, this is because the limit of an MP's influence on behalf of a constituent is the limit of the power of public opinion – or the threat of it – to compel. Whilst effective on occasion, this system is unsound as a *general* enforcer of executive respect for civil rights simply because, faced by an obstinate minister, an MP lacks the capacity either to insist on a revelation of the facts or to compel any form of restitution if it can be shown that a constituent has suffered an injustice. The system is arbitrary in its dependence on the investigative skill and persistence of MPs and on the voluntary willingness of Departments or other executive

agencies to make amends where faults have occurred. In short, even though parliamentarians may play a valuable role in first airing an individual problem or grievance, this method of defending civil liberties lacks both universal reliability and certain remedies.

☐ Administrative Law

Administrative Tribunals

Tribunals are a very important part of the British system of administrative justice. They are normally established by legislation and cover a wide range of functions, many of them in the field of welfare. Thus, there are tribunals for national insurance, pensions, housing, education, the National Health Service (NHS) and immigration. Claims arising out of injuries at work, industrial disputes, unfair dismissal and redundancy are dealt with by industrial tribunals. Tribunals are usually composed of a chairman with legal qualifications (often a solicitor) and two lay-members representing interests related to the concerns of the particular tribunal. They are independent and not subject to political or administrative interference from the Departments under whose aegis they usually work. Their functions may be described as quasi-judicial: to hear appeals against initial decisions of government agencies or, sometimes, disputes between individuals and organisations. Their role is to establish the facts of each case and then apply the relevant legal rules to it, i.e. in the majority of instances to decide what the statutory rights and entitlements of the aggrieved actually are. Except where the parties request privacy, tribunals hear cases in public. They provide simpler, cheaper, speedier, more expert and more accessible justice than the ordinary courts in their specific sphere of responsibility. It is possible to appeal against their decisions – normally to a superior court, tribunal or a minister. For a small number of tribunals, however, including the National Health Service Tribunal, the Social Security Commissioners and the Immigration Appeal Tribunal, no appeal is available.

The mode of operation of tribunals is determined by the Tribunals and Inquiries Act, 1971. Under this Act, a Council on Tribunals has the functions of reporting on the tribunals under its supervision (to the lord chancellor and secretary of state for Scotland, and ultimately to Parliament); of hearing and investigating complaints against tribunals for members of the public; and of being consulted by the responsible minister before procedural rules for tribunals and inquiries are made. A second important provision of the Act concerns the giving of reasons for tribunals' decisions, another matter supervised by the Council on Tribunals. Most of the tribunals listed in the first schedule of the Act are required to supply oral or written reasons for their decisions (unless exempted by order of the chancellor after consultation with the Council). But tribunals are only required to give reasons if requested and are not obliged to inform the parties of their right to request them.

The general trend of the last quarter of a century has been towards making the procedure of tribunals more judicial, but without forfeiting the advantages of tribunals over ordinary courts. These are greater informality, specialisation, capacity to conduct their own investigations and flexibility in terms of the formulation of reasonable standards in their own spheres. The Franks Committee on Administrative Tribunals and Inquiries, 1957 recommended that tribunals move towards 'greater openness, fairness and impartiality'. Proceedings should be held in public and reasons for decisions should be given; the parties before tribunals should know in advance the case they had to meet, should have the chance to put their own case either personally or through representatives, and should be able to appeal against decisions; finally, proceedings should not only be impartial, through stronger safeguards regulating their composition, but also be seen to be impartial by no longer being held on the premises of Government Departments. Under the supervision (since 1958) of the Council of Tribunals, the procedures of administrative tribunals have become both more uniform and more fair in many of the ways recommended by Franks, such as proper notice of hearings and of

the case to be answered, rights to appeal and legal representation at hearings. Outstanding problems in the system relate primarily, although not solely, to the lack of appeal from certain tribunals (already noted); its limited extension (not all tribunals are included); and the particular condition (on request only) of the obligation to give reasons even if, in practice, tribunals do provide reasons.

Statutory Inquiries

The standard method for giving a hearing to objectors to a Government proposal is the **statutory inquiry**. Virtually all legislation concerned with planning and land use makes provision for holding an inquiry. Most often, inquiries arise about new towns, housing, town and country planning, road, aviation and other transport developments, agriculture and health. Inquiries are usually held, then, within the context of government policy: notable examples are individual appeals against a compulsory purchase order for the acquisition of land for a specific purpose or against the refusal of planning permission by a local authority. Procedure before, during and after the inquiry is regulated by rules laid down by the Tribunals and Inquiries Act, 1971. Decisions of inquiries may be challenged either on the grounds of procedure or the substance of the decision in the High Court within six weeks of the decision. Whilst affected third parties in land-use cases do not have legally enforceable rights, legislation governing planning usually protects their interests to a certain degree. Proposals have to be adequately publicised, for instance, and third parties have to be afforded the opportunity to state their cases before decisions are taken.

Whilst realising the need not to impose unnecessary delays on inquiry procedure, the courts in hearing appeals from inquiry decisions have sought to safeguard the rights of the public. For example, they have ruled that objectors at an inquiry should be able to take 'an active, intelligent and informed part in the decision-making process' (1977) and that they must be given 'a fair crack of the whip' (1976) in putting their case. The courts have received important support in this regard from the Council on Tribunals which not only raises specific questions relating to inquiries with the chancellor but also (as with tribunals) reports on their working, has the right to be consulted before procedural rules are made for them, and receives public complaints about them. How successful the courts and Council had been in bolstering the inquiry system as a bastion of democracy became a matter of increasing controversy, however, during the 1980s mainly as a result of disquiet about government handling of issues arising out of its proposals for the management of nuclear waste. Keen to avoid the delays and furore surrounding the 340-day Inquiry into the Sizewell-B Nuclear Reactor (1985), the Government in late 1985 proposed to limit the terms of reference to the Inquiry relating to the Dounreay Fast-Breeder Reactor to the question of where to dump the waste rather than to allow the Inquiry to enter the debate about whether to dump or, as its critics preferred, store it. In 1994, after the Government had given the go-ahead to the Thorp nuclear re-processing plant, the High Court rejected an attempt by environmentalists to force a public inquiry.

☐ *The Ombudsman*

As well as legal rights, citizens have a more general right to a good standard of administration. Despite difficulties of precise definition, this right is still a significant element in administrative justice. In 1967, after rising public concern that traditional parliamentary channels were inadequate to protect the citizen against administrative abuse by government departments and agencies, the Parliamentary Commissioner for Administration (ombudsman) was established by Act of Parliament. His brief is to investigate and, if possible, remedy complaints by individuals and corporate bodies who feel that they have experienced 'injustice in consequence of maladministration' at the hands of central government.

Appointed by the Crown on the advice of the lord chancellor, the ombudsman enjoys an independent status similar to that of a high court judge. His salary is fixed by statute and charged on the Consolidated Fund; he holds office 'during good behaviour' and can be removed on addresses from both Houses of Parliament. He has a staff of about fifty-five, largely drawn from the civil service. During his investigations, which are conducted in private, he can call for the relevant files of the Department concerned; as a matter of course, he informs the head of Department, and any civil servant involved, of his investigation. He possesses the powers to investigate a matter thoroughly: he can administer oaths and compel the attendance of witnesses as well as the presence of documents. His brief covers maladministration which can embrace a wide range of faults: as de Smith and Brazier put it

> corruption, bias, unfair discrimination, harshness, misleading a member of the public as to his rights, failing to notify him properly of his rights or to explain the reasons for a decision, general high-handedness, using powers for a wrong purpose, failing to consider relevant materials, taking irrelevant material into account, losing or failing to reply to correspondence, delaying unreasonably before making a tax refund or presenting a tax demand or dealing with an application for a grant or license, and so on. (de Smith and Brazier, 1990, p. 649)

Complainants have no right of direct access to the Parliamentary Commissioner for Administration (PCA) but must approach him through an MP. Nonetheless, most people do complain directly to him (he received over 1000 direct complaints in 1990) and these he offers to refer to an MP if the complainant wishes. In 1991, over 800 complaints were referred to the Ombudsman by MPs but only about one-quarter of these were accepted for investigation. All told, administration leading to injustice is found in about 10 per cent of cases referred (Table 17.1).

The PCA issues a report on each investigation to the referring MP, with a copy to the Department involved. Where maladministration is found, a Department will be expected to correct it – e.g. by issuing an apology or financial recompense to the aggrieved person – but the Ombudsman has no power to compel it to do so. Where, as occasionally happens, the Department refuses to correct an injustice, the PCA may first bring pressure to bear on it by means of the Commons Select Committee on the PCA, and if this fails, he can lay a Special Report pointing out the unresolved injustice before both Houses of Parliament.

Initially limited to the investigation of maladministration in central government, the ombudsman system was later enlarged by the addition of ombudsmen for Northern Ireland (1969), the National Health Service (1973), and Local Government in England and Wales (1974) and Scotland (1976). No ombudsman was established for the police. Unlike the position with regard to the PCA, direct access to these Ombudsmen is allowed (in the case of local government, only since 1988), and both the health and the local government commissioners receive a much larger volume of complaints than the PCA (Table 17.1). As with the PCA, however, neither local nor health commissioners have any enforcement powers, although in Northern Ireland, a complainant does have legal redress where a legitimate grievance is found, being able to apply to the county court for an appropriate remedy. If a local authority in mainland Britain chooses not to comply with an adverse report by a local ombudsman after various efforts (report, informal meeting with senior officers and councillors, further report) have been made to persuade it, the Ombudsman can require it to publicise the reasons for non-compliance. (Thompson, 1993, pp. 19–20).

The ombudsmen have made a less dramatic impact on British public administration than their early advocates hoped. There are many areas excluded from the jurisdiction of the PCA – government contractual and commercial transactions, for example. The public have no direct access to the PCA and for this and other reasons such as lack of public awareness of his existence, rather a small number of complaints actually reach him. The only powers of the ombudsmen against a recalcitrant public authority are those of publicity. Even where cases of maladministration leading to injustice are found, the complainant

	1976	1991
Complaints to the Parliamentary Commissioner for Administration		
Received during the year	815	801
Dealt with during the year		
Rejected	505	580
Discontinued after partial investigation	29	6
Reported upon Maladministration leading to injustice found	139	87
Total dealt with during the year	863	769
Complaints to the Health Commissioner		
Received during the year	582	1 176
Dealt with during the year		
Rejected	413	987
Discontinued after partial investigation	13	24
Reported upon Containing failures in service/ maladministration leading to injustice found	61	243
Total dealt with during the year	546	1 142
Complaints to the Commissioners for Local Administration		
Received during the year	1 335	14 057
Dealt with during the year		
Rejected/discontinued after partial investigation	772	11 976
Reported upon Maladministration leading to injustice found	143	330
Total dealt with during the year	1 057	12 392

Source: Extracted from *Social Trends* (1993, p. 160).

Table 17.1   *Complaints to ombudsmen*

has no legal remedy available (except in Northern Ireland).

On the other hand, the ombudsmen *have* been more – sometimes much more – than 'ombudsmice'. Most of their recommendations, in fact, are accepted and implemented by the Departments and authorities concerned.

On occasion even, the PCA has achieved considerable success. One of the best-known successes occurred over the famous **Sachsenhausen case** (1967) when the PCA found that the Foreign Office (FO) was responsible for procedural maladministration in its handling of an application by former prisoners of war for compensation for their sufferings in a Nazi prisoner-of-war camp, and the FO paid compensation.

A more recent case was the PCA's discovery of significant maladministration leading to injustice in five areas of the Department of Trade and Industry's handling of the Barlow Clowes investment group when the Government, without accepting the finding of maladministration, agreed to pay huge compensation to aggrieved investors (1989). But these are exceptional cases. More usually, after a report by the PCA, a Department simply rescinds a decision or, in the case of the Inland Revenue, modifies a tax claim in the interest of the aggrieved.

The European Court of Human Rights

The European Court of Human Rights has played an important part in upholding and enlarging civil liberties in Britain since 1965. It does so in a somewhat roundabout way which nonetheless deserves careful attention. The United Kingdom ratified the European Convention on Human Rights in 1951 (Exhibit 17.4). Although these are not legal rights in Britain and therefore not enforceable in British law, they have turned out to be an important influence on civil rights. British Courts can take note of the convention and presume Parliament did not intend to legislate inconsistently with it. Moreover, the UK Government normally complies with judgements of the European Court. However, these rights are not enforceable in British Law because, although Britain renews its ratification of the Convention every year, unlike the other countries who have

Figure 17.1   *Referrals to and judgements of European Court of Human Rights to September 1991–The six worst offenders*

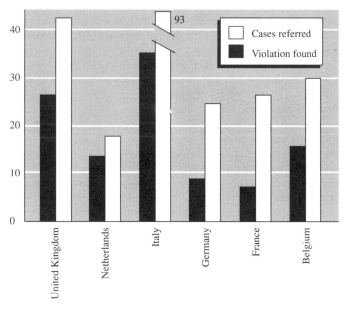

Source: Adapted from *The Guardian,* 24 September 1991.

signed the document, *it has never incorporated the Convention into British law*. Hence, British citizens cannot use the Convention to appeal to British courts when their rights are infringed. They can appeal to the European Court, but only after they have tried and failed to find remedies in the British courts. Complaints go to the *European Commission* at Strasbourg in the first instance. The Commission then decides whether the case is 'admissible' to the European Court; normally cases go before the Court only after the Commission has first failed to achieve a friendly settlement between the parties concerned. Every year the Commission opens about 800 provisional files on complaints by British citizens – more than from any other country. Of these, a small number are declared 'admissible'. If 'admissible', cases are registered and in 1986, about one-quarter (140 out of 533) of registered cases were from the UK.

In all, the Court pronounced on 96 cases between 1955 and 1985; 14 of these were from the UK, and of these judgments all except two went against the British Government. The other 17 member states which permit individual petitions had had 39 violations recorded against them.

Exhibit 17.3 gives some major examples of cases in which the 'rights' of British citizens have been upheld by the European Court. No other signatory state except Italy has lost so many cases before the European Court as the United Kingdom (Figure 17.1). The decisions of the European Court are not, strictly speaking, enforceable in the United Kingdom. But the UK Government, like other countries which have signed the Convention, has agreed to respect the decisions made by the Court and, in practice, its verdicts are observed, normally by changing British law accordingly.

Exhibit 17.3　European Court *decisions bearing on the rights of British citizens*

The European Court:

- has criticised treatment of suspected terrorists interned in Northern Ireland by the UK Government;
- allowed prisoners their right to correspond with their lawyers, MPs and the newspapers;
- condemned corporal punishment in schools;
- ruled against inhuman conditions in solitary confinement;
- criticised undue interference with a free press in the *Sunday Times* thalidomide case against Distillers:
- upheld the rights of workers against closed shops;
- condemned as inadequate the review procedure for life-sentence prisoners recalled after release;
- declared British immigration rules to be unlawful because they discriminated against women; the rules allowed foreign men with full residency rights in the UK to bring in their wives or fiancees, but did not allow women with residency rights to bring in their husbands;
- criticised the ineffective judicial protection of a detained mental patient; it ruled that *habeas corpus* provided inadequate redress against wrongful confinement in this instance;
- condemned the legal ban obtained by the government on press disclosure of documents used in evidence in court;
- ruled that a group of shareholders in shipbuilding and aircraft companies nationalised in 1977 had been inadequately compensated;
- ruled that the UK Government's ban on three British newspapers for disclosing evidence of M15 wrong-doing contained in *Spycatcher* was invalid because the book had already been published in the USA.

Exhibit 17.4		*Rights under the European Convention on Human Rights and its Protocols*

Convention

Article	2	Right to life
"	3	Freedom from torture or inhuman or degrading treatment or punishment
"	4	Freedom from slavery or forced labour
"	5	Right to liberty and security of person
"	6	Right to a fair trial by an impartial tribunal
"	7	Freedom from retroactive criminal laws
"	8	Right to respect for private and family life, home and correspondence
"	9	Freedom of thought, conscience and religion
"	10	Freedom of expression
"	11	Freedom of peaceful assembly and association, including the right to join a trade union
"	12	Right to marry and found a family
"	13	Right to an effective remedy before a national authority
"	14	Freedom from discrimination

Protocol No. 1

Article	1	Right to peaceful enjoyment of possessions
"	2	Right to education. Parental right to the education of their children in conformity with their religious and philosophical convictions must be respected.
"	3	Right to take part in free elections by secret ballot.

Protocol No. 4

Article	1	Freedom from imprisonment for debt
"	2	Freedom of movement of persons
"	3	Right to enter and remain in one's own country
"	4	Freedom from collective expulsion

The situation is by no means ideal. The Strasbourg Court will hear a case only if domestic attempts to find a settlement are exhausted; no legal aid is available; and the Court takes a long time to reach its judgments – it now takes an average of five years for a case to move through the entire process. Nonetheless, the Court has bolstered the rights of prisoners, immigrants, women, mental patients, journalists, expropriated shareholders and workers who may not want to join a union in as effective a way as circumstances allow. It is in order to render such protection even more effective that many concerned about the state of civil liberties in the UK call for a British Bill of Rights.

■ A Bill of Rights for Britain?

No single document enumerating the rights of the citizen exists in the United Kingdom. This absence of a single written code does not mean that the individual lacks civil rights. These rights and the way they are secured – in general by a mixture of common and statute law – are set out in Exhibit 17.1. However, over the past two decades many have come to doubt whether civil liberties in Britain are sufficiently secure. These doubts have surfaced for a number of reasons. The primary reason is the growth of concern about the capacity of **Parliament** to protect individual liberties either positively by espousing the causes of aggrieved citizens or negatively by not actually invading individual rights. How many MPs see one of their major roles as that of serving as a one-person ombudsman or, assuming they do, have the time, energy, capacity and resources for such a role? Again, Parliament – by means of legislation pushed through by the governing party with the aid of its majority – may invade civil liberties as much as protect them. The clamour for a Bill of Rights first surfaced in the 1970s, being raised by Conservatives who saw Labour legislation as a threat, especially legislation on trade unions and nationalisation. However, Labour could with equal legitimacy point to the Conservatives' use of the Official Secrets Act in the 1980s in a number of instances as invasions of individual rights. Again, **judicial review** of administrators' discretionary powers and the work of the **Ombudsman** are only encouraging up to a point. Gaps in the protection of civil liberties include:

- the difficulty of challenging Ministerial discretionary powers in the courts on the grounds of *ultra vires* because of the broad subjective way in which such powers are framed;
- the difficulty of protecting certain kinds of rights (e.g. to supplementary benefits) in the courts because of problems over interpreting individual need;
- the fact that challenge of administrative decisions depends on reasons being given yet the statutory obligation upon administrators to give reasons is far from universal;
- the failure of the courts to develop damages as a remedy for unlawful administrative action.

One critic, Lord Scarman, has pointed to the inability of the common law – i.e. the ordinary courts – to guarantee rights and liberties in four key areas: *(i)* welfare; *(ii)* the environment; *(iii)* industrial relations; and *(iv)* Britain's international obligations under the European Convention.

In addition, civil libertarians have expressed concern about the way in which individual liberties in Britain have been eroded by a combination of Government legislation and legal judgements during the 1980s. Two authors writing in 1990 concluded that 'civil liberties in Britain are in a state of crisis. We have charted the unprecedented extension of police powers; a far-reaching statute for the interception of communications by the state; wide-ranging restrictions on the freedom of assembly and public protest; the growth of a national security consciousness used to justify major limitations on press freedom in particular; the extension of the powers of the security service and the lack of any effective accountability for the way these powers are exercised; and, finally, the assumption of quite extraordinary powers to deal with the north of Ireland, admittedly an issue of immense complexity' (Ewing and Gearty, 1990, p. 255). These writers do not see the remedy as lying in a Bill of Rights but rather as in the development of a more democratic culture. But many individuals and groups do advocate one, including the Liberal Democrats, some Labour and Conservative MPs, Charter 88, Liberty, the Institute for Public Policy Research, and several leading judges, including Lord Chief Justice Taylor. Their arguments, together with those of their opponents, are set out in Exhibit 17.5.

There are three ways of enacting a Bill of Rights:

1. By drawing up a list of individual rights and providing for their constitutional entrenchment by an Act of Parliament. The courts would have the authority to strike down any subsequent Act of Parliament or administrative action which conflicted with it. This way of proceeding would destroy parliamentary sovereignty since, once enacted, the Bill of Rights would take precedence over all subsequent legislation and would in all cases have to be upheld by the courts.
2. (A modified form of 1, preserving parliamentary sovereignty.) Legislation could enact a Bill of Rights which the courts would uphold unless otherwise directed by parliament, and which would remain in place until amended or even superseded by subsequent rights legislation.

The first has the merit of greater security for rights at the expense of parliamentary sovereignty as

Exhibit 17.5   *A British Bill of Rights: for and against*

For	*Against*
• Greater clarity: a code would make clear governmental responsibilities, enable citizens to know their rights more easily and provide courts with a well-defined set of freedoms to protect.	Difficulty of defining rights *(a)* socialists and most liberals would include social and economic rights, Conservatives seek to limit to civil and political rights; *(b)* If social and economic rights are included, these are likely to fluctuate, e.g. Labour in 1970s legislated in favour of closed shop, Conservatives in 1980s against it.
• Courts superior to parliament at protecting civil rights: (a) courts are independent of the Government not aspiring to be part of it, like MPs; (b) a Bill of Rights would make available to British citizens civil rights which at present have to be sought at the European Court, but more speedily and cheaply; (c) A Code of rights would have a moral force lacking in present law, and thereby be harder to flout by, for example, government or big interest groups.	Courts *not* better than parliament at protecting civil rights: (a) unlike MPs, judges unelected and unaccountable, and have undeclared rather than explicit political biases; (b) certain issues – e.g. race relations, industrial relations, press freedoms, privacy, police powers and national security – *are* inherently political and therefore need to be decided openly by politicians, not covertly by judges; (c) Judges might interpret rights narrowly, whittle them down rather than guarantee them; anyway, unwise to *politicize* judges.
• Bill of Rights backed by courts works well in other countries, e.g. USA, where Supreme Court judgement against racial segregation (1954) played key part in eventually gaining civil rights for the black minority.	Institutions do not necessarily transplant well, e.g. US Bill of Rights works in context of very different separation of powers system. British system is based on parliamentary sovereignty – better to reform rather than transform it, e.g. by extending powers of Ombudsman, restricting coverage of Official Secrets Act, increasing investigative powers of MPs, introducing freedom of information. Under parliamentary sovereignty, a Bill of Rights (or part of it) could be overturned by a later parliament.
• Educational value of Bill of Rights; great need in Britain is for understanding of rights to be well-grounded in political culture, and this would be facilitated by a specific code.	Nothing in present situation regarding rights to prevent spread of understanding of them. Rights well-supported in political culture.
• Bill of Rights can be *extended* according to changing circumstances by addition of Protocols e.g. European Convention on Human Rights.	Bill of Rights inflexible because contain social values at the time of their enactment.

well as a certain rigidity; with the second, rights are rather less secure but parliamentary sovereignty as well as a greater flexibility remains.

3. By incorporating the European Convention on Human Rights into British law. This would give Britons the right to seek redress in British courts against infringements of their liberties as set out in that code.

Two attempts in the mid-1980s to legislate a British Bill of Rights both took this form, Lord Broxbourne's Human Rights and Fundamental Freedoms Bill in 1985; and Sir Edward Gardner's bill in 1987.

Summary

Law underpins politics in various ways, two very important ones being the provision of guiding principles such as the rule of law and of a courts system for the orderly settlement of disputes, including disputes between the citizen and the state.

Administrative law regulates the behaviour of public authorities and is of central concern in considering citizen rights and redress of grievances.

Civil liberties, which are extensive in Britain, derive from, and are limited by a complex variety of procedures and laws largely emanating from statute and common law, but not from a single written document. Protected by a number of political and judicial methods with varying degrees of adequacy, civil rights came to seem less secure in recent decades than formerly.

In circumstances in which British citizens often and successfully appealed to the European Court of Human Rights, a significant body of opinion advocated a Bill of Rights for Britain; however, there are difficulties as well as potential benefits in this course.

Questions

1. Discuss the effectiveness of the various methods of protecting individual rights in Britain.

2. What do you understand by the 'rule of law'?

Assignment

State the case for and against a Bill of Rights in Britain.

Further reading

Cumper, P. (1991) 'Human Rights in Europe', *Talking Politics*, 4:1, autumn.

Davis, H. (1993) 'The Political Role of the Courts', *Talking Politics*, 6: 1, autumn.

de Smith, S. and Brazier, R. (1990) *Constitutional and Administrative Law*, 6th edn (London, Penguin) Parts 4–6 especially.

Ewing, K.D. and Gearty, C. (1990) *Freedom under Thatcher: Civil Liberties in Modern Britain* (Oxford: Clarendon).

Griffith, J.A.G. (1991) *The Politics of the Judiciary*, 4th edn (London: Fontana).

Loveland, I. (1993) 'Redefining Parliamentary Sovereignty? A New Perspective on the Search for the Meaning of Law', *Parliamentary Affairs*, 46:3, July.

Marshall, G. (1984) *Constitutional Conventions* (Oxford: Clarendon).

Norton, P. (1993) 'A Bill of Rights: The Case Against', *Talking Politics*, 5: 3, summer.

Oliver, D. (1993) 'Citizenship in the 1990s', *Politics Review*, 3: 1, September.

Savage, S. (1992) 'The Judiciary: Justice with Accountability?', in B. Jones and L. Robins (eds) *Two Decades in British Politics* (Manchester University Press).

Thompson, K. (1993) 'Redressing Grievances: The Role of the Ombudsman', *Talking Politics*, 6: 1, autumn.

■ *Chapter 18* ■

The Secret State

The Security Services
Issues of Control and Accountability,
  Competence and Scope

State Secrecy in Britain
Reform of the Official Secrets Acts
Freedom of Information

In recent decades, issues of national security and defence have attained considerable prominence in British politics. Government prosecutions of two civil servants, Sarah Tisdall and Clive Ponting, for revealing State secrets; its banning of trade unions at GCHQ; and its sustained campaign in the courts to prevent the publication of *Spycatcher*, the memoirs of a former MI5 man, in Britain – these along with numerous other episodes involving the security services kept state security firmly in the public arena. This chapter deals with some central questions arising out of these episodes, focusing particularly upon the character of state secrets, the nature and accountability of the intelligence agencies and the controversy generated by government reforms in this sphere after 1988. In broad terms, it is concerned both with the 'secret state' – the non-elected institutions which exercise considerable power in substantial freedom from democratic control together with the legislation and practices by which governments preclude public discussion of purportedly secret matters – and with pressures for greater 'openness'. These pressures emanate from the values and norms of liberal constitutionalism, in particular, those of political accountability (executive responsibility to Parliament), civil liberties and the freedom of the press.

■ The Security Services

Britain has four main security and intelligence-gathering agencies. These are MI5, the domestic security service; Special Branch, the internal political police; MI6, the overseas intelligence service; and GCHQ, the Government Communications Headquarters, responsible for international surveillance. Basically, these services have two main tasks: at home, to gather information on individuals, groups and organisations considered to be a threat to the state, and to counter those threats; abroad, to gather intelligence of all kinds e.g. economic, political, military about potential enemies and competitors, with a special focus on threats to political stability (terrorism, weapons developments) (Exhibit 18.1).

▐ Issues of Control and Accountability, Competence and Scope

In the 1980s, a series of allegations about the security services, a major spy scandal and continuing developments in the technology of electronic eavesdropping led to intense public debate about their control and accountability, competence and scope (breadth of surveillance).

Key roles in the control and coordination of the security services are played by the prime minister, the home secretary and the Cabinet Office. The precise constitutional position is by no means clear-cut. The home secretary holds overall responsibility for MI5 and Special Branch whilst MI6 is formally answerable to the foreign secretary. However, ultimate responsibility for national security is held by the prime minister as is clear from occasional statements by prime

---

Exhibit 18.1 *Britain's security services*

MI5 (Security Service)
Director-General: Stella Rimington
Headquarters: Millbank
Established: 1909 (to counter German spies)
Staff: 2000, over half of them women
Budget: £160 million (estimated)
Functions: now mainly counter-terrorism (which currently absorbs 70% of its resources) but also counter-espionage (25%) and counter political subversion (5%). Took overall control of anti-IRA terrorist activities in 1992 and is seeking to expand intelligence-gathering into drugs and fraud. Also concerned with political 'vetting'.

Police Special Branch
Senior officer: Deputy Assistant Commissioner, Metropolitan Police (Peter Phelan, 1988); chief constables, local forces
Headquarters: Top Floor, New Scotland Yard; provincial police HQs
Established: 1883 (to counter the Irish Republican Brotherhood – successors to the Fenians)
Staff: 1800 (1988)
Budget: £19.5 million (Met SB – 1988)
Functions: assisting MI5 to combat terrorism, espionage, sabotage and subversion (in addition to intelligence-gathering, makes arrests for MI5) Also concerned with protecting VIPs, watching ports and airports, vetting naturalisation applicants and enforcing Official Secrets and Prevention of Terrorism Acts.

MI6 (Secret Intelligence Service)
Chief: Sir Colin McColl
Headquarters: new HQ on Thames (Formerly Century House, near Lambeth North Tube station)
Established: 1909 (also to counter German spies) 'MI' stood for Military Intelligence
Staff: 2000
Budget: £150 million (estimated)
Functions: gathering political, military and economic intelligence in foreign countries through agents attached to British embassies and high commissions. Works closely with the Defence Intelligence Staff (DIS) – established 1965, current staff over 600 – whose main role is to provide worldwide military threat analyses and assessments.

Government Communications Headquarters (GCHQ)
Director: Sir John Adye
Headquarters: Cheltenham
Established: developed out of Government Code and Cypher School at Bletchley in Second World War. Operates under secret UK–USA treaty (1947) by which UK and USA, assisted by Canada, Australia and New Zealand, share responsibility for monitoring international communications.
Staff: 7000 (at GCHQ); 3000 military personnel throughout Britain.
Budget: £500 million (estimated)
Functions: interception and decoding of international communications – diplomatic, military, commercial and private – by means of spy satellites and listening posts. It cooperates closely with the US National Security Agency at Fort Meade, Maryland. In 1984, following the involvement of GCHQ staff in industrial action in 1981 – which had led to the USA expressing concern about the tightness of British security – the Thatcher Government banned trade union membership at GCHQ, Cheltenham.

ministers in the House of Commons; the PM chairs the Cabinet Committee on the Security and Intelligence Services (IS) and the heads of MI5, MI6 and GCHQ along with the chairman of the Joint Intelligence Committee have direct access to the PM. Only the prime minister sees the true security services budget.

An important role in the day-to-day coordination of the security and intelligence services operations and budgets is played by the **Cabinet Office**: one of its six secretariats is specifically concerned with security and intelligence (**Joint Intelligence Organisation**); it contains a key official, the **Co-ordinator of Intelligence and Security**, who reports directly to the PM; and the Cabinet secretary chairs a range of important committees concerned not only with internal Whitehall security but also with general oversight of security services budgets (the **Permanent Secretaries Committee on Intelligence Services** (PSIS)). The central roles in the processing of intelligence information are shown in Figure 18.1. As can be seen, the **Joint Intelligence Committee** (JIC) serves as the 'central filter'

(Norton-Taylor, 1990) between the expert assessors in the Cabinet Office – themselves drawing upon information provided by the main intelligence-gathering agencies – and key ministers on the Cabinet Overseas Policy and Defence Committee (OPD). The **Security Commission**, set up in 1964, investigates security lapses and advises on vetting procedures at the request of the PM. The overall picture with regard to roles and responsibilities in the control, processing and gathering of intelligence is shown in Figure 18.2.

Three main questions arise about Britain's security and intelligence services.

- How much are ministers told about their operations? The main point at issue here is the adequacy of *political control* over national security.
- Should the security services be accountable to parliament, and if so in what ways?
- How far are security operations a threat to civil liberties? This raises issues of the extent and methods of surveillance of the security services as well as of their legal and political control.

We look at each of these questions in turn.

□ Political Control

A key document here is the 1952 Government directive to the director-general of MI5. This stated that there was a well-established convention whereby ministers '*do not concern themselves with the detailed information which may be obtained by the Security Service in particular cases but are furnished with such information as may be necessary for the determination of any issue on which guidance is sought*'. This is consistent with considerable ministerial – including prime ministerial – ignorance of the day-to-day operations of the security services. The former MI5 officer Peter Wright describes in *Spycatcher* how MI5 built up a file on the then Prime Minister Harold Wilson and tried to undermine and 'de-stabilise' his Government.

Joint Intelligence Organisation

(based in Cabinet Office: prepares daily reports – as well as long-term analyses – on range of international situations; also has coordinating role for security and intelligence services)

Joint Intelligence Committee

(includes heads of security and intelligence agencies: makes assessments for individual ministers and weekly reviews of intelligence information (the 'Red Book') for Cabinet Overseas and Defence Committee)

Cabinet Overseas Policy and Defence Committee (OPD)

(chaired by the prime minister: considers assessments prepared by JIC)

Figure 18.1 *The processing of intelligence information in Britain*

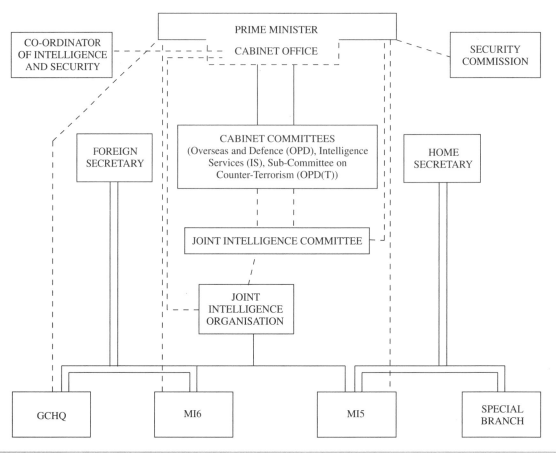

Figure 18.2   *The security services: responsibility, coordination and control*

□ *Political Accountability*

Britain's security services are not democratically accountable. The prime minister and other ministers do from time to time answer questions in Parliament about the services but seek to give away as little as possible – to be in fact 'uniformly uninformative'. The government argues that what can be said publicly about security is very limited – for good security reasons. Margaret Thatcher refused to allow any member of the security services to appear before a Commons Select Committee in 1985 and the Home Secretary Kenneth Clarke forbade the Head of MI5 to appear before the Home Affairs Select Committee in 1993, merely allowing her to take lunch with it. However, this Committee in its report *Accountability of the Security Services* (1993) demanded the right to scrutinise the role of the Security Service (MI5), arguing that such scrutiny would 'meet an important public interest and help to protect against any possible abuse of power'. What it seeks is not oversight of operations but rather of the policy and effectiveness of MI5. It also reiterated an earlier call (by the Liaison Committee in 1982–3) for MI5 to be accountable to a parliamentary committee for its £185 million annual budget. The Home Affairs Committee pointed out that all of Britain's closest allies have a system of independent oversight for their security and intelligence services. For example, the security services are democratically accountable in Canada, Australia and the United States.

Political Surveillance and Civil Liberties

Britain's security services gather information by the interception of communications. Authorisation for these practices is by means of warrants obtained from the home secretary, foreign secretary or the secretaries of state for Scotland or Northern Ireland. Before 1985, the criteria for the issue of warrants were defined by the executive (*Birkett Report*, 1957, *White Paper on Interceptions*, 1980). These were:

- **National security:** there had to be major subversive or espionage activity likely to injure the national interest and, second, the material likely to be obtained by the interception had to be of direct use to the security service in carrying out its specific tasks.
- **Serious crime:** a warrant would be granted only where the crime was really serious, normal methods of investigation had been tried and failed, and there was good reason to believe that the interception would obtain information liable to result in a conviction.

In 1985, however, the issue of warrants for interceptions was given a statutory basis. The Interception of Communications Act (1985) had three major provisions. First, it broadened the criteria upon which warrants could be issued to include: *(i)* National security; *(ii)* preventing or detecting a serious crime; and *(iii)* protecting the economic well-being of the UK. The broadening of the criteria was reflected both in item *(iii)* and in a vaguer notion of 'national security' (item *(i)*), which was no longer equated as previously with 'major subversion or espionage'.

Second, the Act made unauthorised interception of a postal communication or telephone message a criminal offence for the first time. Third, it established a remedy for those aggrieved by what they considered to be improper interception of communications in the form of a right to complain to a tribunal of legally-qualified members.

The tribunal has power to quash improperly issued warrants, to order the destruction of material obtained in an improper manner and to require the secretary of state to pay compensation. However, none of the first 68 complaints to the tribunal was upheld. Critics argue that the powers of the tribunal are *too limited* and, in particular, that it has no power to investigate whether unauthorised interceptions are taking place. They also criticise *the exclusion of the courts* from any role in the scrutiny of illegal or improper behaviour by the security services (Ewing and Gearty, 1990, pp. 72–7). Supervision of the powers exercised by the home secretary and tribunal under the Act is carried out by a security service commissioner.

Intelligence-gathering is done in three main ways: listening in to telephone conversations and opening letters; employing spy satellites to photograph military installations and intercept communication signals; and through human agents using concealed radios to pass back information. The concern of civil libertarians focuses on the first two methods.

Official figures greatly underestimate the extent of telephone tapping (Figure 18.3). This is for two main reasons. First, the published figures do not include warrants issued by the foreign secretary (usually about one-third of the number issued by the home secretary) or those issued by the secretary of state for Northern Ireland. Second, a single warrant can cover a target organisation with thousands of members and may include their friends and relatives. The home secretary refused to comment in 1991 on a *Guardian* report that the security services were tapping 35 000 phones a year.

Even on official figures, telephone tapping increased in the 1980s: the home secretary and Scottish secretary issued 464 warrants in 1980, 539 in 1990 whilst the number of specialist telephone engineers carrying out taps rose from 40 in 1980 to 70 a decade later.

The sheer size of the net cast by the surveillance agencies has led to periodic public outbursts of alarm and controversy. Attention has focused on the 'broad' interpretation of the rules governing the operation of the security services. Details about alleged improper conduct by these services are given in Exhibit 18.2.

Listening in

Warrants issued to intercept telephone calls issued by the home secretary (in England and Wales) and the secretary of state for Scotland during each year.

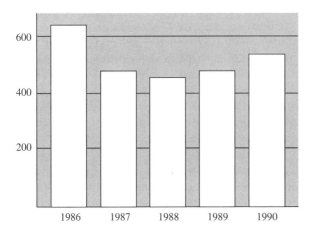

Opening the post

Warrants issued to intercept letters issued by the home secretary and the secretary of state for Scotland during each year.

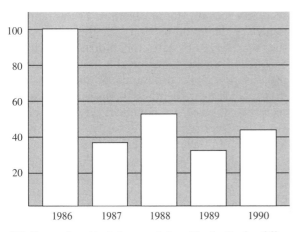

NB: Figures do not include warrants issued by the Foreign Office and the Northern Ireland Office, which are kept secret. One warrant may cover many targets and one target may be covered by many warrants. It is assumed that some phones are tapped without warrants.

Source: *Guardian*, 15 October 1991.

Figure 18.3   *Warrants for telephone-tapping and letter-opening, 1986–90*

The Government's Response to Criticisms of the Security Services

The Government responded to the Massiter allegations by ordering an inquiry by the Chairman of the Security Commission but annoyed the opposition and other critics by restricting its terms of reference to whether ministers since 1979 had operated under official guidelines in authorising telephone tapping. **Lord Bridge's Report** – produced in five days – cleared the Thatcher governments up to that date of issuing warrants for interceptions outside accepted procedures and criteria but did little to allay disquiet. Opposition leaders remained concerned about surveillance without ministerial knowledge or warrant; about blanket surveillance of a whole organisation under a single warrant; about the unauthorised interception of transatlantic communications; and about the possibility that the security services were gathering information on the members of non-subversive organisations.

In 1985, however, the Government was forced to create a statutory framework for the operation of the security services by an adverse judgement in the European Court of Human Rights. The judgement arose in the case of Roger Malone, an antiques dealer whose phone had been tapped – in fact with the authority of a warrant – by the police. The Court ruled that British law was insufficiently clear about the circumstances and conditions under which the authorities would resort to this intrusion into privacy. However, the Interception of Communications Act (1985), for the reasons already outlined, did little to allay public concern, and controversy about the operation of the security services continued. By the late 1980s, following the Spycatcher affair, it would probably not be an exaggeration to say that there was 'a true crisis of confidence in the security services of this country' (Ewing and Gearty, 1990, p. 170).

The Government responded with further legislation, the Security Services Act (1989). This Act placed MI5 (but not MI6) on a statutory footing for the first time; provided for the appointment of a security services commissioner to review the powers of the home secretary to issue warrants for telephone tapping and other

---

Exhibit 18.2   *Informing on the security services*

'MI5's Official Secrets' (1985): a Channel 4 documentary under this title contained allegations by a former MI5 officer, Cathy Massiter, that MI5 had broken its own rules. Massiter disclosed that MI5 tapped the phones of trade union leaders and of leaders of the Campaign for Nuclear Disarmament. Of particular concern was the programme's suggestion that in the late 1970s the phones of union leaders were tapped routinely as well as during industrial disputes. According to one source the phone of a shop steward at the Ford plant in Dagenham was tapped at the request of the Department of Employment in order to discover 'the Ford union's bottom line in the pay negotiations'. Of the 1983 decision to tap the phone of John Cox, a Vice-President of CND and a member of the Communist Party, Massiter stated: '.. we (i.e. MI5) had absolutely no evidence that he was concerned in any criminal activity or that he was engaged in a major subversive or espionage activity that was likely to injure the national interest'. (In 1987 CND lost its case in the High Court that the telephone tap on Cox was unlawful, the judge ruling that the Home Secretary did not act unreasonably in deciding to grant the warrant: although no longer 'communist-dominated', CND was still in 1983 'Communist-penetrated' and Mr Cox was a leading member of the CPGB).

Spycatcher (1987): a retired MI5 agent, Peter Wright, alleged that the organisation committed numerous illegal and treasonable acts including the faking and forging of documents, smear campaigns and illicit 'bugging' and burglaries of political parties and trade unions. For five years he wrote, 'we bugged and burgled our way across London, while pompous bowler-hatted civil servants in Whitehall pretended to look the other way'. In addition to its attempt to destabilise the Wilson government, MI5 had also been involved – according to Wright – in an attempt to assassinate the Egyptian President, Abdul-Gamel Nasser.

Guardian/ITN World in Action 'Defending the Realm' (1991). This programme contained revelations by a former civil servant on the Joint Intelligence Committee, Robin Robison, that Britain's security services engaged in routine spying on EC countries – France, Germany, Italy – to discover the bottom line on Community deals; large-scale commercial spying on major companies such as Rolls-Royce, Marconi and GEC together with major car producers, chemical and oil companies and finance houses; and used information gained from spying on foreign arms deals to assist British arms manufacturers. He also disclosed that he had seen files marked 'Not for Minister's Eyes', a practice he denounced as eroding democratic accountability. The joint World in Action/*Guardian* inquiry also disclosed that GCHQ intercepted the communications of the secretary-general of the Scottish Trades Union Council and that BT tapped the phones of the family of Lieutenant Robert Lawrence, the Falklands war hero, whose story was told in the film 'Tumbledown'. The inquiry revealed how GCHQ through its satellite eavesdropping from its listening post in Cornwall and through its operations at its London office thwarted the rules on the interception of communications.

---

forms of surveillance; and created a tribunal (of 3–5 legally-qualified members) to investigate complaints by persons aggrieved about any action of MI5 in relation to their property. But critics pointed out once more the weakness of these provisions: the wide definition of the powers of MI5 (see Exhibit 18.3); the authorisation of burglary in the form of burglar warrants; and the inadequacy of the review procedures, with the powers of both commissioner and tribunal being strictly limited. The commissioner, for example, has no power to order the cessation of improper practices whilst the tribunal lacks the power to decide whether the service acted reasonably in exercising surveillance over a particular category of persons e.g. trade unions or the Labour Party. Above all, the security and intelligence services remained unaccountable to Parliament.

Exhibit 18.3   *The functions of MI5*

The **Security Service Act** (1989) defined the functions of MI5 as being *'the protection of national security and, in particular, its protection against threats from espionage, terrorism and sabotage, from the activities of agents of foreign powers and from actions intended to overthrow or undermine parliamentary democracy by political, industrial or violent means'; and, also 'to safeguard the economic well-being of the United Kingdom against threats posed by the actions or intentions of persons outside the British Isles'.*

In the continuing absence of proper parliamentary accountability of the security services, questions are still being raised in the early 1990s about the legitimacy of some of their activities. In 1993, for instance, the *Diaries* of Alan Clark, a former minister under Thatcher, suggested that ministers are subject to MI5 surveillance despite the widespread understanding – based on an assurance by Harold Wilson in 1966 – that MPs (and peers) are generally exempt from 'bugging' by the security service. Where such surveillance does occur, it needs the express authorisation of the prime minister and is reported to the House of Commons later. The *Clark Diaries* appeared to confirm earlier statements by MPs Jonathan Aitken and Sir Richard Body (in 1990) that MPs are under MI5 surveillance.

Also subject to scrutiny is the effectiveness of the security and intelligence agencies. Critics point, for example, to intelligence service failures over the Argentinian invasion of the Falklands, the US invasion of the Commonwealth island of Grenada and the Iraqi invasion of Kuwait. Further – and related –questions are how much intelligence information actually finds its way to ministers and the use which is made of that which is received. These questions arose in relation to the collapse of the Bank of Credit and Commerce International (BCCI) about which it was reported that MI5 and MI6 were aware that the bank was being used by drug money launderers and terrorists like Abu Nidal at least two years before the Bank ended; and the collapse of the financial empire of Robert Maxwell, over which the Prime Minister, John Major, in 1992 denied that Ministers had received security service informa-

tion on Maxwell's business dealings in 1989 two years before the tycoon's death.

It was reported in 1993 that in addition to planning legislation to place MI6 and GCHG on a statutory footing, the Government was considering making a Minister answerable to parliament for the security services and that it might make MI5 answerable to a small committee of privy counsellors. The Labour Party ('Charter of Rights', 1991) favours the introduction of an inspector general with access to security services materials and general oversight over their activities and of an intelligence select committee in the House of Commons to which the services would be accountable.

□ *Political Vetting*

Political vetting – as well as control and accountability – has also been a matter of public concern. One aspect is internal vetting within the security services themselves. In 1984, Michael Bettaney, a middle-ranking MI5 officer, was sentenced to 23 years imprisonment on spying charges. His heavy drinking suggested that he was a high security risk and indeed that he ought to have lost his security clearance at an earlier date. Three years later internal vetting procedures once again became the subject of a furore when the Prime Minister disclosed to the House of Commons that Sir Maurice Oldfield, the head of MI6 between 1972 and 1978, had in 1980 admitted to concealing his homosexuality during vetting and as a result had had his internal security clearance withdrawn. At the time of his confession, he had been recalled from retirement to oversee security in Northern Ireland because of severe problems in the relationship between the police, the army and the undercover forces.

Another aspect of political vetting raises the issue of civil liberties. This issue arose in the case of a journalist, Isobel Hilton, who was prevented from joining the BBC because she had been blacklisted by MI5. She had been blacklisted because, as a student, she had been secretary of the Scotland-China Association. The Association, whose members included churchmen, academics and a former governor of Stirling Castle, was regarded as a subversive organisation by MI5, whose negative vetting continued after her resignation from the Association in March 1977. Isobel Hilton's case was turned down by the European Court of Human Rights because she could not provide incontrovertible proof (she was unable to do this because her lawyers did not

have access to MI5 files) but in 1991 three more individuals denied employment because of negative political vetting had taken their cases to the European Court.

■ State Secrecy in Britain

Secrecy is a central characteristic of British government and there exists a variety of constitutional, political, bureaucratic, military, cultural and historical factors which help to explain the obsession with it. (Exhibit 18.4). Its major legislative bulwark down to the late 1980s was the Official Secrets Act of 1911, bolstered further by the Acts of 1920 and 1939. The following examination of the apparatus of secrecy in Britain focuses especially on the workings of this legislation and upon pressures for its reform which culminated in a new Official Secrets Act of 1989.

Exhibit 18.4   *Secrecy and the UK political system*

There are several features of the UK political system which tend to promote government secrecy.

- The lack of a written, codified, constitution, or a Bill of Rights, which outlines the duties of government and the rights of citizens means the public has no 'right to know' laid down in writing. The lack of a Freedom of Information Act is also a factor, although this is as much a result of the predominance of secrecy as its cause.
- A unitary form of government which concentrates political power at Westminster and increases the centralisation of administrative information tends to favour secrecy in the centre.
- For the most part, a two-party system, given its adversarial nature and the wish to keep information from 'the other side', encourages secrecy.
- The doctrine of ministerial responsibility which holds that ministers, not civil servants, are answerable for government decisions promotes secrecy among public officials. The secrecy of the civil service is a mark of its subservience to ministers.
- The civil service also tends to be secretive because of the sheer administrative burdens. In addition, the rivalry for Treasury resources encourages secrecy between the various departments.
- A political culture deferential to strong leadership and pragmatic government, which traditionally has not placed accountability as a priority, has provided a climate for secrecy. The inward-looking administrative culture in the 'Whitehall village' also promotes secrecy.
- Military secrecy, during threats of war and invasion, has led to general government secrecy.
- Historically, government by an elite which regarded openness as unnecessary and undesirable favoured secrecy, as did a lack of commitment to democratic values inside and outside Parliament.

Source: Hunt (1992b).

Our discussion leads inevitably to a consideration of the campaign for freedom of information and to the prospects for greater openness in Britain.

The Official Secrets Act (1911) had two main clauses. Section 1 – the 'spying clause' – made it an offence punishable with fourteen years imprisonment to collect or disclose information which might be useful to an enemy or for any purpose prejudicial to the safety or interests of the State to be within the vicinity of a 'prohibited place' i.e. a military establishment. This section was used against CND leaders in 1964 for demonstrating at an airport occupied by the US Air Force, but generally – unlike section 2 – it operated uncontroversially.

Section 2 of the Act made it a criminal offence for public servants to retain without permission or to communicate without authorisation any information obtained in the course of their employment or for a person to receive such information knowing or having reasonable cause to believe that it had been disclosed in breach of the Act. Such information could be communicated only to someone to whom it was in the interests of the State a duty to disclose it. The main problem with this clause was its *catch-all* nature, its failure to distinguish between sensitive information such as intelligence and certain kinds of defence matters which in the national interest must be kept secret, and more trivial, harmless information. According to one authoritative estimate, section 2 created no fewer than 2324 offences (de Smith and Brazier, 1990, p. 494). Under this section, the government could if it wished prosecute someone for revealing such a trivial matter as the number of cups of tea drunk in a particular government department.

Another problem with the clause is that it provided government with an essentially *arbitrary* weapon. Public servants and people such as journalists habitually in receipt of large quantities of official information found it almost impossible to predict when a prosecution would be launched. As was evident in the Ponting case (see below, p. 344), prosecutions – although initiated by the attorney-general, the government legal officer – may be set in train for *political* reasons, to suit the convenience or to spare the embarrassment of the government of the day.

The key consideration is *authorisation*. Government as a matter of course routinely divulges large quantities of information through ministers who are self-authorising in the matter and through civil servants whose authorisation, more vaguely, is implied. Security classifications – in ascending scale of sensitivity, 'restricted', 'confidential', 'secret' and 'top secret' – play in government terms 'an essential administrative role in handling information' (Exhibit 18.5). But the point is that, no matter how information is classified and no matter how much 'leaks' of classified information have become part of the system by which the media acquire news, government could make the disclosure of any item of *unauthorised* information an offence. The very wide coverage of the Act meant that civil servants and journalists could be in technical breach of the law frequently.

The excessive secrecy of British government has long been the object of criticism. The Fulton Committee (1968) concluded that the administrative process was surrounded by 'too much secrecy' and recommended 'a greater amount of openness'. The Franks Committee (1972) criticised Section 2

Exhibit 18.5 *Whitehall's security classifications*

Category	Consequences of Disclosure:
Top secret	Exceptionally grave damage to the state.
Secret	Serious injury to the interests of the state.
Confidential	Prejudicial to the interests of the state.
Restricted	Undesirable in the interests of the state.

of the Official Secrets Act as a 'catch-all' and 'a mess'. It recommended the repeal of this section and its replacement by a new Official Information Act. Under this Act, only matters of genuine importance to the national interest would be protected against disclosure by the criminal law. These would be:

- Information relating to defence, security, foreign relations, currency and the reserves. Information in this class would be protected (i.e. classified as 'secret' or 'defence-confidential') only if in the Government's view its disclosure would cause *serious* injury to the national interest.
- Information likely to assist criminal activities or impede law enforcement
- Cabinet documents
- Information entrusted in confidence to the government by a private individual or concern.

With regard to the first category, before a prosecution was brought, a minister would have to review the classification personally in order to decide whether it was properly classified at the time of its alleged disclosure; if s/he decided that it was, s/he would issue a certificate to that effect. The Committee recommended the establishment of an advisory committee on matters relating to classification with a similar role to the Defence, Press and Broadcasting ('D' Notice) Committee (Exhibit 18.6).

Attempts at reform of the Official Secrets Acts undertaken by Labour (1978) and the Conservatives (1979) both came to nothing. Both Labour's White Paper and the Conservatives' Protection of Official Information Bill would have been more restrictive than the existing Acts. The revelations contained in Andrew Boyle's book, *A Climate of Treason*, which appeared just as the Conservative bill was under parliamentary consideration, helped to kill it. The book revealed that Anthony Blunt, a distinguished art historian and former officer in MI5, had confessed to being a Soviet spy in 1964, having been granted immunity from prosecution. Critics of the proposed legislation suggested that under its provisions the disclosures about Blunt could never have come to light. After 1978, however, Governments had increasing recourse to the Official Secrets Acts to inhibit publication of materials which in their view endangered the national interest and certain of these widely-publicised prosecutions had the effect of intensifying pressures for reform.

Trials under the Official Secrets Acts in the 1970s and 1980s

Prosecutions under the Official Secrets Acts proceeded at a relatively modest level in the post-war decades, fell away in the 1970s but increased dramatically after 1978. Thus, there were 23 prosecutions involving 34 defendants between

---

Exhibit 18.6   *The 'D' Notice system*

A 'D' Notice is a confidential letter sent by the government to media editors and sometimes to publishers requesting that information be not published because publication would damage national defence or security. The system, which functions on a voluntary basis, constitutes a further inhibition on the publication of 'sensitive' information on defence and security matters: it was used, for example, to block news stories on the spies George Blake (1961) and Kim Philby (1963). The system is managed by the Defence, Press and Broadcasting Committee (comprising senior officials and representatives of the media) which in October 1992 announced a thorough review of 'the purpose scope and operation' of the 'D' Notice system in the light of the end of the Cold War and of 'government policy on greater openness'.

1945–1971 but no fewer than 29 people were prosecuted between 1978–1986. We now survey the most important trials under Section 2 since 1970.

The Sunday Telegraph case (1971)

This involved the prosecution of the editor of the *Sunday Telegraph*, a journalist (Jonathan Aitken, now MP for Thanet South) and a retired general for publishing a report by the Defence Adviser to the British High Commission in Nigeria. The report revealed that British arms supplies to the Federal Government – then engaged in a civil war with Biafra – were far more extensive than publicly stated by the British Government. The judge in his summing up suggested that the government might consider whether it was time for Section 2 to be 'pensioned off'. The defendants were acquitted.

The Tisdall case (1984)

Sarah Tisdall, a junior official in the Foreign Office, was prosecuted and sentenced to six months imprisonment for leaking secret Ministry of Defence documents to *The Guardian* newspaper in October 1983. There were two documents, a Ministry of Defence memorandum marked 'Secret-UK eyes only' which outlined plans by the Defence Secretary to handle the parliamentary and public response to the arrival of Cruise missiles at RAF Greenham Common, and a second document relating to security preparations for the Greenham base. What upset her apparently – she called it 'immoral' – was the evidence contained in the first document of political calculation by the government in its handling of the Cruise issue: it intended to make a statement to Parliament after and not before the arrival of the nuclear missiles.

The Guardian published the first document (although not the second) but lost its case to protect its sources of information and was forced to return the document, possession of which enabled the Government to trace the leak back to Tisdall. Her sentence was considered too harsh by the liberal-minded, the more especially as national security was not endangered by her action, but the political right considered that she deserved her punishment for betraying her trust as an employee of the Crown.

The Ponting case (1985)

Clive Ponting, a senior official in the Ministry of Defence, was prosecuted for leaking official information concerning the sinking of the Argentinian ship, the *General Belgrano*, during the Falklands conflict. Ponting believed that Ministers were deliberately misleading the House of Commons over the circumstances of the sinking and accordingly sent two documents (one unclassified, the second marked 'confidential' but later declassified) to Tam Dalyell, a Labour MP with a strong interest in the matter.

Ponting's defence at his trial was that he had acted in accordance with the national interest, which was to know the truth about this particular event; his broader duty as a citizen overrode his narrower duty as a public official. He believed that the Government had been concerned only with saving itself from political embarrassment.

The prosecution case, upheld by the judge in his instruction to the jury, was that the national interest was the same as the policy of the government of the day. Ponting's duty as a civil servant, therefore, was simply and solely to support the Government's decision to withhold *Belgrano* information from Tam Dalyell. To general surprise, and government consternation, however, Ponting was acquitted.

The 'Zircon affair' (1987)

This episode involved a film made for the BBC's 'Secret Society' series about Britain's proposed spy satellite, Zircon, by the journalist Duncan Campbell. The film was withdrawn by the BBC (it was unclear whether this was after Government pressure) but Campbell then proposed to show the film to MPs (to demonstrate that there was no risk to national security). This, however, was blocked by the Speaker, after a briefing from the Attorney-General.

The Government then pursued Campbell with an injunction to prevent him speaking or writing about his film but the court order was served too late to prevent the contents of the programme appearing in the *New Statesman*. On the authority of a warrant issued under the Official Secrets Act, Special Branch then raided the BBC's Glasgow office and seized the Zircon film along with the other five films in the series. The Government argued that the proposed disclosures would alert the USSR to the existence of the satellite and would endanger cooperation with the USA in gathering intelligence.

Critics riposted that the Government's wish to stifle the programme arose out of its political embarrassment that the project was likely to be delayed. National security, they suggested, was not threatened by the film: the existence of the proposed satellite was more widely known than the Government maintained and, once launched, its position would be easily detected by the Soviet Union. The affair died down: the injunctions against Campbell were lifted and the BBC showed the Zircon film two years later. But the episode had raised worrying questions about Government infringements of media freedom.

Spycatcher (1986–8)

In this long-drawn-out case, the Government obtained injunctions against newspapers in Britain reporting or repeating what they had already reported of the revelations about the security services contained in the book *Spycatcher* by a retired MI5 agent, Peter Wright. On this occasion, the Government based its legal case not on the Official Secrets Acts but on breach of confidence by a servant of the Crown.

At the same time, the Government sought through injunctions to prevent the publication of the book in Australia. It was during the trial in New South Wales that the Cabinet Secretary, Sir Robert Armstrong, caused a considerable public stir by confessing that he had been 'economical with the truth'. The Government argued that publication would damage the confidence of other members of the security service in each other and of other countries in the British security services. But it lost its case both in Britain and in Australia, a decisive point in its defeat being the publication of *Spycatcher* in the United States in July 1987.

Critics pointed out both the illogicality of the Government's position (why continue to ban a book the substance of which from late July 1987 was already in the public domain in Britain or readily obtainable in the US?) and its inconsistency (no action had been taken in the early 1980s against books by Chapman Pincher and Nigel West which contained revelations about the security services). Critics also argued that the seriousness of Wright's allegations – notably, that the British security services had been involved in an attempt to assassinate President Nasser and a plot to destabilise the Wilson Government and that a former head of MI5, Sir Roger Hollis, was a Soviet double-agent – warranted an immediate inquiry, but the Government refused this on the grounds that an Administration does not investigate the conduct of previous Governments.

▌Reform of the Official Secrets Acts

In the aftermath of the Ponting and *Spycatcher* cases, political pressures for reform of the Official Secrets Acts became irresistible. Lord Scarman summed up a widespread opinion in a letter to *The Times* on 7 January 1988 when he urged the Government: 'For heaven's sake legislate now before our law, our courts and our reputation as a free country become the laughing stock of the world'.

In fact, the Government did make clear its own intention to legislate on the matter in January 1988 during parliamentary consideration of a private member's bill to liberalise the secrets law introduced by Richard Shepherd, a Conservative backbencher. Shepherd's Bill would have provided both a prior publication and a public interest defence to those accused of illegal disclosures of information, but Government imposition of a three-line whip ensured it fell before the second reading.

☐ *The Official Secrets Act (1989)*

First, the Act reduces the categories of information protected against disclosure by the criminal law to six, as follows:

* Security and intelligence
* Defence
* International relations
* Information relating to crime and its investigation
* Information about or obtained by activities under warrants issued under the Interception of Communications Act (1985) and the Security Services Act (1989)
* Information provided in confidence by another State or international agency.

Second, it defines the circumstances for each category in which disclosure of information will be considered 'harmful' to the public interest. For example, the disclosure of *defence* information is harmful if it 'endangers the interests of the United Kingdom abroad, seriously obstructs the promotion or protection by the United Kingdom of those interests or endangers the safety of British citizens abroad'. It is also harmful if it damages the capability of the armed forces, results in loss of life or injury to any of their members, or leads to 'serious damage' to military equipment or installations. A jury decides whether any disclosure is sufficiently harmful to justify the application of criminal sanctions.

Third, in the categories of 'security and intelligence' and the interception of communications, the mere disclosure of information is regarded as harmful in itself, and actual or probable harm need not be proved. These are 'absolute offences' under the Act. For example, any unauthorised disclosure of information by a member or former member of the security services is a criminal offence.

Fourth, criminal liability for the disclosure of unauthorised information is not confined to Crown servants and government contractors but extends to e.g. newspaper editors who will be liable to prosecution for printing unlawfully disclosed information.

Fifth, no defence of 'public interest' or 'prior publication' is available to those accused under the Act.

The Act during its passage and afterwards was subjected to strong criticisms. Critics discounted the Government's claim to have 'liberalised' the law on official secrets as misleading. Certainly, the reform of section 2 of the 1911 Official Secrets Act (the counter-espionage provisions of section 1 remained intact) did exclude large quantities of harmless information from the scope of the secrecy law.

But in narrowing the law of secrecy, the 1989 Act also tightened it. For opponents of the Act, this was the Government's real intention: to close up loopholes in the law revealed by the Ponting and *Spycatcher* cases, to eliminate 'whistle-blowers' and further inhibit newspaper editors

---

Exhibit 18.7   *The 1989 Official Secrets Act: a critic's view*

J.A.G. Griffith contends in 'The Official Secrets Act 1989', *Journal of Law and Society*, 16, 2, Autumn 1989 that:

Perhaps the most powerful critic of the (Official Secrets) bill during its passage in the two Houses of Parliament was Lord Hutchinson of Lullington who had appeared as counsel in many leading secrecy cases. On second reading he observed that the bill was 'in no way a liberalising measure'; that in the six areas it introduced 'even greater restrictions' and that in the past thirty years all prosecutions involving leaks to the media had been in the six areas; that the bill did nothing to reduce 'the secret nature of our system of government', not making one piece of official information more available to the citizen, and perpetuating into the twenty-first century the paternalistic state of the nineteenth century.

(Exhibit 18.7). More specific criticisms of the Act included its creation of 'absolute offences' with regard to disclosures by members of the security services and those involved in 'authorised bugging'; the extreme vagueness of the test of 'harm' to the public interest; and the absence of the defences of 'prior publication' and 'public interest'. The ethos of secrecy, critics concluded, had been strengthened rather than eroded.

■ Freedom of Information

The Official Secrets Act (1989) therefore, was seen by many critics as strengthening – rather than weakening – the case for a Freedom of Information Act argued by the Freedom of Information Campaign. The proposed legislation would give individuals the right of access to all official information except for that in certain exempt categories (security, defence, etc). Some limited progress had been made towards this goal by the early 1990s. Thus, the Data Protection Act (1984) provides access to *computerised* personal files; the Local Government (Access to Information) Act (1986) allows access to background papers used in preparing council reports; and the Access to Health Records Act (1990) permits access to manual health records.

The advent of the Major Government, which was pledged to greater 'openness', raised the hopes of campaigners. Early 'open government' initiatives involved the release of details of Cabinet committees and ministerial rules of conduct together with the opening of some previously closed Public Record Office files. A Minister for Public Service (William Waldegrave) was appointed, who quickly identified over 150 statutory restrictions on disclosure.

However, after the failure of private members' Freedom of Information bills in 1992 and 1993, the Minister himself rejected a full-blown Freedom of Information Act but did propose two significant changes in his White Paper 'Open Government' (July 1993). These were a legal right of access both to non-computerised personal files and to information on health and safety; and a new voluntary code of practice laying down the

information government Departments should make available.

But with many areas (defence, international relations, economic management, policing, the security services, immigration, honours, public appointments and 'communications with the Royal Household') still excluded from a non-statutory code, campaigners for greater openness remained unsatisfied.

Summary

The activities, control and accountability of Britain's security and intelligence services became a matter of acute public concern during the 1980s. The revelations of former MI5 officers raised serious questions about the scope and methods of the surveillance agencies, the extent of ministerial knowledge of – and control over – their activities, and the lack of accountability of the security services to Parliament. In addition, the Bettaney spy case revealed a serious failure of internal vetting in MI5.

Government legislation on the interception of communications (1985) and the Security Services (1989) failed to allay public disquiet: this was largely because the first Act broadened the criteria upon which warrants to intercept communications could be issued whilst the second Act defined the functions of MI5 very widely; neither Act – in the view of critics – provided adequate procedures for review.

The extent of official secrecy in Britain and in particular Governments' use of the very widely drawn Section 2 of the Official Secrets Act (1911) to protect it also became a matter of intense political controversy. Once again legislation was the result – a new Official Secrets Act (1989) which both reduced the categories of information protected against disclosure by the criminal law and defined the circumstances in which disclosure might be considered 'damaging' to the national interest. But critics maintained that the Government had tightened rather than 'liberalised' secrecy law. Despite some concessions improving public access to official information in the 1980s and 1990s, campaigners continued to demand a Freedom of Information Act.

Questions

1. How far do you agree that secrecy remains a hallmark of British government?
2. State the case for and against greater freedom of information in the UK.

Assignment

Conduct a brief investigation into the laws and practices relating to *(i)* the political accountability of the security services and *(ii)* official secrets in other democratic countries e.g. Australia, the United States.

Further reading

Birkinshaw, P. (1991) *Reforming the Secret State* (Milton Keynes: Open University Press).

Dorril, S. (1992) *The Silent Conspiracy, Inside the Intelligence Services in the 1990s* (London: Heinemann).

Ewing, K.D. and Gearty, C. (1990) *Freedom under Thatcher: Civil Liberties in Modern Britain* (Oxford: Clarendon).

Griffith, J.A.G. (1989) 'The Official Secrets Act 1989', *Journal of Law and Society*, 16: 2, autumn.

Hunt, S. (1992) 'State Secrecy in the UK', *Politics Review*, 1: 4, April.

Marshall, G. (1984) *Constitutional Conventions*, (Oxford: Clarendon) ch. 7.

Norton-Taylor, R. (1990) *In Defence of the Realm? The Case for Accountable Security Services* (London: Civil Liberties Trust).

Palmer, S. (1990) 'Tightening Secrecy Law:The Official Secrets Act 1989', *Public Law*, summer, pp. 243–25.

Porter, B. (1989) *Plots and Paranoia A History of Political Espionage in Britain 1790–1988* (London: Unwin Hyman).

PART 3
DECISION-MAKING, ISSUES AND POLICIES

■ *Chapter 19* ■

The Policy Process

The Political Agenda	The Policy-Making Process
Policy-Making and Decision-Making	Political Leadership
Decision-Making Theory	Sources of Policy Advice

Earlier chapters in this book have examined the machinery of government and the wider political, social and economic environment within which government operates. Part Three examines how government works in terms of how political issues are processed and the nature of public policy which emerges. How does government make policy? Who participates in policy-making? Why do policy-makers tackle certain political issues whilst ignoring others? How important is leadership? This chapter explores some theoretical approaches which will help in answering these questions.

■ The Political Agenda

At any one time there is a vast number of issues and problems facing people in Britain, yet the Government will attempt to solve only some of them. Some issues will get on to the political agenda and be debated publicly whilst others, which might be just as urgent for those concerned, fail to do so. Why is this? It is because there are factors which both help certain issues emerge whilst suppressing and restricting debate on others.

Firstly, some issues have more *salience* than others as far as the Government is concerned. Salience 'can be regarded as roughly equivalent to the *immediate importance* attributed to an issue or element ... salience can be equated with the *prominence* of the issue' (Frankel, 1970, p. 61). Joseph Frankel has suggested, for example,

that one reason why Britain failed to seize the leadership of Western Europe in the postwar years (see Chapter 7) was because the Attlee Government saw other issues as much more salient. During the late 1940s and 1950s the Labour Government was preoccupied with what it saw as the more important policies of establishing the welfare state (Chapters 21, 22 and 23) and nationalisation (Chapter 10). In his study of environmental politics, Anthony Downs devised a somewhat similar model of the political process in terms of a five stage issue-attention cycle with green issues gaining salience, moving up the political agenda, only to fade away in importance. Downs's model is examined in Chapter 28.

Governments may attempt to reshape the political agenda in order to refocus public attention away from areas of policy failure. For example, the Conservatives used their 1993 Conference to swing public debate away from economic management issues to aspects of public policy such as law and order (Chapter 31) and the future of the welfare state (Chapters 21–3). Deliberately controversial arguments were injected into the debate which were bound to attract and engage the media. A new hard line was taken on crime, with ministers appearing to argue that longer prison sentences would curb increasing lawlessness and that single parent families were both a cause of indiscipline as well as sources of a dependency culture which was a burden on the welfare state. Although the Government cannot normally control the political agenda, it was on this occasion successful in manipulating public debate away from issues concerning the recession, unemployment and poverty on to issues concerning the family and the responsibility of parents, schools and churches in developing social awareness and morality.

Secondly, an issue may be deliberately kept off the political agenda resulting in the absence or sabotage of policy. Peter Bachrach and Morton Baratz have argued that power has 'two faces': one where policy decisions are made and another where non-decisions are made because issues are deliberately suppressed. They have argued that

> non decision-making is a means by which demands for change in the existing allocation of benefits and privileges in the community can be suffocated before they are even voiced; or kept covert; or killed before they gain access to the relevant decision-making arena; or, failing all these things, maimed or destroyed in the decision-implementing state of the policy process (Bachrach and Baratz, 1971, p. 44).

The hidden face of power is explored in Chapter 24 in relation to the political agenda and myths concerning poverty in Britain.

Finally, when governments find that particular policies are failing to attract public support they may argue that the fault lies in the media rather than with ministers. In such cases it will be argued that there is nothing wrong with the *policy* in question, but there are problems with the way in which it is being *presented*. This argument was made by the Thatcher Government during the introduction of the unpopular 'poll tax' (Chapter 11). Ministers argued that there was a sound logic behind the poll tax, but this was not being put across by the media and understood by the public. It was argued that once the public understood the poll tax, they would support it. The Major Government accepted that presentation of the poll tax was negative because the policy was flawed and that the public fully understood this.

Source: Anglia Press.

Figure 19.1   *Problem with policy presentation for MAFF. The Minister feeds his daughter with a beefburger in an attempt to reassure the public that beef is safe despite 'mad cow' disease*

Policy-Making and Decision-Making

Whilst it is important to define terms in the study of government and politics, this is particularly difficult when it comes to *policy-making* and *decision-making*. For example, is it valid to refer to 'opposition party policy' using the same term to describe 'government policy'? There is an important difference between the two in so far as opposition policy is no more than a set of *aspirations* about what the party thinks it might do if in office, whereas Government policy is *operational* since it is generally implemented. Also there are definitional problems with Bachrach and Baratz's concept of a 'non-decision' since deliberately keeping an issue off the political agenda involves making a choice, so a 'non-decision' is also a 'decision'. And finally, what is the difference between a *policy* and a *decision*? The replacement of rates with the community charge, the privatisation of prisons, or putting VAT (Value-added tax) on domestic fuel: were these measures policies or decisions?

Rob Baggott has ventured a definition of policy: 'a policy is a general stance on an issue (or issues), which implicitly or explicitly sets goals and priorities. It may involve the making of plans, and the taking of decisions and actions, but these are not necessary for a policy to emerge or exist' (Baggott, 1991, p. 50).

Richard Snyder and his colleagues defined decision-making as 'a process which results in the selection from a socially defined, limited number of problematical, alternative projects of one project intended to bring about the particular future state of affairs envisaged by the decision-makers' (Snyder, Bruck and Sapin, 1960, p. 155). A more basic distinction is that 'what to do?' answers policy-making questions, and 'how to do it?' answers decision-making questions.

■ Decision-Making Theory

How are decisions actually arrived at? There has been a great deal of research by American political scientists into the process of decision-making. The pioneers in this area of research include Herbert Simon, David Braybrooke, Charles Lindblom, Graham Allison and Amitai Etzioni. Between them, they have devised a number of 'models' or theories to help explain how decisions are made in the real world of politics and government.

❏ *Rational Decision-Making*

Most individuals want others to see them as 'rational'. The term 'rational' is used in a slightly different sense when it comes to decision-making theory. A rational decision is one where decision-makers consider all the possible courses of action, then work out the consequences which would follow each one and finally evaluate all the consequences before selecting the 'best' choice, which is the one most likely to achieve their goals. The definition, quoted already, by Snyder, Bruck and Sapin is of a *rational* decision in which it is assumed that decision-makers are guided by goals.

Herbert Simon, who first defined the rational decision, was criticised because in real life situations politicians rarely have all the information necessary to make rational decisions. Would Margaret Thatcher have pressed ahead with the 'poll tax', rejecting all compromises, had she known all its future political consequences? Even when governments make great efforts to collect all relevant information, rational decisions need not follow. For example, in the 1960s Britain was developing a sophisticated multi-role combat aircraft, the TSR-2, whilst the Americans were developing the rather similar swing-wing F-111 aircraft. A new Labour Government reviewed the TSR-2 project, taking into account all information available at the time concerning the costs of the TSR-2 compared with the F-111, the defence needs of Britain's changing external role, and the likely decline in importance of manned aircraft in the 'age of the missile'. Labour Defence Secretary, Denis Healey, considered all options and took the *rational* decision in 1965 to cancel the TSR-2 and buy the much cheaper F-111, but was it the *right* decision? Subsequent events showed that the F-111 performed poorly, that manned aircraft were to remain important, and that TSR-2 costs were artificially high because they included development costs of the Phantom and Harrier aircraft.

Simon accepted the criticism that decision-makers rarely have total information, and he modified his theory to one of *bounded rationality*. He acknowledged that real-life decision-making is bounded by constraints and that usually a choice has to be made between poorly defined and ambiguous options each with incomplete information. Under these circumstances, decision-makers agree on what is an 'acceptable' decision. This is referred to as *satisficing;* in other words, decision-makers do not select the 'best' rational decision, but one which is satisfactory in terms of being 'good enough'. Given the imperfect information about the TSR-2 and F-111 available to Denis Healey in 1965, his decision to cancel the project seems then a better example of satisficing than of rational decision-making.

Incrementalism

David Braybrooke and Charles Lindblom argued that decision-making could be best understood in terms of what they termed *disjointed incrementalism*. This can be described as 'decision-making through small or incremental moves on particular problems rather than through a comprehensive reform programme. It is also endless, it takes the form of an indefinite sequence of policy moves.' (Braybrooke and Lindblom, 1963, p. 71). In a later article, Braybrooke was to describe his theory as 'the science of muddling through'.

Basically, it was argued that when a particular policy began failing and producing an unsatisfactory or undesirable situation, small changes in policy are made as decision-makers move cautiously towards what they hope will be an improved situation. It is important to note that incremental decision-making tends to move away from an undesirable situation rather than be directed towards predefined policy goals.

Trade union legislation, discussed in Chapter 25, provides an interesting contrast between the policy-making of two Conservative administrations. The Government, led by Edward Heath, attempted to reform trade unions with one far-reaching Act, and failed. In contrast, the step-by-step legislation, expediently taking advantage of union weakness during recession, provided Margaret Thatcher with a successful outcome.

Mixed Scanning

Amitai Etzioni has devised a decision-making model which is basically a compromise between the rational approach and incrementalism. Mixed scanning involves decision-making being done in two distinct phases. In considering a problem, decision-makers first make a broad sweep, or scan, of all the policy options available and assess them in terms of how far each would go toward meeting their objectives. Then decision-making becomes more narrowly focused and incremental in nature as details are agreed on the selected policy option.

How might mixed scanning operate? A chancellor faced with a problem such as a budget deficit may consider a wide range of measures which are available to him. He may decide to do nothing, or to raise taxes, or to cut public spending. Having decided which option or option mix best matches his goals, then attention will focus on the detail of, say, which tax should be raised, by what percentage, and starting from what date, etc.

The Organisation Model

In his study of the Cuban Missile Crisis of 1962, Graham Allison analysed events in terms of alternatives to the rational model. The first of these was the organisation process model in which decisions are seen as the outputs of large organisations functioning according to regular patterns of behaviour. Decisions emerge as the result of negotiation and bargaining between organisations. In the past political scientists have pointed out how the organisation of government in Britain affected decisions concerning Northern Ireland (see Chapter 29). Until 1972 Northern Ireland was governed from Stormont, and Westminster took relatively little interest in the Province's affairs until the 'Troubles' began. Unlike Scotland, there had been no separate government department concerned with its affairs. It is interesting to speculate how different the recent history of Northern Ireland might have been had there been greater Westminster involvement during the 1950s and 1960s.

The Bureaucratic Politics Model

Graham Allison also analysed the Kennedy Administration's decisions in terms of what he called the government politics model, but which in the context of British politics is better understood as a bureaucratic politics model. Allison argued that what happened in 1962 was characterised as the result of various negotiations between those in government with top civil servants playing a key role. Policy emerges from bargains and compromises made by ministers and their civil servants representing different departmental interests and priorities (see Chapter 9). In other words, decisions which emerge are not in the *national interest* but in the interests of particular bureaucracies. For example, Chapter 30 gives details of the large cuts made in Britain's armed forces during the early 1990s. Were these cuts in defence calculated by the Ministry of Defence in response to the reduced international threat resulting from the ending of the cold war? Or, as some Conservative MPs suspected, were the defence cuts insisted on by the Treasury which was determined to reduce spending on defence under the guise of the 'peace dividend'? They suspected that bureaucratic politics resulted in defence cuts providing public spending savings which suited the needs of the Treasury rather than the defence needs of the country.

■ The Policy-Making Process

Having considered decision-making theory, it is timely to examine how and where policies are made in Britain's political system. Figure 19.2 shows a basic representation of the political system, and it should be noted that all the institutions shown have been discussed in earlier chapters.

At the heart of the system lies the Cabinet and Cabinet committee system. Chapter 8 examined power and decision-making within the executive in terms of defining the role of the Prime Minister in the policy process and identifying the constraints on prime ministerial power. Chapter 9 explored the revolution which has taken place within the civil service as well as the power relationship between ministers and their civil servants. What is particularly notable about the British decision-making process is the power of the Treasury to influence the policy proposed in every other ministry through its control over departmental spending.

It is possible to argue that when dealing with technical issues in which the public has little

interest, these small and powerful elites make decisions in a rational manner. This is based on the big assumption, of course, that all members of the elite concerned are highly informed and share similar policy goals. In reality, this would be unlikely. It is normal for political tensions to exist between government departments and between ministers and their civil servants, in which case the organisation model and bureaucratic politics model will be more useful in explaining decision-making than the rational model.

However, once an issue is placed on the political agenda by the mass media (Chapter 16), is discussed in Parliament (Chapter 12), considered by political parties (Chapter 13) and concerns public opinion (Chapter 14), so the issue will become increasingly politicised. Under these circumstances it is very unlikely that those involved in the policy debate will share similar political goals. Even members of the same political party will be divided into competing factions or tendencies, and it is commonplace for members of the same pressure group (Chapter 15) to have different political aspirations. Where policy emerges through the close involvement of sectional interest groups with government departments in a client or corporate relationship, or where policy emerges through a central-local dependency relationship (Chapter 11) then it is likely to have the characteristics of 'muddling through'.

Decisions will be the result of the interaction of participants in a power network. In order to reach agreement on issues they are likely to avoid setting out their political goals in detail, since this would be the cause of conflict. Policies and decisions which are ambiguous and understood differently by participants in the policy process generally contribute towards building a consensus and enabling progress to be made on an issue. In contrast, conviction politics based on explicit political goals generates conflict and maximises opposition. It is for this reason that incrementalism in policy-making has been the general hallmark of contemporary British politics.

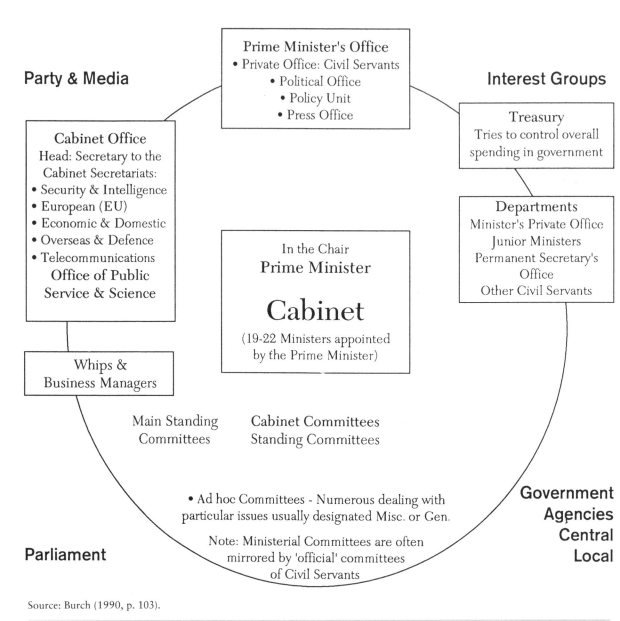

Party & Media

Interest Groups

Prime Minister's Office
- Private Office: Civil Servants
  - Political Office
  - Policy Unit
  - Press Office

Cabinet Office
Head: Secretary to the
Cabinet Secretariats:
- Security & Intelligence
- European (EU)
- Economic & Domestic
- Overseas & Defence
- Telecommunications
**Office of Public
Service & Science**

Treasury
Tries to control overall
spending in government

Departments
Minister's Private Office
Junior Ministers
Permanent Secretary's
Office
Other Civil Servants

In the Chair
Prime Minister

Cabinet

(19-22 Ministers appointed
by the Prime Minister)

**Whips &
Business Managers**

Main Standing
Committees

Cabinet Committees
Standing Committees

- Ad hoc Committees - Numerous dealing with
particular issues usually designated Misc. or Gen.

Note: Ministerial Committees are often
mirrored by 'official' committees
of Civil Servants

**Government
Agencies
Central
Local**

Parliament

Source: Burch (1990, p. 103).

Figure 19.2 *The policy-making process*

■ Political Leadership

Political scientists have paid considerable attention to the significance of leadership style in policy-making. In particular there has been lengthy debate about the development of the office of prime minister into a presidential role. A recent contribution to this debate from Michael Foley considered issues such as the changing ways in which prime ministers and modern presidents communicate with the electorate and relate with other elements of government. A feature of the

American political system is the political distance presidents put between themselves and Washington politics, a strategy which

> allows a president to remain an integral and even central part of government, whilst at the same time affording him the opportunity of detaching himself from government and, thereby, relinquishing responsibility for much of what it does. Paradoxically, it might even be said that this sort of spatial detachment has become one of the most effective ways for a president to maintain his central position in government. (Foley, 1993, pp. 24–5)

In British politics, Prime Minister Margaret Thatcher frequently acted like an outsider in Number Ten, becoming engaged in a struggle against her Cabinet and Whitehall over the direction and content of policy. The outsider role enabled Thatcher to campaign against her own Government ministers, implying that they lacked her vision and generally were not up to the job, whilst at the same time detaching herself from their policy failures and allowing her to dominate the machinery of government.

Leadership involves qualities in the exercise of power which are over and above prime ministerial and presidential styles. Within a given power structure, leadership can be exercised in a number of qualitatively different ways. For example, some prime ministers have played a 'hands-off' role regarding policy-making and issues of government, intervening only when a major problem arose or if a specific policy was failing consistently. As prime minister, Sir Alec Douglas-Home adopted a **laissez-faire form of leadership**. He explained his leadership style in an interview, stating that 'a good prime minister, once he had selected his ministers and made it plain to them he was always accessible for comment or advice, should interfere with their departmental business as little as possible'.

Other prime ministers have played a more positive role in leading the government, making sure that policy kept the backbenchers relatively content. Sometimes this might involve the prime minister acting as broker to make compromises in policy; other times it might involve the prime minister as a wheeler dealer satisfying one party faction in one policy area and another faction in another policy area. Sometimes this type of leadership is referred to as *transactional*, and Harold Wilson as prime minister provides an example of power being exercised in this manner.

Finally, some prime ministers have led in ways which were initially at odds with the wishes of their followers but which won their support in the course of time. Charisma, personality and inspiration have frequently been important factors in gaining the support of others in the party who come to share the leader's vision of what sort of society should be created. This type of leadership is referred to as **transformational**. Margaret Thatcher's dislike of lengthy cabinet discussions, which she saw as a waste of time, her distaste for consensus politics, which were at odds with her strong political convictions, together with her personal domination of the cabinet and wider party, were preconditions for the **Thatcher revolution**, a contemporary example of transformational leadership in practice.

The way in which leadership is exercised has a considerable impact on the policy-making process. The *laissez-faire* approach tends to result in strong continuity in policies which are made at departmental level. The prime minister's thinking is guided by the 'if it ain't broke, don't fix it' rule. Only when one Department's policy works against other Departments' policies or is failing in some other way, will the prime minister intervene in order to find a solution. Such a government's policies will reflect different departmental views, tend to be pragmatic in nature, and, although coordinated at cabinet level, are unlikely to be unified through being based on the same ideological beliefs.

Prime ministers leading in a transactional way will play a much greater 'hands on' role in managing policy-making. Harold Wilson once described the role of prime minister as being like the conductor of an orchestra; talented and ambitious players, many of whom will want to star as soloists, have to be brought together to play the same tune in harmony. In political terms, this means rewarding some people, disappointing others, whilst still keeping the support of as many as possible. Policy emerges heavily influenced by patronage and compromise. For example, prime minister Harold Wilson created a new ministry, the Department of Economic Affairs (DEA), as a long-term thinking counterweight to the short-term thinking Treasury. Clearly this initiative had the potential for making a considerable impact on Labour's economic policy-making as well as challenging the Treasury's influence on other departments' policy-making. But many suspected that Wilson created the DEA simply to provide his troublesome deputy, George Brown, with an apparently important role whilst preventing him from being Foreign Secretary, which was the job George Brown really wanted. If this suspicion was true, then policy-making was influenced by the way in which personal political ambitions in cabinet were satisfied and rewarded. It had little to do with counter-balancing the Treasury.

Transformational leadership is very much a 'hands on' approach to government, with the political vision of the inspirational leader providing the basis of all policy-making. Departmental policies should be unified since they are all derived from the same ideological source. For example, Margaret Thatcher's convictions about the enterprise economy and competition, and her strong preference for free-market solutions, provided the basis not only for economic policy, but also for education reforms, health service reforms, civil service reforms and local government reforms. The main danger for the transformational leader is policy which deviates from the vision. This happened for Thatcher when her Chancellor took Britain into the ERM (see Chapter 20), a policy she believed doomed to failure since 'you can't buck the market' by having strict foreign currency controls. The main danger for others is that the ideology is flawed. If markets fail, if they produce too many losers who rebel against government, if people are not motivated by the profit motive, or if market forces result in corruption, then there would be massive policy failure. Policy would be characterised by what political scientists refer to as 'unintended consequences' which beyond a certain point result in a 'policy mess' at the level of implementation.

■ Sources of Policy Advice

Parties competing for office have wanted to win support on the basis of what has become known as the 'Big Idea'. In many ways, Thatcherism was the Big Idea which inspired a number of policy initiatives which prevented Conservative administrations from looking exhausted at successive general elections. Labour has conducted a policy review which has eliminated its traditional big idea – socialism – from its manifesto in favour of more centrist policies.

The Conservatives have been assisted in policy formulation by a constant stream of proposals from right-wing think-tanks such as the Institute of Economic Affairs, the Centre for Policy Studies, the Adam Smith Institute, Policy Search and the Social Affairs Unit. The importance of these groups was that they were able to 'think the unthinkable' since their activities were conducted outside the party. If one of the think-tanks floated a policy proposal which was widely criticised, it did not damage the reputation of the Conservative Government. Damage was done, however, if a flawed think-tank policy was adopted and implemented by government. The latter occurred when the Adam Smith Institute's idea of financing local government with a 'poll tax' was adopted by Mrs Thatcher.

In the past Labour had the reputation of being a 'thinking party' capable of producing radical policies, but in recent years Labour's policy-making has been criticised for lacking fresh ideas. The Fabians have not played a very vigorous role in generating new ideas, nor have there been individuals able to do this as Anthony Crosland did in the past. However, the recently formed Commission on Social Justice holds the possibility of injecting new, but not necessarily welcome, ideas into Labour's policy-making process.

It has been argued that civil servants, unlike their partisan counterparts in the United States, are poor sources of policy ideas. British civil servants are frequently portrayed as amateurs and generalists, living in a Whitehall village which is cut off from the real world of industry, commerce and those at the delivery end of the public sector (see Chapter 9). What civil servants are able to do skilfully, it is argued, is take on board policy advice from specialists – scientists, professional specialists and others with specific expertise – and blend it with what is politically feasible as the basis of advice for their ministers.

Many pressure groups as well as the think-tanks have established networks which include Whitehall contacts. Groups with insider status frequently have the opportunity of influencing policy at the formulation stage, whilst less favoured outsider groups have to rely on influencing public opinion in their attempts to shape policy (Chapter 15). The involvement of pressure groups in Whitehall can be seen as a feature of consensus politics, and it is therefore not a surprise that pressure groups played a smaller role in policy-making during the Thatcher years. Indeed, one of her ministers attacked pressure groups, describing them as 'strangling serpents' which increased the workload of ministers and got in the way of good government.

Finally, Britain's membership of the European Union (see Chapter 7) is an increasingly important source of policy. However, with the Conservative Party deeply divided on the prospects of greater federalism and policy harmonisation, European policies are likely to present the Government with many problems. Indeed, such policies may be approached in terms of a damage limitation exercise; much emphasis will be put on presentation, subsidiarity will be emphasised, with the comforting knowledge that there is little that backbenchers can do to change such policies.

Summary

Decision-making is a complex process. In politics, decision-making can be understood more clearly by applying a number of theoretical perspectives such as rational decision-making and incrementalism. All the theories have some use in explaining how decisions are made but it is not easy to make generalisations. Nevertheless, given the institutional context within which policy is made in Britain, there is a strong case for arguing that incrementalism most typifies the policy process.

Questions

1. Herbert Simon argued that the task of decision-makers was 'to select that one of the strategies which is followed by the preferred set of consequences'. To what extent is the Government made up of rational decision-makers?

2. Explain the nature of incremental decision-making. Evaluate its usefulness in explaining how policy is made in Britain.

3. How would you assess whether or not a particular issue was on the 'political agenda'?

4. In what ways might different styles of political leadership affect the policy-making process?

Assignment

Thatcherism and policy change

There is no doubt that 1979 was a watershed in British politics since the old policies of the postwar consensus began being replaced by radical Thatcherite policies. New thinking by the Thatcher governments resulted in policies which no previous postwar government had followed with any vigour. The old policies of the 1970s had failed and were swept aside. Corporatism was replaced by monetarism. Large tracts of the nationalised industries were privatised. Millions of council tenants were given the chance to become home-owners, and many seized the opportunity. The old debilitating 'dependency' culture was replaced by an energetic 'enterprise culture'.

Thatcherism and policy continuity

Margaret Thatcher's policies appeared different because of her robust personality and clever rhetoric when presenting them. Essentially her policies were based on those pursued by previous governments. Thatcherism was no more than a recycling and repackaging of old, mostly Labour, policies. For example, monetarism was not new since the Labour Chancellor had been applying monetary controls since 1976. Thatcher's key policy of privatisation was not new: the previous Labour Government had sold part of its shareholding in British Petroleum. Nor was the sale of council houses new – it had been taking place on a small scale since the 1920s. Finally, there was no 'enterprise culture'. Poll after poll showed that the electorate favoured greater public spending on health, education and social benefits.

Consider the contrasting accounts of Thatcherite policies. How could each version be explained in terms of decision-making models? Which version and which model appear to be most useful in explaining Thatcherite policy-making? To what extent would additional information on the role of trade unions and local government provide support for the choices you have made?

Further reading

Baggott, R. (1990–1) 'The Policy-Making Process in British Central Government', *Talking Politics*, 3: 2, winter, pp. 50–56.

Burns, B. (1978) *Leadership* (New York: Harper & Row).

Foley, M. (1993) *The Rise of the British Presidency* (Manchester University Press).

Greenaway, J., Smith, S. and Street, J. (1992) *Deciding Factors in British Politics: A Case-Studies Approach* (London: Routledge).

McGrew, A. and Wilson, M. (eds) (1982) *Decision Making: Approaches and Analysis* (Manchester University Press).

■ *Chapter 20* ■

Management of the Economy

The Tools of Economic Management   Managing the Economy

Britain was the first country to have an industrial revolution and to develop a capitalist economy. Over 40 per cent of the world's trade involved British goods. Two hundred years later Britain has an ailing economy and a 6 per cent share of world trade. For many years the British economy has been in relative decline with Britain seeming unable to shake off the reputation of being the 'sick man of Europe'. Successive governments seemed content to manage Britain's decline so as to soften the blows and mitigate its worst effects. Some were critical of this fatalistic attitude and argued that there was nothing inevitable about Britain's decline. They believed that Thatcherite economics would reverse Britain's fortunes. Were they justified in thinking this? Was there an economic miracle during the Thatcher years? What went wrong?

■ The Tools of Economic Management

The state of the economy and how it affects them personally is an important issue in influencing the way people vote. Because of this political factors play a central role in the way that government manages the economy. Past governments have been criticised for 'stop-go' economic policies which 'go' for growth during the period in the run-up to a general election, winning the approval of the electorate, but then 'stop' once the election has been held in order for the economy to cool down. In political terms it may represent a successful economy strategy, but businessmen are critical of the damage done to the economy through the instability and uncertainty

that 'stop-go' creates. (Figure 20.1) What, then, are the major tools available to government for managing the economy?

☐ *Intervention*

Governments can manage the economy through direct controls and intervention. In directing the wartime economy, the Government led by Winston Churchill assumed massive powers of intervention in controlling the labour force, deciding on the location of industry, requisitioning economic assets, rationing the supply of raw materials to factories, and so on. These controls largely disappeared during the 1950s but nevertheless peacetime governments have attempted since to control aspects of the economy through intervention. For example, in the fight against inflation Labour and Conservative governments have implemented prices and incomes policies. In 1961 a Conservative Chancellor, Selwyn-Lloyd, introduced the 'pay pause', a nine-month long incomes policy designed to hold down pay awards. Between 1965 and 1969 Labour pursued a prices and incomes policy, and the Conservative government which followed converted an informal incomes policy into a statutory policy which controlled all incomes between 1972 and 1974. The Labour Government returned to office in 1974 developed a voluntary incomes policy – known as the 'social contract' – which, under the leadership of James Callaghan finally broke down in the 'Winter of Discontent' of 1978–79. The industrial disputes during Labour's winter of discontent were an important factor in the Conservative election victory which saw Margaret

362

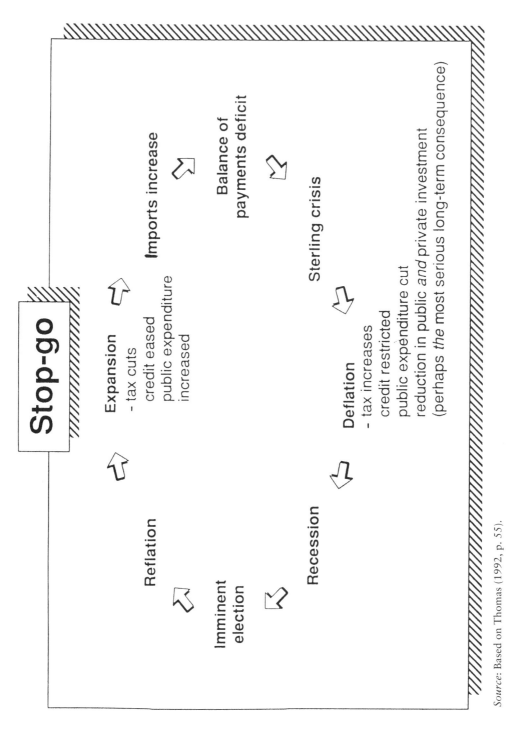

Source: Based on Thomas (1992, p. 55).

Figure 20.1 Stop-go

Thatcher enter Number Ten promising economic management which would rely much more on market forces and far less on government intervention.

During Thatcher's years in office her governments gained a reputation for thinking that 'industry doesn't matter' within the context of Britain having a successful economy. Previous governments, Labour and Conservative, had taken a different view and had implemented industrial policies designed to achieve growth and improve productivity.

Impressed by the success of economic planning in France, a Conservative Government set up the National Economic Development Council (NEDC) – also known as 'Neddy' – in 1962 as a forum in which governments and both sides of industry discussed plans to improve Britain's industrial efficiency and international competitiveness. Later Labour governments set up other interventionist bodies – the Industrial Reorganisation Corporation (IRC) in 1966 and the National Enterprise Board (NEB) in 1975 – with a view to restructure and strengthen Britain's industrial base. By the 1990s all of these interventionist bodies had been abolished.

Economically depressed areas of Britain can be stimulated and improved through an interventionist regional policy which attempts to attract new investment though grants and other financial incentives. Britain's industrial base would have been in an even worse state had it not been for the foreign investment – some £40 billion between 1988 and 1993 – which has created new manufacturing jobs. Some believe that by the year 2000 one in five of Britain's manufacturing jobs will be in a foreign-owned factory.

☐ *Fiscal Policy*

Fiscal policy involves the government managing the economy through taxation and public spending. If the economy is depressed with high levels of unemployment, the government may *(i)* reduce taxes in order to stimulate the economy. Income tax may be reduced so that employees will have more money to spend, or other taxes such as VAT or car tax may be reduced in order to make goods cheaper and thereby encourage more people to buy them; *(ii)* increase public spending on, for example, new roads, hospitals and schools, in order to create new jobs which, as these new workers start spending more, will create yet more new jobs.

Other economic problems, such as a balance of payments deficit or a budget deficit, may be tackled by the government raising taxes and attempting to reduce public spending. Government may pursue other policies through taxation, such as promoting good health through taxing cigarettes or improving the environment through lower taxation of lead-free petrol.

Until 1992 governments announced taxation and spending plans as two separate but related exercises, but from thereon the budget and autumn statements were merged. In 1992, in the depths of a recession, the Government was borrowing a massive £50 billion a year. Governments frequently spend more than they raise in taxes, and so have to borrow to fill this gap. The sum borrowed is known as the Public Sector Borrowing Requirement (PSBR).

☐ *Monetary Controls*

Monetary policy is carried out by the Bank of England and the Treasury in attempting to control the volume of money and purchasing power in the economy, and thereby influencing movements in the inflation rate and the level of consumer spending. The main tool of monetary control is the minimum lending rate (MLR), usually referred to by politicians and the public as simply the 'interest rate'. The level of interest rate determines the cost of borrowing money – a high interest rate will make borrowing expensive and so will lower the demand for credit. It will also mean that mortgages will become more expensive and so take more money out of the home buyers' pockets, which also means that they in turn will have less money available to spend on goods. A low interest rate will mean that money will be cheap to borrow, encouraging consumers to purchase goods on credit. Lower mortgage payments will also mean that home-buyers will have more money available for consumer goods.

Interest rates gained a greater significance when Britain joined the Exchange Rate Mechanism (ERM) of the European Monetary System (EMS). Some believe that the EMS is the first step towards the economic and monetary union which would be necessary for a federal European Union, whilst others see it as simply providing the currency stability necessary for the single market to operate successfully. The ERM involved fixing the exchange rates of Community members so that they could move only marginally against each other. If sterling's international value slipped, then interest rates would be raised in order to make the pound more attractive and thereby increase its value on the foreign exchanges. Should demand for sterling push its value towards the upper limit of its ERM band, then the interest rate would be lowered in order to depress demand.

Margaret Thatcher was persuaded in 1990 that Britain should enter the ERM, although she did not believe in fixed exchange rates since 'you can't buck the market'. Her scepticism was justified to some extent on Wednesday 16 September 1992 when, within hours, interest rates were raised from 10 to 15 per cent to defend the falling pound, then reduced again to 10 per cent with the pound being withdrawn from the ERM. Furthermore, almost all Britain's foreign reserves had been spent in this unsuccessful defence of sterling.

■ Managing the Economy

Some have argued that the most distinctive features of Thatcherism were to be found in the economic policy followed during the 1980s. In basic terms, previous postwar governments had identified **unemployment** as the biggest economic evil to be tackled, and thus they gave high priority to policies which reduced the number of people out of work. The Thatcher governments identified **inflation** as the biggest economic evil, and so governments followed policies which were

designed to 'squeeze' inflation out of the economy. These policies were referred to as 'monetarism', and involved measures to reduce the levels of public spending, placing greater reliance on free market forces, and tighter control on the money supply. The latter measure, controlling the growth of the money supply, comprised a series of targets which was sometimes known as the 'Medium Term Financial Strategy' (MTFS). As the Thatcher years progressed, so control of the money supply was given less prominence, and privatisation took over as the main element of economic policy. That, in turn, was replaced by Britain's entry into the ERM as forming the basis of the Government's economic policy. Under the leadership of John Major, and with the ERM policy in tatters, the Thatcher priorities were abandoned and the creation of jobs became the central, if elusive, goal of economic policy.

□ The Monetarist Experiment

Monetarist policies were implemented during the period 1979–82. The Chancellor lowered the rate of income tax, doubled the level of VAT, and used high interest rates to limit the growth in the money supply. Inflation eventually began to fall but the high interest rate crippled many firms and caused a massive rise in unemployment. By 1982, one in five jobs in manufacturing had disappeared.

Some believed that mass unemployment was being used as a political weapon to curb trade union power. Previous governments which had used interventionist tools of economic management frequently relied on the co-operation of trade unions. But trade unions were not in a strong position to 'deliver' on deals made with the government. For what often seemed an acceptable agreement to trade union leaders was rejected by the rank and file. The attraction of monetarist policies to the Government was that they could be implemented without the co-operation or consent of the trade unions. Since the goodwill of the trade unions was no longer necessary to implement economic policy, the Government felt able to erode the power and privileges until then enjoyed by unions.

Unemployment weakened trade unions, particularly in the old traditional industries of the North most noted for their union militancy.

Others were concerned that monetarist policies, which they saw as weakening Britain's manufacturing industries, were only possible because of the large revenues earned by North Sea oil. A controversial House of Lords Select Committee *Report on Overseas Trade* (1985) was concerned that continued de-industrialisation posed 'a grave threat to the standard of living and to the economic and political stability of the nation'. The Report argued that unless policies were changed, even more manufacturing industries would disappear in the future. In addition it was argued that national output would get even smaller since no other industries such as banking or entertainment would expand to fill the gap in the nation's wealth caused by the collapse of manufacturing; that the very high levels of unemployment would become a permanent feature of the British economy; that fewer firms and fewer people in jobs would result in the government collecting less tax so that drastic real cuts would have to be made in public spending; and that as the economy stagnated and North Sea oil

ran out, so the value of sterling would fall, causing the cost of imported raw materials to rise, with consequent high inflation. By the early 1990s it appeared that their Lordships' predictions could be recognised in the form of a severe recession.

□ *The 'Economic Miracle'*

By 1985 the attempt to control growth in the money supply, the MTFS, had been abandoned. As Fig. 20.2 shows, the money supply (M3) frequently rose above the targets which had been set for it even when the Treasury set newer and higher targets. It can be seen how far the 1985 target was reset above the 1980 target, and yet even the 1985 target was overshot by the actual growth in the money supply.

The Government maintained monetarist rhetoric and talked as if Chancellor Lawson was pursuing policies similar to those of Chancellor Howe. But in reality the economy was being managed in a 'stop-go' manner. The economy was stimulated in the run-up to the 1983 General Election and again, in a much more determined

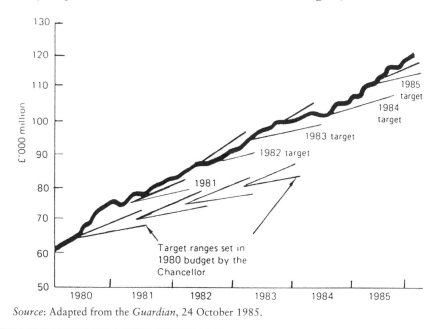

Source: Adapted from the *Guardian*, 24 October 1985.

Figure 20.2   *Monetary targets, 1980–5*

way, in the run-up to the 1987 General Election. The economy was reflated with a mixture of public spending increases, tax cuts, and low interest rates. A lengthy consumer boom was fired by cheap credit and the willingness of people to borrow money to spend as the value of their homes rose sharply.

For a brief period the principal economic indicators were moving in the right direction: unemployment was falling, inflation was falling, interest rates were falling and economic growth was rising. This was the 'economic miracle' and it was accompanied by much heady and unrealistic talk of Britain having overtaken Japan and Germany in terms of economic performance. Looking back at the 1980s, Will Hutton commented:

> The 1980s, the decade of the economic miracle, was in reality 10 years of wild economic mismanagement and monstrous self-delusion. Britain over-consumed and under-produced to an astonishing degree and has been left with its finances – private, public and external – in such disarray that it may take the whole of the 1990s to recover. And even that is not certain (*The Guardian*, 18 March 1993).

This gloomy assessment remains when the Thatcher economic record is compared with the records of other postwar governments. Table 20.1 shows that no economic miracle took place. Indeed, a comparison of macroeconomic indicators reveals that other governments, both Labour and Conservative, have considerably better records in managing the economy.

Some from the radical Right have argued that the relatively poor record of the Thatcher years

resulted from the fact that monetarism, including the MTFS, was cast aside. In other words, they argued that had subsequent chancellors stuck faithfully to monetarism then the final record of the Thatcher years would have been much better. Others disagreed with this view and argue that the poor Thatcher record was a result of policies conducted between 1979 and 1982 and, had these policies not been abandoned, then the situation at the end of the 1980s would have been even worse than it was. For them, monetarism was the cause, not the cure, of Britain's poor economic performance.

☐ *From Miracle to Crisis*

In the spring of 1988 the Chancellor, Nigel Lawson, was being described as 'the greatest chancellor of the century' but interest rates were to rise nine times before the end of the year and there was speculation that the Chancellor was in danger of being sacked. The economy was overheating; the Chancellor wished to slow down economic activity and bring an end to the consumer boom without causing a recession. Britain's economy now faced a massive balance of payments crisis accompanied by rising inflation and rising interest rates.

After a bitter row with Mrs Thatcher, Nigel Lawson resigned from the Cabinet and was replaced, briefly, by John Major. His task was to bring about what was referred to as a 'soft landing' in which the economy slowed down without sliding into recession. Sterling entered the

Table 20.1   *The main economic indicators under postwar governments*

	Growth of GDP (%)	Inflation (%)	Unemployment (%)
Conservatives: 1951–64	3.2	3.5	1.7
Labour: 1964–70	2.4	5.2	2.0
Conservatives: 1970–74	2.4	11.7	3.1
Labour: 1974–79	1.8	21.2	4.7
Conservatives: 1979–88	2.0	8.4	9.5

Note: Figures show annual averages based on data in *The Guardian* (26 April 1989).

ERM and it was recognised that this would cause some economic hardship in the short term, particularly if inflation made British goods uncompetitive abroad, but longer term benefits of ERM membership would be low inflation and low interest rates. The Government was taken by surprise by the depth and length of the recession which began in the late 1980s. At first it was described as a 'blip' in the economy; later it was clear that Britain was in the middle of the deepest recession since the 1930s. From December 1990 Chancellor Lamont began observing the 'green shoots of recovery' and reassured the public that the recession would be 'relatively short-lived and relatively shallow'.

By 1993 some economists were worried that Britain's recession was turning into a slump which was bankrupting or closing a firm every six minutes. The Government argued that Britain's recession was not unique since the economies of all European countries were undergoing a prolonged period of recession. But critics argued that Britain's economy was experiencing both a longer and a deeper recession than our European partners.

After the dramatic events of September 1992, referred to above, some economists believed that Britain's withdrawal from the ERM and subsequent devalued pound would stimulate the economy and bring about a recovery. The failure of free-market Thatcherism, the collapse of the ERM policy, and the frightening prospect of mass unemployment on a scale not yet experienced in Britain, have resulted in some economists arguing that John Major's Government has no option but to follow a basically Keynesian economic policy. However, this will be a difficult strategy to pursue since the Chancellor is penned in by both a massive trade deficit and a huge budget deficit, as well as commitments not to raise taxes. The cure for the economy will be unpalatable in political terms; once-rejected tools for economic management will have to be adopted and past election pledges will have to be ignored.

Summary

Different governments have given different priorities to the management of the British economy. During the early post-war years, governments intervened in the economy in order to maintain high levels of employment but during the 1980s governments intervened far less in order to expand the working of the free market. Their primary aim became to reduce inflation. Since Britain left the ERM, the economy has experienced a patchy recovery with falling unemployment and low inflation but with higher levels of taxation to help reduce the large budget deficit.

Questions

1. The rot set in with the country's readiness to accept the sham panacea of Thatcherism way back in 1979; and it spread throughout the 1980s. It was madness to start the battle against inflation in 1979 by doubling it; it was madness to argue that possession of North Sea oil meant that manufacturing did not matter; and it was madness to obliterate up to a quarter of the manufacturing base in an attempt to conquer inflation ....

Explain the reasons behind William Keegan's opposition to Thatcherite economic thinking.

2. 'Chancellors require two characteristics in their audience: gullibility and amnesia. They want us to believe everything they say now, and to forget everything they said before.' How far do you agree or disagree with this statement?

3. 'Governments no longer have the freedom to manage their countries' economies.' How valid is this statement with regard to management of the British economy?

4. 'There will be stop-go economic policies as long as governments want to be reelected.' How accurate is this statement?

Assignments

1. *Thatcherism and the economy*
   The following material concerns the impact of Thatcherite economics on Britain's manufacturing base. Consider the political implications involved. Write briefing notes for candidates in a forthcoming by-election which (i) support the Government's policy and are optimistic about the future of British manufacturing and (ii) attack the Government's record and present a pessimistic view of the future.

   The graph demonstrates the principal manifestation of Britain's recent economic difficulties, the strong association between reflation (represented here by monetary expansion) and a rising balance of payments deficit. Once again we seem to have encountered a familiar problem; that British manufacturers are unable to take advantage of expansions of the domestic market and earn enough foreign currency through exporting. Critics of the Thatcher regime point to alarming statistics which imply that the British economy as a whole is now considerably worse off than it was in 1979. Gross domestic product grew less in the 1980s than in any decade since the last war; net investment in manufacturing was down by 67 per cent compared to the 1970s; and, consequently, a £5 billion trade surplus in manufactures in 1979 was turned into a £5 billion *deficit* 10 years later. In response, Thatcherites would point to the fact that, despite the above, by the end of the decade British manufacturing had surpassed its record output levels of 1974. They would also defend themselves by arguing that manufacturing is only one aspect of the economy; most people are employed and most wealth earned elsewhere. This brings us closer to the heart of the debate on Thatcherite economics: have they created the wrong sort of economy? The second Thatcher recession was brought about when Chancellors Lawson and Major applied the classic 'stop' tactics to end the 'go' their previous policies had generated. Interest rates were raised continuously from the first quarter of 1988, when they stood at 8.5%, to 15% by the third

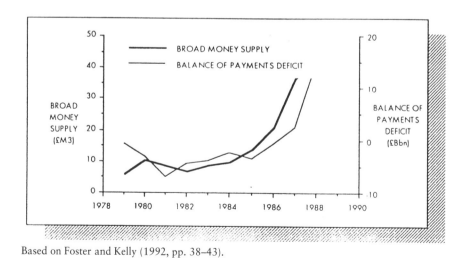

Based on Foster and Kelly (1992, pp. 38–43).

Figure 20.3   *Balance of payments deficit and monetary expansion*

quarter of 1989 in order to take unwanted demand out of the economy. Only in the third quarter of 1990 did they begin to fall. The effects – in terms of business failures and home repossessions – are now so well known that a few statistics will suffice.

- Manufacturing investment stopped growing after 1989, falling by 15% in 1991.
- From its record high of 3 million in 1986, unemployment fell every year to 1990 when it reached 1.6 million. However, by 1991 it had risen once again to 2.25 million.
- From a low of 1% in the first quarter of 1989, company failures rose continually to almost reach the 2.5% mark by the end of 1991. They are still rising.

2. *The first Unified Budget, November 1993.*
   The Chancellor's budget was based on a mixture of tax-raising and public spending reductions which pleased his backbenchers. Norman Lamont's spring budget raised an extra £6.7 billion in taxes, and Kenneth Clarke's unified budget raised an additional £1.7 billion in new taxes as well saving £3.5 billion through cuts in planned spending. The combined effect of the two budgets was the largest tax increase made in postwar Britain. If the extra tax had been raised through income tax rather than through indirect taxes, it would have added up to the basic rate going up by an extra 7 pence in the pound. Overall, tax relief on mortgages was to be limited further, VAT was extended to domestic fuel bills, and petrol, air travel and insurance premiums also went up in price.

   There was much political skill in the Chancellor's budget insofar as he reduced planned spending and introduced new taxes in a way which kept the different wings of the Conservative Party happy. But will the budget be as successful in keeping the electorate happy? Political commentators are divided on what they see as the likely electoral impact of Kenneth Clarke's budget strategy:

- Some argue that traditional Conservative supporters will be hard hit by this budget; the married, mortgaged, and motoring voters are going to be considerably less well off because of this budget. Furthermore, the budget is like a tax 'time bomb' which will explode just before the next general election in 1996 or 1997, when the full impact of the new taxes will be felt. It is argued that traditional Conservative voters will protest and use the next general election to punish the Government.
- Others disagree, and argue that traditional Conservative voters are realistic and understand that there is a public spending problem which the Government had to solve. They realise that tough decisions had to be made and, against the background of the economic recovery, will continue to support the Government and vote Conservative.

(i) 'Budgets can make or break politicians. Public approval increased rapidly for President Clinton after he got his budget through the House and Senate. Kenneth Clarke's successful budget has increased his chances of becoming prime minister.' Discuss.

(ii) Outline the economic problems faced by the Chancellor and estimate his chances of political success in solving them. Discuss the likely electoral impact of budget measures.

Further reading

Gamble, A. (1994) *The Free Economy and the Strong State*, 2nd edn (London: Macmillan).

Maynard, G. (1988) *The Economy under Mrs Thatcher* (Oxford: Blackwell).

Thain, C. (1992) 'Government and the Economy' in B. Jones and L. Robins (eds) *Two Decades in British Politics* (Manchester University Press).

Thomas G.P. (1992) *Government and the Economy Today* (Manchester University Press).

■ *Chapter 21* ■

Education

This chapter examines the ideological struggle between left and right which has taken place throughout the education system from the corridors of Whitehall to the school classroom. For education is a highly political issue. This is because many believe that the shape of society in the future depends on today's education system. Whilst some argue that a more egalitarian society would be fairer, others believe that a structured and differentiated society would offer greater stability.

■ The Current Crisis in Education

A recent survey conducted by the Organisation for Economic Co-operation and Development compared education systems in the OECD's 24 member countries. It found that the UK spends less of its gross domestic product (GDP) on education than other members, with other findings reflecting this financial fact, such as Britain having one of the highest teacher–pupil ratios, being one of the poorest providers of nursery education, and having one of the lowest proportions of young people going on to full-time tertiary education.

Britain's poor performance in providing education for its young people is not a recent development. Britain has a long history of spending less, providing less and getting less from education than other industrialised countries. In an article lamenting this situation, Corelli Barnett quoted from a Schools Inquiry Royal Commission which reported in 1868:

We are bound to add that our evidence appears to show that our industrial classes have not even the basis of a sound general education on which alone technical education can rest. In fact our deficiency is not merely a deficiency in technical education but in general intelligence. (The *Sunday Times*, 26 May 1991)

The style of language used in the Royal Commission of 1868 and the OECD report of 1992 may differ, but the message remains much the same over a century and a quarter – namely, that Britain lags behind its industrial competitors in providing an effective education system. The problems which were present in the last century are still present today, although they have become more acute in recent years as Britain's economic performance has teetered towards disaster. Clearly, then, one of the central goals of any government, whether Labour or Conservative, has been to raise the standard of education in Britain. Whilst there may be consensus on this general goal, the political Left and Right have disagreed very much on the means by which it might be achieved.

■ The Politics of Progressive Education

The Education Act of 1944 – the 'Butler Act' – was a milestone in the history of education in Britain, but by the 1960s its implementation was recognised as being both flawed and damaging to the interests of most children. Essentially the Act led to selective education – a bipartite division in most parts of the country – where the results of an 'eleven plus' examination sealed the fate of the pupils who sat it. The 20 per cent who 'passed' the eleven plus continued their secondary education in prestigious grammar schools, whilst the 80 per cent who 'failed' mainly went on to secondary modern schools.

The solution to the deficiencies of the 1944 Act, promoted in the Department of Education and Science (DES) circular 10/65, was an invitation to local education authorities (LEAs) to submit plans to reorganise secondary schools into a comprehensive system. Since it was a Labour Minister at the DES, and since it was Conservative-controlled LEAs which resisted pressures to go comprehensive, education began to become much more of a party political issue. Ironically, the original initiative for comprehensive schooling came from a liberal-minded Conservative Education Minister, Edward Boyle, and some Conservative-controlled LEAs such as Leicestershire. By the mid-1960s, however, comprehensive education was seen as a Labour policy. This was in many ways inevitable since comprehensive education was more consistent as a concept with Labour's egalitarian ideals than with the values of one-nation Toryism.

The educational left developed a radical philosophy of education, together with the necessary principles for implementation, which went far beyond the original concept of comprehensive schools. Egalitarian methods, which were expected to increase educational opportunity and thereby raise standards, had a place in the classroom. The left argued, for example, that selection in any form was undesirable. Thus streaming within a school was seen as just as iniquitous as the practice of the eleven plus in dividing pupils between schools. Mixed-ability teaching was the method advocated as consistent with the comprehensive ideal.

Traditional methods were based on an essentially élitist power structure in which reward and progress depended upon the individual effort of pupils, whilst progressive methods were more democratic with the skills of participation and cooperation as important as individual effort.

In terms of equalizing educational opportunity, comprehensive schools were probably the most effective reform to date. But in terms of educational standards, comprehensive schools and progressive methods seemed to lag behind traditional schooling. The decline in standards comprised one of the central themes of the *Black Papers*, written by right-wing academics who had become disenchanted with modern educational reforms.

The attack on education mounted by the Right struck a chord with many parents and employers, and by the mid-1970s there was widespread anxiety and dissatisfaction with state education in Britain. In 1976 Labour Prime Minister James Callaghan delivered a speech at Ruskin College, Oxford, which opened what is sometimes referred to as the 'great education debate'. The Prime Minister raised questions about levels of literacy and numeracy, the purpose of the school curriculum and the needs of industry, and expressed unease about certain teaching methods:

> there is the unease felt by parents and teachers about the new informal methods of teaching which seem to produce excellent results when they are in well qualified hands but are much more dubious in their effects when they are not ... There is no virtue in producing socially well adjusted members of society who are unemployed because they do not have the skills. (Quoted in Bash and Coulby (eds) 1989)

Thus education standards were now a major political issue, and the political right and centre were challenging the effectiveness of the 1960s reforms. By chance, the educational left which had promoted many progressive reforms, were caught unguarded and produced no real defence for the changes which had taken place. This was because the left was somewhat disillusioned by the relative lack of impact comprehensives and progressive methods had had in terms of social engineering. Pupils left comprehensives to take their predestined roles in what was still a class-based society; in short, 'open schools' did not produce an 'open society'. Egalitarian education, it seemed, was failing in this respect. Disenchantment on the left enabled the right to take the initiative on education and largely take control of shaping the political agenda. Radical right-wing groups such as the Hillgate Group, the Adam Smith Institute, and the Institute for Economic Affairs, took charge of the 'great debate' and in so doing redefined the purpose and means of schooling in Britain.

■ A Market-Led Education System

The political right argued that education had been subverted to the cause of social engineering rather than the pursuit of high academic standards. To repair the situation, the right argued that the influence of those responsible for causing the damage, those with professional vested interests, must be reduced. At the same time the influence of those with the greatest interest in raising educational standards, parents and employers, must be increased. This, it was argued, could be best accomplished by making education more responsive to market forces. As Stewart Ranson stated, the

> failures of education, it is argued, derive from professionals and (local) politicians appropriating control of the service from its proper source – the parents. The 'producers' have taken over and pursue their own purposes at the expense of the needs of the 'consumers' of the service ... The professionals create a technical language which serves only to bamboozle ordinary people and they organize the system for their convenience rather than to respond to the demands of consumers ... For consumers to fulfil their allotted role as quality controllers in the market place they require some diversity of product, information about the scope of choice and the quality of performance, as well as the opportunity to choose. (Ranson, 1990)

The radical right argued that a market-led system in education would mean that schools would have to compete with each other for 'customers', and that this competition would lead to a general rise in standards. The creation of a market, however, meant that the 'producer' monopoly must be curtailed. Firstly, it was argued, the influence of teachers must be reduced. Secondly,

the influence of local education authorities must reduced. In the event this occurred through delegating more financial and managerial responsibilities to individual schools and through providing opportunities for schools to 'opt out' from local authority control. Having reduced the influence of the 'producers', the right argued that the creation of a market in education rested only on increasing the role of 'consumers' in terms of providing greater choice and control. Parental influence was increased through open enrolment, the provision of more information by schools, and a bigger role in the management of individual schools.

The issues which concerned the right were not solely about the creation of an education marketplace. Some groups, such as the Hillgate Group, were determined that schools should play a role in preserving Britain's traditional culture and (Christian) values. The right was concerned that traditional values were being eroded by the multicultural and equal opportunities approaches of many LEAs, invariably Labour-controlled, in the inner cities. If 'traditional values' encompassed prejudices of one type or another, then it was inevitable that an equal opportunities policy together with a multicultural policy would result in conflict between right and left. As Coulby stated,

> urban LEAs phrased their policies with extra clarity and directness and implemented them with appropriate urgency. Of course, these were precisely the LEAs that were Labour-controlled and that, as such, were opposed to many aspects of central government policy. It was perhaps inevitable, but nonetheless regrettable, that equal opportunities policies were dragged into the arena of party politics. If the Labour-controlled urban LEAs were in favour of equal opportunities in education, it almost seemed as if the Conservative-controlled DES had to be against them. (Bash and Coulby, 1989, p. 13–14)

Having acknowledged the considerable influence over education policy exerted by the Right, the Education Acts of the 1980s were not simply legislative expressions of right-wing thinking. The Acts contained contradictions, ambiguities, and even measures which won support from the educational Left.

The 1980 Education (no. 2) Act

This Act introduced the Assisted Places Scheme which was designed to allow a relatively small number of parents on modest incomes to send their children to private schools. This policy was in line with the goal of increasing parental choice, although its critics saw it as simply a way of subsidising private schools with government money.

The 1986 Education (no. 2) Act

The 1944 Act required all state schools to have a body of governors, on which parents could be represented although it was not mandatory for them to be so. Also 'it was possible for a single governing body to govern many different schools ... In the period 1965–9, for instance, a quarter of English and Welsh LEAs had only one governing body for all their schools' (Deem, 1990, p. 154). The 1986 Act provided for an increased number of parent governors on schools' governing bodies which, with other changes, reduced the number of local authority governors to a minority position. This was done by

> increasing parental governor representation in schools of over 600 pupils from two to five and proportionately in smaller schools, decreasing LEA representation (with minor local authority representation going altogether in secondary schools) and increasing co-opted membership (intended to bring wider community involvement, and more particularly people representing the business community). (Deem, 1990, p. 156)

The Act provided for the secret postal ballot of all eligible parents for the election of parent governors. To be eligible, a parent must have a child attending the school at the time of the election. The period of office is four years, but a parent governor can continue to serve if his or her child leaves before the term ends.

The 1988 Education Reform Act

The 1986 Act enlarged the responsibilities of school governors, and the 1988 Act built further on this through introducing Local Management of Schools (LMS). The central purpose of LMS, with greater parental and community involvement, was to ensure that individual schools were effectively managed and responsive to 'customer' needs.

The Act also specified that a national curriculum be taught to pupils until they reached the age of 16. A core curriculum would include English, maths and science, together with seven foundation subjects covering history, geography, technology, art, music, physical education and a foreign language. Religious education would also be taught as well as certain cross-curricular themes such as citizenship. The Act also introduced the national testing of pupils at four key stages of 7, 11, 14 and 16 years old.

In line with increasing parental choice, the Act introduced open enrolment and the possibility of schools opting out of LEA control and assuming grant maintained status. In line with reducing the influence of progressive forces in education, including an emphasis on multiculturalism and equal opportunities, the Act abolished the Inner London Education Authority (ILEA).

■ Contradictions and Ambiguities

The Butler Act of 1944 represented a major advance in state education based on political consensus; the legislation of the 1980s, particularly the Education Reform Act, represented a success for conservative forces in the reconstruction of state education. As Richard Johnson observed, the Bill 'was forced through by a parliamentary majority against the wishes of unions, teachers, educationists, organised parent groups and most LEA politicians' (R. Johnson 1991, p. 63). But it would be wrong to see the 1980, 1986 and 1988 Acts as being a direct legislative expression of radical right policy on education. There was disagreement among right-wing thinkers on the principal weaknesses of the existing school system and hence an absence of consensus on what was needed to put things right.

Essentially the Acts represented a series of compromises, and as such embraced inconsistencies and contradictions. Leslie Bash and David Coulby have explored some of the tensions, political and educational, that can be detected both in the legislation and its implementation. Firstly, they explored the contradiction between 'vocationalism' and 'traditional education' and cited Margaret Thatcher speaking to the 1987 Conservative Party Conference:

> We want education to be part of the answer to Britain's problems, not part of the cause. To compete successfully in tomorrow's world – against Japan, Germany and the United States – we need well-educated, well-trained, creative young people. If education is backward today, national performance will be backward tomorrow.

Yet, apart from technology, the 1988 Act contained no reference to vocational education within the curriculum. The emphasis was on the traditional form of knowledge promoted by the right.

Secondly, the creation of greater parental choice is likely to have some undesirable unintended consequences. Government policy has led to ending the LEA monopoly on state schooling, and extended choice through the creation of different types of school. These schools, with open enrolment, will have to compete with one another for pupils; and according to radical right theory such competition will result in higher standards. But Bash and Coulby feared that 'schools in less privileged areas will see their pupil numbers dwindle as more privileged parents airlift their children out to CTCs or to opted-out schools. The slum school is about to be created. It will be the province of the local authority sector which will then doubtless be vulnerable to further attacks on account of poor standards'.(Bash and Coulby, 1989, p. 113). Competition, then, will raise educational standards for the better-off, but

leave behind the poor in what Ted Wragg described as 'cheap, cheerless, third-class schools run by clapped-out and impoverished authorities' (The *Observer*, 17 May 1992).

Thirdly, there is a contradiction between increased parental power, LMS and the increased new powers taken on by the Secretary of State for Education. The loss of the local authority role in education puts parents and schools in a very weak position *vis-à-vis* the now more powerful minister. As Richard Johnson argued, 'an individual school can hardly be said to counterbalance a national state ... so the effect of the "devolutionary" erosion of LEA competence is to reduce the local power overall, especially as a counterbalance to the centre' (R. Johnson, 1991, p. 68).

Fourthly, Bash and Coulby have pointed out the contradiction within the national curriculum between nationalist and internationalist aspirations. For example, the national curriculum requires secondary pupils to study one modern language for five years. Yet there is no recognition that many children from ethnic minority backgrounds are already bilingual.

Finally, a point made by Richard Johnson concerned the contradiction between creating a market-led system of education which transmitted a centrally controlled uniform curriculum. For if education was a free market, then choice would extend to variety and choice being present in the curriculum. There would be no national curriculum, but freedom of choice and competition between many local curriculums.

Summary

Harold Laswell once defined politics as 'who gets what, when and how'. In many ways education could be defined in a similar way. The 'great education debate' was dominated by the political right, with arguments about standards given priority over concern about social engineering. The 1980s were a period in which many market mechanisms were proposed and introduced in order to raise standards. However, these mechansms risk having unintended consequences when fully implemented, which include recreating the undesirable social consequences of education of fifty years ago.

Questions

1. To what extent is it possible to 'keep politics out of education'?

2. 'A highly educated young workforce will improve Britain's economic performance.' How valid is this statement?

3. To what extent have educational reform measures been shaped by political philosophies?

4. Write a short report on Labour and Liberal Democrat education policy, pointing out the main differences from Conservative policy.

Assignments

1. The following extract is taken from the National Commission on Education Briefing Number 6 (August 1992). The article, 'Open-

ing Wide the Doors of Higher Education', was written by Professor A.H. Halsey at the very time when polytechnics were granted university status.

Gender and social class

The proportion of all students who were women was less than a quarter before World War Two, began to rise significantly after the mid sixties, and became 42.8 per cent in 1989. Those who consult the facts will accordingly have mixed emotions. In the polytechnics sexual equality of opportunity is established. And, as is clear from Table 21.1, the growth in full-time university undergraduate places has accommodated more women both absolutely (83 000 extra women compared with 33 000 men) and relatively (122 per cent increase for women compared with 20 per cent increase for men). But the evidence of differential relative expansion is also there. Women have gained on men but their advance has been disproportionately in the newer forms of higher education. All part-time categories have risen faster for women than for men over the two decades.

For social classes the general tendency towards inequality of educational attainment persists. General Household Survey data show that, measured in relative terms, the proportions of those entering higher education from manual working families have scarcely shifted by comparison with those from the professional and managerial classes.

Table 21.1   *Expansion of higher education in United Kingdom by type of establishment, sex and mode of attendance, 1970–90*

		Universities			Polytechnics & colleges			Open University		
		1970/71 000s	1989/90 000s	% rise	1970/71 000s	1989/90 000s	% rise	1970/71 000s	1989/90 000s	% rise
Full-time	Men	167	200	20	107	170	59			
	Women	68	151	122	114	169	48			
Part-time	Men	18	31	72	110	159	45	14	47	236
	Women	6	23	283	12	103	758	5	42	740

Source: Education Statistics for the United Kingdom (HMSO).

For degree holders in 1974 whose fathers were professionals or managers, the ratio was 2.75, i.e. they were graduating at nearly 3 times the rate that would obtain if degree-holding were randomly distributed. At the other extreme the children of semi-skilled and unskilled workers had a ratio of 0.28 and the children of skilled manual workers 0.52. By 1985 these ratios had moved to 2.05, 0.36 and 0.50 respectively. The numbers of entrants to higher education from manual social origins had risen absolutely but not relatively to their numbers in the population. This is cold comfort for those who seek the 'classless society'. Moreover, the movement from grants towards loans inaugurated in 1989, and the logic of education as a 'positional good', might well produce greater class inequality in British higher education in the future.

(i)   Describe gender and class patterns in the growth of higher education places.
(ii) To what extent is higher education working towards the creation of a classless society?

2.   Education Vouchers

One idea supported by the Radical Right which, it was argued, would create something close to a real marketplace in education was the use of **vouchers**. It was envisaged that parents could purchase an education for their children by passing the necessary vouchers over to schools which in turn could convert them into appropriate resources. The more vouchers a school received, the more resources it would have. The "best" schools would receive more vouchers than "poorer" schools. Being in a marketplace, poor schools would have to raise their standards in order to survive. Parents who wanted their children to attend private schools would be able to "top up" their vouchers with cash to the fee levels charged. In this way, vouchers would create **a market which stretched across the state and private sector of education**. It was argued that competition for vouchers would mean that the generally superior standards in private schools would pull up standards in state schools. Although the concept of education vouchers has remained popular with the Radical Right, and has been discussed with Ministers, it has never been included in any legislation since it has always been viewed as impractical by the Government. The rejection of vouchers has been a great disappointment to the Right.

(i)   Write a letter to the Education Secretary which explains the merits of education vouchers and urges the adoption of a vouchers scheme for secondary education.
(ii) Imagine that you are a civil servant at the Department of Education and have been given responsibility to draft a reply to such a letter which explains the disadvantages of the voucher system.

Further reading

Barnett, C. 'The Education Battle Begins, 120 years too Late', *Sunday Times*, 26 May 1991.

Bash, L. and Coulby, D. (1989) *The Education Reform Act: Competition and Control* (London: Cassell).

Education Group II (1991) *Education Limited: Schooling, Training and the New Right in England since 1979* (London: Unwin Hyman).

Flude, M. and Hammer, M. (eds) (1990) *The Education Reform Act 1988: Its Origins and Implications* (London: Falmer).

McVicar, M. (1990) 'Education Policy: Education as a Business?' in S. Savage, and L. Robins (eds) *Public Policy Under Thatcher* (London: Macmillan).

Wragg, T. (1992) 'Seeds of Destruction Being Sown in a Three-Class System', *Observer*, 17 May.

■ *Chapter 22* ■

Health

The National Health Service (NHS) came into existence in 1948 as the only universal national health service where treatment was free at the point of access. The medical profession had to be persuaded by the Labour Minister, Nye Bevan, to accept the NHS but it was an immediate success with the public and has remained popular ever since. Nevertheless, successive governments have been concerned about the expense of the NHS and a number of reforms have aimed to improve management, constrain costs and hopefully, improve services. The last reform, introduced in 1991, which organised health care around an internal market, was the most controversial. This chapter examines the administration and politics of health care. As will be seen, details of the administrative structure of the NHS market have become extremely complex whilst the positive impact of competitive forces remains the subject of a simple political faith.

■ The Health Service Reforms: Rhetoric and Reality

In 1991 the biggest reform of the NHS took place since its foundation in 1948. Labour argued that the new-style self-governing hospital trusts and fund-holding general practices designed by the Conservative Government to work in a market-place represented the creeping privatisation of health care in Britain. Looking back, Labour probably over-stated the case against the Conservative reforms. Central to Labour's objections were, firstly, that opting out would represent the first step by hospital trusts to becoming private

hospitals. Indeed, to the annoyance of the Government, this view was shared by some of the Radical right of the Conservative Party (for example, in the pamphlet *All Private Patients Now*). Secondly, Labour argued that the Conservative reforms would break up the NHS; hospital trusts were opting out of the NHS and a two-tier system of health care would emerge as fund-holding general practitioners (GPs) bought immediate treatment for their patients whilst others faced long waits. The introduction of a 'market mentality', with doctors forces to consider commercial criteria and think like accountants before deciding on recommending treatment or not, would destroy the ethos of compassion and care associated with the NHS. Thirdly, the new freedom granted to hospital trusts would allow them, if they so wished, to end the provision of 'unprofitable' operations or treatments even if it was needed. Hospital trusts would be free to offer 'profitable' treatment, even if there was no local need, and sell such treatment to private patients.

The Prime Minister, John Major, attacked Labour for what he called 'the big lie' on NHS reforms. He argued that 'NHS trust hospitals are and will remain part of the NHS. They will be run by NHS staff and will treat NHS patients just as they have done before – only better' (*Observer*, 19 May 1991). The government argued that the NHS reforms were simply an attempt to modernise the management of the NHS. But it is probably true to say that the Conservatives misled the public about the nature of those reforms in the white paper *Working for Patients* which promised that patients and doctors would enjoy greater freedom of choice. Expectations were created by ministers and their civil servants that the market reforms would result in patients being referred to the specialists and hospitals of their choice. It was argued that the new-style contracts made between the purchasers and providers of health care would mean that 'money followed patients'.

In the event, however, the reforms gave very limited choice to patients and doctors since health authorities made contracts which bought health care 'in bulk' from a limited number of hospitals, resulting in 'patients following money'. Like buying any other product, it is cheaper and more efficient to buy health care in bulk, which health authorities do in order to make their money go further. But it is not possible to reconcile greater efficiency and savings with increased patient choice as did Government rhetoric in *Working for Patients*.

■ The Organisation of the NHS

The NHS is a massive organisation, the biggest employer in the Western world, and its organisation and management is extremely complex. Basically, the **Secretary of State for Health** is accountable to Parliament for the provision of health care services, and he 'discharges his responsibility through Regional Health Authorities, District Health Authorities, Family Health Services Authorities, NHS Trusts, and Special Health Authorities' (Ham, 1991, p. 13). The **Department of Health**, within the wider context of Cabinet government, makes policy for health care at the national level, allocates the resources necessary to implement such policies, and monitors the effectiveness of the NHS through a review process.

There are 14 **Regional Health Authorities** (RHAs) in England which are responsible for planning the provision of health care as set out in national policy guidelines. RHAs allocate resources to **District Health Authorities**, Family Health Services Authorities and fund-holding General Practitioners (GPs), as well as monitor the performance and efficiency of the former. RHAs play a key role in Conservative market-style

reforms since they form the crucial intermediate tier between the Department of Health and the District Health Authorities and the Family Health Services Authorities. Future reforms are likely to reduce the number of RHAs. **District Health Authorities** (DHAs) are 'the bodies responsible for purchasing hospital and community health services for their residents' (Ham, 1991, p. 21) In 1991 there were 189 DHAs in England. **Family Health Services Authorities** (FHSAs) 'manage the services provided by general medical practitioners general dental practitioners, retail pharmacists and opticians' (ibid., p. 24). In 1991 there were 90 FHSAs in England, and their best-known role to the public is that of dealing with complaints made by patients.

NHS **Trusts** are generally hospitals, although they can be other bodies providing patient care which are 'self-governing' units within the health service. 'They are run by boards of directors and are accountable directly to the Secretary of State without any intervention from District or Regional Health Authorities' (ibid., p. 26). Trusts have much greater freedom than hospital managed by DHAs in deciding what staff are employed, their conditions of service and how their resources are to be used generally. 'Each Trust will be required to prepare an annual business plan outlining, amongst other things, its plans for service development and capital investment. These plans will be discussed with the NHS Management Executive but will not be public documents' (ibid., p. 26). Trusts will receive their income from contracts agreed with health authorities, fund-holding GPs, and other purchasers of health care. Hospitals which do not have trust status and remain under the control of DHAs are known as **Directly Managed Units** (DMUs), and whilst they do not have the freedom to manage themselves enjoyed by Trust hospitals they are nevertheless managed 'at arm's length' by the DHAs.

Finally, **Special Health Authorities** (SHAs supervise specific services such as health education and postgraduate teaching. Strictly speaking SHAs are not part of the NHS but are accountable directly to the Secretary of State.

The Market Reforms

In the White Paper, *Working for Patients*, the Government argued that although the NHS was a monolithic organisation which provided health care to the public, it played two distinctive roles. On the one hand it 'provided' health care, but this health care had to be paid for, so on the other hand the NHS was also a 'purchaser' of health care. Being both a provider and a purchaser of health care would not have become a problem for the NHS, it was argued, had it not been for the fact that the NHS had become 'producer orientated'. In much the same way as state education had been seen by the Government to have fallen into the hands of producers (LEAs, teachers' unions) rather than serving the interests of consumers (pupils, parents) so too the NHS was seen as working to serve the needs of the producers (the medical profession) rather than the needs of the consumers (the patients).

The Government believed that the grip of the professionals, be they teachers or doctors, could be broken by the introduction of market forces which would operate in ways which would mean that the respective service would become shaped by the needs of the 'consumer'. At the same time, the increased competition resulting from the working of the market would increase efficiency in education and health at a time when costs were rising fast.

Before April 1991 DHAs were responsible for channelling resources for the provision of health care and they served both the 'provider' and 'purchaser' functions. However, after April 1991 there was a split between these functions and under the new system

District Health Authorities (DHAs), together with budget-holding GP practices, have become purchasers of health services from suppliers such as hospitals, community services and ambulance services (the providers). The new purchasing units are able to draw up contracts with any hospitals and other provider units both within and outside their own district. Their stated objective will be to achieve the best value for money available within the constrains of the budget handed down to them from the Regional Health Authority to which they belong. (Bartlett, 1991, p. 56)

Figure 22.1 outlines the provider market of Trusts, DMUs including those in other DHAs as well as private institutions competing for patients. A provider which successfully bids for business will draw up a service contract with the purchaser. It is this system of decentralised contracts which replaced the bureaucratic method of organising health care which existed up until 1991. There are three types of contracts which can be drawn up between provider and purchaser: block contracts, cost-as volume contracts and cost-per-case contracts. Under the block contract 'the purchaser pays the provider an annual fee in return for access to a defined range of services' (Bartlett, 1991, p. 57). This block contract can involve considerable risks for the provider since there will always be much uncertainty about what resources are needed overall. For example, as the BMA argued, admittance to hospital of a number of young adults with a hernia condition would require much less overall treatment than an equivalent number of elderly, unstable diabetics with the same condition.

Cost-per-case contracts, which can be set on an 'average' cost, can place a greater risk on the purchaser because of the uncertainty involved in forecasting the upper limit on the number of cases to be treated. This type of contract will be used to treat referrals which are not covered in any block contract. Finally, cost-and-volume contracts will be made between purchaser and provider which are essentially a mixture of the block contracts and the cost-per-case contracts; they will fund 'a baseline of activity to be undertaken by the provider beyond which all funding is at a cost-per-case basis' (Bartlett, 1991, p. 59)

The internal market of the NHS will comprise thousands of purchasers and hundreds of providers which, in the main, will conduct business in terms of block contracts. But is this internal market a 'real' market? Bartlett refers to the internal market of the NHS as a 'quasi-market' since 'this is not a normal market in which

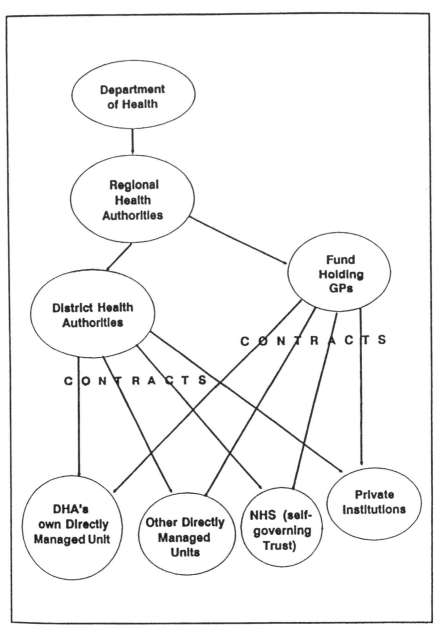

Source: Adapted from Harrison, S., Hunter D. J. and Pollit, C. (1990) *The Dynamics of British Health Policy* (London, Hyman).

Figure 22.1   *The purchaser/provider split: financial flows in the National Health Services*

consumer choice is reflected directly by individuals' decisions to purchase varying levels of service, but rather a quasi-market in which consumers' decisions are mediated through a variety of intervening specialized agents (the DHA and the budget-holding GP practice) who purchase services on their behalf' (Bartlett, 1991 p. 56). It is assumed that the forces of the quasi market will lead to keener competition an mergers of DHAs and FHSAs in an effort t increase their power in the purchasing of service This argument underlines the original criticism c

Working for Patients: namely that the market-like reform mechanisms were always likely to lead to some improvement in efficiency, although some academics doubt this, but to no increase in patient choice.

■ The Politics of Health

The NHS has emerged as an important issue in recent general elections. Large-scale intervention by the state, which is involved in running a national health service, did not appear consistent with Margaret Thatcher's determination to 'roll back the state' and privatise previously state-owned concerns. To quell public anxiety, Conservatives assured the electorate that the NHS was 'safe in our hands' but nevertheless health care remained an issue where Labour was trusted most by the electorate. Nationally during election campaigns, and locally, with news of a ward or hospital closure, political controversy has been intense and even emotional. But because of the complexity and political sensitivity of the NHS, sorting out the 'facts' from the 'politics' is very difficult.

□ *Health Statistics*

NHS statistics are subject to political manipulation and 'spin control' when they are presented to the public. For example, the minister might announce that ten new NHS building projects are to be started next week, which many party supporters and members of the public might assume to mean that new hospitals or clinics are about to be built. In fact, the minister might be referring to ten existing hospital car parks which are about to be resurfaced. Or again, the minister might announce that, in line with the *Citizen's Charter*, no individual will be on a waiting list for more than two years before treatment. But it would be possible for 'pre-waiting lists' to be operated whereby an individual might have to wait for a year before being put on to the official waiting list. Through this type of manipulation the patient might wait as long as three years for treatment but only two of those years would have been spent on a waiting list.

□ *Health Spending*

The amount of money which is being and should be devoted to financing the NHS is a major issue of disagreement between the Labour and Conservative parties. And yet these are not easy figures to calculate. For example, the actual money spent on the NHS by the government of the day has to be adjusted for inflation (in order to calculate 'real' rises and falls). This is more difficult than it might appear since health care inflation is generally higher than the general cost-of-living inflation reported in the media. Also health spending ought to take into account the changing demands made on the NHS through, for example, demographic and technological changes. If these sorts of considerations are taken into account when calculating health spending under recent Labour and Conservative governments, it appears that under Labour (1974–79) spending rose on average by 2.2 per cent a year whilst under the Conservatives it rose by an average of 0.3 per cent a year. If it is accepted that the NHS budget needs to increase by 3 per cent a year just to keep pace with treating the increasing number of elderly people as well as paying for technological advances in medicine, then neither major party maintained health spending in real terms, although Labour came closer to doing this than the Conservatives.

□ *Rationing Health Care*

It has been argued that the public's demand for health care is infinite. In other words, the entire national wealth of Britain could be spent on providing health care. Since this is not going to happen, the limited resources which have been and will be allocated to the NHS mean that health care has to be rationed. This can be achieved through patients paying for treatment through, for example, charging for prescriptions, dental and eye check-ups, or through becoming private patients.

Since the 1991 reforms, health care rationing has become a pressing political issue. At its most visible, health care rationing takes place in processing what are termed 'extra-contractual referrals' (ECRs). People seeking treatment at hospitals where no block contract exists may be accepted as an ECR once their treatment has been approved. ECRs are commonly used for relatively non-urgent operations such as tattoo removals, *in vitro* fertilisation and treatment for varicose veins. Resources devoted to ECRs tend to be used up quickly, and this can generate opposition from the public who do not like the idea of rationing. But there is another objection to what is becoming seen as an ECR lottery: 'ECR decision-making is rife with personal lobbying by GPs and consultants on behalf of their patients' (Salter, 1992, p. 31). This can lead to unfairness as treatment may depend not on the needs of patients but the influence of GPs. Also there have been occasions when seriously ill patients, not ECR referrals, have died because they received no treatment whilst lengthy negotiations took place in the internal market.

There have also been cases of 'overload', that is, simply too many patients requiring treatment, which has led to more imaginative forms of coping than simple rationing. For in some hospitals, higher than anticipated demand for treatments meant that contracts were completed as much as four months ahead of schedule. Academics observed that when put under the strain of insufficient resources, 'solutions' devised within the NHS included *(i)* trying to limit the demand for health care through persuading individuals that treatment was unnecessary, *(ii)* redirecting some patients to local authority care if their problems seemed more 'social' than 'medical', and *(iii)* spreading health services thinly so that all patients received some level of attention.

It is the case that there has always been rationing of health care. What the internal market reforms have done is make this more visible, and consequently raised the issue of rationing in the public's mind.

Private or Privatised Health Care?

Margaret Thatcher's governments encouraged people to use private health care. As Prime Minister, Thatcher was portrayed as a strong supporter, and user, of private medicine. In contrast her successor, John Major, has portrayed himself as a supporter and user of the NHS. To some extent this change of image has taken some of the political sting out of the controversy surrounding the existence of private medicine alongside the NHS. The political right argued that individuals should have the freedom of choice to spend their money as they wished, whilst the left argued that wealth should not be able to purchase treatment ahead of those in greater need.

The Conservative reforms of 1991 focused political debate on the privatisation of the NHS. Labour argued that the new self-governing hospital trusts were outside the NHS and represented the first step towards hospital privatisation. Those who opposed the privatisation of health care were also concerned at the increasing involvement of the private sector in running the NHS, from competitive tendering for hospital cleaning and catering services to the treatment of NHS patients in private hospitals.

Labour's Alternative?

Labour's alternative programme for organising health care was set out in the party's 1990 document *A Fresh Start for Health*. According to this policy document 'Labour will abolish the market' in health by bringing Trust hospitals back under the control of DHAs and ending the GP fund-holding status. The internal market would be replaced by a decentralised structure with a 'Strategic Board' supervising each DHA. These Strategic Boards would agree 'performance targets' with hospitals organised into 'Operational Boards', which would set out both the quality and volume of treatment to be undertaken.

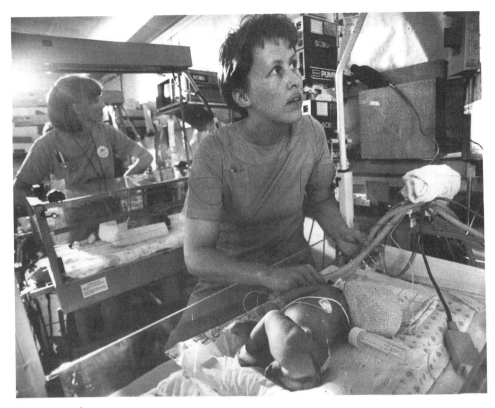

Source: Guardian.

Figure 22.2 *A midwife monitors the condition of a baby in the special care unit at St. Thomas's Hospital, London*

Even friendly critics of Labour have argued that the proposals contained in *A Fresh start for Health* bear a surprising resemblance to those contained in the Conservative White Paper *Working for Patients*. The Strategic Boards look very much like purchasers, the Operational Boards look like providers, and the performance agreements seem very much like contracts. The only significant difference appears to be the strong Conservative commitment to competition as the driving force of the NHS, and Labour's rejection of it in favour of traditional bureaucratic management.

Summary

This chapter examined the politics of health care primarily in terms of recent Conservative reforms. Do these reforms represent the creeping privatisation of the NHS? Can an internal market work effectively in delivering care to patients? What happens when contracts expire earlier than planned and health care has to be rationed?

Criticisms of the NHS were considered, but always against the backcloth of the NHS enduring as one of Britain's most popular institutions.

It is clear that Conservative reforms will change the original purpose of the NHS to provide treatment of similar quality of all users. As the NHS becomes based on a quasi-market so competition, which will include the private sector, will lead to differentiation in the treatment and care of patients. The NHS, which began as a monolithic, centralised, state-provided institution will, in the 1990s, be part of a mixed economy in health care.

Questions

1. 'In 1985, Britain devoted 6.1 per cent of GDP to health, compared with 10.7 per cent in the USA and an OECD average of 7.3 per cent.' (C. Pierson in Dunleavy *et al.* (1993)) Discuss the argument that the problem facing the NHS is not administrative inefficiency but 'wholesale underspending'.

2. Critically examine the case for and against the 1991 reforms of the NHS.

Assignments

1. Controversy over the NHS

Strengths of the NHS

Access	• equal access, based on medical need for treatment
	• a public service with a lot of public accountability
	• organised systems for investigating complaints
Quality	• doctors have no incentive to overtreat patients (as they receive annual salaries rather than fees for each little piece of activity they undertake)
	• clinical autonomy of doctors is not interfered with by managers or politicians
Costs	• cheap system to administer (USA spends four times as much on overheads, for example)
	• fixed public expenditure budgets has kept the total costs of the NHS under control
	• most services, and all hospital services, are free to the patient and met from public funds
	• very high public support for the NHS ensures its future

Weaknesses of the NHS

Access	• long waiting lists, particularly for hospital treatment (in Germany and the USA access is virtually instant)
	• the health gap between the classes has not narrowed
Quality	• low capital investment in new technologies and treatments
	• poor amenities and inconsiderate treatment of patients
	• only a limited emphasis on health education, health promotion and illness prevention
Costs	• staff are poorly paid
	• history of tense industrial relations at all levels – doctors to porters
	• no stability due to constant political uncertainty

Source: B. Wood (1992, pp. 33–7).

Draft a brief speech for either the Minister for Health or the Opposition's Shadow Health Minister. Select appropriate points listed in the boxes as well as material in the rest of the chapter when constructing your arguments for or against current changes. Exchange your speech with a class member who has written for the opposite side of the debate. Discuss the politics of health care mentioning how easy or difficult you found it to attack or defend the Government's record.

2. Public spending on health – interpreting the figures.

Figure 22.3 Public expenditure on health 1960–90

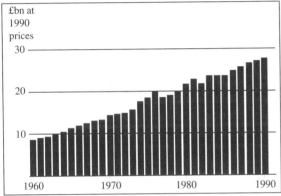

Based on Hogwood, *Trends in Public Policy* (Milton Keynes: Open University Press, 1992).

In the period between 1979/80 and 1992/93 expenditure on the NHS in England increased from £9.25 billion to an estimated £29.5 billion. Between 1980/81 and 1989/90, NHS expenditure grew by an average of 8% each year – more than the increase in GDP. So, can Labour claim the NHS has been underfunded? (Talking Politics)

Write a brief paragraph which explains the complexity of interpreting health service spending figures.

Further reading

Ham, C. (1991) *The New National Health Service Organisation and Management* (Oxford: Radcliffe Medical).

Kendall, I. and Moon, G. (1990) 'Health policy' in S. Savage and L. Robins (eds) *Public Policy Under Thatcher* (London: Macmillan).

Klein, R. (1989) *The Politics of the NHS* (London: Longman).

Wood, B. (1992) *The Politics of Health* (Manchester: Politics Association).

■ *Chapter 23* ■

Housing

Housing is different from other social policies such as health or education. For whilst the overwhelming majority of the population rely on the services of the NHS and state education, an overwhelming majority rely on private owner-occupation for housing. Whilst a failure in health policy or education policy would threaten the wellbeing of many of the electorate, a failure in housing policy would affect only a minority. Government could, then, afford to be less sensitive to the plight of the socially housed, the poorly housed and homeless than to the demands of patients and parents. This chapter examines the nature of the housing crisis, the major pieces of legislation and the implementation of housing policy reforms.

■ The Housing Crisis

Providing sufficient good quality housing for the population of Britain would appear to be a simple goal to achieve in a relatively rich, technologically advanced society. Indeed, much progress was made in tackling the housing problem in the postwar years. Mistakes were made, such as the popularity of building high-rise flats in the 1960s, but generally speaking slums were cleared and replaced by improved housing. The growth of owner-occupation was supported by both Labour and Conservative governments and encouraged through subsidising mortgage payments with tax relief. Local authorities provided accommodation with subsidised rents for the less affluent people in society.

The Thatcher governments of the 1980s adopted a more ideological approach to the housing problem which was based on free-market principles and the wish to limit local authority involvement. Owner-occupation was boosted by the biggest of all privatisation measures, the 'right to buy', which enabled council tenants to buy their own homes. Efforts were made to revive the once-important role of the private landlord in providing accommodation. Finally, the Government preferred housing associations to local authorities in providing 'social housing' for the less well-off. How successful have these reforms been in tackling the housing problem?

During the 1980s Britain's housing problem developed into the proportions of a housing crisis. Groups of homeless people and cardboard cities are now commonplace sights in British towns. Shelter has estimated that 1.7 million individuals are now squatting or staying with friends, with young people being the fastest growing group amongst the homeless. On top of this, many families endure a bleak bed-and-breakfast existence, whilst many vulnerable people with histories of mental illness wander the streets each night in search of hostel accommodation. Others, in their own homes, become unemployed, default on their mortgages, and have their homes repossessed by the building societies. Others simply live in very poor accommodation. Together, these are the victims of policy failure which make up Britain's army of the homeless and poorly housed.

	Owner-occupied	Rented from local authorities	Rented from private landlords
	%	%	%
1971	52	29	19
1986	65	26	8

Table 23.1 *Housing tenure in England and Wales*

Table 23.1 shows changes in housing tenure in England and Wales, with private landlords playing a decreasing role and owner-occupiers playing an increasing role. The impact of the 'Right to Buy' legislation can be traced in the changing trend in the role of local authority housing. The decline of private renting has reduced the amount of cheap accommodation which is available. Obtaining a council house can be a lengthy process, and virtually impossible for people deemed to have a low housing priority need. Owner-occupation has grown in popularity, since it generally offers greater security as well as better housing conditions.

Part of Britain's housing problem results from the old age of many houses. Over six million homes, which is almost a third of all homes, were built before the end of the First World War. Many if these homes are in need of modernisation and major repair work. More than a million council homes were built between the wars – these are now fifty or sixty years old – and so are approaching an age when major refurbishing and repair will be necessary.

A Change of Direction in Housing Policy

Conservative legislation on housing was based on a number of principles found in legislation on, for example, education or health. Reforms aimed to reduce the role of local authorities, encourage the growth of private sector involvement, increase competition and choice, whilst containing public spending.

☐ *The Housing Act 1980*

In 1979 Parliament was informed that the new Thatcher Government intended to fulfil an old political ambition held by many Tories:

> Thousands of people in council houses and new towns came out in support of us for the first time because they wanted a chance to buy their own homes. We will give every council tenant the right to purchase his own home at a substantial discount on the market price and with 100% mortgages for those who need them. This will be a giant stride towards making a reality of Anthony Eden's dream of a property owning democracy.

The most significant part of the Act which was to accomplish this gave council tenants the 'right to buy' their homes. This measure was very popular with voters who lived in council houses. The Act ensured that councils would provide mortgages where necessary with tenants able to buy their homes at a discount. For those tenants who had lived in council houses for a long time, the discount was 50 per cent, later rising to 60 per cent. For long-term flat tenants the discount was 70 per cent. For many council tenants, then, the purchase of their homes from the council represented a bargain. By 1989 a million council homes had been sold to sitting tenants, with some local authorities having sold over a third of their council houses (such as Havant, Corby, Bracknell, Crawley and Bromley).

From the Government's perspective the sale of council homes represented its largest privatisation policy. In fact, 43 per cent of all privatisation proceeds from the first decade of Thatcherism came from council house sales. Opponents saw the sale of council houses as 'asset-stripping' in order to buy votes from the working-class electorate. It was argued that council houses were provided for families in greatest need but under the 'right to buy' council houses were being bought by better-off tenants at bargain discount prices. Critics argued that once a council house became privately owned, it would never again be used to house the poorest members of society.

Labour critics were particularly annoyed that councils could only spend a proportion of the money they received from house sales in building new homes to let.

The Housing and Planning Act 1986

The sale of council houses began to decline during 1985. The Government decided to revive council house sales through what Jonathan Stearn has described as the 'stick and carrot' approach. The Housing and Planning Act 1985 was the carrot which 'boosted publicity and increased discounts to flat owners. Coupled with the profits to be made from soaring house prices buying your council house had its attractions for sitting tenants who had yet to experience owner occupation' (Stearn, 1989, p. 17). The Act also allowed councils to transfer their homes to other landlords, such as a housing association.

The Housing Act 1988

If the 1986 Act was the carrot, then this Act was the stick. As Stearn argued, the 1988 Act 'raised the spectre of private landlords taking over estates. The policy worked. In 1988/89 the second highest number of homes were sold in England (140,127) after the initial surge in 1982/83 when 176,456 homes were bought' (ibid). Furthermore, the sale of council flats soared from being 2 per cent of all sales in 1980/81 to 15 per cent in 1988–9.

The Act introduced the 'Tenants' Choice' which involved the possibility of transferring council houses to other landlords such as private landlords, housing associations or tenants' cooperatives. Private landlords would be able to bid for council properties, with over 50 per cent of tenants having to vote against to prevent such a transfer (abstentions by tenants would be counted as a vote in favour of a transfer).

The 1988 Act also established Housing Action Trusts (HATs) which were designed to take over running the most deprived council estates with dilapidated houses, high unemployment and high crime rates. It was intended that HATs, more efficiently than local authorities, would tackle all the problems of urban blight, improve council estates, then pass them back to the local authorities or on to another, possibly private, landlord. The minister responsible saw HATs as the 'cutting edge of government's inner city regeneration' and they were to be based on the model of Urban Development Corporations (see Chapter 10).

Originally council tenants were *informed* that a HAT would take over managing their estate, and while 'tenants welcomed the possibility of improvements to their estates which had been starved of funds .... they were equally suspicious of HATs. It smacked of change from above, and this non-democratic feature was undoubtedly its most serious flaw' (Dennis, 1990, p. 14). This suspicion resulted in the right of tenants to vote on a transfer to a HAT being introduced into the committee stage of the Act. Despite this concession, there remained considerable opposition to HATs and some of the initial HATs were abandoned.

Why did HATs fail? Ferdinand Dennis argued that the main reason that the HATs policy failed was that, although many tenants were less than satisfied with the council as landlord, 'better the devil you know ...'. Although HATs promised great improvements, tenants were suspicious about promises to return estates to local councils after improvements had been made: 'A local authority could make a policy statement that it would repurchase housing stock from a HAT if possible. Such a statement is of little use as it would not bind future councils and the HAT could not be forced to sell back to the authority' (ibid., p. 15).

The Local Government and Housing Act of 1989

This Act contained a number of financial provisions, including ending the possibility of local authorities to subsidise council rents from rates. The consequence of this was rent increases for many council tenants.

Housing and Urban Development Act 1993

Many previous Acts contained provisions intended to stimulate the role of the private sector in housing. For example, the Housing Act 1980 eased rent and eviction restrictions for private landlords in order to encourage the growth of privately rented accommodation. Later legislation created new 'regulated tenancies' which reduced the security of tenure in order to revive private sector involvement through making the renting of private property a more attractive proposition. At the same time, some feared that too large a role for the private sector landlord could bring back the evil of what was called 'Rachmanism' during the late 1950s where a ruthless landlord exploited and bullied the vulnerable tenants of his dilapidated properties.

The aspects of the 1993 Act concerned with housing policy were opposed by some private landlords, since they included plans to allow leaseholders of property the right to buy the freeholds of their homes. Some Conservatives, including the Duke of Westminster who is reputed to be Britain's richest landlord, opposed the legislation on the grounds that government should not interfere with contracts entered into freely between leaseholders and freeholders.

The new Approach in Action

Council tenants who decided not to buy their council homes did not welcome the prospects of their homes being owned by private landlords, and it was fears such as these which resulted in the failure of the HAT experiment. However, tenants were far less worried about estates leaving councils to be run by housing associations. Housing associations are non-profit-making bodies supervised by a quango, the Housing Corporation. Housing associations can gain estates through the CCT (compulsory competitive tendering) process, or new associations can be set up through large-scale voluntary transfers (LSVTs). CCT for housing management means

that councils set up Direct Service Organisations (DSOs) to bid for contracts against bids from housing associations and private sector management organisations. Although 'competitive', David Brown has argued that the contracts marketplace is biased against DSOs:

> Housing associations competing for council contracts will be bidding from a secure base. Their own housing management is not subject to CCT. Their staff are therefore assured of the work of managing the association's own stock. CCT work is just an optional extra. Private sector housing management organisations will also enjoy an important advantage over DSOs. Whereas DSOs are allowed to bid only for their own council's contracts, private-sector companies will have no constraints on their choice of what to bid for. DSOs, in contrast, are doomed to be shrinking organisations. If there is a single council contract and the DSO loses it, the DSO will not be around to bid again next time. (D. Brown, 1993, p. 14)

Others are less worried about DSOs than they are about the problems which housing associations may soon be facing. Housing associations were established with the purpose of providing affordable housing for people in low income jobs. The Government believes that housing associations, and not councils, will be the principal providers of social housing in the future. But there is concern outside government that housing associations have no experience in running very large estates. Typically housing association accommodation comprises small blocks of flats, very small estates and individual houses. Furthermore, as a consequence of borrowing from private sector rather than public sector sources, housing association rents have risen to an average of £46 a week, which is not affordable to people on low incomes. The least well-off receive 100 per cent housing benefit, which pays full rent, but this frequently results in social problems if all accommodation is devoted to housing the poorest. Richard Best has argued that 'New developments housing 150 homeless, with high levels of child density and a common characteristic of poverty, can create instant – even if architect designed – ghettoes, shunned by their neighbours' (Best, 1992, p. 22).

Finally, however, there has been some reassuring research concerning the quality of housing management by housing associations and local authorities. Although tenants had a poor understanding of the nature of housing associations, generally speaking, tenants reported that

> Accessibility to housing officers and services had improved in most cases. One association was housed in customer-friendly, purpose-built offices. One had set up a local office and future plans in another included introducing decentralised services ... Tenants reported no major disasters since the transfer. Most said that they received the same or better housing service as before and they welcomed the provision of more social housing. (Riseborough, 1992, p. 14)

Despite these findings, putting housing management out to CCT is not popular with tenants. Above all, they fear the loss of local accountability and large rent increases as the profit motive is put before the social service motive.

Summary

During the 1980s many social problems were tackled by governments which were committed to simple market reforms. By the 1990s the failure of this approach became increasingly evident. The Thatcher governments over-relied on home ownership as the solution to the housing problem. For home ownership is an option only for those who are relatively well-off. The less well-off will need to be housed in rented accommodation, and for them the prospects of a free market which could result in their being transferred to a private landlord is not welcomed.

Whilst the 'right to buy' was politically popular, and adopted as policy by Labour, the severe limitations on local authorities to use sales receipts to build replacement homes for renting was an error in the judgement of many critics. Many housing experts doubt whether housing associations will be able to replace local authorities in the provision of new social housing. Furthermore, the privately rented sector has proved very difficult to revive. Until the demand

for housing is matched by the supply of homes, the homeless will be a permanent feature of contemporary British society.

Questions

1. Assess the impact of privatisation policies on housing.

2. 'The right to buy policy was a political success but a failure in terms of solving the housing crisis.' Evaluate this statement.

3. 'The Conservative dream of a property-owning democracy has been turned into nightmare by the impact on housing of a lengthy economic recession. Over 70,000 homes a year are being repossessed, thousands of home-owners are falling behind with their mortgage repayments, whilst thousands more are trapped in properties which are worth much less than the mortgages they are paying off.' How valid is this view? How can government help home-owners who are facing economic difficulties?

Assignment

Since 1979 the Conservative Government of Margaret Thatcher has, in one sense, pursued a coherent and politically successful housing policy, based on cuts in public expenditure on the housing programme and the expansion of home ownership. However it has been suggested that this is merely a tenure policy, not a housing policy, although it is possible to go further and to argue that the Government has been pursuing an anti-housing policy. The charge that the Government has merely a tenure policy is based on the centrality of the council tenants' right to buy, which is about transferring the ownership for existing dwellings, having little or nothing to do with the key housing policy issues of quantity and quality. Moreover, the sale of council houses is a policy aimed at providing benefits for people who are already well housed, doing nothing for those in greatest need. A key feature of current tenure policy is its unfairness, best illustrated by the imposition of a strictly means tested housing benefit scheme for tenants (a scheme which has been a target for spending cuts), while the inverted means test of tax relief on mortgage interest is defended despite escalating cost. In addition the tenure policy accusation rests on the observation that for the individual household the achievement of home ownership is assumed to represent the end of their housing problem. A theme running through a number of chapters in this book is that this assumption is deeply flawed.

The idea that the Thatcher Government has pursued an anti-housing policy goes beyond the attack on council housing to recognise the contradictions between housing and economic policy objectives. First, it is clear that the housing programme bore the brunt of the cuts in public expenditure in the early 1980s, not for any carefully argued housing reasons but for political and economic reasons. Second, the use of high interest rates and high unemployment as tools of economic policy, at the same time as relying on further growth of home ownership, is highly contradictory. Economic policy has frustrated the achievement of housing policy objectives by raising the cost of mortgages.

Extract from Malpass (ed.), 1990, pp. 232–3.

(i)   To what extent did the Thatcher governments pursue a 'tenure' policy rather than a 'housing' policy?

(ii)   Explain the author's opinion on the 'Right to Buy' legislation.

(iii)   Outline reasons why some critics have accused the Thatcher governments of pursuing an 'anti-housing' policy.

(iv)   Construct a brief argument which challenges the criticisms made in the extract and which supports the Thatcher government's housing policy.

Further reading

Atkinson, R. and Durden, P. (1990) 'Housing Policy in the Thatcher Years' in S. Savage and L. Robins (eds) *Public Policy Under Thatcher* (London: Macmillan).

Kemp, P. (1992) 'Housing' in Marsh, D. and Rhodes, R.A.W. (eds) *Implementing Thatcherite Policies* (Buckingham: Open University Press).

Malpass, P. (1990) *Reshaping Housing Policy* (London, Routledge).

Malpass, P. (ed) (1990) *The Housing Crisis* (London: Croom Helm).

■ *Chapter 24* ■

Inequality in Britain

Rich Britain: Poor Britain
Inner City Deprivation

Poverty: Political Myths and the Political
Agenda
The Counter-Arguments

In December 1992 a birthday went almost unnoticed: the Beveridge Report was 50 years old. Sir William Beveridge set out a blueprint for the government to follow which would banish the 'giant evils' of Want, Disease, Squalor, Ignorance and Idleness from Britain. Half a century later, and despite the creation of a welfare state, Britain remains a society plagued by social and economic problems. Why is Britain a 'one-third/two-thirds' society in which the majority enjoy lifestyles based on a decent standard of living but alongside a significant minority who are materially poor and disadvantaged in terms of having poorer health, poorer education, and less chance of employment than the rest? The arguments of the 'poverty lobby', that poverty is an issue for government to tackle, are contrasted with the New Right critique of welfare, which is blamed for creating a 'dependency culture'. The development of poverty in contemporary Britain is considered along with the implications for society of the emerging underclass. The chapter concludes with an exploration of political myths and realities which influence government policy concerning the poor.

■ Rich Britain: Poor Britain

Britain is a society characterised by great inequalities in terms of wealth and income. The most wealthy 5 per cent of the population own 37 per cent of the country's wealth. The most wealthy 50 per cent own 93 per cent of the country's wealth or, to put it another way, the poorest half

of the population own 7 per cent of the country's wealth. This pattern of inequality is reflected in the incomes households receive. For example, the poorest 20 per cent receive 7.6 per cent of all incomes, whilst the wealthiest 20 per cent receive 40.1 per cent of all incomes.

According to official statistics the situation of the poorest section of society has deteriorated since 1979 (Table 24.1). For example, in 1979 the poorest fifth of the population received 9.6 per cent of all incomes and not the 6.9 per cent they received in 1989. In 1989 one in four children were living in poverty; the equivalent figure for 1979 was one in ten. Around 12 million people were living on an income below half of the national average in 1989; in 1979 the equivalent number was 5 million. What do these poverty statistics mean in human terms? Paul Wilding has described the plight of the poorest:

Six and a half million people lacked household goods which the mass of the population saw as essential – a fridge, a telephone or carpets in the living area of their homes. Twenty one million people could not afford hobbies, holidays or celebra-

Table 24.1   *Distribution of household income*

	Bottom fifth of the population	Top fifth of the population
	(% after housing costs)	
1979	9.6	35.3
1989	6.9	41.1

tions at times like birthdays or Christmas. Thirty one million – more than half the population – live without what might reasonably be regarded as minimal financial security [such as the ability to save £10 per month or insure the contents of their home] (Wilding, 1993).

The purpose of the Beveridge Report was to combat poverty and the social ills which accompanied it. Postwar governments of the 1950s, 1960s and 1970s accepted in general terms that a redistribution of resources in society from the better-off to the poor should be the principle that underlay social policy. Although governments, and the electorate, accepted that there would inevitably be rich people and poor people in society, it was also accepted that reducing these inequalities was politically and socially beneficial. Taxation was progressive, with the better-off paying much greater percentages of their incomes in tax than the less well-off. Tax revenues were used by governments to provide a welfare state – the equivalent of 'social wages' – to provide free education, free health care and other benefits to those who would not otherwise have been able to afford these basic needs. Local authorities provided subsidised housing. Although the redistributive principle did not always operate in the way intended, it was assumed that welfare benefits would have been financed disproportionately by the better-off members of society but drawn disproportionately by the less well-off. Through such a redistribution of resources, it was intended that the worst impact of poverty would be softened and that even the poorest members of the society would be able to lead dignified lives in which they or their children, would enjoy some equality of opportunity despite their relative poverty.

New Right thinking increasingly influenced Conservative policy-making from the 1970s onwards. The result was that the assumptions shared by earlier Conservative and Labour governments – that poverty was an evil which should be tackled by government – were no longer held with such certainty. Indeed it was argued that the high levels of taxation which was needed to finance the welfare state actually reduced people's incentive to be enterprising and

to work hard. Furthermore, it was argued that a high level of welfare had a negative impact on the poor. For it produced a 'dependency culture' which sapped their determination and ability to lead independent lives. Cutting taxes and reducing welfare would, it was argued, release enterprise and energy which would result in the creation of more wealth. The fear of poverty, no longer cushioned by generous welfare benefits, would encourage many poor people to reassess their lot and see them move back into the job market. Once in employment, the opportunity to keep more of their income by paying less tax would encourage them to work harder. In this way, it was argued, the existence of poverty has a beneficial effect on society through eventually creating more wealth. Even those in poverty who, for whatever reason, could not redirect their lives, would benefit from the 'trickle down' of prosperity from the richest to the poorest. In other words, the New Right argued that the creation of wealth was more socially beneficial than the redistribution of wealth.

Government policies have not always resulted in their intended impact and reduced poverty. For example, it was frequently middle-class people who benefited disportionately from the welfare state and not the poorest section of society. Chapter 21 illustrated how middle-class parents could ensure that their children went to well-equipped comprehensives in the leafy suburbs whilst inner city pupils were destined to attend 'sink' schools. Nor did the poor benefit from the trickle down of wealth in Mrs Thatcher's enterprise culture. Indeed, the poorest 10 per cent of the population were 6 per cent worse off in real terms in 1989 than they were a decade earlier. The poor, in other words, had become poorer.

■ Inner City Deprivation

Has a new social class emerged in contemporary Britain? Whilst some academics and politicians claim that it is not so, others argue that in Britain, as in the United States, a sub-working-class stratum of individuals disconnected from mainstream society now forms a distinct 'underclass'. This underclass is characterised by poverty, crime, poor education, drug abuse, ill health, and alienation from the political system. Serious crimes committed by young teenagers in deprived areas of Manchester, Liverpool, Newcastle and other large cities, have generated a public debate about the links between underclass poverty, mental illness, suicide and crime.

An example will help to illuminate the issues.

Meadow Well has been described as a 'sink estate' located in Tyneside in one of Britain's most deprived areas. Poverty is the norm. In 1991 the Meadow Well estate had an unemployment rate of 40 per cent, but this rose to 80 per cent in some streets. Every one of the 252 children attending the Meadow Well primary school received a clothing allowance. Visitors to the estate have reported that its fabric is in a poor condition, with houses which look drab and neglected. Most gardens are overgrown and some houses have windows which are boarded over. In September 1991 the Meadow Well estate erupted into violence with fire-bomb attacks, rioting, looting and ram-raiding. What are the causes of this and similar urban unrest?

Theories from the liberal left recognise an inextricable link between an environment of poverty and lawlessness. It is not argued that all poor people are potential criminals, but that poverty increases the vulnerability of some people to committing crime. It has been argued, for example, that the increase in poverty during the 1980s went hand-in-hand with the increase in reported crime from 2.2 million offences in 1979 to 5 million in 1991. Robert Reiner argued that the pattern of crime reflected the state of local economies, and that 'the 1980s were the first time when the Government held out no hope for the poor' (*Observer,* 15 September 1991).

The political right tends to dismiss explanations which link poverty with crime. There may be agreement with the left on the existence of a new underclass, but no agreement that the criminality of the underclass is caused by its poverty. The right argues that poverty was more severe earlier in this century than it is now, yet it was not accompanied by lawlessness. Hence poverty in itself does not result in criminality. The

principal cause of criminality is immorality. Christie Davies has argued that an

> earlier generation of Britons succeeded in changing the character of their people and reducing the many forms of deviance that have reappeared and flourished in our own time, because they saw them as constituting not a social but a moral problem whose solution lay in the reform of personal conduct (Davies, 1993).

To support this view – that poverty is not a direct cause of crime – the right is able to point out that the Meadow Well estate, then known as the Ridges estate, experienced riots in the 'affluent' 1960s. The lack of moral guidance rather than material poverty is recognised to be the main cause of lawlessness, and the right tends to attribute the decline in moral guidance to the increase in one-parent families.

The controversy surrounding the question 'what impact does poverty have on society?' is unlikely to be settled. The attention of the left is focused on improving employment opportunities, improving education and providing more and better housing as the immediate solutions to urban poverty. The left has faith in believing that less poverty will result in less crime. The right is concerned with a decline in morality which is generally recognised to be a consequence of changing family structures, particularly those which result from illegitimacy or broken marriages in which there is no 'authority' from a father. Many on the right believe that the increase in one-parent families is linked with increased anti-social behaviour, and it is argued that social policies should discourage the break-up of the traditional family structure and thereby reduce crime.

Poverty: Political Myths and the Political Agenda

It might be expected that the increase in poverty, the emergence of an underclass, the growth of 'cardboard cities' in many towns, together with an associated culture of crime and drug abuse, would be issues at the top of any government's political agenda. Yet in Britain this is not so. How can this be?

Firstly there has been a political debate on the meaning of 'poverty' in contemporary Britain. What the left recognises as 'poverty' the right sees as 'inequality'. The right argues that the least well-off are not poor; they are just not as well off as the rest of society. It is argued that no one in Britain experiences genuine absolute poverty as do many people living in Ethiopia, Somalia or Bangladesh. In Britain those who are relatively poor never go hungry and may own many possessions associated with affluence such as cars, videos, fridges and telephones. John Moore, once Secretary of State for Health and Social Security, attacked the left's claim that poverty existed in Britain since,

according to the left's definition of poverty, there would be 'poverty in paradise'. Paul Wilding has argued that this New Right argument which redefines 'poverty' as no more than 'inequality' is no more than a political convenience: since it lifts responsibility for action from the shoulders of government since 'inequality is not a matter for government ... responsibility for this so-called poverty is personal' (Wilding, 1993).

Wilding further contends that there are additional beliefs about the nature and causes of poverty which block poverty from being a priority issue. One of these is encouraging people to believe that the unemployed were really work-shy

---

Exhibit 24.1 *The Myth of the Work-Shy*

The crudest form of this is Norman Tebbit's 'on your bike' statement, which is a good example of the popular confusion between 'All ...' and 'Some ...'. The most tough-minded and fast-talking politician could not sustain for ten seconds the proposition that *all* unemployed people are able-bodied and mentally fit bicycle-owners, and this is probably not what Mr Tebbit intended to say. But it was crude, for all that, and in less crude forms, the philosophy is enduring and pervasive: a form of tunnel vision which ignores the realities of mass unemployment – the lack of jobs, the waste of skills, the dashed hopes, and the pathetically restricted horizons – and leads to the conclusion that 'the poor' could perfectly well help themselves if they wanted to; all they need is to 'get up and go'.

It was the spirit of the 1834 Poor Law. The threat of the work-house seared the minds of successive generations. Anyone who is over 70 today (and that means more than six million people in England and Wales alone) was approaching 30 when the Poor Law was finally abolished in 1948. It was the spirit of the Majority Report of the Royal Commission on the Poor Laws of 1905–9; and yet the Commission's own research staff provided overwhelming evidence that most poverty was not due to the failure of able-bodied males to support themselves. A statistical survey in Part II of the report demonstrates beyond argument that only a quarter of paupers were male – the rest were women and children. The age breakdown was even more telling. In the 15–25 age-group, only 3.3 per thousand were unemployed. The figure rose steadily, with a quantum leap around the edge of retirement, to 353 per thousand (more than one in three) over the age of 85.

This statistical picture of the increasing proportion in successive age-groups unable to work (whether through disability or through inability to find a job) should have been enough to kill the myth of the 'work-shy' for all time.

But the myth survives, rippling along at some subliminal level in the public consciousness until it is needed, and then surfacing again. It disappears in times of full employment, when it is not needed (though those are the periods in which any physically and mentally fit person of either sex who is available for work and refuses to work might well be called a lay-about); and it surfaces in times of high unemployment, when it is least true. The women, the children, the old people, and the disabled or handicapped are forgotten. The jobs are assumed to be there for the taking (though everybody knows that they are not).

From K. Jones (1991, pp. 36–7).

Figure 24.1   *Work-shy street beggar or homeless member of the underclass?*

Source: Lynton Robins.

and that job vacancies existed if only they would get 'on their bikes' in search of them (Exhibit 24.1). Another is that the welfare state actually encouraged people to get into the position of needing help – the 'perverse incentive' – by which it was argued by the Right, for example, that young single females chose to become pregnant in order to obtain a council house. Wilding commented that 'blaming the victim' is an approach adopted by all governments when they are either unable or unwilling to tackle poverty, and the 'perverse incentive' argument is used to support the belief that any government policies to tackle poverty will be ineffective.

There is also the belief that inequality stimulates people into working harder and that low wages for some workers help keep Britain competitive in international trade. It is argued that high wages for all, together with the costs of a large welfare state, would make Britain uncompetitive.

Finally, the Government does little to tackle poverty because it believes that 'it can get away with inaction. The so-called poor are unorganised and powerless. They don't matter much as voters and, more importantly, poverty does not matter much to other voters' (Wilding, 1993).

■ The Counter-Arguments

Poverty has not been an important issue for recent Conservative governments, but Wilding argued that for a variety of reasons it should have been. He pointed out that any government committed to maximising freedom should fight poverty since 'poverty is the great unfreedom, the great limitation on people's capacity to behave as free and autonomous beings' (Wilding, 1993).

Secondly, poverty creates attitudes and behaviours which can damage society at large. Quoting Beveridge 'Misery generates hate', Wilding adds that 'hate is a very dangerous feeling to have around'. Following this, government will find it easier to maintain order in a society based on greater social justice than in a society containing much poverty which has created an alienated underclass. Finally, governments should do something about poverty because they 'can do something'. Government allowed poverty to increase during the 1980s, and although it may not be able to eradicate it from society, it could lessen it.

Summary

Politicians and academics from the political left and right do not agree on whether a condition called 'poverty' exists in Britain or not. The left recognises 'poverty' as a state which debilitates people and reduces their equality of opportunity to lead full and decent lives. A comprehensive welfare state is seen as the means by which the evil effects of poverty can be overcome. The right recognises 'inequality' in society as inevitable but something which has a generally positive impact on society. The right believes that welfare encourages the creation of a culture of dependency which traps people rather than liberates them.

Why does the British electorate tolerate poverty, cardboard cities and the existence of a distressed underclass? There are a number of arguments about the nature of poverty and the motives of poor people which have led to recent governments doing less for the poor than their opponents have urged.

Questions

1. 'The poor are always with us.' Can politics and government eliminate poverty?

2. What is the possible impact of a 'one-third/two-thirds' society on voting behaviour? Why has poverty failed to become an election issue?

3. Explain how the political left and right differ in their views on how the welfare state works.

Assignment

The following is an extract from *Poverty*, the Journal of the Child Poverty Action Group (CPAG). Use the material to write a brief article for a tabloid newspaper which is sympathetic to the poor, and another article which is hostile to the poor. Exchange your articles with other members of your class and discuss how easy or difficult it was to write from the different perspectives. Decide which type of story is the most interesting to read, and why.

Facts & Figures

□ *Poverty*

Just before MPs went off for the summer recess, the government published the 'poverty' figures. *Households Below Average Income: a statistical analysis 1979–1988/89* contains key figures on how many people are living in poverty in the UK and who they are.

How many people are living in poverty?
We use 50 per cent of average income after housing costs as one commonly-used definition of poverty. In 1988/89, 12 million people (22 per cent of the population) were living in poverty. This is well over double the figure in 1979, when 5 million (9 per cent of the population) were living in poverty (see Table 1).

How many children are living in poverty?
In 1988/89, 3.1 million children (25 per cent of all children) were living in poverty. This is over double the figure in 1979, when 1.4 million (10 per cent of all children) were living in poverty (see Table 2).

Growing divisions
Looking at the period between 1979 and 1988/89, the poorest have not only fallen behind the rest of the population; but there is also some evidence to show that their real incomes after housing costs have actually fallen. The bottom 10 per cent have seen a drop in their real income of some 6 per cent between 1979 and 1988/89 after housing costs, compared to a rise of 30 per cent for the population as a whole.

Source: Department of Social Security, *Households Below Average Income: a statistical analysis 1979–1988/89*, Government Statistical Service, HMSO, 1992. The new edition incorporates a number of methodological changes which mean that the new figures are not directly comparable to earlier ones.

Facts & Figures—continued

Table 1   Numbers and proportions of individuals living below 50% of average income before and after housing costs

	Before housing costs Nos: millions	%	After housing costs Nos: millions	%
1979	4.4	8	5.0	9
1981	4.7	9	6.2	11
1987	8.7	16	10.5	19
1988/89	10.4	19	12.0	22

Table 2   Numbers and proportions of children living below 50% of average income before and after housing costs

	Before housing costs Nos: millions	%	After housing costs Nos: millions	%
1979	1.2	9	1.4	10
1981	1.7	12	2.2	16
1987	2.5	20	3.0	24
1988/89	2.8	22	3.1	25

(*Note:* figures for people include children)

Table 3   Unemployment rates by sex, age and ethnic origin: average, spring 1989 to spring 1991

	White	Ethnic minority groups	of whom W Indian/ Guyanese	Indian	Pakistani/ Bangladeshi	All other groups
Men						
All aged 16 and over	7	13	15	10	21	11
16 to 24	12	22	•	•	•	•
25 to 44	6	11	•	8	19	10
45 to 64	7	12	•	•	•	•
65 and over	6	•	•	•	•	•
Women						
All aged 16 and over	7	12	12	10	24	11
16 to 24	9	19	•	•	•	•
25 to 44	7	10	•	•	•	•
45 to 64	5	•	•	•	•	•
65 and over	4	•	•	•	•	•

• Sample too small
Source: House of Commons *Hansard*, 21 May 1992, cols 247–8.

☐ *Women's employment patterns*

The *General Household Survey* contains a great deal of information about women's working patterns. The latest edition shows that in 1990:

- 41% of women of working age with the youngest dependent child aged 0–4 were in paid work – 13% were working full-time and 28% were working part-time;

- 67% of women of working age with the youngest dependent child aged 5–9 were in paid work – 19% were working full-time and 47% were working part-time;
- 78% of women with the youngest dependent child aged 10 or over were in paid work – 32% were working full-time and 46% were working part-time.

Overall, 60 per cent of women with dependent children were in paid work. This compares to 52 per cent in 1979 and 47 per cent in 1973.

Source: OPCS, *General Household Survey 1990*, HMSO, 1992, Table 9.5.

□ *Child abuse*

Child Abuse Trends in England and Wales 1988–1990, published by the NSPCC, identifies a number of stress factors which may lead to children being abused. While the interaction between these factors is complex, the figures show that in 1988–1990:

- over half the families of children on the 'at risk' register were in receipt of income support;
- 70% of families of neglected and emotionally abused children were in receipt of income support.

The NSPCC concludes: 'It would seem indisputable that poor and cramped housing conditions, financial difficulties and unemployment are bound to have an impact on family life which may lead to children being harmed. If we are to prevent child abuse, consideration must be given to alleviating such pressures on families.'

Source: Susan J. Creighton, *Child Abuse Trends in England and Wales 1988–1990, and an overview from 1973–1990*, NSPCC, 1992.

Further reading

Boyson, R. (1971) *Down with the Poor* (Enfield: Churchill).

Hutton, J. *et al.* (eds) (1991) *Dependency to Enterprise* (London: Routledge)

Mack, J. and Lansley, S. (1985) *Poor Britain* (London: Allen & Unwin).

Oppenheim, C. (1990) *Poverty: The Facts* (London: CPAG).

Wilding, P. (1993) 'Poverty and Government in Britain in the 1980s', *Talking Politics*, 5(3).

■ *Chapter 25* ■

The Unions, Unemployment and Industrial Relations

Trade Unionism and Monetarism
The Impact of Unemployment

Unions and Government
The New Realism

During the 1970s, it seemed that union power had grown to the point where union leaders were amongst the most influential political figures in the country. Indeed, in opinion polls, leaders of the largest unions ranked alongside the prime minister and members of the Cabinet in terms of power and influence. Union leaders were regularly observed to-ing and fro-ing from Number Ten in their attempts to negotiate industrial peace over 'beer and sandwiches'. The Governments of the 1970s led by Wilson, Heath and Callaghan all lost public support to some extent because they did not appear to be able to cope with the unions. Some blamed Heath's electoral defeat in 1974 on his Government's failure to handle the miners' strike and the 'Winter of Discontent' seemed to inflict similar damage on the Callaghan Government in 1979. Yet, within a few years, the situation changed dramatically, with the unions suffering an enormous loss of power. In 1983, a popular newspaper described the trade unions as 'Like columns of a defeated army struggling to a prisoner of war camp' and continued 'Not long ago their battalions looked to be invincible.' A decade later even the Labour Party was thinking the unthinkable and considering measures which would weaken its links with the unions. What reasons, then, lay behind the unions' fall from power?

■ Trade Unionism and Monetarism

The first point to bear in mind is that the portrayal of union power in the tabloid press and in public opinion was somewhat exaggerated. Although there has been an undeniable loss in trade union power, the unions were never as powerful in the 1970s as some thought, nor in the 1990s are they as weak as some would believe. Nor, as we shall see, was the beginning of the first Thatcher Government the point at which the unions moved from their position of relative strength to one of relative weakness. Although the influence of the unions has declined during the Thatcher governments, the process of decline began years before under a Labour Government.

Part of the Butskellite postwar consensus in British politics was the commitment by governments to full or high levels of employment. This was part of a bargain struck between the unions and governments that relied on interventionist techniques to manage the economy: the Government would maintain high levels of employment in exchange for the unions delivering their part of the bargain such as pay restraint. But too often it appeared that the unions were not able to deliver their side of the bargain, not even to Labour Governments. Whilst union leaders made agreements with the government of the day, they could not make their mass memberships keep to those agreements. In the eyes of the public, the unions became more and more unpopular as they 'had their cake and ate it'.

The most remarkable feature of Margaret Thatcher's governments in this respect was that they did not need any agreements or bargains with the unions in order to implement economic policy. Unlike all previous postwar governments, Thatcher could ignore the trade unions. This was possible in the main because her monetarist policies had no role for the unions to play. The Governments' prime economic aim of squeezing inflation out of the system no longer relied on winning agreements from the unions on limiting pay demands, but on the control of interest rates, reductions in public spending and control of the money supply. And none of these techniques relied on union support or cooperation.

■ The Impact of Unemployment

The Conservatives fought the 1979 General Election with the campaign slogan 'Labour isn't working' in the now-famous dole-queue poster, yet, by the time of the next election in 1983, the rate of unemployment had risen from 5 per cent to 13 per cent. After peaking at a total of 3.3 million, the unemployment total levelled off in 1986 and by the end of the year began to fall. Within two years, however, unemployment was to begin a relentless rise back towards the 3 million level.

Of particular concern to trade unionists was the pattern of unemployment in British manufacturing industries since this is an area of the economy in which trade unions are highly organised. As Figure 25.1 shows, the trend is that fewer and fewer workers are employed by industrial businesses. The recession which began in 1989 increased in intensity during the 1990s as the pace of factory closures and redundancies quickened until by 1992 around five and a half thousand jobs were being lost every week. Since

Margaret Thatcher came to power in 1979, the number of workers in industry had declined by 36 per cent. The disastrous impact of de-industrialisation on manufacturing employment was occurring well in advance of the Thatcher governments, but the process accelerated after Margaret Thatcher and then John Major entered Number Ten. For example, of the 4 million jobs lost between 1966 and 1984, over 3 million were from the manufacturing sector. Although many new jobs have been created in the economy they did not compensate for the old jobs lost since the new jobs tend to be in non-unionised areas or areas where union organisation is weak. Thus each worker lost by manufacturing industry more or less represents a member lost by a trade union.

Table 25.1 shows the membership losses experienced over the last decade by the larger trade unions. It can be seen, for example, that the membership of Britain's largest union, the Transport and General Workers' Union (TGWU), has fallen by a staggering 40 per cent. Of particular

Table 25.1 *Membership of the biggest trade unions, 1979 and 1989*

	Membership	
Union	1979	1989
Transport & General Workers Union	2 086 281	1 270 776
GMB	967 153	823 176
National & Local Gov. Officers Association	753 226	750 502
Amalgamated Engineering Union	1 509 607	741 647
Manufacturing Science & Finance Union	691 054	653 000
National Union of Public Employees	691 770	604 912
Union of Shop Distrib. & Allied Workers	470 017	375 891
Elec. Electronic Telecomm. & Plumbing Union	443 621	367 411
Royal College of Nursing	161 962	285 548
Union of Construction Allied Trades & Technicians	348 875	258 342
National Union of Teachers	290 740	213 482
Confederation of Health Service Employees	212 930	209 344
Union of Communication Workers	203 452	202 500

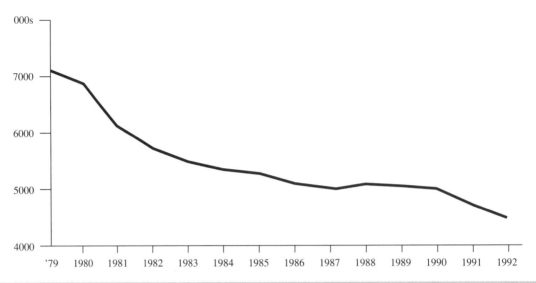

Figure 25.1 *Numbers employed in UK manufacturing industries, June 1979–June 1992*

political significance during the 1980s and 1990s was the shrinking membership of the National Union of Mineworkers (NUM) to the point where it is no longer a large union. It is hard to believe that earlier this century there were over a million miners, and perhaps harder still to believe that the rundown of the coal industry was planned so that by the end of the century Britain's coal would be mined from less than twenty pits. The decline in NUM membership was caused in part by a massive programme of pit closures, and in part by the political divisions among miners which led to the establishment of the rival Union of Democratic Mineworkers.

■ Unions and Government

In the years following the Second World War, the unions maintained the close links that they had developed when cooperating with government during the war. The unions had, as it were, become 'respectable' with their influence no longer stemming from mass rallies in Trafalgar Square but from the quiet persuasion exercised in the corridors of Whitehall. Unions were invited to serve on important committees by both Labour

and Conservative governments, and political scientists during the 1960s talked of a corporate state developing in Britain. It seemed as if policy was forged from a consensus amongst ministers, employers and union leaders on how the economy should develop. In exchange for participating in government through bodies such as the National Economic Development Council ('Neddy') and influencing policy, union leaders were expected to deliver their members' agreement and cooperation. However, with considerable publicity being given to a rash of 'wildcat' strikes, particularly in the car industry, it seemed that union leaders wielded little control over their members. In short, the lesson to be learnt from Britain's industrial relations front was that union leaders 'could not deliver'.

A Labour Government headed by Harold Wilson attempted to introduce legislation which would have changed the power structure of unions to the advantage of union leaders. The White Paper, *In Place of Strife*, was introduced by Barbara Castle in January 1969 and initially received a fairly favourable response from the Trades Union Congress (TUC). However, opposition to the proposals developed during the year, resulting in the Parliamentary Labour Party (PLP) threatening to oppose the Government if it proceeded with *In Place of Strife*. The Government capitulated, withdrew legislation based on the White Paper and accepted a face-saving 'Solemn and Binding Agreement' from the TUC as an alternative. The first attempt to take union power from the 'militant' rank-and-file and place it in the hands of 'moderate' leaders ended in sound defeat.

Included in the Conservative manifesto of 1970 was a proposal to 'put unions on a legal footing', and in 1971 the Heath Government passed its Industrial Relations Act. The Act represented an all-out assault on union privileges and generated vigorous opposition from 'moderate' and 'militant' unionists alike. In practice the Act was clumsy and soon abandoned as unworkable. Thus the second attempt to reform the unions through the use of legislation came to grief and was formally repealed by a subsequent Labour Government in 1974.

The period from 1974 to 1979 is seen by some political scientists as the time when union leaders exercised great influence, almost control, over the Labour governments. The Labour Government and unions had drawn up a social contract which represented a bargain with commitments on both sides. Other political scientists, however, see the period 1974–9 in a more qualified light. At first, the TUC was influential and in 1974–5 the social contract did appear to work in favour of the unions. In particular, a string of legislation – the Trade Union and Labour Relations Act 1974, the Employment Protection Act 1975, and the Health and Safety at Work Act 1975 – improved the position of trade unionists. However, from 1975 onwards, the advantage of the social contract ran in favour of the Government, since it was implemented to work in the same manner as an incomes policy. In 1976 the unions were not only accepting pay restraint but were also having their opposition to public spending cuts dismissed by the Government. Thus for most of its life the social contract was mainly an incomes policy and, as Marsh and King commented, 'based first on the active cooperation, and subsequently on the acquiescence, of the unions. In the end it collapsed in the "Winter of Discontent" of 1978–9

as the TUC could no longer deliver the support of its member unions and union leaders could no longer deliver the support of their members' (Marsh and King, 1987, p. 216).

The 'Winter of Discontent' provided the mass media with a long-running, frequently exaggerated story which nevertheless included workers placing the poor, the sick and the elderly at risk. To many who had not thought so beforehand, the unions now deserved to be disciplined by the government. The Conservatives came to power in 1979 pledged to reform the unions, and the stage was set for a political struggle. But union leaders found the fight against the Thatcher Government more difficult to organise than their successful campaigns against Wilson and Heath. The new trade union legislation was unlike previous attempts in that it did not consist of one major attempt to restrict union activity, but rather it was a step-by-step approach that gradually eroded union power.

The new industrial relations legislation, which was to be implemented against a backcloth of high unemployment and correspondingly weak union position, had four main purposes. Whilst it attempted to reform an outmoded system of industrial relations, it pursued four aims by which to achieve this:

(1) to weaken collectivism and the role of trade unions in industrial relations;
(2) to strengthen the right to manage amongst employers;
(3) to regulate and reduce union power and influence in the labour market; and
(4) to depoliticise trade unions and industrial relations.

(Farnham, 1990, p. 60)

Margaret Thatcher's governments were particularly hostile towards the unions, and the corporate politics of 'beer and sandwiches at Number Ten' came to a sharp end with the 1979 Conservative election success. In the eyes of many Conservatives, the irresponsibility of the unions was largely to blame for Britain's relatively poor postwar economic performance, since acting together unions wielded more than sufficient power to prevent markets from working freely. Legislation was passed which worked towards achieving the four aims of Government industrial relations reform.

The first major piece of legislation was the Employment Act 1980, which curbed picketing, secondary picketing and the use of the closed shop. Picketing was restricted to a person's own workplace with changes outlawing mass picketing but allowing picket-lines of six. The Act also made it easier for workers to avoid joining closed shops on grounds of conscience. The Employment Act 1982 introduced further restrictions on closed-shop agreements, as well as making unions liable for members' actions and outlawing strikes which were political in nature. As Marsh and King observe:

> The resurrection of the spirit of Taff Vale renders the unions no longer the beneficiaries of immunities they have enjoyed since 1906. The Act makes them liable to claims of damages of up to £250 000 from any person whose business is damaged by 'unlawful means', within the new, narrower, concept of a trade dispute. The autonomy of shop stewards and full-time union officials is thus circumscribed by an Act which makes the unions responsible for those actions. (Marsh and King, 1987, p. 219)

The Trade Union Act 1984 focused on the internal workings of unions: it required secret ballots of all members for strikes and elections both for union executives and for the existence of political funds. The latter provision was designed to reduce unions' political influence by cutting links with the Labour Party, but in the event no union membership voted against the existence of a political fund. The Employment Act 1988 represented another significant move in weakening the collectivist power of the unions through an increase in the individual freedom of union members. Amongst a number of provisions, the Act gave union members 'the right to apply to the courts for an order restraining their union from inducing them to take any kind of industrial action without a properly conducted secret ballot, with majority support'. Also, under the Act

union members have the statutory right not to be unjustifiably disciplined by their union ... Previously, union members could be disciplined for working during a strike or other industrial action. Under the present law, union disciplinary action for this is unjustifiable and individuals have the choice whether to work during a dispute or not. (Farnham, 1990, pp. 68–9)

Finally, the Act also established a Commissioner for the Rights of Trade Union Members which was given powers to assist individual members in dispute with their respective unions.

To what extent were the four aims of Conservative policy achieved? David Marsh has made an assessment of how far Conservative manifesto commitments, which embraced the four aims, were put into practice (Table 25.2). He concluded that the unions had been weakened as the result of a cumulative process, but was cautious in stating that this was a deliberately calculated 'step-by-step' approach with each piece of new legislation built upon previous legislation. Although the manifesto commitments were honoured by the Government, he stated, 'It is very difficult to assess whether Government legislation or macroeconomic developments have had more influence on the trade unions' and he doubted whether industrial relations at shopfloor level had changed to any great extent (Marsh, 1992a, p. 49).

Economic policy under John Major's governments has had contradictory implications for the trade union movement. On the one hand, the Chancellor dismayed union leaders by his pronouncement that unemployment was a price worth paying for low inflation. Union leaders were aware that continuing high levels of unemployment would continue to erode union strength. Also the 'Neddy' system was scrapped by the Government in 1992, ending the last vestige of the 'beer and sandwiches' approach which had, since the 1960s, brought union leaders into a network of communication with, and possibly influence upon, government economic policy-makers. The Government argued that 'Neddy' belonged to a past era of corporatism and had no place in a modern, diversified and decentralised free market economy.

Table 25.2 *Conservative manifesto commitments and legislative action on trade union reform, 1979–90*

1979 Manifesto commitments	Enacted?	1983 Manifesto commitments	Enacted?	1987 Manifesto commitments	Enacted?
1. Removal of immunities in relation to picketing	1. Immunity for secondary picketing removed in 1980 Employment Act	1. Removal of immunity if no secret ballot before strike	1. Secret ballots before strikes required in 1984 Trade Union Act	1. Empower individual members to stop unions from calling them out on strike without holding a secret ballot	1. Enacted in 1988 Employment Act
2. Restrictions on closed shop	2. Yes. Restrictions in both 1980 and 1982 Employment Acts	2. Require secret ballots for the election of union executives	2. Required in 1984 Trade Union Act	2. Protect trade union members from union disciplinary action if refused to join strike	2. Enacted in 1988 Employment Act
3. Encouragement of wider use of secret ballots by unions	3. Public funds allocated for union secret ballots in 1980 Employment Act	3. Require periodical political fund ballots	3. Required in 1984 Trade Union Act	3. Require secret ballots for elections for all members of union governing body	3. Enacted in 1988 Employment Act
4. Restriction on benefits for strikers	4. Reduced benefits in 1980 Social Security Act	4. Introduce contracting in to political levy	4. Dropped – the one Trade Union victory	4. Further limit to closed shop	4. Abolished in 1988 and 1990 Employment Acts
		5. Curb the use of strikes within the public sector	Not proceeded with	5. Establish new Trade Union Commissioner	5. Established in 1988 Employment Act

Source: D. Marsh and R.A.W. Rhodes (eds) (1992, p. 34).

On the other hand, there were other developments from which the unions could draw some comfort. As unemployment pushed Britain's three-year recession towards becoming a fully fledged slump, the Government withdrew sterling from the Exchange Rate Mechanism and changed its economic priorities. Although lip-service continued to be paid towards the goal of low inflation, the Government's top priority became the so-called 'dash for growth' in order to stem and then reverse the trend of unemployment. Although the unions did not agree with the details of the Government's policy for growth, their leaders were relieved by the prospects of lower unemployment and the improvements which this would bring to unions' circumstances. At the same time, the Department of Trade and Industry indicated that it was to take a more interventionist role in the economy, and that the fate of firms and companies experiencing difficulties would no longer be decided in the marketplace. Finally, and significantly, the Government indicated that it had postponed plans to introduce further trade union legislation. Although the political situation is complex, and it seems most unlikely that the trade union movement will regain the influence enjoyed during the 1960s and 1970s, its prospects for the 1990s seem far less bleak politically than in the Thatcher era of union-bashing.

■ The New Realism

In 1983, the unions pinned their hopes on a Labour election victory which would be followed by an improvement in their position. Defeat for Labour in 1983, and again in 1987 and 1992, with a future Labour victory seeming a distant prospect, forced union leaders to reappraise their role on the more realistic basis that Thatcherism was here to stay. Union leaders also had to square up to the evidence that many of the Conservatives' union reforms were popular with their trade union members. But individual trade unions responded to these changed circumstances in different ways. Some unionists did not like the new laws but accepted that they had to come to terms with a Government which would be in power until the next general election, and perhaps beyond. These were the views of leaders often described as 'moderates' or 'new realists'. Opposed to them were unionists who so opposed the new laws that they were prepared to ignore them and thereby challenge the Government. These were the views of leaders sometimes described as 'militants' or 'old fundamentalists'.

The defeat of the NUM came as a blow to the old fundamentalists who had argued that they could not learn to live with Thatcherism, whilst the birth of a new pit union, the UDM, represented the new realists amongst mineworkers, who argued that union values had to adapt to new circumstances. These divisions caused tensions within the TUC and conflict between individual unions. The most notable split emerged in the newspaper industry between the electricians (Electrical, Electronic Telecommunication and Plumbing Union – EETPU) and the printworkers (National Graphical Association – NGA) as production utilised new technologies. In a controversial move, News International changed from old printing methods in Fleet Street to new production methods at Wapping. The old craft union, the NGA, appeared to the public to be almost Luddite as it refused to enter realistic negotiations whereas the EETPU which took over News International printing projected an image of being progressive and forward-looking. Some of the old guard in the trade unions accused the new realists in unions such as the EETPU of forming right-wing 'bosses' unions' in which the rank-and-file were more like clients than participating members. The new realists rejected this sort of accusation and replied that whilst they rejected class as the basis for union action, the real difference was one of attitudes towards new technology and competition.

Some unions pressed ahead with single-union strike-free deals (so-called 'sweet heart' deals) with employers. David Marsh played down the significance of this sort of new realism, arguing that 'it is difficult to see "new realism" as a key aspect of industrial relations except in a very minimalist sense of the term ... Single union agreements and strike-free deals are almost exclusively confined to green-field sites ... the attitudes and behaviour of unions and management have not been transformed. "New realism" reflects a realistic assessment by unions of the changes in their bargaining position rather than a permanent transformation in union attitudes or a new style of industrial relations' (Marsh, 1992a, pp. 40, 49)

Summary

Monetarist policies contained no positive role for the trade unions to play and when implemented in tandem with a world recession further weakened the position of unions through creating mass unemployment.

Conservative Governments in the 1980s imposed a legal framework on the organisation and conduct of trade union activities. Much of the new legislation stressed individual rights over and above the collectivist tradition of unions. Trade unions disagreed on how to cope with the prospect of Conservative government for the foreseeable future. Some favoured continued opposition and were prepared to struggle against Thatcherism, whilst others argued that the only future for trade unionism lay in complying with the new laws.

Questions

1. In what ways did the Thatcher governments' approach to trade unions differ from that of previous governments?

2. Analyse the effects of unemployment on trade union activity.

3. How far have the new realists in trade unions departed from traditional union values?

Assignment

Strikes: Working days lost

1976	3 284 000	1981	4 266 000	1986	1 921 000
1977	10 142 000	1982	5 313 000	1987	3 547 000
1978	9 405 000	1983	3 754 000	1988	3 703 000
1979	29 474 000	1984	27 135 000	1989	4 128 000
1980	11 964 000	1985	6 402 000	1990	1 903 000
				1991	761 000

Tasks

(i) Investigate reasons for and explain the high figures for 1979 and 1984.

(ii) Locate and retrieve information from publications such as the *Employment Gazette* which enables you to bring the table up to date. Attempt to explain any patterns which emerge.

(iii) Discuss whether it is necessary to take other trends into account, such as rising levels of unemployment, when interpreting the statistical data above.

Further reading

Farnham, D. (1990) 'Trade Union Policy, 1979–89: Restriction or Reform?' in S. Savage and L. Robins (eds) *Public Policy Under Thatcher* (London, Macmillan).

Marsh, D. (1992a), 'Industrial Relations' in D. Marsh and R.A.W. Rhodes (eds) *Implementing Thatcherite Policies: Audit of an Era* (Buckingham: Open University Press).

Marsh, D. and King, J. (1987) 'The Unions Under Thatcher', in L. Robins (ed.) *Political Institutions in Britain* (London, Longman).

Pimlott, B. and Cook, C. (eds) (1991) *Trade Unions in British Politics: The First 250 Years*, 2nd edn (London: Longman).

Taylor, A.J. (1989) *Trade Unions and Politics: A Comparative Introduction* (London: Macmillan).

■ *Chapter 26* ■

Ethnic Minority Politics

Black and British   Racism and Discrimination
Race Relations   The Political Response

Black people tend to be portrayed as a 'problem' in British politics – the problems of controlling immigration numbers, and of maintaining law and order in the black populated inner cities, and the problems posed by the disadvantages of black people in areas such as housing, education and employment. How justified is this problem image of Britain's black population? Could the real problem be white racism, explicitly and implicitly present in the mainstream culture, rather than in black shortcomings? And how have politics and the political system worked to resolve or exacerbate the situation? This chapter explores these questions.

■ Black and British

Britain has experienced considerable demographic change in terms of immigration and emigration. Numerous groups have settled in Britain – Irish, Jewish, Polish, Chinese, among others – whilst British-born people have set up new homes in countries such as Canada, Australia, New Zealand, South Africa and the former Rhodesia. Britain has a long history of immigration and emigration but a new pattern of immigration was established after the Second World War. The British Nationality Act 1948 allowed citizens of the Commonwealth to settle in Britain and this facilitated a new era in which most of those people who made new homes in Britain were black.

New Commonwealth immigrants formed numerous ethnic communities based on common language, religion and race. But, unlike previous immigrants from countries such as Ireland or Poland who could 'blend in' with the way of life, immigrants from Pakistan, India and the West Indies remained visibly distinctive through skin colour. In other words, they were visible as 'strangers' and because of this many British people formed hostile attitudes towards them which, in turn, made it more difficult still for the new black immigrants to adapt to Britain's traditional culture. It was hoped that in the course of time, British-born blacks would not experience the isolation of their immigrant parents but a survey conducted by the Runnymede Trust in 1986 found this was not the case. It was reported that fewer than 5 per cent of black schoolchildren had been invited into a white home and, although over 40 per cent said they had white friends at school, most felt that British society at large did not like them.

The use of 'black' as a shorthand term in both everyday language and the social sciences can be misleading. At the immediate level, it is obvious that 'blacks' are no more black than 'whites' are white. But just as the term white can embrace widely differing cultures, so the term black disguises the diversity that exists amongst people from a relatively small number of countries in the new Commonwealth. Although general distinctions are made between the Afro-Caribbean and Asian communities, far greater diversity exists than is implied by this simple two-fold categorisation with some ethnic communities having surprisingly little in common. In Leicester, for example, one resident in five is a member of what is popularly known as the 'Asian community'. Yet this community is actually made up of numerous groups based on seven main languages further divided into numerous dialects. Some groups have to resort to a second language, such as English, in order to communicate at anything more than the most basic level with other groups. The Asian community is further fragmented by different religions, values, cultural practices and castes, as well as by the political tensions found in the politics of the Indian subcontinent. For our purposes, then, 'black' is a general label or political colour which covers members of all ethnic communities who are located in a broadly similar position in society (Figure 26.1).

Figure 26.1   *Britain's ethnic minorities*

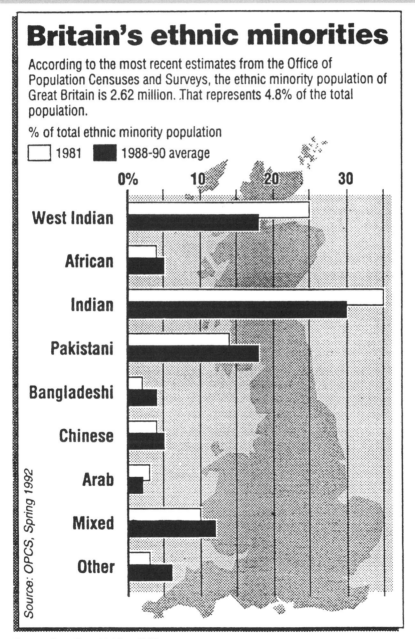

Source: *Guardian*, 19 May 1992.

■ Race Relations

It is a sad fact that many individuals have negative attitudes towards others purely on the grounds of racial difference. Racial prejudice can be expressed by whites against blacks, blacks against whites or, indeed, between ethnic groups, as in the case of Asian prejudice against West Indians. Clearly, the most politically significant prejudice is that expressed by the white majority against the black minority. On occasions in the past that prejudice could be activated lawfully into racial discrimination for example, with lodging houses displaying 'No Blacks' signs in their front windows. There is little doubt that deliberate acts of racial discrimination still take place in British society which are beyond the remit of law. Sometimes, however, racial discrimination has been unintentionally practised by organisations in the public and private sectors which have operated policies which contain a hidden bias against black people. Many bodies now practise race-monitoring in specific areas as a check against unintentional discrimination.

In the late 1950s Britain experienced its only major race riots – as opposed to gang skirmishes – when whites attacked blacks in Notting Hill and Nottingham. These riots came as an unexpected shock and the government adopted both a tough and tender response. The former represented a response to public anxiety about black immigration to Britain whilst the latter was an attempt to promote racial harmony within Britain.

The Commonwealth Immigrants Act 1962 was the first of a number of Acts which restricted the entry of black first-time immigrants and their families to Britain. A second Commonwealth Immigrants Act was rushed through Parliament in 1968 to tighten up the 1962 Act, which did not apply to East African Asians. The Immigration Act 1971 tightened controls still further, although its restrictions were waived on humanitarian grounds to allow Asians expelled from Uganda to enter Britain freely. A new Nationality Act in 1981 represented even tighter restrictions. All this legislation, passed by both Conservative and Labour governments, has been criticised for being founded on racist principles. The prime goal has been not the restriction of immigrants who have claims to be British, but the restriction of *black* immigrants who have claims to British status.

Illiberal immigration policies towards blacks living outside Britain have been accompanied by liberal policies towards those already resident within Britain. The Race Relations Acts of 1965, 1968 and 1976 outlawed direct and indirect discrimination in widening areas of public life and provision such as housing, employment and education. What is sometimes called the 'race relations industry' was established with complaints taken to the Race Relations Board, later replaced by the Commission for Racial Equality, with Community Relations Councils operating at local level. The view expressed by many liberal-minded individuals of the time was that the 'race' problem would eventually wither away. It was felt that the children of immigrants would not suffer from the cultural problems and disadvantages of being newcomers and, given time, economic growth would provide benefits to all Britain's citizens. The blacks, at the end of the queue for prosperity, would be served in due course. How far have these early beliefs been justified by subsequent developments and trends?

■ Racism and Discrimination

A recent NOP poll revealed that a majority of the white, Afro-Caribbean and Asian individuals sampled agreed that Britain is a 'fairly' or 'very' racist society. Whilst most Britons saw themselves as being 'fair minded', they recognised that a minority of the white population was deeply racist and agreed that many institutions of the state, such as the courts and the police, as well as many employers, discriminate against black people. In what ways can such discrimination be reduced and eventually eliminated so that a 'fair minded' society develops in Britain?

Some on the left have argued that Britain should follow the American practice of 'affirmative action'. They cite Northern Ireland as an example of using positive action in order to penalise employers who discriminate on religious grounds by refusing to employ Catholics. It is argued that in much the same way, positive action could be used on the mainland to combat racial discrimination in the job market. The Commission for Racial Equality supports the idea that employers in the public and private sectors should be obliged by law to monitor the ethnic composition of their various workforces in order to strengthen the working of the 1976 Race Relations Act. The political right tends to dislike affirmative action on the grounds that it lowers the self-esteem of the ethnic minority communities; a minister recently argued against positive action because it had not worked well in the United States, and added 'People dislike it intensely. It doesn't do much for your morale if you think that you have been chosen for a job because you are black rather than because you are good. What people want is fair treatment.' (*Independent on Sunday*, 7 July 1991)

These contrasting attitudes towards positive action reflect two distinct philosophies towards equal opportunities in Britain. The minister's viewpoint places the emphasis on equal treatment for all people so that no one is discriminated against. In the example of individuals applying for a job, no person should be discriminated against, with the job being offered to the 'best' candidate. As Dave Russell has stated, this liberal approach 'insists that equal opportunity laws and policies require people to be judged *as individuals* without regard to racial/ethnic group membership but only on his or her own qualities and performance. All individuals should be treated equally in a meritocratic, "colour-blind", non-discriminatory manner.' In other words, fair treatment is seen as the absence of racial discrimination.

In contrast to the liberal approach is what Russell refers to as the 'radical' approach to equal opportunities, which is more concerned with a fair distribution of resources than with fair procedures. The radical approach is more concerned with 'who gets what' in terms of different ethnic groups getting their fair proportional share of society's resources (jobs, houses, education etc.) As Russell stated

This perspective puts the case for racial explicitness, arguing that people should be treated with regard to *group membership*, therefore directly going against the liberal principle of 'blind justice' whereby everyone is treated as an individual .... It also understands fairness to exist where members of different racial/ethnic groups are distributed in *proportion* to their presence in the wider population and in order to provoke a yardstick by which to measure the success for such a *redistributive* approach, equality '*targets*' or '*quotas*' are often established. This might involve some deliberate manipulation of selection procedures and standards in pursuit of proportionality whereby individuals can be selected for a job partly on the basis of group membership rather than because they are the best qualified candidate. (Russell, 1990, p. 11; see Exhibit 26.1)

Legislation concerning equal opportunities and anti-discrimination has embraced both the liberal and radical approaches. How effective has it been? The 1976 Race Relations Act included two important developments. The first was the introduction of the concept of **indirect discrimination**, based on the American model of affirmative action. This made unlawful actions which had an unintended adverse effect on members of ethnic minority communities even when formally they were being treated the same as everyone else. The second development was the setting up of the Commission for Racial Equality with its wide powers to impose sanctions against unlawful discrimination. It is fair to say that these two measures looked far more promising on paper than they have turned out to be in practice. Removing indirect discrimination has proved to be very difficult, and consequently this part of the 1976 Act has done little in removing racial inequalities from society. The Commission for Racial Equality has been attacked from a number of different directions. In practical terms its success rate in combating discrimination has been low. Also right-wing critics have argued that the Commission follows **multicultural policies** which stress the differences between various groups rather than the similarities.

	Exhibit 26.1 *Liberal and radical approaches to equal opportunities*		
	EQUAL WHAT?	PRINCIPLES	APPROACH
LIBERAL	Equal TREATMENT of individuals from different groups	People should be treated as individuals WITHOUT regard to group membership	Regulatory and procedural
		Fairness = absence of racial discrimination	Prohibition of discriminatory forms of behaviour
		Free competition between individuals Blind justice	Concern for processes
RADICAL	Equal SHARES of scarce goods (jobs, housing)	People should be treated WITH regard to group membership	Positive discrimination
		Fairness = proportionality	Targeting particular groups who will benefit – setting quotas
		Social justice	Concern for outcomes

Source: Russell (1990, p. 11).

■ The Political Response

The most controversial contribution from the Conservative right came in a speech made by Enoch Powell in 1968 when he called for a halt to black immigration and for moves to repatriate blacks already settled in Britain. In a widely publicised section of his speech he stated: 'As I look ahead I am filled with foreboding. Like the Roman I seem to see the River Tiber foaming with much blood.' He was immediately sacked from his post in the Shadow Cabinet by the Tory leader, Edward Heath. Conservative nationalism, such as that expressed by Powell, stressed the continuity of Britain's institutions and culture. The nation is seen as being founded on the race, so, by definition, black newcomers to Britain who are excluded from its history cannot be included in its present or future. There is an unwillingness

to accept Britain as a multiracial society since that is seen as breaking with the past and Britain's strengths lie in its continuity with the past. Only once in public has Margaret Thatcher appeared to be influenced by this sort of nationalism when in 1978 as new Conservative leader she told a radio audience that she understood fears that the British character might be 'swamped' by people of a different culture. As Prime Minister, Thatcher distanced herself from those on the Tory right who supported repatriation and called for the dismantling of the 'race relations industry'.

A well-publicised deplorable incident, condemned by senior Tories, concerned the selection of a black candidate, John Taylor, to fight the Cheltenham seat in the 1992 General Election. Taylor was the subject of outright racial abuse from some local Tories as well as the thinly coded message that he was unacceptable in Cheltenham because 'he was not a local man'. In the event, his position as the Conservative candidate was confirmed although he failed to win the seat. He was one of eight Conservative candidates from ethnic minority backgrounds who fought in the 1992 Election.

Labour's political image is one of being 'soft' on immigration but this does not conform to Labour's tough policy when in government. For example, Labour severely restricted new Commonwealth immigrants in the 1968 Act and its alternative to the Conservative Nationality Act 1981, whilst sounding more liberal, would have worked in much the same way.

Labour in the 1980s and 1990s has been posed the politically interesting problem of how to accommodate increasing demands for black influence within the party. Whilst recent general elections have revealed that Labour has been losing working-class support, the black vote has remained largely loyal. A Labour subcommittee investigated the issue of black participation and recommended the establishment of black sections, but the NEC and conference rejected this proposal. The leadership argued that black sections were unnecessary because black candidates had been selected as parliamentary candidates and returned to Westminster. Also, it was argued that having black sections was unacceptable because it would segregate people according to their racial origin, an action which had more in common with apartheid than with socialism. Members from the unofficial black sections that already existed at constituency level argued that the establishment of black sections was vital because they provided a way in which the ethnic minority communities could participate in the Labour Party.

The growth of the black electorate has been important for the Labour Party, since it has had an important impact upon parliamentary candidates contesting urban seats. Zig Layton-Henry stressed this point, stating that 'as the Labour party's support has declined among the white working class in the 1980s so the importance of black voters for Labour party MPs has risen.' (Z. Layton-Henry, 1992)

□ 'Race' Politics

The rise of the far right in Europe – in France and Germany in particular – has been accompanied by displays of considerable violence towards foreigners and refugees. Naturally there were fears in Britain of a fascist revival with a new wave of racist hostility being directed towards the ethnic minorities. Although fascist parties have done poorly in general elections since the war, there have been occasions when support soared in local elections.

The New British National Party won 27 per cent of the vote in Southall in 1963 and in 1976 the combined vote of the National Party and the National Front reached the 44.5 per cent level in Deptford. In September 1993 the British National Party (BNP) candidate won a local government by-election victory in Millwall. Although parties such as the National Front published a manifesto which included policies on a variety of issues, race relations and immigration were the issues they campaigned on. As Steve Hunt argued,

> The NF [National Front] also maintained that it represented the 'majority view' on the issues of black immigration and race relations. To this end the party took full advantage of Enoch Powell's infamous 'River of Blood Speech' in 1968 in which he forewarned that future immigration would result in widespread racial conflict. The NF's opposition to immigration was clearly racist – highlighting a negative prejudice against blacks on the basis of perceived racial and cultural differences. But the party were prepared to go further and in doing so displayed a clear Nazi ideological orientation. The influx of 'non-whites' was regarded as a threat to the 'authentic British community' which was designated 'superior' by a pseudo-scientific logic. (Hunt, 1992a, p. 24)

Far right-wing and fascist groups which campaigned on the 'race' issue, then, have failed to make significant electoral impact except in a limited number of areas where 'race' was at the top of the local agenda. There is a fear that because these groups have failed in the area of conventional politics, they are now becoming increasingly involved in organising racial violence of one type or another. Why did their 'race' manifestos generally fail to win support? There is no simple answer to this question but the following points are important in helping to explain the political failure of British fascism.

Firstly, whilst it can be recognised that there is much racism and discrimination at large in British society, there are limits to how far these attitudes and behaviours extend. In other words, whilst there may be many in Britain who are not 'fair minded' regarding race relations, they are not the race bigots of the type which joins fascist organisations. Secondly, the far right remains weak because of constant internal disputes and factionalism. Thirdly, the first-past-the-post electoral system discriminates against minority and fringe parties. Finally, the rise in influence of the radical Right inside the Conservative Party, with its anti anti-racism platform, weaned some support away from the periphery of British politics into the fringe of the Conservative Party. Dr Roger Eatwell has put this point more strongly:

> The BNP and NF are now desperately short of people who are experienced local campaigners so in electoral terms they are non-starters. But when one looks at the NF you have to look at other things that indicate they are active. Under Thatcher, there was no political space for the NF and she hijacked a lot of their policies. In 1979, there was a clear play for the NF vote by adopting policies on law and order and strict immigration controls. Major's rule, with a more caring face presented and this idea of the one nation, may open the way for a more extreme right wing. (*Guardian*, 27 April 1991)

Other groups have formed to promote good race relations and to defend the position of the ethnic minorities in Britain. One of the most notable was the Anti-Nazi League (ANL), relaunched in 1992 in response to the rise in fascism in continental Europe. Originally the ANL was organised to mobilise young people to 'rock against racism' during a time when the National Front had done better than expected in a few local elections. The talented rock guitarist, Eric Clapton, made a long rambling speech in which he seemed to encourage support for Enoch Powell on the race issue. The ANL was launched to counter any influence Clapton and any other like-minded musicians might have with young people, and represented a political alliance of various groupings in which the Socialist Workers Party (SWP) played the leading role. A rival anti-racist group, the Anti-Racist Alliance (ARA), co-chaired by Labour MP Ken Livingstone, was set up to involve greater representation from the black community as well as to exclude the risk of manipulation by the SWP. Ironically, then, disputes within the anti-racist left have resulted in the factionalism typical of the racist far right.

The ethnic minorities have organised politically in order to participate in Britain's political life and promote their special interests. One of the most publicised groups within the Muslim community has been the Muslim Institute in Britain, led by Dr Kalim Siddiqui. He has established a Muslim parliament to represent a 'non-territorial Islamic state' in Britain. Essentially the non-elected parliament is a forum in which Muslim views are expressed and get reported to a wider public. Proponents of the parliament argue that Muslim views, particularly on race issues, are not well represented by the national parliamentary parties nor reflected in national political debate. Therefore a separate Muslim organisation is needed to put forward in a robust way the distinctive Muslim viewpoint on issues, otherwise Muslims will be ignored. It can be argued that all Siddiqui is arguing for is recognition that Britain is a pluralist society, and that attempts to portray him as a militant are unfounded. Certainly the Muslim parliament is controversial, raising fears in other sections of the Muslim community that fascist groups will make political capital from the publicity it receives. Dr Hesham el-Esawy, President of the Islamic Society for the Promotion of Religious Tolerance, voiced this anxiety when he opposed the Muslim parliament on the grounds that it 'will give ammunition to people who hate Islam'.

Summary

Many white British people have found it hard to accommodate to the reality that new black ethnic communities now exist in Britain. Governments have found it necessary to pass legislation outlawing racial discrimination internally whilst operating racially biased immigration policies towards people external to the United Kingdom.

There is disagreement amongst social researchers about both the scope and nature of such disadvantages. There is, however, a commonly accepted stereotype existing amongst the population at large which associates ethnicity with criminality. Unfortunately, the way in which the tabloid press sometimes presents news reinforces this misleading impression.

Although there are now some black MPs, the role of the political parties is not particularly successful in terms of channelling and responding to black aspirations.

Questions

1. In what ways are some ethnic minorities disadvantaged in Britain?

2. Consider the case for and against major political parties having constitutions which guarantee black representation on policy-making committees.

3. To what extent is the failure of fascist groups to make a political impact proof that Britain is a fair and tolerant society?

Assignments

1. The graph shown opposite is from the *Guardian* (19.5.92) and shows the percentage of unemployed people in the white and ethnic minority population of Britain.

 Unemployed

Unemployed within each group (spring figures)

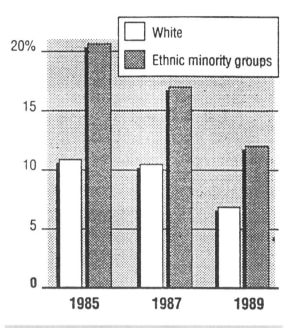

Figure 26.2 *Sharing the misery*

(i) Describe the pattern of unemployment from spring 1985 to spring 1989.

(ii) Explain possible reasons for unemployment levels being higher amongst ethnic minorities than amongst the white population.

(iii) What measures have governments taken to increase equal employment opportunities, and what further measures are available for governments to take in pursuit of this goal?

(iv) In what ways have far right and fascist groups made political capital from a high level of unemployment in the economy?

2. East Enders

The East End of London has two contrasting traditions. The first is one of accepting and assimilating new groups of immigrants which in the past included German, Irish, Chinese and Jewish families. The second tradition is one of fascism and racial intolerance, and in 1936 it was the area for marches chosen by Sir Oswald Mosley and his British Union of Fascists because they had strong support in areas like Shoreditch and Bethnal Green.

In a local government by-election in Millwall the BNP candidate, Derek Beackon, won by seven votes to become the party's first councillor. How was the BNP's victory to be interpreted?

- was it a sign that racism and fascism was on the march in Britain in the same way as in France and Germany? For example, Jean Marie Le Pen's Front National controls 30 town councils and Germany's Republikaner and neo-fascist NPD parties have a considerable number of councillors although they do not control any councils.
- was it simply a by-election protest vote against the poor social conditions in the Isle of Dogs generally? The area is one of high unemployment, poor housing and pressure of numbers on local schools which is made worse by the proximity of 'yuppie Docklands'. Although Millwall does experience racist violence, it is these social issues which best explain the BNP's victory.

- was it a by-election protest against the failure of the local Labour Party which has got out of touch with local needs? Some ex-Labour supporting members of the ethnic minorities stated that they voted for the BNP rather than the 'loony left'. Others accused mainstream opposition parties, especially the Liberal Democrats, of also playing the 'race' card in the campaign.

(i) Explain possible reasons for the BNP victory in Millwall.
(ii) 'Britain's poor and deprived will always turn to the extreme Right, and never to the extreme Left.' How valid is this statement?
(iii) Should anti-democratic parties be permitted to operate within democratic systems?

Further reading

Coxall, B. (1992) 'The Social Context of British Politics: Class, Gender and Race in the Two Major Parties, 1970–1990' in B. Jones and L. Robins (eds) *Two Decades in British Politics* (Manchester University Press).

Layton-Henry, Z. (1992) *Immigration and 'Race' Politics in Post-War Britain* (Oxford: Blackwell)

Lupton. C. and Russell, D. (1990) 'Equal Opportunities in a Cold Climate' in S. Savage and L. Robins (eds) *Public Policy under Thatcher* (London: Macmillan).

McIlroy, J. (1989) 'The Politics of Racism' in B. Jones (ed.) *Political Issues in Britain Today* (Manchester University Press).

■ *Chapter 27* ■

Women, Inequality and Politics

The Women's Movement
Women's Issues

Women in Political Office
Women's 'Invisible' Political Activity

In the past, an understanding of women's role in political life was gained from the research of male political scientists. Recently female political scientists have challenged the familiar portrayal of women and successfully modified the way in which women are seen to act politically. This chapter examines the new portrayal of 'political woman', explores the feminist perspective and considers the women's movement as a force for change in society. We shall see that women do occupy many political roles, but the pattern is uneven. Why is this so?

In the past many assumed that the rough-and-tumble world of politics was more suited to men than women. This was because men alone were seen as having the personal qualities – ambition and aggression – needed to survive in political life. Political scientists, who are mostly men, were influenced by this view. Their research often reinforced the biased belief that women were unsuited for political careers or public service. Political scientists were blind to the contribution that women made to politics in the past, not recognising, for example, their part in the food riots of the seventeenth and eighteenth centuries and the anti-Poor Law demonstrations of the nineteenth century. It was argued by political scientists that boys were socialised into behaving like men and therefore would take an interest in politics, whereas girls were socialised into behaving like women and as a consequence would be much less interested in politics. In modern voting studies, where daughters and fathers or wives and husbands were found voting for the same party, it was inevitably assumed that the female's vote in each case was a reflection of the male's. Few researchers even considered the possibility of daughters influencing the way their fathers voted or wives influencing the way their husbands voted.

Today, the study of political science is much more conscious of its male bias and the false assumptions that were made about women and politics in the past. This new awareness to the role of women has been triggered by the explosion of feminist literature and by the activity of women in the real world of politics. Political science and politics in society are still, as we shall see, 'a man's world' but far less so now than even twenty years ago.

■ The Women's Movement

All contemporary societies are to varying degrees male-dominated. In Britain, as in other Western countries, prestige is attached to 'men's work', be it the glamour of a professional career or the *machismo* of manual labour, whilst women's place of work is seen as in the home. The difference is reflected in rewards; men's work earns a salary or wage whilst women's domestic labour is unpaid. When women enter paid employment, their average incomes are lower than men's. Part-time, unskilled and low-paid jobs are filled overwhelmingly by women. Despite the fact that women account for approximately 40 per cent of Britain's total labour force, women receive far less promotion and career advancement than men. Also, the very nature of women's jobs makes them most vulnerable to automation, and it is women's jobs that are most likely to be lost first as a direct result of the introduction of new technologies.

The women's movement is not a formal political organisation in the sense that it has a national, regional and local structure which recruits members who, in turn, elect officials. It is informally organised and highly factionalised. The women's movement is made up of a network of small localised groups, some of which work within established organisations such as trade unions or political parties. At the beginning of the century, the first wave of the movement exhibited 'moderate' and 'radical' wings and these survive today. The struggle to obtain the vote was waged by the 'respectable' suffragists and the 'militant' suffragettes. The Housewives' League, led by Irene Lovelock, was an example of a 'moderate' postwar protest against 'women's lot', which was made up of rationing, queueing and austerity.

The contemporary women's movement has been studied by Vicky Randall and in *Women and Politics* (1987) she has identified at least three major strands or factions:

1. **Radical feminists** are the most militant within the women's movement and include extremists such as the political lesbians. Generally speaking, radical feminists emphasise the extent to which women are physically oppressed and dominated by men. They point to wife-battering, rape and pornography as manifestations of male oppression.

2. **Marxist feminists** also have a conflict view of society, but believe that the struggle of the working class and the struggle of women are not necessarily one and the same. The class struggle is recognised as the more significant of the two, but it is also believed that female inequality will still exist after the overthrow of the capitalist system and that a separate struggle will still lie ahead for female emancipation. Marxist feminists do not shun collaboration with men, as does the radical element, and they work with Left-wing and trade union organisations in order to improve the lot of women. The second-wave radical

and Marxist feminists are often lumped together by the mass media and described as 'Women's Lib'.

3. **Reformist feminists**, the heirs of the constitutionally minded suffragists, form the third strand. It is probably true to say that most people, male and female, would accept the arguments of reformist feminists as constituting the 'reasonable face of feminism'. Reformists argue that generally speaking women suffer from a series of handicaps and disadvantages in society, and that all of these can be eliminated over time by equal rights legislation.

Reformist feminists argue that much of the battle against female inequality has been won. The Equal Pay Act 1970 stipulated equal pay for equal work and the Sex Discrimination Act 1975 ended discrimination against women in employment, education, housing, as well as in other service areas. The Act also established the **Equal Opportunities Commission**, a body to investigate infringements of the Equal Pay and Sex Discrimination Acts. Residual inequalities – in areas such as retirement and taxation – can be eliminated by future legislation.

The women's movement has also made legislative advances in the area of abortion reform. The abortion issue is of great importance to feminists since it symbolises a woman's reproductive self-determination. As a result, some feminists have taken an extremely hard line on abortion and have been accused of displaying a fascist disregard for human life. On the other hand, many women, including Roman Catholics, put the 'right to life' above 'the woman's right to choose'.

The women's movement is not without its critics. Some of them point out that, despite feminist claims that sex is the fundamental division in society and causes inequalities above and beyond those caused by social class or race, the women's movement itself *is* a very middle-class political phenomenon. It has failed to appeal to or to mobilise those women who suffer greatest social disadvantage, namely those found in the working class. It is argued that this proves that social class is a greater cause of inequality in society than is sex. In addition, critics contend that the women's movement has failed to win the support of all middle-class women.

Some critics of the women's movement argue that feminists undervalue the traditional role of women in society and underestimate the political influence already wielded by women. For example, it is argued that feminists neither recognise the responsibilities involved in child-rearing nor do they understand the extent to which mothers shape the personalities and views of their children be they boys or girls.

■ Women's Issues

All the major political parties have attempted to win the support of the 'female' vote. This is usually attempted through crude, and frequently ineffective, measures to increase the number of women standing for office, or by campaigning on what are seen as issues of immediate concern to women, such as equal opportunities or welfare policies. At the same time and in different ways, feminists are defining a distinctive perspective on a wide range of issues which include those of obvious interest to women as well as others which have in the past been recognised as 'male' issues which are of little or no concern to women. This perspective is

Figure 27.1   *Images of glamour and domesticity: how far does such sex-stereotyping restrict women's activities?*

Source: Guardian.

Source: News Team.

explored below in the contrasting contexts of community care, which is a traditional 'female' issue, and transport, which has been recognised as an issue of greater interest to men.

☐ *Community Care*

Between 1957 and 1981 the number of people employed in health care, welfare provision and education grew from 1.3 million to 3.4 million. Those employed in this 'social welfare industry' were predominantly female; for example, of those who were involved in local authority social services, 90 per cent were women. Being employed in the welfare services can be very hard work, as Sally Baldwin and Julia Twigg have pointed out. 'Caring work is often repetitive and carried out over long hours. Indeed, there are usually no limits circumscribing its performance; the obligations are continuous and open-ended.' (Baldwin and Twigg, 1991, pp. 122–3) The sexual division of labour, with mostly women involved in welfare, results from women's more general role in society as being carers and nurturers. The image of the 'female carer' can lead to multiple disadvantage and even exploitation. For example, those women employed to look after the frail and elderly are frequently part-time and low-paid workers. Feminists have complained rightly that such work undertaken by women is undervalued and underpaid. However, feminists have become even more alarmed at the prospect of the elderly and frail being moved out of institutions into the community. What, they ask, does community care really mean? Care in the community 'means care by the family, which largely, although not exclusively, still means care by women' (Land, 1991, p. 9). Thus, what on the surface appears to be a liberal and humane policy of looking after people in the community rather than in large institutions will result in the further subordination of women. The point was made by Hilary Land with a case-study drawn from the *Independent* (28 June 1989) which focused on a woman who gave up her job to look after her dying sister for five years. By doing this, the woman lost £80 000 in terms of her own income whilst saving the state

at least £20 0000 by looking after her sister at home. Despite this, new benefit rules made her ineligible for a £50 a week welfare payment until she found a job after her sister's death. The woman in question had dutifully performed the female caring role and yet, having saved the state a substantial sum of money, was denied a meagre level of support from the state until she reorganised her own life. This and similar case-studies illustrate the reasons behind feminist opposition to community care.

☐ *Women and Transport*

Women are almost invisible in the eyes of the transport policy-makers and frequently they have to endure poorer services and are exposed to greater danger than men. Kristine Beuret's research has revealed that there are great differences in the ways in which men and women travel; Table 27.1 shows that the most common method for women is walking whilst for men it is driving. Yet in transport planning and policy, the most common method of travel for women is underestimated. As Kristine Beuret argues, walking

> is a form of transport widely ignored in many travel surveys and much available data are unsatisfactory. This is because there is a tendency for the Department of Transport to discount short walk trips of less than a mile ... it is still the norm that local authority transport policy plans ignore walking as a method of transport. (Beuret, 1991, pp. 63, 66)

The result of this official blindness towards walkers is that provision for pedestrians is made in terms of what is convenient to motorists rather than what meets pedestrians' needs. Road safety measures may not always be in the immediate interests of the mainly female walking public. For example, whilst car seatbelt legislation has led to a decline in the number of road deaths, 'less well publicized, however, are the ways in which pedestrian deaths have increased, probably as a result of faster driving speeds resulting from the confidence gained from wearing a seatbelt' (Beuret, 1991, p. 65)

	Per cent of all journeys by					Journeys
	Walk/cycle	Car driver	Car passenger	Public transport	Other	(000s)
Men aged 21–64	25	57	7	9	2	144
Women aged 21–59	42	21	23	14	1	122
Men 65 and over	52	25	6	16	1	100
Women 60 and over	50	6	19	25	1	100

Source: 1978–9 National Travel Survey from S. Potter (1982) 'The transport policy crisis' Unit 27 of the Open University Course D202, *Urban Change and Conflict*, Milton Keynes, p. 63, cited in Beuret (1991, p. 61).

Table 27.1   *Travel methods according to age/sex of adult*

On average three-quarters of all bus passengers are women. Yet bus travel has not developed in ways which provide its major customers with the level of service which they need. Many women, particularly the disabled, those with small children and those carrying shopping, find travelling by bus difficult. The phasing-out of bus conductors means that there is no longer anyone to assist those who need help in getting on and off buses. One survey found that some women 'chose (reluctantly) to walk long distances rather than struggle to use the bus' (Beuret, 1991, p. 66). Also, many women find that their main form of public transport, buses, are dangerous at night. And on top of all these problems, deregulation of the bus transport industry has resulted in a much poorer and less reliable level of service being made available. Rail travel, which is less important to women than to men, receives a greater government subsidy than bus travel, which is more important to women than to men.

In transport policy, as pedestrians or bus passengers, it is possible to detect a distinct tendency to treat women as second-class citizens. The same might be argued in the case of community care policy. This bias may be unintended in the sense that there is no deliberate 'anti-women' policy-making in central and local government. Rather such a bias may result from old fashioned stereotypes and assumptions which still get reflected in administrative practices. Although the female perspective on policies and issues can be uncomfortable and not always welcomed by policy-makers, there can be little

doubt that feminists are right in revealing, and challenging, disadvantage and unfairness to women.

■ Women in Political Office

Women form 52 per cent of the electorate in Britain yet only 9 per cent of MPs are female. It is perhaps, a little misleading to focus on Britain's longest-serving modern Prime Minister since for long periods Margaret Thatcher was the only woman in her Cabinet. Of course MPs are elected to represent their constituencies and not a particular social group. Whilst the composition of MPs in Parliament is not expected to reflect the composition of society at large, on commonsense grounds alone it is clear that women are underrepresented. As its name suggests, the 300 Group has been set up to increase female membership of the Commons so that the number of women in the House is more or less half the total number of MPs. The position is somewhat better in local government; in 1977, 17 per cent of local councillors were women.

The House of Commons has been described as 'the best gentlemen's club in the world'. The working of the Westminster system is certainly designed to meet the comfort and convenience of its male members. The daily routines of an MP in the House – including late-night sittings – are not organised in a way to help female MPs who have young children. In a study of the 1974 Parliament, it was revealed that only two of the twenty-seven female MPs had children under the age of

10. There is a tendency for women MPs to be either single or divorced. The higher proportion of women in local government reflects greater opportunity to combine the domestic role with the public role than is available in national government. Some women have campaigned for reforms in retiming and relocating meetings so that more women would be able to play an active role in politics, but so far their demands for change have gone unheeded.

It has been argued that the biggest barrier to women holding political office lies in the belief held by many that they will not be successful. In other words, because many women feel that they stand little chance of being selected, they do not allow themselves to be put forward as candidates. In addition, even if a woman is selected as a candidate, there is a view that 'the electorate don't like voting for a woman'. If a potential woman candidate expects there to be a slim chance of being selected by the party in the first place to fight an election, and then sees her sex as an electoral liability if the candidates put forward by rival parties are men, we cannot be surprised that there are so few women in Parliament and on local councils.

Women's 'Invisible' Political Activity

It has been argued that women make a contribution to political life through informal, less conventional means and, furthermore, that this contribution goes largely unrecorded by political scientists and journalists. For example, women have campaigned on numerous moral issues which have failed to attract sustained media attention. In the past, women were highly influential in the Temperance movement; during the 1970s, the 'Mothers of Peace' movement lit a brief glimmer of hope in Northern Ireland, and in the 1980s women played a large role in the Peace Movement.

What all these campaigns have in common is a loosely structured organisation. Their activities are only 'newsworthy' when dramatic newsreel can be filmed; otherwise, their activities go un-

noticed. Frequently, women organise 'protest politics' at local or community level regarding the provision of facilities, and this too tends to be ignored by the media. Women are prominent in tenants' groups, childcare campaigns, health campaigns, and anti-poverty lobbies. Women combine self-help projects – such as meeting the needs of the single-parent family – with pressure-group activity.

Furthermore, some women's groups which are often defined as apolitical in nature do, in fact, attempt to influence government policies. Women's Institutes, Townswomen's Guilds, the Mothers' Union and the Women's Royal Voluntary Service (WRVS) have an estimated membership of 3 million. They have participated in campaigns and lobbying on issues such as the payment of Child Benefit, taxation policy, local planning decisions, closure of local schools and the provision of public transport in rural areas.

It is possible, therefore, to conclude that women still play a minor role in the formal institutions of Britain – Parliament, local councils, political parties, public bodies and established interest groups. If, however, female political activity is explored in informal political settings – community groups, moral campaigns, the women's movement network, and the political activities of organisations such as the Women's Institute, a very different picture emerges. In areas which are free from male prejudices and arbitrary constraints which discourage women, and which allow them to combine domestic roles with public roles, there is a great deal of female political activity. There is enough, certainly, to question the commonly held assumption that 'politics is a man's world'.

Summary

The political role of women is being increasingly appreciated although it is still largely absent from many formal political institutions with the House of Commons as the most important example. The women's movement provides an interesting case-study of an informally structured political organisation with mainly middle-class participation.

Frequently, female participation in politics takes unorthodox form since this allows women to reconcile their traditional domestic roles with practical roles. There is, however, an increasing awareness that many political issues affect men and women in different ways.

Questions

1. 'Where power is, woman is not.' Is this an accurate reflection of women's role in British politics?

2. Comment upon the successes and failures of the women's movement.

Assignment

Women and PR

At present 9% of MPs are female, this compares with 38% in Sweden, 34% in Norway, 31% in Denmark, 16% in Germany and 13% in Italy, Spain and Luxembourg. Only France (6%) and Greece (5%) have less female representation than Britain. The next election will increase the number of women MPs, but only marginally.

It is argued that Britain's electoral system is one of the causes of low female representation. Firstly, FPTP results in a confrontational style of politics which is unattractive to many women who prefer the partnership style associated with PR and coalition building. Secondly, single-member constituencies make it difficult for women to get selected as candidates. As Geraldine Ellis argued: 'local selection committees tend to play safe and work with an image of the prospective candidate as a white man in a grey suit.' But when a list of candidates is being selected for a multi-member constituency, it is easier to insist on a quota for women.

More, perhaps, out of a sense of frustration with the present system than with serious intent, Conservative MP Teresa Gorman has argued for a male and female MP to be elected from half as many constituencies. She stated 'I would ensure that 50 per cent of MPs were women simply by making each constituency elect a man and a woman; if we doubled the size of the constituencies, the number of MPs would remain the same. But this policy is not likely to be adopted while men predominate.'

(i) Explain possible reasons why Britain's present electoral system deters women from standing for Parliament.

(ii) 'If the only advantage of PR was that it resulted in more women entering Parliament, that would be sufficient reason for its introduction'. Do you agree? Could more women be encouraged into playing active roles in national and local politics through other means?

(iii) Evaluate the proposal made by Teresa Gorman MP, giving reasons why you would support or oppose her proposal.

Further reading

Culley, L. (1985) *Women and Power* (Leicester: Hyperion).

Hunt, K. 'Women and Politics', in B. Jones (ed.) *Political Issues in Britain Today* (Manchester: Manchester University Press).

Lupton, C. and Russell D. (1990) 'Equal Opportunities in a Cold Climate' in S. Savage and L. Robins (eds) *Public Policy Under Thatcher* (London: Macmillan).

Maclean, M. and D. Groves (eds) (1991) *Women's Issues in Social Policy* (London: Routledge).

Oakley, A. (1972) *Sex, Gender and Society* (Hounslow: Temple Smith).

Randall, V. (1987) *Women and Politics*, 2nd edn (London: Macmillan).

■ *Chapter 28* ■

Politics and the Environment

What is meant by the term 'green politics'? How is it possible for the environment to have emerged as an important issue with the public, yet for the Green Party to have failed to win a single parliamentary seat? The major political parties now claim to have policies for the environment; how valid is this claim? The chapter concludes with an assessment of the EU's impact on Britain's environmental policy-making.

■ The Environment Debate

In his book *The Closing Circle* Barry Commoner spelt out the 'laws of ecology': everything is connected to everything else; everything must go somewhere; Nature knows best; and, finally, there is no such thing as a free lunch. We tend to see the simple acts which fill our everyday lives as inconsequential, even trivial, without realising how the laws of ecology operate and draw them together with what can be awesome impact. A simple example of changing the battery of a transistor radio makes the point. The old battery is thrown into the dustbin, is collected along with other domestic rubbish and taken to the council incinerator. 'But', asked Professor Commoner, 'where does it really go?' The battery contains a heavy metal element, mercury, which cannot be destroyed but can only be combined with other elements. As the battery is heated in the incinerator it

produces mercury vapour which is emitted by the incinerator stack, and mercury vapour is toxic. Mercury vapour is carried by the wind, eventually brought down to earth in rain or snow. Entering a mountain lake, let us say, the mercury condenses and sinks to the bottom. Here it is acted on by bacteria which convert it to methyl mercury. This is soluble and taken up by fish; since it is not metabolised, the mercury accumulates in the organs and flesh of the fish. The fish is caught and eaten by a man and the mercury becomes deposited in his organs. (Commoner, 1971, pp. 33–46)

The interconnection of seemingly unrelated yet commonplace acts – changing a battery and eating a fish; the fact that the mercury did not disappear but simply moved from one place to another; that man-made changes were detrimental to the environment; and that the benefits of a battery-operated radio are gained at the cost of pollution and possible ill-health – together illustrate the working of ecological laws. These laws are working across such a wide range of behaviours with such adverse effects that some scientists talk of there being an 'ecological crisis'. They believe that great damage has already been done to the thin skin of earth, water and air that clothes 'Planet Earth' with yet greater damage in store. The air is polluted by carbon dioxide resulting from the burning of coal and oil, and this is producing the 'greenhouse effect' as the atmosphere slowly heats up because excessive carbon dioxide absorbs heat that previously would have radiated away. Some believe that this will result in climatic changes which will melt the polar ice-caps and transform the world's most fertile areas into deserts. Burning coal and oil also produces large quantities of sulphur dioxide in the atmosphere resulting in acid rain which kills forests and water life. Nitrogen fertilisers used in increasing quantities by farmers have now been washed from the land and have found their way into drinking water causing a major health hazard for young children. Nuclear testing has put radioactive substances into the bones of children for the first time in human history. Exposure to another heavy metal – lead – put into the atmosphere by car exhausts has resulted in the impaired mental development of many urban children. Cancers have been caused through exposure to asbestos. The thinning in the ozone layer which surrounds the Earth has concerned the scientific community. This layer of gas acts as a vital filter which protects animals and plants from the Sun's ultraviolet rays and it has almost disappeared altogether over Antarctica. This list of potential disasters seems endless, so why is global society not in a state of panic?

Environmentalists argue that many of the major ecological threats are recent, and their effects have not yet been fully understood or felt. They sometimes use the analogy of a pond which is gradually being covered by a weed. The area covered by the weed doubles each day, so that by the twelfth day half the pond is covered. Suddenly, on the thirteenth day, the pond will be totally covered by weed. Environmentalists see a crisis creeping up on mankind and taking governments by surprise in a similar way. How has the political system responded to the relatively new environmental lobby and with what results?

The Political Agenda and the Political Process

Much of the postwar consensus was built on the assumption common to both Labour and Conservative that it would be economic growth which would provide the extra resources needed to provide an expanding welfare state. Economic growth would improve the lives of the less well-off in society without having to tax and redistribute wealth from the better off. The major parties competed with each other principally in terms of which would be the most competent in managing the economy and maximising its growth. Many commentators look back at the period from the mid-1950s onwards as the 'age of affluence', with newspapers capturing the feeling of the times when they reported Conservative Prime Minister Harold Macmillan as having told an election rally, 'You've never had it so good'.

It was at the very time Macmillan's words were being spoken that the modern environmental debate began, in a modest, undramatic way, with the publication of Rachel Carson's book *Silent Spring* in 1962. However, it was not until the 1970s that the 'first wave' of environmental concern challenged the assumptions which underlay the consensus about economic growth providing a politically painless way of meeting the rising expectations of the electorate. A report by the Massachusetts Institute of Technology for the Club of Rome, *The Limits to Growth*, examined patterns of growth for various elements, including industrialism and the consumption of non-renewable natural resources. The investigation concluded that (like the surface of the pond discussed earlier) within a short time period a situation of great abundance can turn into one of scarcity.

The 'second wave' of environmental concern emerged during the 1980s as a response to a number of issues including Britain's greater dependence on military and civil nuclear power (the latter being a response to the energy crisis) with the risk of accidents demonstrated by the near-miss at Three Mile Island and the Chernobyl disaster; pollution and acid rain damage; the depletion of the ozone layer through CFC (chlorofluorocarbons) damage and the risks of global warming through increased carbon dioxide in the atmosphere.

The first and second wave of environmental concern differed in one important way. As McCulloch has argued, the debate over the environment was transformed in two respects between the 1970s and 1980s: 'First, a broadening of the way in which the concept of "the environment" has been used, and second, a tendency for the environment to become rather less an issue and rather more the basis for an ideology' (McCulloch, 1988, p. 15). However, in another way, the first and second wave of environmentalism shared a similar political fate. After a period of intense debate, the issue slipped down the political agenda in terms of public concern.

In the United States Anthony Downs argued that political concern about the environment would pass through a five stage process (Exhibit 28.1). Downs's model has proved to be generally accurate in so far as public concern for environmental issues and governmental response has passed through the five stage cycle twice; once with the first wave of environmental concern in the 1970s and again with the second wave in the 1980s. No doubt there will be a third wave of public concern in the future with every chance that it too will pass through five stages.

■ Green Ideology

Green politics has been described as 'new politics' in so far as it does not fit into the framework of conventional parliamentary politics. Yet many aspects of green politics connect with aspects of pre-existing belief systems. In this sense, green politics is not really new. As Robinson has stated 'Environmentalist rhetoric has drawn inspiration from such diverse ideological wells as Christian, Buddhist, Hindu, Taoist and Pagan religious belief systems, Anarchist, Marxist and Conservative political ideologies, the critical rationalist tradition in science from ecology to quantum physics, and the romantic reactions to post Enlightenment social changes from Keats to Kerouac' (Robinson, 1992, p. 34).

Figure 28.1   *The Greenpeace Ship Moby Dick in a campaign to draw attention to the threat to dolphins and porpoises in Cardigan Bay*

Source: *Guardian*.

Exhibit 28.1 *Political concern about the environment: the five-stage cycle*

- **Stage 1: The pre-problem stage**. The problem exists and may be severe but the public is unaware, the media uninterested and only interest groups are alarmed.
- **Stage 2: Alarmed discovery and euphoric enthusiasm**. The problem is suddenly discovered as a result of some particular event; the public call for solutions and the politicians promise action.
- **Stage 3: Realising the cost of significant progress**. This comes slowly and follows disclosure about the sacrifices necessary and the uncertainty of successful technological solutions.
- **Stage 4: Gradual decline of public interest**. Public concern falls either through boredom or rejection of the scale of the changes necessary or the costs involved.
- **Stage 5: Post-problem stage**. The public forgets about the issue but most original problems remain; a few institutions devoted to the problem may survive but on severely reduced funding.

Source: Bradbeer (1990).

Environmentalism is then, an eclectic ideology which is drawn from numerous and diverse sources. It rejects 'industrialisation' and policies of economic growth which remain at the heart of both Conservative and Labour programmes. Environmentalists argue that the economy should produce no more than is necessary to meet people's essential needs, and in a society where people live simpler lives such needs will be met by local production (rather than by multinational companies). Seven basic principles underlie contemporary environmentalism:

- **A world approach**. All human activity should reflect appreciation of the world's finite resources and easily damaged ecology.
- **Respect for the rights of our descendants**. Our children have the right to inherit a beautiful and bountiful planet rather than an exhausted and polluted one.
- **Sufficiency**. We should be satisfied with 'enough' rather than constantly seeking 'more'.
- **A conserver economy**. We must conserve what we have rather than squandering it through pursuit of high growth strategies.
- **Care and share**. Given that resources are limited we must shift our energies to sharing what we have and looking after all sections of society properly.

- **Self-reliance**. We should learn to provide for ourselves rather than surrendering responsibility to experts and specialised agencies.
- **Decentralise and democratise**. We must form smaller units of production, encourage co-operative enterprises and give people local power over their own affairs. At the same time international integration must move forward rapidly. (B. Jones, 1989–90 p. 51)

Finally, some commentators have pointed to the strong links between environmentalism and the women's movement. They have argued that there is a parallel between the domination of nature by men and the domination of women by men. Environmentalism, they claim, cannot be based on traditional masculine values such as economic rationality, competitiveness and individualism. Rather it must be based on traditional female values such as caring, cooperation and intuition. Because of this relationship there is an overlap between many environmentalist and feminist goals.

■ The Greening of Political Parties

How far have green ideas influenced policy-making in the major parties? All of them claim to have coherent environmental policies, but some critics argue that their policies are designed merely to reassure public opinion that problems are being tackled rather than offering real solutions.

There is a close relationship between 'green' and 'red' politics, since both are opposed to capitalist systems which are driven by the profit motive. Environmentalists have long argued that a rational use of resources will mean that 'the socialisation of the country's economy is essential' (Barry Commoner in the *Observer*, 12 March 1972). But, of course, Labour is not a socialist party but one which is committed to industrial policies designed to expand the economy, increase consumption and create more jobs. Basically this means that environmentalism is not amongst Labour's top priorities although, on the other hand, it is not ignored by Labour. For example, Labour published a policy document *The Politics of the Environment* as early as 1973 and a year earlier one of its MPs, Dr Jeremy Bray, had called for creation of a 'Pollution Control Service'. And in the 1990s Labour's willingness to intervene and bring the water and electricity industries back under public sector control, as well as the party's opposition to nuclear power development, was in line with green policies.

What is the relationship between 'green' and 'blue' politics? Can there be such a thing as 'green capitalism', or is it a contradiction in terms? Some companies now conduct green audits in order to check that their production process does as little damage to the environment as possible, and many consumers prefer to buy green products. But some green critics take a cynical approach to such developments and see them as no more than efforts to disguise capitalism's profit motive with green intentions. They argue that so-called green capitalism still damages the environment and exploits the population of the Third World. Companies which appear environment-friendly only do so, it is claimed, because it is a gimmick which sells more products and makes more profit.

In 1988 as Prime Minister, Margaret Thatcher made a speech to the Royal Society in which she appeared a convert to the green cause. Later she declared

It's we Conservatives who are not merely Friends of the Earth – we are its guardians and trustees for generations to come. No generation has a freehold on this earth, all we have is life tenancy – with a full repairing lease. This government intends to meet the terms of that lease in full.

Her words surprised many commentators since they seemed at odds with her own political instincts. Thatcherism was, after all, committed to cutting back on government and bureaucracy and giving the free market more freedom to operate.

The Liberal Party was the first of the established parties to go green and furthermore it was a darker shade of green than achieved by either Conservative or Labour. However, the party's green policies were undermined and weakened during its alliance with the pro-nuclear Social Democratic Party (SDP). Since its emergence in 1989, however, the Liberal Democrat party has again developed green policies considerably in advance of the two other major parties.

In his study of green politics, Robinson concludes that the

> main political parties are still chained to the idea that the natural ecosystem exists primarily as a resource for man's exploitation. Although, as a review of environmental policy documents of recent years show, the parties have begun to address issues of resource planning, future energy policy, recycling and the nascent concept of sustainability, the sacred cow of economic growth has not been sacrificed, nor is it likely to be in the near future. (Robinson, 1992, p. 217)

Hence, the 'greenness' of the major parties is very different from that of the Green Party.

■ The Green Party

Britain's Green Party has not enjoyed the electoral success of its European counterparts. For example in Germany the Green Party won seats with only 5.6 per cent of the vote. Yet with nearly 15 per cent in 1989, the British Greens failed to win a single seat in the European Parliament. The Greens are a party opposed to conventional politics, yet their failure to win representation in traditional parliaments has resulted in resignations and divisions within the party. Even at the height of its electoral success in 1989 the Green Party was suffering an internal crisis.

Greens are divided on both the strategy and goals of their party. Was the Green Party an orthodox political party interested in winning political power or not? Some Greens saw the European election results as evidence that their party had 'taken off' and they believed that they could gradually build up and improve upon their 15 per cent level of support until they began winning seats. When this failed to happen and their support tailed off, 'Green 2000' was set up to relaunch the party as a real contender for power. But not all Greens agreed with this initiative, since they did not believe that the Green Party could operate within the conventional party political system. Dark green fundamentalist party members saw Green 2000 as a sell-out to what they saw as the already failed system of power politics.

Legislating for the Environment

Much legislation contains elements which concern aspects of the environment. However, there have also been a number of Acts centrally concerned with the environment. In 1956 the Clean Air Act was passed in order to solve the problem of choking urban smog (smog = SMoke + fOG) particularly in London. Also concerned with cleaning up the environment was the 1974 Control of Pollution Act. In 1981 the Wildlife and Countryside Act was overwhelmingly concerned with environmental issues. More recently the 1990 Environment Protection Act, containing 120 clauses, covered a wider range of environmental issues than any prior Act.

Has recent legislation shown that, at last, the Government is responding positively to environmental issues? The reaction from the green lobby to recent legislation has been mixed. On the one hand there has been satisfaction, even relief, that the environment is recognised as a complex issue which is now receiving legislative attention. On the

other hand, the green lobby has been disappointed in individual Acts which frequently contain delays in implementation, loopholes of one kind or another, often address the more superficial issues, and are marked by a timid approach containing all the hallmarks of retreat and compromise. In this sense environmental legislation has played a symbolic role which reassures the electorate that 'something is being done about the environment' whilst avoiding the radical and unpopular policies that promise to bring real solutions.

The European Union

Britain's membership of the European Union (EU) has been an important influence on environmental policy. EU Directives have been designed to harmonise environmental policies throughout member states, especially important in equalising commercial costs in the single market. Although EU Directives are binding on member governments, their impact can in effect be avoided through blocking and delaying tactics. Nevertheless, the government has responded positively to many Directives and, where it has not, it has been embarrassed by the publicity which results. Directives on the quality of drinking water and bathing water around Britain's coasts received much publicity in the media. The Commission can bring pressure on national governments if it believes that Directives are being ignored. But some commentators believe that the EU's influence on environmental policy will decline in the future. This is because of the principle of subsidiarity, much favoured by the British Government, which will return responsibility for much environmental policy back to national governments.

Summary

Green ideology has been described as a cocktail of beliefs because of its diversity of origins. This diversity, as well as lack of electoral success, has led to a crisis in the Green Party. The Greens have also been undermined by the major parties which have convinced many voters that they too are green.

Although the influence of the EU on environmental policy is likely to decline, it can be anticipated that environmental issues will get on to the agenda of future governments.

.Questions

1. What is meant by the term 'green politics'?

2. To what extent can it be argued that environmental concern is 'non-political' and above party politics since everyone suffers from the consequences of environmental deterioration?

3. Assess the impact of the Green Party on British politics.

4. How compatible are the economic policies of the Conservative and Labour parties with concern for the environment?

5. Explain how the public can be anxious about green issues one year, yet be unconcerned about them in another.

Assignment

A local environmental group has approached you for advice on how to stop heavy vehicles from taking a short-cut through a housing estate. Refer back to Chapter 15 and consider the different ways in which groups can attempt to influence decision-makers. Your advice should be presented in a brief report.

Further reading

Bradbeer, J. (1990) 'Environmental Policy' in S. Savage and L. Robins (eds) *Public Policy under Thatcher* (London: Macmillan).

Dobson, A. (1993) 'Ecologism' in R. Eatwell and A. Wright (eds) *Contemporary Political Ideologies* (London: Pinter).

Jones, B. (1989–90) 'Green Thinking', *Talking Politics*, 2: 2, pp. 50–54.

Porritt, J. (1984) *Seeing Green* (Oxford: Blackwell).

Robinson, M. (1992) *The Greening of British Party Politics* (Manchester University Press).

Rudig, W., Bennie, L. and Franklin, M. (1992) 'Flash Party Dynamics – The Rise and Fall of the British Green Party', APSA Paper, Chicago.

■ *Chapter 29* ■

Northern Ireland

Background to the Crisis
The Roots of Conflict
The Vocabulary of Conflict

The Search for a Solution
The Talks Process

It is often said that Northern Ireland is 'a place apart'. Its people do things differently from the way things are done on the mainland; the people of Northern Ireland live in a distinctive political culture, support different political parties, and face a unique constitutional problem yet to be resolved. For within Northern Ireland live two minorities; the Catholic minority which feels threatened by the Protestant majority, and the Protestant minority which feels threatened by the Catholic majority should the North reunite with the South. This chapter examines the background and nature of the conflict as well as considering the future of this deeply troubled part of the United Kingdom.

Figure 29.1 *The Falls Road, Belfast*

Source: *Guardian*.

■ Background to the Crisis

Protestants from England and Scotland were settled in Ireland over 300 years ago, and they formed distinct communities from the native Catholic population. The history of Ireland includes much mistrust, fear and hatred between these communities, made worse by violent conflict and disasters such as the Great Famine in which over a million people starved to death. There was considerable pressure from the Catholic population to free Ireland from British rule. Liberals, under the leadership of Gladstone, supported a policy of **Home Rule** which would give Ireland its independence. Conservatives opposed this policy and were committed to defending the **Union** – the political link between Ireland and mainland Britain.

Protestants also opposed Home Rule since they believed that it would end in 'Rome rule' and the loss of their privileges and way of life under Catholic domination. A Home Rule Act was passed but the First World War prevented its implementation, which frustrated militant nationalists. The armed struggle for Irish independence, now symbolised by the Easter Rising of 1916, convinced many British politicians that the Catholic nationalists were treacherous and that the 'Irish question' had to be resolved.

The solution to the Irish question was seen to lie in the **partition** of Ireland, a settlement in which Protestants received six counties within the province of Ulster situated in the north-east of Ireland and the remaining twenty-six counties became an independent country known initially as the Irish Free State (Figure 29.2).

Northern Ireland was to remain with the United Kingdom unless, at some future date, a majority of its electorate decided otherwise. Furthermore Article 2 of the constitution of the **Republic of Ireland** lays claim to the whole island of Ireland, including Northern Ireland, as being its national territory. Since no other part of the United Kingdom is in this constitutional position, in political terms Northern Ireland is 'a place apart'. Northern Ireland was governed by a devolved parliament based in **Stormont**.

The years following the end of the Second World War were relatively peaceful ones in Northern Ireland. It was commonly assumed that conflict between Protestants and Catholics was being diluted by their shared interest in increasing affluence. Although Catholics remained discriminated against in terms of employment, welfare and political rights, they were better off than their counterparts to the South. The Irish Republican Army (IRA) waged an unsuccessful campaign in the late 1950s and this too was taken as evidence that Catholics now accepted the political status quo in return for improving living standards.

The appointment of Captain Terence O'Neill as Prime Minister in March 1963 would, it was assumed, lead to continued tranquillity in the politics of Northern Ireland. For O'Neill was a 'liberal conservative' committed to reforms which would modernise the political system and break down further the ancient hatreds between the rival communities.

O'Neill's brand of progressive Unionism was opposed by many Ulster loyalists who were worried about the direction his reforms were leading towards. Conservative loyalists became more determined to resist change and a more militant attitude was taken towards the Catholic minority.

The position of Prime Minister O'Neill weakened, but nevertheless he pushed ahead with his reforms and, long overdue, provided for universal adult suffrage in local government elections. Soon afterwards his position became untenable and he resigned to be replaced by Major James Chichester-Clark. Fire-bombings and street rioting continued to the point where Westminster sent in troops to end sectarian violence and protect Catholics from militant Unionists. Initially British troops were welcomed by Catholics, but inevitably their strong-arm role was to become identified with supporting the Protestant state rather than defending the Catholic minority. The political condition of Northern Ireland moved close to a state of revolution. Chichester-Clark resigned in 1971 to be replaced by Brian Faulkner, an old hard-line opponent of O'Neill.

Source: Arthur (1984).

Figure 29.2 *Ireland, showing the boundary between Northern Ireland and the Republic*

Violence against Catholics led them into accepting the IRA as their defence force, particularly true regarding the newly formed more militant provisional wing of the IRA. The position of the IRA was strengthened by the policy of **internment**, a practice sometimes referred to as the 'recruiting officer for the IRA', since it involved the imprisonment of suspected terrorists which included many innocent Catholics. The troubles were to become yet more intense in January 1972 when, in controversial circumstances, British paratroopers appeared to overreact on the streets and kill 13 unarmed individuals in a tragedy which has come to be known as 'Bloody Sunday'. British Prime Minister Edward Heath announced that Stormont was to be suspended and from April 1972 Northern Ireland would come under **Direct Rule** from Westminster.

■ The Roots of Conflict

The sources of contemporary conflict in Northern Ireland are extremely complex and change in nature from time to time. Nevertheless, some progress towards understanding can be made by exploring three basic propositions.

Firstly, how far is the conflict between Protestants and Catholics a religious struggle? Steve Bruce has argued that Protestantism and Roman Catholicism 'were not *any two* different religions. They stood in opposition to each other. The former began as a "protest" against features of the latter and, after they separated, each developed elements which most clearly distinguished it from the other'. (Bruce, 1986, p. 6). He continued by speculating how different the history of Ireland would have been had the original settlers from England and Scotland also been Catholic: 'Differences of power, status, and wealth between settler and native would have remained, of course, but a common religious culture would have encouraged intermarriage and eroded the ethnic boundaries' (ibid.). In the 1990s religious differences still keep the two communities apart and, unlike on mainland Britain, church attendance is high and there are other institutions working to maintain the link between religion and politics. For example, on the Protestant side the 'link between religion and politics within the Unionist Party continued to be provided and maintained by the Orange Order' (Wichert, 1991, p. 69). The Orange Order is a semi-secret fraternal organisation having the support of around two-thirds of Protestant males. On the Catholic side religious and political links are sustained through segregated schooling which provides the children of the Catholic community with an Irish identity.

Secondly, can the conflict in Northern Ireland be compared in very general terms with colonial struggles? Although the native populations enjoyed rising living standards under minority rule, they still demand the return of land taken by the settlers and majority rule. The beleaguered settler population includes fundamentalists who are not willing to compromise. There is a struggle, often bloody, between the majority who want independence and a minority who want to maintain the power and privileges enjoyed under the old system of exploitation.

Finally, is the conflict in Northern Ireland no more than a class struggle distorted by the labels of Ulster Protestantism and Irish Catholicism? In other words, has the ruling class maintained its position of power by manipulating members of the working class into fighting each other? According to this analysis the Protestant working class 'have been duped into thinking they enjoy (economic) advantage' over Catholics (Bruce, 1986, p. 254). Because they believed that they were better off than Catholics, the Protestant working class remained loyal to the state and were unwilling to unite with the Catholic working class in order to advance their common class interests. The usefulness of this sort of explanation has been eroded by recent events. For example, the economic gap between members of the Protestant and Catholic working class in employment has diminished, and a common culture of poverty afflicts Protestants and Catholics alike who are without work and rely on welfare.

■ The Vocabulary of Conflict

The majority of the Protestant community supports **Unionist** or **Loyalist** political parties. This is an expression of their loyalty to the Union between Northern Ireland and the British monarch who is at the head of the Protestant Church. Most Protestants oppose the idea of Northern Ireland being reunited with the South and being governed from Dublin under a Catholic-influenced constitution. There are and have been numerous groups and organisations which reinforce general Unionist beliefs amongst Protestants; some of these groups are permanent, others come and go whilst some are set up as rivals to existing groups which may be seen as either too moderate or too extreme. Examples include the influential **Orange Order** (see above) and the **Ulster Volunteer Force (UVF)** whose motto was 'For God and Ulster' and which was absorbed into the paramilitary **Ulster Defence Association**.

Although there are political divisions within the Protestant community it is assumed that if faced with a crisis of survival these divisions would disappear and Protestant leaders would be able to resist change by 'playing the Orange card' which would involve organising mass civil unrest. The **Reverend Ian Paisley** emerged as a Protestant leader during the era of O'Neill's liberal reforms and was initially associated with the UVF. Paisley, the 'big man', is a remarkable figure in the politics of Northern Ireland, having founded both his own **Free Presbyterian Church of Ulster** in 1951 and his populist **Democratic Unionist Party** in 1971 which commands the support of half of Unionist voters. The other main unionist party is the more middle class **Official Unionist Party** which is led by **James Molyneux**.

Security, law and order have long been important and sensitive issues. Many Catholics see the **Royal Ulster Constabulary (RUC)** as a Protestant force despite the fact that it is open to Catholic recruits. A part-time arm of the RUC, the **B Specials**, were exclusively Protestant but these were disbanded and replaced by the **Ulster Defence Regiment**.

Irish Nationalists support the reunification of Ireland, which would involve the withdrawal of Britain and the dissolution of Northern Ireland. The nationalist cause is expressed by a variety of organisations all of which receive Catholic support. Moderate constitutional nationalism is pursued by the **Social Democratic and Labour Party**, which has an open membership but is supported mainly by Catholics. The SDLP was formed in 1970 to pursue the goal of reunification but based on majority consensus. More militant nationalism is expressed in the shape of **republicanism** and is symbolised by the Tricolour rather than the Union Jack of the Unionists. **Sinn Fein**, led by **Gerry Adams**, represents Republicanism in Northern Ireland. Many believe that Sinn Fein has direct links with the IRA, although this

is denied by its members. Sinn Fein has put candidates forward in local and parliamentary elections, the most dramatic being the success in a Fermanagh and South Tyrone by-election of **Bobby Sands** who eventually died on hunger strike in an **H-Block** prison.

The **Irish Republican Army** is the paramilitary wing of republicanism which has committed terrorist acts in Northern Ireland and mainland Britain. The IRA has experienced internal divisions which have resulted in breakaway factions such as the **Provisional IRA** (the 'Provos') and the **Irish National Liberation Army**. For a period the British government tolerated the existence of **no go areas** in which the Catholic population was under republican control.

Finally, there have been political initiatives which have attempted to end the polarisation of politics in Northern Ireland. In 1976 the **Peace People**, a peace movement organised by women after three children were killed in an incident, organised successfully and for a time their message found echoes of support on both sides of the divide. Another attempt to integrate the two communities has been made by the **Campaign for Equal Citizenship**, which wants the electorate to have the opportunity to support Labour, Conservative and Liberal Democratic parties rather than the parties of Northern Ireland which, after all, contribute to Northern Ireland's problems rather than help solve them.

■ The Search for a Solution

Direct Rule from Westminster was not seen by the British government as a long-term future for Northern Ireland. The ultimate goal of the Conservative administration led by Edward Heath was the re-establishment of some form of devolved government for Northern Ireland in the hope that this would find widespread acceptance in both communities. The Secretary of State, William Whitelaw, proposed the setting up of an assembly elected by proportional representation which would gradually assume greater policy responsibilities. The assembly would have a power-sharing executive with Unionist and SDLP representatives. Also a Council of Ireland would be established with its membership drawn from the assembly as well as from the parliaments in Westminster and Dublin. The elections to the assembly fragmented the Unionist vote with ten representatives elected on an anti-power-sharing platform. This experiment was ended in 1974 by a general strike organised by the Ulster Workers Council which brought the province to a standstill. The 'Orange Card' had been played to great effect.

A later Conservative Secretary of State, James Prior, conducted a rather similar experiment with 'rolling devolution'. Once again an assembly was to be elected which would in time gain greater and greater responsibility for policy-making. As before there was relatively little support for the idea, which was made unworkable in practice, and the assembly was dissolved after four years. Yet again the devolution experiment ended in failure.

The New Ireland Forum, a conference made up from nationalist parties north and south of the border published its conclusions on future possibilities for the province. The first option was that of a unitary Irish state with special protection for the Protestant minority. Secondly, there could be a federal or confederal state which would allow for a degree of self-government for 'Northern Ireland' within a United Ireland. Thirdly, there could be arrangements for joint authority in which the governments of London and Dublin would have equal responsibility for administering Northern Ireland.

Despite Prime Minister Thatcher's rejection of the New Ireland Forum, the Anglo-Irish Agreement signed by her and Charles Haughey, the Irish Taoiseach, bore some similarities to the third option contained in the Forum report. The agreement (or 'accord' as it is sometimes described) involved provision for much co-operation between Britain and Ireland, including greater crossborder co-operation to defeat terrorism, with Dublin consulted routinely on Northern Ireland affairs. Unionists were outraged by this provision which they saw as constitutionally unique – that is, a foreign government given the power to influence domestic policy in a part of the United Kingdom. 'Ulster Says No' was the slogan of Unionist parties. Sinn Fein also, but for different reasons, apposed the agreement. The SDLP was in favour, as were the front benches of all Britain's major parties.

■ The Talks Process

There have been two sets of talks, which have raised hopes of peace in Northern Ireland – firstly, the **Hume–Adams** talks and, secondly, the **Anglo–Irish Declaration**, based on talks between **John Major** and **Albert Reynolds** (the Irish Taoiseach). Much secret diplomacy prepared the ground for the Anglo–Irish Declaration, which stated:

> The British Government agree that it is for the people of the island of Ireland alone, by agreement between the two parts respectively, to exercise their right of self-determination on the basis of consent, freely and concurrently given, North and South, to bring about a united Ireland if that is their wish.

For some time Britain has acknowledged that the IRA could not be beaten militarily, and it appears that the IRA accepts that it cannot win by the use of terrorism. Also Sinn Fein has developed into an electoral party which would represent Republicanism at any negotiating table once it became clear that terrorism had ended. The Official Unionists, led by James Molyneaux, have responded to the Declaration in a cautious but positive way. In contrast, Ian Paisley has condemned it as a 'sell-out'.

The Anglo–Irish Declaration has not brought peace, but it might bring the opportunity for peace. Only time will tell.

Summary and Conclusion

Recent developments have included 'talks about talks' and speculation about Northern Ireland's future being settled in the context of an evolving EU. This chapter concludes with a brief consideration of the most talked about options:

- **Keep things as they are in Northern Ireland.** The status quo would be maintained with Northern Ireland being governed directly by the Secretary of State and the Northern Ireland office. The Anglo–Irish agreement, unpopular with the Unionists, would remain in force.

- **British withdrawal resulting in united Ireland.** This is the solution sought by Sinn Fein and other nationalists, but it would be unacceptable to the Unionists. In fact there would be the danger that British withdrawal would be resisted by Unionists 'playing the Orange Card', leading to a higher level of conflict than experienced at present.

- **Devolution and Power-Sharing.** The experience of some local councils in Northern Ireland proves that nationalists and Unionists can share power and work together for the good of the Province. Many nationalists oppose power-sharing solutions because they do not go far enough in the direction of creating a United Ireland.

- **Redraw the boundary around Northern Ireland.** Some argue that Lloyd George made a mistake with the partition of Ireland in 1920, since the border was drawn so as to include a third of the population who were opposed to Northern Ireland. A new border could create a smaller and more 'British' Northern Ireland, with the Catholic communities concentrated in the West and South becoming part of the Republic. To some, however, a repartition could lead to all the horrors and violence of 'ethnic cleansing'.

- **Independent Ulster.** Some Unionists, particularly in the 1970s, called for the creation of an 'Ulster Free State' rather than joining with the South to form a United Ireland. But Unionists would lose one of their main political goals with an independent Ulster: their links with Britain. This solution, whilst still discussed, finds little support today.

- **Creation of a joint authority to govern Northern Ireland.** This solution involves sovereignty over Northern Ireland being shared by Britain and the Irish Republic and could be implemented through a 'beefing up' of the Anglo–Irish agreement. Basically, Northern Ireland would be governed by an executive, known as a 'Joint Authority', made up from representatives of the governments of Britain and the Republic of Ireland, plus elected representatives from Northern Ireland. People living in Northern Ireland would be full citizens of both states. This solution represents a compromise for both Nationalists and Unionists, neither side would get all that it wanted, but both would make some gains. Nationalists would not get a united Ireland, and Unionists would have to accept that the Republic had a role to play in running the North. Gains for each side would include the protection afforded through full membership of their preferred nation state – Britain or the Republic of Ireland.

Questions

1. ' "Catholic" and "Protestant" are terms used to describe the opposing sides. The conflict in Northern Ireland is not, however, primarily about religious faith *per se*' (Collins and McCann).

   'The Northern Ireland conflict is a religious conflict. Economics and social differences are crucial, but it was the fact that the competing populations in Ireland adhered and still adhere to competing religious traditions which has given the conflict its enduring and intractable quality' (Bruce, 1986).

   Evaluate the above claims and discuss other sources of conflict between the two communities.

2. 'The political problems facing Northern Ireland are unique.' How valid is this statement? Compare and contrast Northern Ireland with either the conflict between Afrikaners

and the African National Congress (ANC) in South Africa, the Tamil Tigers and the government of Sri Lanka, or the ethnic struggle in former Yugoslavia.

3. 'Northern Ireland is a problem which has no solution.' Discuss the strengths and weaknesses of any two solutions put forward to end conflict in the province.

Comment on the extent to which the statistics opposite justify Protestant beliefs that they are better off than Catholics. What other factors, apart from economic ones, might lead to working-class Protestants feeling that they are an advantaged group?

Assignment

Table 29.1   Class and religion in Northern Ireland

Social class	Catholic population (%)	Protestant population (%)
A	2.5	6.4
B	8.0	11.4
C1	22.0	26.1
C2	29.8	26.7
D	30.7	25.6
E	7.0	3.8

Adapted from Moxon-Browne (1983).

Further reading

Arthur, P. and Jeffrey, K. (1988) *Northern Ireland Since 1968* (Oxford: Blackwell).

Aughey, A. (1989a) 'The Politics of Equal Citizenship in Northern Ireland', *Talking Politics*, 2: 1, autumn.

Aughey, A. (1989b) *Under Siege: Ulster Unionism and the Anglo-Irish Agreement* (London: Hurst).

Bruce, S. (1986) *God Save Ulster! The Religion and Politics of Paisleyism* (Oxford: Oxford University Press).

Wichert, S. (1991) *Northern Ireland Since 1945* (London: Longman).

■ *Chapter 30* ■

Foreign and Defence Policy

Within the memory span of many middle-aged adults, Britain has moved from being a major world power to being a middle-sized regional power. What factors led to this decline? How has Britain adapted in international politics to its new, reduced circumstances? This chapter examines how Britain's policy-makers adapted to change and moved, falteringly, their focus from an Atlanticist to a European outlook. The conclusion considers the opportunities for British influence in the 'New World Order'.

■ The Differing Nature of External Policy

External policy, such as foreign and defence policy, differs from internal or domestic policies in three important areas. Firstly, foreign policy tends to be **reactive** rather than **pro-active**. The government has far greater control over areas such as education or health, where it can direct policy through legislation and financial support. The day-to-day conduct of foreign policy tends to be in reaction to international politics made up of the actions of other governments and international organisations. As one diplomat stated, 'most important decisions are often made, not as part of a concerted and far-sighted policy, but under the urgent pressure of some immediate crisis' (quoted in Sampson (1962) p. 311).

Secondly, public opinion tends to divide less on foreign policy issues than on domestic issues. On issues such as the economy, education or health, government policy tends to create 'winners' and 'losers'. A situation of **zero-sum politics** may exist in which the gains made by one section of society are at the direct expense of the losses incurred by another section. This is rarely the situation when government faces a foreign crisis or threat from abroad, when all sections of society feel the need to support their own government against the common foe. If armed conflict arises, as between British and Argentinian troops in 1982 over control of the Falklands, even to question the wisdom of one's own government may appear treacherous in the eyes of others.

Thirdly, foreign and defence policy issues tend to interest only a small minority of the population. As a consequence pressure groups, parties and the media play a minor role compared with their influence in shaping domestic policy. Even Parliament's role, despite the energetic work of various party groups and select committees in scrutinising policy, is limited. William Wallace argued that in Britain 'as in other democratic countries, there is a long-established parliamentary tradition that foreign policy ought to be insulated from the rough-and-tumble of domestic debate' (Wallace, 1975, p. 1).

This situation can be explained in part by the fact that much foreign policy is concerned with the security of the country and it is crucial that many issues remain secret. David Vital has confirmed how few participate in the foreign policy community: 'the making of foreign policy ... is the business of the Executive, and for almost all practical purposes the Executive is unfettered in its exercise of this function' (Vital, 1968, p. 49). Generally speaking, then, the making of foreign policy is dealt with as a technical matter by a small élite of decision-makers. Foreign policy making is not an open process characterised by pluralism.

■ The Making of Foreign Policy

Figure 30.1 shows the institutional framework of contemporary foreign policy-making. It is useful to compare it with Figure 19.2, which refers to the general policy-making process which is bedded much more firmly in the wider context of parties, media, pressure groups and various other agencies such as local government. In constitutional terms, responsibility for the conduct of foreign policy lies with the secretary of state for foreign affairs. Normally there is close liaison between his Department, the Foreign and Commonwealth Office (FCO) and the Ministry of Defence, the FCO's 'closest cousin in Whitehall' (M. Clarke, 1992, p. 84). The FCO also works with other Departments on issues of common interest, in which case 'the Foreign Secretary or his officials formulate policy in consultation with those Departments. These policies are implemented by the FCO, either directly or through the agency of British embassies and missions abroad'. (Wallace, 1975 p. 21)

Most academics have recognised the close political relationship between the foreign secretary and the Prime Minister. Of course, in many cases the prime minister has previously held the post of foreign secretary, such as James Callaghan and John Major, and this may explain why in the past so many prime ministers intervened in the work of the FCO. But perhaps the main reason for intervention lies in the fact that the prime minister is expected to be a statesman on the international stage and so has to have a command of foreign policy issues. As Prime Minister, Margaret Thatcher was noted for her long-running hostility towards the FCO and occasional bitter battles with the Foreign Secretary. There were complex reasons for this antagonism, but of central importance amongst them was the clash between Thatcher's **Atlanticist** foreign policy outlook and the **Europeanism** of the FCO.

Whatever foreign policy is pursued by ministers or their civil servants, it will inevitably be accompanied by claims that this decision or that treaty is 'in the national interest'. Yet as we have seen in Chapter 7, some Labour and Tory MPs supported the Maastricht Treaty because closer involvement in a potentially federal structure was in Britain's 'national interest'. Yet other Labour and Tory MPs opposed Maastricht because they believed that it threatened Britain's sovereignty and therefore was against 'the national interest'. What, then, is meant by the term 'national interest'? As Joseph Frankel has stated, ' "National interest" is a singularly vague concept. It assumes a variety of meanings in the various contexts in which it is used and, despite its fundamental importance, these meanings often cannot be reconciled'. (Frankel, 1970, p. 15).

■ The Basis of Britain's Foreign Policy

Looking back, it is remarkable that until the 1960s this small country was one of the leading world powers. Britain was an independent nuclear power, held a permanent seat on the Security Council of the United Nations, and was responsible for policing much of the world. Britain, it was argued, had a unique contribution to make to world politics since it wielded influence in three distinct areas. Winston Churchill described Britain's role in terms of being at the intersection of 'three majestic circles'. The first was the Commonwealth circle which, being the legacy of Britain's imperial power, embraced much of Africa and Asia as well as the dominions of Canada, New Zealand and Australia. The second was Britain's 'special relationship' with the United States, and the third was Britain's close relationship with Western Europe, where armed forces were based as part of the defence against the Soviet threat. But changes abroad such as the rise of nationalism in developing countries, as well as changes at home resulting from Britain's declining economic strength, have meant that Britain has had to adapt and make far-reaching changes in each of its 'foreign policy circles'.

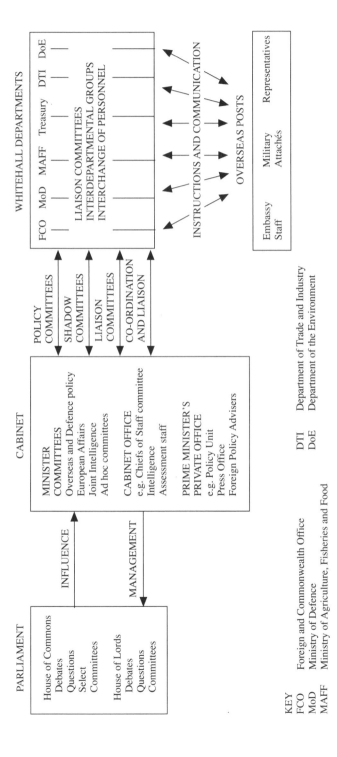

Source: Sanders, 1990, (Macmillan), based on the original in M. Clarke, 'The Policy-Making Process' in M. Smith , S. Smith and B. White (eds) (1988) *British Foreign Policy* (London: Unwin Hyman) p. 86.

Figure 30.1 *The British foreign policy making process*

■ The Commonwealth

The process of decolonisation, the transformation of the British Empire into the Commonwealth of Nations, began in the 1940s with India, Pakistan and Ceylon (Sri Lanka) gaining independence. In the 1960s what Prime Minister Harold Macmillan described as the 'wind of change' was to sweep through Britain's African colonies. Country after country became **self-determining**, with the exception of Rhodesia, which emerged as a problem when an experiment in multiracial government (the Central African Federation) failed, and South Africa, which left the Commonwealth in 1961. Britain retained its global military presence in its former colonies in order to (*i*) deter the Soviets from intervening, as in the Gulf (*ii*) defend countries against insurgency, as in Malaya, and (*iii*) defend Western trade routes, from bases such as Simonstown in South Africa. But the international role encapsulated by the Commonwealth 'circle' was to decline, and many historians see the Suez fiasco of 1956 as critical in eventually changing the direction of British foreign and defence policies.

Anthony Eden was a Foreign Office minister during the 1930s and had learnt the lesson that policies of **appeasement** were not successful in containing the ambitions of dictators. The only language that rulers like Hitler seemed to understand was that of military force. Twenty years later, as Prime Minister, Eden was involved in diplomacy with Egypt over a number of issues including running the Suez Canal which formerly had been a British responsibility. Egypt's leader, Colonel Nasser, outraged the British Prime Minister when he suddenly nationalised the Suez Canal. Eden believed that Nasser was another Hitler, and should be dealt with accordingly. Along with France, and in conspiracy with Israel which attacked Egypt to provide the excuse for intervening, Britain invaded Egypt in order to regain control of the canal.

Figure 30.2   *HMS Ark Royal: a symbol of Britain's world role legacy*

Source: *Guardian.*

In military terms the operation appeared to be going successfully when Britain withdrew its troops. The French Government was shocked by Britain's U-turn, but within a few days French troops, without British support, also withdrew. What went wrong for Britain? Firstly, the United States was vigorous in its opposition to British action and was joined by the Soviet Union in condemning Britain at the United Nations. But most importantly, the Suez invasion had caused a massive run on sterling which placed Britain in a grave financial situation. The lesson of 1956 was, bluntly, that Britain could no longer sustain its old imperial world role. In the years which followed, Britain progressively withdrew from the Commonwealth circle.

Between 1950 and 1966 Britain was involved in 85 military operations around the world; for example, it was involved in Kenya, 1952–6; Cyprus 1954–9; Jordan and Lebanon, 1958; Congo, 1960–1; British Guiana, 1962–6, Malaysia, 1962–6; and the Beira patrol off Mozambique in 1966. It was normal for Britain to be involved in five or six operations at the same time.

Labour Prime Minister Harold Wilson faced the familiar political problem of having to reduce public expenditure and in 1968 his Cabinet decided that big savings must be made in the defence budget. Britain had 220 000 soldiers, 125 000 airmen and 95 000 sailors. Substantial costs would be saved, it was decided, by withdrawing British forces which were garrisoned **East of Suez**. This involved Britain pulling out of Singapore, Malaysia and the Gulf. Along with this the Defence Secretary, Denis Healey, emphasised the growing importance of Europe in strategic thinking: 'our army is well trained and superbly equipped, and has more recent and varied fighting experience than any other European army ... We shall thus be able to contribute to the security of NATO on a scale corresponding with our efforts to forge closer political and economic links in Europe'.

The reduction in Britain's involvement in the Commonwealth circle continued during the 1970s and 1980s as rebellious white Rhodesia found independence as black-majority-ruled Zimbabwe. Britain's responsibilities now involved only a handful of commitments: namely, Hong Kong until its handback to China in 1997, Gibraltar and the Falklands. In 1981 a Defence White Paper announced, in line with Britain's reduced maritime defence needs, that large cuts were to be made in the Navy. Ironically, its publication was followed by Argentina's invasion of the Falklands which necessitated the assembly of a large naval Task Force in order to regain the islands. However, the Falklands War should not be seen as evidence that the Commonwealth circle was regaining its past importance in British foreign policy. Rather it was an aberration which resulted from Argentina's General Galtieri interpreting Britain's military withdrawal from the South Atlantic as a sign that Britain would not challenge his seizure of the Falklands.

In 1990 a Defence review, *Options for Change*, argued that the end of the Cold War presented a further opportunity for cuts in defence spending. The so-called 'peace dividend' included further cuts to the Navy and the overall reduction of uniformed military personnel from 312 000 to 255 000 over five years.

■ The Special Relationship with the United States

The history, institutions and culture of Britain and the United States (US) are intertwined, and out of the close cooperation during the Second World War developed the 'special relationship'. Labour Foreign Secretary Ernest Bevin drew the US into a post-war European defence commitment with the establishment of the North Atlantic Treaty Organisation (NATO). America continued to contribute directly to British defence forces when, after the failure of Britain's own nuclear weapons system, the US provided Britain with the most modern systems in the shape of *Polaris* and *Trident*.

The special relationship was strained during the Suez crisis and weakened considerably during the 1960s and 1970s. Withdrawal of forces East of Suez meant that Britain was unable to play its traditional role of junior world policeman alongside the US. Britain refused to provide troops to fight alongside Americans in Vietnam and Atlantic ties appeared less important as Prime Ministers Wilson, Callaghan and Heath looked increasingly towards Europe.

Margaret Thatcher did not share the deep Europeanism of her predecessor and re-established the special relationship on a personal level with President Reagan. Both leaders held similar New Right views; both saw the Soviet Union, to use Reagan's words, as the 'evil Empire'; and both got along well together in personal terms. There were disagreements, of course, particularly over trade issues but Britain resumed patrolling the Gulf and facilitated US strikes against Libya, and the US lent support to Britain during the Falklands War. Allied action in the Gulf War against Iraq was led by the US with Britain playing a major supporting role.

It is hard to predict where the dynamics of international politics will lead, but there is a logic that points to a loosening of Atlantic ties in the future. Firstly, NATO was troubled by political tensions even during the most bitter years of the Cold War. The removal of the Soviet threat seems likely to weaken such links as were forged through facing a common foe. Secondly, the US and the European Community (EC) have been highly critical of each other's trade policies and progress towards liberalisation of agricultural trade through GATT (General Agreement on Tariffs and Trade) negotiations has been extremely difficult to achieve. Once the US, along with Mexico and Canada, operate within NAFTA, the North American Free Trade Agreement, a rival to the EC will have been created which in turn, is certain to generate increased political tension between America and Europe.

☐ *Britain in Europe*

As the Commonwealth circle declined and the special relationship was redefined more faintly, so Britain adapted by giving greater prominence to the European circle. Britain's reluctant acceptance that its future lay in Europe generally and in the EC in particular has been examined in Chapter 7.

Britain first attempted without success to negotiate a wide free trade area in Europe, then established EFTA (the European Free Trade Association), before eventually deciding to apply for membership of the EEC.

■ The New World Order

The democratic revolutions which swept through Eastern Europe ended the ideological division of Europe which had existed since 1917. The old bipolar certainties of the Cold War disappeared very rapidly; Germany was reunited, the communist Warsaw Pact dissolved, and President Yeltsin announced that he wanted Russia to join NATO. History was moving fast and seemed to be leading to a New World Order. But the Iraqi invasion of Kuwait, civil conflict in former Yugoslavia, and the potential for ethnic turmoil within the Commonwealth of Independent States meant that aggression, instability and suffering remained the familiar ingredients of international politics.

There is now only one superpower – the USA – and the very reason for establishing NATO – the Soviet threat – has now disappeared. The conventional force reduction and strategic arms reduction process accelerated into producing the 'peace dividend'. What sort of institutions might develop and operate within the post-Cold War environment?

Some commentators argue that NATO has to rethink its purpose, since both its rationale and strategy are now obsolete. They believe that NATO will develop a more political role in the future in terms of crisis management. Others believe that NATO will be replaced by the Conference on Security and Co-operation in Europe (CSCE), a large organisation which includes all European states as well as the US, and is developing both a permanent bureaucracy and a parliament. Again, the principal function of CSCE would be crisis management within the European theatre.

Rather than the CSCE developing as the major framework for European security issues, some believe that an enlarged EU with a common defence and foreign policy will become the dominant force. Indeed it is argued that a larger and stronger EU, less closely tied to the US, is likely to play a world role outside Europe. In other words, if the EU develops into a superpower then it will inevitably begin acting like one.

Summary

Britain has moved from world power status to regional power status and this has forced policy-makers into sometimes taking painful decisions. Europe has become the most important focus of Britain's external policy, and here new opportunities and threats have resulted from the end of the Cold War.

Questions

1. 'Domestic policy-making is a pluralist process: Foreign policy-making is an élitist process.' Discuss.

2. How valid is it to argue that having lost its Empire, Britain has not yet found a role in international politics?

3. Should Britain retain its nuclear deterrent? What security threats does Britain face in the 1990s?

4. What, if any, are the disadvantages of the 'peace dividend'?

Assignment

Problems for the Mid-1990s

The most pressing will almost certainly be the economic and political crisis in eastern Europe and the former Soviet Union. The nationalist and ethnic tensions released by the collapse of communism, compounded by the accumulated effects of years of economic failure, constitute an explosive cocktail that will need to be handled with considerable finesse, as well as compassion. The development of militant Islam, especially when it is combined with the likelihood of nuclear proliferation, will similarly require close monitoring and sensitive diplomacy. As far as the present British government is concerned, these are problems for the industrialised world as a whole, not just for Europe. This is why it insists on the need for Europe to maintain its strong Atlantic connections. It is why it resists any developments within the EC that might strengthen the ever-present isolationist tendencies in American foreign policy. For the Major government, global problems require global, not just European, solutions. In its view, American disengagement from the affairs of Europe would be disastrous because it would not only risk damaging Euro–American trade but also substantially reduce the opportunities for successful Euro–American collaboration in global crisis-management in the future. It is therefore very keen to support the Clinton Administration's commitment to resolving problems in Eastern Europe and the former Soviet Union, and to warn against the negative consequences of any protectionist moves in America.

There is, however, a further dimension to Britain's concern to maintain the Atlantic connection. The emergence of Germany as the pivotal European power presents Britain with a major problem within the EC, for British policy for many years has been predicated on the need to prevent the continent from being dominated by a single power. The fact that Germany is already beginning to take a more aggressive diplomatic stance, as was seen in its pre-emptive recognition of Croatia and Bosnia at the start of 1992, only serves to make this problem more pressing. Indeed, the clear danger is that the EC could become little more than a German zone. In these circumstances, maintaining the Atlantic connection gives Britain the option of releasing itself from a European arena in which power imbalances have become substantial.

It is for these reasons that London clings both to the 'special relationship' and to its 'world role' even though the Soviet threat which nurtured them both has now disappeared and Britain has, for a very long time indeed, lacked the relative economic strength to sustain either of them. In spite of the end of the Cold War, Britain's foreign policy-makers still seem to be committed to Realist modes of thinking. As a result, the UK looks set to carry on 'muddling through' in its foreign and defence policies throughout the 1990s.

Source: Sanders (1993, pp. 303–4).

(i) Explain the nature of the 'explosive cocktail' which exists in Europe and how it might affect Britain.
(ii) Why does the author believe that Atlantic ties remain important for British foreign policy?
(iii) Explain how foreign and defence policy-makers are 'muddling through'. How far is 'muddling through' typical of all Government policy-making?

Further reading

Berridge, G.R. (1992) *International Politics: States, Power and Conflict Since 1945* (London: Harvester Wheatsheaf).

Byrd, P. (ed.) (1991) *British Defence Policy: Thatcher and Beyond* (London: Philip Allan)

Clarke, M. (1992) *British External Policy-Making in the 1990s* (London: Macmillan/RIIA).

Sanders, D. (1990) *Losing an Empire, Finding a Role: British Foreign Policy Since 1945* (London: Macmillan).

Chapter 31

The Politics of Law and Order

The Role of the Police
Crime, Policing and the Criminal Justice
   System

Parties' Approaches and Policies Towards
   'Law and Order'

The issue of law and order rose to the forefront of British politics in the 1980s and public concern about it became even more intense in the 1990s. Encompassed within it are questions of police operations, accountability and control, the working of the criminal justice system and rising levels of crime. This chapter focuses on these themes.

■ The Role of the Police

The broader context for the discussion which follows is twofold: first, the monopoly of the legitimate use of violence held by the State and second, its obligation in a liberal democracy to control the law-enforcement agencies and ensure that they operate according to certain rules. Two public needs have to be balanced – *(i)* the need to protect society from the activities of criminals, especially violent criminals; and *(ii)* the need to ensure that the process of bringing suspects to justice takes place within the law, with the officers of the law fully accountable to elected representatives.

There is also a delicate balancing act required by the second proposition. Police impartiality is a central element in the rule of law yet the police must be ultimately accountable to democratic representatives themselves subject to political pressures. How to ensure that the police service is both independent *and* politically accountable is a recurring theme in discussions of policing.

☐ Police Organisation, Accountability and Control

Most European countries have a national police force under the control of the central government. In Britain, however, there is no single national police force; the police are locally organised in 43 separate forces. This number reflects a very considerable reduction from the 117 local forces in 1963 and came about as a result of the restructuring of police forces by the 1964 Police Act. The sole exceptions to local control of the force are the Metropolitan Police and (since 1973) the Royal Ulster Constabulary, which are responsible to the home secretary.

The question of whether Britain should have a national police force accountable to parliament was aired in 1963–4. Supporters of the idea argued that there was too little democratic control in the existing system. They pointed to the Metropolitan Police, which – they claimed – had not been politicised, as a possible model. Opponents feared that a national police force would inevitably degenerate into a very partisan force under government control. In fact, the system of control and accountability which has existed since the 1964 Act has been a tripartite one, dividing power and responsibilities for policing between local police authorities, chief constables, and the home secretary.

The **police authorities**, or 'committees', on which elected councillors are in a majority (two-third councillors, one-third magistrates), are responsible for the maintenance of their forces – i.e. ensuring that they have sufficient resources such as adequate premises, equipment and so on, and for determining the 'establishment' (number of each person of each rank) of their forces. They are also empowered to appoint chief constables, deputy and assistant chief constables; to require senior officers to retire in the interests of efficiency (subject to the approval of the home secretary); to receive an annual report from the chief constable on the policing of the area; and to request reports on specific issues.

Operational decisions are in the hands of **chief constables**, who are accountable only to the law, not to any political authority: they cannot be ordered to do anything regarding policing policy and operations; in the control and direction of their forces they are independent. However, this operational independence should not be taken to mean political unaccountability: the police authority which appoints, can also dismiss; and – rather more remotely – chief constables must have some regard for public opinion.

The final factor is the **home secretary**, who has wide powers to influence the nature of policing. His authority covers pay, conditions of service, and approval of the police authorities' decisions regarding the appointment and dismissal of chief constables, and their decisions in relation to resources. He provides an annual grant equal to approximately half of each force's budget. The home secretary supervises the efficiency of the police service through his control of Her Majesty's Inspectors of Constabulary, who carry out inspections of each force. As police authority for the large (20 000+) Metropolitan Police Force, the home secretary can encourage policing practices for other authorities to follow.

In recent decades, very important issues have surfaced with regard to the control and accountability of Britain's system of policing. These relate to two main areas – political and legal, including the handling of complaints and internal discipline.

Political Control and Accountability

The first 'problem area' concerns the relationship between local police authorities and chief consta-

bles. There is no precise definition of this relationship in the 1964 Act and difficulties have arisen because the local (county or regional) authorities have on occasion wished to concern themselves with law enforcement and this has been resisted by chief constables, who zealously guard their independence in operations matters and take the view that their police committees have no right to intervene.

Several police authorities during the 1980s were in public dispute with their chief constables. Moderate commentators believe that the police committees do, in fact, have a legitimate interest in police operations which 'concern the public interest', such as public order questions, but it seems probable that the problem of the precise responsibilities of these local police authorities can be clarified only by legislation.

Labour has argued for the strengthening of the local police authorities first, by making them entirely elected (i.e. removing the unelected magistrates) and second, by increasing their powers in relation to chief constables. But critics point out that such measures are in danger of further accentuating trends towards the 'politicisation' of the police and further that they run the risk of subjecting the police to control by local party caucuses. The question of the accountability of the police force to local police authorities remains unresolved but plans announced by the Home Secretary in 1993 suggest a further weakening of local control (see below).

Some commentators argue that developments in recent decades have created in Britain a national police force in all but name. These developments may be briefly summarised as follows:

- **Trends in policing:** in order to combat modern crime, the police have had to develop national data storage and retrieval systems such as the Police National Computers (PNC), on which is recorded national information such as missing persons, stolen vehicles, vehicle owners, names of criminals, fingerprints and so on; have had to develop specialised units – most of them run by the Metropolitan Police – to deal with e.g. drugs, serious crime, terrorism, and disturbances; and have been required to coordinate large-scale policing activities across county boundaries as done by the National Reporting Centre at Scotland Yard during the miners' strike. National coordination of police forces also comes about through the work of ACPO – the Association of Chief Police Officers.

- **The power of the home secretary:** the home secretary's powers in relationship to policing are now very extensive. In addition to the powers already mentioned, the authority of the home secretary extends over all law-enforcement activities. A stream of Home Office guidelines, directions and circulars exercise a continuing influence over policing practice, notwithstanding the autonomy of chief constables.

The home secretary's general power to call for reports from chief constables contrasts with the power of the local police authority, which is entitled to receive an annual report but whose further request for other reports may, with the home secretary's consent, be turned down by a chief constable. He has powers of inspection, and should a force be refused a certificate of efficiency – as occurred in the case of Derbyshire Constabulary in 1992 and 1993 – the home secretary's options include amalgamating the force with another, sacking the chief constable or imposing a commissioner. Certain incidents in the 1980s brought out the extent to which his power now 'dwarfs' that of the local police authorities (de Smith and Brazier, 1990, p. 392).

The home secretary has, then, very extensive powers over the police force, but the dilemma over political accountability arises precisely because these seem not to be matched by any corresponding obligation (except in the case of London) to answer to parliament for the police. As de Smith and Brazier point out: 'Home Secretaries still take a very restricted view of their obligations to answer parliamentary questions about law enforcement outside the Metropolis' (ibid., p. 393). Further, it remains unclear whether anyone is entitled to give a chief constable instructions as to the performance of any of his duties, or to what extent the home secretary is politically answerable for decisions taken by chief constables outside the Metropolis (ibid., p. 389).

Legal accountability, the handling of complaints and internal discipline

The police have to keep within the law of the land (although this – as in the case of powers of arrest – is not always easily ascertainable). The police can be prosecuted in the criminal courts for offences such as assault and can be made the subject of civil actions for damages or wrongful arrest.

The main issue here is how far people from outside the force should be involved in investigating complaints against the police. The system since the **Police and Criminal Evidence Act 1984** has been as follows. Any complaint against the police by a member of the public goes to the chief constable who decides whether it should be formally investigated; in pursuing his investigation, he may if he wishes seek the assistance of a police officer from another area. All serious complaints must be referred to the **Police Complaints Authority** (PCA), a completely independent institution none of whose members is or has been a police officer. The PCA then supervises the investigation at the end of which it reports to the chief constable, who must then decide what action to take.

The decision usually amounts to a choice between *(a)* a recommendation that the case go forward to the Director of Public Prosecutions (DPP), who initiates all prosecutions of particular officers; *(b)* internal disciplinary procedure; or *(c)* no further action. The PCA can direct the chief constable to refer a matter to the DPP if he decides not to do so, or to commence internal disciplinary measures, if he decides against that. In the event of internal disciplinary proceedings, two members of the PCA sit with the chief constable on a tribunal to decide whether the charge is proved. The PCA also has general powers of supervision of police disciplinary procedure. It may require the submission to it of any complaint not referred by a chief constable. It presents an annual report to the home secretary.

Although an improvement on the preceding situation, the Police Complaints Authority has been the subject of criticism. Some critics have wondered why the decisions of chief constables themselves were excluded from its remit by the

1984 Act. Others have worried that the PCA itself is insufficiently independent and lacks 'teeth'. In 1992, it received 19 289 complaints against the police and considered 9 200 cases (some cases involved a number of complaints). 904 cases – 9.8 per cent – resulted in disciplinary proceedings and 97 in criminal charges. None of the 73 complaints of racially discriminatory behaviour was upheld. The chairman, Sir Leonard Peach, reported the PCA's concern that too many police officers were escaping disciplinary action by retiring early on medical grounds; he also stated that there had been a rise in the tactical use of complaints by defendants in criminal cases.

Critics argue that an ombudsman for the police would have greater independence, be more effective and enjoy higher public confidence. They point to the way in which certain cases involving serious charges against the police almost failed on account of lack of sufficient police cooperation, e.g. the alleged assaults on youths in Holloway Road by officers from a police patrol van. This case culminated in the gaoling of three officers for assault and two for conspiracy to pervert the course of justice, but only after a public outcry after an initial police cover-up (1986). Prosecutions of constables arising out of the disorders during the Wapping printing dispute collapsed on account of delay (1987). The PCA should have its own staff, say critics, in order to enable it to conduct properly independent investigation into allegations of police misdemeanours.

Crime, Policing and the Criminal Justice System

The 1990s have seen rising public concern about:

- Continuing large increases in recorded crime despite constant rises in expenditure on the police.
- An apparent deterioration in police–community relations: concerns here involved police relations with black people, police interrogation procedures and treatment of people in custody, and cases involving police corruption.
- Conditions in prisons following serious prison disturbances in 1990.

- The operation of the criminal justice system after several cases involving serious miscarriages of justice.

□ Rising Crime Figures

The crime figures showed a constantly upward trend with the number of recorded offences rising from 0.5 million in 1950 to 1.6 million in 1971 to 2.5 million in 1980 and to 5.25 million in 1991. Over 90 per cent of crime is against property, the two largest categories being theft and burglary (Table 31.1). The average clear-up rate continued to fall – it was 29 per cent in 1991. Within this average, clear-up rates varied considerably according to the offence: it was much higher for violent crimes against the person (77 per cent) and sexual offences (76 per cent) than for burglary (23 per cent) robbery (23 per cent) and criminal damage (19 per cent).

The figures need to be taken seriously but also handled with caution. One point to notice is the difference between all crime and recorded crime i.e. the crime recorded by the police. Many

Table 31.1 *Notifiable offences recorded by the police in England and Wales, 1971–91 (thousands)*

	England & Wales	
	1971	1991
Notifiable offences recorded		
Violence against the person	47.0	190.3
Sexual offences, of which,	23.6	29.4
rape and attempted rape	0.8	4.0
Burglary	451.5	1,219.5
Robbery	7.5	45.3
Drugs trafficking	..	11.4
Theft and handling stolen goods	1,003.6	2,761.1
of which, theft of vehicles	167.6	581.9
Fraud and forgery	99.8	174.7
Criminal damage	27.0	821.1
Other notifiable offences	5.6	23.2
Total notifiable offences	1,665.7	5,276.2

Source: Extracted from *Social Trends* (1993), p. 164.

offences are not reported to the police and many offences which are reported are not – for a variety of reasons – recorded.

The *British Crime Survey* gives a fuller account of all crime based on interviews with the public. This is not, however, very reassuring since it suggests that much more crime is committed than appears in the police statistics.

On the other hand, the recorded figures may exaggerate the increase in crime, some of which may be explained by the expansion in the number of police officers and by the pressure from insurance companies on individuals to report crimes. As well as being handled with caution, the crime statistics need to be seen in perspective. Crime has increased considerably world-wide since the 1950s. According to the International Crime Survey, the crime rate in France, Norway and Switzerland is lower than in Britain; it is broadly similar in Spain, West Germany, Sweden and Italy; and worse in Australia, New Zealand, Holland, Canada and the United States.

However, what has disappointed public and politicians alike in Britain is the continuing rise in the crime rate despite the large sums expended on policing. Since 1979 expenditure on the criminal justice system (police, courts and prisons) has escaped cuts and has in fact almost doubled in real terms to £9 billion by 1992; of this money, £5.4 billion was spent on the police.

□ *Police–Community Relations*

Police relations with certain sections of the community deteriorated in the 1980s. The police became distrusted by blacks in the inner cities, as evidenced by the 1981 riots at Toxteth, Brixton, Moss Side, Handsworth and Bristol, and by miners, after being used to contain the picket-lines during the 1984–5 miners' strike.

The police were already facing heavy criticism for lack of sympathy towards blacks as a result of their heavy-handed treatment of black suspects, detention of blacks under the 'sus' law and predominantly white recruitment, when the riot occurred on the Broadwater Farm estate in Tottenham (6 October 1985) which ended in the murder of a police constable, a tragedy which

itself followed the tragic deaths of two black women during police searches of their homes.

In the late 1980s, problems still existed. On the one hand, the police pointed out that responsibility for the urban deprivation and racial prejudice that underlay much inner-city crime was not at root theirs. They felt that they were making serious efforts to improve relations with the black community by for example the issue of documents such as the *Police Code of Behaviour* (1985), which included reference to the need to treat people of all races with courtesy and understanding. On the other hand, critics pointed to the small numbers of black policemen – only 356 black officers in the 'Met' in 1987, just over 1 per cent of the force, and to the inadequacy of police efforts to investigate racial attacks in East London and the dissatisfaction of members of the Asian community with that response.

Other public concerns about police conduct in the 1980s focused on:

- apparent malpractices in interrogation of suspects and in care of people whilst in custody,
- police corruption, especially in the Metropolitan Police.

With regard to malpractice, public worries that the judges' rules in questioning suspects were being flouted were dramatically highlighted during the Blakelock trial (1987). Although the Commons Home Affairs Select Committee found no evidence to support general claims of police brutality to individuals in custody in 1980, accusations and cases of police brutality continued throughout the 1980s.

With reference to police corruption, accusations, which had surfaced in the 1970s in relation to the Metropolitan Police and the CID (Criminal Investigation Department) and appeared to have been largely eradicated in the 1980s, emerged again in the early 1990s.

In 1991, there were allegations that police officers at Stoke Newington Police Station had been corruptly involved with drugs, and in 1993, following an investigation by the BBC 'Panorama' programme, an inquiry into allegations of corruption involving three police officers, one from the

National Criminal Intelligence Service, was launched.

By the early 1990s, public anxieties about the low clear-up rate for crimes had become predominant. A substantial report, *Operational Policing Review*, produced by the police staff associations in 1990, revealed a discrepancy between the views of the public and the police about what constituted 'good policing'. The police emphasis was on 'the firm law enforcer' but the public wanted a greater emphasis on 'a more localised and preventive style of policing'.

☐ Prison Disturbances

A series of major disturbances flared through Britain's prisons in early 1990, leaving two prisoners dead (at Strangeways and Dartmoor), many more prisoners and prison officers injured and much damage to prison buildings and property. The disturbances highlighted the problems of a system which was in crisis, suffering from severe overcrowding with prison population exceeding prison capacity by many thousands of places in the late 1980s.

Critics argued that British penal policy made too much of imprisonment, imprisoning for example a larger proportion of its population than other EC countries (Figure 31.1). They also argued that for lesser crimes greater use could be made of alternatives to prison, such as community service, and that for minor crimes sentences were too long.

The Government responded to the prison disturbances by appointing Lord Justice Woolf to conduct an inquiry. The main goal set out in his report was the progressive improvement of prison conditions leading before the end of the century to a statutory establishment of national standards. The Government accepted the main proposals in his Report in a White Paper (1991), which involved among other things seeking improvements in relations between prisoners and prison officers and providing constructive programmes for prisoners to improve their chances of employment on release. However, this policy appeared to be reversed in 1993 when the Home

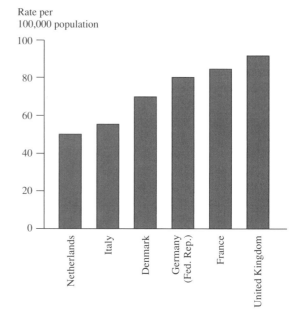

Rate per 100,000 population

Source: Cited in Social Trends (1993, p.174).

Figure 31.1 *Prison population: some international comparisons, 1991*

Secretary announced plans for six more privately built prisons and called for a more 'austere' prison regime.

☐ Miscarriages of Justice

Beginning in 1989, there occurred a series of astonishing releases of prisoners from British gaols, as verdicts were overturned in cases involving, it became clear, serious miscarriages of justice. In quick succession, the verdicts in the three largest IRA terrorist trials ever staged in Britain – the convictions of the Guildford Four, Maguire Seven and Birmingham Six – were all quashed between 1989 and 1991. The Birmingham Six had, it appeared, been wrongfully imprisoned for 16 years. Other cases involving the release of prisoners after the quashing of verdicts followed, including the Tottenham Three, the Cardiff Three, Judith Ward – imprisoned in 1974 for a terrorist offence – Stefan Kiszko, and others.

The Government responded to the grave crisis facing the British criminal justice system by setting up a **Royal Commission on Criminal Justice** under Lord Runciman (1991) following the release of the Birmingham Six. The Royal Commission's Report (July 1993) proved immediately controversial. Most controversial of all was the Commission's recommendation that the right to jury trial should be removed for a wide range of offences, including theft, burglary and criminal damage.

Among the Commission's 352 other proposals were: an independent authority to look into miscarriages of justice; defendants to be expected to disclose the basis of their defence before trial (their right to silence would remain); uncorroborated confessions to be allowed as evidence although judges should direct juries about how to interpret them; a new forensic science council to keep a watch on standards; and a requirement that cell corridors and police custody offices should be videoed.

Some critics felt that a Commission originally established to offer radical proposals for the reform of criminal justice had been overtaken by a public mood less concerned with a long list of miscarriages of justice caused by 'faulty, fabricated or withheld evidence, uncorroborated confessions, biased comments by judges, police misbehaviour and the reluctance of the Court of Appeal to overturn jury verdicts' than with anxieties about the climbing crime rate (*The Economist*, 10 July 1993).

Parties' Approaches and Policies Towards 'Law and Order'

Traditionally, there have been sharp divisions on law and order between the parties, with policy differences flowing inexorably from contrasting ideological perspectives. The Conservative approach is readier to sympathise with the victims of crime than to search for explanations of crime or ways of reforming criminals. To Conservatives, crime is rather the result of inborn psychological factors such as envy, greed, malice

and hatred than of social factors like poverty, unemployment and bad housing. Hence, it is remediable, if at all, more by changes in moral attitudes produced, for example, by more care and discipline in the home, than by improvements in the physical environment. The Conservatives emphasise individual responsibility: the criminal could have chosen otherwise; nothing is inevitable or predetermined. They believe in deterrence; and their policing and penal policy focuses on enhancing the likelihood of capturing wrongdoers by raising police pay and numbers; on deterring wrongdoers by tougher sentences; and on protecting society by using imprisonment as the predominant form of punishment.

Whilst also sympathising with the victims and condemning crime, especially violent crime, Labour and the Liberal Democrats (Liberals/Alliance) have laid their emphasis on the social roots of crime in material deprivation and racist attitudes and look for remedies in policies which tackle these evils. Their policing policy stresses crime prevention whilst their penal policies lay importance on rehabilitation and the investigation of alternatives to imprisonment.

In the wake of the 1992 General Election, Labour's Shadow Home Secretary Tony Blair sought to capture law and order – traditionally a strong Conservative issue – for Labour. Without abandoning Labour's historical belief in attacking the causes of crime, he placed equal emphasis on being 'tough on crime'. His 1993 Conference speech stressed both measures to improve police morale (no short-term contracts or performance-related pay, the extension of witness protection throughout the country, ending court delays) *and* the need to rebuild strong local communities and eradicate the culture of alienation.

As for the Conservatives, their policies since 1979 of a larger police force, tougher sentences for violent crimes and young offenders, and wider powers for the police and courts had failed to turn back the rising tide of crime. Undeterred, the Home Secretary stressed that 'back to basics' in the field of law and order meant giving greater priority to protecting the public than to crime prevention, rehabilitating offenders, or improving conditions in prison.

Source: Times Newspapers Ltd.

Figure 31.2   *Police testing the controversial Arwen Ace – a weapon which shoots plastic bullets*

Two law and order bills were announced in the Queen's Speech of November 1993. Included in the Criminal Justice Bill would be the abolition of the defendant's right to silence in criminal trials together with new procedures enabling the police to take tougher action against hunt saboteurs, New Age travellers and 'raves'. The police section of the Police and Magistrates' Court Bill would implement in part the Sheehy Report (June 1993) on police pay and conditions: three police ranks would be abolished with the loss of up to 3 000 jobs; and there would be fixed-term contracts for senior officers together with a form of performance-related pay for constables. The Bill would also introduce new 16-member police authorities containing only eight elected councillors and pave the way for a reduction in police forces from 43 to about 30. However, both these pieces of legislation encountered severe opposition in the House of Lords and elsewhere in early 1994.

Summary

The police force in Britain is still organised on a local basis (except in London and Northern Ireland) but in recent decades there have been clear trends towards the creation of a more national force.

Problems have arisen in police accountability and complaints procedure and these remain unresolved. Steady increases in the recorded crime figures accompanied by decreases in the clear-up rate, deteriorations in police–community relations, serious miscarriages of justice, and the emergence of grave problems in the prisons have led to mounting public anxiety over 'law and order'.

The political parties have traditionally presented contrasting approaches to this issue, with the Conservatives stressing capture, detention and punishment, and the opposition parties, prevention and rehabilitation. With Labour beginning to combine a new tough approach with its traditional stress on removing the causes of crime, the Conservative Government in late 1993 reaffirmed its commitment to public protection against the criminal and an 'austere' regime in prisons.

Questions

1. Critically review the present system of police accountability and complaints procedure.

2. Why has 'law and order' become such an important political issue?

Assignment

Compare the Conservative, Labour and Liberal Democrat proposals on 'law and order' in their 1992 manifestos (*The Times Guide to the House of Commons 1992* contains the manifestos). Account for the differences and similarities you find.

Further reading

de Smith, S. and Brazier, R. (1990) *Constitutional and Administrative Law*, 6th edn (London: Penguin).

Marshall, G. (1989) 'The Police: Independence and Accountability' in J. Jowell and D. Oliver (eds) *The Changing Constitution*, 2nd edn (Oxford: Clarendon).

Reiner, R. (1985) *The Politics of the Police* (Brighton: Wheatsheaf).

Robertson, D. (1993) 'Preserving Order and Administering Justice: Other Faces of Government in Britain' in I. Budge and D. McKay (eds) *The Developing British Political System: The 1990s*, 3rd edn (London: Longman).

■ PART IV ■

ANALYSING BRITISH POLITICS

Chapter 32

Power in Britain

British Social and Political Élites	Criticisms of 'Power Élite', 'Ruling Class' and
Ruling Class, Power Élite or Competing	Pluralist Theories
Élites?	The Constitution and the Political Process

In the final two chapters, we aim to bring together the concerns of Parts I–III of the book, focusing in this chapter upon ideological approaches to understanding the political system, and in the final chapter upon the main trends in post-Thatcherite British politics in the 1990s.

The first theme of this chapter is the relations between politics and society. It begins with a consideration of the social background of the people who make and influence the major political decisions and then proceeds to an analysis of the main **interpretations** of this evidence – the **theories of the ruling class, power élite and competing élites.**

Having considered theories of the *informal* distribution of power in society, the chapter moves to a discussion of recent constitutional change. This second section explores contrasting ideological perceptions – **Conservative, liberal-pluralist** and **Marxist** – of the formal allocation of political power as embodied in the constitution.

■ British Social and Political Élites

Élites are the very small minority of people who play the key role in making decisions in their respective sectors and, if they are politicians, for society as a whole. The main point of studying them is to assess to what extent entrance to positions of power and social esteem is influenced by the class structure. How far, for example, do power-holders in the various sectors reflect a broad cross-section of society? How far is society in practice as well as in theory a meritocracy?

A subsidiary but important question is the degree to which élite positions are changing. Are they, for example, becoming – however gradually – open to all comers? This needs to be asked not only in relation to their accessibility to the working class but also to women and ethnic groups. The essential context to remember when considering the following analysis is the approximate percentage of the population which is privately educated (7 per cent), university-educated (10 per cent) and belongs to such occupational groupings as employer/proprietor (under 4 per cent), managerial/administrative (about 11 per cent) and higher professional (about 4 per cent).

The most striking point to notice about Figure 32.1 is the contemporary predominance of professional and business groups in Parliament as a whole. These two groups alone have accounted for over three-fifths of the 'political class' since the war. Moreover, middle-class domination of the House of Commons is even more pronounced when it is borne in mind that professional groups such as political organisers, political researchers and journalists form a significant proportion of the 'miscellaneous white collar' category.

A second important observation is the rise in the proportion of university-educated MPs between the interwar period – when half of Conservative MPs and under one-fifth of Labour MPs were university educated – and the postwar period, when the proportion of university-educated MPs in both parties has increased, most sharply in Labour. (Figure 32.2).

That said, the two main parties present sharp contrasts. Labour is now largely and the Con-

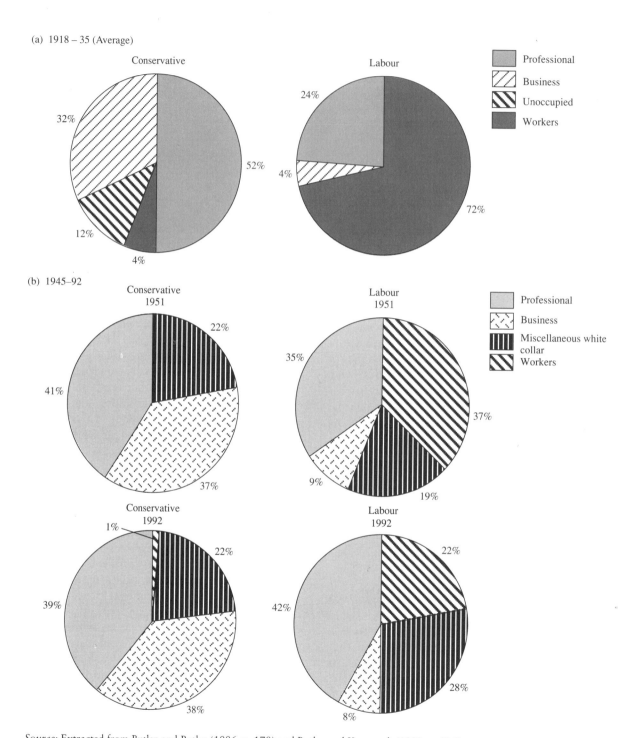

Source: Extracted from Butler and Butler (1986, p. 178) and Butler and Kavanagh (1992, p. 226).

Figure 32.1 *The social background of MPs in the two major parties, 1918–92 (percentages)*

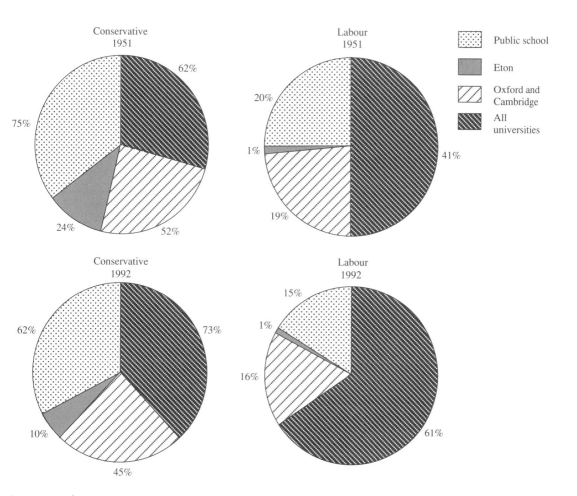

Conservative
1951

62%

75%

24%   52%

Labour
1951

Public school

Eton

Oxford and
Cambridge

All
universities

20%

1%   41%

19%

Conservative
1992

62%   73%

10%

45%

Labour
1992

15%

1%

16%

61%

Source: Data from Butler and Pinto-Duschinsky (1970, p. 303) and Butler and Kavanagh (1992, p. 224).

Figure 32.2   *The educational background of MPs in the two major parties, 1951–92 (percentages)*

servative party almost totally middle class in composition, but each is made up of a different sector of the middle class. Over three-fifths of Tories were educated at public schools, the vast majority of Labour MPs attended state schools. Over 60 per cent of Conservative graduates went to Oxford or Cambridge; over 70 per cent of Labour graduates received their higher education at other universities. The Conservatives contain a sizeable proportion of businessmen (38 per cent) but an infinitesimal number of working-class MPs, whereas Labour contains very few business-men but a significant proportion (nearly 22 per cent) with working-class backgrounds.

Whereas Conservative professionals are drawn mainly from the private sector and traditional professions (lawyers form 18 per cent of the party), Labour professionals generally have public sector occupations, with teachers and lecturers predominant (28 per cent of the Parliamentary Labour Party (PLP)).

Certain important trends are discernible over the century. A declining proportion of Conservatives have had public school educations, with the fall in the number of Old Etonians (over one-quarter of the party in the interwar period) particularly marked. The Tories have become less privileged in their recruitment, with the upper middle class drifting away from the party and from political careers in general.

During the same period, the Labour Party has moved sharply away from its working-class origins towards becoming a predominantly white collar, university-educated, middle-class party. But this apparent convergence of the parties should not be pressed too far. Over 50 per cent of Labour MPs in the 1979–83 Parliament were the children of manual workers. As has been pointed out: 'No other élite group, and few high status occupations, contains such a high proportion of members upwardly mobile from the working class' (Moran, 1989, p. 158).

The social composition of the Cabinet (Table 32.1) reveals a tendency towards the growing embourgeoisement of party leaderships as well as a continuing contrast between the two party élites. Thus, since the early part of the century, Conservative Cabinets have become more middle class and *less aristocratic*, Labour Cabinets, more middle class and *less working class*.

But there are still sharp contrasts. Whereas the public school/Oxbridge element has increased in both Conservative and Labour Cabinets in the postwar period and also constitutes a higher proportion of them than it does of the respective parliamentary parties, it is much more pronounced in Conservative Cabinets. Thus, Tory Cabinets in the post-1945 era have been overwhelmingly

composed of people of middle-class *origins*, but Labour Cabinets have been fairly evenly divided between ministers with working-class and those with middle-class backgrounds.

A brief comparison between the Cabinet and Shadow Cabinet in early 1994 underlines these trends and differences. Both élites were largely university-educated (90 per cent), but whereas the overwhelming majority of Major's Cabinet was educated at public school and Oxbridge (over 70 per cent), only one-third of the Labour Shadow Cabinet attended independent schools and all except three went to universities other than Oxbridge.

The Conservative Cabinet is mainly drawn from the worlds of law, commerce, finance, and career politics; the Labour Shadow Cabinet contains eight former teachers, tutors and lecturers. Labour has five lawyers (the Tories also have five) but collectively, the Labour élite has minimal experience of finance, commerce and industry. About two-thirds of the Shadow Cabinet hail from Wales, Scotland and the North of England.

The political élite – predominantly white, male and middle class – is therefore only a feeble reflection of society as a whole. The House of Commons elected in 1992 contains a mere 9.2 per cent women MPs (although this is more than ever before), 1 per cent from the ethnic minorities (who compose nearly 5 per cent of the popula-

Table 32.1   *Education and class origins of Cabinet ministers, 1916–84*

| | Background of Cabinet Ministers (%) | | | |
| | *1916–1955* | | *1955–1984* | |
	Conservative	*Labour*	*Conservative*	*Labour*
All public schools	76.5	26.1	87.1	32.1
Eton, Harrow	45.9	7.6	36.3	3.5
Oxbridge	63.2	27.6	72.8	42.8
Elem/Sec	4.0	50.7	2.5	37.5
All Universities	71.4	44.6	81.6	62.5
Aristocrat	31.6	6.1	18.1	1.8
Middle Class	65.3	38.4	74.0	44.6
Working Class	3.0	55.3	2.6	41.0
No Data	–	–	4.0	12.6
Number	98	65	77	56

Source: Extracted from Burch and Moran (1985).

	UK (%)	EC (average) (%)	EC (highest) (%)
Women in Parliament (lower and upper chambers)	7.4	13.2	33.0
In lower house	9.2	12.0	33.0
In upper house	6.5	9.4	28.0
In national governments	7.0	11.1	24.0

Table 32.2   *Women in political élites (1993)*

tion) and 10 per cent with a 'manual worker' background (manual jobs still constitute approximately half of all employment).

Britain compares poorly with the EC in terms of women's membership of the political élite (Table 32.2) but relatively well with regard to manual worker representation in the House of Commons (Adonis, 1993, pp. 51–2).

□ *Other Élites*

We now turn to the educational background of other élites. Tables 32.3 and 32.4 show the proportion of a range of élites receiving private education between the late 1930s and the 1980s together with the percentage of the administrative elite which was recruited from Oxbridge over a slightly longer period. Table 32.3 shows that the **higher administrative grade** of the civil service has drawn decreasing proportions of its entrants from people educated at fee-paying schools as the century has progressed. The proportion of higher grade entrants from Oxbridge has also declined, but again not uniformly: overall decline is compatible with a significant increase in the recruitment of the Oxbridge-educated to this grade in the 1980s (Table 32.4).

The civil service is more open than all other élites except the Air Force and the Navy. Table 32.3 reveals that the top posts in **the diplomatic service, the judiciary and the army** remain dom-

Table 32.3   *Percentage of selected administrative élites 1939–83 who had been educated at fee-paying schools*

	1939 %	1950 %	1960 %	1970 %	1983 %
Ambassadors	73.5	72.6	82.6	82.5	76.3
High Court Judges	80.0	84.9	82.5	80.2	79.0
Major Generals and above	63.6	71.3	83.2	86.1	78.9
RAF Vice-Marshals and above	66.7	59.1	58.4	62.5	41.1
Civil Servants, Under-Secretary and above	84.5	58.7	65.0	61.7	58.8

Sources: Columns 1–4 calculated from D. Boyd, *Elites and their Education* (1973), pp. 93–5; column 5 from *Whitaker's Almanack and Who's Who*. Cited in Moran (1989, p. 166).

Table 32.4   *Higher education of 'open competition' entrants to the administrative class/administrative trainee grade of the home civil service (percentages)*

	1921–32	1933–9	1949–50	1961–5	1971–5	1981	1982–3	1985
Oxbridge-educated	84	89	74	80	50	56	66	64

Sources: Data from Moran (1989, p. 163); Drewry and Butcher (1991, p. 71).

inated by people educated in the private sector, and in the Army this predominance actually increased in the half-century down to the 1980s. In contrast, by the early 1980s, both the Air Force and the civil service at the highest levels drew upon state-educated people to a significant extent and, in the Air Force, the majority of top officers were non-public school.

In considering the **business élite**, it is useful to distinguish between a financial élite and an industrial/commercial élite. The **financial élite** consists of the directors of the Bank of England together with the chairmen of the major clearing banks and leading merchant banks and the chairmen of the 12 largest insurance companies. The **industrial/commercial élite** may be defined narrowly as the chairmen or chief executives of the leading industrial and retailing enterprises and more broadly to include the directors as well as the chairmen/chief executives.

Studies of the financial élite suggest its social exclusivity. It is overwhelmingly privately and Oxbridge educated, with a particularly high proportion having been to Eton and other top public schools. Thus, in 1983, according to Moran, 81 per cent of the financial élite had been educated at fee-paying schools (32 per cent at Eton) and 68 per cent had gone to Oxbridge (Moran, 1989, p. 169).

An important reason for the closed nature of the financial élite is the rules of property inheritance which enable the transmission of wealth from one generation to the next, thereby protecting and preserving the positions of the top families.

Studies of the industrial/commercial élite reveal a similar educationally privileged background for the **chairmen of large companies** down to the 1970s although a rather less socially exclusive education for the directors of large industrial firms (Stanworth and Giddens, 1974).

However, there are signs that the domination of boardrooms by those educated at public school may be diminishing. An article in the **Financial Times** found that whereas nearly three-fifths (58 per cent) of the chairmen of the top 50 companies had been educated at leading public schools in 1979, by 1989 under one quarter (24 per cent)

had received such an education, and 70 per cent had attended either grammar schools (40 per cent) or other state schools (30 per cent). The writer also revealed that, compared with the situation a decade earlier, fewer top chairmen in 1989 had Oxbridge degrees (32 per cent), and a smaller proportion were non-graduate (only 28 per cent) (**Financial Times**, November 3 1990).

The social and educational background of the **trade union élite** stands in total contrast to other élites in British society in being entirely working and lower middle class and entirely educated in state schools. This is the case whether we limit our attention to trade union leaders (general secretaries and presidents) or extend our concern to include the officials who make up trade union bureaucracies. Trade union bureaucracies in any case are small and in the trade union movement as a whole there are only about 3000 full-time officials. The tendency is for trade union leaders and officials to have left school at the minimum leaving age, worked in manual or white-collar jobs and risen to their union posts through work in the union itself. Despite the increasing tendency in some – especially white collar – unions, to look for their officers amongst the university-educated, the overwhelming majority of union leaders and officials in the 1990s still reflect the class and educational experiences of the bulk of the population.

Bill Jordan, President of the Amalgamated Engineering Union in 1993, typifies the general norm. Son of a furnaceman in Birmingham, he was educated at secondary modern school, which he left at 15 to take up an apprenticeship with an engineering firm (GKN). He worked there until 1977, when he was elected to the post of Midlands organiser of his union. Thus, from a background of early-school-leaving and manual work on the shop-floor until the age of 40, he moved via his post as union organiser to be president of the AUEW. Only in joining the trade union élite did his experience deviate from that of the working class in general.

This brief survey has shown varying degrees of exclusivity in the social background of British élites. Put another way, it may be said that élite recruitment in the various sectors of politics and society reflects differentially the principle of meritocracy. At one end of the privilege/meritocracy scale are groups such as the core financial élite, – upper middle class in composition and educated at top public schools and Oxbridge. Close to this élite in terms of privileged social backgrounds are leading diplomats, judges and generals, and, only a short distance away again, top industrialists and the Conservative Party, both of which groups have become more meritocratic in recent years. The Conservatives' concessions to the principle of merit notably include their declining recruitment from public schools – especially top public schools such as Eton – and their election of leaders of working and lower middle class origins (the last three being the children respectively of a carpenter, a grocer and a circus artiste).

At the other end of the scale are the top trade unionists – working and lower middle class in background and entirely educated at state schools – and, some way away from them, élite groups such as the Labour Party (mixed working/lower middle, largely university-educated), and the upper ranks of the Royal Air Force (RAF) and home civil service (lower middle class, mainly state-educated and, in the case of the civil service, graduate).

Ruling Class, Power Élite or Competing Élites?

There are three distinct approaches to the empirically observable fact that the highest positions in British society and politics are in general recruited from a small and unrepresentative section of the population. These take the form of three models –

the 'ruling class' theory (Marxist), the 'power élite' theory (Élitist) and the 'pluralist' theory (liberal). We consider and criticise each one in turn.

The Ruling Class Theory (Marxist)

'Ruling class' theory holds that a single cohesive ruling class exists in Britain. Its power rests in the control and ownership of capital. Thus, although a number of élites exist in various sectors of society, they are bound together by a set of common interests into a homogeneous ruling class. The main interests they share consist of the maintenance of property, support for the capitalist system, the limitation of effective democratic control and social reform, and the perpetuation of their own wealth and privilege. Divisions of interest may from time to time appear between sections of this ruling class – between finance capital (the City) and manufacturing industry, for example. Ultimately, however, the common interest of such groups in the continued existence and strength of capitalism takes precedence over apparently divergent interests.

This ruling class encompasses not only those most obviously involved in the ownership of wealth in all its forms (fixed and liquid assets, land, property and shares) but also those élites (Conservative politicians, judges, ambassadors, military chiefs) which possess a common privileged upper-class origin, education and life style. Leading civil servants, too, belong to the upper class since they are 'filtered by a long promotion process' to ensure their identification with the interests of capital (Coates, 1984, p. 236).

Exhibit 32.1 *Élites in Britain: a summary*

Perhaps the most remarkable long-term feature of the social structure of elites in Britain is the limited scale of change in patterns of recruitment, and the slow pace at which that change has been accomplished. Change there has nevertheless been, the end result of which is a perceptible widening in the social origins of many, though not all, elite groups'.

(Moran, 1989, p. 181)

The fact that the ruling class is not particularly visible to people as they go about their everyday lives (it does not pose for a group photograph which then appears in television and the newspapers) does not mean, say Marxists, that it does not exist. On the traditional Marxist view, since the State is always and invariably under the domination of a capitalist ruling class, the apparatus of democracy – the holding of periodic elections, party competition for power, the political influence of pressure groups – makes no difference to the realities of power. It is a mere facade for the class rule of the big owners of property and capital.

☐ *Power Élite Theories*

'Power élite' theorists consider democratic institutions a sham for different reasons. For them, the reason why oligarchy (the rule of the few) always triumphs over democracy is psychological. This theory was developed in the early twentieth century by the Italian sociologists Vilfredo Pareto and Gaetano Mosca and the German sociologist, Robert Michels. The postwar American C. Wright Mills wrote *The Power Elite* (1956) – which argued that an oligarchy of business, political and military chiefs controlled the USA – in this tradition.

From an examination of the practice of organisations, élite theorists concluded that, whatever the ideals purporting to guide behaviour, power invariably passed away from the control of members into the hands of the few. This was because a small minority simply were more able, ruthless, manipulative and willing to give their time to the organisation than the rest.

During the 1950s, a British version of power élite theory drew attention to the existence in Britain of an 'Establishment', a cohesive political class which pursues its own self-serving ends irrespective of the results of elections. This power élite or Establishment is held together less by shared economic interest (although its members do tend to possess similar socio-economic backgrounds) than by a common culture which separates it sharply from the rest of society. Sheltering

behind the traditional rituals, norms of 'moderation' and strong adherence to confidentiality of British political culture, the Establishment governs Britain no matter which party is nominally in power. A permanent and pervasive psychological attitude characterises the 'Establishment'. New people – aspiring working-class and lower middle-class politicians, for example – may enter it but never in sufficient numbers to change or dilute its enduring power and always at the price of the abandonment of radical principles. This is the way in which, historically, radicals and socialists who would challenge social inequality have been contained, tamed and ultimately absorbed. In the final analysis, this shared attitude comes down to a determination to remain in political control, come what may.

☐ *Pluralist Theories*

Pluralists disagree with both these theories. According to pluralist theory, what matters about the distribution of power in society is not that it is uneven – since unevenness characterises all societies and is probably inevitable – but three other vital features:

- Whilst élites undoubtedly exist, they are to varying degrees open and relatively accessible to able people from below, rather than sealed into closed hierarchies. Pluralists do not deny that certain élite groups in Britain – the Conservative Party, the judiciary, the diplomatic service and the financial community in particular – are difficult to enter for those not born into the wealthy upper middle (some would simply say 'upper') class. They argue, however, that élites vary greatly in composition. To set against those parts of society still dominated by upper-class individuals, there are other sectors in which people with working- and lower middle-class backgrounds can reach the top on merit. These include the Labour Party, the home civil service, local government, the police, the Royal Air Force and the trade union movement. Nor is it the case that the Conservative Party, judiciary, diplomatic service and the world of finance are exclusively upper-class preserves at the highest level. Change – however slow it may seem to reformers – has taken place in these sectors, as witness the fact, for example, that the last three leaders of the Conservative Party have come from modest social origins.

- Pluralists maintain no single ruling class or cohesive power élite exists. Rather, they argue, a number of élites compete for influence. Competition between a series of power blocs representing diverse interests rather than the rule of a single monolithic Establishment or ruling class is 'the name of the game'. Resources which can be deployed to influence decisions (money, numbers, organisational skills) are in practice widely dispersed. Thus, élite groups representing sectoral and occupational interests influence policy-making selectively within their specialised fields of concern (industrial, financial, military, academic). Moreover, since disagreements appear from time to time within élites, rank-and-file participation is possible as appeals for members' views have to be made. This type of wider appeal beyond the boundaries of the élite itself occurs quite frequently within political parties and trade unions. In parties, it tends to happen in the wake of electoral defeat, as in 1975 when Margaret Thatcher replaced Edward Heath as Conservative leader after he had suffered two successive election defeats within one year. Both the two major parties and trade unions – the first by reforming themselves, the second by legislation – have become more democratic since the 1960s.

- Pluralists argue that, although many élites can be influential from time to time, the political élite, consisting largely of members of the Cabinet and top civil servants, is supreme. In their model, the power structure is rather like a range of mountain peaks among which one – the political – is discernibly higher than all the rest. Unlike the other two theories, which tend to locate power with hidden, behind-the-scenes manipulators, for pluralism, real power lies

where it ostensibly lies or is supposed to lie – with the political élite. The political élite predominates over the leading business, financial, labour and other groups by virtue of the special authority afforded it by the democratic system of government. Moreover – and this point is fundamental in pluralist analysis – the governing élite acts within the powerful constraints of regular elections, and, between elections, of the countervailing influence of public opinion. Included in public opinion are political institutions such as the civil service and the House of Lords and pressure groups, like the Confederation of British Industry (CBI), the Trades Union Congress (TUC) and the City. Far from considering democratic political machinery a mere facade, pluralists take it seriously. They maintain that although far from perfect it does ensure enough popular control, choice and participation to be regarded as a working or viable system. Whilst it is the case that in some important parts of the system, participation is low – only about 5 per cent of the electorate are members of political parties and an even smaller proportion are party activists – on the other hand, participation is high elsewhere in the system, and increasing. Minor parties now provide a wider base for political participation than was the case in the 1960s, and there has been a huge upsurge in pressure group activity, with participation in the environmental and women's movements becoming a major social phenomenon. In the view of pluralists, the present liberal democratic system, although élitist, is neither deliberately nor irremediably so, and has demonstrated a proven capacity to adapt over time in response to changing social needs and demands.

Criticisms of 'Power Élite', 'Ruling Class' and Pluralist Theories

To many critics, the British variant of power élite theory – the idea of a socially and culturally cohesive Establishment – has declined in plausibility since it was first asserted in the 1950s. The Establishment, they argue, has been eroded by major social and political changes.

Greater Openness and Less Secrecy

Although to many critics the process still has far to go, British government became more open and less secretive. Until the advent of the 1992 Conservative Government, this process happened more by inadvertence than design and was usually resisted by governments of the day. Nonetheless, by the 1980s, the public were far more aware of what went on in the inner counsels of the Cabinet and in the 'Whitehall village' than was the case a generation previously. This had happened as a result of such events as the publication of politicians' diaries and memoirs (Crossman, Castle), 'leaks' by civil servants (Tisdall, Ponting), revelations of goings-on inside secret institutions such as MI5 (Peter Wright), the decreasing anonymity of bureaucrats, and the light shed on the workings of government by the select committees.

Greater Democracy

Certain important sectors of British society became more democratic. In political parties, members played an increasingly important part in the election of leaders and the selection of party candidates; in trade unions, balloting on the choice of leaders and on strike decisions became the norm. Television contributed both to greater openness and greater democracy by providing continual public demonstrations that, far from being cohesive and united, the so-called Establishment spoke with many, often sharply divergent, voices.

Less Deference

Britain became a less deferential society. The willing submission to a social and political élite – and to authority figures generally – by the larger part of society virtually disappeared in the 1970s. A new populism emerged. This profound cultural change, it has been argued, dealt a severe blow to Britain's formerly secure Establishment (Beer, 1982, chaps. 4 and 5 esp.).

The Sudden Weakening of the Monarchy

From being the most widely respected institution in British society, the Royal Family lost credit dramatically in the early 1990s. This was the consequence in part of the collapse of the royal marriages, in part of the critical intrusiveness of the 'tabloid' press and in part also of the failure of the monarchy to participate in voluntary reforms, especially with regard to such matters as the payment of tax (by the Queen) and royal claims on the civil list. Since the monarchy is centrally embedded in the traditional core of the Establishment – the Church of England, the Lords, the landowners, the top military men, the horse-racing world, the very wealthy – this crumbling of the mystique of the Royal Family seems likely to further undermine the Establishment as a whole (see Peele, 1993, pp. 38–9).

However, a survey of individuals in top jobs in 1992 by *The Economist* provided ammunition for those who argued that the Establishment had survived these changes. The journal's survey compared the social backgrounds of a cross-section of top people (drawn from politics, business, the City, the learned professions and the arts) with those of their counterparts in 1972. It found that 66 per cent had attended public school (cf. 67 per cent, in 1972), 54 per cent were Oxbridge-educated (cf. 52 per cent, in 1972) and that only 4 per cent (cf. 2 per cent in 1972) were women. There were fewer Etonians in top posts (8 per cent, cf. 14 per cent in 1972) and fewer in such jobs who had not received higher education (11 per cent, cf. 22 per cent). In general, however, very little had changed. The old establishment had not given way to meritocrats. The 'social revolution' had 'not even started' (*The Economist*, 19 December 1992).

What of the arguments of the early twentieth century élite theorists? How valid are they today? It can be admitted that there is a tendency in all organisations for power to slide towards a few people – those with more than average commitment, capacity and energy – and for such élites to escape control by the membership. However, it is problematic whether this is inevitable, as Michels suggested with his notion of the 'iron law of oligarchy'.

In practice, élite theorists paid too little attention to the dynamics of the leader–follower relationship and to the context, in democratic systems, of that relationship. In effect, leaderships – in parties and trade unions, for example – have to be rather more responsive to the wishes of their memberships than élite theory suggests. In democracies, moreover, membership of social organisations is voluntary, and members accordingly expect to be consulted, at least on major decisions and over the medium and long term.

The assumptions of élite theorists are also relevant. Their starting-point was pessimism about the possibility of democracy. They specifically wrote to refute what they saw as the false Utopianism of the democratic ideal of mass participation in decision-making. Beginning by simply assuming that people were selfish, ignorant and apolitical, they also posed a question – 'Who really rules?' – that invited an answer in terms of an undemocratic élite. It was scarcely surprising that they ended both by finding an élite and by relegating the majority of people to political powerlessness as its dupes. They considered neither the possibility that people would grow in political understanding as society developed nor the possibility that it might make sense for ordinary members of organisations to delegate responsibility for decisions to a few, so long as *ultimate* control remained with the membership. At best, their case remains unproven (perhaps even impossible to establish). At worst, it consists of a sweeping generalisation which requires continual testing by reference to *specific* decisions and often disintegrates when faced by such a test.

'Ruling class' theory – to pluralist analysts – faces a similar methodological problem to 'power élite' theory. This is the difficulty of showing that all decisions are under the control of and in the interests of a specific group – in this case, a capitalist ruling class. How is it possible to prove the existence of power that is by definition *covert*?

For liberal pluralists, ruling class theorists pay too little consistent attention to empirical questions of how decisions are actually made. Thus, a Marxist survey of the post war period can accept that the political system is sufficiently open for lower-class people both to gain certain élite positions and as a class to negotiate benefits from it in the form of the welfare state. On the other hand, its author sees these gains as in effect illusory since they merely serve to stabilise the system and to consolidate the power of the capitalist class. The Conservative working-class vote is explained in terms of the penetration of working-class consciousness by a whole set of official orthodoxies reflecting 'the interests and preoccupations of the ruling strata' (Coates, 1984, pp. 114, 233, 151–2).

To liberal pluralists, this explanation itself seems élitist as totally contemptuous of the working class, whose actual thoughts and wishes are not seen as in any sense their own but rather as a simple reflection of the ruling-class ideology. Just as in right-wing European élitist theory, an oligarchy invariably rules and the lower classes end up as its dupes. Liberal pluralists perceive the ruling-class model as overly determinist and as too prone simply to *assume* the ideological cohesion and socio-economic uniformity of the capitalist class.

Empirically, then, there seem to be better grounds for accepting the pluralist model – that different élites compete for influence with an over-arching political élite; that élites are to some extent and differentially responsive to memberships; and, above all, that elections matter as a mechanism by which real power may change hands peaceably.

However, the pluralist model can itself be criticised. First, with its focus on élite competition rather than any wider distribution of power, it is itself élitist. Hence, the **pluralist élitist model** might be considered a more appropriate term for it than simply 'pluralist'. Second, proponents of the other theories might argue, pluralism – with its emphasis on detailed decision-making – fails 'to see the wood for the trees'. It exaggerates both rather minor disagreements between élites and relatively small changes in their composition. It ignores the extent to which all the élites share a common interest: the perpetuation of people like themselves in power (power élite theory) or of the capitalist system (ruling-class theory). Evidence from Britain in the 1980s and early 1990s – e.g. *The Economist* survey (above p. 468) or the large-scale increase in social inequality or the huge pay rises taken by directors of the largest firms – can be read as pointing to the continued existence, social irresponsibility and political unaccountability of a power élite or ruling class.

Underlying the debate about the distribution of power in society are **ideological** disagreements about ultimate values and **methodological** differences.

With reference to ideology and values, proponents of the power élite were 'mass society' theorists who regarded the majority as incompetent and apathetic 'masses'. They sought to refute the Marxist idea that the ruling class is doomed to be overthrown and replaced by a classless society by showing the inevitability of rule by a political élite in all societies at all times. In turn, the notion of the 'ruling class' represented an ideological response to what was perceived as classical liberalism's neglect of the vital role of economic power in society. Finally, pluralism as a form of political analysis developed out of a very liberal perception and endorsement of the cultural and economic complexity of modern societies which make it both inevitable and desirable that power is dispersed among a multiplicity of interests and élites.

With regard to **methodology**, the question with which one begins an inquiry into the source of power in society plays a key role in shaping one's conclusion. Thus, to ask the question 'Who rules?' invites an answer in terms of a power élite or ruling class. Similarly, to ask the question' Who made that *decision*? or 'Which people and/or groups influenced a particular decision?' invites a pluralist answer in terms of competing groups and interests, and even of the dispersion of power beyond an élite.

Thus far this chapter has explored ideological approaches to the social location of power. But the formal distribution of power in Britain – the organisation of the state – became a subject of intense political controversy in the early 1990s, with appeals to pluralist values playing a key role in this debate too. The rest of this chapter focuses on current disagreements about the **political system**, beginning with the Marxist approach.

The Constitution and the Political Process

☐ *The Marxist approach*

To Marxists, the Constitution is simply a facade concealing the operation of capitalist institutions.

Exhibit 32.2	*Models of power in society: a summary*
Pluralist	Power distributed between competing élites infused to varying degrees with meritocracy and forming checks upon each other. Democratically elected political élite predominates.
Power élite	Rule by an élite dedicated to preservation of its own power and privileges inevitable in modern societies. Democracy thereby reduced to a sham. The 'Establishment' – the idea that whatever the changes in government an unaccountable social élite drawn largely from the public schools is always in power – is a British variant of this theory.
Ruling class	Political control by a cohesive economic class (the owners of the means of production) which shares a common capitalist ideology.

They argue that the British system of government is more appropriately entitled 'capitalist democracy' than 'liberal democracy'. The stress, moreover, is upon the word 'capitalist' rather than 'democracy'. This is because, in their view, economics takes precedence over politics. For them, the central fact bearing upon the working of the political system derives directly from the nature of the economic system. This is the inequality of wealth and income which flows from the workings of capitalism, a system whose essence is the accumulation of capital in the hands of the few. Such concentrations of wealth, in fact, place massive power in the hands of big financiers, financial institutions and the multinational corporations. Thus, constitutional and political rights and freedoms guaranteed to all by the liberal pluralist system are not really 'rights' and 'freedoms' at all, so long as glaring inequalities exist and the life-chances of the many are so overshadowed by the privileges of the few. Devolution, the strengthening of Parliament in relation to the government of the day and a Bill of Rights cannot affect the substance of social power and inequality. They cannot give the unemployed jobs, or the low-paid higher incomes, or prune the power of the financial and business élites.

To Marxists, elections are simply a ritual which confer neither real power nor even ultimate control on voters, merely the illusion of influence. As Ralph Miliband writes: ' a permanent and fundamental contradiction "exists" between the promise of popular power, enshrined in popular suffrage, and the curbing or denial of that promise in practice' (Miliband, 1984, p. 1). Capitalism as an economic system requires the containment of 'pressure from below' and whilst the Conservatives might be expected to endorse such a goal enthusiastically, the Labour Party in practice has fallen in behind it also. It is formally committed to internal party democracy but in fact its parliamentary leadership has waged relentless war against the left-wing activists in the constituency parties and systematically ignored Conference decisions which it found distasteful. In reality, the word 'labourism' is a more accurate description of its

practice than 'socialism'. In power, Labour has done nothing to weaken, let alone to destroy, capitalism; it exists merely to win concessions for the working class, concessions which, by making for a more contented labour force, strengthen rather than undermine the system. The formal rule by a particular party then is simply that – a formality which serves to conceal the fact that the ruling class is always in power. The same analysis is extended to the world of pressure groups. However diverse the character and activities of the groups appear to be, the diversity is only apparent. What seems to be the ebb and flow of influence between government and groups is just shadow-boxing. Behind governments of all complexions stands capitalism, national and international. Ultimately, whatever guise they may assume (the big banks, the finance houses, the insurance companies, the multinationals) capitalists always ensure that the major decisions promote the interests of capital.

Marxists perceive the state as inherently biased in favour of the middle class and against the working class. In its most unequivocal expression, this view holds that the State through its agents – judges, policemen and soldiers – is simply an instrument for ruling–class suppression of the working class; according to Marx, it is the executive arm of the bourgeoisie. The liberal or pluralist claim that the law-enforcement agencies are neutral between classes cannot be true; the law exists to protect property – hence, by definition, its agents are biased towards the possessing classes and against those with little or no property. Second, the legal profession (judges, barristers and solicitors) largely comes from privileged and wealthy backgrounds and finds it hard to understand or sympathise with ordinary people. Finally, it is expensive to obtain justice; legal fees are high and, since legal aid is granted only to those on very modest incomes, pursuing one's rights in the courts is a privilege largely confined to the rich. 'Equality before the law' and 'the legal rights of the citizen' are mere phrases with scant reference to reality for the majority of the population. Marxists point to contemporary historical experience as further endorsement of their viewpoint. They argue that the challenges to the UK state from Roman Catholics in Northern Ireland, from deprived youth and blacks in the inner cities (the 1981 riots) and from the industrial working class (the miners' strike, 1984–5) have revealed the hard authoritarian core and the naked class interest of the UK state beneath its veneer of impartiality.

☐ *The pluralist debate*

For pluralists the political debate about the British Constitution in recent years has focused upon the two interlinked issues of representation and executive concentration and centralisation. The particular form taken by representative democracy in the UK – the simple plurality electoral system producing and validating a powerful executive government – has given rise to intensely contested debate. This controversy over the rules of the constitution came about largely for two reasons: first, because the political pendulum ceased to swing after 1979, leading to one-party rule; and second, because executive power was first reasserted and then used to make the distribution of power in the political system even more centralised.

The main explanation for the first occurrence was the displacement of predominantly two-party competition by multi-partyism in the 1970s. This had the effect of dividing the opposition to the Conservatives, enabling the party to win four elections in a row after 1979. If the party remains in power until 1997, it will have been in government for eighteen consecutive years. British history since 1867 has been several periods of one-party dominance (the Conservatives, 1886–1906 and 1922–45, Labour 1964–79) but not such a lengthy period of uninterrupted rule by the same party. This situation was compounded by – and was itself in large part both the symptom and the cause of – the demoralisation of the main party of opposition. Labour's effort to turn itself into a credible alternative government by ideological realignment and internal reorganisation is far from complete in 1993. In consequence, the only moderately effective opposition to Conservative Government came from within their own party in the Commons and from the House of Lords, an institution which these Governments could also dominate if they needed to by calling up their full – normally passive – support.

Second, the reassertion of the power of the executive by Conservative governments came about in part as a response to the 'ungovernability' crisis of the 1970s. But it was also a reflection of the authoritarian temper and the 'conviction', anti-consensual politics of the Prime Minister, Margaret Thatcher. Government became more ideological, which made it less disposed to compromise, or to admit to error, and more willing to act blatantly to benefit its own clientele – the City and the well-off in general – and to destroy the ideology and undermine the social base of its main party rival. Greater centralisation and uniformity flowed from the Government's determination to achieve a long-lasting victory over the vested interests which it perceived as blocking the efficient use of resources in both the public and private sectors. Thus, the power of the central state was increased against all subordinate institutions and groups, including the Civil Service, local government, the trade unions, public sector professionals, and the BBC. Internally, as one academic has observed, 'the idea of sovereignty as the ultimate legislative authority has come to mean unlimited jurisdiction and unrestricted power' (Beetham, 1993, pp. 358–9). Only with regard to Europe were Governments prepared – albeit grudgingly and contentiously – to concede increments of power to the European Community.

Conservatives – the sole beneficiaries of one-party government – legitimated their actions by straightforward appeals to the traditional Constitution. Margaret Thatcher always argued that her Governments had acted in accordance with the Constitution, deriving their authority from the electoral process, working through Parliament, and exercising their legitimate powers under the doctrine of parliamentary sovereignty.

The Conservatives used the notion of the electoral mandate in two ways to justify their use of political power. First, when in conflict with institutions like the BBC or groups like the trade unions, they invoked their own accountability to the electorate as affording them superior legitimacy. Second, they believed victory in elections entitled them to implement their party manifestos in full.

They fully endorse the simple plurality system, arguing that British elections are about power – which party shall form the government – rather than the precise representation of every strand of political opinion, a fact which is well understood by voters. The system provides for strong, stable government, and this is exactly what the Conservatives have given the country since 1979. Thus, they conclude, there was nothing novel about British politics in the 1980s in the constitutional sense. The party simply operated the political system in accordance with the British constitutional tradition, which is a Tory tradition, combining democracy with unfettered executive authority.

Increasingly, in recent years, the Conservatives have appealed to certain notions of liberty and democracy in their health and education legislation and especially in the citizen's charters. The notion of liberty involved is economic liberty or market freedom, with citizens perceived as consumers of services, customers or clients, rather than patients, parents, rail users and so on. The notion of democracy is that of empowerment, with the charters designed to 'empower' customers against the providers of the services they use. However, the charters can hardly be spoken of in constitutional terms because although containing statements of *legal* rights, they do not generally increase them.

Critics of the Conservative position (Liberal Democrats, Labour increasingly, academics and journalists) draw upon the **liberal pluralist tradition** of political thought. They point out that it is insufficient to argue, as Conservatives do, that the constitutional rules are being observed to the letter when the complaint is that their spirit is being broken; nor is it valid to argue that the Constitution is being adhered to when it is precisely the Constitution which is in dispute. Liberal pluralists appeal in particular to the concepts and values of fairness; to the idea of intermediary groups and institutions as checks on the executive; and to the notion of political and constitutional accountability.

First, they argue that the way in which the party system functions at present results in continual unfairness to the anti-Conservative majority, both in the UK as a whole, where 58 per cent of electors voted against the winning party in 1992, and in Scotland and Wales, with their permanent anti-Tory majorities. This did not happen in the pre-1970 period when the victorious party normally gained close to 50 per cent of the total vote. In those days, it was reasonable for the electoral winner to claim a 'mandate to govern', especially in the context of consensus politics and fairly regular alternations in power. Now, however, the system delivers just 'the rule of the minority over the majority'. Only the introduction of some system of proportional representation can correct this anomalous situation.

Second, liberal pluralists argue, Conservative Governments have used their parliamentary majority to impose an excessive degree of centralisation and uniformity on the country. They have drastically weakened the main centres of countervailing power, thereby destroying any remaining belief in a balanced constitution. Local government – the only major elective governing institution other than central government itself – has had its powers severely pruned and largely transferred to non-elective centrally controlled agencies. The Thatcherite attack on the top civil service was aimed at producing pliant, uncritical – albeit energetic – executors of ideologically generated change rather than independent-minded public servants. Whilst it may be hard to tell how successfully this goal was carried out, little is heard today of the liberal-bureaucratic and power-bloc theories which stress potential civil service obstructiveness.

In pluralist theory, a publicly funded broadcasting institution such as the BBC has a public service role which may legitimately involve it in broadcasting views critical of the government.

However, the BBC was also subjected to heavy pressure by Conservative governments which equated their own political views automatically with the national interest and saw criticism as the undermining of elected authority. The Conservative determination to challenge producer interests – e.g. educational and health service professionals, public sector workers, and especially the trade unions – had the simultaneous effect of weakening legitimate interests occupying an intermediate role between the state and the individual *and* of undermining political support for Labour.

These developments, liberal pluralists conclude, have a twofold importance. First, they reveal the extreme feebleness of constraints on executive power in Britain. Traditionally, checks on this power have been seen to derive from four sources: public opinion; legally established rights; formal constitutional checks embodied in Parliament; and the potential for resistance in sub-national and national political institutions and social groups. None of these alleged restraints proved effective in the 1980s. Parliament, despite frequent well-publicised opposition from Conservative backbenchers or from the House of Lords, proved no more than a minor irritant to a determined Government. An unpopular measure such as the 'poll tax' was enacted without difficulty and, what is more, with minimal discussion and consultation with interested groups. Moreover, in a series of cases involving public order, national security and terrorism, the common law proved too flexible and judges often too executive-minded to provide adequate protection for the civil liberties of individuals and minority groups.

Second, pluralists believe, such measures as the transference of many responsibilities to non-elected 'quangos' and the 'hiving-off' of large parts of the civil service to executive agencies severely diminish political and constitutional accountability and undermine democracy, creating a 'democratic deficit'. At the present time, it has been argued, Britain 'is witnessing a revolution in public life which will quadruple the number of unelected agencies running key services and hand them responsibility for dispensing nearly a quarter of all government spending by 1996'. (*The Guardian* 19 November 1993) Under Conservative Governments power has been shifted from democratically-elected bodies to agencies administered by people appointed directly or indirectly by Ministers. An unelected and unaccountable 'new magistracy' is now responsible for large and growing areas of British life. (Chapter 10) In sum, Britain has degenerated into an 'elective dictatorship', a situation only remediable by radical constitutional reform, including such measures as the strengthening of Parliament against the executive, a Bill of Rights, devolution and the reinvigoration of the elective principle.

Summary

British elites are generally drawn from privileged social backgrounds although some élites do contain significant minorities of working and lower middle class origin. Business and the professions predominate in the political élite – at parliamentary and Cabinet levels, and all but a small minority of Conservative Cabinet ministers have been educated privately rather than in the state system. Whilst most élites have become more open during the twentieth century, change has been only gradual, and in some traditional élites remarkably small. Models of the distribution of power in British society are influenced by the particular questions they ask and by their ideological assumptions. The pluralist concept of competition for power between and within élites gets closer to political realities than the notions of a ruling class or power élite but is not beyond criticism.

Serious political controversy has emerged over the formal constitutional distribution of power in Britain. The Conservatives defend their record in terms of restoring the traditional authority of government and of empowering citizens; liberal pluralists criticise the electoral system for permitting 'minority one-party government' and attack recent governments for centralising and concentrating power at the expense of intermediary groups and institutions and civil liberties;

and Marxists believe that the most important feature of political life is the power placed by the capitalist system in the hands of the major financial institutions and multinational corporations and the need for this power to be controlled in the interests of the majority.

Questions

1. 'Intermediate institutions between the state and the individual have been gravely weakened in Britain.' Has this happened? If so, does it matter and why?

2. Examine the view that an 'Establishment' exists in Britain.

Assignment

Give a short summary of the arguments for and against the idea that to have more poor people, women and blacks in Parliament would make a real difference to decision-making.

Further reading

Baker, D., Gamble, A. and Ludlam, S. (1992) 'More "Classless" and Less "Thatcherite"? Conservative Ministers and New Conservative MPs after the 1992 Election', *Parliamentary Affairs*, October.

Brown, C. (1989) 'Pluralism – A Lost Perspective?', *Talking Politics*, 1: 3, summer.

Burch, M. and Moran, M. (1985) 'The Changing British Political Élite, 1945–1983', *Parliamentary Affairs*, 38, winter.

Coates, D. (1984) *The Context of British Politics* (London: Hutchinson).

Coxall, B. (1992) 'The Social Context of British Politics: Class, Gender and Race in the Two Major Parties, 1970–1990' in B. Jones and L. Robins (eds) *Two Decades in British Politics* (Manchester: Manchester University Press).

Dunleavy, P., Gamble, A., Holliday, I. and Peele, G. (eds.) (1993), *Developments in British Politics 4* (London: Macmillan) (see especially the contributions by G. Peele 'The Constitution' and D. Beetham, 'Political theory and British politics'.)

Judge, D. (1993) *The Parliamentary State* (London: Sage).

Miliband, R. (1984) *Capitalist Democracy in Britain* (Oxford: Oxford University Press).

Moran, M. (1989) *Politics and Society in Britain*, 2nd edn (London: Macmillan).

■ *Chapter 33* ■

From Thatcher to Major

The Thatcher record
The Post-Thatcher Years: A New Consensus?

The 1992 General Election
After the 1992 General Election

At the time of writing the first edition of this book, Margaret Thatcher was still in power. Analysis of the record of her premiership was necessarily incomplete and comment on the nature of her probable political legacy inevitably tentative. With a clearer perspective now available, we analyse the 'pros' and 'cons' of her record before turning to a consideration of how far a new policy 'consensus' had emerged in the 1990s. We next examine contemporary Conservatism, focusing on the problems facing the Major Government after the 1992 General Election, and on prospects for the future. We begin with the record of the three Thatcher governments 1979–90, couched in the form of a debate between a supporter and a critic of Thatcherism.

■ The Thatcher Record

□ *Foreign Policy*

Margaret Thatcher restored British prestige in the world. She put the 'great' back into Great Britain.

Margaret Thatcher suffered from the same delusions about Britain's international importance as her predecessors in the post war period.

Anti-Soviet Communism

Thatcher's tough anti-Soviet Communist stance based on intensified nuclear deterrence, higher defence spending and renewed close relationship

with the USA helped achieve first détente and then the collapse of the USSR. She flexibly softened her 'Iron Lady' image in the mid-80s to act as a valuable intermediary between Reagan and Gorbachev and to restrain the US 'Star Wars' programme.

The main external architect of Soviet disintegration was the US not the UK. Thatcher's renewed emphasis on military strength increased Britain's problem of excessive defence spending in relation to size of the economy compared with other middle-ranking powers. The Anglo-US relationship was, in fact, too close, leaving Britain unable to protest effectively over the US invasion of Grenada (1983) or to resist US use of air bases in Britain for air strikes on Libya (1986). Thatcher's influence in the US declined swiftly in the period after the Cold War and the collapse of the USSR.

The Falklands War (1982)

Victory in the Falklands was a superb demonstration of British military skill and courage which 'finally laid the ghost of Suez' (Nigel Lawson,1988). The feat would have been inconceivable without Thatcher and placed her in the tradition of Churchill as a great war leader. Blame for the war lay primarily with the Argentinian President, General Galtieri. The war led to increased respect for Britain abroad.

The War was an unnecessary one to which the Government's diplomatic mistakes made a significant contribution: the withdrawal of HMS

476

Endurance, the South Atlantic ice-patrol ship in early 1982, sent the wrong signals to the Argentinian junta; also, Thatcher failed to send Galtieri an ultimatum in the week before the invasion. A diversion from the long-term search for a negotiated settlement over the Falklands with Argentina, the war was a very dangerous if not reckless enterprise which owed its narrow success to US support (intelligence and Ascension Island facilities) as well as the courage and skill of the British military forces. The price of victory was 255 British dead and 777 wounded. Seen by most of the rest of the world as 'a bizarre imperial hangover' (Reynolds 1991, p. 261), the war unleashed an unpleasant strain of British chauvinism and led to huge expenditure (£5 billion) to defend 'Fortress Falklands'.

Colonial settlements (i.e. Rhodesia and Hong-Kong)

These showed Thatcher to be a more flexible and pragmatic politician than generally believed.

The settlements occurred against her instincts, owed most to her Foreign Ministers (Carrington and Howe respectively) and merely continued an inevitable decolonisation process.

The European Community (EC)

Thatcher successfully negotiated a large budget rebate for Britain, and in doing so focused EC attention on budget reform.

In the late 1980s, having signed the Single European Act (1986), Thatcher resisted closer European integration in the cause of the preservation of national sovereignty and an alternative vision of a looser free-market-based Community of independent states.

Thatcher's success on the budget was a short-term one on a minor issue; moreover, it was won at the cost of alienating Britain's partners by her confrontational style. Thatcher's attitude in the late 1980s only delayed without diverting progress towards EC goals whilst at the same time contributing further towards the isolation of

Britain on the continent as a reluctant European. A more cooperative attitude – backed by the 'realpolitik' practised by other EC states – would have served British interests better.

☐ The Economy

Thatcher's anti-statist, anti-corporatist, monetarist, supply-side economic policies were a necessary reaction against the Keynesianism which had led only to 'stag-flation' and industrial paralysis in the 1970s. These radical policies administered a vital shock to the economy, and underlay a rapid growth in labour productivity in British manufacturing industry. The rate of this productivity growth between 1979 and 1989 not only far exceeded that of the previous period (1973–9) but also put Britain ahead of the G7 (group of major industrial countries) average and of most of the rest of Europe. In terms of overall economic growth, Britain was enjoying higher growth rates than her major competitors between 1987 and 1989 and over the whole period (1979–90) the gap between Britain and other advanced industrial countries narrowed (Figure 33.1 and Tables 33.1, 33.2).

Table 33.1 *Britain's economic record under Thatcher: historical comparisons*

Rates of change in GDP

1951	1.9	1961	2.7	1971	1.7	1981	−1.2
1952	0.8	1962	1.4	1972	2.8	1982	1.7
1953	3.9	1963	4.0	1973	7.4	1983	3.8
1954	4.2	1964	5.6	1974	−1.5	1984	1.8
1955	3.6	1965	2.9	1975	−0.8	1985	3.8
1956	1.4	1966	1.9	1976	2.6	1986	3.6
1957	1.7	1967	2.2	1977	2.6	1987	4.4
1958	−0.2	1968	4.4	1978	2.9	1988	4.7
1959	4.0	1969	2.5	1979	2.8	1989	2.1
1960	5.6	1970	2.0	1980	−2.0	1990	0.5
						1991	−2.5

Average 1964–70 2.6   1974–9 2.0 1980–91 1.7

Source: CSO Blue Book, cited in Guardian, 12 March 1992.

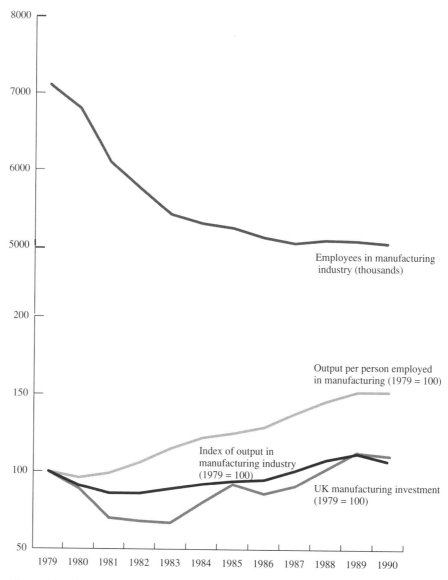

Source: Data from *Economic Trends* annual supplement cited in *Guardian*, 12 March, 1992.

Figure 33.1   *Britain's economic record under Thatcher: manufacturing and productivity*

The Thatcherite monetarist experiment was a failure, and was quietly abandoned in the mid-1980s but not unfortunately before it had driven the British economy into a much more severe recession than experienced elsewhere. The consequence was the loss of 2 million jobs in manufacturing and a serious loss of manufacturing capacity so that output rose little between 1979 and 1992. The abandonment of all macro economic policy objectives except for the control of inflation constitutes an abdication of the state's responsibility for the overall development of the economy. The productivity gains were probably once-for-all, and despite the benefits of North Sea

Annual growth rates per head in UK and other countries						
	USA	Japan	France	WGmy	Italy	UK
79	0.9	4.7	2.7	4.1	5.7	2.7
80	−1.3	2.8	0.9	0.7	4.0	−2.3
81	1.2	2.8	0.6	0.0	0.4	−1.4
82	−3.6	2.5	1.7	−0.9	0.0	1.8
83	2.9	2.0	0.3	1.9	0.6	3.6
84	6.2	3.6	1.1	3.2	2.4	2.0
85	2.8	4.3	1.4	2.2	2.3	3.3
86	2.2	2.0	2.0	2.1	2.8	3.7
87	2.5	3.6	1.7	1.4	2.9	4.5
88	3.5	5.8	3.4	3.1	3.9	4.0
89	1.8	4.2	3.1	2.3	2.9	2.0
90	−0.1	5.3	2.1	2.8	1.7	0.5
Average 79–90...	1.6	3.5	1.7	1.7	2.2	1.9

Source: Adapted from *Guardian*, 12 March 1992.

Table 33.2 *Britain's economic record under Thatcher: comparisons with leading industrial countries*

oil, Britain's growth rate in the 1980s (1980–88) was lower than for earlier periods. (Table 33.1). If her predecessors bore a share of the responsibility for the early 1980s recession, the blame for the late 1980s recession was hers alone.

Thatcher's most important achievements were:

- **The encouragement of popular capitalism** by cutting taxes on income and capital, increasing the number of individual shareholders (from 7 per cent to 21 per cent of the adult population) and raising home ownership (from 52 per cent to 66 per cent of all households). Her period in office also saw increased company formation and a large expansion in self-employment.

- **Pushing back the frontiers of the state** by a massive privatisation programme, the reduction of public expenditure from 44 per cent to 39 per cent of GDP, and an arm's length attitude to powerful interest groups.

- **Curbing the power of the trade unions** by amongst other things abolishing the closed

shop, outlawing secondary picketing and making pre-strike ballots compulsory. Thatcher's government also won bruising battles against the steel unions (1982) and (especially) the miners' union (1984–5). The result was a steady fall in the number of strikes in the late 1980s and overall a marked improvement in Britain's strike record compared with the 1960s and 1970s (Figure 33.2).

- *Popular capitalism is a misnomer since Thatcher tax cuts (from 80 per cent to 40 per cent in top rate, 33 per cent to 25 per cent in basic rate) benefited the rich vastly more than the poor, with 21 per cent of the total income tax cuts going to the top 0.1 per cent on over £70000 a year whilst a mere 2 per cent of the cuts went to the bottom 11 per cent on under £5000 a year. Moreover, cuts in income tax were more than offset by increases in indirect taxes such as VAT and in national insurance contributions. The tax burden as a percentage of gross domestic product (GDP) actually increased from 34 per cent to 37 per cent, 1979–90. The Government believed as an article of faith that tax cuts improve incentives whereas in practice there is no clear-cut relationship between government tax-cutting and individuals working harder. Finally, 60 per cent of the 11 million shareholders held only one share and many bought shares for quick resale profits: 'casino capitalism' is a more appropriate description of the Government's policy.*

- *The Conservatives sold national assets too cheaply, and failed to give sufficient attention to the restructuring and break-up of large corporations pre-privatisation with the result that private sector monopolies were created out of the former nationalised utilities. The Government also forfeited control in areas of key national interest such as energy policy. Public expenditure as a proportion of GDP proved difficult to reduce (it actually rose over the first five years of Thatcher's premiership) and did not decline until the economic boom of the late 1980s. Government spending as a*

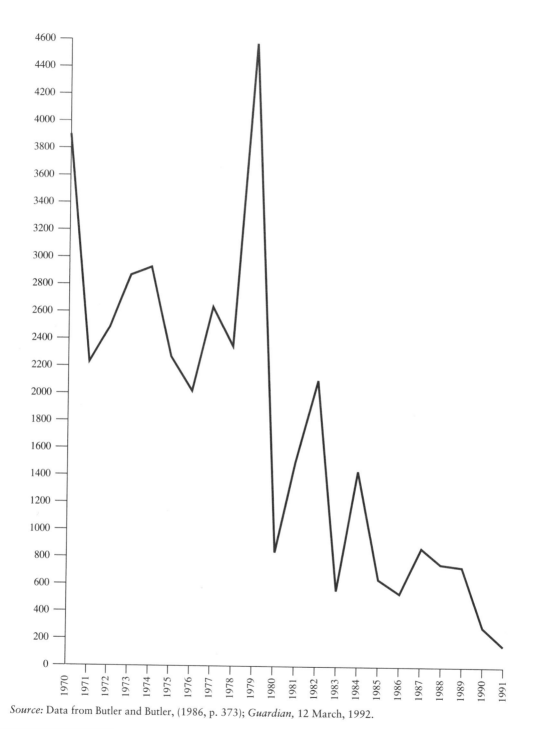

Source: Data from Butler and Butler, (1986, p. 373); *Guardian,* 12 March, 1992.

Figure 33.2   *Strikes: number of stoppages beginning in each year, 1970–91*

proportion of GDP was 43.2 per cent in 1978–9, 46.8 per cent in 1982–5, and 39.5 per cent in 1990–1. It rose to 45 per cent in 1993–4. The late 1980s reduction in public spending as a proportion of GDP was socially harmful, leading to an impoverishment of the public services and infrastructure and to the emergence of a significant gap between UK public spending and the other EC countries.

- *Britain's strike record certainly improved in the 1980s compared with the 1960s and 1970s but this achievement looks less impressive when international comparisons are introduced as strike activity declined in most advanced industrial countries in this period, often to lower levels than in Britain. Unemployment (over 3 million by mid-1986) was more responsible for reducing union membership and strike activity than trade union legislation. The labour law reforms were not accompanied by the improvement of employment rights of workers which remain weak by international standards.*

☐ *The Welfare State*

Margaret Thatcher's drive for greater efficiency and value for money in the welfare services, increased targeting of help to those most in need and a greater role for private provision and voluntary sector involvement were a necessary response to the late 1970s' crisis comprising increasing public demand in the sphere of welfare, weak economic growth, and the domination of the provision of services by the public sector professionals and manual worker unions. Unable to launch a frontal attack on the welfare state because of continuing public support, Thatcher was obliged to proceed more gradually and indirectly than she wished. The major steps were:

- encouraging private provision in education, pensions, health insurance and housing;
- launching efficiency drives to ensure 'value for money' in public provided services such as the NHS;

- making provision for the 'contracting out' of certain services within, e.g., health and education by competitive private tendering;
- making savings at the margin by, e.g., scaling down formula for pension increases, uprating some benefits by less than the rate of inflation;
- encouraging voluntary provision by charities (some of which received government grants);
- encouraging housing associations and housing trusts to provide low-cost rented accommodation in place of local authorities.

More fundamental reforms have been:

- the move away from universal towards targeting help where it is most needed by freezing child benefit and channelling resources towards poor families by income support (which replaced supplementary benefit) and family credit (which replaced family income supplement);
- attacking the 'dependency culture' by denying benefits to 16–17-year-olds who refuse a place on the Youth Training Scheme;
- a very large-scale restructuring of health and education after 1988 involving notably the establishment of 'internal markets'.

New Right attacks on the welfare state and (less radical) Government action failed to shift the consensus in favour of public provision of health, education and pensions. In fact, state social expenditure in real terms increased by about 20 per cent after 1979 despite the prioritisation of defence (to mid-80s) and law and order. Public expenditure on health and social security actually rose as a proportion of GDP (the latter mainly as a result of the rise in unemployment), education spending also rose in real terms whilst holding steady as a proportion of GDP but public spending on housing dropped sharply in real terms and as a proportion of GDP (Table 33.3). The Government's worst failure – compounded by its ideological preference for 'targeting' benefits on the poorest – was the huge rise in poverty: between 1979 and 1985, the number of people at or below the official poverty line (the supplementary benefit level) rose by 55 per cent from 5.1 million to 9.4 million, representing 17 per cent of the population. This constituted by far the largest increase in the EC. With the numbers on income support and one-parent benefit rising by over 2 million during the 1980s, the Conservatives signally failed to eliminate the 'dependency culture'. Overall, the Thatcher governments missed the golden opportunity provided by enhanced revenues from North Sea oil and privatisation to improve the welfare state.

The Post-Thatcher Years: A New Consensus?

What has been the impact of Thatcherism on British politics? In particular, how far has it brought about permanent changes in public opinion and the policies of the main political parties on the role of the state? To what extent is a new post-Thatcherite political consensus discernible in the early 1990s?

A series of 'State of the Nation' polls carried out by ICM for the *Guardian* provides valuable data on the state of public opinion on a range of central social and economic issues. These polls broadly confirm Ivor Crewe's conclusion in 1989 that 'there has been no Thatcherite transformation of attitudes or behaviour among the British public'. On the welfare state, the evidence is more clear-cut than on the economy. There is widespread support for the principle of state-funded education and health services and considerable doubts about the trustworthiness of Conservative governments to run them (Table 33.4). This ICM

Table 33.3 *Government spending, 1979–1990: main items* (as % of total government expenditure and of GDP)

Housing		
	1979–1980	1989–1990
% of total	7.3	2.9
% of GDP	2.7	0.9
Defence		
	1979–1980	1989–1990
% of total	11.9	11.7
% of GDP	4.7	4.0
Social Security		
	1979–80	1989–90
% of total	25.9	29.7
% of GDP	9.6	10.2
Education and science		
	1979–1980	1989–1990
% of total	14.5	14.6
% of GDP	5.4	5.0
Health		
	1979–1980	1989–1990
% of total	12.1	13.8
% of GDP	4.5	4.7
Law and order		
	1979–1980	1989–1990
% of total	4.1	5.6
% of GDP	1.5	1.9

Source: Data extracted from the *Guardian*, 12 March 1992, derived and recalculated from Public Expenditure Analyses to 1994–95, HM Treasury.

Table 33.4 *Public opinion poll, 1993*

HEALTH SERVICE
The NHS is safer in Mr Major's hands

	Now	92	91	90	Men	Wom	Con	Lab	Ldm
agree	13	27	30	18	14	13	43	4	6
disagree	75	53	49	68	76	75	40	91	85
difference	−62	−26	−19	−50	−62	−62	+3	−87	−79
neither	8	11	13	9	7	8	12	3	6
don't know	4	9	8	5	3	4	5	2	2

STATE EDUCATION
State schools are safer in Mr Major's hands

	Now	92	91	90	Men	Wom	Con	Lab	Ldm
agree	18	33	36	22	19	16	51	6	8
disagree	69	47	44	61	69	70	31	89	79
difference	−57	−14	−8	−39	−50	−54	+20	−83	−71
neither	8	10	12	11	7	9	14	3	8
don't know	5	10	9	6	5	5	4	3	5

Source: ICM 'State of the Nation' poll published in the *Guardian* 17 September, 1993.

finding is underlined by an NOP survey during the 1992 General Election campaign which revealed the dissatisfaction with the Government's 'internal market' health and education reforms. A large majority (56 per cent to 30 per cent) favoured scrapping the recent changes to the way the National Health Service was run whilst more respondents disapproved (42 per cent) than approved (37 per cent) of the policy of helping more schools to opt out of local authority control. (*The Independent*, 26 March 1992).

Further confirmation of the public's 'collectivist' attitudes to welfare provision is the consistent lead on pensions, health and education enjoyed by Labour in the polls.

But public spending on the welfare state and taxation are interlinked. How do people respond when pollsters ask questions which make this connection? The polls suggest a steady movement of public opinion during the 1980s against tax-cutting and in favour of more spending on state education and the NHS. There was an exactly equal division in May 1979 between those who favoured tax cuts even if it meant some reduction in state health, education and welfare services and those who considered that these services should be extended even if it meant some increase in taxes; however, by April 1989, the latter group very considerably outnumbered the former (tax-cutting) group (Gallup, cited in Kavanagh, 1990, p. 297).

However, this finding is more ambiguous than it seems. Table 33.5 reveals a division between personal and public interest in people's minds when they consider the tax cuts versus public spending issue. When thinking of the national interest, more people prefer public spending to tax cuts but when thinking of their personal and family interest, more people (just) favour tax cuts over public spending. Moreover, in deciding how to vote, a far larger number are influenced by their personal interest than are swayed by the national interest.

However, the Liberal Democrat proposal of a tax increase for a specific purpose (a rise of 1p in the pound to be spent on education) received a favourable response. According to NOP, 78 per cent approved the proposal to earmark or 'hypothecate' taxation in this way as compared with only 15 per cent who disapproved of it (*The Independent*, 26 March 1992). Overall, then, the polls evidence suggests continuing public support for 'collective' – as opposed to private – provision of welfare services, but serious divisions of opinion when taxes are brought into the picture.

On economic issues, a majority favours an anti-Keynesian and Thatcherite stance on government borrowing to invest (Table 33.6) and the Thatcherite arm's-length policy towards the political role of the trade unions also enjoys majority support (Table 33.7). Public opinion has been consistent on these issues since the mid-

Table 33.5   *Tax cuts versus public spending – the personal/public interest division*

	Voting intention				Social class			
	All voters	Con	Lab	Alli	AB	C1	C2	DE
What matters more to you and your family?								
To reduce taxes	47 (46)	61 (61)	36 (33)	42 (45)	55 (57)	48 (51)	48 (47)	41 (36)
To increase public spending	45 (46)	30 (32)	57 (59)	53 (48)	38 (38)	46 (41)	44 (44)	50 (54)
What is more important for the country as a whole?								
To reduce taxes	37 (34)	45 (43)	33 (29)	30 (25)	36 (35)	33 (33)	38 (35)	39 (34)
To increase public spending	54 (55)	42 (46)	60 (64)	65 (66)	59 (55)	56 (57)	53 (53)	50 (56)
Whose interests will be more important in determining how your friends vote?								
Theirs and their families'	59	57	63	59	57	60	62	55
The country's as a whole	19	21	16	22	25	18	17	19

Source: Marplan, *Guardian*, 13 March 1987.

GOVERNMENT BORROWING
The economy would be stronger if the Government
borrowed more money and used it for investment

	Now	92	91	90	Men	Wom	Con	Lab	Ldm
agree	33	33	31	28	31	37	28	39	31
disagree	44	37	44	43	46	40	51	38	45
difference	–11	–4	–13	–15	–15	–3	–23	+1	–14
neither	14	14	13	17	12	15	15	12	15
don't know	10	17	12	13	6	14	6	11	9

Source: As Table 33.4.

Table 33.6 *Public opinion poll, 1993*

TRADE UNIONS
Trade unions should have more say in the running of
industry and the economy

	Now	92	91	90	Men	Wom	Con	Lab	Ldm
agree	39	35	35	31	40	39	18	61	32
disagree	49	47	50	51	51	47	76	29	56
difference	–10	–12	–15	–20	–11	–8	–58	+32	–24
neither	9	10	10	10	8	9	5	9	11
don't know	3	8	6	6	2	5	3	2	1

Source: As Table 33.4.

Table 33.7 *Public opinion poll, 1993*

1980s. On other issues, however, it has fluctuated, apparently in response to particular circumstances. Thus, in 1985 (high unemployment) only 32 per cent agreed and 57 per cent disagreed – that it was more important for the Government to control inflation than to reduce unemployment (Marplan); in 1990 (lower unemployment), a majority emphasised controlling inflation over cutting unemployment; whilst in 1993 (higher unemployment) the pendulum of opinion had swung once more in favour of reducing unemployment (Table 33.8).

Similarly, on nationalisation/privatisation, public opinion has fluctuated over time. Thus, between 1964 and 1983, support for privatisation increased, but it seems to have declined steadily from the mid-1980s : 39 per cent favoured selling off profitable state industries to the

private sector in 1985, but only 18 per cent did so in 1993 (Table 33.9). Initial support for Thatcherite policies in this sphere has therefore waned, no doubt reflecting the unpopularity of later privatisations such as water and the railways. Finally, a somewhat surprising feature of the 1993 ICM poll was the 46–28 per cent vote in favour of 'more socialist planning'.

In general, then, although making some inroads into public opinion in areas such as taxation, government borrowing and reducing the political influence of the trade unions, Thatcherite social and economic priorities are a long way from dominance. Public opinion has swung strongly away from privatisation and in favour of prioritising the reduction of unemployment over controlling inflation. A majority of voters (58 per cent) voted for parties which

Table 33.8 *Public opinion poll, 1993*

INFLATION
It is more important for the Government to control
inflation than to reduce unemployment

	Now	92	91	90	Men	Wom	Con	Lab	Ldm
agree	34	34	40	45	35	33	58	25	29
disagree	52	46	43	31	50	52	27	64	53
difference	–18	–12	–3	+14	–15	–19	+31	–39	–24
neither	11	11	11	16	11	12	14	8	15
don't know	3	9	6	7	3	4	1	3	2

Source: As Table 33.4.

Table 33.9 *Public opinion poll, 1993*

PRIVATISATION
Profitable state industries should be sold off and run as
private companies

	Now	92	91	90	Men	Wom	Con	Lab	Ldm
agree	18	22	26	22	19	17	41	8	11
disagree	71	58	58	58	70	70	46	85	77
difference	–53	–36	–32	–36	–51	–53	–5	–77	–66
neither	7	10	9	11	8	7	10	4	8
don't know	4	10	7	6	3	5	2	4	2

Source: As Table 33.4.

favoured tax increases of one kind or another in 1992. Finally, support for 'collective' provision of the 'core' welfare services (education, health and pensions) has remained firm throughout the 1980s and early 1990s.

Arguably, Thatcherism had a greater impact on élite opinion than on public opinion. Thus, Labour had already accepted council house sales and much Conservative trade union legislation before 1987 and this movement to the right on the role of the state continued in the Policy Review (1987–9). With Major trimming to the left after 1990 with calls for a more compassionate society and pushing through the Citizen's Charters for greater quality in the public services, many argue that by the 1992 General Election, Britain had returned to a 'social democratic consensus'. One academic commentator has written:

> The 1992 election was the first since 1966 to be fought by three centrist parties; arguably there were fewer policy differences between the Conservative and Labour parties than at any time this century. The centre ground has shifted, however: the new consensus is not the old post-war settlement of welfare Keynesianism within the Atlantic Alliance but a post-Thatcher settlement of the 'social market' within the European Community, in which the state's role is limited to the supply side of the economy and selective, targeted welfare. (Crewe, 1993, p. 110–11).

Another commentator agrees that the new consensus is based upon the idea of the 'social market', arguing further that perhaps 'the European dimension' is the 'central feature' of this new consensus. It is, he continues, 'broadly post-Keynesian and neo-welfarist', standing 'somewhere between post-war social democracy and the Thatcherism of the 1980s' (Heywood, 1991–2, p. 74).

The idea of the 'social market' consensus has much to commend it, the main factor making it 'post-Thatcherite' arguably being the European dimension. But convergence between the parties, although real, should not be exaggerated. Europe apart, the Major Government's economic prospectus is pure Thatcherism and his 'social liberalism' insufficient to make him reconsider

any turning back on the Thatcherite injection of 'market disciplines' into the health and education services. By contrast, Labour's 1992 manifesto did propose (modest) increases in tax and national insurance contributions, a return of water and the National Grid to the public sector, and no more privatisations.

■ The 1992 General Election

Post-election analysis of the result suggested several key factors in the Conservative victory. First, the Conservatives had a very considerable advantage on the leadership issue, with 52 per cent supporting Major but only 23 per cent endorsing Kinnock as likely to make the 'best Prime Minister' (Gallup, 10–11 April 1992). Second, whilst Labour enjoyed a significant advantage over the Conservatives with regard to education, health and unemployment, this was more than offset by the Conservative lead on economic competence: 53 per cent to 35 per cent according to a BBC/NOP exit poll.

Although concerned about the recession and falling living standards, the public attributed the main blame for the poor state of the economy either to world economic conditions or to Margaret Thatcher's Government. Finally, several other factors played a small but important role: the Conservative assault on Labour as the party of higher taxation; the Conservative tabloid press's vitriolic attack on Labour, especially on Neil Kinnock; and the final week Conservative squeeze on the Liberal Democrat vote by talking of it as the 'Trojan Horse' of a Labour Britain.

Labour after its fourth consecutive defeat faced a policy/strategy dilemma summarisable as a choice between undertaking a 'fundamental rethink' and simply placing its faith in 'one more heave'. What a 'fundamental rethink' might produce is hard to predict but suggestions have included the following: abandoning the present electoral system in favour of proportional representation and more positive cooperation with the Liberals; embracing environmentalism more whole-heartedly; taking a stronger line on the promotion of women within the party and of 'women's issues'; abandoning 'Labourism', which would involve the removal of the privileged position of the trade unions within the party; and becoming a social democratic party in the mainstream of the European left by dispensing with the largely symbolic but electorally damaging commitments to 'socialism' in its rhetoric and in clause iv of its constitution.

Supporters of 'one more heave' argue that Labour's traditional commitments to Labourism and socialism should be preserved rather than ditched out of misguided understandings of electoral expediency. They point to gradual increases in the Labour vote and parliamentary representation between 1983 and 1992 and to its large lead in the polls (18 per cent, September 1993) as obviating the need for fundamental changes in the nature of the party, its strategy and its policies.

■ After the 1992 General Election

British politics continued to revolve around the major issues of Europe, the economy and government spending.

□ *Europe*

The Conservative Government enjoyed only the briefest respite after its 1992 General Election victory before the re-emergence of political difficulties over Europe. These arose first over Britain's membership of the European Exchange Rate Mechanism (ERM) and second over the ratification of the Maastricht Treaty.

'Black Wednesday' 16 September 1992

Membership of the ERM was the central means for attaining the goal of zero inflation which was Thatcher's principal legacy to her successor. When she finally agreed to join the ERM in October 1990, she had insisted on sterling's entry at a rate of DM2.95.

Major consistently reiterated his determination to keep Britain within the ERM at this parity until a wave of speculative trading in the financial markets in September 1992 finally led to Britain's exit from the ERM in dramatic circumstances. This removed the central plank of the Government's macroeconomic policy. The goal of 'bearing down' on inflation remained, but the main means for its attainment had disappeared. The Major Government's delay in bringing forward new economic policy proposals undermined public confidence at an early stage. However, the effective devaluation of the pound – which all parties had categorically ruled out only a few months before – was widely expected to boost exports and enhance Britain's prospects of recovery from the recession.

Political speculation now switched to the timing – and circumstances – in which Britain might re-enter the ERM. In Autumn 1993, this moment seemed to have been deferred to the late 1990s, with John Major assuring Conservative Euro-sceptics during the third reading of the Maastricht Bill that Britain's opt-out on monetary union (EMU) meant that there was no obligation to re-enter the ERM 'unless and until we decide to seek to enter a single European currency', i.e. in 1997 or 1999. Major also confirmed that Britain would retain control of its monetary policy throughout stages two and three of the Maastricht economic union process 'for so long as we don't participate in a single monetary policy'. For Euro-enthusiasts, the Government's apparent decision not to make a firm commitment to rejoin the ERM as soon as possible at a more realistic parity revived the spectre of European 'fast-track' countries (West Germany, France, Benelux) going ahead to monetary union without Britain, thereby creating a 'two-tier' EU with an uninfluential Britain relegated to the sidelines.

The Maastricht Treaty

Policy towards the European Community had divided the Conservative Party from the mid-1980s. It underlay Thatcher's difficulties with her Chancellor of the exchequer, Nigel Lawson, and her Foreign Secretary, Sir Geoffrey Howe, both of whom were pressing for Britain to join the ERM.

Ultimately, differences over Europe led to Howe's resignation (November 1990) and a bitter resignation speech which fatally undermined Thatcher's leadership, setting in train the sequence of events which resulted in her downfall.

The EC Maastricht Summit

Shortly before the EC Summit met to consider steps towards deepening the Community, Thatcher called for the Government to agree to hold a referendum on British participation in a single European currency, a demand that underlined the possible difficulties from Conservative Euro-sceptics facing Prime Minister Major as he began the negotiations. The Treaty on European Union (agreed at the December 1991 Summit, signed in February 1992 and finally ratified in November 1993) had two main aspects – economic and monetary; and political. First, member states agreed to adopt a single currency by 1 January 1999 at the latest, this move constituting the third and final stage of European Monetary Union (EMU). A largely independent European Central Bank (ECB) will be in control of monetary policy, and strict 'convergence' conditions – specifying exchange-rate stability, low inflation and interest rates, and small budget deficits and government debt/GDP ratios – will have to be met before member states can join the single currency. Second, the political clauses changed the character of the EC by making citizens of member states into citizens of a European Union with rights to live, work, vote and become candidates in municipal and European elections in any country within the Union, and to petition the European Parliament. In addition, the Treaty strengthened the powers of the European Parliament, established a Committee of the Regions and extended the scope of the Community within certain policy areas, including public health, the environment, culture and education, and transport and communications. Finally, it created several new 'pillars' of the European Union outside the EC in the spheres of foreign policy, defence, fighting crime and, most controversially, social policy (Exhibit 33.1).

The British Prime Minister's negotiating efforts were devoted successfully to persuading his EC partners to permit the UK to 'opt out' of the third stage of monetary union leading to a single currency. Britain will join in the second stage of EMU but will be under no obligation to proceed to the final stage; however, it may do so if it wishes. His stance reflected the distaste felt by many in his party for a single currency – involving the extinction of sterling – and the subordination of national control over the economy to the decisions of the European Central Bank.

Second, John Major resisted the inclusion of a 'social chapter' within the Maastricht Treaty, thereby forcing his EC partners to agree a social policy protocol outside the Treaty. The 'social chapter' to which Britain objected involved measures to improve working conditions within the EC such as limiting working hours, providing workers with more information and establishing equality between the sexes at work. The main objections to these measures were that they would impede free market competition and reverse the trade union legislation of the 1980s. But the UK has a high proportion of working women and part-time workers and sets no statutory limit to the length of the working day. A powerful underlying reason for the Government's opposition to the 'social chapter' was that it would raise wage costs, thereby making the country a less attractive venue for inward investment, especially from Japan.

Opposition criticisms of the deal struck by the Government focused on the emerging danger of a 'two-tier' Europe; the advantages of EMU which Britain had sacrificed, including the possibility of having the European Central Bank situated in the UK; and the 'message' implicit in the Government's attitude to the 'social chapter' that Britain had become a 'cheap labour economy' unwilling to offer the same protection of workers' rights as the poorest members of the European Community.

After early post-General Election expressions in May and June 1992, discontent within the Conservative Party on Europe resurfaced in the wake of Britain's forced departure from the ERM. Emboldened by referendums in Denmark (defeat for Maastricht) and France (narrow

Exhibit 33.1   *The Maastricht Treaty programme for economic and monetary union (agreed December 1991)*

Stage I
1 July 1990
- Currency linkage through EMS
- Abolition of all controls over capital movements
- Initiate convergence process towards four criteria
  - Inflation within 1.5% of three lowest
  - Interest rates within 2% of three lowest
  - Budget deficit not excessive
  - No downward devaluation over past two years
- Process monitored by Council of Ministers, Economic and Finance Ministers (ECOFIN)
- Completion of Single European Market (SEM)

Stage II
1 January 1994
- Creation of European Monetary Institute (EMI) to replace Committee of Central Bank Governors and to implement EMU
- Convergence monitored with greater vigour
- Report on progress by ECOFIN on 31 December 1996 detailing EMU membership and timetable

Stage III
1 January 1999 (unless otherwise specified)
- Creation of European System of Central Banks (ESCB) comprising the European Central Bank (ECB) and the national Central Banks
- ECB and national banks to become fully independent
- ESCB objective is 'price stability'
- ECU becomes common currency in substitution for national currencies
- Procedures for controlling budget deficits strengthened
- Official foreign exchange reserves to be managed by ECB

Source: Maastricht Treaty; see extracts in Gros and Thygesen (1992, pp. 427–59) cited Wilks (1993, p. 230).

victory for the Treaty) which suggested serious popular reservations about the programme on the Continent, Conservative Euro-sceptics mounted fierce antagonism to the Treaty at the annual conference, and dissident backbenchers continued the protest in Parliament through the ratification process. Not until July 1993 was the Bill's progress through the House of Commons complete. Bitter divisions over Europe are likely to continue to bedevil the Conservatives.

☐ *The Economy*

Thatcher's legacy to Major was an economy already in recession with rising unemployment, declining growth, high inflation, and adverse balances on trade and payments. The immediate cause of these economic difficulties was the excessive expansion of the economy under Nigel Lawson in 1987–8; Lawson's tax cuts combined with the effects of economic liberalisation throughout the 1980s (which the Government underestimated) led to an unsustainable boom.

In order to counter the overheating in the economy the Government raised interest rates sharply from 7.5 per cent in May 1988 to 15 per cent in October 1989. The base rate was still at 14.5 per cent when Major took over from Thatcher. He immediately appointed Norman Lamont, who had run his campaign for the leadership, as Chancellor of the Exchequer. Table 33.10 gives the main economic statistics for the 1990–3 period.

Recovery from the recession was handicapped by the very large indebtedness of consumers following the late 1980s 'boom' and by the large amount of 'negative equity' held by householders. Moreover, once a fragile expansion had begun during 1993, rapid growth was precluded not only by the weakening of European markets as the Continent slid into recession but also by the shrinkage in Britain's industrial base. Figures released in 1992 revealed that manufacturing output in Britain rose by a mere 5 per cent between 1979 and 1992, cf. over 60 per cent in Japan, over 30 per cent in the United States, just over 25 per cent in Germany and 20 per cent in Italy. A report on the competitiveness of British industry by the Department of Trade and Industry in 1993 pointed out the continuing weaknesses in the supply side of Britain's economy: lower spending on research and development than leading industrial competitors, lower manufacturing productivity (despite the gains of the 1980s), a lower skills base in the workforce (which pointed to deficiencies in industrial training) and lower overall standards of educational attainment (including lower staying-on rates post-16) than in competitors.

The shrinkage of Britain's manufacturing base and the trade deficit in manufactured goods (which the country has had since 1983) have been described as 'the time-bomb for the 1990s' (Wilks, 1993, p. 244).

Political debate after the débacle of 'Black Wednesday' focused unremittingly on the Government's competence to govern, especially with regard to the economy. The reputation of the Chancellor was damaged severely (as was the Prime Minister's) by Britain's humiliating exit from the ERM. Critics alleged that the Government wasted billions of pounds in their attempt to maintain sterling at an unsustainable rate. The Government riposted that the size of the speculative attack on sterling was unpredictable. Few doubted that the departure was an important turning-point in Britain's macro economic policy, giving British governments greater freedom in economic policy-making for the foreseeable future.

The Government's announcement in mid-October 1992 that it had accepted British Coal's decision to close 31 pits with the loss of 30 000 jobs led to public uproar. The pressure from national opinion and from its own backbenchers forced the Government to put the closure programme on hold pending an internal Board of Trade review. The internal review (March 1993) recommended the saving of only 12 pits, and by June 1993 the remaining 19 pits had been closed down. The Government reiterated the need for market forces to determine the future of coal as opposed to government intervention; critics

Table 33.10 *The UK economy, 1990–3*

	Inflation (%)	Unemployment (millions)	Growth (%)	Balance of Payments (£ billion)	Public Sector Borrowing Requirement (£ billion)
1990	9.5	1.66	0.6	−14.5	0.5
1991	5.9	2.29	−2.4	−4.5	13.8
1992	3.7	2.77	−0.5	−12	35
1993 est.	3.75	3.25	1.25	−17.5	50

pointed to the large state subsidy given to the nuclear power industry and argued that the market was 'rigged' against coal. Government plans to privatise the remaining pits together with the Post Office and British Rail are likely to remain a subject of political controversy into the mid-1990s.

From early in 1993, national political debate focused on the large £50 billion Public Sector Borrowing Requirement and the Government's proposals to handle it. Chancellor of the Exchequer Lamont in what turned out to be his last Budget in March 1993 announced planned tax increases of £10.3 billion over five years, beginning with £500 million in 1993. The higher burden would fall on indirect taxation – VAT (value-added tax) on domestic heating would rise by 8 per cent in April 1994 – and national insurance contributions would increase by 1 per cent at the same time. Lamont continued the Conservative policy of reducing direct taxes by extending the 20 per cent income tax band to a further 1 million lower income tax-payers. The political controversy surrounding these proposals stemmed from the possibly crucial role that Labour's tax proposals had had during the 1992 General Election together with the Prime Minister's denial at that time that he had any plan to increase VAT.

A further source of angry dispute between the parties was over economic statistics, with the Shadow Chancellor Gordon Brown accusing Lamont of deliberately massaging downwards Government borrowing forecasts – from £40 billion for 1993–4 (unpublished Treasury estimate) to £32 billion (pre-election Budget figure) – in order to help win the 1992 General Election.

The Government's immediate promise of special payments to help poor people with their higher heating bills did little to allay public dissatisfaction with its proposals. Within months, the Government had lost the seat of Newbury on a 28 per cent swing to the Liberal Democrats in a by-election and had suffered severe reverses – the loss of a Conservative majority on 15 shire councils – in the May county elections. In late May, in a Cabinet reshuffle which took Michael Howard to the Home Office, Major replaced Lamont with Kenneth Clarke as Chancellor. But

Lamont's dilemma of how to cut the £50 billion public sector deficit in the least politically damaging way remained to face his successor.

Summary

From the vantage point of the 1990s, it is clear that despite some important achievements, the Thatcher governments failed in their aim of 'turning Britain round'. However, they unquestionably transformed the terms of political debate and provided a political agenda for the present decade. The rightward policy shifts of the main opposition parties together with a trimming towards the centre by John Major have led political commentators to speak of the emergence of a new 'social market', pro-European consensus in Britain.

The politics of the mid-1990s are likely to be dominated by a continuing debate on ways of improving the international competitiveness of Britain's economy and of maximising the provision of welfare within tight budgetary constraints. The increasing impact of Europe on British institutions and society will form a continuing refrain. Political problems associated with the future of the ERM including the timing of Britain's rejoining it and of its handling of welfare and privatisation measures will preoccupy the Government; Labour will be concerned with its internal debate on how to improve its electability in 1996–7 (or before).

Questions

1. What do you consider the overall impact of Thatcherism on British politics to have been?

2. How far has a new political consensus emerged in the 1990s?

3. What are the main social, economic and political problems facing John Major as Prime Minister and how successfully has he dealt with them?

Assignment

Using the Tables 33.4–33.9, compare the opinions of party supporters on the main issues of social and economic policy in the period 1990–3.

Further reading

Budge, I. and MacKay, D. (1993) *The Developing British Political System: the 1990s*, 3rd edn London; Longman.

Crewe, I. (1992) 'Why did Labour Lose (Yet Again)?', *Politics Review*, 2: 1, September.

Dunleavy, P. *et al.* (1993) *Developments in British Politics 4* (London: Macmillan), especially the contributions by P. Dunleavy, 'Political parties', N. Nugent, 'The European Dimension', S. Wilks, 'Economic Policy' and C. Pierson, 'Social Policy'.

The Economist, 'A Survey of Britain', 24 October 1992.

Gilmour, I. (1992) *Dancing with Dogma: Britain under Thatcherism* (London: Simon and Schuster).

Heywood, A. (1991–2) 'British Politics in the 1990s: The Return of Consensus?', *Talking Politics*, 4: 2, winter.

Michie, J. (ed.) (1992) *The Economic Legacy 1979–1992* (London: Academic).

Oxford Review of Economic Policy (1991), vol. 7, no. 3.

Kavanagh, D. (1990) *Thatcherism and British Politics: The End of Consensus?* 2nd edn, (Oxford: Oxford University Press).

Riddell, P. (1991) *The Thatcher Era and its Legacy*, 2nd edn (Oxford: Blackwell).

For continuing discussion of the state of British politics, see the quality dailies – *The Times, Guardian, The Independent* – and weeklies such as *The Economist*.

Bibliography

Abercrombie, N. and Warde, A. (1988) *Contemporary British Society* (Cambridge: Polity).

Addison, P. (1987) 'The Road from 1945' in P. Hennessy and A. Seldon (eds) *Ruling Performance* (Oxford: Blackwell).

Adonis, A. (1993) *Parliament Today*, 2nd edn (Manchester: Manchester University Press).

Alderman, G. (1989) *Britain A One-Party State?* (London: Croom Helm).

Almond G. and Verba, S. (1965) *The Civic Culture* (Boston and Toronto: Little, Brown).

Almond, G. and Verba, S. (eds) (1980) *The Civic Culture Revisited* (Boston: Little, Brown).

Anderson, B. (1985) *Imagined Communities* (London: Verso).

Annual Abstract of Statistics (London: HMSO).

Arthur, P. (1984) *Government and Politics of Northern Ireland* (London: Longman).

Arthur, P. and Jeffrey, K. (1988) *Northern Ireland Since 1968* (Oxford: Blackwell).

Atkinson, R. and Durden, P. (1990) 'Housing Policy in the Thatcher Years' in S. Savage and L. Robins (eds) *Public Policy under Thatcher* (London: Macmillan).

Aughey, A. (1989a) 'The Politics of Equal Citizenship in Northern Ireland', *Talking Politics*, 2: 1, autumn.

Aughey, A. (1989b) *Under Siege: Ulster Unionism and the Anglo-Irish Agreement* (London: Hurst).

Bachrach, P. and Baratz, M. (1971) *Power and Poverty: Theory and Practice* (London: Oxford University Press).

Baggott, R. (1990–1) 'The Policy-Making Process in British Central Government', *Talking Politics*, 3: 2 winter.

Baggott, R. (1992a) 'Pressure Groups and the British Political System: Change and Decline' in B. Jones and L. Robins (eds) *Two Decades in British Politics* (Manchester University Press).

Baggott, R. (1992b) 'The Measurement of Change in Pressure Group Politics', *Talking Politics*, 5: 1, autumn.

Baker, D., Gamble, A. and Ludlum, S. (1992) 'More "Classless" and Less "Thatcherite"? Conservative Ministers and New Conservative MPs After the 1992 General Election', *Parliamentary Affairs*, October.

Baker, D., Gamble, A. and Ludlum, S. (1993) 'Whips or Scorpions? The Maastricht Vote and the Conservative Party', *Parliamentary Affairs*, April.

Baldwin, S. and Twigg, J. (1991) 'Women and Community Care' in M. Maclean and D. Groves (eds) *Women's Issues in Social Policy* (London: Routledge).

Ball, M., Gray, F. and McDowell, L. (1989) *The Transformation of Britain* (London: Fontana).

Barker, A. (ed.) (1982) *Quangos in Britain* (London: Macmillan).

Barnett, C. (1986) *The Audit of War* (London: Macmillan).

Barnett, C. (1991) 'The Education Battle Begins, 120 Years too Late', The *Sunday Times*, 26 May.

Barr, G. (1992) 'The Anti-Poll Tax Movement: An Insider's View of an Outsider Group', *Talking Politics*, 4: 3, summer.

Barron, J., Crawley, G. and Wood, T. (1991) *Councillors in Crisis* (London: Macmillan).

Bartlett, W. (1991) 'Quasi-markets and Contracts: A Markets and Hierarchies perspective on NHS reforms', *Public Money and Management*, autumn.

Bash, L. and Coulby, D. (1989) *The Education Reform Act: Competition and Control* (London: Cassell).

Beer, S. (1982) *Britain Against Itself: The Political Contradictions of Collectivism* (London: Faber & Faber).

Beetham, D. (1993) 'Political Theory and British Politics' in P. Dunleavy, A. Gamble, I. Holliday and G. Peele (eds) *Developments in British Parties 4* (London: Macmillan).

Beharrell, P. and Philo, G. (eds) (1977) *Trade Unions and the Media* (London: Macmillan).

Berridge, G.R. (1992) *International Politics: States, Power and Conflict since 1945* (London: Harvester Wheatsheaf).

Berry, S. (1993) 'Lobbying: A Need to Regulate?', *Politics Review*, 2: 3, February.

Best, R. (1992) 'The Tail Wags the Dog', *Housing*, September.

Beuret, Kristine (1991) 'Women and Transport' in M. Maclean and D. Groves (eds) *Women's Issues in Social Policy* (London: Routledge).

Birch, A.H. (1979) *Political Integration and Disintegration in the British Isles* (London: Allen & Unwin).

Birkinshaw, P. (1991) *Reforming the Secret State* (Milton Keynes: Open University Press).

Bolton, R. (1990) *Death on the Rock and Other Stories* (London: W.H. Allen).

Borchardt, K-D. (1990) *European Unification: The Origins and Growth of the European Community* (Luxembourg: Office for Official Publications of the European Communities).

Boyd, D. (1973) *Elites and their Education* (Windsor: NFER).

Boyle, A. (1979) *The Climate of Treason* (London: Hutchinson).

Boyson, R. (1971) *Down with the Poor* (Enfield: Churchill).

Bradbeer, J. (1990) 'Environmental Policy' in S. Savage and L. Robins (eds) *Public Policy under Thatcher* (London: Macmillan).

Brandt, W. (1985) *World Armament and World Hunger*, trans. Anthea Bell (London: Gollancz).

Braybrooke, D. and Lindblom, C. (1963) *A Strategy of Decision* (New York: Free Press).

Brazier, R. (1988) *Constitutional Practice* (Oxford: Clarendon Press).

Brazier, R. (1991) *Constitutional Reform* (Oxford: Clarendon).

Britain 1992 An Official Handbook (London: HMSO).

Britain 1993 An Official Handbook (London: HMSO).

Brown, C. (1989) 'Pluralism – A Lost Perspective?', *Talking Politics*, 1: 3, summer.

Brown, D. (1993) 'Who Wants to be a DSO?', *Housing*, February.

Bruce, S. (1986) *God Save Ulster: The Religion and Politics of Paisleyism* (Oxford: Oxford University Press).

Budge, I. and McKay, D. (1993) *The Developing British Political System: The 1990s*, 3rd edn (London: Longman).

Burch, M. (1990a) 'Cabinet Government', *Contemporary Record*, 4: 1 September.

Burch, M. (1990b) 'Power in the Cabinet System', *Talking Politics*, 2: 3, spring.

Burch, M. and Moran, M. (1985) 'The Changing British Political Élite, 1945–83: MPs and Cabinet Ministers', *Parliamentary Affairs*, 38, winter.

Burns, B. (1978) *Leadership* (New York: Harper & Row).

Butcher, T. (1991–2) 'Rolling Back the State: The Conservative Governments and Privatisation, 1979–91', *Talking Politics*, 4: 2, winter.

Butler, D. and Butler, G. (1986) *British Political Facts, 1900–1985* (London: Macmillan).

Butler, D. and Kavanagh, D. (1988) *The British General Election of 1987* (London: Macmillan).

Butler, D. and Kavanagh, D. (1992) *The British General Election of 1992* (London: Macmillan).

Butler, D. and Pinto-Duschinsky, M. (1970) *The British General Election of 1970* (London: Macmillan).

Butler, D. and Stokes, D. (1974) *Political Change in Britain*, 2nd. edn (London: Macmillan).

Byrd, P. (ed.) (1991) *British Defence Policy: Thatcher and Beyond* (London: Philip Allan).

Cairncross, A. (1981) 'The Post-War Years, 1945–77' in R. Floud and D. McCloskey (eds) *The Economic History of Britain Since 1700*, vol. 2 (Cambridge: Cambridge University Press).

Callaghan, J. (1987) *Time and Chance* (London: Collins).

Campbell, A., Converse, P., Miller, W. and Stokes, D. (1960) *The American Voter* (New York: Wiley).

Castle, B. (1980) *The Castle Diaries 1974–1976* (London: Weidenfeld & Nicolson).

Chalmers, M. (1985) *Paying For Defence* (London: Pluto Press).

Charvet, J. (1982) *Feminism* (London: Dent).

Chester, Sir N. (1979) 'Fringe Bodies, Quangos and All That', *Public Administration*, 57: 1.

Civil Servants and Ministers: Duties and Responsibilities (1986) Government Response to the Seventh Report from the Treasury and Civil Service Committee, Cmnd. 9841 (London: HMSO).

Civil Service Statistics (1992) (London: HMSO).

Clarke, M. (1992) *British External Policy-Making in the 1990s* (London: Macmillan/RIIA).

Clarke, P. (1992) *A Question of Leadership* (Harmondsworth: Penguin).

Coates, D. (1984) *The Context of British Politics* (London: Hutchinson).

Collins, N. and McCann, F. (1989) *Irish Politics Today* (Manchester: Manchester University Press).

Commission of the European Communities (1991) *The European Community 1992 and Beyond* (Brussels: ECSC-EEC-EAEC).

Commoner, B. (1971) *The Closing Circle* (London: Jonathan Cape).

Community Relations Commission (1975) *Participation of Ethnic Minorities in the General Election of 1992* (London: CRC).

Connelly, J. (1993) 'The Single Transferable Vote: Some Questions and Answers', *Talking Politics*, 5: 2, winter.

Cook, C. (1993) *A Short History of the Liberal Party 1900–1992*, 4th edn (London: Macmillan).

Cox, A. (1987) 'The Politics of Privatisation' in L. Robins (ed.) *Politics and Policy-Making in Britain* (London: Longman).

Coxall, B. (1992) 'The Social Context of British Politics: Class, Gender and Race in the Two Major Parties, 1970–1990' in B. Jones and L. Robins (eds) *Two Decades in British Politics* (Manchester University Press).

Creighton, S. (1992) *Child Abuse Trends in England and Wales, 1988–90, and an overview from 1973 to 1990* (London: NSPCC).

Crewe, I. (1985) 'Great Britain' in I. Crewe and D. Denver (eds) (1985) see below.

Crewe, I. (1992) 'Why did Labour Lose (Yet Again)?', *Politics Review*, 2: 1, September.

Crewe, I. (1993) 'Parties and Electors' in I. Budge and D. McKay (eds.) *The Developing British Political System: the 1990s*, 3rd edn (London: Longman).

Crewe, I. and Denver, D, (eds) (1985) *Electoral Change in Western Democracies* (London: Croom Helm).

Crick, B. (1973) *Basic Forms of Government: A Sketch and a Model* (London: Macmillan).

Crick, B. (ed.) (1991) *National Identities* (Oxford: Blackwell).

Crick, B. (1993) *In Defence of Politics*, 4th edn (Harmondsworth: Penguin).

Crosland, A. (1956) *The Future of Socialism* (London: Jonathan Cape).

Crossman, R. (1979) *The Crossman Diaries*, ed. A. Howard, condensed version (London: Methuen).

Crouch, C. and Marquand, D. (eds) (1992) *Towards a Greater Europe? A Continent without an Iron Curtain* (Oxford: Blackwell).

Culley, L. (1985) *Women and Power* (Leicester: Hyperion).

Cumper, P. (1991) 'Human Rights in Europe', *Talking Politics*, 4: 1, autumn.

Curran, J. and Seaton, J. (1990) *Power without Responsibility: the Press and Broadcasting in Britain* (London: Routledge).

Curtice, J. and Gallagher, T. (1990) 'The Northern Irish Dimension' in Jowell *et al.* (eds) *British Social Attitudes: The 7th Report* (Aldershot: Gower).

Curwen, P. (1992) *Understanding the UK Economy*, 2nd edn (London: Macmillan).

Davies, C. (1993) 'The Loss of Virtue', Social Affairs Unit, reproduced in *The Sunday Times*, 21 February.

Davis, H. (1993) 'The Political Role of the Courts', *Talking Politics*, 6: 1, autumn.

Deem, R. (1990) 'The reform of school-governing bodies: the power of the consumer over the producer?' in M. Flude and M. Hammer (eds.) *The Education Reform Act 1988 Its Origins and Implications* (London: Falmer).

de Smith, S. (1983) *Constitutional and Administrative Law*, 4th edition (Harmondsworth: Penguin).

de Smith, S. and Brazier, R. (1990) *Constitutional and Administrative Law*, 6th edn (Harmondsworth: Penguin).

Dennis, F. (1990) 'HATS – Who Needs Them?', *Housing*, November.

Denver, D. and Hands, G. (1990) 'A New Gender Gap: Sex and Party Choice Among Young People', *Talking Politics*, 2: 3, spring.

Denver, D. and Hands, G. (1992) 'The Political Socialisation of Young People' in B. Jones and L. Robins, (eds) *Two Decades in British Politics* (Manchester: Manchester University Press).

Denver, D. (1989) *Elections and Voting Behaviour* (London: Philip Allan).

Denver, D. (1992) 'The 1992 General Election: In Defence of Psephology', *Talking Politics*, 5: 1, autumn.

Dicey, A.V. (1905) *Lectures on the Relation Between Law and Public Opinion in England* (London: Macmillan).

Digby, A. (1989) *British Welfare Policy* (London: Faber & Faber).

Dobson, A. (1993) 'Ecologism' in R. Eatwell and A. Wright (eds) *Contemporary Political Ideologies* (London: Pinter).

Donaldson, P. and Farquhar, J. (1988) *Understanding the British Economy* (Harmondsworth: Penguin).

Donoughue, B. (1987) *Prime Minister* (London: Jonathan Cape).

Donoughue, B. (1988) 'The Prime Minister's Diary', *Contemporary Record*, 2, 2.

Dorey, P. (1991) 'The Cabinet Committee System in British Government', *Talking Politics*, 4: 1, autumn.

Dorey, P. (1992) 'Much Maligned: Much Misunderstood: The Role of the Party Whips', *Talking Politics*, 5: 1, autumn.

Dorril, S. (1992) *The Silent Conspiracy: Inside the Intelligence Services in the 1990s* (London: Heinemann).

Drewry, G. (ed.) (1985) *The New Select Committees*, 1st edn. (Oxford: Clarendon).

Drewry, G. (1988) 'Legislation' in M. Ryle and P. Richards (eds) *The Commons under Scrutiny* (London: Routledge).

Drewry, G. (ed.) (1989) *The New Select Committees* 2nd edn (Oxford: Clarendon).

Drewry, G. and Butcher, T. (1991) *The Civil Service Today*, 2nd edn (Oxford: Blackwell).

Dunleavy, P. (1980) *Urban Political Analysis* (London: Macmillan).

Dunleavy, P. (1990) 'Government at the Centre' in Dunleavy, Gamble and Peele (eds) (1990) (see below).

Dunleavy, P., Jones, G.W. and O'Leary, B. (1990) 'Prime Ministers and the Commons: Patterns of Behaviour, 1868–1967', *Public Administration*, 68, spring.

Dunleavy, P., Gamble, A. and Peele, G. (eds) (1990) *Developments in British Politics 3* (London: Macmillan).

Dunleavy, P., Gamble, A., Holliday, I. and Peele, G. (eds) (1993) *Developments in British Politics 4* (London: Macmillan).

Dunn, J. (ed.) (1992) *Democracy: The Unfinished Journey 508 BC to AD1993* (Oxford: Oxford University Press).

Dunn, M. and Smith, S. (1990) 'Economic Policy and Privatisation' in S. Savage and L. Robins (eds) *Public Policy Under Thatcher* (London: Macmillan).

Eatwell, R. and Wright, A. (eds) (1993) *Contemporary Political Ideologies* (London: Printer).

Eccleshall, R. (1986) *British Liberalism* (London: Longman).

Eccleshall, R., Geoghegan, V., Jay, R. and Wilford, R. (eds) (1984) *Political Ideologies* (London: Hutchinson).

The Economist (1992) 'A Survey of Britain', 24 October.

Education Group II (1991) *Education Limited: Schooling, Training and the New Right in England since 1979* (London: Unwin Hyman).

Efficiency Unit (1988) *Improving Management in Government: The Next Steps* (The Ibbs Report) (London: HMSO).

Engels, F. [1884] (1942) *The Origins of the Family, Private Property and the State* (London: Lawrence & Wishart).

Ewing, K.D. and Gearty, C. (1990) *Freedom under Thatcher: Civil Liberties in Modern Britain* (Oxford: Clarendon).

Farnham, D. (1990) 'Trade Union Policy, 1979–89: Restriction or Reform?' in S. Savage and L. Robins (eds) *Public Policy under Thatcher* (London: Macmillan).

Figes, E. [1970] (1986) *Patriarchal Attitudes* (London: Macmillan).

Financial Management in Government Departments (1983) Cmnd. 9058 (London: HMSO).

Finer, S.E. (1979) *Five Constitutions* (Harmondsworth: Penguin).

Firestone, S. [1970] (1980) *The Dialectic of Sex* (London: Women's Press).

Floud, R. and McCloskey, D. (1981) *The Economic History of Britain Since 1700, vol. 2 1860 to the 1970s* (Cambridge: Cambridge University Press).

Flude, M. and Hammer, M. (eds) (1990) *The Education Reform Act 1988 Its Origins and Implications* (London: Falmer).

Foley, M. (1993) *The Rise of the British Presidency* (Manchester: Manchester University Press).

Foote, G. (1986) *The Labour Party's Political Thought* (London: Croom Helm).

Foster, S. and Kelly, R. (1992) 'Understanding Thatcherism: Economics over Politics?', *Talking Politics*, 5: 1, autumn.

Fourth Report from the Defence Committee (1986): *Westland plc: The Government's Decision-Making*, HC519 (London: HMSO).

Frankel, J. (1970) *National Interest* (London: Pall Mall).

Franklin, M. (1985) *The Decline of Class Voting in Britain* (Oxford: Oxford University Press).

Franks Report (1957) *Report of the Committee on Administrative Tribunals and Inquiries*, Cmnd. 218 (London: HMSO).

Franks Report (1972) *Report of the Departmental Committee on Section 2 of the Official Secrets Act 1911*, Cmnd. 5104, (London: HMSO).

Fulton Report (1968) *The Civil Service vol. 1 Report*, Cmnd. 3638 (London: HMSO).

Galbraith, J.K. (1992) *The Culture of Contentment* (London: Sinclair Stevenson).

Gamble, A. (1990) *Britain in Decline*, 3rd edn (London: Macmillan).

Gamble, A. (1994) *The Free Economy and the Strong State: The Politics of Thatcherism*, 2nd edn (London: Macmillan).

Garner, R. and Kelly, R. (1993) *British Political Parties Today* (Manchester: Manchester University Press).

Garrett, J. (1992) *Westminster: Does Parliament Work?* (London: Gollancz).

Gearty, C. (1991) *Terror* (London: Faber & Faber).

Gibbins, J.R. (ed.) (1989) *Contemporary Political Culture* (London: Sage).

Gilmour, I. (1992) *Dancing with Dogma: Britain under Thatcherism* (London: Simon & Schuster).

Glasgow Media Group (1976) *Bad News*, vol. 1 (London: Routledge & Kegan Paul).

Glasgow Media Group (1980) *More Bad News* (London: Routledge).

Golding, P. (1974) *The Mass Media* (London: Longman).

Gowing, M. (1974) *Independence and Deterrence*, vol. 1, (London: Macmillan).

Grant, W. (1989) *Pressure Groups, Politics and Democracy in Britain* (London: Philip Allan).

Greenaway, J.R. (1992) 'The Civil Service: Twenty Years of Reform' in B. Jones and L. Robins (eds) *Two Decades in British Politics* (Manchester University Press).

Greenaway, J.R., Smith, S. and Street, J. (1992) *Deciding Factors in British Politics: A Case-Studies Approach* (London: Routledge).

Greenleaf, W.H. (1983) *The British Political Tradition, vol. 2. The Ideological Heritage* (London: Methuen).

Greenwood, J. and Wilson, D. (1989) *Public Administration in Britain Today*, 2nd edn (London: Unwin Hyman).

Greenwood, J. (1991–2) 'Local Government in the 1990s: the Consultation Papers on Structure, Finance and Internal Management', *Talking Politics*, 4: 2, winter.

Greer, G. (1970) *The Female Eunuch* (London: Granada).

Griffith, J.A.G. (1989) 'The Official Secrets Act 1989', *Journal of Law and Society*, 16: 2, autumn.

Griffith, J.A.G. and Ryle, M. (1989) *Parliament* (London: Sweet and Maxwell).

Griffith, J.A.G. (1991) *The Politics of the Judiciary*, 4th edn (London: Fontana).

Gros, D. and Thygesen, N. (1992) *European Monetary Integration* (London: Longman).

The Guide to the House of Commons New Parliament: A Guardian Book (1992) (London: Fourth Estate).

Gyford, J. (1991) *Citizens, Consumers and Councils: Local Government and the Public* (London: Macmillan).

Halsey, A.H. (ed.) (1988) *Trends in British Society since 1900* (London: Macmillan).

Halsey, A.H. (1992) 'Opening Wide the Doors of Higher Education', National Commission on Education Briefing no. 6, August.

Ham, C. (1991) *The National Health Service: Organisation and Management* (Oxford: Radcliffe Medical Press).

Hanson, A.H. (ed.) (1963) *Nationalisation: A Book of Readings* (London: Allen & Unwin).

Harden, I. and Lewis, N. (1987) *The Noble Lie: The British Constitution and the Rule of Law* (London: Hutchinson).

Harrison, M. (1985) *TV News: Whose Bias?* Hermitage, Policy Journals.

Harrison, S. (1991) 'Working the Markets: Purchaser/Provider Separation in English Health Care', *International Journal of Health Services*, 21: 4.

Harrison, S., Hunter, D. and Pollitt, C. (1990) *The Dynamics of British Health Care* (London: Unwin Hyman).

Hayek, Friedrich von (1944) *The Road to Serfdom* (London: Routledge and Kegan Paul).

Heath, A. and Topf, R. (1987) 'Political Culture' in R. Jowell, S. Witherspoon and L. Brook (eds) *British Social Attitudes: The 5th Report* (Aldershot: Gower).

Heath, A., Jowell, R. and Curtice, J. (1985) *How Britain Votes* (Oxford: Pergamon).

Heclo, H. and Wildavsky, A. (1974) *The Private Government of Public Money* (London: Macmillan).

Heffernan, R. and Marqusee, M. (1992) *Defeat from the Jaws of Victory: Inside Kinnock's Labour Party* (London: Verso).

Hennessy, P. (1986) *Cabinet* (Oxford: Blackwell).

Hennessy, P. (1987) 'Mediaeval Relic or Mighty Oak?', *The Listener*, 5 November.

Hennessy, P. (1990) *Whitehall*, rev. edn (London: Fontana).

Hennessy, P. and Seldon, A. (eds) (1987) *Ruling Performance* (Oxford: Blackwell).

Heywood, A. (1991–2) 'British Politics in the 1990s: The Return of Consensus?', *Talking Politics*, 4: 2, winter.

Heywood, A. (1992) *Political Ideologies: An Introduction* (London: Macmillan).

Heywood, A. (1993) 'The Dominant-Party System: A Threat to Democracy?', *Talking Politics*, 5: 2, winter.

Himmelweit, H., Humphreys, P. and Jaeger, M. (1984) *How Voters Decide* (Milton Keynes: Open University Press).

Hoffman, S. (ed.) (1960) *Contemporary Theory in International Relations* (Englewood Cliffs: Prentice-Hall).

Holland, R. (1991) *The Pursuit of Greatness: Britain and the World Role, 1900–1970* (London: Fontana).

Holliday, I. (1993) 'Organised Interests after Thatcher' in Dunleavy *et al.* (eds) *Developments in British Politics*, 4 (London: Macmillan).

Holme, R. and Elliott, M. (1988) *1688–1988 Time for a New Constitution* (London: Macmillan).

Hood, C. (1981) 'Axeperson, Spare that Quango...' in C. Hood and M. Wright (eds) (see below).

Hood, C. and Wright, M. (eds) (1981) *Big Government in Hard Times* (Oxford: Martin Robertson).

Horton, S. (1990) 'Local Government 1979–89; A Decade of Change' in S. Savage and L. Robins (eds) *Public Policy Under Thatcher* (London: Macmillan).

House of Lords, (1984–5) *Report from the Select Committee on Overseas Trade*, HL238-1.

Hunt, K. (1987) 'Women and Politics' in B. Jones (ed.) *Political Issues in Britain Today* (Manchester University Press).

Hunt, S. (1992a) 'Fascism and the "Race Issue" in Britain' *Talking Politics*, 5: 1, autumn.

Hunt, S. (1992b) 'State Secrecy in the UK', *Politics Review*, 1: 4, April.

Hutton, J., Hutton, S., Pinch, T. and Shiell, A. (eds) (1991) *Dependency to Enterprise* (London: Routledge).

Ingle, S. (1989) *The British Party System*, 2nd edn (Oxford: Blackwell).

Ingle, S. (1993) 'Political Parties in the 1990s', *Talking Politics*, 6: 1, autumn.

James, S. (1992) *British Cabinet Government* (London: Routledge).

Johnson, N. (1982) 'Accountability, Control and Complexity: Moving Beyond Ministerial Accountability' in A. Barker (ed.) *Quangos in Britain* (London: Macmillan).

Johnson, R. (1991) 'A new road to serfdom? A critical history of the 1988 Act' in Education Group II *Education Limited: Schooling, Training and the New Right in England since 1979* (London: Lawrence and Wishart).

Johnson, R.J. and Pattie, C.J. (1990) 'Tactical voting in Great Britain in 1983 and 1987: an alternative approach', *British Journal of Political Science*, 3, January.

Jones, B. (ed.) (1987) *Political Issues in Britain Today* (Manchester: Manchester University Press).

Jones, B. (1989–90) 'Green Thinking', *Talking Politics*, 2: 2, winter.

Jones, B. and Robins, L. (eds) (1992) *Two Decades in British Politics* (Manchester: Manchester University Press).

Jones, G. and Stewart, J. (1989) 'The Role of a Council Member Needs to be Refocused', *Local Government Chronicle*, 14 April.

Jones, G.W. (1989) 'A Revolution in Whitehall? Changes in British Central Government since 1979', *West European Politics*, 12.

Jones, G.W. (1990) 'Mrs Thatcher and the Power of the Prime Minister', *Contemporary Record*, 3: 4.

Jones, K. (1991) 'Mythology and Social Policy' in J. Hutton *et al.* (eds) *Dependency to Enterprise* (London: Routledge).

Jordan, A.G. (ed.) (1991) *The Commercial Lobbyists* (Aberdeen: Aberdeen University Press).

Jordan, A.G. and Richardson, J.J. (1987) *Government and Pressure Groups in Britain* (Oxford: Clarendon).

Jowell, J. and Oliver, D. (eds) (1989) *The Changing Constitution*, 2nd edn (Oxford: Clarendon).

Jowell, R. and Topf, R. (1988) 'Trust in the Establishment' in R. Jowell *et al.* (eds) (1988).

Jowell, R. and Airey, C. (eds) (1984) *British Social Attitudes: the 1984 Report* (Aldershot: Gower).

Jowell, R., Witherspoon, S. and Brook, L. (eds) (1987) *British Social Attitudes: the 5th Report* (Aldershot: Gower).

Jowell, R., Witherspoon, S. and Brook, L. (eds) (1988) *British Social Attitudes: the 6th Report* (Aldershot: Gower).

Jowell, R., Witherspoon, S. and Brook, L. (eds) (1989) *British Social Attitudes Special International Report* (Aldershot: Gower).

Jowell, R., Witherspoon, S. and Brook, L. (eds) (1990) *British Social Attitudes: the 7th Report* (Aldershot: Gower).

Judge, D. (1992) 'Disorder in the "Frustration" Parliaments of Thatcherite Britain', *Political Studies*, 40: 3, September.

Judge, D. (1993) *The Parliamentary State* (London: Sage).

Kavanagh, D. (1971) 'The Deferential English: a Comparative Critique' in Kavanagh, D. (1990) *Politics and Personalities* (London: Macmillan).

Kavanagh, D. (1980) 'Political Culture in Great Britain: the Decline of the Civic Culture' in G. Almond and S. Verba (eds) *The Civic Culture Revisited* (Boston: Little Brown).

Kavanagh, D. (1974) 'The Monarchy in Contemporary Political Culture' (with R. Rose) in Kavanagh, D. (1990) *Politics and Personalities* (London: Macmillan).

Kavanagh, D. (1990) *Politics and Personalities* (London: Macmillan).

Kavanagh, D. (1990) *Thatcherism and British Politics*, 2nd edn (Oxford: Oxford University Press).

Kavanagh, D. (1991) 'Prime Ministerial Power Revisited', *Social Studies Review*, 6: 4, March.

Keegan, W. (1992) 'Towering folly of the Thatcherite Dream', *The Observer*, 31 May.

Kellner, P. and Crowther-Hunt, Lord (1980) *The Civil Servants* (London: Macdonald).

Kelly, R. (1989) 'Party Conferences: Do They Matter?', *Talking Politics*, 2: 1, autumn.

Kelly, R. and Foster, S. (1991) 'Power in the Labour Party', *Politics Review*, 1: 1, September.

Kelly, R. (1992) 'Power in the Conservative Party', *Politics Review*, 1: 4, April.

Kemp, P. (1992) 'Housing' in D. Marsh and R.A.W. Rhodes (eds) *Implementing Thatcherite Policies* (Buckingham: Open University Press).

Kendall, I. and Moon, G. (1990) 'Health Policy' in S. Savage and L. Robins (eds) *Public Policy under Thatcher* (London: Macmillan).

King, A. (1985) *The British Prime Minister* (London: Macmillan).

King, A. (ed.) (1992) *Britain at the Polls* (Oxford: Oxford University Press).

Klein, R. (1989) *The Politics of the NHS* (London: Longman).

Laffan, B. (1992) *Integration and Cooperation in Europe* (London: Routledge).

Land, H. (1991) 'Time to Care' in M. Maclean and D. Groves (eds) *Women's Issues in Social Policy* (London: Routledge).

Layton-Henry, Z. (1988) 'Black Participation in the General Election of 1987', *Talking Politics*, 1: 1, autumn.

Layton-Henry, Z. (1992) *Immigration and 'Race' Politics in Post-War Britain* (Oxford: Blackwell).

Leach, R. (1991) *British Political Ideologies* (London: Philip Allan).

Leftwich, A. (ed.) (1984) *What is Politics?* (Oxford: Blackwell).

Linton, M. (ed.) (1992) *The Guide to the House of Commons New Parliament* (London: Fourth Estate).

Loveland, I. (1993) 'Redefining Parliamentary Sovereignty? A New Perspective on the Search for the Meaning of Law', *Parliamentary Affairs*, 46: 3, July.

Lucas, J.R. (1985) *The Principles of Politics*, paperback edn (Oxford: Oxford University Press).

Lupton, C. and Russell, D. (1990) 'Equal Opportunities in a Cold Climate' in S. Savage and L. Robins (eds) *Public Policy under Thatcher* (London: Macmillan).

McAuslan, P. and McEldowney, J. (1985) *Law, Legitimacy and the Constitution* (London: Sweet & Maxwell).

McCulloch, A. (1988) 'Politics and the Environment', *Talking Politics*, 1: 1, autumn.

McDowell, L., Sarre, P. and Hamnett, C. (eds) (1989) *Divided Nation: Social and Cultural Change in Britain* (London: Hodder & Stoughton).

McGrew, A. and Wilson, M. (eds) (1982) *Decision-making: Approaches and Analysis* (Manchester: Manchester University Press).

McIlroy, J. (1989) 'The Politics of Racism' in B. Jones (ed.) *Political Issues in Britain Today* (Manchester University Press).

McKenzie, R.T. (1964) *British Political Parties*, 2nd edn (London: Mercury Books).

Mack, J. and Lansley, S. (1985) *Poor Britain* (London: Allen & Unwin).

Maclean, M. and Groves, D. (eds) (1991) *Women's Issues in Social Policy* (London: Routledge).

McLellan, D. (1980) *The Thought of Karl Marx* (London: Macmillan).

Macpherson, C.B. (1966) *The Real World of Democracy* (Oxford: Clarendon).

McQuail, D. (1987) *Mass Communications Theory* (Beverly Hills: Sage).

McVicar, M. (1990) 'Education Policy: Education as a Business?' in S. Savage and L. Robins (eds) *Public Policy under Thatcher* (London: Macmillan).

Madgwick, P. (1991) *British Government: The Central Executive Territory* (London: Philip Allan).

Malpass, P. (ed.) (1990) *The Housing Crisis* (London: Croom Helm).

Malpass, ` P. (1990) *Reshaping Housing Policy* (London: Routledge).

Mancuso, M. (1993) 'The Ethical Attitudes of British MPs: A Typology', *Parliamentary Affairs*, 46: 2, April.

Marquand, D. (1987) *The Unprincipled Society* (London: Fontana).

Marsh, D. (1992a) 'Industrial Relations' in D. Marsh and R.A.W. Rhodes (eds) (1992) see below.

Marsh, D. (1992b) *The New Politics of British Trade Unionism* (London: Macmillan).

Marsh, D. and King, J. (1987) 'The Unions under Thatcher' in L. Robins (ed.) *Political Institutions in Britain* (London: Longman).

Marsh, D. and Rhodes, R.A.W. (eds) (1992) *Implementing Thatcherite Policies* (Milton Keynes: Open University Press).

Marshall, G. (1984) *Constitutional Conventions* (Oxford: Clarendon).

Marshall, G. (1989a) 'The Police: Independence and Accountability' in J. Jowell and D. Oliver (eds) *The Changing Constitution* (Oxford: Clarendon).

Marshall, G. (ed.) (1989) *Ministerial Responsibility* (Oxford: Oxford University Press).

Marshall, G. and Moodie, G. (1967) *Some Problems of the Constitution* (London: Hutchinson).

Marshall, G., Newby, H., Rose, D. and Vogler, C. (1988) *Social Class in Modern Britain* (London: Hutchinson).

Maynard, G. (1988) *The Economy under Mrs. Thatcher* (Oxford: Blackwell).

Meadows, D.H., Meadows, D.L. and Randers, J. (1972) *The Limits to Growth* (New York: Universe Books).

Michie, J. (ed.) (1992) *The Economic Legacy 1979–1992* (London: Academic).

Middlemas, K. (1979) *Politics in Industrial Society* (London: Deutsch).

Miles, R. (1989) 'Racism and Class Structure: Migrant Labour in Contemporary Capitalism', in L. McDowell, P. Sarre and C. Hamnett, *Divided Nation: Social and Cultural Change in Britain* (London: Hodder and Stoughton).

Miliband, R. (1973) *The State in Capitalist Society* (London: Quartet).

Miliband, R. (1984) *Capitalist Democracy in Britain* (Oxford: Oxford University Press).

Mill, J.S. [1869] (1975) *Three Essays* (including *The Subjection of Women*) edited and with an introduction by R. Wollheim (Oxford: Oxford University Press).

Miller, W.L., Clarke, H., Harrop, M., Leduc, L. and Whiteley, P. (1990) *How Voters Change* (Oxford: Clarendon).

Millett, K. [1970] (1977) *Sexual Politics* (London: Virago).

Mills, C. Wright (1956) *The Power Elite* (New York: Oxford University Press).

Mishler, W., Hoskin, M. and Fitzgerald, R. (1989) 'British Parties in the Balance: A Time Series Analysis of Long-Term Trends in Labour and Conservative Support', *British Journal of Political Science*, 19: 2.

Mitchell, J. (1971) *Women's Estate* (Harmondsworth: Penguin).

Moran, M. (1989) *Politics and Society in Britain*, 2nd edn (London: Macmillan).

Morgan, K. (1990) *The People's Peace: British History 1945–1989* (Oxford: Oxford University Press).

Mosley, Sir Oswald (1932) *The Greater Britain* (London: BUF Publication).

Moxon-Browne, E. (1983) *Nation, Class and Creed in Northern Ireland* (Aldershot: Cramer).

Murdoch, G. and Golding, P. (1977) 'Beyond Monopoly – Mass Communications in an Age of Conglomerates' in P. Beharrell and G. Philo (eds) *Trade Unions and the Mass Media* (London: Macmillan).

Nisbet, R. (1986) *Conservatism* (Milton Keynes: Open University Press).

Noël, E. (1992) *Working Together – The Institutions of the European Community* (Luxembourg: Office for Official Productions of the European Community).

Norton, P. (1981) *The Commons in Perspective* (London: Longman).

Norton, P. (1990a) ' "The Lady's Not For Turning" But What About the Rest? Margaret Thatcher and the Conservative Party, 1979–89', *Parliamentary Affairs*, 43: 1, January.

Norton, P. (1990b) 'Public Legislation' in M. Rush (ed.) *Parliament and Pressure Politics* (Oxford: Oxford University Press).

Norton, P. (1991a) *New Directions in British Politics* (Aldershot: Edward Elgar).

Norton, P. (1991b) 'Reforming the House of Commons', *Talking Politics*, 4: 1, autumn.

Norton, P. (1992) 'The House of Commons: from overlooked to overworked' in B. Jones and L. Robins (eds) *Two Decades in British Politics* (Manchester: Manchester University Press).

Norton, P. (1993) 'A Bill of Rights: The Case Against', *Talking Politics*, 5: 3, summer.

Norton, P. and Aughey, A. (1981) *Conservatives and Conservatism* (London: Temple Smith).

Norton-Taylor, R. (1990) *In Defence of the Realm? The Case for Accountable Security Services* (London: Civil Liberties Trust).

Nugent, N. (1991) *The Government and Politics of the European Community*, 2nd edn (London: Macmillan).

Oakeshott, M. (1981) *Rationalism in Politics and other Essays* (New York: Routledge Chapman and Hall).

Oakley, A. (1972) *Sex, Gender and Society* (Hounslow: Temple Smith).

O'Gorman, F. (1986) *British Conservatism* (London: Longman).

Oliver, D. (1993) 'Citizenship in the 1990s', *Politics Review*, 3: 1, September.

Office for Official Publications of the European Communities (1986) *The Court of Justice of the European Community* (Luxembourg: OPEC)

Oppenheim, C. (1990) *Poverty: the Facts* (London: CPAG).

O'Sullivan, N. (1983) *Fascism* (London: Dent).

Oxford Review of Economic Policy (1991) 7: 1 (Oxford: Oxford University Press and the Oxford Review of Economic Policy Ltd).

Palmer, S. (1990) 'Tightening Secrecy Law: The Official Secrets Act 1989', *Public Law*, summer.

Parry, G. and Moyser, G. (1990) 'A Map of Political Participation in Britain' *Government and Opposition*, 25: 2.

Parry, G. and Moyser, G. (1993) 'Political Participation in Britain', *Politics Review*, 3: 2, November.

Parry, G., Moyser, G. and Day, N. (1992) *Political Participation and Democracy in Britain* (Cambridge: Cambridge University Press).

Peele, G. (1993) 'The Constitution' in P. Dunleavy, A. Gamble, I. Holliday and G. Peele (eds) *Developments in British Politics 4* (London: Macmillan).

Pierson, C. 'Social Policy' in P. Dunleavy, A. Gamble, I. Holliday and G. Peele (eds) *Developments in British Politics 4* (London: Macmillan).

Pimlott, B. and Cook, C. (eds) (1991) *Trade Unions in British Politics: the first 250 years*, 2nd edn (London: Longman).

Pliatzky, L. (1982) *Getting and Spending* (Oxford: Blackwell).

Pliatzky Report (1980) *Report on Non-Departmental Public Bodies*, Cmnd. 7797 (London: HMSO).

Plowden, W. (ed.) (1987) *Advising the Rulers* (Oxford: Blackwell).

Porritt, J. (1984) *Seeing Green* (Oxford: Blackwell).

Porter, B. (1989) *Plots and Paranoia: A History of Political Espionage in Britain, 1790–1988* (London: Unwin Hyman).

Pulzer, P. (1967) *Political Representation and Elections in Britain* (London: Allen & Unwin).

Punnett, R.M. (1992) *Selecting the Party Leader: Britain in Comparative Perspective* (London: Harvester Wheatsheaf).

Pyper, R. (1991) 'Governments, 1964–90: A Survey', *Contemporary Record*, 5: 2, autumn.

Pyper, R. (1992) 'A New Model Civil Service?', *Politics Review*, 2: 2, November.

Radice, L., Vallance, E. and Willis, V. (1987) *Member of Parliament* (London: Macmillan).

Randall, V. (1987) *Women and Politics*, 2nd end (London: Macmillan).

Ranson, S. (1990) 'From 1945 to 1988: Education, Citizenship and Democracy' in M. Flude and M. Hammer (eds) *The Education Reform Act 1988 Its Origins and Implications* (London: Falmer).

Rayner, Sir D. (1982) *The Scrutiny Programme-a note of guidance* (revised) (London: Management and Personnel Office).

Reeve, A. and Ware, A. (1992) *Electoral Systems – A Comparative and Theoretical Introduction* (London: Routledge).

Reiner, R. (1985) *The Politics of the Police* (Brighton: Wheatsheaf).

Renwick, A. and Swinburn, I. (1990) *Basic Political Concepts*, 3rd edn (London: Stanley Thornes).

Research Volume 1 (1986) *The Political Organisation of Local Authorities*, Cmnd. 9798 (London: HMSO).

Reynolds, D. (1991) *Britannia Overruled: British Policy and World Power in the Twentieth Century* (London: Longman).

Rhodes, R.A.W. (1981) *Control and Power in Central — Local Relations* (Farnborough: Gower).

Rhodes, R.A.W. (1992a) 'Local Government' in B. Jones and L. Robins (eds) *Two Decades in British Politics* (Manchester University Press).

Rhodes, R.A.W. (1992b) 'Local Government Finance' in D. Marsh and R.A.W. Rhodes (eds) *Implementing Thatcherite Policies* (Buckingham: Open University Press).

Riddell, P. (1991) *The Thatcher Era and its Legacy*, rev. edn of *The Thatcher Decade* (1989) with new postscript (Oxford: Blackwell).

Ridley, F.F. (1988) 'There is no British Constitution: A Dangerous Case of the Emperor's Clothes', *Parliamentary Affairs*, 41: 3, July.

Ridley, F.F. (1991) 'Using Power to Keep Power: The Need for Constitutional Checks', *Parliamentary Affairs*, 44: 4, October.

Ridley, F.F. (1992) 'What Happened to the Constitution under Mrs. Thatcher?' in B. Jones and L. Robins (eds) *Two Decades in British Politics* (Manchester University Press).

Ridley, F.F. and Doig, A. (1992) 'It's Not All Politics', *Politics Review*, 2: 2, November.

Riseborough, M. (1992) 'Life on the Transfer Market', *Housing*, October.

Roberts, K., Cook, F.G., Clark, S.C. and Semeonoff, E. (1977) *The Fragmentary Class Structure* (London: Heinemann).

Robertson, D. (1993) 'Preserving Order and Administering Justice: Other Faces of Government in Britain' in I. Budge and D. McKay (eds) *The Developing British Political System: The 1990s*, 3rd edn (London: Longman).

Robins, L. (ed.) (1982) *Topics in British Politics* (London: Politics Association).

Robins, L. (ed.) (1987a) *Policy-Making in Britain* (London: Longman).

Robins, L. (ed.) (1987b) *Political Institutions in Britain* (London: Longman).

Robins, L., Brennan, T. and Sutton, J. (1985) *People and Politics in Britain* (London: Macmillan).

Robinson, M. (1992) *The Greening of British Party Politics* (Manchester: Manchester University Press).

Robinson Report (1977) *Remuneration of Councillors*, vol. 1 Report, Cmnd. 7010 (London: HMSO).

Rose, R. (1982) *Understanding the United Kingdom* (London: Longman).

Rose, R. and McAllister, I. (1990) *The Loyalties of Voters* (London: Sage).

Routh, G. (1987) *Occupations of the People of Great Britain 1801–1981* (London: Macmillan).

Rudig, W., Bennie, L. and Franklin, M. (1992) 'Flash Party Dynamics – The Rise and Fall of the British Green Party', APSA Paper, Chicago.

Rush, M. (1989) 'The Education, Science and Arts Committee' and 'The Social Services Committee' in G. Drewry (ed.) *The New Select Committees* 2nd edn (Oxford: Clarendon Press).

Rush, M. (ed.) (1990) *Parliament and Pressure Politics,* (Oxford: Clarendon).

Rush, M. (1991) 'The Departmental Select Committees: Into the 1990s', *Talking Politics*, 3: 3, summer.

Russell, D. (1990) 'Equal Opportunities and the Politics of Race', *Talking Politics*, 3: 1, autumn.

Ryle, M. and Richards, P. (eds) (1988) *The Commons Under Scrutiny* (London: Routledge).

Salter, B. (1992) '*Heart of the Matter*', Health Service Journal, 1 October.

Sampson, A. (1962) *Anatomy of Britain* (New York: Harper & Row).

Sampson, A. (1993) *The Essential Anatomy of Britain Democracy in Crisis* (London: Coronet).

Sanders, D. (1990) *Losing an Empire, Finding a Role* (London: Macmillan).

Sanders, D. (1993) 'Foreign and Defence Policy' in P. Dunleavy *et al.* (eds) *Developments in British Politics 4* (London: Macmillan).

Savage, S. (1992) 'The Judiciary: Justice with Accountability?' in B. Jones and L. Robins (eds) *Two Decades in British Politics* (Manchester University Press).

Schattschneider, E.E. (1960) *The Semi sovereign People* (New York: Holt, Rinehart and Winston).

Sedgemore, B. (1980) *The Secret Constitution* (London: Hodder & Stoughton).

Seldon, A. (1990) 'The Cabinet Office and Coordination', *Public Administration*, 68: 1, spring.

Seldon, A. (ed.) (1990) *UK Political Parties since 1945* (London: Philip Allan).

Seyd, P. (1987) *The Rise and Fall of the Labour Left* (London: Macmillan).

Seyd, P. and Whiteley, P. (1992) *Labour's Grass Roots: The Politics of Party Membership* (Oxford: Clarendon).

Seventh Report From the Treasury and Civil Service Committee (1986) *Civil Servants and Ministers: Duties and Responsibilities*, HC92 (London: HMSO).

Seymour-Ure, C. (1974) *The Political Impact of the Mass Media* (London: Constable).

Shell, D. (1992a) 'The House of Lords: the best second chamber we have got?' in B. Jones and L. Robins (eds) *Two Decades in British Politics* (Manchester: Manchester University Press).

Shell, D. (1992b) *The House of Lords* 2nd edn (London: Philip Allan).

Skidelsky, R. (1975) *Oswald Mosley* (London: Macmillan).

Smith, A.D. (1979) *Nationalism in the Twentieth Century*, (Oxford: Martin Robertson).

Smith, A.D. (1991) *National Identity* (Harmondsworth: Penguin).

Smith, D. (1989) *North and South: Britain's Economic, Social and Political Divide* (Harmondsworth: Penguin).

Smith, K. (1989) *The British Economic Crisis* (Harmondsworth: Penguin).

Smith, M., Smith, S. and White, B. (eds) (1988) *British Foreign Policy* (London: Unwin Hyman).

Smith, Martin J. (1992) 'CAP and Agricultural Policy' in D. Marsh and R.A.W. Rhodes (eds) *Implementing Thatcherite Policies* (Milton Keynes: Open University Press).

Snyder, R.C., Bruck, H.W. and Sapin, B. (1960) 'Decision-Making as an Approach to the Study of International Politics' in S. Hoffman (ed.) *Contemporary Theory in International Relations* (Englewood Clifs, NJ: Prentice-Hall).

Social Trends (London: HMSO).

Stanworth, P. and Giddens, A. (1974) *Elites and Power in British Society* (Cambridge: Cambridge University Press).

Stearn, J. (1989) 'Stripping the Assets', *Housing*, October.

Steed, M. (1986) 'The Core–Periphery Dimension of British Politics', *Political Geography Quarterly*, supplement to 5: 4, October.

Stevenson, G. (1993) *Third Party Politics since 1945* (Oxford: Blackwell).

Stoker, G. (1991) *The Politics of Local Government* (London: Macmillan).

Tapper, T. and Bowles, N. (1982) 'Working-class Tories: The Search for Theory' in L. Robins (ed.) *Topics in British Politics* (London: Politics Association).

Taylor, A.J. (1989) *Trade Unions and Politics: A Comparative Introduction* (London: Macmillan).

Thain, C. (1992) 'Government and the Economy' in B. Jones and L. Robins (eds) *Two Decades in British Politics* (Manchester University Press).

Theakston, K. (1991–2) 'Ministers and Mandarins', *Talking Politics*, 4: 2, winter.

Thomas, G.P. (1992) *Government and the Economy Today* (Manchester: Manchester University Press).

Thompson, K. (1993) 'Redressing Grievances: The Role of the Ombudsman', *Talking Politics*, 6: 1, autumn.

Thurlow, K.C. (1986) *Fascism in Britain: A History 1918–85* (Oxford: Blackwell).

The Times Guide to the House of Commons, April 1992 (1992) (London: Times Newspapers).

Tivey, L. and Wright, A. (eds) (1989) *Party Ideology in Britain* (London: Routledge).

Topf, R., Mohler, P. and Heath, A. (1989) 'Pride in One's Country: Britain and West Germany' in R. Jowell *et al.* (eds) (1989).

Topf, R. (1989) 'Political Change and Political Culture in Britain, 1959–1987' in Gibbins, J.R. (ed.) *Contemporary Political Culture* (London: Sage Publications).

Townsend, P., Davidson, N. and Whitehead, M. (1990) *The Health Divide* (Harmondsworth: Penguin).

Training Agency (1989) 'TECs: What's in it for Employers', Sheffield.

Training Agency (1990) 'A Challenging Role for British Business', Sheffield.

Trenaman, J. and McQuail, D. (1961) *Television and the Political Image* (London: Methuen).

United Kingdom Balance of Payments (1987) London, Central Statistical Office.

United Kingdom National Accounts 'Blue Book' (1991) London, Central Statistical Office.

Van Mechelen, D. and Rose, R. (eds) (1986) *Patterns of Parliamentary Legislation* (Aldershot: Gower).

Vital, D. (1968) *The Making of British Foreign Policy* (Oxford: Oxford University Press).

Wade, H.W.R. [1977] (1988) *Administrative Law*, 6th edn, (Oxford: Clarendon).

Wallace, W. (1975) *The Foreign Policy Process in Britain* (London: Royal Institute for International Affairs).

Wass, D. (1983) *Government and the Governed* (London: Routledge and Kegan Paul).

Watts, D. (1993) 'Lobbying Europe', *Talking Politics*, 5: 2, winter.

Welfare, D. (1992) 'An Anachronism with Relevance: The Revival of the House of Lords in the 1980s and its Defence of Local Government', *Parliamentary Affairs*, April.

Whale, J. (1977) *The Politics of the Media* (London: Fontana).

Widdicombe Report (1986) *The Conduct of Local Authority Business*: Report of the Committee of Inquiry into the Conduct of Local Authority Business, Cmnd. 9797 (London: HMSO).

Wichert, S. (1991) *Northern Ireland since 1945* (London: Longman).

Wilding, P. (1993) 'Poverty and Government in Britain in the 1980s', *Talking Politics*, 5: 3, summer.

Wilkinson, P. (1986) *Terrorism and the Liberal State*, 2nd edn (London: Macmillan).

Wilks, S. (1993) 'Economic Policy' in P. Dunleavy *et al.* (eds) *Developments in British Politics 4* (London: Macmillan).

Willetts, D. (1987) 'The Role of the Prime Minister's Policy Unit', *Public Administration*, 65.

Wilson, D. (1990) 'More Power to the Centre? The Changing Nature of Central Government/Local Authority Relationships', *Talking Politics*, 3: 1, summer.

Wollstonecraft, M. [1792] (1982) *Vindication of the Rights of Woman*, (ed.) M. Kramnick (Harmondsworth: Penguin).

Wood, A.H. and Wood, R. (1992) *The Times The House of Commons April 1992* (London: Times Books).

Wood, B. (1992) *The Politics of Health* (Manchester: Politics Association).

Wood, T. and Crawley, G. (1987) 'Equal Access to Political Power – A Principle in Danger', *Local Government Chronicle*, 21 August.

World Tables 1993 (Baltimore and London: Johns Hopkins, for the World Bank).

The World in 1992 (1991) (London: *The Economist* Publications).

Wragg, T. (1992) 'Seeds of Destruction Being Sown in a Three-Class System', The *Observer*, 17 May.

Wright, A. (1983) *British Socialism* (London: Longman).

Young, H. (1990) *One of Us*, expanded edn with new epilogue (London: Pan in association with Macmillan).

Index

£ 3.00

KT-164-980

SV

Wolfgang Koeppen
Drei Romane

Tauben im Gras
Das Treibhaus
Der Tod in Rom

Suhrkamp Verlag

Erste Ausgabe 1972
Copyright dieser Gesamtausgabe
Suhrkamp Verlag Frankfurt am Main 1972
Tauben im Gras
© 1951 by Scherz & Goverts Verlag GmbH Stuttgart
Das Treibhaus
© 1953 by Scherz & Goverts Verlag GmbH Stuttgart
Der Tod in Rom
© 1954 by Scherz & Goverts Verlag GmbH Stuttgart
Alle Rechte vorbehalten
Satz und Druck: Hieronymus Mühlberger, Augsburg
Printed in Germany

Inhalt

Tauben im Gras

Pigeons on the grass alas

Gertrude Stein

»Tauben im Gras« wurde kurz nach der Währungsreform geschrieben, als das deutsche Wirtschaftswunder im Westen aufging, als die ersten neuen Kinos, die ersten neuen Versicherungspaläste die Trümmer und die Behelfsläden überragten, zur hohen Zeit der Besatzungsmächte, als Korea und Persien die Welt ängstigten und die Wirtschaftswundersonne vielleicht gleich wieder im Osten blutig untergehen würde. Es war die Zeit, in der die neuen Reichen sich noch unsicher fühlten, in der die Schwarzmarktgewinner nach Anlagen suchten und die Sparer den Krieg bezahlten. Die neuen deutschen Geldscheine sahen wie gute Dollars aus, aber man traute doch mehr den Sachwerten, und viel Bedarf war nachzuholen, der Bauch war endlich zu füllen, der Kopf war von Hunger und Bombenknall noch etwas wirr, und alle Sinne suchten Lust, bevor vielleicht der dritte Weltkrieg kam. Diese Zeit, den Urgrund unseres Heute, habe ich geschildert, und ich möchte nun annehmen, sie allgemeingültig beschrieben zu haben, denn man glaubte, in dem Roman »Tauben im Gras« einen Spiegel zu sehen, in dem viele, an die ich beim Schreiben nicht gedacht hatte, sich zu erkennen wähnten, und manche, die ich nie in Verhältnissen und Bedrückungen vermutet hatte, wie dieses Buch sie malt, fühlten sich zu meiner Bestürzung von mir gekränkt, der ich nur als Schriftsteller gehandelt hatte und nach dem Wort Georges Bernanos' »das Leben in meinem Herzen filterte, um die geheime, mit Balsam und Gift erfüllte Essenz herauszuziehen«.

(Vorwort zur 2. Auflage)

Flieger waren über der Stadt, unheilkündende Vögel. Der Lärm der Motoren war Donner, war Hagel, war Sturm. Sturm, Hagel und Donner, täglich und nächtlich, Anflug und Abflug, Übungen des Todes, ein hohles Getöse, ein Beben, ein Erinnern in den Ruinen. Noch waren die Bombenschächte der Flugzeuge leer. Die Auguren lächelten. Niemand blickte zum Himmel auf.

Öl aus den Adern der Erde, Steinöl, Quallenblut, Fett der Saurier, Panzer der Echsen, das Grün der Farnwälder, die Riesenschachtelhalme, versunkene Natur, Zeit vor dem Menschen, vergrabenes Erbe, von Zwergen bewacht, geizig, zauberkundig und böse, die Sagen, die Märchen, der Teufelsschatz: er wurde ans Licht geholt, er wurde dienstbar gemacht. Was schrieben die Zeitungen? *Krieg um Öl, Verschärfung im Konflikt, der Volkswille, das Öl den Eingeborenen, die Flotte ohne Öl, Anschlag auf die Pipeline, Truppen schützen Bohrtürme, Schah heiratet, Intrigen um den Pfauenthron, die Russen im Hintergrund, Flugzeugträger im Persischen Golf.* Das Öl hielt die Flieger am Himmel, es hielt die Presse in Atem, es ängstigte die Menschen und trieb mit schwächeren Detonationen die leichten Motorräder der Zeitungsfahrer. Mit klammen Händen, mißmutig, fluchend, windgeschüttelt, regennaß, bierdumpf, tabakverbeizt, unausgeschlafen, alpgequält, auf der Haut noch den Hauch des Nachtgenossen, des Lebensgefährten, Reißen in der Schulter, Rheuma im Knie, empfingen die Händler die druckfrische Ware. Das Frühjahr war kalt. Das Neueste wärmte nicht. *Spannung, Konflikt,* man lebte im Spannungsfeld, östliche Welt, westliche Welt, man lebte an der Nahtstelle, vielleicht an der Bruchstelle, die Zeit war kostbar, sie war eine Atempause auf dem Schlachtfeld, und man hatte noch nicht richtig Atem geholt, wieder wurde gerüstet, die Rüstung verteuerte das Leben, die Rüstung schränkte die Freude ein, hier und dort horteten sie Pulver, den Erdball in die Luft zu sprengen, *Atomversuche in Neu-Mexiko, Atomfabriken im Ural,* sie bohrten Sprengkammern in das notdürftig geflickte Gemäuer der Brücken, sie redeten von Aufbau und bereiteten den Abbruch vor, sie ließen weiter zerbrechen, was schon angebrochen war: Deutschland war in zwei Teile gebrochen. Das Zeitungspapier roch nach heißgelaufenen Maschinen, nach Unglücksbotschaften, gewaltsamem Tod, falschen Urteilen, zynischen Bankrotten, nach Lüge, Ketten und Schmutz. Die Blätter klebten verschmiert aneinander, als näßten sie Angst. Die Schlagzeilen schrien: *Eisenhower inspiziert in Bundesrepublik, Wehrbeitrag gefordert, Adenauer gegen Neutralisierung, Konferenz in Sackgasse, Vertriebene klagen an, Millionen Zwangsarbeiter, Deutschland größtes Infanteriepotential.* Die Illustrierten lebten von den Erinnerungen der Flieger und Feldherren, den Beichten der strammen Mitläufer, den Memoiren der Tapferen, der Aufrechten, Unschuldigen, Überraschten, Übertölpelten. Über Kragen mit Eichenlaub und Kreuzen blickten sie grimmig von den Wänden der Kioske. Waren sie Akquisiteure der Blätter, oder warben sie ein Heer? Die Flieger, die am Himmel rumorten, waren die Flieger der andern.

Der Erzherzog wurde angekleidet, er wurde hergestellt. Hier ein Orden, da ein Band, ein Kreuz, ein strahlender Stern, Fangschnüre des Schicksals, Ketten der Macht, die schimmernden Epauletten, die silberne Schärpe, das Goldene Vlies, Orden del Toison de oro, Aureum Vellus, das Lammfell auf dem Feuerstein, zum Lob und Ruhm des Erlösers, der Jungfrau Maria und des heiligen Andreas wie zum Schutz und zur Förderung des christlichen Glaubens und der heiligen Kirche, zur Tugend und Vermehrung guter Sitte gestiftet. Alexander schwitzte. Übelkeit quälte ihn. Das Blech, der Tannenbaumzauber, der gestickte Uniformkragen, alles schnürte und engte ihn ein. Der Garderobier fummelte zu seinen Füßen. Er legte dem Erzherzog die Sporen an. Was war der Garderobier vor den blankgewichsten Schaftstiefeln des Erzherzogs? Eine Ameise, eine Ameise im Staub. Das

elektrische Licht in der Umkleidekabine, diesem Holzver-
schlag, den man Alexander anzubieten wagte, kämpfte mit
der Morgendämmerung. Was war es wieder für ein Morgen!
Alexanders Gesicht war käsig unter der Schminke; es war ein
Gesicht wie geronnene Milch. Schnäpse und Wein und ent-
behrter Schlaf gärten und gifteten in Alexanders Blut; sie
klopften ihm von innen den Schädel. Man hatte Alexander
in aller Frühe hierhergeholt. Die Gewaltige lag noch im Bett,
Messalina, seine Frau, das Lustroß, wie man sie in den Bars
nannte. Alexander liebte sein Weib; wenn er an seine Liebe
zu Messalina dachte, war die Ehe, die er mit ihr führte, schön.
Messalina schlief, aufgeschwemmt das Gesicht, die Augentu-
sche verwischt, die Lider wie von Faustschlägen getroffen,
die grobporige Haut, ein Droschenkutscherteint, vom Trunk
verwüstet. Welche Persönlichkeit! Alexander beugte sich vor
der Persönlichkeit. Er sank in die Knie, beugte sich über die
schlafende Gorgo, küßte den verqueren Mund, atmete den
Trunk, der nun wie ein reines Spiritusdestillat durch die Lippen drang: »Was ist? Gehst du? Laß mich! Oh, mir ist
schlecht!« Das war es, was er an ihr hatte. Auf dem Weg zum
Badezimmer trat sein Fuß in Scherben. Auf dem Sofa schlief
Alfredo, die Malerin, klein, zerzaust, hingesunken, niedlich,
Erschöpfung und Enttäuschung im Gesicht, Krähenfüße um
die geschlossenen Augen, mitleiderregend. Alfredo war amü-
sant, wenn sie wach war, eine schnell verbrennende Fackel;
sie sprühte, witzelte, erzählte, girrte, scharfzüngig, erstaun-
lich. Der einzige Mensch, über den man lachen konnte. Wie
nannten die Mexikaner die Lesbierinnen? Es war was wie
Maisfladen, Tortilleras, wohl ein flacher gedörrter Kuchen.
Alexander hatte es vergessen. Schade! Er hätte es anbringen
können. Im Badezimmer stand das Mädchen, das er aufge-
gabelt, das er mit seinem Ruhm angelockt hatte, mit dieser
schiefen Visage, die jedermann kannte. Schlagzeilen der Film-
blätter: *Alexander spielt den Erzherzog, der deutsche Superfilm, der Erzherzog und die Fischerin*, die hatte er gefischt,
aufgefischt, abgetischt. Wie hieß sie noch? Susanne! Susanne
im Bade. Sie war schon angezogen. Billiges Konfektionskleid.
Strich mit Seife über die Laufmasche im Strumpf. Hatte sich

mit dem Guerlain seiner Frau begossen. War mißmutig. Maulig. Das waren sie nachher immer. »Na, gut bekommen?« Er wußte nicht, was er sagen sollte. Eigentlich war er verlegen. »Dreckskerl!« Das war es. Sie wollten ihn. Alexander, der große Liebhaber! Hatte sich was! Er mußte sich duschen. Das Auto hupte unten wie verrückt. Die waren auf ihn angewiesen. Was zog denn noch? Er zog noch. *Alexander, die Liebe des Erzherzogs.* Die Leute hatten die Nase voll; sie hatten genug von der Zeit, genug von den Trümmern; die Leute wollten nicht ihre Sorgen, nicht ihre Furcht, nicht ihren Alltag, sie wollten nicht ihr Elend gespiegelt sehen. Alexander streifte den Schlafanzug ab. Das Mädchen Susanne sah neugierig, enttäuscht und böse auf alles, was an Alexander schlapp war. Er dachte ›schau dir es an, erzähl, was du willst, sie glauben es dir nicht, ich bin ihr Idol‹. Er prustete. Der kalte Strahl der Dusche schlug seine schlaffe Haut wie eine Peitsche. Schon wieder hupten sie unten. Die hatten es eilig, sie brauchten ihren Erzherzog. In der Wohnung schrie ein Kind, Hillegonda, Alexanders kleines Mädchen. Das Kind schrie »Emmi!« Rief das Kind um Hilfe? Angst, Verzweiflung, Verlassenheit lag in dem Kinderschrei. Alexander dachte ›ich müßte mich um sie kümmern, ich müßte Zeit haben, sie sieht blaß aus‹. Er rief: »Hille, bist du schon auf?« Warum war sie so früh schon auf? Er prustete die Frage ins Handtuch. Die Frage erstickte im Handtuch. Die Stimme des Kindes schwieg, oder sie ging unter im wütenden Hupen des wartenden Wagens. Alexander fuhr ins Atelier. Er wurde angekleidet. Er wurde gestiefelt und gespornt. Er stand vor der Kamera. Alle Scheinwerfer leuchteten auf. Die Orden glitzerten im Licht der Tausendkerzenbirnen. Das Idol spreizte sich. Man drehte den Erzherzog *Eine deutsche Superproduktion.*

Die Glocken riefen zur Frühmesse. Hörst-du-das-Glöcklein-läuten? Teddybären hörten zu, Puppen hörten zu, ein Elefant aus Wolle und auf roten Rädern hörte zu, Schneewittchen und Ferdinand der Stier auf der bunten Tapete vernahmen das traurige Lied, das Emmi, die Kinderfrau, langgezogen und klageweibisch sang, während sie den mageren Körper des kleinen Mädchens mit einer rauhen Bürste schrubbte. Hillegonda dachte ›Emmi du tust mir weh, Emmi du kratzt mich, Emmi du ziepst mich, Emmi deine Nagelfeile sticht mich‹, aber sie wagte der Kinderfrau, einer derben Person vom Lande, in deren breitem Gesicht die einfache Frömmigkeit der Bauern böse erstarrt war, nicht zu sagen, daß ihr weh getan wurde und daß sie litt. Der Gesang der Kinderfrau, hörst-du-das-Glöcklein-läuten, war eine immerwährende Mahnung und hieß: klage nicht, frage nicht, freue dich nicht, lache nicht, spiele nicht, tändele nicht, nütze die Zeit, denn wir sind dem Tod verfallen. Hillegonda hätte lieber noch geschlafen. Sie hätte lieber noch geträumt. Sie hätte auch gern mit ihren Puppen gespielt, aber Emmi sagte: »Wie darfst du spielen, wenn dich Gott ruft!« Hillegondas Eltern waren böse Menschen. Emmi sagte es. Man mußte für die Sünden der Eltern büßen. So begann der Tag. Sie gingen zur Kirche. Eine Straßenbahn bremste vor einem jungen Hund. Der Hund war struppig und ohne Halsband, ein herrenloser, verlaufener Hund. Die Kinderfrau drückte Hillegondas kleine Hand. Es war kein freundlicher, beistehender Druck; es war der feste unerbittliche Griff des Wächters. Hillegonda blickte dem kleinen herrenlosen Hund nach. Sie wäre lieber hinter dem Hund hergelaufen als mit der Kinderfrau in die Kirche gegangen. Hillegonda preßte die Knie zusammen, Furcht vor Emmi, Furcht vor der Kirche, Furcht vor Gott bedrückte ihr kleines Herz; sie machte sich schwer, sie ließ sich ziehen, um den Weg zu verzögern, aber die Hand des Wächters zerrte sie weiter. So früh war es noch. So kalt war es noch. So früh war Hillegonda schon auf dem Wege zu Gott. Die Kirchen haben Portale aus dicken Bohlen, schwerem Holz, eisernen Beschlägen und kupfernen Bolzen. Fürchtet sich auch Gott? Oder ist auch Gott gefangen? Die Kinderfrau faßte die kunstgeschmiedete Klinke und öffnete spaltbreit die Tür. Man konnte gerade zu Gott hineinschlüpfen. Es duftete bei Gott wie am Weihnachtstag nach Wunderkerzen. Bereitete sich hier das Wunder vor, das schreckliche, das angekündigte Wunder, die Vergebung der

Sünden, die Lossprechung der Eltern? ›Komödiantenkind‹ dachte die Kinderfrau. Ihre schmalen, blutlosen Lippen, Asketenlippen in einem Bauerngesicht, waren wie ein scharfer, für die Ewigkeit gezogener Strich. ›Emmi ich fürchte mich‹, dachte das Kind. ›Emmi die Kirche ist so groß, Emmi die Mauern stürzen ein, Emmi ich mag dich nicht mehr, Emmi liebe Emmi, Emmi ich hasse dich!‹ Die Kinderfrau sprengte Weihwasser über das zitternde Kind. Ein Mann drängte durch den Spalt der Tür. Fünfzig Jahre Mühe, Arbeit und Sorge lagen hinter ihm, und nun hatte er das Gesicht einer verfolgten Ratte. Zwei Kriege hatte er erlebt. Zwei gelbe Zähne verwesten hinter seinen immer flüsternden Lippen; er war in ein endloses Gespräch verstrickt; er sprach zu sich: wer sonst hätte ihm zugehört? Hillegonda folgte auf ihren Zehen der Kinderfrau. Düster waren die Pfeiler, das Mauerwerk war von Splittern verwundet. Kälte, wie aus einem Grab, wehte das Kind an. ›Emmi verlaß mich nicht, Emmi Hillegonda Angst, gute Emmi, böse Emmi, liebe Emmi‹, betete das Kind. ›Das Kind zu Gott führen, Gott straft bis ins dritte und vierte Glied‹, dachte die Kinderfrau. Die Gläubigen knieten. Sie sahen in dem hohen Raum wie verhärmte Mäuse aus. Der Priester las den Meßkanon. Die Wandlung der Elemente. Das Glöcklein läutete. Herr-vergib-uns. Der Priester fror. Wandlung der Elemente! Macht, der Kirche und ihren Dienern verliehen. Vergeblicher Traum der Alchimisten. Schwärmer und Schwindler. Gelehrte. Erfinder. Laboratorien in England, in Amerika, auch in Rußland. Zertrümmerung. Einstein. Blick in Gottes Küche. Die Weisen von Göttingen. Das Atom photographiert: zehntausendmillionenfache Vergrößerung. Der Priester litt unter seiner Nüchternheit. Das Flüstern der betenden Mäuse rieselte wie Sand über ihn. Sand des Grabes, nicht Sand des Heiligen Grabes, Sand der Wüste, die Messe in der Wüste, die Predigt in der Wüste. Heilige-Maria-bitt-für-uns. Die Mäuse bekreuzten sich.

Philipp verließ das Hotel, in dem er die Nacht verbracht, aber kaum geschlafen hatte, das Hotel Zum Lamm, in einer Gasse der Altstadt. Er hatte wach auf der harten Matratze

gelegen, dem Bett der Handlungsreisenden, der blumenlosen
Wiese der Paarung. Philipp hatte sich der Verzweiflung hingegeben, einer Sünde. Das Schicksal hatte ihn in die Enge
getrieben. Die Flügel der Erinnyen schlugen mit dem Wind
und dem Regen gegen das Fenster. Das Hotel war ein Neubau; die Einrichtung war fabrikfrisch, gelacktes Holz, sauber, hygienisch, schäbig und sparsam. Ein Vorhang, zu kurz,
zu schmal und zu dünn, um vor dem Lärm und dem Licht
der Straße zu schützen, war mit dem Muster einer Bauhaus-
tapete bedruckt. In regelmäßigen Abständen flammte der
Schein eines Leuchtschildes, das Gäste für den gegenüberliegenden Ecartéklub anlocken sollte, ins Zimmer: ein Kleeblatt entfaltete sich über Philipp und entwischte. Unter dem
Fenster schimpften Spieler, die ihr Geld verloren hatten. Betrunkene torkelten aus dem Bräuhaus. Sie pißten gegen die
Häuser und sangen die-Infanterie-die-Infanterie, verabschiedete, geschlagene Eroberer. Auf den Stiegen des Hauses war
ein fortwährendes Kommen und Gehen. Das Hotel war ein
Bienenstock des Teufels, und jedermann in dieser Hölle schien
zur Schlaflosigkeit verdammt. Hinter den windigen Wänden
wurde gejohlt, gerülpst und Dreck weggespült. Später war
der Mond durch die Wolken gebrochen, die sanfte Luna, die
Leichenstarre.
Der Wirt fragte ihn: »Bleiben Sie noch?« Er fragte es grob,
und seine kalten Augen, todbitter im glatten ranzigen Fett
befriedigter Freßlust, gesättigten Durstes, im Ehebett sauer
gewordener Geilheit, blickten Philipp mißtrauisch an. Philipp war am Abend ohne Gepäck in das Hotel gekommen.
Es hatte geregnet. Sein Schirm war naß gewesen, und außer
dem Schirm hatte er nichts bei sich gehabt. Würde er noch
bleiben? Er wußte es nicht. Er sagte: »Ja, ja.« »Ich zahle
für zwei Tage«, sagte er. Die kalten, todbitteren Augen ließen ihn los. »Sie wohnen hier in der Fuchsstraße«, sagte der
Wirt. Er betrachtete Philipps Meldezettel. ›Was geht es ihn
an‹, dachte Philipp, ›was geht es ihn an wenn er sein Geld
bekommt.‹ Er sagte: »Meine Wohnung wird geweißt.« Es
war eine lächerliche Ausrede. Jeder mußte merken, daß es
eine Ausrede war. ›Er wird denken ich verstecke mich, er

17

wird sich genau denken was los ist, er wird denken daß man mich sucht.‹

Es regnete nicht mehr. Philipp trat aus der Bräuhausgasse auf den Böttcherplatz. Er zögerte vor dem Haupteingang des Bräuhauses, am Morgen einem geschlossenen Schlund, aus dem es nach Erbrochenem dunstete. Auf der anderen Seite des Platzes lag das Café Schön, der Klub der amerikanischen Negersoldaten. Die Vorhänge hinter den großen Spiegelfenstern waren zur Seite gezogen. Die Stühle standen auf den Tischen. Zwei Frauen spülten den Unrat der Nacht auf die Straße. Zwei alte Männer kehrten den Platz. Sie wirbelten Bierdeckel, Luftschlangen, Narrenkappen der Trinker, zerknüllte Zigarettenpackungen, geplatzte Gummiballons auf. Es war eine schmutzige Flut, die mit jedem Besenstoß der Männer Philipp näher rückte. Hauch und Staub der Nacht, der schale tote Abfall der Lust hüllten Philipp ein.

Frau Behrend hatte es sich gemütlich gemacht. Ein Scheit prasselte im Ofen. Die Tochter der Hausbesorgerin brachte die Milch. Die Tochter war unausgeschlafen und hungrig. Sie war hungrig nach dem Leben, wie es ihr Filme zeigten, sie war eine verwunschene Prinzessin, zu niederem Dienst gezwungen. Sie erwartete den Messias, die Hupe des Erlöserprinzen, den Millionärssohn im Sportwagen, den Fracktänzer der Cocktail-Bar, das technische Genie, den vorausschauenden Konstrukteur, den Knock-out-Sieger über die Zurückgebliebenen, die Feinde des Fortschritts, Jung-Siegfried. Sie war schmalbrüstig, hatte rachitische Gelenke, eine Bauchnarbe und einen verkniffenen Mund. Sie fühlte sich ausgenutzt. Ihr verkniffener Mund flüsterte: »Die Milch, Frau Obermusikmeister.«

Geflüstert oder gerufen: die Anrede zauberte das Bild schöner Tage. Aufrecht schritt der Musikmeister an der Spitze des Regiments durch die Stadt. Aus Fell und Blech dröhnte der Marsch. Schellen rasselten. Die Fahne hoch. Die Beine hoch. Die Arme hoch. Herrn Behrends Muskeln stemmten sich gegen das Tuch der engen Uniform. Die Platzmusik im Waldpavillon! Der Meister dirigierte den Freischütz. Unter dem Befehl seines ausgestreckten Stabes stiegen Carl Maria von Webers romantische Klänge pianissimo gedämpft in die Wipfel der Bäume. Frau Behrends Brust hob und senkte sich, den Wogen des Meeres gleich, am Gartentisch der Wirtschaft. Ihre Hände ruhten in Filethandschuhen auf dem buntgewürfelten Leinen der Kaffeetafel. Für diese Stunde der Kunst sah sich Frau Behrend aufgenommen in den Kreis der Damen des Regiments. Leier und Schwert, Orpheus und Mars verbrüderten sich. Frau Major bot liebenswürdig das Mitgebrachte an, das Selbstgebackene, die Schichttorte aus dreierlei Mus, in den Ofen geschoben, während der Major auf dem Pferde saß, den Kasernenhof kommandierte, das Auf-marsch-marsch, und dazu die Paukenwirbel der Wolfsschlucht.

Konnten sie uns nicht in Frieden lassen? Frau Behrend hatte den Krieg nicht gewollt. Der Krieg verseuchte die Männer. Beethovens Totenmaske musterte bleich und streng die enge Mansarde. Ein bronzebärtiger und barettierter Wagner balancierte vergrämt auf einem Stoß klassischer Klavierauszüge, der vergilbenden Hinterlassenschaft des Musikmeisters, der sich in irgendeiner vom Führer besetzten und dann wieder verlorenen Gegend Europas an eine bemalte Schlampe gehängt hatte und nun in Gott weiß was für Kaffeehäusern für Neger und Veronikas »Wenn-ich-nach-Alabama-komm'« spielte.

Er kam nicht nach Alabama. Er entwischte nicht. Die Zeit der Gesetzlosigkeit war vorbei, die Zeit, die meldete *Gruppenführer als Rabbiner in Palästina, Barbier Direktor der Frauenklinik.* Die Akteure waren eingefangen; sie saßen, saßen hinter Gittern ihre neuen, viel zu milden Strafen ab: Kazettler, Verfolgte, Deserteure, Doktortitelschwindler. Es gab wieder Richter in Deutschland. Der Musikmeister zahlte die Mansarde, er zahlte das Scheit im Ofen, die Milch in der Flasche, den Kaffee im Topf. Er zahlte es vom Alabama-Sündenlohn. Ein Tribut an die Ehrbarkeit! Was hilft's? Alles wird teurer, und wieder sind es Schleichwege, die zu den Annehmlichkeiten des Daseins führen. Frau Behrend trank Maxwell-Coffee. Sie kaufte den Kaffee beim Juden. Beim

19

Juden — das waren schwarzhaarige, gebrochenes Deutsch
sprechende Leute, Unerwünschte, Ausländer, Hergewehte,
die einen vorwurfsvoll aus dunkelschimmernden, nachtver-
wobenen Augen ansahen, von Gas und Grabgräben wohl
sprechen wollten und Hinrichtungsstätten im Morgengrauen,
Gläubiger, Gerettete, die mit dem geretteten Leben nichts
anderes zu beginnen wußten, als auf den Schuttplätzen der
zerbombten Städte (warum mit Bomben beworfen? mein
Gott, warum geschlagen? für welche Sünde gestraft? die fünf
Zimmer in Würzburg, Heim am Südhang, Blick über die
Stadt, Blick über das Tal, der Main schimmernd, die Morgen-
sonne auf dem Balkon, *Führer beim Duce*, warum?) in kleinen schnell errichteten Buden, den windigen Notläden, Un-
verzolltes und Unversteuertes zu verkaufen. »Sie lassen uns
nichts«, sagte die Lebensmittelhändlerin, »nichts, sie wollen uns zugrunde richten.« In der Villa der Lebensmittelhändlerin wohnten die Amis. Sie wohnten seit vier Jahren
in dem beschlagnahmten Haus. Sie gaben die Wohnung aneinander weiter. Sie schliefen in dem Doppelbett aus ge-
flammter Birke, dem Schlafzimmer der Aussteuer. Sie saßen
im Altdeutschen Zimmer in den Ritterstühlen, inmitten der
Pracht der achtziger Jahre, die Beine auf dem Tisch, und
leerten ihre Konservenbüchsen, die Fließbandnahrung *Chi-
kago packt tausend Ochsen pro Minute*, ein Jubel in ihrer
Presse. Im Garten spielten die fremden Kinder, tütenblau,
dottergelb, feuerrot, angezogen wie Clowns, siebenjährige
Mädchen, die Lippen wie Huren geschminkt, die Mütter in
Schlosserhosen, die Waden aufgekrempelt, fahrende Leute,
unernste Menschen. Der Kaffee im Laden der Händlerin ver-
schimmelte, verzollt und übersteuert. Frau Behrend nickte.
Sie vergaß nie den Respekt, den sie der Krämerin schuldete,
die Furcht, anerzogen in der harten Schule der Markenzeit
Aufruf zweiundsechzigeinhalb Gramm Weichkäse. Nun gab
es wieder alles. Bei uns jedenfalls. Wer konnte es kaufen?
Vierzig Mark Kopfgeld. Sechs Prozent Aufwertung des Ersparten und vierundneunzig Prozent in den Wind geschrieben. Der eigene Bauch am nächsten. Die Welt war hart. Sol-
datenwelt. Soldaten packten hart zu. Bewährung. Das Ge-

wicht stimmte wieder. Für wie lange? Zucker verschwand
aus den Geschäften. In England fehlte Fleisch. Wo ist der
Sieger, ich will ihn bekränzen? *Bacon* heißt Speck. *Ham* ist
dasselbe wie Schinken. Fett lag das Geräucherte im Fenster
des Schlächters Schleck. »Bitte vom Mageren.« Das Schläch-
termesser trennte das gelblich weißliche schwabbelnde Fett
von der rötlichen Faser des Kerns. Wo ist der Sieger, ich will
ihn bekränzen? Die Amis waren reich. Ihre Automobile glichen Schiffen, heimgekehrten Karavellen des Kolumbus. Wir
haben ihr Land entdeckt. Wir haben ihren Erdteil bevölkert.
Solidarität der weißen Rasse. Es war schön, zu den reichen
Leuten zu gehören. Verwandte schickten Pakete. Frau Behrend schlug das Heft auf, in dem sie gestern vor dem Einschlafen gelesen hatte. Eine spannende Geschichte, ein lebens-
wahrer Roman: *Das Schicksal greift nach Hannelore.* Frau
Behrend wollte wissen, wie es weiterging. Der Dreifarben-
titel zeigte das Bild einer jungen Frau, brav, rührend und
unschuldig, und im Hintergrund versammelten sich die Schur-
ken, gruben ihre Gruben, Wühlmäuse des Schicksals. Gefährlich war das Leben, voll Fallgruben der Weg der Anständigen. Das Schicksal griff nicht nur nach Hannelore. Aber im
letzten Kapitel triumphieren die Guten.

Philipp kam mit der Zeit nicht zurecht. Der Augenblick war
wie ein lebendes Bild, der possierliche Gegenstand einer Erstarrung, das Dasein in Gips gegossen, ein Rauch, der Husten hervorrief, umschwebte es wie eine karikierende Ara-
beske, und Philipp war ein kleiner Junge im Kieler Anzug,
S. M. Schiff Grille auf dem Mützenband, und er saß in einer
Kleinstadt auf einem Stuhl im Deutschen Saal, und die Damen des Luisenbundes führten auf der Bühne in einer Wald-
kulisse Bilder aus der vaterländischen Geschichte vor, Germania und ihre Kinder, das liebte man damals, oder man
gab vor, es zu lieben, die Tochter des Rektors hielt die Pfanne
mit dem brennenden Pech, das der Szene wohl etwas Feier-
liches, Dauerndes, dem Tag Entrücktes geben sollte. Die
Tochter des Rektors war schon lange tot. Eva, er hatte ihr
Kletten ins Haar geworfen. Die Jungens waren tot, alle, die

neben ihm auf den Stühlen des Deutschen Saales gesessen hatten. Die Stadt war eine tote Stadt wie so viele Städte im Osten, eine Stadt irgendwo in Masuren, doch man konnte nicht mehr zum Bahnhof gehen und eine Fahrkarte nach diesem Ort verlangen. Die Stadt war ausgelöscht. Merkwürdig: niemand war auf der Straße. Die Klassenzimmer des Gymnasiums waren stumm und leer. In den Fenstern nisteten die Krähen. Das hatte er geträumt, das hatte er in den Schulstunden geträumt: das Leben war in der Stadt gestorben, die Häuser waren leer, die Straßen, der Markt stumm und leer, und er, als einziger übriggeblieben, war mit einem der verlassen am Straßenrand stehengebliebenen Autos allein durch die tote Stadt gefahren. Die Dekoration des Traums war ins Leben gestellt, aber Philipp agierte nicht mehr auf dieser Bühne. Litt er, wenn er an die Toten dachte, an die toten Stätten, die verscharrten Gefährten? Nein. Die Empfindung versteifte sich wie vor den lebenden Bildern des Luisenbundes, die Vorstellung war irgendwie pompös, traurig und abscheulich, eine Siegesallee aus Stuck und gestanztem Lorbeer, aber vor allem war sie langweilig. Zugleich aber raste dieselbe Zeit, die doch wiederum stillstand und das Jetzt war, dieser Augenblick von schier ewiger Dauer, flog dahin, wenn man die Zeit als die Summe aller Tage betrachtete, den Ablauf aus Licht und Dunkel, der uns auf Erden gegeben ist, glich dem Wind, war etwas und nichts, meßbar durch List, aber niemand konnte sagen, was er da maß, es umströmte die Haut, formte den Menschen und entfloh ungreifbar, unhaltbar: woher? wohin? Aber er, Philipp, stand noch dazu außerhalb dieses Ablaufs der Zeit, nicht eigentlich ausgestoßen aus dem Strom, sondern ursprünglich auf einen Posten gerufen, einen ehrenvollen Posten vielleicht, weil er alles beobachten sollte, aber das Dumme war, daß ihm schwindlig wurde und daß er gar nichts beobachten konnte, schließlich nur ein Wogen sah, in dem einige Jahreszahlen wie Signale aufleuchteten, schon nicht mehr natürliche Zeichen, künstlich listig errichtete Bojen in der Zeitsee, schwankendes Menschenmal auf den ungebändigten Wellen, aber zuweilen erstarrte das Meer, und aus dem Wasser der Unendlichkeit hob sich ein gefrorenes, nichtssagendes, dem Gelächter schon überantwortetes Bild.

In die Engellichtspiele kann man schon am Morgen vor dem Licht des Tages fliehen. »Der letzte Bandit« ist ein Kassenschlager. Der Lichtspielbesitzer telegraphiert die Besucherzahl an den Filmverleiher. Hausrekord, Zahlenakrobatik wie einst die Sondermeldung *Bruttoregistertonnen versenkt.* Wiggerl, Schorschi, Bene, Kare und Sepp standen unter dem Lautsprecher, standen unter der Kaskade von Worten, Sieg und Fanfaren, kleine Hitlerjungen, Pimpfsoldaten, braunes Hemd, kurze Hosen, nackte Schenkel. Sie schüttelten die Sammelbüchsen, rüttelten die Groschen wach, klapperten mit den Abzeichen aus Blech. »Für die Winterhilfe! Für die Front! Für den Führer!« In der Nacht heulte die Sirene. Die Flak schwieg. Jetzt flogen die Jäger auf Jagd. Brillanten zum Ritterkreuz. Minen. Das Licht flackerte. Duck dich! In den Kellerrohren rauschte das Wasser. Im Nebenhaus sind sie ersoffen. Alle sind sie im Keller ersoffen. Schorschi, Bene, Kare und Sepp sitzen vor dem letzten Banditen. Tief graben sich ihre harten Hintern in die ausgefurzten kuhligen Polster des Kinogestühls. Sie haben keine Lehrstelle und keine Arbeit. Sie haben kein Geld, aber doch die Mark für den Banditen; sie flog ihnen zu, Vöglein auf dem Felde. Sie schwänzen die Gewerbeschule, da sie kein Gewerbe haben, oder doch Gewerbe, die man in der Schule nicht lernt, wohl an den Straßenecken, in den Torwegen der Dollarwechsler, den Gassen der Damen, den Alleen der Freunde im Schatten des Justizpalastes, das Gewerbe der flinken Hände, die nehmen und nicht geben, das Handwerk der festen Fäuste, die schlagen und fleddern, und die warme Tour, die Profession des weichen Blicks, der schwingenden Hüften, des wippenden Arsches. Wiggerl ist in der Legion, übers Meer so weit, bei den Annamiten im Busch, Schlangen und Lianen, verfallene Tempel, oder bei den Franzosen im Fort, Mädchen und Wein in Saigon, Brodem der Unterkünfte, die Strafzelle in den Kasematten, Eidechsen in der Sonne. Gleichgültig. Wiggerl kämpft. Er singt: weiter die Fahne hoch. Er fällt. *Soldaten-*

tod ist der schönste Tod. So oft gehört, in der Kindheit eingeprägt, von Vätern und Brüdern vorgelebt, Tränentrost der Mutter, nie wird das Wort vergessen. Schorschi, Bene, Kare und Sepp warten auf den Trommler. Sie warten in der Dämmerung des Kinos. Der letzte Bandit. Sie sind bereit; bereit zu folgen, bereit zu kämpfen, bereit zu sterben. Es braucht kein Gott zu sein, der sie ruft, ein Plakat auf allen Mauern, eine grade gängige Larve, ein Bärtchen mit Markenschutz, kein lächelnder Augur, die Roboter-Maske aus gestanztem Blech, ein Gesicht unter dem Durchschnitt, kein Versprechen in den Augen, leere Wasser, geschliffene Spiegel, die immer nur dich zeigen, Kaliban, von dem die Genien sich abwandten, der synthetische Rattenfänger, sein Ruf: *Bewährung,* Blut, Schmerzen und Tod, ich führe dich zu dir selbst, Kaliban, du brauchst dich nicht zu schämen, ein Scheusal zu sein. Noch steht das Kino; in die Kasse strömt das Geld. Noch steht das Rathaus; die Lustbarkeitssteuer wird verbucht. Noch wächst die Stadt.

Die Stadt wächst. *Zuzugsperre aufgehoben.* Sie strömen zurück, eine Flut, die verebbte, ins Land verrieselte, in die Bauernstuben, als die Städte brannten, als der Asphalt hinschmolz in der täglich durchschrittenen Gasse, stygisches Wasser wurde, ätzend und brennend, dort, wo die kleinen Schuhe zur Schule liefen, wo man als Braut und Bräutigam ging, die Steinheimat bebte, und dann hockten sie in den Dörfern, verloren der Hausrat, verloren das Nest, wo die Brut zur Welt kam, verloren das Immeraufbewahrte, das Was-du-Warst, die in das unterste Fach des Schrankes verbannte Jugend, ein Kinderbild, die Schulklasse, der ertrunkene Freund, die verblaßte Schrift eines Briefes, Leb-wohl-Fritz, Ade-Marie, ein Gedicht, war ich es, der es reimte? —

Der kleine zierliche stramme Körper des Doktors lag, wohltrainiert in behenden leichtathletischen Übungen, auf dem mit Wachstuch bezogenen Tisch, und aus einer Vene des Armes strömte sein Blut nicht sichtbar und nicht nah einem anderen Menschen zu, kein warmer Blick des mit neuem

Lebensfluß Beschenkten dankte dem Spender, Dr. Behude war ein abstrakter Samariter, sein Blut verwandelte sich in eine Ziffer, eine chemische Formel, ausgedrückt durch die Zeichensprache der Mathematik, es strömte in ein Einmachglas, wurde mit einem Schild versehen, Himbeersaft, Erdbeermarmelade, die Blutgruppe stand auf dem Schild, der Saft wurde sterilisiert, und die Konserve konnte verschickt werden, irgendwohin, durch die Luft, über Ozeane weit, dahin wo gerade ein Schlachtfeld war, und das fand sich immer, eine ursprünglich harmlose Landschaft, Natur mit dem Wechsel der Jahreszeiten, ein Acker mit Saat und Ernte, wohin nun Menschen marschiert, gereist und geflogen waren, um sich zu verwunden und zu töten. Da lagen sie blaß auf einer Feldbahre, der Wimpel des Roten Kreuzes flatterte im fremden Wind und erinnerte sie an die Unfallwagen, die mit Sirenenschwall durch die Straßen der verkehrsverstopften Städte eilen, der Städte, aus denen sie kamen, die Tetanusspritze brannte, und Dr. Behudes Blut wurde ihnen in den zerrissenen Leib gepumpt. Der Behude erhielt zehn Mark für die Blutentnahme. Bar wurde das Geld an der Kasse der Klinik ausgezahlt. Die jungen Ärzte, die schon die Soldaten des Zweiten Weltkrieges aufgeschnitten, zersägt, bespritzt und zugenäht hatten und nun in unbezahlten Volontär- und Assistentenstellen erkennen mußten, daß sie überflüssig und zu viele waren, viel zuviel Kriegsmediziner, drängten sich, ihr Blut zu verkaufen, das einzige, was sie zu verkaufen hatten. Auch Dr. Behude brauchte die zehn Mark, aber es war nicht nur der Betrag, Blut gegen Geld, der ihn zu diesem Handel veranlaßte. Dr. Behude kasteite sich. Es war eine mönchische Geißelung, der er sich unterzog, und die Blutentnahme war ein Versuch, wie die Hanteln, die Morgenläufe, die Rumpfbeugen, die Atemübungen, ein Gleichgewicht herzustellen zwischen den Kräften und Forderungen des Körpers und der Seele. Dr. Behude analysierte sich, während er auf dem kühlen Wachstuch des Tansfusionstisches lag. Er war kein Wohltäter, kein Spender; das Blut löste sich von ihm ab, wurde ein Medikament wie andere, man konnte es verschicken, konnte damit handeln, Leben retten, es berührte Dr. Behude nicht; er reinigte sich, er bereitete sich vor. Bald werden sich die Räume seiner Praxis füllen, werden sich mit Leuten füllen, die Kraft und Lebensmut von ihm zapfen wollen. Die Schar der Halbverrückten liebt und bedrängt den Dr. Behude, die Neurotiker, die Lügner, die nicht wissen, warum sie lügen, die Impotenten, die Schwulen, die Pädophilen, die sich in Kinder vergaffen, kurzen Röcken folgen, nackten Beinen, die Literaten, die zwischen allen Stühlen sitzen, die Maler, denen die Farben des Lebens zu geometrischen Strichen zusammenfließen, Schauspieler, die an toten Worten ersticken, Pan war tot, zum zweitenmal gestorben, sie alle kamen, die ihre Komplexe brauchten wie ihr tägliches Brot, die Geängstigten und Untüchtigen, zu untüchtig auch, sich in eine Krankenkasse einzukaufen oder je eine Rechnung zu bezahlen. —

Sie hatten ihr Leben gerettet, ein nutzloses Dasein, sie hausten verbittert in den Flecken, auf Alm und Au, in Hütten und auf den Höfen, der Rauch verzog sich, sie lauschten den Baggern, die in die Trümmer griffen, lauschten von fern, ausgesperrt von Ninive, von Babylon, Sodom, den geliebten Städten, den großen wärmenden Kesseln, Geflohene, zur Sommerfrische verdammt, Touristen, die nicht zahlen konnten, scheel angesehen beim Landvolk, heimwehtoll nach den Steinen. Sie kehrten heim, die Schranke hob sich, die verhaßte Verordnung der Zuzugssperre fiel, aufgehoben war die Ausstoßung, sie strömten zurück, sie fluteten ein, der Pegel stieg *Stadt Brennpunkt des Wohnungsbedarfs*. Sie waren wieder zu Hause, reihten sich ein, rieben sich aneinander, übervorteilten einander, handelten, schufen, bauten, gründeten, zeugten, saßen in der alten Kneipe, atmeten den vertrauten Brodem, beobachteten das Revier, den Paarungsplatz, den Nachwuchs der Asphaltgassen, Gelächter und Zank und das Radio der Nachbarn, sie starben im Städtischen Krankenhaus, wurden vom Bestattungsamt hinausgefahren, lagen auf dem Friedhof an der Ost-Süd-Kreuzung, von Straßenbahnen umbimmelt, benzindunstumschwelt, glücklich in der Heimat. *Superbomber in Europa stationiert.*

Odysseus Cotton verließ den Bahnhof. Am schlenkernden Arm, in der braunen Hand baumelte ein Köfferchen. Odysseus Cotton war nicht allein. Eine Stimme begleitete ihn. Aus dem Koffer kam die Stimme, sanft, warm, weich, eine tiefe Stimme, wohlige Atmung, ein Hauch wie Samt, heiße Haut unter einer alten zerrissenen Autodecke in einer Wellblechhütte, Schreie, Brüllen der Riesenfrösche, Nacht am Mississippi. Richter Lynch reitet über Land, o Tag von Gettysburg, Lincoln zieht in Richmond ein, vergessen das Sklavenschiff, ewig das Brandmal ins Fleisch gesengt, Afrika, verlorene Erde, das Dickicht der Wälder, Stimme einer Negerin. Die Stimme sang *Night-and-day*, sie schirmte mit ihrem Klang den Kofferträger gegen den Platz vor dem Bahnhof, umschlang ihn wie Glieder der Liebenden, wärmte ihn in der Fremde, zeltete ihn ein. Odysseus Cotton stand unschlüssig. Er schaute über die Taxistände, blickte zum Warenhaus Rohn hinüber, sah Kinder, Frauen, Männer, die Deutschen, wer waren sie? was dachten sie? wie träumten und liebten sie? Waren sie Freunde? Feinde?

Die schwere Tür der Telephonzelle schlug hinter Philipp zu. Das Glas isolierte ihn von dem Treiben auf dem Bahnhofsplatz, der Lärm war nur noch ein Rauschen, der Verkehr ein Schattenspiel auf den geriffelten Flächen der Wände. Philipp wußte noch immer nicht, wie er den Tag verbringen sollte. Die Stunde gähnte. Er fühlte sich wie eine der leeren Pakkungen, die der Besen zum Kehricht gefegt hatte, nutzlos, seiner Bestimmung beraubt. Welcher Bestimmung? War er zu etwas bestimmt gewesen, hatte er sich dieser Bestimmung entzogen, und konnte man sich überhaupt, vorausgesetzt, es gab sie, einer Bestimmung entziehen? *Das astrologische Jahrhundert, das Wochenhoroskop, Trumans und Stalins Sterne.* Er hätte heimgehen können. Er konnte nach Hause in die Fuchsstraße gehen. Der Frühling setzte sich durch. Im verwilderten Garten der Villa blühte das Unkraut. Nach Hause? ein Unterstand, in den es hineinprasselte: Emilia würde sich gegen Morgen wohl beruhigt haben. In die Türen würden Schrammen getreten, in die Wände Löcher gestoßen, Porzellan würde zerschlagen sein. Emilia, von ihrem Toben erschöpft, von ihren Träumen ermattet, ihrer Angst geschlagen, lag auf dem rosa Erbbett, dem Totenbett der Urmutter, die noch ein schönes Leben gelebt hatte, Heringsdorf, Paris, Nizza, die Goldwährung und den Glanz des Wirklichen Geheimen Kommerzienrattitels. Die Hunde, die Katzen, der Papagei, eifersüchtig aufeinander und Feind einander, aber in einer gemeinsamen Front des Hasses gegen Philipp vereint, einer Phalanx tückischer Blicke, wie alles in diesem Haus ihn haßte, die Verwandten seiner Frau, die Miterben, die verbröckelnden Mauern, das stumpfe Parkett, die rieselnden, säuselnden Röhren der kaputten Heizung, der lange nicht gerichteten Bäder, die Tiere hielten die Möbel wie Kampftürme besetzt und beobachteten den Schlaf ihrer Herrin aus halbgeöffneten Lidern, den Schlaf ihres Opfers, an das sie gekettet waren und das sie bewachten. Philipp rief Dr. Behude an. Vergebens! Der Psychiater war noch nicht in seine Praxis zurückgekehrt. Philipp versprach sich nichts von einer Begegnung mit Dr. Behude, keine Deutung, keine Erhellung, weder Vertrauen noch Mut, aber es war ihm zu einer Gewohnheit geworden, den Nervenarzt aufzusuchen, sich in das verdunkelte Behandlungszimmer zu legen und den Gedanken freien Lauf zu lassen, einer Flucht von Bildern, die ihn bei Dr. Behude überkam, einem kaleidoskopartigen Wechsel des Ortes und der Zeit, während der Therapeut der Seele ihn mit sanfter einschläfernder Stimme von Schuld und Buße befreien wollte. — Dr. Behude schloß in dem Behandlungszimmer der Klinik sein Hemd. Sein Gesicht schimmerte bleich im weißgerahmten Spiegel an der Wand. Seine Augen, die hypnotische Kraft besitzen sollten, waren trüb, müde und leicht entzündet. Einhundert Kubikzentimeter seines Blutes ruhten in dem Kühlschrank der Klinik.

Night-and-day. Odysseus Cotton lachte. Er freute sich. Er schlenkerte seinen Koffer. Er zeigte kräftige strahlende Zähne. Er hatte Vertrauen. Ein Tag lag vor ihm. Der Tag bot sich allen. Unter dem Vordach des Bahnhofs wartete Josef, der Dienstmann. Die rote Dienstmannsmütze saß streng, militärisch grade auf dem kahlen Haupt. Was hatte Josefs Rücken gebeugt? Die Koffer der Reisenden, das Gepäck der Jahrzehnte, ein halbes Jahrhundert Brot im Schweiß des Angesichts, Adams Fluch, Märsche in Knobelbechern, die Knarre über der Schulter, das Koppel, der Sack mit den Wurfgranaten, der schwere Helm, das schwere Töten. Verdun, Argonnerwald, Chemin-des-Dames, er war heil herausgekommen, und wieder Koffer, Reisende ohne Gewehr, Fremdenverkehr zum Gebirgsbahnhof, Fremdenverkehr zum Hotel, die Olympischen Spiele, die Jugend der Welt, und wieder Fahnen, wieder Märsche, er schleppte Offiziersgepäck, die Söhne gingen ohne Wiederkehr, die Jugend der Welt, Sirenen, die Alte starb, die Mutter der vom Krieg verschlungenen Kinder, die Amerikaner kamen mit bunten Taschen, Bagagesäcken, leichtem Gepäck, die Zigarettenwährung, die neue Mark, das Abgesparte verweht, Spreu, bald siebzig Jahre, was blieb? Der Sitz vor dem Bahnhof, das Nummernschild an der Mütze. Der Leib war zusammengeschrumpft, die Augen blinzelten noch munter hinter der stahlgefaßten Brille, lustige Fältlein liefen vom Lid in das Feld der Haut, strömten ein in das Altersgrau, in die Luftbräune, die Bierröte des Gesichts. Die Kollegenschaft ersetzte die Familie. Sie ließen dem Papa die leichten Kommissionen, die zwischen dem schweren Gepäck anfielen, eine Briefbestellung, eine Blumenbesorgung, das Tragen einer Damentasche. Josef ergatterte die Aufträge in Demut und auch mit List. Er kannte die Menschen. Er wußte für sich einzunehmen. Manche Tasche wurde ihm gereicht, die man ihm nicht hatte geben wollen. Er traute dem Tag. Er sah Odysseus Cotton. Er liebäugelte mit dem Köfferchen, aus dem die Musik klang. Er sagte: »Sie, Mister, ich tragen.« Er störte sich nicht an dem Gesang, der das Zelt um Odysseus baute, er griff in die fremde Welt, *Night-and-day*-Welt, drängte die braune Hand vom Bügel des Koffers, drängte sich klein, bescheiden, standhaft, freundlich gegen den dunklen Riesen, King Kong, der ihn überragte, unergründlich sind die nie geschlagenen, die uralten Wälder. Josef blieb ungebannt von der Stimme, Stimme des breiten, trägen und warmen Stromes, Stimme des Eingewobenseins, Stimme der heimlichen Nacht. Wie Holz auf dem Fluß glitt eins zum andern; Totemtiere um den Kral, ein Tabu um den Abtrünnigen des Stammes, Josef empfand weder Lust noch Unlust, nichts lockte und nichts schreckte ihn: kein libidinöses Verlangen, Odysseus stand in keinem Affektzusammenhang zu Josef, Josef war keine Maske des Ödipus für Odysseus, nicht Haß, nicht Liebe bewegten sie, Josef vermutete Freigebigkeit, er trieb heran, sacht und beharrlich, er sah eine Brotzeit, sah ein Bier *Night-and-day* —

Der Papagei krächzte, ein Liebesvogel, Kama, der Gott der Liebe, reitet auf einem Papagei, die Erzählungen des Papageienbuches, phantastisch und obszön, die Minderjährige nahm sie aus dem Schrank des Vaters, versteckte sie unter dem Bett, der Papagei auf den alten Darstellungen der Heiligen Familie, Symbol der Unbefleckten Empfängnis, es war ein behäbiger Rosellapapagei, rundlich wie eine alte erfolgreiche Schauspielerin, rot, gelb, agavengrün, stahlblau sein Gefieder, das Kleid, das er grimmig schüttelte, die Freiheit war vergessen, war ein vergessener, schon nicht mehr wahrer Traum, der Vogel krächzte, nicht nach Freiheit krächzte er, jammerte nach Licht, nach dem Hochziehen der Jalousie, dem Beiseitestoßen der schweren Vorhänge, dem Zerreißen der Zimmerdunkelheit, dem Ende der künstlich verlängerten Nacht. Auch die Hunde und die Katzen wurden unruhig. Sie sprangen zu der Schlafenden ins Bett, zankten sich, zerrten an der zerschlissenen Seide der Decke, und Daunen wirbelten wie Schnee unsichtbar in der Dunkelheit durch den Raum. Emilia lag noch unter der Decke der Nacht, die draußen schon seit Stunden vergangen war. Ihr Bewußtsein war noch zugedeckt von der Nacht. Ihre Glieder lagen in der Tiefe der Nacht wie in einem Grab. Die rosa Zunge des schwarzen Katers leckte das Ohr der jungen Toten. Emilia regte sich, schlug um sich, wälzte sich vom Bauch auf den Rücken, tastete über den knisternden Pelz der Katze, faßte den Kopf eines Hundes, röchelte »was ist los, was ist denn schon wieder?«, wo kam sie her? aus welchen dunkelen

Abgründen des Schlafs? Sie hörte das ewige Säuseln in den
Röhren des Hauses, das Bröckeln des Verputzes, das Schnau-
ben, Knurren, Tappen und Schweifschlagen der Tiere. Die
Tiere waren ihre Freunde, die Tiere waren ihre Gefährten,
sie waren die Gefährten der glücklichen Kindheit, aus der
Emilia nun vertrieben war, sie waren die Genossen der Einsamkeit, in der Emilia lebte, sie waren Spiel und Freude,
sie waren harmlos, hingebungsvoll und dem Augenblick ergeben, sie waren die harmlose und dem Augenblick ergebene Kreatur ohne Falschheit und Berechnung, und sie kannten nur die gute Emilia, eine Emilia, die zu den Tieren wirklich gut war. Die böse Emilia wandte sich gegen die Menschen. Sie fuhr hoch und rief: »Philipp!« Sie lauschte, die
Züge ihres Gesichtes zwischen Weinen und Erbitterung.
Philipp hatte sie verlassen! Sie knipste die Bettlampe an,
sprang auf, rannte nackt durch das Zimmer, drehte den
Schalter für das Deckenlicht, silberne Kerzenbirnen, die sich
in grünspanbedeckten Mispelzweigen wiegten, Wandarme
entflammten, Licht, das sich in Spiegeln wiederholte, ver-
vielfachte und von Lichtschirmen gefärbt, gelb und rötlich,
wie gelbe und rötliche Schatten auf die Haut der Frau fiel,
auf ihren fast noch kindlichen Leib, die hohen Beine, die
kleinen Brüste, die schmalen Hüften, den glatten elastischen
Bauch. Sie lief in Philipps Zimmer, und das natürliche Licht
des trüben Tages, das hier durch das unverhüllte Fenster
drang, ließ ihre hübsche Gestalt plötzlich erbleichen. Die
Augen glänzten krank, lagen unter Schatten, das linke Lid
hing herab, als wäre es aller Spannkraft beraubt, die kleine
eigensinnige Stirn war gefurcht, Schmutzteilchen staken in
der Haut, die schwarzen Haare baumelten in kurzen Zotteln
ins Gesicht. Sie betrachtete den Tisch mit der Schreibmaschine, das weiße unbeschriebene Papier, die Requisiten der Arbeit, die sie verabscheute und von der sie sich Wunder versprach, Ruhm, Reichtum, Sicherheit, über Nacht gewonnen,
in einer Rauschnacht, in der Philipp ein bedeutendes Werk
schreiben würde, in einer Nacht, doch nicht an vielen Tagen,
nicht in einer Art Dienst, nicht mit dem stetigen Geklapper
der kleinen Schreibmaschine. »Er ist unfähig. Ich hasse

dich«, flüsterte sie, »ich hasse dich!« Er war gegangen. Er
war ihr entlaufen. Er würde wiederkommen. Wo sollte er
hingehen? Aber er war gegangen; er hatte sie allein gelassen. War sie so unerträglich? Sie stand nackend in dem Arbeitsraum, nackt in dem Tageslicht, eine Straßenbahn fuhr
vorüber, Emilias Schultern sackten ein, die Schlüsselbeinkno-
chen traten hervor, ihr Fleisch verlor an Frische, und ihre
Haut, ihre Jugend, war wie mit abgestandener, mit geronne-
ner Milch übergossen, für eine Sekunde käsig, säuerlich, krü-
melig. Sie legte sich auf das rillige Ledersofa, das fest und
kalt wie ein Doktorbett und darum ihr unheimlich war, und
sie dachte an Philipp, zauberte ihn durch Denken herbei,
zwang ihn in den Raum zurück, den Komischen, den Unfä-
higen, den Nicht-Geschäftsmann, den Gefährten, den Geliebten und Gehaßten, den Schänder und Geschändeten. Sie
steckte einen Finger in den Mund, umzüngelte ihn, feuch-
tete ihn an, ein kleines Mädchen, nachdenklich, verlassen,
ratlos, streichele-mich, sie nahm den Finger, spielte an sich,
ließ ihn in sich eindringen und fiel in die tiefe Betäubung
der Lust, die ihr, dem Tag zwar schon preisgegeben und
von seinem Schein schon feindlich überschüttet, noch ein
Stück innerer Nacht gewährte, eine Spanne Heimlichkeit und
Liebe, ein Hinauszögern —

Night-and-day. Odysseus sah herab auf die rote Mütze des
Dienstmannes, auf das vielbefleckte brüchige Tuch, er sah
den militärisch grade über Brille und Augen gesetzten Mützenschirm, er sah die Messingnummer, erkannte die müden
Schultern, die schäbige Wolle des Rockes, die ausgefransten
Bänder der Schürze und erblickte schließlich ein Bäuchlein,
kaum wert, es zu erwähnen. Odysseus lachte. Er lachte wie
ein Kind, das schnell Bekanntschaft schließt, er empfand,
kindlich, den Alten als altes Kind, als Spielgefährten der
Straße. Odysseus freute sich, er war gutmütig, er begrüßte
den Gefährten, er gab ihm etwas ab aus seiner augenblick-
lichen Fülle, gab ihm etwas von der Siegerposition, ließ ihm
den Koffer: die Musik, die Stimme, sie hing in des alten
Dienstmannes Hand. Tapfer, ein kleiner schmächtiger Schat-

ten, schritt Josef neben der hohen breiten Gestalt des Soldaten über den Bahnhofsplatz. Aus dem Koffer gellte, knarrte, quietschte es: Limehouse-Blues. Josef folgte dem schwarzen Mann, er folgte dem Befreier, dem Eroberer, folgte der Schutz- und Besatzungsmacht in die Stadt.

Ein Schrein, ein Altarschrein, ein ernster Schatten, Moder vermeintlicher und wieder verworfener Erkenntnis, eine wahrgenommene und nicht wahrgenommene Bedrohung, Brunnen der Hoffnung, täuschender Quell für die Dürstenden: mit seinen geöffneten Flügeln war der Bücherschrank ein unheiliges Triptychon der Schrift hinter der nackten Emilia. Für wen opferte sie sich, Priesterin und Hirschkuh in einer Gestalt, eine verkommene Iphigenie, von keiner Artemis beschützt, nach keinem Taurien entrückt? Die geerbten Bücher, die Prachteinbände der achtziger Jahre, die unberührten Goldschnittausgaben, die deutschen Klassiker und der Pharus-am-Meere-des-Lebens für den Salon der Dame, der Kampf-um-Rom und Bismarcks-Gedanken-und-Erinnerungen für das Herrenzimmer und dazu das Fach mit dem Kognak und den Zigarren, die Bibliothek der Vorfahren, die Geld verdient und nicht gelesen hatten, stand neben Philipps, des unermüdlichen Lesers, ins Haus getragener Büchersammlung voll Unrast und Zergliederung, das entblößte Herz, der sezierte Trieb. Und vor ihnen, den prächtig gebundenen und den zerlesenen vergebens befragten Bänden, vor ihnen und zu ihren Füßen gewissermaßen ruhte die Unbekleidete, die Erbin, die Hand zwischen den kindlich gebliebenen Schenkeln, und suchte zu vergessen, zu vergessen, was man nun Wirklichkeit nannte und Härte des Lebens und Lebenskampf und soziale Eingliederung, und Behude sprach von der nicht gelungenen Anpassung an die Umwelt, und alles bedeutete doch nur, daß es ein schlechtes Leben war, eine verfluchte Welt und die Sonderstellen verloren das Fein-heraus-Sein durch die glückliche Geburt, den Fall ins wohlbereitete Nest, was war nun am törichten Schmeichelschwall um ihr Kindesalter? ›Du bist reich, Schöne, du erbst, Hübsche, erbst das Großmütterleinvermögen, die Kommer-

zienratsfabrikmillionen, er dachte an dich, der Geheime diät-
lebende Kommerzienrat, der treusorgende *pater familias*,
dachte an seine Enkelin, an die noch nicht geborene, be-
schenkte sie reichlich und reichlich sichernd und vorausschau-
end in seinem Testament, auf daß es dir gut gehe, Kind, und
das Geschlecht blühen möge und immer noch reicher werde,
brauchst nichts zu tun, er tat so viel, brauchst dich nicht zu
mühen, er mühte sich und achthundert Arbeiter, ›für dich,
Täubchen, schwimmst oben‹ (was schwimmt oben? was
schwimmt oben auf einem Teich? Froschlaich, Vogeldreck,
Faulholz, schillernde Farbflecke, unruhige Spektren aus
Schmiere, Schlamm und Verwesung, die Leiche der jungen
Liebenden), ›darfst feiern, Kind, Gartenfeste, du Hübsche,
wirst immer die Ballkönigin sein, Emilia!‹ Sie wollte vergessen, vergessen die entwerteten Hypotheken, die enteigneten
Rechte, die Reichsschatzanweisungen im Girosammeldepot,
Papier, Makulatur, vergessen den unrentablen verfallenden
Hausbesitz, die Bodenlasten, die unverkäuflichen Mauerstei-
ne, die Kettung an die Ämter, die Formulare, die gewährten
und widerrufenen Stundungen, die Anwälte, sie wollte vergessen, wollte dem Betrügenden entlaufen, zu spät, der Materie entkommen, dem Geist nun sich hingeben, dem bisher
nicht geachteten, dem verkannten, er war ein neuer Retter,
seine schwerelosen Kräfte, *les fleurs du mal*, Blumen aus dem
Nichts, der Trost in Dachkammern, wie-hasse-ich-die-Poeten,
die-Pumper, die-alten-Freitischschlucker, Geist Trost in verfallenen Villen, ja-wir-waren-reich, *une saison en enfer: il*
semblait que ce fût un sinistre lavoir, toujours accablé de la
pluie et noir, Benn Gottfried Frühe Gedichte, La Morgue ist
— dunkele-süße — Onanie, *les paradis artificiels* auf den
Holzwegen, Philipp auf den Holzwegen, ratlos im Gestrüpp
in den Fußangeln Heideggers, der Geruch nie wieder ge-
schmeckter Bonbons auf dem Ausflug mit den Freundinnen,
der Lido von Venedig, die Kinder der Wohlhabenden *à la*
recherche du temps perdu, Schrödinger *What is Life?* das
Wesen der Mutation, das Verhalten der Atome im Organismus, der Organismus kein physikalisches Laboratorium, ein
Strom von Ordnung, du entgehst dem Zerfall im anatomi-

schen Chaos, die Seele, ja, die Seele, *Deus factus sum,* die Upanischaden, Ordnung aus Ordnung, Ordnung aus Unordnung, die Seelenwanderung, die Vielheitshypothese, komme-als-Tier-wieder, bin-freundlich-zu-den-Tieren, das-Kalb-am-Strick-das-so-schrie-vor-dem-Garmischer-Schlachthof, das Geworfensein, Kierkegaard Angst tagebuchschreibender Verführer nicht zu Cordelia ins Bett, Sartre der Ekel ich-ekele-mich-nicht, ich treibe dunkele süße Onanie, das Selbst, die Existenz und die Philosophie der Existenz, Millionärin, warmal, es-war-einmal, die Reisen der Großmutter, Wirkliche Geheime Kommerzienrätin, Onanie dunkele süße, Auers Gasglühlicht summt, wenn-sie-alles-in-Gold-angelegt-hätten, Beginn der Sozialversicherung, ich-sollte-kleben-für-mein-Alter, der junge Kaiser, Billioneninflation, hätten-sie-in-Gold, Soforthilfeabgabe fällig, das war Nizza, Onanie, die Promenade des Anglais, die Reiherhüte, in Kairo Shepheards Hotel, Mena House Hotel vor den Pyramiden, die Nierenkur des Wirklichen Geheimen Kommerzienrats, Austrocknung der Verschlammung, Wüstenklima, Photopostkarte, *carte postale* Wilhelm-und-Lieschen-auf-dem-Kamelritt, die Ahnen, Luxor das hunderttorige Theben, die Nekropolis, das Totenfeld, die Totenstadt, ich-sterbe-jung, Admet der junge Gide in Biskra *l'Immoraliste* Liebe ohne Namen, der Wirkliche Geheime starb *pompes funèbres,* Millionen, Millionen-nicht-in-Gold, die Abwertungshypothek, der Ammontempel, Ramses irgendeiner im Schutt, die Sphinx Cocteau: ich-liebe, wer-liebt-mich?, das Gen der Kern des befruchteten Eis, brauch'-mich-nicht-vorzusehen-zwölfmal-regelmäßig, der Mond, kein Arzt, Behude-ist-neugierig, alle-Ärzte-lüstern, mein Schoß, Körper-gehört-mir, kein Leiden, süße-dunkle-Schuftigkeit —

Erschöpfung perlte auf ihrer Stirn, jede Perle ein Mikrokosmos der Unterwelt, ein Gewimmel von Atomen, Elektronen und Quanten, Giordano Bruno sang auf dem Scheiterhaufen das Lied von der Unendlichkeit des Alls, Botticellis Frühling reifte, wurde Sommer, wurde Herbst, war es schon Winter, ein neuer Frühling? ein Embryo eines Frühlings? Wasser sammelte sich in ihren Haaren, sie fühlte sich feucht an, und

vor ihrem glänzenden, im Feuchten schwimmenden Blick
schien Philipps Schreibtisch ihr wieder der Ort des Zauberns,
ein gehaßter Ort freilich, aber die Stätte des möglichen
Wunders zu sein: Reichtum und Ruhm, auch sie in rühm-
lichem Reichtum und in Sicherheit! Sie taumelte. Die Sicherheit, die ihr die Zeit genommen hatte, die ihr das verkündete,
angefallene und entwertete Erbe nun versagte, die ihr die
Häuser nicht mehr gewährten, die Risse in den Mauern,
überall Risse in der Materie, würde ihr diese verlorene, wie
ein Hochstapler aufgetretene und wie ein Hochstapler geplatzte Sicherheit der schwache, mittellose, von Herzklopfen
und Schwindel gequälte Philipp bringen, der, immerhin, das
war neu für sie, mit dem Unsichtbaren in Verbindung stand,
dem Gedanken, dem Geist, der Kunst, der hier sein Sach auf
nichts gestellt, aber dort im Spirituellen vielleicht ein Gut-
haben hatte? Vorerst aber war jede Sicherheit hin. Philipp
sagte, es habe nie eine Sicherheit gegeben. Er log! Er wollte
sein Gut nicht mit ihr teilen. Wie könnte er ohne Sicherheit
leben? Emilia war nicht schuld, daß die alte Sicherheit ein-
gestürzt war, in deren Schoß zwei Generationen sich's gemütlich gemacht hatten. Sie wollte Rechenschaft! Sie forderte ihr
Erbe von jedermann, der älter war als sie. Sie war in der
Nacht durchs Haus gerast, eine kleine schmächtige Furie, von
ihren Tieren gefolgt, den nicht reden könnenden und darum
unschuldigen Lieblingen, gestern, als Philipp sich drückte, als
er ihre Schreie nicht zu ertragen meinte, ihr sinnloses Auf-
begehren treppauf treppab zum Hausmeister in den Keller,
Füße und Fäuste gegen die geschlossene Tür: »Ihr Nazis,
warum habt ihr ihn gewählt, warum habt ihr das Elend gewählt, warum den Abgrund, warum den Untergang, warum
den Krieg, warum das Vermögen in die Luft geschossen, ich
hatte ja Geld, ihr Nazis« (und der Hausmeister lag hinter
der verriegelten Tür, hielt den Atem an, rührte sich nicht,
dachte ›warte es geht vorüber, ein Wetter, es kommt wieder
anders, sie beruhigt sich‹), und die andern Nazis hinter anderen Türen im Haus, ihr Vater hinter der gesicherten
Schloßfalle ein Miterbe »du Nazi, du Tor, Verschleuderer,
mußtest marschieren, mußtest mitmarschieren, mitlaufen, bist

Mitläufer, Hakenkreuz auf der Brust, futsch das Geld, konntet ihr nicht Ruhe geben? mußtet ihr kläffen« (und der Vater saß hinter der Tür, hörte nicht den Schrei, stellte sich nicht der Anklage, gerechtfertigt oder nicht, hielt die Akten vors Gesicht, die Bankpapiere, die Schuldbriefe, die Hinterlegungsscheine, rechnete ›und dies bleibt mir noch und dieser Anteil und jener und dort ein Fünftel vom Nebenhaus und vielleicht die Berliner Hypothek, aber im Ostsektor, wer weiß‹ *USA gegen Präventivkrieg*). Warum sorgte Philipp sich nicht? Vielleicht, weil er von dem mitzehrte, was sie noch hatte, vom Gott der Großeltern, und sein Gott war ein falscher Gott? Wenn man es alles wissen könnte! Das blasse Gesicht zuckte. Sie taumelte, taumelte nackt zum Schreibtisch, nahm ein Blatt vom Stoß des weißen unbeschriebenen Papiers, vom Häufchen der Reinheit der ungeschehenen Empfängnis, spannte es in die kleine Maschine ein und tippte vorsichtig mit einem Finger: ›Sei nicht böse. Ich liebe dich doch, Philipp. Bleib bei mir.‹

Er liebte sie nicht. Warum sollte er sie lieben? Er war nicht weiter stolz auf die Verwandtschaft. Gleichmut erfüllte ihn. Warum sollte er sich gerührt fühlen? Keine besondere Empfindung bedrängte oder weitete die Brust. Die dort unten wohnten, beschäftigten Richard nicht mehr als andere alte Völker: oberflächlich. Er reiste dienstlich; nein, dienstlich, das hätten die unten gesagt, die Kasernenhofsippe, die alten Fürstendiener, er reiste aus Nützlichkeitsgründen, im Auftrag seines Landes und seiner Zeit, und er glaubte, es sei nun die Zeit seines Landes, das Jahrhundert der gereinigten Triebe, der nützlichen Ordnung, der Planung, der Verwaltung und der Tüchtigkeit, und zunächst würde es neben dem Dienst eine Art ironisch-romantischer Welt- und Schloßbesichtigung sein. Was sie von ihm erwarten durften, war Unbefangenheit. Das war ihre Chance. Augustus schiffte sich nicht als Wohltäter der Griechen nach Hellas ein. Die Geschichte zwang Augustus, sich um die verworrenen griechischen Verhältnisse zu kümmern. Er schuf Ordnung. Er gängelte einen Haufen von Fanatikern, Stadtschwärmern und Winkelpatrioten; er unterstützte die Vernunft, die Gemäßigten, das Kapital und die Akademien und nahm die Wahnsinnigen, die Weisen und die Päderasten in Kauf. Es war sein Interesse und ihre Chance. Richard fühlte sich frei von Feindschaft und Vorurteilen, nicht Haß und Verachtung belasteten ihn. Die Mißgefühle waren Giftstoffe, von der Zivilisation überwundene Krankheiten wie Pest, Cholera und Pocken. Richard war geimpft, er war hygienisch erzogen und ausgeschlackt. Vielleicht würde er herablassend sein, ohne herablassend sein zu wollen, denn er war jung, überschätzte das Jungsein und blickte herab, blickte herab auf sie in aller Tatsächlichkeit, herab auf ihre Länder, ihre Könige, ihre Grenzen, ihren Hader, ihre Philosophen, ihre Gräber, ihren ganzen ästhetischen, pädagogischen, gedanklichen Humus, ihre ewigen Kriege und Revolutionen, er blickte herab auf ein einziges lächerliches Schlachtfeld, die Erde lag unter ihm wie auf einem Chirurgentisch: arg zerschnitten. Natürlich sah er es nicht wirklich so; er sah weder Könige noch Grenzen, wo vorläufig nur Nebel und Nacht war, auch sein geistiges Auge stellte es sich nicht vor, sein Schulwissen war es, das den Erdteil so sah. Geschichte war Vergangenheit, die Welt von gestern, Jahreszahlen in Büchern, eine Kindermarter, jeder Tag aber bildete auch wieder Geschichte, neue Geschichte, Geschichte im Präsens, und das bedeutete Dabeisein, Werden, Wachsen, Handeln und Fliegen. Man wußte nicht immer, wohin man flog. Erst morgen würde alles seinen historischen Namen erhalten, mit dem Namen seinen Sinn, würde echte Geschichte werden, in Schulbüchern altern, und dieser Tag, dies Heute, dieser Morgen würde einst für ihn ›meine Jugend‹ sein. Er war jung, er war neugierig, er würde sich's anschauen: das Land der Väter. Es war eine Morgenlandfahrt. Kreuzritter der Ordnung waren sie, Ritter der Vernunft, der Nützlichkeit und angemessener bürgerlicher Freiheit: sie suchten kein Heiliges Grab. Es war Nacht, als sie das Festland erreichten. Am klaren Himmel leuchtete vor ihnen ein frostiges Licht: der Morgenstern, Phosphoros, Luzifer, der Lichtbringer der antiken Welt. Er wurde zum Fürsten der Finsternis. Nacht und Nebel lagen über Belgien, über Brügge, Brüssel und Gent. Der Dom zu Köln hob sich aus dem Morgengrauen. Das Morgenrot löste sich wie eine Eischale von der Welt: der neue Tag war geboren. Sie flogen den Rhein aufwärts. Lieb-Vaterland-magst-ruhig-sein-fest-steht-und-treu-die-Wacht-am-Rhein: Lied des Vaters, als er achtzehn war, Lied des Wilhelm Kirsch in Schulklassen, in Kasernenstuben, auf dem Exerzierplatz, auf Märschen gesungen, Wacht des Vaters, Wacht des Großvaters, Wacht des Urgroßvaters, Wacht am Rhein, Wacht von Brüdern, Wacht von Vettern, Wacht am Rhein, Grab von Ahnen, Grab der Blutsverwandten, Wacht am Rhein, nicht erfüllte Wacht, mißverstandene Wacht, sie-sollen-ihn-nicht-haben, wer? die Franzosen, wer hatte ihn schon? die Menschen am Strom, Schiffer, Fischer, Gärtner, Winzer, Händler, Fabrikherren, Liebende, der Dichter Heine, wer soll ihn haben? wer mag, wer da ist, hatte nun er ihn, Richard Kirsch, Soldat der US-Luftwaffe, achtzehn Jahre alt, der ihn von oben betrachtete, oder war er es gar nun wieder, der die Wacht am Rhein bezog, guten Glaubens wie sie und vielleicht wieder in der Falle eines Mißverstehens des geschichtlichen Augenblicks? Er dachte ›wenn ich etwas älter wäre, vierundzwanzig vielleicht statt achtzehn, dann hätte ich auch mit achtzehn Jahren hier fliegen, hier zerstören und hier sterben können, wir hätten Bomben gebracht, wir hätten Bomben geworfen, wir hätten einen Weihnachtsbaum angezündet, wir hätten einen Teppich ausgelegt, wir wären ihr Tod gewesen, wir wären vor ihren Scheinwerfern in den Himmel getaucht, wo wird das einmal sein? wo werde ich ausüben, was ich lerne? wo werde ich Bomben werfen? wen werde ich bombardieren? hier? diese? weiter vor? andere? weiter zurück? wieder andere?‹ Über Bayern trübte sich das Land ein. Sie flogen über den Wolken. Als sie landeten, roch die Erde feucht. Der Flughafen roch nach Gras, nach Benzin, Auspuffgasen, Metall und nach etwas Neuem, nach der Fremde, es war ein Backgeruch, ein Brotteiggeruch nach Gärung, Hefe und Alkohol, appetitanregend und animierend, es dunstete nach Biermaische aus den großen Brauereien der Stadt.

Sie gingen durch die Straßen, Odysseus voran, ein großer König, ein kleiner Sieger, jung, lendenstark, unschuldig, tierhaft, und Josef hinter ihm, zusammengeschrumpft, gebückt, alt, müde und pfiffig doch, und mit seinen pfiffigen Äuglein durch die billige Krankenkassenbrille schaute er auf den schwarzen Rücken, hoffnungsvoll, mit Vertrauen, die leichte Last, den guten Auftrag in der Hand, das musizierende Köfferchen Bahama-Joe mit seinen Klängen, Bahama-Joe mit seinem Musikgeknatter, Stimmgeschnatter, Bahama-Joe mit den gestopften Trompeten, den Drums, den Schellen, dem Gequietsch, Gejaul und dem Rhythmus, der sich ausbreitete und die Mädchen ergriff, die Mädchen, die dachten ›der Nigger, dieser freche Nigger, der greuliche Nigger, nein, ich tät's nicht‹, Bahama-Joe, und andere dachten ›Geld haben die, so viel Geld, ein schwarzer Soldat verdient mehr als ein Oberinspektor bei uns, US-Private, wir Mädels haben unser Englisch gelernt, Bund Deutscher Mädel, kann man einen Neger heiraten? keine Rassengesetze in USA, Verfemung, kein Hotel nimmt einen auf, die halbschwarzen Kinder, Besatzungsbabies, arme Kleine, wissen nicht, wo sie hingehören, können nichts dafür, nein, ich tät' es nicht!‹ Bahama-Joe, Schnörkel des Saxophons. Eine Frau stand vor einem Schuhgeschäft, sie sah im Spiegel der Scheibe den Neger vorübergehen, sie dachte ›die Sandalen mit dem Keilabsatz, die würden mir gefallen, wenn man mal könnte, die Burschen haben Körper, Manneskraft, sah mal 'n Boxkampf, Vater war nachher erschöpft, der nicht‹ — Bahama-Joe. Sie gingen vorbei an den Trinkbuden, den Stehausschänken, verboten für alliierte Soldaten, und aus den Holzverschlägen krochen sie hervor, die Schlepper, die Wechsler, die Schnapper: »He, Joe, Dollar? Joe, hast du Benzin? Joe, ein Girl?« Sie saßen schon in den Buden, die Ware, bei Limonade, bei Coca-Cola, schlechtem Kaffee, stinkender Brühe, den Bettdunst, den Geruch der Umarmungen von gestern noch nicht abgewaschen, die Hautflecken überpudert, das von Bleiche und Färbung tote Puppenhaar wie gebündeltes Stroh, sie warteten, Geflügel auf Bestellung täglich frisch, blickten durch die Scheiben, was die Schlepper trieben, ob sie winkten. ein Schwarzer, die waren gutmütig, gaben großzügig, gehörte sich so, minderwertige Kerle, zerrissen einem den Unterleib: ›müssen froh sein 'ne weiße Frau zu kriegen, Entwürdigung von uns, schöne widerliche Entwürdigung.‹ »He, Joe, hast du was zu geben?« — »He, Joe, suchst du was zu kaufen?« — »Joe, ich gebe!« — »Joe, ich nehme!« Sie umschwärmten sie: Maden am Speck, käsige Gesichter, hungrige Gesichter, Gesichter, die Gott vergessen hatte, Ratten, Haifische, Hyänen, Lurche, kaum noch mit Menschenhaut getarnt, wattierte Schultern, karierte Jacken, dreckige Trenchcoats, bunte Socken, Wulstsohlen unter den speckigen Wildlederschuhen, Karikaturen einer Revuefilmmode von drüben, arme Schlucker auch, Heimatlose, Verwehte, Opfer des Krieges. Sie wandten sich an Josef, Bahama-Joe: »Braucht dein Nigger deutsches Geld?« — »Wir wechseln deinem Nigger.« — »Will er fikken? Drei Mark für dich. Darfst zugucken, Alter, machst die Musik.« Bahama-Joe, Musik mit ihrem Silberklang. Josef und Odysseus hörten das Gewisper und hörten es nicht. Bahama-Joe: sie ließen die Wisperer stehen, die zischenden Schlangen, Odysseus stieß sie zurück, sanft, gewaltig wie ein Walfisch, drängte sie beiseite, die kleinen mickrigen Gauner, die Pickelgesichter, die Stinknasen, die ausgevögelten Burschen. Josef folgte dem mächtigen Odysseus, watschelte in seinem Sog. Bahama-Joe: sie gingen weiter, gingen an den Neubauten der Kinos *Unsterbliche Leidenschaft gnadenlos ergreifendes Arztschicksal*, an den Neubauten der Hotels *Dachgarten über den Ruinen Cocktailstunde* vorbei, wurden von Kalkstaub berieselt, mit Mörtel beworfen, gingen durch die auf Trümmerfeldern errichteten Ladenstraßen, zur Linken und zur Rechten die ebenerdigen Baracken, blitzend mit Chromleisten, Neonleuchten und Spiegelscheiben: Parfum aus Paris, Dupont-Nylon, Ananas aus Kalifornien, schottischer Whisky, bunte Zeitungsstände: *Zehn Millionen Tonnen Kohle fehlen.* Die Verkehrsampel stand auf Rot und hemmte den Übergang. Straßenbahnen, Automobile, Radfahrer, schwankende Dreiradwagen und schwere amerikanische Heerestrucks strömten über die Kreuzung.

Das rote Licht sperrte vor Emilia den Weg. Sie wollte zum
Leihamt, das schloß am Mittag, dann zu Unverlacht, dem
Althändler im feuchten Gewölbe, er würde ihr unter den
Rock langen, zur jammernden Antiquitätenhändlerin, Frau
de Voss, die würde nichts kaufen, wohnte aber nahe bei
Unverlacht, und schließlich, sie ahnte es, sie wußte es, die
Perlen würden geopfert werden, das geknüpfte mondbleiche
Geschmeide, sie mußte zu Schellack, dem Juwelier. Sie trug
Schuhe von gutem Schnitt aus echtem Schlangenleder, aber
die Absätze waren schiefgetreten. Ihre Strümpfe waren aus
dem allerdünnsten Gewebe, denn Philipp liebte hauchdünne
Strümpfe und wurde zärtlich, wenn sie im Winter bei schar-
fem Frost mit verkühlten Waden nach Hause kam, aber,
o weh, in dem als maschenfest angepriesenen Gespinst lok-
kerten sich die Fäden und stürzten wie rieselnde Bäche vom
Knie zum Knöchel. Der Rock hatte einen Triangelriß im
Saum: wer sollte ihn nähen? Emilias Pelzjacke, zu warm für
die Jahreszeit, war aus feinstem Feh, zerzaust und zerrissen,
was tat's, sie ersetzte den Übergangsmantel, den Emilia
nicht hatte. Ihr junger Mund war geschminkt, die Blässe
der Wangen mit etwas Rouge behoben, die Haare wehten
offen im regennassen Wind. Die Sachen, die sie mitgenommen hatte, waren in ein englisches Reiseplaid gewickelt, dem
Gepäck der Lords und Ladys bei Wilhelm Busch und in den
Fliegenden Blättern. Emilia trug schwer an dem Entzücken
der alten Humoristen. Jede Last machte ihr rheumatische
Beschwerden in der Schulter. Jede Beschwerde machte sie un-
leidlich und erfüllte sie mit Trotz und Verbitterung. Sie
stand mißgelaunt unter der roten Ampel und blickte mißmutig in den Strom des Verkehrs.

Im Wagen des Konsuls, im lautlos und erschütterungsfrei
gleitenden Cadillac, im Gefährt der Reichen auf der Seite
der Reichen, der Staatsmänner, der Arrivierten, der planen-
den Manager, wenn man sich nicht täuschen ließ, in einem
geräumigen schwarzglänzenden Sarg fuhr Mr. Edwin über
die Kreuzung. Er fühlte sich müde. Die Reise, wohl liegend,
doch schlaflos verbracht, hatte ihn angestrengt. Er schaute

entmutigt in den trüben Tag, entmutigt in die fremde Straße. Es war das Land Goethes, das Land Platens, das Land Winckelmanns, über diesen Platz war Stefan George gegangen. Mr. Edwin fror. Er sah sich auf einmal übriggeblieben, allein gelassen, alt, uralt, so alt, wie er war. Er drückte den somit alten, den noch immer jugendschlank gehaltenen Leib in die weichen Polster des Wagens. Es war eine Geste des Verkriechens. Die Krempe seines schwarzen Hutes stieß gegen die Kissen, und er legte den Hut, ein federleichtes Erzeugnis der Bond Street, in den Schoß. Sein edles, Askese, Zucht und Versenkung andeutendes Gesicht wurde böse. Unter den sorgfältig gescheitelten, seidezarten langen grauen Haaren bekam er die scharfen Züge eines alten gierigen Geiers. Der Konsulatssekretär und der literarische Impresario des Amerikahauses, die man zu Mr. Edwins Empfang an die Bahn geschickt hatte, saßen vor ihm auf den Klappsitzen des Wagens, beugten sich zu ihm zurück und fühlten sich verpflichtet, den Berühmten, den Preisgekrönten, das seltene Tier zu unterhalten. Sie deuteten auf angebliche Sehenswürdigkeiten der Stadt, sprachen über die Art, wie sie seinen Vortrag organisiert hatten, schwätzten — es hörte sich an, als schwenkten Scheuerfrauen unermüdlich die nassen Tücher über einen staubigen Boden. Mr. Edwin fand, daß die Herren den Slang der Gewöhnlichkeit sprachen. Das war ärgerlich. Mr. Edwin liebte den Slang der Gewöhnlichkeit, manchmal, wenn er sich der Schönheit gesellte, aber hier bei diesen wohlerzogenen Herren seiner Gesellschaftsklasse ›meine Gesellschaftsklasse? welche Klasse? vorurteilslos gegen jedermann, klassenloser Außenseiter, keine Gemeinschaft, keine‹ war der Slang, das wie Gummi gekaute Amerikanisch, peinlich, bedrückend und verstimmend. Edwin rutschte noch tiefer in die Wagenecke. Was brachte er dem Land mit, Goethe, Winckelmann, Platen, was brachte er mit? Sie würden empfindlich, vielleicht empfänglich sein, die Geschlagenen, sie würden wach sein, schon geweckt vom Unheil, sie würden voll Ahnung sein, näher am Abgrund, vertrauter mit dem Tod. Kam er mit einer Botschaft, brachte er Trost, deutete er das Leid? Er sollte über die Unsterblich-

keit sprechen, über die Ewigkeit des Geistes, die unvergäng-
liche Seele des Abendlandes, und jetzt? jetzt zweifelte er.
Seine Botschaft war kalt, sein Wissen war erlesen. Erlesen im
Doppelsinn, aus Büchern stammend, aber auch ausgewählt,
ein Extrakt aus dem Geist der Jahrtausende, erlesen, aus
allen Zungen erlesen, der Heilige Geist, ausgegossen in die
Sprachen, erlesen, kostbar, die Quintessenz, funkelnd, destilliert, süß, bitter, giftig, heilsam, fast schon die Deutung, aber
die Deutung der Geschichte nur, schließlich auch diese Deutung fragwürdig, die schöngeformten klugen Strophen, sen-
sible Reaktionen, und dennoch: er kam mit leeren Händen,
ohne Gabe, ohne Trost, keine Hoffnung, Trauer, Müdigkeit,
nicht Trägheit, Herzensleere. Sollte er nicht schweigen? Er
hatte schon vorher die Zerstörungen des Krieges gesehen,
wem in Europa waren sie unbekannt?, er hatte sie in London
gesehen, in Frankreich, in Italien, furchtbare unverhüllte
Wunden in den Städten, doch was er hier in dem wohl be-
troffensten Ort seiner Wanderschaft aus dem Fenster des
Konsulatswagens sah, gewiegt auf Gummi, Preßluft und
ingeniöser Federung, vor Staub geschützt, war aufgeräumt,
geordnet, verpflastert, schon wiederhergestellt und grade darum so schrecklich, so hinfällig: es war nie wiedergutzumachen. Er sollte über Europa und für Europa sprechen, aber
wünschte er geheim vielleicht die Zerstörung, die Zertrümmerung des Gewandes, in welcher der geliebte, der im Geist
so sehr geliebte Erdteil sich zeigte, oder war es so, daß er,
Mr. Edwin, spät auf die Reise gegangen, den spät und ach
aus welchem Mißverstehen gekommenen Ruhm zu kassieren,
sich feiern zu lassen, daß er die Bedeutung des Vergehens
kannte, ein Freund des Vogels Phönix war, der ins Feuer
mußte, in die Asche das bunte Gefieder, diese Läden da, die
Menschen, behelfsmäßig alles, das Slanggeschwätz in seinem
Wagen — töricht: was sollte er ihnen sagen? Vielleicht würde
er in dieser Stadt sterben. Eine Nachricht. Eine Notiz in den
Abendausgaben. Ein paar Gedenkartikel in London, in Paris,
in New York. Dieser schwarze Cadillac war ein Sarg. Nun
streiften sie einen Radfahrer ›o weh, er schwankt, er hält
sich‹ —

Er hielt sich im Gleichgewicht. Er balancierte, strampelte, lenkte das Rad in die freie Lücke, Dr. Behude, Facharzt für Psychiatrie und Neurologie, er trat die Pedale, er kam voran, heute abend wird er im Amerikahaus den Vortrag von Mr. Edwin hören, das Gespräch über den abendländischen Geist, die Rede über die Macht des Geistes, Sieg des Geistes über die Materie, Geist bezwingt die Krankheit, Krankheiten seelisch bedingt, Leiden psychisch heilbar. Dr. Behude schwindelte. Die Blutentnahme hatte ihn diesmal geschwächt. Vielleicht ließ er sich zu oft anzapfen. Die Welt brauchte Blut. Dr. Behude brauchte Geld. Sieg der Materie über den Geist. Sollte er vom Weg abbiegen, vom Rad steigen, in eine Kneipe gehen, etwas trinken, fröhlich sein? Er schwamm im Strom des Verkehrs. Er spürte Kopfschmerzen, die er bei seinen Patienten ignorierte. Er radelte weiter auf dem Wege zu Schnakenbach, dem müden Gewerbelehrer, dem begabten Formeltüftler, dem Volkshochschuleinstein, einem pervitin- und benzidrinsüchtigen Schatten. Behude bereute, Schnakenbach gestern die Pillen verweigert zu haben, die den Lehrer wach hielten. Nun wollte er ihm das die Sucht befriedigende, für eine Spanne das klägliche Leben erhaltende und es doch weiter zerstörende Rezept ins Haus bringen. Gern wäre er zu Emilia gefahren. Er mochte sie: er hielt sie für gefährdeter als Philipp ›der wird alles überstehen, er wird sogar seine Ehen überstehen, ein tapferes Herz, Neurosen, gewiß Neurosen, eine Pseudoangina pectoris, gehupft wie gesprungen, aber ein tapferes Herz, man sieht's ihm nicht an‹, doch Emilia kam nicht in seine Sprechstunde und versteckte sich, wenn er Philipp zu Hause besuchte. Er übersah, daß Emilia an der Kreuzung, an der er vorüberradelte, auf das grüne Licht wartete. Er war über die Lenkstange gebeugt, die rechte Hand an der Bremse, den Zeigefinger der linken an der Klingel: ein Fehlläuten konnte töten, eine Fehlleistung entlarven, das Fehlläuten der Nachtglocke, verstand er Kafka? —

Washington Price lenkte die horizontblaue Limousine über die Kreuzung. Sollte er? Sollte er nicht? Er wußte, daß die

Tankwagen in seinem Depot geheime Zapfhähne hatten. Das Risiko war klein. Er brauchte nur mit dem Fahrer des Tanks halbpart zu machen, bei der deutschen Tankstelle, die jeder Benzinkutscher kannte, vorzufahren und sich einige Gallonen abdrehen zu lassen. Gutes Geld war ihm sicher. Er brauchte Geld. Er wollte nicht unterliegen. Er wollte Carla, und er wollte Carlas Kind. Er hatte noch keinen Punkt auf der Strafliste. Er glaubte an Anständigkeit. Jedem Bürger seine Chance. Auch dem schwarzen Mann seine Chance. Washington Price Sergeant in the Army. Washington mußte reich sein. Er mußte wenigstens vorübergehend reich sein; hier und heute mußte er reich sein. Dem Reichtum würde Carla vertrauen. Sie würde dem Geld eher vertrauen als seinen Worten. Carla wollte nicht sein Kind zur Welt bringen. Sie hatte Angst. Mein Gott, warum Angst haben? Washington war der beste, der stärkste, der flinkeste Baseballcrack in der berühmten Mannschaft der Red Stars. Aber er war nicht mehr der Jüngste. Dieses mörderische Laufen um die Base! Es strengte ihn an. Er bekam keine Luft mehr. Aber ein Jahr, zwei Jahre würde er es schon noch aushalten. Er würde noch gut in der Arena sein. Ein rheumatischer Schmerz durchzuckte seinen Arm; das war eine Warnung. Er würde die Sache mit dem Benzin nicht machen. Er mußte zum Central Exchange fahren. Er mußte Carla ein Geschenk kaufen. Er mußte telephonieren. Er brauchte Geld. Gleich —

Gleich aus der Linie sechs in die elf. Sie würde Dr. Frahm noch treffen. Es war gut, wenn sie ein wenig nach der Sprechstunde kam. Frahm hatte dann Zeit. Sie mußte es loswerden. Gleich. Washington war ein guter Kerl. Wie hatte sie sich gefürchtet! Der erste Tag in der Kaserne der Schwarzen. Der Leutnant hatte gesagt: »Ich weiß nicht, ob Sie bleiben werden.« Sie drängten sich vor dem Fenster der Tür, preßten die platten Nasen wie Knetgummi gegen die Scheibe, ein Gesicht neben dem andern. Wer saß im Käfig? wer vertrat die Gattung im Zoo? sie hinter dem Glas? die vor dem Glas? War es ein so weiter Weg vom deutschen Wehrmachtsbüro, Sekretärin des Platzkommandanten, zu den schwarzen

Soldaten der US-Transporttruppe? Sie schrieb, schrieb ganz gut Englisch, beugte den Kopf über die Maschine, nicht das fremde Wesen sehen, nicht die dunkle Haut, nicht diese Geschmeidigkeit in Ebenholz, nicht den Mann, nicht den gutturalen Laut hören, nur den Text, den er diktiert, sie mußte arbeiten, sie konnte nicht bei der Mutter bleiben, nicht bei Frau Behrend, sie gab ihr unrecht in der Verurteilung des Musikmeisters, sie mußte für ihren Jungen sorgen, sein Vater lag an der Wolga, vielleicht ertrunken, vielleicht begraben, verschollen in der Steppe, kein Gruß mehr nach Stalingrad, sie mußte was auftreiben, man war am Verhungern, die schlimmen Jahre fünfundvierzig, sechsundvierzig, siebenundvierzig, am Verhungern, sie mußte, warum sollte sie nicht? waren es nicht auch Menschen? Am Abend war er da. »Ich bringe Sie nach Hause.« Er führte sie durch den Kasernengang. War sie nackt? Die Männer standen im Gang, dunkel im Abendschatten des Ganges, ihre Augen waren wie unruhige weiße Fledermäuse und ihre Blicke wie Haftscheiben an ihrem Leib. Er saß neben ihr am Steuer des Jeeps. »Wo wohnen Sie?« Sie sagte es ihm. Er sprach nicht während der Fahrt. Er hielt vor ihrem Haus. Er öffnete den Wagenschlag. Er reichte ihr Schokolade, Konserven, Zigaretten, sehr viel in jenen Tagen. »Auf Wiedersehen.« Nichts weiter. Jeden Abend. Er holte sie ab aus dem Büro, führte sie durch den Gang mit den wartenden, starrenden, dunklen Männern, brachte sie heim, saß stumm neben ihr im Wagen, schenkte ihr was, sagte: »Auf Wiedersehen.« Manchmal hockten sie wohl eine Stunde in dem Wagen vor ihrem Haus: stumm und ohne sich zu rühren. Auf der Straße lag damals noch der Schutt der zerbombten Gebäude. Der Wind wehte Staub auf. Die Ruinen waren wie ein Totenfeld, außerhalb jeder Wirklichkeit des Abends, waren Pompeji, Herkulaneum, Troja, versunkene Welt. Eine erschütterte Mauer stürzte ein. Neuer Staub legte sich wie eine Wolke über den Jeep. In der sechsten Woche hielt Carla es nicht mehr aus. Sie träumte von Negern. Im Traum wurde sie vergewaltigt. Schwarze Arme griffen nach ihr: wie Schlangen kamen sie aus den Kellern der Ruinen. Sie sagte: »Ich kann nicht mehr.« Er kam mit ihr auf ihr Zimmer. Es war wie ein Ertrinken. War es die Wolga? Nicht eisig, ein glühender Strom. Am nächsten Tag kamen die Nachbarn, kamen die Bekannten, der frühere Wehrmachtchef kam, alle kamen sie, wollten Zigaretten, Konserven, Kaffee, Schokolade »sag deinem Freund, Carla«, »dein Freund kann im Central Exchange, im amerikanischen Kaufhaus, Carla«, »wenn dein Freund mal dran denken würde, Carla, Seife«: Washington Price besorgte, beschaffte, brachte. Die Freunde bedankten sich leichthin. Es war, als liefere Carla einen Tribut ab. Die Freunde vergaßen, daß die Waren im amerikanischen Lager Dollars und Cents kosteten. War es zum Lachen? War es schön? War es, um stolz drauf zu sein? Carla als Wohltäterin? Sie wußte es bald nicht mehr, und Nachdenken strengte sie an. Sie gab die Stellung in der Transportkaserne auf, zog in ein anderes Haus, wo andere Mädchen mit anderen Männern verkehrten, lebte mit Washington zusammen, war ihm treu, obwohl sich ihr nun viele, ja ungezählte Gelegenheiten zum Beischlaf ergaben, denn jedermann, ob Schwarz ob Weiß, Deutscher oder Ausländer, glaubte nun, da sie mit Washington zusammenlebte, daß sie mit allen ins Bett ginge, es geilte sie auf, und Carla war ihres Gefühls nicht sicher und fragte sich ›liebe ich ihn? liebe ich ihn wirklich? fremd, fremd aber ich bleibe ihm treu, treu das bin ich ihm schuldig, keinen andern‹, und im Nichtstun gewöhnte sie sich an die Bilderwelt unzähliger Magazine, die ihr das Damenleben in Amerika zeigten, die automatischen Küchen, die Waschwunder und Spülmaschinen, die alles reinigten, während man im Liegestuhl der Television folgte, Bing Crosby erschien in jedem Heim, die Wiener Sängerknaben jubelten vorm elektrischen Herd, im schwellenden Polster des Pullmanwagens fuhr man von Ost nach West, im Stromlinienauto genoß man am Abend die Lichter- und Palmenpracht am Golf von San Franzisko, Sicherheit jeder Art wurde von Tablettenfabrikanten und Insurancegesellschaften angeboten, keine Angstträume ängstigten mehr, denn *you can sleep soundly tonight* mit Maybels Magnesium Milch, und die Frau war die Königin, der alles dort diente und zu Füßen lag, sie war *the gift that starls the home*, und für die Kinder gab es Puppen, die echte Tränen weinten; es waren die einzigen Tränen, die in diesem Paradies geweint wurden. Carla wollte Washington heiraten. Sie war bereit, ihm in die Staaten zu folgen. Durch ihren ehemaligen Chef, den Platzkommandanten, der jetzt Bürovorsteher in einer Anwaltskanzlei war, ließ sie die Todeserklärung ihres an der Wolga verschollenen Mannes betreiben. Und da kam das Kind, ein schwarzes Wesen, rührte sich in ihrem Leib, kam zu früh, bereitete ihr Übelkeit, nein, sie wollte es nicht, Dr. Frahm mußte ihr beistehen, mußte es nehmen, gleich —

»Das Zentrum, das Sie hier sehen, war vollständig zerstört. Fünf Jahre Aufbau demokratischer Verwaltung und Verständnis der Alliierten machten die Stadt wieder zum blühenden Mittelpunkt des Handels und des Gewerbes« *Marshallplanhilfe auch für Deutschland, ERP-Mittel gekürzt, Senator Taft kritisiert Ausgaben.* Der Autobus mit der Reisegesellschaft der Lehrerinnen aus Massachusetts passierte die Kreuzung. Sie reisten, ohne es zu ahnen, getarnt. Keinem Deutschen, der die Frauen hinter den Scheiben des Autobusses sah, fiel es ein, sie für Lehrerinnen zu halten. Es waren ja Damen, die da auf rotem Leder saßen, wohlgekleidete, schöngeschminkte, jugendlich gehaltene und wirklich junge, jedenfalls, so dachte man, reiche, gepflegte, nichtstuende, sich mit Stadtbesichtigungen die Zeit vertreibende Damen. ›Hättet ihr die Stadt nicht in Brand geworfen, gäb's hier was anderes zu sehen und ihr wäret gar nicht hier, Soldaten, schön, aber auch noch Weiber auf Besatzungskosten, das sind doch lauter Drohnen.‹ Eine amerikanische Lehrerin verdient — was verdient sie? — ach, unendlich viel mehr als ihre deutsche Kollegin in Starnberg, das arme verschüchterte Wesen, ›ja keinen Anstoß erregen, etwas Puder im Gesicht der Herr Vikar könnte es übel vermerken, der Herr Schulrat könnte es in die Personalakten schreiben‹. Erziehung ist in Deutschland eine ernste und graue Angelegenheit, fern jeder Daseinsfreude, ein Pfui dem Mondänen, und es bleibt ewig unvorstellbar, eine Dame auf einem deutschen Schulkatheder zu sehen, geschminkt, parfümiert, zu den Ferien in Paris, auf

Studienreisen in New York und in Boston, Massachusetts, mein Gott, die Haare sträuben sich, wir sind ein armes Land, und das ist unsere Tugend. Kay saß neben Katharine Wescott. Kay war einundzwanzig, Katharine achtunddreißig Jahre alt. »Du bist in Kays grüne Augen verliebt«, sagte Mildred Burnett. ›Grüne Augen Katzenaugen falsche Augen.‹ Mildred war fünfundvierzig und saß vor ihnen. Sie hatten einen Tag für die Stadt und zwei weitere für die amerikanische Besatzungszone in Deutschland. Katharine schrieb alles mit, was der neben dem Fahrer stehende Mann vom American-Express-Büro ihnen erzählte. Sie dachte ›ich kann es im Geschichtsunterricht anbringen, es ist eine historische Stunde, Amerika in Deutschland, die *stars and stripes* über Europa, ich habe es mir angesehen, ich habe es erlebt‹. Kay hatte es aufgegeben, während der Besichtigungsfahrten ein Merkheft zu führen. Man sah ohnedies zuwenig. Erst im Hotel übertrug Kay die wichtigsten Daten aus Katharines Stenogramm in ihr Reisetagebuch. Kay war enttäuscht. Das romantische Deutschland? Es war düster. Das Land der Dichter und Denker, der Musik und der Gesänge? Die Leute sahen aus wie Leute überall. An der Kreuzung stand ein Neger. Ein kleiner Radiokoffer spielte Bahama-Joe. Das war wie in Boston; wie in einer Vorstadt von Boston. Das andere Deutschland war wohl eine Erfindung des Professors für Germanistik im College. Er hieß Kaiser und hatte bis zum Jahre dreiunddreißig in Berlin gelebt. Man hatte ihn vertrieben. ›Vielleicht hat er Heimweh‹, dachte Kay, ›es ist ja seine Heimat, er sieht das anders als ich, er mag Amerika nicht, er hält sie hier alle für Dichter, sie sind nicht so geschäftstüchtig wie die Leute bei uns, aber sie haben ihn vertrieben, warum? er ist ein netter Mann, in Amerika haben wir auch Dichter, Kaiser sagt, es sind Schriftsteller, bedeutende Schriftsteller, aber er macht da einen Unterschied, immerhin: Hemingway, Faulkner, Wolfe, O'Neill, Wilder, Edwin lebt in Europa, wandte uns den Rücken, auch Ezra Pound, in Boston hatten wir Santayana, die Deutschen haben Thomas Mann, aber der ist bei uns, komisch, auch vertrieben, sie hatten, sie hatten Goethe, Schiller, Kleist, Hölderlin, Hofmannsthal, Hölderlin und

Hofmannsthal sind Dr. Kaisers Lieblingsdichter, Rilkes Elegien, Rilke starb sechsundzwanzig, wen haben sie jetzt? sitzen auf den Trümmern Karthagos und weinen, ich müßte unserer Reisegesellschaft entwischen, vielleicht würde ich jemand kennenlernen, einen Dichter, ich würde mit ihm sprechen, ich, eine Amerikanerin, ich würde ihm sagen, er soll nicht traurig sein, aber Katharine paßt auf mich auf, lästig, ich bin erwachsen, sie wollte nicht daß ich *Across-the-river* lese ein Buch das nie hätte gedruckt werden dürfen sagte sie, warum eigentlich nicht? wegen der kleinen Contessa? ob ich auch so schnell?‹ — ›Die Stadt ist farblos‹, dachte Mildred, ›und die Frauen sind schlecht angezogen.‹ Katharine notierte: Noch immer sichtbar die Unterdrückung der Frau, keine dem Mann gleichwertige Stellung. Sie würde darüber in Massachusetts im Frauenklub sprechen. Mildred dachte ›es ist blöd mit lauter Weibern zu reisen, wir müssen stinken, die Frau das schwache Geschlecht, ermüdend diese Fahrt, was sieht man? nichts, jedes Jahr lass' ich mich wieder darauf ein, die gefährlichen Krauts, die Judenschinder, jeder Deutsche unterm Stahlhelm, ich seh' nichts, friedliche Leute, arm wohl, ein Soldatenvolk, *Warnung vor Ohne-uns-Propaganda*, Katharine mag den Hemingway nicht, stellte sich an, die Gans, als Kay das Buch lesen wollte, ein furchtbares Buch, Komtesse geht mit altem Major ins Bett, Kay ginge auch mit Hemingway ins Bett, ist aber kein Hemingway da, dafür Schokolade als Betthupfer von Katharine, Kay-Liebling, ihre grünen Augen, haben es ihr angetan, was seh' ich? natürlich ein Pissoir, nie seh' ich Denkmäler, immer nur so was, ob ich mich mal analysieren lasse? wozu? zu spät, in Paris an diesen Orten Wellblech wie kurze Hottentottenschürzen, daß sich die Kerle nicht genieren?‹

Grünes Licht. Messalina hatte sie entdeckt. Alexanders lustwütiges Weib. Emilia wollte ihr entwischen, wollte sich verstecken, aber die Flucht in die Retirade mißglückte: es war ein Männerpissoir gerade an der Straßenecke, und Emilia merkte es erst, als ihr Herren entgegentraten, die sich die Hose schlossen. Emilia erschrak, stolperte und wäre, nun auch

noch von dem strengen Ammoniakdunst und Teergeruch benommen, mit dem schweren Plaid, dem lustigen komischen
Plaid der Karikaturisten beinahe gegen die urinierenden Rük-
ken gefallen, die Rücken, über die sich ihr Köpfe zuwandten,
sinnend ins Leere gerichtete Augen, einfältige Gesichter, die
langsam den Ausdruck des Staunens annahmen. Messalina
hatte von dem erspähten Opfer nicht gelassen; sie hatte ihr
Taxi verabschiedet, das Mietsauto, das sie zum Friseur bringen sollte, zum Bleichen und Aufplustern der Haare: nun
wartete sie vor der Retirade. Emilia kam mit feuerrotem
Kopf aus der Männerzuflucht gerannt, und Messalina rief:
»Emilykind suchst du Strichjungenbekanntschaften, ich kann
dir Hänschen empfehlen, er ist der Freund von Jack, du
weißt doch, wer Jack ist, sie treffen sich bei mir. Tag, wie
geht's dir denn, laß dich küssen, du hast einen so frischen
Teint, ganz rot. Du treibst es zuwenig, komm heut abend
zu mir, ich geb' eine Party, vielleicht kommt Edwin der
Dichter, er soll in der Stadt sein, ich kenn' ihn nicht, weiß
nicht, was er geschrieben hat, er hat einen Preis bekommen.
Jack bringt ihn vielleicht mit, er soll Hänschen kennenlernen, es wäre doch nett!« Emilia krümmte sich, wenn Messalina sie Emilykind nannte, sie haßte es, wenn Philipp von
Messalina erwähnt wurde, alle Bemerkungen Messalinas
verletzten sie und machten sie verlegen, aber da sie in Alexanders nach Dämonenart hergerichtete Frau mit der Ring-
kämpferfigur ein Riesenmiststück sah, dem nicht zu entkommen war, eine gewaltige und gewalttätige Dame, das
pompöse groteske Denkmal einer Dame, war Emilia immer
wieder von ihr eingeschüchtert und begegnete ihr, dem Denkmal, fast wie ein kleines Mädchen, knicksend und zur Denk-
malshöhe emporblickend, was wiederum Messalina aufs neue
begehrlich machte, in schwindelnder Bewunderung mit aus-
gesuchter Höflichkeit. Messalina dachte ›sie ist reizvoll, warum lebt sie mit Philipp? sie liebt ihn, es ist nicht anders möglich, komisch, ich konnte es lange nicht begreifen, vielleicht
hat er sie entjungfert, es gibt solche Bindungen, der erste
Mann, ich trau' mich nicht sie zu fragen, ärmlich, alles an
ihr ist abgerissen, eine feine Gestalt ein feiner Kopf, sieht

immer gut aus, dieser räudige Pelz, Feh, Lumpenprinzessin, ob sie im Bett was kann? ich glaube es, Jack ist scharf auf sie, Knabenkörper, wenn sie mit Alexander? aber sie kommt nicht zu mir, oder sie kommt mit Philipp, er ruiniert das Mädchen, man müßte sie retten, er nützt sie aus, ein Nichtskönner, Alexander bat ihn um einen Film, was schrieb er? nichts, lachte verlegen, ließ sich nicht wieder sehen, undurchschaubar, verkanntes Genie Kaffeehausliterat in Berlin im Romanischen Café, in Paris im Dome, dabei ernst, die wahre Vogelscheuche, schade um die hübsche Kleine, hat einen sinnlichen Mund‹. Und Emilia dachte ›was ist es für ein Pech, daß ich sie treffen mußte, immer wenn ich mit Sachen unterwegs bin treffe ich jemand, ich schäme mich, das dumme Plaid, natürlich merkt sie daß ich was verkaufen muß daß ich auf dem Weg zum Leihamt bin zu den Althändlern sie sieht es mir an, ein Blinder muß es sehen, die anzüglichen Fragen nach Philipp, gleich wird sie sich nach seinem Buch erkundigen, die leeren weißen Seiten liegen zu Haus, ich schäme mich, ich weiß er könnte ein Buch schreiben und er kann nicht, *Angriff bedeutet Weltkrieg*, was versteht sie? Edwin ist für sie ein Name aus der Zeitung, keine Zeile hat sie von ihm gelesen, sie sammelt Berühmtheiten, Wunderdoktor Gröning war bei ihr, ob es wahr ist, daß sie Alexander prügelt wenn er mit anderen Frauen, was versteht sie? ich muß mich beeilen, das grüne Licht.‹ —

Das grüne Licht. Sie gingen weiter, Bahama-Joe. Josef blinzelte zum alten Wirtshaus »Zur Glocke« hinüber; es war bis auf die Grundmauern abgebrannt und nun als Bretterhütte wiedererstanden. Josef zupfte seinen schwarzen Herrn am Ärmel: »Mister vielleicht Bier trinken wollen? Hier sehr gutes Bier.« Er blickte hoffnungsvoll. »Oh, *beer*«, sagte Odysseus. Er lachte, Bahama-Joe, das Lachen hob und senkte die breite Brust: Wellen des Mississippi. Er schlug Josef auf die Schulter; der sackte in die Knie. »*Beer!*« — »Bier!« Sie gingen hinein, gingen in die berühmte alte zerstörte wiederauferstandene »Glocke«, Arm in Arm, Bahama-Joe, tranken: der Schaum lag wie Schnee auf ihren Lippen.

Vor dem Schreibmaschinengeschäft zögerte Philipp. Er betrachtete die Auslage. Das war falsch. Er traute sich nicht hinein. Die dürre Gräfin Anne — sie war eine überaus geschäftstüchtige, gewissensfreie, herzlose und aller Welt bekannte Dame aus der politischen Kulissenfamilie, die Hitler auf den Reichskanzlerstuhl half, wofür dann Hitler, zur Macht gekommen, die Familie bis auf die dürre Anne ausrottete, eine Nazistin mit dem Opfer-des-Faschismus-Ausweis, das eine von Natur, den Ausweis besaß sie zu Recht — die dürre Gräfin Anne hatte Philipp, den Verfasser eines im Dritten Reich verbotenen und nach dem Dritten Reich vergessenen Buches, traurig in einem traurigen Café getroffen, und da sie immer unternehmungslustig und zu einem Gespräch aufgelegt war, hatte sie auch mit Philipp eine Unterhaltung begonnen. Einseitig, sehr einseitig, ›mein Gott, was will sie?‹ — »Sie dürfen sich nicht treiben lassen«, hatte sie gesprochen, »Philipp, wie sieht das aus! Ein Mann mit Ihrem Talent! Sie dürfen sich nicht von ihrer Frau ernähren lassen. Sie müssen sich aufraffen, Philipp. Warum schreiben Sie keinen Film? Sie kennen doch Alexander. Sie haben doch Beziehungen. Messalina erwartet viel von Ihnen!« Doch Philipp dachte ›welchen Film soll ich schreiben? Wovon redet sie? Filme für Alexander? Filme für Messalina? *Erzherzogliebe im Atelier*, ich kann das nicht, sie wird es nicht begreifen, aber ich kann das nicht, ich verstehe es nicht, *Erzherzogliebe*, was sagt mir das? die falschen Gefühle, die echten falschen Gefühle, kein Organ dafür, wer will so was sehen? alle, so sagt man, ich glaube es nicht, ich weiß es nicht, ich will nicht!‹ — »Aber wenn Sie nicht wollen«, sagte die Gräfin, »dann tun Sie was anderes, Philipp, verkaufen Sie einen leichtabsetzbaren Artikel, ich habe die Vertretung für einen Patentkleber, jedes Geschäft braucht ihn, hausieren Sie doch mit ihm. Keine Verpackung ist heute ohne den Patentkleber denkbar, er spart Zeit und Material, Sie brauchen nur in den erstbesten Laden zu gehen, und schon haben Sie zwei Mark verdient. Zwanzig, dreißig Packungen können Sie am Tag verkaufen — rechnen Sie sich das aus!« So das Gespräch mit Anne, der dürren, der geschäftstüchtigen, ein suggestives Geschwätz, nun saß er in der Tinte, nein, stand da mit dem Kleister — er öffnete die Tür. Eine Alarmvorrichtung schrillte und erschreckte ihn. Er zuckte zusammen wie ein Dieb. Seine Linke umkrampfte in der Manteltasche den Patentkleber der Gräfin. Die Schreibmaschinen blitzten im Neonlicht, und Philipp hatte die Empfindung, daß ihre Tastaturen ihn angrinsten: die Buchstabenfront wurde zu einem höhnenden offenen Maul, in dem das Alphabet mit bleckenden Zähnen nach ihm schnappte. War Philipp nicht Schriftsteller? Herr der Schreibgeräte? Ein gedemütigter Herr! Wenn er den Mund aufmachte, ein Zauberwort aussprächte, würden sie losklappern: willige Diener. Philipp wußte das Zauberwort nicht. Er hatte es vergessen. Er hatte nichts zu sagen. Er hatte den Leuten, die draußen vorübergingen, nichts zu sagen. Die Leute waren verurteilt. Er war verurteilt. Er war in anderer Weise verurteilt als die vorübergehenden Leute. Aber er war auch verurteilt. Die Zeit hatte diesen Ort verurteilt. Sie hatte ihn zu Lärm und Schweigen verurteilt. Wer redete, was redete man denn? *Wie Emmy Hermann Göring kennenlernte,* die grellen Plakate schrien es von allen Wänden. Lärm für ein Jahrhundert. Was sollte Philipp hier? Er war überflüssig. Er war feige. Er hatte nicht den Mut, dem Geschäftsmann im eleganten Anzug, viel neuer als Philipps Anzug war, den gräflichen Patentkleber anzubieten, einen, wie es Philipp nun vorkam, völlig lächerlichen und unnützen Gegenstand. ›Mir fehlt der Sinn für die Wirklichkeit, ich bin eben kein ernster Mann, der Geschäftsmann hier ist ein ernster Mann, ich kann das, was alle treiben, einfach nicht ernst nehmen, ich finde es komisch, dem Mann etwas zu verkaufen, gleichzeitig bin ich zu feige dazu, soll er seine Pakete verkleben womit er will, was geht es mich an? warum klebt er Pakete? um seine Maschinen zu verschicken, warum verschickt er sie? um Geld zu verdienen, um gut zu essen, um sich gut zu kleiden, weil er gut schlafen will, Emilia hätte diesen Mann heiraten sollen, und was tun die Leute mit den Maschinen, die sie bei ihm gekauft haben? sie wollen mit ihnen Geld verdienen und gut leben, sie stellen Sekretärinnen an, schauen ihnen auf die Waden und diktieren Briefe »Sehr geehrte

Herren wir bestätigen Ihr Gestriges und geben unser Heutiges«, ich möchte ihnen ins Gesicht lachen, dabei lachen sie mich aus, sie haben recht, ich bin der Reingefallene, ein Verbrechen an Emilia, unfähig, feige, überflüssig bin ich: ein deutscher Schriftsteller.‹ — »Was darf ich dem Herrn zeigen?« Der elegant gekleidete Geschäftsmann verbeugte sich vor Philipp, auch er ließ sich's sauer werden. Philipps Blick schweifte über die Stellagen mit den blanken geölten Maschinen, den boshaften zu jedem Schabernack bereiten Erfindungen, denen der Mensch seine Gedanken, seine Mitteilungen, seine Botschaften, die Kriegserklärungen anvertraute. Dann sah er das Diktiergerät. Es war ein Tonaufnahmekoffer, wie er ihn von zwei Rundfunklesungen kannte, die er aufs Magnetophonband gesprochen hatte, und auf dem Apparat stand das Wort Reporter. Reporter heißt Berichterstatter. ›Bin ich ein Berichterstatter?‹ dachte Philipp. ›Ich könnte mit diesem Gerät Bericht erstatten, berichten, daß ich zu feige und zu unfähig bin, einen Kleister zu verkaufen, daß ich mich zu erhaben fühle, für Alexander einen Film nach dem Geschmack der Leute zu schreiben die draußen vorübergehen, und daß ich mir's nicht zutraue, den Geschmack der Leute zu ändern, daran liegt es, überflüssig und komisch bin ich, und ich finde mich überflüssig und komisch, aber ich sehe die andern, etwa diesen Geschäftsmann, der sich einbildet, er könne mir was verkaufen, während ich mich nicht traue, ihm einen Kleister anzudrehen, ich finde ihn nicht weniger überflüssig und komisch als mich!‹ Der Ladenbesitzer sah Philipp erwartungsvoll an. »Ich interessiere mich für das Diktaphon da«, sagte Philipp. »Es ist die beste Konstruktion auf dem Markt«, entgegnete der elegante Herr. Er war sehr beflissen. »Ein erstklassiges Gerät. Es macht sich von selbst bezahlt. Überall, auf Reisen, im Auto, im Bett können Sie Ihre Briefe diktieren. Probieren Sie es bitte —.« Er schaltete an dem Kasten und reichte Philipp ein kleines Mikrophon. Das Tonband lief von der einen Spule auf die andere. Philipp sprach in das Mikrophon: »Das Neue Blatt will, daß ich Edwin interviewe. Ich könnte den Apparat hier mitnehmen, und er würde unser Gespräch aufzeichnen. Ich werde verlegen sein, als

Berichterstatter zu Edwin zu kommen. Wahrscheinlich fürchtet er Journalisten. Er wird sich verpflichtet fühlen, was Allgemeines und Verbindliches zu sagen. Es wird mich kränken. Ich werde mich genieren. Natürlich kennt er mich nicht. Andererseits freue ich mich auf Edwin. Ich schätze ihn. Vielleicht wird es eine gute Begegnung. Ich könnte mit Edwin im Park spazierengehen. Oder soll ich doch lieber den Kleister —« Er hielt erschrocken inne. Der Geschäftsmann lächelte verbindlich und sagte: »Der Herr sind Journalist? Schon viele Journalisten haben unsern Reporter —« Er schaltete das Band zurück, und Philipp hörte nun seine eigene Stimme seine Gedanken über das Interview mit Edwin wiedergeben. Die Stimme befremdete ihn. Was sie sagte, beschämte ihn. Es war eine Exhibition, eine intellektuelle Exhibition. Er hätte sich auch nackt ausziehen können. Seine eigene Stimme, die Worte, die sie sprach, erschreckten Philipp, und er floh aus dem Laden.

— wie Schnee auf den Lippen. Sie wischten sie ab und tauchten wieder in die irdenen Krüge, der Bock stieg in sie ein, rieselte süß bitter klebrig aromatisch die Kehle hinunter »*Beer*« — »Bier«: Odysseus und Josef prosteten einander zu. Der kleine Radioapparat stand auf dem Stuhl neben Josef. Er spielte jetzt Candy. *Candy-I-call-my-sugar-candy*. Irgendwo meilenfern lief die Platte ab, stumm und unsichtbar lief der Klang durch die Luft, und hier auf dem Wirtshausstuhl sang nun eine schmalzige Stimme, die Stimme eines fetten mit seiner Schmalzstimme gut verdienenden Mannes den Text *Candy-I-call-my-sugar-candy*. Die »Glocke« war gut besucht. In Loden gekleidete Leute vom Lande, die in der Stadt was kaufen wollten, und Geschäftsleute, die ihren Laden in der Nähe hatten und den Leuten vom Lande etwas verkaufen wollten, aßen Weißwürste. Der Friseur Klett pellte mit den Fingern die Haut von der weißen Fülle und steckte sich die Wurst prall und voll in den Mund. *Candy-I-call-my-sugar-candy*. Klett schmatzte und grunzte genüßlich. Eben waren noch seine Hände in Messalinas Haaren gewesen. ›Messalina Frau des Schauspielers. Alexander spielt *Erzher-*

zogliebe, wird bestimmt ein wunderbarer Film‹. »Haar etwas spröde, gnädige Frau, vielleicht eine Ölmassage. Herr
Gemahl in Uniform, ich freu' mich schon, *Erzherzogliebe*,
deutsche Filme sind doch die besten, das können sie uns nicht
nehmen.« Jetzt saß Messalina unter der Trockenhaube. Noch
fünf Minuten. Ob er noch eine Weißwurst? Das zarte Fleisch,
der Saft an den Fingern. *Candy-I-call-my-sugar-candy.* An
einem Tisch würfelten Griechen. Sahen aus, als wollten sie
sich an die Gurgel springen. Theater! »He, Joe, willst du
setzen? fünfmal den Einsatz?« — »Das sind schlechte Menschen, Mister, haben Messer.« Josef hob das Gesicht aus dem
Bierkrug und blinzelte treu Odysseus den Herrn an. Odysseus' Brust schüttelte das Lachen, Mississippiwellen, wer konnte ihm was? »*Beer*« — »Bier«. Die »Glocke« war gemütlich. Italienische Händler maßen Stoffballen ab, schnitten
mit einer kleinen flinken Schere Coupons von den Ballen:
Zellwolle mit englischen Stempeln. Zwei fromme Juden ver-
stießen gegen Moses Gesetz. Sie aßen unkoscher, aber sie aßen
nichts Schweinernes, vergeben, vergeben auf der Reise, vergeben auf der Wanderschaft, immer auf der Wanderschaft, immer auf dem Weg nach Israel, immer im Schmutz. *Kämpfe
am See Genezareth, Arabische Liga beansprucht Jordanien.*
Ein Mann erzählte einem andern von der Landung in Nar-
wik unter Dietl »wir waren am Polarkreis«, der andere berichtete aus der Cyrenaika, aus der Libyschen Wüste »die
Sonne Rommel«, sie waren in der Welt herumgekommen,
siegreich voran, alte Kameraden, es drängte hoch aus dem
Vergessen, da war einer bei der SS »in Tarnopol Mensch
wenn der Scharführer pfiff ich sag euch die sprangen.« —
»Halt die Fresse sauf's aus und Scheiße.« Sie legten die
Arme einander über die Schulter und sangen: das-war-ein-
Edelweiß. »*Beer*« — »Bier«. Mädchen strichen herum, dick-
liche Mädchen, rauhgesichtige Mädchen *Candy-I* —

call-the-States! In einer gepolsterten Telephonzelle im großen
Postraum des Central Exchange stand Washington Price. Er
schwitzte in der geschlossenen Zelle. Er wischte sich den
Schweiß von der Stirn, und sein Taschentuch flatterte unter

der matten elektrischen Birne der Zelle wie ein aufgeregter weißer Vogel in einem Käfig. Washington sprach mit Baton Rouge, seiner Heimatstadt im Staate Louisiana. In Baton Rouge war es vier Uhr früh, die Sonne war noch nicht aufgegangen. Die Glocke des Telephons hatte sie aus dem Schlaf geschreckt, so früh, das war nichts Gutes, eine Unglücksbotschaft, sie standen furchtsam im Gang des kleinen sauberen Hauses, die Bäume in der Allee rauschten, der Wind rauschte in den Wipfeln der Ulmen, Züge fuhren zu den Getreidesilos, Weizenkähne glitten zum Kai, ein Schlepper schrie, Washington sah sie, die beiden Alten, ihn im gestreiften Schlafanzug, sie hatte eine Schürze schnell übergeworfen, er sah sie im Geist, wie sie zögerten, wie sie sich fürchteten, er die Hand schon ausgestreckt hatte nach dem Hörer und sie ihre Hand, um seine zurückzuhalten, Morgenbotschaft Unkenruf im bewahrten mühsam gesicherten Haus, Onkel Toms Hütte, ein Steinhaus, Haus eines farbigen Bürgers, eines achtbaren Mannes, aber das Telephon mit seiner Stimme von fern, Ruf aus der weißen Welt, der feindlichen Welt, aufschreckende Stimme und doch so ersehnte Stimme, sie wußten es, noch bevor es in der Hörmuschel rauschte und wahr wurde, seine Stimme, die Stimme des Sohnes, warum blieb er? verlorener Sohn, kein Kalb war zu schlachten, er selbst geschlachtet, blieb über den Krieg hinaus, über die Pflicht hinaus, blieb bei der Army, was ging es ihn an? Deutschland, Europa, wie fern ihr Gezänk, die Russen, warum nicht die Russen? unser Sohn Sergeant, sein Bild in Uniform auf dem Buffet neben dem Neusilberkrug, neben dem Radio, *Rote Offensive, Kinder lieben Ludens Drops,* was will er? ach, sie ahnen es, und er weiß es, daß sie es ahnen: Verstrickung. Der Alte nimmt den Hörer und meldet sich, der Vater, Oberaufseher im Getreidesilo, Washington spielte im Getreide, erstickte fast, ein Kind in rotweißgestreiften Overalls, ein schwarzer Kobold, im Überfluß, in einem Meer von gelbem Korn: Brot. »Hallo!« Jetzt muß er es sagen: Carla, die weiße Frau, das Kind, er kommt nicht heim, er wird die weiße Frau heiraten, er braucht Geld, Geld, um zu heiraten, Geld, um das Kind zu retten, das kann er ihnen nicht sagen, Carla

droht mit dem Arzt, Washington will Geld vom Ersparten
der Alten, er kündigt ihnen die Heirat an, das Kind, was wissen sie? Sie wissen. Verstrickung, der Sohn in Not. Nichts
Gutes: Sünde. Oder nicht Sünde vor Gott, aber vor den Menschen. Sie sehen die fremde Tochter im Negerviertel von
Baton Rouge, sehen die Andershäutige, die Frau von drüben,
Frau von jenseits des Grabens, sehen das Abteil für Farbige,
die Straße der Apartheid, wie will er leben mit ihr? wie sich
freuen, wenn sie weint? zu eng das Haus, das Haus im Ghetto,
Onkel Toms saubere Hütte und das Rauschen der Bäume in
der Allee, das gemächliche Treiben des Flusses, breit und
tief, und in der Tiefe Frieden, Musik aus dem Nachbarhaus,
das Raunen der Stimmen, der dunklen Stimmen am Abend,
zuviel für sie, zuviel Stimmen und doch nur eine Stimme, zu
eng zu dicht zu nah zu dunkel, Schwärze und Nacht und die
Luft und die Leiber und die Stimmen sind wie ein schwerer
Vorhang aus Samt, der mit tausend Falten über den Tag
fällt. Wenn es Abend wird — führt er sie zum Tanz in Napoleon's Inn? Washington weiß es, weiß es so gut, wie sie es
wissen, die Alten, die guten Alten im Gang des Hauses unter den rauschenden Bäumen am raunenden Fluß in den
Samtfalten der Nacht, vor Napoleons Schenke wird eine Tafel stehen am Abend vor dem Tanz, vor der Feindfrau der
Feindfreundin der Feindgeliebten, die nicht erbeutet, die
erdient wurde, wie Jakob um Rahel warb, keiner wird das
Schild sehen, und alle werden es lesen, in jedem Auge wird
es zu lesen sein *Weiße unerwünscht*. Washington telephoniert, spricht über den Ozean, seine Stimme eilt der Morgen-
röte voraus, und die Stimme des Vaters entflieht unfroh der
Nacht, und das Schild, das einmal an der Zellentür hing, die
Washington hinter sich geschlossen hat, hieß *Für Juden verboten*. Präsident Roosevelt hörte damals von diesem Schild,
die Diplomaten und die Journalisten berichteten es ihm, und
er erzählte vom Leidensstern Davids am Kamin, und die
Rede am Kamin strahlte durch den Äther und strahlte aus
dem Klangkasten neben dem Neusilberkrug in Onkel Toms
Hütte und entfaltete sich in den Herzen. Washington wurde
Soldat und zog in den Krieg, *vorwärts christliche Soldaten*,

und in Deutschland verschwanden die infamen Gebote, und abgerissen, verbrannt und versteckt wurden die Tafeln des Ungesetzes, die jeden Menschen beschämten. Washington wurde dekoriert, aber im Vaterland, das ihn auszeichnete mit den Bändchen und den Medaillen für Tapferkeit, im Vaterland behaupteten sich die Schilder des Hochmuts, die Denkweise des Aftermenschen, ob plakatiert oder nicht, blieb stehen *Für Schwarze verboten*. Verstrickung, Washington ist verstrickt. Er träumt, während er mit den Eltern von seiner Liebsten spricht (ach liebenswert! ist sie liebenswert? ist es Hochmut? Hochmut von ihm? Washington **gegen** alle? Washington Ritter gegen Vorurteil und Verfemung?), er träumt, und im Traum besitzt er ein kleines Hotel, eine nette gemütliche Bar, und *niemand ist unerwünscht* steht in einem Kranz von immer brennenden bunten Glühbirnen an der Tür geschrieben — das wäre Washington's Inn. Wie soll er es ihnen begreiflich machen? fern er in Deutschland, fern sie am Mississippi, und weit ist die Welt und frei ist die Welt, und böse ist die Welt und Haß ist in der Welt, und voller Gewalt ist die Welt, warum? weil alle sich fürchten. Washington trocknet das schweißnasse Gesicht. Der weiße Taschentuchvogel flattert gefangen im Käfig. Sie werden das Geld senden, die guten Alten, das Hochzeitsgeld, das Kindbettgeld: Es ist Mühsal, es ist Schweiß, es sind schwere volle Schaufeln, Schaufeln voll Korn, es ist Brot, und neue Verstrickung, und Unheil ist unser Gefährte —

Da aber das Kind in ihrem Leib sich regte, fürchtete auch sie sich vor sichtbaren und unsichtbaren Schildern, Nebukadnezarträumen, Belsazarschriften, die sie aus dem Paradies der automatischen Küchen und der Pillensicherheit vertreiben könnten, *Weiße unerwünscht, Schwarze unerwünscht*, es traf sie beides, und für *Juden unerwünscht* war, ohne daß er es wußte oder besonders wollte, der Vater ihres Sohnes in den Krieg gezogen. Unerwünscht war ihr das neue Kind, das dunkle, das gesprenkelte, in seiner Höhle noch ahnungslos, daß es Wildfrucht sein sollte, verworfen vom Gärtner, mit Schuld und Vorwurf beladen, bevor es Schuld und Vorwurf

sich zuziehen konnte, und sie stand im Untersuchungszim-
mer, was wollte er noch untersuchen? sie wußte es ja, es war
unnötig, sich auf den Stuhl zu setzen, sie wollte den Eingriff,
die Auskratzung, er sollte es wegbringen, war er ihr nicht
verpflichtet? was hatte er bekommen? Kaffee, Zigaretten,
den teuren Whisky zu einer Zeit, als es weder Kaffee, Zigaretten noch Schnaps gab, nicht den schäbigsten Fusel, wofür
hatte er es genommen? für Spülungen, Befühlungen, Mittel-
chen ›er faßte meine Brüste an, nun soll er was für mich
tun‹. Und er, Dr. Frahm, Facharzt für Frauenheilkunde und
Chirurgie, wußte, was er tun sollte, wußte es, ohne daß sie
es aussprach, wußte, was der vorgestreckte Bauch bedeutete,
und er dachte ›Eid des Hippokrates, kein Leben sollst du nehmen, was geben sie jetzt an mit diesem Eid, wer ist wohl
drauf gekommen? Kater nach den Euthanasieprozessen,
Mord an Geisteskranken, Mord an Ungeborenen, bei mir
hängt das in gotischer Fraktur im Gang vor dem Sprech-
zimmer, es ist etwas dunkel im Gang, und der Spruch macht
sich da sehr gut, was ist Leben? die Quanten und das Leben, die Physiker quälen sich jetzt mit der Biologie, ich kann
ihre Bücher nicht lesen, zu viel Mathematik Formelkram ab-
straktes Wissen Gehirnakrobatik, ein Leib ist kein Leib mehr,
Auflösung der Gegenständlichkeit in den Bildern der neuen
Maler, das sagt mir nichts, ich bin Doktor, vielleicht zu ungebildet, habe auch keine Zeit, kaum für die Fachblätter, immer wieder was Neues, ich bin müde am Abend, meine Frau
will ins Kino, Film mit Alexander, ich halte ihn für einen
Schnösel, aber die Frauen? Leben schon im Sperma? das Ei?
dann auch Gonokokkenschutz, die Priester sagen natürlich
die Seele, sollten sich das mal aufgeschnitten ansehen, Hippokrates, war er Kassenarzt? hatte er eine Großstadtpraxis?
die Spartaner warfen die Mißgestalten in die Schluchten des
Taygetos, Militärdiktatur totaler Staat sicher verwerflich, lieber Athen Philosophie und Knabenliebe, aber Hippokrates?
er sollte mal zu mir kommen und sich's anhören »ich bring'
mich um« — »wenn Sie's Herr Doktor nicht machen« —
»ich will's weghaben«, und zu wissen wo sie dann hingehen,
die Pfuschaborte, sterben zu Tausenden, Ladenmädchen, Se-

kretärinnen, können sich selber kaum erhalten, und zu was wächst so was heran? Wohlfahrtssuppen Heimbetreuung Familienpflegschaft Arbeitslosigkeit Gefängnis Krieg, ich war Feldarzt, was fiel da rot auf den Tisch, noch mal wie geboren, die Glieder schon weggerissen, zum Tod geboren, Achtzehnjährige, besser nie geboren, was erwartet das Negerkind? man müßte ihnen den Koitus verbieten, aussichtslos, sie werden es nie lassen, hätte nichts gegen Entvölkerung, Malthus, wenn man sieht was so in die Sprechstunde kommt, müßte mir einen anderen Beruf suchen, Krankenkassenesel, für die Kasse Verwaltungspaläste für uns die Pfennige, der gute Onkel Doktor, mein Vater fuhr im Pferdewagen über Land, das Pferd trug im Sommer einen Strohhut, was gab mein Vater ihnen denn? klopfte ihnen den Bauch und verordnete Lindenblütentee, heute verschreibt jeder eine chemische Formel die niemand lesen oder aussprechen kann, Geheimzeichen der Medizinmänner im Busch, Opposition dagegen, die Psychotherapeuten auch so Brüder, Amenorrhöe der Gattin weil der Mann im Büro auf den Laufjungen scharf ist und sich nicht traut, die alte Warzenbesprechung, Patienten wollen immer das Neueste, heute Ultraschall morgen was mit Atomspaltung, kommt von den Illustrierten, hab' das Zeug im Wartezimmer, all die Apparate, das blitzt und funkelt, Krankenbehandlung am Fließband, wer zahlt es? der Onkel Doktor, Tribut an die Industrie, die Raten für den Wagen, sie wird Spaß mit ihrem Neger haben, in Paris sollen sie wie verrückt drauf sein, *Vernegerung*, Kriegspropaganda im Völkischen Beobachter, *Rassenverrat*, wohin kamen sie mit ihrer Rassenreinhaltung? eine Bunkerwohnungsrasse, soziale Indikation macht Schwierigkeiten, eugenische Indikation nicht zugelassen, Schwarz und Weiß gibt auch hübsche Kinder, was meine Frau sagen würde wenn ich eins annehmen wollte? medizinische Indikation‹ — »lassen Sie mal sehen« — ›gesund, wir brauchen einen Namen, *Einbruch in ärztliche Schweigepflicht*‹ — »dauerndes Erbrechen?« — ›kaum noch mit der Spritze, bei Schulte in der Klinik mit Komfort, ordentliche Schwestern, arbeite gern mit ihnen, muß über das Honorar reden, nur-die-Lumpe-sind-bescheiden, sag es

63

mit Goethe.‹ — »Frau Carla, am besten machen wir es gleich
in der Klinik.« —

›Das Beste für Carla.‹ Washington war im großen Verkaufs-
raum des Central Exchange. Er ging zu den Damenartikeln
hinüber. Was wollte er? ›Das Beste für Carla.‹ Die deutschen
Verkäuferinnen waren freundlich. Zwei Frauen wählten
Nachthemden. Es waren Frauen von Offizieren, und die
Nachthemden waren lange Gewänder aus rosa und schilf-
grünem Crêpe de Chine. Die Frauen würden wie üppige grie-
chische Göttinnen im Bett liegen. Die Verkäuferin ließ die
Frauen bei den Hemden allein. Sie wandte sich Washington
zu und lächelte. Was wollte er? Ein Sausen war in der Luft.
Ihm war noch immer, als habe er die Telephonmuschel am
Ohr und höre Worte, die über den Ozean gesprochen wurden.
Durch technischen Zauber war er zu Hause in Baton Rouge.
Durch welchen Zauber stand er im Central Exchange einer
deutschen Stadt? Was wollte er? Es war gut, und es war
schändlich: er wollte heiraten. Wem wollte er Kummer bereiten, wen unglücklich machen? War jeder Schritt gefährlich?
Auch hier? In Baton Rouge hätten sie ihn totgeschlagen. Die
Verkäuferin dachte ›er ist schüchtern, diese Riesen sind immer
schüchtern, sie suchen Wäsche für ihre Freundinnen und trau-
en sich nicht zu sagen was sie wollen‹. Sie legte ihm vor, was
sie in diesem Fall für passend hielt, Höschen und Hemdchen,
leichte zarte Schleier, die richtige Nuttenwäsche, ›das richtige
für die Fräuleins‹, schattenfein, mehr zur Anreizung als zur
Verhüllung. Die Verkäuferin trug dieselbe Wäsche. ›Ich
könnt's ihm zeigen‹, dachte sie. Washington wollte die Wäsche nicht. Er sagte »Kinderwäsche«. Die Verkäuferin dachte
›o weh, er hat ihr schon ein Kind gemacht‹. — ›Sie sollen gute
Väter sein‹, dachte sie, ›aber ich möchte kein Kind von ihnen
haben.‹ Er dachte ›man muß jetzt an die Kindersachen denken, man muß alles rechtzeitig besorgen, aber Carla müßte
es aussuchen, sie wird wütend sein wenn ich es aussuche und
mitbringe‹. — »Nein. Doch keine Kinderwäsche«, sagte er.
Was wollte er? Er deutete unentschlossen auf die leichten
Gewebe der erotischen Verführung. Die Offiziersfrauen hat-

64

ten ihre Nachthemden gefunden und blickten Washington böse an. Sie riefen nach der Verkäuferin. ›Er läßt sie mit dem Kind sitzen‹, dachte die Verkäuferin, ›er hat schon eine neue Braut, der schenkt er die Reizwäsche, so sind sie, Schwarze wie Weiße.‹ Sie ließ Washington stehen und schrieb den Verkaufszettel für die Offiziersfrauen aus. Washington legte seine große braune Hand auf ein Stück gelber Seide. Die Seide verschwand wie ein gefangener Schmetterling unter seiner Hand. Die schwarze Hand des Negers und die gelblichen schmutzigen Hände der Griechen nahmen die Würfel, schleuderten sie auf das Tuch, ließen sie hüpfen, springen und rollen. Odysseus hatte gewonnen. Josef zupfte ihn an der Jacke: »Mister, wir gehen, schlechte Menschen.« Die Griechen drängten ihn weg. Josef hielt den Musikkoffer fest in der Hand. Er hatte Angst, man könnte das Köfferchen stehlen. Die Musik schwieg für eine Weile. Eine Männerstimme sprach Nachrichten. Josef verstand nicht, was der Mann sagte, aber manche Worte verstand er doch, die Worte Truman Stalin Tito Korea. Die Stimme in Josefs Hand redete vom Krieg, redete vom Hader, sprach von der Furcht. Wieder fielen die Würfel. Odysseus verlor. Er blickte verwundert auf die Hände der Griechen, Taschenspielerhände, die sein Geld einsteckten. Die Bläserkapelle in der »Glocke« begann ihre Mittagsarbeit. Sie bliesen einen der beliebten dröhnenden Märsche. ›Die macht uns keiner nach.‹ Die Leute summten den Marsch mit. Einige schlugen mit ihren Bierkrügen den Takt. Die Leute hatten die Sirenen vergessen, hatten die Bunker vergessen, die zusammenbrechenden Häuser, die Männer dachten nicht mehr an den Schrei des Unteroffiziers, der sie in den Dreck des Kasernenhofs jagte, nicht an den Graben, die Feldverbandplätze, die Trommelfeuer, die Einkesselung, den Rückzug, sie dachten an Einmärsche und Fahnen. ›Paris wenn da der Krieg aus gewesen wäre, es war ungerecht daß er da nicht aus war.‹ Sie waren um ihren Sieg betrogen worden. Odysseus verlor zum zweitenmal. Die Würfel fielen gegen ihn. Die Taschenspielerhände zauberten. Es war ein Trick. Odysseus wollte hinter den Trick kommen. Er ließ sich nicht blenden. *Kein neuer Militarismus aber Ver-*

teidigungsbereitschaft. Josef hob im Lärm der Blaskapelle Odysseus' Musikkasten an sein Ohr. Hatte die Stimme im Kasten eine Botschaft für Josef den Dienstmann? Die Stimme war jetzt sehr eindringlich, ein eindringliches Rauschen. Josef verstand nur hin und wieder ein Wort, Städtenamen, ferne Namen fremde Namen, fremdländisch ausgesprochene Namen Moskau, Berlin, Tokio, Paris —

In Paris schien die Sonne. Paris war unzerstört. Wenn man seinen Augen trauen wollte, konnte man meinen, der Zweite Weltkrieg habe nicht stattgefunden. Christopher Gallagher war mit Paris verbunden. Er stand in der Zelle, aus der Washington Price mit Baton Rouge telephoniert hatte. Auch Christopher hielt ein Taschentuch in der Hand. Er rieb sich mit dem Tuch die Nase. Die Nase war großporig und etwas gerötet. Seine Gesichtshaut war rauh. Sein Haar rot. Er sah aus wie ein Seemann; er war aber Steueranwalt. Er sprach mit Henriette. Henriette war seine Frau. Sie wohnten in Santa Ana in Kalifornien. Ihr Haus stand am Stillen Ozean. Man konnte sich einbilden, aus den Fenstern des Hauses nach China hinüberzublicken. Jetzt war Henriette in Paris. Christopher war in Deutschland. Christopher vermißte Henriette. Er hatte vorher nicht gedacht, daß er sie vermissen würde. Sie fehlte ihm. Er hätte sie gern bei sich gehabt. Er hätte sie besonders gern in Deutschland bei sich gehabt. Er dachte ›wir sind so förmlich miteinander, woran liegt das wohl? ich liebe sie doch.‹ Henriette saß in ihrem Zimmer in einem Hotel am Quai Voltaire. Vor dem Hotel floß die Seine. Drüben am anderen Ufer lag der Tuileriengarten, ein oft gemaltes, ein öfter noch photographiertes, ein immer wieder berückendes Bild. Christopher hatte eine laute Stimme. Aus der Hörmuschel klang seine Stimme wie ein Brüllen. Er brüllte immer wieder dieselben Sätze: »Ich verstehe dich; aber glaube mir, es würde dir gefallen. Es würde dir sicher gefallen. Es würde dir sehr gut gefallen. Mir gefällt es auch sehr gut.« Und sie sagte immer wieder dieselben Worte: »Nein. Ich kann nicht. Du weißt es. Ich kann nicht.« Er wußte es, aber er verstand es nicht. Oder er verstand es, aber so wie man eine Traumerzählung versteht und dann sagt: »Vergiß es!« Sie sah, während sie mit Christopher sprach, die Seine, sie sah die Tuilerien in der Sonne liegen, sie sah den lieblichen Pariser Frühlingstag, die Landschaft vor dem Fenster glich einem Renoir, aber ihr war es, als ob durch die Grundierung ein anderes Bild durchbräche, ein dunkleres Gemälde. Die Seine verwandelte sich in die Spree, und Henriette stand am Fenster eines Hauses am Kupfergraben, und drüben lag die Museumsinsel, lagen die preußisch-hellenischen Tempel, an denen ewig und ewig gebaut wurde, und sie sah ihren Vater am Morgen ins Amt gehen, er schritt wie eine Menzelsche Figur aufrecht, korrekt, stäubchenfrei, den schwarzen steifen Hut grade über den goldenen Kneifer gesetzt, über die Brücke in sein Museum. Er war kein Kunsthistoriker, er hatte nicht unmittelbar mit den Bildern zu tun, wenn er sie natürlich auch alle kannte, er war Oberregierungsrat in der Generaldirektion, ein Verwaltungsmann, der die Ordnung im Hause unter sich hatte, aber für ihn war es sein Museum, das er selbst an den Feiertagen nicht aus den Augen ließ und dessen jeweiligen kunsthistorischen Leiter er als einen Unmündigen ansah, als einen für die Unterhaltung der Besucher engagierten Artisten, dessen Tun und Angabe nicht weiter ernst zu nehmen war. Er lehnte es ab, in die Wohngegenden des neuen Westens zu ziehen, aus dem Blick des Museums, er blieb in der Wohnung am Kupfergraben, wo es karg und preußisch zuging (blieb da auch nach seiner Entlassung und bis zu dem Tag, als sie ihn holten, ihn und die schüchterne Frau, Henriettes Mutter, die im Schatten von so viel Preußentum unselbständig und willenlos verkümmert war). Henriette spielte als Kind auf den Stufen des Kaiser-Friedrich-Museums unter dem Denkmal des kriegerisch zu Pferd sitzenden Dreimonatskaisers mit den schmutzigen, lauten und herrlichen Gören der Oranienburger Straße, den Rangen vom Monbijouplatz, und später, als sie, nach der Lyzeumszeit, Schauspielschülerin bei Reinhardt am Deutschen Theater war und über die Brücke zur Karlstraße ging, riefen die Halbwüchsigen, die einstigen Spielgefährten, die sich jetzt unter den Hufen des Kaiserpferdes zu heimlichen Um-

armungen trafen, ihr zärtlich »Henri« zu, und sie winkte
entzückt zurück und rief »Fritz« und »Paule«, und der korrekte stäubchenfreie Oberregierungsrat sagte: »Henriette,
das geht nicht.« Was ging, und was ging nicht? Es ging, daß
sie in Berlin den Reinhardt-Preis als beste Schülerin ihres
Jahrgangs bekam; aber es ging nicht, daß sie in Süddeutsch-
land, wohin sie verpflichtet war, die Liebhaberin in den Frei-
ern von Eichendorff spielte. Es ging, daß sie beschimpft wurde; es ging nicht, daß sie engagiert blieb. Es ging, daß sie
ein Wanderleben führte und mit einer Emigrantentruppe in
Zürich, Prag, Amsterdam und New York tingelte. Es ging
nicht, daß sie irgendwo eine unbefristete Aufenthaltsbewilligung, die Arbeitserlaubnis oder für irgendein Land ein Dau-
ervisum bekam. Es ging, daß sie mit anderen Mitgliedern
der Tingeltruppe aus dem Deutschen Reich ausgebürgert
wurde. Es ging nicht, daß der korrekte Oberregierungsrat
weiter im Museum arbeitete. Es ging, daß ihm das Telephon und die Bank in den Anlagen verboten wurde. Es ging,
daß sie in Los Angeles in einer Speisewirtschaft die Teller
abwusch. Es ging nicht, aus Berlin der Tochter Geld zu schik-
ken, damit sie in Hollywood auf eine Filmrolle warten konnte. Es ging, daß sie, aus dem Tellerwischjob entlassen, auf
der Straße stand, einer sehr fremden Straße, und daß sie
hungrig die Einladung eines fremden Mannes annahm, der
zufälligerweise ein Christ war. Er heiratete sie, Christopher
Gallagher. Es ging nicht, daß ihr Vater seinen Namen Friedrich Wilhelm Cohen behielt; es ging, daß er Israel Cohen
genannt wurde. Bereute Christopher seine Ehe? Er bereute
sie nicht. Es ging nicht, daß die Menzelsche Erscheinung, der
preußische Beamte und seine schüchterne Frau länger in ihrer Geburtsstadt Berlin blieben. Es ging, daß sie zu den ersten Juden gehörten, die abtransportiert wurden: zum letztenmal traten sie aus dem Haus am Kupfergraben, in der Abend-
dämmerung, sie stiegen in ein Polizeiauto, und Israel Friedrich Wilhelm, korrekt, stäubchenfrei, ruhig in frideriziani-
scher Zucht, half ihr hinauf, Sarah Gretchen, die weinte, und
dann schloß sich die Tür des Polizeiautos, und man hörte
nichts mehr von ihnen, bis man nach dem Krieg alles hörte,

nichts Persönliches zwar, nur das Allgemeine, die Gesichts-
losigkeit des Schicksals, die Landläufigkeit des Todes — es
genügte. Christophers laute Stimme brüllte: »Du bleibst also in Paris?« Und sie sagte: »Versteh mich.« Und er rief:
»Gewiß, ich verstehe dich. Aber es würde dir gefallen. Es
würde dir gut gefallen. Es hat sich alles geändert. Mir gefällt es gut.« Und sie sagte: »Geh mal ins Bräuhaus. Gegenüber ist ein Café. Das Café Schön. Da lernte ich meine
Rollen.« Und er schrie: »Gewiß. Sicher will ich hingehen.
Aber es würde dir gefallen.« Er war wütend, weil sie in
Paris blieb. Sie fehlte ihm. Liebte sie Paris? Sie sah nun
wieder den Renoir, sah die Seine, die Tuilerien, das heitere
Licht. Gewiß, sie liebte den Blick, das Unzerstörte, aber das
Zerstörte drängte sich in Europa ins Unversehrte, trat zu-
tage, war ein Mittagsgespenst: die hellenisch-preußischen
Tempel auf der Museumsinsel in Berlin lagen ausgeraubt
und zertrümmert. Sie hatte sie mehr geliebt als die Tuilerien.
Sie empfand keine Genugtuung. Sie haßte nicht mehr. Sie
fürchtete sich nur. Sie fürchtete sich, nach Deutschland zu
fahren, und sei es nur für drei Tage. Sie sehnte sich fort aus
Europa. Sie sehnte sich zurück nach Santa Ana. Am Stillen
Ozean war Frieden, war Vergessen, war Frieden und Vergessen für sie. Die Wellen waren das Symbol der ewigen
Wiederkehr. Im Wind war der Atem Asiens. Sie kannte
Asien nicht, *Asien Weltproblem Nummer Eins*, aber die Pa-
zifische See gab ihr etwas von der Ruhe und Sicherheit der
Kreatur, die sich dem Augenblick hingibt, ihre Trauer wurde
eine in die offene Weite hinausschwingende Melancholie,
der Ehrgeiz, als Schauspielerin bewundert zu werden, starb,
es war nicht Zufriedenheit, es war Bescheidung, was sie erfüllte, etwas wie Schlaf, die Bescheidung auf das Haus, auf
die Terrasse, auf den Strand, auf diesen einen durch Glück,
Zufall oder Bestimmung erreichten Punkt in der Unendlichkeit. »Grüße Ezra«, sagte sie. »Er ist großartig«, brüllte
er. »Er kann sich mit deinem Deutsch verständigen. Er über-
setzt mir alles. Du würdest Spaß haben. Es würde dir gut
gefallen.« — »Ich weiß«, sagte sie. »Ich verstehe dich. Ich
warte auf euch. Ich warte in Paris auf euch. Wir fahren dann

nach Hause. Es wird herrlich sein. Zu Hause wird es herrlich
sein. Sag das auch Ezra! Sag ihm, daß ich auf euch warte.
Sag ihm, er soll sich alles ansehen. Sag Ezra —«
Ezra saß in Christophers geräumigem, mit mahagonifarbe-
nem Holz verschaltem Wagen. Der Wagen sah aus wie das
ältere Modell eines Sportflugzeuges, das man zum Boden-
dienst degradiert hatte. Ezra machte Rundflüge über den
Platz. Er gab es ihnen aus allen Bordwaffen. Er feuerte lustig in die Straße. Eine Panik bemächtigte sich der Menge,
des Gewimmels aus Spaziergängern und Mördern, dieses
Haufens von Jägern und Verfolgten. Sie sackten in die Knie,
sie beteten und winselten um Gnade. Sie wälzten sich am
Boden. Sie hielten die Arme schützend vor den Kopf. Sie
flohen wie aufgescheuchtes Wild in die Häuser. Die Schaufenster der großen Geschäfte zersplitterten. Die Kugeln flogen in leuchtender Spur in die Läden. Ezra stürmte im Tief-
flug auf das Denkmal los, das den Mittelpunkt des amerikanischen Parkplatzes vor dem Central Exchange bildete.
Auf den Stufen des Denkmals saßen Jungen und Mädchen,
so alt wie Ezra. Sie schwätzten, johlten und spielten Kopf und
Schrift; sie handelten, tauschten und stritten sich um kleine
Mengen amerikanischer Waren; sie neckten einen struppi-
gen jungen Hund; sie prügelten und versöhnten sich. Ezra
schüttete eine Garbe seiner leuchtenden Munition über die
Kinder. Die Kinder lagen tot oder verwundet auf den Stufen des Denkmals. Der junge Hund kroch in einen Gully.
Ein Junge schrie: »Das war Ezra!« Ezra überflog das Dach
des Central Exchange und stieg steil in die Höhe. Als er hoch
über der Stadt war, warf er eine Bombe. *Wissenschaftler
warnen vor Anwendung.*
Ein kleines Mädchen wischte den Staub vom horizontblauen
Lack einer Limousine. Das kleine Mädchen arbeitete eifrig;
man konnte meinen, es putze das himmlische Fahrzeug eines
Engels. Heinz hatte sich versteckt. Er war auf den Sockel des
Denkmals geklettert und hockte unter dem Pferd des Kur-
fürsten. Die Geschichtsschreiber nannten den Kurfürsten den
Frommen. In den Religionskriegen war er für den rechten
Glauben ins Feld gezogen. Seine Feinde kämpften ebenso für

den rechten Glauben. In der Frage des Glaubens gab es dann auch keinen Sieger. Vielleicht war der Glaube allgemein besiegt worden, indem man um ihn kämpfte. Der fromme Kurfürst aber war durch den Krieg ein mächtiger Mann geworden. Er war so mächtig geworden, daß seine Untertanen nichts zu lachen hatten. Heinz kümmerte sich nicht um den Glaubensstreit und die Macht des Fürsten. Er beobachtete den Platz. Es war eine Nation von Autofahrern, die sich breitmachte. Die Wagen parkten in langen Reihen. Wenn ihnen das Benzin ausginge, würden sie hilflose Kutschen sein, Hütten für Schäfer, wenn man nach dem nächsten Krieg Schafe weiden sollte, Verstecke für Liebespaare, wenn man sich nach dem Tod noch zur Liebe verstecken mochte. Jetzt waren die Wagen, blank und flink, eine stolze Automobilausstellung, ein Triumph des technischen Jahrhunderts, eine Saga von der Herrschaft des Menschen über die Kräfte der Natur, ein Symbol der scheinbaren Überlistung der Trägheit und des Widerstandes im Raume und in der Zeit. Vielleicht würden die Wagen eines Tages zurückgelassen werden. Sie würden wie Leichen aus Blech auf dem Platz bleiben. Man würde sie nicht fahren können. Man würde sich 'rausnehmen, was man brauchen konnte, ein Polster für den Hintern. Der Rest würde rosten. Frauen, Frauen modisch und burschikos gekleidet, Frauen damenstolz und jungenhaft, Frauen in olivgrünen Uniformen, weibliche Leutnants und weibliche Majore, keß geschminkte Backfische, sehr viel Frauen, dann Zivilangestellte, Offiziere und Soldaten, Neger und Negerinnen, sie alle gehörten zur Besatzung, sie bevölkerten den Platz, sie riefen, lachten, winkten, sie lenkten die schönen das Lied des Reichtums summenden Automobile geschickt zwischen die schon parkenden Fahrzeuge. Die Deutschen bewunderten und verabscheuten den rollenden Aufwand. Einige dachten ›unsere marschierten‹. In ihrer Vorstellung war es anständiger, in einem fremden Land zu marschieren, als zu fahren; das Marschieren kam ihrer Auffassung vom Soldatentum entgegen; es entsprach besser den ihnen eingeprägten Spielregeln, von Landsern als von Herrenfahrern bewacht zu sein. Die Herrenfahrer waren wohl freundlicher, die Landser

mochten rauher sein; darauf kam es nicht an; es ging um
die Spielregeln, um die Einhaltung der bei Krieg, Sieg und
Niederlage überlieferten Gepflogenheiten. Deutsche Offizie-
re, die sich als Stadtreisende durchschlugen und mit ihrem
Musterköfferchen auf die Straßenbahn warteten, ärgerten
sich, wenn sie gewöhnliche amerikanische Soldaten wie reiche
Touristen in bequemen Polstern grußlos an ihren Vorge-
setzten vorüberfahren sahen. Das war Demokratie und Unordnung. Die luxuriösen Wagen gaben der Besatzung einen
Anstrich von Übermut, Frevel und Sybaritentum.
Washington näherte sich seiner horizontblauen Limousine.
Er war der Engel, für den das kleine Mädchen das himmlische Gefährt blankgerieben hatte. Die Kleine knickste. Sie
knickste und wischte mit ihrem Tuch über den Wagenschlag.
Washington schenkte ihr Schokolade und Bananen. Er hatte
die Schokolade und die Bananen für das kleine Mädchen
gekauft. Er war Stammkunde des kleinen Mädchens. Heinz
unter dem Pferd des frommen Kurfürsten feixte. Er wartete,
bis Washington abgefahren war, dann kletterte er vom Sok-
kel.
Er spuckte gegen die Tafel mit dem in Erz gegossenen Verzeichnis der Siege des Kurfürsten. Er sagte: »Das war der
Nigger meiner Mutter.«
Die Kinder guckten Heinz respektvoll an. Er imponierte ihnen, wie er dastand, spuckte und sagte: »Das war der Nigger
meiner Mutter.« Das fleißige kleine Mädchen war zum
Denkmal gekommen und aß nachdenklich eine vom Neger-
seiner-Mutter geschenkte Banane. Der junge Hund beschnup-
perte die weggeworfene Bananenschale. Das kleine Mädchen
beachtete den Hund nicht. Der Hund trug kein Halsband.
Man hatte ihm einen Bindfaden umgebunden. Er schien gefangen, aber herrenlos zu sein. Heinz prahlte: er habe die
Amiwagen schon gelenkt, er könne das alle Tage, wenn er
nur wolle: »Meine Mutter geht mit einem Neger.« Der
dunkle Freund, der schwarze Ernährer der Familie, die ga-
benspendende und dennoch fremde und störende Erscheinung
in der Wohnung beschäftigte ihn unaufhörlich. An manchen
Tagen log er den Neger aus seinem Leben weg. »Was macht

euer Neger?« fragten die Jungen. »Weiß nicht. Gibt keinen Nigger«, sagte er dann. Ein andermal trieb er eine Art Kult mit Washington, beschrieb seine enorme Körperkraft, seinen Reichtum, seine Bedeutung als Sportsmann, um am Ende den Kameraden den letzten Trumpf entgegenzuschleudern, der alle Leistungen des bedeutenden schwarzen Mannes erst in das rechte persönliche Licht rückte, den Trumpf, daß Washington mit seiner Mutter lebe. Die Gefährten kannten die oft berichtete Geschichte, sie erzählten sie selber zu Hause weiter, aber sie warteten dennoch immer wieder mit einer Spannung wie im Kino auf die Pointe, diesen nicht zu schlagenden Trumpf: er geht mit meiner Mutter, er ißt bei uns am Tisch, er schläft in unserem Bett, sie wünschen, daß ich Dad zu ihm sage. Das kam aus Tiefen der Lust und der Pein. Heinz konnte sich an seinen an der Wolga verschollenen Vater nicht erinnern. Eine Photographie, die den Vater in grauer Uniform zeigte, sagte ihm nichts. Washington konnte ein guter Vater sein. Er war freundlich, er war freigebig, er strafte nicht, er war ein bekannter Sportler, er trug eine Uniform, er gehörte zu den Siegern, er war für Heinz reich und fuhr einen großen horizontblauen Wagen. Aber gegen Washington sprach die schwarze Haut, das auffallende Zeichen des Andersseins. Heinz wollte sich nicht von andern unterscheiden. Er wollte genau wie die andern Jungen sein, und die hatten weißhäutige einheimische überall anerkannte Väter. Washington war nicht überall anerkannt. Man redete mit Mißachtung von ihm. Einige machten sich über ihn lustig. Manchmal wollte Heinz Washington verteidigen, aber dann wagte er nicht, eine andere Meinung als die vielen zu haben, die Erwachsenen, die Landsleute, die Gescheiten, und er sagte: »Der Nigger!« Man sprach häßlich über Carlas Beziehung zu Washington; man scheute sich nicht, in Gegenwart des Kindes gemeine Bezeichnungen zu gebrauchen; doch am meisten haßte es Heinz, wenn man ihm mit falschem Mitleid über den Kopf strich und plärrte »armer Junge, du bist doch ein deutscher Junge«. So war Washington, ohne es zu ahnen (doch vielleicht ahnte er es, wußte es sogar und ging Heinz aus dem Wege, scheu und den Blick

ins Leere gerichtet), Sorge für Heinz, Ärger, Leid und ein
dauernder Konflikt, und es kam, daß Heinz Washington
mied, nur noch widerstrebend seine Geschenke annahm und
selten und ohne Lust in dem bewunderten und prächtigen
Auto fuhr. Er trieb sich herum, er redete sich ein, die Schwarzen und die Amis, sie alle zusammen zu verabscheuen, und
um sich für eine Haltung, die er im Grunde für feige hielt,
zu quälen und um zu beweisen, daß er's selber aussprechen
konnte, womit die anderen meinten ihn unterzukriegen, kräh-
te er unermüdlich sein »Sie geht mit einem Nigger«. Als
er sich von Ezra aus dem einem Flugzeug so sehr ähnelnden
Wagen beobachtet fühlte, brüllte er in ziemlich geläufigem
Englisch (das er von Washington und nur zu dem Zweck
gelernt hatte, um die Gespräche seiner Mutter mit dem Neger zu belauschen, um zu hören, was sie vorbereiteten, was
ja auch ihn anging, die Reise nach Amerika, die Ausund-
heimwanderung, von der er, Heinz, nicht wußte, ob er sie
antreten wollte oder nicht, vielleicht würde er darauf drängen, mitgenommen zu werden, vielleicht würde er sich verstecken, wenn alles gepackt war): »*Yes, she goes with a nigger.*«
Heinz hielt den Hund am Bindfaden. Der Junge und der
Hund waren wie zusammengebunden. Sie waren wie zwei
verurteilte zusammengebundene arme Schlucker. Der Hund
zerrte von Heinz weg. Ezra beobachtete Heinz und den
Hund. Es war ihm, als träume er alles. Der Junge, der rief:
»*Yes, she goes with a nigger*«, der an den Bindfaden gefes-
selte Hund, das Reiterdenkmal aus gründunklem Erz waren
unwirklich, sie waren kein wirklicher Junge, kein wirklicher
Hund, kein wirkliches Denkmal; sie waren Ideen; sie hatten die leichte schwindlig machende Transparenz der Traum-
figuren; sie waren Schatten, und zugleich waren sie er selbst,
der Träumer; es war eine innige und böse Verbundenheit
zwischen ihnen und ihm, und das beste wäre es, mit einem
Schrei zu erwachen. Ezra hatte fuchsrotes kurzgeschnittenes
Haar. Seine kleine Stirn krauste sich unter der fuchsroten
Kappe. Er hatte das Gefühl, zu Hause in Santa Ana im Bett
zu liegen. Der Stille Ozean brandete mit eintönigem Rauschen gegen den Strand. Ezra war krank. In Europa war

Krieg. Europa war ein ferner Erdteil. Es war das Land der armen Alten. Es war der Erdteil der grausamen Sagen. Es gab da ein böses Land, und in dem bösen Land gab es einen bösen Riesen *Hitler Aggressor*. Auch Amerika war im Krieg. Amerika kämpfte gegen den bösen Riesen. Amerika war großmütig. Es kämpfte für die Menschenrechte. Was waren das für Rechte? Besaß Ezra sie? Hatte er das Recht, seine Suppe nicht zu essen, seine Feinde, die Kinder vom Nordstrand, zu töten, dem Vater zu widersprechen? Die Mutter saß an seinem Bett. Henriette sprach deutsch mit ihm. Er verstand die Sprache nicht, und er verstand sie doch. Dieses Deutsch war die Muttersprache, das war wörtlich zu nehmen, es war die Sprache der Mutter, älter, geheimnisvoller als das übliche und im Hause allein schickliche, das alltägliche Amerikanisch, und die Mutter weinte, im Kinderzimmer weinte sie, sie weinte seltsamen Menschen nach, Verschwundenen, Geraubten, Entführten, Geschlachteten, und der jüdisch-preußische Oberregierungsrat und sein stilles sanftes Sarah-Gretchen, abgeführt *im Zuge der Liquidierung*, wurden am Bett eines kranken Kindes in Santa Ana, Kalifornien, zu Gestalten aus Grimms deutschen Kinder- und Hausmärchen, genauso wahr, genauso lieb, genauso traurig wie König Drosselbart, wie Däumling und Großmütterchen und der Wolf, und so unheimlich war's wie die Geschichte vom Machandelbaum. Henriette lehrte ihren Jungen die Muttersprache, indem sie ihm deutsche Märchen vorlas, aber wenn sie dachte, daß er schlafe, dann erzählte sie für sich, seinen Fieberschlaf bewachend und um ihn in Sorge, das Märchen von den Großeltern, und wie das Summen der neuesten Sprachlehrgrammophone, die einen im Schlaf die fremden Laute lehren, senkten sich die deutschen Leidworte, die Murmel- und Tränenworte Ezra ins Gemüt. Nun war er im Dickicht, im unheimlichen Zauberwald des Traumes und des Märchens — der Parkplatz war der Wald, die Stadt war das Dickicht: der Luftangriff hatte nichts genützt, Ezra mußte am Boden den Kampf bestehen. Heinz hatte lange blonde Haare, einen verwilderten Schopf. Er sah mit Mißfallen den kurzen neumodischen amerikanischen Haarschnitt, Ezras revidierte Bar-

75

rasfrisur. Er dachte ›der ist hochnäsig, dem will ich's geben‹.
Ezra fragte: »Wollen Sie den Hund verkaufen?« Aus sprach-
licher Unsicherheit fand er es angebracht, Sie statt du zu
sagen. Heinz empfing das Sie als neuen Beweis des Hochmuts dieses fremden Jungen, der zu Recht in dem interes-
santen Auto saß (nicht wie Heinz im Auto Washingtons in
fragwürdiger Position), es war eine Zurückweisung, ein In-
Distanz-Halten (vielleicht, vielleicht war das Sie wirklich als
Schranke gedacht, Schutzwehr für Ezra, und nicht sprachliche
Verwirrung), und er, Heinz, gebrauchte es nun auch, dies
Sie, und die beiden Elfjährigen, die beiden in der Kriegs-
furcht gezeugten Kinder, unterhielten sich steif wie altfrän-
kische Erwachsene. »Wollen Sie den Hund kaufen?« sagte
Heinz. Er wollte den Hund gar nicht verkaufen. Es war auch
nicht sein Hund. Der Hund gehörte der Kinderbande. Aber
vielleicht konnte man ihn doch verkaufen. Man mußte im
Gespräch bleiben. Heinz hatte die Empfindung, daß sich hier
etwas ergeben würde. Er wußte nicht was, aber etwas würde
sich ergeben. Ezra war gar nicht darauf aus, den Hund zu
kaufen. Für eine Weile hatte er zwar das Gefühl, er müsse
den Hund retten. Aber dann war die Hunderettung schon
vergessen, war nicht das Wesentliche, das Wesentliche war
das Gespräch und etwas, was sich zeigen würde. Man sah es
noch nicht. Der Traum war noch nicht soweit. Der Traum
fing erst an. Ezra sagte: »Ich bin Jude.« Er war Katholik. Er
war wie Christopher katholisch getauft und erhielt katholi-
schen Religionsunterricht. Aber es gehörte zum Stil des Märchens, daß er Jude war. Er schaute Heinz erwartungsvoll an.
Heinz wußte mit Ezras Bekenntnis nichts anzufangen. Es
verblüffte ihn als undurchsichtiger Zug des anderen. Es hätte
ihn auch verblüfft, wenn Ezra erzählt hätte, er sei Indianer.
Wollte er sich interessant machen? Juden? Das waren Händler, unreelle Geschäftsleute, sie mochten die Deutschen nicht.
War es das? Womit handelte Ezra? Im Flugzeugauto war
keine Ware. Vielleicht wollte er den Hund billig kaufen und
ihn später teuer verkaufen. Das würde er ihm versalzen! Für
alle Fälle wiederholte Heinz sein eigenes Bekenntnis: »Meine Mutter, müssen Sie wissen, lebt mit einem Neger.« Drohte

Heinz mit einem Neger? Ezra hatte keine Berührung mit Negern. Aber er wußte von weißen und schwarzen Kinderbanden, die sich bekämpften. Heinz gehörte einer Negerbande an, das war überraschend. Ezra mußte vorsichtig sein. »Was wollen Sie für den Hund haben?« sagte er. Heinz antwortete: »Zehn Dollar.« Das konnte man machen. Für zehn Dollar konnte man es machen. Wenn der blöde Junge zehn Dollar zahlte, war er 'reingefallen. Der Hund war keine zehn Mark wert. Ezra sagte: »Gut.« Er wußte noch nicht, wie er's machen würde. Aber er würde es machen. Es würde schon gehen. Er mußte Christopher was vorlügen. Christopher würde es nicht verstehen, daß es nur ein Traumgeschehen und nicht wirklich war. Er sagte: »Ich muß mir die zehn Dollar erst besorgen.« Heinz dachte ›Scheißkerl, möchtest du wohl‹. Er sagte: »Erst wenn Sie mir das Geld geben, bekommen Sie den Hund.« Der Hund zerrte, unbeteiligt an dem Handel, am Bindfaden. Das kleine Mädchen hatte ihm ein Stück Schokolade vom Neger-von-Heinz'-Mutter zugeworfen. Die Schokolade lag in einer Pfütze und löste sich langsam auf. Der Hund konnte die Pfütze nicht erreichen. Ezra sagte: »Ich muß meinen Vater fragen. Er wird mir das Geld geben.« — »Jetzt?« fragte Heinz. Ezra dachte nach. Wieder furchte sich seine kleine Stirn unter der fuchsroten Kappe seines kurzgeschnittenen Haares. Er dachte ›hier geht es nicht‹. Er sagte: »Nein, heute abend. Kommen Sie zum Bräuhaus. Mein Vater und ich sind heute abend im Bräuhaus.« Heinz nickte. Er rief: »Okay!« In der Bräuhausgegend kannte er sich aus. Am Bräuhausplatz war der Klub der Negersoldaten. Heinz stand oft vor dem Lokal und beobachtete, wie seine Mutter und Washington aus der horizontblauen Limousine stiegen und an dem schwarzen Militärpolizisten vorbei in den Klub gingen. Er kannte alle Dirnen, die um den Platz herumstrichen. Zuweilen schenkten ihm die Dirnen Schokolade, die sie von den Negern bekommen hatten. Heinz brauchte die Schokolade nicht. Aber es befriedigte ihn, die Schokolade von Dirnen zu nehmen. Er konnte dann zu Washington sagen: »Ich mag keine Schokolade.« Er dachte: ›Du kriegst deinen Hund, dir bin ich schon entwischt.‹

77

Odysseus entwischte ihnen. Er entwischte den Griechen, entwischte den flinken, wie flinke gelbe Eidechsen übei den Biertisch huschenden Händen. Der Wurf war für sie. Sie rafften die Würfel, reichten sie Odysseus; Odysseus verlor; sie krallten sie wieder in die Hand, schleuderten sie hin, das Glück auf ihrer Seite; es ging um Mark und Dollar, um Mannesmark und Flitscherldollar, es ging um das, was sie Leben nannten, es ging um die Füllung des Bauches, es ging um den Rausch, um die Lust, um das Taggeld ging es, denn was sie den Tag ertragen ließ, kostete Geld, das Fressen, das Saufen, das Lieben, alles kostete Geld, Mark oder Dollar, hier wurden sie aufs Spiel gesetzt: was waren die Griechen, was war König Odysseus ohne Geld? Er hatte Wildtöteraugen. Die »Glocken«-Kapelle spielte Ich-schieß-den-Hirsch-im-wilden-Forst. Alle in der »Glocke« jagten den weißen Hirsch ihrer Wünsche und Illusionen. Das Bier hatte sie auf imaginäre Pferde gesetzt; sie waren stolze Jäger zu Pferde. Ihre Triebe machten Treibjagd, Lustjagd auf den weißen Hırsch des Selbstbetruges. Der Gebirgsschütze sang das Lied der Kapelle mit, der Afrikakämpfer, der Ostfrontmann fielen ein. Josef, durch die Machenschaften der Griechen von seinem schwarzen Tagesherrn weggedrängt, hörte aus Odysseus' Musikkasten einen Vortrag über die Lage in Persien *Fallschirmjäger nach Malta,* und weiter war es nur ein Lautrauschen für Josef und weiter nur eine Brandung der Geschichte, eine Brandung aus dem Äther zu ihm gespült, unverständliche erlebte gärende Geschichte, ein Sauerteig, der aufging. Namen wurden hineingerührt, Namen immer wieder Namen, oft gehörte Namen, die Namen der Weltstunde, die Namen der großen Spieler, die Namen der Manager, die Namen der Schauplätze, Konferenzplätze, Schlachtplätze, Mordplätze, wie wird der Sauerteig aufgehen? was für Brot werden wir morgen essen? »Wir waren die ersten in Kreta«, rief der Rommelsoldat, »erst waren wir in Kreta eingesetzt. Wir sprangen einfach in sie hinein.« Da war der Hirsch! Jetzt hatte er's durchschaut, Wildtöteraugen! Die schwarze Hand war flinker als der Zaubertrick der gelben Eidechsen. Odysseus griff zu. Er hatte die Würfel. Diesmal waren es die rechten, die gezinkten, die ausgeheckten, die das Glück brachten, die listig immer wieder vertauschten. Er schlug sie aufs Holz: Sieg! Er warf sie aufs neue und warf wieder das Glück. Er stieß mit den Ellbogen. Die Griechen wankten zurück. Odysseus' Rücken deckte den Tisch. Der Tisch war die Front. Er feuerte Serien ins Holz, ein Bombardement des Glücks: Häuptling Odysseus König Odysseus General Odysseus Generaldirektor Mister Odysseus Cotton Esquire. »Wir säuberten die Weißen Berge. Wenn wir ins Tal 'runtergingen, brauchten wir geballte Ladungen, im Gestrüpp das Messer, Tommys und Rosinenkacker. Wir haben das Kretaschild bekommen.« — »Scheiß drauf!« — »Sagst du —« — »Ich sage scheiß drauf. Krieg war in Rußland. Alles andere sind Jungengeschichten. Zehnerlhefte mit bunten Deckeln. Romantik, Mensch! Bunte Deckel! Mal 'ne nackte Hur und mal 'n Fallschirmspringer mit Todesblick. Dasselbe, Mensch! Ich werd' meinem Jungen den Arsch versohlen, wenn er's nach Hause bringt.« Die Stimme im Musikkoffer sagte: »Zypern.« Zypern war strategisch wichtig. Die Stimme sagte: »Teheran.« Die Stimme sagte nicht Schiras. Die Stimme erwähnte nicht die Rosen von Schiras. Die Stimme sagte nicht Hafis. Die Stimme kannte Hafis den Dichter nicht. Hafis hatte für diese Stimme nie gelebt. Die Stimme sagte: »*Oil.*« Und wieder war Rauschen, Lautrauschen, dumpfes Silbengeplätscher, der Strom der Geschichte rauschte vorüber, Josef saß am Ufer des Stroms, der Alte, der Müde, der Abgekämpfte, noch blinzelnd nach Abendglück, unverständlich war der Strom, unverständlich das Geplätscher, einlullend das Silbenrauschen. Die Griechen trauten sich nicht an ihre Messer. Der weiße Hirsch war ihnen entwischt. Der schwarze Odysseus war ihnen entkommen: listiger großer Odysseus. Er gab Josef Geld, das Bier zu bezahlen. »Zuviel, Mister«, sagte Josef. »Nix zuviel *money*«, sagte Odysseus. Die Kellnerin steckte den Schein ein: Glanz und Gnade von Odysseus. »Komm«, rief Odysseus. »Appell an den Haag«, sagte die Stimme. Die Stimme wurde von Josef getragen, *Wilhelm II. Friedenskaiser stiftet für den Haag*, von Josef geschüttelt, er schüttelte mit seinem Altmännergang das Geriesel der großen Worte. Der Strom der Geschichte floß. Zuweilen trat der Strom über die Ufer. Er überschwemmte das Land mit Geschichte. Er ließ Ertrunkene zurück, er ließ den Schlamm zurück, die Düngung, das stinkende Mutterfeld, eine Fruchtbarkeitslauge: wo ist der Gärtner? wann wird die Frucht reif sein? Josef folgte klein und blinzelnd, auch er im Schlamm, noch immer im Schlamm, schon wieder im Schlamm, folgte dem schwarzen Gebieter, dem Herrn, den er sich für diesen Tag erwählt hatte. Wann war Blütezeit? Wann kam das Goldene Zeitalter, die hohe Zeit —

Er war ein Hochzeiter. Die horizontblaue Limousine hielt vor dem Mietshaus, in dem Carla wohnte. Washington hatte Blumen gekauft, gelbe Stengel. Als er aus dem Wagen stieg, drang die Sonne durch den verhangenen Himmel. Das Licht reflektierte in der Karosserie der Limousine und ließ die Blumen schwefelgelb blühen. Washington fühlte, wie man ihn aus den Fenstern des Mietshauses beobachtete. Die kleinen Bürger, die hier in vielen Parteien wohnten, in jedem Raum drei, vier Menschen, jedes Zimmer ein Käfig, im Zoo hauste man geräumiger, die kleinen Bürger drückten sich gegen die oft gestopften und immer wieder gestärkten Gardinen und stießen einander an. »Blumen bringt er ihr. Siehst die Blumen. Daß er sich nicht —.« Aus irgendeinem Komplex erboste es sie, daß Washington Blumen ins Haus brachte. Washington allein wurde verhältnismäßig wenig beachtet; er war ein Mensch, wenn auch ein Neger. Beachtet wurden die Blumen, gezählt wurden die Pakete, die er trug, erbittert wurde das Auto betrachtet. Das Auto kostete in Deutschland mehr als ein kleines Haus. Es kostete mehr als das Häuschen am Stadtrand, nach dem man sich ein Leben lang vergeblich sehnte. Max sagte es. Max mußte es wissen. Max arbeitete in einer Garage. Die horizontblaue Limousine vor der Haustür war eine Herausforderung.

Ein paar alte Frauen hatten sich über das Treiben in der Wohnung im dritten Stock beschwert. Die Welz mußte Beziehungen zur Polizei haben. Die Polizei griff nicht ein, *Krebsschäden der Demokratie.* In Wahrheit sah die Polizei nur keinen Grund zum Einschreiten. Sie konnte nicht über-

all einschreiten, wo etwas faul in der Stadt war. Überdies
hätten die alten Frauen das Eingreifen der Polizei sehr bedauert. Die Polizei hätte sie um das einzige Schauspiel gebracht, das sie sich leisten konnten.

Washington ging die Treppe hinauf: Dschungeln umgaben
ihn. Hinter jeder Tür standen sie und lauschten. Sie waren
domestizierte Raubtiere; sie witterten noch das Wild, aber
die Zeit war nicht günstig, die Zeit erlaubte es der Herde
nicht, sich auf die fremde, in das Revier der Herde einge-
drungene Kreatur zu stürzen. Die Welz öffnete die Tür. Die
Frau war strubbelhaarig, fett, hängeärschig, schmutzig. Für
sie war wiederum Washington ein gezähmtes Haustier: nicht
gerade eine Kuh, aber noch immerhin eine Ziege, ›ich melk’
den schwarzen Bock‹ — »Is nich da«, sagte sie. Sie wollte
ihm die Pakete abnehmen. Er sagte: »Oh, macht nichts.«
Er sagte es mit der freundlichen unpersönlichen Stimme der
Schwarzen, wenn sie zu Weißen sprechen, aber die Stimme
hatte einen gepreßten und ungeduldigen Unterton. Er wollte
die Frau loswerden. Er verabscheute sie. Er ging durch den
düsteren Korridor zu Carlas Zimmern. Aus einigen Türen
beobachteten ihn die Mädchen, die sich bei Frau Welz mit
den Soldaten trafen. Washington litt unter dieser Wohnung.
Aber er konnte es nicht ändern. Carla fand keine anderen
Zimmer. Sie sagte: »Mit dir finde ich keine anderen.« Auch
Carla litt unter der Wohnung, aber sie litt weniger unter ihr
als Washington, dem sie unermüdlich versicherte, wie sehr
sie leide, wie unwürdig das alles für sie sei, und das hieß
unausgesprochen, wie sehr sie sich verschenke, wie tief sie
sich herablasse, tief zu ihm, und daß er durch immer neue
Liebe, neue Geschenke, neue Aufopferung es ein wenig gut-
machen müsse, ein ganz klein wenig nur. Carla verachtete
und beschimpfte Frau Welz und die Mädchen, aber wenn
sie allein war, wenn sie sich langweilte, wenn Washington
in der Kaserne arbeitete, biederte sie sich mit den Mädchen
zusammen, lud sie ein, tratschte mit ihnen den Mädchen-
tratsch, den Hurenschwatz, oder sie saß bei Frau Welz in der
Küche, trank am Herd den Mischkaffee aus dem stets auf
dem Feuer brodelnden Topf und erzählte alles, was Frau

Welz (die es dann an die Nachbarinnen weitergab) wissen wollte. Die Mädchen im Gang zeigten Washington, was sie hatten; sie öffneten ihre Kleiderschürzen, richteten sich die Strumpfbänder, wedelten Duftwolken aus dem gefärbten Haar. Es war ein Wettstreit unter den Mädchen, ob es einer einmal gelänge, Washington ins Bett zu bekommen. Da sie Neger nur im Zustand der Brunst kannten, schloß ihr kleines Hirn, daß alle Neger geil seien. Sie verstanden Washington nicht. Sie begriffen nicht, daß er kein Bordellgänger war. Washington war für ein glückliches Familienleben geboren; doch leider war er durch unglückliche Zufälle vom Wege und in diese Wohnung, war er in Schlamm und Dschungeln geraten. Washington hoffte im Wohnzimmer eine Botschaft zu finden, die Carla vielleicht hinterlassen hatte. Er glaubte, Carla würde bald zurückkehren. Vielleicht war sie zum Friseur gegangen. Er suchte auf der Spiegelkommode nach einem Zettel, der ihm sagen sollte, wohin sie gegangen sei. Auf der Kommode standen Flaschen mit Nagellack, Gesichtswasser, Cremetöpfchen und Puderschachteln. Im Rahmen des Spiegels steckten Photographien. Ein Bild zeigte Carlas verschollenen Ehemann, der jetzt seiner Todeserklärung, seinem amtlichen Tod entgegenging, von dem die Fessel genommen wurde, die ihn und Carla in dieser Welt verband bis-daß-der-Tod-euch-scheide. Er war in feldgrauer Uniform. Auf seiner Brust war das Hakenkreuz zu sehen, gegen das Washington zu Feld gezogen war. Washington betrachtete den Mann gleichmütig. Gleichmütig betrachtete er das Hakenkreuz auf der Brust des Mannes. Das Kreuz war bedeutungslos geworden. Vielleicht hatte das Rassenkreuz dem Mann nie etwas bedeutet. Vielleicht hatte Washington nie gegen dieses Kreuz gekämpft. Vielleicht waren sie beide betrogen worden. Er haßte den Mann nicht. Der Mann beunruhigte ihn nicht. Er war nicht eifersüchtig auf seinen Vorgänger. Zuweilen beneidete er ihn darum, daß er's hinter sich hatte. Das war so ein dunkles Gefühl; Washington verdrängte es immer. Neben ihrem Gatten hing Carla im Rahmen des Spiegels im Hochzeitsschmuck und mit weißem Schleier. Sie war achtzehn Jahre alt, als sie heiratete. Zwölf Jahre war es her. In diesen

Jahren war die Welt zusammengebrochen, in der Carla und ihr Mann lange und sicher zu leben glaubten. Freilich war ihre Welt nicht mehr die Welt der Eltern gewesen. Carla war schwanger, als sie zum Standesamt ging, und der weiße Schleier auf der Photographie war Lüge und doch nicht Lüge, weil niemand belogen wurde oder belogen werden konnte, denn der weiße Schleier hatte schon lange nur noch schmükkenden Sinn und wurde eine peinliche dem Spott ausgelieferte Maskerade, wenn man ihn für das Zeichen der unverletzten Scham nahm, und keinesfalls war es frivol, daß man so dachte, denn die Zeit war eher geneigt, die Vorstellung, daß der Bräutigam nach vollzogener öffentlicher Zuführung und Feier sich auf die Braut stürze, auf das weiße Lamm, mit dem er das Hymenopfer vollzog, als frivol und schamlos zu empfinden, dennoch bedurfte es der Trauung, des Ordentlichen und der Amtlichkeit des Zusammentuns, des Segensspruches der Gemeinschaft, der Kinder wegen bedurfte es dies alles, der Kinder, die der Gemeinschaft geboren werden sollten und selbst mit Werbung ins Leben gelockt wurden, *Besucht das schöne Deutschland,* und Carla und ihr Mann, die eben Getrauten, glaubten damals an ein Reich, dem man Kinder schenken konnte, vertrauensvoll, pflichtgemäß und verantwortungsbewußt, *Kinder Reichtum der Nation, Ehestandsdarlehen für junge Leute.* Carlas Eltern hingen auch im Rahmen des Spiegels. Frau Behrend hatte sich mit Blumen im Arm aufnehmen lassen, der Musikmeister war in Uniform, aber statt des Dirigentenstabes hielt seine linke Hand den Griff einer Geige, die er im Sitzen gegen die Schenkel stützte. So waren Herr und Frau Behrend als poetisch und musisch gesonnenes Paar friedlich vereint. Heinz war als Säugling photographiert. Er stand aufrecht im Kinderwagen und winkte. Er wußte nicht mehr, wem er zugewinkt hatte, irgendeiner erwachsenen Person wahrscheinlich; die Person war sein Vater gewesen, der hinter der das Bild aufnehmenden Kamera gestanden hatte, und bald darauf war Vater in den Krieg gezogen. Ein Bild, das von größerem Format als die übrigen war, zeigte nun gar ihn selbst, Washington Price: Er war im Baseballdreß mit der weißen

Schirmmütze, den Fanghandschuhen und dem Schläger. Sein
Gesichtsausdruck war würdig und ernst. Das war Carlas Familie. Washington gehörte zu Carlas Familie. Für eine Weile
starrte Washington stumpfsinnig auf die Bilder. Wo mochte
Carla sein? Was sollte er hier? Er sah sich mit seinen Blumen und den Paketen im Spiegel. Es war komisch, wie er in
diesem Zimmer stand vor den Familienbildern, dem Toilet-
tenkram und dem Spiegel. Für einen Augenblick hatte Washington das Gefühl, sein Leben sei sinnlos. Ihm schwindelte
vor seinem Spiegelbild. Aus einem Zimmer der Mädchen
klang Radiomusik. Der amerikanische Sender spielte die
kummervoll erhabene Melodie Negerhimmel von Ellington.
Washington hätte weinen mögen. Während er die Melodie
hörte, ein Heimatlied aus einem Hurenzimmer in der Fremde (und wo war nicht Fremde?), empfand er die ganze Häß-
lichkeit des Daseins. Die Erde war kein Himmel. Die Erde
war bestimmt kein Negerhimmel. Aber gleich eilte sein Lebensmut einer Fata Morgana entgegen, er klammerte sich
an den Gedanken, daß bald ein neues Bild im Spiegel stekken würde, das Bild eines kleinen braunen Kindes, des Kindes,
das er und Carla der Welt schenken wollten.
Er trat in die Küche an den Herd zu Frau Welz, zu den brodelnden Töpfen, und sie gab ihm zu verstehen, eine Hexe in
Wolken von Rauch, Dampf und Gerüchen, daß sie wohl wisse, wo Carla sei, er möge beruhigt sein, es sei doch nicht in
Ordnung mit Carla, es hätte doch was gegeben, er wisse
schon, man passe ja mal nicht auf, wenn man wen liebhabe,
passe man nicht auf, sie kenne sich aus, man sehe es ihr wohl
nicht mehr an, aber sie wisse Bescheid, und die Mädchen
hier, sie wüßten alle Bescheid, ja mit Carla, das sei nicht
schlimm (er verstand nicht, er, Washington, verstand nicht,
verstand nicht das deutsche Hexeneinmaleins, eine böse Frau,
was wollte sie? was war mit Carla? warum sagte sie nicht,
sie sei beim Friseur, sei ins Kino gegangen? warum das Gemurmel? so viel üble Worte), gar nicht schlimm sei es also,
wo sie doch einen so guten Doktor habe und immer für den
Doktor gesorgt habe in der schlechten Zeit, »ich sagte ja
zu Carla, es ist zuviel, Carla, aber Carla wollte ihm das Beste

bringen, nun weiß man, wozu es gut war, daß Carla ihm das
Beste brachte«, gar kein Anlaß zur Sorge sei gegeben,»Washington, Dr. Frahm wird es schon machen«. Dies verstand er. Er
verstand den Namen Dr. Frahm. Was war? War Carla krank?
Washington erschrak. Oder war sie des Kindes wegen zum Arzt
gegangen? Aber das konnte nicht sein, das konnte nicht sein.
Das konnte sie nicht tun, grade dies konnte sie nicht tun —

Es war ein Scherz. Irgend jemand hatte sich den Scherz gemacht, Emilia an zu viel Besitz zu binden. Aber vielleicht
war es nicht einmal ein Scherz, vielleicht war Emilia jeder
Macht, jeder Planung, jeder Überlegung, jeder guten oder
bösen Fee, dem Geist des Zufalls so gleichgültig, daß es nicht
einmal zu einem Scherz gereicht hatte, und sie war mit ihrem
Besitz zusammen in den Abfall geworfen worden, ohne daß
irgendwer sie hatte dahin werfen wollen, zufällig war's geschehen, gewiß zufällig, aber es war ein völlig geistloser, ein
dummer, ein ganz bedeutungsloser Zufall, der sie an Güter
gebunden hatte, die ihr von anderen und dann auch von den
eigenen Wünschen immerfort als Mittel zu einem herrlichen
Leben beschrieben wurden, während das Erbe in Wahrheit
nur noch eine Bohemeexistenz ermöglichte mit Unordnung,
Ungewißheit, Bettelgängen und Hungertagen, eine Bohemeexistenz, die grotesk mit Kapitalverwaltung und Steuertermi-
nen gekoppelt war. Nicht mit Emilia hatte die Zeit etwas
geplant, weder im Guten noch im Bösen etwas mit ihr vorge-
habt, Emilias Erbe nur war dem Zeitgeist und seiner Planung verfallen, das Kapital wurde gesprengt, in manchen
Ländern war es schon gesprengt, in anderen würde es gesprengt werden, und in Deutschland lockerte die Stunde wie
Scheidewasser den Besitz, fraß mit Ätzung auf, was sich an
Reichtum angesammelt hatte, und es war töricht von Emilia,
die Spritzer der Ätzung, soweit sie die scharfe Lösung traf,
persönlich zu nehmen, sie für eine ihr persönlich zugedachte
Ranküne des Schicksals zu halten. Niemand dachte ihr etwas
zu. Das Leben, das Emilia nicht meisterte, war Wendezeit,
Schicksalszeit, aber dies nur im Großen gesehen, und im
Kleinen konnte man weiterhin Glück und Unglück haben,

und Emilia hatte das Pech, sich hartnäckig und ängstlich
an das Entschwindende zu klammern, das in einer verzerr-
ten, ungeordneten, anrüchigen und auch ein wenig lächerlichen Agonie lag; doch war die Geburt der neuen Weltzeit
nicht weniger vom Grotesken, Ungeordneten, Anrüchigen
und Lächerlichen umrandet. Man konnte auf der einen und
auf der anderen Seite leben, und man konnte auf dieser und
jener Seite des Zeitgrabens sterben. »Große Glaubenskriege
werden kommen«, sagte Philipp. Emilia verwechselte das
alles, sie sah sich durch Geldschwierigkeiten in die Schicht
der Boheme versetzt, sah sich zu Leuten gesetzt, die bei Emilias Eltern zwar Freitisch und Narrenfreiheit, aber nicht Achtung genossen hatten, und die Großeltern, die den Familien-
reichtum so fruchtbar mehrten, hätten diese Windigen überhaupt nicht empfangen. Emilia haßte und verachtete die Boheme, die mittellosen Geistigen, die lebensuntüchtigen
Schwätzer, die Träger ausgefranster Hosen und ihre hier
schon aus zweiter Hand gekleideten, nach längst vergangener Pariser Tabu-Keller-Mode angezogenen billigen Freundinnen, mit denen sie nun auf demselben Kehricht lag, während Philipp die Schicht, die Emilia so verabscheute, einfach
mied, weil er sie als Boheme nicht anerkannte, die Boheme
war schon lange tot, und das Volk, das so tat, als gäbe es noch
die jungen Intellektuellen, die Revoluzzer und Kunsttheore-
tiker im Kaffeehaus, das waren für den Abend Maskierte,
die sich in hergebrachter Weise amüsieren wollten, während
sie am Tage, lange nicht so untüchtig, wie Emilia dachte,
als Gebrauchsgraphiker arbeiteten, Reklametexte schrieben,
beim Film und Rundfunk verdienten und, die Tabu-Mäd-
chen, brav hinter Schreibmaschinen saßen, die Boheme war
tot, sie war schon gestorben, als das Romanische Café in Berlin von Bomben getroffen brannte, sie war schon tot, als der
erste SA-Mann das Café betrat, sie war genaugenommen
schon vor Hitler von der Politik erwürgt worden. Der Züri-
cher Bohemien Lenin hatte, als er nach Rußland abreiste,
die Tür des Literatencafés für die nächsten Jahrhunderte geschlossen. Was nach Lenin im Café blieb, war im Grunde
konservativ, war konservative Pubertät, konservative Liebe

zu Mimi, war konservativer Bürgerschreck (wobei noch zu bedenken war, daß Mimi, die geliebt, und der Bürger, der erschreckt werden sollte, daß sie beide auch schon gestorben und Figuren des Märchens geworden waren), bis die Boheme endlich in gewissen Barlokalen ihr Grabmal fand, von einer konservativen zu einer konservierten Angelegenheit wurde, ein Museumsstück, eine Attraktion für den Fremdenverkehr. Diese Lokale nun, die *boîtes*, die Mausoleen der *Scènes-de-la-vie-de-bohème* wurden allerdings wieder groteskerweise von Emilia, die sich auf die gehaßte Bohemetour das Geld dazu verschaffen mußte, gerne besucht, während sie Philipp mit ihren Tanzgeschöpfen und dem Glas-Wein-Mäzenatentum der Geschäftsleute geradezu ein Greuel waren. »Wir gehen nirgendwohin«, rief Emilia dann, »du vergißt, daß ich jung bin.« Und er dachte ›ist deine Jugend so verdorrt, daß sie dieses Gusses bedarf, dieses Gusses aus Rausch, Alkohol und Synkopen, braucht dein Gefühl die Luft der Ungefühle, dein Haar den Wind schläfst-du-mit-mir-heutnacht »aber dann rasch ich muß früh 'raus«?‹ Emilia stand von allen Seiten bedroht im Niemandsland. Sie war reich und war ausgestoßen von der Nutznießung des Reichtums, sie war von Pluto nicht mehr angenommen worden, sie war nicht aufgenommen, war nicht sein Kind, aber sie war auch nicht aufgenommen und nicht angenommen von der arbeitenden Welt, und dem, daß man früh-'raus-mußte, stand sie mit blinder, kalter, aber vollkommen unschuldiger Ablehnung gegenüber. Jetzt war sie vorangekommen, sie war fortgeschritten, sie hatte ein Stück des schottischen Plaidweges hinter sich gebracht. Emilia war im Leihhaus gewesen. Sie hatte in der Halle des Städtischen Leihamtes unter den Armen gestanden. Die Halle war mit Marmor verkleidet und glich einem Schwimmbassin, aus dem man das Wasser abgelassen hatte. Die Armen schwammen nicht. Sie waren untergegangen. Sie waren nicht oben. Sie waren unten. Oben, das Höhere, das Leben, ach, dieser Glanz, ach, diese Fülle, das Leben war jenseits der Marmorwände, war über dem Glasdach, das die Halle deckte, über den milchigen Scheiben, diesem Nebelhimmel über dem Teich der Versunkenen. Sie waren am Grund des Daseins und trieben ein gespenstisches Wesen. Sie standen vor den Schaltern und hielten ihren Besitz von früher im Arm, die Habe eines anderen Lebens, das mit ihrem gegenwärtigen Leben gar nichts mehr zu tun hatte, eines Lebens, das sie geführt hatten, bevor sie ertrunken waren, und das Gut, das sie zum Schalter brachten, kam ihnen wie fremder Besitz vor, wie Diebesgut, das sie versetzen wollten, und sie benahmen sich scheu wie schon ertappte Diebe. War es aus mit ihnen? Es ging zu Ende, aber noch war es nicht aus. Die Habe verband sie noch mit dem Leben, so wie Gespenster sich an vergrabene Schätze klammern; sie gehörten zur Halbwelt des Styx, noch gab es Aufschub, der Schalter lieh sechs Mark für den Mantel, drei für die Schuhe, acht für das Federbett, die Ertrunkenen schnappten nach Luft, sie wurden noch einmal ins Leben entlassen, für Stunden, für Tage, Begünstigte für Wochen *Verfallfrist vier Monate.* Emilia hatte silberne Fischbestecke in den Schalter gereicht. Das Renaissancemuster des Besteckes wurde nicht betrachtet, die Kunst des Silberschmiedes nicht geachtet, es wurde nach dem Silberstempel gesehen, und dann wurde das Besteck auf die Waage geworfen. Der Fischgang vom reichen Kommerzienratsmahl lag auf der Waage des Leihhauses. »Exzellenz, der Salm!« Dem General des Kaisers wurde zum zweitenmal vorgelegt. *Volldampf voraus, Kaiserworte zur Jahrhundertwende.* Das Besteck wog nicht viel. Die silbernen Griffe waren hohl. Hände von Kommerzienräten, Bankiers und Ministern hatten die Griffe gehalten, hatten sich mit Salm, Stör und Forelle bedient: fette Hände, ringgeschmückte Hände, verhängnisvolle Hände. »Majestät erwähnte in seiner Rede Afrika. Ich sage Kolonialpapiere —« — ›Toren! In Gold hätten sie's anlegen und vergraben sollen, Toren, in Gold wäre alles gerettet worden, ich stände nicht hier!‹ Das Leihamt leiht drei Pfennig für ein Gramm Silberbesteck. Emilia wurden achtzehn Mark und der Pfandschein aus dem Schalter gereicht. Die im stygischen Bassin Ertrunkenen beneideten sie. Noch gehörte Emilia zur Elite der Schatten, noch war sie die Prinzessin im Lumpenpelz. Und weiter war sie fortgeschritten, Kalvariengang, vorange-

kommen im Lumpenprinzessinnenpelz und mit dem Waren-
packen im komischen schottischen Reiseplaid: sie stand vor
dem Gewölbe des Herrn Unverlacht, auch dies ein Eingang
zur Unterwelt, glitschige Stufen führten hinab, und hinter
schmutzigen Scheiben sah Emilia im Licht von Alabaster-
lampen, schweren birnenförmigen opalisierenden Leucht-
glocken, die er einmal aus dem Nachlaß eines Selbstmörders
gekauft hatte und bis jetzt nicht wieder losgeworden war,
Unverlachts gewaltige Glatze glänzen. Er war von unter-
setzter breitschultriger Gestalt; wie ein Möbelpacker sah er
aus, der eines Tages entdeckt hatte, daß es leichter und einträglicher sei, mit altem Hausrat zu handeln, statt ihn zu
tragen, auch wie ein stämmiger Dicker, der in einer Ring-
kämpfertruppe den bösen Mann mimt, doch sicher war er
weder Packer noch Ringkämpfer gewesen, vielleicht ein
Frosch, ein hinterhältiger plumper Frosch, der in seinem Gewölbe auf Fliegen wartete. Emilia stieg hinab, öffnete die
Tür, und schon grauste es sie. Ihre Haut zog sich zusammen.
Das war kein Froschkönig, der zur Tür blickte, mit kalten
wässerigen Augen, Unverlacht war wie er war, unverzaubert,
und keine Entzauberung war zu erwarten, kein Prinz würde
je aus dem Froschkleid springen. Ein Musikmechanismus,
durch Emilias Eintritt in Bewegung gesetzt, spielte Ein-feste-
Burg-ist-unser-Gott. Das war bedeutungslos, kein Bekenntnis. Unverlacht hatte den Mechanismus wie die Lampen billig erworben und wartete nun auf einen Käufer für diese
Schätze. Was die Lampen betraf, war es dumm von ihm, sie
verkaufen zu wollen: sie gaben mit ihrem Alabasterschein
seinem Gewölbe den echten Hadesschimmer. »Na, Sissy, was
bringst du?« sagte er, und die Froschflossenhand (wirklich,
die Finger waren wie mit hornschuppigen Schwimmhäuten
zusammengewachsen) hielt Emilia schon am Kinn gefaßt,
ihr kleines Kinn glitt in die Wölbung der Froschhand wie in
einen Schlund, während Unverlachts andere Hand ihren jungen und strammen Hintern betastete. Aus einem nicht klaren
Grund nannte Unverlacht Emilia Sissy; vielleicht erinnerte
sie ihn an eine wirkliche Trägerin dieses Namens, und Emilia und die unbekannte, vielleicht lange schon begrabene Sis-

sy verschmolzen in dem Gewölbe zu einem Wesen, dem der
Besitzer mit geiler Zärtlichkeit begegnete. Emilia drängte
sich von ihm los. »Ich will über Geschäfte reden«, sagte sie.
Auf einmal wurde ihr schlecht. Der Gewölbedunst benahm
ihr den Atem. Sie ließ ihr Plaid zu Boden fallen und warf
sich in einen Stuhl. Der Stuhl war ein Schaukelstuhl, der
durch den Schwung, mit dem sie in ihn geplumpst war, in
heftige Schwingungen geriet. Emilia war es, als reise sie in
einem Boot über das Meer; das Boot schaukelte auf hoher
See; ein Ungeheuer hob sein Haupt aus den Wellen; ein
Schiffbruch drohte; Emilia fürchtete seekrank zu werden.
»Hör auf, Sissy«, rief Unverlacht. »Ich hab' kein Geld. Was
denkst du? Das Geschäft geht nicht.« Er betrachtete die auf
und ab wippende Emilia; er sah sie vor sich, unter sich, hingestreckt im Schaukelstuhl, ihr Rock war hochgerutscht, er sah
über den Strümpfen die nackten Oberschenkel; ›Kinderschenkel‹, dachte er; er hatte eine dicke und eifersüchtige Frau. Er
war mißmutig. Emilia erregte ihn, die Kinderschenkel erregten ihn, das müde verzogene Gesicht eines müden und verzo-
genen kleinen Mädchens hätte ihn betören können, wenn er
begabt gewesen wäre, einem anderen als dem Impuls der
Gewinnsucht zu folgen. Emilia war für Unverlacht was Feines, ›diese gute Familie‹, dachte er, er begehrte sie, aber er
begehrte sie nicht wirklicher als ein Bild in einem Magazin,
an dem man sich erregt, und er wollte nicht mehr als sie betatschen, aber schon das Betatschen konnte das Geschäft stören: er wollte wohl von Emilia kaufen, er tat nur so, als ob er
kein Geld habe, das gehörte zum Handel, es waren gute Sachen, die Emilia anbot ›aus so feiner Familie aus so reichem
Haus‹, und sie gab sie billig her, hatte keine Ahnung von ihrem Wert, ›was für 'ne kleine Hose sie anhat, es ist als ob sie
gar keine anhat‹, aber jede Sekunde konnte Frau Unverlacht,
eine fettkrustige böse Kröte, in das Gewölbe treten. »Hör
mit der Schaukelei auf! Was bringst du, Sissy?« Er duzte Emilia; es machte ihm Freude, sie wie ein kleines verhurtes Gas-
sengör zu duzen, und wieder dachte er ›die feine Familie, so
eine feine Familie‹. Emilia raffte sich auf. Sie öffnete das
Plaid. Ein kleiner Gebetsteppich kam zum Vorschein; er war

zerrissen, aber man konnte ihn stopfen. Emilia breitete ihn
aus. Philipp liebte diesen Teppich, liebte sein feines Muster,
die schwingende blaue Ampel auf rotem Grund, und Emilia
hatte grade diesen Teppich mitgenommen, sie hatte ihn mitgenommen, weil Philipp ihn liebte und weil sie Philipp strafen wollte, weil er kein Geld hatte, und weil sie aufs Leihamt
und zu Unverlacht gehen mußte, und weil es ihm gleichgültig
zu sein schien, daß er geldlos war und sie mit Bettlerdemut
ihre Sachen verschleudern durfte, manchmal sah Emilia Philipp als einen Oger, doch dann wieder als den ihr geschickten
Retter, von dem alles zu erwarten war, Überraschung,
Schmerz, aber auch Glück, Ruhm und Reichtum, und es tat
ihr leid, daß sie ihn quälte, und am liebsten wäre sie nun auf
dem Gebetsteppich niedergekniet und hätte gebetet, hätte
Gott und Philipp um Verzeihung gebeten für ihr Schlimm-
sein (sie gebrauchte den Kinderausdruck), aber wo war Gott
und wo lag Mekka, wohin sollte sie sich mit ihrem Gebet
wenden? Unverlacht, von keiner Reue belästigt, von keinen
religiösen Skrupeln gepeinigt, stürzte sich geschäftig auf die
Risse im Teppich. Sie begeisterten ihn zu Triumphschreien:
»So ein Fetzen! Nur Löcher! Diese Risse! Wertlos, Sissy,
morsch, brüchig, wertlos!« Er knüllte die Wolle zusammen,
hielt sie sich an den kahlen Schädel, legte das Ohr an den
Teppich, schrie: »Er singt!« — »Was tut er?« fragte Emilia, für eine Weile verblüfft. »Er singt«, sagte Unverlacht,
»er knistert, er ist brüchig, ich will dir fünf Mark geben,
Sissy, weil du's bist und weil du ihn hergeschleppt hast.« —
»Sie sind verrückt«, sagte Emilia. Sie bemühte sich, ihrem
Gesicht den Ausdruck kalter Uninteressiertheit zu geben. Unverlacht dachte ›hundert ist er wert‹, zwanzig würde er
schlimmstenfalls zahlen. Er sagte: »Zehn in Kommission;
ich lad' mir da was auf, Sissy.« Emilia dachte ›ich weiß, daß
er ihn für hundert verkauft‹. Sie sagte: »Dreißig bar.« Ihre
Stimme klang fest und entschlossen, aber ihr Herz war müde.
Sie hatte bei Unverlacht die Finten des Handels gelernt.
Manchmal überlegte sie, wenn es ihr gelänge, ein Haus zu
verkaufen (aber nie würde es gelingen, nie würde es geschehen: wer kauft Häuser? verfallene Mauern? wer lädt sich

Lasten auf? wer stellt sich unter die Vormundschaft der Ämter, läßt sich mit Steuerbehörden und Wohnungskontrolleuren ein? wer schafft sich Plagen? bietet sich dem Gerichtsvollzieher an? wer will sich mit ständig auf teure Reparaturen versessenen Mietern streiten, mit Mietern, deren Zins man zum Finanzamt tragen muß, statt wie die alten Hauswirte der Märchenzeit selbstzufrieden, gemütlich, die Hände im Schoß von der Miete zu leben?), wenn es gelänge! — es war einer ihrer größten Träume, endlich einmal eins ihrer Häuser loszuwerden, aber die Käufer wollten die schlechte jedem Zugriff des Staates preisgegebene Geldanlage kaum geschenkt haben — vielleicht würde Emilia dann auch einen Altwarenhandel eröffnen und wie Unverlacht vom Reichtum der Vergangenheit und von den Nachlässen der Toten zehren. War das die Verwandlung, die Entzauberung? Nicht Unverlacht entsprang als Prinz dem Froschkleid, sondern sie, die liebreizende Emilia, die schöne junge Erbin des Kommerzienratsvermögens, die Lumpenprinzessin, wollte in die Unterwelt des niedrigsten Feilschens reisen, in den Keller der kleinen Habgier steigen, aus bloßer Zukunftsangst die Maske des Frosches tragen, der kalten Kreatur, die auf arme Fliegen wartet. War das ihr wahres Wesen, das träge Tümpelleben, der lauernde zuschnappende Mund? Aber bis zum Althandel war es noch weit, kein Hauskäufer war zu sehen, und Philipp würde bis dahin sein Buch geschrieben, und die Welt würde sich geändert haben.

Philipp hatte sie schon vorher gefürchtet, und seine Furcht hatte die Mißverständnisse vielleicht herbeigelockt, wie das Aas Fliegen anzieht, oder wie man auf dem Lande meint, es lade das Wetter ein, wenn man nach den Wolken gucke. Er war in einen Strudel lächerlicher, nur ihm bestimmter, nur auf seinen Weg wie Fallen gelegter Verwechselungen geraten, als er Edwin im Auftrage des Neuen Blattes (gern, und doch von Schüchternheit gehemmt, und das grade durch den Auftrag der Zeitung, der anderen Mut gegeben hätte) besuchen wollte. Das Abendecho, das die Namen von Dichtern nur nannte, wenn sie durch irgendwelche Verleihungen Personen des öffentlichen Lebens geworden, nicht länger zu übersehen und überdies gestorben waren, eine Erwähnung, die dann in der Spalte Ferner-ereignete-sich geschah, in der Rubrik des kleinen Klatsches *Kater des argentinischen Konsuls entlaufen, André Gide gestern verschieden,* dieses literarisch so überaus interessierte Blatt hatte eine Redaktionselevin in Mr. Edwins Hotel geschickt, um den berühmten Schriftsteller zu interviewen, ihn für die Leser des Abendechos zu fragen, ob er an den dritten Weltkrieg noch in diesem Sommer glaube, was er von der neuen Badekleidung der Damen halte und ob es seine Meinung sei, daß die Atombombe den Menschen wieder zum Affen zurückwerfen werde. Aus irgendeiner falschen Überlegung nun, vielleicht weil Philipp bekümmert aussah und weil man der jungen Schreibbeflissenen, der sich übenden Nachrichtenjägerin, gesagt hatte, das zu erlegende preisgekrönte Tier sei ein ernster Mann, hielt sie Philipp, den Unberühmten und immerhin wesentlich Jüngeren, für Edwin und stürzte sich mit dem Englisch der Oberschule, gemischt mit dem Barslang einer amerikanischen Bekanntschaft vom letzten Fasching, auf ihn, während zwei frech und herrisch blickende junge Männer, Begleiter der Reporterin und wie sie Vertreter der Pressemacht, schwer an gefährlich aussehenden Geräten trugen und Philipp mit Blitzlicht beleuchteten.

Die aufsehenerregende, blitzbeleuchtete, für Philipp so peinliche und ihn in mancher Weise beschämende Szene (Beschämungen, die den Umstehenden entgingen, es war eine Philipp innerlich peinigende Scham) hatte zur Folge, daß andere Besucher der Hotelhalle, neugierig geworden, erfuhren, daß eine Verwechslung geschehen sei, ein Versehen, das den berühmten Mr. Edwin betraf, ein immer noch nicht ganz aufgeklärtes Mißverständnis, und man war nun geneigt, Philipp für Edwins Sekretär zu halten und ihn, voll plötzlicher Teilnahme am Leben des Dichters, mit Fragen zu bestürmen, wann der Meister zu sprechen, auszufragen, zu sehen und zu photographieren sein werde. Ein Mann in einem vielgurtigen Wettermantel, der eben in wichtiger Mission um den Erdball geflogen zu sein schien, doch während des Fluges nichts erlebt und nur ein Kreuzworträtsel gelöst hatte, dieser gegen mögliche Wetterunbilden und geistige Anfechtungen Wohlgewappnete erkundigte sich bei Philipp, ob der bekannte Mr. Edwin wohl willens sei, zu einer dann in allen Illustrierten Zeitungen erscheinenden Photographie zu erklären, daß er ohne den Genuß einer bestimmten, von dem Wettergegürteten vertretenen Zigarettenmarke nicht leben und nicht dichten könne. Half Philipp sich hier noch mit Schweigen und eiligem Weitergehen, so sah er sich von der Gruppe der Lehrerinnen aus Massachusetts doch eingefangen und zur Rede gestellt. Miß Wescott hielt Philipp fest, blickte ihn durch ihre breitgefaßte Hornbrille wie eine freundliche, gepflegte Eule an und fragte ihn, ob er nicht Edwin bitten könne, der Reisegesellschaft der Lehrerinnen und, wie man wohl behaupten könne, Edwin-Verehrerinnen eine kleine Vorlesung zu halten, ein stilles Privatissimum, ihnen eine Einführung in sein doch allzu schwer zugängliches, allzu dunkles, der Deutung bedürfendes Werk zu geben. An dieser Stelle, noch ehe Philipp zu Wort kommen und seine Unzuständigkeit erklären konnte, unterbrach Miß Burnett Miß Wescott. Privatissimum hin und Verehrung her, meinte Miß Burnett, Edwin werde anderes zu tun haben, Besseres, Unterhaltsameres, als sich mit reisenden Schulweibern abzugeben, aber Kay, ihre Jüngste, der Benjamin der Gruppe sozusagen, die Junge und Hübsche, beinahe hätte Miß Burnett gerufen »die mit den grünen Augen«, schwärme nun wirklich und in aufrichtiger, unverbildeter und jüngerhafter Weise für die Dichter, für Edwin natürlich besonders, und vielleicht, Philipp der Sekretär müsse es einsehen, würde es den Gefeierten erfrischen, ihn von der Reise und in der Fremde erfrischen, von so viel junger Anmut angeschwärmt zu werden, kurz, Philipp solle es doch wagen, Kay zu Edwin zu führen, damit er ihr eine Widmung, ein Gedenken an den Tag ihrer Begegnung in Deutschland in ihr Exemplar seiner Gedichte schreiben könne, einen Band, den sie in der flexiblen Dünndruckausgabe bei sich habe. Miß Burnett schob Kay ins Licht, und Philipp sah sie mit Rührung an. Er dachte ›ich würde so empfinden, wie diese energische Dame meint, daß Edwin empfinden wird, wenn die junge Anbeterin erscheint‹. Kay wirkte so unbefangen, so frisch, sie war von einer Jugend, wie man sie hier kaum noch sieht, sie war unbeschwert, das war es wohl, sie kam aus anderer Luft, aus herber und reiner Luft, wie es Philipp schien, aus einem anderen Land mit Weite, Frische und Jugend, und sie verehrte die Dichter. Edwin freilich war aus dem Land geflohen, aus dem Kay kam: war er vor der Weite oder vor der Jugend des Landes geflohen, doch nein, vor Kay war er wohl nicht auf Nimmerwiederkehr davongereist, vielleicht vor Miß Wescott, der freundlichen Eule mit der Brille, doch auch diese war wohl nicht so schrecklich, man konnte schwer urteilen, warum Edwin geflohen war, wenn man das Land nicht kannte, ihm, Philipp, war die Neue Welt, im Augenblick durch Kay vertreten, sympathisch. Er beneidete Edwin. Aber um so peinlicher war es nun für ihn, daß er nichts für die reizende, aus dem weiten und jungen Amerika gekommene Verehrerin der Poesie tun konnte und daß es allzu lächerlich und allzuschwer sein würde, nun von sich zu reden und all die Verwechselungen und Mißverständnisse zu erklären, die hier am skurril boshaften Werk waren. Er versuchte den älteren Damen zu offenbaren, daß er keineswegs Edwins Sekretär und selber nur gekommen sei, Edwin zu sprechen, aber schon war hiermit ein neuer Irrtum geboren, denn jeder faßte Philipps Worte so auf, daß er Edwins Freund sei, ein vertrauter Genosse, Edwins deutscher Freund, sein deutscher Kollege, in Deutschland ebenso berühmt wie Edwin in der Welt, und die Lehrerinnen entschuldigten sich gleich, sie waren höflich und hatten Lebensart (sie waren viel höflicher und hatten viel mehr Lebensart als deutsche Lehrerinnen), daß sie Philipp nicht kannten, sie baten um seinen Namen, und Burnett schob gar Kay noch näher an Philipp heran und sagte »er ist auch ein Dichter, ein deutscher Dichter«. Kay reichte Philipp die Hand und äußerte Bedauern, nicht auch ein Buch von Philipp bereit zu haben, um ihn um seine Widmung bitten zu können. Kay duftete nach Reseda. Philipp liebte die Blütenwasser nicht, er mochte Parfüme aus künstlichen unbestimmten Ingredienzen, aber der Resedaduft paßte gut zu Kay, er war ein Attribut ihrer Jugend, eine Aura ihrer grü-

nen Augen, und er erinnerte Philipp an etwas. Im Garten des
Rektors hatte Reseda geblüht, die wohlriechende Reseda, und
der Wohlgeruch hatte zu den Sommertagen gehört, wenn
Philipp, das Kind, mit Eva, der Rektorstochter, auf dem Rasen lag. Reseda war hellgrün. Und von hellem Grün war Kay.
Sie war ein hellgrüner Frühling. Kay dachte ›er sieht mich
an, ich gefalle ihm, er ist nicht mehr jung aber er ist bestimmt sehr berühmt, ich bin erst Stunden hier und schon
habe ich einen deutschen Dichter kennengelernt, die Deutschen haben so fürchterlich ausdrucksvolle Gesichter, sie tragen Charakterköpfe wie bei uns die schlechten Schauspieler,
das ist wohl so, weil sie ein altes Volk sind und so viel durchgemacht haben, vielleicht war dieser Dichter in einem Bom-
benkeller verschüttet, es soll entsetzlich gewesen sein, mein
Bruder sagt daß es entsetzlich war, er war bei den Fliegern,
er hat hier Bomben geworfen, ich würde es nicht ertragen
bombardiert zu werden, oder doch? vielleicht denkt man nur
vorher man erträgt es nicht, die Dichter in Dr. Kaisers deutscher Literaturgeschichte sehen alle so schrecklich romantisch
aus, wie Leute aus dem Verbrecheralbum, allerdings tragen
sie da Bärte, wahrscheinlich arbeitet er die Nächte durch, da-
her ist er so blaß, oder er ist traurig weil sein Vaterland Unglück hatte? vielleicht trinkt er auch, viele Dichter trinken,
er wird Rheinwein trinken, ich möchte auch Rheinwein trinken, Katharine wird mich nicht lassen, wozu reise ich nur? er
geht in einem Eichenwald spazieren und dichtet, eigentlich
ist ein Dichter komisch, Hemingway glaub' ich ist weniger
komisch, Hemingway angelt, es ist weniger komisch zu an-
geln als im Wald spazierenzugehen, aber ich würde mit dem
deutschen Dichter in seinem Eichenwald spazierengehen
wenn er mich aufforderte, schon um es Dr. Kaiser zu erzählen
würde ich mit ihm spazierengehen. Dr. Kaiser wird sich
freuen wenn ich ihm erzähle daß ich mit einem deutschen
Dichter im Eichenwald spazierengegangen bin, aber der
Dichter wird mich gar nicht auffordern, ich bin zu jung,
vielleicht wird er Katharine auffordern oder Mildred, aber
mich würde er lieben wenn er sich trauen würde eine Amerikanerin zu lieben, mich würde er viel mehr lieben als er

Katharine oder Mildred lieben würde‹. Katharine Wescott
sagte: »Sie kennen Mr. Edwin sicher sehr gut.« — »Seine
Bücher«, erwiderte Philipp. Aber anscheinend verstanden sie
sein Englisch nicht. Mildred Burnett sagte: »Es wäre nett,
wenn wir uns später noch sehen würden. Vielleicht werden
wir uns sehen, wenn Sie bei Mr. Edwin sind. Vielleicht werden wir doch noch Mr. Edwin lästig fallen.« Sie glaubten
immer noch, daß Philipp als vertrauter und erwarteter
Freund zu Edwin gehe. Philipp sagte: »Ich weiß nicht, ob ich
Edwin aufsuchen werde; es ist keineswegs sicher, daß Sie
mich bei Mr. Edwin treffen werden.« Doch wieder schienen
ihn die Lehrerinnen nicht zu verstehen. Sie nickten ihm
freundlich zu und schnatterten im Chor »bei Edwin, bei Edwin«. Kay erwähnte, sie lerne Deutsch bei Dr. Kaiser, deutsche Literaturgeschichte. »Vielleicht habe ich schon etwas von
Ihnen gelesen«, sagte sie. »Ist es nicht komisch, daß ich etwas von Ihnen gelesen habe und Sie jetzt kennenlerne?«
Philipp verneigte sich. Er war verlegen und fühlte sich beleidigt. Er wurde von Fremden beleidigt, die ihn nicht beleidigen wollten. Es war, als würden den Fremden die beleidigen-
den Sätze souffliert, und sie sprachen sie in bester Absicht
gutgläubig als Schmeichelei und Achtungsworte nach, und
nur Philipp und der unsichtbar bleibende boshafte Souffleur
verstanden die Kränkung. Philipp war wütend. Aber er wurde auch angelockt. Er wurde angelockt von dem jungen Mädchen, von ihrer frischen, aufrechten und unbefangenen Achtung vor Werten, die auch Philipp achtete, Qualitäten, die
er besessen und verloren hatte. Ein bitterer Reiz lag in allem
Mißverständnis mit Kay. Etwas erinnerte ihn Kay auch an
Emilia, nur daß Kay eine unbefangene, eine unbeschwerte
Emilia war und daß sie, es tat wohl, ihn nicht kannte und
nichts von ihm wußte. Aber dennoch blieb es peinlich, daß
ihm auf so anrüchige hinterhältig höhnende Weise Achtung
bezeigt wurde, daß ein Philipp geachtet wurde, den es gar
nicht gab, den es aber leicht hätte geben können, ein Philipp,
der er hatte werden wollen, ein bedeutender Schriftsteller,
dessen Werk selbst in Massachusetts gelesen wurde. Und
gleich war er sich darüber klar, daß dies ›selbst in Massa-

chusetts‹ ein dummer Gedanke war, denn Massachusetts war
genauso fern und genauso nah wie Deutschland, vom Schriftsteller aus gesehen natürlich, der Schriftsteller stand in der
Mitte, und die Welt um ihn war überall gleich fern und nah,
oder der Schriftsteller war außen, und die Welt war die Mitte,
war die Aufgabe, um die er kreiste, etwas nie zu Erreichen-
des, niemals zu Bewältigendes, und es gab keine Ferne und
keine Nähe; vielleicht saß auch in Massachusetts ein dummer
Literat und wünschte sich, ›selbst in Deutschland‹ gelesen zu
werden, für dumme Menschen war die geographische Entfernung immer die Wüste, die Unkultur, das Ende der Welt,
der Ort, wo die Füchse sich gute Nacht sagen, und Licht war
nur, wo man selber im Dunkeln tappte. Doch leider war
Philipp kein bedeutender Schriftsteller geworden, er war
schließlich nur jemand, der sich Schriftsteller nannte, weil er
in den Einwohnerakten als Schriftsteller geführt wurde: er
war schwach, er war auf der Walstatt geblieben, auf der sich
die schändliche Politik und der gemeinste Krieg, Wahnsinn
und Verbrechen ausgetobt hatten, und Philipps kleiner Ruf,
der erste Versuch, sein erstes Buch war im Lautsprecherbrül-
len und im Waffenlärm untergegangen, war von den
Schreien der Mörder und Gemordeten übertönt worden, und
Philipp war wie gelähmt, und seine Stimme war wie erstickt, und schon sah er mit Grauen, wie der verfluchte
Schauplatz, den er nicht verlassen konnte, vielleicht auch
nicht verlassen mochte, für ein neues blutiges Drama hergerichtet wurde.
Nach den Mißverständnissen in der Hotelhalle, nach dem
Gespräch mit den reisenden Lehrerinnen war es Philipp unmöglich, noch wirklich zu Edwin zu gehen. Er mußte dem
Neuen Blatt den Auftrag, Edwin zu besuchen, zurückgeben.
Es war wieder ein Mißerfolg. Philipp wollte aus dem Hotel
fliehen. Er schämte sich aber, jetzt, nachdem er Aufsehen
erregt hatte, vor allen Blicken wieder hinauszugehen, fortzu-
schleichen wie ein geprügelter Hund. Vor allem schämte er
sich vor Kays grünen Augen. Er ging die Treppe hinauf, die
zu den Hotelzimmern führte, aber er hoffte irgendwo eine
Hintertreppe zu finden, die er wieder hinuntergehen konnte,

um dann einen Notausgang zu erreichen. Auf der Haupt-
treppe aber traf er Messalina. »Ich beobachte Sie schon lange«, rief die Gewaltige und stellte sich Philipp breit in den
Weg. »Sie besuchen Edwin?« fragte sie. »Wer ist die Kleine
mit den grünen Augen? Sie ist süß!«»Ich besuche niemand«,
sagte Philipp. »Was machen Sie dann hier?« — »Treppen-
gehen.« — »Sie täuschen mich nicht.« Messalina machte einen
Versuch, ihm kokett auf die Schulter zu schlagen. »Hören Sie
zu, wir geben eine Party heute abend, und ich möchte gern
Edwin dafür haben. Es wird schick. Es wird auch für Edwin
nett sein. Jack kommt und Hänschen. Sie wissen schon, was
ich meine, alle Schriftsteller sind so.« Ihr frisch onduliertes
Haar zitterte wie Himbeergelee. »Ich kenne Mr. Edwin
nicht«, sagte Philipp erbost. »Ihr seid verrückt. Alle bringt
ihr mich mit Edwin in Verbindung. Was soll das? Ich bin
zufällig im Hotel. Ich habe hier zu tun.« — »Vorhin sagten
Sie, Sie seien Edwins Freund. Wollen Sie die Grünäugige
verführen? Sie sieht Emilia ähnlich. Emilia und das Mädchen wären ein schönes Paar.« Messalina blickte in die Halle
hinunter. »Es ist alles ein Mißverständnis«, sagte Philipp.
»Ich kenne auch das Mädchen nicht. Ich werde sie nie wiedersehen.« Er dachte ›schade ich würde dich gern wiedersehen, aber würde ich dir gefallen?‹ Messalina blieb hartnäk-
kig: »Was machen Sie also wirklich hier, Philipp?« — »Ich
suche Emilia«, sagte er verzweifelt. »Ach! Kommt sie her?
Ihr habt hier ein Zimmer?« Sie rückte ihm näher. ›Es war
falsch, es war falsch ihr das zu sagen‹, dachte Philipp. »Nein«,
sagte er, »ich suche Emilia hier nur. Sie kommt aber bestimmt nicht hierher.« Er versuchte an dem Denkmal vorbei-
zukommen, doch das Himbeergelee zitterte allzu gefährlich,
jeden Moment konnte es ins Gleiten geraten, eine Wolke
werden, eine rote sich in roten Nebel auflösende Wolke, ein
Rauch, in dem Philipp sterben würde. »Lassen Sie mich
doch«, rief er verzweifelt. Aber sie flüsterte nun, das breite
trunkverwüstete Gesicht gegen sein Ohr gepreßt, als habe sie
ihm Vertrauliches mitzuteilen: »Was macht der Film? Der
Film für Alexander. Er fragt immer, wann Sie wohl den Film
bringen werden. Er freut sich schon so darauf. Wir könnten

uns alle in Edwins Vortrag treffen. Sie bringen Emilia und die kleine Grüne mit. Wir gehen vor der Party in Edwins Vortrag, und nachher hoffe ich —«—»Hoffen Sie nichts«, unterbrach Philipp sie brüsk. »Es gibt nichts zu hoffen. Es gibt überhaupt keine Hoffnungen mehr. Und für Sie erst recht nicht.« — Er eilte die Treppe hoch, bereute auf dem Treppenabsatz seine Aufrichtigkeit, wollte umkehren, fürchtete sich dann und öffnete eine Tür, die an Wäschekammern vorbei zu einem absteigenden Gang und schließlich in die berühmte im Reisehandbuch mit Sternen hervorgehobene Küche des Hotels führte.

Hatte Edwin die Lust an Küchenfreuden verloren? Das Essen schmeckte ihm nicht. Nicht appetitlos, nein angewidert verschmähte er die Erzeugnise des berühmten Herdes, die leckeren Gaumenspezialitäten des Hauses, die man ihm in silbernen Töpfen und porzellanenen Schüsseln ins Zimmer gebracht hatte. Er trank ein wenig Wein, Frankenwein, von dem er gelesen, gehört und auf den er neugierig gewesen war, aber der aus der bauchigen Flasche hell sprudelnde Trunk deuchte ihm dann allzu herb für diese Mittagsstunde eines trüben Tages. Es war ein Sonnenwein, und Edwin sah keine Sonne, der Wein schmeckte nach Gräbern, er schmeckte, wie alte Friedhöfe bei nassem Wetter riechen, es war ein Wein, der sich anpaßte, der die Heiteren lachen und die Traurigen weinen machte. Entschieden, Edwin hatte einen schlechten Tag. Er ahnte nicht, daß unten in der Halle ein anderer für ihn unfreiwillig stellvertretend die belanglosen mit dem Ruhm des Pressebildes kommenden Lästigkeiten und kleinen Huldigungen empfing und erduldete, Annäherungen und Schmeicheleien, die Edwin ebenso zuwider waren, wie sie Philipp peinlich quälten, der sie ertragen mußte und dem sie nicht galten. Philipps Mißgeschick hätte noch weiter zu Edwins Verstimmung beigetragen; Edwin hätte sich nichts von Philipp abgenommen gesehen, er hätte nur das Fragwürdige und Komische der eigenen Existenz durch Philipps Auftritt wie durch einen Schatten vergrößert, gezeichnet und verraten gefunden. Aber Edwin erfuhr nichts von Philipp. Er schritt in schwarzroten Lederhausschuhen,

in einen buddhistischen Mönchsmantel, sein Arbeitskleid, gehüllt, um den zierlichen Tisch herum, auf dem die ver-
schmähten Eßgenüsse dampften und dufteten. Die unberührte Tafel ärgerte ihn; er fürchtete den Koch zu kränken, einen
Meister, dessen Kunst Edwin normalerweise geschätzt hätte.
Er entfernte sich mit schlechtem Gewissen von dem Speise-
tisch und schritt die Umrandung des Teppichs ab, in dessen
Muster Götter und Prinzen, Blumen und Fabeltiere geknüpft
waren, so daß die Wollmalerei einer Illustration zu einer
Schachtelgeschichte aus Tausendundeiner Nacht glich. Der
Bodenbelag war so prächtig märchenorientalisch, so blumig
mythenreich, daß der Dichter das Knüpfwerk nicht richtig
querüber betreten mochte und sich, obwohl in Hausschuhen
und wie ein Weiser Indiens gekleidet, respektvoll am Rande
hielt. Die echten Teppiche waren neben der guten Küche der
Stolz des alten von den Zerstörungen des Krieges im wesent-
lichen verschont gebliebenen Hauses. Edwin liebte altmodi-
sche Unterkünfte, die Karawansereien des gebildeten Europas, Betten, in denen Goethe oder Laurence Sterne gelegen,
nette etwas wacklige Schreibkommoden, die vielleicht Platen,
Humboldt, Herman Bang oder Hofmannsthal benutzt hatten. Er zog die von alters her wohlberufenen Gasthöfe bei
weitem den neuerrichteten Palästen, den Behausungsmaschi-
nen einer Corbusier-Architektur vor, den blinkenden Stahl-
rohren und bloßstellenden Glaswänden, und so geschah es,
daß er auf seinen Reisen manchmal unter einer nicht funk-
tionierenden Heizung oder zu kühlem Badewasser zu leiden
hatte, Unbequemlichkeiten, die er nicht bemerken wollte, auf
die aber seine große, überaus empfindliche Nase mit einem
Schnupfen zu reagieren pflegte. Mr. Edwins Nase hätte Wärme und technischen Komfort dem Geruch des Holzwurm-
mehls in den antiken Sekretären, dem Dunst von Motten-
mitteln, Menschenschweiß, Unzucht und Tränen, der aus
dem Gewebe der alten Tapisserien stieg, vorgezogen. Aber
Edwin lebte nicht für seine Nase und nicht für sein Wohlbe-
hagen (obwohl er Behaglichkeit liebte, sich ihr aber niemals
ganz hingeben konnte), er lebte in Zucht, in der strengen
Zucht des Geistes und in den Sielen tätiger humaner Tradi-

tion, einer höchst sublimen Tradition, versteht sich, zu deren
Bild und Bestand auch die alten Herbergen gehörten, der
Elefant, das Einhorn und die Jahreszeiten, am Rande natürlich, doch im übrigen verzehrte ihn Unruhe, denn der in der
Neuen Welt geborene Dichter zählte sich (mit unbestreitba-
rem Recht) zur europäischen Elite, der späten und, wie immer mehr zu fürchten war, letzten des geliebten abendländischen Erdteils, und nichts empörte und verletzte Edwin mehr
als der Barbarenschrei, die Genie und Größe leider nicht er-
mangelnde und darum nur um so erschreckendere Voraussage,
der Ruf dieses Russen, des Heilig-Kranken, des Besessenen,
des großen Unweisen, unweise im Sinn der aufgeklärten
Griechen, wie Edwin behauptete, doch auch des Sehers und
Urdichters, wie Edwin gestehen mußte (eines Dichters, den
er verehrte und mied, denn er selbst fühlte sich nicht den
Dämonen verbunden, sondern der hellenisch-christlichen Ratio, die Übersinnliches — in Maßen — nicht ausschloß; aber
schon schienen die vertriebenen Gespenster des Grausam-Ab-
surden wiederaufzutauchen), das Wort von der kleinen,
Asien vorgelagerten Halbinsel, die nach drei Jahrtausenden
der Selbständigkeit, der Frühreife, der Ungezogenheit, des
Ordentlich-Unordentlichen, des Größenwahns zur Mutter
Asien zurückkehren oder zurückfallen werde. War es soweit?
Hatte die Zeit sich wieder erfüllt? Edwin hatte sich, von der
Reise ermüdet, hinlegen wollen, aber Ruhe und Schlaf waren
ihm ferngeblieben, und das Mahl, verschmäht und mit Widerwillen betrachtet, hatte ihn nicht erfrischen können. Die
Stadt erschreckte ihn, die Stadt bekam ihm nicht, sie hatte zu
viel durchgemacht, sie hatte das Grauen erlebt, das abgeschla-
gene Haupt der Medusa gesehen, frevelige Größe, eine Parade von aus ihrem eigenen Untergrund heraufgekommenen
Barbaren, die Stadt war mit Feuer gestraft worden und mit
Zerschmetterung ihrer Mauern, heimgesucht war sie, hatte
das Chaos gestreift, den Sturz in die Ungeschichte, jetzt hing
sie wieder am Hang der Historie, hing schräg und blühte,
war es Scheinblüte? was hielt sie am Hang? die Kraft eigener
Wurzeln (wie unheimlich das Schlemmermahl auf dem zierlichen Tisch an diesem Ort)? oder hielt sie die dünne Fessel,

die sie mit allerlei Interessen verknüpfte, mit den vorübergehenden und sich widersprechenden Interessen der Sieger,
die lockere Bindung an die Tagespläne der Strategie und des
Geldes, der Glaube Aberglaube Afterglaube an die Einfluß-
sphären der Diplomatie und die Positionen der Macht? nicht
Historie Wirtschaft, nicht die verwirrte Klio Mercurius mit
dem gefüllten Beutel beherrschte die Szene. Edwin sah in
dieser Stadt ein Schauspiel und ein Beispiel, sie hing, hing
am Abgrund, war in der Schwebe, hielt sich in gefährlicher
mühsamer Balance, sie konnte ins Alte und immerhin Bewährte, sie konnte ins Neue und Unbekannte schwanken,
konnte der überlieferten Kultur treu bleiben, doch auch in
vielleicht nur vorübergehende Kulturlosigkeit absinken, vielleicht als Stadt überhaupt verschwinden, vielleicht ein Mas-
senzuchthaus werden, in Stahl, Beton und Übertechnik die
Vision des phantastischen Gefängnisses von Piranesi erfüllen,
des merkwürdigen Kupferstechers, dessen römische Ruinen
Edwin so liebte. Die Bühne war zur Tragödie hergerichtet,
aber was sich im Vordergrund abspielte, vor der Stunden-
rampe, die persönlichen Weltberührungen blieben vorläufig
possenhaft. Im Hotel warteten Leute auf Edwin. Man hatte
sie ihm gemeldet, Journalisten, Photographen, eine Ausfra-
gerin hatte ihr Anliegen hinaufgeschickt, unsinnige Fragen,
ein Schwachsinngespräch. — Edwin mied nicht immer die
Öffentlichkeit und ihre Vertreter, sie strengten ihn zwar an,
freilich, es kostete ihn Überwindung, zu Fremden zu sprechen, aber zuweilen, ja oft, hatte er es schon getan, hatte es
vollbracht, hatte mit einem Scherz die Torheit befriedigt und
sich die Sympathien der Meinungsmacher erworben, aber
hier in dieser Stadt fürchtete er die Journalisten, er fürchtete
sie, weil er hier, wo Erde und Zeit schon gebebt hatten und
gleich ins Nichts brechen konnten oder ins Neue, ins Andere,
in die unbekannte Zukunft, von der man nichts wußte, hier
würde er nicht scherzen können, nicht leicht das gute geistvoll
tändelnde Wort finden, das man von ihm erwartete. Und
wenn er die Wahrheit sagen würde? Kannte er denn die
Wahrheit? O älteste Frage: was war Wahrheit? Er hätte nur
von Befürchtungen reden können, unsinnigen Ängsten viel-

leicht, der Melancholie Lauf lassen, die ihn hier überkommen hatte, aber Furcht und Trauer schienen ihm hier in die Keller verbannt zu sein, in die Keller, über die Häuser gestürzt waren, und dort ließ man sie nun eine Weile. Der Geruch dieser zugeschütteten Keller lag über der Stadt. Niemand schien es zu merken. Vielleicht vergaß man die Grüfte ganz. Sollte Edwin erinnern?

Die Stadt zog ihn an. Trotz allem zog sie ihn an. Er legte das seidene Mönchsgewand ab und kleidete sich, der Welt angepaßt, zeitgenössisch schicklich. Vielleicht verkleidete er sich so. Vielleicht war er kein Mensch. Er eilte die Treppe hinunter, den leichten schwarzen Hut aus der Londoner Bond Street ein wenig schräg in die Stirn gezogen. Er sah überaus vornehm und etwas wie ein alter Zuhälter aus. Auf dem Treppenabsatz vor der Halle bemerkte er Messalina. Sie erinnerte ihn an eine entsetzliche Person, an ein Gespenst, das in Amerika als Gesellschaftsjournalistin arbeitete, ein Berufsklatschweib, und Edwin lief die Treppe wieder empor, suchte die Tür zu einem Hinterausgang, ging an Wäschekammern vorbei, an kichernden Mädchen, sie schwangen Bettücher Leintücher Totentücher, Hüllen für die Leiber und Hüllen für die Liebe, für Umarmung, Zeugung und letzte Atemzüge, er eilte durch eine Frauenwelt, durch Randbezirke des Mütterreiches, und, nach anderer Luft dürstend, öffnete er eine Tür und fand sich in der geräumigen und berühmten Küche des Hotels. Fatal! Fatal! Das unberührte Mahl in seinem Zimmer bedrückte ihn wieder. Wie gerne hätte Edwin sich sonst mit dem Chef über *Physiologie-du-goût* unterhalten und hätte den hübschen Küchenjungen zugesehen, die sanfte wie Gold glänzende Fische schuppten. So stürmte er durch Fleischsuppendampf und scharfen Grünzeugdunst zu einer weiteren Tür, die hoffentlich endlich ins Freie führte — doch auch sie führte nicht wirklich ins Freie. Edwin stand nun im Hof des Hotels vor einem eisernen Gestell, das die Fahrräder des Personals, der Köche, Kellner, Pagen und Hausdiener, barg, und hinter dem Gestell stand ein Herr, den Edwin in der Verwirrung einer Sekunde für sich hielt, für sein Spiegelbild, für seinen Doppelgänger, eine sympathisch-unsympathische Erscheinung, doch dann sah er, daß es natürlich Täuschung war, gedankliche Absurdität, nicht sein Ebenbild stand da, sondern ein jüngerer, ihm nicht einmal entfernt ähnlich sehender Herr, der aber dennoch verwandt sympathisch-unsympathisch blieb und etwa einem Bruder zu vergleichen war, den man nicht mochte. Edwin begriff: der Herr war ein Schriftsteller. Was tat er hier hinter den Fahrrädern? Lauerte er ihm auf? Philipp erkannte Edwin, und nach dem ersten Augenblick der Überraschung dachte er ›dies ist die Gelegenheit ihn zu sprechen‹. — ›Wir können unser Gespräch führen‹, dachte er. ›Edwin und ich, wir wollen uns unterhalten, wir werden uns verstehen; vielleicht wird er mir sagen, was ich bin.‹ Aber schon floh Philipp die Hoffnung, die Verwirrung triumphierte, die Verblüffung, Edwin hier im Hof des Hotels zu sehen, und er dachte ›es ist lächerlich, ich darf ihn jetzt nicht ansprechen‹, und statt vorzutreten, ging er einen Schritt zurück, und auch Edwin trat zurück und dachte dabei ›wenn dieser Mann jung wäre, könnte er ein junger Dichter sein, ein Verehrer meines Werkes‹, und es war ihm nicht bewußt, wie lächerlich der Gedanke und seine Formulierung war, zu Papier gebracht, hätte Edwin den Satz nie gelten lassen, er wäre errötet, doch hier im Unsichtbaren Schwebenden des gerade buhlenden Gedankens siegte nicht Überlegung, sondern der Wunsch, ja, er hätte es begrüßt, in dieser Stadt einen jungen Dichter zu treffen, einen Strebenden, einen Nacheifernden, er hätte gern einen Jünger gefunden, einen Dichter aus dem Lande Goethes und Platens, aber der hier war ja kein Jüngling mehr, kein strahlend Gläubiger, der eigene Zweifel, die eigene Trauer, die eigene Sorge standen dem andern im Gesicht geschrieben, und beide dachten sie im Hof des Hotels, geflohen vor der Gesellschaft der Menschen, ›ich muß ihn meiden‹. Philipp war schon eine Weile im Hofe. Er konnte nicht hinaus. Er zögerte vor dem Personalausgang des Hotels, er fürchtete sich, an einer Kontrolluhr und dem Portier vorbeizugehen. Der Türhüter würde ihn für einen Dieb halten. Wie sollte er seinen Wunsch, unbemerkt aus dem Haus zu verschwinden, erklären? Und Edwin? Auch er schien ratlos zu sein. Aber im Vordergrund des

Hofes stehend, fiel Edwin mehr auf als Philipp, und der Portier trat aus seinem Verschlag und rief: »Was wünschen die Herren?« Beide Dichter schritten nun, scheu zueinander Distanz wahrend, zum Ausgang, sie gingen an der Kontrolluhr vorüber, dem mechanischen Sklavenhalter, einem Stundenmesser und Arbeitszähler, dem sie beide sich nie unterworfen hatten, und der Portier hielt sie für Männer, die wegen einer Frauengeschichte den Personalausgang benutzen mußten, und dachte ›Pack‹ und ›Nichtstuer‹.

Nichtstuend schwätzend träumend, kleine flache gefällige Träume in einem ewigen Halbschlummer, einem Schlummer des Glücks, träumend, *Fesche Endvierzigerin sucht Herrn in gesicherter Position*, saßen die Frauen, die von Staatspensionen, geglückten Auszahlungen bei Todesfall, Scheidungsrenten und Trennungsgeldern leben, im Domcafé. Auch Frau Behrend liebte die Stätte, den bevorzugten Versammlungsort gleichgeseelter Genossinnenschaft, wo man bei Kaffee und Sahne sich wohlig der Erinnerung an Ehefreuden, wohlig dem Schmerz des Verlassenseins, wohlig der Bitternis der Enttäuschung hingeben konnte. Carla hatte es noch nicht zu Pension und Rente gebracht, und Frau Behrend sah die Tochter mit Furcht und Unbehagen aus dem Schatten des Domturmes in das bonbonrosa gefärbte Ampellicht, in diesen gemächlichen Hafen des Lebens, in die still plätschernde Bucht, in das Gehege der freundlich Versorgten, treten: eine Verlorene. Carla war verloren, sie war das Opfer, ein Opfer des Krieges, sie war einem Moloch hingeworfen, man mied die Opfer, sie war für die Mutter verloren, für die wohlanständigen Kreise der Mutter verloren, für alle Herkunft und Sitte verloren, dem Elternhaus entrissen. Aber was machte es schon? Es gab kein Elternhaus mehr. Als das Haus durch Bombenwurf zerstört wurde, hatte die Familie sich aufgelöst. Die Bande waren gesprengt. Vielleicht hatte die Bombe nur gezeigt, daß es lockere Bande gewesen waren, der aus Zufall, Irrtum, Fehlentscheidung und Torensinn geknüpfte Strick der Gewohnheit. Carla lebte mit einem Neger, Frau Behrend in einer Mansarde mit den vergilbenden Noten der Platzkon-

zerte, und der Musikmeister spielte, an ein Flitscherl wegge-
worfen, den Nutten auf. Als sie Carla gesehen hatte, blickte
Frau Behrend beunruhigt in die Runde, ob Freundinnen,
Feindinnen, Freundfeindinnen, Bekannte in der Nähe saßen.
Sie zeigte sich nicht gern mit Carla in der Öffentlichkeit
(wer weiß? vielleicht erschien auch noch ihr Neger, und die
Damen im Café würden die Schande sehen), aber noch mehr
fürchtete Frau Behrend Gespräche mit Carla in der Einsamkeit der Mansarde. Mutter und Tochter hatten sich nichts
mehr zu sagen. Und Carla, die in dem Café, das sie als Nach-
mittagssitz der Mutter kannte, Frau Behrend gesucht hatte,
in dem Gefühl, sie sehen zu müssen, bevor sie in die Klinik
ging, um sich die unerwünschte Frucht der Liebe abtreiben
zu lassen, der Liebe? ach, war es Liebe? war es nicht nur
Zweisamkeit, Verzweiflung der in die Welt Geworfenen, das
warme Mensch-bei-Mensch-Liegen? und das nah-fremde
Wesen in ihrem Leib, war es nicht nur Frucht der Gewöhnung, der Gewöhnung an den Mann, seine Umarmung, sein
Eindringen, Frucht des kleinen Ausgehaltenseins, Frucht der
Furcht, des Nichtalleinbestehenkönnens, die wieder neue
Furcht gezeugt hatte, wieder Furcht gebären wollte? Carla
sah die Mutter fischgesichtig, flunderhäuptig, kalt fischig abweisend, ihre Hand mischte mit dem kleinen Löffel Kaffee
und Rahm und war wie die Flosse eines Fisches, die ein wenig zitternde Flosse eines bedauernswerten Fisches in einem
Zimmeraquarium, so sah es Carla, war es verzerrende Vision?
war es das wahre Gesicht der Mutter? ein anderes wohl hatte
sich über Carlas Wiege gebeugt, und erst dann, später, viel
später, als nichts im Kleinen zu sorgen und zu tun war, war
der Fisch durch die Haut getreten, das Flunderhaupt, und
Carlas Gefühl, das sie hergetrieben hatte, die Mutter zu sehen, ein Zueinanderreden zu versuchen, starb, als sie Frau
Behrends Platz im Café erreichte. Frau Behrend hatte für
einen Augenblick die Empfindung, daß nicht ihre Tochter,
sondern der Domturm erdrückend vor ihr stünde.

Odysseus und Josef hatten den Turm bestiegen. Josef war
außer Atem und sog die Höhenluft ein, als sie endlich nach

Überwindung von bröckelnden Gemäuerstufen und steilen Leitern die oberste Bühne des Turms erreicht hatten. Das Musikköfferchen schwieg. Es war eine Sendepause eingetreten. Man hörte nur den jappenden Atem, vielleicht das müde pochende Herz des alten Dienstmannes. Sie blickten über die Stadt, über die alten Dächer, über die romanischen, gotischen, barocken Kirchen, über die Ruinen der Kirchen, über die neuerrichteten Dachstühle, über die Wunden der Stadt, die Freiflächen der gesprengten Gebäude. Josef dachte, wie alt er geworden sei, immer hatte er in dieser Stadt gelebt, nie war er verreist gewesen, bis auf den Ausflug in den Argonnerwald und zum Chemin-des-Dames, er hatte immer nur die Koffer der Leute, die verreisten, getragen, doch im Argonnerwald hatte er ein Gewehr getragen und am Chemin-des-Dames Handgranaten, und vielleicht, das hatte er sich damals im Unterstand gedacht, während einer Todesstunde, während des Trommelfeuers, vielleicht schoß er auf Reisende und bewarf Reisende mit Explosivstoffen, Leute, die ihm zu Hause als fremde Reisende ein gutes Trinkgeld gegeben hätten, warum also verbot es die Polizei nicht, daß er schoß und mit Würfen mordete? es wäre so einfach gewesen, er hätte gehorcht: Krieg polizeilich verboten; aber die waren ja verrückt, alle waren sie verrückt, selbst die Polizei war verrückt geworden, duldete das Morden, ach, man durfte nicht denken, Josef hielt sich daran, das Trommelfeuer verging, man war des Tötens müde geworden, das Leben, die Koffer der Reisenden, die Brotzeit und das Bier waren wieder in ihre Rechte getreten, bis alle zum zweitenmal verrückt wurden, es war wohl eine Krankheit, die immer wiederkehrte, die Pest hatte den Sohn erwischt, sie hatte ihm den Sohn genommen, und für heute hatte sie ihm einen Neger gegeben, einen Neger mit einem sprechenden und musizierenden Koffer, und nun hatte ihn der Neger auf den Domturm geschleppt, noch nie war Josef auf dem Turm gewesen; auf den Einfall, den Turm zu besteigen, konnte auch nur ein Neger kommen. ›Er ist doch ein sehr fremder Herr‹, dachte Josef, während er blinzelnd in die Ferne blickte. Er fürchtete sich sogar ein wenig vor Odysseus, und er überlegte ›was tue ich, wenn der schwarze Teufel mich plötzlich hinunterwerfen will?‹ Ihm schwindelte vor so viel Denken und vor so viel Weite. Odysseus blickte zufrieden über die Stadt. Er stand oben. Sie lag unter ihm. Er wußte nichts von der alten Geschichte der Stadt, er wußte nichts von Europa, aber er wußte, daß dies eine Hauptstadt der weißen Leute war, eine Stadt, aus der sie gekommen waren und dann Orte wie New York gegründet hatten. Die Black Boys waren aus dem Wald gekommen. War hier nie Wald gewesen, immer nur Häuser? Natürlich, auch hier war Wald gewesen, dichter Urwald, grünes Gestrüpp, Odysseus sah gewaltige Dschungeln unter sich wachsen, Gestrüpp, Farne, Lianen überwucherten die Häuser; was gewesen war, konnte immer wieder kommen. Odysseus schlug Josef auf die Schulter. Der alte Dienstmann taumelte unter dem Schlag. Odysseus lachte, lachte sein breites König-Odysseus-Lachen. Wind regte sich in der Höhe. Odysseus streichelte eine gotische Dämonenfratze des Turmvorsprunges, eine Steinfigur des Mittelalters, das die Teufel auf die Türme verbannte, und Odysseus holte einen Rotstift aus seiner Jacke und schrieb quer über den Dämonenleib stolz seinen Namenszug: Odysseus Cotton aus Memphis-Tennessee, USA.

Was brachten einem die Amerikaner? Es war schimpflich, daß Carla sich mit einem Neger verbunden hatte; es war fürchterlich, daß sie von einem Neger geschwängert war; es war ein Verbrechen, daß sie das Kind in sich töten wollte. Frau Behrend weigerte sich, weiter darüber nachzudenken. Das Schreckliche konnte man nicht aussprechen. Wenn etwas geschah, was nicht geschehen durfte, mußte man schweigen. Hier war nicht Liebe, hier waren Abgründe. Das war nicht das Liebeslied, wie es Frau Behrend im Radio hörte, das war nicht der Film, den sie gerne sah, hier ging es nicht um die Leidenschaft eines Grafen oder eines Chefingenieurs wie in den Romanheften, die so erhebend zu lesen waren. Hier gähnten nur Abgründe, Verlorensein und Schande. ›Wenn sie nur schon in Amerika wäre‹, dachte Frau Behrend, ›Amerika soll zusehen, wie es mit der Schande fertig wird, wir haben hier keine Neger, aber Carla wird nie nach Amerika fahren, sie wird mit ihrem schwarzen Bankert hierbleiben, sie wird mit dem schwarzen Kind auf dem Arm in dieses Café kommen.‹ — ›Ich will nicht‹, dachte Carla, ›woher weiß sie es? hat der Fischkopf Seheraugen? ich wollte es ihr sagen aber ich habe es ihr nicht gesagt, ich kann ihr gar nichts sagen.‹ — ›Ich weiß alles‹, dachte Frau Behrend, ›ich weiß, was du mir sagen willst, du bist 'reingefallen, du willst was Schlechtes tun, du willst Rat wo ich nicht raten kann, tu nur das Schlechte, lauf zum Arzt, es bleibt dir gar nichts anderes übrig, als das Schlechte zu tun, ich will dich hier nicht mit dem Negerkind‹ —

Er wollte das Kind. Er sah das Kind seiner Liebe in Gefahr. Carla war nicht glücklich. Er hatte Carla nicht glücklich gemacht. Er hatte versagt. Sie waren in Gefahr. Wie sollte Washington es sagen? Wie konnte er sagen, was er fürchtete? Dr. Frahm war widerwillig in den Korridor getreten. Das Behandlungszimmer wurde gesäubert. Die Tür stand offen. Eine Frau wischte mit einem feuchten Tuch über den Linoleumbelag des Bodens. Das feuchte Tuch fuhr über die weißen Beine des großen Untersuchungsstuhles. Dr. Frahm war beim Essen gestört worden. Er war vom Tisch aufgestanden. Er hielt eine weiße Serviette in der Hand. Auf der Serviette war ein frischer roter Fleck: Wein. Ein Geruch von Karbol drang aus dem Behandlungszimmer, ein alter Wundreinigungsdunst wurde von der Frau, die das Zimmer wischte, in die Luft gescheucht. Wie sollte Washington es dem Arzt sagen? Carla war hiergewesen. Dr. Frahm sagte es. Er sagte, es sei alles in Ordnung. Was fehlte Carla dann? Warum war sie hiergewesen, wenn alles in Ordnung war? »Eine kleine Störung«, sagte Frahm. Bahnte sich hier Ärger an? Das war er also, der schwarze Vater. Ein schöner Mann, wenn man sich an die Haut gewöhnte. »Wir erwarten ein Kind«, sagte Washington. »Ein Kind?« fragte Frahm. Er blickte Washington erstaunt an. Er dachte ›ich spiele den Naiven‹, Dr. Frahm hatte die befremdende Vorstellung, daß der Neger in dem dunklen Korridor, er stand gerade unter dem gerahmten

Spruch, diesem sogenannten Eid des Hippokrates, blaß wurde. »Hat sie es Ihnen nicht gesagt?« fragte Washington. »Nein«, sagte Frahm. Was war mit diesem Neger los? Frahm legte die Serviette zusammen. Der rote Fleck verschwand in den weißen Falten. Es war, als schlösse sich eine Wunde. Die Sache war nicht zu machen. Carla sollte ihr Kind zur Welt bringen. Der kleine Neger wollte leben. Hier drohte Schande.

Frau Behrend schwieg, schwieg beharrlich, beleidigt und flunderhäuptig, und Carla erriet weiter ihre Gedanken. Es waren Gedanken, die Carla erraten und begreifen konnte, ihr eigenes Denken bewegte sich nicht fern von den Mutter-Gedanken, vielleicht war es Schande, war es Verbrechen, was sie tat und tun wollte, Carla hielt nichts von ihrem Leben, sie hätte ihr Leben gern verleugnet, sie litt es, sie führte es nicht, sie glaubte sich entschuldigen zu müssen, und sie meinte die Entschuldigung der Zeit für sich zu haben, die Entschuldigung der unordentlich gewordenen Zeit, die Verbrechen und Schande gebracht hatte und ihre Kinder verbrecherisch und schändlich machte. Carla war keine Rebellin. Sie glaubte. An Gott? An die Konvention. Wo war Gott? Gott hätte vielleicht den schwarzen Bräutigam gebilligt. Ein Gott für alle Tage. Gott war aber schon bei ihrer Mutter nur ein Feiertagsgott gewesen. Carla war nicht zu Gott geführt worden. Man hatte sie bei der Kommunion nur bis zu seinem Tisch gebracht.

Sie wollte sie zu Gott führen. Emmi, die Kinderfrau, wollte das ihr anvertraute Kind zu Gott führen; sie sah es als die ihr von Gott gestellte Aufgabe an, Hillegonda, das Schauspielerkind, das Sündenkind, das Kind, um das sich die Eltern nicht kümmerten, in der Furcht vor Gott zu erziehen. Emmi mißachtete Alexander und Messalina; sie war bei ihnen angestellt und wurde von ihnen bezahlt, sehr gut bezahlt, aber sie mißachtete sie. Emmi meinte das Kind zu lieben. Aber man durfte Hillegonda nicht Liebe, man durfte ihr nur Strenge zeigen, um sie der Hölle zu entreißen, der sie durch ihre Geburt schon verfallen war. Emmi sprach zu Hillegonda

111

vom Tod, um ihr die Nichtigkeit des Lebens zu beweisen, und sie führte sie in die hohen dunklen Kirchen, um ihren Sinn auf die Ewigkeit zu lenken, aber die kleine Hillegonda schauderte vor dem Tod und fror in den Kirchen. Sie standen in der Seitenkapelle des Doms vor dem Beichtstuhl. Im Pfeiler, den Hillegonda betrachtete, war ein Bombenriß notdürftig mit schlechtem Mörtel verschmiert und zog sich wie eine kaum vernarbte Wunde bis zur steinernen Blätterkrone des Pfeilerhauptes hin. ›Das Kind zu Gott führen‹, das Kind mußte zu Gott geführt werden. Emmi sah, wie klein, wie hilflos das Kind neben dem wuchtigen mörtelverschmierten Pfeiler stand. Gott würde Hillegonda helfen. Gott würde ihr beistehen. Er würde sich der Kleinen und Hilflosen, der unschuldig schuldig mit Sünde Beladenen annehmen. Hillegonda sollte beichten. Noch vor dem Beichtalter sollte sie beichten, um von den Sünden losgesprochen zu werden. Was sollte sie beichten? Hillegonda wußte es nicht. Sie fürchtete sich nur. Sie fürchtete sich vor der Stille, sie fürchtete sich vor der Kälte, vor der Größe und Erhabenheit des Kirchenschiffs, sie fürchtete sich vor Emmi und vor Gott. »Emmi Hand halten.« Die Sünden der Eltern? Was waren das für Sünden? Hillegonda wußte es nicht. Sie wußte nur, daß ihre Eltern Sünder und von Gott verstoßen waren. ›Schauspielerkind, Komödiantenkind, Filmkind‹, dachte Emmi. — »Ist Gott böse?« fragte das Kind.

»Prächtig! Großartig! Hervorragend!« Der Erzherzog wurde ausgezogen, das Goldene Vlies wurde abgelegt. »Prächtig! Großartig! Hervorragend!« Der Produktionschef hatte die Muster gesehen: die Aufnahmen des Tages waren prächtig, großartig und hervorragend. Der Produktionschef lobte Alexander. Er lobte sich selbst. Ein *Superfilm*. Der Produktionschef fühlte sich als Schöpfer eines Kunstwerkes. Er war Michelangelo, der mit der Presse telephonierte *Erzherzogliebe läuft an, Großstaffel im Einsatz.* Alexander spürte Sodbrennen. Die Schminke war vom Gesicht gewischt. Er sah wieder käsig aus. Wo mochte Messalina sein? Er hätte sie gern angerufen. Er hätte ihr gern gesagt: »Ich bin müde.

112

Heute abend gibt es kein Fest, keine Gesellschaft. Ich bin müde. Ich will schlafen. Ich muß schlafen. Ich werde schlafen. Verdammt noch mal. Ich werde schlafen!« Am Telephon hätte er es gesagt. Er hätte Messalina gesagt, wie müde, leer und elend er sich fühlte. Am Abend würde er es nicht sagen.

Sie saß in der Bar des Hotels und trank einen Pernod. Pernod, das war so verrucht, das pulverte auf: ›Pernod Paris, Paris die Stadt der Liebe, *Öffentliche Häuser geschlossen, schädigen Frankreichs Ansehen.*‹ Messalina blätterte in ihrem Notizbuch. Sie suchte nach Adressen. Sie brauchte Frauen für den Abend, Mädchen, hübsche Mädchen für ihre Gesellschaft. Daß Emilia kommen würde, war unwahrscheinlich. Philipp würde sie nicht kommen lassen. Auch die kleine Grüne würde er nicht zu ihr bringen, die kleine reizende Amerikanerin mit den grünen Augen. Man mußte aber Mädchen auf dem Fest haben. Wer sollte sich entkleiden? Nur die Epheben? Es gab auch noch Heterosexuelle. Ob man wieder Susanne aufforderte? Immer wieder Susanne? Sie war langweilig. Sie entflammte nicht. Es gab keine Mädchen mehr. Susanne war nur eine dumme Nutte.

›So viele Nutten gibt es‹, dachte Frau Behrend, ›und ausgerechnet auf Carla muß er sich stürzen, und sie muß ja sagen, muß auf ihn 'reinfallen, daß es sie nicht graust, mich würde es grausen, warum ging sie in die Kaserne, warum ging sie zu den Negern? weil sie nicht bei mir bleiben wollte, weil sie's nicht mit anhören konnte wie ich über ihren Vater jammerte, damals jammerte ich noch über sein Verbrechen, sie mußte ihn verteidigen, mußte ihn mit seinem Flitscherl verteidigen, sie hat das von ihm, das Musikerblut, sie sind Zigeuner, nur die Wehrmacht hielt sie in Zucht, sie und ihn, was war er für ein Mann wenn er dem Regiment voranschritt, der Krieg machte ihn schlecht.‹
Es war nicht so schlimm. Die Zeitungen hatten übertrieben. Hier jedenfalls schien der Krieg nicht so schlimm getobt zu haben, und grade von dieser Stadt hatten die Berichterstatter geschrieben, daß die Kriegsfurie sie besonders heimgesucht

habe. Richard, der im Autobus des Flughafens in die Stadt
fuhr, enttäuschte das sich ihm bietende Bild der Zerstörungen. Er dachte ›da bin ich so weit geflogen, gestern war ich
noch in Amerika, heute bin ich in Europa, im Herzen Europas würde der gute Wilhelm sagen, und was seh' ich? kein
Herz seh' ich, ein welkes Licht, ich hab' Glück, daß ich nicht
hierbleiben muß‹. Richard hatte ungeheure Verwüstungen zu
sehen erwartet, mit Trümmern verschüttete Straßen, Bilder,
wie sie gleich nach der deutschen Kapitulation in der Presse
erschienen waren, Aufnahmen, die er als Knabe neugierig
betrachtet und über die sein Vater geweint hatte. Das Stück
Werg, mit dem der Vater sich die Augen gewischt, war mit
Putzöl getränkt gewesen, und die Augenlider waren, verschmiert, wie von Faustschlägen gezeichnet. Richard Kirsch
fuhr durch eine Stadt, die gar nicht so sehr verschieden von
Columbus, Ohio, war, und Wilhelm, der Vater, hatte in Columbus, Ohio, doch gerade den Untergang dieser Stadt be-
klagt. Was war hier untergegangen? Ein paar alte Häuser
waren zusammengebrochen. Sie waren längst untergangsreif
gewesen. Die Lücken im Straßenzug würden sich schließen.
Richard dachte, er möchte hier Baumeister sein; für eine
Weile, und ein amerikanischer Baumeister natürlich. Was
für Hochhäuser würde er ihnen auf die Schutthalden setzen!
Die Gegend würde ein fortschrittlicheres Gesicht bekommen.
Er verließ den Bus und schlenderte durch die Straßen. Er
suchte die Straße, in der Frau Behrend wohnte. Er blickte in
die Schaufenster, er sah reiche Auslagen, *Lebenshaltungs-
index gestiegen*, eine Warenfülle, die ihn überraschte, es
fehlte hier und dort an Reklame, aber sonst sahen die Läden
genau wie die Läden zu Hause aus, ja oft waren sie geräumiger und prächtiger als des Vaters Waffengeschäft in Columbus.
Diese Geschäftsstraße war nun die Grenze, das Grenzland,
das Richard schützen sollte. Von der Höhe, vom Flugzeug sah
alles einfacher, flächiger aus, man dachte in weiten Räumen,
dachte geographisch, geopolitisch, unmenschlich, zog Fronten
durch Erdteile wie einen Bleistiftstrich über eine Landkarte,
doch unten in der Straße, unter den Menschen, die alle etwas
Albernes und Erschreckendes hatten, wie es Richard schien,

lebten sie in einem kranken Ungleichmaß zwischen Trägheit und Hetze, in ihrer Gesamtheit sahen sie arm, im einzelnen doch wieder reich aus, Richard hatte das Gefühl, daß hier verschiedenerlei nicht stimme, in der ganzen Konzeption nicht stimme, und daß diese Menschen für ihn undurchschaubar waren. Wollte er sie schützen? Sie sollten sehen, wie sie mit ihrem europäischen Wirrwarr zurechtkamen. Er wollte Amerika verteidigen. Wenn es sein mußte, würde er Amerika auch in Europa verteidigen. Der alte Reichswehrsoldat Wilhelm Kirsch hatte sich nach zehnjähriger Dienstzeit von Deutschland abgesetzt. Er hatte sich noch rechtzeitig mit seiner Dienstentschädigung über den Ozean zurückziehen können. Nachher kam Hitler, und mit Hitler kam der Krieg. Wilhelm Kirsch wäre ein toter Held oder ein General geworden. Vielleicht wäre er als General von Hitler oder nach dem Kriege von den Alliierten als Kriegsverbrecher gehängt worden. Allen historischen Möglichkeiten, der Ehre und dem Hängen, war Wilhelm durch seine rechtzeitige Auswanderung nach Amerika entrückt. Doch nicht ganz entkommen war er der Schmach. Richard, der seinen Vater von den ersten Schritten an, die taumelnd in den Laden führten, immer mit Waffen hatte hantieren sehen, mit den festen Griffen, den kühlen töten könnenden Läufen der Handfeuerwaffen, Richard hatte es verwundert, als hätte eine Kugel aus einem der Gewehre ihn getroffen, daß der Vater nicht, wie die Väter der Schulgefährten, mit der Armee ins Feld gezogen war, sondern sich als alter Waffenmeister auf einen mit Frontdienstbefreiung verbundenen Fabrikposten setzte. Richard irrte sich: sein Vater war kein Feigling, es war ihm nicht darum gegangen, sich den Strapazen, Leiden und Gefahren des Krieges zu entziehen, auch nicht Gleichgültigkeit gegen das neue erwählte Vaterland ließ ihn in den Staaten bleiben, eher noch Scheu und Zögern, das alte verlassene Vaterland der Geburt anzugreifen, aber der wirkliche Grund, aus dem Wilhelm Kirsch sich dem Krieg versagte, war seine Erziehung in der Reichswehr, war der scharfe Schliff, die Seecktsche Schulung, die Beibringung der glatten, raschen Art, den Feind zu töten, die Wilhelm Kirsch überzeugt hatten, daß alle Gewalt abscheulich und jeder Konflikt besser durch Aussprache, Verhandlung, Kompromißbereitschaft und Versöhnung als durch Pulver zu lösen sei. Amerika war für den ausgewanderten Reichswehrsoldaten Wilhelm Kirsch das Land der Verheißung gewesen, das neue Reich der Friedfertigen, die Stätte der Toleranz und des Verzichtes auf die Gewalt, Wilhelm Kirsch war mit dem Glauben der Pilgerväter in die Neue Welt gereist, und der Krieg, den Amerika führte, mochte er selbst gerecht sein, war eine Erschütterung seines in einer deutschen Kaserne errungenen Glaubens an Vernunft, Verständnis und friedliche Gesinnung, und schließlich zweifelte Wilhelm Kirsch an der Wahrheit der alten Ideale Amerikas. Der alte deutsche Reichswehrsoldat war, eine Sonderlichkeit, die das Leben mit sich brachte, ein mit Handfeuerwaffen handelnder Pazifist geworden, aber Richard, sein in Amerika geborener Sohn, dachte wieder anders über Soldatentum und Krieg, und fast schien es dem Vater, als gleiche sein Sohn den jungen Offizieren der Reichswehr der zwanziger Jahre, und jedenfalls meldete sich Richard, sobald es sein Alter erlaubte, zur amerikanischen Luftwaffe. Wilhelm Kirsch hatte nicht im Krieg gekämpft. Richard Kirsch war bereit, für Amerika zu kämpfen.

Schnakenbach wollte nicht kämpfen. Er lehnte den Krieg als Mittel menschlicher Auseinandersetzungen ab, und er verachtete den Soldatenstand, den er als Überbleibsel barbarischer Zeiten, als einen unwürdigen Atavismus in der fortgeschrittenen Zivilisation betrachtete. Er hatte den Zweiten Weltkrieg still für sich gewonnen und verloren. Er hatte seinen Krieg, den berechtigten, gefährlichen und fintenreichen Krieg gegen die Musterungskommissionen, gewonnen, aber er war invalid aus dem Kampf zurückgekommen. Schnakenbach hatte eine Idee gehabt, eine wissenschaftliche Idee, denn alles richtete sich bei ihm nach wissenschaftlichen Prinzipien, und er wäre vielleicht auch bereit gewesen, wissenschaftlich Krieg zu führen, einen Krieg ohne Soldaten, einen globalen Krieg der Gehirne, deren einsame Träger Todesformeln ausbrüten, sich hinter Schalttafeln setzen und mit einem Finger-

116

druck auf irgendeine Taste in einem fernen Erdteil das Leben vernichten. Schnakenbach war im Zweiten Weltkrieg nicht in die Versuchung gekommen, eine Todestaste nieder zudrücken, und dieser Krieg war eben nicht sein Krieg gewesen, aber er hatte Pillen geschluckt. Es waren Wachhaltepillen, die er schluckte, Pillen, die ihn, in genügender Menge genommen, Tage, Wochen, Monate fast ohne Schlaf verbringen ließen, so daß er endlich durch den dauernden Schlafentzug in einen solchen Zustand des körperlichen Verfalls geraten war, daß ihn selbst ein Militärarzt als untauglich von der Musterung wieder nach Hause schicken mußte. Schnakenbach verfiel nicht dem Kommiß, nicht diesem Atavismus der Menschenentwürdigung, aber er blieb, auch als der Krieg zu Ende war, den Drogen verfallen. Seine Hypophyse, die Nebenniere steuerten verkehrt, die Organe traten gegen die Konkurrenz der Chemie in Streik und streikten beharrlich weiter, als die Musterungskommission aufgelöst und die Gefahr, Soldat zu werden, in Deutschland für eine Weile nicht vorhanden war. Schnakenbach war schlafsüchtig geworden; der Schlaf rächte sich an ihm, ein tiefer Schlaf war über ihn gekommen, er schlief, wo er ging und stand, und er brauchte ungewöhnlich große Dosen von Pervitin und Benzidrin, um für einige Stunden am Tag wenigstens den Zustand des Halbschlummers zu erreichen. Die Belebungsmittel waren rezeptpflichtig, und da Schnakenbach sie nicht mehr ausreichend bekam, bestürmte er Behude um Verschreibungen, oder er versuchte, als begabter Chemiker, sich die Pülverchen herzustellen. Aus seiner Stellung wegen Schlafsucht entlassen, sein weniges Geld für wissenschaftliche Versuche ausgebend, wohnte der verarmte Schnakenbach im Keller des Hauses einer Baronin, einer Patientin von Behude, die, seit sie vor Jahren eine Vorladung zum Arbeitsamt erhalten hatte, an der Vorstellung litt, zum Straßenbahndienst eingezogen zu sein, und die nun jeden Tag in aller Frühe ihre schöne Wohnung verließ und acht Stunden mit einer bestimmten Linie der Straßenbahn sinnlos durch die Stadt fuhr, was sie täglich drei Mark kostete und sie, was schlimmer war, »energvierte«, wie sie zu Behude sagte, den sie um Dienstbefreiungsatteste anging, die er ihr aber nicht ausstellen konnte, da sie ja zu keinem Dienst verpflichtet war. Behude versuchte Straßenbahnfahren auszureden. Er hatte im Leben der Achtder Patientin durch eine Analyse ihrer frühen Kindheit das jährigen inzestuöse, dem Vater, einem Kommandierenden General, geltende und auf einen Trambahnschaffner übertragene Neigungen festgestellt. Aber Behudes Aufdeckung der verschütteten Vergangenheit hatte die Baronin erst einmal ihren imaginären Dienst versäumen lassen, wodurch sie, wie sie Behude erzählte, große Unannehmlichkeiten gehabt hatte. Behude fand Schnakenbach nicht in seinem Keller. Er fand ein ungemachtes, kohlenstaubverschmutztes Lager, er fand des Gewerbelehrers zerrissene Jacken und Hosen auf dem Boden liegen, er sah auf einem Gartentisch die Gläser, Retorten und Kocher der Giftküche stehen, und überall, auf Bett, Boden und Tisch verstreut, fand er Zettel mit chemischen Formeln, chemische Strukturzeichnungen, die wie stark vergrößerte Mikroaufnahmen von Krebsgeschwülsten aussahen, sie hatten etwas Wucherndes, gefährlich Krankes und immer Weiterfressendes, aus Punkten und Kreisen zweigten immer neue Punkte und Kreise ab, Kohlenstoff, Wasserstoff und Stickstoff teilten, vereinten und vermehrten sich in diesen Bildern aus Tintenstrichen und Klecksen und sollten mit Phosphor und Schwefelsäure Schnakenbachs Schlaf bannen und die ersehnte Belebungsdroge geben. Behude dachte, als er die Formelzeichnungen betrachtete, ›so sieht Schnakenbach die Welt, das All, so sieht er sich selbst, alles in seiner Vorstellung ist abstrakt und wächst aus den kleinsten Teilen zu gigantischen Rechnungen‹. Behude legte eine Packung Pervitin auf den Gartentisch. Er hatte ein schlechtes Gewissen. Er schlich sich aus dem Keller wie ein Dieb.

Die Kellnerin räumte den Tisch ab. Frau Behrends Stammsitz im Domcafé war für heute frei. Mutter und Tochter waren gegangen. Sie hatten sich vor der Tür des Cafés im Schatten des Domturms getrennt. Was sie sich vielleicht sagen wollten, war ungesagt geblieben. Flüchtig hatten beide das Verlangen nach gegenseitiger Umarmung gespürt, aber nur kalt hatten sich ihre Hände für eine Sekunde gestreift. Frau Behrend dachte ›du hast es so gewollt, du mußt deinen Weg gehen, laß mich in Frieden‹, und das hieß ›stör mir mein Domcafé nicht, meine Ruhe nicht, meine Bescheidung nicht, meinen Glauben nicht‹, und ihr Glaube war, daß anständige Frauen wie sie irgendwie erhalten werden mußten, daß die Welt niemals so aus den Fugen geraten konnte, daß nicht ihr der Nachmittagsplausch mit Damen ihrer Art als Trostpreis bleibe. Und Carla dachte ›sie weiß nicht, daß es ihre Welt nicht mehr gibt‹. Welche Welt aber gab es? Eine dreckige Welt. Eine ganz und gar gottverlassene Welt. Die Domuhr schlug eine Stunde. Carla mußte sich beeilen. Sie wollte, bevor Washington vom Baseballspiel nach Hause kam, ihre Sachen packen und in die Klinik gehen. Das Kind mußte weg. Washington war wahnsinnig, daß er sie bewegen wollte, sein Kind in die Welt zu setzen. Die andere Welt, die schöne bunte Welt der Magazine, der mechanischen Küchen, der Fernsehapparate und der Wohnung im Hollywoodstil, paßte nicht zu diesem Kind. Aber war es nicht schon gleichgültig? War nicht selbst dieses Kind, seine Geburt oder sein Tod, schon gleichgültig? Carla zweifelte jetzt, ob sie die schöne Traumwelt der amerikanischen Magazine jemals erreichen würde. Es war ein Fehler gewesen, sich mit Washington zu vereinen. Carla war in den falschen Zug gestiegen. Washington war ein guter Kerl, aber er saß leider im falschen Zug. Carla konnte nichts dafür, sie konnte es nicht ändern, daß er im falschen Zug saß. Alle Neger saßen im falschen Zug. Selbst die Leiter der Jazzkapellen saßen im falschen Zug; sie saßen im Luxusabteil des falschen Zuges. Wie dumm war Carla gewesen. Sie hätte auf einen weißen Amerikaner warten sollen. ›Ich hätte auch einen Weißen haben können, auch ein Weißer wäre zufrieden gewesen, hängen die Brüste? sie hängen nicht, sie sind stramm und rund, wie nannte sie der Kerl? Milchäpfel, sind noch Milchäpfel, der Leib ist weiß, etwas zu dick, aber sie lieben volle Schenkel, das Mollige, ich bin mollig, im Bett bin ich immer mollig, macht Spaß, hätt' ich kein Vergnügen haben sollen? was hat man schon? Bauchweh, aber ich hätt' auch einen Weißen bekommen.‹ Carla hätte in den richtigen

Zug steigen können. Es war nie wiedergutzumachen. Nur der Zug der weißen Amerikaner führte in die Traumwelt der Magazinbilder, in die Welt des Wohlstandes, der Sicherheit und des Behagens. Washingtons Amerika war dunkel und schäbig. Es war eine Welt, so dunkel, so schäbig, so dreckig, so von Gott aufgegeben wie die Welt hier. ›Vielleicht sterbe ich‹, dachte Carla. Vielleicht würde es das beste sein zu sterben. Carla drehte sich um, sie schaute zurück über den Platz, blickte noch einmal nach ihrer Mutter aus, doch Frau Behrend hatte feige mit schnellen, das Unheil fliehenden Schritten und ohne sich noch einmal nach der Tochter umzusehen den Domplatz schon verlassen. Aus der Kirche, aus ihren noch nicht wieder eingesetzten Fenstern grollte unter den Händen des übenden Organisten die Orgel, erhob sich das Stabat-mater.

Stormy-weather: die Musik der Kinoorgel wehte, wogte, bebte und rasselte. Sie wehte, wogte, bebte und rasselte aus allen Lautsprechern. Synchron mit den Lautsprechern wehten, wogten, bebten und rasselten die Töne aus dem Musikkoffer, den Josef neben sich auf die Bank gestellt hatte. Er kaute an einem Sandwich. Er kaute schwer an dem dicken vielschichtigen Brot. Er mußte seinen Mund bis zum äußersten aufreißen, um von dem dicken Sandwich etwas abbeißen zu können. Es war ein fader Geschmack. Auf den Schinken hatte man eine süßliche Paste geschmiert. Der Schinken schmeckte wie verdorben. Der süßliche Geschmack störte Josef. Es war, als wäre der Schinken verdorben und man hätte ihn dann parfümiert. Auch die grünen Salatblätter, die man zwischen den Schinken und das Brot gelegt hatte, waren nicht nach Josefs Geschmack. Das Sandwich war wie das Grab einer Schinkensemmel, mit Efeu bepflanzt. Josef würgte mit Widerwillen an dem Brot. Er dachte an seinen Tod. Er aß die fremde, fremdländisch schmeckende Speise nur aus anerzogenem Gehorsam. Er durfte Odysseus, seinen Herrn, nicht beleidigen. Odysseus trank Coca-Cola. Er setzte die Flasche an den Mund und trank sie leer. Er spuckte den letzten Schluck unter die vordere Bank. Er traf genau die untere Leiste der vorderen Bank. Josef hatte sich drücken können. Vor dem Coca-Cola hatte er sich drücken können. Er mochte das neumodische Zeug nicht.

Washington rannte. Er hörte das Abschlagen und Aufklatschen des Balles. Er hörte das Wehen, Wogen, Beben und Rasseln der Kinoorgel. Er hörte Stimmen, die Stimmen der Menge, Stimmen der Sportgemeinde, Rufe, Pfiffe und Gelächter. Er rannte um das Spielfeld. Er keuchte. Er war in Schweiß gebadet. Das Stadion sah mit seinen Tribünen wie eine riesige gerippte Muschel aus. Es war, als ob die Muschel sich schließen, als ob sie ihm für immer den Himmel nehmen, als ob sie sich zusammenpressen und ihn erdrücken wolle. Washington rang nach Atem. Die Kinoorgel schwieg. Der Sprecher am Mikrophon lobte Washington. Die Lautsprecher sprachen die Worte des Reporters mit. Der Reporter sprach aus Odysseus' Koffer. Washingtons Name füllte das Stadion. Er hatte den Lauf gewonnen. Der Name des Siegers stemmte sich gegen die Muschel und hinderte sie am Zuklappen. Für eine Weile hatte Washington die Muschel besiegt. Sie würde nicht zuklappen, sie würde ihn nicht erdrücken, würde ihn in diesem Augenblick nicht fressen. Immer wieder mußte Washington siegen.

›Er ist nicht in Form‹, dachte Heinz. Er sah es Washington an, daß er nicht in Form war. Er dachte ›den nächsten Lauf wird er verlieren, wenn er den nächsten Lauf verliert werden sie ihn fressen‹. Es ärgerte Heinz, daß sie Washington auspfeifen, über ihn lachen und ihn verhöhnen würden. Es konnte jeder mal nicht in Form sein. Waren sie denn in Form? ›Rotzbibben.‹ Er schämte sich. Er wußte nicht recht, warum er sich schämte. Er sagte: »Den nächsten schafft er nicht.« — »Wer schafft ihn nicht?« fragten die Jungens. Sie hatten die Karten für das Stadion vom amerikanisch-deutschen Jugendklub bekommen. Sie hatten den kleinen herrenlosen Hund an seinem Bindfaden mit auf die Tribüne genommen. »Na, der Nigger meiner Mutter«, sagte Heinz, »der Nigger schafft's nicht mehr.«

Richard hatte zum Haus der Frau Behrend gefunden. Er sprach mit der Tochter der Hausbesorgerin. Die Tochter der

121

Hausbesorgerin redete von oben herab mit ihm, von oben herab in aller Tatsächlichkeit, denn sie stand zwei Treppenstufen höher als Richard, aber auch von oben herab im übertragenen Sinn. Richard war nicht der Strahlende, der Erfolgsmensch, der Held, auf den das häßliche Mädchen wartete. Richard war zu Fuß gekommen; die Lieblinge der Götter kamen im Auto. Richard, sie sah es, war ein einfacher Soldat, wenn auch ein Flieger. Die Flieger waren natürlich etwas Besseres als die gewöhnlichen Soldaten, der Ruhm des Ikarus erhöhte sie, aber die Tochter der Hausbesorgerin wußte nichts vom Ikarus. Wenn Richard im Flugzeug auf der Treppe gelandet und mit Blumen im Arm herausgesprungen wäre, dann hätte er vielleicht der erwartete Bräutigam des reizlosen Geschöpfes sein können; doch nein, er hätte der Bräutigam nicht sein können: ihm hätte selbst dann noch das Ritterkreuz gefehlt. Das Mädchen lebte in einer Welt entsetzlicher Standesvorurteile. Sie hatte sich eine Hierarchie der Stände ausgedacht, steifere und strengere Sitten als zu des Kaisers Zeit herrschten in ihrem Kopf, und unüberbrückbar war die Kluft, die den einen Stand vom anderen trennte. Die Vorstellung einer sozialen Leiter mit oben und unten ließ die Tochter der Hausbesorgerin ihre niedrige Stellung im Haus, niedrig nach ihrer Meinung, ertragen, denn um so schöner lockte, was ihr beschieden war, der soziale Aufstieg, den ihr das Horoskop des Abendechos verkündete: gerade ihr würde gelingen, was kaum einem gelang, sie war unten, freilich, aber ein Prinz würde kommen oder ein Chef und sie auf die ihr zugedachte Sprosse von Rang und Ansehen führen. Der Prinz oder der Chef hielten sich aus Schicksalsgründen vorübergehend und vielleicht verkleidet im gesellschaftlichen Unterreich auf, aber sicher würde der Prinz oder der Chef sie in den Glanz des Oberreiches geleiten. Zum Glück wußte die Hausbesorgerstochter, daß sie die Verkleideten gleich erkennen würde; so konnte es keinen Irrtum geben. Richard war kein verkleideter Höhergestellter, sie sah es, er gehörte zu den Leuten unten und mußte so behandelt werden. Alle Amerikaner gehörten zu den geringen Leuten. Sie taten nur manchmal so, als gehörten sie zur besseren Schicht.

Aber wenn sie auch reich sein mochten, die Tochter der Hausbesorgerin durchschaute sie: es waren Leute, die unten standen. Die Amerikaner waren keine richtigen Prinzen, keine richtigen Offiziere, keine richtigen Chefs. Sie glaubten nicht an die Hierarchie: *Demokratischer Gedanke in Deutschland gefestigt.* Das Mädchen schickte Richard mit schnippischer Geste zur Lebensmittelhändlerin. Vielleicht sei Frau Behrend bei der Händlerin. Richard dachte ›was hat die? sie ist so komisch, mag sie uns nicht?‹ Das Mädchen blickte ihm mit starren Augen nach. Sie hatte die starren Augen und die mechanischen Bewegungen einer Puppe. Sie hatte den Mund geöffnet, und ihre Zähne standen etwas vor. Sie glich einer schäbigen, häßlichen Puppe, die jemand auf der Treppe stehengelassen hatte.

Diesmal war Washington nicht schnell genug. Er verlor den Lauf. Er keuchte. Seine Brust hob und senkte sich wie ein auf und nieder gedrückter Blasebalg in einer Schmiede. Er verlor den Lauf. Der Mann am Mikrophon war nicht länger Washingtons Freund. Aus allen Lautsprechern schimpfte der Reporter. Er schimpfte aufgeregt aus dem kleinen Koffer zwischen Josef und Odysseus. Odysseus schleuderte eine Coca-Cola-Flasche auf das Spielfeld. Josef schaute sich blinzelnd ängstlich nach einem Polizisten um. Er wollte nicht, daß Odysseus abgeführt würde. Auf allen Tribünen wurde gejohlt und gepfiffen. ›Jetzt haben sie ihn, jetzt machen sie ihn fertig‹, dachte Heinz. Er sträubte sich dagegen, daß sie Washington verjohlten und ihn fertigmachten. Aber auch er johlte und pfiff. Er heulte mit den Wölfen: »Der Nigger kann nicht mehr. Der Nigger meiner Mutter kann nicht mehr.« Die Kinder lachten. Selbst der kleine herrenlose Hund heulte. Ein dicker Junge sagte: »Ist recht, dem geben sie's!« Heinz dachte ›dir geb' ich's, Rotzbibbe widerliche‹. Er heulte, johlte und pfiff. Es war ein Spiel der Red Stars gegen eine Gastmannschaft. Die Sympathien der Zuschauer waren auf der Seite der Gäste.
Ezra hatte weder für die eine noch für die andere Mannschaft irgendwelche Sympathien. Das Spiel auf dem Baseball-

feld langweilte ihn. Die eine Partei würde siegen. Das war immer so. Immer siegte eine Partei. Aber nach dem Spiel schüttelten sie sich die Hände und gingen zusammen in die Garderoben. Das war langweilig. Man mußte mit seinen wirklichen Feinden kämpfen. Er kniff seine kleine Stirn zusammen. Selbst die Kappe seines kurzgeschorenen roten Haares runzelte sich. Er hatte den Jungen mit dem Hund wiedergesehen, den Jungen und den Hund vom Parkplatz vor dem Central Exchange. Das Problem beschäftigte ihn. Das war kein Spiel, das war Kampf. Er wußte nur immer noch nicht, wie er es machen sollte. Christopher fragte: »Was hast du? Du schaust nicht zu!« — »Ich mag Baseball nicht«, sagte Ezra. Christopher ärgerte sich. Er ging gern zum Baseball. Er hatte sich gefreut, auch in Deutschland ein Spiel sehen zu können. Er hatte geglaubt, Ezra eine Freude zu machen, als er mit ihm ins Stadion ging. Er war verstimmt. Er sagte: »Wenn es dir nicht gefällt, so können wir ja gehen.« Ezra nickte. Er dachte ›so muß es gemacht werden‹. Er sagte: »Kannst du mir zehn Dollar geben?« Christopher wunderte sich, daß Ezra zehn Dollar haben wollte. »Zehn Dollar sind viel Geld«, sagte er, »willst du was kaufen?« — »Ich will das Geld nicht ausgeben«, sagte Ezra. Er blickte nach der Tribünenseite, auf der die Kinder mit dem Hund saßen. Christopher verstand Ezra nicht. Er sagte: »Wenn du das Geld nicht ausgeben willst, warum soll ich es dir geben?« Ezra quälten Kopfschmerzen hinter der kleinen gefurchten Stirn. Wie schwer Christopher alles begriff! Man konnte es ihm nicht erklären! Er sagte: »Ich brauche die zehn Dollar, weil ich doch verlorengehen könnte. Ich könnte mich doch verirren.« Christopher lachte. Er sagte: »Du sorgst dich zuviel. Du sorgst dich genau soviel wie deine Mutter.« Aber dann fand er Ezras Gedanken ganz vernünftig. Er sagte: »Schön. Ich werde dir die zehn Dollar geben.« Sie standen auf und drängten sich durch die Reihe. Ezra stieg noch schnell mit einem Flugzeug auf und ließ eine Bombe auf das Spielfeld fallen. In beiden Mannschaften gab es Verluste. Ezra sah noch einmal zu Heinz und dem Hund hinüber und dachte ›ob er heut' abend kommen wird? es wäre zum Kotzen wenn er nicht käme‹.

»Frau Behrend würde sich freuen«, sagte die Lebensmittel-händlerin. »Wenn Frau Behrend jetzt käme, würde sie sich freuen!« Sie drängte Richard in die Ecke des Ladens, wo, unter Einwickelpapier versteckt, der Sack mit dem schon wieder knappen Zucker stand. Richard fühlte sich auf einmal hungrig und durstig. Er sah zwischen sich und der Händlerin auf einer Platte einen Schinken liegen, und ein Kasten mit Bier stand neben seinen Füßen. Die Luft in Deutschland oder die nach alten Speisen riechende Luft in diesem Laden schien durstig und hungrig zu machen. Richard hätte die Händlerin gerne gebeten, ihm eine Flasche Bier und eine Scheibe von dem Schinken zu verkaufen. Doch die Frau bedrängte ihn zu sehr. Er fühlte sich in der Ladenecke wie gefangen. Es kam ihm vor, als solle er wie der Zucker in Verwahrung genommen und nach Gutdünken oder Wohlwollen ausgegeben werden. Es ärgerte ihn, daß er der sentimentalen Idee seines Vaters gefolgt war und Frau Behrend, eine ferne Verwandte, der man kurz nach dem Kriege Pakete schickte, aufgesucht hatte. Gerade sprach die Händlerin von den Paketen. Sie schilderte die Not der ersten Nachkriegszeit, und dabei beugte sie sich über den Schinken, auf den Richard immer verlangender blickte. »Alles hatten sie uns genommen, rein gar nichts war da«, sagte die Händlerin, »und Neger haben sie uns geschickt, Sie stammen ja auch von Deutschen, Sie werden es verstehen, mit Negern mußten wir uns einlassen, um nicht zu verhungern. Das ist ja der große Kummer von Frau Behrend!« Sie sah Richard erwartungsvoll an. Richard beherrschte die deutsche Sprache nur unvollkommen. Was war hier mit Negern los? In der Luftwaffe hatten sie Neger. Die Neger flogen in denselben Maschinen wie die anderen Flieger. Richard hatte nichts gegen Neger. Sie waren ihm gleichgültig. »Die Tochter«, sagte die Händlerin. Sie senkte ihre Stimme und beugte sich noch weiter zu Richard hinüber. Der Ansatz ihrer Schürze berührte den Fettrand des Schinkens. Richard wußte nichts von einer Tochter der Frau Behrend. Frau Behrend hatte die Tochter in ihren Briefen an Wilhelm Kirsch nicht erwähnt. Richard überlegte, ob Frau Behrend eine Tochter von einem Neger bekommen habe, dem sie sich vor Hunger hatte hingeben müssen. Aber sie war doch zu alt, als daß sie sich hätte für Brot verkaufen können. Hatte Richard noch Appetit auf den Schinken? Er dachte an die Tochter der Frau Behrend und sagte: »Ich hätte Spielsachen mitgebracht.« — »Spielsachen?« Die Händlerin verstand Richard nicht. War dieser junge Mann, in Amerika geboren, aber doch von einem deutschen Vater gezeugt, so amerikanisiert, daß er das Gefühl für Sitte und Anstand verloren hatte? Wollte er sich über die deutsche Not und Verirrung lustig machen? Sie fragte streng: »Für wen Spielsachen? Mit der Tochter verkehren wir nicht mehr.« Sie nahm an, daß auch Richard nicht mit der Tochter von Frau Behrend verkehren würde. Richard dachte ›was geht es mich an? was geht mich die Tochter der Frau Behrend an? es ist, als ob ich in etwas versinke, es ist die Herkunft, das alte Zuhause des Vaters, die hier beheimatete Familie, die Enge, es sind Sümpfe‹. Er riß sich vom Anblick des Schinkens los und befreite sich aus den Umstrickungen dieses Ladens, der eine merkwürdige Mischung aus Not und fetten Speisen, aus Mißgunst, Mangel und Illusionen war. Sein Fuß stieß gegen das Bier. Er sagte, er würde am Abend im Bräuhaus sein, sein Vater habe ihm geraten, dort hinzugehen, Frau Behrend könne ihn dort suchen, wenn sie wolle. Es lag ihm gar nichts daran, Frau Behrend zu sehen — Frau Behrend und ihre Neger-Tochter.

»Es ist kein Bett bestellt. Es ist kein Bett für Sie bestellt worden«, sagte die Schwester. Die Schwester hatte die monotone Stimme einer Schallplatte des Fernsprechdienstes die, wenn man ihre Nummer gewählt hat, immer ein und dieselbe Auskunft wiederholt. »Es ist nichts bestellt. Es ist nichts bekannt«, sagte die Stimme. »Aber Dr. Frahm sagte doch —« Carla war ratlos. »Es muß ein Irrtum sein, Schwester. Dr. Frahm sagte mir, er würde anrufen. — »Es ist nichts bekannt. Dr. Frahm hat nicht angerufen.« Die Schwester hatte das Gesicht einer Steinfigur. Sie sah wie eine Steinmetzarbeit an einem öffentlichen Brunnen aus. Carla stand mit einem kleinen Koffer im Aufnahmeraum der Schulteschen

Klinik. Im Koffer war Wäsche, war ein Gummibeutel mit Kosmetika, waren die neuesten amerikanischen Magazine; die bunten Bildermagazine, die das häusliche Glück der Holly-woodschauspieler beschrieben. Mit dem Glück aus Holly-wood ausgerüstet, war Carla bereit, sich das Kind nehmen zu lassen, das Kind des schwarzen Freundes, des Freundfein-des aus dem dunklen Amerika, töten zu lassen. »Es muß ein Bett für mich bestellt sein. Dr. Frahm versprach es. Ich soll operiert werden. Es ist dringend«, sagte sie. »Es ist nichts bestellt worden. Es ist kein Bett bestellt.« Die Steinfigur würde höchstens durch ein Erdbeben zu erschüttern sein, und nur auf die Weisung eines Arztes würde sie den Weg zu dem Abtreibungsbett freigeben. »Ich werde auf Dr. Frahm war-ten«, sagte Carla. »Ich sage Ihnen doch, Schwester, es ist ein Irrtum.« Sie hätte weinen mögen. Sie hätte der Schwester von den vielen Geschenken erzählen mögen, die sie Dr. Frahm in der Zeit, als es nichts gab, keinen Kaffee, keinen Schnaps, keine Zigaretten, gebracht hatte. Sie setzte sich auf eine har-te Bank. Die Bank war hart wie eine Armesünderbank. Die Schwester bediente das Telephon und sprach genau wie eine Schallplatte der Post: »Bedauere, es ist nichts frei. Bedauere, es ist kein Bett frei.« Monoton, gleichgültig, mechanisch, fertigte die Schwester die unsichtbaren Hilfesuchenden ab. Die Betten dieser Klinik schienen sehr begehrt zu sein.

Josef schlief. Er war im Sitzen eingeschlafen. Er war im Sit-zen auf der Tribüne des Stadions eingeschlafen, aber es war ihm, als schlafe er in einem Bett. Er war harte Betten ge-wohnt, aber dies war ein Spitalbett, in dem er schlief, ein Bett in einem Armenspital, ein besonders hartes Bett, sein Sterbebett. Es war das Ende seiner Lebensreise. Der im Sta-dion und im Dienst, im Dienstmannsdienst, im Dienst bei einem fremden aus fremder Ferne hergereisten Herrn ein-geschlafene Josef, umgeben vom Lautsprecherschwall eines sinnlosen Rasenspiels, sinnlos angesprochen von demselben Lärm und Schwall, der leiser und an ihn persönlich mit einer sinnlosen Botschaft gerichtet noch einmal aus dem kleinen Koffer, den er heute zu tragen und zu bewahren hatte, drang, der schlafende Josef wußte, daß dies sein letzter Dienst gewesen war, der Transport dieses Köfferchens, das Tragen des kleinen Musikkoffers, ein leichter, ein eigentlich amüsanter Dienst bei einem großen und freigebigen, wenn auch schwarzen Herrn. Josef wußte, daß er sterben würde. Er wußte, daß er auf diesem Spitalbett sterben würde. Wie konnte es auch anders sein, als daß er am Ende seines Lebensweges im Armenspital sterben würde? War er vorbereitet zu gehen, gerüstet, die große Reise anzutreten? Er dachte ›Gott wird mir verzeihen, er wird mir die kleinen Listen des Fremdenverkehrs vergeben, die Fremden kommen ja her, damit man sie ein wenig betrüge, damit man sie ein wenig weiterführe, als sie geführt werden wollen‹. Es gab sonderbare Schwestern in diesem Spital. Sie gingen in Baseballtracht umher und hielten Schläger in der Hand. War Gott doch böse mit Josef? Sollte Josef geschlagen werden? An der Pforte des Spitals stand Odysseus. Aber es war nicht der freundliche, freigebige Odysseus der Stadtwege. Es war der Odysseus vom Domturm, ein gefährlicher und zu fürchtender Teufel. Er war eins mit der Teufelsfratze des Turmvorsprungs geworden, der Teufelsfratze, auf die er seinen Namen und seine Herkunft geschrieben hatte; ein schwarzer Teufel war Odysseus, wirklich, ein böser schwarzer Teufel; er war nichts als ein ganz gewöhnlicher fürchterlicher Teufel. Was wollte der Teufel von Josef? War Josef nicht immer brav gewesen, bis auf die kleinen zum Gewerbe gehörenden Listen des Fremdenverkehrs? Hatte er nicht jedermanns Koffer getragen? War er nicht in den Krieg gezogen? Oder war doch gerade das In-den-Krieg-Ziehen Sünde gewesen? War die Pflichterfüllung Sünde gewesen? Die Pflicht Sünde? die Pflicht, von der alle redeten, schrieben, schrien und sie verherrlichten? Hatte man ihm nun die Pflicht angekreidet, stand sie auf der Tafel bei Gott angekreidet, wie nicht bezahltes Bier auf der Tafel des Wirtes? Es war wahr! Josef hatte es immer gequält. Insgeheim hatte es ihn gequält. Er hatte nicht gern daran gedacht: er hatte getötet, er hatte Menschen getötet, er hatte Reisende getötet; er hatte sie getötet am Chemin-des-Dames und im Argonnerwald. Es waren die einzigen Ausflugsziele seines

Lebens gewesen, Chemin-des-Dames, Argonnerwald, keine schönen Gegenden, und dorthin war man ausgeflogen, um zu töten und um getötet zu werden. ›Herr, was sollte ich tun? was konnte ich tun, Herr.‹ War es gerecht, daß er nun für diese angekreidete und nie gestrichene Schuld des erzwungenen Tötens dem Teufel übergeben wurde, dem schwarzen Teufel Odysseus? ›He! He! Holla!‹ Schon wurde er geschlagen. Schon schlug der Teufel zu. Josef schrie. Sein Schrei ging in anderen Schreien unter. Er wurde auf die Schulter geschlagen. Er schreckte auf. Er schreckte ins Leben zurück. Odysseus der Teufel, Odysseus der Freundliche, König Odysseus der freundliche Teufel schlug Josef auf die Schulter. Dann sprang Odysseus auf die Tribünenbank. Er hielt eine Coca-Cola-Flasche wie eine wurfbereite Handgranate. Die Lautsprecher brüllten. Das Stadion johlte, pfiff, trampelte, schrie. Die Stimme des Reporters drang heiser aus dem kleinen Radiokoffer. Die Red Stars hatten gesiegt.

Er hatte gesiegt. Washington hatte gesiegt. Er hatte die meisten Läufe gewonnen. Er hatte den Sieg für die Red Stars aus seinen Lungen geholt. Die Muschel klappte nicht zu. Noch klappte die Muschel nicht zu. Vielleicht würde die Muschel nie über Washington zusammenklappen, nie ihm den Himmel nehmen. Das Stadion fraß ihn nicht. Washington war der Held der Tribünen. Sie riefen seinen Namen. Der Radiosprecher hatte sich mit Washington versöhnt. Washington war wieder der Freund des Sprechers. Alle jubelten Washington zu. Er keuchte. Er war frei. Er war ein freier Bürger der Vereinigten Staaten. Es gab keine Diskriminierung. Wie er schwitzte! Er würde immer weiter laufen. Er würde immer weiter und immer schneller um das Spielfeld laufen. Der Lauf machte frei, der Lauf führte ins Leben. Der Lauf schuf Platz für Washington in der Welt. Er schuf Platz für Carla. Er schuf Platz für ein Kind. Wenn Washington nur immer ordentlich laufen, immer schneller laufen würde, hätten sie alle Platz in der Welt.

»War doch in Form.« — »Natürlich war er in Form.« — »War doch in Form, der Nigger.« — »Sag nicht Nigger.« — »Ich sag', daß er in Form war.« — »Er war großartig in

Form.« — »Du hast gesagt, er wär' nicht.« — »Ich hab'
gesagt, er wär'. Washington ist immer in Form.« — »Du
hast gesagt, der Nigger deiner Mutter wär' nicht.« — »Halt's
Maul, Depp.« — »Wetten? Du hast gesagt.« — »Ich sag',
halt's Maul, Lump, krummer.« Sie prügelten sich am Ausgang des Stadions. Heinz schlug sich für Washington. Er
hatte nie gesagt, daß Washington nicht in Form sei. Washington war großartig in Form. Er war überhaupt großartig.
Schorschi, Bene, Kare und Sepp umstanden die Kinder, die
sich prügelten. Sie sahen zu, wie sich die Kinder ins Gesicht
schlugen. »Gib's ihm!« rief Bene. Heinz hörte auf zu schlagen. »Wegen dir nicht, Strizzi.« Er spuckte Blut aus. Er
spuckte es Bene vor die Füße. Bene hob die Hand. »Laß ihn«,
sagte Schorschi. »Wirst dich aufregen! Laß ihn, den Deppen.« — »Selber 'n Depp«, schrie Heinz. Doch er wich etwas
zurück. »Das Spiel war fad«, sagte Sepp. Er gähnte. Die
Burschen hatten die Karten vom amerikanisch-deutschen Jugendklub bekommen. Die Karten hatten sie nichts gekostet.
— »Was machen wir jetzt?« fragte Kare. »Weiß nicht«,
sagte Schorschi. »Weißt du's?« fragte er Sepp. »Nee. Weiß
nicht.« — »Kino?« meinte Kare. »Ich kenn' schon alles«,
sagte Schorschi. Er kannte alle laufenden Kriminalfilme und
Wildweststreifen. »Mit'm Kino ist nichts.« — »Wenn's schon
Abend wäre«, sagte Bene. »Wenn's schon Abend wäre«,
echoten die andern. Sie setzten irgendwelche Hoffnungen auf
den Abend. Sie zogen, nach vorne übergebeugt, die Hände
in den Jackentaschen, die Ellbogen nach außen gestemmt,
mit müden Schultern, wie nach schwerer Arbeit, aus dem Stadion. Die goldene Horde. »Wo 's der Köter?« schrie Heinz.
Während er sich prügelte, hatte Heinz den Bindfaden losgelassen. Der herrenlose kleine Hund war weggelaufen. Er
war im Gedränge verschwunden. »Verdammt«, sagte Heinz,
»ich brauch' den Köter heut' abend.« Er wandte sich wütend
an seine Gefährten. »Ihr hättet auch aufpassen können, ihr
Rotzbibben. Der Köter war zehn Dollar wert!« — »Hättest
selber aufpassen können, Niggerbankert, dreckiger.« Sie prügelten sich wieder.
Washington stand unter der Brause in den Duschräumen

130

des Stadions. Der kalte Strahl ernüchterte ihn. Sein Herz zuckte. Für einen Augenblick blieb ihm die Luft weg. Scharfer Schweiß spülte mit dem Wasser von ihm 'runter. Er war noch gut in Form. Sein Körper war noch gut in Form. Er reckte die Muskeln, hob seine Brust, Muskeln und Brust waren in Ordnung. Er befühlte seine Geschlechtsteile. Sie waren gut und in Ordnung. Aber das Herz? Aber die Atmung? Sie machten ihm zu schaffen. Sie waren nicht in Ordnung. Und dann der Rheumatismus! Vielleicht würde er doch nicht mehr lange aktiv sein können. Auf dem Sportplatz würde er nicht mehr lange aktiv sein können. Zu Haus und im Bett würde er noch lange aktiv sein. Was konnte er tun? Was konnte er für sich, für Carla, für das Kind tun, und vielleicht auch für den kleinen Jungen, den Heinz? Er hatte genug gebraust. Er trocknete sich ab. Er konnte den Dienst quittieren, die horizontblaue Limousine verkaufen, noch ein Jahr als Sportsmann arbeiten und dann vielleicht in Paris ein Lokal aufmachen. In Paris hatte man keine Vorurteile. Er konnte in Paris sein Lokal aufmachen: Washington's Inn. Er mußte mit Carla reden. Er konnte mit Carla in Paris leben, ohne daß sie mit jemand wegen ihres Lebens Differenzen kriegen würden. Sie konnten in Paris das Lokal aufmachen, sie konnten sein Schild 'raushängen, konnten es mit bunten Glühbirnen beleuchten, sein Schild *niemand ist unerwünscht*. In Paris würden sie glücklich sein; sie würden alle glücklich sein. Washington pfiff ein Lied. Er war glücklich. Er verließ pfeifend den Duschraum.

Dr. Frahm wusch sich. Er stand im Waschraum der Schulteschen Klinik und wusch sich die Hände. ›In Unschuld alter Pontius Pilatus ein schönes Gefühl‹, er wusch die Hände mit einer guten Seife und schrubbte die Finger mit einer scharfen Bürste. Er fuhr mit den Borsten der Bürste unter die Nägel der Finger. Er dachte ›Hauptsache keine Infektion‹, er dachte ›muß mir schon wieder die Nägel schneiden, Semmelweis, den verfilmen sie nun auch, hab's in der Zeitung gelesen, ob sie eine Metritis zeigen? wär' doch ganz schön, in Großaufnahme, könnt' abschrecken, könnt' von allem möglichen abschrecken, mein Leben wird niemand verfilmen, ist mir auch recht‹. Er sagte: »Es geht nicht. Tut mir leid, Frau Carla, es ist nicht zu machen.« Carla hielt sich neben ihm, sie stand neben dem Becken, über dem er sich unter dem kräftigen Strahl des aus dem Nickelhahn fließenden Wassers die Hände schrubbte. Carla blickte auf den Nickelhahn, sie blickte auf das Wasser, sie blickte auf den Seifenschaum, auf die von der Seife, von der Bürste und von dem warmen Wasser krebsroten Hände des Arztes. Sie dachte ›Metzgerhände, richtige Metzgerhände‹. Sie sagte: »Das können Sie doch nicht machen, Herr Doktor.« Ihre Stimme klang unsicher und gepreßt. Der Arzt sagte: »Ihnen fehlt nichts. Sie sind schwanger. Wahrscheinlich im dritten Monat. Das ist alles.« Carla fühlte, wie ihr übel wurde. Es war die widerliche würgende Übelkeit der Schwangeren. Sie dachte ›warum kommen wir so zur Welt?‹ Sie hätte sich den Leib schlagen mögen, diesen wieder anschwellenden, wie ein Kürbis wachsenden Leib. Sie dachte ›ich muß mit ihm reden, ich muß doch mit ihm reden, aber ich kann jetzt nicht mit ihm reden‹. Sie sagte: »In Ihrer Praxis sagten Sie doch, ich solle kommen.« Der Arzt sagte: »Ich habe gar nichts gesagt. Sehen Sie, der Vater will das Kind haben. Ich kann da gar nichts machen.« Sie dachte ›er war hier, der schwarze Schuft war hier, er hat mir den Arzt vermiest, jetzt will der Frahm nicht mehr, jetzt will er nicht mehr und was hab' ich ihm alles gegeben‹. Es reute sie, daß sie dem Arzt so viel Kaffee, Zigaretten und Schnaps gegeben hatte. Ihr wurde immer übler. Sie mußte sich am Becken festhalten. Sie dachte ›ich muß mich übergeben, ich kotz' ihm über seine Hände, über seine widerlichen roten Metzgerhände, wo diese Hände einem überall hinlangen, immer kurzgeschnittene Fingernägel, langen einem direkt ins Leben 'rein‹. Sie sagte: »Ich will aber nicht! Verstehen Sie, ich will nicht!« Sie würgte und brach in Tränen aus. ›Ihr wird gleich schlecht werden‹, dachte Frahm. ›Sie sieht käsig aus.‹ Er schob ihr einen Stuhl hin. »Setzen Sie sich!« Er dachte ›hoffentlich wird sie nicht auch noch hysterisch, würd' mich schön in die Nesseln setzen wenn ich ihr's wegmache‹. Da er den Stuhl angefaßt hatte, mußte er sich noch einmal die Hände einseifen. ›Werd' ihr mal zureden‹, dachte er, ›hilft bei den Weibern immer, weinen sich aus und nachher sind sie glückliche Mütter.‹ Er sagte: »Nun seien Sie doch vernünftig. Ihr Freund ist ein guter Kerl. Ich sag' Ihnen, der wird ein prima Vater. Der wird für Sie und für das Kind sorgen. Passen Sie nur auf, was das für ein hübsches Kind gibt. Verständigen Sie mich nur rechtzeitig; ich mach' Ihnen die Geburt. Wir machen's schmerzlos. Sie spüren nichts, und nachher haben Sie das Baby.« — ›Ich werd's ihr an die Brust legen‹, dachte er, ›hoffentlich wird sie's liebhaben, sieht nicht so aus, armes Wesen, noch im Dunkeln und schon gehaßt, aber wenn der Vater drauf besteht, was kann ich tun? der Vater müßte das Leben doch kennen.‹ Sie dachte ›Washington dieser Schuft, Frahm dieser Schuft, das haben die beiden Schufte sich so ausgedacht, ich kann dabei draufgehen‹. Sie sagte: »Ich geh' zu irgendwem.« Sie dachte ›zu wem? Frau Welz kennt sicher jemand, die Huren kennen sicher jemand, ich hätte den Huren die Zigaretten und den Kaffee geben sollen‹. — »Das werden Sie nicht tun«, sagte Frahm. »Nun machen Sie Schluß, Frau Carla. Das ist viel gefährlicher, als Sie denken. Nachher kann Ihnen niemand mehr helfen. Meinen Sie, ich schrubb' mir die Pfoten zum Vergnügen? Oder weil mich ekelt? Mich ekelt schon lange nicht mehr.« Er wurde allmählich schlechter Laune. Die Frau hielt ihn auf; er konnte ihr nicht helfen. Sie dachte ›ich kotz' ihm doch noch über seine Hände, da hätt' er was Feines, hätt' was Feines auf seinen Metzgerhänden, da könnt' er schrubben‹. — »Ist alles nicht so tragisch«, sagte Frahm. ›Es ist der Tod‹, dachte Carla.

›Es ist entsetzlich‹, dachte Frau Behrend. Was sie für ein Pech hatte! Da war sie ausgegangen, um im Domcafé friedlich gemütlich mit den Damen zu plauschen, da war sie von der verlorenen Tochter gestört und aufgeregt worden, kein friedlich gemütlicher Plausch hatte sich ergeben, nur Schande und Verlorensein, Schande der Zeit und Verlorensein in Unordnung, Irrwegen und moralischen Abgründen, und während ihr so Unangenehmes widerfuhr und die Schande sie streifte — hätte sie nicht zu Hause bleiben können? in der

Mansarde wäre es friedlich gemütlicher gewesen, in die Mansarde wäre Carla nicht gekommen –, war Besuch aus Amerika dagewesen, ein Verwandter, der Sohn vom Wilhelm, der ihr Pakete geschickt hatte. Was war es für ein Pech! Die Lebensmittelhändlerin erzählte es ihr. Sie hatte Frau Behrend in den Laden gewinkt. Der junge Kirsch war dagewesen. Er hatte von den Paketen gesprochen. Und die Händlerin, das klatschsüchtige mißgünstige Weib – oh, Frau Behrend sah es ihr an, sie kannte sich aus –, die hatte natürlich alles ausgeschwätzt, hatte von Carla erzählt und von ihrem Neger, hatte sicher alles erzählt, was Frau Behrend ihr erzählt hatte, und dabei waren sie drüben in Amerika so streng mit den Negern, *Rassenschande, arischer Nachweis,* ob Neger oder Jude, es war dasselbe, daß Carla das tun mußte, nie war so etwas vorgekommen in ihrer Familie, der Ariernachweis war lückenlos gewesen, und nun diese Schande! »Er erwartet Sie im Bräuhaus«, sagte die Händlerin. Im Bräuhaus? Das war doch Ausrede, Flucht und Abwendung. Der junge Kirsch kam von Amerika gereist, um Frau Behrend zu besuchen, um die deutsche Verwandte zu sehen, und dann bestellte er sie ins Bräuhaus. Das stimmte doch nicht! Die Händlerin wußte es! Sie hatte ihr den reichen amerikanischen Verwandten nicht gegönnt. Alle Amerikaner waren reich. Alle weißen Amerikaner waren reich. Die Händlerin hatte ihr schon die Lebensmittelpakete nicht gegönnt. Der junge Kirsch war sicher schon abgereist, war enttäuscht zurückgereist in den Reichtum und in die Anständigkeit Amerikas. Plötzlich gab Frau Behrend Carla die Schuld am Verschwinden des jungen Kirsch. Der junge Kirsch war vor der Unmoral geflohen, er war davongelaufen vor der Schande und der Verkommenheit. Er hatte sich von Carlas Verkommenheit und Schande zurückgezogen. Er hatte sich mit dem Reichtum Amerikas von der alten in Schande und Verkommenheit gesunkenen Familie in Deutschland losgesagt. Carla war schuld; sie allein war schuld. Die Händlerin hatte recht getan, als sie es erzählte. Die Händlerin war eine brave Frau. Die Händlerin gehörte zu den anständigen Leuten. Frau Behrend würde es auch erzählt haben, wenn sie eine solche Schande von jemandem gewußt hätte. Sie beugte sich weit über den Ladentisch. Ihre Brust streifte die Käseglocke, unter der ein Mainzer Handkäse langsam zerfloß. Frau Behrend flüsterte: »Sie haben es ihm gesagt?« — »Was denn?« fragte die Händlerin. Sie stemmte die Arme auf und blickte Frau Behrend herausfordernd an. Sie dachte ›paß auf, daß du bei mir noch deinen Zucker kriegst‹. Frau Behrend wisperte: »Das mit Carla.« Die Händlerin richtete ihren strengen entrüsteten Blick auf Frau Behrend, den Blick, mit dem sie schon viele Kunden gebändigt hatte, arme Kunden, Markenkunden, Normalverbraucher. ›Denkt ja nicht es könnte nicht wiederkommen, *Bauernverband gegen neue Bewirtschaftung, Gewerkschaften erwägen Kontrolle der wichtigsten Nahrungsmittel.*‹ Die Händlerin sagte: »Was meinen Sie, Frau Behrend, wo werd' ich denn!« Frau Behrend richtete sich wieder auf. Sie dachte ›sie hat es ihm erzählt, natürlich hat sie es ihm erzählt‹. Die Händlerin lüftete die Käseglocke; die Zersetzung war schon fortgeschritten; ein Fäulnisgestank erhob sich.

Philipp dachte an die Oderbrücke. Es war eine Brücke unter Glas. Der Zug fuhr über die Brücke wie durch einen gläsernen Tunnel. Die Reisenden erbleichten. Das Licht fiel wie durch Milch gefiltert in den Tunnel; aus der Sonne wurde ein blasser Mond. Philipp rief: »Jetzt sind wir unter der Käseglocke!« Philipps Mutter seufzte: »Wir sind wieder im Osten.« Die Brücke über die Oder war für Philipps Mutter der Übergang vom Westen zum Osten. Sie haßte den Osten. Sie seufzte, weil sie im Osten leben mußte, fern vom Glanz der Hauptstadt oder von den Festen des südlich-westlichen Faschings. Für Philipp bedeutete der Osten das Kinderland; er bedeutete Winterfreuden, die Katze am Ofen, Bratäpfel im Rohr; er bedeutete Frieden, er bedeutete Schnee, er bedeutete schönen, sanften, stillen, kalten Schnee vor dem Fenster. Philipp liebte den Winter. Dr. Behude strengte sich an, eine Glocke aus Optimismus und Sommerfreuden über Philipp zu bauen. ›Es wird ihm nie gelingen mich zurückzuführen, es wird ihm nicht gelingen mich zu ändern.‹ Philipp lag auf dem Patientenbett in Behudes verdunkeltem Behandlungszimmer. Er fuhr immer wieder über die Oder. Immer wieder saß er in einem Zug unter der Glocke der Brücke in einem bleichen verwandelten Licht. Seine Mutter weinte, aber Philipp fuhr in sein Kinderland, er reiste der Kälte, dem Frieden, dem Schnee entgegen. Behude sagte: »Es ist ein schöner Sommertag. Sie haben Urlaub. Sie liegen auf einer Wiese. Sie haben nichts zu tun. Sie sind ganz entspannt.« Behude stand im verdunkelten Zimmer wie eine sanfte Traumfigur über den liegenden Philipp gebeugt. Die Traumfigur hatte ihre Hand sanft auf Philipps Stirn gelegt. Philipp lag auf dem Bett des Arztes in einer Anspannung von Lachlust und Gereiztheit. Da strengte sich der liebe gute Behude so an, verbrauchte sein bißchen Kraft und dachte sich Ferien aus. Philipp machte sich nichts aus schönen Sommertagen. Er hatte keinen Urlaub. Er hatte noch nie in seinem Leben Urlaub gehabt. Das Leben beurlaubte Philipp nie. Man konnte es so sehen. Immer wollte Philipp etwas tun. Er dachte immer an eine große Arbeit, die er beginnen und die ihn vollkommen erschöpfen würde. Er bereitete sich in Gedanken auf diese große Arbeit vor, die ihn anzog und erschreckte. Er konnte mit Recht sagen, die Arbeit lasse ihn nicht los; sie quälte und beglückte ihn, wo er ging und wo er stand und selbst wenn er schlief; er fühlte sich zu dieser Arbeit aufgerufen; aber er tat nie oder nur sehr selten wirklich etwas; er versuchte es nicht einmal. Und so betrachtet, war sein Leben bisher ein einziger langer Urlaub gewesen, ein schlecht verbrachter Urlaub, ein Urlaub bei schlechtem Wetter, in schlechten Unterkünften, in schlechter Gesellschaft, ein Urlaub mit zu wenig Geld. »Sie liegen auf einer Wiese −«. Er lag auf keiner Wiese. Er lag auf dem Patientenbett bei Behude. Er war nicht verrückt. Wie viele Irre, wie viele Hysteriker und Neurotiker mochten schon vor ihm auf diesem Entspannungsbett gelegen haben? Immer hatte Behude seinen Patienten schöne Urlaubstage vorgeträumt: Urlaub vom Wahn, Urlaub von der Einbildung, Urlaub von der Angst, Urlaub von der Sucht, Urlaub von den Konflikten. Philipp dachte ›soll ich träumen? ich träume nicht Behudes Traum, Behude sucht auf dem Grunde unseres Seins einen normalen

136

Angestellten zu finden, ich hasse Wiesen, warum soll ich auf einer Wiese liegen? ich liege nie auf einer Wiese, die Natur ist mir unheimlich, die Natur beunruhigt, ein Gewitter beunruhigt mit dem Wechsel der elektrischen Spannung auf der Haut und in den Nerven, es gibt nichts Böseres als die Natur, nur der Schnee ist schön, der leise der freundliche der sanft fallende Schnee«. Behude sagte: »Sie sind nun völlig entspannt. Sie ruhen aus. Sie sind glücklich. Keine Sorgen können Sie erreichen. Keine schweren Gedanken belasten Sie. Sie fühlen sich richtig wohl. Sie schlummern. Sie träumen. Sie träumen nur angenehme Träume.« Behude zog sich auf Zehenspitzen von Philipp zurück. Er ging in das nicht abgedunkelte Nebenzimmer, in das Zimmer der von Behude nur ungern angewandten, der gröberen psychiatrischen Methoden. Schalttafeln und Elektrisiermaschinen hätten hier Emilia erschreckt, die eine entsetzliche Furcht vor Ärzten hatte und sie alle für Sadisten hielt. Behude setzte sich an seinen Schreibtisch und nahm Philipps Blatt aus der Patientenkartei. Er dachte an Emilia. Er dachte ›sie sind kein normales Ehepaar aber sie sind doch ein Ehepaar, ich halte ihre Ehe sogar für ganz unlöslich obwohl sie zunächst betrachtet mehr eine Perversität als eine Ehe ist, von Philipp und von Emilia war es pervers sich auf eine Ehe einzulassen, aber grade daß sie beide nicht für eine Ehe taugen kittet sie zusammen, ich möchte sie gern zusammen psychotherapeutisch beeinflussen, gemeinsame Heilung des einen durch den andern, aber wozu? wovon will ich sie heilen? sie sind ja so wie sie sind glücklich, wenn ich sie geheilt hätte würde Philipp eine Stellung an einer Zeitung annehmen und Emilia würde mit andern Männern schlafen, lohnte das die Behandlung? ich müßte mehr Sport treiben, ich denke zuviel an Emilias infantile Reize, mit mir wird sie nicht schlafen, bis sie geheilt ist schläft sie nur mit Philipp, Emilia und Philipp leisten sich die Perversität einer normalen Ehe mit Eifersucht Bindung und Treue‹.

Emilia erkannte Edwin gleich. Sie wußte, daß dieser Mann mit dem schönen schwarzen Hut, der etwas von einem alten

Lord an sich hatte, etwas von einem alten Geier und etwas von einem alten Zuhälter, einer von Philipps Dichtern war. Sie erinnerte sich dann an eine Photographie Edwins, die Philipp eine Zeitlang an seinem Arbeitsplatz über dem Stoß des weißen unbeschriebenen Papiers an die Wand geheftet hatte. Emilia dachte ›das ist also Edwin der große preisgekrönte Schriftsteller, so einer wie Edwin möchte Philipp werden, vielleicht wird er es, ich hoffe und ich fürchte es, wird Philipp dann wie Edwin aussehen? so alt? so vornehm? ich glaube er wird weniger vornehm aussehen, er wird weniger wie ein Lord und auch weniger wie ein Geier aussehen, wie ein alter Zuhälter wird er vielleicht aussehen, früher sahen die Dichter anders aus, ich möchte nicht daß Philipp Erfolg hat, wenn er Erfolg hätte, könnte er mich verlassen, ich möchte aber doch daß er Erfolg hätte, er müßte so viel Erfolg haben daß wir wegfahren könnten und immer Geld hätten, wenn wir aber auf diese Weise zu Geld kämen hätte Philipp das Geld, ich möchte nicht daß Philipp das Geld hat, ich möchte das Geld haben‹. Emilia kannte sich ganz gut. Sie wußte, daß sie Philipp, wenn es ihr doch noch gelänge, eins ihrer Häuser zu verkaufen, daß sie dann Philipp ein reichliches Taschengeld geben, daß sie ihn aber immer bei seinen verzweifelten Versuchen, zu arbeiten und das lange geplante Buch zu schreiben, stören würde. ›Ich würde vor keiner Gemeinheit zurückschrecken, ich würde so schlimm wie noch nie sein, ich würde ihm keine ruhige Stunde lassen, der arme Philipp, er ist so gut‹. Oft überfiel sie Rührung, wenn sie an Philipp dachte. Sie überlegte, ob sie versuchen sollte, Edwin kennenzulernen. Es war eine Gelegenheit, die sich Messalina nicht hätte entgehen lassen. ›Sie hätte versucht ihn auf ihre Party zu schleppen, armer Edwin‹, Emilia würde Edwin auf kein Fest führen. Aber sie dachte, daß es Philipp verblüffen würde, wenn sie ihm erzählen könnte, daß sie Edwin kennengelernt hätte. Edwin kramte im Laden von Frau de Voss unter den Antiquitäten. Er betrachtete Miniaturen. Er hatte feine lange, am Ansatz des Gelenks stark behaarte Hände. Er betrachtete die Miniaturen durch eine Lupe, was ihm noch mehr das Gesicht eines Geiers gab. Frau de Voss zeigte

Edwin eine Rosenholzmadonna. Die Madonna hatte Philipp gehört. Emilia hatte sie Frau de Voss verkauft. Edwin betrachtete die Madonna durch die Lupe. Er fragte nach dem Preis der kleinen Madonna. Frau de Voss flüsterte den Preis. Emilia sollte den Preis nicht hören. ›Sie wird wahnsinnig aufgeschlagen haben‹, dachte Emilia. Edwin stellte die schöne Rosenholzplastik wieder auf den Tisch. Emilia dachte ›er ist geizig‹. Frau de Voss wandte sich, von Edwin enttäuscht, an Emilia: »Was bringen Sie, Kindchen?« Sie nannte Emilia immer Kindchen. Frau de Voss begegnete Kunden, die etwas verkaufen wollten, mit der Herablassung einer früheren Hofdame und der Strenge einer Lehrerin. Emilia stotterte etwas. Sie schämte sich, vor Edwin das lächerliche schottische Plaid zu öffnen. Dann dachte sie ›warum schäm' ich mich? wenn er mehr Geld hat als Philipp hat er eben Glück gehabt‹. Sie reichte Frau de Voss eine Tasse. Es war eine Tasse der Berliner Manufaktur. Die Tasse war innen vergoldet und zeigte außen ein Miniaturbildnis Friedrichs des Großen. Frau de Voss nahm die Tasse und stellte sie auf ihren Schreibsekretär. Emilia überlegte ›jetzt handelt sie nicht mit mir, sie muß jetzt ihr freundliches Gesicht zeigen weil Edwin da ist, erst nachher wird sie mir ihr wahres Gesicht zeigen‹. Edwin fand unter den Antiquitäten nichts, was ihn interessiert hätte. Alles in diesem Laden war zweitrangig. Die kleine Madonna war zu teuer. Edwin kannte die Preise. Er war kein Sammler, aber hin und wieder kaufte er eine Altertümlichkeit, die ihm gefiel. Er war aus Langeweile in den Laden der Frau de Voss gekommen. Er hatte sich in dieser Stadt plötzlich gelangweilt. Wenn man am Nachmittag durch ihre Straßen ging, war die Stadt weder besonders traditionsreich noch abgründig. Sie war gewöhnlich, eine Stadt mit gewöhnlichen Menschen. Vielleicht würde Edwin den Nachmittag in dieser Stadt in seinem Tagebuch beschreiben. Das Buch sollte nach seinem Tode erscheinen. Es sollte die Wahrheit enthalten. Im Licht der Wahrheit würde der Nachmittag in dieser Stadt nicht mehr gewöhnlich sein. Edwin nahm Emilias Tasse in die Hand. Er betrachtete das Bild Friedrichs des Großen. Die Tasse gefiel ihm. ›Ein schönes Gesicht‹, dachte Edwin, ›Geist und Kummer, seine Gedichte seine Kriege und seine Politik waren Krampf, aber er hat Voltaire ausgehalten, und Voltaire hat recht böse über ihn geschrieben.‹ Er erkundigte sich nach dem Preis der Tasse. Frau de Voss machte eine verlegene Geste zu Emilia hin und versuchte Edwin in eine Art Alkoven hinter den Laden zu ziehen. Emilia dachte ›sie ärgert sich, wenn ich erfahre was Edwin zahlt, kann sie mich schlecht mit dem abspeisen was sie mir geben will‹. Die Verlegenheit der Händlerin belustigte Emilia. Sie dachte ›komisch, daß Edwin so auf die Sachen aus ist die Philipp gefallen‹. Edwin durchschaute das Spiel der Händlerin. Es interessierte ihn nicht. Aber er ging nicht mit Frau de Voss in den Alkoven. Er stellte die Tasse wieder auf den Sekretär; wie plötzlich von ihr angewidert, stellte er sie wieder auf den Sekretär. Er wandte sich zum Gehen. Emilia überlegte, ob sie die Tasse nehmen und sie Edwin auf der Straße anbieten sollte. Aber sie dachte ›das ist Bettelei und die de Voss würde das ewig verstimmen, jetzt wird sie mir sehr wenig geben, schon aus Wut, aber Edwin hat mich überhaupt nicht beachtet, er hat mich sowenig beachtet wie man einen alten häßlichen Stuhl beachtet, ich war für Edwin nichts als ein alter häßlicher Stuhl, ich hasse die Literaten, die arroganten Kerle‹. Edwin dachte, schon auf der Straße, ›sie war arm, sie hatte Angst vor der Händlerin, ich hätte der jungen Frau helfen können, aber ich half ihr nicht, warum stand ich ihr nicht bei? das wäre zu untersuchen‹. Edwin wird die Tasse und Emilia in seinem Tagebuch erwähnen. Es wird im Licht der Wahrheit geschehen. Im Licht der Wahrheit wird Edwin untersuchen, ob er an diesem Nachmittag ein guter oder ein böser Mensch war. Das Licht der Wahrheit wird in jedem Fall Edwin, Emilia und Friedrich den Großen verklären.

Keine Verklärung, keine Aufklärung, kein Licht der Wahrheit. Wo lag Philipp? Im verdunkelten Zimmer. ›Er läßt mich träumen, kleiner Traumdoktor kleiner Psychotherapeut, sitzt nebenan und füllt meine Karteikarte aus, meine Traumkarte, kleiner Psychobürokrat, trägt ein: Philipp träumt, träumt von Wiesen, Urlaub und Sommerglück, laß doch die

Wiesen, ich bin bei Frau Holle eingeladen, sie schüttelt den Schnee aus den Betten den kühlen sanften den stillfrohen den friedlichen Schnee, der gemütliche Kachelofen, eine Katze buckelt und schnurrt, die Bratäpfel brutzeln im Rohr, ich kleide Puppen für das Theater an, ich kleide sie für meine kleine Bühne auf der Ofenbank an, es ist schön Theater zu spielen, aber das Wichtigste ist doch das Zurechtmachen der Puppen, eine Puppe wird wie Emilia angezogen, eine Puppe wie die kleine Amerikanerin mit den grünen Augen, sie könnte den Don Gil spielen den Don Gil von den grünen Hosen, keck grüne Hosen grüne Augen frisch munter *Sanella immer frisch* einen Degen in der Hand, mein kleiner Liebhaber, oder bist du der Junge der auszog das Fürchten zu lernen? zum Jungen fehlt dir ein kleines Ding, Trauer für deine Freundinnen, aber das Fürchten kannst du lernen, wie soll man Emilia kleiden? sie ist Ophelia das-arme-Kind-von-ihren-Melodien-hinunter-gezogen-in-den-schlammigen-Tod, als ich vierzehn war, sagte ich mir den Hamlet auf, sterben-schlafen-vielleicht-auch-träumen Pubertätsschmerz, nun träum' ich beim kleinen Behude, soll ich ihm meinen Hamlet zeigen? er erwartet immer Unanständiges erotische Konfessionen, möchte ein kleiner Beichtvaterersatz sein, ich kann den Hamlet noch, ich habe ein gutes Gedächtnis, für alles, was damals war, habe ich ein vorzügliches Gedächtnis, der See vor unserm Haus, er war zugefroren vom Oktober bis Ostern, die Bauern fuhren mit ihren Holzschlitten über den See holten die schweren Bäume aus den Wäldern gefällte Riesen, Eva, ihre Pirouetten auf dem Eis, die frostklirrende Sonne, Eva lief für mich ohne Strümpfe, es regte mich auf, ihre Mutter war empört, fürchtete eine Eierstockentzündung, sagte es natürlich nicht, dachte wir wüßten nicht was das sei, vergaß das Lexikon, sie sah wie eine Gluckhenne aus putt-putt-putt, Emilia geht nicht aufs Eis, findet Sport albern, lachte sich tot als Behude ihr sagte sie solle Tennis spielen, Emilia läuft durch die Stadt, Lene-Levi-lief-besoffen-nächtlich: wo gehört? in der prähistorischen Zeit am Kurfürstendamm, später marschierte SA, Katzen sollen die Welt anders sehen als wir: nur braun oder gelb, Emilia sieht eine Althändlerstadt eine schmutzfarbene Stadt mit schmutzigen Händlern, sie ist auf der Geldjagd, ihr Dämon hockt ihr im Nacken, sie schleppt ihr Lord-Reise-Plaid zu den Tandlern steigt in ihre Keller steigt hinunter zu Schlangen Fröschen und Lurchen, Herkules schlug die Hydra, Emilias Hydra hat mehr als neun Köpfe, sie hat dreihundertfünfundsechzig Köpfe im Jahr, dreihundertfünfundsechzigmal gegen das Ungeheuer Geldlosigkeit, sie verkauft was in unserer Wohnung steht, läßt sich von den Lurchen anlangen, es ekelt sie, aber sie treibt Geld auf, nachher vertrinkt sie's, steht im Stehausschank wie jeder Süffel, immer noch ein Gläschen, »Prost, Herr Nachbar«, die andern Süffel halten sie für 'ne Nutte, »schlechtes Geschäft heute auf der Straße?« — »schlechtes Geschäft« — »bei dem Wetter« — »bei dem Wetter« — »wie wär's denn?« — »wär' was?« — »mit uns beiden« — »geht nicht« — »bist du?« — »bin« — »Scheißleben« — »trink einen«, bald wird sie wie Messalina aussehen, kleiner, zarter, aber doch wie Messalina die Suffvisage die großporige fleckige Haut, Messalina lockt Emilia zu ihren Parties, will sie Alexander vorwerfen dem Erzherzogfrauentraum oder den kessen Vätern, wundert sich daß Emilia nicht kommt, Emilia macht sich nichts aus Orgien sie macht sich nichts aus Messalinas Verzweifelten, Emilia ist für sich verzweifelt braucht keine andere Verzweiflung, sie sagt sie renne für mich durch die Stadt, damit ich mein Buch schreiben könne, haßt mich dafür wenn sie nach Hause kommt, wenn ich was geschrieben hätte würd' sie's zerreißen, Emilia meine Ophelia: *o-pale-Ophélia-belle-comme-la-neige*, ich liebe dich aber du trenntest dich besser von mir, du wirst auch allein untergehen, du wirst von deinen Häusern erschlagen werden, du liegst schon lange unter deinen Häusern begraben, du bist nur noch ein kleines zartes tobendes versoffenes Gespenst der Verzweiflung, meine Schuld? ja, meine Schuld, jedermanns Schuld, alte Schuld, Urväterschuld, Schuld von weither, wenn sie tobt schreit sie ich sei ein Kommunist, hat es dazu gelangt? es hat nicht dazu gelangt, ich hätte Schriftsteller sein können, ich hätte auch Kommunist sein können, alles verfehlt, Kisch sagte im Romanischen Café »Genosse«

zu mir, ich sagte »Herr Kisch«, ich mochte ihn: Kisch rasender Reporter wohin raste er? ich verabscheue die Gewalt, ich verabscheue Unterdrückung, ist das Kommunismus? ich weiß es nicht, die Gesellschaftswissenschaft: Hegel Marx die Dialektik die marxistisch-materialistische Dialektik — nie begriffen, Gefühlskommunist: immer auf der Seite der Armen sinnlos empört, Spartakus Jesus Thomas Münzer Max Hölz, was wollten sie? gut sein, was geschah? man tötete sie, kämpfte ich in Spanien? mir schlug die Stunde nicht, ich drückte mich durch die Diktatur, ich haßte aber leise, ich haßte aber in meiner Kammer, ich flüsterte aber mit Gleichgesinnten, Burckhardt sagte mit Leuten seiner Art sei kein Staat zu machen, sympathisch, aber mit Leuten dieser Art ist auch kein Staat zu stürzen, keine Hoffnung, für mich nicht mehr, Behude sagt für mich gäbe es Hoffnung, Rilke-Lyrik: von-einer-Kirche-die-im-Osten-steht, verschwommen, kein Weg, der Osten in mir: die Kinderlandschaft, meine *recherche-du-temps-perdu*, suchet-so-werdet-ihr-finden, Gerüche, die Bratäpfel, Geräusche, das knisternde Fell der Katze, das Knirschen der Kufen der Holzschlitten auf dem Eis, die einsam auf dem See ihre Pirouetten tanzende nacktbeinige Eva: Schnee Frieden Schlaf —‹

Schlaf, aber keine Heimkehr, keine Einkehr, ein Fall, ein Gefälltwerden. Wie ein schwerer Stein ins Wasser, massig, empfindungslos, sank Alexander in seiner Wohnung in Schlaf. Im Darsteller des Erzherzogs lebte kein Traum. Er hatte sich unausgezogen auf ein Sofa geworfen; hier hatte in der Nacht die tribadische Alfredo gelegen; in Alexander war keine Wollust. Er war nur müde. Er hatte es satt. Satt die Erzherzogrolle. Satt die blödsinnige Sprechwalze des Erzherzogs. Satt das geborgte Heldentum. Was tat er im Krieg? Er spielte. Er war reklamiert. Was spielte er? Ritterkreuzheldenflieger. Er stürzte viermal glücklich ab, nachdem seine Feinde und Rivalen weniger glücklich im Staub zerschmettert lagen. Er hatte nie in einem fliegenden Flugzeug gesessen. Er fürchtete sich schon, wenn er eine Verkehrsmaschine benutzen sollte. Als die Bomben fielen, hockte er im Adlon-

Diplomaten-Bunker. Das war ein Bunker für feine Leute. Landser auf Urlaub wurden nicht 'reingelassen. Der Bunker hatte zwei Etagen. Alexander saß in der zweiten: der Krieg rückte fern. Nach dem Angriff räumten Hitlerjungen auf der Straße den Schutt weg. Im Schutt gruben die Jungen nach Verschütteten. Sie baten Alexander um ein Autogramm. Sie baten Alexander den Helden, Alexander den Tollkühnen. Man verwechselte Alexander mit seinem Schatten. Es machte ihn schwindlig. Wer war er? Ein draufgängerisch-treu-sentimental-kühner-Helden-Potenter? Er hatte es satt. Er war müde. Er war ausgeheldet. Er war wie ein ausgenommener Kapaun: fett und hohl. Sein Gesicht trug den Ausdruck der Dummheit: es war abgeschminkt, es war leer. Sein Mund stand offen, und durch das blendend-weiße Gebiß der Jacketkronen drang ein Schnarchen aus Dumpfheit und Übelkeit, aus träger Verdauung und mattem Stoffwechsel. Hundertsechzig Pfund Menschenfleisch lagen auf dem Sofa, noch hingen sie nicht am Haken des Metzgers, aber für den Augenblick, da der Witz abgeschaltet war, der Strom der Geistreichelei und des Witzelns, der in diesem Leib die Funktionen der Seele übernommen hatte, war Alexander nicht mehr als Metzgerfleisch, und davon hundertsechzig Pfund. Hillegonda kam in das Zimmer getrippelt. Sie hatte das Auto mit Alexander vorfahren hören, und für eine Weile brachte sie den Mut auf, sich von Emmis Hand zu lösen und allein in die Welt voll Sünde zu gehen. Hillegonda wollte Alexander fragen, ob Gott wirklich böse sei, ob Gott auf Hillegonda, auf Alexander und auf Messalina böse sei. Auf Emmi sei Gott nicht böse. Aber vielleicht war es eine Lüge von Emmi. »Pappi, darf Emmilein lügen?« Das Kind erhielt keine Antwort. Vielleicht war Gott gerade auf Emmi böse. Emmi war immer vorgeladen bei Gott. Schon ganz früh, wenn der Tag dämmerte, mußte sie in Gottes dunkle Gerichtssäle gehen. Alexander war auch mal vorgeladen. Zur Steuer war er vorgeladen gewesen. Er hatte Angst gehabt. Er hatte gerufen »die Rechnung stimmt ja nicht!« Stimmte vielleicht Emmis Rechnung nicht? Das Kind quälte sich. Es hätte mit Gott gerne besser gestanden. Es konnte doch sein, daß Gottes

Verstimmung gar nicht Hillegonda galt. Aber der Vater sagte nichts. Er lag da wie tot. Nur das Röcheln, das Schnarchen,
das aus dem offenen Mund drang, zeigte, daß er lebte. Hillegonda wurde von Emmi gerufen. Sie mußte zurück an Emmis Hand. Emmi war wieder vorgeladen. Sie mußte schon
wieder niederknien, auf Fliesen knien, auf kalten harten
Fliesen, sie mußte sich vor Gott in den Staub beugen.

Die Heiliggeistkirche gab dem Heiliggeistplatz, dem Heiliggeistspital und der Heiliggeistwirtschaft den Namen. Die
Wirtschaft war verrufen. Wo waren sie hingeraten? Als Josef
noch klein war, hatten sich Marktleute in der Wirtschaft
getroffen. Die Marktleute kamen mit Pferd und Wagen in
die Stadt gefahren, und Josef half ihnen beim Aus- und
Einspannen. Damals war das alte Viertel um die Heiliggeistkirche das Herz der Stadt gewesen. Später hatte sich das
Stadtzentrum verlagert. Die alte Gegend starb. Der Markt
starb. Der Platz, die Häuser, das Spital, die Kirche wurden
im Krieg bombardiert, als sie schon lange gestorben waren.
Ruinen blieben. Niemals würde jemand das Geld haben, diese
Ruinen wiederherzurichten. Die Gegend wurde ein Schlupfwinkel. Die kleinen Diebe trafen sich hier, die schäbigen Zuhälter, die billigen Dirnen. Wo waren sie hingeraten? Es war
Josefs Erzheimat, sein Spielviertel, sein Kinderarbeitsviertel,
die Kirche seiner ersten Kommunion. Wo waren sie hingeraten? Sie saßen in der Wirtschaft. Die Wirtschaft war voll,
lärmvoll; eine schwere warme Luft aus Dunst, Gestank und
Rauch füllte den Raum, blähte sich im Raum wie Gas in
einem halbschlaffen Ballon. Wo waren die Marktleute geblieben? Die Marktleute waren tot. Sie lagen in ihren Gräbern
auf ihren Dorffriedhöfen neben den weißen Kirchen. Ihre
Pferde, die Josef schirrte, hatte der Schinder geholt. Josef
und Odysseus tranken Schnaps. Odysseus nannte den Schnaps
Gin. Der Schnaps war Steinhäger. Es war ein fuseliger ver-
fälschter Steinhäger. Im Musikkoffer auf Josefs Schoß sang
ein Chor *she-was-a-nice-girl*. Wie kamen sie hierher? Was
wollten sie hier? Der kleine Josef hatte um Milch gebettelt.
Die Bäuerin hatte ihm Milch in den Krug gefüllt. Josef war

über den Platz gelaufen und hingefallen. Der Krug war zerbrochen. Die Milch war verschüttet. Josefs Mutter schlug Josef. Sie schlug ihm mit harten Schlägen die Ohren. Das Leben der Armen ist hart; sie machen sich das Leben immer noch härter. *She-was-a-nice-girl*. Was wollten sie hier? Sie rechneten ab. Odysseus entlohnte Josef. Er zog seine Brieftasche. Die Griechen hatten ihn nicht betrügen können. Odysseus gab Josef fünfzig Mark: großer herrlicher König Odysseus. Josef betrachtete den Schein blinzelnd durch seine Brille. Er faltete das Geld zusammen, legte es sorgsam zwischen die Seiten eines schmutzigen Notizbuches und steckte das Buch in die Brusttasche seiner Dienstmannsbluse. Der Fremdenverkehr hatte sich wieder einmal gelohnt. Es wurde ausgemacht, daß Josef noch bis zum Abend Odysseus begleiten sollte, daß er ihm den Musikkoffer tragen sollte, bis Odysseus mit einem Mädchen in der Nacht verschwinden würde. *She-was-a-nice-girl*. Großer Odysseus. Er blickte in den Nebel aus Schweiß, Unsauberkeit, Bratwurstrauch, Tabakschwaden, Alkoholdunst, Pißgeruch, Zwiebelbeize und schalem Menschenatem. Er winkte Susanne heran. Susanne war eine Blüte von Guerlainduft in einer Unratgrube. Sie wollte in der Grube sitzen. Sie wollte heute richtig in der Unratgrube sitzen, in die sie gehörte. Sie war von den feinen Leuten enttäuscht. Verdammte ekelhafte geizige Schweine. Alexander hatte sie eingeladen, der berühmte Alexander. Wer glaubte es ihr? Niemand. War er zu ihr gekommen, hatte er sie erwählt aus der Schar der Mädchen, er, von dem die Frauen träumen? Wer glaubte es? Hatte sie mit Alexander geschlafen? Ein Grunzen, *Erzherzogliebe ein Erlebnis auch für Sie,* die Schweine hatten gesoffen, sie hatten gesoffen wie die Schweine. Und dann? Kein Gott, der sich offenbarte. Kein Alexander, der sie umarmte. Kein Held, der sie rettete. Frauen. Susanne war geschlagen worden. Frauen hatten sie geschlagen. Und weiter? Küsse Streicheln Berührungen Hände an ihren Schenkeln. Frauen hatten sie geküßt gestreichelt berührt, Frauenhände lagen heiß und trocken auf ihren Schenkeln. Und Alexander? Erloschen trägeschwer lidverschwollen, Blicke aus toten gläsernen Augen. Sahen die Augen etwas? nahmen sie

146

etwas wahr? Wo lachte und liebte Alexander? wo diente er
Frauen und hob sie zu sich empor? Im Thaliapalast, Ecke
Schillerplatz und Goethestraße, fünf Vorstellungen am Tag.
Wo schnarchte Alexander? wo hing er wie leblos über dem
Sessel und hing sein Fleisch? Zu Hause, wenn er sich Mädchen eingeladen hatte. Was schenkte man Susanne nach dieser Nacht? Man vergaß es, ihr was zu schenken. Susanne
dachte ›nach Alexander ein Nigger, ich bin nicht schwul, ich
bin ganz gesund‹. Sie ging träge, die Zigarette in der Hand,
zu Odysseus hinüber. Der Parfümduft aus Messalinas Flasche begleitete sie in der schweren gestankdünstenden Luft
des Lokals wie eine isolierte und isolierende, andersartig
schwere anderweis dünstende Wolke. Susanne schob Josef
und den singenden Koffer auf der glatten von vielen Hintern
abgewetzten und glatt und blank gescheuerten Bank beiseite.
Sie drängte den Koffer und den alten Mann wie zwei tote
Dinge zur Seite, und der alte Mann war die wertlosere Sache. Den Koffer konnte man verkaufen. Josef konnte man nicht
mehr verkaufen. Susanne war Kirke und die Sirenen, sie war
es in diesem Augenblick, sie war es eben geworden, und vielleicht war sie auch noch Nausikaa. Niemand im Lokal merkte, daß andere in Susannes Haut steckten, uralte Wesen;
Susanne wußte nicht, wer alles sie war, Kirke, die Sirenen und
vielleicht Nausikaa; die Törichte hielt sich für Susanne, und
Odysseus ahnte nicht, welche Damen ihm in dem Mädchen
begegneten. Junge Haut umspannte Susannes Arm. Odysseus fühlte den Puls, er fühlte den Blutschlag dieses Arms in
seinem Nacken. Der Arm war kühl und sommersprossig, ein
Knabenarm, doch die Hand, die nach der Umschlingung des
Nackens Odysseus' Brust berührte, war warm, weiblich und
geschlechtlich, *she-was-a-nice-girl* —

Sie liebte Juwelen. Der Rubin ist das Feuer die Flamme, der
Diamant das Wasser der Quell die Welle, der Saphir die
Luft und der Himmel, und der grüne Smaragd ist die Erde,
das Grün der grünenden Erde, das Grün der Wiesen und der
Wälder. Emilia liebte den funkelnden Glanz, sie liebte die
schillernde Pracht der kalten Brillanten, das warme Gold, die

Götteraugen und die Tierseelen der Farbsteine, die Märchen des Orients, das Stirndiadem der heiligen Elefanten, *Aga Khan mit Edelsteinen aufgewogen, Tribut der Gläubigen, Industriediamanten kriegswichtig.* Es war nicht die Höhle, die Aladin fand. Keine Wunderlampe brannte. Herr Schellack, der Juwelier, sagte: »Nein.« Sein gewaltiges Kinn war mit Puder geglättet. Er hatte ein Gesicht wie ein Mehlsack. Hätte Emilia die Wunderlampe des hübschen Aladin besessen, der Sack wäre geplatzt, ein böser Geist, der Wächter der Schätze, entschwunden. Was hätte Emilia getan? Sie hätte das Plaid mit Gold und Edelsteinen gefüllt. Keine Angst, ihr Juweliere, es gibt keinen Zauber; es gibt Pistolen und Totschläger, doch Emilia wird sie nicht gebrauchen, auch habt ihr eure Alarmanlagen, die aber nicht vor dem Teufel schützen, der euch holen wird. Herr Schellack blickte wohlwollend auf Kay, eine vielversprechende Kundin, eine junge Amerikanerin, vielleicht Rockefellers Enkelkind. Sie betrachtete Korallen und Granaten. Der alte Schmuck lag auf Samt gebettet. Er erzählte von den Familien, die ihn besessen, von den Frauen, die ihn getragen hatten, er berichtete von der Not, die ihn verkaufen mußte, es waren kleine Maupassantgeschichten, die er erzählte, aber Kay hörte nicht zu, sie dachte nicht an unter der Wäsche in der Kommode versteckte Schmuckschatullen, nicht an Geiz, Erbschaften und Leichtsinn, nicht an den Hals schöner Frauen, nicht an ihre vollen Arme, ihre feinen Handgelenke, nicht an die einst gepflegten Hände, die manikürten Fingernägel, nicht an den Hunger, der mit Augen das Brot im Fenster des Bäckers verschlingt, sie dachte ›wie schön ist die Kette, wie funkelt der Reif, wie glitzert der Ring, wie leuchtet das Geschmeide‹. Mondbleich, aus Perlen, Email und diamantenen Rosen gefügt, lag das Geschmeide vor Schellack, dem Gepuderten, und wieder sagte er, wieder zu ihr gewandt, der Glanz des Wohlwollens, der für Kay geleuchtet hatte, war erloschen, wie ausgeknipst, eine ausgeknipste mattierte Glühbirne, wieder: »Nein.« Herr Schellack wollte das Geschmeide nicht kaufen. Das sei Großmutterschmuck, sagte er. Es war Großmutterschmuck, Geheimer Kommerzienratsschmuck; Großmutterschliff, Großmutterfassung, Geschmack der achtziger Jahre. Und die Diamantrosen? »Nichts wert! Nichts wert!« Herr Schellack hob die kurzen Arme, die dicken Hände, Hände wie zwei fette Wachteln; es war eine Geste, die fürchten ließ, Herr Schellack würde versuchen zu fliegen, er würde versuchen, vor lauter Bedauern und Enttäuschung davonzufliegen. Hörte Emilia ihm zu? Sie hörte ihm nicht zu. Sie sah ihn nicht mal an. Seine Gesten entgingen ihr. Sie dachte ›wie nett sie ist, sie ist sehr nett, sie ist ein wirklich nettes Mädchen, sie ist das nette Mädchen das ich vielleicht hätte werden können, sie freut sich daß alles so schön rot ist, rot wie Wein rot wie Blut rot wie junge Lippen daß es so glitzert und funkelt, noch überlegt sie nicht daß sie nichts für den Schmuck bekommen wird wenn sie ihn einmal verkaufen muß, ich weiß Bescheid, ich kenne mich aus, ich bin ein alter Handelsmann, ich liebe die bunten Steine aber ich würde sie mir nie kaufen, sie sind eine unsichere Anlage zu sehr der Mode unterworfen, nur Brillanten geben einige Sicherheit, der neueste Schliff der Parvenügeschmack triumphiert, und Gold eben, reines Gold, das sich hinzulegen hat Sinn, solange ich Gold und Brillanten habe brauche ich nicht zu arbeiten, ich will nicht vom Wecker geweckt werden, ich will nie sagen »verzeihen Sie, Herr Bürovorsteher, entschuldigen Sie, Herr Werkmeister, ich habe die Straßenbahn versäumt«, dann hätte ich die Straßenbahn versäumt, wenn ich das je sagen müßte, die Bahn meines Lebens, nie! nie! nie! und du meine Schöne und Nette, du mit deinen Korallen und Granaten, Herr Schellack wird viel von dir verlangen für die Ringlein und Kreuzlein, für die Kettchen und die Anhänger, aber geh mal zu ihm, meine Süße, komm mal und biete ihm dasselbe Ringchen, dieselbe Kette an, tu's doch, biet sie ihm an, er wird dir sagen, daß deine hübschen Granaten und Korallen nichts wert sind, gar nichts, da lernst du's, da weißt du's, du Unschuldslamm, du Unverschämte aus Amerika‹. Emilia nahm ihr Geschmeide vom Ladentisch zurück. Herr Schellack sagte mit trägem Lächeln: »Ich bedaure, gnädige Frau.« Er dachte, sie würde gehen. Er dachte ›schade, so kommt die Kundschaft herab, ihre Großmutter hat den

Schmuck bei meinem Vater gekauft, sie wird zweitausend Mark gezahlt haben, zweitausend in Gold.‹ Emilia aber ging nicht. Sie suchte die Freiheit. Für einen Augenblick wenigstens wollte sie frei sein. Sie wollte frei handeln, eine freie Tat tun, die von keinem Zwang und keiner Notwendigkeit bestimmt und mit keiner Absicht verbunden war, außer der Absicht, frei zu sein; doch auch dies war keine Absicht, es war ein Gefühl, und das Gefühl war eben da, ganz absichtslos. Sie ging zu Kay und sagte: »Lassen Sie die Korallen und Granaten. Sie sind rot und hübsch. Aber diese Perlen und Diamanten sind hübscher; auch wenn Herr Schellack behauptet, sie seien zu altmodisch. Ich schenke sie Ihnen. Ich schenke sie dir, weil du nett bist.« Sie war frei. Ein unerhörtes Gefühl von Glück durchströmte Emilia. Sie war frei. Das Glück würde nicht währen. Aber für den Augenblick war sie frei. Sie befreite sich, sie befreite sich von Perlen und Diamanten. Im Anfang hatte ihre Stimme gezittert. Aber jetzt jubelte sie. Sie hatte es gewagt, sie war frei. Sie legte Kay den Schmuck an, sie knüpfte ihr die Kette im Nacken zu. Und auch Kay war frei, sie war ein freier Mensch, unbewußter als Emilia, war sie vielleicht um so selbstverständlicher frei, sie trat zum Spiegel, betrachtete sich lange mit dem ihr umgetanen Geschmeide, beachtete nicht Schellack, der offenen Mundes protestieren wollte und nicht die Worte fand, und sagte: »Ja. Es ist herrlich! Die Perlen, die Diamanten, das Geschmeide. Es ist wunderschön!« Sie wandte sich zu Emilia und sah sie mit ihren grünen Augen an. Kay war unbefangen, während Emilia doch etwas erregt war. Aber beide Mädchen hatten die herrliche Empfindung zu rebellieren, sie fühlten das wunderbare Glück, gegen Vernunft und Sitte zu rebellieren. »Du mußt auch etwas von mir nehmen«, sagte Kay. »Ich hab' keinen Schmuck. Vielleicht nimmst du meinen Hut.« Sie nahm ihren Hut vom Kopf, es war ein spitzer Reisehut mit einer bunten Feder, und setzte ihn Emilia auf. Emilia lachte, blickte in den Spiegel und rief entzückt: »Jetzt sehe ich wie Till Eulenspiegel aus. Genau wie Till Eulenspiegel.« Sie schob den Hut in den Nacken, dachte ›besoffen, sieht besoffen aus, aber ich schwör's, ich hab' noch keinen

150

Schluck getrunken, Philipp würd' mir's nicht glauben‹. Sie
lief zu Kay. Sie umarmte Kay, sie küßte Kay, und als sie
Kays Lippen berührte, dachte sie ›herrlich, so schmeckt die
Prärie‹ —

— ›wie in einem Wildwestfilm‹, überlegte Messalina. Sie
hatte Susanne in ihrer Wohnung nicht gefunden, aber man
hatte ihr gesagt, daß sie in der Wirtschaft am Heiliggeistplatz zu finden sei. ›Wie in einem Wildwestfilm, aber wir
drehen keine mehr, unkünstlerischer Klamauk.‹ Sie trat
selbstbewußt in den Dunst, in die stinkende grausame Magie des Lokals, in dem man früher seinen Schoppen getrunken hatte, bevor man zur Hexenverbrennung auf den Markt
ging. Messalina war schüchtern. Man sah es noch auf dem
Bild, das sie als Kommunikantin zeigte, in weißem Kleid,
eine Kerze in der Hand. Aber schon damals, als dieses Bild
aufgenommen wurde, im Atelier eines der letzten Photographen, die noch Samtjacken trugen und große schwarze
Schmetterlingsschleifen und die »bitte recht freundlich« riefen (Messalina hatte kein freundliches Gesicht gemacht: ein
schüchternes, aber schon ein schüchternes, das mit Trotz und
Gewaltsamkeit gegen die Schüchternheit ankämpfte), schon
damals wollte sie nicht schüchtern sein, nicht diese Rolle
spielen, nicht gegen die Wand gedrückt werden, und es war
der Tag der Kommunion, der Ausgangspunkt ihres Wachs-
tums, ihre Blutung kam, und sie wuchs und nahm zu an
Laster und Gemeinheit und Fleischesfülle, sie wurde zum
lästerlichen gemeinen Denkmal, wo sie ging und wo sie stand,
sie war ein Denkmal, das erschreckte oder begeisterte: wer
wußte, daß sie schüchtern geblieben war? Dr. Behude wußte
es. Aber Dr. Behude war noch viel schüchterner als Messalina, und da er seine Schüchternheit nie wie sie ins Überdi-
mensionale ausgeglichen hatte, wagte er, aus Schüchternheit,
Messalina nicht zu sagen, daß sie schüchtern sei, und dabei
wäre dies, hätte es Behude gesagt, ein Zauberwort gewesen,
ein Wort der Denkmalzerstörung, und Messalina wäre in
den schüchternen reinen Zustand der Vorkommunion zurückgekehrt. Alle betrachteten Messalina, die kleinen Nutten und

die kleinen Zuhälter, die kleinen Diebe allzumal und auch
der kleine Kriminalagent, der hier, von jedem als Kriminaler
gekannt, verkleidet saß: Messalina schüchterte alle ein. Nur
Susanne schüchterte sie nicht ein. Susanne dachte ›das Aas,
wenn sie mir den Nigger vermasselt‹. Sie wollte denken ›dann
kratze, beiße, schlage, trampele ich‹, aber sie dachte es nicht,
sie war nicht eingeschüchtert, aber sie fürchtete sich, sie fürchtete Messalinas Schläge, denn sie hatte Messalinas Schläge
gespürt. Susanne erhob sich. Sie sagte: »Moment, Jimmy.«
Zwei Wolken des gleichen Parfüms, Guerlain Paris, vereinten
sich, hielten stand gegen Schweiß, Pisse, Zwiebel, Wurstbrühe,
gegen Bierdunst und Tabakrauch. Susanne wurde aufgefordert, am Abend zu Alexander zu kommen, und sie dachte
›ich wär' schön blöd wenn ich's täte, ein schlechtes Geschäft,
wenn aber Alexander doch mit mir schliefe? ja, er schläft,
aber nicht bei mir, er kann nicht mehr, und wenn er könnte,
wer glaubt es mir, und wenn mir es keiner glaubt, ist mir der
Nigger am Arsch lieber, der kann, wenn ich auch gar nicht
drauf aus bin, aber die unbefriedigten Weiber? ohne mich,
*Erste Legion warnt vor Ohne-mich-Parole, Justizminister
sagt wer Frau und Kind nicht verteidigt, ist kein Mann‹.*
Doch empfand es Susanne als unpassend, einer Dame, Dame
der Gesellschaft, Überdame einer von Susanne unklar empfundenen Denkmalhaftigkeit, eine Einladung abzuschlagen.
Sie sagte, sie käme, natürlich, gern, geehrt und mit Freuden,
und sie dachte ›du kannst lange warten, leck mich, aber leck
mich aus der Ferne, meine Ruh' will ich haben, meinst, du
bist was Besseres als ich? ich möchte mich mit dir noch lange
nicht vergleichen‹. Messalina hatte sich im Lokal umgesehen.
Sie hatte Susannes freien Platz neben Odysseus entdeckt, und
sie sagte: »Bring doch einen Schwarzen mit, wenn du willst.«
Sie dachte ›vielleicht ist er was für die Schwulen‹. Susanne
wollte antworten, wollte eine Ausrede finden, wollte sagen,
daß sie mit dem Neger nichts zu tun habe, oder sie konnte
auch für den Jimmy oder den Joe zusagen, es war ja egal,
sie ging ja doch nicht hin, da erhob sich Geschrei und Gewalt.
Odysseus war bestohlen worden, sein Geld war verschwunden, weg waren die Dollars und die deutschen Scheine, der

Musikkoffer spielte Jimmys-Boogie-Woogie, König Odysseus war gekränkt, er war beleidigt, er griff sich den Nächsten, langte sich einen Zuhälter oder einen Dieb oder den kleinen Kriminalagenten, beschuldigte ihn, schüttelte ihn, »seht den Gorilla, King Kong, Ficker, schmeißt ihn 'raus, den Niggerficker, 'raus«, die Meute sprang auf, die Herde setzte sich durch, Kameradschaft siegte, *Gemeinnutz geht vor Eigennutz*, sie stürzten sich auf ihn, sie nahmen Bierseidel, Stuhlbeine, feststehende Messer, sie stürzten sich auf den großen Odysseus, die Schlacht brandete, tobte, ruckte, Odysseus war in Feindesland, es ging um sein Leben, der Tisch schlug um, Josef hielt den Musikkoffer, er hielt ihn über sich, schützend hielt er Jimmys-Boogie-Woogie über sich, die Töne rasselten, die Synkopen fauchten, es war wie im Unterstand, da war wieder das Trommelfeuer, der Chemin-des-Dames, der Argonnerwald, doch Josef nahm nicht teil am Kampf, er entsühnte sich, er tötete nicht, er trieb in den Wellen eines fernen Stroms, floh mit Odysseus, der sich freigekämpft hatte, umflossen von der Musik des Stromes des fernen Erdteils, Jimmys-Boogie-Woogie. Messalina stand allein, innerlich verschüchtert und äußerlich ein Denkmal, im Trubel. Ihr geschah nichts. Der Kampf bewegte sich um das Denkmal herum. Niemand beleidigte Messalina. Sie stand inmitten des Lokals wie ein allgemein respektiertes Monument, das hierhergehörte. Susanne aber folgte dem neuen Freund. Es wäre klug gewesen, es nicht zu tun. Es wäre klug gewesen zu bleiben. Vielleicht wäre es sogar klug gewesen, mit Messalina zu gehen. Aber da Susanne Kirke und die Sirenen und vielleicht noch Nausikaa war, mußte sie Odysseus folgen. Sie mußte ihm gegen alle Vernunft folgen. Sie war mit Odysseus verstrickt. Sie hatte es gar nicht so recht gewollt. Sie hatte nicht widerstehen können, sie war dumm gewesen, und jetzt war sie töricht. Odysseus und Josef liefen über den Heiliggeistplatz. Susanne lief hinterher. Sie folgte Jimmys-Boogie-Woo-

Die Glocken der Heiliggeistkirche läuteten. Auf den Fliesen knieten Emmi und Hillegonda. Es roch in der Kirche nach gie.

altem Weihrauch und frischem Mörtel. Hillegonda fror. Sie fror mit ihren nackten Knien auf den kalten Fliesen. Emmi schlug das Kreuz und-vergib-uns-unsere-Sünden. Hillegonda dachte ›was ist denn nur meine Sünde? wenn es mir nur jemand sagen täte, ach, Emmi, ich fürchte mich‹. Und Emmi betete: »Herr, du hast diese Stadt zerstört, und du wirst sie wieder zerstören, denn sie gehorchen dir nicht und mißachten dein Wort, und ihr Geschrei ist ein Greuel vor deinen Ohren.« Hillegonda hörte von draußen gellende Rufe, und es war, als ob Steine gegen die Tür der Kirche geworfen würden. »Emmi, hörst du? Emmi, was ist das? Man will uns was tun, Emmi!« — »Es ist der Teufel, Kind. Der Teufel geht um. Bete nur! Ach-Herr-erlöse-uns!«

Sie lagen hinter Mauerschutt und Steinen aus dem Bombeneinschlag der Kirche. Die Meute ging gegen sie vor, Susanne dachte ›worauf lass' ich mich ein? ich bin verrückt daß ich mich darauf einlasse, aber die haben mich gestern verrückt gemacht bei Alexander, und jetzt lass' ich mich drauf ein‹. Jimmys-Boogie-Woogie. »Geld«, sagte Odysseus. Er brauchte Kapital. Er war im Krieg. Er war wieder im alten Krieg Weiß gegen Schwarz. Auch hier wurde der Krieg geführt. Er brauchte Geld zum Kriegführen. »Geld! Schnell!« Odysseus packte Josef. Josef dachte ›es ist wie am Chemin-des-Dames, der Schwarze ist nicht der Teufel, er ist der Reisende den ich getötet habe, er ist der Turko der Senegalese den ich getötet habe auf meinem Ausflug in Frankreich‹. Josef wehrte sich nicht. Er erstarrte nur. Vor seinen alten Augen verwandelte sich das Bild seiner Kinderlandschaft noch einmal in ein europäisches Schlachtfeld mit außereuropäischen Kämpfern, fremden Reisenden, die töten wollten oder getötet wurden. Josef hielt krampfhaft den Koffer fest. Der Koffer war sein Dienst. Für das Tragen des Koffers war er bezahlt worden. Er mußte ihn festhalten. Jimmys Boogie-Woogie —

Sie standen sich gegenüber, Freunde? Feinde? Gatten? sie standen sich in Carlas Zimmer gegenüber, in der Hurenwohnung der Frau Welz, in einer Welt der Unzucht und

Verzweiflung, und da sie in einer Welt der Unzucht und Verzweiflung lebten, schrien sie einander an, und Frau Welz verließ die Hexenküche, den Herd mit den brodelnden Dämpfen, schlich durch den Korridor und zischte durch die spaltbreit geöffneten Türen der Mädchenzimmer, wo sie sich bereitmachten, nackend, in Höschen, in schmierigen Schlafmänteln, bei der Toilette aufgeschreckt, beim Anlegen der Schönheit für den Abend, nicht fertig geformte, erst halb gepuderte Gesichter, sie vernahmen das Wirtinnengezisch, den geilen Jubel in der Stimme, daß Böses geschah: »Jetzt prügelt er sie, der Nigger. Jetzt schlägt er sie. Jetzt zeigt er's ihr. Ich hab' mich schon lange gewundert, daß er's ihr nicht zeigt.« Washington schlug sie nicht. Gegen seine Brust schlugen Teller und Tassen, zu seinen Füßen lagen die Scherben: die Scherben seines Glücks? Er dachte ›ich kann gehen, wenn ich meine Mütze nehme und gehe wird das alles hinter mir liegen, vielleicht werde ich es vergessen, es wird gar nicht gewesen sein‹. Carla schrie, ihr Gesicht war tränenverschwollen: »Du hast mir den Doktor vermiest. Du falscher Kerl! Du bist bei Frahm gewesen. Meinst, ich will deinen Bankert haben? Meinst, ich will ihn haben? Mit Fingern würden sie auf mich weisen. Ich pfeif' auf dein Amerika. Auf dein dreckiges schwarzes Amerika. Ich bleib' hier. Ich bleib' hier ohne deinen Bankert, und wenn ich bei draufgehe, ich bleib'!« Was hielt ihn zurück? Warum nahm er nicht seine Mütze? Warum ging er nicht? Vielleicht war es Trotz. Vielleicht war es Verblendung. Vielleicht war es Überzeugung, vielleicht Glaube an den Menschen. Washington hörte, was Carla schrie, aber er glaubte ihr nicht. Er wollte das Band, das nun zu reißen drohte, das Band zwischen Weiß und Schwarz, nicht lösen, er wollte es fester knüpfen durch ein Kind, er wollte ein Beispiel geben, er glaubte an die Möglichkeit dieses Beispiels, und vielleicht forderte auch sein Glaube Märtyrer. Für einen Augenblick dachte er wirklich daran, Carla zu schlagen. Es ist immer die Verzweiflung, die prügeln will, aber sein Glaube überwand die Verzweiflung. Washington nahm Carla in seine Arme. Er hielt sie fest in seinen kräftigen Armen. Carla zappelte in seinen Armen wie

155

ein Fisch in der Hand des Fischers. Washington sagte: »Wir lieben uns doch, warum sollen wir's nicht durchstehen? Warum sollen wir's nicht schaffen? Wir müssen uns nur immer lieben. Wenn alle andern uns beschimpfen: wir müssen uns liebhaben. Noch als ganz alte Leute müssen wir uns lieben.«

Odysseus schlug mit dem Stein, oder ein Stein, den die Meute geworfen hatte, schlug gegen Josefs Stirn. Odysseus riß das Geld, den Schein, den er Josef gegeben hatte, König Odysseus, aus dem Notizbuch des Dienstmannes, aus dem abgegriffenen Heft, in das Josef seine Botengänge und seine Einnahmen eingetragen hatte. Odysseus rannte. Er rannte um die Kirche herum. Die Meute rückte nach. Sie sahen Josef am Boden liegen und sahen das Blut auf seiner Stirn. »Der Nigger hat den alten Josef totgeschlagen!« Da wimmelte der Platz voll Gestalten, die aus Kellern, Verschlägen und Gemäuer kamen, jeder im Viertel hatte ihn gekannt, den alten Josef, den kleinen Josef, er hatte hier gespielt, er hatte hier gearbeitet, er war in den Krieg gezogen, er hatte wieder gearbeitet, und jetzt war er ermordet worden: er war um seinen Lohn ermordet worden. Sie umstanden ihn: eine graue Wand armer und alter Leute. Im Musikkasten neben Josef erklang ein Negro-Spiritual. Marian Anderson sang, eine schöne, volle und weiche Stimme, eine Vox humana, eine Vox angelica, Stimme eines dunklen Engels; es war, als ob die Stimme den Erschlagenen versöhnen wolle. ›Ich muß weg‹, dachte Susanne, ›ich muß schleunigst hier weg, ich muß weg bevor die Polente kommt, die MP wird kommen, und die Funkstreife wird kommen‹. Sie drückte ihre rechte Hand gegen die Bluse, wo sie das Geld fühlte, das sie Odysseus aus der Tasche gezogen hatte. ›Warum hab' ich's nur getan‹, dachte sie, ›ich hab' doch nie so etwas getan, die haben mich schlecht gemacht, die Schweine bei Alexander haben mich schlecht gemacht, ich wollte mich rächen, ich wollte mich an den Schweinen rächen, aber man rächt sich immer nur an den Falschen.‹ Susanne schritt durch die graue Wand der Alten und Armen, die sich vor ihr öffnete. Die Alten und Armen ließen Susanne passieren. Sie gaben Susanne die

156

Mitschuld an den Ereignissen, eine Frau war immer bei einem Unglück dabei, aber sie waren keine Psychologen und keine Kriminalisten, sie dachten nicht ›cherchez la femme‹, sie dachten ›auch sie ist arm, auch sie wird alt werden, sie gehört zu uns‹. Erst als die Wand sich hinter Susanne wieder geschlossen hatte, schrie ein Bengel »Ami-Hur'!« Ein paar Frauen schlugen das Kreuz. Ein Priester kam und beugte sich über Josef. Der Priester legte sein Ohr auf Josefs Brust. Der Priester war grauhaarig, und sein Gesicht war müde. Er sagte: »Er atmet noch.« Aus dem Spital kamen vier Dienende Brüder mit einer Bahre. Die Dienenden Brüder sahen arm und wie gescheiterte Verschwörer in einem klassischen Drama aus. Sie legten Josef auf die Bahre. Sie trugen die Bahre in das Heiliggeistspital hinüber. Der Priester folgte der Bahre. Hinter dem Priester ging Emmi. Sie zog Hillegonda hinter sich her. Man ließ Emmi und Hillegonda in das Spital gehen. Man dachte wohl, daß sie zu Josef gehörten, und dann vernahm man die Sirenen, die Sirenen der Funkstreife und der Militärpolizei. Von allen Seiten näherten sich die Sirenen dem Platz.

Es war der Moment, die Stunde am Abend, da die Radfahrer durch die Straßen sausen und den Tod verachten. Es war die Zeit der niederfallenden Dämmerung, die Zeit des Schichtwechsels, des Ladenschlusses, die Stunde der Heimkehr der Werktätigen, die Stunde des Ausschwärmens der Nachtarbeiter. Die Polizeisirenen kreischten. Die Überfallwagen drängten sich durch den Verkehr. Die blauen Lampen verliehen ihrem Rasen einen geisterhaften Schein: Gefahr verkündende Sankt-Elmsfeuer der Stadt. Philipp liebte die Stunde. In Paris war es die *heure bleue*, die Stunde des Träumens, eine Spanne relativer Freiheit, der Augenblick des Freiseins von Tag und Nacht. Die Menschen waren freigelassen von ihren Werkstätten und Geschäften, und sie waren noch nicht eingefangen von den Ansprüchen der Gewohnheit und dem Zwang der Familie. Die Welt hing in der Schwebe. Alles schien möglich zu sein. Für eine Weile schien alles möglich zu sein. Aber vielleicht war dies eine Einbildung von Philipp, dem Außenstehenden, der von keiner Arbeit zu keiner Familie heimkehrte. Der Einbildung würde die Enttäuschung auf dem Fuße folgen. Philipp war an Enttäuschungen gewöhnt; er fürchtete sie nicht. Der Abendschein verklärte. Der Himmel brannte in südlichen Farben. Er war ein Ätna-Himmel, ein Himmel wie über dem alten Theater in Taormina, ein Feuer wie über den Tempeln in Agrigent. Die Antike hatte sich erhoben und lächelte einen Gruß über die Stadt. Die Konturen der Gebäude standen wie ein scharfer Stich vor diesem Himmel, und die Sandsteinfassade der Jesuitenkirche, an der Philipp vorüberging, war von tänzerischer Anmut, sie war ein Teil des alten Italiens, sie war human, klug und von karnevalistischer Ausgelassenheit. Wohin aber hatten Humanität und Klugheit und schließlich noch Ausgelassenheit geführt? Das Abendecho rief das Unheil des Tages aus *Rentner wählte den Tod, Sowjets beißen auf Granit, Wieder ein Diplomat verschwunden, Deutsche Wehrverfassung kommt, Explosion ließ Hölle sehen.* Wie ernst und wie dumm das war! Ein Diplomat war übergelaufen, er war zum Feind seiner Regierung übergelaufen, *Verrat aus Idealismus.* Die offizielle Welt bemühte sich noch immer, in hohlen Phrasen zu denken, in längst jeden Begriffes baren Schlagworten. Sie sahen feste, unverrückbare Fronten, abgesteckte Erdstücke, Grenzen, Territorien, Souveränitäten, sie hielten den Menschen für ein Mitglied einer Fußballmannschaft, der sein Leben lang für den Verein spielen sollte, dem er durch Geburt beigetreten war. Sie irrten: die Front war nicht hier und nicht dort und nicht nur bei jenem Grenzpfahl. Die Front war allüberall, ob sichtbar oder unsichtbar, und ständig wechselte das Leben seinen Standort zu den Milliarden Punkten der Front. Die Front ging quer durch die Länder, sie trennte die Familien, sie lief durch den Einzelnen: zwei Seelen, ja, zwei Seelen wohnten in jeder Brust, und mal schlug das Herz mit der einen und mal mit der anderen Seele. Philipp war nicht wetterwendischer als andere; im Gegenteil, er war ein Sonderling. Aber selbst er hätte mit jedem Schritt und mehr als tausendmal am Tag seine Meinung zu den Verhältnissen in der Welt ändern können.

›Überschaue ich es denn‹, dachte er, ›kenne ich die Rechnung der Politik? die Geheimnisse der Diplomaten? ich freue mich, wenn einer zum andern flieht und die Karten etwas durcheinanderbringt, die Macher werden dann das Gefühl haben, das wir haben, das Gefühl der Hilflosigkeit, kann ich die Wissenschaft noch verstehen? kenne ich die letzte Formel des Weltbildes, kann ich sie lesen?‹ Alle, die da auf der Straße gingen, radelten, fuhren, Pläne machten, Sorgen hatten oder den Abend genossen, alle wurden sie ständig belogen und betrogen, und die Auguren, die sie belügen und betrügen, waren nicht weniger blind als die einfachen Leute. Philipp lachte über die Dummheit der politischen Propaganda. Er lachte über sie, obwohl er wußte, daß sie ihn das Leben kosten konnte. Aber die andern auf der Straße? Lachten sie auch? War ihnen das Lachen vergangen? Hatten sie im Gegensatz zu Philipp keine Zeit zu lachen? Sie erkannten nicht, wie schlecht das Futter war, das man ihnen vorwarf, und wie billig man sie kaufen wollte. ›Ich bin leidlich immun gegen Verführungen‹, überlegte Philipp, ›und doch, ich höre einmal hier ein Wort, das mir gefällt, und manchmal von der anderen Seite einen Ruf, der noch besser klingt, ich spiele immer die lächerlichen Rollen, ich bin der alte Tolerante, ich bin für das Anhören jeder Meinung, wenn man schon auf Meinungen hören will, aber die ernsten Leute regen sich nun auf beiden Seiten auf und brüllen mich an, daß meine Toleranz gerade die Intoleranz fördere, es sind feindliche Brüder, beide intolerant bis auf die Knochen, beide einander gram und nur darin sich einig, daß sie meinen schwachen Versuch, unbefangen zu bleiben, begeifern, und jeder von ihnen haßt mich, weil ich nicht zu ihm gehen und gegen den andern bellen will, ich will in keiner Mannschaft spielen, auch nicht im Hemisphärenfußball, ich will für mich bleiben.‹ Es gab noch Hoffnung in der Welt: *Vorsichtige Fühler, kein Krieg vor dem Herbst* —

Die Lehrerinnen aus Massachusetts gingen in Zweierreihen wie eine Schulklasse durch die Stadt. Die Klasse war auf dem Wege in das Amerikahaus. Sie genoß artig den Abend. Die

159

Lehrerinnen wollten den Vortrag von Edwin hören und vorher noch etwas vom Leben der Stadt sehen. Sie sahen nicht viel. Sie sahen so wenig vom Leben dieser Stadt, als die Stadt vom Leben der Lehrerinnen sah. Nichts. Miß Wescott hatte die Führung übernommen. Sie schritt der Klasse voran. Sie führte die Kolleginnen nach dem Stadtplan des Reisehandbuchs. Sie führte sie sicher und ohne Umwege. Miß Wescott war verstimmt. Kay war verschwunden. Sie hatte sich am Nachmittag aus dem Hotel entfernt, um sich die Auslagen der Läden anzusehen. Sie war zur verabredeten Stunde nicht zurückgekehrt. Miß Wescott machte sich Vorwürfe. Sie hätte Kay hindern müssen, allein in die fremde Stadt zu gehen. Kannte man die Leute? Waren es nicht Feinde? Konnte man ihnen trauen? Miß Wescott hatte eine Nachricht im Hotel zurückgelassen, daß Kay sich sofort ein Taxi nehmen und ins Amerikahaus fahren solle. Miß Wescott verstand Miß Burnett nicht. Miß Burnett sagte, Kay würde jemand kennengelernt haben. War das Kay zuzutrauen? Sie war jung und unerfahren. Es konnte nicht sein. Miß Burnett sagte: »Sie wird jemand kennengelernt haben, der sie besser unterhält, als wir es können.« — »Und da bleiben Sie so ruhig?« — »Ich bin nicht eifersüchtig.« Miß Wescott kniff die Lippen zusammen. Diese Burnett war unmoralisch. Und Kay war einfach ungezogen. Sonst war es nichts. Kay hatte sich verlaufen oder die Zeit vertrödelt. Die Lehrerinnen gingen über den großen Platz, eine von Hitler entworfene Anlage, die als Ehrenhain des Nationalsozialismus geplant war. Miß Wescott machte auf die Bedeutung des Platzes aufmerksam. Im Gras hockten Vögel. Miß Burnett dachte ›wir verstehen nicht mehr als die Vögel von dem was die Wescott quatscht, die Vögel sind zufällig hier, wir sind zufällig hier, und vielleicht waren auch die Nazis nur zufällig hier, Hitler war ein Zufall, seine Politik war ein grausamer und dummer Zufall, vielleicht ist die Welt ein grausamer und dummer Zufall Gottes, keiner weiß warum wir hier sind, die Vögel werden wieder auffliegen und wir werden weitergehen, hoffentlich läßt unsere Kay sich auf keine Dummheit ein, es wäre dumm wenn sie sich auf eine Dummheit einließe, der Wescott kann ich das nicht sagen die würde verrückt werden, aber Kay lockt die Verführer an, sie kann nichts dafür, sie lockt sie an wie die Vögel den Jäger oder den Hund‹. »Was ist mit Ihnen?« fragte Miß Wescott Miß Burnett. Miß Wescott war befremdet; Miß Burnett hörte ihr nicht zu. Miß Wescott fand, daß die Burnett das Gesicht eines ausgehungerten Jagdhundes hatte. »Ich schau' mir nur die Vögel an«, sagte Miß Burnett. »Seit wann interessieren Sie sich für Vögel?« fragte Miß Wescott. »Ich interessiere mich für uns«, sagte Miß Burnett. »Das sind Spatzen«, sagte Miß Wescott, »gewöhnliche Spatzen. Achten Sie lieber auf die Weltgeschichte.« — »Das ist dasselbe«, sagte Miß Burnett, »es spielt sich alles unter Spatzen ab. Auch Sie sind nur ein Spatz, liebe Wescott, und unser Spätzchen, die Kay, fällt grade aus dem Nest.« — »Ich verstehe Sie nicht«, sagte Miß Wescott spitz, »ich bin kein Vogel.«

Philipp ging in den Saal des Alten Schlosses, in dem der Staat einen Weinausschank eingerichtet hatte, um den Absatz des heimatlichen Weinbaus zu fördern. Der Saal war um diese Zeit sehr besucht. Die Beamten der zahllosen Ministerien und Staatskanzleien tankten hier ein wenig Fröhlichkeit, bevor sie nach Hause gingen, nach Hause zu ihren Frauen, zu ihren herzlosen Kindern, zu dem lieblos aufgewärmten Essen. Es war eine Männerwelt. Es waren wenig Frauen da. Nur zwei Redakteurinnen waren da. Aber das waren keine richtigen Frauen. Sie gehörten zum Abendecho. Sie löschten im Wein den Brand ihrer Schlagzeilen. Philipp dachte, daß er heimgehen, daß er zu Emilia gehen müsse. Aber er wollte doch auch zu Edwin gehen, obwohl die Begegnung mit Edwin so peinlich verlaufen war. ›Wenn ich jetzt nicht zu Emilia gehe, kann ich heute überhaupt nicht mehr nach Hause gehen‹, dachte Philipp. Er wußte, daß Emilia sich betrinken würde, wenn sie ihn am Abend nicht zu Hause fände. Er dachte ›ich würde mich in unserer Wohnung allein mit all den Tieren auch betrinken, ich würde mich betrinken wenn ich mich überhaupt betrinken würde, ich betrinke mich schon lange nicht mehr‹. Der Wein, den es im Alten Schloß gab, war gut. Aber Philipp mochte auch keinen Wein mehr. Er war sehr begabt, sich zu freuen, aber er hatte die Lust an fast allen Freuden verloren. Er war fest entschlossen, zu Emilia zu gehen. Emilia war wie Dr. Jekyll und Mr. Hyde in der Geschichte von Stevenson. Philipp liebte Dr. Jekyll, eine reizende und gutherzige Emilia, aber er haßte und fürchtete den widerlichen Mr. Hyde, eine Emilia des späten Abends und der Nacht, die ein wüster Trunkenbold und eine geifernde Xanthippe war. Wenn Philipp jetzt nach Hause ginge, würde er noch den lieben Dr. Jekyll treffen, besuchte er aber Edwins Vortrag, würde der entsetzliche Mr. Hyde auf ihn warten. Philipp überlegte, ob er sein Leben mit Emilia nicht anders führen, ob er es nicht ganz anders gestalten könnte. ›Es ist meine Schuld, wenn sie unglücklich ist, warum verschaffe ich ihr kein Glück?‹ Er dachte daran, aus dem Haus in der Fuchsstraße auszuziehen, aus der verfallenen Villa, die Emilia so bedrückte. Er dachte ›wir könnten in eins ihrer unverkäuflichen Landhäuser ziehen, die Häuser sind mit Mietern besetzt, die Mieter gehen nicht 'raus, schön, dann bauen wir uns eben eine Hütte im Garten, andere haben es auch getan‹. Er wußte, daß er nichts bauen würde, keine Hütte, kein Haus im Freien. Emilia würde aus der Fuchsstraße nicht ausziehen. Sie brauchte die Luft des Familienzwistes, den Anblick des immer nahen Geldverhängnisses. Und auch Philipp würde nie aufs Land ziehen. Er brauchte die Stadt, auch wenn er in der Stadt arm war. Er las manchmal Gartenbücher und bildete sich ein, im Züchten von Pflanzen Frieden zu finden. Er wußte, daß es eine Einbildung war. Er dachte ›auf dem Lande, in der selbstgebauten Hütte, wenn wir sie bauten, würden wir uns zerfleischen, in der Stadt lieben wir uns noch, wir tun nur so als ob wir uns nicht liebten‹. Er zahlte den Wein. Leider hatte er am Tisch der Abendecho-Damen den Redakteur des Neuen Blattes übersehen. Der Redakteur machte Philipp Vorwürfe wegen des unterlassenen Interviews. Er erwartete, daß Philipp nun wenigstens zu Edwins Vortrag gehen und über ihn für das Neue Blatt berichten würde. »Gehen Sie doch«, sagte Philipp. »Nee, wissen Se«, antwortete der Redakteur, »für

162

den Schmonzes hab' ich Sie. Da müssen Sie mir schon den Gefallen tun.« — »Zahlen Sie mir ein Taxi?« fragte Philipp. »Schreiben Sie's auf die Spesen«, sagte der Redakteur. »Gleich«, sagte Philipp. Der Redakteur holte einen Zehnmarkschein aus einer Tasche und reichte ihn Philipp. »Wir verrechnen es nachher«, sagte er. ›So weit ist es mit mir gekommen‹, dachte Philipp, ›ich verkaufe mich und Edwin.‹

Von der Schlägerei am Heiliggeistplatz erschreckt, von den Polizeisirenen verwirrt und begleitet, eilte Messalina in die stille Bar des Hotels. Messalina war so mit Spannung geladen, daß sie meinte, in der Stille zerplatzen zu müssen. ›Ist denn niemand hier?‹ dachte sie. Alleinsein war schrecklich. Messalina war aus dem Dirnenlokal zurück in die Bezirke der ihrer Meinung nach guten Gesellschaft geflohen, der guten Gesellschaft, an deren Rande sie gern räuberte. Messalina trennte sich nie ganz von der Gemeinschaft der gesitteten Klasse. Sie gab nichts auf. Sie wollte etwas dazuhaben. Die Gemeinschaft der gesitteten Klasse war ein Halt; von dort aus konnte sie sich mit der ungesitteten verbrüdern, eine vorübergehende Sinnenverbrüderung mit der Schicht treffen, die sie für das Proletariat hielt. Die Ahnungslose! Sie hätte nur Philipp zu fragen brauchen. Philipp hätte beredte Klage darüber geführt, wie puritanisch gesonnen das Proletariat war. Philipp war kein besonders ausschweifender Mensch. Messalina hielt ihn für einen Mönch. Aber das war was anderes. Philipp klagte oft: »Ein puritanisches Jahrhundert zieht herauf!« Er berief sich dabei in etwas unklarer Weise auf Flaubert, der das Aussterben des Freudenmädchens bedauerte. Das Freudenmädchen war gestorben. Philipp hielt den Puritanismus der Arbeiterschaft für ein Unglück. Philipp wäre sehr für die Aufhebung des Eigentums, aber er wäre entschieden gegen die Einengung der Freude gewesen. Übrigens machte er einen Unterschied zwischen Freuden- und Trauermädchen; zu den Trauermädchen zählte Philipp die gesamte landläufige Prostitution. ›Was für hemmungslose Menschen‹, dachte Messalina, ›sie prügelten sich.‹ In Messalinas Haus wurde nur in ästhetisch schicklicher Weise nach gemessenem Ritus geschlagen. Messalina sah sich um. Die Bar schien wirklich leer zu sein. Doch nein, in der hintersten Ecke saßen zwei Mädchen: Emilia und die kleine Amerikanerin mit den grünen Augen. Messalina stellte sich auf Zehenspitzen. Das große Denkmal, das sie war, schwankte gefährlich. Sie wollte die Kleinen beschleichen. Die Mädchen tranken, lachten, sie umarmten und küßten sich. Was ging da vor? Was für einen komischen Hut hatte Emilia auf? Sie hatte nie einen Hut getragen. Wie die meisten unsicheren Menschen glaubte Messalina gern, daß andre sich gegen sie verschworen, daß sie Geheimnisse hatten, von denen Messalina ausgeschlossen blieb. Die kleine grünäugige Amerikanerin war beunruhigend. Mit Philipp hatte die Grünäugige gesprochen, und nun wurde sie in Umarmungen und Küssen, es waren kleine Mädchenpensionatsküsse, mit Emilia überrascht. Wer war die kleine Reizende? Wo hatten Philipp und Emilia sie aufgetrieben? ›Vielleicht kommen sie doch auf meine Party, dann werden wir weiter sehen‹, dachte Messalina. Aber da sah sie Edwin, und sie stellte sich wieder auf die Füße. Vielleicht konnte sie Edwin gewinnen. Edwin war der größere, wenn auch weniger wohlschmeckende Fisch. Edwin kam mit schnellen Schritten in die Bar und eilte zur Theke. Er flüsterte mit dem Mixer. Der Mixer goß Edwin den Kognak in ein großes Rotweinglas. Edwin trank das Glas aus. Er hatte Lampenfieber, Vortragsfieber. Er bekämpfte die Erregung mit Kognak. Vor dem Hotel wartete schon der Wagen des Konsulats. Edwin war ein Gefangener seiner Zusage. Ein entsetzlicher Abend! Warum hatte er sich nur drauf eingelassen? Eitelkeit! Eitelkeit! Eitelkeit der Weisen. Warum war er nicht in seiner Klause geblieben, der behaglichen mit Büchern und Antiquitäten vollgestopften Wohnung? Neid auf den Ruhm der Schauspieler, Neid auf den Beifall, mit dem man den Protagonisten überschüttete, hatte ihn hinausgetrieben. Edwin verachtete die Schauspieler, die Protagonisten und die Menge, von der sie lebten und mit der sie lebten. Aber ach, es war eine Verführung, der Beifall, die Menge, die Jugend, die Jünger, sie waren Lockung und Verführung, wenn man so lange wie Edwin am Schreibtisch gesessen und sich einsam um Erkenntnis und Schönheit, aber auch um Anerkenntnis gemüht hatte. Da war die gräßliche Gesellschaftsjournalistin, das Treppenweib wieder, dieser Geschlechtskoloß, sie starrte ihn an, er mußte fliehen. Und Kay rief zu Emilia: »Da ist Edwin! Siehst du ihn nicht? Komm mit! Ich muß zu seinem Vortrag. Wo ist der Zettel von der Wescott? Komm doch mit! Bald hätt' ich's vergessen!« Emilia blickte Kay auf einmal böse an: »Geh mir mit deinem Edwin! Ich verabscheue die Literaten, diese Schießbudenfiguren! Ich rühr' mich nicht!« — »Aber er ist ein Dichter«, rief Kay, »wie kannst du so was sagen!« — »Philipp ist auch ein Dichter«, sagte Emilia. »Wer ist das, Philipp?« fragte Kay. »Mein Mann«, sagte Emilia. ›Sie ist verrückt‹, dachte Kay, ›was will sie? sie ist verrückt, sie ist doch gar nicht verheiratet, sie kann doch nicht erwarten, daß ich hier sitzen bleibe, ich bin schon ganz betrunken, ich habe genug verrückte Weiber in meiner Reisegesellschaft, aber sie ist entzückend, diese kleine verrückte Deutsche.‹ Sie rief: »Wir sehen uns noch!« Sie warf Emilia eine Kußhand zu, eine letzte flüchtige Geste. Sie wirbelte zu Edwin. Sie hatte Whisky getrunken; jetzt würde sie Edwin ansprechen; sie würde ihn um das Autogramm bitten; sie hatte Edwins Buch nicht mehr in der Hand, wo war es nur? wo lag es wohl? aber Edwin konnte das Autogramm auf den Block des Mixers schreiben. Doch Edwin eilte schon fort. Kay rannte ihm nach. Emilia dachte ›es geschieht mir recht, jetzt kommt auch noch Messalina‹. Messalina schaute empört hinter Edwin und Kay drein. Was war das schon wieder? Warum stürmten die fort? Hatten sie sich gegen Messalina verschworen? Emilia würde es ihr erklären müssen. Aber Emilia war auch verschwunden, sie war durch eine Tapetentür verschwunden. Auf dem Tisch lag neben den leeren Gläsern nur der komische Hut, den Emilia aufgehabt hatte. Er lag da wie eine erlittene Enttäuschung. ›Es ist Hexerei‹, dachte Messalina, ›es ist die reine Hexerei, ich bin ganz allein auf der Welt.‹ Sie wankte, eine für den Augenblick Gebrochene, zur Theke. »Einen Dreifachen«, rief sie. »Was soll's denn sein, gnädige Frau«, fragte der Mixer. »Ach irgendwas. Ich bin müde«. Sie war

wirklich müde. So müde war sie lange nicht gewesen. Sie
war auf einmal furchtbar müde. Aber sie durfte nicht müde
sein. Sie mußte ja noch zum Vortrag, sie mußte ja noch so
viel für die Party organisieren. Sie griff nach dem hohen
Glas, über das wasserhell der Schnaps schwippte. Sie gähnte.

Der Tag war müde. Das Abendlicht des Himmels, die unter-
gehende Sonne schien direkt in die horizontblaue Limousine
hinein, und für einen Augenblick blendete das Licht Carla
und Washington. Das Licht blendete, aber es reinigte und
verklärte auch. Carla und Washington hatten erleuchtete
Gesichter. Erst nach einer Weile stellte Washington den
Blendschutz ein. Sie fuhren langsam am Ufer des Flusses
entlang. Gestern hätte Carla noch geträumt, sie würden auf
dem Riverside-drive in New York oder am Golden Gate in
Kalifornien so spazierenfahren. Jetzt hatte ihr Herz sich
beruhigt. Sie fuhr keiner Magazin-Traum-Wohnung entgegen mit Liegestühlen, Fernsehapparatur und mechanischer
Küche. Es war ein Traum gewesen. Ein Traum, der Carla
gequält, weil sie in ihrem innersten Herzen immer gefürchtet
hatte, das Traumland nicht zu erreichen. Die Last dieser
Sehnsucht war nun von ihr genommen. In ihrem Zimmer
hatte sie sich wie erschlagen gefühlt. Als Washington sie zum
Auto führte, war sie nicht mehr als ein Sack an seinem Arm
gewesen, ein schwerer Sack mit irgendeiner toten Füllung.
Jetzt war sie befreit. Sie war nicht von dem Kind befreit,
aber von dem Traum an die faule Glückseligkeit des Daseins,
an den Schicksalsbetrug durch einen Knopf, an dem man
drehen konnte. Sie glaubte wieder. Sie glaubte Washington.
Sie fuhren am Fluß entlang, und Carla glaubte an die Seine.
Die Seine war nicht so weit wie der Mississippi, sie war nicht
so fern wie der Colorado. An der Seine würden sie beide zu
Hause sein. Sie würden beide Franzosen werden, wenn es
sein mußte, sie, eine Deutsche, würde Französin werden, und
Washington, ein schwarzer Amerikaner, würde Franzose werden. Die Franzosen freuten sich, wenn einer bei ihnen leben
wollte. Carla und Washington würden das Lokal errichten,
Washington's Inn, die Wirtschaft, in der niemand uner-

wünscht ist. Ein Wagen überholte sie. Christopher und Ezra saßen in dem Wagen. Christopher freute sich. Er hatte in einem Antiquitätengeschäft eine Tasse der Berliner Porzellanmanufaktur gekauft, eine Tasse mit dem Bild eines großen preußischen Königs. Er würde die Tasse mit an die Seine nehmen. Er würde sie im Hotel an der Seine Henriette schenken. Henriette würde sich über die Tasse mit dem Bild des preußischen Königs freuen. Henriette war eine Preußin, wenn sie jetzt auch eine Amerikanerin war. All diese Nationalitäten sind Unsinn‹, dachte Christopher, ›wir sollten Schluß damit machen, natürlich ist jeder auf seinen Heimatort stolz, ich bin stolz auf Needles am Colorado, aber deshalb schlag' ich doch noch keinen tot.‹ — ›Wenn's nicht anders geht, schlag' ich ihn tot‹, dachte Ezra, ›ich nehm' einen Stein und schlag' ihn tot und dann schnell in das Auto hinein, der Hund muß vorher schon in das Auto hinein, die Dollar kriegt er nicht der Kraut, wenn Christopher bloß schnell und genügend Gas gibt.‹ Ezras kleine Stirn war schon seit Stunden in besorgte Falten gelegt. Christopher hatte Ezra die zehn Dollar gegeben. »Nun wirst du also nicht verlorengehen«, hatte er gescherzt, »oder wenn du verlorengehst, wirst du mit Hilfe der zehn Dollar wieder zu mir finden.« — »Ja, ja«, hatte Ezra gesagt. Die Sache schien ihn nicht mehr zu interessieren. Er hatte die zehn Dollar gleichgültig eingesteckt. »Kommen wir rechtzeitig ins Bräuhaus?« fragte Ezra. »Was willst du nur im Bräuhaus?« erkundigte sich Christopher. »Andauernd fragst du, ob wir rechtzeitig hinkommen.« — »Nur so«, sagte Ezra. Er durfte nichts verraten. Christopher würde dagegen sein. »Aber wenn wir die Brücke erreicht haben, kehren wir um«, bohrte Ezra. »Natürlich kehren wir dann um. Warum sollten wir nicht umkehren?« Christopher wollte noch schnell die Brücke sehen, von der es im Reisehandbuch hieß, daß sie einen romantischen Blick über das Flußtal biete. Christopher fand Deutschland schön.

Behude konnte in drei Stehausschänke gehen. Von draußen sahen sie alle gleich aus. Es waren die gleichen Behelfsbauten, sie hatten die gleichen Flaschen im Fenster, die gleichen Prei-

se auf der Tafel stehen. Der eine Ausschank gehörte einem
Italiener, der andere einem alten Nazi und der dritte einer
alten Dirne. Behude wählte den Ausschank des alten Nazis.
Emilia trank manchmal beim alten Nazi ein Glas. Es war
Masochismus von ihr. Behude lehnte sein Fahrrad an die
bröckelnde aus Preßmüll gefertigte Mauer des Ausschanks.
Der alte Nazi hatte schlaffe Wangen, und eine dunkle Brille
verdeckte seine Augen. Emilia war nicht da. ›Ich hätte doch
zur alten Dirne gehen sollen‹, dachte Behude, aber nun war
er schon beim alten Nazi. Behude verlangte einen Wodka.
Er dachte ›wenn er keinen Wodka hat, kann ich wieder ge-
hen‹. Der alte Nazi hatte Wodka. ›Eigentlich bin ich der
Typ für Mineralwasser‹, dachte Behude, ›Sportsmann, hätte
nicht Psychiater werden sollen, ruiniert einen.‹ Er trank den
Wodka und schüttelte sich. Behude mochte keinen Alkohol.
Aber zuweilen trank er ihn aus Trotz. Er trank nach der
Sprechstunde. Er dachte ›und-der-Beutel-schlapp-und-leer‹.
Es war ein Studentenlied. Behude hatte es nicht gesungen.
Er hatte überhaupt keine Studentenlieder gesungen. Aber
der Beutel war schlapp und leer. Er selber war schlapp, leer,
er, Dr. Behude, nach jeder Sprechstunde war er schlapp und
leer. Und der Beutel war es auch. Zwei Patienten hatten
Behude wieder angepumpt. Behude konnte sie nicht abweisen.
Er behandelte ja die Leute wegen Lebensuntüchtigkeit. ›Dieser Nazi ist auch schlapp und leer‹, dachte er. Er bestellte
noch einen Wodka. »Nun wird's bald wieder losgehen«,
sagte der Nazi. »Was denn?« fragte Behude. »Nun, Tschin-
dradada«, sagte der Nazi. Er tat, als ob er eine Pauke schlü-
ge. ›Sie haben wieder Oberwasser‹. dachte Behude, ›was auch
geschehen mag, es treibt sie nach oben.‹ Er trank den zweiten
Wodka und schüttelte sich wieder. Er zahlte. Er dachte ›wäre
ich nur zur alten Dirne gegangen‹, aber sein Geld reicht
nicht mehr zur alten Dirne.

Emilia stand im Stehausschank der alten Dirne. Sie hatte
nach Hause gehen wollen. Sie hatte nicht betrunken nach
Hause kommen wollen, weil Philipp dann schimpfte oder
manchmal auch weinte. Philipp war in letzter Zeit hysterisch.

168

Es war verrückt von ihm, Emilias wegen besorgt zu sein. »Ich vertrage schon einen Stiefel«, sagte Emilia. Sie kannte die Zweiteilung Dr. Jekyll und Mr. Hyde, die Philipp mit ihr vornahm. Sie wäre gern als Dr. Jekyll zu ihm gekommen, als der liebe gute Doktor. Sie hätte Philipp dann gesagt, daß noch etwas von dem Geld des Leihamtes, etwas von dem Geld der Königstasse, etwas von dem Geld des Gebetteppichs übriggeblieben sei. Man würde wieder einmal die Lichtrechnung zahlen können. Sie hätte Philipp dann von dem Schmuck erzählt, den sie verschenkt hatte. Philipp hätte das verstanden. Er hätte auch verstanden, warum sie sich, als sie der grünäugigen Amerikanerin den Schmuck umhängte, so frei gefühlt hatte. Aber im ganzen war es doch ärgerlich gewesen. Philipp würde es ihr gleich sagen »du hättest weglaufen müssen. Du hättest ihr den Schmuck umhängen und dann weglaufen müssen.« Philipp war ein Psychologe. Das war wunderbar, und das war ärgerlich. Man konnte Philipp nichts verbergen. Es war besser, man erzählte ihm alles. ›Warum bin ich nicht weggelaufen? weil ihr Mund so gut schmeckte, weil er so frisch und frei nach Prärie schmeckte, mach' ich mir was aus Mädchen? nein ich mach' mir gar nichts aus Mädchen, aber vielleicht hätt' ich so ein bißchen geflirtet wie mit einem hübschen Schwesterlein, Streicheln, Küsse und komm-doch-noch-gut-Nacht-sagen, sie hatte auch Lust dazu, der blöde Edwin, jede menschliche Beziehung ist blöd, wär' ich gleich davongelaufen hätte ich mich heute wohl gefühlt, ich hätte nie mit dieser Amerikanerin sprechen dürfen, ich hasse sie jetzt!‹ Aber der Kummer hatte Emilia diesmal nicht zur alten Dirne getrieben. Emilia hätte der Lust, bei der alten Dirne einzukehren, widerstanden. Aber sie war verführt worden. Sie hatte kurz hinter dem Hotel den herrenlosen Hund mit dem nachschleppenden Bindfaden getroffen. »Du Armer«, hatte sie gerufen, »du kannst überfahren werden.« Sie hatte den Hund an sich gelockt. Der Hund witterte Emilias andere Tiere, und sofort zeigte er, daß er hier auf Stellungssuche ging; Emilia war für ihn ein guter Mensch, und seine Nase trog ihn nicht. Emilia sah, daß der Hund Hunger hatte. Sie hatte ihn in den Ausschank der alten Dirne geführt und ihm eine Wurst gekauft. Da sie schon im Ausschank war, trank Emilia einen Kirsch. Sie trank das scharfe kernbittere Kirschwasser. Sie trank es aus Lebensbitternis und wegen der Bitterkeit des Tages, der Bitterkeit der Schmuckaffäre, der Bitterkeit mit Philipp und der Bitterkeit des Fuchsstraßenheims. Die alte Dirne war freundlich, aber auch bitter. Emilia trank mit der alten Dirne. Emilia lud die alte Dirne zum Trinken ein. Die alte Dirne war wie ein gefrorener Wasserstrahl. Sie hatte einen großen Hut auf, der wie der erstarrte Wasserkranz eines Springbrunnens war, und dann hatte sie jettbesetzte Handschuhe an. Das Jett auf den Handschuhen klirrte bei jeder Bewegung der Hände wie Eis; es klirrte wie kleine Eisstückchen in einem Becher, den man schüttelt. Emilia bewunderte die alte Dirne. ›Wenn ich so alt bin wie sie, werde ich lange nicht so gut aussehen, ich werde nicht halb so gut aussehen, ich werde auch keinen Stehausschank haben, ich werde mein Geld in ihrem Stehausschank gelassen haben, sie hat ihr Geld zusammengehalten, sie hat nie auf eigene Kosten getrunken, sie hat immer nur auf Kosten der Männer getrunken, ich werde nicht aufhören, auf eigene Kosten zu trinken.‹ Der Hund wedelte. Er war sehr klug. Man sah es ihm nicht an, aber er war klug. Er ahnte, daß er das menschliche Wesen, das sich nun seiner angenommen hatte, rühren konnte. Er würde die Frau beherrschen. Die Aussicht zu herrschen war hier viel günstiger als bei den Kindern, die unberechenbare launische Götter waren. Die neue Göttin war eine gute Göttin. Der Hund war, wie der Psychiater Behude, der Meinung, daß Emilia ein guter Mensch sei. Emilia wird den Hund nicht enttäuschen. Schon ist sie entschlossen, ihn mit nach Hause zu nehmen. »Du bleibst bei der Tante«, sagte sie. »Ja, mein Guter, ich weiß, wir trennen uns nicht mehr.«

Im Stehausschank des Italieners beugte sich Richard über die Theke. Wo war er hingeraten? Er war da so 'reingegangen. Die Tür hatte offengestanden. Er hatte den Laden für einen Drugstore gehalten. Er hatte gedacht ›vielleicht ist ein Mädchen dort, es wäre nett, wenn ich am ersten Abend

in Deutschland ein deutsches Mädchen hätte‹. Jetzt war er
auf ein Schlachtfeld geraten. Flaschen, Gläser und Korkenzieher wurden zu Bastionen und rollenden Panzern, Zigarettenpackungen und Zündholzschachteln zu Luftgeschwadern.
Der italienische Besitzer des Stehausschankes war ein wüten-
der Stratege. Er zeigte dem jungen amerikanischen Flieger,
wie man Europa verteidigen müsse. Von der geglückten Verteidigung ging er zum Angriff über und löschte den Osten
aus. »Nehmt doch ein paar Bomben«, rief er. »Nehmt ein
paar Bomben, und ihr habt gesiegt!« Richard trank einen
Wermut. Er merkte verwundert, daß der Wermut bitter
schmeckte. Er schmeckte wie bitteres Zuckerwasser. ›Vielleicht hat der Kerl recht‹, dachte Richard, ›es ist so einfach,
ein paar Bomben, vielleicht hat er recht, warum kommt Truman nicht auf die Idee? ein paar Bomben, warum macht man
es im Pentagon anders?‹ Aber dann fiel Richard etwas ein;
es fiel ihm etwas aus der Geschichtsstunde ein, oder aus den
Zeitungen, die er gelesen, oder aus den Reden, die er gehört
hatte. Er sagte: »Das hat doch Hitler schon getan, das haben
doch die Japaner schon gemacht: einfach angreifen, so einfach über Nacht angreifen —« — »Hitler hat recht gehabt«,
sagte der Italiener. »Hitler war ein großer Mann!« —
»Nein«, sagte Richard, »er war ein abscheulicher Mann.«
Richard wurde blaß, weil es ihm peinlich war, sich zu streiten, und weil er sich ärgerte. Er war nicht hergekommen,
um sich zu streiten. Er konnte sich nicht streiten; er wußte
nicht, was hier vorging. Vielleicht sahen hier die Leute alles
ganz anders an. Er war aber auch nicht hergekommen, um
seine amerikanischen Grundsätze zu verleugnen; die Grundsätze, auf die er so stolz war. »Ich bin nicht hier, um wie
Hitler zu handeln«, sagte er. »Wir werden niemals wie
Hitler handeln.« — »Sie werden müssen«, sagte der Italiener. Er warf wütend die Bastionen, die Panzer und die Luft-
geschwader durcheinander. Richard brach das Gespräch ab.
»Ich muß ins Bräuhaus«, sagte er. Er dachte ›man verliert
hier jeden Halt‹.

Der Krieger, der kein Krieger hatte sein wollen, der Töter, der nicht hatte töten wollen, der Erschlagene, der von einem gemächlicheren Tod geträumt hatte, er lag auf dem harten Bett im Heiliggeistspital, er lag in einer weißgekalkten Kammer, in einer Mönchszelle, er lag unter einem Kreuz mit dem Gekreuzigten daran, eine Kerze brannte zu seinem Haupt, ein Priester kniete neben ihm, eine Frau kniete mit einem viel strengeren Gesicht als der Geweihte Gottes hinter dem Priester, die Vertreterin einer unerbittlichen Religion, die selbst das Sterben noch als Sünde betrachtete, so verhärtet war ihr Herz, ein kleines Mädchen stand vor ihm und starrte ihn an, und immer mehr Polizeibeamte drängten sich wie Statisten in die enge Kammer. Auf der Straße heulten die Polizeisirenen. Das Viertel wurde durchsucht. Die deutsche Polizei und die amerikanische Militärpolizei suchten den großen Odysseus. Der Todesengel hatte längst die Hand auf Josef gelegt. Was gingen ihn die Sirenen an? Was kümmerten ihn die Polizisten zweier Nationen und zweier Erdteile? Als Josef arbeitete, war er der Polizei aus dem Wege gegangen. Die Polizei brachte nie etwas Gutes. Sie brachte Stellungsbefehle oder Vermahnungen. Am besten war es gewesen, wenn niemand nach Josef fragte. Wenn man nach ihm rief, wollte man etwas von ihm; man wollte dann immer etwas Unangenehmes von ihm. Jetzt brachte sein Sterben die ganze Stadt in Aufruhr. Der alte Dienstmann hatte das nicht gewollt. Er kam noch einmal zu sich. Er sagte: »Es war der Reisende.« Er sagte es nicht, um anzuklagen. Er war froh, daß es der Reisende gewesen war. Die Schuld war beglichen. Der Priester sprach die Absolution. Emmi bekreuzte sich und murmelte ihr Vergib-uns-unsere-Sünden. Sie war eine grimmige kleine Gebetsmühle. Hillegonda überlegte: da war ein alter Mann; er sah lieb aus; er war tot; der Tod sah lieb aus; der Tod war gar nicht zu fürchten; er war lieb und still; aber Emmi meinte, der alte Mann sei in Sünden gestorben und Sünden müßten ihm vergeben werden; es schien Emmi noch gar nicht sicher zu sein, daß dem alten Mann seine Sünden vergeben würden; Gott war noch nicht entschlossen, sie zu vergeben; er würde die Schuld bestenfalls gnadenweise verzeihen; Gott war sehr streng; es gab kein Recht vor Gott; man konnte sich auf nichts vor Gott berufen, alles war Sünde; aber wenn alles Sünde war, dann war es doch ganz gleich, was man tat; wenn Hillegonda schlimm war, dann war es Sünde, aber wenn sie brav war, dann blieb es immer noch Sünde; und warum war der Mann so alt geworden, wenn er ein Sünder war; warum hatte Gott ihn nicht früher schon gestraft, wenn er ein Sünder war; und warum sah der alte Mann so lieb aus? man konnte also verbergen, daß man ein Sünder war; man sah es keinem an, wer er war; man konnte keinem trauen. Und wieder regte sich bei Hillegonda ein Mißtrauen gegen Emmi: konnte man Emmi trauen, der frommen betenden Emmi, war nicht die Frömmigkeit vielleicht eine Maske, die den Teufel verbarg? Wenn Hillegonda nur mit ihrem Vater hätte darüber reden können, aber der Vater war so dumm, er sagte, daß es keine Teufel gebe, vielleicht meinte er auch, daß es keinen Gott gebe: oh, er kannte Emmi schlecht, es gab den Teufel. Man war ihm immer ausgeliefert. Die vielen Polizisten: waren das nun die Polizisten Gottes oder die Polizisten des Teufels? Sie holten den toten alten Mann, um ihn zu bestrafen; Gott wollte ihn bestrafen, und der Teufel wollte ihn bestrafen. Es kam am Ende auf dasselbe 'raus. Es gab keinen Ausweg für den toten alten Mann. Er konnte sich nicht verbergen. Er konnte sich nicht wehren. Er konnte nicht mehr davonlaufen. Hillegonda tat der alte Mann leid. Er konnte doch gar nichts dafür. Hillegonda trat zu dem toten Josef und küßte ihm die Hand. Sie küßte die Hand, die so viele Koffer getragen hatte, eine runzelige Hand mit Rillen voll Erde, voll Schmutz, voll Krieg und Leben. Der Priester fragte: »Du bist seine Enkelin?« Hillegonda brach in Tränen aus. Sie barg ihren Kopf in der Soutane des Priesters und schluchzte bitterlich. Emmi unterbrach ihr Gebet und sagte ärgerlich: »Sie ist ein Schauspielerkind, Hochwürden. Lüge, Verstellung und Komödie liegen ihr im Blut. Strafen Sie das Kind, retten Sie seine Seele!« Aber noch ehe der Priester, der erschrocken aufhörte, Hillegonda zu streicheln, der Kinderfrau antworten konnte, erhob sich unter Josefs Spitalbett und Totenbahre eine Stimme. Odysseus' Musikkoffer, der unter dem Bett abgestellt war und eine Weile geschwiegen hatte, sprach wieder. Er sprach diesmal mit einer englischen Stimme, weich, leise, schwingend, eine schöne, eine gebildete, eine etwas gezierte Oxfordstimme, die Stimme eines Philologen, und sie wies auf Edwins Bedeutung und seinen Vortrag im Amerikahaus hin. Die Stimme schilderte es als ein Glück für Deutschland, daß Mr. Edwin, ein Kreuzfahrer des Geistes, in die Stadt gekommen sei, um hier für den Geist, die Tradition, für die Unvergänglichkeit des Geistes, für das alte Europa zu zeugen, das seit den Tagen der Französischen Revolution, die Stimme zitierte Jacob Burckhardt, in seiner gesellschaftlichen und geistigen Ordnung erschüttert und in einem Zustand des andauernden Zuckens und Bebens sei. War Edwin gekommen, die Erschütterung zu bannen, die Unordnung zu ordnen und, freilich im Sinne der Tradition, neue Tafeln eines neuen Gesetzes zu errichten? Der Priester, der Josefs Leben überdachte, den die Unruhe bewegte, die der Tod des alten Dienstmannes im Sprengel hervorrief, und der seltsam berührt war von der finsteren Frömmigkeit der Kinderfrau, von ihrem jeder Wärme, jeder Freude baren steinernen Gesicht und gerührt vom Schluchzen des kleinen Mädchens, dessen Tränen in den Schoß seines Priesterkleides fielen, der geistliche Herr hörte beiläufig der englischen Stimme zu, der Stimme aus dem Musikkoffer unter dem Totenbett, und er hatte die Empfindung, die Stimme spreche von einem falschen Propheten.

Schnakenbach, der Schläfer, der entlassene Gewerbelehrer, der nicht genug gebildete Einstein, hatte den Nachmittag im Lesesaal der Amerikanischen Bibliothek verbracht. Er hatte sich im Halbschlaf zum Amerikahaus geschleppt und war, wie von einem Engel behütet, noch einmal den Straßenbahnen, den Automobilen und den Radfahrern entgangen. Im Lesesaal der Bibliothek hatte er alle erreichbaren chemischen und pharmakologischen Publikationen um sich aufgestapelt. Er wollte sich über den neuesten Stand der Forschung in Amerika unterrichten; er wollte sehen, wie weit sie in dem großen Amerika mit der Herstellung schlafhindernder Mittel

vorangekommen seien. In Amerika schien es viele Schlaf-
süchtige zu geben. Die Amerikaner beschäftigten sich einge-
hend mit dem Problem, wach zu bleiben. Schnakenbach lernte von ihnen. Er machte sich Notizen. Er schrieb und zeichnete mit winziger Schrift Formeln und Strukturen auf; er
rechnete; er beachtete den Spiegel der Moleküle; er bedachte,
daß es linksdrehende und rechtsdrehende Verbindungen gab
und daß er herausfinden mußte, ob sein Leben, dieser Teil
des allgemeinen Lebens, diese Ich denkende Zusammensetzung chemischer Kräfte, die er, Schnakenbach, für eine Weile
war, bevor er wieder in die große Retorte getan wurde, sich
nach links oder nach rechts drehe. Bei dieser Überlegung
übermannte ihn sein Feind, sein Leiden, der Schlaf. Man
kannte Schnakenbach im Lesesaal. Man störte seinen Schlaf
nicht; man entriß ihn nicht seinem Feind. Die Bibliothekarin
hatte seltsame Kunden. Der Lesesaal übte eine ungeheure
Anziehungskraft auf Obdachlose, Wärmeschinder, Sonder-
linge und Naturmenschen aus. Die Naturmenschen kamen
barfuß, in handgewebtes Linnen gehüllt, mit langem Haupt-
haar und wildem Bart. Sie verlangten Werke über Hexen
und böse Blicke, Kochbücher für Rohkostspeisen, Broschüren
über das Leben nach dem Tode und über die Übungen indi-
scher Fakire, oder sie vertieften sich in die letzten Veröffent-
lichungen der Astrophysik. Sie waren kosmologische Geister
und knabberten Wurzeln und Nüsse. Die Bibliothekarin sagte: »Ich erwarte immer, daß sich einer bei mir die Füße
wäscht; aber sie waschen sich nie.« Die Amerikanische Bibliothek war eine herrliche Einrichtung. Ihre Benutzung war
völlig kostenlos. Die Bibliothek stand jedermann offen, fast
war sie Washington's Inn, fast das Lokal, das der Neger und
amerikanische Bürger Washington Price in Paris eröffnen
wollte, das Lokal, in dem niemand unerwünscht ist.
Schnakenbach schlief. Während er schlief, füllte sich der
große Vorlesungssaal des Hauses. Viele kamen, um Edwin
zu hören. Studenten kamen, junge Arbeiter kamen, ein paar
Künstler kamen, die aus existentiellen Gründen Vollbärte
trugen und ihre Baskenmützen nicht vom Kopf nahmen, es
kam die Philosophieklasse des Priesterseminars, Bauernge-

175

sichter, die sich zum Geist, zur Strenge oder zur Einfalt wandelten, es kamen zwei Straßenbahnschaffner, ein Bürgermeister und ein Gerichtsvollzieher, der Literaten zu seiner Klientel zählte und so auf die schiefe Bahn geraten war, und außerdem kamen sehr viele gutangezogene und wohlgenährte Leute. Edwins Vortrag war ein gesellschaftliches Ereignis. Die gutangezogenen Leute waren beim Rundfunk oder beim Film angestellt, oder sie arbeiteten in der Reklamebranche, soweit sie nicht das Glück hatten, Volksvertreter, höherer Ministerialbeamter, gar Minister selbst oder Besatzungsoffizier und Konsularagent zu sein. Sie alle waren an Europas Geist interessiert. Die Kaufleute der Stadt schienen am Geiste Europas weniger interessiert zu sein; sie hatten keinen Vertreter geschickt. Erschienen jedoch waren die Modeschöpfer, feminine wohlriechende Herren, die ihre Vorführpuppen mitgebracht hatten, schöngewachsene Mädchen, die man ihnen unbesorgt anvertrauen durfte. Behude hatte sich zu den Priestern gesetzt. Es war eine kollegiale Geste. Er dachte ›wir können jederzeit psychiatrischen und geistlichen Beistand leihen, nichts kann passieren‹. Messalina und Alexander hielten Hof. Sie standen in der Nähe des Podiums und wurden von den Pressephotographen mit Blitzlicht beleuchtet. Jack war bei ihnen. Er hatte eine verdrückte amerikanische Offizierssommerhose und einen buntgestreiften Sweater an. Er war ungekämmt und sah aus, als wäre er eben, durch ein Klingeln erschreckt, aus dem Bett gesprungen. Neben ihm hielt sich Hänschen, sein Freund, ein semmelblonder, leicht geschminkter Sechzehnjähriger in einem blauen Konfirmandenanzug, sehr artig. Er blickte mit kalten wasserhellen Augen auf die Modeschöpfer und ihre Puppen, Hänschen, Hänschen klein, war Hans im Glück: er wußte, wo was zu holen war. Jetzt erschien auch Alfredo, die Bildhauerin. Ihr angestrengtes, müdes, enttäuschtes Gesicht, das Spitzgesicht einer Katze von den Inschriften der Pyramiden, war gerötet, als hätte sie sich selber geohrfeigt, um Mut und Frische für den Abend zu gewinnen. Gegen Messalina wirkte Alfredo so zierlich und klein, daß man wünschte, Messalina möge Alfredo auf den Arm nehmen, damit sie alles gut sehen könne.

Alexander wurde beglückwünscht. Ein paar Wichtigtuer und ein paar Speichellecker beglückwünschten ihn. Sie hofften, mit auf die Blitzlichtaufnahmen und in die Zeitungen zu kommen: *Alexander im Gespräch mit Pippin dem Kleinen, Bund erwägt Kulturpfennig stiftet Akademie.* Sie sprachen von der *Erzherzogliebe, Bessere Filme im neuen Deutschland, liegt es am Drehbuch, Dichter an die Filmfront.* »Es soll ein so wundervoller Film sein«, schwärmte eine Dame, deren Mann den »Gerichtskurier« herausgab, *Vampir in Frauenkleidern,* und damit genug Geld verdiente, um seine Frau bei den femininen Modeschöpfern anziehen zu lassen. »Ein Schmarren«, sagte Alexander. »Wie witzig Sie wieder sind«, flötete die Dame. ›Natürlich‹, dachte sie, ›natürlich ist es ein Schmarren, aber warum sagt er's so laut? ist es vielleicht doch kein Schmarren? dann ist es sicher ein ernster und langweiliger Schmarren‹, *Neorealismus nicht mehr gefragt.* Die Lehrerinnen aus Massachusetts saßen in der vordersten Reihe. Sie hatten ihre Merkbücher in der Hand. Sie hielten die im Blitzlicht Stehenden für Koryphäen des europäischen geistigen Lebens. Sie hatten das Glück gehabt, keine Filme mit Alexander zu sehen. »Es ist ein sehr interessanter Abend«, sagte Miß Wescott. »Ein Zirkus«, sagte Miß Burnett. Sie schielten beide zur breiten Eingangstür, ob nicht Kay endlich noch käme. Sie waren beide sehr besorgt um Kay. Edwin wurde durch eine kleine besondere Pforte auf das Podium geführt. Die Photographen knieten wie Schützen nieder und feuerten ihr Blitzlicht ab. Edwin verneigte sich. Er hatte die Augen geschlossen. Er zögerte den Moment hinaus, da er in sein Auditorium blicken mußte. Ihm war ein wenig schwindlig. Er glaubte, er würde kein Wort sprechen können, keinen Ton aus der Kehle bekommen. Er schwitzte. Er schwitzte vor Angst, aber er schwitzte auch vor Glück. So viele waren gekommen, ihn zu hören! Sein Name hatte sich durchgesetzt in der Welt. Er wollte es sich nicht überschätzen. Aber die Menschen kamen, um seinen Worten zu lauschen. Edwin hatte sein Leben den geistigen Bemühungen geweiht, er war zum Geist gekommen, er war Geist geworden, und nun konnte er den Geist weitergeben: Jünger empfingen ihn in jeder Stadt, der Geist würde nicht sterben. Edwin legte sein Manuskript auf den Lesetisch. Er rückte die Lampe zurecht. Er räusperte sich. Aber noch einmal wurde die breite Tür geöffnet, und Philipp und Kay liefen die Stufen hinunter, die in den Saal führten. Philipp hatte Kay vor der Tür getroffen. Der Ordner wollte sie nicht mehr hineinlassen, aber Philipp hatte die Pressekarte des Neuen Blattes wie einen Zauber gezückt, und der Ordnungsmann hatte die Tür freigegeben. Philipp und Kay setzten sich abseits des Auditoriums auf zwei Klappstühle, die bei Theateraufführungen für den Feuerwehrmann und den Polizisten reserviert waren. Zu Edwins Vortrag war kein Feuerwehrmann und kein Polizist gekommen. Miß Wescott stieß Miß Burnett an: »Sehen Sie das?« flüsterte sie. »Es ist dieser deutsche Dichter, ich weiß seinen Namen nicht«, sagte Miß Burnett. »Sie hat sich mit ihm herumgetrieben.« Miß Wescott war entrüstet. »Wenn sie weiter nichts getan hat«, sagte Miß Burnett spitz. »Es ist furchtbar«, stöhnte Miß Wescott. Sie wollte aufspringen und zu Kay gehen; sie hatte das Gefühl, daß man die Polizei rufen müsse. Aber wieder räusperte sich Edwin, und Stille senkte sich über den Saal. Edwin wollte mit der griechischen und lateinischen Antike beginnen, er wollte die Christenheit erwähnen, die Verbindung biblischer Tradition mit der Klassik, er wollte von der Renaissance sprechen und Lob und Tadel an den französischen Rationalismus des achtzehnten Jahrhunderts wenden, aber leider drang statt der Worte nur Geräusch zu seinen Zuhörern, ein Gurgeln und Knacken und Raspeln wie von Jahrmarktspritschen. Edwin, am Lesepult, merkte zunächst nicht, daß die Lautsprecheranlage des Saales in Unfunktion geraten war. Er spürte Unruhe im Raum und ein der geistigen Konzentration ungünstiges Klima. Er sprach noch ein paar Worte von der Bedeutung der Halbinsel, die dem eurasischen Kontinent vorgestreckt liegt, als ihn Scharren und Rufe, lauter und deutlicher zu sprechen, unterbrachen. Edwin war wie einem Hochseilgänger zumute, der mitten auf dem Seil merkt, daß er nunmehr weder vorwärts noch rückwärts gehen kann. Was wollten die Leute? Waren sie gekommen, ihn zu verhöhnen? Er schwieg und hielt sich am Pult fest. Man rebellierte. Die Technik rebellierte gegen den Geist, die Technik, das vorlaute, entartete, schabernacksüchtige, unbekümmerte Kind des Geistes. Ein paar Eifrige stürzten vor, um die Mikrophone zu verrücken. Der Fehler lag aber an der Lautsprecheranlage des Hauses. ›Ich bin hilflos‹, dachte Edwin, ›wir sind hilflos, ich habe mich auf diesen dummen und bösen Sprechtrichter verlassen, hätte ich ohne diese Erfindung die mich nun lächerlich macht vor sie hintreten können? nein, ich hätte es nicht gewagt, wir sind keine Menschen mehr, keine ganzen Menschen, ich hätte nie wie Demosthenes direkt zu ihnen sprechen können, ich brauche Blech und Draht die meine Stimme und meine Gedanken wie durch ein Sieb pressen.‹ Messalina fragte: »Siehst du Philipp?« — »Ja«, sagte Alexander, »ich muß mit ihm über das Manuskript reden. Ihm wird nichts eingefallen sein.« — »Quatsch«, sagte Messalina, »er schreibt doch nie was. Aber das Mädchen. Die Niedliche. Eine Amerikanerin. Die verführt er. Was sagst du nun?« — »Nichts«, sagte Alexander. Er gähnte. Er würde einschlafen. Mochte doch Philipp verführen, wen er Lust hatte. ›Er muß schön potent sein‹, dachte Alexander. »Idiot«, flüsterte Messalina. Das Krachen in der Lautsprecheranlage des Hauses war auch im Lesesaal zu hören und hatte Schnakenbach geweckt. Auch er hatte zu Edwins Vortrag gehen wollen, auch er interessierte sich für den europäischen Geist. Er sah, daß es schon spät war und daß der Vortrag schon begonnen hatte. Er taumelte hoch und torkelte in den Saal. Irgend jemand hielt Schnakenbach für den erwarteten Haustechniker, der wohl im Keller geschlafen hatte, und reichte ihm versehentlich das Mikrophon. Schnakenbach sah sich plötzlich vor eine Zuhörerschaft gestellt; er glaubte, schlafbenommen wie er war, vor der Klasse zu stehen, die er geleitet hatte, bevor er sein Amt als Gewerbeschullehrer aufgeben mußte, und so schrie er in das Mikrophon die große Sorge, die ihn erfüllte: »Schlaft nicht! Wacht auf! Es ist Zeit!«

Es war Zeit. Heinz beobachtete den Platz zwischen dem Bräuhaus und dem Klub der Negersoldaten. Es war viel Polizei auf dem Platz; es war viel zuviel Polizei auf dem

Platz. Die Wache der Militärpolizei vor dem Klub war verstärkt worden. Die Militärpolizisten waren besonders große, besonders schön gewachsene Neger. Sie trugen weiße Gamaschen, weiße Koppel und weiße Handschuhe. Sie sahen wie nubische Legionäre des Cäsar aus. Heinz wußte noch immer nicht, wie er es anstellen sollte. Das beste würde es sein, die Dollar zu nehmen und in die Ruinen zu laufen. In den Ruinen würde der amerikanische Junge ihn nicht finden. ›Aber wenn er den Hund sehen will? natürlich wird er den Hund sehen wollen, bevor er mit seinem Schein 'rausrückt.‹ Es war dumm, daß der Hund weggelaufen war. Es konnte das Geschäft gefährden. Aber es wäre gelacht, wenn Heinz sich deshalb schon vom Geschäft zurückzöge, weil der Hund ausgekniffen war. Heinz hatte sich gut versteckt. Er stand im Eingang der Broadway-Bar. Die Bar war geschlossen. Der Eingang war dunkel. Der Besitzer der Bar hatte es vorgezogen, zum wirklichen Broadway zu fliehen. In der neuen Welt war Sicherheit. In der Alten Welt konnte man sterben. In der Neuen Welt konnte man auch sterben, aber man starb in größerer Sicherheit. Der Besitzer der Broadway-Bar hatte in Europa Ängste, Schulden, Finsternis und nackte Mädchen zurückgelassen. Er hatte auch Gräber zurückgelassen, ein großes Grab, in dem seine erschlagenen Verwandten lagen. Die Bilder der nackten Mädchen klebten in der Dunkelheit des Ganges vergessen und verworfen an der schmutzigen Mauer. Die Mädchen lächelten und hielten mit neckischer Gebärde kleine Schleier vor ihre Scham. Ami-Huren — ein Entrüsteter hatte es hingeschrieben. Die Mädchen lächelten, sie blieben neckisch, sie hielten sich neckisch die kleinen Schleier vor. Ein Nationalist hatte Deutschland-erwache an die Wand gemalt. Die Mädchen lächelten. Heinz pißte gegen die Mauer. Susanne ging am dunklen Eingang der Bar vorüber. Sie dachte ›die Schweine pissen überall hin‹. Susanne ging zum Klub der Negersoldaten. Die schwarzen Militärpolizisten prüften Susannes Ausweis. Sie hielten den Ausweis in ihren blendendweiß behandschuhten Händen. Der Ausweis war in Ordnung. Ein Sirenenwagen der weißen Militärpolizei fuhr beim Klub vor. Die weißen Militärpolizisten riefen ihren schwarzen

180

Kameraden eine Botschaft zu. Die weißen Polizisten sahen nicht so elegant aus wie die schwarzen. Sie sahen gegen die schwarzen Polizisten schäbig aus. Susanne verschwand in der Tür des Klubs. Einer der weißen Polizisten dachte ›diese Nigger haben die hübschesten Mädchen‹.

Im Klub spielte eine deutsche Kapelle. Der Klub war arm. Eine amerikanische Kapelle war zu teuer gewesen. Nun spielte eine deutsche Kapelle, und die deutsche Kapelle war auch ganz gut. Es war die Kapelle des Obermusikmeisters Behrend. Die Kapelle spielte alle Jazzstücke, und zuweilen spielte sie den Hohenfriedberger Marsch oder den Spanischen Walzer von Waldteufel. Der Marsch gefiel den schwarzen Soldaten sehr. Waldteufel gefiel ihnen weniger. Kapellmeister Behrend war zufrieden. Er spielte gern in den Klubhäusern der amerikanischen Armee. Er fand, daß er gut bezahlt wurde. Er war glücklich. Vlasta machte ihn glücklich. Er blickte zu Vlasta hinüber, die an einem kleinen Tisch neben der Kapelle saß. Vlasta war über eine Näharbeit gebeugt. Zuweilen schaute sie auf, und Vlasta und Herr Behrend lächelten einander zu. Sie hatten ein Geheimnis: sie hatten sich gegen die Welt gestellt und sich behauptet; sie hatten sich jeder gegen die eigene Umwelt und ihre Anschauungen gestellt, und sie hatten den Kreis des Vorurteils, der sie einengen wollte, gesprengt. Der Obermusikmeister der deutschen Wehrmacht hatte das kleine Tschechenmädchen im Protektorat Böhmen und Mähren kennengelernt und geliebt. Mit Mädchen schliefen viele. Aber sie verachteten die Mädchen, mit denen sie schliefen. Nur wenige liebten das Mädchen, mit dem sie schliefen. Der Obermusikmeister liebte Vlasta. Er hatte sich erst gegen die Liebe gewehrt. Er hatte gedacht ›was will ich mit dem Tschechenmädel?‹ Aber dann hatte er sie geliebt, und die Liebe hatte ihn verwandelt. Sie hatte nicht nur ihn verwandelt, sie hatte auch das Mädchen verwandelt, auch das Mädchen war eine andere geworden. Als man in Prag die deutsche Wehrmacht wie freigegebenes Wild jagte, versteckte Vlasta Herrn Behrend in der Truhe, und später floh sie mit ihm aus der Tschechoslowakei. Vlasta hatte sich von allem losgesagt; sie hatte sich von ihrem Vaterland losgesagt; und Herr Behrend hatte sich von vielem losgesagt; er hatte sich von seinem ganzen bisherigen Leben losgesagt: sie fühlten sich beide losgelöst, sie waren frei, sie waren glücklich. Sie hätten es vorher nicht für möglich gehalten, daß man so frei und so glücklich sein könne. Die Kapelle spielte Dixieland. Unter der Stabführung des Musikmeisters spielte sie eine der ersten Jazzkompositionen, deutsch und romantisch in der Weise des Freischütz.

Susanne fand die Kapelle langweilig. Die blassen Idioten schlugen ein zu gemächliches Tempo an. Die Kapelle entsprach nicht dem, was Susanne schräge Musik nannte. Sie wollte Wirbel, sie wollte Rausch; sie wollte sich dem Wirbel und dem Rausch hingeben. Es war dumm, daß alle Neger sich ähnlich sahen. Wer kannte sich da aus? Nachher ging man mit dem Falschen mit. Susanne hatte ein Kleid aus gestreifter Seide an. Sie trug das Kleid wie ein Hemd auf der bloßen Haut. Sie hätte jeden haben können. Jeder im Saal wäre mit ihr fortgegangen. Susanne suchte Odysseus. Sie hatte ihm Geld gestohlen, aber da sie Kirke und die Sirenen und vielleicht auch Nausikaa war, mußte sie wieder zu ihm gehen und konnte ihn nicht in Ruhe lassen. Sie hatte ihm sein Geld gestohlen, aber sie würde ihn nicht verraten. Nie würde sie ihn verraten; sie würde nie verraten, daß er Josef erschlagen hatte. Sie wußte nicht, ob Odysseus Josef mit dem Stein erschlagen hatte, aber sie glaubte es. Susanne tat es nicht leid, daß Josef gestorben war, ›wir müssen alle sterben‹. Aber sie bedauerte, daß Odysseus nicht einen anderen erschlagen hatte. Er hätte Alexander oder Messalina erschlagen sollen. Aber wen er auch erschlagen hatte: Susanne mußte zu ihm halten, ›wir müssen gegen die Schweine zusammenhalten‹. Susanne haßte die Welt, von der sie sich ausgestoßen und mißbraucht fühlte. Susanne liebte jeden, der sich gegen diese hassenswerte Welt wandte, der ein Loch in ihre kalte grausame Ordnung schlug. Susanne war treu. Sie war ein zuverlässiger Kamerad. Auf Susanne konnte man sich verlassen. Man brauchte keinen Polizisten zu fürchten.

Heinz drückte sich gegen die Mauer mit den nackten Mädchen. Ein deutscher Polizist schlenderte am Eingang der Bar vorüber. Die deutschen und die amerikanischen Polizisten waren an diesem Abend wie aus ihrem Nest aufgeschreckte Wespen. Ein Neger hatte einen Taxichauffeur umgebracht oder einen Dienstmann. Heinz wußte es nicht genau. In der Altstadt sprach man davon. Die einen meinten, es sei ein Taxifahrer gewesen, die andern sagten ein Dienstmann. ›Ein Dienstmann hat doch kein Geld‹, dachte Heinz. Er lugte aus dem Gang und sah Washingtons horizontblaue Limousine vor dem Negerklub vorfahren. Washington und Carla stiegen aus. Sie gingen in den Klub. Heinz wunderte sich. Washington und Carla waren lange nicht im Klub gewesen. Carla hatte nicht mehr hingehen wollen. Sie hatte sich geweigert, mit den Nutten zusammenzukommen, die im Klub verkehrten. Wenn Washington und Carla wieder in den Klub gingen, mußte sich etwas ereignet haben. Heinz wußte nicht, was sich ereignet haben konnte, aber es mußte bedeutungsvoll sein. Es beunruhigte ihn. Wollte das Paar nach Amerika fahren? Sollte er mitfahren? Sollte er nicht mitfahren? Wollte er überhaupt mitfahren? Er wußte es nicht. Er wäre jetzt am liebsten nach Hause gegangen, um im Bett darüber nachzudenken, ob er nach Amerika fahren solle. Vielleicht hätte er im Bett geweint. Vielleicht hätte er auch nur Old Shatterhand gelesen und Schokolade gegessen. Konnte man Karl May trauen? Washington sagte, Indianer gebe es nur noch in Hollywood. Sollte er nach Hause gehen? Sollte er zu Bett gehen? Sollte er über all diese Probleme nachdenken? Da kam das Auto, das einem Flugzeug so ähnlich sah, auf den Platz gefahren. Der Parkwächter wies das Auto ein. Christopher und Ezra stiegen aus. Ezra guckte sich um. Er war also gekommen. Er wollte das Geschäft machen. Heinz konnte nicht mehr zurück. Er konnte nicht mehr ins Bett gehen. Es wäre feige gewesen, sich jetzt vom Geschäft zurückzuziehen. Christopher ging ins Bräuhaus. Ezra ging langsam hinter Christopher her. Er schaute sich immer wieder um. Heinz dachte ›ob ich ihm ein Zeichen gebe?‹ Aber er überlegte ›nein, es ist noch zu früh, sein Vater, der alte Ami, muß erst beim Bier sitzen‹.

›Was für ein junger Kerl er ist, was für ein junger Ami‹,
dachte das Fräulein, ›es ist sein erster Abend in Deutschland,
und schon habe ich ihn kennengelernt.‹ Das Fräulein war
hübsch. Es hatte dunkle Locken und blanke Zähne. Das
Fräulein hatte sich von Richard in der Hauptstraße ansprechen lassen. Es hatte gesehen, daß Richard Lust hatte, ein
Mädchen anzusprechen, und daß er zu schüchtern war, es zu
tun. Das Fräulein hatte es Richard leichtgemacht. Das Fräulein hatte sich ihm in den Weg gestellt. Richard merkte, daß
sie es ihm leichtmachte. Sie gefiel ihm, aber er dachte ›wenn
sie nun krank ist?‹ Man hatte ihn in Amerika gewarnt. Man
warnte in Amerika die ausreisenden Soldaten vor den Fräuleins. Aber er dachte ›ich will ja gar nichts von ihr, und vielleicht ist sie auch gar nicht krank‹. Sie war nicht krank. Sie
war auch kein Straßenmädchen. Richard hatte Glück gehabt.
Das Fräulein verkaufte im Warenhaus am Bahnhof Socken.
Das Warenhaus verdiente an den Socken. Das Fräulein verdiente wenig. Es gab das Wenige zu Hause ab. Es hatte aber
keine Lust, am Abend zu Hause zu sitzen und die Radiomusik zu hören, die der Vater bestimmte: Glühwürmchen-
flimmere, das ewige tödlich langweilige Wunschkonzert, das
zäheste Erbe des Großdeutschen Reiches. Der Vater las, während das Glühwürmchen flimmerte, die Zeitung. Er sagte:
»Bei Hitler war's anders! Da war Zug drin.« Die Mutter
nickte. Sie dachte an die alte ausgebrannte Wohnung; da war
Zug drin gewesen; es war Zug in den Flammen gewesen. Sie
dachte an die immer gehütete und dann verbrannte Aussteuer. Sie konnte den Linnenschrank der Aussteuer nicht
vergessen, aber sie wagte dem Vater nicht zu widersprechen:
der Vater war Portier in der Vereinsbank, ein angesehener
Mann. Das Fräulein suchte nach den Socken und nach der
Glühwürmchen-Musik etwas Heiterkeit. Das Fräulein wollte
leben. Es wollte sein eigenes Leben. Es wollte nicht der Eltern
Leben wiederholen. Das Leben der Eltern war nicht nach-
ahmenswert. Die Eltern waren gescheitert. Sie waren arm.
Sie waren unheiter, unglücklich, vergrämt. Sie saßen vergrämt in einer grämlichen Stube bei grämlich munterer
Musik. Das Fräulein wollte ein anderes Leben, eine andere

Freude, wenn es sein sollte, einen anderen Schmerz. Die amerikanischen Jungen waren dem Fräulein lieber als die deutschen Jungen. Die amerikanischen Jungen erinnerten das Fräulein nicht an das grämliche Zuhause. Sie erinnerten das Fräulein nicht an alles, was es bis zum Überdruß kannte: die ewige Einschränkung, das ewige Nach-der-Decke-Strecken, die Wohnungsenge, die völkischen Ressentiments, das nationale Unbehagen, das moralische Mißvergnügen. Um die amerikanischen Jungen war Luft, die Luft der weiten Welt; der Zauber der Ferne, aus der sie kamen, verschönte sie. Die amerikanischen Jungen waren freundlich, kindlich und unbeschwert. Sie waren nicht so mit Schicksal, Angst, Zweifel, Vergangenheit und Aussichtslosigkeit belastet wie die deutschen Jungen. Auch wußte das Fräulein, was ein Kommis im Warenhaus verdient; es kannte die Entbehrungen, die er litt, um sich einen Anzug kaufen zu können, einen Anzug im schlechten Geschmack der Konfektion, in dem er unglücklich aussah. Das Fräulein würde einmal einen überarbeiteten, enttäuschten, schlechtangezogenen Mann heiraten. Das Fräulein wollte das heute vergessen. Es wäre gern tanzen gegangen. Aber Richard wollte ins Bräuhaus gehen. Auch das Bräuhaus war lustig. Ging man also ins Bräuhaus. Aber man spielte auch im Bräuhaus die Glühwürmchen-Musik.

Die Säle waren überfüllt. Die Volks- und Völkergemeinschaft, die viel gerühmte, die oft besungene Gemütlichkeit des Bräuhauses tobte. Aus großen Fässern strömte und schäumte das Bier; es strömte und schäumte in ununterbrochenem Fluß; die Zapfer drehten die Spünde nicht ab; sie hielten die Maßkrüge unter den Strom, rissen sie vom Bier zurück, schnitten sie ab vom Naß und hielten schon den nächsten Krug unter den Fluß. Kein Tropfen ging verloren. Die Kellnerinnen schleppten acht, zehn, ein Dutzend Krüge zu den Tischen. Das Fest des Gottes Gambrinus wurde gefeiert. Man stieß an, man trank aus, man legte den Krug auf den Tisch, man wartete auf die zweite Füllung. Die Oberländer-Kapelle spielte. Es waren alte Herren in kurzen Lederhosen, die haarige gerötete Knie zeigten. Die Kapelle spielte das Glüh-

würmchen, sie spielte Sah-ein-Knab'-ein-Röslein-stehn, und
alle im Saal sangen das Lied mit, sie faßten sich unter, sie
standen auf, sie stellten sich auf die Bierbänke, sie hoben die
Krüge und brüllten langgezogen gefühlsbetont Röslein-auf-
der-Hei-hei-den. Man setzte sich wieder. Man trank wieder.
Väter tranken, Mütter tranken, kleine Kinder tranken; Greise
umstanden den Waschbottich und suchten nach Biereigen
in den abgestellten Krügen, die sie durstig gierig hinunter-
spülten. Man sprach von der Ermordung des Taxifahrers.
Ein schwarzer Soldat hatte einen Taxifahrer ermordet. Es
war Josefs Tod, von dem gesprochen wurde; aber die Fama
hatte aus dem Dienstmann einen Taxifahrer gemacht. Ein
Dienstmann schien der Fama ein zu armes Opfer für einen
Mord zu sein. Die Stimmung war den Amerikanern nicht
günstig. Man schimpfte, man raunzte; man hatte zu klagen.
Bier hebt in Deutschland das nationale Bewußtsein. In andern Ländern regt Wein, in manchen vielleicht Whisky den
Nationalstolz an. In Deutschland ist das Bier der die Vater-
landsliebe belebende Stoff: ein dumpfer, ein nicht erhellen-
der Rausch. Den einzelnen Angehörigen der Besatzung, die
sich in den Hexenkessel des Bräuhauses verirrt hatten, begegnete man nachbarlich freundlich. Viele Amerikaner liebten das Bräuhaus. Sie fanden es großartig und gemütlich. Sie
fanden es noch großartiger und noch gemütlicher als alles,
was sie darüber gelesen oder gehört hatten. Die Oberländer-
Kapelle spielte den Badenweiler Marsch, den Lieblingsmarsch
des toten Führers. Man brauchte der Kapelle nur eine Lage
zu spendieren, und sie spielte den Marsch, der den Einzug
Hitlers in die Versammlungssäle der Nationalsozialisten begleitet hatte. Der Marsch war die Musik der jungen und ver-
hängnisvollen Geschichte. Der Saal hob sich wie eine einzige
geschwellte Brust der Begeisterung von den Plätzen. Es waren nicht Nazis, die sich da erhoben. Es waren Biertrinker.
Die Stimmung allein machte es, daß alle sich erhoben. Es
war nur eine Gaudi! Warum so ernst sein? warum an Ver-
gangenes, Begrabenes, Vergessenes denken? Auch die Amerikaner wurden von der Stimmung mitgerissen. Auch die
Amerikaner erhoben sich. Auch die Amerikaner summten

den Marsch des Führers, schlugen mit Füßen und Fäusten den Takt. Amerikanische Soldaten und davongekommene deutsche Soldaten umarmten sich. Es war eine warme rein menschliche Verbrüderung ohne politische Absicht und diplomatischen Handel. *Fraternization verboten, Fraternization freigegeben, Die Woche der guten Nachbarschaft.* Christopher fand es wunderbar. Er dachte ›Warum sträubt Henriette sich dagegen? Warum kann sie nicht vergessen? Sie sollte das hier sehen, es ist wunderbar, es sind prächtige Leute‹. Ezra beobachtete die Kapelle, er beobachtete die Menschen. Seine Stirn hatte sich noch mehr gekraust; ganz eng, ganz klein war sie. Er hätte schreien mögen! Er war in einem finsteren Wald. Jeder Mann war hier ein Baum. Jeder Baum war eine Eiche. Und jede Eiche war ein Riese, der böse Riese des Märchens, ein Riese mit einer Keule. Ezra ahnte, daß er den Aufenthalt in diesem Wald nicht lange ertragen konnte. Er würde die Furcht nicht lange mehr bannen können. Wenn der Junge mit dem Hund nicht bald kam, würde Ezra schreien. Er würde schreien und davonlaufen. Frau Behrend drängte sich durch die Reihen. Sie suchte Richard, den jungen amerikanischen Verwandten, den Sohn des Paketeschickers, man konnte nicht wissen, vielleicht kam wieder eine schlechte Zeit, *Konflikt verschärft sich,* Verwandte mußten zusammenhalten. Welch eine Dummheit von dem Jungen, sie in das Bräuhaus zu bestellen! Fast an jedem Tisch saß ein Amerikaner. Sie saßen da wie unsere Soldaten, fast wie die Soldaten der Wehrmacht; sie saßen nur in schlechterer Haltung, sie saßen bequem und nicht zackig da. ›Zu viel Freiheit verwildert‹, dachte Frau Behrend. Sie sprach junge Amerikaner an: »Bist du es, Richard? Ich bin Tante Behrend!« Sie erntete Verständnislosigkeit oder Gelächter. Einige riefen »setz dich, Alte« und schoben ihr den Bierkrug hin. Ein dicker Kerl, ein Faß fast, klapste ihr den Hintern. ›Was die für Soldaten haben, es sind nur ihre Autos und ihre Flugzeuge die gesiegt haben.‹ Frau Behrend eilte weiter. Sie mußte Richard finden! Richard durfte nicht nach Hause berichten, was die giftige Lebensmittelhändlerin ihm erzählt hatte. Frau Behrend mußte Richard finden. Sie sah ihn mit einem Mädchen sitzen, einem schwarzlockigen ganz hübschen Flitscherl. Die beiden tranken aus einem Krug. Die linke Hand des Mädchens lag auf der rechten Hand des jungen Mannes. Frau Behrend dachte ›ist er das? er könnte es sein, dem Alter nach könnte er es sein, aber er kann es nicht sein, es ist unmöglich daß er es ist, er wird doch wenn er mit seiner Tante verabredet ist nicht sein Flitscherl mitbringen‹. Richard merkte, daß die Frau ihn beobachtete. Er erschrak. Er dachte ›das ist sie wohl, die Frau mit dem Fischgesicht ist die Tante mit der Negertochter, ich bin nicht neugierig, ich will mich nicht aufdrängen‹. Er wandte sich seinem Mädchen zu, er nahm das Fräulein in die Arme und küßte es. Das Fräulein dachte ›ich muß aufpassen, er ist stürmischer als ich dachte, ich fürchtete er würde mich erst vorm Haus küssen‹. Des Fräuleins Lippen schmeckten nach Bier. Auch Richards Lippen schmeckten nach Bier. Das Bier war sehr gut. ›Er ist es nicht‹, dachte Frau Behrend, ›er würde sich nie so benehmen, auch wenn er in Amerika groß geworden ist, würde er sich nie so benehmen.‹ Sie setzte sich auf eine Bank und bestellte sich zögernd ein Bier. Das Bier war eine unnötige Ausgabe. Frau Behrend machte sich nichts aus Bier. Aber sie war durstig, und sie war auch zu erschöpft, um den Kampf mit der Kellnerin, den Kampf mit dem Saal aufzunehmen und nichts zu bestellen.

Carla und Washington waren in den Negerklub gegangen, um die Zukunft zu feiern, die Zukunft, in der niemand mehr unerwünscht ist. An diesem Abend glaubten sie an die Zukunft. Sie glaubten, daß sie diese Zukunft erleben würden, die Zukunft, in der niemand, wer er auch sein mochte und wie er leben würde, unerwünscht wäre. Carla war musikalisch. Noch ehe sie ihn sah, hatte sie an seiner Art, den Jazz zu spielen, ihren Vater, den alten Freischütz-Dirigenten, erkannt. Gestern wäre es Carla noch peinlich gewesen, den Musikmeister in einem Negerklub zu treffen, und fürchterlich wäre es ihr erschienen, von ihm dort mit Washington gesehen zu werden. Jetzt berührte sie die Begegnung anders. Sie waren Menschen. Menschen dachten anders. In einer

Musikpause begrüßte Carla den Vater. Herr Behrend freute sich, Carla zu sehen. Er war etwas verlegen, aber er bekämpfte die Verlegenheit und machte Carla mit Vlasta bekannt. Auch Vlasta war verlegen. Sie waren alle drei verlegen. Aber sie dachten nichts Böses voneinander. »Da sitzt mein Freund«, sagte Carla. Sie deutete auf Washington. »Wir gehen nach Paris«, sagte sie. Der Musikmeister wäre auch beinahe einmal nach Paris gegangen. Er sollte im Krieg nach Paris versetzt werden. Er wurde aber nach Prag versetzt. Herr Behrend überlegte ›ob es recht von Carla ist, einen Neger zu lieben?‹ Er wagte die Frage nicht zu beantworten. Der Neger war wohl ein guter Mensch, wenn Carla mit ihm lebte. Einen Augenblick regte sich in allen das Gift des Zweifels. Sie dachten ›wir verkehren miteinander, weil wir alle deklassiert sind‹. Aber weil sie sich an diesem Abend froh fühlten, hatten sie die Kraft, den Zweifel zurückzudrängen, die hämischen Empfindungen zu töten. Sie blieben freundlich und liebten sich. Herr Behrend sagte: »Jetzt wirst du staunen. Du wirst sehen, daß dein Vater auch *hot* spielen kann, einen richtigen Hot-Jazz.« Er ging wieder auf das Podium. Carla lächelte. Auch Vlasta lächelte. Der arme Vater. Er bildete sich ein, richtigen Jazz spielen zu können. Den richtigen Jazz konnten nur die Schwarzen spielen. Die Kapelle des Herrn Behrend fing an, mit Blech zu rasseln und die Trommeln zu rühren. Dann setzten die Trompeten ein. Es war laut, und es war auch schön. Susanne hatte Odysseus gefunden. Er hatte sich in den Klub gewagt. Er hatte sich ihretwegen aus Verstecken hervor an Polizeischlingen vorbei in den Klub gewagt, Susanne hatte gewußt, daß Odysseus kommen würde; sie hatten sich mit einem Wort, einem Ruf verständigt, und er war gekommen. Susanne, die Kirke und die Sirenen und vielleicht auch Nausikaa war, hielt Odysseus umschlungen. Zur Hot-Weise des Musikmeisters glitten sie wie ein Leib im Tanz über das Parkett, wie eine vierfüßige sich windende Schlange. Sie waren beide erregt. Alles, was sie heute erlebten, hatte sie erregt. Odysseus hatte fliehen, Odysseus hatte sich verstecken müssen, man hatte ihn nicht gefangen, der große listenreiche Odysseus war den Häschern entkommen, er hatte

189

Susanne Kirke die Sirenen betört, oder sie hatten ihn betört, und vielleicht hatte er Nausikaa erobert. Wenn das nicht erregte? Es erregte. Es erregte sie beide. Die Schlange mit den vier Beinen, die so geschmeidig sich windende Schlange wurde von allen bewundert. Nie würden sie sich aus dieser Umschlingung lösen. Die Schlange hatte vier Beine und zwei Köpfe, ein weißes und ein schwarzes Gesicht, aber nie würden die Köpfe sich gegeneinander wenden, nie die Zungen gegeneinander geifern: sie würden sich nie verraten, die Schlange war ein Wesen gegen die Welt.

Er war nicht die Rote Schlange, er war Wildtöter. Der rothaarige Amerikanerjunge war die Rote Schlange. Wildtöter beschlich die Rote Schlange. Heinz war in die Ruine eines Geschäftshauses geklettert. Vom Stumpf der gesprengten Mauer konnte er in den Saal des Bräuhauses blicken. Die Prärie wogte. Büffelherden zogen durch das Gras. Das Licht der Saallampen, an riesige Wagenräder gehängte Leuchten, verdämmerte in der Ausdünstung der Menschen und des Bieres wie in einem Nebel. Heinz konnte niemand erkennen. Wildtöter mußte die Blauen Berge verlassen. Er mußte sich auf Schleichwegen durch die Prärie bewegen. Er duckte sich unter Tische und Bänke. Da entdeckte er einen Feind, den er hier nicht vermutet hatte. Frau Behrend saß überraschenderweise im Bräuhaus und trank Bier. Heinz mochte die Großmutter nicht. Frau Behrend wollte Heinz in eine Erziehungsanstalt geben. Frau Behrend war eine gefährliche Frau. Was tat sie im Bräuhaus? War sie jeden Abend hier? Oder war sie nur heute hier, um Heinz aufzulauern? Ahnte sie, daß er auf dem Kriegspfad war? Heinz durfte sich nicht sehen lassen. Aber es lockte ihn, Frau Behrend einen Streich zu spielen. Es war eine Mutprobe. Er durfte sich ihr nicht entziehen. Die Kapelle spielte Fuchs-du-hast-die-Gans-gestohlen. Der Saal hatte sich wieder erhoben. Alle hatten sich untergefaßt und sangen das Lied. Frau Behrend war von zwei kahlköpfigen Geschäftsleuten untergefaßt und sang gib-sie-wieder-her. Heinz wollte Frau Behrend das Bier ausschütten. Er drängte sich hinter Frau Behrend und die dicken kahlköpfigen Geschäftsleute. Aber als er dicht hinter Frau Behrend stand, traute sich Heinz nicht mehr, den Krug zu nehmen und das Bier auszuschütten. Er nahm nur das volle Schnapsglas, das neben dem Krug stand, und schüttete den Schnaps in das Bier. Dann entwischte er. Er war wieder Wildtöter, der die Rote Schlange suchte.

Ezra schwitzte. Er zitterte. Er glaubte zu ersticken. Auch sein Vater war nun ein Riese geworden, einer der deutschen Riesen in dem deutschen Zauberwald. Christopher stand neben den andern und sang sonst-wird-dich-der-Jäger-holen-mit-dem-Schießgewehr. Er kannte die Worte nicht, er konnte sie nicht aussprechen, aber er bemühte sich, sie zu singen, und zuweilen unterstützte ihn sein deutscher Nachbar, stieß ihn an und sang die Worte deutlicher silbentrennend und belehrend Schieß-ge-wehr, und Christopher nickte und lachte und hob den Bierkrug gegen den Nachbar, und dann bestellten Christopher und der Nachbar Würste und Rettiche, und sie aßen zusammen Würste und Rettiche, und Christopher ahnte nicht, daß sein Kind sich fürchtete. Wildtöter hatte sie gefunden. Er suchte den Blick der Roten Schlange und machte ihr ein Zeichen. Es war soweit. Ezra konnte dem Kampf nicht ausweichen. Der deutsche Junge war sein ihm von den Riesen des Waldes erwählter Gegner. Mit ihm mußte er sich messen. Mit ihm mußte er ringen. Wenn er den Jungen besiegte, hatte er den Wald besiegt. »Ich geh' zum Auto«, sagte Ezra. Christopher sagte: »Was willst du im Wagen? Bleib hier.« — »Ich sitz' lieber im Auto«, sagte Ezra. »Komm auch bald. Wir müssen nach Hause fahren. Wir müssen ganz schnell nach Hause fahren.« Christopher dachte ›Ezra hat recht, es gefällt ihm nicht, es ist nichts für einen Jungen, er ist noch zu klein, ich werde mein Bier austrinken, und dann werde ich ihn ins Hotel fahren, ich kann ja noch mal zurückkommen wenn ich noch weiter Bier trinken will, wenn Ezra schläft kann ich zurückkommen und weiter Bier trinken‹. Es gefiel ihm. Das Bräuhaus gefiel ihm sehr. Es gefiel ihm zu denken, daß er zurückkommen und weiter Bier trinken würde.

Die Fama erreichte Frau Behrend. Ein Neger hatte gemordet, Neger waren Verbrecher, die Polizeisirenen kreischten, man suchte den Neger. »Es ist eine Schande«, sagte Frau Behrend. »Sie sind wie die wilden Tiere. Sie sind wie wilde reißende Tiere. Man sieht es ihnen ja an. Ich könnte Ihnen Geschichten erzählen.« Der Geschäftsmann zur Linken von Frau Behrend verdächtigte sie im stillen, seinen Schnaps ausgetrunken zu haben. Er dachte ›sieh mal an, die Alte, ganz munter, trinkt heimlich meinen Schnaps und tut, als sei nichts gewesen‹. Aber er fand, daß Frau Behrend eine anständige Gesinnung hatte. Mochte sie den Schnaps getrunken haben, sie hatte eine anständige Gesinnung, er würde ihr noch einen bestellen. Frau Behrend dachte ›ich könnte es nicht erzählen, ich brächte es nicht über mich, aber wenn ich es erzählen könnte —‹. Sie malte sich das Erstaunen und die Entrüstung der Geschäftsleute aus. Sie dachte ›der Vater mit einem ausländischen Flittscherl und die Tochter mit einem Neger‹. Und der amerikanische Neffe? Der Neffe hatte sich gedrückt. Er hatte sie genarrt. Er war nicht im Bräuhaus erschienen. Frau Behrend tat ergrimmt einen tiefen Zug aus ihrem Krug. Mit den Ausländern kannte man sich nicht aus. Bei den Steinkrügen sah man nicht, wieviel man noch drin hatte. Sollte sie wirklich schon das Bier ausgetrunken haben? Es war wahr; der Saal, die Musik, die Menschen, das Singen, die Erregung, der Ärger, die Verbrechen der Neger — alles machte einen durstig. Auch der andere Geschäftsmann dachte, daß Frau Behrends Gesinnung gut sei. Ihr Krug war leer. Er würde sie zu einem weiteren Bier einladen. Die Frau sah noch ganz gut aus. Aber vor allem hatte sie die richtige Gesinnung. Darauf kam es an. Was wollten die Neger hier? Es war eine Schande! Die Geschäftsleute hatten keine schwarzen Kunden.

»Wo ist der Hund?« fragte Ezra, »ich will ihn sehen.« Die Rote Schlange wollte den Hund sehen. Wildtöter hatte es gefürchtet. Es konnte alles noch an dem verdammten, ausgekniffenen Hund scheitern. Heinz mußte Zeit gewinnen. Er sagte: »Kommen Sie in dieses Haus. Ich werde Ihnen

dann den Hund zeigen.« Die Kinder begegneten einander
steif und mit Würde. Sie sprachen miteinander, als ob sie
die Sätze aus einem Reisediktionär für vornehme Leute gelernt hätten. Heinz führte Ezra in das zerstörte Geschäfts-
haus. Er kletterte auf den Mauerstumpf. Ezra folgte ihm.
Er wunderte sich nicht, daß Heinz ihn in eine Ruine führte.
Auch Ezra wollte Zeit gewinnen. Auch er hatte noch immer
keinen festen Plan. Er sorgte sich, ob Christopher rechtzeitig
zum Auto kommen würde. Er mußte rechtzeitig zum Auto
kommen und schnell davonfahren. Alles hing davon ab, daß
Christopher rechtzeitig davonfahren würde. Sie saßen auf
dem Mauerstumpf und blickten in den Saal des Bräuhauses.
Für eine Weile fanden sie sich ganz nett. ›Wir könnten uns
eine Schleuder machen und Steine in das Fenster schießen,
Steine in die Prärie, Steine auf die Büffel‹, dachte Heinz.
›Von hier draußen sehen die Riesen nicht so furchtbar aus‹,
dachte Ezra. ›Es hat keinen Zweck, es länger hinauszuzö-
gern‹, dachte Heinz. Er hatte wahnsinnige Angst. Er hätte
sich lieber nicht drauf einlassen sollen. Aber da er sich nun
mal drauf eingelassen hatte, mußte er es auch durchführen.
Er fragte:»Haben Sie die zehn Dollar bei sich?« Ezra nickte.
Er dachte ›jetzt geht es los, ich muß siegen‹. Er sagte:»Wenn
ich Ihnen das Geld zeige, rufen Sie dann den Hund?« Heinz
nickte. Er rückte etwas zum Rand der Mauer. Von dort konnte er leicht abspringen. Wenn er das Geld gepackt hatte,
konnte er abspringen. Er konnte auf eine niedrigere Mauer
springen und dann durch die Ruine zur Bäckergasse laufen.
Der amerikanische Junge würde ihm nicht folgen. Er würde
in der Ruine hinfallen. Er würde Zeit verlieren und ihn in
der Bäckergasse nicht mehr erwischen. Ezra sagte:»Wenn
Sie ihn gerufen haben, kann ich dann den Hund mit in das
Bräuhaus nehmen und ihn meinem Vater zeigen?« Er dachte
›wenn ich den Hund habe, müssen wir weg, Christopher muß
dann losfahren‹. Heinz sagte:»Erst müssen Sie mir die zehn
Dollar geben.« Er dachte ›zeig du was du willst, dir zeig' ich
es schon‹. Ezra sagte:»Erst muß mein Vater den Hund sehen.« — »Sie haben das Geld gar nicht«, schrie Heinz. »Ich
habe das Geld, aber ich kann es Ihnen erst geben, wenn mein

Vater den Hund gesehen hat.« — ›Falscher Hund‹, dachte
Heinz. Der war schlau. Die Rote Schlange war schlauer, als
Heinz gedacht hatte. »Sie bekommen den Hund nicht, bevor
ich nicht das Geld habe.« — »Dann ist nichts zu machen«,
sagte Ezra. Seine Stimme bebte. Heinz schrie wieder: »Sie haben das Geld nicht!« Er war dem Weinen nahe. »Ich habe
es!« rief Ezra. Seine Stimme überschlug sich. »Dann zeigen
Sie es! Zeig's doch, blöder Hund, Hund blöder, zeig's doch,
wenn du's hast!« Heinz hielt die Spannung nicht länger aus.
Er fiel aus dem vornehmen Konversationston und packte
Ezra. Ezra stieß ihn zurück. Die Knaben rangen. Sie rangen
auf der Ruinenmauer, die unter den Bewegungen ihres erbitterten Ringens, unter der Erschütterung ihrer wütenden
Stöße zu bröckeln begann. Der von der Hitze des Brandes
ausgedörrte Mörtel rieselte aus allen Fugen zwischen den
Steinen, und die Mauer stürzte mit den kämpfenden Jungen
ein. Sie schrien. Sie schrien um Hilfe. Sie schrien deutsch und
englisch um Hilfe. Die Polizisten auf dem Platz hörten die
Schreie. Die deutschen Polizisten hörten die Schreie, und die
amerikanischen Militärpolizisten hörten die Schreie. Auch die
Negerpolizisten hörten die Schreie. Die Sirene des amerikanischen Polizeijeeps schrillte. Die Sirenen der deutschen Strei-
fenwagen antworteten.

Die Schreie der Sirenen drangen in den Bräuhaussaal und
entzündeten die Biergeister. Die Fama, die allmächtige Unheil webende Fama erhob aufs neue ihr Haupt und kündete
ihre Mär. Die Neger hatten ein neues Verbrechen begangen.
Sie hatten ein Kind in die Ruinen gelockt und es erschlagen.
Die Polizei war am Tatort. Die verstümmelte Leiche des Kindes war gefunden worden. Die Volksstimme gesellte sich der
Fama. Die Fama und die Volksstimme sprachen im Chor:
»Wie lange wollen wir das noch mit ansehen? Wie lange
wollen wir uns das noch gefallen lassen?« Vielen war der
Negerklub ein Ärgernis. Vielen waren die Mädchen, die
Frauen, die sich mit Negern einließen, ein Ärgernis. Die Ne-
ger in Uniform, ihr Klub, ihre Mädchen, waren sie nicht ein
schwarzes Symbol der Niederlage, der Schmach des Besiegt-

seins, waren sie nicht das Zeichen der Erniedrigung und der Schande? Noch einen Augenblick lang zögerte die Menge. Der Führer fehlte. Ein paar Burschen brachen als erste auf. Dann folgten sie alle, folgten mit roten Gesichtern, schwer atmend und erregt. Christopher wollte gerade zum Wagen gehen. Er fragte: »Was ist los? Warum rennen sie alle?« Der Mann, mit dem Christopher Rettich gegessen hatte, sagte: »Die Nigger haben ein Kind umgebracht. Ihre Nigger!« Er stand auf und sah Christopher herausfordernd an. Christopher rief: »Ezra!« Er lief mit der Menge auf den Platz und rief: »Ezra!« Sein Ruf ging unter im Geheul der erregten Stimmen. Er konnte sich zu seinem Auto nicht durchdrängen. Er dachte ›warum ist keine Polizei auf dem Platz?‹ Der Eingang zum Negerklub war unbewacht. Hinter den großen Fensterscheiben leuchteten rote Vorhänge. Man hörte Musik. Die Musik des Herrn Behrend spielte Hallelujah. »Schluß mit der Niggermusik«, schrie die Volksstimme. »Schluß, Schluß«, rief Frau Behrend. Die beiden kahlköpfigen Geschäftsmänner stützten sie. Frau Behrend schwankte ein wenig, aber ihre Gesinnung war vorzüglich. Man mußte sie stützen. Man mußte die gute Gesinnung stützen. In einem Auflauf weiß man nie, wer den ersten Stein wirft. Wer den ersten Stein wirft, weiß nicht, warum er es tut, es sei denn, man habe ihn dafür bezahlt. Aber einer wirft den ersten Stein. Die andern Steine fliegen dann schnell und leicht. Die Fenster des Negerklubs zerbrachen unter den Steinen.

›Alles zerbricht‹, dachte Philipp, ›wir können uns nicht mehr verständigen, nicht Edwin redet, der Lautsprecher spricht, auch Edwin bedient sich der Lautsprechersprache, oder die Lautsprecher, diese gefährlichen Roboter, halten auch Edwin gefangen: sein Wort wird durch ihren blechernen Mund gepreßt, es wird zur Lautsprechersprache, zu dem Weltidiom, das jeder kennt und niemand versteht.‹ Immer wenn Philipp einen Vortrag hörte, mußte er an Chaplin denken. Jeder Redner erinnerte ihn an Chaplin. Er war auf seine Weise ein Chaplin. Im ernstesten und traurigsten Vortrag mußte Philipp über Chaplin lachen. Chaplin bemühte sich, seine Gedanken zu äußern, Erkenntnisse zu vermitteln, freundliche und weise Worte in das Mikrophon zu sprechen, aber die freundlichen und weisen Worte stürzten wie Fanfarenstöße, wie laute Lügen und demagogische Parolen aus den Schalltrichtern. Der gute Chaplin am Mikrophon hörte nur seine Worte, er hörte die freundlichen und weisen Worte, die er in das Tonsieb sprach, er hörte seine Gedanken, er lauschte seinem Seelenklang, aber er vernahm nicht das Brüllen der Lautverstärker, es entgingen ihm ihre Simplifikationen und ihre dummen Imperative. Am Ende seiner Ansprache glaubte Chaplin sein Auditorium zur Besinnlichkeit geführt und es lächeln gemacht zu haben. Er war peinlich überrascht, wenn die Leute aufsprangen, Heil riefen und sich zu prügeln begannen. Edwins Zuhörer würden sich nicht prügeln. Sie schliefen. Die Leute, die sich vielleicht gerauft hätten, schliefen. Wer nicht schlief, würde sich auch nicht raufen. Es waren die Sanften, die nicht schliefen. Bei einem andern Chaplin hätten die Wilden nicht geschlafen, und die Sanften wären eingenickt. Die Wilden hätten dann die Friedfertigen unsanft geweckt. In Edwins Vortrag würde niemand geweckt werden. Der Vortrag würde völlig folgenlos bleiben. Als erster war Schnakenbach eingeschlafen. Behude hatte ihn von den Mikrophonen weggeführt. Er hatte Schnakenbach zwischen sich und die Philosophieklasse des Priesterseminars gesetzt. Er dachte ›weder sie noch ich können ihm helfen, wir erreichen ihn nicht‹. Gab es Schnakenbach überhaupt? Für Schnakenbach war der Saal, waren der vorlesende Dichter und seine Zuhörer ein nicht zu rechter Reaktion kommender chemisch-physikalischer Prozeß. Schnakenbachs Weltbild war unmenschlich. Es war völlig abstrakt. Seine Schulmeisterausbildung hatte Schnakenbach noch ein äußerlich intaktes Weltbild, das Weltbild der klassischen Physik, vermittelt, in der alles schön kausalgesetzlich zuging und in der Gott in einer Art Austragsstübchen, belächelt, aber geduldet, wohnte. In dieser Welt hätte sich auch noch Schnakenbach einrichten können. Seine Jahrgangskollegen richteten sich ein. Sie fielen im Krieg und hinterließen Frauen und Kinder. Schnakenbach wollte nicht in den Krieg ziehen. Er war unverheiratet. Er fing an nachzudenken, und er fand, daß das ihm überlieferte Weltbild nicht mehr stimmte. Vor allem entdeckte er, daß es schon Gelehrte gab, die wußten und verkündeten, daß dieses Weltbild nicht stimmte. Schnakenbach, um der Kaserne zu entgehen, schluckte Schlafentzugsmittel und studierte Einstein, Planck, de Broglie, Jeans, Schrödinger und Jordan. Er sah nun in eine Welt, in der Gottes Austragsstüblein aufgehoben war. Entweder gab es Gott gar nicht oder Gott war tot, wie Nietzsche behauptet hatte, oder, auch dies war möglich und war so alt wie neu, Gott war überall, doch er war gestaltlos, kein Gottvater mit Bart, und der ganze Vaterkomplex der Menschheit von den Propheten bis Freud erwies sich als selbstquälerischer Irrtum des Homo sapiens, Gott war eine Formel, ein Abstraktum, vielleicht war Gott Einsteins allgemeine Theorie der Schwerkraft, war das Kunststück der Balance in einer sich immer ausdehnenden Welt. Wo Schnakenbach auch war, er war die Mitte und der Kreis, er war der Anfang und das Ende, aber er war nichts Besonderes, jeder war Mitte und Kreis, Anfang und Ende, jeder Punkt war es, das Schlafkorn in seinem Auge, die ihm reichlich zugemessene Gabe des Sandmanns, war noch ein zusammengesetztes Ding, ein Mikrokosmos für sich mit Atomsonnen und Trabanten, Schnakenbach sah eine mikrophysikalische Welt, bis zum Bersten angefüllt mit dem Kleinsten, und, freilich, sie barst, barst fortwährend, explodierte in die Weite, entfloh in den unbeschreibbaren, den endlich unendlichen Raum. Der schlafende Schnakenbach war in dauernder Bewegung und Verwandlung; er empfing und verströmte Kräfte; aus den fernsten Teilen des Alls kamen sie zu ihm und flohen ihn, sie reisten mit Überlichtgeschwindigkeit und reisten Milliarden Lichtjahre, es kam auf die Betrachtungsweise an, erklären ließ es sich nicht, es ließ sich vielleicht in ein paar Zahlen aufnotieren, vielleicht konnte man es auf die abgerissene Hülle einer Pillenpackung schreiben, vielleicht brauchte man ein Elektronengehirn, um eine Annäherungsziffer zu finden, die wahre Summe würde unbekannt bleiben, vielleicht hatte der Mensch abgedankt. Edwin sprach von der Summa theologiae der Scholastik. *»Veni creator*

197

spiritus, komm Schöpfer Geist, bleib Schöpfer Geist, nur im Geiste sind wir.« Edwin rief die großen Namen Homer, Vergil, Dante, Goethe. Er beschwor die Paläste und die Ruinen, die Dome und die Schulen. Er sprach von Augustin, Anselm, Thomas, Pascal. Er erwähnte Kierkegaard, die Christenheit sei nur noch ein Schein, und doch, sagte Edwin, sei dieser Schein, der vielleicht letzte Abendschein des müden Europas, das einzige wärmende Licht in der Welt. Die Modeschöpfer schliefen. Ihre Puppen schliefen. Alexander, der Erzherzogdarsteller, schlief. Sein Mund stand offen; Leere strömte ein und aus. Messalina kämpfte mit dem Schlaf. Sie dachte an Philipp und die reizende Grünäugige, und ob man nicht vielleicht doch noch Edwin für die Party gewinnen könne. Miß Wescott schrieb nach, was sie nicht verstand, aber für bedeutend hielt. Miß Burnett dachte ›ich habe Hunger, immer wenn ich einen Vortrag höre, kriege ich furchtbaren Hunger, mit mir muß was nicht stimmen: ich fühle mich nicht erhoben, ich fühle mich hungrig‹. Alfredo, die zarte ältliche Lesbierin, hatte die Wange auf Hänschens Konfirmandenanzug gelegt und träumte etwas furchtbar Unanständiges. Hänschen dachte ›ob sie Geld hat?‹ Er war eine kleine Rechenmaschine; aber er war noch unerfahren, sonst hätte er wissen müssen, daß die arme Alfredo kein Geld hatte. Er hätte seinen Arm, auf den sie sich stützte, zurückgezogen. Hänschen war brutal. Jack versuchte, sich alles zu merken, was Edwin sagte. Jack war ein Papagei. Er sprach gern nach. Aber die Rede war zu lang. Sie ermüdete und verwirrte. Jack konnte sich immer nur für eine kleine Weile konzentrieren. Er hatte Sorgen. Er dachte an Hänschen. Hänschen wollte schon wieder Geld haben. Aber auch Jack hatte kein Geld. Kay war vom Whisky, den sie mit Emilia getrunken hatte, benommen. Sie verstand ihren Dichter nicht. Was er sprach, war schön und weise; aber es war wohl zu hoch, Kay verstand es nicht. Dr. Kaiser hätte es wohl verstanden. Sie saß unbequem auf ihrem Feuerwehrsitz, und sie legte sich in den Arm des deutschen Dichters, der hart auf dem Polizeistuhl saß. Sie dachte ›vielleicht ist der deutsche Dichter leichter zu verstehen, er wird nicht so klug wie Edwin sein, aber vielleicht hat er mehr Herz, die deutschen Dichter träumen, sie besingen den Wald und die Liebe‹. Philipp dachte ›sie schlafen, und doch ist Größe in seinem Vortrag, hatte der Irre nicht recht, als er uns wecken wollte? es ist einer von Behudes Patienten, Edwins Bemühung rührt mich, ich verehre ihn, jetzt verehre ich ihn, sein Vortrag ist eine vergebliche Beschwörung, er empfindet sicher auch wie vergebens die Beschwörung ist, vielleicht rührt mich das, Edwin ist einer von den rührenden hilflosen gequälten Sehern, er sagt uns nicht was er sieht, was er sieht ist furchtbar, er versucht einen Schleier vor sein Gesicht zu ziehen, nur manchmal lüftet er den Schleier vor dem Grauen, vielleicht gibt es kein Grauen, vielleicht ist nichts hinter dem Schleier, er spricht nur für sich, vielleicht spricht er noch für mich, vielleicht für die Priester, ein Augurengespräch, die andern schlafen‹. Er drückte seinen Arm fester um Kay. Sie schlief nicht. Sie wärmte ihn. Sie war warmes frisches Leben. Immer wieder empfand Philipp Kays freiere Existenz. Nicht das Mädchen, die Freiheit verführte ihn. Er betrachtete ihren Schmuck, ein mondbleiches Geschmeide aus Perlen, Email und diamantenen Rosen. ›Es paßt nicht zu ihr‹, dachte er, ›wo mag sie es herhaben, vielleicht hat sie geerbt, sie sollte keinen Schmuck tragen, dieser alte Schmuck stiehlt ihr etwas von ihrer Frische, vielleicht sollte sie Korallen tragen.‹ Der Schmuck kam ihm bekannt vor, aber er erkannte ihn nicht als Emilias Schmuck. Philipp hatte keinen Sinn für Juwelen und kein Gedächtnis für ihre Form und Gestalt und außerdem vermied er es, Emilias Preziosen zu betrachten; er wußte, daß die Steine, die Perlen und das Gold Tränen herbeilockten, Tränen, die ihn bedrückten; Emilia mußte ihren Schmuck verkaufen, sie weinte, wenn sie ihn zum Juwelier trug, und von dem Erlös der Kostbarkeiten und der Tränen lebte auch Philipp. Es gehörte zu den Kalamitäten seiner Existenz, daß er allein, ohne Emilia, viel einfacher leben und sich erhalten konnte, aber da er Emilia liebte und mit ihr lebte, mit ihr die Tafel teilte und das Lager, beraubte er sie ihres Gutes und war, wie ein Vogel an der Rute, der Luxusboheme des Kommerzienratserbes verleimt und konnte seine natürlichen Schwingen zu den kleinen Flügen, die ihm bestimmt waren und die ihm sein Futter gegeben hätten, nicht mehr rühren. Es war eine Fesselung, Liebesfesselung, Bande des Eros, aber der Lebenslauf führte in die Abhängigkeit von der schlechten Verwaltung eines in Trümmer gesunkenen Vermögens, und das war eine andere Fesselung, eine ungewollte, die sich drückend auf das Empfinden der Liebe legte. ›Ich werde nie wieder frei sein‹, dachte Philipp, ›ich habe mein Leben lang die Freiheit gesucht, aber ich habe mich verlaufen.‹ Edwin erwähnte die Freiheit. Der europäische Geist, sagte er, sei die Zukunft der Freiheit, oder die Freiheit werde keine Zukunft mehr in der Welt haben. Hier wandte sich Edwin gegen einen Ausspruch der seinen Zuhörern völlig unbekannten amerikanischen Dichterin Gertrude Stein, von der erzählt wird, daß Hemingway bei ihr zu schreiben gelernt habe. Gertrude Stein und Hemingway waren Edwin gleichermaßen unsympathisch, er hielt sie für Literaten, Boulevardiers, zweitrangige Geister, und sie wieder gaben ihm die Nichtachtung reichlich zurück und nannten ihn ihrerseits einen Epigonen und sublimen Nachäffer der großen toten Dichtung der großen und toten Jahrhunderte. Wie Tauben im Gras, sagte Edwin, die Stein zitierend, und so war doch etwas von ihr Geschriebenes bei ihm haftengeblieben, doch dachte er weniger an Tauben im Gras als an Tauben auf dem Markusplatz in Venedig, wie Tauben im Gras betrachteten gewisse Zivilisationsgeister die Menschen, indem sie sich bemühten, das Sinnlose und scheinbar Zufällige der menschlichen Existenz bloßzustellen, den Menschen frei von Gott zu schildern, um ihn dann frei im Nichts flattern zu lassen, sinnlos, wertlos, frei und von Schlingen bedroht, dem Metzger preisgegeben, aber stolz auf die eingebildete, zu nichts als Elend führende Freiheit von Gott und göttlicher Herkunft. Und dabei, sagte Edwin, kenne doch schon jede Taube ihren Schlag und sei jeder Vogel in Gottes Hand. Die Priester spitzten die Ohren. Bearbeitete Edwin ihren Acker? War er nichts als ein Laienprediger? Miß Wescott hörte auf, die Rede mitzuschreiben. Hatte sie, was Edwin jetzt sagte, nicht schon einmal vernommen? Waren es nicht ähnliche Gedanken, die Miß Burnett auf dem

Platz der Nationalsozialisten geäußert hatte, hatte nicht auch sie die Menschen mit Tauben oder mit Vögeln verglichen und ihr Dasein als zufällig und gefährdet geschildert? Miß Wescott blickte überrascht auf Miß Burnett. War der Gedanke, daß der Mensch sich gefährdet und als Objekt des Zufalls empfand, so allgemein, daß ihn der verehrte Dichter und die viel weniger verehrte Lehramtskollegin fast gleichzeitig äußern konnten? Miß Wescott verwirrte das. Sie war keine Taube oder sonst ein Vogel. Sie war ein Mensch, eine Lehrerin, sie hatte ein Amt, auf das sie sich vorbereitet hatte und immer wieder vorbereitete, sie hatte Pflichten, und sie suchte sie zu erfüllen. Miß Wescott fand, daß Miß Burnett hungrig aussah; ein seltsam hungriger Ausdruck lag in Miß Burnetts Gesicht, als habe die Welt, als hätten Edwins Erleuchtungen sie schrecklich hungrig gemacht. Philipp dachte ›jetzt wendet er sich Goethe zu, es ist fast deutsch, wie Edwin sich jetzt auf Goethe beruft, auf das Gesetz-nach-dem-wir-angetreten, und er sucht wie Goethe die Freiheit in diesem Gesetz: er hat sie nicht gefunden‹. Edwin hatte sein letztes Wort gesprochen. Die Lautsprecher knirschten und knackten. Sie knirschten und knackten weiter, als Edwin geendet hatte, und das wortlose Knirschen und Knacken in ihren zahnlosen Mündern riß die Zuhörer aus Schlaf, Traum und abwegigem Denken.

Die Steine, die Steine, die sie geworfen hatte, das klirrende Glas, die fallenden Scherben erschreckten die Menge. Die Älteren fühlten sich an etwas erinnert; sie fühlten sich an eine andere Blindheit, an eine frühere Aktion, an andere Scherben erinnert. Mit Scherben hatte es damals begonnen, und mit Scherben hatte es geendet. Die Scherben, mit denen es endete, waren die Scherben ihrer eigenen Fenster gewesen. »Hört auf! Wir müssen es doch bezahlen«, sagten sie. »Wir müssen's doch immer bezahlen, wenn etwas kaputtgeht.« Christopher hatte sich vorgedrängt. Er wußte nicht recht, um was es ging, aber er hatte sich vorgedrängt. Er stellte sich auf einen Stein und rief: »Seid doch vernünftig, Leute!« Die Leute verstanden ihn nicht. Aber da er die Arme so schützend ausgebreitet hielt, lachten sie und sagten, es sei der heilige Christophorus. Auch Richard Kirsch war vorgelaufen. Sein Fräulein hatte gemahnt »kümmere dich nicht darum, misch dich nicht ein, es geht dich nichts an«, aber er war doch vorgelaufen. Er war bereit, mit Christopher zusammen Amerika zu verteidigen, das schwarze Amerika, das hinter ihm lag, das dunkle Amerika, das sich hinter zerbrochenen Fenstern und wehenden roten Vorhängen versteckte. Die Musik hatte aufgehört zu spielen. Die Mädchen kreischten. Sie riefen um Hilfe, obwohl ihnen niemand etwas tat. Der Luftzug, der durch die zersplitterten Fenster drang, legte sich wie eine Lähmung auf die schwarzen Soldaten. Sie fürchteten nicht die Deutschen. Ihr Schicksal, das sie verfolgte, die lebenslängliche Verfolgung, die sie auch in Deutschland nicht freigab, verfinsterte und lähmte sie. Sie waren entschlossen, sich zu verteidigen. Sie waren entschlossen, sich auf dem Boden des Klubs zu verteidigen. Sie würden kämpfen, sie würden in ihrem Klub kämpfen, aber die Lähmung hinderte sie, sich in das Meer zu stürzen, in das Meer der weißen Menschen, in diese weiße See, die meilenweit um ihre kleine schwarze Insel brandete. Die Sirenenwagen der Polizei rückten an. Man hörte ihre gellenden Rufe. Man hörte Pfiffe, Geschrei und Gelächter. »Komm«, sagte Susanne. Sie kannte einen Ausweg. Sie nahm Odysseus an die Hand. Sie führte ihn durch einen dunklen Gang, an Mülltonnen vorbei über einen Hof und zu einer niedrigen eingestürzten Mauer. Susanne und Odysseus kletterten über die Mauer. Sie tasteten sich durch eine Ruine und erreichten eine verlassene Gasse. »Schnell!« sagte Susanne. Sie eilten die Gasse entlang. Das Geräusch ihrer Schritte wurde übertönt vom unaufhörlichen Heulen der Sirenen. Die Polizei drängte die Menge zurück. Ein Kordon der Militärpolizei stellte sich vor den Eingang des Klubs. Wer den Klub verlassen wollte, wurde kontrolliert. Christopher fühlte sich von einer kleinen Hand von seinem Stein gezerrt. Vor ihm stand Ezra. Sein Anzug war zerrissen, seine Hände und sein Gesicht waren verschrammt. Hinter Ezra stand ein fremder Junge; auch seine Kleider waren zerrissen, auch sein Gesicht und seine Hände waren verschrammt. Ezra und Heinz waren auf die Steine der einstürzenden Mauer gefallen. Sie hatten sich weh getan. In der ersten Angst hatten sie um Hilfe gerufen. Aber dann, als sie die Polizeisirenen hörten, hatten sie sich gegenseitig von den Steinen aufgeholfen und waren zusammen in die Bäckergasse geflohen. Von dort hatten sie den Platz wieder erreicht. Sie wollten nichts mehr voneinander. Sie vermieden es, sich anzusehen. Sie waren aus Märchen und Indianergeschichten erwacht und schämten sich. »Frag nicht«, sagte Ezra zu Christopher, »frag nicht, ich möchte nach Hause fahren. Es ist nichts. Ich bin hingefallen.« Christopher drängte durch die Menge zu seinem Wagen. Aus dem Klub kamen Washington und Carla. Sie gingen zu ihrem Auto. »Da ist er!« rief Frau Behrend. »Wer ist das?« riefen die kahlköpfigen Geschäftsmänner. Frau Behrend schwieg. Sollte sie ihre Schande hinausschreien? »Ist es der Taximörder?« fragte der eine Kahlkopf. Er leckte sich die Mundwinkel. »Da geht der Taximörder«, rief der zweite Kahlkopf. »Die Frau sagt, es ist der Taximörder. Sie kennt ihn!« Dem zweiten Kahlkopf stand der Schweiß im Gesicht. Eine neue Welle der Wut schäumte aus der Menge. Die zerbrochenen Fenster hatten sie ernüchtert, aber da sie menschliches Wild sahen, erwachten ihre Jagdinstinkte, die Verfolgungswut und das Tötungsgelüste der Meute. Pfiffe gellten, »der Mörder und seine Hure« wurde gerufen, und wieder flogen die Steine. Die Steine flogen gegen die horizontblaue Limousine. Sie trafen Carla und Washington, sie trafen Richard Kirsch, der hier Amerika verteidigte, das freie, brüderliche Amerika, indem er den Gefährdeten beistand, die ruchlos geworfenen Steine trafen Amerika und Europa, sie schändeten den oft berufenen europäischen Geist, sie verletzten die Menschheit, sie trafen den Traum von Paris, den Traum von Washington's Inn, den Traum *Niemand ist unerwünscht*, aber sie konnten den Traum nicht töten, der stärker als jeder Steinwurf ist, und sie trafen einen kleinen Jungen, der mit dem Schrei »Mutter« zum horizontblauen Wagen gelaufen war.

Der kleine Hund schmiegte sich dicht an Emilia an. Noch

fürchtete er sich. Er fürchtete sich vor den anderen Hunden der Fuchsstraßenvilla, er fürchtete sich vor den Katzen und vor dem kreischenden Papagei, er fürchtete sich vor der kalten und toten Luft dieses Hauses. Aber die Tiere taten ihm nichts. Sie beruhigten sich. Sie hatten geknurrt, gejault, gekreischt, sie hatten ihn beschnuppert, und dann beruhigten sie sich. Sie wußte, der neue Hund würde bleiben. Er war ein neuer Gefährte, ein neuer Kollege, mochte er bleiben. Es war genug Essen für die Tiere in diesem Haus, wenn es auch für die Menschen nicht mehr reichte. Der Hund würde sich an die kalte und tote Luft gewöhnen, und Emilia war ihm ein Versprechen von Freundschaft und Wärme. Emilia aber fror. Sie hatte gehofft, daß Philipp in der Wohnung auf sie warten würde. Noch war sie Dr. Jekyll. Sie hatte noch nicht viel getrunken, sie wollte Dr. Jekyll bleiben. Dr. Jekyll wollte nett zu Philipp sein. Aber Philipp war nicht da. Er hatte sich ihr entzogen. Er hatte den lieben Dr. Jekyll nicht liebgehabt. Wie Emilia das Haus haßte, aus dem sie niemals für immer fortgehen würde! Das Haus war ein Grab, aber es war das Grab der lebenden Emilia, und sie konnte es nicht verlassen. Wie haßte sie die Bilder, die Philipp aufgehängt hatte! Ein Kentaur mit einem nackten Weib auf dem Pferderücken, die Nachbildung eines pompejanischen Wandgemäldes, starrte sie mit höhnischem Lächeln an. In Wahrheit war das Gesicht des Kentauren ausdruckslos. Es war so ausdruckslos wie alle Gesichter auf den pompejanischen Bildern, aber Emilia schien es, daß der Kentaur sie verhöhnte. Hatte nicht auch Philipp sie entführt, nicht gerade auf einem Pferderücken, aber jung und nackt hatte er sie aus dem Glauben an den Besitz, aus dem schönen unschuldigen Glauben an das ewige Recht des Besitzes gerissen und sie in das Reich der Intellektualität, der Armut, des Zweifels und der Gewissensnot geführt. In einem dunklen Rahmen hing ein Stich des Piranesi, das Gemäuer des alten Aquäduktes in Rom, eine Mahnung an Untergang und Verfall. Nur Moder umgab Emilia, Stücke der Kommerzienratserbschaft, tote Bücher, toter Geist, tote Kunst. Dieses Haus war nicht zu ertragen. Hatte sie nicht Freunde? Hatte sie nicht Freunde unter den Lebenden? Konnte sie nicht zu Messalina und Alexander gehen? Bei Messalina gab es Musik und Getränke, bei Messalina wurde getanzt, bei Messalina gab es Vergessen. ›Wenn ich jetzt gehe‹, sagte sie sich, ›werde ich als Mr. Hyde nach Hause kommen‹. ›Schön‹, sagte sie sich, ›Philipp ist nicht hier. Wenn er es anders wollte, wäre er hier. Soll ich hier auf ihn warten? Bin ich eine Witwe? Will ich wie ein Eremit leben? Und wenn Philipp hier wäre? Was wäre dann? Nichts wäre! Keine Musik, kein Tanz. Wir würden uns düster gegenübersitzen. Die Liebe bliebe uns noch, die erotische Verzweiflung. Warum soll ich nicht trinken, warum nicht Mr. Hyde sein?‹ Philipp führte Kay aus dem Saal. Er sah noch, wie Edwin sich verneigte, wie lange er sein Gesicht zu Boden senkte, schamvoll die Augen schloß, als wäre der Dank, der ihm nun zuteil wurde, der Beifall um den er geheim die Schauspieler und die Protagonisten der Zeit beneidet hatte, etwas Sichtbares und Gräßliches, aus reinem Mißverstehen entstanden, ein brutaler Niederschlag, der dem Nichtverstehen folgte, eine Befreiung der Zuhörer, die nichts von Edwins Worten begriffen hatten und die nun mit dem Beifallsklatschen ihrer Hände noch den zarten und zärtlichen, den schon durch den Lautsprecher vergröberten und, als er sie erreichte, schon gestorbenen, schon toten, ja zu Staub und Moder gewordenen Anhauch seines Geistes als lästige Spinnwebe von sich streiften: es war eine Beschämung, und weil sie als Hohn und Beschämung und Sieg der Rührigkeit, der bloßen Konvention, des unrühmlichen Ruhmbetriebes und des Ungeistes von ihm erfaßt wurde, schloß der Dichter schamvoll die Augen. Philipp verstand ihn. Er dachte ›mein unglücklicher Bruder, mein lieber Bruder, mein großer Bruder‹. Emilia hätte gesagt: »Und mein armer Bruder? Das verschweigst du.« — »Gewiß. Auch mein armer Bruder«, hätte Philipp erwidert, »aber das ist unbedeutend. Was du arm nennst, ist das Herz des Dichters, um das sich Glück, Liebe und Größe der dichterischen Existenz legen, wie Schnee um den Kern der Lawine. Ein kaltes Bild, Emilia, aber Edwin, sein Wort, sein Geist, seine Botschaft, die in diesem Saal ohne sichtbare Wirkung blieben und keine wahrnehmbare Erschütterung hinterließen, zählen zu den großen Lawinen, die ins Tal unserer Zeit rollen.« — »Und zerstören«, hätte Emilia hinzugesetzt, »und Kälte verbreiten.« Aber Emilia war ja nicht da, sie war wohl zu Hause und schuf aus Schnaps und Wein den fürchterlichen Mr. Hyde, der die Besitzzerstörung beweinte, der über die Zerstörung des Besitzes zum Süffel wurde und mit Zerstörung im kleinen, mit dem irren Toben des Betrunkenen gegen die große Zerstörung der Zeit kämpfte. Philipp führte Kay aus dem Saal. Sie entkamen den Lehrerinnen; sie entwischten Alexander und Messalina. Die kosmetisch gepflegten, gutangezogenen und vergleichsweise wohlsituierten amerikanischen Lehrerinnen standen arm wie verschüchterte deutsche Lehrerinnen im Vortragssaal. In ihre Merkbücher hatten sie tote Wörter geschrieben, eine Aufzählung toter Wörter, Grabzeichen des Geistes; Wörter, die sie nicht zum Leben, die sie zu keinem Sinn erwecken würden. Es erwartete sie eine Autobusheimfahrt ins Hotel, ein kalter Imbiß im Hotel, das Briefeschreiben nach Massachusetts wir-haben-eine-deutsche-Stadt-besichtigt, wir-haben-Edwin-gehört-es-war-wundervoll, es erwartete sie das Herbergsbett, und es war nicht viel anders als das Bett an anderen Orten der Reise.

Was blieb? Der Traum blieb. Und dann die Enttäuschung mit Kay; die Reizende, die Schamlose, sie war mit dem deutschen Dichter, von dem man nicht mal wußte, wer er war und wie er hieß, davongelaufen, und es war sehr zu überlegen, ob man nicht die Polizei verständigen sollte, aber Miß Burnett war dagegen, und sie schüchterte Miß Wescott mit dem Skandal ein, den es wohl gäbe, wenn die Militärpolizei mit ihren Sirenenwagen die kleine treulose Kay suchen müßte. Das Amerikahaus, ein Führerbau des Nationalsozialismus, lag hinter Philipp und Kay. Das Haus sah, aus seinen symmetrisch aneinandergereihten Fenstern in die Nacht leuchtend, wie gewisse Museen aus, wie ein kolossales Grabmal der Antike, wie ein Bürogebäude, in dem der Nachlaß der Antike verwaltet wird, der Geist, die Heldensagen, die Götter. Kay wollte Philipp nicht begleiten, aber etwas in ihr sträubte sich nicht, ihn doch zu begleiten, und dieses Etwas riß die Kay, die nicht mit Philipp gehen wollte, mit, so stark

206

war es, und es war Sehnsucht nach Romantik, Sehnsucht nach dem Ungewöhnlichen, Sehnsucht nach Erfahrung, nach besonderem Erleben, nach Abenteuer, nach Alter, nach Degeneration und Untergang, nach Opfer, Hingabe und Iphigenienmythe, es war Trotz, es war Überdruß an der Reisegesellschaft, es war die Erregung der Fremde, die Eile der Jugend, es war Emilias Whisky, es war, daß sie der schwärmenden, hemmungsvollen Liebe der Damen Wescott und Burnett müde war. Kay dachte ›er wird mich in seine Wohnung führen, ich werde die Wohnung eines deutschen Dichters sehen, das wird Dr. Kaiser interessieren, vielleicht wird der deutsche Dichter mich in seiner Wohnung verführen, Edwin wollte mich nicht verführen, ich hätte mich natürlich lieber von Edwin verführen lassen, aber Edwins Vortrag war langweilig, wenn ich ehrlich sein soll, war er kalt und langweilig, ich werde die einzige von unserer Reisegesellschaft sein, die zu Hause erzählen kann wie es ist wenn einen ein deutscher Dichter verführt‹. Sie stützte sich auf Philipps Arm. Die Stadt war erfüllt vom Schrei der Polizeisirenen. Kay dachte ›es ist ein Dschungel, in dieser Stadt passieren sicher viele Verbrechen‹. Und Philipp dachte ›wo kann ich mit ihr hingehen? ich könnte in die Fuchsstraße gehen, aber Emilia ist vielleicht schon betrunken, sie ist Mr. Hyde, wenn sie Mr. Hyde ist kann sie keinen Gast empfangen, soll ich mit der Amerikanerin in das Hotel Zum Lamm gehen? das Hotel ist schäbig, es ist deprimierend, das hieße, das Lämmchen zum Lamm bringen, was will ich von ihr? will ich mit ihr schlafen? vielleicht könnte ich mit ihr schlafen, für sie ist es Reiseromantik, ich bin für sie so etwas wie ein ältlicher Strichjunge, das Gedicht über die Porta Nigra von George: fühle ich den Hochmut des alten Strichjungen? Kay ist reizend, aber ich bin gar nicht versessen darauf, ich will gar nicht sie, ich will das andere Land, ich will die Weite, ich will die Ferne, einen anderen Horizont, ich will die Jugend, das junge Land, ich will das Unbeschwerte, ich will die Zukunft und das Vergängliche, den Wind will ich, und da ich nichts anderes will wäre das andere ein Verbrechen?‹ Nach ein paar Schritten dachte Philipp ›ich will das Verbrechen‹.

Sie lagen zusammen, weiße Haut, schwarze Haut, Odysseus Susanne Kirke die Sirenen und vielleicht Nausikaa, sie schlängelten sich, schwarze Haut weiße Haut, in einer Kammer, die sich windig auf ein paar Balken stützte und fast wie ein kleiner Balkon über der Tiefe schwebte, denn die Grundmauern des Hauses waren an dieser Seite fortgerissen, eine Bombe hatte sie zur Seite gerissen, und nie würden sie wieder errichtet werden. Die Wände der Kammer waren mit Schauspielerbildern beklebt, die meistbetrachteten, die repräsentativen Gesichter der Zeit blickten mit ihrer dummen Wohlgeformtheit, mit ihrer leeren Schönheit auf sie herab, die auf den Kissen lagen, schwarz und weiß, auf den Kissen, die wie Tiere, wie Teufel und langbeinige Vamps geformt waren, nackt weiß und schwarz, sie lagen wie auf einem Floß, im Taumel der Vermischung lagen sie wie auf einem Floß, nackt und schön und wild, sie lagen unschuldig auf einem Floß, das in die Unendlichkeit segelte.

»Eine Unendlichkeit! Aber eine Unendlichkeit zusammengefügt aus allerkleinsten Endlichkeiten, das ist die Welt. Unser Körper, unsere Gestalt, das, von dem wir denken, daß wir es sind, das sind nur lauter Pünktchen, kleine aller-allerkleinste Pünktchen. Aber die Pünktchen, die haben es in sich: das sind Kraftstationen, allerallerkleinste Kraftstationen von allergrößter Kraft. Alles kann explodieren! Aber die Milliarden Kraftstationen sind für den kleinsten Augenblick, für unser Leben, wie Sand in diese Form geweht, die wir unser Ich nennen. Ich könnte Ihnen die Formel aufzeichnen.« Schnakenbach wankte im Halbschlaf, auf Behudes Arm gestützt, nach Hause. Sein armer Kopf sah wie ein gerupftes Vogelhaupt aus. ›Es ist blödsinnig‹, dachte Behude ›aber was kann ich ihm entgegnen? Es ist Blödsinn, aber vielleicht hat er recht, wir kennen uns weder im Kleinen noch im Großen aus, wir sind gar nicht mehr zu Hause in dieser Welt, die Schnakenbach mir in einer Formel deuten will, wußte Edwin eine Deutung? Er wußte keine, sein Vortrag ließ mich kalt, er führte auch nur in eine kalte finstere und ausweglose Gasse.‹

Edwin hatte sich aller Gesellschaft entzogen, wie ein alter
Aal hatte er sich allen Einladungen entwunden, auch der
Heimfahrt im Konsulatswagen war er entkommen; über die
Treppen des Amerikahauses, die breiten Marmorstufen des
Führerbaus, war er in die Nacht, in die Fremde und in das
Abenteuer entwischt. Ein Dichter altert nicht. Sein Herz
schlägt jung. Er war in die Gassen gegangen. Er ging ohne
Plan, seiner Nase nach, seine große Nase führte ihn. Er fand
die finsteren Gassen um den Bahnhof, die Anlagen um den
Justizpalast, die Gassen der Altstadt, das Revier von Oscar
Wildes goldenen Nattern. Edwin war in dieser Stunde Sokrates und Alkibiades. Er wäre gern Sokrates in Alkibiades' Leib
gewesen, aber er war Alkibiades in Sokrates' Körper, wenn
auch aufrecht und wohlgekleidet. Sie erwarteten ihn. Bene,
Kare, Schorschi und Sepp erwarteten ihn. Sie hatten schon
lange auf ihn gewartet. Sie sahen nicht Sokrates und Alkibiades. Sie sahen einen alten Freier, einen alten Deppen,
eine alte wohlhabende Tante. Sie wußten nicht, daß sie schön
waren. Sie ahnten nicht, daß es ein Verfallensein an die
Schönheit gibt und daß der Liebhaber im Geliebten, im
Körper eines rüden Burschen, den Abglanz des ewig Schönen, das Unsterbliche lieben kann, die Seele, wie Plato sie
anbetete. Bene, Schorschi, Kare und Sepp hatten auch Platen
nicht gelesen wer-die-Schönheit-angeschaut-mit-Augen-ist-
dem-Tode-schon-anheimgegeben. Sie sahen einen eleganten
reichen Freier, ein komisches Geschäft, das ihnen nicht einmal ganz verständlich, das aber, wie sie aus Erfahrung wußten, mitunter einträglich war. Edwin sah ihre Gesichter. Er
dachte ›sie sind stolz und schön‹. Er übersah nicht ihre Fäuste, ihre großen und grausamen Fäuste, aber hielt sich an ihre
Gesichter, stolz und schön.

Es war ein Fest ohne Stolz und Schönheit. War es ein Fest?
Was feierten sie? Feierten sie das Nichts? Sie sagten: »Wir
feiern!« Aber sie ließen nur ihre trüben Sinne laufen. Sie
tranken Champagner, und sie ließen die Trostlosigkeit leben,
sie füllten die Lebensleere mit Geräuschen, sie jagten die
Angst mit Mitternachtsmusik und schrillem Lachen. Es war

ein scheußliches Fest. Es kam keine Stimmung auf; nicht einmal die Stimmung der Lust kam auf. Alexander schlief. Er schlief mit offenem Mund. Auch Alfredo schlief, ein spitzmäuliges, enttäuschtes, schlecht träumendes Kätzchen. Messalina tanzte mit Jack. Jack unterlag widerwillig in einem Freistilringen. Hänschen sprach mit Emilia von Geschäften. Er wollte wissen, ob der Besatzungsdollar eingezogen würde. Er wollte sich Bruchgold kaufen. Er wußte, daß Emilia etwas vom Handel verstand. Die kleine Rechenmaschine Hänschenklein schnurrte. Emilia trank. Sie trank Champagner und scharfen brennenden Gin, sie trank hochprozentigen Kognak und schwere Pfälzer Spätlesen. Sie füllte sich voll. Sie trank alles durcheinander. Sie baute den Mr. Hyde auf. Sie baute ihn böse und systematisch auf. Sie trank, um Messalina zu schädigen. Sie tanzte mit niemand. Sie ließ sich von niemand berühren. Sie war ein keuscher Süffel. Sie füllte hinein, was hineinging. Was kümmerte sie die Gesellschaft. Sie war hergekommen, um zu trinken. Sie lebte für sich. Sie war die Kommerzienratserbin. Das war genug. Man hatte die Erbin bestohlen; die Menschen hatten das Erbe angetastet. Das genügte ihr. Das genügte ihr von den Menschen. Mehr brauchte sie über die Menschen nicht zu wissen. Wenn sie ausgetrunken hatte, würde sie gehen. Sie hatte genug getrunken. Die Orgie interessierte sie nicht. Sie ging. Sie ging heim zu ihren Tieren. Sie ging heim, um zu toben, heim, um anzuklagen. Der feige Philipp würde sich dem Mr. Hyde nicht stellen, er würde sich dem Toben entziehen, sie mußte gegen den Hauswart toben, sie mußte gegen die verschlossenen Türen schreien, gegen die Türen, hinter denen nur Berechnung und Kälte wohnten.

Er schloß die Tür des Zimmers, und er sah, daß sie fror. Das häßliche Einbettzimmer, der schäbige Raum mit den billigen Schleiflackmöbeln, diese geschmacklose Einrichtung aus der Fabrik, war das die poetische Behausung, das Heim des deutschen Dichters? Er sah sie an, ›sie denkt, es ist eine Absteige‹. Er durfte jetzt nicht versuchen, zärtlich zu sein; er mußte sie niederwerfen, wie ein Kalb im Hof des Schlächters; er mußte sie niederwerfen, ›damit sie was von der Absteige hat‹. Verdorrt. Erstarrt. Er fühlte sich alt und fühlte sein Herz erkalten. Er dachte ›ich will nicht böse werden: kein Herz aus Stein‹. Er öffnete das Fenster. Die Hotelluft war dumpf und säuerlich. Sie atmeten die Nacht ein. Sie standen am Fenster des Hotels Zum Lamm und atmeten die Nacht ein. Ihr Schatten sprang in die Straße. Es war der Schatten der Liebe, eine flüchtige, vorüberhuschende Erscheinung. Sie sahen das Leuchtschild des Ecartéklubs aufflammen und das Kleeblatt des Glücks sich entfalten. Sie hörten die Sirenenwagen der Polizei. Sie hörten einen Hilferuf. Eine schrille englische Stimme rief um Hilfe. Es war nur ein kurzer kleiner Schrei, und dann starb der Schrei. »Das war Edwins Stimme«, sagte Kay. Philipp erwiderte nichts. Er dachte ›es war Edwin‹. Er dachte ›welche Sensation für das Neue Blatt‹. Selbst das Abendecho würde einen überfallenen Dichter von Weltruhm auf die erste Seite setzen. Philipp dachte ›ich bin ein schlechter Reporter‹. Er rührte sich nicht. Er dachte ›kann ich noch weinen? habe ich noch Tränen? würde ich weinen, wenn Edwin tot wäre?‹ Kay sagte: »Ich möchte gehen.« Sie dachte ›er ist arm, wie arm er ist, er geniert sich, weil er so arm ist, wie arm ist dieses Zimmer, er ist ein armer Deutscher‹. Sie hakte den Schmuck ab, das mondbleiche Geschmeide aus Perlen, Email und diamantenen Rosen, den alten Großmutterschmuck, den Emilia ihr geschenkt hatte. Sie legte Emilias Versuch, eine freie und absichtslose Tat zu tun, auf die Fensterbank. Philipp verstand die Geste. Er dachte ›sie hält mich für einen Hungrigen‹. Die kleine Kay sah das Kleeblatt, das aufflammende Neonlicht und dachte ›das ist sein Wald, sein Eichenhain, sein deutscher Wald, in dem er wandelt und dichtet‹.

Mitternacht schlägt es vom Turm. Es endet der Tag. Ein Kalenderblatt fällt. Man schreibt ein neues Datum. Die Redakteure gähnen. Die Druckformen der Morgenblätter werden geschlossen. Was am Tage geschehen, geredet, gelogen, erschlagen und vernichtet war, lag in Blei gegossen wie ein flacher Kuchen auf den Blechen der Metteure. Der Kuchen

211

war außen hart, und innen war er glitschig. Die Zeit hatte den Kuchen gebacken. Die Zeitungsleute hatten das Unheil umbrochen, Unglück, Not und Verbrechen; sie hatten Geschrei und Lügen in die Spalten gepreßt. Die Schlagzeilen standen, die Ratlosigkeit der Staatenlenker, die Bestürzung der Gelehrten, die Angst der Menschheit, die Glaubenslosigkeit der Theologen, die Berichte von den Taten der Verzweifelten waren vervielfältigungsbereit, sie wurden in das Bad der Druckerschwärze getaucht. Die Rotationsmaschinen liefen. Ihre Walzen preßten auf das Band des weißen Papiers die Parolen des neuen Tages, die Fanale der Torheit, die Fragen der Furcht und die kategorischen Imperative der Einschüchterung. Noch wenige Stunden, und müde, arme Frauen werden die Schlagzeilen, die Parolen, die Fanale, die Furcht und die schwache Hoffnung ins Haus des Lesers tragen; verfrorene, mißmutige Händler werden den Morgenspruch der Auguren an die Wände ihrer Kioske hängen. Die Nachrichten wärmen nicht. *Spannung, Konflikt, Verschärfung, Bedrohung.* Am Himmel summen die Flieger. Noch schweigen die Sirenen. Noch rostet ihr Blechmund. Die Luftschutzbunker wurden gesprengt; die Luftschutzbunker werden wiederhergerichtet. Der Tod treibt Manöverspiele. *Bedrohung, Verschärfung, Konflikt, Spannung.* Komm-du-nunsanfter-Schlummer. Doch niemand entflieht seiner Welt. Der Traum ist schwer und unruhig. Deutschland lebt im Spannungsfeld, östliche Welt, westliche Welt, zerbrochene Welt, zwei Welthälften, einander feind und fremd, Deutschland lebt an der Nahtstelle, an der Bruchstelle, die Zeit ist kostbar, sie ist eine Spanne nur, eine karge Spanne, vertan, eine Sekunde zum Atemholen, Atempause auf einem verdammten Schlachtfeld.

Das Treibhaus

*Gott allein weiß, wie kompliziert die Politik ist
und daß Hirne und Herzen der Menschen
oft nur wie hilflose Hänflinge in der Schlinge flattern.
Doch wenn wir uns über ein großes Unrecht
nicht genügend empören können, werden wir
niemals rechtschaffene Taten vollbringen.*

HAROLD NICOLSON

Der Prozeß der Geschichte ist ein Verbrennen.

NOVALIS

Der Roman *Das Treibhaus* hat mit dem Tagesgeschehen, insbesondere dem politischen, nur insoweit zu tun, als dieses einen Katalysator für die Imagination des Verfassers bildet. Gestalten, Plätze und Ereignisse, die der Erzählung den Rahmen geben, sind mit der Wirklichkeit nirgends identisch. Die Eigenart lebender Personen wird von der rein fiktiven Schilderung weder berührt noch ist sie vom Verfasser gemeint. Die Dimension aller Aussagen des Buches liegt jenseits der Bezüge von Menschen, Organisationen und Geschehnissen unserer Gegenwart; der Roman hat seine eigene poetische Wahrheit.   W. K.

I

Er reiste im Schutz der Immunität, denn er war nicht auf
frischer Tat ertappt worden. Aber wenn es sich zeigte, daß
er ein Verbrecher war, ließen sie ihn natürlich fallen, liefer-
ten ihn freudig aus, sie, die sich das Hohe Haus nannten,
und welch ein Fressen war es für sie, welch ein Glück, welche
Befriedigung, daß er mit einem so großen, mit einem so un-
vorhergesehenen Skandal abging, in die Zelle verschwand,
hinter den Mauern der Zuchthäuser vermoderte, und selbst
in seiner Fraktion würden sie bewegt von der Schmach sprechen, die sie alle durch ihn erlitten (sie alle, sie alle Heuchler),
doch insgeheim würden sie sich die Hände reiben, würden
froh sein, daß er sich ausgestoßen hatte, daß er gehen mußte,
denn er war das Korn Salz gewesen, der Bazillus der Unruhe
in ihrem milden trägen Parteibrei, ein Gewissensmensch und
somit ein Ärgernis.
Er saß im Nibelungenexpreß. Es dunstete nach neuem Anstrich, nach Renovation und Restauration; es reiste sich gut
mit der Deutschen Bundesbahn; und außen waren die Wagen
blutrot lackiert. Basel, Dortmund, Zwerg Alberich und die
Schlote des Reviers; Kurswagen Wien Passau, Fememörder
Hagen hatte sich's bequem gemacht; Kurswagen Rom Mün-
chen, der Purpur der Kardinäle lugte durch die Ritzen ver-
hangener Fenster; Kurswagen Hoek van Holland London,
die Götterdämmerung der Exporteure, die Furcht vor dem
Frieden.
Wagalaweia, rollten die Räder. Er hatte es nicht getan. Er
hatte nicht gemordet. Wahrscheinlich war es ihm nicht gegeben zu morden; aber er hätte morden können, und die bloße
Vorstellung, daß er es getan hatte, daß er das Beil gehoben
und zugeschlagen hatte, diese Annahme stand so klar, so
lebendig vor seinen Augen, daß sie ihn stärkte. Die Mord-

gedanken liefen wie Ströme hochgespannter Energie durch Leib und Seele, sie beflügelten, sie erleuchteten, und für eine Weile hatte er das Gefühl, es würde nun alles gut werden, er würde alles besser anpacken, er würde zupacken, er würde sich durchsetzen, er würde zur Tat gelangen, sein Leben ausschöpfen, in neue Reiche vorstoßen — nur leider hatte er wieder nur in seiner Phantasie gemordet, war er der alte Keetenheuve geblieben, ein Träumer *von des Gedankens Blässe angekränkelt.*

Er hatte seine Frau beerdigt. Und da er sich im bürgerlichen Leben nicht gefestigt fühlte, erschreckte ihn der Akt der Grablegung, so wie ihn auch Kindtaufen und Hochzeiten entsetzten und jedes Geschehen zwischen zwei Menschen, wenn die Öffentlichkeit daran teilnahm und gar noch die Ämter sich einmischten. Dieser Tod schmerzte ihn, er empfand tiefste Trauer, würgenden Kummer, als der Sarg in die Erde gesenkt wurde, das Liebste war ihm genommen, und wenn auch das Wort durch Millionen Trauerkarten glücklicher Erben entwertet war, ihm war das Liebste genommen, die Geliebte wurde verscharrt, und das Gefühl *für immer für immer verloren ich werde sie nicht wiedersehen nicht im Himmel und auf Erden ich werde sie suchen und nicht finden* das hätte ihn weinen lassen, aber er konnte hier nicht weinen, obwohl ihn nur Frau Wilms auf dem Friedhof beobachtete. Frau Wilms war seine Aufwartefrau. Sie überreichte Keetenheuve einen Strauß geknickter Astern aus dem Schrebergarten ihres Schwagers. Zur Hochzeit hatte Frau Wilms einen ähnlichen Strauß geknickter Astern gebracht. Damals sagte sie: »Sie sind ein schönes Paar!« Jetzt schwieg sie. Er war kein schöner Witwer. Immer fiel ihm Komisches ein. In der Schule hatte er, statt dem Lehrer zuzuhören, an Lächerliches gedacht, in den Ausschüssen, im Plenum sah er die würdigen Kollegen wie Clowns in der Manege agieren, und selbst in der Lebensgefahr war ihm das immer auch Groteske der Situation nicht entgangen. Witwer war ein komisches Wort, ein schaurig komisches Wort, ein etwas verstaubter Begriff aus einer geruhsameren Zeit. Keetenheuve entsann sich, als Kind einen Witwer gekannt zu haben, Herrn Possehl. Herr

216

Possehl, Witwer, lebte noch in Eintracht mit einer geordne-
ten Welt; die kleine Stadt respektierte ihn. Herr Possehl
hatte sich eine Witwertracht zugelegt, einen steifen schwarzen Hut, einen Schwalbenschwanzrock, gestreifte Hosen und
später eine immer etwas schmutzige weiße Weste, über die
sich eine goldene Uhrkette spannte, an der ein Eberzahn
hing; ein Symbol, daß das Tier besiegt sei. So war Herr
Possehl, wenn er beim Bäcker Labahn sein Brot kaufte, eine
lebendige Allegorie der Treue über den Tod hinaus, eine
rührende und achtbare Gestalt der Verlassenheit.
Keetenheuve war nicht achtbar, und er rührte auch niemand.
Er besaß weder einen steifen noch einen gewöhnlichen Hut,
und zur Beerdigung hatte er seinen windig modischen
Trenchcoat angezogen. Das Wort Witwer, das Frau Wilms
nicht gesprochen hatte, das ihm aber bei Frau Wilms' ge-
knickten Astern eingefallen war, verfolgte und verbitterte
ihn. Er war ein Ritter von der traurigen, er war ein Ritter
von der komischen Gestalt. Er verließ den Friedhof, und
seine Gedanken eilten seinem Verbrechen zu.
Er handelte diesmal im Denken nicht intellektuell, er handelte instinktmäßig, wutgemäß, und Elke, die ihm stets vor-
geworfen hatte, daß er nur in der Welt der Bücher lebe,
Elke würde sich gefreut haben, wie geradewegs und folge-
richtig er auf seine Tat zuging und dabei noch auf Sicherheit bedacht war, wie der Held eines Filmes. Er sah sich die
Althändlergasse durchstreifen, sah sich in Kellern und Winkeln die Witwertracht kaufen. Er erstand die gestreifte Hose,
den Schwalbenschwanzrock, die weiße Weste (schmutzig wie
bei Herrn Possehl), den steifen würdigen Hut, eine goldene
Uhrkette, und nur den Eberzahn vermochte er nicht aufzu-
treiben und so auch keinen Sieg über das Tier zu erringen.
Im großen Kaufhof trug ihn die Rolltreppe in die Abteilung
für Berufskleidung, und er erwarb einen weißen Mantel, wie
ihn die Viehtreiber brauchen. Auf einem Holzplatz stahl er
das Beil. Es war ganz einfach; die Zimmerleute vesperten,
und er nahm das Beil aus einem Haufen Späne und ging
langsam davon.
Ein weitläufiges, vielbegangenes Hotel mit mehreren Aus-

gängen war der Schlupfwinkel des Mörders. Hier stieg er ab, *Keetenheuve Abgeordneter des Bundestages Possehl Witwer aus Kleinwesenfeld*. Er verkleidete sich. Er hüllte sich vor dem Spiegel in die Witwertracht. Er wurde Possehl ähnlich. Er war Possehl. Er war endlich achtbar. Am Abend ging er aus, den Viehtreibermantel und das Beil unter dem Arm. In der tristen Straße leuchtete grün der Skorpion aus dem schwarzen Glas des Lokalfensters. Es war das einzige Licht in der Gegend, ein Moorlicht aus einer düsteren Geschichte. Hinter den geschlossenen verrosteten Jalousien schlummerten die kleinen Milchläden, die Gemüsehandlungen, die Bäckerei. Es roch muffig, faulig und säuerlich; es roch nach Dreck, nach Ratten, nach keimenden Kellerkartoffeln und nach dem angesetzten Hefestück des Bäckers. Aus dem »Skorpion« lockte Schallplattenmusik. Rosemary Clooney sang »Botch-a-me«. Keetenheuve stellte sich in eine Toreinfahrt. Er zog den Viehtreibermantel an, er nahm das Beil in die Hand — ein Metzger, der auf den Bullen wartet.

Der Bulle kam, die Wanowski erschien, garstig borstige Krüllhaare auf dem Bullenschädel, ein Weib, das als Schläger gefürchtet war und sich Gewalt über die Tribaden verschafft hatte; ihnen wurde wohlig weh, wenn die Wanowski auftauchte, und sie nannten sie die Landesmutter. Sie trug einen Männeranzug, den Anzug eines dicken Mannes, stramm wölbte sich das Gesäß, die überhöhten, mit Watte gepolsterten Schultern waren ein Gleichnis des Penisneides, lächerlich und furchtbar zugleich, und zwischen den schwellenden Lippen unter dem mit Kork abgebrannten Bartflaum kaute sie am häßlichen zerknatschten Stummel einer bitteren Zigarre. Kein Mitleid! Kein Mitleid mit dem Oger! Und kein Gelächter, das versöhnt! Keetenheuve hob das Beil, er schlug zu. Er schlug in das Struppwerk, in das Krüllhaar hinein, diese Matratze, mit der er sie überall bedeckt glaubte, er spaltete dem Bullen den Schädel. Der Bulle sackte ab. Er sackte zusammen. Das Bullenblut färbte den Viehtreibermantel.

Mantel und Beil warf er in den Fluß, der Witwer Possehl, er beugte sich übers Geländer der Brücke, Mantel und Beil sanken in den Flußgrund, sie waren beseitigt, das Wasser glättete sich, *Wasser von den Bergen Schneeschmelze Gletscherschutt blanke wohlschmeckende Forellen.*

Niemand hatte ihn gesehen, niemand hatte ihn sehen können, denn leider hatte er die Tat nicht getan, er hatte wieder nur geträumt, am hellen Tage geträumt und sich nicht aufgerafft, er hatte gedacht, statt zu handeln, es war ewig, ewig das alte Lied. Er hatte versagt. Vor jeder Lebensaufgabe versagte er. Er hatte neunzehnhundertdreiunddreißig versagt und neunzehnhundertfünfundvierzig versagt. Er hatte in der Politik versagt. Er hatte im Beruf versagt. Er bewältigte das Dasein nicht, wer tat das schon, Dummköpfe, es war wie ein Fluch, aber dies ging ihn allein an, er hatte auch in seiner Ehe versagt, und jetzt, da er traurig an Elke dachte, mit dem echten und gar nicht mehr lächerlichen Schmerz des Witwers, an Elke unter der Friedhofserde und schon dem Unbekannten ausgeliefert, der Verwandlung, die entsetzlich war, wenn es das Nichts war, und die entsetzlich blieb, wenn es mehr als nichts war, da schien es ihm, als könne er nicht lieben und nicht hassen, und alles war nur eine geile Fummelei, ein Betasten von Oberflächen. Er hatte die Wanowski nicht erschlagen. Sie lebte. Sie saß im »Skorpion«. Sie herrschte, sie trank, sie kuppelte unter den Tribaden. Sie hörte dem Schallplattengesang der Rosemary Clooney zu, »botch-a-me, botch-a-me« — und da legte es sich wie ein Reif um sein Herz, denn er hatte doch gemordet!

Wagalaweia, heulte die Lokomotive. Elke war zu ihm gekommen, als sie hungrig war, und er hatte damals Konserven, ein warmes Zimmer, Getränke, einen kleinen schwarzen Kater und nach langem Fasten Appetit auf Menschenfleisch, eine Formulierung, die Novalis für die Liebe gebraucht.

Er hatte nie aufgehört, sich als Deutscher zu fühlen; aber in jenem ersten Nachkriegssommer war es für einen, der elf Jahre weg gewesen war, nicht leicht, sich zu orientieren. Er hatte viel zu tun. Nach langer Brache faßte die Zeit nach ihm und nahm ihn ins Getriebe, und er glaubte damals, daß sich in der Zeit etwas erfüllen würde.

An einem Abend schaute er aus dem Fenster. Er war müde.

Es dunkelte früh. Wolken drohten am Himmel. Der Wind wehte Staub auf. Da sah er Elke. Sie schlüpfte in die Ruine, die gegenüber lag. Sie schlüpfte in den Spalt in der geborstenen Mauer, in die Höhlen aus Schutt und Geröll. Sie war wie ein Tier, das sich verkriecht.

Regen schüttete herab. Er ging hinunter auf die Straße. Der Regen und der Sturm schüttelten ihn. Der Staub stürmte ihm in den Mund und in die Augen. Er holte Elke aus den Trümmern. Sie war durchnäßt und dreckig. Das besudelte Kleid klebte auf der bloßen Haut. Sie hatte keine Wäsche am Leib. Sie war nackt gegen den Staub, den Regen, die harten Steine gestellt. Elke kam aus dem Krieg und war sechzehn Jahre alt. Er mochte ihren Namen nicht. Er stimmte ihn mißtrauisch. Elke, das war ein Name aus der nordischen Mythologie, er erinnerte an Wagner und seine hysterischen Helden, an eine verschlagene, hinterlistige und grausame Götterwelt, und siehe, Elke war die Tochter eines Gauleiters und Statthalters des Herrn.

Der Gauleiter und seine Frau waren umgekommen. Sie hatten die kleine Todeskapsel des Für-alle-Fälle geschluckt, und Elke hatte die Nachricht vom Tod der Eltern im Wald gehört. Sie hörte die Nachricht (und mehr als eine Nachricht war es nicht, denn die Zeit hatte den Tag gleichsam chloroformiert, und Elke empfand alle Stöße, als wäre sie in Watte gebettet und würde in einer Wattekiste von groben Händen herumgeworfen) aus einem schnaubenden, von Geheimzeichen und Hilferufen echauffierten Rundfunkempfänger in einer Gruppe deutscher Soldaten, die sich ergeben hatten und auf ihren Abtransport in die Gefangenschaft warteten.

Zwei Neger bewachten sie, und Elke konnte sie nicht vergessen. Die Neger waren große schlaksige Burschen, die in einer seltsamen und überaus sprungbereit wirkenden Balance auf ihren Fersen hockten. Das war eine Urwaldhaltung. Die Gewehre der Zivilisation ruhten auf ihren Knien. An ihren Patronengurten hingen lange, verknotete Lederpeitschen. Die Peitschen waren viel eindrucksvoller als die Gewehre.

Zuweilen standen die Neger auf und verrichteten ihre Notdurft. Sie verrichteten ihre Notdurft mit großem Ernst und

ohne den Blick ihrer kugeligen weißunterlaufenen Augen
(die irgendwie treuherzig waren) von den Gefangenen zu
lassen. Die Neger pißten in zwei hohen Strahlen in das Gras
unter den Bäumen. Die Peitschen baumelten, während sie
pißten, gegen ihre langen schönen Schenkel, und Elke fiel
der Neger Owens ein, der in Berlin im olympischen Kampf
gesiegt hatte. Die deutschen Soldaten stanken nach Regen,
Erde, Schweiß und Wunden, sie stanken nach vielen Straßen,
nach Schlaf in Kleidern, nach Siegen und nach Niederlagen,
nach Furcht, nach Überanstrengung, Überdruß und Tod, sie
stanken nach dem Wort Unrecht und nach dem Wort Vergeblich.

Und hinter dem bewachten Bezirk tauchten auf Wildpfaden,
schüchtern hinter dem Gestrüpp, noch voll Angst vor den
Soldaten, noch mißtrauend den Negern, Gespenster auf, ab-
gezehrte Leiber, gebrochene Skelette, Hungeraugen und Lei-
densstirnen, sie kamen aus Höhlen, wo sie sich versteckt
hatten, sie brachen aus den Lagern des Todes aus, sie schweif-
ten umher, soweit sie die abgemagerten, die geschlagenen
Füße trugen, der Käfig war offen, es waren die Verfolgten, die
Eingesperrten, die Gehetzten der Regierung, die Elke eine
schöne Kindheit beschert hatten, *Spiele auf dem Statthalter-
gut des Vaters, Falter schwirren über den Blumen auf der
Terrasse, eine Gefangene deckt den Frühstückstisch, Gefangene harken den Kies auf den Wegen des Parkes, Gefangene
sprengen den Rasen, das Pferd wird zum Morgenritt vorgeführt, Vaters blankgewichste hochschäftige Stiefel blitzen, ein
Gefangener bürstete sie, das Sattelzeug knarrt, das wohlgenährte, das schön gestriegelte Pferd schnauft und scharrt mit
den Hufen* — Elke wußte nicht, wie sie weitergewandert war;
mal mit dem und mal mit jenem Troß.

Keetenheuves kleiner Kater war es, der Elke zutraulich stimmte. Das Mädchen und die Katze, sie waren jung, und sie
spielten zusammen. Sie liebten es, Keetenheuves Manuskript-
blätter zu Bällen zu zerknüllen und sich zuzuwerfen. Wenn
Keetenheuve von seinen vielen Beschäftigungen, in die er
sich immer weiter verstrickte und die ihn immer mehr enttäuschten, nach Hause kam, rief Elke: »Herrchen kommt!«

Herrchen war Keetenheuve wohl auch für sie. Aber bald langweilte Elke das Treiben mit dem Kater, sie wurde übellaunig, wenn Keetenheuve am Abend bei seinen Papieren saß, damals besessen von dem Gedanken, zu helfen, aufzubauen, Wunden zu heilen, Brot zu schaffen, und da ihre Freundschaft so Schiffbruch litt, ließen sie sich trauen.

Die Ehe komplizierte alles. In allen Fragebogen, die, von den Nationalsozialisten erfunden, doch erst von ihren Besiegern vollkommen entwickelt waren, in allen Fragebogen war Keetenheuve nun der Schwiegersohn des toten Gauleiters. Das befremdete viele, aber ihn scherte es nicht, denn er war gegen Sippenhaftung in allen Fällen, und so auch in dem seiner Frau. Schlimmer war es, daß die Ehe ihn innerlich befremdete. Er war ein Junggeselle, ein Alleingänger, vielleicht ein Wollüstling, vielleicht ein Anachoret, er wußte es nicht, er schwankte zwischen den Daseinsformen, aber sicher war, daß er sich mit der Ehe auf eine Erfahrung eingelassen hatte, die ihm nicht bestimmt war und die ihn überflüssig belastete. Er hatte überdies (mit Vergnügen) ein Kind geheiratet, das den Jahren nach seine Tochter sein konnte, und er mußte nun angesichts ihrer Jugend feststellen, daß er nicht erwachsen war. Sie paßten für die Liebe zusammen, doch nicht für das Leben. Er konnte begehren, aber er konnte nicht erziehen. Er hielt auch nicht viel von Erziehung, aber er sah, wie Elke unglücklich wurde vor einem Übermaß an Freiheit. Sie wußte mit der Freiheit nichts anzufangen. Sie verlor sich in ihr. Das anscheinend pflichtlose Leben war für Elke wie ein ungeheures Wasser, das sie landlos umspülte, ein Ozean der Leere, dessen unendliche Öde allein vom Gekräusel der Lust, vom Schaum des Überdrusses, vom Wind aus vergangenen Tagen belebt wurde. Keetenheuve war ein Wegweiser, der wohl an Elkes Lebenspfad gestellt war, doch nur, um sie in die Irre zu führen. Und dann erlebte Keetenheuve, was für ihn neu und (ihm nicht bestimmt) niederdrückend war, das Todtraurigsein nach vielen Vereinigungen, das Todsündegefühl der Frommen. Aber erst mal stillte er seinen Appetit. Elke brauchte viel Liebe. Sie war sinnlich, und einmal erwacht, war ihr Verlangen nach Zärt-

lichkeit maßlos. Sie sagte: »Halte mich fest!« Sie führte
seine Hand. Sie sagte: »Fühle mich!« Sie bekam heiße
Schenkel, der Leib brannte, sie gebrauchte grobe Worte, sie
rief: »Nimm mich! Nimm mich!« Und er war hingerissen,
er entsann sich seines Hungers, des Wanderns durch die
Straßen fremder Städte, in die ihn der Abscheu vor Elkes
Eltern getrieben hatte, er dachte an die Schaufenster tau-
sendfacher Verführung, an die werbenden Puppen, ihre naiv
lasziven Haltungen, an ausgebreitete Wäsche, an die Plakat-
damen, die ihre Strümpfe hoch zu den Schenkeln hinaufzo-
gen, an Mädchen, deren Sprache er nicht sprach und die wie
Eis und Feuer in einem an ihm vorübergingen. Die wirkliche
Wollust war ihm bisher nur im Traum erschienen, im Traum
hatte er die Leiblichkeit empfunden, nur im Traum die vielen Reize der Haut, im Traum die Verschmelzung, den fremden Atem, die heißen Gerüche. Und die genossene schnelle
Lust in Absteigequartieren, auf Parkbänken, in Altstadtwin-
keln, was war sie gegen die erschöpfende Verführung der
aneinandergereihten Sekunden, gegen die Kette der Minuten, den Ring der Stunden, das Rad der Tage, Wochen und
Jahre, eine Verführung in Ewigkeit und dazu die ständige
Gelegenheit des Ehebundes, die einem aus Entsetzen vor so
viel Dauer das Äußerste einfallen ließ?
Elke streichelte ihn. Es war die Zeit der Stromsperren. Die
Nächte bedrückten und waren dunkel. Keetenheuve hatte
sich für seine Arbeit eine Batterielampe besorgt. Elke schaltete die Lampe neben dem Bett ein, und das Licht fiel grell
auf die Liegenden, wie der Strahl eines Scheinwerfers auf
nächtlicher Straße ein nacktes Paar umfängt. Elke betrachtete Keetenheuve lange und aufmerksam. Sie sagte: »Mit
zwanzig mußt du hübsch gewesen sein.« Sie sagte: »Du
hast viele Mädchen geliebt.« Er war neununddreißig. Er
hatte nicht viele Mädchen gehabt. Elke sagte: »Erzähle mir
was.« Sie fand sein Leben bewegt und bunt, an ihr unver-
ständlichen Sprüngen reich, fast die Biographie eines Aben-
teurers. Es war ihr alles fremd. Sie begriff nicht, nach welchem Stern er sich richtete. Als er ihr sagte, warum er der
Politik der Nationalsozialisten ausgewichen und ins Ausland

gegangen war, sah sie keinen Grund für solches Verhalten, es sei denn einen unsichtbaren, einen jedenfalls nicht greifbaren; er war eben moralisch. Sie sagte: »Du bist ein Schullehrer.« Er lachte. Aber vielleicht lachte nur sein Gesicht. Vielleicht war er immer ein alter Schullehrer gewesen, ein alter Schullehrer und ein alter Schulknabe, ein ungezogener Schüler, der die Aufgaben nicht konnte, weil er die Bücher liebte. Elke haßte mit der Zeit Keetenheuves viele Bücher, sie eiferte gegen die zahllosen Schriften, Papiere, die Hefte, die Journale, die Ausschnitte und Entwürfe, die überall herumlagen und Keetenheuve aus ihrem Bett entführten in Bezirke, zu denen sie den Weg nicht fand, in Reiche, die für sie kein Tor hatten.

Keetenheuves Beschäftigungen, seine Mitarbeit am Wiederaufbau, sein Eifer, der Nation neue Grundlagen des politischen Lebens und die Freiheit der Demokratie zu schaffen, hatten es mit sich gebracht, daß er in den Bundestag gewählt wurde. Er war bevorzugt aufgestellt worden und hatte sein Mandat bekommen, ohne sich als Wahlredner anstrengen zu müssen. Das Kriegsende hatte ihn mit Hoffnungen erfüllt, die noch eine Weile anhielten, und er glaubte, sich nun einer Sache hingeben zu müssen, nachdem er so lange abseits gestanden hatte. Er wollte Jugendträume verwirklichen, er glaubte damals an eine Wandlung, doch bald sah er, wie töricht dieser Glaube war, die Menschen waren natürlich dieselben geblieben, sie dachten gar nicht daran, andere zu werden, weil die Regierungsform wechselte, weil statt braunen, schwarzen und feldgrauen jetzt olivfarbene Uniformen durch die Straßen gingen und den Mädchen Kinder machten, und alles scheiterte wieder mal an Kleinigkeiten, an dem zähen Schlick des Untergrundes, der den Strom des frischen Wassers hemmte und alles im alten stecken ließ, in einer überlieferten Lebensform, von der jeder wußte, daß sie eine Lüge war. Keetenheuve stürzte sich zunächst mit Eifer in die Arbeit der Ausschüsse, es trieb ihn, die verlorenen Jahre einzuholen, und *wie in Blüte wäre er gewesen wenn er mit den Nazis marschiert wäre denn das war der Aufbruch der verfluchte Irrbruch seiner Generation und jetzt war all sein Eifer der*

Verdammnis preisgegeben der Lächerlichkeit eines grau wer-
denden Jünglings er war geschlagen als er anfing.
Und was er in der Politik verlor, was ihm abgekämpft wurde
und was er aufgeben mußte, das verlor er auch in der Liebe,
denn Politik und Liebe, sie waren beide zu spät zu ihm
gekommen, Elke liebte ihn, aber er reiste mit dem Freifahrschein der Parlamentarier Phantomen nach, dem Phantom
der Freiheit, vor der man sich fürchtete und die man den
Philosophen zu unfruchtbarer Erörterung überließ, und dem
Phantom der Menschenrechte, nach denen nur gefragt wurde, wenn man Unrecht erlitt, die Probleme waren unendlich
schwierig, und man konnte wohl verzagen. Keetenheuve sah
sich bald wieder in die Opposition gedrängt, aber die ewige
Opposition machte ihm keinen Spaß mehr, denn er fragte
sich: kann ich es ändern, kann ich es besser machen, weiß
ich den Weg?
Er wußte ihn nicht. An jeder Entscheidung hingen tausend-
fache Für und Wider, Lianen gleich, Lianen des Urwalds,
ein Dschungel war die praktische Politik, Raubtiere begegneten einem, man konnte mutig sein, man konnte die Taube
gegen den Löwen verteidigen, aber hinterrücks biß einen
die Schlange. Übrigens waren die Löwen dieses Waldes zahn-
los und die Tauben nicht so unschuldig, wie sie girrten, nur
das Gift der Schlangen war noch stark und gut, und sie
wußten auch im richtigen Moment zu töten. Hier kämpfte
er sich durch, hier irrte er. Und im Dickicht vergaß er, daß
eine Sonne ihm leuchtete, daß ihm ein Wunder widerfahren
war, eine liebte ihn, Elke mit ihrer schönen jungen Haut,
sie liebte ihn. Kurz waren die Umarmungen zwischen den
Zügen, und er eilte wieder auf Wanderschaft, ein törichter
Ritter gegen die Macht, die so versippt war mit den alten
Urmächten, daß sie über den Ritter lachen konnte, der gegen
sie anging, und manchmal stellte sie ihm, fast aus Freundlichkeit, um seinem Eifer ein Ziel zu bieten, eine Windmühle
in den Weg, gut genug für den altmodischen Don Quichotte,
und Elke fiel zu Hause der Hölle in den Schoß, der Hölle
des Alleinseins, der Hölle der Langeweile, der Hölle der In-
teresselosigkeit, der Hölle täglicher Filmbesuche, wo der Teu-

fel einem in molliger Dunkelheit das Leben gegen ein Pseudoleben tauscht, die Seele von Schatten vertrieben wird, der Hölle der Leere, der Hölle einer qualvoll empfundenen Ewigkeit, die Hölle des bloßen vegetativen Daseins, das gerade noch die Pflanzen ertragen können, ohne den Himmel zu verlieren. »Die Sonne? Eine Täuschung«, sagte sich Elke, »das Licht ist schwarz!« *Und schön war schließlich nur die Jugend die Jugend sie kommt nicht wieder und die war abgebrochen im Mai gesenst und Keetenheuve ein guter Kerl er gehörte zu den Mähern sie hatte keinen Schullehrer gehabt jetzt hatte sie einen Schullehrer in Bonn und er gab ihr keine Aufgaben sie würde auch keine Aufgaben erfüllen wie kam sie dazu das Statthalterkind Gefangene harkten den Park,* und da kam die Wanowski zu ihr, die Wanowski mit ihren breiten gepolsterten Schultern, eine pervertierte Frauenschaftsführerin, die Wanowski mit ihrer groben tiefen befehlenden Stimme *sie erinnerte an zu Hause sie war das Elternhaus seltsam verwandelt zwar aber sie war das Elternhaus sie war die Stimme des Vaters sie war die Stimme der Mutter sie war wie die Bierabende der alten Kämpfer in die der Gauleiter geschniegelt heraufgekommen hinuntertauchte wie in ein verjüngendes Schlammbad die Wanowski sagte »komm Kind«* und Elke kam, sie kam in die Arme der Tribade, da war Wärme, da war Vergessen, da war Schutz vor der Weite, Schutz vor der Sonne, Schutz vor der Ewigkeit, da wurden einfache Worte gesprochen, keine Abstrakta geredet, da war nicht die entsetzliche, die bedrückende, fließende, springende, sprudelnde, nie zu fassende Intellektualität Keetenheuves *der sie geraubt hatte als sie schwach war ein Schulmeister er ein Drache sie die Prinzessin nun rächte sie sich rächte sich an Keetenheuve rächte sich an dem Drachen rächte sich an dem Vater der nicht gesiegt hatte und feige gestorben war und sie den Drachen überließ rächte sich an diesem verfluchten Dasein rächte sich mit den schwulen Weibern sie waren die Höllenhunde ihrer Rache,* sie rächte sich nicht nur mit der Wanowski, denn die Wanowski befriedigte nicht nur, sie kuppelte auch und warb Jüngerinnen zum unheiligen Vestalinnendienst, sie verachtete die Männer

Waschlappen alle Waschlappen Schlappschwänze zum Glück
so konnte sie die gepolsterten Schultern zeigen, den prallen
Arsch in der Männerhose, die Zigarre als letztes Glied noch
im Mund, sie hätte den zu Unrecht gut ausgestatteten un-
fähigen Priapen gern die Frau überhaupt geraubt, ein Oger
des Geschlechtsneides, eine bös und dick gewordene Penthesi-
lea der Budiken, die ihren Achill versäumt hatte. Was die
Wanowski Elke bot, war eine unwiderstehliche Bestechung,
war Zweisamkeit und Bier. Elke fühlte sich nicht mehr verlassen, wenn Keetenheuve in Bonn weilte. Sie trank. Sie trank
mit den verbitterten Tribaden, die darauf warteten, daß Elke
betrunken wurde. Sie trank Flasche nach Flasche. Sie bestellte das Bier durch das Telephon, und es kam in sogenannten
Gebinden, viereckigen eisernen Flaschenkörben, ins Haus.
Wenn Keetenheuve von der Reise zurückkam, huschten die
kessen Väter mit höhnischem Grinsen wie gesättigte Ratten
durch die Tür. Er schlug nach ihnen; sie huschten in ihre
Verstecke. Im Zimmer stank es nach Weiberschweiß, nach
fruchtloser Erregung, sinnloser Ermattung und nach Bier
Bier Bier. Elke war blöd vom Bier, ein Kretin, der lallte. Der
Speichel tropfte aus dem hübschen, dem rotgeschminkten,
dem liebenswerten Mund. Sie lallte: »Was willst du hier?«
Sie lallte: »Ich hasse dich!« Sie lallte: »Ich lieb ja nur
dich.« Sie lallte: »Komm ins Bett.« *Die Sonne war schwarz.*
Konnte er kämpfen? Er konnte nicht kämpfen. Die Weiber
saßen in den Rattenlöchern. Sie beobachteten ihn. Und im
Bund saßen andere — Männer — in den Verstecken, und auch
sie beobachteten ihn. Er beugte sich über Elkes Mund, der
Biergeist, Sankt Spiritus, der Flaschenteufel stieg ihm mit
ihres Atems Hauch entgegen, es ekelte ihn, und doch fühlte
er sich angezogen, und schließlich war er es, der sich dieser
Schwäche hingeben mußte. Am Morgen versöhnten sie sich.
Meist war es ein Sonntagmorgen. Die Glocken riefen zur
Kirche. Keetenheuve war es recht, daß die Glocken riefen, ihn
riefen sie nicht, und vielleicht bedauerte er es sogar, daß sie
ihn nicht ansprachen, aber Elke fühlte sich von jeder Aufforderung wie von einem Fordern bewegt, der Anspruch von
etwas Absolutem trat mit dem Klang der Glocken gegen sie

auf, und sie wehrte sich dagegen. Sie rief: »Ich hasse das Bimmeln. Es ist gemein, so zu bimmeln.« Er mußte sie beruhigen. Sie weinte. Sie fiel in Düsternis. Sie fing an, Gott zu beschimpfen. Elkes Gott war ein böser Gott, ein Ungeheuer mit der Wollust des Quälens. »Es ist kein Gott da«, sagte Keetenheuve, und er nahm ihr den letzten Trost, den Glauben an einen blutigen Götzen. Sie sangen im Bett Kinderlieder, sprachen Abzählverse. Er liebte sie. Er ließ sie fallen. Ihm war ein Mensch überantwortet, und er ließ ihn fallen. Er reiste den Gespinsten nach, rang in den Ausschüssen um nebelhafte Menschenrechte, die nicht erkämpft wurden, es war ganz überflüssig, daß er in den Ausschüssen agierte, er würde für niemand etwas erreichen, aber er reiste hin und ließ Elke, das einzige Wesen, das ihm anvertraut, das seine Aufgabe war, in Verzweiflung verfallen. Die kessen Väter töteten sie. Das Bier tötete sie. Einige Drogen kamen hinzu. Aber eigentlich hatte sie die Verlassenheit erstickt, eine Ahnung von Ewigkeit und Nichtewigkeit, das All, so endlich und so unendlich, das All in seinem schwarzen Licht, mit seinem schwarzen unbegreiflichen Himmel jenseits aller Sterne. *Keetenheuve Schulmeister, Keetenheuve Mädchenräuber, Keetenheuve Drache aus der Sage, Keetenheuve Possehl Witwer, Keetenheuve Moralist und Lüstling, Keetenheuve Abgeordneter, Keetenheuve Ritter der Menschenrechte, Keetenheuve Mörder*

In einer Zeitung das Antlitz des Weisen ein alter Mann ein gütiges Gesicht unter schlohweißem Haar eine Gestalt in eines Gärtners vielgetragener Kluft Einstein der ein Irrlicht jagte und ein Irrlicht fand und die klare schöne Formel der letzten Gleichung Vergattung der Erkenntnisse Harmonie der Sphären die einheitliche Feldtheorie der Naturgesetze der Gravitation und der Elektrizität zurückgeführt auf den gemeinsamen Ursprung der Gleichung IV

Wagalaweia. Sanft, heißt es, sei der Schlaf des Gerechten. Doch kann er schlafen? Im Schlaf kamen die Träume, die keine Träume waren, Angst und Gespenster. Im Zuge ostwestlich gebettet, die geschlossenen Augen gen Westen gerichtet, was hätte Keetenheuve sehen können? Die Saar, das

schöne Frankreich, die Benelux-Staaten, das ganze Klein-
europa, die Montanunion. Und Waffenlager? Waffenlager.
Man umschlich die Grenzen. Man tauschte Noten aus. Man
schloß Verträge. Man spielte wieder. Das alte Spiel? Das alte
Spiel. Die Bundesrepublik spielte mit. Man korrespondierte
mit den Amerikanern in Washington und rieb sich an den
Amerikanern in Mannheim. Der Kanzler saß an manchem
runden Tisch. Gleichberechtigt? Gleichberechtigt. Was lag
hinter ihm? Verteidigungslinien, Flüsse. Verteidigung am
Rhein. Verteidigung an der Elbe. Verteidigung an der Oder.
Angriff über die Weichsel. Und noch? Ein Krieg. Gräber.
Vor ihm? Ein neuer Krieg? Neue Gräber? Rückzug auf die
Pyrenäen? Die Karten wurden neu gemischt. Wer nannte
den Außenminister einer Großmacht einen gelackten Affen?
Ein alter Hase aus der Wilhelmstraße. Er fühlte sich schon
wieder auf dem Wege zur Großmacht, hetzte die alte Renn-
strecke, nun durch die Koblenzer Straße, die Zunge heraus,
und am Anfang und am Ende, da saßen der Swinegel und
seine Frau. Auf dem Rhein kämpfte ein Schleppzug müde
gegen die Strömung. Im Nebel glitten die Kohlenkähne wie
tote Wale durch das Wasser.

Hier hatte der Hort gelegen, unter den Wellen das Gold, in
einer Felsenhöhle, der verborgene Schatz. Er wurde geraubt,
gestohlen, unterschlagen, verflucht. List, Hinterlist, Lug, Trug,
Mord, Tapferkeit, Treue, Verrat und Nebel in Ewigkeit,
Amen. Wagalaweia, sangen die Töchter des Rheins. Verdauung, Verwesung, Stoffwechsel und Zellerneuerung, nach
sieben Jahren war man ein anderer, doch auf dem Feld der
Erinnerung lagerten Versteinerungen — ihnen hielt man die
Treue.

Wagalaweia. In Bayreuth schwebten die Mädchen in Schau-
keln über die Bühne, glitzernde Huldinnen. Den Diktator
hatte der Anblick belebt, warm war es ihm ins Mark gestiegen, die Hand überm Koppelschloß, das Schmachthaar
in die Stirn, die Mütze geradegerückt, aus dumpfem Brüten
entfaltete sich Zerstörung. Und schon empfing man die Hohen Kommissare, die Arme geöffnet, an die Brust! an die
Brust! Tränen flossen, Tränen der Rührung, Salzbächlein des

Wiedersehens und des Verzeihens, grau geworden war die Haut, ein wenig Wangenrot schwamm mit den Tränen mit, und Wotans Erbe war wieder gerettet.

Fahnen bieten sich immer, zerknitterte Prostituierte. Die Fahnen zu hissen, ist jeweils Pflicht. *Ich hisse heute diese Fahne und morgen die andere Fahne ich erfülle meine Pflicht.* Die Fahnen klirren im Wind. O Hölderlin, was klirrt denn so? Die scheppernde Phrase, die hohlen Knochen der Toten. Die Gesellschaft harrte mal wieder aus, hohe Aufgaben waren zu erfüllen, das Vermögen zu retten, Tuchfühlung zu halten, der Besitz zu wahren, der Anschluß nicht zu verlieren, denn das Dabeisein ist alles, in den Schöpfungen der Haute Couture und im gebügelten Frack und, wenn es anders nicht geht, mit dem Marschtritt der langschäftigen Stiefel. Es kleidet der Frack den Träger, aber schmuck und prall sitzt die Uniform. Sie verleiht Größe, sie gibt Sicherheit. Keetenheuve machte sich nichts aus Uniformen. Machte er sich auch nichts aus Größe, nichts aus Sicherheit?

Er hatte geträumt. In unruhigen Schlaf gefallen, hatte er geträumt, er reise zu einer Wahlversammlung. Der kleine Bahnhof lag in einem Tal. Niemand war erschienen, den Abgeordneten zu begrüßen. Von Fahrzeugen leer liefen die Schienen ins Unendliche. Neben den Schwellen dorrte Gras. Disteln umrankten den Schotter. Vier Hügel waren der Ort, auf den Hügeln der katholische Dom, die protestantische Kirche, das Kriegerdenkmal aus unfruchtbarem Granit, das Gewerkschaftshaus lieblos und schnell errichtet aus rohem Holz. Die Bauten standen einsam wie die griechischen Tempel in der traurigen Landschaft von Selinunt. Sie waren Vergangenheit, Staub der Geschichte, Klios erstarrte Losung, kein Mensch kümmerte sich um sie, doch ihm war befohlen, einen der Hügel hinauf, zu einer der Stätten zu laufen, anzuklopfen und zu rufen: Ich glaube! Ich glaube!«

Ihm war heiß. Irgend jemand mußte die Heizung im Wagen angedreht haben, obwohl die Nacht warm war. Er schaltete das Licht ein. Er sah auf die Uhr. Es war fünf. Der Sekundenzeiger kreiste rot über dem Blatt mit den phosphoreszierenden Ziffern wie eine Warnung vor Überdruck und

Explosionsgefahr. Keetenheuves Zeit lief ab. Sie verrann phosphoreszierend, wie zu sehen war, und sinnlos, was weniger zutage trat. Die Räder des Zuges führten ihn sinnlos unleuchtenden Zielen zu. Hatte er seine Zeit genützt? Nützte er den Tag? Lohnte es sich? Und war die Frage nach einem Lohn der Zeit nicht schon wieder eine Äußerung menschlicher Perversion? »Einen Zweck gibt es nur in der Verderbtheit«, hatte Rathenau meditiert, und so fühlte Keetenheuve sich verderbt. Er hatte, älter geworden, die Empfindung, noch gar nicht richtig auf die Bahn der Zeit gesetzt und doch schon am Ende seines Lebenspfades zu sein. Es war so viel passiert, daß er meinte, er sei immer nur stehengeblieben und nie vorangekommen; die Katastrophen, die er erlebt hatte, das turbulente Weltgeschehen, Geschichtsuntergänge, Aufbrüche neuer Epochen, deren Abendfeuer und Morgenrot (wer wußte es?) auch sein Gesicht färbte und gerbte, dies alles ließ ihn mit fünfundvierzig Jahren wie einen Jungen zurück, der einen Räuberfilm gesehen hatte und sich die Augen rieb, töricht hoffnungsvoll, töricht enttäuscht und töricht lasterhaft. Er streckte die Hand aus, um die Heizung abzustellen; doch der Hebel stand über dem Zeichen *Kalt.* Vielleicht mußte man die Heizung von einem ferneren Hebel lenken, vielleicht bestimmte ein Zugführer die Temperatur in den Wagen; vielleicht war aber auch gar keine Heizung eingeschaltet, und es war nur die Nacht, die Keetenheuve bedrückte. Er legte sich auf das Polster zurück und schloß wieder die Augen. Auf dem Gang regte sich nichts. Die Fahrgäste lagen in ihren Pferchen, dem Vergessen überliefert.

Und wenn er nicht wiedergewählt wurde? Ihm graute vor der Ochsentour der Wahlschlacht. Immer mehr scheute er Versammlungen, die häßliche Weite der Säle, den Zwang, durch das Mikrophon sprechen zu müssen, die Groteske, die eigene Stimme in allen Winkeln verzerrt aus den Lautsprechern bullern zu hören, ein hohlklingendes und für Keetenheuve schmerzlich hohnvolles Echo aus einem Dunst von Schweiß, Bier und Tabak. Als Redner überzeugte er nicht. Die Menge ahnte, er zweifele, und das verzieh sie ihm nicht.

Sie vermißten bei Keetenheuves Auftritt das Schauspiel des Fanatikers, die echte oder die gemimte Wut, das berechnete Toben, den Schaum vor dem Maul des Redners, die gewohnte patriotische Schmiere, die sie kannten und immer wieder haben wollten. Konnte Keetenheuve ein Protagonist des Parteioptimismus sein, konnte er die Kohlköpfe im abgesteckten Beet der Parteilinie nach der Sonne des Programms ausrichten? Phrasen sprangen vielen wie quakende Frösche vom Mund; aber Keetenheuve grauste es vor Fröschen.

Er wollte wiedergewählt werden. Gewiß, das wollten sie alle. Aber Keetenheuve wollte wiedergewählt werden, weil er sich für einen der wenigen hielt, die ihr Mandat noch als eine Anwaltschaft gegen die Macht auffaßten. Aber was war dazu zu sagen? Sollte er die Hoffnung malen, den alten Silberstreifen aufziehen, der vor jeder Wahl aus der Kiste geholt wird wie der Baumschmuck zu Weihnachten (die Partei verlangte es), die Hoffnung, daß alles besser wird, diese Fata Morgana für Einfältige, die sich nach jedem Plebiszit in Rauch auflöst, als wären die Stimmzettel in des Hephaistos Esse geworfen? Doch konnte er es sich leisten, sich nicht anzupreisen? War er eine gesuchte Ware, ein Star des politischen Kintopps? Die Wähler kannten ihn nicht. Er tat, was er tun konnte, aber das meiste tat er in den Ausschüssen, nicht im Plenum, und die Arbeit der Ausschüsse geschah geheim und nicht vor den Augen der Nation. Korodin von der anderen Partei, sein Gegner im Ausschuß für Petitionen, nannte Keetenheuve einen Menschenrechtsromantiker, der Verfolgte suchte, Geknechtete, um ihnen die Ketten abzunehmen, Leute, denen Unrecht widerfahren, Keetenheuve war immer auf der Seite der Armen und der Sonderfälle, er stand den Unorganisierten bei und nie den Kirchen und Kartellen, doch auch den Parteien nicht, nicht unbedingt selbst der eigenen Partei, und das verstimmte die Parteifreunde, und manchmal schien es Keetenheuve, als ob Korodin, sein Gegner, ihn am Ende noch besser verstand als die Fraktion, mit der er sich verbunden hatte.

Keetenheuve lag ausgestreckt und gerade unter dem Betttuch. Bis zum Kinn zugedeckt, sah er wie eine Mumie des alten Ägyptens aus. Im Abteil stagnierte Museumsluft. War Keetenheuve ein Museumsstück?

Er hielt sich für ein Lamm. Aber er wollte vor den Wölfen nicht weichen. Diesmal nicht. Fatal war, daß er faul war; faul, auch wenn er sechzehn Stunden am Tag arbeitete, und das nicht schlecht. Er war faul, weil er ungläubig, zweifelnd, verzweifelt, skeptisch war, und sein eifriges und aufrichtiges Vertreten der Menschenrechte war nur noch ein letzter eigensinnig spielerischer Rest von Oppositionslust und Staatswiderstand. Ihm war das Rückgrat gebrochen, und die Wölfe würden es nicht schwer haben, ihm alles wieder zu entreißen. Was konnte Keetenheuve sonst beginnen? Er konnte kochen. Er konnte ein Zimmer saubermachen. Er hatte hausfrauliche Tugenden. Sollte er sein Gewissen pflegen, Artikel schreiben, Kommentare in den Äther sprechen, eine öffentliche Kassandra werden? Wer würde die Artikel drucken, wer die Kommentare senden, wer wird auf Kassandra hören? Sollte er revoluzzen? Wenn er's recht bedachte, würde er lieber kochen. Vielleicht konnte er den Mönchen in einem Kloster das Mahl bereiten. Korodin würde ihn empfehlen. Korodin war Ehemann und Vater, Enkel würden ihm heranwachsen, er hatte seinen Glauben, er besaß ein beträchtliches Vermögen und schöne Geschäftsbeteiligungen, er war ein Freund des Bischofs und stand sich gut mit den Klöstern.

Manche in der Hauptstadt erhoben sich früh. Es war fünf Uhr dreißig. Der Wecker schellte. Frost-Forestier war mit dem Läuten wach. Aus keinem Traum, aus keiner Umarmung hatte er sich zu lösen, kein Alp hatte ihn gequält, keine Messe rief ihn, er war nicht in Furcht verstrickt.

Frost-Forestier schaltete das Licht ein, und es wurde hell in einem enormen Raum, einem prächtigen Festsaal des neunzehnten Jahrhunderts mit Stuckplafond und gedrechselten Säulen, dies war Frost-Forestiers Schlafkammer, Eßraum, Arbeitszimmer, Salon, Küche, Laboratorium, Bad. Keetenheuve erinnerte sich an die schweren Vorhänge vor den hohen Fenstern, sie waren generalsrot und standen, ständig geschlossen, wie ein Feuerwall gegen die Natur. Leise nur war das Zwitschern zu hören, das Jubelsingen, das Erwachen der Vögel

233

draußen im Park, und was sich im Saal ereignete, war der Arbeitsbeginn in einer Fabrik, die Ankurbelung eines Fließbandes, ein Ablauf ausgeklügelter wohlberechneter Bewegungen, rationell und präzise, und Frost-Forestier war das Werk, das in Gang gesetzt wurde. Er eiferte den elektronischen Gehirnen nach.

Das war ein Knipsen und Schalten! Ein großer Funkkasten sprach Nachrichten aus Moskau. Ein kleiner Bruder des großen glühte und wartete auf seine Zeit. Eine Kaffeemaschine erhitzte sich. Aus dem Boiler stürzte das Wasser in die Brause. Frost-Forestier stellte sich unter den Strahl. Der Plastikvorhang der Duschecke blieb beiseite geschoben. Frost-Forestier übersah, während er duschte, sein strategisches Feld. Es berieselte ihn heiß und kalt. Er war ein trainierter, ein proportionierter Mann. Er frottierte sich mit einem rauhen olivgrünen Handtuch amerikanischer Herkunft, ein nackter Mann auf einem leeren Kasernenhof. Seine Haut rötete sich. In Moskau nichts Neues. Aufrufe an das Sowjetvolk. Frost-Forestier setzte die Musen ein, schaltete Musik herbei. Neben der Duschkammer war ein Reck. Frost-Forestier ging in Grundstellung; saubere Hände auf sauberen Schenkeln. Er sprang an das Reck, Aufschwung und Abschwung. Er stand wieder in Grundstellung. Sein Gesicht war ernst. Sein Geschlecht hing ruhig, wohlproportioniert zwischen den trainierten Beinen. Der Kontakt des elektrischen Rasierapparates wurde in die Dose gesteckt. Frost-Forestier rasierte sich bei leisem Schnurren. Im großen Radio gab es Störungen. Frost-Forestier stellte das große Radio ab. Der Einsatz der Musen war vorbei. Er nahm einen Wattebausch und tupfte mit einem scharfen brennenden Rasierwasser sein Gesicht ab. Der Wattebausch verschwand unter der Patentklappe eines hygienischen Eimers. Im Gesicht traten ein paar Bläschen hervor. Er zog einen Hausmantel über den Leib, ein härenes Gewand; er knüpfte es mit einem roten Schlips zu. Die Stunde des kleinen Radios war gekommen. Es knisterte und sagte: »Dora braucht Windeln.« Frost-Forestier lauschte. Das kleine Radio wiederholte: »Dora braucht Windeln.« Mehr hatte das kleine Radio nicht zu sagen.

Die Kaffeemaschine zitterte und dampfte. Ein Pfiff eilte durch ihren Flötenmund, die Fabriksirene meldete den Schichtbeginn. Frost-Forestier ließ den Kaffee in die Tasse rinnen. Die Tasse war aus altem preußischen Porzellan, eine Ziertasse für freundliche Sammler. Keetenheuve kannte die Tasse, ihr Henkel war abgebrochen. Frost-Forestier verbrannte sich, als er die gefüllte Tasse anfaßte. Auch als Keetenheuve bei ihm war, hatte sich Frost-Forestier an der Tasse verbrannt. Er verbrannte sich jeden Morgen die Finger. Die Tasse zeigte ein buntes Bild Friedrichs des Großen. Der König blickte mit dem Ausdruck eines melancholischen Windhundes von seiner Tasse in das Zimmer. Frost-Forestier nahm ein Papiertaschentuch, legte es um das Porzellan und den König und schlürfte nun endlich sein heißes schwarzes Morgengetränk. Im ganzen war keine Viertelstunde seit dem Läuten des Weckers vergangen. Frost-Forestier öffnete das Kombinationsschloß eines Panzerschrankes. Keetenheuve amüsierte sich über den Schrank. Der Schrank war ein Geschenk an die Neugier. Dokumente, Akten, Lebensläufe, Briefe, Pläne, Filme und Tonbänder warteten hier *wie lieblich duftete dem Knaben das Eingemachte im Schrank der alten Tante,* und mancher hätte sich gern was 'rausgenommen. Auf dem Tisch aus rohem Holz, einem langen Brett, das auf vier Böcken ruhte, standen Tonaufnahmegeräte. Auch lag eine winzig kleine und eine größere photographische Kamera da. Diebesgerät! Man stahl die Sache nicht mehr, die blieb an ihrem Ort, man stahl ihren Schatten. Auch die Stimme des Menschen konnte man stehlen.

Keetenheuve ließ immer so viel herumliegen. Er war unordentlich. Frost-Forestier, ein Mann in einer politischen Stellung, setzte sich an den Schreibtisch. Er begann zu denken, er begann zu arbeiten. Drei Stunden lagen vor ihm, drei ungestörte Stunden, die wichtigsten des Tages, er konzentrierte sich, er bewältigte viel. Er legte ein Band in das Magnetophon und schaltete auf Wiedergabe. Er hörte seine eigene Stimme und eine andere Stimme aus dem Magnetophon sprechen. Hingegeben, versunken hörte Frost-Forestier den Stimmen zu. Zuweilen regten sie ihn zu einer Notiz an

Frost-Forestier hatte rote, grüne und blaue Schreibhefte. Er schrieb einen Namen auf ein Blatt. War es Keetenheuves Name? Frost-Forestier unterstrich den Namen. Er unterstrich ihn mit dem roten Stift.

General Yorck schloß die Konvention von Tauroggen. Sein König rehabilitierte ihn. General Scharnhorst rekrutierte. General Gneisenau reformierte. General Seeckt erwog, daß aus dem Osten das Licht kommt. General Tuchatschewski wollte den Teppich der Welt aufrollen. General de Gaulle war für Panzer, er wurde nicht gehört und hatte recht. General Speidel reiste zu seinen alliierten Kollegen. General Paulus saß noch immer in Rußland. General Jodl lag in seinem Grab. General Eisenhower war Präsident. Wer war der große Informator der Roten Kapelle? Frost-Forestier erinnerte sich gern seiner Tätigkeit im OKH. Er liebte Soldatenausdrücke. Er sagte einmal zu Keetenheuve: »Ich spür's im Urin.« Was spürte er im Urin? Daß sie zusammenkommen würden?

Der Morgen drängte sich durch das Rouleau. Keetenheuve lüpfte die Decke. Zugwind traf ihn *Freud oder das Unbehagen in der Kultur. Im Berliner Café diskutierte man die Schulen der Psychoanalytiker. Tulpe war Kommunist. Keetenheuve war Bürger. Es war die Zeit, als Bürger und Kommunisten noch miteinander sprachen. Gut so. Sinnlos. Vergeblich. Mit Blindheit geschlagen? Mit Blindheit geschlagen.* Es war Erich, der Keetenheuve in ein Gewerkschaftshaus geführt hatte. Erich wollte ihn zu etwas einladen, und Keetenheuve mußte die Einladung annehmen, obwohl er nicht hungrig war. Ein kleiner verhärmter Mann mit einem großen Schnauzbart, der für sein eingefallenes Gesicht zu gewaltig war, um Respekt einzuflößen, brachte ihnen schwarzverbrannte Kartoffelpuffer und eine Brauselimonade, die nach künstlichem Pudding schmeckte. Als Keetenheuve die Puffer gegessen und die Limonade getrunken hatte, fühlte er sich revolutionär. Er war jung. Die Stadt war klein, stumpfsinnig, engherzig, und das Gewerkschaftshaus galt als Feste des Aufruhrs. Doch nie kam es zu der Erhebung, von der die Knaben träumten, nie, nie, nie, was blieb und immer wiederkehrte, waren die schwarzverbrannten Kartoffelpuffer der Armut, war der mattrosa Trank der Evolution, eine Limonade aus synthetischen Säften, aufbrausend, wenn man die Flasche öffnete, und aufstoßend, wenn man sie getrunken hatte. Erich war umgekommen. In der kleinen Stadt hatte man später eine Straße nach ihm genannt; aber die Leute, stumpfsinnig, engherzig, vergeßlich wie eh und je, nannten die Gasse weiter die Kurze Reihe. Keetenheuve fragte sich immer wieder, ob Erich wirklich für seine Überzeugung gestorben war, denn er mußte den Glauben der Jugend damals schon verloren haben. Vielleicht aber hatte Erich sich im Augenblick seines Todes wieder zu dieser Hoffnung bekannt, und das nur, weil die Menschen der kleinen Städte in jenen Tagen gar so entsetzlich waren. Die Gesetzlosigkeit schlug Erich auf dem Markt, aber der Ekel war es, der ihn tötete. Keetenheuve klappte den Deckel der Waschgelegenheit hoch, Wasser floß in das Becken, er konnte sich waschen, konnte die Reinigung des Pontius Pilatus vornehmen, wieder einmal, wieder einmal aufs neue, gewiß, er war unschuldig, ganz unschuldig am Lauf der Welt, aber gerade weil er unschuldig war, stand vor ihm die uralte Frage, was ist Unschuld, was Wahrheit, o alter Statthalter des Augustus. Er sah sich im Spiegel.

Die Augen, der Brille ledig, blickten gutmütig, und einen gutmütigen Trottel hatte ihn der Kollege vom »Volksblatt« genannt, am letzten Abend, als er ihn zum letzten Male sah. Das war vor zwanzig Jahren gewesen, an dem Tag, an dem der Komissar in das »Volksblatt» einzog. Die jüdischen Redakteure flogen gleich, kluge Leute, gewandte Leitartikler, hervorragende Stilisten, die alles falsch vorausgesehen, alles falsch gemacht hatten, ahnungslose Kälber im Gatter des Schlachthofes; die anderen bekamen die Chance, sich zu bewähren. Keetenheuve verzichtete auf die Bewährung. Er holte sein Gehalt und reiste nach Paris. Er reiste freiwillig, und niemand hinderte ihn. In Paris fragte man verwundert: Was wollen Sie eigentlich bei uns? Erst als die Soldaten über die Champs Elysées marschierten, hätte Keetenheuve es erklären können. Aber da war er auf dem Wege nach Kanada; zusammen mit deutschen Juden, zusammen mit deutschen An-

tifaschisten, deutschen Nationalsozialisten, jungen deutschen
Fliegern, deutschen Seeleuten und deutschen Handlungsge-
hilfen schwamm er tief unten im Bauch eines Schiffes von
England nach Kanada. Der Kommandant des Dampfers war
ein gerechter Mann; er haßte sie alle gleichermaßen. Und
Keetenheuve war es nun, der sich fragte: Was will ich hier,
was tue ich hier, nur nicht teilhaben, nur die Hände in Unschuld waschen, ist das genug?
Keetenheuves Kopf saß, wo er hingehörte, kein Fallbeil hatte
ihn vom Rumpf getrennt. Sprach das gegen Keetenheuve,
oder sprach es, wie einige meinten, gegen die Gewerkschaft
der Henker in der Welt? Keetenheuve hatte viele Feinde,
und es gab keinen Verrat, dessen man ihn nicht zieh. So hätte
mich Georges Grosz gemalt, dachte er. Sein Gesicht trug nun
schon sehr den Ausdruck der herrschenden Schicht. Er war
des Kanzlers getreuer Abgeordneter und Oppositioneller in
Ergebenheit; ach ja, in Ergebenheit.
Halbakt eines Managers — so stellte ihn der Spiegel dar.
Spiegelein, Spiegelein an der Wand, fleischig war er nun, die
Muskeln ungeübt, die Haut schimmerte weiß mit einem
blauen Unterton wie Magermilch in den Kriegen, entrahm-
te Frischmilch hieß es, o schönes Wort des staatlichen Euphe-
mismus, man zählte zu den Gemäßigten, man fand sich ab,
man richtete sich ein, man vertrat behutsame Reformen im
Rahmen der Tradition, man hatte Kreislaufstörungen und
war lüstern *(kiss me) you will go*. Er war ein stattlicher
Mann. Er verdrängte mehr Luft, als er je erwartet hatte,
Luft zu verdrängen. Wie war der Geruch um ihn? Lavendel-
wasser, eine Erinnerung an das Empire, die langen Gänge
des Hier-ist-England *(kiss me) you will go*. Keetenheuve war
keine durchschnittliche Erscheinung der parlamentarischen
Elite. Das konnte er mit diesen Augen schon nicht sein; sie
waren eben zu gutmütig. Wer wollte gutmütig geschimpft
werden und in den Ruf des Trottels kommen? Und dann der
Mund — er war zu schmal, zu verschlossen *Schulmeister
Schulmeister* er war nicht gesprächig, er beunruhigte, und so
war Keetenheuve nie ganz enträtselt; »he was a handsome
man and what I want to know is how do you like your blue-

eyed boy Mr. Death«. Keetenheuve war ein Kenner und
Liebhaber der zeitgenössischen Lyrik, und manchmal belustigte es ihn, während er im Plenum einem Redner zuhörte,
daran zu denken, wer im Saal außer ihm wohl Cummings
gelesen habe. Das unterschied Keetenheuve von der Fraktion,
bewahrte ihm Jugend und machte ihn unterlegen, wenn es
hieß, rücksichtslos zu sein. Die schmalen Zeitschriften, gegründet gestorben, die Blätter, der Dichtkunst geweiht, rieben sich an den Akten in Keetenheuves Handtasche, seltsamerweise, ja seltsam fürwahr, die Gedichte des experimentie-
renden Dichters E. E. Cummings scheuerten in der Aktenmappe eines deutschen Bundestagsabgeordneten die gefärbten Pappen der Schnellhefter *Vertraulich, Dringend, Geheim
(kiss me) you will go*
Keetenheuve trat in den Gang hinaus. Viele Wege führten
zur Hauptstadt. Auf vielen Wegen wurde zur Macht und zur
Pfründe gereist.
Sie kamen alle, Abgeordnete, Politiker, Beamte, Journalisten, Parteibüffel und Parteigründer, die Interessenvertreter
im Dutzend, die Syndiken, die Werbeleiter, die Jobber, die
Bestecher und die Bestochenen, Fuchs, Wolf und Schaf der
Geheimdienste, Nachrichtenbringer und Nachrichtenerfinder,
all die Dunkelmänner, die Zwielichtigen, die Bündlerischen,
die Partisanwahnsinnigen, alle, die Geld haben wollten, die
genialen Filmer zu *Heidelberg am Rhein auf der Heide in
der Badewanne für Deutschland am Drachenstein*, die
Schnorrer, Schwindler, Quengler, Stellenjäger, auch Michael
Kohlhaas saß im Zug und Goldmacher Cagliostro, Fememörder Hagen witterte ins Morgenrot, Kriemhild hatte Renten-
ansprüche, das Geschmeiß der Lobby lugte und horchte, Generäle noch im Anzug von Lodenfrey marschierten zur Wiederverwendung auf, viele Ratten, viele gehetzte Hunde und
viele gerupfte Vögel, sie hatten ihre Frauen besucht, ihre
Frauen geliebt, ihre Frauen getötet, sie hatten ihre Kinder in
den Eisladen geführt, sie hatten dem Fußballspiel zugesehen,
sie waren im Meßgewand dem Priester zur Hand gegangen,
sie hatten Diakonissendienste geleistet, sie waren von ihren
Auftraggebern gescholten worden, von ihren Hintermännern

angetrieben, sie hatten einen Plan entworfen, eine Marsch-route aufgestellt, sie wollten ein Ding drehen, sie machten einen zweiten Plan, sie hatten am Gesetz gearbeitet, in ihrem Wahlkreis gesprochen, sie wollten oben bleiben, an der Macht bleiben, beim Geld bleiben, sie strebten der Hauptstadt zu, der Hauptstadt der Kleinstadt, über die sie witzelten, und sie begriffen nicht das Wort des Dichters, daß die innerste Hauptstadt jeden Reiches nicht hinter Erdwällen liegt und sich nicht erstürmen läßt.

Freie Bahn dem Volksvertreter, Spott aus dem billigsten Ramschladen, schon zu des Kaisers Zeit mit Bart verkauft *ein Leutnant und zehn Mann Deutschland erwache an die Latrine geschrieben,* man sah vor lauter Bart den Witz nicht mehr. Was meinte das Volk, und wer war das eigentlich, das Volk, wer war es im Zug, wer auf der Straße, wer auf den Bahnhöfen, war es die Frau, die nun in Remagen die Betten ins Fenster legte, Geburtsbetten Kopulationsbetten Sterbe-betten, Granatsplitter hatten das Haus getroffen, war es die Magd mit dem Melkeimer, die zum Stall wankte, so früh schon auf so früh schon müde, war er, Keetenheuve, das Volk? Er sträubte sich gegen den simplifizierenden Plural. Was sagte das schon, das Volk, war es eine Herde, zu scheren, zu scheuchen, zu leiten, setzte es sich aus Gruppen zusammen, die je nach Bedarf und nach der Sprechweise der Planer ein-zusetzen waren, in die Schlacht zu werfen, ins Grab zu trei-ben, der deutsche Junge im Einsatz, das deutsche Mädchen im Einsatz, oder waren Millionen von einzelnen das Volk, Wesen ein jedes für sich, die für sich dachten, die selber dachten, die sich voneinander fort dachten, auseinander dach-ten, zu Gott hin dachten, zum Nichts hin oder in den Irrsinn hinein, die nicht zu lenken, nicht zu regieren, nicht einzuset-zen, nicht zu scheren waren? Keetenheuve wäre es lieber ge-wesen. Er gehörte einer Partei an, die auf die Mehrheit setzte. Was meinte also das Volk? Das Volk arbeitete, das Volk bezahlte den Staat, das Volk wollte vom Staat leben, das Volk schimpfte, das Volk frettete sich so durch.

Es sprach wenig von seinen Deputierten. Das Volk war nicht so artig wie das Volk im Schullesebuch. Es faßte den Abschnitt Staatsbürgerkunde anders als die Verfasser auf. Das Volk war neidisch. Es neidete den Abgeordneten den Titel, den Sitz, die Immunität, die Diäten, den Freifahrschein. Würde des Parlaments? Gelächter in den Schenken, Gelächter auf den Gassen. Die Lautsprecher hatten das Parlament in den Stuben des Volkes entwürdigt, zu lange, zu willig war die Volksvertretung ein Gesangverein gewesen, ein einfältiger Chor zum Solo des Diktators. Das Ansehen der Demokratie war gering. Sie begeisterte nicht. Und das Ansehen der Diktatur? Das Volk schwieg. Schwieg es in weiterwirkender Furcht? Schwieg es in anhänglicher Liebe? Die Geschworenen sprachen die Männer der Diktatur von jeder Anklage frei. Und Keetenheuve? Er diente der Restauration und reiste im Nibelungenexpreß.

Nicht alle Abgeordneten reisten im Bundesbahnbett. Andere kamen im Auto zur Hauptstadt gefahren, quittierten das Kilometergeld und standen sich gut dabei; sie waren die schärferen Hechte. Auf der Rheinstraße brausten die schwarzen Mercedeswagen neben dem Wasser stromabwärts. Stromabwärts der Schlick, stromabwärts das Treibholz, stromabwärts Bakterien und Kot und die Laugen der Industrie. Die Herren hockten neben ihrem Fahrer, sie hockten hinter ihrem Fahrer, sie waren eingenickt. Die Familie hatte einen strapaziert. Körperabwärts, unter dem Mantel, der Jacke, dem Hemd, lief der Schweiß. Schweiß der Erschöpfung, Schweiß der Erinnerung, Schweiß des Schlummers, Schweiß des Sterbens, Schweiß der Neugeburt, Schweiß des Wohingefahrenwerdens und wer weiß wohin, Schweiß der nackten, der bloßen Angst. Der Fahrer kannte die Strecke und haßte die Gegend. Der Fahrer konnte Lorkowski heißen und aus Masuren sein. Er kam aus den Tannenwäldern; da lagen Tote. Er gedachte der Seen in den Wäldern; da lagen Tote. Der Abgeordnete hatte ein Herz für die Vertriebenen. Das soll hier nun schön sein, dachte Lorkowski, ich scheiß' doch auf den Rhein. *Er schiß auf den Rhein, Lorkowski, Abgeordnetenfahrer aus Masuren, Lorkowski, Leichenfahrer aus dem Gefangenenlager, Lorkowski, Sanitätsfahrer von Stalingrad, Lorkowski, NSKKfahrer aus Kraftdurchfreudetagen, alles*

Scheiße, Leichen Abgeordnete und Verstümmelte dieselbe Ladung, alles Scheiße, er schiß nicht nur auf den Rhein.

»Puppe.«

Der Interessenvertreter verließ den Abort, schlenkerte das Hosenbein, nichts Menschliches war ihm fremd. Er trat zu den anderen Interessenvertretern in den Vorraum des Wagens, ein Mann unter Männern.

»Bißchen blaß ist sie.«

»Macht nichts.«

»Durchgeschüttelt, durchgerüttelt, durchgerollt.«

»Zu lange unten gelegen.«

Wagalaweia.

Das Mädchen kam wehenden Gewandes, Engel des Schienenstranges, ein Nachtengel, wehenden Nachtgewandes, Spitzen streiften den Staub Rotz und Dreck des gefirnißten Ganges, Brustspitzen, pralle Knospen rieben die Gewandspitzen, die Füße trippelten in zierlichen Pantöffelchen, Bändergeschnür, *die Füße der Salome die wie kleine weiße Tauben sind,* die Zehennägel leuchteten rot, verschlafen war das Kind, launisch, mürrisch, viele Mädchen trugen den Ausdruck des Mürrischen im hübschen Puppengesicht, es war eine Mädchenmode, mürrisch zu sein, im Hals kratzte der Raucherhusten, die Männer sahen zu, wie das Mädchen trippelnd, lackiert, hochbeinig, hübsch und mürrisch auf den Lokus ging. Parfum kitzelte die Nasen und mischte sich hinter der Tür mit des Interessenvertreters strengem Ablauf am Abend genossener Bockbiere — an ihm war Hopfen und Malz nicht verloren.

»Feinen Koffer haben Sie da. Richtige Diplomatenkiste. Wie neu aus dem AA. Schwarzrotgoldene Streifen.«

»Schwarzrotmostrich, wie wir früher sagten.«

Wagalaweia.

Der Rhein schlängelte sich nun, ein gewundenes, silbernes Band, durch flache Ufer. Fern aus dem Frühdunst wölbten sich Berge. Keetenheuve atmete die milde Luft, und schon spürte er, wie sehr sie ihn traurig stimmte. Verkehrsvereine, Fremdenlockbetriebe nannten das Land die rheinische Riviera. Ein Treibhausklima gedieh im Kessel zwischen den

Bergen; die Luft staute sich über dem Strom und seinen Ufern. Villen standen am Wasser, Rosen wurden gezüchtet, die Wohlhabenheit schritt mit der Heckenschere durch den Park, knirschenden Kies unter dem leichten Altersschuh, Keetenheuve würde nie dazu gehören, nie hier ein Haus haben, nie Rosen schneiden, nie die Edelrosen, die Nobiles, die Rosa indica, er dachte an die Wundrose, Erysipelas traumaticum, Gesundbeter waren am Werk, Deutschland war ein großes öffentliches Treibhaus, Keetenheuve sah seltsame Floren, gierige, fleischfressende Pflanzen, Riesenphallen, Schornsteinen gleich voll schwelenden Rauches, blaugrün, rotgelb, giftig, aber es war eine Üppigkeit ohne Mark und Jugend, es war alles morsch, es war alles alt, die Glieder strotzten, aber es war eine Elephantiasis arabum. Besetzt, stand auf der Klinke, und hinter der Tür pinkelte das Mädchen, hübsch und mürrisch, die Schwellen an.

Jonathan Swift, Dechant von St. Patrick zu Dublin, hatte sich zwischen Stella und Vanessa gesetzt und war empört, daß sie Leiber hatten. Keetenheuve hatte im alten Berlin den Doktor Forelle gekannt. Forelle unterhielt eine Kassenpraxis in einer Mietskaserne am Wedding. Er ekelte sich vor den Körpern, arbeitete seit Jahrzehnten an einer psychoanalytischen Studie über Swift und legte am Abend Watte um seine Türschelle, um ja nicht zu einer Geburt geholt zu werden. Nun lag er mit all den verabscheuten Leibern zusammen unter den Trümmern der Mietskaserne. Die Interessenvertreter mit entleerter Blase, befreitem lebensfrohem Gedärm schnatterten, schnodderten, sie waren ihres Appetites sicher.

»Gehen Sie man zu Hanke. Hanke war schon immer im RWM. Sagen Sie ihm, Sie kommen von mir.«

»Kann ihm schließlich keine Bockwurst vorsetzen.«

»Essen im Royal. Dreihundert. Aber wirklich erste Klasse. Rentiert sich immer.«

»Sonst sagen Sie eben dem Hanke, daß wir den Artikel dann nicht mehr herstellen können.«

»Soll sich doch der Minister um die Bürgschaft kümmern. Wozu ist er Minister?«

»Plischer war bei mir in der Fachschaft.«

»Dann verlass' ich mich auf Plischer.«

»Weiche Knie.«

Wagalaweia.

Das Mädchen, hübsch und mürrisch, trippelte ins Bett zurück. Das Mädchen, hübsch und mürrisch, war für Düsseldorf bestimmt, es konnte noch einmal ins Bett kriechen, und die Geilheit der Männer schlüpfte mit ihr, der Hübschen und Mürrischen, unter die Decke. Die Geilheit wärmte. Das Mädchen war in der Mode tätig, Mannequinkönigin irgendeiner Wahl. Das Mädchen war arm und lebte, nicht schlecht, von den Reichen. Von Timborn öffnete die Tür seines Abteils, von Timborn wohlrasiert, von Timborn korrekt, von Timborn schon jetzt wie in Downing Street akkreditiert.

»Guten Morgen, Herr Keetenheuve.«

Woher kannte er ihn? Von einem Bankett der ausländischen Presse. Man prostete sich zu und belauerte einander. Keetenheuve erinnerte sich nicht. Er wußte nicht, wer ihm begegnete. Er nickte einen Gruß. Aber Herr von Timborn hatte ein rühmliches Personengedächtnis, und er trainierte es um seiner Karriere willen. Er stellte seinen Koffer auf das Gitter der Gangheizung. Er beobachtete Keetenheuve. Timborn schob die Lippe etwas vor, ein schnüffelndes Kaninchen im Klee. Dem Abgeordneten gab es vielleicht der Herr im Schlaf. Das Kaninchen hörte das Gras nicht wachsen, aber das Flüstern im Amt. Keetenheuve spurte schlecht, er war nicht zu lenken, er war unbequem, er eckte an, er war in seiner Fraktion das Enfant terrible, so was bekam einem im allgemeinen schlecht, konnte einem schaden, für Timborn wäre es das Ende aller Hoffnung gewesen, aber diese Außenseiter, man konnte es nie wissen, die machten mit ihren Fehlern ihr Glück. Es gab schöne Posten, Druckposten, Bundesposten, Abstellposten, fern von Madrid, und Timborn war wieder mal genasführt, trottend auf dem schmalen Pfad nicht grade der Tugend, aber des Avancements, Schritt für Schritt, Stufe für Stufe, aufwärts oder abwärts, das wußte man in dieser Zeit nicht so genau, immerhin, man saß wieder in der Zentrale, vor acht Jahren saß man in Nürnberg, vor weiteren acht Jahren hatte man auch in Nürnberg gesessen, damals auf der

Tribüne, die Nürnberger Gesetze wurden verkündet, die ersten, immerhin, die Katastrophenversicherung auf Gegenseitigkeit funktionierte, man war wieder im Amt, und alles war drin, und viel konnte geschehen. Und wenn Herr Keetenheuve nun auf die Wahlen setzte, vielleicht ein Portefeuille erwartete? Dann würde Keetenheuve sich wehren. Wie dumm — Gandhi melkte nicht mehr seine Ziege. Keetenheuve und Gandhi, sie hätten Hand in Hand am Ganges spazieren können. Gandhi wäre ein Magnet für Keetenheuve gewesen. Timborn zog die Lippe wieder ein und blickte träumend über den Rhein. Er sah Keetenheuve unter Palmen — keine gute Figur. Timborn würde der Tropenanzug besser sitzen. Das Tor nach Indien war geöffnet. Alexander tötete den Freund mit dem Speer.

Der Zug hielt in Godesberg. Herr von Timborn lüftete den Hut, den korrekten, kleidsamen Mister-Eden-Filz. In Godesberg wohnten die feinen Leute, die Bruderschaft vom Protokoll. Herr von Timborn schritt elastisch über den Perron. Der Lokomotivführer fluchte. Was war das für eine Strecke! Dampf geben und drosseln. Schließlich fuhr er einen Expreß. Durch Godesberg und Bonn war man mal durchgerast. Jetzt hielt man. Die Interessenvertreter blockierten die Tür. Sie waren Ellbogenritter und die ersten in der Hauptstadt. Schulkinder liefen die Tunneltreppe herauf. Man roch die Provinz, das Muffige enger Gassen, verbauter Stuben, alter Tapeten. Der Bahnsteig war überdacht und grau —

und da vor der Sperre, in der nüchternen Halle, er betrat die Hauptstadt, hetz ihn, faß ihn, o Gott Apollon o, da packten sie ihn wieder, überkamen ihn, fielen über ihn her, da hatten ihn Schwindel und Atemnot, ein Herzkrampf schüttelte ihn, und ein eiserner Reif legte sich ihm um die Brust, wurde festgeschmiedet, wurde geschweißt, vernietet, jeder Schritt schmiedete, nietete mit, der Auftritt seiner nun steifen Beine, seiner nun tauben Füße war wie ein Hammerschlag, der Nieten in ein Wrack hämmerte auf eines Teufels Werft, und so ging er, Schritt für Schritt (wo war eine Bank, sich zu setzen? eine Mauer, sich anzuklammern?), ging, obwohl er des Gehens nicht mehr fähig zu sein glaubte, nach einem

245

Halt wollte er tasten, obwohl er es auch wieder nicht wagte,
die Hand nach einem Halt auszustrecken, Leere, Leere dehn-
te sich gewaltig in seinem Schädel aus, preßte, stieg an wie
in allzuferner verschwindender abschiednehmender die Erde
verlassender Höhe der Innendruck in einem Ballon, aber wie
in einem Ballon, der mit dem reinsten Nichts gefüllt war,
einem Nichtstoff, einem Unstoff, etwas Unbegreiflichem, das
den Drang hatte zu wachsen, das aus Knochen und Haut
dringen wollte, und schon vernahm er, vernahm er, noch ehe
es soweit war, vernahm er wie Eiswind das Zerreißen der
Seide, und dies war der extreme Augenblick, eine unsicht-
bare, selbst in der Geheimschrift der Mathematik nicht mehr
zu bezeichnende Wegmarke, wo alles aufhörte, ein Weiter
gab es nicht, und hier war die Deutung, sieh!, sieh!, du wirst
sehen, frage!, frage!, du wirst hören, und er senkte den Blick,
feig, feig, feig, geschlossen blieb der Mund, arm, arm, arm,
und er klammerte sich an, klammerte sich fest an sich selbst,
und der Ballon war eine enttäuschende schmutzige Hülle, er
war schrecklich entblößt, und dann begann der Sturz. Er
zeigte den Fahrausweis vor, und seine Empfindung war, daß
der Sperrenwächter ihn nackt sah, so wie Gefängniswärter
und Feldwebel den ihnen ausgelieferten Menschen vor seiner
Einkleidung zu Haft und Sterben sehen.

Schweiß stand auf seiner Stirn. Er ging zum Zeitungsstand.
Die Sonne war zu Besuch, kam durch ein Fenster und warf
ihr Spektrum über die neuesten Nachrichten, über das Guten-
bergbild der Welt, es war ein irisierendes, ein ironisches Flim-
mern. Keetenheuve kaufte die Morgenblätter *Kein Treffen*
mit den Russen. Natürlich nicht. Wer wollte wen treffen oder
nicht treffen? Und wer kam schon gerannt, wenn er gepfiffen
wurde? Wer war ein Hund? Eine Verfassungsklage — war
man sich uneinig? Wer konnte nicht lesen? Das Grundgesetz
war geschaffen. Bereute man die Bemühung? Was tat sich in
Mehlem? Der Hohe Kommissar war auf der Zugspitze gewesen. Er hatte einen wunderbaren Fernblick gehabt. Der
Kanzler war leicht erkrankt, aber er waltete seines Amtes.
Sieben Uhr früh — er saß schon an seinem Schreibtisch. In
Bonn arbeitete nicht nur Frost-Forestier. Keetenheuve war

seiner Beklemmung noch nicht Herr geworden. Der Haupt-
saal des Bahnhofsrestaurants war geschlossen. Keetenheuve
ging in den Nebenraum, Schulkinder hockten am runden
Tisch, reizlos angezogene Mädchen, Jungen, die schon Beam-
tengesichter hatten, verstohlen rauchten, auch sie waren fleißig, wie der Kanzler, hatten Bücher aufgeschlagen, lernten,
strebten (wie der Kanzler?), eine Jugend verbissenen Gesichts, was für vernünftig galt, was dem Vorankommen diente, steuerte ihr Herz, sie dachten an den Stundenplan und
nicht an die Sterne. Die Kellnerin meinte, man müsse hier
Flügel haben, Keetenheuve sah sie schweben, ein Butt mit
Schwingen, der Betrieb war dem Andrang nicht gewachsen,
dem Auswurf der großen Züge, die Interessenvertreter
schimpften, wo blieben ihre Eier, Keetenheuve bestellte ein
Helles. Er verabscheute Bier, aber der bittere prickelnde
Trank beruhigte diesmal sein Herz. Keetenheuve schlug die
Lokalseite der Zeitung auf. Was gab es Neues in Bonn? Er
war der Kurgast, der, allzulang in einen trostlosen Badeort
verbannt, schließlich dem Dorfklatsch lauscht. Sophie Mergentheim hatte sich zum Wohle von Flüchtlingen mit Wasser bespritzen lassen. Sieh, sie schaffte es immer. Auf einem
Empfang für Gott weiß wen hatte sie sich mildtätig unter
die Gießkanne gebeugt. Sophie, Sophia, ehrgeizige Gans, sie
rettete das Capitol nicht. Wer zahlte, durfte spritzen. Schöne
Tulpe. Die Zeitung brachte das Bild der Sophie Mergentheim, naß im durchnäßten Abendkleid, bis in die Hose naß,
naß bis auf die duftbetupfte, die puderbestreute Haut. Kollege
Mergentheim stand hinter dem Mikrophon und starrte durch
seine dicke schwarze Hornbrille mutig ins Blitzlicht. Zeig mir
deinen Uhu! *Nichts Neues in Insterburg. Ein Hund hat gebellt.*
Mergentheim war Spezialist für jüdische Witze; am alten
»Volksblatt« hatte er den Humor des Tages redigiert. *Was,
wer bellte in Insterburg? Gestern? Heute? Wer bellte? Juden?
Schweigen. Hundewitz.* Im Kino — Willy Birgel reitet für
Deutschland. *Der widerliche Schaum des Bieres auf den Lippen.
Elke, ein Name aus der nordischen Mythologie. Die Nornen
Urd, Werdandi und Skuld unter dem Baum Yggdrasil. Blank-
gewichste Stiefel. Der Tod in Kapseln. Bier über ein Grab.*

247

II

Korodin verließ am Bahnhof die Straßenbahn. Ein Schutzmann spielte Schutzmann in Berlin am Potsdamer Platz. Er
gab die Bonner Straße frei. Es wimmelte, es schwirrte,
quietschte, klingelte. Automobile, Radfahrer, Fußgänger,
asthmagequälte Trams strebten aus engen Gassen auf den
Bahnhofsplatz. Hier waren Equipagen gerollt, Viergespanne,
von königlichen Kutschern gelenkt, Prinz Wilhelm war zur
Universität und so ein paar Meter näher zum holländischen
Asyl gefahren, er trug einen Cutaway, das Corpsband der
Saxoborussen und ihren weißen Stürmer. Der Verkehr ver-
knäuelte sich, von Bauzäunen, Kabelgräben, Kanalrohren,
Betonmischern, Teerkochern bedrängt und behindert. Das
Knäuel, das Labyrinth, der Knoten, das Verschlungene, das
Geflecht, Sinnbilder des Verirrens, des Irrens überhaupt, der
Verknotung, des Unlösbaren, des Verflochtenen, schon die
Alten hatten den Fluch gespürt, die Tücke erkannt, die List
gemerkt, waren in Fallen gefallen, hatten's erfahren, bedacht und geschildert. Die nächste Generation sollte klüger
sein, sie sollte es besser haben. Seit fünftausend Jahren! Nicht
jedem war ein Schwert gegeben. Und ein Schwert, was nützt
es? Man kann mit ihm fuchteln, man kann mit ihm töten,
und man kann durch das Schwert umkommen. Aber was ist
gewonnen? Nichts. Man muß zur rechten Zeit in Gordium
erscheinen. Die Gelegenheit macht den Helden. Als Alexander
aus Mazedonien kam, war der Knoten seines Trotzes müde.
Überdies war das Ereignis belanglos. Indien wurde sowieso
nicht erobert; nur die Randgebiete waren ein paar Jahre besetzt, und zwischen der Besatzung und der Bevölkerung ent-
wickelten sich Tauschgeschäfte.

Was ist am wirklichen Potsdamer Platz? Ein Drahtverhau,
eine neue und recht kräftige Grenze, ein Weltende, der Eiserne Vorhang; Gott hatte ihn fallen lassen, Gott allein wußte,
wozu. Korodin eilte zur Haltestelle des Oberleitungsbusses,
des hauptstädtisch stolzen, des modernen Vehikels, das zwischen den weit voneinander entfernt liegenden Regierungs-

vierteln Massen transportieren konnte. Korodin hätte es nicht nötig gehabt, sich an der Haltestelle in die Schlange der Wartenden zu reihen. Er hatte zwei Automobile in der Garage seines Hauses. Es war ein Akt der Bescheidenheit und der Kasteiung, daß Korodin in öffentlichen Verkehrsmitteln zur Politik fuhr, während der Chauffeur, bequem und morgenmunter, Korodins Kinder im Wagen zur Schule brachte. Korodin wurde gegrüßt. Er dankte. Er war ein Volksmann. Aber der Gruß der Unbekannten machte ihn nicht nur dankbar; er machte ihn auch verlegen. Der erste Bus kam. Sie drängten sich hinein, und Korodin trat zurück, in Bescheidenheit und in Selbstkasteiung trat er zurück, aber es ekelte ihn auch (ein sündiger Gedanke) vor diesen hastenden, um ihr Brot kämpfenden Menschen. Da fuhr die Fuhre zum Bundeshaus, zu den Ministerien, in die Unzahl der Ämter, wie Sardinen waren sie zusammengepackt, die Schar der Sekretärinnen, das Heer der Angestellten, die Kompanien der mittleren Beamten, Fische desselben Fanges, Emigranten aus Berlin, Emigranten aus Frankfurt, Emigranten aus den Höhlen der Wolfsschanze, mit den Ämtern mitgewandert, mit den Akten mitgebündelt, dutzendweise waren sie in die Wohnungen der neuen Schnellbaublöcke gepreßt worden, hellhörige Wände trennten ihr Bett kaum von anderen Betten, immer waren sie beobachtet, nie waren sie allein, immer lauschten sie, immer wurden sie belauscht, wer ist im Eckzimmer zu Besuch, was wird geredet, spricht man über mich, sie schnupperten, wer hat Zwiebel gegessen, wer badet so spät, Fräulein Irmgard, die wäscht sich mit Chlorophyllseife, wird es nötig haben, wer kämmte sein Haar ins Becken, wer benutzte mein Handtuch, gereizt, vergrämt, versauert, verschuldet waren sie, von ihren Familien getrennt, sie trösteten sich, aber sie trösteten sich nicht oft, überdies waren sie am Abend zu müde, sie rackerten sich ab, sie tippten die Gesetze, sie schufteten Überstunden, sie opferten sich auf für den Chef, den sie haßten, den sie belauerten, gegen den sie hetzten, dem sie anonyme Briefe schrieben, dem sie den Kaffee wärmten, dem sie Blumen ans Fenster stellten — und stolz schrieben sie nach Hause, schickten blasse Boxbilder, die sie im Garten des Ministeriums zeigten, oder kleine Leicaschüsse, die der Chef im Büro geknipst hatte: sie waren bei der Regierung tätig, sie verwalteten Deutschland. Korodin fiel ein, daß er noch nicht gebetet hatte, und er entschloß sich, aus dem Strom zu gleiten und eine Teilstrecke zu Fuß zu gehen.

Keetenheuve hatte seine Wohnung im Bonner Abgeordneten-Getto an diesem Morgen nicht aufgesucht, für ihn war sie ein bloßes Pied-à-terre der Unlust, eine Puppenstube der Be-engung *morgen Kinder wird's was geben morgen werden wir uns freun,* was sollte er da; was er brauchte, trug er bei sich in der Aktenmappe, und selbst dies war noch Ballast auf der Wanderschaft. Auch Keetenheuve hatte den Bus verschmäht. Auf dem Münsterplatz traf Keetenheuve Korodin, den Be-scheidenen. Korodin hatte zum heiligen Cassius und zum hei-ligen Florentius gebetet, den Beschützern dieser Stätte, er hatte ihnen die Sünde des Hochmuts bekannt *ich danke dir Gott daß ich nicht bin wie diese hier,* und er hatte sich selbst und vorläufig und für diesen Tag von der Schuld absolviert. Daß Keetenheuve ihn zur Münstertür hinaustreten sah, machte Korodin aufs neue verlegen. Waren die Heiligen durch das Gebet des Abgeordneten nicht versöhnt worden, und straften sie nun Korodin, indem sie ihm Keetenheuve in den Weg stellten? Vielleicht aber war die Begegnung auch das schöne Walten der Vorsehung und ein Zeichen, daß Koro-din in Gnade stand.

Es galt als ungewöhnlich, wenn Abgeordnete einander feind-licher Parteien, mochten sie auch in den Ausschüssen zusam-menarbeiten, gelegentlich sogar zusammenhalten, selbzweit spazierten. Für jeden war es anrüchig, mit dem andern gese-hen zu werden, und für die Parteileiter war es ein Anblick, als wandele einer aus ihrer Herde öffentlich mit einem Strich-jungen und zeige schamlos seine perverse Veranlagung. Die Fama vermutete bei jedem Gelegenheitsgespräch, das viel-leicht dem drückenden Wetter, den noch bedrückenderen Herzkrankheiten gegolten hatte, die Fama vermutete Ver-schwörung, Parteiverrat, Ketzerei und Kanzlersturz. Überdies, es wimmelte von Journalisten in der Stadt, und das Bild der Friedlichen konnte am Montag im »Spiegel« stehen und Anlaß zu größtem Unfrieden geben. All dies bedachte Korodin wohl, aber Keetenheuve war ihm (beinahe hätte er »hol's der Teufel« gesagt) nicht unsympathisch, deshalb haßte er ihn auch manchmal mit einem geradezu persönlichen Haß, nicht nur mit der kalten, routinemäßigen Ablehnung der Parteigegnerschaft, denn er hatte (»hol's doch der Teufel«), in auffälliger, nicht zu übersehender, nicht zu unterdrückender Weise das Gefühl, daß hier eine Seele zu retten sei, daß man Keetenheuve noch auf den rechten Weg bringen könne, man durfte ihn am Ende vielleicht sogar bekehren. Korodin, die beiden großen teuren Automobile meist in der Garage, umschwärmte aufrichtigen Herzens eine neue Priestergeneration, die Arbeitergeistlichen des nahen Reviers. Das waren verknurrte Männer in groben Schuhen, von denen sich Korodin einbildete, daß sie Bernanos und Bloy gelesen hätten, während nur er es war, der von diesen Geistern, und das sprach für ihn, beunruhigt wurde, und so empfingen die verknurrten Männer zuweilen einen Scheck von Korodin und fanden im übrigen, daß er menschlich nicht viel hergab. Für Korodin aber war dieses Scheckgeschenk Urchristentum, reine Opposition gegen die bestehende Ordnung, gegen die eigene Schicht und gegen die teuren Automobile, und tatsächlich hatte er schon Schwierigkeiten wegen seiner »roten Neigungen«, erhielt sanfte Vorwürfe, und der Bischof, sein Freund, der, wie Korodin, Bernanos gelesen hatte, aber sich durchaus nicht beunruhigt, sondern nur befremdet fühlte, der Bischof hätte den Scheck lieber in einer anderen Opferlade gesehen.

Korodin, der immer alles wußte, immer eine Liste von Geburtstagen im Kopf hatte, sie im Gedächtnis bewahrte, schon um in seiner weitverzweigten und begütert verschwägerten Familie keinen zu kränken, Korodin wollte Keetenheuve sein Beileid aussprechen, und vielleicht hoffte er dabei, daß der andere in einem Augenblick der Erschütterung der Bekehrung zugänglicher sein möge, daß der Verlust sterblichen irdischen Glückes ihm den Sinn auf die Freuden der Unsterblichkeit gelenkt habe, aber dann, als er dicht vor Keetenheuve stand, schien Korodin eine Kondolation hier doch unangebracht, ja taktlos und von verwerflicher Intimität zu sein, denn fragwürdig blieb schließlich einem Menschen wie Keetenheuve gegenüber alles, was in Korodins Kreisen selbstverständlich war, das Aussprechen des Mitgefühls beispielsweise, trauerte Keetenheuve überhaupt, man wußte es nicht, man sah es nicht, kein Trauerflor bedeckte den Arm, kein schwarzer Streifen kennzeichnete das Revers, und keine Tränen standen dem Witwer in den Augen, aber das machte den Mann auch wieder anziehend, vielleicht trauerte er nicht auf offenem Markt, und so sagte Korodin, indem er den Blick senkte und auf das Pflaster des Münsterplatzes starrte: »Wir stehen hier auf einem Gräberfeld aus fränkisch-römischer Zeit.« Doch so war es nun — der Satz, schon losgelassen, nicht mehr ein bloßer unverbindlicher Verlegenheitsgedanke, eine Assoziation, die sich aufgedrängt hatte, der Satz war dümmer als jede Kondolation, und Keetenheuve mochte ihn als Anspielung auf seine Trauer und zugleich als ein banal zynisches Darüberhinwegschreiten auffassen. So sprang Korodin nun aus reiner Verlegenheit von dem Gräberfeld mitten in die Frage, um die er sonst lange herumgeschlichen wäre und die er am Ende vielleicht gar nicht erwähnt hätte, denn schließlich war es eine Aufforderung zum Verrat, wenn auch zum Verrat an einer schlechten Partei.

Er fragte: »Können Sie Ihre Haltung nicht ändern?«

Keetenheuve verstand Korodin. Er verstand auch, daß Korodin ihm hatte kondolieren wollen, und er war ihm dankbar, daß er es nicht getan hatte. Natürlich konnte er seine Haltung ändern. Er konnte sie wohl ändern. Jeder Mensch konnte jede Haltung ändern, aber mit Elke hatte Keetenheuve den einzigen intimen Kenner seiner alten Haltung verloren, den Zuschauer seiner Unruhe, und so konnte er diese Haltung nicht und nie mehr ändern. Er konnte sie von sich aus nicht ändern, denn diese Haltung war er, war ein Urabscheu in ihm, und er konnte sie erst recht nicht ändern, wenn er an Elkes kurzen von Verbrechen und Krieg verstörten Lebensweg dachte, und Korodin hatte ihm die Antwort schon zugeschoben, mit seinem Gräberfeld aus fränkisch-römischer Zeit.

Keetenheuve sagte:»Ich will kein neues Gräberfeld.«
Er hätte auch sagen können, er wolle kein europäisches oder
kleineuropäisches Gräberfeld; doch das hatte ihm zu pathe-
tisch geklungen. Natürlich ließ sich mit dem Gräberfeld, gegen das Gräberfeld argumentieren. Das wußten sie beide.
Auch Korodin wollte kein Gräberfeld. Er war kein Militarist.
Er war Reserveoffizier. Er wollte jedoch das mögliche Gräberfeld, an das Keetenheuve dachte, wagen, um das Aufschau-
feln eines anderen, noch viel größeren und ihm sonst sicher
erscheinenden Feldes (in das er selber sinken würde mit
Autos, Frau und Kindern), wenn's anging, zu verhindern.
Was ließ sich aber verhindern? Die Geschichte war ein tol-
patschiges Kind oder ein alter Blindenführer, der allein wußte, wohin der Weg ging, und deshalb rücksichtslos vorantrieb. Sie spazierten dem Hofgarten zu und verweilten vor
dem Spielplatz. Zwei kleine Mädchen schaukelten auf der
Wippe. Das eine kleine Mädchen war dicklich; das andere
kleine Mädchen war mager und hatte hübsche lange Beine.
Die Dicke mußte sich vom Boden abstoßen, wenn sie mit der
Wippe hochschnellen wollte.
Korodin sah ein Gleichnis. Er sagte:»Denken Sie an die Kinder!« Er fand selbst, daß es salbungsvoll klang. Er ärgerte
sich. So würde er Keetenheuve nicht bekehren.
Keetenheuve dachte an die Kinder. Er wäre gern zur Wippe
gegangen, um mit dem hübschen Mädchen zu spielen. Keetenheuve war auch ein Ästhet, und der Ästhet war ungerecht.
Er war ungerecht gegen das dicke Mädchen. Die Natur war
ungerecht. Alles war ungerecht und unergründlich. Jetzt
sehnte er sich nach einem bürgerlichen Hausstand, nach einer
Frau, die auch Mutter war. Nach einer hübschen Frau natürlich, nach einem reizvollen Kind. *Er hob ein kleines Mädchen
auf eine Schaukel, er stand im Garten, die schöne Frau und
schöne Mutter rief zum Mittagessen, Keetenheuve Hausvater,
Keetenheuve Kinderfreund, Keetenheuve Heckenschneider.*
Es waren unverbrauchte, verdorbene zärtliche Gefühle in
ihm.
Er sagte:»Ich denke an die Kinder!«
Und er sah ein Bild, das ihm immer wieder vor Augen kam,

an das er sich immer wieder erinnerte als an einen Augenblick unheimlicher prophetischer Schau. Keetenheuve hatte,
als er freiwillig das Vaterland verließ, von niemand gedrängt
als von einem Gefühl tiefer Ablehnung des Gegenwärtigen
und des Kommenden, Keetenheuve hatte, als er nach Paris
reiste, in Frankfurt übernachtet, und am Morgen hatte er vor
dem Schauspielhaus in Frankfurt, von der Terrasse eines
Cafés aus, wo er knusprige Hörnchen aß und Himalajablü-
tentee trank, einen Aufmarsch der Hitlerjugend beobachtet,
und da hatte sich vor seinen Augen der Platz aufgetan, der
weite bunte Platz, und alle, alle waren sie mit Fahnen, mit
Wimpeln, mit Flöten, Trommeln und Dolchen in ein breites
tiefes Grab marschiert. Es waren Vierzehnjährige, die ihrem
Führer folgten, und neunzehnhundertneununddreißig waren
sie zwanzigjährig, waren sie die Sturmtruppe, die Flieger, die
Matrosen — sie waren die Generation, die starb. Korodin
blickte zum Himmel auf. Die Wolken schwärzten sich. Er
ahnte ein Gewitter. An der Stelle, wo sie standen, war ein
Kind vom Blitz erschlagen worden, und Korodin fürchtete
nun doch wieder den Zorn des Himmels. Er winkte ein zufällig des Weges kommendes Taxi herbei. Er haßte Keetenheuve. Er war eben doch ein Verlorener, ein Mann ohne Verantwortung, ein Vagabund, der keine Kinder hatte. Am lieb-
sten hätte Korodin Keetenheuve in der Allee stehenlassen.
Mochte der Blitz ihn erschlagen! Und vielleicht gefährdete
Korodin sich und das Taxi, indem er den Verworfenen zur
Mitreise einlud. Aber dann siegte doch Korodins gute Erziehung über Angst und Abwendung, und mit gefrorenem
Lächeln ließ er Keetenheuve in den Wagen klettern.
Sie saßen stumm nebeneinander. Es tropfte und blitzte, und
Regenschleier legten sich wie Nebel über die Häupter der
Bäume, aber der Donner grollte kraftlos und matt, als wenn
das Gewitter schon müde oder noch fern wäre. Es roch inten-
siv nach Feuchtigkeit, Erde und Blüten, dabei wurde es immer wärmer, man schwitzte, das Hemd klebte am Leib, und
wieder hatte Keetenheuve die Vorstellung, sich in einem großen Treibhaus zu befinden. Sie fuhren an der Rückseite des
Präsidentensitzes, an der Front der Kanzlervilla vorbei,

schmiedeeiserne Tore standen offen. Posten bewachten die freie Einfahrt, man sah Beete, weite grüne Flächen, Rabatten, Blumen leuchteten, ein Dackel und ein Wolfshund gingen, ein größenungleiches Paar, wie in Gespräche vertieft, langsam über Kieswege. Eine botanische Landschaft, ein botanischer Garten, Prinzessinnen hatten hier gewohnt und Zuckerfabrikanten, Hochstapler waren bei ihnen zu Gast gewesen, sie hatten das Vermögen nicht kleingekriegt. Ein paar Bomben waren auch gefallen. Da ragten geschwärzte Mauerstümpfe aus dem dichten Grün. Die Bundesfahne wehte. Ein Herr ging, einen kleinen Damenknirpsschirm trotz des Regens geschlossen an einer Schlaufe am Handgelenk, langsam ins Amt. Ein ehemaliger, ein zukünftiger, ein wiederverwendeter Gesandter? Statisten der politischen Bühne wanderten durch die Alleen, und mit ihnen wanderten ihre Biographien, ihre gedruckte Wahrheit, eine Dirne in vielen Gassen. Man sah die Statisten. Wo weidete der Regisseur? Wo fraß der Protagonist sein Gras? Es hatte ja nie Regisseure und Protagonisten gegeben. Das Taxi begegnete lauter Verhütern, die Schlimmeres verhütet hatten. Es regnete gerade; sonst hätten sie sich in ihrem Ruhm gesonnt.

Sie hielten vor dem Bundeshaus. Korodin zahlte den Wagen. Er wehrte ab, daß Keetenheuve an den Kosten der kleinen Fahrt partizipiere, aber er ließ sich vom Fahrer eine Quittung geben, Korodin wollte dem Staat nichts schenken. Er verabschiedete sich hastig mit erforenem Lächeln, ängstlich, es blitzte wieder, von Keetenheuve. Er eilte fort, als habe das Gesetz ihn und gerade ihn gerufen und berufen. Keetenheuve wollte in die Pressebaracken schauen, aber Mergentheim würde noch nicht auf sein, er hatte seine anstrengende Sophie zu Haus und war nicht matinal. Keetenheuve zögerte, in sein Büro zu gehen. Da sah er, daß sich auswärtige Besucher, in Autobussen herangeschleppt, Besichtigung der Bundeshauptstadt, Besichtigung des Bundesparlaments, das Mittagessen im Bundeshausrestaurant, zu einer Führung versammelt hatten, und wie ein alter Berliner wohl mal auf den Einfall kam, an Käses Rundfahrt teilzunehmen, schloß sich Keetenheuve der gerade aufbrechenden Schar an. Wie merk-

würdig! Der Hausbeamte in dunkler Dienstkleidung, der die
Neugierigen führte, sah genau wie der Kanzler aus. Er hatte
ein etwas verkniffenes Gesicht, trocken, listig, mit Falten der
Humorigkeit, er sah wie ein kluger Fuchs aus, und er sprach
mit dem Dialektanklang des bedeutenden Staatsmannes. (In
monarchistischer Zeit trugen die treuen Diener die Barttracht
der Könige und Kaiser.) Sie gingen die Treppe zum Plenarsaal hinauf, und ihr Führer, dessen Ähnlichkeit mit dem
Kanzler wohl nur Keetenheuve aufgefallen war, denn niemand beachtete ihn sonderlich, der Führer erklärte nun, daß
der Bau, den sie begingen, eine pädagogische Akademie gewesen sei, und leider ließ er sich's entgehen, nun, deutsch
gebildet weltanschaulich, goethisch zu werden und auf die
pädagogische Provinz hinzuweisen, die von hier sich ausbreiten konnte. Wußte der Kanzler-Kanzlist, daß es seinem Parlament an Philosophen mangelte, von hier aus geistig päd-
agogisch zu ackern?
Zum erstenmal stand Keetenheuve auf der Galerie des Ple-
narsaals und sah die ungepolsterten, die dem Volk und der
Presse vorbehaltenen Sitze. Unten war alles Gestühl schön
grün aufgeplustert, selbst die Kommunisten durften sich der
grünen Bequemlichkeit des Polsters erfreuen. Der Saal war
leer. Ein leeres großes Klassenzimmer mit aufgeräumten
Schülerpulten. Der Katheder des Herrn Lehrers war erhöht,
wie es sich gehörte. Der Kanzler-Kanzlist erwähnte das Be-
merkenswerte. Er sagte, der Saal habe tausend Meter Neon-
röhren. Schwerhörige Abgeordnete, sagte der Kanzler-Führer,
könnten sich einer Kopfhöreranlage bedienen. Ein Witzkopf
wollte wissen, ob man den Kopfhörer auf Musik schalten
konnte. Der Kanzler-Cicerone überhörte den Zwischenruf mit
überlegener Ruhe. Er deutete auf die Abstimmungstüren des
Hauses und erwähnte die Gepflogenheit des Hammelsprun-
ges. Keetenheuve hätte hier mit einer Anekdote zur Unterhaltung der Gäste beitragen können, mit einer reizenden
kleinen Anekdote aus dem Leben eines Parlamentariers. Keetenheuve, der Hammel, war einmal falsch gesprungen. Das
heißt, er wußte nicht, ob er falsch gesprungen war, ihm waren auf einmal Zweifel gekommen, und er war durch die Ja-

Tür gehüpft, während seine Fraktion sich zum Nein entschlossen hatte. Die Koalition hatte ihm applaudiert. Sie irrte
sich. Korodin hatte den ersten Erfolg seines Bekehrungs-
wahns gesehen. Er irrte sich. Im Fraktionszimmer hatte man
Keetenheuve erregt gerügt. Auch dort irrten sie sich. Keetenheuve hatte die Frage, über die abgestimmt wurde, ziemlich
belanglos gefunden und nach der Intuition des Augenblicks
gehandelt, ein Jasager und kein Neinsager, der einer unwich-
tigen Regierungsvorlage zustimmte. Warum sollte die Regierung nicht in manchen Fragen recht haben? Es schien ihm
töricht, das zu verneinen und eine Opposition der Starrköp-
figkeit zu treiben oder der politischen Grundsatztreue, was
genau dasselbe war. Keetenheuve sah Schulbuben unten sitzen, Bauernbuben, Quadratschädel, zänkisch und gotterge-
ben, zänkisch und aufmuckend, zänkisch und trägen Verstandes, und unter ihnen ein paar Streber. »Quasselbude«,
sagte ein Besucher. Keetenheuve sah ihn an. Der Besucher
war der üble Typ des Bierbanknationalisten, der sich mit
Wollust von einem Diktator knechten ließ, wenn er nur selbst
ein Paar Stiefel bekam, um nach unten zu treten. Keetenheuve sah ihn an. In die Fresse, dachte er. »Na, meinen Sie
etwa nicht?« sagte der Mann und blickte Keetenheuve herausfordernd an. Keetenheuve hätte erwidern können: Ich
weiß nichts Besseres, selbst dieses Parlament ist das kleinere
Übel. Er sagte aber: »Halten Sie hier Ihr verfluchtes Maul!«
Das Gesicht des Mannes lief rot an, dann wurde er unsicher
und kuschte feige. Er drückte sich von Keetenheuve weg.
Wenn er den Abgeordneten Keetenheuve erkannt hätte, würde er denken: Ich merk' Sie mir, Sie stehen auf der Liste, am
Tage X, im Sumpf und auf der Heide. Aber niemand kannte
Keetenheuve, und der Kanzler-Kanzlist führte seine Schar
wieder ins Freie.
Die Journalisten arbeiteten in zwei Baracken. Die Baracken
lagen lang hingestreckt und einstöckig, dem Bundeshaus gegenüber; sie sahen von außen wie Militärbauten aus, wie
eine für Kriegsdauer (und Kriege dauern lange) errichtete
Unterkunft der Stäbe und der Verwaltung eines neuen Trup-
penübungsplatzes. Innen aber war in jedem Stockwerk ein

Mittelgang, der an den Korridor eines Schiffes erinnerte, nicht gerade an das Luxusdeck, aber doch an die Touristenklasse, wo links und rechts des Ganges Kabine an Kabine geschichtet wurde, und das Geklapper der Schreibmaschinen, das Ticken der Fernschreiber, das unaufhörliche Schrillen der Telephone gab die Vorstellung, daß hinter den Zimmern der Redaktionen die erregte See war mit Möwengekreisch und Dampfersirenen, und so waren die Pressebaracken zwei Kähne, die, von den Wogen der Zeit getragen, geschaukelt und erschüttert wurden. Wie Flut und Ebbe liefen über einen Tannenholztisch am Eingang die »Mitteilungen an die Presse«, blasse und verwischte Informationen auf billigem Papier, die dort achtlos hingeworfen wurden von den gemächlichen Boten der vielen Regierungsstellen, die sich mit den Anpreisungen des Tuns der Ämter, mit der Unterrichtung der Öffentlichkeit, mit der Bundespropaganda, der Verhüllung, Vernebelung und Verschweigung von Ereignissen, der Beschwichtigung, den Dementis von Lügen und Wahrheiten beschäftigten und zuweilen gar ins Horn der Entrüstung bliesen. Das Auswärtige Amt gibt bekannt, das Bundesministerium für den Marshallplan gibt bekannt, das Bundesministerium für Finanzen, das Statistische Bundesamt, Post und Bundesbahn, die Besatzungsämter, der Polizeiminister, die Justiz, sie alle gaben viel oder wenig bekannt, waren redselig oder schweigsam, zeigten die Zähne oder ein ernstes besorgtes Gesicht, und einige hatten auch ein Lächeln für die Öffentlichkeit, das aufmunternde Lächeln einer zugänglichen Schönen. Das Bundespresseamt gab bekannt, daß an der Behauptung einer Oppositionspartei, eine Regierungspartei habe den französischen Geheimdienst um Wahlhilfe gebeten, kein wahres Wort sei. Hier war man nun ernstlich böse, man drohte, den Staatsanwalt zu bemühen, denn der Wahlfonds, die Parteigelder waren tabu, ein immer heikles Kapitel; man brauchte Geld wie jedermann, und wo sollte es herkommen, wenn nicht von reichen Freunden. Korodin hatte reiche Freunde, aber wie das bei Wohlhabenden Sitte ist, sie waren geizig (Korodin verstand es) und wollten für ihr Geld etwas haben.

Das Presseschiff schunkelte an diesem Morgen bei leichter Brise dahin. Keetenheuve spürte, daß nichts Besonderes los war. Die Planken zitterten nicht, keine Tür wurde aufgerissen und dröhnend zugeschlagen; doch gibt es Stürme, die plötzlich und unvermutet, von keiner Wetterwarnung gemeldet, hereinbrechen. Keetenheuve klopfte bei Mergentheim an. Mergentheim vertrat in der Hauptstadt ein Blatt, das sich mit Recht zu den »angesehenen« des Bundes zählte (doch was war mit den andern? wurden sie nicht angesehen, oder waren sie nicht angesehen? arme Mauerblümchen öffentlicher Volkstänze!), und an großen Tagen sprach er im Rundfunk gefällige eingängige Betrachtungen, die keineswegs unkritisch waren und selbst schon unwirsche Beschwerden der mimosenhaft empfindlichen und zigeunerhaft eifersüchtigen Parteien herausgefordert hatten. Keetenheuve und Mergentheim — waren sie Freunde, Feinde? Sie hätten die Antwort nicht gewußt: Freunde waren sie wohl kaum, und keiner hätte vom andern mit dem Stolz der Schuljungen gesprochen: mein Freund Mergentheim, mein liebster Freund Keetenheuve. Aber zuweilen zog es sie wohl zueinander, denn sie waren Anfänger und Kollegen zu einer Zeit gewesen, als alles noch hätte anders kommen können, und wenn die Geschichte anders gelaufen wäre (gewiß war dies unvorstellbar), ohne den österreichischen Irren, ohne die monströse Erhebung, ohne Frevel, Hybris, Krieg, Tod und Zerstörung, vielleicht hätten Keetenheuve und Mergentheim noch Jahre zusammen im selben dunklen Hofzimmer des alten »Volksblattes« gesessen (Keetenheuve hätte es gewünscht, doch Mergentheim wohl kaum) und hätten wirklich, sie waren jung, das Gefühl gleichen Strebens, ähnlicher Ansichten und der Freundschaft gehabt. Aber dreiunddreißig trennte sich's wie in Scheidewasser. Keetenheuve, gutmütiger Trottel geschimpft, wanderte ins Exil, und Mergentheim begab sich erfolgreich auf den Pfad der Bewährung, der ihn Chefredakteur, man sagte Hauptschriftleiter, des gewandelten Blattes werden ließ. Später allerdings mußte das »Volksblatt« trotz gehorsamer Angleichung, mit der es die Leser verlor, sein Erscheinen einstellen, oder es war von der Arbeitsfront geschluckt worden, man wußte es nicht so genau, und lebte noch eine Zeitlang als Untertitel fort mit einem Parteigenossen als Chef, und Mergentheim setzte sich als Korrespondent nach Rom ab. Gerade rechtzeitig! Der Krieg kam, und in Rom war es angenehm. Später in der oberitalienischen Mussolini-Republik schien's auch für Mergentheim kritisch zu werden, Kugeln der SS oder Kugeln der Partisanen drohten, und nah war die Gefangenschaft, aber wieder konnte Mergentheim sich noch rechtzeitig absetzen, und so war er mit leidlich weißer Weste ein gesuchter und geförderter Mann des Wiederaufbaus geworden. Keetenheuve freute sich jeweils, Mergentheim im Büro zu sehen, denn solange Mergentheim hinter seinem Tisch saß, solange er sich nicht aufs neue absetzte, etwa Korrespondent in Washington wurde, schien Keetenheuve der Staat sicher und der Feind fern zu sein. Mergentheim hatte Keetenheuve gänzlich aus seinem Gedächtnis verloren, und als er ihn als Abgeordneten in Bonn bemerkte, einen Wilderer in seinem Revier, war er ehrlich erstaunt. »Ich dachte, du seist tot«, stammelte er, als Keetenheuve ihn zum erstenmal aufsuchte, und er glaubte sich ertappt und meinte, zur Rechenschaft gezogen zu werden. Zur Rechenschaft wofür übrigens? Konnte er etwas dafür, daß alles so gekommen war? Er war der Mann volkstümlich erklärender Betrachtungen, nicht unkritisch, wenn es nicht direkt den Kopf oder die Stelle kostete, und schließlich hatte er den Beruf des Zeitungsmannes und nicht den des Märtyrers gewählt. Doch bald fing sich Mergentheim wieder. Er sah, daß Keetenheuve freundlich freundschaftlich gekommen war, aus sentimentalen Motiven der Erinnerung und keineswegs vorwurfsvoll. So wunderte sich Mergentheim am Ende nur, daß auch Keetenheuve von der Woge der Zeit emporgetragen war, und mehr noch, daß er es verstanden hatte, sich hochtragen zu lassen und das Glück (so faßte Mergentheim es auf) beim Schopf zu packen. Doch als er im Laufe der ersten Unterhaltung merkte, daß Keetenheuve nicht, wie Mergentheim vermutet hatte, mit einem britischen oder panamanesischen Paß heimgekehrt war und daß er gar zu Fuß zu ihm, dem alten Kollegen, gewandert war, da verwandelte sich Mergentheim aus einem Furchtsamen in einen Gönner, packte Keetenheuve in seinen verchromten Dienstwagen und fuhr ihn in sein Heim, zu Sophie.

Sophie, lockend, duftend, im Hauskleid eines Düsseldorfer Diors und durch das Telephon anscheinend vom Kommen des Gastes unterrichtet (wie hatte Mergentheim das wieder geschafft?), begrüßte Keetenheuve mit einem vertraulichen »Wir kennen uns ja« und einem Augenaufschlag, der den Gedanken weckte, er habe mit ihr geschlafen. Das war unwahrscheinlich. Aber dann entpuppte sich's, daß Sophie einmal Bürolehrling im Vertrieb des »Volksblattes« gewesen war, und wenn Keetenheuve sich auch nicht an sie erinnern konnte, Mergentheim mußte sie später entdeckt haben, wenn nicht sie ihn aufgespürt hatte, und der Aufstieg zur Frau Hauptschriftleiter hatte ihrem gesellschaftlichen Ehrgeiz Appetit gemacht; sie war die Muse, die Mergentheim auf der Bahn des Erfolges, der Karriere und der rechtzeitigen Anpassung beriet, vorantrieb und stützte.

Nein, Keetenheuve hatte nicht mit ihr geschlafen, vielleicht hätte er es tun können, Sophie gab sich bedeutenden und einflußreichen Leuten ohne Wollust hin, die Wollust empfand sie erst, wenn über die Kopulation geredet wurde, Jünglinge und bloß schöne Männer verschmähte sie, und wenn Keetenheuve auch nicht der Konzertmeister in seiner Partei war, so spielte doch auch er dort die erste Geige und wäre ihres Bettes wert gewesen. Aber nie war es zu Umarmung, Kuß und Beischlaf gekommen; Keetenheuve reagierte lustlos, und da er am gesellschaftlichen Leben der Bundeskreise konsequent nicht teilnahm, war er für Sophie auch kein lokkendes Wild, sondern bald nur ein Trottel. Das Epitheton gutmütig fehlte diesmal, ornierte nicht, und auch Mergentheim fügte es der Kennzeichnung des alten Freundes nicht hinzu, denn da Keetenheuve es zum Abgeordneten gebracht hatte, mochte er wohl ein Trottel sein, aber daß er gutmütig sei, war nun unwahrscheinlich und nicht länger erwähnenswert.

Zu einer Verstimmung, die aus der lockeren Freundschaft beinahe Feindschaft gemacht hätte, kam es aber, als Mergentheim im Handbuch des Bundestages entdeckt hatte, daß Keetenheuve verheiratet sei. Da prickelte die Neugier Sophie. Wer war die Frau, die Keetenheuve nicht zeigte? War sie so schön, war sie so häßlich, daß er sie verbarg? War sie eine reiche Erbin, und fürchtete er, sie könne ihm geraubt werden? Darauf kam's wohl hinaus, und Sophie verkuppelte im Geiste Elke schon an junge Gesandtschaftssekretäre, nicht um Keetenheuve zu schaden, sondern um die natürliche Ordnung wiederherzustellen, denn Keetenheuve verdiente keine schöne junge Erbin. Schließlich begegneten die Frauen einander und fanden sich dann garstig. Elke benahm sich ungezogen, maulte, wollte nicht auf die Redoute gehen (was Keetenheuve entzückte, er wollte auch nicht gehen, konnte auch nicht gehen, denn er besaß keinen Frack), aber schließlich setzte Sophie doch ihren Willen durch, und Elke fuhr mit Mergentheim zum Ball, nachdem sie Keetenheuve noch zugeflüstert hatte, Sophie trage ein Korsett (was Keetenheuve genierte). Auf dem Fest war es dann furchtbar geworden. Beide Frauen dachten aus nicht zu ergründender Abneigung voneinander: blöde Nazistin (so können sich Frauen täuschen), und Elke hielt sich nicht an die Gesandtschaftssekretäre, sondern an den Gesandtschaftsgin, der zollfrei eingeführt und vorzüglich war, und als ihr der Alkohol den Kopf verwirrt hatte, verkündete sie der überraschten Gesellschaft, die sie als eine Versammlung von Gespenstern bezeichnete, daß Keetenheuve die Regierung stürzen werde. Sie nannte Keetenheuve den Mann der Revolution, der die sich ausbreitende und festigende Restauration verachte; so viel hielt Elke von ihrem Gatten, und wie sehr mußte sie sich allmählich von ihm enttäuscht fühlen. Aber als das Erstaunen über ihre Verkündigung sich gelegt hatte und Elke nun doch von einem Attaché, den sie, statt ihn zu umarmen, beschimpfte, im Wagen heimgebracht wurde, nützte der dumme Vorfall komischerweise dem Ansehen des Abgeordneten, denn Elke hatte nicht verraten (sie hätte es auch nicht zu sagen gewußt), welche Art von Regierungssturz Keetenheuve vorbereite, von welcher Seite, mit welcher Hilfe, mit welchen Waffen und zu welchem Ziel er die Regierung beseitigen wolle, und so betrachteten nach diesem Abend viele Keetenheuve mißtrauisch und werbend als einen Politiker, mit dem man vielleicht rechnen mußte. Mergentheim saß wie ein aufgeplusterter melancholischer Vogel hinter seinem Schreibtisch, sein Gesicht wurde immer breiter, die Augen ständig verschleierter, die Gläser dicker, die Hornfassung der Brille schwärzer und schwerer, so verstärkte sich der Eindruck, einer Eule, einem Uhu gegenüberzutreten, einem Gebüsch- und Ruinenvogel, der teure Maßanzüge trug, und vielleicht war er recht zufrieden, lustig und vergnügt, krächzte nur ein wenig vor aufgeplusterter Geschäftigkeit, war nur etwas erschöpft von den Nachtflügen der antreibenden Gefährtin, und die Annahme, die der Ornis angehörende Wesenheit sei melancholisch, war vielleicht ein Irrtum in der von Fehldeutungen ausgehenden Vorstellung des Besuchers. Mergentheim schickte seine Sekretärin weg, etwas zu besorgen. Er bot Keetenheuve Zigarren an. Er wußte, Keetenheuve rauchte nicht, aber Mergentheim tat, als habe er es vergessen. Keetenheuve sollte sich nur nicht zu wichtig nehmen. Mergentheim wickelte eine schwarze Tabakrolle aus knisterndem Stanniol und zündete sie an. Er betrachtete Keetenheuve durch blauen Dunst. Mergentheim wußte, daß Elke gestorben war, man munkelte, unter mysteriösen Umständen, Klatsch reiste schnell, aber gleich Korodin fand auch Mergentheim kein Wort des Beileids für Keetenheuve, auch er fühlte, daß die Erwähnung familiären Unglücks, persönlichen Leides Keetenheuve gegenüber unangebracht sei, taktlos und aufdringlich; Mergentheim hätte nicht sagen können, warum — Keetenheuve war nun mal so. Mergentheim fühlte diesmal recht! Keetenheuve war kein Familienmensch, er konnte lieben, er war sinnlich, aber er hatte so wenig Zweisames mitbekommen, daß er nicht mal zum Ehemann getaugt hatte. Keetenheuve war ein Mensch ohne Kontakte, der sich zuweilen nach Kontakten sehnte, und das führte ihn in seine Partei, in Schwierigkeiten und Verwirrungen. Die Ehe, nicht die Liebe, war für Keetenheuve eine perverse Lebensform gewesen, und vielleicht war er doch ein in die Irre gelaufener Mönch, ein in den Käfig geratener Landstreicher, am Ende gar ein Märtyrer, der das Kreuz verfehlt hatte. Mergentheim dachte: Armer Kerl. Elkes Tod war Keetenheuve bestimmt nahegegangen, und Mergentheim erklärte es sich so (und nicht ganz falsch), Keetenheuve war entwurzelt aus dem Exil zurückgekehrt, und Elke war sein verzweifelter Versuch gewesen, hier wieder Wurzeln zu schlagen, hier Liebe zu gewinnen und zu lieben. Der Versuch war gescheitert. Was würde der Mann nun tun? Ein unvermutetes Glück (so faßte es Mergentheim unentwegt auf) hatte Keetenheuve nach oben getragen, in den Bereich der großen politischen Entscheidungen, und durch verschiedene Umstände, die Keetenheuve nicht absichtlich herbeigeführt oder angestrebt hatte, war er in eine Schlüsselposition geraten, in der er zwar nicht durchsetzte, was er vielleicht wollte (und was wollte er?), in der er aber ein Stein im Weg sein konnte. Das war gefährlich! Vielleicht wußte Keetenheuve wirklich nicht, wie gefährlich seine Stellung war. Vielleicht war er doch ein Tor, ein gutmütiger Trottel geblieben. Dann war er, zumindest unter Parlamentariern, ein Unikum, und Mergentheim betrachtete ihn mit neuem Wohlwollen.

»Sieh dich vor«, sagte Mergentheim.

»Warum?« Es interessierte Keetenheuve eigentlich nicht. Warum sollte er sich vorsehen? Was wollte Mergentheim? Was wollte er hier, er Keetenheuve, was wollte er hier? Das Zimmer im alten »Volksblatt« war heimischer gewesen. Es war in Trümmer gefallen. *Vergiß es!* Was wollte Keetenheuve in dieser Baracke, wo es an allen Wänden mit hysterischer Betriebsamkeit pochte? Keetenheuve war es allmählich gleichgültig geworden, ob es regnete oder schön Wetter war. Er hatte seinen Trenchcoat.

»Du könntest schlachtreif sein«, sagte Mergentheim.

Das war wahr! Er war schlachtreif. Er fühlte es selbst. Er war der Wollust des Fressens verfallen. Vielleicht wollte er all die Armensuppen einholen, die er gegessen hatte. Sie waren nicht einzuholen. Aber er war dick geworden. Träg schlief das Fett unter der Haut. Mergentheim war viel dicker. Aber dem stand's; ihm nicht. Nun gut, er würde kämpfen.

Er fragte: »Was weißt du?«

»Nichts«, sagte Mergentheim. »Ich denk' mir nur was.«

Der Uhu machte ein schlaues Gesicht. Er hüllte sich in Rauch.
Die dicken Brillengläser beschlugen vor den verschleierten
Augen. So sahen die Eulen auf den alten Bildern der Hexen
aus. Eigentlich sahen sie dumm aus.

»Spiel nicht die Pythia. Was ist los?« Ach, er war gar nicht
neugierig. Er trieb heut so hin. *Schlecht*

Mergentheim lachte: »Wer einen Hund hängen will...«
Ein Hund hat gebellt in Insterburg

»Ich hab' aber keinen Haken«, sagte Keetenheuve; »für die
nicht!«

»Herr Major...«

»Sei nicht blöd. Das ist eine zu dumme Lüge.«

»Die Wahrheit ist oft nur eine Frage der Aufmachung«,
sagte Mergentheim.

Also das war es! So wollten sie ihn stumm machen. Es war
ein alter stinkender Hut, unter dem er verschwinden sollte.
Schon bald nach seiner Rückkehr hatte sich um Keetenheuve
das Gerücht verbreitet, er habe während des Krieges in England die Uniform eines britischen Majors getragen; und natürlich fanden sich Leute (wann finden die sich nicht?), die
ihn in fremdem Tuch gesehen haben wollten. Es war vollkommener Unsinn, so leicht zu widerlegen, daß Keetenheuve
keine Lust hatte, sich zu verteidigen, und für jeden, der Keetenheuve kannte, war es ein lächerlicher Gedanke, ihn als
Major wandeln zu sehen, wenn auch als britischen, das Pa-
radestöckchen unterm Arm, es war absurd, denn Keetenheuves echte Schwäche war es (und stur war er in diesem Punkt),
daß er ehrlich stolz darauf war, nie eine Uniform getragen
zu haben, wenn er auch in abstrakter Überlegung meinte
(und mit einem Schluß, der für ihn praktisch überhaupt nicht
in Frage gekommen war), daß im Fall Hitler die britische
Uniform der deutschen vorzuziehen war — aus ethischen
Gründen, die Keetenheuve weit über die nationalen stellte,
die er für atavistisch hielt. Kein Toter nützt seinem Vaterland, und die Menschen fallen bestenfalls für Ideen, die sie
nicht begreifen und deren Konsequenz sie nicht übersehen.
Die geschundenen Krieger auf den Schlachtfeldern, die ge-
plagten Völker waren die Opfer zänkischer, überaus eigen-

sinniger, rechthaberischer und gänzlich unfähiger Denker, die in ihrem verdrehten armen Kopf keine Klarheit schaffen konnten und die sich außerdem gegenseitig nicht verstanden und nicht ausstanden. Vielleicht waren die Heere aber auch verworrene Schöpfungsgedanken Gottes, die gegeneinander losgingen. Wohl dem, der da nicht mitmachte! Noch wohler dem, der Halt gebot!

Keetenheuve machte eine müde Bewegung der Abwehr. »Das ist doch Quatsch, warum erzählst du mir das?«

»Ich weiß nicht«, sagte Mergentheim, »nenn es Quatsch, natürlich warst du nicht Royal Officer, meinst du, ich glaub' das, aber die Behauptung prägt sich gut ein und gibt der Menge ein anschauliches Bild von dir. Keetenheuve Abgeordneter und britischer Major. Da stimmt doch was nicht, nicht wahr? Da ist was faul. Wir wissen, es ist eine Lüge, eine gänzlich aus der Luft gegriffene Geschichte. Aber erst steht sie mal in der Zeitung. Wenn du Glück hast, vergißt man sie. Aber dann setzt man die Mär wieder in die Zeitung. Von politischer Verleumdung verstand Hitler wirklich etwas, und was lehrt er in seinem Fachbuch? Die ständige, ermüdende Wiederholung der Verleumdung. Einer heißt Bernhard. Man nennt ihn Itzig. Immer wieder. Immer wieder. Das ist das Rezept.«

»Soweit sind wir noch nicht.«

»Du hast recht. Soweit sind wir noch nicht. Aber vielleicht hat jemand, vielleicht hat Freund Frost-Forestier eine Photographie von dir gefunden. Du erinnerst dich nicht. Aber vielleicht stehst du auf dieser Photographie hinter dem Mikrophon des BBC, man sieht die Buchstaben, und wenn man sie nicht sieht, man kann da nachhelfen, und jeder sieht sie dann und jeder kennt sie. Ahnst du was? Und vielleicht hat jemand, vielleicht wieder Frost-Forestier, ein altes Tonband aufgetrieben, vielleicht noch aus Abwehrkisten, aus Gestapobeständen, und man kann dich heute wieder hören, wie du zu deinen Wählern sprachst, als sie im Keller saßen . . .«

Hier ist England. Hier ist England. Die langen Korridore des Sendehauses. Die verdunkelten Fenster. Die blaubeschmierten Lampen. Der Geruch nach Karbol und nach ver-

266

schimmeltem Tee. Er ging nicht in den Keller, wenn Alarm
war. Die verdunkelten Scheiben zitterten. Die blauver-
schmierten Glühbirnen zitterten und zuckten. Das Herz! Das
Herz! Er kam aus den Wäldern . . .
Er kam aus den Wäldern Kanadas. Er hatte als Internierter
beim Holzfällen geholfen. Körperlich war es keine schlechte
Zeit gewesen: die einfache kräftige Nahrung, die kalte ozon-
reiche Luft, Handarbeit, Schlaf in Zelten . . .
Aber für Keetenheuve kein Schlaf! Was tu' ich hier? Was will
ich hier? Nur nicht mitmachen? Nur nicht dabeisein? Nur
abseits bleiben? Die Unschuld päppeln, die gepflegte, die
täuschende Unschuld? Ist das genug? Schnee fiel auf die
Zelte im Winter, fiel lautlos durch den hohen Wald, schüttete
ein ruhmloses stilles Grab aus sanftem fremdem Schnee, denn
hatte er es nicht so weit kommen lassen, war es nicht seine
Schuld, hatte er sich nicht immer schon abseits gehalten, mi-
mosenhaft verzärtelt, im Elfenbeinturm, vornehm, hungernd,
obdachlos, elend, von Land zu Land gewiesen, aber immer
abseits, immer erduldend, nie kämpfend, war er nicht die
Wurzel aller Greuel, die nun wie blutig eitrige Geschwüre in
der Welt aufbrachen . . .
Nach Monaten trennte man im kanadischen Waldlager die
schwarzen von den weißen Schafen, und Keetenheuve reiste
auf Bürgschaft und Anforderung eines Quäkers nach London zurück.
Er sprach in England. Er kämpfte hinter dem Mikrophon,
und er kämpfte nicht zuletzt für Deutschland, wie er meinte, für Tyrannensturz und Frieden; es war ein guter Kampf,
und nicht er mußte sich schämen. Ein Ende dem Wahnsinn,
hieß die Losung, und ein früheres Ende wäre von größtem
Nutzen für die Welt gewesen und von allergrößtem für
Deutschland. Keetenheuve fühlte sich einig mit allen Wider-
ständischen, einig selbst mit den Militärs unter ihnen, mit
den Männern des zwanzigsten Juli. Er sagte es Mergentheim.
Doch der erwiderte: »Ich bin nicht Missionar. Ich bin Journalist. Hier schau dir das Jahrbuch des Hohen Hauses an!
Den Widerstand haben deine Kollegen schon wieder aus ih-

rem Lebenslauf gestrichen. Ich habe die neueste Auflage. Du scheinst noch bei der alten zu stehen. Und die ist schon eingestampft! Begreif es doch! Sei du friedlich! Viele meinen, daß man mit deinem Chef verhandeln könne, aber mit dir kann man nicht reden. Knurrewahn war Unteroffizier. Du verwirrst ihn. Sie nennen dich schon seinen bösen Geist. Du machst ihn schwanken.« Keetenheuve sagte: »Das wäre schon etwas. Dann hätte ich etwas erreicht. Wenn Knurrewahn zweifelt, wird er anfangen zu denken. Und das Denken wird ihn noch stärker an seiner Politik zweifeln lassen.« Mergentheim unterbrach ihn ungeduldig. »Du bist verrückt«, rief er. »Dir ist nicht zu helfen. Aber das will ich dir noch sagen: Du verlierst. Du verlierst mehr, als du ahnst. Denn diesmal kannst du auch nicht mehr emigrieren. Wohin denn? Deine alten Freunde denken heute wie wir, und alle Erdteile, ich sage dir, alle Erdteile sind durch Vorhänge des Mißtrauens geschlossen. Du bist vielleicht nur eine Mücke. Aber die Elefanten und die Tiger fürchten sich vor dir. Und deshalb hüte dich vor ihnen.«

Der Schiffsgang zwischen den Pressezimmern schwankte nicht sonderlicher als je unter seinen sich entfernenden Schritten. Er hatte kein Gefühl von Untergang oder persönlicher Gefährdung. Was Mergentheim gesagt hatte, beunruhigte Keetenheuve nicht. Es stimmte ihn nur trauriger, der schon traurig war; aber es erschütterte nicht, bestätigt zu hören, was man lange schon weiß und fürchtet, hier die nationale Restauration, den restaurativen Nationalismus, auf den alles hinauslief. Die Grenzen öffneten sich nicht. Sie schlossen sich wieder.

Und wieder saß man in dem Käfig, in den man hineingeboren war, dem Käfig des Vaterlandes, der zwischen anderen Käfigen mit anderen Vaterländern diesmal an einer Stange hing, die von einem der großen Käfig- und Menschensammler weiter in die Geschichte getragen wurde. Natürlich liebte Keetenheuve sein Land, er liebte es so gut wie jeder, der's laut beteuerte, vielleicht sogar mehr noch, da er lange weg gewesen, sich zurückgesehnt und mit dem Sehnen das Land aus der Ferne idealisiert hatte. *Keetenheuve Romantiker.*

Aber er wollte nicht in einem Käfig sitzen, dessen Tür von Bereitschaftspolizei bewacht wurde, die einen nur mit einem Paß hinausließ, um den man den Käfigobersten bitten mußte und dann ging's weiter, man stand zwischen den Käfigen, dort, wo kein Hausen war, man rieb sich in diesem Stand an allen Gittern, und um in einen anderen Käfig hineinzukommen, brauchte man wieder das Visum, die Aufenthaltsbewilligung von diesem Käfigherrscher. Die Erlaubnis wurde ungern gegeben. In allen Käfigen zeigte man sich über den Rückgang der Bevölkerung besorgt, aber Freude herrschte nur über den Zugang, der aus dem Schoß der Käfigbewohnerinnen kam, und das war ein furchtbares Bild der Unfreiheit auf der weiten Erde. Hinzu kam, daß man diesmal an der Stange des großen Käfigträgers baumelte. Wer wußte, wohin er ging? Und gab es eine Wahl? Man kam mit seinem ganzen Käfig nur an die Stange des anderen großen Käfigträgers, der genauso unberechenbar wie der erste (und wer weiß von welchem Dämon, von welcher fixen Idee getrieben) in die Irre ging — eine Anabasis, mit der man die Nachkommen wieder in ihren Schulen quälen würde. Am Ausgang des Pressehauses, des Nachrichtenschiffes, am Tannentisch der Mitteilungen traf Keetenheuve Philip Dana, der, ein lieber Gott der wahren Gerüchte, erhaben über Flut und Ebbe amtlicher Verlautbarungen, unwirsch im dürftigen Futter wühlte. Dana nahm Keetenheuve bei der Hand und führte ihn in sein Zimmer.

Der Nestor der Korrespondenten war ein Greis und schön. Er war der schönste unter den schönen und geschäftigen Greisen der Politik. Mit schlohweißem glänzendem Haar und seiner frischen geröteten Haut sah er aus, als käme er immer gerade aus dem Wind, den er sich in der Welt hatte um die Ohren wehen lassen. Man wußte nicht, ob Dana von sich aus eine Persönlichkeit war, oder ob er nur so bedeutend wirkte, weil er mit Berühmtheiten und mit Berüchtigtheiten gesprochen hatte, die vielleicht sich und der Welt nur darum das Schauspiel des großen Mannes bieten konnten, weil Philip Dana sie für würdig befunden hatte, mit ihnen zu telephonieren. Im Grunde verachtete er die Staatsmänner, die er interviewte; er hatte zu viele von dieser Sorte aufsteigen, glänzen, fallen und manchmal am Galgen hängen sehen, was für Dana insgeheim ein erfreulicherer Anblick war, als sie rüstig und rechthaberisch in Präsidentensesseln oder mit dem befriedigten Lächeln des sanften Alterstodes im fetten Gesicht in Staatssärgen aufgebahrt zu erblicken, während ihre Völker ihnen fluchten. Dana war seit vierzig Jahren bei allen Kriegen und allen Konferenzen, die den Schlachten folgten und den neuen Angriffen vorangingen, dabeigewesen; er hatte die Dummheit der Diplomaten mit Schaufeln geschluckt, er hatte Blinde als Führer gesehen und hatte Taube vergeblich vor heranbrausenden Katastrophen gewarnt, er hatte tollwütige Hunde erlebt, die sich Patrioten schimpften, und Lenin, Tschiangkaischek, Kaiser Wilhelm, Mussolini, Hitler und Stalin hatten vor ihm im weißen Kleid der Engel gestanden, die Taube auf der Schulter, den Palmenwedel in der Hand, und gesegnet sei der Frieden des Erdkreises. Dana hatte mit Roosevelt getrunken und mit dem Negus gespeist, er hatte Menschenfresser und wirkliche Heilige gekannt, er war Zeuge aller Aufstände, Revolutionen, Bürgerkämpfe unserer Epoche gewesen, und stets hatte er die Niederlage des Menschen konstatiert. Die Besiegten waren ihrer Sieger würdig; sie waren nur für eine Weile sympathischer, weil sie die Besiegten waren. Die Welt, der Dana den Puls gefühlt hatte, wartete auf seine Memoiren, aber es war sein Geschenk an die Welt, daß er sie nicht schrieb — er hätte nur Greuel berichten können. So saß er sanft und anscheinend weise zu Bonn in einem Schaukelstuhl (er hatte ihn sich teils der Bequemlichkeit und teils der Symbolik halber in sein Büro gestellt) und beobachtete wippend den Pendelschlag der Weltpolitik in einem kleinen, aber neuralgischen Verhältnis. Dieses Bonn war Danas Altenteil; vielleicht sein Grab. Es war nicht so anstrengend wie Korea, aber man hörte auch hier die Saat des Unverstandes aufgehen, das Gras der Uneinsicht und des Unabänderlichen wachsen. Keetenheuve kannte Dana aus alten »Volksblatt«-Tagen. Dana hatte eine Reportage Keetenheuves über den großen Berliner Verkehrsstreik, der Nazis und Kommunisten zu einer merkwürdigen, verwirrenden und hochexplosiven Einheitsfront zusammengeführt hatte, aus dem »Volksblatt« in seinen internationalen Nachrichtendienst übernommen und Keetenheuve so Leser auf der ganzen Erde verschafft. Später sah Keetenheuve Dana in London wieder. Dana schrieb ein Buch über Hitler, das er als Bestseller plante und als Bestseller absetzte; so brachte ihm sein Abscheu viel Geld ein. Keetenheuve hatte sein Antipathie für alles Braune nur arm und flüchtig gemacht, und er bewunderte Danas Tüchtigkeit nicht ganz neidlos und mit der kritischen Einschränkung, daß Danas Verführerbuch doch eben nur ein Bestseller sei, seicht und geschickt aufgemacht.

Der liebe Gott war freundlich. Er reichte Keetenheuve ein Blatt eines Nachrichtendienstes, mit dem er in Tauschverkehr stand. Keetenheuve entdeckte sofort die Meldung, auf die es Dana ankam, eine Nachricht aus dem Conseil Supérieur des Forces Armées, ein Interview mit englischen und französischen Siegergenerälen, die, Führer in der geplanten Europaarmee, im wahrscheinlichen und nun durch Verträge zu unterbauenden Lauf der Politik die Verewigung der deutschen Teilung sahen und in dieser Teilung den leider einzigen Gewinn des letzten großen Krieges. Diese Äußerung war im Bund reines Dynamit. Sie mußte von bedeutender Sprengkraft sein, wenn sie im Parlament im richtigen Moment als Bombe platzen würde. Daran war nicht zu zweifeln. Nur war Keetenheuve kein Bombenwerfer. Aber mit dieser Nachricht konnte er Knurrewahn, der davon träumte, der Mann der Wiedervereinigung zu werden (und davon träumten viele), stärken und standhaft machen. Aber hatten die Zeitungen die Meldung nicht schon aufgegriffen und grell herausgestellt, so daß die Dementis der Regierung jedem Handeln zuvorkamen? Dana verneinte. Die Bundespresse, meinte er, würde das Interview nur klein und beiläufig bringen, wenn überhaupt. Die Freude der Generäle war ein zu heißes Eisen, ein wahrer Rammbock für die Regierungsvorlage, und so würde sie höchstens schlecht placiert erscheinen, um übersehen zu werden. Keetenheuve hatte sein Dynamit. Aber er mochte keine Sprengkörper. Alle Politik war schmutzig, sie glich den Gangsterkämpfen, und ihre Mittel waren dreckig und zerreißend; selbst wer das Gute wollte, wurde leicht zu einem anderen Mephistopheles, der stets das Böse schafft; denn was war gut und was war böse auf diesem Feld, das sich weit in die Zukunft ausdehnte, weit in ein dunkles Reich? Keetenheuve blickte traurig durch das offene Fenster in den neuerlich wie Dampf sprühenden Regen. Durch das Fenster drang wieder feuchtwarm Erddunst und Pflanzengeruch eines botanischen Gartens, und bleiche Blitze durchzuckten das Treibhaus. Selbst das Gewitter schien künstlich zu sein, ein Kunst- und Unterhaltungsgewitter in den Restaurationsbetrieben des Hauses Vaterland, und Dana, der sanfte schöne und vielerfahrene Greis, war trotz des Donnergrollens ein wenig eingeschlafen. Er lag in seinem leicht bewegten Schaukelstuhl, ein wippender Beobachter, ein Schläfer und ein Träumer. Er träumte von der Göttin des Friedens, aber leider erschien ihm die Göttin im Traum in Gestalt der Irène, eines annamitischen Puffmädchens, das Dana vor gut fünfundzwanzig Jahren in Saigon besucht hatte, weich waren ihre Arme gewesen, munter wie kleine reißende Flüsse, nach Blüten duftete die Haut. Dana schlief in Irènes der Friedlichen Armen friedlich ein, und später hatte er bittere Tabletten zu schlucken bekommen. So war es mit der Göttin des Friedens. Wir spielen. *Wir spielen Räuber und Gendarm Räuber und Gendarm immer wieder immer wieder*

Keetenheuve hatte sich in sein Büro im Neubau des Bundeshauses, in dem der Pädagogischen Akademie angebauten Trakt, begeben. Die Korridore und die Zimmer der Abgeordneten waren mit staubfrei gewachstem Linoleum bedeckt. Sie erinnerten in ihrer blinkenden Sauberkeit an die aseptische Abteilung einer Klinik, und vielleicht war auch die Politik, die hier am kranken Volk geübt wurde, steril. Keetenheuve war in seinem Arbeitsraum dem Himmel näher, aber nicht der Klarheit; neue Wolken, neue Gewitter zogen herauf, und der Horizont hüllte sich in bläuliche und in giftig gelbe Schleier. Keetenheuve hatte, um sich zu konzentrieren, das Neonlicht eingeschaltet und saß, wo Tagesschimmer und künstlicher Schein sich brachen, im Zwielicht. Der Tisch lag voll Post, voll Bitten, voll Hilferufe; er lag voll von Beschimpfungen und unlösbaren Problemen. Unter der Neonleuchte guckte Elke ihn an. Es war nur ein kleines Bild von ihr, das da stand, ein Gelegenheitsphoto mit zerzaustem Haar in einer Trümmerstraße (und ihm lieb, weil er sie so gefunden hatte), aber jetzt kam es ihm vor, als ob sie im Neonlicht groß wie ein flimmernder Schatten auf einer Kinoleinwand da wäre und ihn, das Haar diesmal glatt gebürstet, mit freundlichem Spott betrachte, so, als riefe sie ihm zu: »Da hast du deine Politik und deine Händel, und von mir bist du befreit!« Es schmerzte Keetenheuve, sie so reden zu hören, zumal es ja eine Stimme aus dem Grab war, die zu ihm sprach und unwiderruflich war. Er nahm Elkes Bild und legte es weg. Er legte Elke zu den Akten. Aber was hieß das, zu den Akten? Die Akten waren unwichtig, und was wichtig war, ob in Akten dokumentiert oder nicht, blieb gegenwärtig, war ganz von selber da, bis in den Schlaf, bis in den Traum, bis in den Tod hinein. Keetenheuve wandte sich noch nicht der Post zu, nicht den Bitten und nicht den Beschimpfungen, nicht den Briefen von Berufsbettlern, Quenglern, Geschäftsleuten und Wahnsinnigen, nicht dem Schrei der Verzweiflung — er hätte gerne alle Briefe an den Abgeordneten vom Tisch gefegt. Er nahm ein Blatt seines MdB-Papiers und schrieb »Le beau navire«, »Das schöne Schiff«, auf die Seite, denn an dieses herrliche Gedicht des Frauenlobs hatte ihn nun Elke erinnert, so sollte sie in seinem Gedächtnis leben, und er versuchte, die ewigen Verse Baudelaires aus der Erinnerung zu übersetzen, »je veux te raconter, o molle enchanteresse«, ich werde dir sagen, ich werde dir erzählen, ich werde dir beichten ..., das gefiel ihm, er wollte Elke beichten, daß er sie liebe, daß sie ihm fehle, er suchte das richtige Wort, den adäquaten Ausdruck, er sann, er kritzelte, er strich aus, er verbesserte, er versank in ästhetisch wehmütigen Gefühlen. Log er? Nein, er empfand so; die Liebe war groß und die Trauer tief, aber mit schwang ein Unterton aus Eitelkeit und Selbstmitleid und der Verdacht, daß er in der Poesie wie in der Liebe dilettiere. Er beklagte Elke, aber ihm graute auch vor der Vereinsamung, die er sein Leben lang herausgefordert hatte, und die ihn nun ganz umfing. Er übersetzte aus den »Blumen des Bösen«, »o molle enchanteresse«, mein süßes, mein weiches, mein warmes Entzükken, *o mein weiches, mein schmeichelndes, mein entzücktes Wort;* — er hatte niemand, dem er schreiben konnte. Hundert Briefe lagen auf seinem Tisch, Jammerlaute, ratloses Gestammel und Verwünschungen, aber niemand erwartete einen Brief von ihm, der nicht ein Anliegen betraf. An Elke hatte Keetenheuve seine Briefe aus Bonn geschrieben, und wenn sie vielleicht auch an die Nachwelt gerichtet waren, so war Elke doch weit mehr als eine Adresse gewesen; sie war das Medium, das ihn sprechen ließ und das ihm Kontakt gab. Bleich wie ein Verdammter saß Keetenheuve im Bundeshaus, bleiche Blitze geisterten vor dem Fenster und über dem Rhein, Wolken geladen mit Elektrizität, beladen mit dem Auspuff der Essen des Industriegebiets, dampfende trächtige Schleier, gasig, giftig, schwefelfarben, die unheimliche ungezähmte Natur zog sturmbereit über Dach und Wände des Treibhauses und pfiff Verachtung und Hohn dem Mimosengewächs, dem trauernden Mann, dem Baudelaireübersetzer und Abgeordneten im Neonbad hinter dem Glas des Fensters. So verging ihm die Zeit, bis Knurrewahn ihn rufen ließ.

Sie lebten in Symbiose, in dem Zusammenleben ungleicher Lebewesen zu gegenseitigem Nutzen; aber sie waren nicht sicher, ob es ihnen nicht schade. Knurrewahn hätte sagen können, er nehme durch Keetenheuve Schaden an seiner Seele. Doch Knurrewahn, der sich vor dem Ersten Weltkrieg selbst gebildet und mit einer schon damals nicht mehr ganz neuen Literatur fortschrittsgläubiger Naturerkenntnis vollgestopft hatte (die Welträtsel schienen gelöst zu sein, und nachdem er den unvernünftigen Gott vertrieben hatte, brauchte der Mensch nur noch alles sachlich zu ordnen), leugnete das Dasein der Seele. So war das Unbehagen, das Keetenheuve ihm bereitete, dem Ärger eines gewissenhaften Unteroffiziers an einem Einjährigen zu vergleichen, der das Exerzierreglement nicht begreift, schlimmer noch, es nicht ernst nimmt. Leider brauchte die Armee Einjährige, und die Partei brauchte Keetenheuve, der (dies ahnte Knurrewahn) vielleicht gar kein Offizier, kein Offiziersaspirant, sondern einfach ein Hochstapler war, ein Vagabund, der aus irgendeinem Grund, vielleicht wegen seines arroganten Betragens, für einen Offizier gehalten wurde. Hier irrte Knurrewahn; Keetenheuve war nicht arrogant, er war unkonventionell, und das schien Knurrewahn die vollendete Form der Arroganz zu sein, und so war er es am Ende doch, der Keetenheuve für den Offizier hielt, während dieser selbst ohne weiteres zugegeben hätte, irgend etwas, vielleicht ein Stromer zu sein. Er achtete Knurrewahn, den er den Meister nach altem Schrot und Korn nannte, was nicht ohne Spott, doch nicht gehässig gemeint war, während die Äußerung Knurrewahns Ohren, ihnen zugetragen, wieder ärgerlich überheblich klang. Er war aber wirklich ein Mann nach altem Schrot und Korn, ein Handwerker aus einer Handwerkerfamilie, der früh nach Wissen, dann nach Gerechtigkeit und später, weil sich Wissen und Gerechtigkeit als unsichere Begriffe entpuppt hatten, schwer zu bestimmen und immer relativ zur unbekannten Größe, nach Herrschaft und Macht gestrebt hatte. Auch Knurrewahn wollte der Welt seinen Willen nicht geradezu aufzwingen, aber er hielt sich für den Mann, sie zum Guten zu lenken. Hierzu brauchte er Mitstreiter und war an Keetenheuve geraten, der ihn nicht stärkte, sondern verwirrte. Keetenheuve war kein vierter Mann beim Skat und kein Biertrinker, und das schloß ihn aus einer warmen Runde von Männern aus, die sich abends um Knurrewahn versammelten, die den Krug hoben und die Karten auf den Tisch klopften, Männer, die das Schicksal der Partei bestimmten, mit denen aber kein Staat zu machen und nicht einmal ein Hund zu locken war.

Knurrewahn hatte viel durchgemacht; aber er war nicht weise geworden. Sein Herz war gut gewesen; nun hatte es sich verhärtet. Er war aus dem Ersten Weltkrieg mit einem Steckschuß heimgekehrt und hatte zum Erstaunen der Ärzte weitergelebt; das war zu einer Zeit gewesen, als die Mediziner noch nicht glauben wollten, daß man mit einem Herzsteckschuß weiterleben könne, und Knurrewahn war als lebender Leichnam von Klinik zu Klinik gewandert, bis er klüger als seine Ärzte geworden war, einen Posten in seiner Partei annahm und sich durch zähen Fleiß und ein wenig mit Hilfe des wunderlichen Steckschusses, der sich auf Wahlplakaten empfahl, zum Reichstagsabgeordneten hochdiente. Neunzehnhundertdreiunddreißig warfen Frontsoldaten unter Berufung auf die Frontkameradschaft Knurrewahn, der das Fronterlebnis aus Blei im Herzen trug, in das Lager. Sein Sohn, bestimmt, den Aufstieg seiner Familie akademisch weiterzuführen, kam wieder nach altem Familienbrauch in die Tischlerlehre, und verbittert über die Deklassierung und aus Trotz gegen den Vater, der politisch eben leider falsch lag, und im Wahn, sich bewähren zu müssen (denn überall im Lande bewährte sich's furchtbar), meldete er sich zur Legion Condor nach Spanien, wo er als Bordwart fiel. Auch Keetenheuve hatte daran gedacht, sich nach Spanien zu melden, auch er, sich dort zu bewähren, doch auf der anderen Seite (er hatte es nicht getan, und er machte sich zuweilen noch Vorwürfe, auch hier versagt zu haben), und leicht hätte es so geschehen können, daß Keetenheuve aus einer Flakstellung um Madrid Knurrewahns Sohn vom südlichen Himmel geschossen hätte. So kreuz und quer und mitten durch die Länder liefen die Fronten, und die meisten, die da flogen oder schossen, wußten gar nicht mehr, wie sie gerade auf diese Seite der Front geraten waren. Knurrewahn begriff es nie. Er war ein nationaler Mann, und seine Opposition gegen die nationale Politik der Regierung war sozusagen deutschnational. Knurrewahn wollte der Befreier und Einiger des zerrissenen Vaterlandes werden, schon sah er sich als Bismarckdenkmal in den Knurrewahnanlagen stehen, und er vergaß darüber den alten Traum, die Internationale. In seiner Jugend hatte diese Internationale mit roten Fahnen noch die Menschenrechte vertreten. Neunzehnhundertvierzehn war sie gestorben. Die neue Zeit zog nicht mit ihr, die marschierte hinter ganz anderen Fahnen drein, und was es noch gab und sich Internationale nannte, das waren Verbände mit Ordnungsziffern hinter dem stolzen Namen, Spaltgruppen, Sekten, die kein Beispiel des Friedens boten, sondern vor aller Welt den Hader symbolisierten, indem sie sich andauernd heftig in den Haaren lagen. Vielleicht fürchtete Knurrewahn so mit Recht einen alten Fehler. Nach seiner Meinung war die Partei in der ersten deutschen Republik nicht national genug aufgetreten; sie hatte in der schon gespaltenen Internationale keinen Beistand gefunden, und in der Nation hatte sie die Massen verloren, die der eingängigen Parole des primitiven nationalen Egoismus folgten. Diesmal wollte sich Knurrewahn den nationalen Wind nicht aus dem Segel nehmen lassen. Er war für ein Heer, gebranntes Kind scheut nicht immer das Feuer, aber er war für eine Truppe von Patrioten (die große Französische Revolution legte ihm die Binde der Torheit vor die Augen, und Napoleon war vielleicht schon wieder geboren), er war für Generale, aber sie sollten sozial und demokratisch sein. Narr, meinte Keetenheuve, die Generale, diese, wenn's um ihre Karriere ging, gar nicht dummen, diese geriebenen Brüder würden Knurrewahn eine schöne Komödie vorspielen, die versprachen ihm alles, die legten sich hin und machten die Beine breit, die wollten ihre Stäbe zusammenkriegen, ihre Ranglisten aufstellen und ihre Sandkästen bauen. Was dann kam, wußte niemand. Schneider wollten nähen. Und mit dem nationalen Auftrieb war es überhaupt so eine Sache. Dieser Wind hatte

277

sich vielleicht sogar gelegt, die nationale Regierung, schlauer, fuchsiger, segelte ein wenig mit der internationalen Brise, und Knurrewahn saß in der Flaute, wenn er national aufkreuzen wollte, statt vielleicht international das Rennen zu machen, ein Rennen mit dem Segel neuer Ideale zu neuen Ufern. Er sah sie leider nicht. Er sah weder die neuen Ideale noch das neue Ufer. Er begeisterte nicht, weil ihn nichts mehr begeisterte. Er glich sich den Volksbiedermännern aus einer billigen patriotisch sozialen Traktätchenliteratur an, er wollte ein von Hysterie und Unmoral gereinigter Bismarck, ein Arndt, ein Stein, ein Hardenberg und ein wenig ein Bebel sein. Lassalle war ein Porträt des Abgeordneten als junger Mann. Der junge Mann war tot; er hatte den Ärzten recht gegeben und den Herzsteckschuß nicht überlebt. Heute stand Knurrewahn der Schlapphut, den er nicht trug. Er polterte eigensinnig, nicht nur beim Skat, polterte eigensinnig wie der märkische Soldatenkönig und wie der alten Hindenburg, und so lief auch im politischen Leben alles wild durcheinander, die Winde wehten kreuz und quer durch die Parteien, und nur Wetterkarten, die keiner verstand, rätselhafte Verbindungslinien zwischen Punkten gleicher Wärme (die weit voneinander entfernt liegen konnten) zeigten die Fronten und warnten vor dem Tief und dem Sturm. In solcher Lage kannte Knurrewahn sich nicht mehr aus, und er klammerte sich an Keetenheuve (den Mephistopheles des guten Willens), damit er unter dem sternenlosen verhangenen Himmel das Besteck aufnehme und in Nacht und Nebel den Kurs des Schiffleins bestimme.

Knurrewahn hatte sich fortschrittlich eingerichtet, in einem Stil, den er für radikal hielt und der den Anschauungen einer soliden Kunstzeitschrift entsprach. Die Möbel waren praktisch, die Sessel bequem; Möbel, Sessel, Lampen und Vorhänge erinnerten an das Schild »Modernes Chefzimmer« im Schaufenster eines Innenarchitekten gemäßigt moderner Richtung, und der von der Sekretärin gekaufte und gepflegte Strauß roter Blumen stand, genau wo er hingehörte, unter der in kraftlosen Farben gemalten Weserlandschaft. Keetenheuve überlegte, ob Knurrewahn in seinem Stuhl manchmal

Indianergeschichten lese, aber der Fraktionsführer hatte keine Zeit für private Lektüre. Er hörte Keetenheuves Bericht, und mit den Generalen des Conseil Supérieur des Forces Armées traten Glanz und Falschheit in sein Zimmer, Arroganz und Perfidie der schlechten Welt, er sah die fremden Militärs in Reitstiefeln mit silbernen Sporen über den Teppich aus deutschem Garn schreiten, die Franzosen mit ausgebuchteten kokottenhaften roten Hosen und die Engländer mit kleinen Stöckchen, bereit, auf den Tisch zu trommeln. Knurrewahn war entrüstet. Er empörte sich, während Keetenheuve das Wort der Generale von der Verewigung der deutschen Teilung als dürftigen Gewinn des letzten Krieges aus dem Spezialistentum der Herren verständlich fand, das Urteil des Fachmannes war immer begrenzt, und hier war es eine Generalsmeinung, also sowieso beschränkten Verstandes. Knurrewahn teilte diese Ansicht nicht; ihn beeindruckten Generale, die Keetenheuve höchstens als Feuerwehrmänner gelten ließ. Knurrewahn brannte seine Kugel im Herzen, ihn brannte das mit seinem Fleisch verwachsene Blei, und es war ein Jünglingsschmerz, der ihn belebte und verjüngte. Er haßte. Es war zudem ein Haß, den sich der Leiter einer sozialen Friedenspartei leisten durfte, er haßte zweifach und war so doppelt legitimiert und versichert, er haßte den Landesfeind und den Klassenfeind, die sich diesmal in den gleichen Personen seiner Wut darboten. Im Grunde war es die seinen Ohren arrogant klingende Bezeichnung ihrer Körperschaft, war es der Ausdruck Conseil Supérieur des Forces Armées, der Knurrewahn reizte und den Keetenheuve ihm absichtlich elegant hingehalten hatte wie ein Torero das rote Tuch dem Stier.

Keetenheuve liebte es, Knurrewahn so erregt zu sehen. Was für ein prächtiger Mann war er doch, mit seinem breiten Schädel, und sicher hatte er in seinem Schreibtisch verschämt in einer Blechschachtel das Eiserne Kreuz und das Verwundetenabzeichen aus dem Grabenkrieg liegen, eingewickelt vielleicht in den Entlassungsschein aus dem Konzentrationslager und den Abschiedsbrief des Sohnes, bevor er zur Legion Condor ging und fiel. Aber nun mußte Keetenheuve auf-

passen, daß Knurrewahn ihm nicht davonlief. Der Parteifüh-
rer wollte das Interview der Generale, die deutsche Meinung
der Chefs der Europaarmee plakatieren. Er wollte die Worte
Ewige Teilung an die Mauern schlagen lassen und so sich
an das Volk wenden:»Seht, wir sind verraten und verkauft,
dahin führt der Kurs der Regierung!« Eine solche Aktion
hieß aber die Bombe für das Parlament entschärfen; sie würde dem Kanzler die Dementis liefern oder Beistandserklärun-
gen der europäischen Regierungen, bevor der Fall im Plenum überhaupt zur Sprache kam, und gemein und perfide
würde am Ende nur der Plakateur genannt werden. Die
mögliche Erregung im Volk war nicht hoch einzusetzen; die
Regierung würde sich durch die Volksmeinung nicht stören
lassen. Knurrewahn dachte, die Sätze der Generale, die sich
in einem Conseil Supérieur so erfreut über die deutsche Teilung geäußert hatten, ließen sich nicht einfach dementieren,
aber Keetenheuve wußte, daß die Staatsmänner in England
und Frankreich ihre Generale berichtigen würden. Sie würden sie zur Ordnung rufen, denn (hier war Keetenheuve
wieder voreingenommen) fremde Generale ließen sich zu-
rechtweisen, sie waren Staatsdiener, wenn auch nicht sympathisch, während deutsche Generale sofort wieder die tatsäch-
liche Macht im Staat verkörpern und die ihnen natürlich
scheinende Ordnung, den Primat des Militärischen über das
Politische, herstellen würden. Der deutsche General war für
Keetenheuve ein Krebs des deutschen Volkes, und an dieser
Meinung änderte auch die Achtung nichts, die er für die
von Hitler ermordeten Generale empfand. Er verabscheute
die alten Kommißköpfe, die mit der Miene väterlicher Bie-
dermänner die erwachsenen Bürger des Staates mit »meine
Jungens« oder »meine Söhne« anzureden wagten, um dann
diese Jungen und Söhne in das Maschinengewehrfeuer zu
jagen. Keetenheuve hatte das Volk an der Generalskrankheit
leiden und sterben sehen; und wer, wenn nicht die Generale,
hatten den Braunauer Bazillus großgezogen! Die Gewalt hatte immer nur Unglück gebracht, nur Niederlagen, und Keetenheuve setzte auf die Gewaltlosigkeit, die, wenn nicht das
Glück, doch zumindest den moralischen Sieg sichern mußte.

Ob das dann der berühmte Endsieg war? So war Keetenheuve mit Knurrewahn, der ehrlich von einem deutschen Volksheer und einem deutschen Volksgeneral träumte, der, ein schlichter sportlicher Mann in grauer Bergsteigertracht, mit seinen Soldaten dieselbe Suppe aß, die er auch, immer ein braver sorgender Vater, mit seinen Gefangenen teilen würde, in diesem Punkt nur auf Zeit verbunden. Er wollte, daß niemand mehr gefangen wurde, und so brauchte er Knurrewahn, um gegen die Armeeidee des Kanzlers zu frondieren, aber der Tag würde kommen, wo er sich gegen des Freundes noch viel gefährlichere Volksheerpläne wenden mußte. Keetenheuve war für reinen Pazifismus, für ein endgültiges Die-Waffen-Nieder! Er wußte, welche Verantwortung er auf sich nahm, sie bedrückte ihn und ließ ihn nicht schlafen, aber, wenn er sich auch ohne Bundesgenossen sah, ohne Freund in West und Ost und verkannt hier wie dort, die Geschichte schien ihn zu lehren, daß der Verzicht auf Wehr und Gewalt niemals zu solchem Übel führen konnte, wie ihre Anwendung. Und wenn es keine Heere mehr gab, würden die Grenzen fallen; auf die zur Zeit der Flugzeuge ganz und gar lächerlich gewordene Souveränität der Länder (man flog dem Schall davon, respektierte aber von Irrsinnigen in die Luft hineingedachte Korridore) würde verzichtet werden und der Mensch würde frei und freizügig, ja wahrhaft vogelfrei sein. Knurrewahn gab nach. Ihm deuchte zwar, er gebe zu oft und zu viel nach, aber er gab wieder nach, dämmte seinen Zorn zurück, und sie beschlossen, daß Keetenheuve die kleine Siegrede der Generale in der Debatte über die Sicherheitsverträge überraschend zitieren solle.

Er ging zurück in sein Zimmer. Er setzte sich zurück ins Neonlicht. Er ließ die Röhren weiterleuchten, obwohl der Himmel jetzt klar und hell war und die Sonne für einen Augenblick alles in ein gleißendes Licht tauchte. Der Rhein funkelte. Ein Ausflugdampfer mühlte weiß in der spritzenden Gischt seiner Wasserräder vorbei, und die Passagiere deuteten mit Fingern auf das Bundeshaus. Keetenheuve war geblendet. Die Übersetzung des »Beau navire«, des »Schönen Schiffes«, sie blieb unvollendet zwischen den ungeöff-

281

neten Briefen liegen, und neue waren schon wieder hinzuge-
kommen, neue Schreiben, neue Notschreie, neue Klagen, neue
Beschwerden, neue Verwünschungen an den Herrn Abgeordneten, das strömte wie draußen das Wasser des Flusses, von
Briefträgern und Boten treulich geschöpft, auf den Tisch und
riß nicht ab. Keetenheuve war der Adressat einer Nation von
Briefschreibern; es saugte ihn aus, und nur die Intuition des
Augenblicks rettete ihn vor dieser Flut, in der er sonst zu
ersticken meinte. Er entwarf die Rede, die er im Plenum
halten wollte. Er würde glänzen! Ein Dilettant in der Liebe,
ein Dilettant in der Poesie und ein Dilettant in der Politik —
er würde glänzen. Und von wem soll das Heil kommen, wenn
nicht von einem Dilettanten? Die Fachmänner marschierten
auf alten Wegen in die alten Wüsten. Sie hatten noch nie
woanders hingeführt, und nur der Dilettant schaute wenigstens nach dem Gelobten Land aus, nach dem Reich, in dem
Milch und Honig fließen würde. Keetenheuve schenkte sich
einen Kognak ein. Der Gedanke, daß irgendwo Honig fließen sollte, war ihm unsympathisch. Auch die Beschreibung
des Gelobten Landes durfte man nicht wörtlich nehmen;
darum fanden es die Kinder auch nicht, wurden müde, wuchsen auf und ließen sich als Fachanwälte für Steuerrecht nieder, was alles über den Zustand der Welt sagt. Aus dem
Paradies war man vertrieben worden. Das stand fest. Gab
es einen Weg zurück? Zu sehen war auch nicht der schmalste
Pfad, aber vielleicht war er unsichtbar, und vielleicht gab es
Millionen und aber Millionen unsichtbarer Steigen, die ständig vor jedem lagen und nur darauf warteten, begangen
zu werden. Keetenheuve mußte nach seinem Gewissen handeln; doch auch das Gewissen war sowenig zu sehen und zu
greifen wie der rechte Weg, und nur zuweilen glaubte man
es pochen zu hören, was wiederum mit Kreislaufstörungen
erklärt werden konnte. Das Herz schlug unregelmäßig, und
seine Schrift auf dem glatten MdB-Papier verschnörkelte.
Frost-Forestier rief an und fragte, ob Keetenheuve mit ihm
essen wolle. Er würde ihm seinen Wagen schicken. War es
die Kriegserklärung? Keetenheuve meinte es. Er nahm die
Einladung an. Es war soweit. Sie wollten ihn abtun. Sie woll-

ten ihm die Pistole auf die Brust setzen, ihn erpressen. Mergentheim hatte es schon gewußt. Nun gut, er würde kämpfen. Er ließ die Briefe, er ließ die Akten, er ließ die Baudelaireübertragung, seine Notizen zur Debatte und das Blatt des Nachrichtendienstes, das Dana ihm gegeben hatte, er ließ alles offen im Neonlicht liegen, das er zu löschen vergaß, denn noch schien die Sonne und brach sich in tausend Prismen im Spiegel des Flusses und in den Wassertropfen auf den grünen Blättern in den Wipfeln der Bäume. Es leuchtete, blendete, glitzerte, funkelte, blitzte.

Die Automobile der Regierung sehen wie amtliche schwarze Särge aus, sie haben etwas phantasielos Zuverlässiges, sind von gedrungenem Bau, kosten viel, stehen jedoch in dem Ruf, solid und sparsam, dazu noch repräsentabel zu sein, und Minister, Räte und Beamte fühlen sich gleichermaßen zur Solidität, zur Sparsamkeit und zum Repräsentativen hingezogen. Frost-Forestiers Amt lag vor der Stadt, und Keetenheuve wurde solid, sparsam und repräsentabel durch kleine Rheindörfer gefahren, die verfallen waren, ohne historisch, enggassig, ohne romantisch zu sein. Die Dörfer sahen verkommen aus, und Keetenheuve vermutete hinter den bröckelnden Mauern mißmutige Menschen; vielleicht verdienten sie zuwenig; vielleicht drückten sie Abgaben; vielleicht waren sie aber nur deshalb mißmutig und ließen ihre Häuser verkommen, weil so viele schwarze Wagen mit wichtigen Persönlichkeiten vorüberfuhren. Und zwischen den alten, verfallenen Dörfern, verloren, einsam, zerstreut, auf Kohläckern, Brachen und mageren Weiden standen die Ministerien, die Ämter, die Häuser der Verwaltung, sie waren in alten Hitlerbauten untergekrochen, schrieben ihre Akten hinter Speerschen Sandfassaden und kochten ihre Süpplein in alten Kasernen. Die hier geschlafen hatten, waren tot, die man hier geschunden hatte, waren gefangen, sie hatten's vergessen, sie hatten's hinter sich, und wenn sie lebten und frei waren, bemühten sie sich um Renten, jagten Stellungen nach — was blieb ihnen übrig? Es war das Regierungsviertel einer Exilregierung, durch das Keetenheuve im Regierungswagen fuhr, Wächter wachten hinter sinnlos ins Feld gesteckten Zäunen, es war ein Gouvernement, das auf Gastfreundschaft und Wohlwollen angewiesen war, und Keetenheuve dachte: Es ist ein Witz, daß ich der Regierung nicht angehöre; es wäre meine Regierung — exiliert von der Nation, exiliert vom Natürlichen, exiliert vom Menschlichen (doch träumte er von der Menschen Brüderschaft). Auch Uniformierte wanderten auf der Straße zu Frost-Forestier. Sie hatten ihre Unterkunft in der Gegend; aber sie gingen einzeln fürbaß mit dem Schritt der Staatsangestellten und marschierten nicht schon in Haufen wie richtige Soldaten. Waren sie Bereitschaftspolizisten, waren sie Grenzschützler? Keetenheuve wußte es nicht; er war entschlossen zu jeder Charge, sollte er sie erkennen, »Herr Oberförster« zu sagen.

Frost-Forestier saß in einer alten Kaserne und herrschte über ein Heer; doch war es ein Heer von Sekretärinnen, das er in Atem hielt. Hier wurde in Stachanowschichten gearbeitet, und Keetenheuve wurde schwindlig, als er sah, wie eine Sekretärin gleich zwei Telephonapparate auf einmal bediente. Welche Scherze für Kinder waren hier möglich, und welche Partner konnte man miteinander verbinden! Wenn die Nation an Keetenheuve schrieb, die Welt telephonierte mit Frost-Forestier. War Paris am Apparat, Rom, Kairo, Washington? Rief man aus Tauroggen schon an? Was wollte der Dunkelmann aus Basel am Draht? Hatte er sich verfangen? Oder sangen Geschäftspartner, die in Bonn im Hotel Stern warteten, ihr Lied aus der Telephonmuschel in die Ohrmuschel der Damen? Es scheppterte, bimmelte, summte in Dur und Moll, ein andauerndes Armsünderläuten, ein fortwährendes Beichtstuhlgeflüster, und immer wieder wisperten die Mädchenstimmen, »nein, Herr Frost-Forestier bedauert, Herr Frost-Forestier kann nicht, ich werde es Herrn Frost-Forestier ausrichten« — Herr Frost-Forestier hatte keinen amtlichen Titel.

Der Vielverlangte ließ den Gast nicht warten. Er kam sofort, begrüßte Daniel in der Löwengrube und lud ihn ins Casino ein. Keetenheuve stöhnte. Der Feind rückte mit schweren Waffen an. Das Casino, ein scheunenartiger Raum, in dem es penetrant nach ranzigem Fett, heiß nach verbranntem Mehl dunstete, war gefürchtet. Es gab Deutsches Beefsteak

Esterhazy auf Püree, Fleischbällchen mit Bohnengemüse auf Püree, Schellrippchen mit Sauerkraut auf Püree, und ganz unten auf der Speisekarte stand »Schnullers Feinschmekkersuppen geben jedem Essen eine festliche Note«. Es war Taktik von Frost-Forestier (eine billige Taktik), den Abgeordneten, dessen gourmandise Neigungen bekannt waren, in das Casino zu bitten. Er wollte Keetenheuve an die dürftigen Schüsseln erinnern, zu denen man hinabsinken konnte. Links und rechts saßen an wachstuchüberzogenen Tischen Sekretärinnen und Angestellte und aßen das Deutsche Beefsteak Esterhazy. Was hat Esterhazy den Köchen getan, daß sie alle verbrannten Zwiebelgerichte nach ihm nennen? Keetenheuve wollte sich erkundigen. Frost-Forestier gab zwei Blechmarken für ihr Essen ab. Sie bestellten Matjesfilet mit grünen Bohnen, Specktunke und Kartoffeln. Der Matjes war ein alter Salztonnenbewohner. Die Specktunke war schwarz und hatte schleimige Mehlbatzen. Auch die Kartoffeln waren schwarz. Frost-Forestier speiste mit Appetit. Er aß den Hering auf, quetschte die schwarzen Kartoffeln in die schwarze Sauce und ließ auch von den strohfädigen Bohnen nichts auf dem Teller. Keetenheuve staunte. Vielleicht täuschte ihn alles, und Frost-Forestier aß nicht mit Appetit und war kein Mensch; vielleicht war er eine Hochleistungsmaschine, ein raffiniert konstruierter Allesschluckmotor, der sich zu bestimmter Zeit mit Brennstoff füllen mußte und in der Notwendigkeit kein Vergnügen sah. Während er sich vollstopfte, erzählte er Geschichten vom Klassenkampf und von der Hierarchie in den Ämtern und deutete unbefangen auf die Beispiele, die herumsaßen. Der Sachbearbeiter für Stahl sprach außer Dienst nicht mit dem Referenten für Gußeisen, und das Fräulein, das englisch stenographierte, aß die Schellrippchen auf Sauerkraut und Püree nicht am Tisch des armen Wesens, das nur die deutsche Kurzschrift gelernt hatte. Schönheit war aber selbst hier begehrt und bevorzugt, und Frost-Forestier berichtete von trojanischen Kriegen, die zwischen den Büros entbrannten, wenn der Personalchef ein hübsches Mädchen anzubieten hatte, und Helena durfte, beneidet, befeindet, mit dem Berichterstatter für Flurschäden Fleischbällchen auf

Püree verzehren. *Auch ein Hermaphrodit ein lieblicher war da zu sehen* Was war? Er fühlte sich an einen Sänger erinnert, an einen Flüsterer. *Ein Hermaphrodit ein lieblicher. Wo war das? Am Meer, am Strand? Vergessen. Sagesse, ein Gedicht von Verlaine. Weisheit, schön und melancholisch. Ich küsse Ihre Hand, Madame. Ein Sänger. Weibisch. Strandgut. Ich küsse Ihre Hand. Flüsterer. Wie hieß er? Paul. Küsse Ihre Hand, Herr Paul. Monsieur Frost. Frost-Forestier, der Matjesmotor, die Specktunkenhochleistungsmaschine. Das Denkelektron. Zweitonbändermann. Stahlgymnast. Männlich. Ruhiges Membrum. Was will er? Der Hering wird abserviert. Armer Fisch. Witwer. In Salz gelegt. Frost-Forestier Junggeselle. Leidenschaftslos. Unbestechlich. Frost-Forestier der Unbestechliche. Robespierre. Keine große Revolution. Weit und breit nicht. Spürt's im Urin. Was? Einen Kitzel? Gefährlich leben. Latriniert mit Landsern. Latrinenparolen. Informiert Dunkelmänner. Kohlenklau Feind hört mit. Dunkler Ätherdschungel. Latrinen. Pißt Wellen in den Äther. Latrinen. Hakenkreuz an der Wand. Die Interessenvertreter. Kennen ihren Referenten. Bockbier. Pisse.* Er sagte: »Gibt es hier was zu trinken?« *Nein. Es gab nicht. Nicht für ihn. Kaffee und Limonade. Kaffee beschleunigte den Herzschlag. Ging nicht. Schlug schon beschleunigt. Schlug schon im Hals. Die blasse Limonade der Evolution aufbrausend und aufstoßend. Was also?* Frost-Forestier bestellte einen Kaffee. *Was also?* Was wollte er?

Frost-Forestier fragte ihn was. Er sah ihn an. »Kennen Sie Mittelamerika?« fragte er. Er fügte hinzu: »Ein interessantes Land.« *Nein meine Schlange nicht aus dem Pfeffergebüsch, wüßtest es doch, wenn ich dort gewesen wäre, hättest es bei den Akten. Hilft dir nichts. Ich helfe dir nicht. Jetzt hilft wieder nur der britische Major. Sir Felix Keetenheuve, Commander, Member of Parliament, Royal Officers Club, warf Bomben auf Berlin.*

»Nein. Ich war nicht in Mittelamerika. Ich hatte einmal einen honduranischen Paß, wenn Sie darauf anspielen. Den habe ich gekauft. Man konnte das. Ich durfte mich mit dem

Paß überall sehen lassen, nur nicht in Honduras.« *Warum verrat' ich's ihm? Butter auf sein Brot. Gleichgültig. Keetenheuve Paßfälscher. Ich ließ mich in Scheveningen sehen. Weißt du, das Meer, der Strand, die Sonnenuntergänge? Ich saß vor dem Café Sport, und der Sänger setzte sich zu mir. Er setzte sich zu mir, weil er allein war, und ich ließ ihn bei mir sitzen, weil ich allein war. Die jungen Mädchen gingen vorüber, Prousts »jeunes filles en fleurs« vom Strand von Balbeck. Albertine, Albert. Die jungen Männer gingen vorüber. Mädchen und Jünglinge promenierten über den Seeboulevard, sie schwammen durch das Abendlicht, ihre Körper glühten, der versinkende Sonnenball funkelte durch ihre dünnen Kleider. Die Mädchen hoben die Brüste. Wer waren sie? Verkäuferinnen, Handelsschülerinnen, Modistinnen. Der Friseurlehrling von der Haager Plein. Sie war nur eine Verkäuferin in einem Schuhgeschäft — auch das hatte der Sänger in seiner guten Zeit auf Schallplatten geflüstert, sanft und tantig. Er wurde umgebracht. Wir blickten den Mädchen und den Burschen nach, und der Sänger sagte: Sie sind geil wie Affenscheiße.* Was war? Er mußte sich zusammenreißen, er hatte nicht zugehört. Frost-Forestier sprach nicht mehr von Mittelamerika, er redete von Keetenheuves Partei, die bisher zu kurz gekommen sei bei der Verteilung der diplomatischen Posten, nun, auch die Regierung denke verständlicherweise zuerst an ihre Freunde, freilich sei so zu verfahren nicht immer gerecht, andererseits fehle es Keetenheuves Gruppe an geeigneten Leuten, und wenn sich einer fände, nun, kurz und gut, Frost-Forestier fühlte vor, er zeigte, was er gesponnen hatte, noch war alles inoffiziell natürlich, der Kanzler wußte nichts, aber sicher, er würde zustimmen — Frost-Forestier bot Keetenheuve die Gesandtschaft in Guatemala an. »Ein interessantes Land«, wiederholte er. »Etwas für Sie! Interessante Menschen. Eine linke Regierung. Aber keine kommunistische Diktatur. Eine Republik der Menschenrechte. Ein Experiment. Sie wären der Mann, die Entwicklung für uns zu beobachten und die Beziehungen zu pflegen.«

Keetenheuve Gesandter Keetenheuve Exzellenz. Er war verblüfft. Aber die Ferne lockte ihn, und vielleicht war es die

Lösung aller Probleme. All seiner Probleme! Es war Flucht. Es war wieder Flucht. Es war die letzte Flucht. Sie waren nicht dumm. Aber vielleicht war es auch die Freiheit; und er wußte, daß es die Pensionierung war. *Keetenheuve Staatspensionist.* Er sah sich in Guatemala-City von der säulengeschmückten Veranda eines spanischen Hauses die unter der Sonne glühende staubige Straße, die staubbedeckten Palmen, die staubschweren verdorrten Kakteen beobachten. Wo die Straße sich zum Platz weitete, dämpfte der Staub in der Anlage die obszönen Farben der Kaffeeblüten, und das Denkmal des großen Guatemalteken schien in der Hitze zu schmelzen. Üppige lautlose Automobile, ratternde feuerrote Motorräder sprangen aus dem Sonnendunst, fuhren vorüber und lösten sich wie Visionen im Glast wieder auf. Es stank nach Benzin und nach Verwesung, und hin und wieder peitschte ein Schuß. Vielleicht war es die Rettung, vielleicht war es die Chance, alt zu werden. Er würde Jahre auf dieser säulengeschmückten Terrasse verweilen und Jahre die heiße staubige Straße beobachten. Er würde in Abständen einen Bericht nach Hause senden, den niemand lesen würde. Er würde unendlich viel bitteres gasiges Sodawasser trinken, und am Abend würde er den fauligen Geschmack des Wassers mit Rum vermischen. Er würde die Übersetzung des »Beau navire« vollenden, er würde in Gewitternächten zu Elke sprechen, vielleicht auch die Briefe an den Abgeordneten beantworten, was keinem mehr nützte, und eines Tages würde er sterben — auf dem Regierungsgebäude von Guatemala und vor den spanischen Veranden der anderen diplomatischen Vertretungen wird man halbstock flaggen. *Exzellenz Keetenheuve der Deutsche Gesandte sanft entschlafen*

Frost-Forestier drängte. Seine Sekretärinnen riefen ihn, seine Telephonapparate, seine Magnetophone. Keetenheuve schwieg. War der Speck nicht fett genug? Scheute die Maus noch die Falle? Frost-Forestier erwähnte, daß Keetenheuve als Gesandter in den diplomatischen Dienst übernommen war. Was für Aussichten! Wenn Keetenheuves Partei bei den Wahlen siegte, war Keetenheuve Außenminister. »Und wenn die Regierung wieder wechselt, werden Sie unser Botschafter

in Moskau!« Frost-Forestier glaubte nicht an den Wahlsieg
der Opposition.

Keetenheuve sagte:»Ich wäre Persona ingrata.«
Frost-Forestier lächelte schmalmündig:»Vielleicht arbeitet
die Zeit für Sie.« Spürte er's wieder im Urin? Kamen sie
noch zusammen?

Er ging zurück in seine Kaserne, zurück zu den zwitschern-
den Mündern seiner Sekretärinnen, zu den summenden Dräh-
ten, zur geheimnisvollen drahtlosen Verständigung aus der
Luft. Keetenheuve ließ sich nach Godesberg fahren, in die
Stadt der, wie die Sage ging, fünfzig pensionierten Oberbürgermeister, die alle nun einem großen Vorbild nachstreb-
ten und wie Morgensterns Polyp erkannt hatten, wozu sie in
die Welt gesetzt, zur Staatsführung natürlich, und sie übten
sie am Familientisch. Über den Napfkuchen stülpte sich
schon unsichtbar der Ehrendoktorhut. Wenn er nach Guatemala ging, würde man Keetenheuve wohl einen schwarzen
Regierungswagen mit auf die Reise geben, vielleicht sogar
das neue Modell, bei dem die Repräsentation ganz über die
Sparsamkeit gesiegt hatte. Keetenheuve strebte Godesberg
zu, weil er nach dem salzigen Hering und der wenn auch
inoffiziellen Ernennung zur Exzellenz nach Diplomatenart
speisen wollte, und wo konnte man das besser als auf der
berühmten Rheinterrasse der großen diplomatischen Blama-
ge? Er war allein in der Halle, allein auf dem Teppich, der
Teppich war neu; vielleicht hatte der Führer den alten Perser
zum Frühstück verspeist, weil Chamberlain und die Herren
vom Foreign Office sich verspätet hatten und seine Neur-
asthenie das Warten nicht vertrug. Jetzt mochten sich Manager hier erholen. Der Führer war eine Fehlinvestition gewesen, oder war er es nicht gewesen? Ein Dilettant soll nicht
urteilen. Vielleicht hatte sich der Retter rentiert. Wieviel Millionen Tote? Die Essen rauchen. Die Kohle wird gefördert.
Die Erzöfen brennen. Weiß glüht der Stahl. Auch Keetenheuve sah wie ein Manager aus. Er hatte seine Aktenmappe
bei sich; die gewichtige Aktenmappe des Abgeordneten. Gedichte von Cummings, Verlaine, Baudelaire, Rimbaud, Apol-
linaire — er trug sie im Kopf. *Keetenheuve Manager, Keeten-*

heuve Exzellenz, Keetenheuve Sir, Keetenheuve Verräter, Keetenheuve der Mann, der das Gute will. Er ging auf die Terrasse. Er setzte sich an den Rhein. Vier Kellner beobachteten
ihn. Dunst. Gewitterdunst. Treibhausluft. Sonnenglast. Die
Fenster des Treibhauses waren schlecht geputzt; die Lüftung
funktionierte nicht. Er saß in einem Vakuum, dunstumgeben,
himmelüberwölbt. Eine Unterdruckkammer für das Herz.
Vier Kellner näherten sich leise; Todesboten, feierlich in Fräk-
ken, eine erste Aufwartung, eine Offerte? »Einen Kognak,
bitte.« Ein Kognak regt an. »Einen Kognak Monnet!« Was
treibt auf dem Rhein? Stahl, Kohle? Die Flaggen der Nationen über schwarzen Kähnen. Tief in den Strom gesargt, im
Bett neuer Sagen schwimmend, sagenhafte Bilanzen, die
Volksmärchen der Abschreibungen, die Substanz unangeta-
stet, Umstellung eins zu eins, immer davongekommen, das
Erz, die Kohle, von Hütte zu Hütte, vom Ruhrrevier nach
Lothringen, von Lothringen zurück ins Revier, Ihr Europa,
meine Herren *Besuchen Sie die Kunstschätze der Villa Hügel,* und die Hosen der Rheinschifferfrau, Hosen von Woolworth aus Rotterdam, Hosen von Woolworth aus Düsseldorf,
Hosen von Woolworth aus Basel, Hosen von Woolworth aus
Straßburg, die Hosen hängen an der Leine über dem Deck,
baumeln im Westwind, die mächtigste Flagge der Erde, rosa
rosenrot über den tückischen Kohlen. Ein kleiner Spitz, weiß
und energisch, ein kleiner Spitz, sehr von sich eingenommen,
wedelt deckauf und deckab. Drüben am anderen Ufer gähnt
die Siesta der pensionierten Rosendörfer.
Er bestellte Salm, einen Salm aus dem Rhein, und gleich bereute er's, im Geiste sah er die Kellner springen, die feierlichen
befrackten Empfangsherren des Todes, albern übereifrig wie
tolpatschige Kinder, albern überwürdig wie tolpatschige Greise torkelten sie zum Ufer, stolperten über Stock und Stein
der Flußlände, hielten Käscher in den Strom, deuteten zu
Keetenheuve zur Terrasse hinauf, nickten ihm zu, wähnten
sich seines Einverständnisses sicher, fingen den Fisch, reckten
ihn hoch, den schönen, den goldschuppenen Salm in glän-
zender Rüstung, wie Gold und Silber schwuppte er ins Netz,
von Lemuren aus seinem starken Element gerissen, aus sei-

ner guten Welt des murmelnden, Geschichten erzählenden Wassers — o das Ertrinken in Licht und Luft, und wie hart blitzt in der Sonne das Messer! Keetenheuve wurde der Salm geopfert. *Keetenheuve Gott dem sanfte Fische geopfert werden.* Er hatte es wieder nicht gewollt. Versuchung! Versuchung! Was tat der Anachoret? Er mordete die Heuschrecken. Der Fisch war tot. Der Wein war mäßig. Exzellenz Keetenheuve aß sein Diplomatenmahl mit gemäßigtem Appetit.

Er führte diplomatische Gespräche. Wer waren seine Gäste? Herr Hitler, Führer, Herr Stendhal, Konsul. Wer servierte? Herr Chamberlain, Ehrenwert.

Hitler: Diese Luft ist eine milde; die Rheinlandschaft ist eine historische; diese Terrasse ist eine anregende. Schon vor neunzehn Jahren —

Stendhal: Meine Bewunderung und meine Verehrung! O jung zu sein, als Sie von dieser Terrasse nach Wiessee aufbrachen, um Ihre Freunde zu killen! Wie bewegt mich das Schicksal der Jünglinge. Wie erregen mich die Romane unter Ihrer Ägide. Als Intendanturrat wäre ich Ihrem Heerbann gefolgt. Ich hätte Mailand wiedergesehen, Warschau und die Beresina. Mit Mann und Roß und Wagen hat sie der Herr geschlagen. Sie zitierten das Gedicht nach Ihrem Sieg über Polen. Sie sprachen im Reichstag. Sie belehnten Ihre Heerführer mit Marschallstäben und mit Liegenschaften in Westpreußen. Ein paar ließen Sie hängen. Andere erschossen sich gehorsam. Einem schickten Sie Gift. Und all Ihre strahlenden Jünglinge, Ihre Helden der Luft, Ihre Helden der See, Ihre Helden im Panzer, und Ihre Knaben in Berlin, Herr Hitler! Was machen Ihre Literaten, Herr Keetenheuve? Sie übertragen Baudelaire. Wie schön, wie tapfer! Aber Narvik, die Cyrenaika, der Atlantik, die Wolga, alle Richtstätten, die Gefangenenlager im Kaukasus und die Gefangenenlager in Iowa. Wer schreibt das? Die Wahrheit interessiert, nichts als die Wahrheit —

Keetenheuve: Es gibt hier überhaupt keine Wahrheit. Nur Knäuel von Lügen.

Stendhal: Sie sind ein impotenter Gnostiker, Herr Abgeordneter.

Die Lügenknäuel formieren sich in der Luft über dem Rhein zu einem Ballett und zeigen schmutzige Reizwäsche.

Hitler: Jahre kämpfte ich in meinen Tischgesprächen für das Germanisch-Historische Institut der Vereinigten Illustrierten Zeitschriften für eine Säuberung der deutschen Kultur von erstens jüdischen, zweitens christlichen, drittens moralisch sentimentalischen und viertens kosmopolitisch international pazifistisch blutrünstigen Einflüssen, und ich kann Ihnen heute versichern, daß mein Sieg ein globaler ist.

Über den Rhein rollen sechs Erdkugeln. Sie sind bewimpelt und bewaffnet. Lautsprecher brüllen: Die Fahne hoch! Chamberlain zittern die Hände. Er schüttet die zerlassene Butter auf das Tischtuch und sagt: Peace in our time.

Aus dem Wasser hebt sich der Leichnam der Tschechoslowakei und stinkt. Die Vorsehung ist im Bauch des Leichnams gefangen und wandert ratlos auf und ab. Drei Lautsprecher kämpfen gegeneinander. Der eine schreit: Planmäßig! Der andere brüllt: Plansoll! Der dritte singt den Chor aus der Dreigroschenoper: Ja, mach nur einen Plan. Lautsprecher eins und Lautsprecher zwei fallen wütend über Lautsprecher drei her und verprügeln ihn.

Senator McCarthy schickt zwei Lügendetektoren herüber, um den Fall zu untersuchen.

Der erste Lügendetektor wendet sich an Hitler: Herr Hitler, haben Sie jemals der Kommunistischen Partei angehört?

Hitler: Als unbekannter Gefreiter entschloß ich mich, Politiker zu werden und den bolschewistischen Untermenschen, der nie wieder, das können Sie mir glauben, sein Haupt erheben wird . . .

Der Zeiger des Lügendetektors wedelt freundlich.

Hitler aber sieht ihn an, unterbricht sich und schreit aufgebracht: Zeigen Sie mir mal Ihren arischen Nachweis!

Der erste Lügendetektor ist sehr verwirrt. Eine Sicherung brennt in ihm durch, und er muß sich verstört zurückziehen.

Der zweite Lügendetektor wendet sich an Keetenheuve: Waren Sie Mitglied der Kommunistischen Partei?

Keetenheuve: Nein. Niemals.

Der zweite Lügendetektor: Haben Sie am neunten August

neunzehnhundertachtundzwanzig aus der Berliner Staatsbibliothek »Das Kapital« von Karl Marx entliehen und haben Sie am Abend zu Ihrer damaligen Freundin Sonja Busen geäußert, sie solle ihr Hemd anbehalten, es sei nun wichtiger, »Das Kapital« zu studieren?

Keetenheuve erschrickt und schämt sich. Der Zeiger des Lügendetektors schlägt heftig nach links. Aus dem Rhein heben sich die Rheintöchter. Sie tragen die horizontblauen, erotisierenden Uniformen der Luftstewardessen und singen: Wagalaweia, du kommst nicht nach Amerika, wagalaweia, du bleibst da.

Keetenheuve ist zerknirscht.

Stendhal versucht, Keetenheuve zu trösten: Guatemala ist auch nicht langweiliger als Civitavecchia, wo ich Konsul war. Fahren Sie nicht in Urlaub. Da trifft Sie der Schlag.

Keetenheuve sieht Chamberlain vorwurfsvoll an und sagt: Aber Beck und Halder wollten doch putschen! Bedenken Sie, Beck und Halder wollten ihm an die Kehle!

Hitler schlägt sich belustigt aufs Knie und lacht mit nachtwandlerischer Sicherheit.

Chamberlain blickt furchtbar traurig auf die Reste des Fisches, die er abräumt. Er flüstert: Ein General, der putschen will, ist kein Partner für das Vereinigte Königreich; der General, der erfolgreich geputscht hat, mag am Hof von St. James aufwarten.

Er mußte gehen. Es war Zeit. Die vier Kellner umstanden ihn. Bald würden sie wieder Generalen servieren. Es war wohl unvermeidlich. Die Rosendörfer am anderen Ufer erwachten aus ihrer Siesta. Man rüstete den Kaffeetisch. Auch an ihn würden Generale geladen werden. Die Rosendörfer wollten ihre Generale wiederhaben. Sie fühlten sich wie Rosenblätter auf einem schwarzen Tümpel. Was konnte nicht alles aus der Tiefe heraufsteigen? Kröten, Algen, getötete Frühgeburten. Vielleicht sprang eine Kröte aufs Rosenblatt, hüpfte an den Tisch und sagte: »Ich übernehme den Haushalt.« Da war es gut, wenn ein General seinen Säbel hatte. Die Kellner verneigten sich. Er gab immer zu hohe Trinkgelder, und es war gut, daß er zu hohe Trinkgelder gab, denn so entließen ihn die Empfangsherren des Todes für diesmal noch gnädig.

Frost-Forestiers schwarzer Regierungswagen hatte auf Keetenheuve gewartet. Frost-Forestier wollte Keetenheuve weiter an die Annehmlichkeiten gewöhnen, die der Bund und das Leben den hohen Beamten und den Gesandten gewähren. Als er in den Wagen stieg, sah Keetenheuve das Haus der französischen Hohen Kommission, und auf dem Dach des Hauses wehte die Trikolore. »Le jour de gloire est arrivé!« War er da, der Tag des Ruhmes? War er immer wieder da? Seit hundertfünfzig Jahren ein Tag des Ruhmes nach dem andern? Es war noch nicht lange her und schien doch vor so langer Zeit gewesen zu sein. Es war noch nicht lange her, und die Trikolore wehte in Amerika, man errichtete der Freiheit eine Statue »qu'un sang impur abreuve nos sillons«. Seit einhalb Jahrhunderten schrien die Nationen nach unreinem Blut, tränkten sie die Furchen. Sie konnten gar nicht genug unreines Blut auftreiben, um den ungeheuren Bedarf zu decken: deutsches, russisches, englisches, französisches, italienisches, spanisches, amerikanisches Blut, Blut vom Balkan und Blut aus Asien, Negerblut, Judenblut, Faschistenblut, Kommunistenblut, ein entsetzlicher Blutsee, der Zufluß versiegte nicht, so viele Menschenfreunde hatten an den Blutkanälen gebaut, so viele, die das Gute wollten, die Enzyklopädisten, die Romantiker, die Hegelianer, die Marxisten und all die Nationalisten. Keetenheuve sah die Bäume rot mit rotem Laub, er sah die Erde, den Himmel rot, und der Gott der Philosophen betrachtete sein Werk und sah, daß es nicht gut war. Da rief er die Physiker auf den Plan, sie dachten in Wellen und Korpuskeln, es gelang ihnen, das Atom zu spalten, und sie töteten in Hiroshima.

Kinder begegneten seinem Auto. Französische Kinder, deutsche Kinder, amerikanische Kinder. Die Kinder gingen oder spielten nach den Nationen geschieden. Die Gruppen sprachen kein Wort miteinander. Keetenheuve fuhr durch das amerikanische Dorf. Es war ein amerikanisches Dorf am Rhein. Eine kleine amerikanische Kirche war so gebaut, wie sie amerikanische Siedler der Pionierzeit am Rande der Prärie bauten, nachdem sie die Indianer getötet oder vertrieben hatten. In der Kirche wurde zu einem Gott gebetet, der die Erfolgreichen liebte. Der amerikanische Gott hätte Keetenheuve nicht geliebt. Er war nicht erfolgreich und hatte nie eine Prärie erobert.

Sie kamen nach Mehlem, erreichten das Haus des amerikanischen Hohen Kommissars, und Keetenheuve stieg aus dem Wagen. Das amerikanische Kommissariat war ein Pfahlbau im Wald, eine nüchterne Konstruktion aus Beton, Stahl und Glas und doch, wie es da stand, ein romantisches Schloß aus dem deutschen Märchen, ein Wolkenkratzer, vom Broadway hierherverschlagen und auf Betonklötze gesetzt, als fürchte er, der Rhein werde aus seinem Bett steigen, ihn zu verschlingen, und die vielen Automobile, die unter dem Haus zwischen den Betonpfählen parkten, wirkten wie zu eiliger Abfahrt bereitgehaltene Rettungsboote. Obwohl es Tag war, brannten im ganzen großen Gebäude Tausende von Leuchtröhren, und sie erhöhten den unwirklichen, den magischen Eindruck, den der Pfahlbau im Wald machte. Das Kommissariat war wie der Palast eines mächtigen Zauberers, und es war auch wie ein ungeheurer Bienenkorb, in dem die neonerleuchteten Fenster wie aneinandergeschichtete Waben wirkten. Keetenheuve hörte das Haus summen. Die Bienen waren emsig. Keetenheuve ging mutig in das Zauberreich, stürzte sich tapfer in den magischen Schein. Er zeigte einer Wache einen Ausweis, und die Wache ließ ihn passieren. Aufzüge stiegen und fielen durch das Gebäude wie der Blutkreislauf eines Lebewesens. Herren und Damen ließen sich geschäftig mit kleinen Akten in der Hand hinauf- und herunterpumpen, Bakterien, die diesem Körper zu eigen waren, ihn am Leben erhielten, ihn kräftigten und schwächten. Vielleicht hätte ein Mikroskop verraten, ob sie aufbauende oder abbauende Teile waren. Auch Keetenheuve stieg in einen der Aufzüge und fuhr himmelwärts. Er stieg in einem Mittelgeschoß aus dem Fahrstuhl und ging einen langen neonerleuchteten Gang entlang. Der Gang war geisterhaft, unwirklich und angenehm, und die gekühlte Luft aus einer Klimaanlage berieselte ihn freundlich. Er klopfte an eine

Tür und trat in ein neonzwielichtiges Zimmer. Das Zimmer war wie ein künstlich erhelltes Aquarium bei Sonnenschein, und Keetenheuve entsann sich, daß er selber gern in einem ähnlich zwielichtig erleuchteten Aquarium arbeitete. Was waren sie doch für gezüchtete, in Aquarien und Treibhäuser gesetzte Wesen! Hier traf er zwei deutsche Sekretärinnen. Er fragte nach einem Amerikaner, und eine Sekretärin sagte, daß der Amerikaner irgendwo im Haus sei, aber sie wisse nicht, wo er sei. Es habe auch keinen Zweck, den Amerikaner zu suchen, sagte die andere Sekretärin; man würde den Amerikaner nicht finden, und dann sei die Sache, für die Keetenheuve sich einsetze, auch noch nicht entschieden, sie werde gerade von anderen Amerikanern, höheren als dem Chef dieses kleinen Aquariums, geprüft. Keetenheuve bedankte sich für die Auskunft. Er trat wieder in das unzwielichtige, das reine Neonlicht des Ganges hinaus, und die Sinnlosigkeit seines Tuns war ihm klar. Trüber Fleck auf dieser schönen klaren Sinnlosigkeit waren irgendwo Menschen, die auf die Entscheidung des Falles warteten. Keetenheuve erreichte einen Fahrstuhl. Er fuhr weiter himmelwärts. Er kam in eine Dachkantine, von der man weit über den Rhein blicken konnte, und zugleich betrat er ein Kellercafé im verzweifeltsten Paris. Die in den Gängen und den Fahrstühlen so geschäftigen Damen und Herren verweilten hier bei Kaffee, Zigaretten und Problemen — sie kratzten an der Existenz. Existierten sie? Sie schienen es zu meinen, weil sie Kaffee tranken, rauchten und sich gedanklich oder tatsächlich aneinander rieben. Sie dachten über ihre Existenz und ihre Existenz im Verhältnis zu allen anderen Existenzen nach, sie betrachteten die Existenz des Hauses, die Existenz des Hohen Kommissariats, die Existenz des Rheines, die Existenz dieses Deutschlands, die Existenz der anderen Rheinstaaten und die Existenz Europas, und in all diesen Existenzen bohrte der Wurm, war Zweifel, Unwirklichkeit und Ekel. *Und Thor drohte mit dem Riesenhammer!* »Amerika ist das vielleicht letzte Experiment und zugleich die größte Chance der Menschheit, um ihre Sendung zu erfüllen«, Keetenheuve hatte das Wort in der Keyserling-Gesellschaft gehört, und er

296

dachte darüber nach. Er wäre gern nach Amerika gereist. Er hätte gern das neue Rom gesehen. Wie war Amerika? Groß? Frei? Sicher war es anders, als man es sich am Rhein vorstellen konnte. Dies Haus war nicht Amerika. Es war ein vorgeschobenes Büro, ein Außenposten, vielleicht ein besonderes Experiment in einem besonderen Vakuum. »Amerika ist nicht, es wird«, das hatte der Redner gesagt. Keetenheuve war sehr für neues Werden; er hatte bisher nur Untergänge gesehen. Die Mädchen im Dachcafé hatten dünne Nylonstrümpfe an, die sich, von ihrem Fleisch durchatmet, wie eine zweite, geile Haut das Bein hochzogen und lockend unter dem Rock verschwanden. Die Männer trugen Knöchelsocken, und wenn sie die Beine übereinanderschlugen, sah man ihre behaarten Waden. Sie arbeiteten miteinander, die geschäftigen Herren und Damen, schliefen sie auch zusammen? Keetenheuve sah, während Thor donnerte, ein düsteres Bacchanal der Vermischung in diesem Saal, und geschäftig, wie mit den Akten in den Fahrkörben und Gängen, waren sie nun in einer allseitigen Geschlechtlichkeit, von der Keetenheuve ausgeschlossen blieb wie überhaupt von ihrer Betriebsamkeit, er neidete sie ihnen einen Augenblick lang, und doch wußte er, daß es nicht Liebe und Leidenschaft war, was sie bewegte, sondern nur die hoffnungslose Befriedigung eines immer wiederkehrenden Juckreizes. Er trank seinen Kaffee im Stehen, und er beobachtete die hübschen nettbestrumpften Mädchen, und er beobachtete die jungen Männer in kurzen Socken, die wie unzufriedene Engel aussahen, und dann erkannte er, daß ihre schönen Gesichter gezeichnet waren, gezeichnet von Leere, gezeichnet von bloßem Dasein. *Es war nicht genug*

IV

Keetenheuve hatte sich verspätet, der Diplomat hatte gespeist, der Träumer war herumgeirrt, und die Mitglieder des Ausschusses guckten ihn nun vorwurfsvoll an. Die Fraktionskollegen Heineweg und Bierbohm blickten mit dem Ausdruck der Strenge und der Mißbilligung auf den Eintretenden. Ihre Mienen sagten, daß Keetenheuve in diesem Gremium, in dem er noch keine Stunde versäumt hatte, in diesem Beratungszimmer, in dem er fleißig und produktiv gewesen war, ihre Partei nun in nicht wiedergutzumachender Weiße bloßgestellt und geschädigt habe.

Auch Korodin schaute Keetenheuve an, aber es war weniger Vorwurf als Erwartung in seinem Blick. Aufs neue überlegte Korodin, ob Keetenheuve sich vielleicht gewandelt, ob er vielleicht in einer Kirche, Gott um Erleuchtung bittend, die Zeit verloren habe und nun vor sie hintreten und bekennen würde: Der Herr hat sich mir offenbart, ich bin ein anderer. Korodin hätte ein Gespräch mit Gott als Begründung der Verspätung anerkannt und Keetenheuve verziehen. Aber Keetenheuve sprach von keiner Erleuchtung, er murmelte nur eine unverständlich unverbindliche Entschuldigung und setzte sich auf seinen Platz. Er setzte sich aber (nur sie merkten es nicht) beschämt auf seinen Platz, beschämt wie ein schlechter Schüler, dem keine Entschuldigung für seine Faulheit einfallen will. Er hatte sich heute treiben lassen. Wie ein altes Boot, das seinen Halt verloren hat, war er auf des Tages unsteten Strömungen dahingeglitten. Er dachte nach. Er mußte auf sich achten. Was war sein Halt gewesen, den er verloren hatte? Er hatte Elke verloren, die Gauleiterstochter, die Waise des Krieges, und er dachte an sie jetzt nicht wie an eine Frau, er sah sie wie ein Kind, das ihm anvertraut war und das er nicht gehütet hatte. Das Kind oder die Bande der zärtlichen Empfindung waren sein Halt gewesen, ein fester Punkt in der zerfließenden Flut, der Anker seines Bootes auf der, wie sich nun zeigte, öde gewordenen See des Lebens, und der Anker war hinabgesunken, er hatte sich vom

Boot getrennt, die Kette war gerissen, der Anker blieb für
immer unten, blieb in der grausigen, der unbekannten, der
entsetzlichen dunklen Tiefe. Armer kleiner Anker! Er hatte
ihn schlecht geputzt. Er hatte ihn rosten lassen. Was war aus
Elke an seiner Seite geworden? Eine Trinkerin. Wohin war
sie betrunken gefallen? In die Arme der Lesbierinnen, in die
Arme der durch und durch Verdammten der Liebe. Er hatte
Elke nicht gehütet. Er begriff es nicht. Er hatte Ausschüsse
besucht, er hatte hunderttausend Briefe geschrieben, er hatte
im Parlament gesprochen, er hatte Gesetze redigiert, er begriff es nicht, er hätte bei Elke bleiben können, an der Seite
der Jugend, und vielleicht wäre es, wenn er nicht alles falsch
gemacht hätte, die Seite des Lebens gewesen. Ein Mensch
genügte, dem Leben Sinn zu geben. Die Arbeit genügte
nicht. Die Politik genügte nicht. Sie schützten ihn nicht vor
der ungeheuren Öde des Daseins. Die Öde war sanft. Die
Öde tat ihm nichts. Sie griff nicht nach dem Abgeordneten
mit langen Gespensterarmen. Sie würgte ihn nicht. Sie war
nur da. Sie blieb nur. Die Öde hatte sich ihm gezeigt, sie
hatte sich mit ihm bekannt gemacht, und nun waren ihm die
Augen geöffnet, nun sah er sie, überall, und nie wieder würde die Öde verschwinden, nie wieder würde sie seinen Augen
unsichtbar werden. Wer war sie? Wie sah sie aus? Sie war
das Nichts, und sie hatte kein Aussehen. Sie sah wie alle
Dinge aus. Sie sah wie der Ausschuß aus, wie das Parlament,
wie die Stadt, wie der Rhein, wie das Land, alles war die
Öde, war das Nichts in einer schrecklichen Unendlichkeit, die
unzerstörbar war, denn selbst der Untergang berührte das
Nichts nicht. Das Nichts war die wirkliche Ewigkeit. Und
Keetenheuve empfand zugleich sehr deutlich sein Sein, er war
da, er war etwas, er wußte es, er war vom Nichts umlagert
und durchdrungen, und doch war er ein Teil für sich, ein Ich,
allein und einsam gegen die Öde gestellt, und hierin war ein
wenig Hoffnung, eine winzige Chance für David gegen Go-
liath — aber David war nicht traurig. Keetenheuve war von
Traurigkeit erfüllt. Korodin hätte ihm sagen können, daß
die Traurigkeit eine Todsünde sei. Aber was hätte es Keeten-

heuve geholfen, das zu wissen? Und überdies wußte er es ja. Er war nicht dümmer als Korodin.

Keetenheuve verstand die Ausschußsprache nicht mehr. Was redeten sie? Chinesisch? Sie sprachen das Ausschußdeutsch. Er beherrschte es doch! Er mußte es wieder verstehen. Er schwitzte. Er schwitzte vor Anstrengung, die Beratung zu verstehen; aber die anderen schwitzten auch. Sie wischten den Schweiß mit Taschentüchern auf; sie wischten sich über das Gesicht, sie wischten über die blanken Glatzen, sie wischten den Nacken, steckten das Taschentuch hinter den aufgeweichten Hemdkragen. Es roch im Zimmer nach Schweiß und nach Lavendel, und Keetenheuve roch wie sie: immer verweste etwas, und immer wieder versuchte man, mit Duftwasser den Geruch der Verwesung zu verstecken.

Jetzt sah er die Mitglieder des Ausschusses wie Spieler an einer Roulettetafel sitzen. Ach, wie vergebens ihr Hoffen, die Kugel sprang, das Glück enteilte! Heineweg und Bierbohm sahen wie kleine Spieler aus, die mit geringem Einsatz, ein jeder nach seinem System, vom Glück das Tagegeld erpressen wollten. Dabei ging das Spiel um Menschen, um große Summen und um die Zukunft. Es war ein wichtiger Ausschuß, er hatte wichtige Fragen zu beraten, er sollte den Menschen Häuser bauen. Aber wie kompliziert war das schon! Durch gefährliche Strudel mußte jeder Vorschlag gelenkt werden, brachte man ihn gar als Antrag zu Papier, leicht scheiterte das Papierschifflein, strandete an einem der tausend Riffe, wurde leck und sank. Ministerien und andere Ausschüsse mischten sich ein, Fragen des Lastenausgleichs, des Kapitalmarkts, des Steuerrechts wurden berührt, die Zinspolitik war zu bedenken, die Eingliederung der Vertriebenen, die Entschädigung der Ausgebombten, das Recht der Besitzenden, die Versorgung der Verstümmelten, man konnte am Ländergesetz und am Städterecht anecken, und wie sollte man den Armen etwas geben, wenn niemand etwas hergeben wollte, wie durfte man enteignen, wenn das Grundgesetz das Eigentum bejahte, und wenn man sich dennoch entschloß, in bestimmten Fällen behutsam zu enteignen, so war wieder neuem Unrecht die Möglichkeit gegeben zu sein; ge-

riet ein Ungeschickter in den Verhau der Paragraphen, war
vielem Mißbrauch das Tor geöffnet. Keetenheuve vernahm
Zahlen. Sie waren wie das Rauschen einer Wasserleitung
vor seinem Ohr, eindrucksvoll und doch nichtssagend. Sechs-
hundertfünfzig Millionen aus öffentlichen Mitteln. So viel
aus zentralem Aufkommen. Sondermittel für Versuche; das
waren nur fünfzehn Millionen. Aber dann gab es noch den
Einlauf aus den Umstellungsgrundschulden. Korodin las die
Zahlen vor, und zuweilen guckte er Keetenheuve an, als erwarte er von ihm einen Einspruch oder eine Zustimmung.
Keetenheuve schwieg. Er konnte sich auf einmal zu Korodins
Zahlen sowenig äußern wie der Zuschauer einer Zaubervor-
stellung zu den rätselvollen und eigentlich langweiligen Vor-
gängen auf der Bühne; er weiß, daß ein Trick angewandt
und er getäuscht wird. Keetenheuve war von der Nation in
diesen Ausschuß gesetzt, um aufzupassen, daß niemand hin-
tergangen werde. Dennoch — für ihn war die Beratung jetzt
nur noch ein verblüffender Zahlenzauber! Niemand würde
die Millionen sehen, von denen Korodin sprach. Niemand
hatte sie jemals gesehen. Selbst Korodin, der den Zahlenspuk
vorführte, hatte die Millionen nicht gesehen. Sie standen auf
dem Papier, wurden auf dem Papier weitergereicht, und nur
auf dem Papier wurden sie verteilt. Sie liefen durch unendlich viele Rechenmaschinen. Sie hetzten durch die Rechenmaschinen der Ministerien, der Rechnungshöfe, der Ober-
ämter und der Nebenstellen, sie erschienen in den Konto-
rahmen der Banken, tauchten in den Bilanzen auf, vermin-
derten sich, zerrannen, aber sie blieben Papier, eine Ziffer auf
Papier, bis sie sich endlich irgendwann materialisierten und
vierzig Mark in einer Lohntüte wurden und fünfzig gestoh-
lene Pfennige für ein Indianerbuch in einer Knabenhand.
So recht begriff es keiner. Selbst Stierides, der Bankier der
Reichsten, begriff das magische Spiel der Zahlen nicht; aber
er war Meister in einem Yoga, das seine Konten wachsen
ließ. Keetenheuve wollte sich zu Wort melden. Konnte man
nicht etwas tun? Konnte man nicht die doppelte Größe durch
die Rechenmaschinen laufen lassen, einen zweimal so großen
Betrag als den vorgeschlagenen, und würden dann nicht auf

einmal achtzig statt vierzig Mark in der Lohntüte liegen? Aber Keetenheuve wagte es nicht, so zu reden. Wieder blickte ihn Korodin erwartungsvoll, ja aufmunternd an, aber Keetenheuve wich seinem Blick aus. Er fürchtete sich vor seinen Fraktionsgenossen, er fürchtete Heineweg und Bierbohm, ihre Verwunderung und ihre Entrüstung. Keetenheuve sah Straßenbahnen über den Beratungstisch fahren, und die Straßenbahnen klingelten: Auch wir verdoppeln, wir verdoppeln unsern Tarif; und er sah die Bäcker demonstrieren: Doppelter Preis für das Brot; und er sah die Gemüsehändler die Preisschilder ändern für Kraut und Rüben. Die Verdoppelung der Papierzahlen nützte nichts. Die Lohntüte blieb immer schwach gefüllt. Das war ein ökonomisches Gesetz oder das eine Gesicht der Relativität. Keetenheuve hätte so gern mehr in die Lohntüte hineingetan; aber auch er sah nicht, wie es zu machen sei, und ihn schwindelte. Den ganzen Tag schon hatte er unter Schwindelanfällen gelitten.

Sie sprachen von Bergarbeiterwohnungen auf neuem Siedlungsland bei den Halden, und ein Sachverständiger hatte die Quadratmeter errechnet, die jedem Siedler zugebilligt werden sollten, und ein anderer Sachverständiger hatte sich ausgedacht, wie primitiv und wie billig man die Mauern ziehen könne. Korodin gehörten Anteile an den Gruben. Die Arbeiter förderten die Kohle zutage, und auf geheimnisvolle Weise verwandelte ihre Anstrengung Korodins Bankkonto. Die Arbeiter fuhren in den Schacht, und Korodin las seinen neuen Saldo. Die Arbeiter gingen müde heim. Sie gingen durch die Vorstadt, gingen vorbei an den Halden, die immer noch wuchsen wie die Gebirge in der Urzeit, schwarze Tafelberge, die das Gesicht der Landschaft veränderten und auf deren staubigen Kuppen schmutzige Kinder Mörder und Detektiv, Winnetou und Old Shatterhand spielten. So sah Keetenheuve den Bergmann das Siedlungshaus erreichen, das sie im Ausschuß berieten, das sie durchrechneten, das sie Gesetz werden ließen und für das sie die Mittel, die stolzen **Ziffern** auf dem Papier bewilligten. Der Bergmann betrat die von den Sachverständigen geforderten Mindestquadratmeter. Er teilte sie mit seiner Frau und seinen Kindern und mit Verwandten, die das Schicksal, Unglück und Arbeitslosigkeit plötzlich zu ihm getrieben hatten, und mit Schlafgängern, deren Geld er brauchte, um die Raten für die abscheulichen, die unpraktischen, die viel zu großen und zu großspurigen Möbel zu zahlen, für das Schlafzimmer »Erika«, das Wohnzimmer »Adolf«, diese Schreckenskammern und Hausfrauenträume in den Schaufenstern der Abzahlungsgeschäfte. Der Bergmann war zu Hause. Da summte es und sprach es, schrie, knarrte und quakte es aus Mündern und Lautsprechern, drang als Geschrei, Gekeif, Fluch, Klatsch und Gebuller, drang als Iphigenie auf Tauris und Totoansage durch des Sachverständigen Billigstmauern, und der Bergmann denkt zurück an die Grube, denkt sich zurück in den tiefen Schacht, denkt: Vor Ort, wenn die Preßluftbohrer surren, wenn das Gestein knirscht und bricht, ist es in dem Geratter still. Und viele zogen willig in den Krieg, weil sie ihren Alltag haßten, weil sie das häßliche enge Leben nicht mehr ertragen konnten, weil der Krieg mit seinen Schrecken auch Flucht und Befreiung war, die Möglichkeit des Reisens, die Möglichkeit des Sich-Entziehens, die Möglichkeit, in Rothschilds Villa zu wohnen. Überdruß erfüllte sie, ein verschwiegener Überdruß, der manchmal als Totschlag in Erscheinung trat, als Freitod, als scheinbar unbegreifliches Familiendrama, und doch war es nur der Überdruß am Lärm der Siedlungen, der Unmut über so viel Nähe, der Ekel vor den Gerüchen des Essens und der Verdauung, vor den Ausdünstungen der vielgetragenen Kleider und der eingelaugten Wäsche im Zuber, dem Bergmann wurde übel vor dem Schweiß der Frau (er liebte sie), vor den Ausscheidungen der Kinder (er liebte sie) und wie ein Orkan umdröhnte ihn das unaufhörliche Gequatsch ihrer Lippen.

Heineweg und Bierbohm waren's zufrieden. Sie stimmten den Vorschlägen der Sachverständigen bei; sie bewilligten die Mindestkosten, die Mindestquadratmeter, die Mindestwohnung. Die Wohnung würde gebaut werden. Heineweg und Bierbohm waren für das Schrebergartenglück. Sie sahen kleine Giebelhäuser entstehen und hielten sie für gemütlich; sie sahen zufriedene Arbeiter klassenbewußt auf eigener

Scholle säen, und durch das geöffnete Fenster drang aus dem Lautsprecher des Radios eine aufmunternde Rede Knurrewahns. *Unser die Zukunft, unser die Welt.* Und Korodin war's zufrieden. Er stimmte den Vorschlägen der Sachverständigen bei; er bewilligte die Mindestkosten, die Mindestquadratmeter, die Mindestwohnung. Die Wohnung würde gebaut werden. Auch Korodin war für das Schrebergartenglück der Arbeiter, auch ihn erfreuten romantische Giebelhäuser im Grünen; er sah aber die Türen und Fenster an Fronleichnam mit Birken geschmückt, aus dem Lautsprecher drang die Predigt des Bischofs, und zufriedene Arbeiter knieten im Vorgarten, fromm auf eigener Scholle, vor dem Allerheiligsten, das in der Prozession vorübergetragen wurde. *Der Herr ist mein Hirte, mir wird nichts mangeln.* Sie waren für Beschwichtigung. Heineweg, Bierbohm und Korodin, sie waren feindliche Brüder. Sie wußten es nicht, daß sie Brüder im Geiste waren. Sie hielten sich für Feinde. Aber sie waren Brüder. Sie berauschten sich an der gleichen wässerigen Limonade. Was wollte Keetenheuve? Jedes Dach war besser als keins. Er wußte es. Er kannte Barackenlager und Nissenhütten, er kannte Bunkerwohnungen, Trümmerunterkünfte, Notherbergen, er kannte auch die Slums in London und die Kellergelasse im Chinesenviertel des Rotterdamer Hafens, und er wußte, daß die Mindestwohnung, die der Ausschuß bauen wollte, ein Fortschritt gegen dieses Elend war. Aber er mochte die Beschwichtigung nicht. Er sah kein Schrebergartenglück. Er meinte die Situation zu durchschauen: sie barg Gift und Bazillen. Was waren denn diese Siedlungen anders als die nationalsozialistischen Siedlungen der Kinderreichen, als SA- und SS-Siedlungen, nur billiger, nur enger, nur schäbiger, nur dürftiger? Und wenn man die Blaupausen betrachtete, es war der Nazistil, in dem weitergebaut wurde, und wenn man die Namen der Baumeister las, es waren die Nazibaumeister, die weiterbauten, und Heineweg und Bierbohm hießen den braunen Stil gut und fanden die Architekten in Ordnung. Das Programm des nationalsozialistischen Bundes der Kinderreichen war Heinewegs und Bierbohms Programm, es war ihre Bevölkerungsbeschwichtigung, es war ihr sozialer Fortschritt. Was wollte also Keetenheuve? Wollte er die Revolution? Welch großes, welch schönes, welch in Staub gestürztes Wort! Keetenheuve wollte die Revolution nicht, weil er sie gar nicht mehr wollen konnte — es gab sie ja nicht mehr. Die Revolution war tot. Sie war verdorrt. Die Revolution war ein Kind der Romantik, eine Krise der Pubertät. Sie hatte ihre Zeit gehabt. Ihre Möglichkeiten waren nicht genützt worden. Jetzt war sie ein Leichnam, ein trockenes Blatt im Herbarium der Ideen, ein toter Begriff, ein antiquiertes Wort aus dem Brockhaus, ohne Existenz in der täglichen Sprache, und nur ein enthusiastischer Jüngling mochte noch für eine Weile von der Revolution schwärmen, und sie war dann auch nichts als ein Schwarm- und Traumbegriff, eine duftlose Blume — nun ja, die blaue Herbariumsblume der Romantik. Die Zeit des zärtlichen Glaubens an Freiheit, Gleichheit, Brüderlichkeit, sie war vergangen *der Morgen Amerikas Walt Whitmans Gesänge die Kraft und die Genialität und dann war es Onanie die schwächte und zufrieden legte sich der Epigone ins breite Ehebett der gesetzlichen Ordnung den Kalender mit den fruchtbaren und den unfruchtbaren Tagen der Frau auf dem Nachttisch neben dem Gummischutz und der Enzyklika aus Rom.* Korodin hatte über die Revolution gesiegt, und er ahnte, daß er etwas verloren hatte. Heineweg und Bierbohm hatten über die Religion gesiegt, und sie ahnten, daß sie etwas preisgegeben hatten. Gemeinsam hatten sie die Religion und die Revolution entmannt. Der Teufel hatte jede soziale Gemeinschaft geholt und hielt sie fest in seinen Krallen. Es gab wohl noch Putsche, man teilte sie in heiße und kalte wie Punsch, aber der Trank wurde aus immer billigeren Surrogaten gebraut und machte den Völkern nur Kopfweh. Keetenheuve war nicht für Beschwichtigung. Er war dafür, der Gorgo ins Gesicht zu sehen. Er wollte den Blick vor dem Grauen nicht senken. Aber er wollte behaglich wohnen und dem Teufel etwas ablisten. Er war für das Glück in der Verzweiflung. Er war für Glück aus Komfort und Einsamkeit, er war für ein jedermann zugängliches einsames komfortables und verzweifeltes Glück in der nun einmal geschaffenen technischen Welt. Es war nicht nötig, daß man, wenn man traurig war, auch noch fror; es war nicht nötig, daß man, wenn man unglücklich war, auch noch hungerte; es war nicht nötig, daß man durch Schmutz wandelte, während man an das Nichts dachte. Und so wollte Keetenheuve den Arbeitern neue Häuser bauen, Corbusier-Hausungs-Maschinen, Wohnburgen der technischen Zeit, eine ganze Stadt in einem einzigen Riesenhaus mit künstlichen Höhengärten, künstlichem Klima, er sah die Möglichkeit, den Menschen vor Hitze und Kälte zu schützen, ihn von Staub und Schmutz zu befreien, von der Hausarbeit, vom Hauszank und allem Wohnungslärm. Keetenheuve wollte zehntausend unter ein Dach bringen, um sie voneinander zu isolieren, so wie die großen Städte den Menschen aus der Nachbarschaft heben, ihn allein sein lassen, ein einsames Raubtier, ein einsamer Jäger, ein einsames Opfer, so sollte jeder Raum in Keetenheuves Riesenbau gegen jeden anderen schallabgedichtet sein, und jeder sollte sich in seiner Kammer das ihm gemäße Klima einstellen, er konnte allein sein mit seinen Büchern, allein mit seinem Denken, allein mit seiner Arbeit, allein mit seinem Nichtstun, allein mit seiner Liebe, allein mit seiner Verzweiflung und allein in seiner menschlichen Ausdünstung.

Keetenheuve wollte aufstehen. Er wollte zu ihnen sprechen. Er wollte sie überzeugen, und vielleicht wollte er sie nur reizen, denn er glaubte nicht mehr, daß er sie überzeugen konnte. Er wünschte, daß neue Architekten, junge begeisterte Baumeister, neue Pläne zeichneten, eine mächtige Wohnstadt, welche die häßliche Landschaft der Halden, der Auswürfe der Gruben, des Kotes der Industrie, der Schrottplätze, der Abfallager in ein einziges strahlendes lichtfunkelndes Riesenhaus verwandeln sollte, das alle Kleinleutlichkeit der Stadtrandsiedlungen, ihre Enge, ihre Dürftigkeit, ihren lächerlichen Besitzwahn, der gehätschelt wurde zur Beschwichtigung des sozialen Neides, die Versklavung der Frau an die Hausarbeit, die Versklavung des Mannes an die Familie, aufnehmen und aufheben mußte. Er wollte ihnen von seinem Turm berichten und von den tausend ingeniös und komfortabel ausgestatteten Wohnungen der bewußten Einsamkeit, der stolz getragenen Verzweiflung. Keetenheuve wollte das profane Kloster bauen, die Eremitenzellen für den Massenmenschen. Er sah die Menschen, und er sah, daß sie sich an Illusionen festklammerten, an die sie schon lange nicht mehr glaubten. Eine dieser Illusionen war das Familienglück Und dabei grauste es selbst Korodin heimzufahren (von Heineweg und Bierbohm zu schweigen, die Dreizimmerwohnungen hatten, von Hausrat und Menschen vollgestopft), heim in sein großes ererbtes Haus, heim zu den Gesellschaften, den schwachsinnigen und ermüdenden Orgien der Falschheit, die seine Frau, von einem Kobold genarrt, arrangierte und die ihn langweilten, heim zu der Selbstsucht seiner halberwachsenen Kinder, die ihn quälten und entsetzten, die behütet und doch wie Wildlinge aufwuchsen und die mit ihren kalten mitleidlosen Gesichtern ihm entgegentrotzten, ein Antlitz, hinter dem sich Abscheu, Gier und Schmutz verbargen, und wie enttäuschten ihn selbst seine berühmten Bilder, die hochversicherten Holländer, ihre Landschaften mit tumben Stieren auf fetten Weiden, ihre geputzten blinkenden Interieurs, die Winterszenen mit Eislauf, Nebel und überfrorenen Wasserrädern, auch ihn ließen sie frieren, und so trieb er sich lieber in der Politik herum (aus einem guten Glauben, etwas tun zu müssen, denn seine Arbeit hatte man ihm genommen, in den Werken und Fabriken herrschten die Manager, die wußten, wie man die Belegschaft behandelt und wie man Rohlinge walzt, Korodin wußte es nicht) oder saß beunruhigt in Kirchen, besuchte den Bischof, gab sich mit Leuten wie Keetenheuve ab und ging abends gern über Friedhöfe. Sie würden Keetenheuve nicht verstehen. Sie würden seinen Turm für einen Turm zu Babel halten. Er schwieg. Korodin schaute ihn noch einmal auffordernd und über sein Schweigen enttäuscht an, und Heineweg und Bierbohm schauten ihn wieder an, auch sie enttäuscht und vorwurfsvoll, und sie dachten, was aus ihm geworden war, ein Wrack, ein schwer herzkranker Mann, wie schrecklich hatte er sich verändert, es war, als ob die Arbeit im parlamentarischen Kreis seine Kraft erschöpft habe, und sie erinnerten sich des früheren Keetenheuve, der, wie sie, mit ernstem Eifer das

Notwendige getan hatte, der mitgeholfen hatte, die Opfer des grausamen Krieges zu nähren, sie zu kleiden, sie wieder in Häuser zu bringen, ihnen neue Hoffnung zu geben — was half's, und so beschlossen sie, alles Zahlenwerk neuerlich zu prüfen, alle Pläne noch einmal den Sachverständigen vorzulegen, und Heineweg sagte abschließend mit einem milden Blick auf Keetenheuve: »Ich glaube, wir sind heute wieder ein gutes Stück vorangekommen.«

Keetenheuve ging durch die Gänge des Parlaments, er ging über Treppen in sein Büro, und hin und wieder begegneten ihm Aktenträger, die wie Gespenster aussahen. Die Stenotypistinnen hatten das Haus schon verlassen. Nur ein paar Streber schlichen durch das Gebäude. Keetenheuve dachte: das Labyrinth ist leer, der Stier des Minos wandelt verehrt unter dem Volk, und ewig irrt Theseus durch die Gänge. Sein Schreibtisch war, wie er ihn verlassen hatte. Das Blatt des Nachrichtendienstes, das Dana ihm gegeben hatte, lag offen über den Briefen des Abgeordneten, offen über des Abgeordneten Kritzeleien zum »Beau navire« von Baudelaire. Guatemala oder nicht — das war die Frage. Die Interviews der Generale aus dem Conseil Supérieur des Forces Armées standen zwischen ihm und Guatemala. Wenn Keetenheuve Danas Anregung folgte und die Interviews morgen im Plenum erwähnte, dann konnte er sich nicht mehr zurückziehen, und sie würden ihn hier abschießen und ihm nicht mehr das Gnadenbrot Guatemala gewähren. Es war ein schlauer Mann, der diesen Speck ihm hinhielt. Eigentlich war's ein schäbiger Bissen! Guatemala — wer sagte sich dort gute Nacht? Füchse? — Die grüßen sich am Rhein. Guatemala war Frieden, Guatemala war Vergessen, Guatemala war Tod. Und das wußte, wer's ihm anbot, genau, der wußte, daß er gerade darauf anbeißen würde, auf Frieden, auf Vergessen, auf den Tod. Sonst hätten sie ihm den Haag freigehalten, Brüssel, Kopenhagen, vielleicht Athen, so viel war er noch wert; aber Guatemala, das war die Terrasse in der brütenden Sonne, das war der Platz mit verstaubten Palmen, das war die langsame und sichere Verwesung. Sie kannten ihn! Knurrewahn, zur Regierung gekommen, hätte ihm Paris offeriert, um ihn loszuwerden. Knurrewahn kannte ihn nicht. Paris war die Verpflichtung, herumzustümpern und mitzuspielen; Guatemala war die Auflösung, eine zynische Hingabe an den Tod. Es war, als ob man vorm Herrn Tod die Hosen herunterließ; und dieser Vergleich hätte Frost-Forestier gefallen.

Über dem Rhein war ein Regenbogen erschienen. Er spannte sich von Godesberg, von Mehlen, vom Haus der Amerikaner hinüber nach Beuel, wo er neben der Brücke hinter einer Mauer verschwand, auf der das Wort *Rheinlust* geschrieben stand. Der Regenbogen hing wie Aufstieg und Abstieg einer Himmelsleiter über dem Strom, und es war leicht, sich vorzustellen, daß Engel über das Wasser gingen und Gott nahe war. Bedeutete der Regenbogen Versöhnung, bedeutete er Frieden, brachte er Freundlichkeit? Der Präsident in seinem Palais mußte nun auch den Regenbogen sehen, den freundlichen Friedensbogen von Godesberg nach Beuel, vielleicht stand der Präsident auf blumenbewachsener Terrasse und blickte über den Fluß, schaute in die Abendluft, die still wie ein altes Bild in dieser Stunde war, und vielleicht war der Präsident traurig und wußte nicht warum, und vielleicht war der Präsident enttäuscht und wußte wieder nicht warum. Und Keetenheuve, der am Fenster stand, am Fenster seines Büros im Parlamentsgebäude, dachte sich einen Mann aus, der Musäus hieß und Butler beim Präsidenten war. Wahrscheinlich hatte der Präsident gar keinen Butler, aber Keetenheuve gab ihm nun einen, Musäus mit Namen, und Musäus sah dem Präsidenten ähnlich. Er war so alt wie der Präsident, er sah so aus wie der Präsident, und er hielt sich für den Präsidenten. Seine Beschäftigungen ließen ihm Zeit dazu. Musäus hatte das Handwerk eines Friseurs gelernt und war »zu Hof gegangen«, davon sprach er manchmal, das vergaß er nicht, er war in jungen Jahren im Frack »zu Hof gegangen«, den jungen Fürsten zu rasieren, mit dem er, während er ihn einseifte, freimütig über die Not des Volkes gesprochen hatte, und als der Fürst neunzehnhundertachtzehn abdankte, wollte Musäus keinen mehr rasieren und wurde Diener in einer Staatskanzlei, dann wurde er Diener bei Hindenburg und dann bewies er Charakter und diente dem Braunauer nicht. Er schlug sich mühsam durch Diktatur und Krieg, bis der neue Staat sich seiner entsann und ihn zum Butler beim Präsidenten ernannte. Nun gut, nun schön; er war verwirrt, der gute Musäus. Er las zuviel Goethe, den er sich in den prächtigen Bänden der Sophien-Ausgabe aus der Bibliothek des Präsidenten lieh, und am Abend, wenn der Regenbogen die Ufer des Rheines verband, stand auch Musäus an rosenumrankter Brüstung, hielt sich für den Präsidenten, schaute weit ins Land und freute sich, daß in der ringsum blühenden Pädagogischen Akademie, die ihm zu Füßen lag, alles zu best stand, gedieh und lebte. Aber irgendwo in seinem Herzen nistete ein Unbehagen, war es ihm, als habe er etwas vergessen, was er besessen hatte, als er noch »zu Hof gegangen« war, die Stimme des Volkes, das Raunen des Volkes, das unbedeutende eintönige Gemurmel, das er mit dem Seifenschaum dem jungen Fürsten um den Bart geschmiert hatte, das vernahm er nicht mehr, und es störte ihn, daß es nicht mehr da war. Musäus wollte gut sein, ein guter Landesvater, vielleicht hatte er schon damals den Fürsten zu einem guten Landesvater erziehen wollen, aber der Fürst hatte nicht lange regiert, und nun herrschte Musäus und hatte die Erziehungsregeln für Fürsten leider vergessen. So konnte Musäus nicht richtig regieren, man zog ihn in Kuhhändel hinein, so dachte Musäus verärgert, und der führende Staatsmann, so dachte Musäus am Abend, der fütterte Musäus zu gut, so daß er fett und taub und träge wurde und schließlich gar nichts mehr hörte vom Volksgeraune oder gar falsche Stimmen hörte, ein nachgeahmtes Volksgemurmel, wie in einer Schallplattenfabrik aufgenommen, wer wußte es, Musäus konnte es nicht mehr unterscheiden, früher hätte er es gekonnt, und dann nahm er sich vor, Diät zu halten, wenig zu essen, wenig zu trinken, er hungerte drei Tage, der gute Musäus, er durstete drei Tage, der gute Musäus, aber dann — der Posten war zu gut, und Küche und Keller waren zu wohl bestellt, Musäus aß ein Ripple, trank ein Fläschchen und nährte und beschwichtigte so sein seelisches Unbehagen. Keetenheuve verzichtete auf Guatemala. Er verzichtete auf die spanisch koloniale Sterbeveranda. Auch am Rhein gab es Terrassen. Er war entschlossen, sich nicht abschieben zu lassen. Er würde bleiben. Er würde an seinem Schreibtisch bleiben, er würde im Parlament bleiben; er würde nicht auf die Barrikade, aber auf die Tribüne steigen. Er würde mit heiligem Zorn gegen die Politik der Regierung sprechen. Ihm sollte jedes Mittel recht sein. Sein Ziel war Friede. Sein Ziel war Freundlichkeit unter den Menschen. War's nicht ein lockendes Ziel? Vielleicht würde er's erreichen. Er gab es auf, seine Rede auszuarbeiten. Er wollte frei sprechen, mit Eifer und aus dem Herzen. Keetenheuve *Gesandter a. D. Redner Volkstribun* verließ als einer der letzten an diesem Tag das Bundeshaus. Ein Wächter schloß ihm den Ausgang auf. Keetenheuve ging für eine Weile beflügelten Schrittes in den Abend. Was ließ er zurück? Die unvollendete Übersetzung eines Gedichtes, einen Tisch voll unbeantworteter Briefe, eine nicht ausgearbeitete Rede, *und mit ihm ging die neue Zeit* Aber bald merkte er, daß er schwitzte. Der Abend blieb schwül, obwohl der Regenbogen prangte. Aus einer Senkgrube drang Gestank. Aus den Gärten Rosenduft. Ein Rasenmäher ratterte über den Grasteppich. Gepflegte Hunde wandelten durch die Allee. Der große diplomatische Verhinderer von Schlimmerem machte, den kleinen Knirpsdamenschirm kokett in der Hand, seinen Abendweg und dachte über ein neues Kapitel seiner lukrativen Memoiren nach, wie auch andere Statisten der politischen Bühne und Gassenhauersänger der Wahrheit gemächlich von Besitz zu Besitzung schritten. Keetenheuve begrüßte den Verhinderer, den er nicht kannte, und der große Memoirist dankte geschmeichelt. »Durchschaut! Durchschaut!« Keetenheuve hätte es ihm gern zugerufen und ihm auf die Schulter geklopft. Bismarck kannte die Brüder: »Die Eitelkeit ist eine Hypothek, die auf jedem Politiker lastet.« Sie waren eitel, sie waren alle eitel, Minister, Beamte, Diplomaten, Abgeordnete und selbst der Portier, der die Tür im Amt öffnete, war eitel, weil er im Amt die Tür öffnete, weil er zur Regierung gehörte und hin und wieder in der Zeitung erwähnt wurde, weil ein Journalist beweisen wollte, daß er auch wirklich im Ministerium gewesen sei und den Portier gesehen habe. Sie alle hielten sich für Persönlichkeiten der Geschichte, für öffentliche Größen, nur weil sie ein Amt hatten, weil ihre Gesichter durch die Presse liefen, denn die Presse will ihr Futter haben, weil ihre Namen durch den Äther sprangen, denn auch die Funkstationen brauchten ihr tägliches Heu, und dann sahen die Gattinnen die großen Gatten und kleinen Begatter entzückt von der Kinoleinwand winken und mit dem Grinsen der Anbiederung dastehen, das sie den Amerikanern abgeguckt hatten, die wie Mannequins vor den Photographen posieren. Und wenn die Welt auch nicht viel von den beamteten Weltgeschichtlern hielt, so raschelte sie doch ständig mit ihnen, um zu beweisen, daß der Vorrat an Nichtigkeiten und Schrecken nicht erschöpft, daß Geschichte noch immer da sei. Wer wollte denn, daß Geschichte sei? Und wenn sie schon unvermeidlich war, ein unvermeidliches Übel, warum dann das Gackern beim Legen von Windeiern? Der Minister fährt nach Paris. Nun schön. Was tut er da? Er wird von einem anderen Minister empfangen. Na, wunderbar. Die Minister frühstücken zusammen. Herrlich. Herrlich. Hoffentlich war schönes Wetter. Die Minister ziehen sich zu einer Aussprache zurück. Bravo! Und nun? Sie trennen sich wieder. Na, und nachher? Der eine Minister bringt den andern zum Bahnhof oder zum Flugplatz. Ja, aber was ist nun? Nichts ist. Der Minister fliegt nach Hause, und der andere Minister wird ihn bald besuchen. Und die ganze Reise, der Bahnhof hin, der Flugplatz her, das Frühstück und das Händeschütteln auf Zeitungsseiten mit Balkenüberschriften, auf Kinoleinwänden und Fernsehschirmen und in den Lautsprechern in jeder Kammer — wozu geschehen? Man wußte es nicht. Fahrt doch mal leise nach Paris!! Amüsiert euch still. Es wäre viel wohltuender. Ein Jahr lang Schweigen um diese Leute! Ein Jahr soll ihrer nicht gedacht werden. Vergessen wollen wir ihre Gesichter, und an ihre Namen wollen wir uns nicht erinnern. Vielleicht werden sich Sagen bilden. Sie werden wesentlich sein. *Keetenheuve Held der Sage.* Er zerdachte die Welt, die ihn trug, denn wie wollte er Minister werden, wenn man nicht täglich mit allen Mitteln der Propaganda der

Erde einredete, daß sie Minister brauche? *Keetenheuve Minister mit Bismarcks Hypothek der Eitelkeit belastet* — Er schwitzte sehr. Er war in Schweiß gebadet. Alles erregte ihn. Das Hemd klebte. Er fühlte sich wieder beengt und bedrückt. Er streckte die Hand in den Hemdschlitz, legte sie auf die Haut, fühlte die Nässe, fühlte heiße borstige Haare, *Keetenheuve kein Knabe, Keetenheuve ein männliches Tier, Mann mit Bockgeruch, Haare auf der Brust, verdeckt durch Kleider, verdeckt durch Zivilisation, domestiziertes Tier, der Bock war nicht zu sehen* — darunter pochte das Herz, eine Pumpe, die es nicht mehr schaffte. Er hatte ihnen entgegentreten wollen: das Herz hatte freudig geschlagen. Er war ihnen begegnet (und sich selbst): das Herz ging unruhig, verzagt, japste, ein gehetztes Weidtier. Fürchtete er sich? Er fürchtete sich nicht. Aber er war wie ein Schwimmer, der gegen eine starke Strömung zum Ufer schwimmt und weiß, er wird es nicht schaffen, er wird abgetrieben, er kommt nicht voran, die Anstrengung ist sinnlos, und schöner wär's man ließe sich treiben, schaukelte ins Grab.

Er kam an Baustellen vorüber. Man werkte über den Feierabend. Die Regierung baute, die Ämter bauten, die Bauaufsichtsbehörde baute, der Bund und die Länder errichteten Repräsentationshäuser, fremde Gesandtschaften mauerten sich hoch, Kartelle, Industrieverbände, Bankvereine, Ölgesellschaften, Stahlgewerke, Kohlenkontore, Elektrizitätswerke stellten hier ihre Verwaltungsgebäude hin, als brauchten sie in der Regierungssonne keine Steuern zu zahlen, Versicherungsgesellschaften stockten auf und bauten vor, und Versicherungsgesellschaften, bei denen sich Versicherer für den Versicherungsfall versicherten, konnten nicht Räume genug finden, ihre Policen zu verwahren, ihre Anwälte unterzubringen, ihre Lebenserwartungsstatistiker zu beherbergen, ihre Gewinne zu verputzen, ihren Reichtum zu zeigen. Alle wollten sie so schnell wie nur möglich in Regierungsnähe unter Dach kommen; es war, als fürchteten sie, die Regierung könne ihnen davonlaufen, würde eines Tages nicht mehr da sein, und in ihren schönen neuen Häusern sollte das Grauen wohnen. Lebte Keetenheuve in einer neuen Gründerzeit? Es war eine untergründige, eine hintergründige, eine begründet grundlose Zeit *auf flüchtigem Sande habt ihr gebaut. Keetenheuve Verdisänger in Bonn, vorn an der Rampe meisterte er den Belcanto auf flüchtigem Sande ach wie so trügerisch habt ihr gebaut. Kleiner Abgeordneter arm zwischen Sicherheitspalästen. Der Wurm im Holz. Der Nagel zu ihrem Sarg. Kranker Wurm. Krümmte sich. Verrosteter Nagel. Nun gut, die Versicherungen würden ihn überleben. Er war nicht versichert. Starb so. Eine lästige Leiche. Kein Denkmal für Keetenheuve. Befreite die Menschheit von nichts. Tastete sich durch Baugruben. Fallen. Blind. Ein Maulwurf.* Er kam zu dem Spielplatz, und wieder saßen, wie am Morgen, zwei Mädchen auf der Wippe. Es waren Dreizehnjährige. Als Keetenheuve sie beschaute, ließen sie ihr Auf- und Niederwippen, die eine hockte unten, die andere hing oben auf dem Schwebebalken. Sie kicherten. Sie tuschelten sich etwas zu. Die eine zupfte am Röckchen, zog den Stoff über den Schenkel. Verdorben. Verdorben. Und du? Lockte dich nicht die Jugend, die glatte, die sanftkühle Haut? Ein Haar, das noch nicht nach Tod roch? Ein Mund, der noch nicht die Verwesung atmete? Es duftete nach Vanille. Im Ruinenhaus schmorte jemand Mandeln und Zucker in einem Kupferkessel. *Eßt die gebrannten Riesenmandeln* rief ein regendurchwaschenes Transparent. Keetenheuve kaufte für fünfzig Pfennig gebrannte Riesenmandeln und aß sie. Er dachte: es ist das letzte Mal, jetzt esse ich zum letztenmal gebrannte Mandeln. Sie schmeckten bitter. Die Zuckerkruste knackte zwischen den Zähnen. Auf der Zunge lag eine bröcklig klebrige Masse. Die gebrannten Riesenmandeln schmeckten nach Pubertät, nach Knabenlüsternheit in dunklen Tageskinos: auf der Leinwand schwellen schmutzig fleckig weiß die Brüste der Lya de Mara, man lutscht Konfekt, und im Blut regt sich ein neues Weh. Keetenheuve stand kauend vor einem Schaufenster mit Studentenutensilien. Auch der Besitzer dieses Schaufensters lebte von Pubertätsgefühlen. Es war alles wieder da, die Zeit lief zurück, die Kriege waren nie gewesen. Keetenheuve sah weiße Stürmer, bunte Mützen, Korpsbänder, Kneipjacken, er betrachtete Fechtausrüstungen, Schläger,

Bierhumpen mit der Verbindungsschutzmarke auf dem Dekkel, Kommersbücher mit goldenen Nägeln im Einband und mit geschmiedeten Verschlüssen. Das wurde hergestellt, das war zu verkaufen, das brachte die Miete für das Schaufenster und den Laden ein und nährte den Geschäftsmann. Wirklich, die Gründerjahre waren wiedergekehrt, ihr Geschmack, ihre Komplexe, ihre Tabus. Die Söhne der bauwütigen Direktoren fuhren am Steuer ihres Wagens zur Universität, aber am Abend setzten sie sich Narrenmützen auf, ahmten ihre Großväter nach und taten, was sehr komisch sein mußte, sie rieben einen Salamander; Keetenheuve verband dies mit der unsympathischen Vorstellung von jungen Männern, die von Bier, Dummheit und unklaren, manchmal nationalen Gefühlen bewegt, singend häßliche Krötentiere zwischen Kneiptisch und Humpen zerrieben. Keetenheuve warf den Rest der gebrannten Mandeln in die Gosse. Die spitze Tüte platzte, und die Zuckermandeln hüpften wie Marbeln über das Pflaster. *Keetenheuve Kind spielt mit Achatkugeln am Straßenrand. Bonner Versicherungsdirektor Kösener Verband CC stürmt mit weißer Mütze Korpsband und Schläger auf Keetenheuve los. Direktor ersticht Keetenheuve. Keetenheuve nimmt eine gebrannte Mandel, stopft sie dem Direktor in den Mund. Er zieht an des Direktors Jacke, und Groschen fallen aus dem Ärmel auf die Straße. Kleine Mädchen kommen und sammeln die Groschen auf: Sie rufen: mehr, mehr, mehr, und immer mehr Groschen fallen, hüpfen, springen über die Straße. Keetenheuve lacht. Der Direktor ist böse und sagt: Ernst der Situation —* Keetenheuve ging über den Markt. Die Marktweiber wuschen ihre Stände. *Witz für Mergentheim: Ein Blinder geht über den Fischmarkt, sagt: »Girls«. Schlafzimmer bei Mergentheims. Sophie zieht sich für die Party an, CD in Godesberg, sie spannt ein durchsichtiges Mieder über den erschlafften Leib. Mergentheim ist nicht erregt. Er ist müde. Er sagt: »Keetenheuve war bei mir.« Das Mieder drückt Sophie. Sie möchte den Saum aufschneiden. Ihr ist heiß. Mergentheim sagt: »Ich sollte mich nicht länger mit ihm duzen.« Sophie denkt: Was quatscht er, das Mieder zwickt mich, Nylonseide,*

315

durchsichtig und straff, ich könnte den Saum aufreißen, ich
zieh mich doch nicht aus. Mergentheim sagt: »Ich bin sein
Feind. Ich sollte es ihm sagen. Ich sollte sagen: ›Herr Keeten-
heuve, ich bin Ihr Feind.‹ « Sophie denkt: Wozu trage ich
das durchsichtige Korsett? Wenn François-Poncet mich so
sähe, man sieht doch alles, Falten, das träge Fett. Mergent-
heim sagt: »So ist es gemein.« Keetenheuve ging durch den
Abfall des Marktes, Fauliges, Stinkendes, Verwesendes, Ran-
ziges, Verdorbenes lag unter seinen Füßen, er glitschte hinein, *in eine Orange, eine Banane, eine schöne Frucht unnütz*
gereift, sinnlos gepflückt, geboren in Afrika, gestorben auf
dem Markt in Bonn, nicht einmal verspeist, reiste nicht durch
den gierigen Menschen, verwandelte sich nicht. Wurst, Fleisch
Käse, Fische und überall Fliegen. Schwere Brummer. Maden
im Leib. Ihre Waffe. Wurst auf der Platte zerstört. Das essen
wir. Das essen sie im Hotel Stern. Ich könnte hineingehen.
Jobber in der Halle, Feldspaten für den Grenzschutz, Patent
des Düsenwasserwerfers, künstliche Diamanten, sie warten
noch immer auf den Anruf des Ministers. Der schickt seinen
Wagen. Her mit den Diamanten, her mit dem Wasserwurf-
patent, den Spaten her, netter zusammenklappbarer Westen-
taschenspaten, unauffällig unter dem Anzug zu tragen, macht
beliebt in jeder Gesellschaft, einmalige Leistung, sechshun-
dert Kubikmeter deutsche Erde in der Stunde, Massengräber,
Kamerad gräbt Kamerad ein. Wartet auf die Weisungen der
Regierung. Hier ist England. Hier ist England. Sie hören die
Stimme Amerikas. Diesmal würde Keetenheuve nicht spre-
chen. Er würde nicht im Äther kämpfen. *Keetenheuve un-*
bekannter Soldat an unbekannter Front. Schuß nach vorn?
Schuß nach hinten? Wer Nerven hat, schießt in die Luft.
Vorsicht, die Geschwader! Ja, keinen Vogel abschießen! Kee-
tenheuve guter Mensch, kein Jäger. Weiße Hände. Dichter.
Auf dem Balkon des Sternhotels stand ein Abgeordneter der
Bayernpartei. Er sah ins Mangfalltal. Kühe zogen von den
Weiden. Die Kuhglocken bimmelten. Das Jahr reifte. Die
Pensionen waren mit Preußen belegt: Ave Maria. Die Bayern-
partei konnte wie alle kleinen Parteien das Zünglein an der
Waage sein. Sie wurde umworben. Wenn's ernst wurde,

stimmte sie für die Regierung, aber mit föderalistischer Reservatio mentalis.

Die Menschen standen vor einer Kinokasse an. Was erwartete sie? Das große deutsche Lustspiel. Keetenheuve stellte sich in die Reihe. Ariadne führte ihn, Theseus, der sich ins Dunkel wagte, Ariadne sagte:»Nachrücken zur Mitte!« Ihre Stimme war hochnäsig piepsig. Sie war als Ordnerin über eine ungezogene Menschheit gesetzt, die nicht rechtzeitig zur Mitte rückte. Keetenheuve saß, und er saß in der seiner Zeit gemäßen Haltung, er war Objekt, es wurde über ihn verfügt. Jetzt war er ein Objekt der Werbung. Auf der Leinwand wurden ihm Rasierapparate, Führerscheine, Binden, Kleiderstoffe, Lippenstifte, Haarfärbemittel, eine Reise nach Athen angeboten. *Keetenheuve Käufer und Konsument, Normalverbraucher. Nützlich.* Keetenheuve kaufte sechs Hemden im Jahr. Fünfzig Millionen Bundesdeutsche kauften dreihundert Millionen Hemden. Von einem ungeheuren Ballen rollte der Stoff in die Nähmaschinen. Stoffschlangen umwanden den Bürger. *Gefangen.* Schulstunde: Einer raucht zehn Zigaretten am Tag, dann raucht er im Jahr wieviel Zigaretten, also verrauchen fünfzig Millionen Raucher sechsmal den Kölner Dom, wenn er aus Tabak wäre. Keetenheuve rauchte nicht. *Entwischt!* Er freute sich. Es kam die Wochenschau. Ein Minister übernahm eine Brücke. Er zerschnitt ein Band. Er stelzte über die Brücke. Andere Stelzer stelzten hinter dem Minister drein. Der Präsident besuchte die Ausstellung. Ein Kind begrüßte ihn. *Unser Führer liebt die Kinder.* Ein Minister reiste ab. Er wurde zum Zug gebracht. Ein Minister kam an. Er wurde abgeholt. Miß Loisach wurde gewählt. Bikini auf der Alm. Netter Hintern. Großer Atombombenpilz über der Wüste von Nevada. Skirennen auf künstlichem Schnee am Strand von Florida. Wieder Bikinis. Großer Auftrieb. Noch nettere Hintern. In Korea: Zwei ernst blickende Feinde treffen sich; sie gehen in ein Zelt; sie trennen sich wieder; der eine klettert ernst in einen Hubschrauber, der andere noch ernster in sein Auto. Schüsse. Bomben auf irgendeine Stadt. Schüsse. Bomben in ein Dschungel. Miß Makao wird gewählt. Bikini. Sehr netter chinesisch-portugiesischer Hintern. Der Sport versöhnt die Völker. Zwanzigtausend starren auf einen Ball. Es ist höchst langweilig. Aber dann holt das Teleobjektiv der Filmkamera einzelne Gesichter aus den Zwanzigtausend heraus: erschreckende Gesichter, verkrampfte Kinnladen, haßverzerrte Münder, Mordgier im Blick. *Wollt ihr den totalen Krieg?* ja ja ja Keetenheuve beobachtete von seinem Sitz im verdunkelten Zuschauerraum die von den tückischen Fernrohrobjektiven aus ihrer Geborgenheit in der Masse und Anonymität grausam herausgerissenen und aller Fassung entblößten Gesichter, die nun vom Licht (nach Newton ein unwägbarer Stoff, der kalt und hochmütig über der gebundenen Materie schwebt) auf die Leinwand wie auf einen Seziertisch geworfen wurden, und er fürchtete sich. War dies des Menschen Antlitz? War so erschreckend des Zeitgenossen Gesicht? Wohin war man verschlagen, und welchem Zufall verdankte er es *Keetenheuve Pharisäer*, daß nicht auch er verrührt war in diesen Brei der Zwanzigtausend (Minister saßen auf den Bänken und wurden vom Kameraaauge erfaßt, Minister waren volksverbunden, sie waren es, oder sie taten so: hervorragende Mimiker) und mit verklemmten Kiefern den Ball verfolgte? Ihm klopfte das Herz hier nicht, sein Blut pulste nicht schneller, er empfand nicht die Wut: an die Kehle dem Schiedsrichter, schlagt den Hund, Schiebung, ein Elfmeter, kein Elfmeter, Pfiffe! Keetenheuve stand abseits. Er stand außerhalb des echten Spannungsfeldes dieser Versammlung der Zwanzigtausend. Sie waren vereint, sie akkumulierten, sie waren eine gefährliche Häufung von Nullen, eine explosive Mischung, zwanzigtausend erregte Herzen und zwanzigtausend hohle Köpfe. Natürlich warten sie auf ihren Führer, auf die Nummer Eins, auf den, der sich positiv mit ihnen konfrontiert und sie erst zur gewaltigen Ziffer macht, zum Volk, zum neuen Golem des Mischbegriffs ein Volk, ein Reich, ein Führer, ein totaler Haß, eine totale Explosion, ein totaler Untergang. Keetenheuve war der Masse negativ entgegengestellt. Er war allein. Das war die Position des Führers. *Keetenheuve Führer.* Aber Keetenheuve konnte die Menge nicht berücken. Er setzte die Masse nicht in Bewegung. Er entzündete sie nicht. **Er** konnte das Volk nicht einmal betrügen. Als Politiker war er ein Heiratsschwindler, der impotent wurde, wenn er mit Frau Germania ins Bett gehen sollte. Aber in seiner Vorstellung und auch oft tatsächlich und mit ehrlichem Bemühen vertrat gerade er immer das Recht des Volkes! Auf der Leinwand warb nun das Kino für das Kino; es wurden kurze Schnitte aus den konfektionierten Träumen des nächsten Programms gezeigt. Zwei alte Männer spielten Tennis. Es waren aber diese alten Knaben die jugendlichen Liebhaber des nächsten Filmes, neckisch in kurze Höschen gekleidet, und sie konnten leicht Keetenheuves ältere Brüder sein, denn schon als er noch halbwüchsig war, hatte Keetenheuve die Herren im Flimmerspiel agieren sehen. Sie waren aber nicht nur Tennisspieler, sie waren auch Gutsbesitzer, denn es war ein Zeitfilm, der hier angekündigt wurde *erschütternd und aufwühlend,* und die Herren Gutsbesitzer hatten alles verloren, jeglichen Besitz dem Sturm der Welt geopfert, nur das Gut war ihnen geblieben, Gutsschloß und Feld und Wald und der Tennisplatz und die kurzen feschen Hosen und selbstverständlich ein paar edle Pferde, um wieder für Deutschland zu reiten. Eine Tonbandstimme sprach: »Zwischen den verschworenen Freunden steht eine bezaubernde Frau. Wer wird sie erringen?« Eine Matrone tollte im Backfischkleid an das Netz. Großmütterchens Zeitvertreib, und alles spielte sich in der besten Gesellschaft ab, in einer Welt, die es so fein gar nicht mehr gab. Und Keetenheuve zweifelte, ob es diese feine Welt je gegeben hatte. Was war das? Was wurde hier gespielt? Eine beliebte deutsche Volksschriftstellerin nannte einen ihrer vielen Romane *Highlife;* sie oder ihr Verleger setzten den englischen Titel auf das deutsche Buch, und Millionen, die gar nicht wußten, was das Wort *Highlife* bedeutete, verschlangen den Band. Highlife — vornehme Welt, ein Zauberspruch, was war das, wer gehörte dazu? Korodin? Nein. Korodin war nicht Highlife. Der Kanzler? Auch er nicht. Der Bankier des Kanzlers? Der hätte solche Leute 'rausgeschmissen. Wer war Highlife denn? Gespenster waren es, Schatten. Die Schauspieler auf der Leinwand waren es, sie, die Highlife spielen sollten, waren auch die einzigen Ver-

treter dieser vornehmen Welt, sie und ein paar Reklame-
figuren der Illustrierten und der Werbung, der Mann mit
dem gepflegten Schnurrbart, der Sekt einschenkt in unnach-
ahmlicher Würde, der Mann, der jedermanns Straßenbahn-
zigarette im Polodreß raucht, und der blaue Dunst schlängelt
sich um den schönen Hals des Pferdes. Nie wird ein Mensch
so den Sekt einschenken, nie wird jemand so auf dem Pferd
sitzen, und warum sollte man es auch tun — aber diese
Gestalten waren echte Schattenkönige des Volkes. Ein zweiter Vorspann warb für einen Farbfilm. Die Tonbandstimme
rief:»Amerika im Bürgerkrieg! Der heiße Süden, das Land
der glühenden Seelen! Eine entzückende Frau zwischen zwei
verschworenen Freunden!« Zwei verschworene Freunde und
eine entzückende Frau — das schien diesseits und jenseits des
Ozeans eine fixe dramatische Idee der Drehbuchverfasser zu
sein. Die entzückende Frau saß diesmal auf einem ungesat-
telten Mustang und ritt in drei Farben, daß Keetenheuve die
Augen weh taten. Die Freunde schlichen — auch sie in drei
Farben — durch das Gehölz und schossen aufeinander. Die
Tonbandstimme kommentierte:»Tollkühne Männer!« Keetenheuve hatte keinen Freund, auf den er schießen konnte.
Sollte er auf Mergentheim anlegen und Mergentheim auf
ihn? Vielleicht keine schlechte Idee. Man müßte Sophie zur
entzückenden Frau ernennen. Sie würde mitmachen. War
kein Spielverderber. Jetzt kam das deutsche Lustspiel. Keetenheuve war erschöpft. Das Lustspiel flimmerte. Es war Ge-
spensterspuk. Der Liebhaber verkleidete sich. Er ging als Dame aus. Nun gut, es gab Transvestiten. Aber Keetenheuve
fand es nicht komisch. Der Transvestit setzte sich in eine Badewanne. Auch Transvestiten müssen mal baden. Was war
daran komisch? Eine Dame überraschte den nun schicklich
Nackten und nicht länger unschicklich Verkleideten in der
Wanne. Man lachte neben Keetenheuve, man lachte vor und
lachte hinter ihm. Warum lachten sie? Er verstand es nicht.
Es erschreckte ihn. Er war ausgestoßen. Er war aus ihrem
Gelächter ausgeschlossen. Er hatte nichts Komisches gesehen.
Einen nackten Schauspieler. Eine dreimal geschiedene Dame,
die den Schauspieler in der Badewanne fand. Das waren doch

eher traurige als komische Vorfälle! Sie lachten aber rings um Keetenheuve. Sie lachten schallend. War Keetenheuve ein Ausländer? War er unter Menschen gereist, die anders weinten, anders lachten, die anders waren als er? Vielleicht war er ein Ausländer des Gefühls, und das Gelächter aus der Dunkelheit, die ihn umgab, schlug schmerzhaft wie eine allzu kräftige Woge über ihn und drohte ihn zu ersticken. Er tastete sich hinaus aus diesem Labyrinth. Er verließ eilig das Kino. Es war eine Flucht. Ariadne piepste hinter ihm drein: »Rechts halten! Zum Ausgang rechts halten!« *Theseus auf der Flucht Minotaurus lebt*

Der Tag verdämmerte. Am Himmel war noch ein letzter Widerschein der untergehenden Sonne. Es war Abendbrotzeit. Sie saßen in ihren dumpfen Stuben, sie saßen vor den gemachten Betten, sie nährten sich, und sie lauschten kauend träge der Lautsprecherberieselung: Nimm mich mit Kapitän auf die Reise, Heimat deine Sterne. Nur wenige Menschen bevölkerten die Straße. Es waren Menschen, die nicht wußten, wohin sie gehen sollten. Sie wußten nicht wohin, auch wenn sie ein Zimmer hatten, auch wenn ihr Bett gemacht war, das Bier und die Wurst auf sie warteten, sie wußten nicht, wohin. Es waren Menschen wie Keetenheuve, und doch waren sie wieder anders als Keetenheuve — sie wußten auch mit sich nichts anzufangen. Vor dem Kino standen Halbwüchsige. Sie gingen zweimal in der Woche in das Kino hinein, und an den anderen Tagen standen sie vor dem Kino. Sie warteten. Worauf warteten sie? Sie warteten auf das Leben, und das Leben, auf das sie warteten, blieb aus. Das Leben erschien nicht zum Rendezvous vor dem Kino, oder wenn es erschien und neben ihnen stand, dann sahen sie es nicht, und die Lebensgefährten, die sich später einfanden und zu sehen waren, das waren nicht die erwarteten. Man hätte sich gar nicht hingestellt, wenn man gewußt hätte, daß nur sie kommen würden. Die Burschen warteten für sich. Die Langeweile hauste in ihnen wie eine Krankheit, und in ihren Gesichtern war schon zu lesen, daß sie langsam an dieser Krankheit sterben würden. Die Mädchen standen abseits. Sie waren weniger langeweilekrank als die Buben. Sie waren fickrig und kaschierten das, indem sie die Köpfe zusammensteckten, tuschelten und sich aneinander rieben. Die jungen Männer betrachteten zum hundertstenmal die Filmphotographien. Sie sahen den Darsteller in der Badewanne sitzen, und sie sahen ihn Frauenkleider tragen. Was stellte der Darsteller dar? Einen Schwulen? Sie gähnten. Ihr Mund wurde ein rundes Loch, der Eingang eines Tunnels, in dem die Leere aus und ein ging. Sie steckten Zigaretten in das Loch, stopften die Leere, bissen die Lippen über dem Tabak zusammen und bekamen hämische wichtigtuerische Gesichter. Sie konnten einmal Abgeordnete werden; aber wahrscheinlich würde sie vorher das Militär holen. Keetenheuve hatte keine Vision: er sah sie nicht im Feldgrab liegen, er sah sie nicht auf Kinderwagenrädern beinlos zur Bettelfahrt rollen. In dieser Stunde hätte er sie nicht einmal bedauert. Die Gabe der Vorhersicht war ihm genommen, und das Mitgefühl war gestorben. Ein Bäckerlehrling beobachtete die Kinokasse. Die Kassiererin saß im Kassenkasten wie die Wachsbüste einer Dame im Schaufenster eines Friseurs. Die Kassiererin lächelte starr und süß wie die Wachsbüsten und trug dünn und stolz ihr onduliertes Perückenhaar. Der Bäckerlehrling überlegte, ob er die Kassiererin berauben könne. Sein Hemd war tief bis zum Nabel geöffnet, und seine sehr kurze Backstubenhose bedeckte gerade seinen Hintern. Seine Brust und seine nackten Beine waren mehlbestäubt. Er rauchte nicht. Er gähnte nicht. Seine Augen waren wach. Keetenheuve dachte: Wenn ich ein Mädchen wäre, ich würde mit dir ans Ufer gehen. Keetenheuve dachte: Wenn ich die Kassiererin wäre, ich würde mich vorsehen.

Es begegneten ihm Einsame, die einen verzweifelten Bummel durch die Stadt machten. Was dachten sie? Was litten sie? Waren sie sinnlich? Quälte es sie? Suchten sie Partner für die Geilheit, die in ihnen gärte? Sie würden die Partner nicht finden. Die Partner waren überall. Sie gingen aneinander vorüber, Männer und Frauen, sie tränkten sich mit Bildern, und in der gemieteten Kammer, in dem gemieteten Bett würden sie sich der Straße erinnern und sich selbst befriedigen. Einige hätten sich gern betrunken. Sie hätten gern ein

Gespräch geführt. Sie blickten sehnsüchtig in die Fenster der Wirtschaften. Aber sie hatten kein Geld. Der Lohn war verteilt; er war für Miete, Wäsche, für die notwendige Verpflegung, ein Aliment, eine Unterstützung verteilt; sie mußten froh sein, wenn sie den Job behielten, der das Geld, das verteilt werden mußte, einbrachte. Sie stellten sich vor die Schaufenster und betrachteten teure photographische Apparate. Sie überlegten, ob die Leica oder die Contax besser sei, und sie konnten sich keine Kinderbox leisten. Keetenheuve ging in die Weinstube mit den getäfelten Wänden. Es war still, es war angenehm; nur die Hitze war in der Stube stehengeblieben; er schwitzte. Ein alter Herr saß bei seinem Wein und las die Zeitung. Er las den Leitartikel. Der Artikel war überschrieben *Wird der Kanzler siegen?* Keetenheuve hatte den Artikel gelesen; er wußte, daß sein Name in dem Aufsatz als ein Stein auf dem Weg des Kanzlers erwähnt war. *Keetenheuve Stein des Anstoßes.* Er bestellte einen Ahrwein, der hier gut war. Der alte Herr streichelte, während er sich über die Aussichten des Kanzlers unterrichtete, einen alten Dackel, der neben ihm manierlich auf der Bank hockte. Der Dackel hatte ein kluges Gesicht; er sah wie ein Staatsmann aus. Keetenheuve dachte: So werde auch ich einmal sitzen, alt, allein, auf die Freundschaft eines Hundes angewiesen. Aber es war noch die Frage, ob er das haben würde, einen Hund, ein Glas Wein und irgendwo in der Stadt ein Bett.

Ein Priester kam in die Weinstube. Ein kleines Mädchen begleitete den Priester. Das kleine Mädchen war wohl zwölf Jahre alt und hatte rote Söckchen an. Der Priester war groß und stark. Er sah wie ein Landmann aus, aber er hatte den Kopf eines Gelehrten. Es war ein guter Kopf. Der Priester reichte dem kleinen Mädchen die Weinkarte, und das kleine Mädchen las schüchtern die Namen der Weine. Das kleine Mädchen fürchtete, es würde Limonade bekommen; aber der Priester fragte sie, ob sie Wein trinken wolle. Er bestellte für das kleine Mädchen ein Achtel und für sich ein Viertel. Das kleine Mädchen faßte das Weinglas mit beiden Händen an und trank mit kleinen vorsichtigen Schlucken. Der Priester fragte: »Schmeckt er dir?« Das kleine Mädchen sagte: »Guut!« Keetenheuve dachte: Du brauchst nicht schüchtern zu sein; er ist froh, daß du bei ihm bist. Der Priester zog eine Zeitung aus seiner Soutane. Es war eine italienische Zeitung, es war eine vatikanische, es war der Osservatore Romano. Der Priester setzte eine Brille auf und las den Leitartikel des Osservatore. Keetenheuve dachte: Die Zeitung ist nicht schlechter als andere, wahrscheinlich ist sie besser. Keetenheuve dachte: Der Artikel ist gut geschrieben, sie sind Humanisten, sie können denken, sie vertreten mit guten Gründen eine gute Sache, aber sie unterdrücken die Ansicht, daß man mit genauso guten Gründen eine gegenteilige Sache vertreten kann. Keetenheuve dachte: Es gibt keine Wahrheit. Er dachte: Es gibt den Glauben. Er überlegte: Glaubt der Redakteur des Osservatore, was in seinem Blatt steht? Ist er Geistlicher? Hat er die Weihen empfangen? Wohnt er im Vatikan? Keetenheuve dachte: Ein schönes Leben; am Abend die Gärten, am Abend der Spaziergang am Tiber. Er sah sich als Priester am Ufer des Tiber wandeln. Er trug eine saubere Soutane und einen schwarzen Hut mit einem roten Band *Keetenheuve Monsignore. Kleine Mädchen knicksten und küßten ihm die Hand.* Der Priester fragte das kleine Mädchen: »Willst du einen Sprudel zum Wein?« Das kleine Mädchen schüttelte den Kopf. Es trank seinen Wein rein mit genießerischen kleinen Schlucken. Der Priester faltete den Osservatore zusammen. Er nahm die Brille ab. Seine Augen waren klar. Sein Gesicht war ruhig. Es war kein leeres Gesicht. Er schmeckte den Wein wie ein Weinbauer. Die Söckchen des kleinen Mädchens hingen rot unter dem Tisch. Der alte Herr streichelte seinen klugen Dackel. Es war still. Auch die Kellnerin saß still an einem Tisch. Sie las in einer Illustrierten den Fortsetzungsbericht *Ich war Stalins Freundin.* Keetenheuve dachte: Ewigkeit. Er dachte: Erstarrung. Er dachte: Verrat. Er dachte: Glauben. Er dachte: Der Friede trügt. Und er dachte weiter: Die Hitze hier, die Stille hier, das ist ein Moment der Ewigkeit, und eingeweckt in diesen Moment der Ewigkeit sind wir, der Priester und der Osservatore Romano, das kleine Mädchen und seine roten Söck-

chen, der Herr und sein Hund, die Kellnerin, die sich aus-
ruht, Stalin und seine treulose Freundin und ich, der Abgeordnete, ein Proteus, aber krank, aber schwach, doch wenigstens noch unruhig.

Auf einmal zahlten sie alle. Der Priester zahlte. Der alte
Herr zahlte. Keetenheuve zahlte. In der Weinstube war Feierabend. Wohin? Wohin? Der alte Herr und sein Hund gingen nach Hause. Der Priester brachte das kleine Mädchen
nach Hause. Hatte der Priester kein Zuhause? Keetenheuve
wußte es nicht. Vielleicht besuchte der Priester Korodin. Vielleicht übernachtete er in einer Kirche, verbrachte die Nacht
im Gebet. Vielleicht hatte er ein schönes Heim, ein breites
Barockbett mit gedrechselten Schwänen, alte Spiegel, eine
bedeutende Bibliothek, Franzosen des siebzehnten Jahrhunderts, vielleicht schmökerte er noch ein wenig, vielleicht schlief
er auf kühlem Linnen ein, und vielleicht träumte er von roten Söckchen. Keetenheuve trug kein Verlangen, nach Hause
zu gehen; seine Abgeordnetenabsteige war ein Pied-à-terre
der Unlust, eine Puppenstube der Angst, in der er nur eines
fühlen würde — wenn er dort stürbe, niemand würde trau-
ern. Den ganzen Tag fürchtete er sich schon vor dieser traurigen Stube.

Die Straßen des Viertels waren leer. Nutzlos brannten die
Lampen in den Schaufenstern der Konfektionäre. Keetenheuve betrachtete das Leben der Schaufensterfamilien. Eine
Rundfunkstation hatte die ideale Familie gesucht. Hier war
sie. Der Konfektionär hatte sie längst gefunden. Ein grin-
sender Vater, eine grinsende Mutter, ein grinsendes Kind
starrten verzückt auf ihre Preisschilder. Sie freuten sich, weil
sie billig gekleidet waren. Keetenheuve dachte: Wenn es dem
Dekorateur einfiele, den Mann in eine Uniform zu stecken,
wie wird er grinsen, wie werden sie ihn grinsend bewundern;
sie werden ihn bewundern, bis im Druck der Explosionen die
Scheiben platzen, bis im Feuersturm das Wachs wieder schmelzen wird. Auch die Dame im Nebenfenster, die eine mon-
däne Frisur, einen lüsternen Mund und einen netten frech
herausgestreckten Unterleib hatte, freute sich ihrer preis-
werten Drapierung. Es war eine Idealbevölkerung, die da

stand, ideale Väter, ideale Hausfrauen, ideale Kinder, ideale Freundinnen *Fortsetzungsbericht* Ich war Keetenheuves Schaufensterpuppe *Keetenheuve Persönlichkeit der Zeitgeschichte, Keetenheuve Sittenbild der Illustrierten,* sie grinsten Keetenheuve an. Sie grinsten aufmunternd. Sie grinsten: Greif zu! Sie führten ein ideales, sauberes und billiges Leben. Selbst der frech herausgestreckte Unterleib der mondänen Puppe, der kleinen Hure, war sauber und billig, er war ideal, er war synthetisch: in diesem Schoß lag die Zukunft. Keetenheuve konnte sich eine Puppenfamilie kaufen. Eine ideale Frau. Ein ideales Kind. Er konnte seine Abgeordnetenpuppenwohnung mit ihnen bevölkern. Er konnte sie lieben. Er konnte sie in den Schrank legen, wenn er sie nicht mehr lieben mochte. Er konnte ihnen Särge kaufen, sie hineinbetten und sie beerdigen.

Die Stadt bot dem einsamen Wanderer vieles an. Sie bot ihm Automobile an, sie bot ihm Öfen an, Kühlschränke, Fahrräder, Töpfe, Möbel, Uhren, Radioapparate, all diese Güter standen oder lagen in den wie nur für Keetenheuve erleuchteten Schaufenstern in einer auffallenden Vereinsamung, sie waren des Teufels Versuchung, sie waren zu dieser Stunde unwirkliche Automobile, unwirkliche Öfen, Töpfe oder Schränke, sie waren wie in die Form von Verbrauchsgegenständen gebrachte Zaubersprüche oder Flüche. Ein mächtiger Zauberer hatte alles erstarren lassen, es war fest gewordene, in eine Zufallsform gepreßte Luft, und es hatte dem Zauberer Spaß gemacht, auch häßliche Formen zu bilden, und nun freute er sich, daß der Mensch diese Dinge begehrte und für sie arbeitete, für sie mordete, stahl, betrog; ja, der Mensch brachte sich um, wenn er die Wechsel nicht einlösen konnte, die Unterschrift, die er dem Teufel gegeben und mit der er sich die Zaubersachen aufgehalst hatte. Ein Laden mit rotem Licht war reine schwarze Magie. Ein Mensch stand aufgeschnitten in einer Vitrine. Keetenheuve sah das Herz, die Lungen, die Nieren, den Magen des Menschen; sie lagen frei und in natürlicher Größe vor seinen Augen. Die Organe waren durch Glasröhren, durchsichtige Laboratoriumsschlangen miteinander verbunden, und durch die Röhren lief eine

hellrote Limonade, die man mit dem Zaubertrank Sieglinde in Schwung halten sollte. Der aufgeschnittene Mensch trug einen Totenschädel mit geputzten Zähnen, und sein rechter Arm, der von der Haut entblößt war, so daß Muskelstränge und Nervenbahnen aufgedeckt zu sehen waren, sein rechter Arm war zum Faschistengruß erhoben, und Keetenheuve glaubte das »Heil Hitler« zu hören, das dieses Gespenst ihm entgegenschmetterte. Das Wesen hatte keine Geschlechtsmerkmale, es stand impotent in einem Lager hygenischer Artikel, wie sie sich nannten, und Keetenheuve bemerkte Gummiduschen, Präservative, empfängnisverhütende Tabletten, allerlei schmierige Pasten und verzuckerte Pillen, ein Storch aus Kunstharz war zu sehen, und ein Leuchtschild verkündete: *Hier finden Sie das Beste für unsere Kleinen.*
Keetenheuve dachte: Nicht mehr mitspielen, nicht mitmachen, den Pakt nicht unterschreiben, kein Käufer, kein Untertan sein. Keetenheuve träumte für eine Weile in den nächtlichen, in den stillen Straßen der Hauptstadt, die sich jetzt wieder darauf besann, eine Kleinstadt zu sein, den uralten Traum von der Bedürfnislosigkeit. Der Traum gab ihm die Kraft, wie er noch jedem Kraft gegeben hat. Seine Schritte hallten. *Keetenheuve Asket. Keetenheuve Jünger des Zen. Keetenheuve Buddhist. Keetenheuve der große Selbstbefreier.* Aber die Anregung, die er empfand, regte auch die Säfte an, die geistige Beflügelung seiner Schritte weckte auch den Appetit, der große Selbstbefreier spürte Hunger, er spürte Durst, es war nichts mit der Befreiung, die, wenn sie gelingen sollte, jetzt beginnen mußte, jetzt, gleich und sofort. Seine Schritte hallten. Sie hallten hohl in der stillen Straße.
Keetenheuve ging in die zweite Weinstube der Stadt. Die Weinstube war weniger still, die Weinstube war weniger vornehm als die erste, kein Priester verkehrte dort, kein kleines Mädchen in roten Söckchen erfreute den Blick, aber das Lokal war noch offen, es wurde noch ausgeschenkt. Zwei Stammtische debattierten. Es waren dicke Männer, es waren dicke Frauen; sie hatten hier ihre Geschäfte, sie hatten ihr bequemes Auskommen, sie hatten die Schaufenster erleuchtet, sie waren mit dem Teufel im Bund. Keetenheuve bestellte

Wein und Käse. Es befriedigte ihn, daß er Käse bestellte. Der Buddhist wollte nicht, daß für ihn geschlachtet wurde. Der leicht stinkende Käse war eine Gewissensberuhigung. Er schmeckte ihm. An der Wand hing das Vermächtnis des sterbenden Weinhändlers an seine Söhne: Man kann Wein auch aus Trauben bereiten. Der Wein, den Keetenheuve trank, war gut. Und dann kamen die Heilsarmeemädchen in das Lokal.

Nur eines der Mädchen trug die blaurote Uniform und den Schutenhut der Soldaten des Herrn, und von der anderen wußte man nicht, ob sie überhaupt zur Heilsarmee gehörte, ob sie eine noch nicht eingekleidete Novizin oder ob sie nur zufällig mitgegangen war, freiwillig aus Freundschaft oder unfrei durch widergünstige Verhältnisse dazu gezwungen, trotzig oder aus bloßer Neugier. Sie war vielleicht sechzehn Jahre alt. Sie hatte ein zerknittertes Kleid aus einer billigen Kunstfaser an, ihre junge Brust hob den rauhen Stoff, und Keetenheuve fiel ein Ausdruck des Staunens in ihrem Gesicht auf, ein ständiger Zug der Verwunderung, gepaart mit Enttäuschung, Reue und Zorn. Das Mädchen war nicht eigentlich schön, auch war sie klein, aber ihre frische und etwas trotzige Haltung machten sie hübsch. Sie war wie ein junges Pferd, das ins Gespann genommen war, erschreckt ist und sich bäumt. Sie folgte zögernd, die Blätter des »Kriegsrufes« in der Hand, der Uniformierten, die fünfundzwanzig Jahre alt sein mochte, ein blasses, von Heimsuchungen gezeichnetes Gesicht hatte, in dessen bleicher nervös gespannter Fläche streng ein fast lippenloser Mund verschlossen ruhte. Ihr Haar, soweit Keetenheuve es unter der Schute sehen konnte, war kurz geschnitten, und das Mädchen sollte, wenn es die entstellende Kopfbedeckung abnahm, wie ein Knabe aussehen. Keetenheuve fühlte sich von dem Paar angezogen. *Keetenheuve neugierig und empfindsam. Die* Uniformierte hielt dem Stammtisch die Sammelbüchse hin, und die dicken Geschäftsleute warfen mit mißmutiger Miene Fünfpfennigstücke in den verrosteten Schlitz. Ihre dicken Weiber blickten dumm und hochmütig in die Weite; sie schauten, als wären das Heilsarmeemädchen und die Sammelbüchse nicht zu se-

hen. Das Mädchen zog ihre Büchse zurück, und in ihrem Gesicht waren Gleichgültigkeit und Verachtung. Die Bürger sahen nicht zu dem Gesicht des Mädchens auf. Sie vermuteten nicht, daß man sie verachten könne; und das Heilsarmeegeschöpf brauchte sich nicht zu mühen, seine Verachtung zu verbergen. Die mit frommen Spruchbändern geschmückte Gitarre schlug mit hellem Ton gegen Keetenheuves Tisch, und das Mädchen hielt nun ihm verächtlichen Ausdrucks die Büchse hin — ein hochmütiger, finsterer Engel des Heils. Keetenheuve wollte mit ihr reden, aber Schüchternheit hinderte ihn, und er sprach nur in seinen Gedanken zu ihr. Er bat: Singen Sie doch! Singen Sie den Choral! Und das Mädchen sprach in Keetenheuves Gedanken: Es ist nicht der Ort! Und Keetenheuve erwiderte in seinem Denken: Jeder Ort ist der rechte Platz, um den Herrn zu preisen. Und er dachte weiter: Du bist eine kleine Lesbierin, du erinnerst mich, und du hast große Angst, dir könnte etwas genommen werden, was du dir gestohlen hast. Er schob fünf Mark in die Sammelbüchse, und er schämte sich, weil er fünf Mark in den Schlitz steckte. Es war zuviel, und es war zuwenig. Die kleine nichtuniformierte Sechzehnjährige beobachtete Keetenheuve und schaute ihn verwundert an. Und dann schob sich die ein wenig aufgesprungene Unterlippe ihres gewölbten sinnlichen Mundes vor, und in ihrem Gesicht zeigten sich sinnlos aufrichtige Wut und Empörung. Keetenheuve lachte, und das Kind sah sich ertappt und errötete. Keetenheuve hätte die Mädchen gern aufgefordert, sich zu ihm zu setzen. Er wußte, daß es bei den Bürgern ein Aufsehen geben würde; aber das war ihm gleichgültig, ja, es hätte ihn gefreut. Aber er war schüchtern gegen die Mädchen, und bis er es wagte, sie zu sich zu bitten, rief die Uniformierte die Kleine, die unentwegt Keetenheuve anstarrte, energisch zur Tür. Das junge Mädchen bebte wie das Pferd, das den verhaßten Ruf des Kutschers hört und einen festen Griff an der Kandare fühlt; sie wandte von Keetenheuve den Blick und rief: »Gerda, ich komme ja schon.«
Die Mädchen gingen. Die Tür klingelte. Die Tür fiel ins Schloß. Und mit dem Zuschlagen der Tür sah Keetenheuve

London. Er sah einen großen Plan der großen Stadt London mit all ihren ins Land gelegten Vororten an der Wand einer Untergrundbahnstation hängen, und auf dem Plan war in London im Viertel der Docks ein wenig Fliegendreck. Da stand er, Keetenheuve, in London im Viertel der Docks und auf einer Untergrundbahnstation. Der Zug, der ihn ausgeworfen hatte, war weitergefahren; es brauste und zog eisig im Fahrtunnel. Keetenheuve fror auf dem Bahnsteig. Es war Sonntagnachmittag. Es war ein Sonntagnachmittag im November. Keetenheuve war arm, fremd und allein. Auf der Straße regnete es. Es war ein strichelnder, peitschender Regen, der aus niedrigen Wolken tropfte, aus trächtigen Nebelwänden, die wie schwere wollene Mützen auf den Dächern der aussätzig schmutzigen Häuser, der geteerten Schuppen lagen und sich mit dem beißenden trägen Rauch aus alten grindigen Kaminen vollsogen. Der Rauch dunstete nach Mooren, er roch wie schwelender Torfbrand auf nassem Moor. Es war ein bekannter Geruch, es war der Geruch der Hexen Macbeth', und im Wind war ihr Schrei; schön ist wüst, und wüst ist schön! Die Hexen waren mit den Nebelbänken in die Stadt gereist, sie hockten auf den Dächern und Traufen, sie hatten ein Rendezvous mit dem Seewind, sie besichtigten London, sie pißten in die alten Viertel, und dann heulten sie geil auf, wenn der Sturm sie stieß, wenn er sie ins Wolkenbett warf, sie durchschüttelte, sie toll und lüstern umfing. Überall pfiff und stöhnte es. Ringsumher knarrte das Gebälk der Speicher, ächzten die windschiefen Dächer. Keetenheuve stand auf der Straße. Er hörte die Hexen gurren. Die Kneipen waren geschlossen. Männer standen untätig herum. Sie hörten die Hexen. Die warmen Kneipen waren geschlossen. Frauen standen frierend in den Torwegen. Sie lauschten ins Hexenrumoren. Der Gin war in den verriegelten Kneipen eingeschlossen. Die geilen Hexen lachten, heulten, pißten, koitierten. Der Himmel war voll von ihnen. Und da kam aus Nebel und Nässe, aus Torfrauch, Sturm und Hexensabbat die Musik, kam die Heilsarmee mit ihren Bannern, kam mit ihrem »Kriegsruf«, kam mit Pauken und Trompeten, mit Schirmmützen und Schutenhüten, mit Ansprachen und Chor-gesang und versuchte, die Dämonen zu bannen und die Nichtigkeit des Menschen zu leugnen. Der Zug der Heilsarmee formte eine Schnecke, schloß einen Kreis, und da standen sie und riefen, bliesen und paukten ihr *Lobet den Herrn,* und die Hexen lachten weiter, hielten sich den Wolkenbauch, pißten und legten sich vor dem Wind auf den Rücken. Gelbe graue schwarze moorgeschwängerte schwellende wollustwehe Hexenschenkel, Hexenbäuche waren der sturmgerüttelte wolkige Himmel über dem schmutzigen Square zwischen den Docks. Die kleinen gemütlichen Kneipen waren geschlossen, die finsteren, anheimelnden Stehausschänke. Und wären die Kneipen selbst offen gewesen, wer hätte den Shilling gehabt für das leimige dunkelschäumende Bier? So stellten sich die Männer und die Frauen, so stellten sich die Armen des Sonntags, so stellte sich *Keetenheuve armer Emigrant* um die Heilsleute auf, sie hörten der Musik zu, sie hörten stumm dem Singen zu, aber sie hörten die Ansprache nicht, sie hörten die Hexen, sie fühlten, wie es kalt nach ihnen griff, sie fühlten, wie es sie durchnäßte. Und dann gingen sie, ein schultergebeugter, ein frierender, ein trauriger Zug, die Arme verschränkt, die Hände in die Taschen gesteckt. Männer und Frauen, *Keetenheuve Emigrant SA marschiert,* hinter der Heilsarmeefahne her, hinter der Heilsarmeepauke drein, und die Hexen tobten und lachten, und der Wind stieß sie ordentlich, fest, noch einmal noch einmal, du lieber Wind von der See, vom eiskalten Pol, erwärm dich, erhitze dich, wir sind die Hexen vom Moor, wir sind zum Ball im guten alten London ... Sie kamen zu einem Schuppen, und dort mußten sie warten, weil auch die Heilsarmee ihnen zeigen wollte, daß sie arme Leute waren, die zu warten hatten. Und warum sollten sie nicht warten? Es wartete nichts auf sie. Der Schuppen war warm. Es brannten Gaskamine. Sie summten, ihre Flammen leuchteten gelb und rot und blau wie flatternde Irrlichter, und es roch süßlich im Raum, süßlich wie nach einer dumpfen Narkose. Sie setzten sich auf Holzbänke ohne Lehnen, denn für die Armen sind Bänke ohne Lehnen gut genug. Die Armen dürfen nicht müde sein. Die Reichen dürfen sich anlehnen. Hier waren nur Arme. Sie stützten die

Hände auf die Schenkel und beugten sich vor, denn sie waren kreuzmatt vom Stehen, vom Warten, vom Verlorensein. Die Musik spielte »Wacht auf ihr Christen allzumal«, und ein Mann, den sie Oberst nannten und der wie ein Oberst aus dem »Sketch« aussah *Colonel Keetenheuve bei einer Krik-ketpartie auf Schloß Bancquo,* hielt die Predigt. Der Oberst hatte eine Frau (sie sah lange nicht so vornehm aus wie er, dessen Bild im »Sketch« erschien, sie konnte gerade noch seine Waschfrau sein, durfte seine Unterhosen walken) und Frau Oberst forderte, nachdem Herr Oberst gesprochen hatte (Was hatte er gesagt? Keetenheuve wußte es nicht, niemand wußte es), Frau Oberst forderte die Versammelten auf zu bekennen, wie schlecht sie seien. Nun lebt ein Hang zur Ent-blößung in vielen Menschen, auch eine Neigung zum Maso-chismus, und so traten einige vor und klagten sich eitel schlechter Gedanken an, die sie nie gedacht hatten, während sie ängstlich verhüteten, daß die Schlangen aus ihnen spra-chen, das Giftgewürm, das wirklich in ihrer Brust nistete. Die schlechten Taten blieben ungebeichtet. Vielleicht war es klug, sie hier nicht zu erwähnen. Vielleicht saßen Kriminal-beamte im Saal. Und was waren überhaupt schlechte Taten, wenn man sie hier den Menschen und doch wohl auch Gott bekennen sollte? Einen Hund zu quälen, ist eine schlechte Tat. Ein Kind zu schlagen, ist eine schlechte Tat. Aber war es ein schlechter Gedanke, die Bank berauben zu wollen? Oder war es schlecht, einen Anschlag auf einen mächtigen bösen und allseits geehrten Mann zu planen? Wer wußte es? Man brauchte ein sehr waches Gewissen, um das zu ent-scheiden. Hatte der Oberst der Heilsarmee ein solches Gewis-sen? Er sah nicht so aus. Sein vornehmer Stutzbart war martia-lisch, er war mehr Armee als Heil. Und wenn der Oberst die-ses empfindsame Gewissen hätte, was würde es ihm nützen, denn gerade ein entwickelter, ein scharfer, ein zarter Sinn für Gut und Böse wird die Frage, ob ein Bankraub sittlich oder unsittlich sei, überhaupt nicht beantworten können. Nach der Beichte gab es endlich den erwarteten Tee. Er wurde aus einem großen dampfenden Kessel in Aluminium-becher geschöpft. Der Tee war schwarz und war stark gesüßt.

Man verbrannte sich an dem Aluminiumbecher die Lippen, aber wohlig lief der Trank über die Zunge, wohlig und glühend rann er in den Leib. Die Gasflammen summten, und ihre weichen tödlichen Abgase vermischten sich mit dem süßen Duft des Tees, mit Indiens Märchengeruch und mit der strengen Ausdünstung der ungewaschenen Körper, dem Mief der regennassen, nun schwelenden Kleider zu einem Nebel eigener Art, der sich vor Keetenheuves Augen rötete und ihn schwindlig machte. Alle sehnten sich nach draußen, sie sehnten sich nach dem Sturm, sie sehnten sich nach den Hexen — aber die lockenden Kneipen waren noch immer geschlossen. Man wollte auch hier in Bonn schließen. Die Stammtische brachen auf. Die Geschäftsleute reichten sich unter falschem Lächeln die fetten Hände, sie drückten einander die dicken Finger mit den goldenen Ringen, sie wußten, was jeder wert war, sie kannten den gegenseitigen Saldo. Nun gingen sie und löschten die Lampen in ihren Schaufensterfallen. Sie entkleideten sich. Sie entleerten sich. Sie krochen ins Bett, der dicke Geschäftsmann, die dicke Geschäftsmannsfrau, der Sohn wird studieren, die Tochter wird gut heiraten, die Frau gähnt, der Mann furzt. Gute Nacht! Gute Nacht! Wer friert auf dem Feld?

Keetenheuve sah, wie die Lichter in den Fenstern erloschen. Wo sollte er hingehen? Er ging ziellos. Und vor dem Kaufhaus traf er wieder die Heilsarmeemädchen, und diesmal begrüßte er sie wie alte Bekannte. Gerda zerbiß ihre schmalen blutlosen Lippen. Sie war wütend. Wie haßte sie die Männer, die in ihrer Vorstellung durch das unverdiente Geschenk des Penis toll gewordene Dummköpfe waren. Gerda wäre gern davongelaufen, aber sie zweifelte, ob Lena, die kleine Sechzehnjährige, ihr folgen würde, und so mußte sie stehenbleiben und die Nähe des räuberischen Mannes erdulden. Keetenheuve ging mit Lena vor den Schaufenstern des Kaufhauses auf und ab, auf und ab vor dem erloschenen Licht in den Zimmern der Puppen, und er hörte, während Gerda sie verkniffenen Mundes und mit brennenden Augen beobachtete, die Geschichte eines Flüchtlings. Lena erzählte sie ihm mit einem sanften, zärtlich die Silben verschluckenden Dialekt. Sie kam aus Thüringen und war Mechanikerlehrling. Sie behauptete, Zeugnisse zu haben, daß sie Mechaniker sei und schon als Werkzeugmacher gearbeitet habe. Ihre Familie war mit Lena nach Berlin geflogen, und dann waren sie in den Bund geflogen worden und hatten lange in Lagern gelebt. Lena, der kleine Mechaniker, wollte seine Lehrzeit beenden, und dann wollte er als Werkzeugmacher viel Geld verdienen, und dann wollte er studieren und Ingenieur werden, wie man es ihm im Osten versprochen hatte, aber im Westen lachte man ihn aus und sagte ihm, die Drehbank sei hier nichts für Mädchen und das Studieren nichts für Arme. So steckte irgendein Arbeitsamt Lena in eine Küche, steckte sie in die Küche eines Gasthauses, und Lena, der Flüchtling aus Thüringen, mußte die Teller abspülen, die fettigen Reste, die fetten Saucen, die Fetthäute der Würste, die fetten übriggebliebenen Stücke vom Braten, und ihr wurde übel vor so viel Fett, und sie kotzte in das bleiche schwabbelnde Fett hinein. Sie lief aus der Fettküche fort. Sie lief auf die Straße. Sie stellte sich am Wegrand auf und winkte den Automobilen, denn sie wollte das Paradies erreichen, das ihr als eine blanke Fabrik mit geölten Werkbänken und gutbezahlter Achtstundenarbeit vorschwebte. Handlungsreisende nahmen Lena mit. Fette Hände betasteten ihre Brust. Fette Hände langten unter ihren Rock, zerrten am Steg ihrer Hose. Lena wehrte sich. Die Handlungsreisenden schimpften. Lena versuchte es mit den Lastfahrern. Die Lastfahrer lachten über den kleinen Mechaniker. Sie langten Lena unter den Rock. Wenn sie schrie, schalteten sie den Motor 'runter und warfen Lena im ersten Gang aus dem Wagen. Sie kam zur Ruhr. Sie sah die Essen. Die Hochöfen brannten. Die Walzwerke arbeiteten. Die Schmieden schmiedeten. Aber vor den Werktoren saßen die fetten Portiers, und die fetten Portiers lachten, wenn Lena fragte, ob man einen geübten Mechanikerlehrling einstellen wolle. Die fetten Portiers waren viel zu fett dazu, um einem Mechanikerlehrling unter den Rock zu greifen. So war Lena in die Hauptstadt gekommen. Was tut der Obdachlose, was beginnt der Hungernde? Er hält sich am Bahnhof auf, als ob mit den Zügen das Glück käme. Viele sprachen Lena an.

Auch Gerda sprach Lena an. Lena folgte Gerda, dem Heilsarmeemädchen, und sie besah sich die Stadt mit dem »Kriegsruf« in der Hand, und sie wunderte sich über alles, was sie sah. Keetenheuve dachte: Auch Gerda wird deine Brust anfassen. Er dachte: Auch ich werde es tun. Er dachte: Es ist dein Schicksal. Er dachte: Wir sind so, es ist unser Schicksal. Er sagte ihr aber, daß er versuchen wolle, ihr eine Stelle zur Beendigung ihrer Lehre zu verschaffen. Gerdas Mund öffnete sich böse. Sie meinte, das hätten schon viele Lena versprochen, und diese Versprechungen kenne man. Keetenheuve dachte: Du hast recht, ich will Lena wiedersehen, ich will sie anfassen, sie reizt dazu, und mich reizt sie besonders; das ist es. *Keetenheuve ein schlechter Mensch.* Er nahm sich aber dennoch vor, mit Korodin, der Verbindungen zu Fabriken hatte, vielleicht auch mit Knurrewahn oder mit einem in arbeitsamtlichen Verhältnissen erfahrenen Kollegen seiner Fraktion über Lena zu sprechen. Er wollte ihr helfen. Der Mechaniker sollte an seine Werkbank kommen. *Keetenheuve ein guter Mensch.* Er bat Lena, am nächsten Abend wieder in die Weinstube zu schauen. Gerda nahm Lenas Hand. Die Mädchen entschwanden in die Nacht. Keetenheuve blieb in der Nacht zurück.

Nacht. Nacht. Nacht. Kein guter Mond. Ein Wetterleuchten. Nacht. Nacht. Nachtleben. In der Gegend vom Bahnhof versuchte man's. Lemuren. In der Bar glotzten Lemuren auf ein hageres Gespenst, das einen Rekord im Dauerklavierspiel aufstellen wollte. Das Gespenst saß in durchschwitzten Strümpfen an einem alten Flügel und hämmerte, von gefüllten Aschenbechern und geleerten Coca-Cola-Flaschen umgeben, aus den Tasten die Melodien, die jeder Lautsprecher brüllte. Von Zeit zu Zeit trat ein Kellner an das Gespenst heran, steckte ihm mit gleichgültiger Miene eine Zigarette in den Mund oder schüttete ihm gelangweilt ein Glas Coca-Cola in den Schlund. Das Gespenst nickte dann wie der Tod im Kasperle-Theater, was Dankbarkeit und kameradschaftliche Verbundenheit ausdrücken sollte. Nacht. Nacht. Lemuren. Die Rheinuferbahn blitzte. Sie blitzte nach Köln. An der Station im Café Kranzler saßen dicke Männer und san-

gen »Ich hab' noch einen Koffer in Berlin«. Sie blickten zu
dicken Frauen hinüber und sangen »Ich hab' so Heimweh
nach dem Kurfürstendamm«, und die dicken Frauen dachten: Ministerialräte, Regierungsräte, Botschaftsräte, und sie
wackelten mit ihrem Fett auf Berliner Art, Schweineleber
mit Äpfeln und Zwiebeln, schneuzten sich berlinerisch: »So
komm doch Kleener immer de Pfoten mang de Blumen-
töppe«, und die Agenten, die Reisenden, die Antichambrie-
rer dachten: Wat für 'ne Wolke von Weib, jenau wie die
Olle zu Hause, nur zu dufte, dreißig Piepen, die Olle macht's
Sonntag umsonst, muß mir 'n Magazin koofen, verjess sonst,
wie 'n Weib jebaut ist. »Ich passe.« Sie spielten Berliner
Skat und tranken ihre Weiße mit Schuß aus großen Urin-
gläsern. Nacht. Nacht. Lemuren. Frost-Forestier ging zu Bett.
Die Fabrik Frost-Forestier wurde stillgelegt. Er turnte am
Reck. Er stellte sich unter die Brause. Er frottierte den trainierten, den proportionierten Leib. Er trank zwei Schluck
Kognak aus einem hohen Schwenkglas. Der große Funkkasten sprach Nachrichten. In Moskau nichts Neues. Aufrufe
an das Sowjetvolk. Der kleine Funkkasten schrie: »Dora hat
Windeln. Dora hat Windeln.« Auf dem Tisch lag eine Photo-
kopie des Interviews der Generale aus dem Conseil Supérieur
des Forces Armées. Mergentheims Telephonnummer steht auf
dem Streifen. Auf dem Streifen steht: Anfragen wegen Guatemala. Das schwarze Photopapier mit der weißen Schrift
sieht wie ein Corpus delicti aus. Frost-Forestier zieht den
Wecker auf. Er ist auf fünf Uhr dreißig gestellt. Frost-Forestiers Bett ist schmal. Es ist hart. Eine dünne Decke deckt
Frost-Forestier zu. Frost-Forestier schlägt einen Band aus
dem Werk Friedrichs des Großen auf. Er liest. Er liest Friedrichs holpriges Französisch. Er betrachtet einen Stich, ein
Bild des Königs, des Königs mit dem Windhundgesicht. Frost-
Forestier löscht das Licht. Er schläft wie auf Kommando ein.
Hinter den generalsroten Vorhängen draußen im Park schreit
ein Käuzchen. Nacht. Ein Käuzchen schreit. Es bedeutet Tod.
*Ein Hund hat gebellt. Judenwitz. Bedeutet Tod. Keetenheu-
ve abergläubisch.* Nacht. Nacht. Lemuren. Im ersten Stock
wählten sie die Schönheitskönigin der Nacht. Abendkleider

wie wehende Lokusfenstervorhänge. Ein Berufsrheinländer, immer lustig, immer vergnügt, stand am Hausmikrophon und bat die Damen zur Wahl. Kichern der Damen. Verschämte Blicke auf den geölten Fußboden. Der Berufsrheinländer, immer lustig, immer vergnügt, setzte durch, was er durchpeitschen wollte *Keetenheuve Einpeitscher im Haus der Gemeinen.* Der Berufsrheinländer, immer lustig, immer vergnügt, lief unter die Gäste, Sekttische, Weinzwangtische, Sekt-und-Weincommis, faßte die Händchen der Dämchen, führte sie aufs glatte Parkett der Entscheidung, stellte sie vor, stellte sie bloß, stellte sie zur Wahl, entgleiste Hausfrauen, ausgekratzte Mütter, Gewänder aus dem Heimberater *schlicht und strahlend,* wie entferne ich Spermatozoen, was koche ich schlank, fragen Sie Frau Christine sie rät am dümmsten, unfreie, verkrampfte, doch maßlos eingebildete Bewegungen. Keetenheuve stand am Eingang *Keetenheuve schlechter Gast Nassauer Flaschenzwang Flaschenkind nimm den Schnuller* er dachte ans Parlament, zweite Lesung des Gesetzes, das war morgen, kein Gesetz für Schönheitsparaden, Herr Präsident, meine Damen und Herren, eine Entscheidung von säkularer Bedeutung, wir stimmen im Hammelsprung ab, ich springe durch die falsche Tür, ärgert die Fraktion, wir springen hier Hammel, Schäfchen zur Rechten und Schäfchen zur Linken, der Berufsrheinländer, immer lustig, immer vergnügt, auf, auf, marsch, marsch!, er wartet auf die Annahme der Gesetze. Keetenheuve dachte: Was stellst du an, wie wirst du sie kränken, jede dieser des Rupfens nicht werten Gänse hält sich für schön, träumt sich unwiderstehlich, ihre Eitelkeit ist noch größer als ihre Dummheit, sie werden's dir übelnehmen. Den Berufsrheinländer aber, auf auf marsch marsch!, lustig vergnügt, quälten solche Skrupel nicht. Munter blieb er beim einmal begonnenen Werk. Er numerierte seine goldene Schar, bat die verehrten Gäste, bat die Commis, geschwänzte Böcke, die Nummer der Erkorenen, die Nummer der Schönsten auf die im Saal verteilten Wahlzettel zu schreiben. War aber keine Schöne im Saal. Waren alle reizlos. Sie waren häßlich. Sie waren die häßlichen Töchter des Rheins. Wagalaweia, Huldinnen, Blödin-

nen, Ungekürte. Schau noch einmal hin! Eine animalische
Hübsche ist da. Fleisch auf dem Markt. Ein rosiger Rabe.
Keetenheuve wählte sie. *Keetenheuve erfüllte Wahlpflicht.*
Keetenheuve Staatsbürger. Sie hatte geschwungene sinnliche
Lippen, einen Kuhblick, leider, Europa *Keetenheuve Zeus,*
einen runden Busen, straffe Hüften, schlanke Beine, und die
Vorstellung, mit ihr im Bett zu liegen, war nicht unange-
nehm. Warm ist die Nacht. Van de Veldes Vollkommene
Ehe. Liebling, wie soll ich mich drehen und wenden? *Kee-*
tenheuve Van-de-Velde-Gatte. Er war neugierig. Wie stan-
den die Odds? Machte sein Favorit das Rennen? Nur eine
Stimme für die animalisch Hübsche! Sie war die letzte im
Kranz. Ein knochiger Kleiderständer mit Damenfrisur und
Gansgesicht war gewählt; lief unter der Marke »anständiges
Mädchen mit solider Aussteuer«. Hübschheit nicht gefragt.
Im Schlafzimmer schummerige Lampen. Alle Katzen grau.
Tusch der Künstlerkapelle. Der Berufsrheinländer, immer lustig, immer vergnügt, überreichte Schachteln mit klebrigem
Konfekt. Holdes Lächeln der Schönen. *Holdes Mädchen, hör*
mein Flehen. Keetenheuve Sänger im Abgang. Die Commis
klatschten und bestellten die zweite Flasche; angeregte, geschwänzte Böcke. Rührige Vertreter gesucht. Zielbewußte Arbeiter. Arbeitete Keetenheuve zielbewußt? *Wird Keetenheuve*
klug? Nein, er wird nicht klug, Ist er verurteilt? Ja, er ist
verurteilt. Keine Stimme: Ist gerettet? Keine Stimme. Nacht
Nacht. Lemuren. Ein feinerer Ort, eine vornehmere Stätte.
François-Poncet war nicht erschienen. Ging in Paris im Frack
der Akademiker aus. Palmenbestickt. Er arbeitete am Wörterbuch. Saß auf Pétains Stuhl. Sie wußte nicht, in welchem
Arm sie lag, aber es war ein gesellschaftlich vertretbarer
Arm, und der Kopf zu dem Arm gehörte einer Whisky-Re-
klame, King Simpson Old Kentucky Home American Blend,
das forderte Vertrauen, und sie tanzte beim Wetterleuchten auf
einer Terrasse am Rhein, Sophie Mergentheim aus der Ver-
triebsabteilung des alten »Volksblattes« in Berlin. Berliner
Zimmer, Hofzimmer, Dunkelzimmer, beschlagnahmt, ein-
gekerkert, verbrannt, zerstört, sie gehörte zum Schaum auf
dem Pudding, Creme der Creme, rötlicher Fonds, goldener

338

Schaum, karamelliert, Eidotter ins blonde Haar geklatscht. Mergentheim telephonierte. Der Gastgeber verließ diskret den Raum. Diplomat. Was tut er? Er lauscht diskret. Er zapft die Leitung an. Mergentheim telephonierte mit der Redaktion. Er vergewisserte sich. Der Artikel war im Blatt. Das Blatt war rechtzeitig zur Bahn gekommen. Mergentheim schwitzte in seinem Frack. Er dachte: Er ist eben mein Feind, ein Mann mit solchen Ansichten ist mein Feind. Nacht. Nacht. Lemuren. Keetenheuve stieg in den Keller. »Bei mir biste scheen« — das gab es unterirdisch. »Bei mir biste de Scheenste auf der Welt« — das war Katakombenluft, aber nicht die Katakomben unter dem Münster, nicht Korodins Grabstätte aus fränkisch-römischer Epoche, das war Keetenheuves Nachtstätte aus westbündlerischer Zeit, es duftete nicht nach Moder und nicht nach Weihrauch, es roch sehr intensiv nach Zigarettenqualm, nach Schnaps, nach Mädchen und nach Männern, man tanzte Boogie-Woogie und Rheinländer und beides heftig, es war das Lokal der jungen Leute, die keinen Stürmer trugen und keinen Schläger brauchten, um sich zu fühlen, es war eine wirkliche Katakombe, ein Keller des Verstecks, ein Hort der Opposition der Jugend gegen die alten Betten der Stadt, aber die junge Opposition gluckste wie Grundwasser dahin, rumorte für eine Nacht im Brunnen und verrieselte dann in Hörsälen, in Streberseminaren, auf Büroschemeln und am Arbeitsplatz der Laborantin. »Wir kommen alle, alle in den Himmel«, spielte die Studentenkapelle. Keetenheuve stand an der Theke. Er trank drei Schnäpse. Er trank sie schnell hintereinander, kippte sie 'runter. Er fühlte sich alt. Er kam auch nicht in den Himmel. Die jungen Leute wirbelten. Ein dampfender brodelnder Gärteig. Nackte Arme, nackte Beine. Offenstehende Hemden. Nackte Gesichter. Sie vermischten sich. Sie verwischten. Sie sangen: »Weil wir so brav sind, weil wir so brav sind.« Keetenheuve dachte: Ihr werdet euch brav in die verachteten Schlafzimmerbetten der Eltern legen, ihr werdet euch keine neuen Betten bauen, aber vielleicht verbrennen die alten Betten bis dahin, vielleicht verbrennt ihr, vielleicht liegt ihr im Gras. Es war ein Gedränge vor der Theke, aber ihn berührte es nicht. Sie stießen ihn nicht. Er stand wie isoliert. Elke wäre ein Medium gewesen, das Keetenheuve mit der jungen Welt verbunden hätte. So wagte er nicht, sie einzuladen, mit ihm zu trinken. Nicht Jüngling und nicht Mädchen wagte er einzuladen. *Keetenheuve der steinerne Gast.* Er entfernte sich. *Keetenheuve Schuljunge mit dem die andern nicht spielen wollen.* Nacht. Nacht. Lemuren. Korodin betete. Er betete in einer Mansarde. Die Kammer war unmöbliert, bis auf einen Schemel, der vor einem Kruzifix stand, das ernst an der geweißten Mauer hing. Korodin kniete auf dem Schemel. Eine Kerze brannte. Sie flackerte. Das Fenster der Mansarde stand offen. Das Wetterleuchten war stärker geworden, und die Blitze illuminierten die Kammer. Korodin fürchtete sich vor dem Himmelsfeuer, und es war eine Kasteiung, daß er das Fenster nicht schloß. Er betete: Ich weiß, daß ich schlecht bin; ich weiß, daß ich nicht recht lebe; ich weiß, daß ich alles den Armen geben sollte; doch ich weiß auch, daß es sinnlos wäre; kein Armer würde reich, kein Mensch würde besser werden. Herr, strafe mich, wenn ich irre! Der Gekreuzigte, von einem Meister aus Rosenholz geschnitzt, sah im Licht der Blitze schmerzgekrümmt, krank, leidend, er sah verwest aus. Er war ein Sinnbild der Qual. Die Qual blieb stumm. Sie antwortete Korodin nicht. Korodin dachte: Ich sollte weggehen. Ich sollte nichts verschenken. Das ist alles ganz falsch. Das hält nur auf. Das lenkt nur ab. Ich sollte einfach weggehen. Weggehen und immer weitergehen. Ich weiß nicht, wohin. Ich habe kein Ziel — und er ahnte wohl, daß es darauf ankam, kein Ziel zu haben. Das Nichtziel war das wahre Ziel. Aber er fürchtete den Blitz. Er fürchtete den beginnenden Regen. Er betete weiter. Christus blieb stumm. Nacht. Nacht. Lemuren. Am Bahnhof grölten Besoffene. Sie grölten: »Die Infanterie!« Vorbei! Sie grölten: »Wir wollen unsern Kaiser Wilhelm wiederhaben.« Vorbei! In Haustoren standen Strichburschen und boten sich an. Vorbei. Am Bahnhof warteten abdeckerreife Totenrosse der Lust auf einen Reiter. Vorbei. Es blitzte und donnerte. Der Regen fiel. Keetenheuve nahm ein Taxi. Es blieb ihm nichts anderes übrig. Er mußte heimfahren. Heim in die Puppenstube. Heim in das Getto. Heim in das Regierungsgetto, in das Getto der Abgeordneten, in das Getto der Journalisten, das Getto der Beamten, das Getto der Sekretärinnen. Es blitzte und donnerte. Er öffnete das von der niedrigen Zimmerdecke bis zum Fußboden reichende französische Fenster. Das schmale Wandklappbett erwartete ihn 'runtergeklappt, wie er es verlassen hatte. Das Bettzeug war nicht gemacht. Bücher lagen aufgeschlagen herum. Schriften lagen herum. Ein Tisch war mit Papieren bedeckt, mit Skizzen, mit Entwürfen, mit halb konzipierten Reden, Eingaben, Beschlüssen, mit angefangenen Aufsätzen, mit liegengelassenen Briefen. Keetenheuves Leben war ein Entwurf. Es war ein Entwurf zu einem wirklichen Leben; aber Keetenheuve konnte sich das wirkliche Leben nicht mehr vorstellen. Er wußte nicht, wie es aussah; und er würde es bestimmt nicht mehr leben. Ein Brief von Elke lag bei den Papieren. Ihr letzter Brief. Elke war die Chance gewesen, die Chance für ein anderes Leben. Vielleicht. Er hatte die Chance verspielt. Vorbei. Blitze. Blitze über ein Grab. Er sah die traurigen immergrünen Gewächse des Friedhofs im Schein fahler Blitze. Er atmete den Geruch der modrig feuchten Buchsbaumhecken, die süße Verwesung der verfaulten Rosen in den Totenkränzen. Die Friedhofsmauer duckte sich im Licht der Blitze. Furcht und Zittern. Kierkegaard. Kindermädchentrost für Intellektuelle. Schweigen. Nacht. *Keetenheuve furchtsamer Nachtvogel Keetenheuve verzweifelter Nachtkauz Keetenheuve gerührter Wanderer durch Gräberavenuen Gesandter in Guatemala Lemuren begleiten ihn*

Er erwachte. Er erwachte früh. Er erwachte nach unruhigem Schlaf. Er erwachte im Getto.

Jedes Getto war von unsichtbaren Mauern umzogen und lag zugleich offen da, zur Schau gestellt jedem Überblick und jedem Einblick. Keetenheuve dachte: Getto der Hitler und Himmler, Getto der Verschleppten und Getto der Gejagten, die Mauern, der Wall, die Verbrennungsöfen von Treblinka, der Aufstand der Juden in Warschau, alle Lager des Nachkriegs, jede Baracke die uns angeht, alle Nissenhütten, alle Bunker, alle Vertriebenen und alle Geflohenen — die Regierung, das Parlament, die Beamten und der Troß, wir sind ein Fremdkörper im trägen Fleisch unserer Hauptstadt.

Sichtbar waren des Raumes vier Wände, sichtbar Decke, Fenster und Tür des winzigen Zimmers, und zu sehen waren, der Vorhang beiseite, die Jalousie hochgezogen, die Fronten der anderen Gettohäuser, die schnellerrichteten, flachdächigen, weitfenstrigen, stahlgefaßten, hochgetriebenen Baracken. Sie glichen der Wohnstadt eines großen Wanderzirkusses, den Buden einer Ausstellung; sie waren auf Abbruch gebaut. Ein Fräulein Sekretär badete. Das Wasser rauschte in Röhren durch die Wand. Das Fräulein Sekretär wusch sich gründlich, seifte sich ein, spülte sich ab, amtlicher Schmutz löste sich auf, floß über die Brüste, die senkten sich, leider, floß über den Leib, die Schenkel hinunter, schwamm in den Abfluß, fiel in die Unterwelt, vermählte sich dem Kanalwasser, dem Rheinstrom, dem Meer. Die Spülungen der Klosetts ruckten und liefen. Dreck trennte sich von den Menschen. Ein Lautsprecher krächzte: »Eins, zwei, drei, nach links geneigt, eins, zwei, drei, nach rechts gebeugt.« Ein Narr gymnastizierte. Er hüpfte, man hörte es, ein schwerer Körper, nacktleibig, klatschfüßig über die Dielen. Es war Sedesaum, der Froschmensch. Aus einem zweiten Lautsprecher piepste ein Kinderchor: »Lasset uns singen, tanzen und springen.« Die Stimmen der Kinder klangen gedrillt, sie schienen gelangweilt zu sein, der Gesang war dumm. Die Abgeordnete Frau

Pierhelm hörte den Kindern zu. Frau Pierhelm lebte aus der Büchse. Sie bereitete sich einen Kaffee aus der Nesbüchse, mischte ihn mit Büschenmilch und wartete auf die Sendung *Wir Hausfrauen und der Sicherheitspakt.* Frau Pierhelm hatte vor vierzehn Tagen die Sendung in Köln auf das Tonband gesprochen.

Keetenheuve lag auf dem schmalen Klappbett. Er starrte auf zu der Umrandung des Bettes, einem mit Büchern bedeckten Brett, und er starrte weiter zur niedrigen Zimmerdecke hinauf, in der sich die Rillen im kaum getrockneten Verputz zu verschlungenen Linien vereinten, zu einem verworrenen Wegenetz, der Generalstabskarte eines unbekannten Landes. Frau Pierhelm war nun im Radio zu hören: »Wir Hausfrauen dürfen nicht, wir Hausfrauen müssen, wir Hausfrauen vertrauen.« Was durfte Frau Pierhelm nicht, was mußte sie, wem vertraute sie? In der Generalstabskarte rieselte es. Ein neuer Graben wurde aufgerissen. Frau Pierhelm rief aus Köln: »Ich glaube! Ich glaube!« Frau Pierhelm im Äther glaubte. Keetenheuve auf seinem Klappbett glaubte nicht. Frau Pierhelm, Wand an Wand mit Keetenheuve im Gettohaus, Frau Pierhelm, die Tasse mit der Neskaffee-Büchsenmilchmischung, den Aschbecher mit ihrer Morgenzigarette vor sich, die Abgeordnete Frau Pierhelm, ein Vogel Strauß, steckte den Kopf tief in den Schrankkoffer, wo sie frische Wäsche suchte, wer wusch einem das Hemd, wenn man für des Volkes Zukunft werkte, die Politikerin Frau Pierhelm hörte zufrieden der Rednerin Pierhelm zu, die zu dem Schluß kam, daß der Pakt den deutschen Frauen Sicherheit gebe, ein schöner Slogan, der nur allzusehr an die Anzeige einer Fabrik für intime Tampons erinnerte.

Es war noch früh. Keetenheuve war ein Frühaufsteher, und fast alle in Bonn waren matinale Geister. Der Kanzler bereitete sich rosenduftumweht und von der Rheinluft gestärkt, die seine Gegner lähmte, schon auf die Sitzung vor, und Frost-Forestier hätte sich längst wieder wie eine von starken Spannungen bewegte Maschine in Gang gesetzt. Keetenheuve dachte: Wird er sich wieder vortasten, was wird er mir heute anbieten, Kapstadt, Tokio? Aber er wußte, Frost-Forestier

343

würde ihm keine Mission mehr anbieten, und wenn es Abend war, würden sie ihn hetzen.

Keetenheuve war ruhig. Sein Herz schlug ruhig. Ein wenig bedauerte er, daß ihm Guatemala entgehen sollte. Er dachte mit Bedauern an seinen Verzicht auf den Tod in der spanisch-kolonialen Veranda. Guatemala war eine echte Versuchung gewesen. Er war ihr nicht unterlegen. Er hatte sich entschieden. Er würde kämpfen. Die Radios schwiegen. Man hörte nur das sommerliche Morgenlied der Hauptstadt: Grasmäher, die ratternd wie alte Nähmaschinen über den Rasen gezogen wurden.

Sedesaum, der Froschmensch, hüpfte die Treppen hinunter. Auf jeder Stufe erschütterte sein Aufklatsch das leichtgebaute Haus. Sedesaum war Berufschrist, Gott möge ihm verzeihen, und da keine Kapelle in der Nähe war, hüpfte er allmorgendlich in den Milch- und Brötchenladen, ein Werk der Demut und der Publicity zu tun, und die Illustrierten hatten auch schon den volksnahen Volksvertreter *eure Sorgen sind meine Sorgen* mit Milchflasche und Brötchentüte im Arm ins Bild gebracht, und außerdem war, was er hier unternahm, auch noch eine Tat der Toleranz, der Samariter unterstützte seinen gestrauchelten Bruder, und im Jenseits wurde es ihm angerechnet. Sedesaum kaufte sein Frühstück bei Dörflich ein. Dörflich hatte den einzigen Laden weit und breit, somit ein Monopol, man mußte bei ihm kaufen, aber leider war Dörflich auch ein Ärgernis, man konnte ihn mit einem abtrünnigen Priester vergleichen, er war ein aus seiner Fraktion ausgestoßener Abgeordneter, der aber noch nicht die parlamentarischen Weihen verloren hatte. Er war in eine anrüchige und zunächst einträgliche Affäre verwickelt gewesen, für die sich leider die Journalisten interessiert hatten, und die dann, durch Dementis und Ehrenerklärungen aufgerührt, nicht mehr zu vertuschen und nicht mehr vorteilhaft gewesen war; man schickte Dörflich als Sündenbock in die Wüste der Fraktionslosigkeit, wo er zum Entsetzen aller Kollegen im Parlamentariergetto das Milchgeschäft eröffnete. Wollte Dörflich sich mit Kuhmilch weißwaschen, indem er spekulierte, daß seine Kunden von ihm sagen würden, er sei ein ehrenwerter

Mann, oder wollte er nur den Gewinn aus der einträglichen Anrüchigkeit sicherstellen; wie dem auch sei, »non olet«, bei Dörflich stank merkbar nur der Käse, wenn Keetenheuve auch einen aasigen Geruch, der nicht aus der Käseglocke kam, in Dörflichs Nähe zu spüren meinte. Dabei fand Keetenheuve es vernünftig von Dörflich, sich durch den Milchhandel eine Existenz über die Unsicherheit einer Neuwahl hinaus gesichert zu haben. Er teilte die Entrüstung der Parlamentsgenossen nicht, und er dachte sogar: Wir sollten jeder unser Milchgeschäft haben, damit uns nicht der Brotkorb mit unseren gestorbenen Ideen verheiratet. So belustigte es Keetenheuve, aus dem Fenster des Gettohauses zuzusehen, wie Dörflich die Ware aus seinem Abgeordnetenwagen hob, und Keetenheuve nahm es hin, daß der schwarze und vorläufig fraktionslose Volksvertreter sein Handelsgut wahrscheinlich auf Bundeskosten bewegte. Aber von dieser vielleicht unmoralischen Amüsiertheit abgesehen, mochte Keetenheuve Dörflich nicht, und Dörflich seinerseits haßte *Keetenheuve die Intelligenzbestie*. So wurde Keetenheuve, als er einmal bei Dörflich die Milch probierte, mit Fleiß ein sauer gewordener Trunk kredenzt, und Keetenheuve dachte: Wer weiß, wer weiß, vielleicht sehen wir uns im Vierten Reich wieder, Dörflichs Ministersessel steht schon zwischen den Milchkannen verborgen, und mein Todesurteil ist geschrieben.

Keetenheuve blickte zum Fenster hinaus, und er sah die Gegend wie eine photographische Aufnahme, wie die interessante Kameraeinstellung eines Films, ein Stück Rasen war angeschnitten im Bild, und auf dem grünen frischen Teppich stemmte sich ein Mädchen in weißer Dienstschürze, mit weißem Diensthäubchen (ein Mädchen, wie es sie gar nicht mehr gab und wie sie plötzlich Gespenstern gleich in Bonn auftauchten) gegen eine ratternde Grasmähmaschine, und das Keetenheuve gegenüberliegende Gettohaus senkte sich als kühle Fassade aus Beton, Stahl und Glas bis zu Dörflichs Milchladen herab, wo Sedesaum, Milchflasche und Brötchentüte im runden Ärmchen, klein aus dem Schatten der weißblaugestreiften Markise hüpfte, klein, eitel und demütig, klein, fromm und schlau, und so würde er, die Milch und die

Brötchen dann im runden Bäuchlein, klein, demütig und eitel, klein, schlau und fromm, in den Plenarsaal hüpfen, ein Jasager, ein Sänger des Herrn, und der Herr brauchte nicht unbedingt als der Herr Zebaoth über dem Sternenzelt zu wohnen, Sedesaum fand immer die Formel, irdischen und himmlischen Herrendienst vor seinem Gewissen und vor der Welt in Einklang und Wohlklang zu bringen, und jetzt folgte ihm, der über den Platz hüpfte, sein rechter Fuß klatschte eitel, der linke klatschte demütig auf, folgte ihm Dörflich aus dem Schatten der Markise, der für heute sein Milchgeschäft seinem ihm ehelich angetrauten Weibe überließ und sich im blauen Anzug und mit der gestärkten Hemdbrust betont altväterlicher Ehrbarkeit in den von Milchkannen und Brotkörben befreiten Abgeordnetenwagen setzte, um ins Parlament zu fahren und dort sein Mandat auszuüben. Keetenheuve bereitete der Anblick Unbehagen. Es war nicht vorauszusagen, wie Dörflich stimmen würde. Gern marschierte er mit den stärkeren Bataillonen, aber seit er fraktionslos geworden war, redete er lieber zum Fenster hinaus, phrasierte, um Anhänger zu gewinnen, vor den Unzufriedenen im Lande, fischte im trüben, und so war zu fürchten, daß er diesmal mit der Opposition stimmen würde, wenn auch aus unklaren und eigensüchtigen Motiven. Keetenheuve schämte sich eines solchen nach altem Nazismus riechenden und neuem Nazitum zustrebenden Verbündeten (noch hatte sich der Wind nicht recht erhoben), wie überhaupt die Zufallsfronten, die sich ergaben, die Gemeinschaft mit den Sturen, den Verstimmten, den Diktatorialen, den bestenfalls Mediokren, die irgendein Sektenwahn oppositionell und sanft gestimmt hatte, Keetenheuve ärgerten, ihn behinderten und ihn schließlich an seiner Sache zweifeln ließen. Erst als er Frau Pierhelm und Sedesaum gemeinsam — er hüpfte, und sie ging erhobenen Hauptes, entschlossenen Schrittes — das Haus verlassen sah, arme Ritter der alten Union der festen Hand, die kleinen Gefolgsleute der braven staatserhaltenden Gesinnung und des montanunionistisch eifersüchtigen Klüngels (nicht, daß sie Kuxen besaßen, aber sie wußten doch, wo Bartel den Most holt, wo das Quellein

rieselte, wo es in den Wahltopf pinkelte, aber nicht, daß sie
sich verkauften, weiß Gott nicht, die Richtung lag ihnen
eben, sie hatten es noch in der Schule vernommen, und dabei
waren sie stehengeblieben, einfältige Klippschüler der Politik und eitel auf des Herrn Lehrers Gruß), da fühlte sich Keetenheuve wieder berufen, ihnen entgegenzutreten und ihnen,
die wieder Leithammel ins Schlachthaus sein wollten, Bremsen ins Fell zu setzen. Aber der Leithammel, drum ist er's ja,
geht unbeirrt seines Weges, und die Herde, es ist ja ihr Wesen, folgt, von jedem Warnruf nur noch zusätzlich erschreckt,
ängstlich dem Vortier ins Unglück. Der Hirte aber hat seine
eigenen Gedanken über die Bestimmung der Schafe. Er ver-
läßt unabgestochen das Schlachthaus und schreibt fern von
der Blutstätte die »Erinnerungen eines Schäfers«, anderen
Hirten zu Nutz und Frommen.

Das Parlament war an diesem Tag durch Polizei abgeriegelt,
und die Truppe zeigte die hysterische Einsatzbereitschaft
jeder gedrillten Mannschaft, der man auf dem Übungsplatz
das Gespenstersehen beigebracht hat, und sie besetzten und
umzirkelten das Haus des Volkes mit Waffen, Wasserwerfern
und Spanischen Reitern, als ob die Hauptstadt und das Land
sich gegen den Bundestag erheben wolle (und dann wäre er
abgesetzt), während Keetenheuve, der sich immer wieder
aufs neue ausweisen mußte, den Eindruck hatte, daß außer
wenigen Neugierigen und Schausüchtigen nur ein paar billig
Hergefahrene, ein paar preiswert Verfrachtete, arme Cla-
queure mit Rufen demonstrierten, die erst durch den massi-
ven Einsatz ihrer polizeilichen Bekämpfer überhaupt Bedeutung gewannen. Sie schrien, daß sie ihre Abgeordneten
sprechen wollten, und Keetenheuve dachte: Das ist doch ihr
gutes Recht, warum läßt man sie nicht mit ihren Abgeordneten sprechen? Er wäre bereit gewesen, mit den Schreiern
zu sprechen; aber es war fraglich, ob sie ihn meinten, ob sie
ihn sprechen wollten. *Keetenheuve Mann des Volkes kein
Mann des Volkes.* Die eigentlich dürftige Demonstration war
traurig, weil sie etwas von der dumpfen Schicksalsergebenheit
des wirklichen Volkes zeigte, das aus einem Gefühl, es kommt
doch alles wie es kommen soll, wir können da doch nichts

machen, Gesetze und Entscheidungen, die es wohl ablehnte, nicht verhinderte, es nicht einmal versuchte, sondern bereit war, die Folgen zu tragen; — die Würfel waren dann eben wieder einmal gefallen. So erinnerte die Szene vor dem Parlament an die Premiere eines Filmes, eine nicht zu große Menge dummer und schaulustiger Leute, die gerade Zeit haben, hat sich vor dem Lichtspielhaus eingefunden und wartet auf die bekannten Gesichter der Stars. Man raunt, da kommt der Albers, und ein Kritiker, der den Film kennt, möchte den Gassenjungen recht geben, die pfeifen; doch die Bengel flöten ja gar nicht, weil auch sie das Lichtspiel schlecht finden, sie pfeifen, weil das Gellen ihres Pfiffes sie freut, und die strenge Meinung des Kritikers bliebe ihnen unverständlich und wäre ihnen sogar zuwider. Keetenheuve wußte, während er sich dem Bundeshaus näherte, wie verworren und fragwürdig sein Auftrag war. Aber welches System war besser als das parlamentarische? Keetenheuve sah keinen anderen Weg; und die Schreier, die das Parlament überhaupt abschaffen wollten, waren auch seine Feinde. *Quasselbude schließen. Genügt Leutnant mit zehn Mann. Und der Hauptmann von Köpenick.* Gerade darum schämte sich Keetenheuve des Schauspiels, das er sah. Der Präsident des Bundestages ließ sein Haus durch Polizisten bewachen, während jedes echte Parlament bestrebt sein sollte, die bewaffneten Organe der Exekutive seinem Domizil möglichst fernzuhalten, und in den guten Urzeiten der parlamentarischen Idee hätten sich die Abgeordneten geweigert, unter Polizeischutz zu tagen, denn das Parlament war damals, wie es auch zusammengesetzt sein mochte, polizeifeindlich, weil es die Opposition an sich war, die Opposition gegen die Krone, die Opposition gegen der Mächtigen Willkür, die Opposition gegen die Regierung, die Opposition gegen die Exekutive und ihren Säbel, und so bedeutete es eine Pervertierung und Schwächung der Volksvertretung, wenn aus ihrer Mitte die Mehrheit zur Regierung wird und die vollziehende Gewalt an sich reißt. Was heißt dies bei **unglücklicher** Zusammensetzung des Hauses anderes als Diktatur auf Zeit? Die Mehrheit exekutiert ihre Gegner nicht; aber sie ist doch ein kleiner Tyrann, und während sie herrscht, ist die Minderheit ein für allemal geschlagen und zu einer eigentlich sinnlosen Opposition verdammt. Die Fronten standen fest, und leider war es undenkbar, daß ein Redner der oppositionellen Minderheit die regierende Mehrheit überzeugen konnte, daß er einmal recht und sie unrecht habe. Aus der Opposition den Kurs der Regierung zu ändern, gelänge in Bonn selbst Demosthenes nicht; und auch wenn man mit eines Engels Zunge spräche, man predigte tauben Ohren, und Keetenheuve wußte, während er die letzte Sperrkette passierte, daß es genau besehen zwecklos war, daß er hier erschien, um im Plenum zu reden. Er würde nichts ändern. Er hätte ebensogut im Bett bleiben und träumen können. Und so näherte sich der Abgeordnete nicht hochgemut, sondern niedergestimmt dem Quartier seiner Fraktion: *Napoleon der am Morgen der Schlacht weiß wie Waterloo enden wird*

Im Zimmer der Fraktion warteten sie auf ihn; Heineweg und Bierbohm und die anderen Routiniers der Ausschüsse, die Verfahrenshasen, die Geschäftsordnungshengste blickten schon wieder vorwurfsvoll auf Keetenheuve. Knurrewahn hielt Heerschau über die Seinen, und sieh', es fehlte unentschuldigt kein teures Haupt. Sie waren aus der Provinz zur Sitzung gereist, die Luft der Provinz hing in ihren Kleidern, sie brachten sie mit in den Saal, eine dumpfe Luft aus engen Kammern, in denen sie aber anscheinend abgekapselt hausten, denn auch sie vertraten nicht unmittelbar das Volk, dachten nicht mehr wie das Volk, auch sie waren — kleine, ganz kleine — Präzeptoren des Volkes, nicht gerade Lehrer, aber doch Respekts- oder Unrespektspersonen, vor denen die Leute das Maul hielten. Und sie wieder, seine Heerscharen, hielten den Mund vor Knurrewahn, der zuweilen fühlte, daß hier etwas nicht stimme. Er betrachtete seine schweigende Garde, Rundköpfe und Langschädel, brave Kerle, auf die er sich verlassen konnte. Treugebliebene aus der Zeit der Verfolgung, aber alle Befehlsempfänger, eine Mannschaft, die vor dem Feldwebel strammstand, und Knurrewahn, der nun oben saß, als Volksmann, gewiß, aber doch oben im Kreis der Kopfgötter, regierungsnah und einflußreich, Knurrewahn lauschte vergeblich nach einem Sehnsuchtswort von unten, nach einem Freiheitsschrei, nach einem Herzschlag, der aus der Tiefe kam, keine unverbrauchte Kraft, kaum in die Disziplin zu bannen, regte sich, kein ungebärdiger Wille zur Erneuerung, kein Mut zum Sturz der alten toten Werte war zu spüren, seine Sendboten brachten kein Echo der Straßen und Plätze, der Fabriken und der Hütten mit, sie waren es im Gegenteil, die auf Weisungen lauschten, auf Richtungszeichen von der Spitze, auf Befehle von Knurrewahn, sie förderten die Parteibürokratie der Zentrale und waren nichts als Außenposten dieser Bürokratie, und hier lag die Wurzel des Übels, sie würden zurück in ihre Provinzorte reisen und dort verkünden, Knurrewahn will, daß wir uns so oder anders verhalten, Knurrewahn und die Partei wünschen, Knurrewahn und die Partei befehlen, statt daß es umgekehrt gewesen wäre, statt daß die Provinzboten zu Kurrewahn gesagt hätten, das Volk wünscht, das Volk will nicht, das Volk trägt dir auf, Knurrewahn, das Volk erwartet von dir, Knurrewahn — Nichts. Vielleicht wußte das Volk, was es will. Aber seine Vertreter wußten es nicht, und so taten sie so, als ob wenigstens ein starker Parteiwille da sei. Aber wo kam er her? Aus den Büros. Er war impotent. Von den Samensträngen der Volkskraft war der Parteiwille abgeschnitten, die Kraftstränge verliefen im Unsichtbaren, und einmal mußte es irgendwo im Volksbett Pollutionen und Befruchtungen geben, die unerwünscht waren. Die Parteileitung kannte ihre Mitglieder nur als Beitragszahler und, seltener, als Befehlsempfänger. Da funktionierte die Maschine reibungslos. Und wenn Knurrewahn die Auflösung der Partei befohlen hätte, die Ortsgruppen würden die Auflösung vollziehen, wenn Knurrewahn die Selbstentleibung als Opfer an die Nation anordnete — die Partei hatte schon seit neunzehnhundertviezehn ein nationales Herzleiden. Wenige sprangen aus der Reihe (und machten sich dadurch verdächtig). Da war Maurice, der Advokat, und da war Pius König, der Journalist, Knurrewahn brauchte sie, aber eigentlich bereiteten sie ihm Unbehagen, und Keetenheuve machte ihm wirklichen Kummer. Er nahm Keetenheuve am Arm, führte ihn an ein

Fenster und beschwor ihn, in der Debatte nicht zu heftig zu werden, die nationalen Instinkte (Gab es sie? Waren sie nicht Komplexe, Neurosen, Idiosynkrasien?) nicht zu brüskieren, und er erinnerte ihn, daß die Partei nicht bedingungslos und grundsätzlich gegen jede Bewaffnung sei und daß sie nur die jetzt zur Diskussion stehende Form der neuen Rüstung ablehne. Keetenheuve kannte die Weise. Sie stimmte ihn traurig. Er war allein. Er kämpfte allein gegen den Tod. Er kämpfte allein gegen die älteste Sünde, das älteste Übel der Menschheit, gegen die Urtorheit, den Urwahn, daß durch das Schwert das Recht verfochten, daß durch Gewalt irgend etwas gebessert werden könne. Die Sage von Pandora und ihrer Büchse ist ein Gleichnis für das Übel, das aus Weibshörigkeit stammt, aber Keetenheuve hätte dem alten Knurrewahn gern eine Büchse des Mars beschrieben, aus der, wenn man sie öffnete, alle Weltübel, die nur auszudenken waren, breit, kräftig und allwegs vernichtend strömten. Aber Knurrewahn wußte es ja, auch er kannte die Gefahren, aber er meinte (er litt mit seinem Steckschuß besonders an der nationalen Herzkrankheit seiner Partei), das Heer in der Hand der demokratischen Staatsmacht behalten zu können, obwohl Noske das Heer aus dieser demokratischen Hand schon einmal kläglich verloren hatte.

Keetenheuve wurde zum Telephon gerufen, er sprach aus einer Zelle, und er hörte das Zwitschern der geschäftigen Schwatzhelferinnen Frost-Forestiers, bis Frost-Forestier *Magnus* selbst aus der Hörmuschel säuselte und Keetenheuve verkündete, Guatemala würde ihm bewilligt werden, das gehe glatt, was auch geschehen möge; und Keetenheuve, etwas verwundert zwar, hatte deutlich das Empfinden, daß Mephisto am anderen Ende des Drahtes sei, wenn auch ein entlarvter Teufel, von dem man plötzlich wußte, daß er zur Schmiere gehöre. Er wünschte sich einen Moment, um sich konzentrieren zu können, um alles noch einmal zu bedenken, und er mußte weit denken, er mußte bis an die Saar denken und bis zur Oder, er mußte sich an Paris erinnern, an Grünberg in Schlesien und an Ortelsburg in Masuren, er hatte an Amerika und an Rußland zu denken, an gleich-ungleiche

Brüder, Korea, China und Japan, Persien und Israel und die muselmanischen Staaten waren zu betrachten, und vielleicht war Indien das Morgenland, aus dem das Heil kam, die dritte Macht, ausgleichend und versöhnend, und wie klein war das Vaterland, in dem er lebte, das winzige Pult, auf dem er sprechen würde, während Überschallflugzeuge von Kontinent zu Kontinent rasten, Atomgranaten zur Erprobung des großen Sterbens über Wüsten flogen und Todespilze, den zartesten Gehirnen entreift, über einsamen Atollen aufblühten. Da aber trat Maurice, der Advokat, zu Keetenheuve und gab ihm Mergentheims Blatt zu lesen und meinte gutgläubig und advokatisch, daraus könne Keetenheuve doch was für seine Rede gewinnen. Keetenheuve hielt Mergentheims Zeitung in der Hand, und wirklich, er mußte seine Rede umwerfen. Er sah, daß seine Waffe ihm entwunden, daß sein Dynamit stumpf geworden war. Mergentheim brachte in großer Aufmachung einen Bericht über das Interview der Generale aus dem Conseil Supérieur des Forces Armées, und er knüpfte, der Mutige, der mutige Ballzuwerfer, an die Nachricht einen Kommentar, daß man mit Generalen von solcher Siegergesinnung keine deutsch-alliierte Armee aufbauen könne. Ja, Keetenheuves Pulver war naß geworden! Sie hatten die Pressekorrespondenz, die Dana ihm gegeben hatte, in die Hand bekommen, und da nur ein Exemplar dieser im Bund wenig gelesenen Agenturausgabe in Bonn gewesen war, mußten sie's sich von ihm geholt haben, den Schatten natürlich nur, sie hatten's photographiert und waren ihm so zuvorgekommen, und Frost-Forestiers neuer Anruf wegen der spanisch-kolonialen Sterbeveranda in Guatemala war also das freundliche Gnadenbrot, das man selbst noch dem zahnlosen Köter gewähren wollte. Was sich ereignet hatte, war Keetenheuve klar, und was sein würde, war ihm nicht weniger deutlich. Der Kanzler, wahrscheinlich in die Intrige gar nicht eingeweiht und für eine Weile auf Mergentheim erbost, würde heftig auf den Artikel reagieren, er würde die Versicherungen der französischen und der englischen Regierung haben, daß die Äußerungen der Generale bedauerlich und zu dementieren und daß die angestrebte

Militärvereinigung ihrem Wesen nach herzlich und von Dauer sei.

Man läutete zur Sitzung. Sie strömten in den Plenarsaal, Schafe zur Linken und Schafe zur Rechten, und die schwarzen Schafe saßen ganz rechts und ganz links, aber sie schämten sich nicht, sie krakeelten. Keetenheuve konnte von seinem Platz aus den Rhein nicht strömen sehen. Aber er dachte sich sein Strömen, er wußte ihn hinter dem großen Fenster, dem pädagogisch-akademischen, und er wähnte ihn völkerverbindend, nicht völkerscheidend, er sah das Wasser wie einen freundlichen Arm sich um die Länder legen, und das Wagalaweia klang nun wie Zukunftsmusik, ein Abendlied, ein Wiegenlied im Frieden.

Der Präsident war ein Schwergewicht, und da er der Partei der guten Sache angehörte, gab er auch ihr gleich Gewicht. Sein Glöcklein läutete. Die Sitzung war eröffnet.

Spannung liegt über der Fußballarena in Köln. Der Erste Fußballclub Kaiserslautern spielt gegen den Ersten Fußballclub Köln. Es ist belanglos, wer siegt; aber zwanzigtausend Zuschauer beben. Spannung liegt über dem Spielfeld in Dortmund. Der Verein Borussia Dortmund spielt gegen den Hamburger Sportverein. Es ist völlig gleichgültig, wer siegt; niemand wird deshalb hungern, weil Hamburg gewinnt, niemand wird entsetzlich sterben, weil Borussia mehr Tore schießt; aber zwanzigtausend Zuschauer beben. Das Spiel im Plenarsaal erreicht jedermanns Brot, es kann jedermanns Tod sein, es kann diese Unfreiheit und jene Sklaverei mit sich bringen, dein Haus kann einstürzen, deinem Sohn können die Beine weggeschossen werden, dein Vater muß nach Sibirien, deine Tochter gibt sich drei Männern für eine Fleischbüchse, die sie mit dir teilt, du schlingst sie hinab, du hebst Kippen auf, die einer in den Rinnstein spuckte, oder du verdienst an der Aufrüstung, du wirst reich, weil du den Tod ausstattest (Wieviel Unterhosen braucht eine Armee? Errechne den Profit bei der Annahme eines Gewinnes von vierzig Prozent, denn du bist bescheiden), und die Bomben, die Kugeln, die Verstümmelung, der Tod, die Verschleppung erreichen dich erst in Madrid, du bist noch in deinem neuen

Wagen hingekommen, du hast noch einmal bei Horcher gegessen, du hast dich vor dem amerikanischen Konsulat angestellt, vielleicht erreichst du noch Lissabon, wo die Schiffe liegen, aber die Schiffe nehmen dich nicht mit, die Flugzeuge erheben sich ohne dich über den Atlantik, lohnt es sich? Nein, es ist nicht zu schwarz gesehen; aber im Plenarsaal zittert die Spannung nicht, keine Tausend sind bewegt. Mit Recht breitet sich Langeweile aus. Die siebenmal gesiebten Zuschauer sind enttäuscht von dem Spiel. Die Journalisten kritzeln Männchen auf ihr Papier; die Reden bekommen sie im Klischee, und das Ergebnis der Abstimmung steht fest. Man kennt das Torverhältnis zwischen den Gegnern, und niemand wettet auf den Verlierer. Keetenheuve dachte: Warum die Umstände, wir könnten das klägliche Resultat auch ohne jede Rede in fünf Minuten erfahren, der Kanzler brauchte nicht zu sprechen, wir könnten uns die Widerrede und sie sich die Verteidigung schenken, und unser gewichtiger Präsident hätte nur zu sagen, er meine, daß unser Spiel acht zu sechs enden werde, und wer's nicht glauben will, der kann die Hammel ja noch einmal zählen. Dort war die Tür zum Sprung. Da standen die Mädchen mit den Stimmzettelladen. Ach, und schon gähnte einer der Volksvertreter. Ach, und schon schlummerte einer. Ach, und schon schrieb einer nach Hause: Vergiß auch nicht, bei Unhold anzurufen, daß er die Spülung mal nachsieht, sie tropft immer in der letzten Zeit.

Heineweg stellte einen Antrag zur Geschäftsordnung. Eine zänkische, zähe Debatte entwickelte sich, und der Antrag wurde, wie vorauszusehen gewesen, niedergestimmt.

Auf der Tribüne flammten die Scheinwerfer der Wochenschauen auf, die Fernrohrobjektive der Kameras richteten sich auf den Weltstar des Hauses, der in geübter lässiger Haltung das Rednerpult bestieg. Der Kanzler trug sein Anliegen vor. Er war lustlos gestimmt und verzichtete auf Effekte. Er war kein Diktator, aber er war der Chef, der alles vorbereitet, alles veranlaßt hatte, und er verachtete das oratorische Theater, in dem er mitspielen mußte. Er sprach müde und sicher wie ein Schauspieler auf der wegen einer Umbesetzung notwendig gewordenen Durchsprechprobe eines oft gegebenen Repertoirestückes. Der Kanzler-Schauspieler wirkte auch als Regisseur. Er wies den Mitspielern ihre Plätze an. Er war überlegen. Keetenheuve hielt ihn zwar für einen kalten und begabten Rechner, dem nach Jahren ärgerlicher Pensionierung überraschend die Chance zugefallen war, als großer Mann in die Geschichte einzugehen, als Retter des Vaterlandes zu gelten, aber Keetenheuve bewunderte auch die Leistung, die Kraft, mit der ein alter Mann einen einmal gefaßten Plan beharrlich und euphorisch zuversichtlich verfolgte. Sah er nicht, daß sein ganzes Vorhaben am Ende nicht an seinen Widersachern, doch an seinen Freunden scheitern würde? Keetenheuve stritt dem Kanzler nicht den Glauben ab. Es war sein Weltbild, das er verkündete, für ihn brannte die Welt, und er ließ Feuerwehren herbeirufen und Feuerwehren gründen, um den Brand einzudämmen und zu bekämpfen. Aber der Kanzler, fand Keetenheuve, verlor den Überblick, er litt, fand Keetenheuve, an der deutschen Krankheit, unter keinen Umständen von einer einmal gehabten Vorstellung von der Welt zu lassen, und so bemerkte er nicht, fand Keetenheuve, daß von anderen Standorten aus andere Staatsmänner die Welt an anderen Plätzen von anderen Bränden heimgesucht sahen und daß auch sie Feuerwehren herbeiriefen und Löschtrupps ausrüsteten, den Brand einzudämmen und zu bekämpfen. So war die Aussicht groß, daß die verschieden orientierten Feuerwehrmänner beim Löschen einander im Wege stehen und sich schließlich prügeln würden. Keetenheuve dachte: Laßt uns überhaupt keine Weltfeuerwehren aufstellen, laßt uns ausrufen »die Welt brennt nicht«, und laßt uns zusammenkommen und uns unsere Alpdrücke erzählen, laßt uns bekennen, daß wir alle Feuersbrünste sehen, und wir werden die eigene Angst an der Angst der anderen als Wahn erkennen und zukünftig besser träumen. Er wollte von Paradiesen irdischen Glückes träumen, von einer Welt des Überflusses, von einer Erde der bezwungenen Mühe, von einem Reich Utopia ohne Krieg und Not, und er vergaß für eine Weile, daß auch diese Welt vom Himmel verstoßen, unwissend, antwortlos durch das schwarze

All treiben würde, wo hinter den nahen trügenden Sternen vielleicht die großen Ungeheuer wohnen. Niemand außer Korodin schien dem Kanzler zuzuhören, und Korodin lauschte, ob Gott aus dem Staatsführer spräche; aber Korodin hörte Gottes Stimme nicht, statt dessen hatte er zuweilen das irritierende Empfinden, seinen Bankier sprechen zu hören. Heineweg und Bierbohm wagten manchmal einen Zwischenruf. Jetzt riefen sie: »Bestellte Arbeit!« Sie erschreckten Keetenheuve, denn es kam ihm widersinnig vor, was sie da riefen. Erst dann merkte er, daß der Kanzler Mergentheims Arbeit über die Generale des Conseil Supérieur zitierte und den Artikel perfide nannte. Armer Mergentheim! Er würde es hinnehmen. Die Ehrenerklärungen lagen sicher auf dem Rednerpult, und richtig, da wurden sie schon verlesen, die Dementis aus Paris und London, die Treuebotschaften, die Freundesworte, die Bruderschaftsbeteuerungen und bald die Waffenbrüderschaft. Man hatte die Ernennung zum Festlandsdegen so gut wie in der Tasche, und nun konnte man sich rüsten, den Helm aufzusetzen, den Helm, den der Bürger verehrt, den Helm, der zeigt, wer regiert, den Helm, der dem antlitzlosen Staat das Gesicht gibt, und nur in den rechtsradikalen Brüsten saß noch neidisch und tückisch der Wurm vom Erbfeind, und sie dachten an Landsberg, an die Gefängnisse von Werl und Spandau, sie riefen »wir wollen unsere Generale wiederhaben« (und der große Butt hob sich aus dem Wasser und antwortete: Geht nur nach Hause, ihr habt sie schon); und in Knurrewahns Brust brannte der Steckschuß, und Knurrewahn war voll Mißtrauen und Sorge.

Keetenheuve sprach. Auch er stand im Licht der Wochenschauen, auch er würde im Kino zu sehen sein. *Keetenheuve Held der Leinwand.* Er sprach erst im bedächtigen, sorgenden Sinn Knurrewahns. Er erwähnte die Bedenken und Befürchtungen seiner Partei, er warnte vor weitgehenden Verpflichtungen, die unabsehbar seien, er lenkte den Blick der Welt auf das geteilte Deutschland, auf die zwei kranken Zonen, die wieder zusammenzuführen die erste deutsche Aufgabe ist, und während er sprach, hatte er das Gefühl: Es ist zwecklos, wer hört mir zu, wer soll mir auch zuhören, sie wissen, daß ich dies sage und daß ich jenes sagen muß, sie kennen meine Argumente, und sie wissen, daß auch ich kein Rezept habe, nach dem der Patient morgen gesund wird, und so glauben sie weiter an ihre Therapie, mit der sie wenigstens die Hälfte zu retten meinen, die sie für gesund und lebensfähig halten, und zufällig strömt dort der Rhein, zufällig fließt dort die Ruhr, und zufällig erheben sich da die Essen des Reviers.

Der Kanzler hielt den Kopf in die Hand gestützt. Er saß unbeweglich. Hörte er Keetenheuve zu? Man wußte es nicht. Hörte ihm irgend jemand zu? Man konnte es nicht wissen. Frau Pierhelm schleuderte wieder ihren Werbespruch gegen das Rednerpult *Sicherheit für alle Frauen*; aber auch Frau Pierhelm hatte nicht zugehört. Knurrewahn hatte das Haupt zurückgelehnt, mit seinen Bürstenhaaren sah er wie Hindenburg aus oder wie ein Schauspieler, der einen alten General spielt; das Jahrhundert artete seinen Filmschauspielern nach, und selbst ein Bergarbeiter sah schon wie ein Kumpel aus, der dargestellt wird, und Keetenheuve konnte nicht sehen, ob Knurrewahn schlief, ob er nachdachte oder ob es ihm angenehm schmeichelte, seine eigenen Gedanken aus Keetenheuves Mund zu vernehmen. Nur einer hörte Keetenheuve wirklich zu, Korodin; aber Keetenheuve sah Korodin nicht, der wider Willen gefesselt war und wieder daran glaubte, daß der Abgeordnete Keetenheuve vor einer Wandlung stand, die ihn in Gottes Nähe bringen mußte.

Keetenheuve wollte schweigen. Er wollte abtreten. Es hatte keinen Sinn, weiterzureden, wenn ihm niemand zuhörte; es war zwecklos, Worte von sich zu geben, wenn man nicht überzeugt war, einen Weg weisen zu können. Keetenheuve wollte den Weg des Raubtieres verlassen und den Pfad des Lammes gehen. Er wollte die Friedfertigen führen. Wer aber war friedfertig und bereit, ihm zu folgen? Und weiter gedacht, wenn sich alle friedfertig um Keetenheuve scharten, so würden sie zwar nicht auf ein Schlachtfeld geraten, aber es blieb fraglich, ob sie der Schädelstätte entgehen konnten. Zweifellos war es moralisch besser, ermordet zu werden, als in der Schlacht zu fallen, und die Bereitschaft, nicht kämpfend zu sterben, war die einzige Möglichkeit, das Gesicht der Welt zu ändern. Aber wer war bereit, auf das gefährliche, schwindeln machende Hochseil solcher Ethik zu klettern? Sie blieben am Boden, ließen sich eine verdammte Waffe in die Hand drücken und starben verflucht und aufgerissenen Bauches, genauso dumm wie ihre Gegner. Und wenn der entsetzliche Kriegstod, so dachte Keetenheuve, der Wille Gottes war, dann sollte man dem grausamen Gott nicht die Hilfestellung und Tarnung des Kampfes leisten, dann sollte man sich aufrecht und waffenlos ins Feld stellen und schreien: Zeige dein furchtbares Antlitz, zeige es nackt, schlage, morde, wie es dir gefällt, und schiebe die Schuld nicht auf den Menschen. Und da Keetenheuve in die unaufmerksame, in die gelangweilte, die ungerührte Runde blickte, da er den Kanzler wieder sah, gelangweilt, starr, aufgestützten Hauptes, da rief er ihm zu: »Sie wollen das Heer schaffen, Herr Kanzler, Sie wollen bündnisfähig werden, aber welche Bündnisse wird Ihr General schließen? Welche Verträge wird Ihr General brechen? In welcher Richtung wird Ihr General marschieren? Unter welcher Fahne wird Ihr General kämpfen? Kennen Sie das Tuch, Herr Kanzler, wissen Sie die Richtung? Sie wünschen das Heer. Ihre Minister wollen Paraden. Ihre Minister wollen am Sonntag bramarbasieren, wollen ihren *Männern wieder ins Auge sehen.* Schön. Lassen Sie die Dummköpfe, innerlich verachten Sie sie, aber wie ist es mit Ihrem Traum, Herr Kanzler, auf einer Lafette beerdigt zu werden? Sie werden auf einer Lafette beerdigt werden, aber Ihrem Ehrensarg werden Millionen Leichen folgen, die nicht einmal mehr billigstes Tannenholz deckt, die verbrennen, wo sie gerade stehen, die dort von der Erde begraben werden, wo die Erde aufreißt. Werden Sie alt, Herr Kanzler, werden Sie uralt, werden Sie Ehrenprofessor und Ehrensenator und Ehrenrektor aller Universitäten. Fahren Sie mit allen Ehren auf einem Rosenwagen zum Friedhof, aber meiden Sie die Lafette — das ist keine Ehrung für einen so klugen, für einen so bedeutenden, für einen genialen Mann!« Hatte Keetenheuve die Worte wirklich gerufen, oder hatte er sie wieder nur gedacht? Der Kanzler stützte weiterhin ruhig den Kopf in die Hand. Er sah abgespannt aus. Er sah nicht unnachdenklich aus. Der Saal tuschelte. Der Präsident blickte gelangweilt auf seinen Bauch. Die Stenographen hielten gelangweilt ihre Schreibgeräte bereit. Keetenheuve trat ab. Er war in Schweiß gebadet. Seine Fraktion klatschte obligatorisch. Von ganz links gellte ein Pfiff.

Frau Pierhelm stieg aufs Pult: Sicherheit, Sicherheit, Sicherheit. Sedesaum hüpfte aufs Pult, er war kaum zu sehen: Christ und Vaterland, Christ und Vaterland, Christ und Vaterland. Christ und Welt? Dörflich bemächtigte sich des Parlaments und des Mikrophons: Grundsätzliche Gegnerschaft, deutsche Grundsatztreue, Feind bleibt Feind, Ehre bleibt Ehre, Kriegsverbrechen nur auf Feindseite, Ehrenerklärung dringend notwendig. Hieß Dörflich wirklich Dörflich? Man konnte meinen, er heiße Bormann; kein Wunder, daß die Milch bei ihm sauer wurde. Eine Weile tat der Kanzler Keetenheuve leid. Noch immer saß er in unbewegter Haltung, den Kopf in die Hand gestützt. Maurice meldete staatsrechtliche Bedenken an. Korodin sollte noch reden. Er würde das christliche Abendland ins Feld führen, die alte Kultur verteidigen und von Europa schwärmen. Auch Knurrewahn würde noch kurz vor der Abstimmung sprechen. Keetenheuve ging in das Restaurant. Der Plenarsaal mußte sich sehr geleert haben. Es waren mehr Abgeordnete im Restaurant als im Plenum. Keetenheuve sah Frost-Forestier, aber er wich ihm aus. Er wich Guatemala aus. Er wollte kein Almosen. Keetenheuve sah Mergentheim. Mergentheim erholte sich bei einem Kaffee von Rundfunkdurchsagen. Er hielt Cercle. Man gratulierte ihm, daß er dem Kanzler aufgefallen war. Keetenheuve wich ihm aus. Er wollte keine Erinnerungen. Er wünschte keine Erklärungen. Er ging auf die Terrasse hinaus. Er setzte sich unter einen der bunten Sonnenschirme. Er saß wie unter einem Pilz. *Ein Männlein steht im Walde ganz still und stumm.* Er bestellte ein Glas Wein. Der Wein war dünn und gezuckert. Es war ein kleines Glas. Keetenheuve bestellte eine Flasche. Er bestellte sie in Eis. Man würde es bemerken. Man würde sagen: Der Bonze trinkt Wein. Nun gut, er trank öffentlich Wein. Es war ihm gleichgültig. Heineweg und Bierbohm würde der Anblick entsetzen. Es war Keetenheuve gleichgültig. Der Eiskübel würde Knurrewahn kränken. Es war Keetenheuve nicht gleichgültig, aber er schenkte sich ein. Er trank den kalten herben Trank in gierigen Schlucken. Vor ihm lagen Blumenbeete. Vor ihm lagen Kieswege. Vor ihm lag ein an einen Hydranten angeschlossener Feuerwehrschlauch. An der Ecke standen Polizisten mit Hunden. Die Hunde sahen wie ängstliche Polizisten aus. Bei der Senkgrube stand ein Einsatzwagen der Polizei. Der Wagen stand im Gestank. Keetenheuve trank. Er dachte: Ich bin gut bewacht. Er dachte: Ich habe es weit gebracht.

Er dachte an Musäus. Musäus, der Butler des Präsidenten, Musäus, der sich für den Präsidenten hielt, stand auf der rosenumrankten Terrasse des Präsidentenpalais, und auch er sah die Polizisten, die ihre Absperriegel bis zu ihm vorgeschoben hatten, er sah die Polizeiwagen fahren, er sah die Hundegänger bis zu ihm vordringen, und er sah Polizeiboote über den Strom brausen. Da dachte Musäus, daß er, der Präsident, gefangen sei, und die Polizei ließ dichte undurchdringliche Rosenhecken um das Palais wachsen, sie wuchsen, mit Dornen, Selbstschüssen, Fußangeln und Polizeihunden besetzt, hoch um den Präsidentensitz auf, der Präsident konnte nicht entweichen, konnte nicht zum Volk fliehen, und das Volk konnte nicht zum Präsidenten kommen. Das Volk fragte, was macht der Präsident? Das Volk erkundigte sich, was sagt der Präsident? Und man meldete dem Volk: Der Präsident ist alt, der Präsident schläft, der Präsident unterschreibt die Verträge, die der Kanzler ihm vorlegt. Und man sagte dem Volk auch, der Präsident sei sehr zufrieden, und man zeigte dem Volk Bilder des Präsidenten, auf denen der Präsident zufrieden im Präsidentenstuhl saß, und in seiner Hand verglühte weiß und vornehm eine dicke schwarze Zigarre. Aber Musäus wußte, daß er, der Präsident, unruhig war, daß ihm das Herz unruhig schlug, daß er traurig war, daß irgend etwas nicht stimmte, vielleicht die Verträge nicht, vielleicht die Rosenhecken nicht, vielleicht die Polizei mit ihren Wagen und ihren Hunden nicht, und dann wurde Musäus, der Präsident, mißgestimmt, er mochte auf einmal die Landschaft nicht mehr, die still wie ein schönes altes Bild vor seinem Blick lag, nein, Musäus, der gute Präsident, er war zu traurig, um sich länger des Landes zu freuen, er stieg in die Küche hinab, er aß ein Ripple, er trank ein Fläschchen, er mußte es tun — aus Kummer, aus Schwermut, aus Traurigkeit und großer Herzbedrückung.

Keetenheuve ging zurück in den Plenarsaal. Der Saal füllte sich wieder. Bald würde man tun, wozu man hergekommen war, man würde seine Stimme abgeben und sein Geld verdient haben. Knurrewahn sprach. Er sprach aus echter Sorge, ein Patriot, den Dörflich hängen würde, wenn er könnte. Aber auch Knurrewahn wollte sein Heer haben, auch er wollte bündnisfähig werden, aber noch nicht zu dieser Stunde. Knurrewahn war ein Mann des Ostens, und es lag ihm am Herzen, den Osten mit dem Westen wieder zu vereinen, er träumte sich als den großen Vereiner, er hoffte, mit der nächsten Wahl die Mehrheit zu erringen, zur Regierung zu kommen, und dann wollte er das Werk der Einheit vollbringen, danach wünschte er dann das Heer und die Bündnisfähigkeit. Es war merkwürdig, wie leicht zu allen Zeiten der Geschichte die Ältesten bereit waren, die Jugend dem Moloch zu opfern. Dem Parlament war nichts Neues eingefallen. Es wurde namentlich abgestimmt. Die Stimmzettel wurden eingesammelt. Keetenheuve gab seine Stimme gegen die Regierung ab, und er wußte nicht einmal, ob er recht daran tat, ob er politisch klug handelte. Er war aber auch nicht mehr gewillt, klug zu handeln. Wer würde der Regierung im Amt nachfolgen? Eine bessere Regierung? Knurrewahn? Keetenheuve glaubte nicht, daß Knurrewahns Partei die regierungsfähige Mehrheit erringen würde. Vielleicht würde eines Tages eine große Koalition der Unzufriedenen regieren mit Dörflich an der Spitze, und dann waren Tod und Teufel los. Da saßen sie nun und waren am Ende ihres Lateins, die Günstlinge des Suffrage universel, die Jünger Montesquieus, und sie merkten gar nicht, daß sie Torenspiele arrangierten, daß von der Gewaltenteilung, die Montesquieu gefordert hatte, schon lange nicht mehr die Rede war. Die Mehrheit regierte. Die Mehrheit diktierte. Die Mehrheit siegte in einem zu. Der Bürger hatte nur noch zu wählen, unter welcher Diktatur er leben wolle. Die Politik des kleineren Übels, sie war das A und O aller Politik, das Alpha und Omega der Wahl und der Entscheidung. *Die Gefahren der Politik, die Gefahren der Liebe*, man kaufte Broschüren und Schutzmittel, man glaubte, heil davonzukommen, und plötzlich hatte man Kinder und Pflichten oder die Syphilis. Keetenheuve schaute sich um. Sie sahen alle bedeppert aus. Niemand gratulierte dem Kanzler. Der Kanzler stand einsam da. Die Griechen deportierten ihre großen Männer. Gegen Themistokles und gegen Thukydides entschied das Scherbengericht. Thukydides wurde erst in der Verbannung ein großer Mann. Auch Knurrewahn stand einsam. Er faltete Zettel zusammen. Seine Hände zitterten. Heineweg und Bierbohm blickten vorwurfsvoll auf Keetenheuve. Sie blickten vorwurfsvoll, als ob er die Schuld habe, daß Knurrewahns Hände zitterten. Keetenheuve stand völlig verlassen da. Jeder mied ihn, und er ging jedermann aus dem Weg. Er dachte: Wenn wir eine Regenanlage im Saal haben, man sollte sie anstellen, man sollte es heftig regnen lassen, ein grauer Landregen sollte niederprasseln und uns alle durchnässen. *Keetenheuve der große parlamentarische Landregen*

Es war aus. Es war alles zu Ende. Es war nur Theater gewesen; man konnte sich abschminken. Keetenheuve verließ den Saal. Er floh nicht. Er ging langsam. Keine Erinnyen hetzten ihn. Er löste sich Schritt für Schritt aus einem verhexten Dasein. Er wanderte wieder durch die Gänge des Bundeshauses, wieder über die Treppen der Pädagogischen Akademie, wieder durch das Labyrinth, *Theseus der den Minotaurus nicht erschlagen hat*, gleichmütige Wächter begegneten ihm, Bundesreinemachefrauen gingen mit Eimern und Schrubbesen gleichmütig dem Staub zu Leib, gleichmütige Beamte traten den Heimweg an, das Stullenpapier sauber zusammengefaltet in der Aktenmappe, sie wollten es morgen wieder verwenden, sie hatten ein Morgen, sie waren Gestalten der Dauer, und Keetenheuve gehörte nicht zu ihnen. Er kam sich

wie ein Gespenst vor. Er erreichte sein Büro. Er schaltete
wieder das Neonlicht ein. Zwielichtig, zwiegesichtig und
bleich stand der Abgeordnete in der Unordnung seines volks-
vertretenden Lebens. Er wußte, daß es aus war. Er hatte den
Kampf verloren. Die Verhältnisse hatten ihn besiegt, nicht
die Gegner. Die Gegner hatten ihn kaum beachtet. Die Verhältnisse waren das Unabänderliche. Sie waren die Entwicklung. Sie waren das Verhängnis. Was blieb Keetenheuve? Es
blieb ihm, sich dreinzufügen, sich zum Haufen der Fraktion
zu halten, mitzulaufen. Alle liefen irgendwo mit, hängten
sich an die Notwendigkeit, sahen sie ein, hielten sie vielleicht
gar für die Ananke der Alten, und doch war es nur der Trott
der Herde, der Schub der Angst und ein schäbiger Weg zum
Grab. Nimm dein Kreuz, riefen die Christen. Diene, forderten die Preußen. Divide et impera, lehrten schlechtbezahlte
Schullehrer die Knaben. Auf Keetenheuves Tisch lagen neue
Briefe an den Abgeordneten. Seine Hand wischte sie von der
Platte. Es war nun gänzlich sinnlos geworden, ihm zu schreiben. Er wollte nicht mehr mitspielen. Er konnte nicht mehr
mitspielen. Er hatte sich ausgegeben. Er warf seine Abgeord-
netenexistenz mit den Briefen fort. Die Briefe fielen auf den
Boden, und es war Keetenheuve, als höre er sie dort stöhnen
und jammern, sie schimpften und fluchten ihm, da lagen Bitten, und da waren Erbitterung, Drohungen mit Selbstmord
und Drohungen mit Attentaten, das rieb sich, scheuerte, entzündete sich, das wollte leben, wollte Renten, Versorgungen,
ein Dach, das wollte Posten, Befreiungen, Pfründen, Beihil-
fen, Straferlasse, eine andere Zeit und andere Ehepartner
haben, das wollte seine Wut loswerden, seine Enttäuschung
beichten, seine Ratlosigkeit gestehen oder seinen Rat aufdrängen. Vorbei. Keetenheuve konnte nicht raten. Er brauchte keinen Rat. Er nahm Elkes Bild zu sich und die angefan-
gene Übersetzung des »Beau navire«. Die Mappe mit den
Akten, mit der neuen Lyrik, mit den Gedichten von E. E.
Cummings ließ er im Büro *(kiss me) you will go*
Das Neonlicht in Keetenheuves Büro leuchtete die ganze
Nacht. Es leuchtete unheimlich über den Rhein. Es war das
Auge des Drachens aus der Sage.

Aber die Sage war alt. Der Drache war alt. Er hütete keine Prinzessin. Er bewachte keinen Schatz. Es gab keinen Schatz, und es gab keine Prinzessinnen. Es gab unerfreuliche Akten, ungedeckte Wechsel, unbedeckte Schönheitsköniginnen und schmutzige Affären. Wer wollte sie bewachen? Der Drache war ein Kunde des Städtischen Elektrizitätswerkes. Sein Auge leuchtete mit einer Spannung von zweihundertzwanzig Volt und verbrauchte fünfhundert Watt in der Stunde. Seine Magie lebte in der Einbildung des Betrachters. Es war eine seelenlose Welt. Auch der friedliche Rhein war eine bloße Einbildung des Beschauers.

Keetenheuve ging die Rheinuferstraße stadteinwärts. Die Stenographen des Bundestages begegneten ihm. Sie trugen ihre Regenmäntel über dem Arm. Sie schlenderten heim. Sie verweilten am Fluß. Sie hatten es nicht eilig. Sie suchten ihr Spiegelbild im trüben Wasser. Ihre Gestalt schwankte auf trägen Wellen. Sie trieben in einem matten warmen Wind. Es war der matte warme Wind ihrer Existenz. Freudlose Kammern erwarteten sie. Den einen oder den anderen erwartete ein lustloser Schoß. Einige guckten Keetenheuve an. Sie guckten interesselos. Sie hatten gelangweilte leere Gesichter. Ihre Hand hatte Keetenheuves Worte aufgenommen. Ihr Gedächtnis hatte seine Rede nicht bewahrt.

Ein Ausflugsdampfer näherte sich dem Ufer. Über den Decks brannten Lampions. Eine Reisegesellschaft saß beim Wein. Die Männer hatten bunte Mützen auf ihre kahlen Schädel gesetzt. Sie hatten sich lange Nasen vor ihre Knollennasen gesteckt. Die Männer mit den bunten Kappen und den langen Nasen waren Fabrikanten. Sie umarmten häßlich angezogene, häßlich frisierte, streng und süßlich riechende Fabrikantenfrauen. Sie sangen. Die Fabrikanten und die Fabrikantenfrauen sangen »Wo die Möwe fliegt zum Nordseestrand«. Vor dem Wasserrad unter seiner schmutzigen Gischt stand auf einer kleinen Bühne der erschöpfte Koch des Schiffes. Er blickte abgespannt und gelangweilt zum Ufer hinüber. An seinen nackten Armen klebte Blut. Er hatte traurige stumme Karpfen getötet. Keetenheuve dachte: Wäre es eine Existenz für mich, jeden Tag die Nordseemöwe, jeden

Tag die Loreley? *Keetenheuve trauriger Koch der Rhein-dampfergesellschaft, tötet keine Karpfen*
Im Palais des Präsidenten brannte Licht. Alle Fenster standen offen. Der matte warme Wind, der Wind der Stenographen, floß durch die Räume. Musäus, der Butler des Präsidenten, der sich für den Präsidenten hielt, ging von Zimmer zu Zimmer, während der wirkliche Präsident eine seiner gebildeten Ansprachen memorierte. Musäus sah nach, ob die Betten gemacht waren. Wer würde drin schlafen in dieser Nacht? Das Bundesschiff mit dem Präsidenten trieb im matten warmen Wind auf trägen Wellen dahin, aber gefährliche Riffe lagen tückisch unter der sanften Strömung verborgen, und dann wurde der Fluß urplötzlich reißend, zerreißend, Schiffbruch drohte, Zerschellen im Dröhnen eines Falls. Die Betten waren gemacht. Wer würde schlafen? Der Präsident?
Ein Plakat leuchtete, von Scheinwerfern angestrahlt, ein erleuchtetes Zelt war am Rheinufer errichtet, es stank nach Schlick, Verwesung und künstlicher Erhaltung eines Leichnams. *Jonas den Walfisch muß man gesehen haben!* Kinder belagerten das Zelt. Sie schwenkten Papierfahnen, und auf den Fahnen stand: *Eßt Busses vitaminreiche reine Walfettmargarine.* Keetenheuve zahlte sechzig Pfennig und sah sich dem großen Säugetier des Meeres, dem Leviathan der Bibel gegenüber, einem Mammut der Polarseen, einem königlichen Wesen, urweltlich, menschenverachtend und doch eine Harpunenbeute, eine elend geschändete und zur Schau gestellte Größe, ein formalinbespritzter und nicht beerdigter Kadaver. Der Prophet Jona wurde ins Meer geworfen, der Walfisch verschlang ihn (der gute Walfisch, Jonas Retter, Jonas Vorsehung), drei Tage und drei Nächte saß Jona im Leibe des gewaltigen Fisches, das Meer beruhigte sich, die Gefährten, die ihn ins Wasser geworfen hatten, ruderten in die leere Weite, sie ruderten beruhigt dem leeren, uferlosen Horizont entgegen, und Jona betete zu Gott aus dem Bauch der Hölle, aus der Finsternis, die seine Rettung war, und Gott machte sich dem Walfisch verständlich, und er befahl dem braven, dem mißbrauchten, dem an Fastenspeisen gewöhnten mönchischen Tier, den Propheten wieder auszu-

speien. Dies konnte, wenn man das spätere Verhalten des Propheten in Betracht zog, auch eine Magenverstimmung des gutmütigen Fisches gewesen sein. Und Jona ging nach Ninive, in die große Stadt, und er predigte *Es sind noch vierzig Tage, so wird Ninive untergehen,* und da das vor den König von Ninive kam, stand er auf von seinem Thron, legte seinen Purpur ab und hüllte einen Sack um sich und legte sich in die Asche. Ninive tat Buße vor dem Herrn, aber Jona verdroß es, daß sich der Herr Ninives erbarmte und es rettete. Jona war ein großer und begabter, aber er war auch ein kleiner und rechthaberischer Prophet. Er hatte recht: Ninive sollte in vierzig Tagen untergehen. Aber Gott dachte sprunghaft, er dachte nicht nach der Denk- und Dienstvorschrift, nach der Jona, Heineweg und Bierbohm dachten, und Gott freute sich des Königs von Ninive, der seinen Purpur ablegte, und er freute sich des bereuenden Volkes von Ninive, und Gott ließ die Bombe in der Wüste von Nevada sterben, und er freute sich, weil sie in Ninive freundliche kleine Boogies zu seiner Ehre tanzten. Keetenheuve fühlte sich vom Walfisch verschlungen. Auch er saß in der Hölle, auch er saß tief unter dem Meeresspiegel, auch er im Leib des großen Fisches. *Keetenheuve Prophet von alttestamentarischer Strenge.* Aber von Gott gerettet, ausgespien aus dem Bauch des Wales, würde Keetenheuve zwar Ninives Untergang verkünden, aber groß wäre seine Freude, wenn der König seinen Purpur ablegen würde, ablegen den aus einem Maskenverleih geborgten Königsmantel, und Ninive gerettet wäre. Vor dem Zelt standen die Kinder. Sie schwenkten ihre Fahnen *Eßt Busses vitaminreiche reine Walfettmargarine.* Die Kinder hatten blasse, verbitterte Gesichter, und sie schwenkten ihre Papierfahnen mit großem Ernst, wie es die Werbefachleute von ihnen erwarteten.

Ein paar Schritte weiter traf Keetenheuve auf einen Maler. Der Maler war mit einem Wohnauto zum Rhein gefahren. Er saß im Licht seiner Autoscheinwerfer am Ufer des Stromes, er blickte sinnend in den Abend, und er malte eine deutsche Gebirgslandschaft mit einer Hütte, mit einer Sennerin, mit gefährlichen Steilhängen, mit viel Edelweiß und mit drohenden Wolken, es war eine Natur, die Heidegger erfunden haben und die Ernst Jünger mit seinen Waldgängern beschreiten konnte, und das Volk stand um den Maler herum, erkundigte sich nach dem Preis des Kunstwerkes und bewunderte den Meister.

Keetenheuve erstieg eine Fortifikation, den alten Zoll, er sah verwitterte alte Kanonen, die vielleicht noch gemütlich, mit freundschaftlichen Klapsen als Gruß von Souverän zu Souverän auf Paris geschossen hatten, er sah schmächtige, nicht recht gedeihende, schwindsüchtig winkende Pappeln, und hinter ihm stand auf einem würdigen billigen Sockel Ernst Moritz Arndt in präzeptiver redseliger Haltung. Zwei kleine Mädchen kletterten Ernst Moritz Arndt auf die Füße. Sie hatten angerauhte, viel zu große baumwollene Hosen an. Keetenheuve dachte: Ich würde euch gern in nettere Gewänder kleiden. Doch vor ihm hob sich nun mächtig der Strom aus der Landschaft. Aus der Enge seines mittleren Laufes schüttete er sich breit in die niederrheinische Weite, ergab sich dem Handel, der Regsamkeit, dem Gewinn. Das Siebengebirge versank im Abend. Der Kanzler und seine Rosen versanken im Abendschatten. Links schwang sich in hohen Bogen die Brücke nach Beuel. Kandelaber leuchteten auf der Brücke wie Fackeln gegen die Dämmerung. Ein Dreiwagenzug der Straßenbahn schien auf dem Mittelbogen der Brücke stillzustehen. Die Bahn war wie aus jeder Wirklichkeit herausgehoben, für einen Augenblick das überrealistische Abbild eines Verkehrsmittels, ein gespenstisches Abstraktum. Es war eine Todesbahn, und man konnte sich nicht vorstellen, daß sie irgendwohin fuhr. Man konnte sich nicht einmal denken, daß die Bahn ins Verderben fuhr. Die Bahn war so, wie sie auf der Brücke stand, gebannt, versteint, ein Fossil oder ein Kunstwerk, eine Bahn an sich, ohne Vergangenheit und ohne Zukunft. Eine Palme langweilte sich in den Uferrabatten. Es war nicht anzunehmen, daß es eine Palme aus Guatemala war; aber Keetenheuve dachte an die Palmen der Plaza von Guatemala. Eine Hecke wie von einem Friedhof umschloß die Palme in Bonn. Am Ufer standen Pfadfinder. Sie sprachen eine ausländische Sprache. Sie beugten sich über das Geländer des Ufers und blickten in den Fluß. Es waren Jungen. Sie hatten kurze Hosen an. In ihrer Mitte war ein Mädchen. Das Mädchen hatte lange schwarze, sehr enge, Schenkel und Waden nachzeichnende Beinkleider an. Die Jungen hatten ihre Arme auf die Schulter des Mädchens gelegt. In der Vereinigung der Pfadfinder war Liebe. Sie griff Keetenheuve ans Herz. Die Pfadfinder existierten. Die Liebe existierte. Die Pfadfinder und die Liebe existierten an diesem Abend. Sie existierten in dieser Luft. Sie existierten am Ufer des Rheins. Aber sie waren völlig unwirklich! Es war hier alles so unwirklich wie die Blumen in einem Treibhaus. Selbst der matte und heiße Wind war unwirklich.

Keetenheuve schwenkte zur Stadt ein. Er kam in das Viertel, das zerstört war. Aus einem Ruinenfeld, aus Mauerstümpfen, aus einer Kellerlandschaft ragte unversehrt der gelbe Luftschutzrichtungspfeil *Rhein*. Die Bewohner der Stadt waren einst an den Fluß geflohen, um ihr Leben zu retten. Ein großer schwarzer Wagen parkte zwischen den Trümmern. Ein Wagen mit einer ausländischen Nummer strolchte über eine Schuttstraße. Auf einem Warnschild stand das Wort *Schule*. Der ausländische Wagen bremste im Krateracker. Aus den Furchen krochen Gestalten auf ihn zu.

Keetenheuve sah wieder die Schaufenster, er sah die Schaufensterpuppen, er sah die pompösen Schlafzimmer, die pompösen Särge, die vielfachen geschlechtlichen Verkehrs- und Verhütungsapparate; er sah allen Komfort, den die Kaufleute im Frieden vor dem Volk ausbreiten.

Er ging wieder in die weniger vornehme Weinstube. Die Stammtische waren besetzt. Die Stammtische erörterten die Abstimmung im Bundestag. Die Stammtische waren mißgelaunt, und die Abstimmung mißfiel ihnen. Aber ihr Mißfallen und ihre Mißlaune waren steril; sie waren eine Mißlaune und ein Mißfallen wie unter einem Vakuum. Die Stammtische nahmen übel. Auch jedes andere Ergebnis der Parlamentssitzung hätte sie mißgelaunt gemacht und ihnen mißfallen. Sie sprachen vom Bundestag mit einem prinzipiell vorhandenen Ärger; sie sprachen von der letzten Tagung wie von einem Ereignis, das zwar an sich ärgerlich und von angemaßter Macht sei, doch das sie nichts angehe und sie nicht berühre. Was berührte dieses Volk? Sehnten sie sich nach der Peitsche, um »Hurra« schreien zu können? Keetenheuve hielt sich nicht mit den Schoppen auf *Keetenheuve großer Trinker*, er bestellte eine Flasche, ein bauchiges lustvolles Gefäß *Unterleibsflasche Krämerlustflasche* des guten Ahrweins. Dunkelrot, sanft, sämig floß der Wein aus der Flasche ins Glas, floß in die Kehle. Die Ahr war nahe. Keetenheuve hatte gehört, daß ihr Tal lieblich sei; aber Keetenheuve hatte gearbeitet, er hatte geredet und geschrieben, er hatte den Fluß und sein Tal, er hatte die Weinberge nicht besucht. Er hätte hinfahren sollen. Warum war er nicht mit Elke an die Ahr gewandert? Sie wären zur Nacht geblieben. Ihr Fenster hätte offengestanden. Die Nacht war warm. Sie hätten dem Murmeln des Wassers gelauscht. Oder waren es Palmen, die raschelten, dürre, schwertscharfe Blätter? Er saß allein *Gesandter Exzellenz Keetenheuve*, er saß auf der Veranda in Guatemala. Starb er? Er trank hastig den Wein. E. E. Cummings' »handsome man« trank begierig; US-Dichter Cummings' »blueeyed boy« trank begierig in tiefen Zügen; Mr. Death' »blueeyed boy« *Abgeordneter* trank begierig in tiefen Zügen den roten Burgundertraubenwein von der deutschen Ahr. Wer begleitete ihn von Schultagen her, breitete seine Fittiche über ihn, zeigte den scharfen Schnabel, die räuberischen Krallen? Der deutsche Aar. Er putzte sein Gefieder, er plusterte sich, nach der Mauserung der alte Kampfvogel. Keetenheuve liebte alle Kreatur, aber er mochte kein Wappentier. Drohte ein Hoheitszeichen? Stand Erniedrigung bevor? Keetenheuve brauchte kein Hoheitszeichen. Er wollte niemand erniedrigen. In der Tasche trug er Elkes Bild, trug's auf der Brust *links wo das Herz ist*. Als Knabe hatte er gelesen *Der Mensch ist gut. Und jetzt die grausige feuchte dunkle Tiefe des Grabes. Bei mir biste scheen. Schön schön schön.* Der Rundfunklautsprecher über dem Stammtisch wisperte. »Man schenkt sich Rosen in Tirol.« *Schlagerliedrosen, Rosen auch am Rhein, üppige Treibhausluftrosen, weise reiche Rosenzüchter gehen mit der Zuchtschere umher und beschneiden die jungen Triebe, Heckenschneider auf kiesbestreuten Holzwegen, böse alte Rosenzauberer, emsige Hexer werken schwitzen hexen im rheinischen Treibhaus von der Kohle des Reviers befeuert. Bei mir biste scheen, bei mir biste cheil. Geil geil geil. Zuviel geile Politik, zuviel geile Generale, zuviel geiler Verstand, zuviel geile Essen, zuviel volle Schaufenster in der Welt. Bei mir biste de Scheenste auf der Welt.* Ja, die schönste Fassade. »Vergessen Sie die Optik nicht.« »Sie müssen es von der richtigen optischen Seite ansehen.« »Jawohl, Herr Ministerialrat, Optik ist alles! *Schönste Schönheitskönigin. Bikini. Atomversuchsatoll. Schöne Säuferin. Elke verlorenes Trümmerkind. Kaputt. Verlorenes KriegsNSgauleiterkind. Kaputt. Schönste der Tribaden »be-o by-o be-o boo would-ja ba-ba-botch-a-me«.* Der Stammtisch-Lautsprecher singt: »Denn in Texas, da bin ich zu Hause.« *Busses vitaminreiches Schmelzschmalz. Die* Stammtischgeschäftsherren nicken. Sie sind Knaben. Sie sind in Texas zu Haus. Tom Mix und Hans Albers reiten in Gestalt der Geschäftsherrenjugendträume auf ungesatteltem Aschenbecher über den Stammtisch. *Ständer einer Vereinsfahne. Weht. Winkt. Everything goes crazy.* Keetenheuve trank. Warum trank er? Er trank, weil er wartete. Auf wen wartete er in der Hauptstadt? Hatte er Freunde in der Hauptstadt? Wie hießen seine Freunde in der Hauptstadt? Sie hießen Lena und Gerda. Wer waren sie? Sie waren Heilsarmeemädchen.

Sie kamen, Gerda, die Strenge, mit der Gitarre, Lena, der Mechanikerlehrling, mit dem »Kriegsruf«, und Lena verbarg nicht, daß sie zu Keetenheuve gehen wollte, und Gerda stand bleich da und verkniffenen Mundes. Die Mädchen hatten sich gezankt. Das war zu sehen. Du wirst bestohlen werden, dachte Keetenheuve, und er erschrak, weil er grausam war, weil er merkte, es vergnügte ihn, die kleine Lesbierin zu quälen, er war unritterlich (und doch nicht ungerührt), er hätte sie gern die Gitarre nehmen und singen lassen – ein Lied vom himmlischen Bräutigam. Er dachte es sich schön, Lena, den Mechanikerlehrling, um die Taille zu fassen, und Gerda sollte dazu das Lied vom himmlischen Bräutigam singen. Er sah in Gerdas bleiches Gesicht, er sah die Wut in ihrem Gesicht, er sah den verkniffenen Mund, er beobachtete die zitternden schmalen Lippen, das nervöse, gequälte Zucken der Lider, und er dachte: Du bist meine Schwester, wir gehören beide zur selben armen Hundefamilie. Aber er haßte sein Spiegelbild, das närrische Spiegelspiel seiner Vereinsamung. Ein Trinker zertrümmert den Spiegel; er zerschlägt mit dem splitternden Glas den verhaßten Ritter von der schwankenden Gestalt, sein Ebenbild, das sich zur Gosse neigt. Lena setzte sich, aufgefordert, nieder, und Gerda, auch aufgefordert, hockte sich widersam hin, weil sie nicht weichen wollte. Die Stammtischherren schauten auf. Sie saßen in der geschützten Loge und sahen den Raubtierkämpfen des Lebens zu. Keetenheuve nahm die Sammelbüchse der Heilsarmee, stand auf, klapperte mit den Groschen, *Keetenheuve später WHWsammler,* hielt sie den Geschäftsleuten hin. Die rümpften die Nase. Kannten das Büchslein nicht mehr, *keine Spenden für den Führer und seine Wehrmacht.* Sie wandten sich ab, in ihren Knabenträumen gestört. Keetenheuve träumte im Augenblick stärkere Träume. Pueril war er wie sie. *Keetenheuve Kind Pädagoge und Pädophilist. Mann mit entwickeltem pädagogischem Eros. Bekannte sich zur Jugend.* Der Stammtischrundfunklautsprecher plärrte: »Pack die Badehose ein!« Ein Kind sang, quäkte über Wald und Feld und Berg und Tal, ein Tonband verschnurrte. *Ein Hund hat gebellt. Wo? In Insterburg. Judenwitz. Mergentheimwitz. Alter Volksblattwitz. Wer lebt? Wer ist tot? Wir leben noch. Mergentheim und Keetenheuve, Arm in Arm, altes Volksblatt-Denkmal, Dem Schutz der Bürger empfohlen!* Lena wollte Coca-Cola mit Kognak trinken; paßte sich an. Gerda wollte nichts annehmen; sapphische Grundsätze. Keetenheuve sagte: »Ein Kognak würde Ihnen bekommen.« Gerda bestellte Kaffee; sie bestellte Kaffee, um sich das Recht zu sichern, auf alle Fälle im Lokal bleiben zu können. Keetenheuve hatte noch nichts für Lena, den Mechanikerlehrling, getan. Er bedauerte es aufrichtig. Er hatte seinen Tag vertan. Die Kellnerin brachte ihm Briefpapier. Es war das Papier der Weinstube. *Was ist Wein Aufgefangener Sonnenschein* stand auf dem Briefkopf. Der Brief würde auf die Herren Adressaten einen schlechten Eindruck machen. *Keetenheuve Mann ohne*

371

Anstand. Er schrieb einen Brief an Knurrewahn und schrieb einen Brief an Korodin. Er bat Knurrewahn und Korodin, Lena, den Mechanikerlehrling, wieder an die Werkbank zu bringen. Er gab Lena die Briefe. Er sagte zu ihr: »Korodin weiß nicht, ob er an Gott glaubt, und Knurrewahn weiß nicht, ob er nicht an Gott glaubt. Am besten gehst du zu beiden. Einer wird dir helfen.« Er dachte: Du wirst dich nicht abweisen lassen, meine kleine Stachanowa. Er wollte ihr helfen. Aber zugleich wußte er, daß er ihr nicht helfen wollte, daß er es war, der sich gern an sie geklammert hätte; er hätte sie gern mitgenommen, sie konnte bei ihm wohnen, sie sollte bei ihm essen, sie mußte mit ihm schlafen, er hatte wieder Appetit auf Menschenfleisch, *Keetenheuve der alte Oger;* vielleicht konnte er Lena auf die Technische Hochschule schicken, sie würde ihr Examen machen, *Lena Doktor der Ingenieurwissenschaft* — und was dann? Sollte er's wagen? Sollte er Kontakt suchen? Aber was tat man mit einem akademisch gebildeten Brückenbauer? Schlief man mit ihm? Was empfand man, wenn man ihn umarmte? *Die Liebe eine Formel*

Er nahm Lena und führte sie in die Ruinen. Gerda folgte ihnen. Mit jedem ihrer Schritte klopfte die Gitarre gegen ihren männerfeindlichen Leib und brummte. Es war ein monotoner Rhythmus. Es war ein Takt wie von einer Negertrommel, eine Klage von Geschlagensein, von Verlassenheitsgefühl, von Sehnsucht in den dunklen Wald getrommelt. Der schwarze Wagen wartete noch immer vor der Landschaft der Mauerstümpfe. Der ausländische Wagen hielt noch immer auf dem Schuttweg. Der Mond brach durch die Wolken. Auf geborstenen Steinen saß Frost-Forestier. Vor ihm stand, lässig und kühn, in freier Haltung, vom Mondlicht überflossen, in seinem bis zum Nabel geöffneten Hemd, in seinen knappen kurzen Hosen, mit mehlbestäubten nackten Waden und nackten Schenkeln der schöne Bäckerknabe, der die Kassiererin des Kinos berauben wollte. Keetenheuve winkte Frost-Forestier einen Gruß zu; aber die schattengleichen Gestalten des aufrecht auf Trümmern sitzenden Mannes und des stolz vor ihm stehenden Epheben rührten sich nicht. Sie waren wie

versteinerte Visionen, und alles war unwirklich und über-
wirklich zugleich. Aus dem auf dem Schuttweg parkenden
ausländischen Wagen drang ein Stöhnen, und Keetenheuve
war es, als ob Blut unter dem Wagenschlag hervorbräche und
in den Staub der Zerstörung tropfte. Keetenheuve führte
Lena in eine ausgeräumte Bucht aus halben Mauern, die
einmal ein Zimmer gewesen war, man sah sogar noch etwas
von der Tapete, es mochte der Raum eines Bonner Gelehrten
gewesen sein, denn Keetenheuve erkannte ein pompejani-
sches Muster und den verwaschenen wollüstigen Leib eines
weibischen Eroten mit zerrissenen Geschlechtsteilen, die über-
reifen Früchten glichen. Gerda folgte Lena und Keetenheuve
in dieses Gemäuer, das der Mond erhellte, und aus den Höhlen ringsum, aus den verschütteten Kellern, aus den Verstek-
ken der Not und der Verkommenheit wisperte es und kroch
hervor und robbte heran wie zu einem Schauspiel. Gerda
stützte die Gitarre auf einen Stein, und das Instrument antwortete mit einem vollen Akkord. »Spiel doch!« rief Keetenheuve. Er packte Lena, das Mädchen aus Thüringen, er beugte sich über ihr neugieriges erwartungsvolles Gesicht, er
suchte ihre etwas zu geschwungenen, ihre weichen, mittel-
deutsch sprechenden Lippen, trank süßen Speichel, kraftvol-
len Atem und heißes Leben aus ihrem jungen Mund, er
streifte Lenas, des Mechanikerlehrlings, dürftiges Kleid beiseite, er berührte sie, und Gerda, noch bleicher im bleichen
Mondlicht, nahm ihre Gitarre auf, schlug die Akkorde und
sang mit heller Stimme das Lied vom himmlischen Bräutigam. Und aus den Erdlöchern taumelten die Erschlagenen,
aus den Trichtern robbten die Verschütteten, aus dem Mörtel-
grab krochen die Erstickten, aus ihren Kellern wankten die
Unbehausten, und aus den Schuttbetten kam die Liebe, die
sich verkauft, und Musäus kam aufgeschreckt aus seinem
Palais und sah Elend, und die Abgeordneten versammelten
sich zu außerordentlicher nächtlicher Sitzung in ihnen angemessener Weise auf dem Gräberfeld aus nationalsozialistischer Zeit. Der große Staatsmann kam angefahren, und er
durfte in die Werkstatt der Zukunft blicken. Er sah Teufel
und Gewürm, und er sah, wie sie einen Homunkulus schu-

fen. Ein Zug von Piefkes bestieg den Obersalzberg und traf sich mit der Omnibusreisegesellschaft der Rheintöchter, und die Piefkes zeugten mit den Wagalaweiamädchen den Überpiefke. Der Überpiefke schwamm die hundert Meter im Schmetterlingsstil in weniger als einer Minute. Er gewann mit einem deutschen Wagen das Tausend-Meilen-Rennen in Atlanta. Er erfand die Mondrakete und rüstete, da er sich bedroht fühlte, gegen die Planeten auf. Schlote erhoben sich wie pralle erigierte Glieder, ein ekler Rauch legte sich um die Erde, und im schwefligen Dunst gründete der Überpiefke den Superweltstaat und führte die lebenslängliche Wehrpflicht ein. Der große Staatsmann warf eine Rose in den Rauch der Zukunft, und wo die Rose hinfiel, entstand ein Quell, und aus dem Quell floß schwarzes Blut. Keetenheuve lag im ewigen Blutfluß, er lag mit dem Thüringer Mädchen, mit dem Thüringer Mechanikerlehrling im Kreis der Volksvertreter, im Kreis der Staatsmänner, er lag im Blutbett, umgeben von Taggesindel und Nachtgelichter, und Käuzchen kreischten in der Luft, und die Kraniche des Ibykus schrien, und die Geier wetzten am erschütterten Gemäuer ihre Schnäbel. Eine Richtstätte wurde errichtet, und der Prophet Jona kam auf Jonas dem toten und gutmütigen Walfisch geritten und beaufsichtigte mit Strenge die Aufstellung der Galgen. Der Abgeordnete Korodin schleppte ein großes goldenes Kreuz herbei, unter dessen Last er gebückt ging. Er richtete mit großer Mühe das Kreuz neben dem Galgen auf, und er fürchtete sich sehr. Er brach Gold aus dem Kreuz und warf die Goldstücke in den Kreis der Staatsmänner und der Volksvertreter, in die Runde des Nachtgelichters und des Taggesindels. Die Staatsmänner verbuchten das Gold auf ihrem Konto. Der Abgeordnete Dörflich versteckte das Gold in einer Milchkanne. Der Abgeordnete Sedesaum ging mit dem Gold zu Bett und rief den Herrn an. Das Nachtgelichter und das Taggesindel beschimpfte Korodin mit gemeinen Worten. Überall auf den Mauerstümpfen, in hohlen Fenstern, auf der geborstenen Säule aus des Sängers Fluch saßen die gefräßigen heraldischen Tiere, hockten dumme aufgeplusterte mordgierige Wappenadler mit geröteten Schnäbeln, fette selbstzufriedene Schildlöwen mit blutverschmiertem Maul, züngelnde Greife mit dunkelfeuchten Klauen, ein Bär brummte drohend, Mecklenburgs Ochse sagte Muh, und SA marschierte, Totenkopfverbände paradierten, Fememordbataillone rückten mit klingendem Spiel an, Hakenkreuzbanner entfalteten sich aus moorverschmierten Hüllen, und Frost-Forestier, einen durchschossenen Stahlhelm auf dem Haupt, rief: »Die Toten an die Front!« Eine große Heerschau ereignete sich. Die Jugend zweier Weltkriege marschierte an Musäus vorbei, und Musäus nahm bleich die Parade ab. Die Mütter zweier Weltkriege zogen stumm an Musäus vorüber, und Musäus grüßte bleich ihren schwarzumflorten Zug. Die Staatsmänner zweier Weltkriege schritten mit Orden bedeckt zu Musäus hin, und Musäus unterschrieb bleich die Verträge, die sie ihm vorlegten. Die Generale zweier Weltkriege kamen mit Orden übersät im Stechschritt herbei; sie stellten sich vor Musäus auf, zogen ihre Säbel, salutierten und forderten Pensionen. Musäus gewährte bleich die Pensionen, und die Generale packten ihn, führten ihn auf den Schindanger und überlieferten ihn dem Henker. Dann kamen die Marxisten mit roten Fahnen gezogen. Sie schleppten schwer an einem Gipsbild des großen Hegel, und Hegel reckte sich und rief: »Die großen Individuen in ihren partikularen Zwecken sind die Verwirklichung des Substantiellen, welches der Wille des Weltgeistes ist.« Der ausgemergelte Dauerklavierspieler aus dem Nachtlokal spielte dazu die Internationale. Die dürftigen Schönheiten des anderen Nachtlokals tanzten die Carmagnole. Der Polizeiminister kam in einem Wasserwerfer gefahren und lud zu einer Treibjagd ein. Er hetzte dressierte Hunde über das Feld und feuerte sie mit Rufen an: Hetzt ihn, faßt ihn, jagt ihn! Der Minister suchte mit seinen Hunden Keetenheuve den Hundefreund zu fangen. Aber Frost-Forestier breitete schützend eine Weltkarte vor Keetenheuve aus, deutete auf den Rhein und sagte: »Dort liegt Guatemala!« Die Gitarre schlug; ihre Saiten wimmerten. Der Gesang des Heilsarmeemädchens hallte weit über die Trümmer, erhob sich über die Schutthalde voll Elend und Angst. Keetenheuve fühlte Lenas Hin-

gabe, und er empfand alle Hingabe der Jahre seiner Rückkehr, all die verzweifelte Bemühung, sich in den Brei zu
mischen, die unfruchtbar geblieben war und nicht erlöste. Es
war ein Akt vollkommener Beziehungslosigkeit, den er vollzog, und er starrte fremd in ein fremdes, den Täuschungen
der Lust überantwortetes Gesicht. Nur Trauer blieb. Hier war
keine Erhebung, hier war Schuld, hier war keine Liebe, hier
gähnte ein Grab. Es war das Grab in ihm. Er ließ von dem
Mädchen und richtete sich auf. Vor sich sah er den Luft-
schutzrichtungsweiser *Rhein*. Der Luftschutzpfeil stand un-
übersehbar im hellen Mondlicht und wies gebieterisch auf
den Fluß. Keetenheuve brach aus dem Kreis des Gelichters,
das sich hier wirklich versammelt hatte, von dem traurigen
Gesang, von dem schönen Gitarrenklang des Heilsarmeemädchens angelockt. Keetenheuve rannte zum Ufer des Rheins.
Schimpfworte, Gelächter eilten ihm nach. Ein Stein wurde
geworfen. Keetenheuve lief zur Brücke. Aus den erleuchteten
Vitrinen des Kaufhauses am Brückeneck winkten die Schaufensterpuppen. Sie streckten verlangend die Arme nach dem
Abgeordneten aus, der ihrem Zauber für immer entfloh. Vorbei. *Es war vorbei. Die Ewigkeit hatte schon begonnen.*
Keetenheuve erreichte die Brücke. Die Brücke bebte unter
der Fahrt der unwirklich aussehenden Straßenbahnen, und
es war Keetenheuve, als bebe der freischwebende Bogen der
Brücke unter der Last seines Körpers, unter dem Aufsetzen
seiner eilenden Schritte. Die Glocken der gespenstischen Bah-
nen schellten; es war wie ein boshaftes Kichern. In Beuel am
jenseitigen Ufer strahlte aus einem Gewinde von Glühbirnen
das Wort *Rheinlust*. Aus dem ländlichen Garten stieg eine
Rakete auf, zerplatzte, fiel, ein sterbender Stern. Keetenheuve
faßte das Brückengeländer, und wieder fühlte er das Beben
des Steges. Es war ein Zittern im Stahl, es war, als ob der
Stahl lebe und Keetenheuve ein Geheimnis verraten wolle,
die Lehre des Prometheus, das Rätsel der Mechanik, die
Weisheit der Schmiede — aber die Botschaft kam zu spät.
Der Abgeordnete war gänzlich unnütz, er war sich selbst eine
Last, und ein Sprung von dieser Brücke machte ihn frei.

Der Tod in Rom

il mal seme d'Adamo

DANTE *Inferno*

Und noch desselben Tages
empfing eine respektvoll erschütterte Welt
die Nachricht von seinem Tode.

THOMAS MANN *Der Tod in Venedig*

1

Es war einmal eine Zeit, da hatten Götter in der Stadt gewohnt. Jetzt liegt Raffael im Pantheon begraben, ein Halb-
gott noch, ein Glückskind Apolls, doch wie traurig, was später
sich ihm an Leichnamen gesellte, ein Kardinal vergessener
Verdienste, ein paar Könige, ihre mit Blindheit geschlagenen
Generale, in der Karriere hochgediente Beamte, Gelehrte, die
das Lexikon erreichten, Künstler akademischer Würden. Wen
schert ihr Leben? Die Reisenden stehen staunend im antiken
Gewölbe und blicken verlegenen Antlitzes zum Licht empor,
das durch das einzige Fenster des Raumes, die runde Öff-
nung in der einst mit bronzenen Ziegeln gedeckten Kuppel,
wie Regen auf sie fällt. Ist es ein goldener Regen? Danae
läßt sich von Cook und vom Italienischen Staatsverband für
den Fremdenverkehr wohl führen; doch Lust empfindet sie
nicht. So hebt sie auch nicht ihr Kleid, den Gott zu empfangen. Perseus wird nicht geboren. Die Meduse behält ihr Haupt
und richtet sich bürgerlich ein. Und Jupiter? Weilt er, ein
kleiner Pensionär, unter uns Sterblichen? Ist er vielleicht der
alte Herr in der American-Express-Gesellschaft, der Betreute
des Deutsch-Europäischen Reisebüros? Oder haust er hinter
Mauern am Stadtrand, in die Irrenanstalt gesperrt und von
neugierigen Psychiatern analysiert, in die Gefängnisse des
Staates geworfen? Unter dem Kapitol hat man eine Wölfin
hinter Gitter gesetzt, ein krankes verzweifeltes Tier, fern davon, Romulus und Remus zu säugen. Die Gesichter der Touristen sind in dem Licht des Pantheons wie ein Teig. Welcher
Bäcker wird ihn kneten, welcher Ofen ihm Farbe geben?

Falsch klang die Musik, sie bewegte ihn nicht mehr, fast
war sie ihm unsympathisch wie die eigene Stimme, die man,
auf ein Tonband gefangen, zum erstenmal aus dem Laut-

sprecher hört und denkt, das bin nun ich, dieser aufgeblasene Geck, dieser Lügner, Gleisner und eitle Fant, die Geigen vor allem stimmten nicht, sie klangen zu schön, das war nicht der unheimliche Wind in den Bäumen, nicht das Gespräch, das Kinder am Abend mit dem Dämon führen, so war die Furcht vor dem Dasein nicht, sie war nicht so maßvoll, sie war bei weitem nicht so wohltemperiert, inniger quält sie, die uralte Angst, sie erbebt vor dem Grün des Waldes, vor der Himmelsweite, vor den Wolken, die ziehen — dies hatte Siegfried singen wollen, es war ihm ganz und gar mißlungen, und weil seine Kraft nicht ausgereicht hatte, fühlte er sich nun schwach und verzagt, er hätte weinen mögen, doch Kürenberg war guten Mutes und lobte die Symphonie. Siegfried bewunderte Kürenberg, wie er den Noten diente und mit dem Taktstock herrschte; aber es gab Augenblicke, da sich Siegfried von Kürenberg vergewaltigt wähnte. Siegfried ärgerte sich dann, weil er sich nicht wehrte. Er konnte es nicht; Kürenberg wußte und verstand so viel, und Siegfried hatte wenig gelernt und war ihm in der Theorie unterlegen. Kürenberg glättete, gliederte, akzentuierte Siegfrieds Partitur, und was Siegfried wehe Empfindung war, das Suchen eines Klangs, eine Erinnerung an einen Garten vor aller Geburt, eine Annäherung an die Wahrheit der Dinge, die nur unmenschlich sein konnte, das wurde unter Kürenbergs dirigierender Hand human und licht, eine Musik für gebildete Zuhörer, doch Siegfried klang es fremd und enttäuschend, die gebändigte Empfindung strebte zur Harmonie, und Siegfried war unruhig, aber schließlich war er artistisch gesinnt und freute sich der Präzision, der Reinheit der Instrumente, der Sorgfalt, mit der die hundert Künstler des berühmten Orchesters seine Komposition spielten.

Im Saal wuchs Lorbeer aus grünangestrichenen Kübeln, es mochte auch Oleander sein; in Krematorien standen dergleichen Gewächse und ließen selbst zur Sommerzeit an kalte Wintertage denken. »Variationen über den Tod und die Farbe des Oleanders« hatte Siegfried seine erste größere Arbeit genannt, ein Septett, das nicht aufgeführt wurde. Er hatte in der ersten Fassung an den Tod der Großmutter gedacht, der einzigen Person in seiner Familie, die er geliebt hatte; vielleicht weil sie so still und fremd durch das vielbesuchte, von Marschstiefeln widerhallende, laute Haus seiner Eltern gegangen war. Und wie glänzend und traurig war ihre Einäscherung! Die Großmutter war die Witwe eines Pastors, und hätte sie zuschauen können, es wäre ihr nicht recht gewesen, mit wieviel Technik und Komfort, wie hygienisch und bequem, wie kaltschnäuzig und gewandt gepredigt sie aus der Welt geschafft wurde, und auch der Kranz mit der grellen Hakenkreuzschleife, den die Frauenschaft gestiftet hatte, war ihr bestimmt unlieb, wenn sie auch nie dagegen gesprochen hätte. In der zweiten Fassung des Septetts aber hatte Siegfried mit seinen sieben Instrumenten etwas Allgemeineres, Zwielichtiges ausdrücken wollen, geheimen Widerstand, blinzelnde, unterdrückte, romantische und brüchige Gefühle, und in den Sätzen des Trotzes glich sein Versuch einem rosenumwundenen Marmortorso, dem Torso eines jungen Kriegers oder dem Torso eines Hermaphroditen in der brennenden Ruine einer Waffenhandlung; es war Siegfrieds Auflehnung gegen seine Umgebung, gegen das Kriegsgefangenencamp, den Stacheldrahtzaun, die Kameraden, deren Gespräche ihn anödeten, den Krieg, den er seinen Eltern zuschrieb, und das ganze vom Teufel besessene und geholte Vaterland. Sie alle wollte Siegfried ärgern, und er hatte Kürenberg, einen früher auch zu Hause bekannten Dirigenten, von dem er in einer englischen Zeitung gelesen hatte, daß er in Edinburg sei, gebeten, ihm Beispiele der Zwölftonmusik zu senden, einer in Siegfrieds Jugendreich unerwünschten Kompositionsweise, die ihn allein schon deshalb anzog, weil sie von den Machthabern verfemt war, den gehaßten militärischen Erziehern, dem gefürchteten Onkel Judejahn, diesem mächtigen Manne, dessen düsteres Konterfei in verabscheuter Uniform über des verachteten Vaters Schreibtisch gehangen hatte, und Kürenberg hatte Siegfried das Werk von Schönberg und Webern mit einem freundlichen Brief in das Lager geschickt. Es waren ältere Notenhefte der Universaledition, die so zu Siegfried kamen und zu früh in Wien erschienen waren, um Siegfried bekannt zu werden, bevor sie

nach der Vereinigung Deutschlands und Österreichs nicht
mehr verkauft werden durften. So war diese Musik für Siegfried eine neue Welt, ein Tor, das ihn aus einem Käfig ließ,
nicht allein aus dem Stacheldrahtpferch der Kriegsgefangen-
schaft, nein aus bedrückenderer Enge, und er kroch nicht
zurück unter das Joch, wie er es nannte, der Krieg war verloren, und er wenigstens war befreit worden und beugte sich
nicht länger den Anschauungen der Sippe, in die geboren
zu sein er immer nur entsetzlich gefunden hatte.

Das Gesträuch im Saal wirkte staubig und war doch wohl
Lorbeer, denn die Blätter sahen wie getrocknetes Gewürz aus,
das zwar genäßt, doch unverkocht und splitterig in der Suppe
schwimmt. Das Gestrüpp deprimierte Siegfried, der in Rom
nicht traurig sein wollte. Aber das Blattwerk erinnerte ihn
allzusehr an eine Suppe, die ihm nicht geschmeckt hatte, an
den Eintopf der Reichsschule der Partei, in die sein Vater
ihn auf Judejahns Wunsch geschickt hatte, an den Verpfle-
gungskessel der Wehrmacht, zu der Siegfried vor dieser Schule geflohen war; auch in der Junkerschule der Partei hatte
Lorbeer gegrünt und in der Kaserne Eichenlaub mit Ranken
hin zu Orden und zu Gräbern, und stets hatte ein Bild des
verkniffenen verdrückten Kerls, des Führers mit dem Chap-
linbart, wohlwollend auf die Herde der Opferlämmer geblickt, auf die gerade schlachtreifen in Uniform gesteckten
Knaben. Hier unter dem Lorbeer und Oleander der Konzert-
halle, im künstlich frostigen Hain, hing nun ein altes Bildnis
des Meisters Palestrina, nicht wohlwollenden, eher strengen
und vorwurfsvollen Gesichts über den Bemühungen des Orchesters. Das Tridentiner Konzil hatte Palestrinas Musik anerkannt. Der Kongreß in Rom würde Siegfrieds Musik ab-
lehnen. Auch das deprimierte Siegfried, bedrückte ihn schon
auf dieser Orchesterprobe, obwohl er in der Erwartung der
Ablehnung nach Rom gereist war und sich einredete, es sei
ihm gleichgültig.

Ein Graben zieht sich um das Pantheon und war einmal eine
Straße, die vom Tempel aller Götter zu den Thermen des
Agrippa führte, das römische Weltreich brach zusammen,

Verfall deckte den Graben zu, Archäologen hoben ihn aus, Mauerrümpfe ragen verwittert moosbewachsen hervor, und auf den Stümpfen hocken die Katzen. Katzen gibt es überall in Rom, sie sind die älteste Familie der Stadt, ein stolzes Geschlecht wie die Orsini und die Colonna, sie sind wahrlich die letzten echten Römer, aber diese hier sind Gestürzte. Cäsarische Namen! Sie heißen Othello, Caligula, Nero, Tiberio. Kinder scharen sich um sie und rufen und necken die Katzen. Die Kinder haben laute, schrille, schnellsprudelnde, für den Fremden so reizvoll klingende Stimmen. Die Kinder liegen bäuchlings auf der Umfassungsmauer des Grabens. Ihre Schulschleifen verwandeln ihre verrotzten Gesichter in kleine Renoirs. Die Schulschürzen sind hochgerutscht, die Hosen winzig, und die Beine sind anzusehen wie die Glieder gegossener Plastiken unter einer Patina von Sonne und Staub. Das ist die Schönheit Italiens. Jetzt erhebt sich Gelächter. Eine alte Frau wird ausgelacht. Das Mitleid erscheint immer in hilfloser Gestalt. Die Alte wandelt mühsam am Stock und bringt den Katzen Speise. Eine eklig durchfeuchtete Zeitung umschließt den Fraß. Fischköpfe sind es. Auf blutbesudeltem Druckbild reichen sich der amerikanische Staatssekretär und der russische Außenminister die Hände. Kurzsichtig beide. Ihre Brillengläser funkeln. Verkniffene Lippen täuschen ein Lächeln vor. Die Katzen knurren und fauchen sich an. Die alte Frau wirft das Papier in den Graben. Abgemesserte Häupter der Meerleichen, gebrochene Augen, verfärbte Kiemen, opalisierende Schuppen stürzen unter die schweifschlagende mauzende Meute. Aas, ein scharfer Geruch von Ausscheidungen, von Sekret, von Fortpflanzungsgier, ein süßer von Altersfäulnis und Eiter steigt in die Luft und vermischt sich mit den Benzindünsten der Straße und dem frischen anregenden Kaffeeduft aus der Espressobar an der Ecke der Piazza della Rotonda. Die Katzen balgen sich um den Abfall. Es geht um ihr Leben. Unselige Kreatur, warum vermehrte sie sich! Die Katzen sind ausgesetzt zu Hunderten, sie sind hungrig zu Hunderten, sie sind geil, schwanger, kannibalisch, sie sind krank und verloren und so tief gesunken, wie man als Katze nur sinken kann. Ein Kater mit mächtigem

Schädel, schwefelgelb und kurzhaarig, herrscht böse über die Schwächeren. Er tatzt. Er teilt zu. Er nimmt weg. Er trägt die Schrammen der Machtkämpfe im Gesicht. Er hat eine Bißwunde am Ohr — diesen Krieg verlor er. An seinem Fell frißt die Räude. Die Kinder nennen den Kater zärtlich »Benito«.

Ich saß an einem Aluminiumtisch, auf einem Aluminiumstuhl, leicht, als solle mich der Wind forttragen, ich war glücklich, ich redete mir es ein, ich war ja in Rom, in Rom, in Rom, ich saß in Rom draußen vor der Espressobar an der Ecke der Piazza della Rotonda und trank einen Schnaps. Auch der Schnaps war flüchtig, leicht, leichtmetallen, wie aus Aluminium gebraut, ein Grappa, und ich trank ihn, weil ich bei Hemingway gelesen hatte, man trinke ihn in Italien. Ich wollte lustig sein, aber ich war nicht lustig. Mich grämte etwas. Vielleicht grämte mich die elende Katzenschar. Niemand sieht Armut gern, und hier konnte man sich nicht mit Pfennigen loskaufen. Ich weiß dann nie, was ich tun soll. Ich gucke weg. Das machen viele, aber mich quält es. Hemingway scheint nichts von Schnäpsen zu verstehen. Der Grappa schmeckte synthetisch und faulig. Er schmeckte wie ein deutscher Schwarzmarktschnaps aus der Reichsmarkzeit. Ich hatte einmal zehn Flaschen eines ähnlichen Schnapses gegen einen Lenbach getauscht. Der Lenbach war eine Bismarckstudie; ein falscher Kubaner in amerikanischer Uniform erwarb ihn. Der Schnaps war aus dem Antriebssprit von V-2-Raketen destilliert, die London vernichten sollten; man sauste, wenn man ihn trank, in die Luft, aber keine Angst, auch der Lenbach war falsch. Jetzt hatten wir in Deutschland das Wirtschaftswunder und gute Schnäpse. Auch die Italiener hatten gute Schnäpse, aber sie hatten wohl kein Wirtschaftswunder. Ich beobachtete den Platz. Da wurde der Staat betrogen. Ein junges Weib handelte aus schmutziger Schürze mit amerikanischen Zigaretten. Wieder kamen mir die Katzen in den Sinn. Das Weib war die menschliche Schwester der armen Kreatur, zerlumpt, zerzaust, voll offener Schwären. Sie war elend und verkommen; auch ihre Art hatte sich

zu stark vermehrt, und Geilheit und Hunger hatten sie verkommen lassen. Jetzt hoffte das Weib, auf Schleichwegen
reich zu werden. Sie war bereit, das Goldene Kalb anzube-
ten; aber ich weiß nicht, ob das Goldene Kalb sie erhören
wird. Mir fiel ein, das Weib könnte ermordet werden. Ich
stellte sie mir stranguliert vor; während sie sich schon als
feine Geschäftsfrau, eine echte Signora, in einem respektab-
len Kiosk thronen sah. Auf der Piazza ließ sich das Goldene
Kalb herbei, das Weib ein wenig zu lecken. Sie schien hier
wohlbekannt zu sein. Wie eine Boje stand sie im Strom des
dichten Verkehrs, und kleine flinke Fiats steuerten sie geschickt und verwegen an. Wie hier die Bremsen kreischten!
Die Fahrer, schöne Männer, mit gelockten, mit ondulierten,
mit gesalbten Haaren, gecremten, polierten, parfümierten
Glatzen, manikürten Fingernägeln, reichten Geld aus dem
Fenster des Wagens, empfingen ihre Päckchen, und schon
jagte der kleine Fiat anderen Geschäften nach und munter
anderen Weisen, den Staat um das Seine zu bringen. Eine
Jungkommunistin kam gegangen. Ich erkannte sie an dem
grellroten Halstuch über ihrer blauen Windjacke. Ein stolzes
Gesicht! Ich dachte: Warum bist du so hochmütig, du verleugnest alles, du verleugnest die alte Frau, die den Katzen
Futter bringt, und überhaupt verleugnest du das Mitleid. In
einem Torweg lauerte ein Bursche, schmierig, wie durch Öl
gezogen. Er war der Freund der Zigarettenverkäuferin, ihr
Schützling oder ihr Beschützer; vielleicht war er auch ihr
Chef, ein ernster Geschäftsmann mit Absatzsorgen, und jedenfalls meine ich, er war der Teufel, den das Schicksal dieser
Frau mit auf den Weg gegeben hatte. In Abständen traf
sich das Paar wie zufällig auf der Piazza. Sie reichte ihm die
eingenommenen schmutzigen Lirescheine, und er steckte ihr
neue, sauber in Cellophan gehüllte Päckchen zu. Ein Cara-
biniere stand in seiner eleganten Uniform wie sein eigenes
Denkmal da und blickte verächtlich und gelangweilt zum
Pantheon hinüber. Ich dachte: Du und die kleine Kommunistin, ihr werdet ein prächtiges Paar geben, die Katzen werden
Staatskatzen heißen, die mitleidige alte Frau wird in einem
Staatsheim sterben, die Fischköpfe werden volkseigen und

alles schrecklich geordnet sein. Noch aber gab es Unordnung und Sensationen. Händler riefen mit lüsterner, heiserer Stimme die Abendblätter aus. Ich bewundere sie immer. Sie sind die Rhapsoden und Panegyriker der Verbrechen, der Unglücksfälle, der Skandale und der nationalen Erregungen. Die weiße Festung im indochinesischen Dschungel stand vor dem Fall. Es ging in diesen Tagen um Krieg und Frieden, aber wir wußten es nicht. Wir erfuhren die Vernichtung, die uns gedroht hatte, erst viel später und aus Zeitungen, die jetzt noch nicht gedruckt waren. Wer konnte, aß gut. Wir tranken unseren Kaffee, unseren Schnaps; wir arbeiteten, um Geld ausgeben zu können, und wenn es sich ergab, schliefen wir miteinander. Rom ist eine wunderbare Stadt für Männer. Ich interessierte mich für Musik, und es sah so aus, als ob sich auch noch andere in Rom für neue Musik interessierten. Aus vielen Ländern waren sie zum Kongreß in die alte Hauptstadt gekommen. Asien? Asien war fern. Zehn Flugstunden war Asien fern und unheimlich und groß wie die Woge des Hokusai. Diese Woge kam heran. Sie bespülte den Strand von Ostia, wo man die Leiche eines jungen Mädchens gefunden hatte. Die arme Tote ging wie ein Gespenst durch Rom, und Minister erschraken vor ihrem bleichen Spiegelbild; doch konnten sie alles noch einmal zu ihrem Besten richten. Die Woge näherte sich dem Felsen von Antibes. *»Bon soir, Monsieur Aga Khan!«* Wage ich zu sagen, daß es mich nichts angehe? Ich besitze kein Bankkonto, kein Gold und keine Edelsteine, mit nichts werde ich aufgewogen; ich bin frei, ich habe keine Rennpferde und keine Filmmädchen zu verteidigen. Ich heiße Siegfried Pfaffrath. Ich weiß, es ist ein lächerlicher Name. Aber der Name ist auch wieder nicht lächerlicher als viele andere. Warum mißachte ich ihn so sehr? Ich habe ihn mir nicht ausgesucht. Ich rede gern schamlos drein, aber ich schäme mich, ich gebe mich respektlos und sehne mich danach, achten zu können. Ich bin Tonsetzer. Das ist, schreibt man nicht für das Große Wunschkonzert, ein Beruf, so lächerlich wie mein Name. Siegfried Pfaffrath erscheint nun in Konzertprogrammen. Warum wähle ich kein Pseudonym? Ich weiß es nicht. Hänge ich gar an diesem gehaßten

Namen, bleibe ich an ihm hängen? Läßt mich die Sippe nicht los? Und ich glaube doch, daß alles, was geschieht, gedacht, geträumt, verdorben wird, alles im All, selbst das Unsichtbare und das Unfaßliche, mich angeht und mich ruft.

Ein großes Automobil, lackglänzend, schwarz, geräuschlosen Getriebes, ein funkelnder dunkler Sarg, spiegelblank und undurchsichtig die Fenster, war vor dem Pantheon vorgefahren. Der Wagen sah wie ein Gesandtschaftsauto aus, der Botschafter Plutos, der Minister der Hölle oder des Mars mochte drinnen auf schwellenden Polstern sitzen, und Siegfried, der auf der Piazza seinen Schnaps trank und träumte, las hinüberblickend und ein Geschehen betrachtend, das er wohl wahrnahm, doch nicht bemerkenswert fand, die Schrift auf dem Nummernschild für arabische Zeichen. War es ein Prinz aus den Märchen der Tausendundeinen Nacht, der da ankam, ein vertriebener König? Der braungesichtige Chauffeur in militärähnlicher Livree sprang vom Steuersitz, riß die Tür des Coupés auf und hielt sich dicht, dienstbereit, adjutantisch beflissen hinter einem Mann, der in einen bequemen grauen Anzug gehüllt war. Der Anzug war aus englischem Flanell und wohl von einem guten Schneider gearbeitet, aber auf dem gedrungenen Körper des Mannes — wuchtig der Nacken, breit die Schultern, gehoben der Brustkorb, gerundet und elastisch wie ein praller Boxball der Bauch und stämmig die Schenkel — erinnerte der Anzug an eine gebirglerisch bäurische Lodentracht. Der Mann hatte borstiges, kurzgeschorenes ergrautes Haar und trug eine große dunkle Sonnenbrille, die ihm ein allerdings gar nicht bäurisches, viel eher ein geheimnisvolles, listiges, weithergereistes, corpsdiplomatisches oder verwegen steckbrieflich gesuchtes Aussehen verlieh. War er Odysseus, der die Götter besuchen wollte? Er war nicht Odysseus, der verschlagene König Ithakas; dieser Mann war ein Henker. Er kam aus dem Totenreich, Aasgeruch umwehte ihn, er selber war ein Tod, ein brutaler, ein gemeiner, ein plumper und einfallsloser Tod. Siegfried hatte seinen Onkel Judejahn, vor dem er sich als Kind gefürchtet hatte, seit dreizehn Jahren nicht getroffen. Oft hatte man

Siegfried gestraft, weil er sich vor Judejahn versteckte, und der Junge hatte schließlich in Onkel Gottlieb die Verkörperung alles zu Fürchtenden und zu Hassenden gesehen, das Symbol des Zwanges, der Aufmärsche, des Krieges, und noch glaubte er manchmal die polternde, immer schimpfende Stimme des stiernackigen Mannes zu hören, doch erinnerte er sich nur noch undeutlich an des im Lande gefürchteten mächtigen Tribunen zahllose Abbilder aus Zeitungen, von Litfaßsäulen, als Wandschmuck in Schulsälen, als lähmender Schatten auf Kinoleinwänden, die den Gewaltigen böse vorgebeugten Hauptes in aufdringlich schmuckloser Parteiuniform und in stumpfen Marschstiefeln zeigten. So erkannte Siegfried, inzwischen in die Freiheit entkommen, nach Hemingway Grappa trinkend, über den römischen Platz und seine Musik meditierend, die sein einsames Abenteuer war, Gottlieb Judejahn nicht, und er ahnte nicht einmal, daß dies Ungeheuer in Rom erschienen und im Begriff war, von den Toten aufzuerstehen. Siegfried bemerkte nur beiläufig und mit unwillkürlichem Schauder einen korpulenten, vermutlich wohlhabenden, in der Welt etwas vorstellenden und unsympathischen Fremden, der den Kater Benito an sich lockte, ihn am Genick packte und das Tier unter dem Gekreisch der Kinder in sein nobles Auto trug. Der Chauffeur erstarrte eine Sekunde zinnsoldatenstramm und schloß achtungsvoll hinter Judejahn und Benito den Wagenschlag. Lautlos glitt das große schwarze Automobil vom Platz, und Siegfried sah flüchtig in der Sonne des Nachmittags die arabische Schrift auf seinem Nummernschild funkeln, bis sie plötzlich, eine Wolke trat vor die Sonne, in Staub und Dunst sich auflöste und verschwand.

Von Kürenberg, ihrem Gatten, zur Probe geladen, hatte Ilse, von Siegfried unbemerkt, in der letzten Reihe des nur über dem Orchester erhellten Saales neben einem der grünen Kübelbäumchen gesessen und der Symphonie gelauscht. Sie mißfiel ihr. Was sie hörte, waren Dissonanzen, einander feindliche unharmonische Klänge, ein Suchen ohne Ziel, ein unbeharrliches Experiment, denn viele Wege wurden eingeschlagen und wieder verlassen, kein Gedanke mochte weilen, und alles war von Anfang an brüchig, von Zweifel erfüllt und von Verzweiflung beherrscht. Ilse kam es vor, als seien diese Noten von einem geschrieben, der nicht wußte, was er wollte. War er verzweifelt, weil er keinen Weg sah, oder gab es für ihn keinen Weg, weil er über jeden Pfad die Nacht seiner Verzweiflung breitete und ihn ungangbar machte? Kürenberg hatte viel von Siegfried gesprochen, aber Ilse hatte ihn noch nicht kennengelernt. Bisher war er ihr gleichgültig gewesen. Jetzt beunruhigte sie Siegfrieds Musik, und sie wollte nicht beunruhigt werden. Es war ein Ton da, der sie wehmütig machte. Sie hatte aber in ihrem Leben erfahren, daß es besser sei, Leid und Wehmut zu fliehen. Sie wollte nicht leiden. Nicht mehr. Sie hatte genug gelitten. Sie gab Bettlern unverhältnismäßig große Summen, aber sie fragte sie nicht, warum sie bettelten. Kürenberg hätte überall in der Welt, in New York oder in Sydney einträglicher dirigieren können; Ilse hatte ihm nicht abgeraten, Siegfrieds Symphonie für den Kongreß in Rom einzustudieren, aber sie bedauerte ihn nun, weil er sich um Zerfahrenes und Hoffnungsloses bemühte, um eine in ihrer Nacktheit schamlos wirkende Äußerung der reinen nichtswürdigen Verzweiflung.

Nach der Probe gingen Kürenbergs essen. Sie aßen gern; sie aßen oft, sie speisten viel und gut. Zum Glück sah man es ihnen nicht an. Sie vertrugen das viele und gute Essen; sie waren beide wohlproportioniert, nicht fett, gut genährt, nicht üppig, gut beisammen wie wohlgepflegte Tiere. Da Ilse schwieg, wußte Kürenberg, daß ihr die Smyphonie nicht gefallen habe. Es ist schwer, einer Schweigenden zu widersprechen, und Kürenberg lobte schließlich Siegfried als den Begabtesten unter den Neuen. Er hatte Siegfried für den Abend eingeladen. Nun wußte er nicht, ob es Ilse recht sei. Er gestand es beiläufig, und Ilse fragte: »In das Hotel?« Kürenberg sagte: »Ja.« Da wußte Ilse, daß Kürenberg, der selbst auf Reisen, und sie reisten immer, ein leidenschaftlicher Koch war, kochen wollte, und das war ein Zeichen, daß er Siegfried wirklich schätzte und ihn umwarb, und wieder schwieg sie. Doch warum sollte sie Siegfried nicht empfangen? Sie verweigerte sich nicht gern. Auch mochte sie mit Kürenberg nicht hadern. Sie stritten sich kaum. Sie führten eine Ehe ohne Streit und waren zanklos sogar durch Not und Gefahr über Land und Meer gereist. Gut, Siegfried konnte in das Hotel kommen, es würde für ihn gekocht werden, ihr war es recht. Vielleicht stimmte auch, was Kürenberg versprach, und Siegfried war angenehm; aber seine Musik, änderte sie sich zukünftig nicht, und Ilse glaubte nie, daß sie sich ändern könne, denn diese Töne waren, ihr zwar zuwider, in ihrer Art echt und in all ihrer Zerfahrenheit ein Schicksalsbild und damit unabänderlich, diese Musik würde ihr, mochte Siegfried vielleicht sogar nett sein, immer unsympathisch bleiben. Ilse betrachtete Kürenberg, wie er in seinem Anzug aus grobgewebter schottischer Wolle, in knarrenden doppelt gesohlten Schuhen neben ihr ging, ergraut, ziemlich kahl, doch mit hellen Augen in seinem guten festen Gesicht, ein wenig stämmig in der Gestalt, aber sicheren Schrittes und gewandt im unruhigen Gewimmel der römischen Straße. Kürenberg wirkte verschlossen, deutender gesagt, fest in sich ruhend und im Geistigen lebend, nie gab er sich ungeduldig und nie sentimental, und doch glaubte Ilse, daß die Förderung, die er Siegfried angedeihen ließ, gefühlsbetont war; es hatte ihn eben doch bewegt, daß im Jahr vierundvierzig ein deutscher Kriegsgefangener aus einem englischen Lager sich an ihn, den freiwilligen Emigranten und unfreiwillig freiwilligen Langemarckstürmer des Ersten Weltkrieges, gewandt und ihn um Notenbeispiele der neuen Musik gebeten hatte. Für Kürenberg war Siegfrieds Prisoner-of-war-Brief ein Zeichen gewesen, eine Botschaft aus dem barbarisch gewordenen Europa, die Taube, die sagte, die Flut weiche zurück.

Sie setzten sich in die Sonne, genossen die Sonne, setzten sich auf die Terrasse des böse teuren Restaurants an der Piazza Navona, sie genossen es, dort zu sitzen, sie sahen in das beruhigende harmonische Oval der alten Arena, genossen das Glück, daß die Kämpfe vergangen waren, und speisten. Sie speisten kleine knusprige in Butter gesottene Krebse, zartgegrilltes Geflügel, trockene mit Zitronensaft und Öl betropfte Salatblätter, wollüstig rote Riesenerdbeeren, und dazu tranken sie herben anregenden Frascatiwein. Sie genossen den Wein. Sie genossen das Essen. Sie tranken andächtig. Sie aßen andächtig. Sie waren ernste ruhige Esser. Sie waren ernste heitere Trinker. Sie sprachen kaum ein Wort; doch liebten sie sich sehr.

Nach dem Essen fuhren sie mit dem Omnibus zur Bahnhofsgegend, in der sie wohnten. Der Omnibus war, wie immer, überfüllt. Sie standen Leib gegen Leib gepreßt und Leib an Leib mit anderen. Sie standen stumm, ruhig, zufrieden. Am Bahnhof entschlossen sie sich zu einem kurzen Besuch des Nationalmuseums in den Resten der Thermen des Diokletian. Sie liebten die Antike. Sie liebten den festen Marmor, die erhabenen Gestalten, die der Mensch nach seinem Bilde schuf, die kühlen Sarkophage, die verheißende Wölbung der Mischkrüge. Sie besuchten die Eroten, die Faune, die Götter und die Helden. Sie betrachteten die Ungeheuer der Sage und versonnen den schönen Leib der Venus von Cirene und das Haupt der schlafenden Eumenide. Dann schritten sie in die dämmerige, tief zwischen den hohen Häusern liegende schattenkühle Gasse hinter ihrem Hotel, einer langweiligen Allerweltsherberge, in der sie angenehm wohnten, betraten des Schlächters Laden, sahen an grausamen Haken die hängenden aufgeschnittenen Leiber, blutlos, frisch, kühl, sahen die Köpfe von Schaf und Rind, die Geopferten, sanft und stumm, kauften vom sauberen schräggerichteten schönen Marmorbrett des Metzgers zarte abgelagerte Steaks, die Kürenberg mit bohrenden Fingern auf den Grad ihrer Reife hin drückte und prüfte, sie besorgten an offenen Ständen Frucht und Gemüse, sie erwarben in alten Gewölben Öl und Wein, und nach längerem Suchen und nachdem er ihn mit den Zähnen getestet hatte, fand Kürenberg einen Reis, der körnig zu kochen versprach. Beide trugen sie die Pakete und fuhren mit dem Fahrstuhl in ihr großes helles Zimmer, das Staatsgemach des Hauses. Sie waren müde, und sie genossen die Müdigkeit. Sie sahen das breite Bett, und sie genossen im Vorgefühl Kühle und Reinheit des Bettes. Es war heller Nachmittag. Sie verdunkelten das Zimmer nicht. Sie entkleideten sich im Licht und legten sich zwischen die

Tücher und deckten sich zu. Sie dachten an die schöne Venus und dachten an die springenden Faune. Sie genossen ihre Gedanken; sie genossen die Erinnerung; danach genossen sie sich und fielen in tiefen Schlummer, in jenen Zustand eines vorweggenommenen Todes, der ein Drittel unseres Lebens ist; doch Ilse träumte, sie sei die Eumenide, die schlafende Eumenide, die besänftigend die Wohlwollende genannte, die Rachegöttin

Es war Zeit, er mußte hinübergehen, jetzt hatte er sich angesagt, es war die verabredete Stunde, sie erwarteten ihn, und da wollte er nicht, er zögerte, er fürchtete sich. Er, Judejahn, ängstigte sich, und was war sein Leib- und Lebensspruch? »Ich weiß nicht, was Furcht ist!« Die Phrase hatte viele verschlungen, sie hatten ins Gras gebissen, die andern natürlich, er hatte befohlen, sie waren bei sinnlosen Angriffen gefallen, hatten, um einem irrsinnigen Ehrbegriff zu genügen, von vornherein verlorene Stellungen gehalten, hatten sie bis zum letzten Mann gehalten, wie Judejahn dann brustgeschwellt seinem Führer meldete und wer sich fürchtete, hing, baumelte an Bäumen und Laternen, schaukelte mit dem Prangerschild um den zugeschnürten Hals »Ich war zu feige mein Vaterland zu verteidigen« im kalten Wind der Toten. Wessen Vaterland war zu verteidigen? Judejahns? Judejahns Zwingreich und Marschverband, sie waren in die Hölle zu wünschen, man hing nicht nur, man wurde auch geköpft, man wurde gemartert, erschossen, starb hinter Mauern und vor Wällen, der Feind zielte, natürlich, der Feind schoß auch, aber hier sandte der Kamerad die Kugel, einen bessern findst du nit, hier raste der Volksgenosse, der verehrte und hochgepriesene, und der junge Verurteilte konnte sich's zu spät überlegen, wer nun Feind war und wer Kamerad war; Judejahn sprach väterlich »meine Jungens«, und Judejahn sprach ordinär latrinenschnäuzig »killt die Sau«, immer war er volksnah und immer ein Prachtkerl, humorgesegnet, alter Fememörder von Landsberg, Blutprofos der schwarzen Heerlager auf Mecklenburgs Gütern, Totenkopf am Stahlhelm, doch selbst sie, die alten Götter, hatten Ver-

592

rat gepflogen, Ehrhardt, der Kapitän, tafelte mit Literaten und Hirnscheißern, und Roßbach zog mit milchwangigen Knaben durchs Land, führte Mysterienspiele auf zu der Schulmeister und Pfaffen Freude, aber er, Judejahn, er war den rechten Weg gegangen, stur und immer geradeaus, den Weg zu Führer und Reich und vielen Ehren.

Er schritt durch das Zimmer, wanderte über den weichen Teppich, die Wände waren stoffbespannt, Seide schirmte die Lichter der Ampeln, auf dem Damast des Bettes lag Benito, der räudige Kater, schaute Judejahn an, blinzelnd, höhnisch, wollte wohl knurren »du lebst noch« und blickte dann angeekelt auf die gebratene Leber zu Füßen des Bettes auf silbernem Tablett. Warum hatte er das Biest hergebracht? War Magie im Spiel? Judejahn sah nie Gespenster. Er war bloß ein sentimentaler Hund, konnte es nicht mitansehen, hatte sich geärgert, daß so ein Staatstier geneckt wurde. Benito! Diese Rotznasen! Judejahn wohnte in der Via Veneto, er wohnte in einem Botschafter- und Minister-Hotel, in einem Atlantikpaktgeneralsquartier, einem US-Steelpräsidentenhaus, in einem Farbenaufsichtsratsheim, einer Filmbrüstepreisausstellung, Hochstapler und Kokotten hatten hier ihre Käfige, was für Vögel kamen nicht nach Rom, modische Bärte aller Schnitte und Schneidertaillen, mit einer Hand zu umspannen, märchenteure Kostüme, man konnte die Mädchen in der Taille erwürgen, doch griff man fester nach festem Busen und festem Popo, spürte das lockende erregende wippende Fleisch unter der Nylonhaut, den schmalen Reizgürtel, der straff über Bauch und Schenkel zum Schleiergespinst der Strümpfe hinunterstieg — Kardinäle wohnten nicht im Haus. Er hatte seine blaue Brille abgenommen. Wässerige Augen, blauweiß zerronnen. War es leichtsinnig von ihm, hier zu wohnen? Da mußte er lachen. Erstens war er im Recht und war immer im Recht gewesen, und zweitens, wie wehte denn der Wind: Vergeben und vergessen. Es war ein Scherz von Judejahn, und Judejahn scherzte gern, gerade in diesem Hotel abgestiegen zu sein, wenn auch mit einem Paß, in dem sein Name nicht sein Name und sein Geburtsland nicht sein Geburtsland war, aber das Dokument war im übrigen echt, war diplomatisch visiert, er war wer, Judejahn, war immer wer gewesen und war es wieder. Er konnte es sich leisten, hier zu hausen und die Erinnerung an seine großen Tage zu genießen: unter diesem Dach hatte er residiert, von hier hatte er Botschaften in den Palazzo Venezia geschickt, in der Halle des Hauses hatte er befohlen, die Geiseln zu erschießen. Was sollte er anziehen? Er war gut in Schale, er besaß Anzüge von geschickten arabischen Schneidern aus englischem Geweb gebaut, er war weltmännisch geworden, parfümierte sich sogar, bevor er ins Bordell ging, Kraft abzustoßen, das hatte er von den Scheichs gelernt, aber in jedem Tuch blieb er unverkennbar der alte Judejahn, ein infantiler Typ, ein düsterer Knabenheld, der nicht vergessen konnte, daß sein Vater, ein Volksschullehrer, ihn geprügelt hatte, weil er nichts lernen wollte. Vielleicht den dunklen Anzug? Man mußte das Wiedersehen feierlich gestalten. Aber es war wohl nicht angebracht, sich in diesem Fall zu parfümieren. Man stank nicht nach Moschus, wo er hinging. Man verbarg den Bock. Die deutschen Bürger hatten sich wiedergefunden. Waren wieder feine Leute. Ob man ihm ansah, wo er herkam? All die Blutwege und jetzt, das letzte Bild, die Hitze, die Dürre, den Sand?

Er kam von den Schakalen. Nachts heulten sie. Fremde Sterne leuchteten am Himmel. Was gingen sie ihn an? Sie waren Richtungszeichen über der Geländekarte. Sonst sah er sie nicht. Er hörte auch die Schakale nicht. Er schlief. Er schlief ruhig, friedlich, traumlos. Er fiel jeden Abend in den Schlaf wie ein Stein in den tiefen Brunnen. Kein Alp, kein Gewissen drückte ihn, kein Gerippe erschien ihm. Erst die Reveille weckte den Schläfer. Das war vertraute willkommene Musik. Aus der Wüste wehte Sturm. Der Ton des Horns flatterte und starb. Der Hornist war ein schlapper Hund; er war auf Vordermann zu bringen. Sand prasselte gegen die Wand der Baracke. Judejahn erhob sich vom schmalen Feldbett. Er liebte das harte Lager. Er liebte die getünchte Kammer mit dem Schrank aus Eisenblech, dem Klapptisch, dem Waschgestell, den angerosteten klappernden Kannen und Schüsseln. Er hätte in der Königsstadt in einer Villa hausen kön-

nen, Chefausbilder, Heeresreorganisator, gesuchter hochbe-
zahlter Fachmann, der er war. Aber er liebte die Kaserne.
Sie verlieh im Selbstbewußtsein, sie allein gab ihm Sicherheit. Die Kaserne war Heimat, sie war Kameradschaft, sie
war Halt und Ordnung. In Wahrheit hielten ihn Phrasen
zusammen, die Phrasen eines Pennälers. Wem war Judejahn
Kamerad? Er liebte den Blick in die Wüste. Es war nicht ihre
Unendlichkeit, die ihn anzog, es war ihre Kahlheit. Die Wüste
war für Judejahn ein großer Exerzierplatz, sie war die Front,
ein fortwährender prickelnder Reiz, der einen mannbar erhielt. In der Königsstadt hätten ihn leichtsohlige Diener um-
huscht, er hätte warmbäuchige Mädchen beschlafen, sich in
Schößen verloren, er hätte, ein Pascha, in gewürztem Wasser
baden können. Er seifte sich aber im Camp ein, schrubbte
sich die Haut mit der Wurzelbürste rot, rasierte sich mit dem
alten deutschen Apparat, den er in der Hosentasche von der
Weidendammer Brücke bis in die Wüste gebracht hatte. Er
fühlte sich wohl. Er dachte: Wie eine gesengte Wildau. Er
hatte gute Witterung. Er hörte Männergeräusch, Waschge-
plätscher, Kübelklimpern, Pfiffe, Zoten, Flüche, Kommandos,
Stiefelscharren, Türenschlagen. Er roch den Kasernenmief
aus Gefangenschaft, Knechtung, Lederfett, Waffenöl, scharfer
Seife, süßer Pomade, saurem Schweiß, Kaffee, heißem Alu-
miniumgeschirr und Urin. Es war der Geruch der Angst;
aber Judejahn wußte nicht, daß es der Geruch der Angst
war. Er kannte ja die Furcht nicht. Er prahlte es seinem Spiegelbild vor; nackt, dickwanstig stand er vor dem fliegen-
schmutzverdreckten Glas. Er schnallte um. Hierin war er
alte Schule. Überdies drückte der Gürtel den Bauch zurück,
und der Arsch war wie aufgehängt. Trick alter Generale.
Judejahn trat in den Gang hinaus. Menschen schnellten gegen die Wand, machten sich flach, ergebene Schatten. Er sah
sie nicht. Er drängte ins Freie. Die Sonne schwebte blutrot,
wie vom Sandsturm getragen. Judejahn schritt die Front ab.
Sturm zerrte am Khaki der Uniformen. Sand schnitt wie
scharfe Glassplitter ins Fleisch und peitschte wie Hagel gegen
die Panzer. Judejahn belustigte der Anblick. Die Parade der
Wüstensöhne! Er schaute sie an. Was er sah, waren Mandel-

augen, dunkle, glänzende, verräterische, war braune Haut, waren gesengte Gesichter, Mohrenvisagen, Semitennasen. Seine Männer! Seine Männer waren tot. Sie lagen unter Gras, unter Schnee, unter Stein und Sand, sie ruhten am Polarkreis, in Frankreich, in Italien, auf Kreta, am Kaukasus, und einige lagen in Kisten unterm Zuchthaushof. Seine Männer! Nun waren es diese hier. Judejahn hatte wenig Sinn für die Ironie des Schicksals. Er schritt den alten Frontabnahmetrott und schaute ihnen streng und fest in die Mandelaugen, die glänzenden, die verräterischen, die träumenden. Judejahn sah keinen Vorwurf in diesen Augen. Er las keine Anklagen. Judejahn hatte diesen Männern die Sanftmut genommen, die Sanftmut der Kreatur. Er hatte ihnen den Stolz genommen, das natürliche Selbstgefühl der männlichen Haremskinder. Er hatte sie gebrochen, indem er sie eines lehrte: Gehorchen. Er hatte sie gut geschliffen, auch das nach alter Schule. Nun standen sie aufrecht und ausgerichtet wie Zinnsoldaten vor ihm, und ihre Seele war tot. Sie waren Soldaten. Sie waren Menschenmaterial. Sie waren einsatzbereit und konnten verheizt werden. Judejahn hatte seine Zeit nicht vergeudet. Er hatte seine Brotherren nicht enttäuscht. Wo Judejahn befahl, war Preußens alte Gloria, und wo Judejahn hinkam, war sein Großdeutschland. Der Sand der Wüste war noch immer der Sand der Mark. Judejahn war verjagt, aber er war nicht entwurzelt; er trug sein Deutschland, an dem die Welt noch immer genesen mochte, in seinem Herzen. Der Flaggenmast reckte sich hoch in den Sturm, er reckte sich einsam gegen die sandverschleierte Sonne, er reckte sich hoch und einsam in das gottlose Nichts. Es wurde kommandiert. Schreie schlugen wie elektrische Kontakte durch die Soldaten. Sie strafften sich noch straffer, und die Fahne ging wieder einmal hoch! Welch herrliches Symbol der Sinnlosigkeit! Auf grünem Tuch leuchtete nun rot der Morgenstern. Hier konnte man noch Ladenhüter verkaufen, Nationalstaattrug, Mark der Treue und Feindschaft den Israelis, diesen immer nützlichen Brüdern, denen Judejahn auch heute wieder Geld, Ansehen und Stellung verdankte.
Der dunkle Anzug war auch nicht der richtige. Judejahn sah

wie ein fetter Konfirmand aus, und es erboste ihn, wie er nun
daran dachte, daß sein Vater, der Volksschullehrer, ihn gezwungen hatte, so brav gekleidet zum Altar des Herrn zu
schreiten. Das war neunzehnhundertfünfzehn gewesen, er
wollte ins Feld, von der Schule fort, aber man nahm den
kleinen Gottlieb nicht, und dann hatte er sich gerächt, das
Notabitur warf man ihm neunzehnhundertsiebzehn nach,
und er kam zum Offizierskurs, nicht ins Feld, und dann wurde er Leutnant, nicht im Feld, aber dann pfiffen doch noch
Kugeln um Judejahn, Freikorpskrieg, Annabergschlachten,
Spartakuskämpfe, Kapptage, Ruhrmaquis und schließlich die
Genickschußpatrouille im Femewald. Das war seine Boheme,
das war seine Jugend, und schön ist die Jugend, sagte das
Lied, und sie kam nicht wieder. In Hitlers Dienst wurde Judejahn bürgerlich, arrivierte, setzte Speck an, trug hohe Titel,
heiratete und verschwägerte sich mit dem Märzveilchen, dem
immerhin Kappwaffenbruder, dem Nutznießer und Karriere-
schleicher, dem Oberpräsidenten und Oberbürgermeister, dem
Führergeldverwalter und Spruchkammermitläufer und jetzt
wieder Obenauf, altes vom Volk wiedergewähltes Stadtober-
haupt, streng demokratisch wiedereingesetzt, das verstand
sich bei dem von selbst, mit dem also verschwägerte er sich,
mit Friedrich Wilhelm Pfaffrath, den er für ein Arschloch
hielt und dem er sich in einer schwachen Stunde brieflich zu
erkennen gegeben hatte, sie sollten nicht weinen, denn er
sei gut im Kraut; und dann hatte er in dieses idiotische Wiedersehen in Rom gewilligt. Der Schwager schrieb, er wollt's
ihm richten. Was wohl? Die Heimkehr, die Entsühnung, die
Begnadigung und schließlich ein Pöstchen? Gab mächtig an
der Mann. Wollte Judejahn denn heimkehren? Brauchte er
den Schein der Entsühnung, die Freiheit der Begnadigung?
Er war frei; hier lag die Liste seiner Geschäfte. Er hatte Waffen zu kaufen, Panzer, Kanonen, Flugzeuge, Restbestände,
für das kommende große Morden schon unrationell gewordene Maschinen, aber für den kleinen Wüstenkrieg, für
Putsch und Aufstand noch schön verwendbar. Judejahn war
bei Banken akkreditiert, er war bevollmächtigt. Er hatte mit
Waffenschiebern aus beiden Hemisphären zu handeln. Er

hatte alte Kameraden anzuwerben. Er saß im Spiel. Es machte ihm Spaß. Was galt da die Familie? Eine Kackergesell-
schaft. Man mußte hart sein. Aber Eva war ihm treu gewesen, eine treue deutsche Frau, das Musterexemplar, für das
zu leben und zu kämpfen man vorgab; und manchmal glaubte man daran. Er fürchtete sich. Er fürchtete sich vor Eva,
der ungeschminkten und haargeknoteten, dem Frauenschafts-
weib, der Endsieggläubigen; sie war in Ordnung, gewiß,
aber nichts zog ihn zu ihr. Überdies war sie wohl abgekämpft. Und sein Sohn? Eine sonderbare Ratte. Was verbarg sich hinter der unglaublichen Maskerade? In Briefen
wurden Wandlungen angedeutet. Er konnte sie nicht fassen.
Er breitete einen Stadtplan von Rom wie eine Generalstabskarte vor sich aus. Er mußte die Via Ludovisi hinuntergehen,
dann die Spanische Treppe, von deren Höhe er mit einem
Geschütz die Stadt beherrschen würde, ja und dann in die
Via Condotti, zu dem spießbürgerlichen Hotel, in dem sie
alle untergekrochen waren und auf ihn warteten. Natürlich
hatte er auch dort wohnen sollen, im von Deutschen bevorzugten Haus, wie es die Reiseführer nannten, in Heimatenge
und Familiendunst, und Friedrich Wilhelm Pfaffrath, der
allzeit vernünftige Vertreter vernünftiger und durchsetzbarer
nationaler Ansprüche, Pfaffrath, der es wieder geschafft hatte
und sich vielleicht gar als der Klügere fühlte, weil er wieder
an der Krippe saß und bereit war zu neuem deutschem Aufstieg, Schwager Pfaffrath, Oberbürgermeister und angesehener Bundesbürger, hatte ihn wohl unter Dach und Schutz
nehmen wollen, ihn, den vermeintlich Gejagten, so hatte er
es sich wohl ausgemalt, den Umhergetriebenen wollte er an
die Brust ziehen, und ausdrücklich vergeben sei das angerich-
tete Ungemach, Fragebogenangst und Spruchkammerwäsche.
Was husten würde Judejahn ihm, er war zu weit gereist für
dieses Idyll, der Tote oder Totgesagte, der Zertrümmerte von
Berlin, der Vermißte des großen Aufräumens, der in Nürnberg Verurteilte, in contumaciam und von Zweifels wegen,
versteht sich, denn der Hohe Gerichtshof, der über Schicksal,
Verhängnis, Menschenlos und blindes Walten der Geschichte
urteilte und selber im Irrgarten der Historie taumelte, nicht

eine Justitia mit verbundenen Augen, sondern eine Blinde
Kuh spielende Törin, die, da sie Recht auf rechtlosem Grund
sprach, mitgegangen mitgefangen und mitversunken war im
Morast des morallosen Geschehens, der Hohe Gerichtshof hatte keinen Zeugen für Judejahns Tod und keinen für sein irdisches Fortbestehen beigebracht, und so hatte der Hohe Richter über den vor aller Welt als Scheusal angeklagten Judejahn, sorgsam, falls der Unhold im Verborgenen atme, den
Stab gebrochen, das Todeslos ausgeworfen, in Abwesenheit,
wie gesagt, was klug und glücklich war, der Verworfene ent-
kam klug und glücklich dem Strick, mit dem man in jenen
Tagen allzu voreilig umging, und für das Gericht war am
Ende, daß Judejahn nicht gehängt war, ein klug und glücklich vermiedener Fehler, denn Judejahn war als Scheusal
zur Wiederverwendung vorgemerkt, und Krieg ist ein böses
Handwerk. Der Oberbürgermeister war wahrscheinlich mit
eigenem Wagen nach Rom gereist, zu einem Mercedes reichte es wohl wieder, oder die Stadt stellte das Vehikel zur
schönen Fahrt, Italien Land der Sehnsucht Land der Deutschen, und Pfaffrath, der Deutsche, hatte seinen ledergebun-
denen Goethe im Bücherschrank, und die Steuerkommenta-
re, die neben dem Weimarer standen, einem verdächtigen
Burschen, aus Weimar kam nie Gutes, las er genau, und jedenfalls ärgerte es Judejahn, daß er sich den Schwager schon
wieder im Fett vorstellen mußte — war doch Verrat, hunds-
föttischer Verrat, der Kerl hätte krepieren sollen. Aber auch
Judejahn konnte mit einem Wagen aufwarten, so war es
nicht, daß er zu Fuß gehen mußte, nein, er ging freiwillig,
er wollte zu Fuß hinüberwandern, zu Fuß ins bürgerliche
Leben pilgern, das war hier wohl angemessen, angebracht in
der Situation und der Stadt, er wollte Zeit gewinnen, und
Rom, hieß es doch, Rom, wo die Pfaffen sich niedergelassen
hatten und in den Straßen die Priesterröcke wimmelten,
Rom, hieß es, sei eine schöne Stadt, auch Judejahn konnte
sie sich einmal ansehen, das hatte er bisher versäumt, er
hatte hier nur repräsentiert, er hatte hier nur befohlen, er
hatte hier gewütet, jetzt konnte er Rom zu Fuß durchstreifen, konnte mitnehmen, was die Stadt bot an Klimadunst,

an Geschichtsstätten, an raffinierten Huren und reicher Tafel. Warum sollte er es sich versagen? Er war lange in der Wüste gewesen, und Rom stand noch und lag nicht in Trümmern. Ewig nannte man Rom. Das waren Pfaffen und Professoren, die so schwärmten. Judejahn zeigte sein Mordgesicht. Er wußte es besser. Er hatte viele Städte verschwinden sehen.

Sie wartete. Sie wartete allein. Niemand half ihr, zu warten, verkürzte ihr mit Gespräch die Wartezeit, und sie wünschte auch nicht, daß ihr die Zeit verkürzt werde und daß sie sich um sie kümmerten, denn nur sie allein grämte sich, nur sie trug Trauer, und selbst Anna, ihre Schwester, begriff nicht, daß Eva Judejahn nicht um verlorenen Besitz, verlorene Stellung, verlorenes Ansehen weinte, und schon gar nicht Trauer um Judejahn, den sie als Held in Walhall gesehen hatte, bleichte ihr Gesicht, sie trauerte um Großdeutschland, sie beweinte den Führer, beweinte die durch Verrat und Tücke und widernatürliches Bündnis niedergerungene germanische Weltbeglückungsidee, das tausendjährige Dritte Reich. Aus der Halle des Hauses drang Lachen durch Treppengewind und Gänge, aus dem Hof stieg mit Essendunst ein amerikanisches Tanzlied, von einem italienischen Küchenjungen gesungen, zu ihrem Fenster hoch; doch sie erreichten nicht Lachen und lustiger junger Negersong italisch belcantisch erhellt, sie stand schwarzgewandet in ihrem Zimmer, einem Käfig aus Steinen, Wahn, Verkanntheit und dahinschwindender Zeit, stand vergeltungsschwanger wolfsrachig umnachtet in Mythos, dem erschwindelten ertüftelten und geglaubten, den Urängsten preisgegeben, den echten von Wehr und Wolf, das angegraute verblichene strohblonde Haar, Garbe auf dem Felde gebliebenen Weizens, als unter Gewitterdräuen die aufgeschreckten Knechte flohen, dies Haar zu strengem Frauenknoten gebunden über dem bleichen Gesicht Langschädelgesicht Eckkinngesicht Harmgesicht Schreckgesicht ausgezehrt ausgebrannt ein Totenkopfhaupt wie das Zeichen, das Judejahn auf hochgekniffener Dienstmütze getragen und nach dem er angetreten, sie wirkte wie ein Gespenst, keine

Eumenide, ein nordisches Gespenst, ein Nebelgespenst, das ein Verrückter nach Rom gebracht und in ein Hotelzimmer gesperrt hatte.

Es war ein kleines Zimmer, in dem sie sich aufhielt, das billigste des Hauses, sie selbst hatte es so gewollt, denn Schwager Friedrich Wilhelm, der nicht erkennen wollte, daß sie es war, die Schmach vom deutschen Namen tilgen mußte, Schwager Friedrich Wilhelm machte ja ihretwegen die Reise, das sagte auch Anna, und Friedrich Wilhelm Pfaffrath klopfte Eva Judejahn freundlich den Rücken und sprach »na laß man Eva, ist doch selbstverständlich, daß wir den Gottlieb wieder holen«, und sie zuckte zurück und biß sich die Lippen wund, weil er Gottlieb gesagt hatte, das hatte er früher nie gewagt, und es war Verrat, den Standartenführer, SS-General und einen der höchsten Amtsträger der gottlosen Partei Gottlieb zu nennen, denn Judejahn haßte den Namen, den ihm vom Schullehrer verliehenen Pfaffenschleim, er wollte nicht Gott lieb sein und ließ sich in der Familie und unter Freunden Götz rufen, während er dienstlich und amtlich G. Judejahn zeichnete, und Götz war eine freie Ableitung von Gottlieb aus freier wilder Freikorpszeit, aber Friedrich Wilhelm, der Korrekte und Besitzer der in Leder gebundenen Goetheausgabe, hatte Götz unwürdig gefunden, deutsch zwar und kernig, aber doch das berühmte Zitat im Geiste wachrufend, und dann war es ein angemaßter, ein okkupierter Name, man hieß nun einmal, wie man getauft war, und so sagte er jetzt wieder, als er es wagen durfte und sich den Stärkeren glaubte, Gottlieb, obwohl er diesen Namen, auch er, lächerlich und eines Mannes nicht passend fand. Sie wandelte in Schwarz. Wandelte schwarzgekleidet vom Hoffenster bis zum Spiegel über dem Waschbecken, wandelte umher wie in einer Zelle, wie ein gefangenes nicht gezähmtes Tier; sie hatte all die Jahre Trauer getragen, nur im Anhaltelager hatte sie keine Trauer getragen, weil man sie im Reisekostüm verhaftet hatte, aber als sie entlassen war, da nahm sie von ihrer Schwester ein schwarzes Kleid an, denn ihre eigenen Kleider waren verschwunden, die Schränke geplündert, und die Häuser, die Judejahn besessen hatte, waren ihr genom-

men worden. Und als das Lebenszeichen von ihm, dem Tot-
geglaubten, kam, da legte Eva zur Verwunderung der Familie
Pfaffrath die Trauer nicht ab, denn sie hatte ja nicht um den
Gemahl geweint, den totgewähnten Helden, und daß er nun
lebte, erhöhte gar nur den Trauergrund, er würde nach dem
Sohn fragen, sie hatte ihn nicht bewahren können, und vielleicht war Judejahn selber zu Kreuz gekrochen und lebte
fett; sie nahm's ihm nicht übel, daß er mit anderen Frauen
schlief, das hatte er immer getan und immer ihr erzählt, das
gehörte zum Kriegerleben, und wenn er Kinder zeugte, so
zeugte er Kriegerkinder und gute Rasse, Nachwuchs für die
Sturmtruppen und für den Führer, aber daß er sich im Orient
versteckt hatte, das beunruhigte sie, als wenn sie ahnte, daß
auch er Verrat getrieben habe, Rassenverrat und Blutsver-
rat im weichen feindlichen Klima, in rosenduftender Harems-
dunkelheit, in knoblauchstinkenden Höhlen mit Negerinnen
und Semitinnen, die nur auf die Rache gewartet hatten und
gierig nach germanischem Samen lechzten. Eva hätte ein
Heer ausrüsten mögen, um diese Kinder heimzuholen, Jude-
jahns Bastarde; ihre rechte Leibesart war zu prüfen, und als
Deutsche sollten sie leben oder als Mischlinge sterben. Der
Küchenjunge im Hof pfiff sich nun eins, wieder war es ein
Negerlied, grell frech und höhnisch, und das Lachen aus der
Halle polterte fett, gemütlich und manchmal gackernd trepp-
auf und ganglang. Der Oberbürgermeister
Friedrich Wilhelm Pfaffrath saß mit Anna, seiner Frau, und
Dietrich, seinem jüngeren Sohn im Gesellschaftsraum der von
Deutschen bevorzugten Herberge, und schon hatten sie Anschluß an andere Italienreisende gefunden, Landsleute gleicher Schicht und gleicher Ansichten, Davongekommene, einmal vom Schreck Geschüttelte und dann Vergessende wie sie,
Volkswagenbesitzer, Mercedesfahrer, an deutscher Tüchtigkeit Genesene und nun wieder willkommene Devisenbrin-
ger, sie unterhielten sich, tranken auch süßen Wermutwein,
und auf den Tischen lagen Straßenkarten und Reisehandbücher, denn man beratschlagte Ausflüge, wollte nach Tivoli
und nach Frascati, aber auch zur wiederaufgebauten Abtei
von Cassino, die Schlachtfelder waren zu besichtigen und wa-

ren diesen Menschen kein Grauen, und einer würde suchen und finden und rufen »hier stand unsere Batterie, hier spuckten wir 'runter, hier hatten wir uns festgekrallt, hier hielten wir stand«, und dann würde sich's zeigen, was für ein feiner Kerl er war, mit Achtung, denn er bewunderte sich als fairen Krieger, als tötenden Sportsmann sozusagen, würde er vom Tommy sprechen und vom Ami und vielleicht sogar von den polnischen Legionären der Anders-Armee, aber das war nicht sicher, denn Pole blieb Pole, und auf dem Soldatenfriedhof würde man mit allseitig hehrem Gefühl sich selber und die Toten ehren. Die Toten lachten nicht, sie waren tot; oder sie hatten keine Zeit, und es war ihnen gleichgültig, wer da von Lebenden kam, sie waren in der Wandlung, stiegen vom Leben besudelt und schuldbeladen, die vielleicht nicht einmal ihre Schuld war, ins Rad der Geburten zu neuer Sühneexistenz, zu neuem Schuldigwerden, zu neuem vergeblichem Dasein. Friedrich Wilhelm Pfaffrath fand es ungehörig von Judejahn, sie warten zu lassen. Aber vielleicht war er noch nicht in Rom angekommen, vielleicht hatte er Reiseschwierigkeiten gehabt, Paßkalamitäten, sein Fall war immerhin delikat und mit Vorsicht zu behandeln. Man durfte nichts übersürzen, aber Pfaffrath war überzeugt, daß es nun Zeit sei, da der Schwager überraschenderweise am Leben war, den Akt Judejahn still verschwinden zu lassen, behutsam, ohne Aufsehen und ohne Skandal natürlich, noch konnte man sich kompromittieren, ein vaterlandsloser Wicht mochte kläffen, aber die Zeit des Gehängtwerdens war ein für allemal vorbei, für sie wenigstens, die Amerikaner waren zur Vernunft gekommen, hatten nun den richtigen Blick für die deutschen Verhältnisse und die deutsche Brauchbarkeit, und Haßgefühle und Racheurteile waren schon lange nicht mehr klug und fein. Roosevelt war tot und kommunistisch kollaborationsverdächtig. Und wer war Morgenthau? Ein Nebbich! Wer's überlebt hatte, mochte weiterleben. Und für Judejahn fand sich vielleicht eine Stellung im Landwirtschaftlichen Verband, später konnte man weitersehen, und Eva würde aufhören zu spinnen, denn, alles was recht war, er, Friedrich Wilhelm Pfaffrath, war ein nationaler Mann, aber

Fehler waren geschehen, das mußte man einsehen und eben wieder von vorn anfangen. Preußen hatte sich großgehungert! Tat man's im Restland nicht auch? Und hatte man es nicht schon wieder weit gebracht, nicht im Hungern, das war bildlich zu nehmen, eine erbauliche Legende aus vergangener stolzkarger Zeit, denn sonst war das Hungern ein Knurren leerer Mägen nach durch Verrat verlorenen Kriegen, woran man besser nicht dachte, aber an den Wohlstand, der greifbar und gar nicht Legende war, konnte man denken und sich halten, und schließlich: Würde der neue Habenstand nicht auch die Söhne überzeugen, die verlorenen Schafe der Auflösung, die Verscheuchten der glücklich überwundenen Unordnung, so daß sie heimkehrten und wieder nach ihrer Sippe Art lebten? Der deutsche Bund hatte seine demokratischen Schwächen, das war gewiß und vorerst wohl schwerlich zu ändern, aber im ganzen herrschte doch Ordnung im besetzten Land, und alles war vorbereitet für straffere Zügelführung, bald würde man weiter blicken, es sah nicht schlecht aus, und Pfaffraths Vergangenheit war die rechte, sie empfahl ihn ganz selbstverständlich; doch was mit den Söhnen war, ihre Unvernunft, ihre Überspanntheiten, ihre angeblichen Gewissensentscheidungen, so waren das Zeiterscheinungen, Zeitkrankheiten und würden mit der Zeit vorübergehen wie eine zu lange während Pubertät. Friedrich Wilhelm Pfaffrath dachte hier weniger an Adolf Judejahn, seinen Neffen, als an Siegfried, den älteren seiner beiden Söhne, der ihn verlassen hatte, während er mit Dietrich, dem jüngeren, zufrieden sein durfte, der war nun Vandale, war der Burschenschaft des Vaters beigetreten, hatte Komment gelernt, Beziehungen erworben, stand vor dem Referendar und freute sich auf den Schlachtfeldbesuch in Cassino, wie es sich für junge Leute gehörte. Aber Siegfried war aus der Art geschlagen. In Teufels Namen denn — mochte er Kapellmeister werden; es gab auch im Musikfach hochbezahlte Stellungen. Friedrich Wilhelm Pfaffrath war ein unterrichteter Mann, und er hatte erfahren, daß Siegfried in Rom war. Dies schien ihm ein Fingerzeig zu sein, die Möglichkeit zu Aussprache und Versöhnung. Es würde nicht leicht sein, denn

noch schien Siegfried in Sümpfen zu waten, bildlich gesprochen, und das Programm des Musikkongresses verkündete
Surrealismus, Kulturbolschewismus und negroide Neutönerei.
War denn der Junge blind? Aber vielleicht machte man
heute auf diese Weise Karriere, da die Juden wieder im internationalen Geschäft saßen und Ruhm und Preise verteilten?
Pfaffrath hatte auch gelesen, daß Kürenberg Siegfrieds Symphonie dirigieren werde, und er erinnerte sich.»Besinnst du
dich noch«, fragte er seine Frau, »auf Kürenberg, der vier-
unddreißig bei uns Generalmusikdirektor war und der nach
Berlin gehen sollte?«»Der hat doch die Aufhäuser geheiratet« erwiderte Anna. »Ja«, sagte Pfaffrath, »darum
konnte er nicht mehr nach Berlin gehen, und wir konnten
ihn auch nicht halten.« Und irgendwie kam es Pfaffrath
vor, als ob er, der damals, als die Gauleiter noch nicht alle
Macht an sich gerissen hatten, Oberpräsident der Provinz
war, Kürenberg gefördert habe, und das freute ihn nun, denn
so war es natürlich, daß Kürenberg sich dankbar des Vaters
erinnerte, wenn er des Sohnes Werk aufführte und bekannt-
machte. Aber
Eva oben in ihres Zimmers Käfig lauschte auf den Schritt des
Rächers.
Aus der Drehtür gekreist, des Portiers Hand, in weißem
Handschuh Lakaienhand Henkershand Todeshand, hatte
dem Karussell des Eintritts und Ausgangs Schwung verliehen, hochachtungsvoll sehr ergebener Diener stets dem Herrn
zu Wünschen ein Trinkgeldtod, von ihm aus der Drehtür
gekreist, fühlte sich Judejahn aus dem Hotel geworfen, aus
der Sicherheit gestoßen, die Geld und Rang verliehen, aus
der Geborgenheit der Macht, die hinter ihm stand, geborgte
Macht diesmal, fremdländische Macht zwar, fremdrassige
gar, dunkle orientalische Macht, aber immerhin Staatsmacht
mit Souveränität und Flagge — auf einmal war er hilflos.
Es war seit sehr langer Zeit das erste Mal, daß Judejahn als
Mensch unter Menschen trat, ein Zivilist, unbewacht, unbe-
schützt, unbewaffnet, ein stämmiger ältlicher Herr in einem
dunklen Anzug. Es verwirrte ihn, daß niemand ihn beachtete. Vorübergehende berührten ihn, streiften ihn, stießen ihn

und murmelten ein flüchtiges uninteressiertes »Pardon«. Pardon für Judejahn? Er tat ein paar blinde Schritte. Niemand wahrte achtungsvollen Abstand. Judejahn hätte in das Hotel zurückgehen, er hätte die diplomatische Mission seines Auftraggebers anrufen können, und man hätte ihm den Wagen mit der arabischen Nummer geschickt. Auch hätte er nur dem Portier des Hauses, dem Weißbehandschuhten zu winken brauchen, und der Dienstbereite hätte mit einer kleinen schrillen Flöte ein Taxi herbeigepfiffen. Damals — wie stramm hatten sie hier Spalier gestanden! Zwei Reihen schwarzer Gestalten. Zwanzig Pistolen, und vor seinem Automobil ein Schutzwagen voran und ein Schutzwagen hinterher. Er wollte aber zu Fuß gehen. Er war wohl dreißig Jahre nicht zu Fuß durch eine Stadt gegangen. Als Berlin eine glühende Hölle war, als die ganze Welt Judejahn jagte, da war er ein Stück gelaufen, war durch Staub gekrochen, über Leichen gestiegen, durch Zerstörung gerobbt, und dann war er gerettet worden. Wie? Durch Zufall, oder durch die Vorsehung, hätte sein Führer gesagt, gescheitert, benzinübergossen, zu Asche verbrannt und doch nicht gescheitert, sondern die säkulare Erscheinung, schon zeigte sich Auferstehung im Geiste, also die Vorsehung hatte Judejahn gerettet und ins Gelobte Land nicht der Juden, aber anderer dunkler Brüder geführt. Und auch dort war Judejahn nicht zu Fuß gegangen, wohl über den Exerzierplatz gestapft, ein paar Schritte in die Wüste.

Er fing sich, natürlich, ein alter Fürchtenichts, und wenn er stürzte, hier war ein Gitter, sich daran zu halten. Schmiedeeiserne Stangen reckten sich wie hohe Speere in den Himmel — eine Palisade von Macht, Reichtum und Abweisung. Ein großer Wagen glitt über den Kies der Auffahrt. Judejahn erinnerte sich: Hier war auch er vorgefahren, zackiger, knirschender, aber er war hier vorgefahren. Ein Schild belehrte ihn, daß er vor der Botschaft der Vereinigten Staaten stand. Natürlich hatte Judejahn die Amerikaner nicht besucht; sie hatten ihn nicht eingeladen und waren gar nicht hier gewesen, als er hier war, aber er war bestimmt hier gewesen, und es mußte etwas Faschistisches in diesem Gebäude geschehen sein, eine ganz große Oper, und nie hatte man scharf genug durchgegriffen. Was war der Duce? Eine Sentimentalität des Führers. Judejahn verabscheute Südländer. Er verabscheute sie ganz besonders. Er näherte sich den Kaffeehäusern der Via Veneto, und da saßen sie nun, nicht nur die mißgeachteten Südländer, die Allerweltsländler saßen hier, hockten beisammen wie einst am Kurfürstendamm, saßen da, spielten Friede auf Erden und beschmusten sich, die Entwurzelten, die Internationalen, die Unvölkischen, der goldene Treibsand, die nun auf Luftwegen unruhig und beutegierig hin und her eilenden Stadtbewohner, die hochnäsigen Aasgeier, die der deutschen Zucht und Ordnung entsprungen waren. Judejahn hörte vorwiegend englische Rede, die Amerikaner herrschten vor, sie waren die Erben dieses Krieges, aber Judejahn vernahm auch italienische, französische und andere Laute, zuweilen deutsche, hier seltener, die biederten sich anderswo an. Schmutz, Pack, Juden und Judenknechte! Schimpfe speichelte wie grüne Galle in seinem Mund und filzte die Zähne stumpf. Er sah keine Uniformen, keine Abzeichen am Rock, er blickte in eine ranglose ehrvergessene Welt; nur hier und dort leuchtete die betreßte Affenjacke eines Angestellten des gastronomischen Gewerbes auf. Doch welche Formation rückte nun scharlachrot in die Weltausbeutergasse ein, nahm stürmisch den reichen Lungererpfad? War die scharlachrote Truppe ein Symbol der Stärke, ein Sinnbild der Macht, war sie die goldene Schar, die junge Garde, die Giovinezza, die kam, hier zu säubern? Doch es war Trug und Hohn für Judejahn, was da gegangen kam; es waren Talare, die scharlachrot um die mageren Gestalten junger Priester flatterten, und die rote Schar marschierte nicht, sie lief ungeordnet ihres Weges, doch Judejahn schien es nun, als ob sie beschämend weibisch trippelten, denn ihm war, als er herrschte, entgangen, wie männlich und fest Priester unter der Diktatur sterben können, und zu seinem Glück ahnte er nicht, daß die Scharlachroten Alumnen des Germanischen Seminars waren — ihr Anblick hätte ihn noch mehr verstört.

In der Via Veneto regierte das Geld. Aber hatte Judejahn nicht Geld, konnte er nicht auftrumpfen, kaufen, was andere kauften? Vor einer Bar standen äußerst zerbrechlich wirkende gelbe Stühle, sie waren lächerlich, nicht wie zum Sitzen gebaut, sie glichen einem Haufen verrückter Kanarienvögel, die man piepsen zu hören meinte, und Judejahn fühlte sich angezogen von dieser Bar, weil sie aus irgendeinem Grunde zu dieser Stunde ohne Gäste war. Er setzte sich nicht ins Freie, er verschmähte die unsicheren Stühle, er ging in den zur Straße hin weitgeöffneten Innenraum, stellte sich an die Theke, stützte sich auf, er fühlte sich müde, es mußte wohl das Klima sein, das ihn erschlaffte, und er bestellte ein Bier. Ein schöner Mann in einem lila Frack deutete ihm an, daß er sich, wenn er das Bier im Stehen trinken wolle, einen Bon an der Kasse lösen müsse. Hinter der Kasse saß Laura und lächelte. Ihr liebliches Lächeln war in der Straße berühmt, und der Barbesitzer entließ sie nicht um dieses Lächelns willen, das in seinem Lokal leuchtete, ihm einen Schimmer von Freundlichkeit verlieh und die Kasse zu einem Quell der Freude machte, obwohl Laura dumm war und nicht rechnen konnte. Was tat es? Niemand betrog Laura, denn selbst die homosexuellen Männer, die zu später Stunde und an Sonntagnachmittagen in diesem Etablissement verkehrten, fühlten sich durch Lauras stilles Lächeln beschenkt. Auch Judejahn war beeindruckt. Aber Unmenschlichkeit machte ihn blind, und so erkannte er nicht, daß er ein kindliches Wesen vor sich hatte, das sein Bestes umsonst hergab. Er dachte: Eine hübsche Nutte. Er sah Haar schwarz wie Lack, ein Puppengesicht vom Lächeln belebt, er sah den roten Mund, die roten Nägel, er hatte Lust, sie zu kaufen, und in dieser Straße des Reichtums mußte man als Käufer auftreten, wenn man nicht Knecht sein wollte. Aber schon stand er wieder hilflos und tölpelhaft da und wußte nicht, wie er sich benehmen und wie er es sprachlich beginnen sollte, er war ja nicht in Uniform, das Mädchen fürchtete ihn nicht, es war nicht mit bloßem Winken getan. Er war bereit, gut zu zahlen, und in Lire klang jede Summe gewaltig. Aber sollte er deutsch mit ihr reden? Sie würde ihn nicht verstehen. Italienisch sprach Judejahn nicht. Englisch hatte er ein wenig gelernt. Er verlangte aber dann in englischer Sprache nur statt Bier Whisky, einen großen Scotch. Laura reichte ihm lächelnd gedankenlos den Bon und avisierte Judejahn gedankenlos dem schönen Mann im lila Frack: »Einen großen King George.« »Eis?« »Nein.« »Soda?« »Nein.« Die Unterhaltung blieb einsilbig. Judejahn kippte den Whisky hinunter. Er ärgerte sich. Er konnte nur befehlen. Nicht einmal einer Nutte konnte er ein paar freundliche Worte sagen. Vielleicht war sie eine Jüdin? Man konnte sie im Welschland nicht gleich erkennen. Aber er war wieder der kleine Gottlieb, der Sohn des Volksschullehrers; er sollte studieren und kam auf dem Gymnasium nicht recht mit. Er stand da, wie er einst in seines Vaters gewendeten und für ihn umgeschneiderten Anzügen unter seinen reicheren Kameraden gestanden hatte, die Kieler Matrosenblusen trugen. Sollte er noch einen Whisky trinken? Männer tranken Whisky. Große vermögende Lords tranken stumm ihren Scotch, waren Säufer und verloren den Krieg. Judejahn verzichtete auf ein zweites Glas, das er gern getrunken hätte; er fürchtete, der schöne Mann hinter der Bar und das schöne Mädchen hinter der Kasse würden über den stummen Gast, der er war, lachen. Doch wie vielen war vor diesem stummen Gast das Lachen für immer vergangen? Das wollte er doch einmal fragen! Judejahn merkte sich die Bar. Er dachte: Ich krieg' dich noch. Und Laura verschwendete ihr liebliches Lächeln an seinen breiten Rücken. Nichts warnte sie, einen Mörder zu sehen. Sie dachte, falls sie überhaupt etwas dachte, denn Denken war ihr fremd, und sie pflegte dafür ein vegetatives Sinnen: Familienvater, in Geschäften hier, kein Schwuler, Laufkunde, kam zufällig zu uns, gibt an mit der blauen Brille, fand es fad um diese Zeit, wird nicht wiederkommen. Und würde er wiederkommen, würde er ihretwegen wiederkommen, und sie würde merken, daß er ihretwegen kam, sie würde ihn trotz der blauen Brille nicht unsympathisch finden, denn die Homosexuellen, die am Abend hier auftauchten, langweilten Laura und gaben ihr Zutrauen zu jedem Mann, der nach Mann roch, auch wenn sie an sich nichts gegen die Homosexuellen, die sie ernährten, hatte.

Judejahn wandte sich nun doch der Familie, der harrenden,

zu, die ihren vom Tode auferstandenen Helden wiederhaben wollte. Er warf einen Blick auf den Stadtplan, den er gefaltet bei sich trug. Er orientierte sich schnell, das hatte er gelernt; in Wäldern, in Sümpfen und in Wüsten konnte er sich nicht verirren. Er würde sich auch im Dschungel der Stadt nicht verlaufen. Er ging nun die Via di Porta Pinciana entlang, ging neben einer hohen alten Mauer her, hinter der wohl ein großer schöner schattiger Garten lag, der einem der reichen Aristokraten gehören mochte, einem von der Königsclique, die den Duce verraten hatte. Die Luft war warm und roch nach Regen. Ein Windstoß wirbelte Staub auf und erregte Judejahn wie eine elektrische Dusche. An der Gartenmauer klebten Affichen. Ein Jahrgang der Jugend wurde zum Heeresdienst einberufen. Das konnte den Schwächlingen nur guttun. Für Waffen sorgte Onkel Sam. Aber deutsche Ausbilder taten ihnen not. Ohne deutsche Ausbilder war jeder Dollar umsonst ausgegeben. Konnte Onkel Sam nicht mehr rechnen? Ein rotes Plakat der Kommunistischen Partei brannte wie ein Fanal. Judejahn dachte an die Nacht des Reichstagsbrandes. Das war die Erhebung gewesen! Man war angetreten! Eine Epoche hatte begonnen! Eine Epoche ohne Goethe! Was wollte die russisch-römische Kommune? Judejahn vermochte den Text nicht zu lesen. Was brauchte er ihn zu lesen? Er war für an die Wand stellen. Hier an diese Mauer sollte man sie stellen. In Lichterfelde hatte man sie an die Wand gestellt. Nicht nur Rotfront; da hatten noch ganz andere an der Mauer gestanden. Judejahn hatte zum Spaß mitgeschossen. Wer sagte, daß die Menschen Brüder seien? Schwächlinge, die etwas haben wollten! Und wenn man sich mit Moskau geeinigt hätte? In Moskau saßen keine Schwächlinge. Wenn man es unter starken Brüdern ausgehandelt, wenn es zu einem größeren umfassenderen Stalin-Hitler-Pakt gekommen wäre? Judejahn tat sein armer Kopf weh. Versäumte Möglichkeiten, vielleicht noch nicht ganz versäumt, »und die Welt wird unser sein« dann kräftig in einen wieder strahlenden Morgen gekräht. Am Sonntag war irgendein Rennen Rom—Neapel, Neapel—Rom. Gladiatorenspiele für Schwachnervige. Wie hieß der Kämpfer mit Dolch

und Netz, wie der Kämpfer mit dem Schwert? Germanen fochten im Zirkus gegen wilde Tiere. Germanen waren zu gutmütig, wurden überlistet. Auf weißem Grund mit schwarzem Kreuz stand ein kirchlicher Erlaß. Die Kirche siegte immer. Priester blieben schlau im Hintergrund. Ließen andere sich erschöpfen. Nach den Kriegen bauten sie dann ihre Parteien auf. Fledderer. Jesuiten-Jiu-Jitsu. Grünes Papier. Olio Sasso. War wohl alles in Öl. Krieg? Mobilmachung? Noch nicht. Kam auch noch nicht. Traute sich keiner. Kleine Übungen nur auf Versuchsfeldern, in Wüsten, Dschungeln und entlegenen Gebieten. Wie einst in Spanien. Im Parterre eines großspurigen Mietshauses lockte ein Kojote. Der Kojote war ein Präriewolf; Judejahn erinnerte sich an Karl May. Hier war der Kojote eine American Bar. Er hatte viel blankgeputztes Messing an seiner Tür und sah vornehm und teuer aus. Judejahn hatte Geld, aber er traute sich nicht in die Bar. Judejahn hatte Durst, aber er traute sich nicht in den Kojoten. Warum traute er sich nicht? Der kleine Gottlieb stand ihm im Weg, und nur eine Uniform am Leib überwand den kleinen Gottlieb. Judejahn ging weiter. Er fand eine Fiaschetteria. Strohumwundene Flaschen lagen in Haufen da, Wein näßte den Boden. Hier trank das Volk. Das Volk brauchte man nicht zu fürchten. Das Volk konnte man lenken. Mit dem Volk brauchte man nicht zu reden. Das Volk wurde eingesetzt. Der Führer stand über dem Volk. Judejahn verlangte Chianti. Er stürzte ihn hinunter. Der Wein tat ihm gut. Er forderte ein zweites Glas. Er schmeckte den Wein nicht, aber er fühlte sich gestärkt. Mit festem Tritt erreichte er den berühmten Platz vor der Kirche Trinitá dei Monti. Die Kirche hatte zwei spitze Türme. Nonnen vom Kloster du Sacré Cœur standen auf den Stufen, die zur Kirche führten. Judejahn ekelte sich vor ihren langen Röcken, ihren Umhängen, ihren Hauben. Hexen!
Zu seinen Füßen war nun die Spanische Treppe, lag Rom, und im Hintergrund erhob sich mächtig die Kuppel von St. Peter — der alte Feind. Er war nicht geschlagen. Niemand war geschlagen. Die Partie war — durch Verrat — remis ausgegangen; der Führer hatte alle Trümpfe in der Hand ge-

habt, Gnomen hatten sie ihm entwunden, Befehle wurden nicht ausgeführt — nur Judejahn hatte jeden Befehl ausgeführt. Er hatte reinen Tisch gemacht. Hatte er überall reinen Tisch gemacht? Leider nein. Wie es schien, gar nirgends. Die Hydra hatte mehr als neun Köpfe gehabt. Sie hatte Millionen Köpfe gehabt. Ein Judejahn war zuwenig. Nun kehrte er aus dem Kriege heim, kein Eroberer, ein Bettler, namenlos. Er mußte nach der Brüstung greifen. Seine Finger klammerten sich an die bröckelnde Mauerung. Schmerz wühlte ihn auf. Rom schwamm vor seinem Blick, ein Meer von sich auflösenden Steinen, und die Kuppel von St. Peter war eine schaukelnde Luftblase auf dieser wilden See. Schluchzen schüttelte Judejahn. Eine alte vornehme Dame mit blaugepudertem Haar deutete mit ihrem Schirm über die Ewige Stadt, über das große Panorama, das sie bot. Die alte Dame rief: »*Isn't it wonderful!*« Der linke Turm von Trinitá dei Monti läutete einen Segen.

Er stieg hinab. Er stieg die Spanische Treppe hinab, stieg über das malerische Italien, stieg über den Müßiggang des Volkes, das hier auf den Stufen hockte, lag, schlief, spielte, las, lernte, das sich hier unterhielt, sich stritt und sich umarmte. Ein Knabe bot Judejahn Mais an, geröstete gelbe Körner. Er hielt dem Fremden, dem Barbaren aus dem Norden die spitze Tüte hin, sagte mit schmeichelnder Stimme »*cento Lire*«, und Judejahn stieß gegen die Tüte, und der Mais fiel auf die Treppe, und Judejahn zertrat die Körner. Er hatte es nicht gewollt. Es war Ungeschick. Er hätte den Knaben prügeln mögen.

Er überquerte den Platz und erreichte keuchend die Via Condotti. Der Bürgersteig war schmal. Menschen drängten sich in der belebten Geschäftsstraße, drängten sich vor den Schaufenstern, drängten aneinander vorbei. Judejahn stieß und wurde gestoßen. Er wunderte sich. Er staunte, daß keiner ihm Platz machte, niemand vor ihm zurückwich. Es wunderte ihn, daß auch er gestoßen wurde.

Die zweite Gasse suchte er, suchte sie nach dem Plan — aber suchte er sie wirklich? Die Jahre am Wüstenrand erschienen ihm nun wie eine in Narkose verbrachte Zeit, er hatte keinen

Schmerz gefühlt, doch jetzt war ihm übel, er spürte Schmerz und Fieber, empfand die Schnitte, die sein Leben nur noch zu einem bloßen Rest machten, empfand die Schnitte, die diesen Rest aus der breiten Fülle seiner Macht trennten. Was war er? Er war ein Clown seines Einst. Sollte er auferstehen von den Toten, oder sollte er ein Spuk in der Wüste bleiben, ein Gespenst in den Illustrierten Zeitungen des Vaterlandes? Judejahn fürchtete sich nicht, der Welt die Stirn zu bieten Was wollte die Welt von ihm? Sie sollte nur kommen, sie sollte nur kommen in all ihrer Schlappheit, in all ihrer Käuflichkeit, mit all ihren schmutzigen, mit all ihren raubtierhaften Gelüsten, verborgen unter der Maske des Biedermanns. Die Welt sollte froh sein, wenn sie Kerle von seiner Art hatte. Judejahn bangte nicht, gehängt zu werden. Er fürchtete sich, zu leben. Er fürchtete die Befehlslosigkeit, in der er leben sollte; er hatte viel verantwortet, je höher er stieg, um so mehr hatte er verantwortet, und die Verantwortung hatte ihn nie gedrückt, doch seine Rede »auf meine Verantwortung« oder »das verantworte ich« war Phrase gewesen, eine Phrase, an der er sich berauschte, denn in Wahrheit hatte er immer nur gehorcht. Judejahn war mächtig gewesen. Er hatte die Macht ausgekostet, aber um der Macht froh zu werden, brauchte er eine Einschränkung seiner Allmacht, brauchte er den Führer als Verkörperung und weithin sichtbaren Gott der Macht, den Befehlsgeber, auf den er sich berufen konnte vor dem Schöpfer, den Menschen und dem Teufel: Ich habe immer nur gehorcht, ich habe stets nur Befehle ausgeführt. Also hatte er Gewissen? Nein, er hatte nur Angst. Er hatte Angst, man könne dahinterkommen, daß er der kleine Gottlieb war und sich Größe angemaßt hatte. Judejahn hörte insgeheim eine Stimme, nicht die Stimme Gottes, und er vernahm sie nicht als Gewissensruf, es war die dünne, die hungrige und fortschrittsgläubige Stimme des Vaters Volksschullehrer, die flüsterte: Du bist dumm, du hast deine Aufgaben nicht gelernt, du bist ein schlechter Schüler, eine Null, die aufgeblasen wurde. Und so war es gut, daß er sich immer im Schatten eines Größeren gehalten hatte, daß er ein Trabant geblieben war, der glanzvolle Trabant des mächtigsten Ge-

413

stirns, und er begriff noch immer nicht, daß diese Sonne, von der er Licht und die Befugnis zu töten geliehen hatte, auch nur ein Betrüger gewesen war, auch nur ein schlechter Schüler, auch nur ein kleiner Gottlieb, doch des Teufels auserwähltes Werkzeug, eine magische Null, eine Schimäre des Volkes, eine Luftblase, die schließlich platzte.

Judejahn spürte Gier, sich zu füllen. Schon im Freikorps hatte er Anfälle von Gefräßigkeit gehabt und Schlag nach Schlag die Löffelerbsen der Gulaschkanone in sich hineingefüllt. Jetzt roch er am Eingang der gesuchten Gasse Speisegeruch. Ein Garkoch hatte in seinem Schaufenster allerlei Gerichte zur Schau gestellt, und Judejahn ging in den Laden und verlangte gebackene Leber, auf der im Fenster ein Täfelchen »*fritto scelto*« gelegen hatte, und Judejahn forderte die Leber mit dieser Täfelchenbezeichnung »*fritto scelto*«, das hieß aber nur »nach Wahl«, und man brachte ihm aus Mißverständnis und nicht rechtem Hinhören in Teig und Öl gebackene kleine Meertiere. Er schlang sie hinunter; sie schmeckten ihm wie gebackene Regenwürmer, und ihn grauste. Er fühlte, wie sein schwerer Leib sich in Würmer auflöste, er erlebte lebendigen Leibes seine Verwesung, aber um der Auflösung zu begegnen, schlang er gegen alles Grausen weiter hinunter, was auf dem Teller lag. Danach trank er ein Viertel Wein, auch diesen im Stehen, und nun konnte es weitergehen

ein paar Schritte nur noch, und da war das von seinen Landsleuten und von seiner Familie bevorzugte Hotel. Wagen mit dem deutschen D-Schild standen in Reihen geordnet vor dem Haus. Judejahn sah die Symbole des deutschen Wiederaufstiegs, das Stromlinienblech des deutschen Wirtschaftswunders. Es imponierte ihm. Es zog ihn an. Sollte er hineingehen, die Hacken zusammenschlagen, schnarren: »Ich stelle mich zur Verfügung!« Sie würden die Arme ausbreiten. Würden sie die Arme ausbreiten, ihn an die Brust zu ziehen? Etwas stieß ihn auch ab an diesen gelackten Wagen. Der Aufstieg, das Weiterleben, das gute fette und erfolgreiche Weiterleben nach totalem Krieg, nach totaler Schlacht und totaler Niederlage war und blieb auch Verrat, Verrat an den Absichten, der

Vorsehungsschau und dem Testament des Führers, es war und blieb schmähliche Kollaboration mit den westlichen Erbfeinden, die das deutsche Blut, die den deutschen Soldaten gegen den östlichen Teilhaber ihres erschlichenen Sieges brauchten. Wie sollte er sich verhalten? Schon zündete man die Lichter im Hotel an. Fenster nach Fenster erleuchtete sich, und hinter einem saß Eva und wartete. Nach den Briefen, den rätselvollen Wendungen, die von Enttäuschung, die ihn erwarte, von Entartung und Schande sprachen, durfte er nicht hoffen, auch Adolf, seinen Sohn hier zu treffen. Lohnte es sich, heimzukehren? Noch stand ihm die Wüste offen. Noch war das Netz deutscher Bürgerlichkeit nicht über den alten Kämpfer geworfen. Zweifelnd, unsicher schritt er durch die Tür, kam in die getäfelte Halle, und da sah er deutsche Männer, Schwager Friedrich Wilhelm Pfaffrath war unter ihnen, er hatte sich kaum verändert, und die deutschen Männer standen sich nach deutscher Art und Sitte gegenüber, sie hielten ihre Gläser in der Hand, keine Humpen mit deutschem Gerstensaft, Gläser mit welschem Gesöff, aber auch er, Judejahn, soff das Gesöff ja und noch ganz anderes Zeug, kein Vorwurf in der Fremde, und diese Männer, sie waren markig, kernig, er hörte es, sie sangen, sie sangen »Ein feste Burg ist unser Gott«, und dann fühlte er sich beobachtet, nicht von den Sängern, von der Tür her fühlte er sich beobachtet, es war ein ernster, ein suchender, ein flehender, ein verzweifelter Blick, der ihn traf.

Es entsetzte Siegfried nicht, aber es beirrte ihn doch, das breite ungemachte Bett zu sehen, es zog seinen Blick an, den er nicht hinzuwenden sich vergebens bemühte, das breite Bett, das Ehebett stand großmächtig im geräumigen Zimmer, es war sachlich und schamlos, es war ganz unsinnlich und schamlos, es war aufgedeckt, kaltes und reines Linnen, und sprach kalt und rein von Gebrauch, den niemand verbergen wollte, von Umarmungen, deren niemand sich schämte, von tiefem gesundem Schlaf
und auf einmal begriff ich, daß Kürenbergs mir voraus waren, sie waren der Mensch, der ich sein möchte, sie waren

sündelos, sie waren der alte und der neue Mensch, sie waren antik und Avantgarde, sie waren vorchristlich und nachchristlich, griechisch-römische Bürger und Flugreisende über den Ozean, sie waren in Körper gesperrt, aber in saubere gekannte und klug unterhaltene Leiber; sie waren Exkursanten, die sich's in einer vielleicht unwirtlichen Welt wirtlich gemacht hatten und sich des Erdballs freuten.

Kürenberg hatte sich auf Nomadie eingestellt. Er wirtschaftete im Hemd und in weißen Leinenhosen, über die eine Gummischürze gehalftert war, an zwei Extratischen, die das Hotel ihm in sein Zimmer gestellt hatte, und überhaupt fragte ich mich, wie er es sich mit der Direktion arrangierte, denn man mußte ihm Sondersicherungen gebaut haben, in die Stromdosen hatte er Drei- und Vierfachstecker gepreßt, und Leitungsschnüre liefen wie ineinander verschlungene Schlangen zu blinkenden elektrischen Geräten, Grillrosten, Backhauben, Infrarotstrahlern, Dampftöpfen, Schnellkochern, es war die vollkommenste transportable Küche, an der er seine Freude hatte und die mit ihm reiste, und hier bereitete er das Mahl, zu dem er mich geladen, er rührte, schmeckte, klopfte, würzte und hatte ein festes ernstes Männergesicht, das in seiner gesammelten Ruhe anzusehen mit guttat, während Frau Kürenberg, nachdem sie mir freundlich zur Begrüßung die Hand gereicht und ein paar Worte mit mir gesprochen hatte »wie gefällt Ihnen Rom? Sie sind zum erstenmal hier?«, zwitschernde Schwalben einer kleinen Konversation, erdnahe Flüge, den Tisch deckte, beim Decken hin und her lief, ins Badezimmer ging, die Tür stets offenließ, dort Gläser spülte, Blumen in eine Vase tat und den Wein in das laufende Wasser des Brunnens stellte.

Ich wollte nicht müßig stehen. Ich fragte Kürenberg, ob ich helfen könne, und er drückte mir eine Schüssel, eine Reibe und ein Stück Parmesan in die Hände und forderte mich auf, den Käse zu reiben. Erst bröckelte der Käse vom steinharten Klumpen in die Schüssel, und Kürenberg zeigte mir, wie es zu machen sei, und dann fragte er mich, ob ich nie meiner Mutter in der Küche geholfen habe. Ich sagte: »Nein.« Und ich erinnerte mich an die große kalte Küche

416

unseres Hauses, deren Fliesenboden immer von frischem Aufwisch feucht war, und die Stiefel der uniformierten Amtsboten und Dienerschaftsfreunde zeichneten immer wieder neuen Schmutz in den feuchten spiegelnden Fliesengrund zum Ärger des bei uns stets unwirschen, hektisch lauten und hektisch fahrigen Personals. »Wo stammen Sie her?« fragte Kürenberg. Ich nannte ihm den Ort, und ich wollte noch erklären, daß nichts mich an ihn binde, nichts als der Zufall der Geburt, als ich merkte, daß Kürenberg mich überrascht ansah, und dann rief er: »Ilse kommt aus derselben Stadt«, und sie, die Glas trocknete, richtete nun auch den Blick auf mich, aber einen Blick, der durch mich durchsah, und ich dachte, sie sieht die Allee, die alte Allee mit den Cafés und den Bäumen, die jetzt verbrannt sind, aber die Cafés hat man wohl wieder aufgebaut, und Leute sitzen draußen in der Sonne, unter Schirmen vielleicht, weil die Bäume verbrannt sind, oder man hat neue Bäume gepflanzt, schnellwachsende Pappeln, sie sieht das wohl, genau wie ich es sehe, sachlich und doch ein wenig gerührt; weiß sie überhaupt, daß die Bäume verbrannt sind? Ich wollte sie fragen, aber sie ging hinaus, ging wieder beschäftigt ins Bad, und Kürenberg schlug eine Sauce mit dem Schneebesen, ich merkte aber, daß er abgelenkt blieb, gestört war, und dann sagte er, nachdem er zum Badezimmer geblickt hatte, als wolle er sich vergewissern, daß sie nicht in der Nähe sei: »Ich war bei Ihnen am Theater. Sie hatten ein gutes Orchester, gute Stimmen, ein schönes Haus.« »Es ist zerstört«, sagte ich, »man spielt in der Redoute.« Er nickte. Die Sauce war fertig. Er sagte: »Es gab da einen Regierungspräsidenten, er hieß Pfaffrath wie Sie, waren Sie verwandt?« Ich sagte: »Er ist mein Vater; aber jetzt ist er Bürgermeister.« Er beugte sich über einen dampfenden Topf und rief dann: »Ilse, schnell, das große Sieb.« Und sie brachte das Sieb aus dem Badezimmer, ein straffes Geflecht, straff wie sie, und er schüttete den Reis in das Sieb, sprang mit dem Gefäß voll dampfenden Korns zur Wanne, ließ kaltes Wasser darüberschießen, tropfte durch Schütteln das Wasser ab, hängte den Reis in dem Sieb zur Nachquellung und Wiedererwärmung in den Topf über den Wasserdampf und sagte

zu mir: »Ein Rezept aus Batavia, der Reis wird gar und bleibt
körnig.« Sie waren viel herumgekommen, er hatte überall
dirigiert, und sie hatten sich ganz in dieses Leben gefügt, sie
hatten kein Haus, keine feste Wohnung, sie besaßen Koffer,
große schöne Koffer und ein Hotelzimmer hier oder dort und
immer dem ähnlich, in dem ich stand. Und da wußte ich, daß
ich Kürenberg länger gekannt habe, als ich gedacht hatte, ich
erinnerte mich, natürlich war es mir damals nicht bewußt,
ich war ein Kind, ich hatte keinen Einblick in die Vorgänge,
aber jetzt sah ich's wieder, als sei es heute, ich sah meinen
Vater Kürenberg hinausbegleiten, ich spielte in der Diele,
und als mein Vater hinter Kürenberg die Tür geschlossen
hatte, sah ich an seinem geröteten Gesicht, daß er verärgert
war, und er schalt mich, weil ich in der Diele spielte, und ging
zu meiner Mutter hinein, und ich folgte ihm, weil ich nicht
wußte, wohin ich gehen sollte in dem großen Haus, und ich
folgte ihm auch aus Neugierde, obwohl ich wußte, daß er
schlechter Laune war, wie meistens wenn man ihn um Hilfe
gebeten hatte, und die Leute schienen ihn schlecht zu kennen
in unserer Stadt, denn sie baten ihn damals oft um Hilfe, doch
er dachte gar nicht daran, sich für Verlorene einzusetzen,
nicht weil er sie haßte, das nicht, er war nicht verrückt, er
mochte sie nicht, so war es wohl, aber er fürchtete sie nun, da
man sie für aussätzig erklärt hatte, als Aussätzige, und vor
allem fürchtete er damals schon Onkel Judejahn, und ich
hörte ihn jetzt, wie er damals zu meiner Mutter sagte: »Unser Generalmusikdirektor« — er drückte sich immer ge-
schwollen aus, und Titel imponierten ihm — »war bei mir
und wünschte seinen Schwiegervater, den alten Aufhäuser,
freizubekommen. Ich habe ihm geraten, an seine Laufbahn
zu denken und sich scheiden zu lassen —« Und dann sah mein
Vater mich und schickte mich wütend hinaus, und ich weiß
heute, daß der alte Aufhäuser damals zum erstenmal verhaftet war, es war beim ersten kleinen Judenboykottag, doch
erst am großen Judentag zündete man Aufhäusers Kaufhaus
an, ich hatte Ferien von der Junkerschule und sah das Haus
brennen, das erste, das ich lichterloh brennen sah, und Aufhäuser war wieder in Schutzhaft, und mein Vater teilte zu

Hause am Familientisch die Suppe aus, zuweilen gab er sich patriarchalisch, und aus dem Lautsprecher geiferten Göring und Goebbels, und meine Mutter sagte »es kann einem leid tun, um all die schönen Sachen, die verbrannt sind«, und der alte Aufhäuser saß wieder in Schutzhaft, und später beschäftigte ich mich mit seiner Bibliothek, sie lag in ungeordneten Haufen auf dem Dachboden des Hitlerjugendheims, irgend jemand mußte sie dort hingeschleppt und dann vergessen haben, Aufhäuser war ein Bibliophile, und ich fand Erstausgaben der Klassiker und der Romantiker, seltene deutsche und lateinische Drucke der Alten, Erstausgaben des Naturalismus, Erstausgaben der Brüder Mann, die Werke von Hofmannsthal, Rilke, George, Zeitschriften wie die *Blätter für die Kunst* und die *Neue Rundschau* in Sammelbänden, die Literatur des Ersten Weltkrieges, die Expressionisten bis zu Kafka, ich stahl mir was und trug es fort, und später verbrannte, was dort blieb, wurde mit dem Hitlerjugendheim von Bomben zerrissen, und Aufhäuser der Schutzhäftling wurde erschlagen — und sie war nun die Tochter. Konnte ich sie ansehen? Wohin fliehen die Gedanken? Die Gedanken wehrten sich. Sie sagten mir: Sie hat sich gut gehalten, sie muß über vierzig sein, dabei kaum eine Falte. Und der Gedanke wehrte sich weiter: Die Aufhäusers waren reich, ob man sie entschädigt hat? Und dann: Er heiratete nicht ihren Reichtum, die Zeit war schon zu vorgeschritten, er stellte sich gegen das Böse. Und dann: Sie lieben sich, sie haben zueinandergehalten, sie lieben sich noch immer. Und wir gingen zu Tisch, wir setzten uns, Kürenberg tat die Speisen auf, sie schenkte den Wein ein, und sicher war es ein köstliches Mahl, ich hatte den Koch zu loben, aber ich konnte nicht, ich schmeckte nichts, oder doch — Asche schmeckte ich, lebenlose zum Verwehen bereite Asche, und ich dachte: Sie hat ihres Vaters Haus nicht brennen sehen. Und ich dachte: Sie hat auch unsere Häuser nicht brennen sehen. Und ich dachte: Das ist geschehen geschehen geschehen das ist nicht zu ändern nicht zu ändern das ist verdammt verdammt verdammt verdammt. Ganzblätterigen Spinat gab es, in feinstem Öl gesotten, und darüber streuten wir den Käse, den ich gerieben hatte, und die Steaks waren zwei Finger dick, wie in Butter schnitt das Messer, und rot lief das Blut aus dem Mittelstück, und der Wein war kalt und herb wie eine frische Quelle, das spürte ich noch in all der trockenen filzigen Asche auf meiner Zunge, es wurde nicht gesprochen beim Mahl, Kürenbergs beugten sich über ihre Teller und nährten sich ernst, und ich sagte einmal »herrlich«, vielleicht zu zag, niemand antwortete, und dann gab es einen flambierten Auflauf von Himbeeren, tropisch fast und dennoch von deutschem Waldaroma, und Kürenberg sagte: »Den Kaffee soll der Kellner bringen; keine Zubereitung übertrifft das Konzentrat der Espressomaschinen.« Ilse Kürenberg bestellte über das Haustelephon den Kaffee; Kognak kam auf den Tisch, und dann sprachen wir von Rom.

Sie lieben das alte, das antike, das römische Rom, sie lieben die Foren mit ihrer zerschlagenen Größe, sie lieben den Blick am Abend über die alten Hügel, über die Zypressen, die einsamen Pinien, sie lieben die sinnlos gewordenen nichts mehr tragenden Säulen, die Marmorstufen, die nirgendwohin führen, die gespaltenen Bogen über den zugeschütteten Abgründen der Bildung gewordenen Siege, sie lieben das Haus des Augustus und nennen Horaz und Vergil, sie bewundern die Rotunde der Vestalinnen, und sie beten im Tempel des Glücks. Ich höre ihnen zu, wie sie unterrichtet von neuen Funden sprechen, mit Kennerschaft von Ausgrabungen und Museumsschätzen; auch ich liebe sie, liebe die alten Götter, liebe die Schönheit, die, lange in der Erde verborgen, wieder ans Licht kam, liebe das Maß und die glatte kühle Steinhaut der alten Gestalten, aber noch mehr liebe ich Rom, wie es lebt, wie es ist und mir sich zeigt, ich liebe seinen Himmel, Jupiters unergründliches Meer, und ich denke, wir sind versunken, sind Vineta, und droben über dem Element, das uns umschließt, ziehen auf blendender Woge nie von uns gesehene Schiffe, und der Tod wirft sein unsichtbares Netz über die Stadt, ich liebe die Straßen, die Winkel, die Treppen, die stillen Höfe mit Urnen, Efeu und Laren und die lauten Plätze mit den tollkühnen Lambrettafahrern, ich liebe das Volk am Abend vor den Haustüren, seine Scherze, seine aus-

drucksvollen Gesten, seine Begabung für die Komödie, sein
Gespräch, das ich nicht verstehe, ich liebe die rauschenden
Brunnen mit ihren Meergöttern, Nymphen und Tritonen, ich
liebe die Kinder auf dem Brunnenrand aus Marmelstein, die
gaukelnden bekränzten grausamen kleinen Neronen, ich
liebe das Drängen, Reiben, Stoßen, Schreien, Lachen und die
Blicke auf dem Corso und die obszönen Worte, die den Damen im Vorübergehen zugeflüstert werden, und ich liebe die
starre leere Larve des Damenantlitzes, die der Schmutz mit-
formt, und ich liebe ihre Antworten, ihre Beschämungen und
ihre Lust an geiler Huldigung, die sie eingegraben auf
ihrem wirklichen Gesicht, verborgen unter der Straßenmaske,
nach Hause und in ihre Frauenträume tragen, ich liebe die
strahlenden Schaufenster des Reichtums, die Auslagen der
Juweliere und die Vögelhüte der Modistinnen, ich liebe die
kleine hochmütige Kommunistin der Piazza della Rotonda,
ich liebe die lange blanke Espressobar mit der zischenden
dampfspeienden Maschine und die Männer davor, die aus
den kleinen Tassen den heißen starken bittersüßen Kaffee
trinken, ich liebe Verdis Musik, wenn sie in der Passage vor
der Piazza Colonna aus dem Lautsprecher des Fernsehstudios
schallt und ihr Echo zurückschlägt von den Stuckfassaden der
Jahrhundertwende, ich liebe die Via Veneto, die Kaffeehäuser
des Jahrmarkts der Eitelkeit, ihre lustigen Stühle, ihre bunten Markisen, ich liebe die hochbeinigen schmalhüftigen
Modemädchen, ihr brandrot gefärbtes Haar, ihre blassen Gesichter, ihre großen staunenden Augen, Feuer, das ich nicht
greifen kann, ich liebe die wartenden glücklichen dummen
athletischen Gigolos, die von den wohlhabenden Elastikform-
damen eingehandelt werden, ich liebe die würdigen amerikanischen Senatoren, die der Heilige Vater empfängt und die
sich alles kaufen können, ich liebe die weißhaarigen sanften
Automobilkönige, die ihr Vermögen herschenken, die Wissenschaft, die Kunst und die Dichtung zu fördern, ich liebe
die homosexuellen Poeten in engen Röhrenhosen und spitzen
dünnsohligen Schuhen, die von den Stiftungen leben und
ihre klingenden silbernen Armbänder kokett aus den über-
langen Manschetten ihrer Hemden schütteln, ich liebe das

alte faulende Badeschiff, verankert auf dem trüben Tiber vor
der Engelsburg, und seine roten unbeschirmten Glühbirnen
in der Nacht, ich liebe die kleinen heimlichen weihrauch-
durchzogenen, mit Kunst und Schmuck ausgepolsterten Kirchen, obwohl Kürenberg sagt, das barocke Rom sei enttäuschend, ich liebe die Priester in ihren schwarzen, roten, vio-
letten und weißen Gewändern, die lateinische Sprache der
Messe, die Priesterschüler und die Angst in ihrem Gesicht,
die alten Kanoniker in befleckter Soutane und schönem spek-
kigem Monsignorehut mit lustiger roter Kordel und die
Angst in ihrem Gesicht, die alten Frauen, die vor den Beicht-
stühlen knien, und die Angst in ihrem Gesicht, die armen
rilligen Hände der Bettler vor den geschnitzten und geschmiedeten Portalen der Kapellen und ihre Angst dort, wo
die Schlagader zittert im Hals, ich liebe den kleinen Lebens-
mittelhändler in der Straße der Arbeiter, der die großen
Scheiben der Mortadella aufschneidet, als wären sie Blätter
eines Baumes, ich liebe die kleinen Märkte, die Stände der
Fruchthändler grün rot orange, der Fischhändler Bottiche mit
den unverstandenen Wesen der See und alle Katzen Roms,
die längs den Mauern streichen
und sie, zwei feste Schatten, sie waren an das Fenster getreten, an das hohe Fenster, das bis zum Erdboden zu öffnen
und wie die Kanzel eines Turmes war, und sie blickten in den
lichtervollen Graben der Straße, blickten in dieser dem Bahnhof nahen Gegend auf andere Herbergen in hochgestockten
Steinkästen, der ihren ähnlich und Wanderer voll, Leucht-
schilder flammten auf und lockten, und Rom war wie je bereit, erobert zu werden, und Kürenberg dachte an Siegfrieds
Musik, die er morgen für diese Stadt aufs neue straffen, kühlen und im Strom ihres Gefühls komprimieren wollte, und
Ilse stand neben ihm und sah die Dächer der Automobile wie
einen Heerbann großer Wanzen im Grunde der Straße kriechen, sie sah den für eine Weile gebändigten Blitz mit dem
Anschein der Harmlosigkeit an den Kontaktstangen der
Oberleitungsomnibusse flattern, sie durchschaute die Konvention, den Tod nicht zu sehen, das allgemeine Übereinkom-
men, den Schrecken zu leugnen, der Besitz an den Gebäuden,

die sie sah, war im Grundbuch eingetragen, und selbst die
Römer, mit Stätten vernichteter verschütteter Pracht wohl
vertraut, glaubten an die Ewigkeit der gerade jetzt auf der
alten Erde nützlich aufgeschichteten Steine, sie sah die Mysterienspiele des Handels, auch diese auf den Wahn von
Ewigkeit, Vererbbarkeit und Sicherheit gegründet, sie erblickte die aufblühenden und verlöschenden Wunder der
Reklame, bunte Schimmer auch über ihrer Kinderzeit, Mer-
kurlichter oder Unholdskerzen, und wie einfältig war es von
ihrem Vater, zwischen ihrem Mädchenleben und dem Kaufhof eine Mauer aus Büchern, Musik und Kunst zu errichten,
eine Bastion, die trog, einen milden Lampenschein, der für
immer erlosch — es fröstelte sie, und sie dachte, wie kalt alles
sei. Sie dachte: Es ist spät. Und sie dachte: Dieser junge
Mann aus meiner Stadt schreibt Symphonien, und sein Groß-
vater hat vielleicht am Spinett gesessen oder die Flöte gespielt, aber sein Vater hat meinen Vater erschlagen, meinen
Vater, der Bücher sammelte und gern ins Brandenburgische
Konzert ging. Sie nahm Kürenbergs Hand, drängte ihre
Hand, die kalt und für einen Augenblick wie gestorben war,
in die Faust des Dirigenten, die sich warm, trocken, fleisch-
fest und vertrauenswürdig anfühlte. Kürenberg schaute noch
in die Straße hinunter, und er dachte: Man kann ihnen ihre
Zukunft voraussagen. Er war Analytikern, Soziologen, Plan-
wirtschaftlern, Atomspaltern, Völkerrechtlern, Politikern und
Public-Relations-Männern begegnet. Sie waren eine Teufelszunft. Die Teufelszunft war sein Publikum. Sie kamen in
seine Konzerte. Er schloß das Fenster und fragte Siegfried:
»Kennen Sie das Wort des Augustinus von der Musik, der
sich große Männer nach vollbrachter Arbeit hingeben, um
ihre Seele wiederherzustellen?« Siegfried kannte das Wort
nicht. Er kannte Augustinus nicht. So wenig wußte er. So viel
Erkenntnis fehlte ihm. Er errötete. Sind es große Männer,
die ich kenne? fragte sich Kürenberg. Und wenn es diese
nicht sind, wo sind die wirklich großen Männer? Und haben
sie eine Seele, die am Abend durch Musik wiederherzustellen
ist? Kannte Augustinus denn große Männer? Und hielten sie,
die er vielleicht für große Männer hielt, ihn für einen großen

Mann? So viele Fragen! Kürenberg schätzte Siegfrieds Begabung. Er erwartete von Siegfried die Überraschung, eine noch nie gesprochene Sprache. Sie mochte dem allgemeinen Gehör, das hinter dem schnellen Lauf der Zeit zurückgeblieben ist, schrecklich klingen; aber sie würde neue Kunde bringen. Neue Kunde für ein paar Menschen, die neue Botschaft hören konnten. Waren dies die großen Männer, von denen Augustinus sprach? Es drängt uns zu wissen, selbst wenn es uns unglücklich macht. Kürenberg sah Siegfried freundlich an. Aber er sagte ernst: »Ich weiß nicht, für wen Sie Ihre Musik schreiben. Aber ich glaube, daß Ihre Musik eine Funktion in der Welt hat. Vielleicht wird der Unverstand pfeifen. Lassen Sie sich nie von Ihrem Weg bringen. Versuchen Sie nie, Wünsche zu erfüllen. Enttäuschen Sie den Abonnenten. Aber enttäuschen Sie aus Demut, nicht aus Hochmut! Ich rate Ihnen nicht, in den berühmten Elfenbeinturm zu steigen. Um Gottes willen — kein Leben für die Kunst! Gehen Sie auf die Straße. Lauschen Sie dem Tag! Aber bleiben Sie einsam! Sie haben das Glück, einsam zu sein. Bleiben Sie auf der Straße einsam wie in einem abgeschlossenen Laboratorium. Experimentieren Sie. Experimentieren Sie mit allem, mit allem Glanz und allem Schmutz unserer Welt, mit Erniedrigung und Größe — vielleicht finden Sie den neuen Klang!« Und Siegfried dachte an die Stimmen, an die Stimmen der Straße, er dachte an die Stimmen der Roheit, der Angst, der Qual, der Gier, der Liebe, der Güte, des Gebets, er dachte an den Laut des Bösen, an das Geflüster der Unzucht und den Schrei des Verbrechens. Und er dachte: Und morgen wird er mich ducken, wird mir mit den Harmoniegesetzen und schulmeisterlicher Strenge begegnen, ein berühmter Orchesterleiter, ein genauer Notenleser, vielleicht ein Gärtner, der alles beschneidet, und ich bin Wildwuchs und Unkraut. Und Kürenberg sagte, als habe er Siegfried gehört: »Ich glaube an unsere Arbeit. In mir sind Widersprüche, und Widersprüche sind in Ihnen — das widerspricht sich nicht.« Und widerspruchsvoll war das Leben, in das sie geworfen waren, und sie widersprachen der Art.

Judejahn hatte sich beobachtet gefühlt und sich zurückgezogen. Er zog sich zurück, den kantigen Schädel zwischen die
gewölbten Schultern genommen, Flucht oder Taktik, wie die
Patrouille im Niemandsland zwischen den Fronten sich zu-
rückzieht, wenn sie sich entdeckt glaubt, Flucht oder Taktik,
kein Schuß ist gefallen, keine Leuchtspur zieht durch die
Nacht, noch wartet das Schicksal ab, aber man kriecht zurück,
kriecht zurück durch Verhau und Gestrüpp, zurück in die
eigene Stellung und ahnt für einen Augenblick, daß die Position des Gegners uneinnehmbar ist. Aber auch der Mörder,
der gehetzte Verbrecher drückt sich zurück in Schatten,
Dschungel und Stadt, wenn er das Nahen der Spürhunde
fühlt, wenn er sich im Sehfeld des Polizistenauges weiß. Der
Sünder gar flieht das Angesicht Gottes; aber wer Gott leugnet
und nicht die Gnade erfährt, sich als Sünder zu fühlen, wohin
flieht er? An Gott vorbei, und in welche Wüste! Judejahn
wußte nicht, wer ihn beobachtete. Er sah keinen Späher. Nur
ein Priester war im Empfangsraum, die Brüder wimmelten
in Rom, stand seltsam versteint und starrte gleich Judejahn
durch das durchsichtige Glas der Flügeltür und auf die ani-
mierte Tafelrunde, die da saß, redete und zechte. Ein Stammtisch war es, ein deutscher Stammtisch mit deutschem Recht
zufällig und vorübergehend etabliert auf südlichem Breiten-
grad, und gegenständlich genommen trennte nichts als das
Holz und Glas der Flügeltür Judejahn von seinem Schwager
Friedrich Wilhelm Pfaffrath, aber der war sitzengeblieben,
ob er nun hier schwadronierte oder im Stadtrat zu Hause, er
war sitzengeblieben, während Judejahn tapfer vorangeschritten war, tapfer und blind vorangeschritten nach der Losung,
daß Gott tot sei. Er war weiter gegangen als die Bürger in der
Halle, aber sie waren es, die ihm erlaubt hatten, so weit zu
gehen. Sie hatten sein Wandern mit dem Tod gebilligt. Sie
hatten das Blut beschworen, sie hatten ihn gerufen, sie hatten
ihn angefeuert, dem Schwert gehört die Welt, sie hatten Reden geschwungen, kein schönerer Tod als in der Schlacht, sie
hatten ihm die erste Uniform gegeben und hatten sich vor
der neuen Uniform, die er sich schuf, geduckt, sie hatten all
sein Tun gepriesen, sie hatten ihn den Kindern als Vorbild

gezeigt, sie hatten »das Reich« gerufen und Mord und Schlag und Leichenrauch für Deutschland hingenommen, doch selber waren sie an ihrem Stammtisch geblieben in altdeutscher Bierstube, die germanische Phrase auf der geschwätzigen Zunge, die Phrase ihrer Nietzschedeutung im Hirn, und Phrase, an der sie sich berauschten, war ihnen selbst Führerwort und Rosenbergmythus, während sie für Judejahn Aufruf zur Tat gewesen waren, er war vorangeschritten, der kleine Gottlieb hatte die Welt ändern wollen, sieh an, er war ein Revolutionär, und er verabscheute doch Revolutionäre und ließ sie peitschen und hängen, er war dumm, ein dummer Kopf, der kleine Gottlieb, der die Strafe anbetete, der kleine Gottlieb, der Prügel fürchtete und prügeln wollte, der ohnmächtige kleine Gottlieb, der zur Macht gepilgert war, und als er die Macht erreicht hatte und ihr ins Gesicht sehen durfte, was hatte er gesehen? Den Tod. Die Macht war der Tod. Der Tod war der einzige Allmächtige. Judejahn hatte es hingenommen, er war nicht erschrocken, denn der kleine Gottlieb hatte es immer schon geahnt, daß es nur diese eine Macht gab, den Tod, und nur eine wirkliche Machtübung, nur eins, was Klarheit schuf: das Töten. Es gab kein Auferstehen. Judejahn hatte dem Tod gedient. Er hatte ihn reich beliefert. Das entfernte ihn von den Bürgern, von den Italienschwärmern und Schlachtfeldreisenden; sie besaßen nichts, sie hatten nichts außer dem Nichts, saßen fett im Nichts, stiegen auf im Nichts, bis sie endgültig in das Nichts eingingen, ein Teil von ihm wurden, wie sie es immer schon gewesen waren. Aber er, Judejahn, er hatte seinen Tod, den hielt er fest, und höchstens der Priester mochte versuchen, ihn ihm zu stehlen. Doch Judejahn ließ sich nicht bestehlen. Auch Priester konnten erschlagen werden. Wer war der Schwarzrock hier? Ein finniger Junge, übernächtigten Gesichts, ein Stück schmorender Geilheit unter der weibischen Kutte. Auch der Priester blickte auf die Hallengesellschaft, auch ihn schien zu grauen. Aber er war kein Bundesgenosse für Judejahn. Judejahn grauste es vor dem Priester und vor den Bürgern. Er sah, daß die Stellung der Bürger an diesem Tag uneinnehmbar war. Aber die Zeit arbeitete für Jude-

jahn, und so wollte er zurück in die Wüste, Rekruten für den
Tod drillen, und erst wenn Schlachtfelder nicht zu besichtigen, sondern frisch aufzureißen waren, würde Judejahn wieder marschieren.

Er floh aus dem Hotel. Er floh den Anblick der Bürger, floh
den Anblick des Priesters, er floh das Auge des unsichtbaren
Spähers. Es war nicht schändlich, es war nicht feig; es war
ein taktisches Sichabsetzen. Wenn Judejahn in die Halle getreten wäre, wenn Judejahn sich zu erkennen gegeben hätte,
die Bürger wären aufgesprungen, sie hätten ihn umjubelt,
aber es wäre eine Heldenverehrung für einen Abend gewesen, und dann hätten sie ihm das Netz ihrer Bürgerlichkeit
übergeworfen. Hinter einem der erleuchteten Fenster mochte
Eva warten — eine Heldenmutter, wenn sie im Mai der
Schmach gestorben wäre. Sie lebte aber; und Judejahn sah
sich mit ihr in deutscher Stube sitzen, er ging in den Dienst,
den Pfaffrath ihm besorgen würde, er kam aus dem Dienst
heim, den Pfaffrath ihm besorgt hatte, sie konnten Gänse-
braten essen und Rheinwein trinken, das würde der Schwa-
ger-Pfaffrath-Dienst wohl abwerfen, und am Führergeburts-
tag und am neunten November würde Eva die Brosche ans
Kleid stecken, wenn man die Brosche ihr nicht gestohlen
hatte, Besatzungssoldaten waren Wert- und Andenkenjäger,
das wußte Judejahn, die Brosche mit dem goldenen Hakenkreuz, das Führergeschenk, und sie würde ihn anstieren,
wenn aus dem Radio die Nachrichten kamen, wenn Heuss
sprach, wenn Adenauer redete, wenn aus der Nachbarwoh-
nung amerikanischer Niggersong drang, und sie würde stieren und denken: Du lebst du lebst du lebst. Und er würde
leben und an die Wüste denken, an die Wüste, von der aus
Deutschland zu erobern war. Er ging in eine Garküche irgendwo an seinem Weg, der jetzt ziellos war, er trat ein in
Öl- und Teig- und Meergerüche, er stellte sich an das Büfett,
er hätte alles in sich hineinschlingen mögen, ein wahnsinniger Hunger quälte ihn. Da waren dicke weiße Bohnen, ein
deutsches Gericht, ein Schulhauskinderzeitgericht, er deutete
drauf hin, aber die Bohnen waren kalte Speise, kein deutsches Gericht, sie glitschten glatt in Öl, schwammen scharf in

427

Essig, und überdies schmeckten sie fischig, denn was er für
Fleisch gehalten hatte auf seinem Teller, war traniger Fisch,
aber er schlang alles hinunter und hinterher noch eine Pasta,
Nudeln jetzt ganz italienisch, die Tomatensauce schmierte
sich ihm weich und fettig um den Mund, ein welscher Kuß,
die Spaghetti hingen die Lippen abwärts, man hatte ihm
kein Messer gegeben, sie zu schneiden, nun schnaufte er sie
hoch wie eine Kuh das lange Gras, und erst ein neuer halber
Liter Chianti reinigte Judejahn und machte ihn wieder zum
Menschen. Das glaubte er.
Der Mensch erreichte durch Gassengeschlängel die Piazza S.
Silvestro. Er sah die Leuchtschrift des Telephonamtes. Das
war ihm recht. Er ging in das Haus, sah die Zellen mit den
Sprechapparaten, wußte sie nicht zu bedienen, er schrieb den
Namen von Pfaffraths Hotel auf einen Zettel, reichte ihn der
Schalterbeamtin, die suchte für ihn die Nummer aus dem
Verzeichnis, verkaufte ihm eine Telephonmarke, er stand in
der Zelle, er wählte die Ziffern der Drehscheibe, er hörte
»Pronto« rufen, sprach deutsch in die Sprechmuschel, verlangte Pfaffrath, hörte im Ohr Knacken, Sausen und Schritte,
und dann war Pfaffrath da, war in der Leitung, meldete sich
amtlich korrekt und würdebewußt »hier Oberbürgermeister
Pfaffrath, wer dort«, und Judejahn hätte gern »du Arschloch« gerufen, oder sollte er seine Titel abschnarren, die militärischen und die parteiamtlichen oder gar den windig orien-
talisch blumenreichen, den er jetzt trug, sollte er sich als
Obereunuch melden, als Haremsbeschäler, als Wüstenschreck,
oder sollte er piepsen »hier ist Gottlieb«, und schon wurde er
so klein, der kleine Gottlieb, daß er die ganze Sprechappara-
tur nicht mehr erreichen konnte, und so sagte er nur »Judejahn«, aber er betonte den schlichten Namen dergestalt, daß
Macht, Gewalt und Tod mit durch den Draht schwangen.
Nun räusperte sich Pfaffrath, räusperte sich vom Oberbürgermeister zum Schwager hin, überwand wohl auch ein wenig
Schreck und Grauen vor der Stimme des geliebten und gefürchteten Toten, des Familienstolzes und der Familienangst,
je nachdem, den er als Auferstandenen erwartete, brauchte
wohl auch etwas Zeit, um den Mut wieder zu finden, mit

dem er sich jetzt zu Judejahn stellen wollte, und er sprach
aufgeregt »wo bist du denn, wir warten schon auf dich«, und
Judejahn versicherte hoheitsvoll, viele Geschäfte und wenig
Zeit zu haben, und er bestellte sie für den anderen Tag in
sein Hotel, in den großen prächtigen Palast an der Via
Veneto, sie sollten Judejahn in all seinem Glanz sehen, und
er nannte ihm den falschen Namen, den Deck- und Paßna-
men, den er führte, befahl in dem engen Sprechraum, an
dessen Wänden in italienischer Sprache wohl Schweinereien
standen wie in jeder Zelle, und Judejahn dachte, ob zu Hause
schon wieder »erwache« in die Latrinen geschrieben wurde,
befahl ihm »wiederhole den Namen«, und Oberbürgermeister Friedrich Wilhelm Pfaffrath wiederholte brav den
Falschnamen, die Urkundenlüge — er würde nicht mehr in
Gönnerhaltung vor Judejahn treten, er würde strammstehen,
und Judejahns Abschlich aus dem von Deutschen bevorzugten
Haus war keine Flucht, der Abschlich war bewährte hohe
Taktik gewesen.
Und der Mensch fühlte sich wieder obenauf, war wieder Herr
seines Schicksals. Ein Sieger verließ das Telephonamt. Er
wollte über die Piazza S. Silvestro gehen, er wollte Rom erobern, da knisterte und krachte es, und war Lärm wie von
Krieg und Schlacht, es schmetterte und brach, und Entset-
zensgebrüll erhob sich und Todesschrei, ein Neubau war ein-
gestürzt, sein Fundament war falsch berechnet worden, aus
einer Wolke von Staub ragten verbogene Träger, Menschen
rannten kopflos herbei, und Judejahn kommandierte »absperren, zurückbleiben, absperren«, er wollte Disziplin in den
Tod bringen, aber niemand hörte auf seinen deutschen Ruf,
niemand verstand ihn, und dann kamen schon Sirenen und
Glocken, die Polizei kam und Rettungswagen und Feuer-
wehr, und aus der Kirche am Platz kam ein Priester, die
mischten sich überall ein, und Judejahn erkannte, daß er
fremd hier war und lästig und im Wege stand oder bestenfalls unbeachtet blieb, und er trat zur Seite, drängte sich aus
der Menge, und dann fiel ihm ein, daß er in der Schule, dem
verhaßten Gymnasium gelernt hatte, daß die Römer an
Omen glaubten, und dies hier war ein schlechtes Zeichen.

Gellend heulte ein Weib. Hatte sie Angehörige unter den
Trümmern? Die Opfer, die Judejahn dem Tod darbrachte,
hatten nie geheult. Es war merkwürdig, er hatte sie nie
heulen hören.

So trieb er ab, trieb in den Corso hinein, einen langen Darm,
gefüllt mit Wagen und Menschen. Wie Mikroben, wie Maden, wie Stoffwechsel und Verdauung zog es durch den
Längsdarm der Stadt. Judejahn schwemmte der Sog des Verkehrs nach rechts, in die Richtung der Piazza del Popolo, aber
er fühlte, daß es das falsche Ende war, auf das er sich zube-
wegte, und er stemmte sich gegen den Strom, wurde gepufft
und gestoßen, aber er wandte sich um, blickte zurück, und da
sah er es leuchten, Weiß und Gold und von Scheinwerfern
angestrahlt, und jetzt wußte er Bescheid, da war er drauf
zugefahren, den Schutzwagen voran, eine Kraftradfahrer-
eskorte zu beiden Seiten, und viele Wagen hinter ihm drein
mit Deutschen und Italienern, mit den Spitzen der Ämter,
mit den Würdenträgern der Partei und der Wehrmachtsteile.
Er schob sich voran, zurück, er hatte Richtung und Zeit verloren, Gegenwart wurde Vergangenheit, aber das Ziel hielt
er im Auge, die Marmorstufen, den Steinkoloß, das weiße
Ehrenmal an der Piazza Venezia, das Nationaldenkmal des
zweiten Viktor Emanuel, das Judejahn nach irgendeiner
Verwechselung, einer falschen Erklärung für das Kapitol
hielt und zugleich für einen Mussolini-Bau, für ein vom Duce
errichtetes Monument, die Historie zu ehren, die alten Fund-
stätten zu krönen, und dies war die weiß und golden strahlende Verkündigung der Wiederauferstehung des Impe-
riums. Da war er drauf zugefahren. Er eilte drauf zu. Hier
rechts war der Palast des Duce. Keine Wache? Keine Wache.
Gelblich schmutzig lag die Mauer im Schatten der Nacht.
Niemand stand vor dem Tor. Kein Fenster war hell. Hier
war er vorgefahren. Ein alter Besucher kam wieder. Klopf an,
klopf an — der Hausherr ist tot. Die Erben kennen dich nicht
— suche sie unter den Geschäftigen des Corso. Ja, mit dem
Duce war er über diesen Platz geschritten, an seiner Seite war
Judejahn gegangen, den Kranz des Führers am Ehrenmal des
toten Soldaten niederzulegen. Da standen sie noch, die Wa-

chen, standen breitbeinig, stramm und starr. Es war nichts an
ihrer Haltung auszusetzen. Aber Judejahn fühlte nichts —
keine Ehrung, keinen Stolz, keine Trauer, keine Bewegung.
Es ging ihm wie einem Frommen, der in der Kirche nichts
fühlt. Er will beten, und Gott ist nicht da. Er will niederknien, und er denkt: Der Boden ist kalt und schmutzig. Er
sieht die Madonna, und er denkt: Das ist Holz und etwas
Farbe, und der Wurm sitzt drin. Das Volk jubelte nicht. Kein
Vivat erscholl, kein Gesang. Motorroller knatterten vorüber.
Keine Photographen waren erschienen, Judejahn in Blitzlicht
zu tauchen. Ein paar müde Droschkenpferde schauten vom
Rondell zu ihm hinüber. War er ein Gespenst? Er eilte die
Marmorstufen hinauf. Hinter sich hatte er nun die Säulen-
reihe des pompösen Tempels, dessen Errichtung er fälschlich
Mussolini zuschrieb, und die weiße Pracht erinnerte ihn an
etwas, sie erinnerte ihn an eine Torte im Schaufenster des
Konditors Süfke, an eine Torte, die der kleine Gottlieb bewundert und nie bekommen hatte, und vor ihm war das
schwarze Hinterteil von des Königs Pferd, Judejahn wußte
nicht, welcher König da in Eisen ritt, und es war ihm auch
gleichgültig, denn er mochte Italiens Könige nicht, die er sich
seit Kindertagen, durch Witzblätter des Ersten Weltkrieges
dazu verführt, mit Regenschirmen statt mit einem Säbel in
der Faust vorstellte, aber wie er da stand, er oder der kleine
Gottlieb, er empfand Größe, er dachte an den Duce, der dies
alles gebaut und den man geschändet hatte, und er empfand
die Größe der Geschichte, der man Denkmale setzte und hinter der immer der Tod als letzte Weihe war. Viel Licht breitete sich um Judejahn. Rom leuchtete. Aber ihm schien es
eine tote Stadt zu sein, reif zum Abservieren, der Duce war
geschändet, die Geschichte hatte Rom verlassen und mit ihr
der zu rühmende Tod. Nun lebten die Leute hier, wagten es,
nur so zu leben, lebten für ihre Geschäfte, lebten für ihr Vergnügen — gab es Schlimmeres? Judejahn sah auf die Stadt.
Sie dünkte ihm toter noch als tot zu sein.

Am späten Abend ist die Via del Lavatore eine tote Straße.
Der Markt hat seine Stände weggekarrt, und die vor den

kleinen Comestibles heruntergelassenen Rolläden, altersgrau und altersgrün, machen die Front der Häuser blind wie grauer oder grüner Star das altersmüde Auge. In den Seitengassen, den dunklen Sackgängen sind die einfachen Weinschenken des Volkes, das hier in vielen Stockwerken in engen und hohen Kammern wohnt. Sie sitzen auf Bänken und Schemeln an ungedeckten von Resten und Lachen gefärbten Tischen, sie bestellen einen halben Liter roten oder einen halben Liter weißen Wein, *dolce* oder *secco*, und wer essen will, bringt die Speisen mit, in Papier eingeschlagen oder in Töpfen, und breitet sie ungeniert über den Tisch. Fremde finden selten den Weg in diese Winkel. Doch Siegfried sitzt draußen vor einer solchen Schenke im blassen künstlichen Mondlicht der weißen Kugellampe. Ein Mann wirtschaftet am Tisch. Aus einer Zwiebel wird ein Salat bereitet. Siegfried mag den Geschmack der Lauchgewächse nicht, aber der Mann schält und schneidet mit so viel Vorfreude die junge noch grüne Knolle, er mischt die Scheiben so sorgsam mit Essig und Öl und Pfeffer und Salz, er bricht so andächtig sein trockenes Brot, daß Siegfried nicht umhin kann, ihm »*buón appetito*« zu wünschen. Den Mann freut Siegfrieds Teilnahme, und er bittet ihn, doch seinen Wein zu probieren. Siegfried graust es vor dem Glas des Mannes, dessen Zwiebelmund schon ölig und ätherisch den Rand beschmiert hat, aber er überwindet den Ekel und kostet den Wein. Nun bietet Siegfried dem Mann von seinem Wein an. Sie trinken und reden. Das heißt, der Mann redet. Er redet lange schöngebaute und schönverschlungene Sätze, deren Sinn Siegfried, der nur ein paar Floskeln nach dem Wörterbuch stottert, nicht versteht. Aber gerade weil er den Mann nicht versteht, unterhält er sich gern mit ihm. Für einen Augenblick ist Siegfried froh, und die beiden sitzen beisammen wie zwei alte Freunde, von denen der eine viel zu erzählen weiß, während der andere zuhört oder auch nicht zuhört und vielleicht dankbar und freundlich einer Geisterstimme lauscht, die er auch nicht versteht, aber für eine Weile zu begreifen glaubt. Als der Mann die Zwiebel verzehrt hat, stippt er mit dem Rest des Brotes das letzte Öl aus der Kumme. Das fettdurchzogene Brot reicht er der Katze, die ihn schon lange bittend beobachtet hat. Die Katze bedankt sich und geht mit dem Brot in den Torgang; dort hat sie ihre Jungen. Siegfried wünscht »*felice notte*«. Er verneigt sich. Er wünscht die glückliche Nacht dem Mann, der Schenke, der Katze und ihren Jungen. Vielleicht wünscht er die glückliche Nacht auch sich. Er ist zufrieden in dieser Abendstunde. Nun geht er in die Schenke, um einen Fiasco zu kaufen. Vielleicht wird er nicht schlafen können. Es ist gut, wenn man nicht schlafen kann, etwas Wein im Haus zu haben. Siegfried möchte noch eine zweite Flasche Wein kaufen. Er würde sie gern dem Mann schenken, mit dem er gesprochen hat. Siegfried hält den Mann für arm. Vielleicht würde der Wein ihn erfreuen. Aber Siegfried fürchtet, den Mann, weil er arm ist, zu kränken. Er unterläßt es, die zweite Flasche zu kaufen. Beim Hinausgehen verneigt er sich noch einmal vor dem Tischgenossen. Noch einmal »*felice notte*«. Aber hat er recht gehandelt? Warum schämte er sich seines freundlichen Einfalls? Er weiß es nicht. Schon wieder zweifelt er. Es ist schwer, das Rechte zu tun. Und schon ist er nicht mehr froh. Er ist nicht mehr zufrieden.

Siegfrieds Schritte hallen in der nächtlich stillen Via del Lavatore. Sein Schatten läuft ihm voran, sein Schatten kriecht in ihn hinein, sein Schatten verfolgt ihn. Und schon überfällt Siegfried der Lärm und das Rauschen am Platz der Fontana di Trevi. Die Scharen der Fremden stehen am Rande des Wunderbrunnens und reden wie einst in Babel in vielen Sprachen. Reisegesellschaften sind fleißig und absolvieren noch in der Nacht ihren Schnellkurs in Kulturgeschichte und Länderkunde. Photographen lassen ihr Blitzlicht leuchten: auch ich war in Rom. Übernächtigte römische Jugend beugt sich über das Becken der Fontäne und fischt mit langen Stekken das Geld aus dem Wasser, das die Fremden leichtsinnig oder abergläubisch oder aus purem Jux hineinwerfen. Der Reiseführer lehrt, man komme nach Rom zurück, wenn man Geld in den Brunnen geworfen habe. Will der Fremde wiederkommen, will er zurückkehren, fürchtet er in freudloser Heimat zu sterben, will er in Rom begraben werden? Sieg-

fried möchte wiederkommen, er möchte bleiben, er wird nicht bleiben, er wirft kein Geld in den Brunnen. Er möchte nicht sterben. Er möchte nicht zu Hause sterben. Möchte er hier begraben werden? Am Brunnen steht sein Hotel. Schmal und schief spiegelt sich die alte Fassade im Wasser. Siegfried tritt ein. Er geht durch den Windfang. Allein
der alte Mann hinter dem Windfang fror. Er fror an seinem Pult vor dem Schlüsselbrett im zugigen Treppenhaus. Er trug Filzschuhe wegen der Kühle des Steinbodens, er hatte den Mantel nach abgekämpfter Krieger Art über die Schulter geworfen, er deckte seinen kleinen kahlen Schädel nach alter Professoren Weise mit einem schwarzen Schlapphut, er sah wie ein Emigrant aus, wie ein liberaler Exilpolitiker aus einer liberalen Zeit, aber er war nur der Verwalter dieses kleinen Hotels, doch war er als Österreicher geboren, und als Italiener würde er sterben, bald, in wenigen Jahren, und ihm war es gleichgültig, ob er als Italiener oder als Österreicher sterben mußte. Manchmal unterhielten wir uns, und jetzt, als ich heimkam, empfing er mich eifrig: »Ein Priester wartet auf Sie!« »Ein Priester?« fragte ich. Und er sagte: »Ja, er wartet auf Ihrem Zimmer.« Und ich dachte: Es muß ein Irrtum sein, und es ist sonderbar zu dieser Stunde. Ich stieg die Treppe hinauf, die Treppe des alten Hauses, die Steinstufen waren zu kleinen Mulden ausgetreten, das Gemäuer senkte sich, der Boden meines Stockwerks hing schief, ich ging wie bergan und erreichte die schlecht sperrende Tür meines Zimmers. Kein Licht schimmerte durch die breiten Ritzen im aufgesprungenen Holz, und wieder dachte ich: Ein Irrtum. Ich öffnete die Tür, und da sah ich ihn der Tür gegenüber am Fenster stehen, ein hoher schwarzer Schatten, wirklich ein Priester, im Licht der Scheinwerfer, die draußen noch immer die Fontana di Trevi anstrahlten, ihre üppigen Fabelwesen, ihren barocken fleischigen Olymp und ihre ständig strömenden, wie Meeresschlag rauschenden und einschläfernden Wasser. Er war groß und wirkte hager. Sein Gesicht war bleich, aber vielleicht kam das von dem tünchenden Strahl der Scheinwerfer. Ich schaltete das Zimmerlicht an, die unverhüllte Glühbirne, die über dem breiten Bett hing, dem

letto grande des Beherbergungsgewerbes, dem *letto matri-*
moniale, dem Ehebett, das jetzt mir vermietet war, mir
allein, und auf dem ich nackt liegen mochte, bloß, keusch
oder nicht keusch, allein, und die nackte bloße Glühbirne
über mir, allein oder fliegenumsummt, und das Rauschen des
Brunnens und das Gebabel der Stimmen aus aller Herren
Länder, so sagt man, und er, der Priester, wandte sich mir
nun mit einer in sich gehemmten Geste der Begrüßung zu,
die er nicht vollendete, er hob und breitete die Arme, eine
Bewegung, die, da er die Kutte trug, an einen Kanzelredner
denken ließ, und gleich senkte er die Arme wieder, wie verzagt oder als ob er sich der Geste schäme, und seine Hände
versteckten sich wie zwei schüchterne rötliche Tiere in den
Falten seines schwarzen Gewandes. Er rief: »Siegfried!« Und
dann sprach er hastig, sich überstürzend: »Ich habe deine
Adresse ausfindig gemacht, verzeih. Ich will dich nicht stören. Ich störe dich sicher, und ich gehe besser gleich wieder,
wenn ich dich störe.«
Es war Adolf, der groß und hager, verwirrt und im geistlichen Kleid vor mir stand, Adolf Judejahn, der Sohn meines
einst so mächtigen und schrecklichen Onkels, und ich sah
Adolf, wie ich ihn zuletzt gesehen hatte, auf der Ordensburg,
klein, er war jünger als ich, ein kleiner armer Soldat in der
Uniform der Junkerschule, klein in langer schwarzer Militärhose mit roter Biese, klein in dem braunen Parteirock, klein
unter dem schwarzen Schiffchen, das schräg auf das kurzgeschnittene nach Vorschrift gescheitelte Haar gesetzt war, auch
ich war so 'rumgelaufen, und ich hatte es gehaßt, mich wie
die Soldaten oder wie die Bonzen kleiden zu müssen, und
vielleicht hatte auch er den Anzug gehaßt, aber ich wußte es
nicht, ich hatte ihn nicht gefragt, ob er die Ordensburg, den
Dienstbetrieb, die Soldaten und die Bonzen hasse, ich dachte
an Onkel Judejahn, und ich traute Adolf nicht, ich ging ihm
aus dem Weg, und ich dachte gar, daß er wie mein Bruder
Dietrich gern in der Uniform steckte oder seinen Vorteil draus
holte und sich zu Posten drängte, und darum belustigte es
mich, ihn nun im Gewand des Priesters zu sehen, und ich
überlegte, in was für Verkleidungen wir doch auftreten, trau-

rige Clowns in einer mäßigen Verwechselungsposse. Ich sah ihn stehen, und ich sagte: »Setz dich doch.« Und ich schob ihm den schäbigen wackligen Stuhl der Herberge hin, drängte von der Marmorplatte der Kommode Bücher, Zeitungen und Notenblätter zurück, ich holte aus der Schublade den Korkenzieher, öffnete den Wein, den ich mitgebracht hatte, und spülte das Zahnputzglas im Waschbecken aus. Ich dachte: Judejahn ist verschollen, Judejahn hat es erwischt, Judejahn ist tot. Und ich dachte: Wie schade, daß Onkel Judejahn seinen Sohn nicht sehen kann; wie schade, daß er ihn nicht bei mir auf wackligem Stuhl sehen kann; wie schade, denn ich glaube, er wäre geplatzt, und noch heute würde ich ihn gern platzen sehen. Übertrieb ich nicht? Maß ich ihm nicht zuviel Bedeutung zu? Ich schenkte den Wein ein und sagte: »Trink zuerst. Wir müssen aus einem Glas trinken. Ich habe nur ein Glas.« Und er sagte: »Ich trinke nicht.« Und ich: »Als Priester darfst du doch ein Glas Wein trinken. Das ist doch keine Sünde.« Und er: »Eine Sünde ist es nicht. Aber ich danke dir. Ich mag nicht.« Und nach einer Weile sagte er: »Ich bin noch nicht Priester. Ich habe erst die Diakonatsweihe.« Ich trank von dem Wein, schenkte das Glas wieder voll und nahm es mit mir zu dem breiten Bett. Ich legte mich auf das breite Bett, und es war, als wolle ich andeuten, daß ich unkeusch lebe, was in diesem Zimmer gar nicht mal zutraf, und ich weiß auch nicht, was unkeusch ist, oder ich weiß es, aber ich will es nicht wissen, und ich lehnte mich zurück, stützte mich gegen das Kopfkissen und fragte ihn: »Was ist der Unterschied?« Und er sagte: »Ich darf taufen.« Und dann, als ob er sich besonnen hätte, sagte er: »Ich kann noch nicht die Messe feiern. Ich habe noch keine Absolutionsgewalt. Ich kann die Sünden nicht vergeben. Erst wenn mich der Bischof zum Priester geweiht hat, darf ich die Sünden nachlassen.« Ich sagte: »Da wirst du viel zu tun haben.« Und dann ärgerte ich mich, weil ich das gesagt hatte. Es war dumm und witzlos und gemein, und eigentlich mag ich die Priester. Ich mag die Priester, die ich nicht kenne. Ich mag die Priester, die ich sehe, ohne sie zu kennen. Ich mag die Priester von weitem, ich mag sie aus sicherer Entfernung.

Ich mag die Priester, die lateinisch sprechen, weil ich sie dann nicht verstehe. Ich verstehe sie nicht, aber ihre lateinische Sprache gefällt mir, und ich höre ihnen gern zu. Wenn ich sie verstehen könnte, würde ich ihnen gewiß weniger gern zuhören. Vielleicht verstehe ich sie auch, aber nur ein wenig. Vielleicht bilde ich mir bloß ein, sie ein wenig zu verstehen, und es gefällt mir, weil ich sie, genaugenommen, doch nicht verstehe. Vielleicht verstehe ich sie sogar falsch, aber es gefällt mir dann, sie falsch zu verstehen, und es wird schon richtig sein, wenn ich sie falsch verstehe, denn wenn sie recht haben und es gibt Gott, dann wird Gott mir durch ihren Mund das Richtige verkünden, auch wenn der Mund seiner Diener ganz andere Sätze spricht, als ich sie verstehe. Wenn ich die Wörter der Priester so verstehen könnte, wie die Priester sie reden, würde ich sie nicht mehr mögen. Sicher sind auch die Priester dumm und rechthaberisch und eigensinnig. Sie berufen sich auf Gott, um zu herrschen. Judejahn berief sich, als er herrschte, auf Hitler und die Vorsehung. Und Adolf? Auf wen mochte er sich berufen? Ich sah ihn an. Er sah mich an. Wir schwiegen. Die Fremden, keine Pilger, redeten nach Babels Weise. Das Wasser rauschte Vergänglichkeit. Das war draußen. Hier summten Fliegen. Fliegen summten hier. Schmutzige Fliegen.

In dem Keller mochten Ratten nisten, aber es zog Judejahn hinab, es zog ihn von der breiten langweiligen Via Nazionale hinunter in diesen Keller, die feuchten schmutzigen Steinstufen hinab, die Freßlust trieb ihn, der Durst trieb ihn, ein Schild »Deutsche Küche« lockte, ein Schild »Pilsener Bier«, deutsch sei der Mann, deutsch sei das Essen, Pilsen war eine deutsche Stadt, man hatte sie nicht genug verteidigt, Pilsen war eine tschechische Stadt, man hatte sie durch Verrat verloren, die Skodawerke waren kriegswichtig, das Bier war kriegswichtig, Galgen waren kriegswichtig, Verschwörung, Untermenschentum, Ratten, die Fremdarbeiter, Gefahr vom Reichssicherheitshauptamt erkannt und bereinigt, Kamerad Heydrich hatte durchgegriffen, Kamerad Heydrich war tot, war Blut von seinem Blut, war sein Spiegelgesicht — Judejahn

lebte. Immer der gleiche Vorwurf. Es war Eva, die den Vorwurf in ihm dachte. Und er dachte, warum lebt sie, warum
überlebte sie? Denken war nicht seine Art. Das war Treibsand, gefährliches verbotenes Territorium. Literaten dachten.
Kulturbolschewisten dachten. Juden dachten. Schärfer dachte
die Pistole. Judejahn hatte keine Waffe bei sich. Er fühlte
sich wehrlos. Was war mit ihm? Warum ging er nicht gut
gekleidet, mit einem guten Paß ausgestattet, mit Geld reichlich versehen in ein gutes Restaurant, füllte sich den Bauch
bis zum Speien, füllte ihn sich, wie ihn sich die Juden wieder
füllten, füllte ihn sich mit Gänseleber, mit Mayonnaisen, mit
zarten gemästeten Kapaunen, ging dann in ein Dancing, gut
gekleidet, mit Geld versehen, trank sich voll und gabelte für
die Nacht was auf, wohl gekleidet, wohl versehen, geil wie
die Juden, er konnte konkurrieren, er durfte Ansprüche stellen, warum tat er es nicht? Fressen, saufen, huren, das war
Landsknechtsweise, so ging das Landsknechtslied, im Freikorps hatten sie es gesungen, bei Roßbach hatten sie es am
Lagerfeuer gesungen, im Schwarzenreichswehrlager hatte
man es gebrüllt, im Femewald, Judejahn war ein Landsknecht, er war der letzte übriggebliebene Landsknecht, er
pfiff das Lied in der Wüste, er wollte fressen, saufen, huren,
er hatte Lust dazu, Unruhe zwickte seine Hoden, warum
nahm er sich nicht, was er haben wollte, warum die Gar-
küchen, die Stehkneipen, warum dieser Keller? Es zog ihn
hinunter. Es war ein verhängnisvoller Tag. Lähmung lag in
der alten Luft dieser Stadt, Lähmung und Verhängnis. Ihm
war, als könne in dieser Stadt keiner mehr ficken. Ihm war,
als hätten die Priester der Stadt die Hoden abgeschnitten. Er
ging hinunter, Pilsener Bier, stieg in die Unterwelt, tschechische Ratten, Pilsener Fässer, es empfing ihn ein Steinkeller,
groß, gewölbig, ein paar Tische, ein paar Stühle, hinten eine
Theke, oxydierende rostige Bierhähne, Bierschaum wie er-
brochen auf dem Zink. An einem Tisch saßen zwei Männer.
Sie spielten Karten. Sie musterten Judejahn. Sie grinsten. Es
war kein gutes Grinsen. Sie begrüßten ihn: »Sie sind auch
nicht von hier!« Sie sprachen deutsch. Er setzte sich. »Hummel Hummel«, sagte der eine. Der Kellner kam. Judejahn

sagte: »Ein Pils.« Die Männer grinsten. Judejahn sagte: »Eine Runde.« Die Männer grinsten. Mit dem Kellner sprachen sie italienisch. Es waren gesengte Zungen. Der Kellner grinste. Die Männer sagten »Kamerad« zu Judejahn. Einer sagte vom andern: »Der ist mein Kumpel.« Judejahn fühlte sich angezogen. Er kannte die Sorte: Galgenvögel, verlorene Haufen. Ihre Gesichter waren wie die Gesichter von Leichen, die an einer widerlichen Krankheit gestorben waren. Das Bier kam. Es schmeckte stechend. Es schmeckte wie eine mit Gift gemischte Brauselimonade, doch es war kalt. Die Gläser waren beschlagen. Die Männer hoben die frostbeschlagenen Gläser mit dem giftig schmeckenden Bier gegen Judejahn. Sie hatten Komment. Unter dem Tisch preßten sie Knie und Hacken zusammen, auch den Arsch. Judejahn kam nach. Er hatte immer Komment gehabt. Der Kellner servierte Speisen. Die Männer hatten sie wohl bestellt. Braungebrannte Zwiebeln brutzelten auf großen gehackten Steaks. Man aß. Man stopfte sich voll. Die Zwiebeln schmeckten den Männern. Die Zwiebeln schmeckten Judejahn. Man freundete sich an. »Das schmeckt wie zu Haus«, sagte der eine. »Quatsch!« sagte der andere, »wie beim Barras. Ich hab' immer nur beim Barras gut gefuttert.« »Bei welchem Haufen?« fragte Judejahn. Sie grinsten. »Nimm mal die Brille ab«, sagten sie. »Du bist auch kein heuriger Hase.« Judejahn nahm die Brille ab. Er sah die beiden an. Sie waren seine rechten Söhne. Er hätte sie gern gedrillt. Gedrillt waren sie brauchbar. Er dachte: Durchgevögelte Scheißkerle. »Kenne ich dich nicht?« fragte der eine. »Bestimmt habe ich dich schon mal gesehen. Na, macht nichts.« Was machte schon was? Sie nannten eine Formation. Judejahn kannte die Formation gut, eine Truppe verruchter Kerle, ein anrüchiger Verein, Helden, gingen 'ran, wo die Wehrmacht nicht mitzog. Die hatten viele umgelegt. Sie waren Judejahn unterstellt gewesen. Sie hatten Bevölkerungsfragen für den Führer gelöst. Sie hatten Völkermord getrieben. Judejahn fragte nach ihrem Kommandeur, einem fixen Kerl, einer brauchbaren Bestie. Sie grinsten ihn an. Einer zeichnete eine Schlinge in die Luft und zog sie zu. »In Warschau«, sagte der andere. War Warschau nicht erobert worden, war Paris nicht erobert worden, war Rom nicht besetzt? »Was macht ihr?« fragte Judejahn. »Och, wir fahren so 'rum«, sagten sie. »Wie lange schon?« »Lange.« »Woher?« »Wien.« Sie waren keine Germanen, waren ostische Mischrasse, österreichische SS, sie waren überall durchgerutscht. Judejahn betrachtete sie, wie die Kobra die Kröte betrachtet, und sie hielten ihn für den großen Ochsenfrosch. Aber er sah sie auch mit dem Wohlwollen und der Berechnung des Schlangenzüchters an, mit dem Wohlwollen und der Berechnung des Reptiliengärtners, der das Ungetier zu Giftgabe und Vivisektion in die Laboratorien liefert. Judejahn schickte Männer und Jünglinge in das stinkende blutige Labor der Geschichte, er schickte sie in die Versuchsstation des Todes. Sollte er sich zu erkennen geben? Sollte er sie für die Wüste verpflichten? Er fürchtete sich nicht, seinen Namen zu nennen; aber nachdem er mit ihnen gegessen und getrunken hatte, verbot ihm sein Rang, sich zu offenbaren. Der kommandierende Mörder saß nicht mit den Handlangern bei Tisch; das widersprach den Kasinositten. Sie sagten: »Wir haben einen Wagen.« Sie nannten das »organisieren«. Sie hatten zu organisieren gelernt. Sie organisierten noch immer. Judejahn beglich die Rechnung. Es amüsierte ihn, daß sie nun meinten, er würde die Zeche bezahlen. Judejahn zahlte nie die Zeche. Er hatte verschiedene Geldsorten in seiner Brieftasche und kam nicht zurecht mit den großen zerknitterten Scheinen, den aufgeblähten Zahlen einer vom Kriege korrumpierten Währung. Der Krieg, das war Judejahn; und es war ihm, als habe er geholfen, das Geld zu entwerten und die Zahlen aufzublähen; es befriedigte ihn und ekelte ihn. Die Männer standen Judejahn bei, den Kurswert des Geldes zu erkennen; sie organisierten auch im Devisenhandel; sie konnten Geld verschwinden lassen, Dollar gegen Blüten wechseln. Judejahn verachtete das Geld und brauchte viel. Dabei paßte er auf, daß er nicht bestohlen wurde. Der kleine Gottlieb hatte die Reichen immer bewundert, er hatte sie immer gehaßt. Judejahn lebte gern wie die Reichen, aber er achtete ihr Leben nicht. Er hatte versucht, sie zu übertreffen. Die Reichen waren dumm. Sie hatten Judejahn für einen

Lakaien gehalten, der ihre Geschäfte besorgen würde. Aber der Lakai wurde ihr Kerkermeister und hielt sie gefangen. Doch am Ende waren auch diese Gefangenen Judejahn entkommen. Die Reichen waren wieder reich. Sie waren wieder frei. Sie waren wieder klug. Der kleine Gottlieb stand wieder bewundernd und hassend in der Ecke. Zuweilen fiel ein Stück vom Kuchen für ihn ab. Die Konstellationen waren für Judejahn nicht ungünstig. Wallenstein glaubte an die Sterne. Mars, Merkur und Klio hausen in Rattenwinkeln. Erschöpft lustlos zänkisch mißgönnig habsüchtig begehrlich und ewig gierig hören sie nicht auf, einander beizuwohnen. Die Presse zeigt ihre Fehlgeburten an. Judejahn verließ mit den ostisch germanischen, er verließ mit den leichengesichtigen, den grinsenden Mannen, verließ mit den sehr verwendbaren Organisatoren, den ostmärkischen Hummel-Hummel-Brummern, den Seelenbrüdern und Kampfgenossen den Pilsener Keller. Kameraden, Ratten. Ratten stiegen über die Kellerstufen.

Er war erschöpft, und ich bot ihm noch einmal von dem Wein an, und er wehrte noch einmal den Wein ab, und ich dachte, ob er auch so erschöpft sei, wenn er seinen Oberen gebeichtet hatte. Ich war nicht sein Beichtiger, und ich konnte ihm nichts vergeben. Ich sah keine Sünden. Ich sah nur das Leben, und das Leben war keinem zu vergeben. Ich konnte ihm auch nicht raten. Wer darf raten? Es sagte mir nichts, und es sagte mir so viel, daß er rief: »Sie ist doch meine Mutter, er ist doch mein Vater!« Und so erfuhr ich, daß sie in Rom waren, meine Eltern, mein Bruder Dietrich, Tante und Onkel Judejahn, auch er, er lebte, und Adolf saß vor mir, wenn auch nicht ganz, wie ich empfand, denn durch sein Priesterkleid hatte er sich von uns gelöst, er hatte sich befreit, ich wollte nicht wissen, um welchen Preis, wie auch ich mich von ihnen befreit hatte und den Preis nicht wissen wollte. Wohin denn nun fliehen, da sie hier waren, mich verfolgten, denn Adolf war ja ihnen gefolgt, oder ihr, seiner Mutter, die er mir entsetzlich schilderte? Und wenn er mir sagte: »Er ist mein Vater, sie ist meine Mutter« — ich wollte es nicht hören. Ich wollte nicht mehr. Ich hatte mich befreit.

Ich fühlte mich frei. Ich glaubte mich befreit und wollte frei bleiben — und ich war kein Christ. Ich meine, ich war nicht wie Onkel Judejahn kein Christ, ich war kein Christenfeind, ich ging nur nicht in die Kirche, oder ich ging viel in die Kirchen, doch nicht zum Gottesdienst, oder ich ging auch zum Gottesdienst hin, aber nicht zu ihrem, den sie dort feierten. Aber wenn er nun Christ war und Priester, dann gab es für ihn doch das Wort, daß man Vater und Mutter lassen solle — und hatte er sie nicht gelassen?

Er stützte sein Gesicht in die Hände. Er hatte mir das Ende der Ordensschule erzählt, das Ende der nationalsozialistischen Erziehungsburg, in der sie uns schmoren ließen, aus der sie ihren Führernachwuchs holen wollten. Wir hatten schon immer mit Handgranaten geschmissen, mit Übungshandgranaten, die mit einem spitzen Knall und einer spitzen kleinen Flamme auf der Schulwiese explodierten, und dann hatte man ihnen richtige Handgranaten an das Wehrgehenk gegeben, aber es waren nicht genug Granaten für alle Kinder da, und es wurden alte unzuverlässig gewordene Beutehandgranaten griechischer Herkunft hinzugenommen, und einem Jungen hatte eine Granate den Leib zerfetzt, weil die Abzugschnur sich um seinen Schulterriemen gewunden und sich beim Gehen gelöst hatte, so erklärten die Erzieher den Unfall, und die Erzieher hatten ihnen dann Gewehre gegeben, Beutegewehre aus Siegestagen mit verrosteten Läufen, und sie sollten zusammen mit den alten Männern des Volkssturms den Adlerhorst verteidigen, das Refugium der geschlagenen und noch immer blutdürstigen Götter, aber die Götter fraßen zum Glück einander und verloren den Kopf, bevor sie tot waren, und die alten Männer des Volkssturms verdrückten sich in den Wald und in die Berge, oder sie versteckten sich in Heumieten und in Kartoffelkellern, und die forschen Erzieher huschten wie Mäuse umher, denn nun sollten sie für den Speck zahlen, den sie gegessen hatten, nun saßen sie in der Falle, saßen im Netz des Käfigs, den sie Masche für Masche mitgeflochten hatten, und dann hieß es, es gehe noch ein Zug, und die Erzieher schickten die Kinder nach Hause, ohne Gewehr, ohne Handgranaten, aber in der braunen Schuluniform, und das Zuhause war nicht mehr zu erreichen, das Zuhause war eine Erinnerung. Der Zug kam nicht weit. Er wurde von Tieffliegern beschossen. Wie wütende Hornissen stachen die Flieger mit Schußgarben durch splitterndes Glas, Blech und Holz der Abteile. Adolf war unverletzt. Aber der Zug blieb auf der Strecke, ein regloser zur Strecke gebrachter Wurm. Die Kinder gingen zu Fuß den Bahndamm weiter, dem Schotter nach, sie stolperten über die Schwellen, und dann trafen sie den anderen Zug, es war ein Konzentrationslager, das verladen und auf dem Gleis liegengeblieben war. Gerippe guckten die Kinder an. Tote guckten sie an. Die Kinder in der Uniform der Parteischule fürchteten sich. Aber eigentlich wußten sie nicht, warum sie sich fürchteten. Sie waren doch deutsche Kinder! Sie waren sogar auserwählte Kinder! Aber sie flüsterten nun: »Das sind Kazettler!« Und sie flüsterten: »Das sind Juden!« Und die Kinder sahen sich um und flüsterten: »Wo sind die Unsern, wo ist die Wachmannschaft?« Aber es war keine Wachmannschaft mehr da, und der Zug stand zwischen Wald und Wiese, es war ein Frühlingstag, die ersten Blumen blühten, die ersten Falter schwirrten, die Kinder in braunen Jacken standen allein den Häftlingen im blauweißen Sträflingskleid gegenüber, und die Gerippe und die Toten schauten aus tiefliegenden Augenhöhlen wie durch die Parteijunker hindurch, und denen war es auf einmal, als ob sie selbst keine Skelette mehr hätten, kein Knochengerüst, als ob sie nur noch eine braune Parteijacke seien, die durch bösen Zauber in der Frühlingsluft hing. Die Kinder liefen vom Bahnkörper hinunter in den Wald. Sie blieben nicht beisammen. Sie zerstreuten sich. Sie gingen grußlos auseinander. Kein Arm wurde gereckt, kein »Heil Hitler« geschrien. Und Adolf setzte sich vor ein Gebüsch ins Gras, denn er wußte nicht, wohin er gehen sollte. In dem Gebüsch hatte sich aber ein Gespenst versteckt, und das Gespenst beobachtete Adolf. Das Gespenst war genau so alt wie Adolf, aber es hatte nur die Hälfte von Adolfs Gewicht. Adolf weinte. Immer hatte man ihm verboten zu weinen. »Ein deutscher Junge weint nicht«, sprachen die Eltern und Erzieher. Jetzt weinte Adolf. Er wußte aber nicht, warum er weinte. Vielleicht weinte er, weil er zum erstenmal allein war, und weil niemand da war, der zu ihm sagen konnte: »Ein deutscher Junge weint nicht.« Doch als das Gespenst Adolf weinen sah, nahm das Gespenst den Knüppel, der neben ihm lag, und kam aus dem Gebüsch, eine schlotternde Gestalt, ein ausgemergelter Leib, eine verprügelte Haut, ein kahlgeschorener Kinderschädel, ein Totenantlitz, und das Gespenst in seiner blauweißgestreiften Zwangsjacke hob den Knüppel, und seine Nase stand groß und knochig in dem Hungertodgesicht, und Adolf Judejahn erblickte das *Stürmer*-Bild und sah zum erstenmal einen lebenden Juden, wenn der Jude auch kaum noch am Leben war, und das Gespenst, den Knüppel erhoben in der zitternden Hand, schrie nach Brot. Adolf öffnete seinen Rucksack, er hatte Brot und Wurst und Margarine, sie hatten Marschverpflegung bekommen und seltsamerweise ein Pfund Mandeln, weil Mandeln gerade da waren, und Adolf reichte die Verpflegung dem Gespenst, das den Rucksack an sich riß und sich in einiger Entfernung von Adolf niedersetzte und die Wurst und das Brot in großen Stücken in sich hineinstopfte. Adolf sah ihm zu. Er dachte nichts. Er dachte gar nichts. Es war eine absolute Leere in seinem Kopf, es war so, als ob alles, was er bisher gedacht und gelernt hatte, nun ausgeräumt war, um vielleicht einem neuen Denken, einer neuen Lehre Platz zu machen, aber das wußte man noch nicht. Und vorerst war sein Kopf nur leer, ein leerer Luftballon, der schlapp über dem Gras hing. Und das Gespenst, das sah, wie Adolf ihn ansah, warf ihm von der Wurst und vom Brot zu und rief: »Iß auch! Es reicht für uns beide!« Und Adolf aß, ohne Hunger und ohne daß es ihm schmeckte, aber auch ohne Ekel. Als er Adolf essen sah, kam der andere näher. Er setzte sich zu Adolf. Die Mandeln aßen sie zusammen. Die Tüte mit den Mandeln lag zwischen ihnen, und sie langten beide mit etwas abwesenden Bewegungen in die Tüte. »Jetzt kommen die Amerikaner«, sagte der jüdische Junge. »Wo willst du hin?« fragte er. »Ich weiß nicht«, sagte Adolf. »Bist du Nazi?« fragte der jüdische Junge. »Mein Vater«, sagte Adolf. »Mei-

ne Leute sind tot«, sagte der jüdische Junge. Und da dachte
Adolf, daß auch sein Vater tot sein würde, er mußte tot sein;
aber es sagte ihm nichts, daß sein Vater tot war. Wenn er
weinte, dann weinte er um sich, oder nicht einmal um sich,
er wußte nicht, warum er weinte, vielleicht weinte er um die
Welt, aber er weinte nicht um seinen Vater. Hatte er ihn
nicht geliebt? Er wußte es nicht. Hatte er ihn gehaßt? Er
glaubte es nicht. Er sah ihn nur als Bild, als das parteioffi-
ziöse Wandbild — es sagte ihm nichts. Der jüdische Junge
erbrach sich. Er gab die Wurst und das Brot und die Margarine wieder von sich. Er gab auch die Mandeln wieder von
sich. Er klapperte mit den Zähnen, und es war, als klapperten
alle seine durch die bleiche Haut drängenden Knochen. Adolf
zog seine braune Parteijacke aus und legte sie über den Jungen. Er wußte nicht, warum er es tat. Er tat es nicht aus
Mitleid. Er tat es nicht aus Liebe. Nicht einmal aus Scham
deckte er den Jungen zu. Er tat es einfach, weil der andere
zu frieren schien. Nachher tauschten sie ihre Jacken. Adolf
zog die blauweißgestreifte Sträflingsjacke mit dem Juden-
stern an. Das berührte ihn. Sein Herz schlug so, daß er den
Schlag in den Adern spürte. Die Jacke brannte. Er fühlte es.
Später hörten sie auf der Chaussee ein Rollen. »Panzer«,
sagte Adolf. »Die Amerikaner«, flüsterte der Junge. Ihm
war das Leben geschenkt, aber er war zu schwach, um zu den
Panzern zu kriechen. Und Adolf? War ihm das Leben genommen, zerbrach es der Heerbann, der da rollend und ratternd durch deutsches Land zog? Die Jungen legten sich in
das Laub und deckten sich mit Zweigen zu. Sie lagen bei-
einander und wärmten einander in dieser Nacht. Am Morgen gingen sie in das Dorf. Der junge Jude suchte die Amerikaner. Er sagte: »Komm mit!« Aber Adolf ging nicht mit
ihm; er suchte nicht die Amerikaner. Adolf wanderte durch
das Dorf. Man starrte ihn an, einen Jungen in schwarzer
Militärhose mit roter Biese, mit soldatischem Haarschnitt
und in einer Zuchthäuslerjacke. Er setzte sich in die Dorfkirche. Er setzte sich in die Dorfkirche, weil ihr Tor offenstand, und weil sonst kein Tor offenstand, und weil er müde
war, und weil er nicht wußte, wohin er gehörte. So fand ihn

der Priester. Er fand ihn schlafend. War es Berufung? Hatte Gott ihn gerufen? Am Sonntag predigte der Priester: »Wahrlich, wahrlich, ich sage euch, wer mein Wort hört und dem glaubt, der mich gesandt hat, der hat das ewige Leben und kommt nicht ins Gericht, sondern ist schon vom Tod zum Leben übergegangen. Wahrlich, wahrlich, ich sage euch: Es kommt die Stunde, ja sie ist jetzt schon da, in der die Toten die Stimme des Sohnes Gottes hören werden; und die auf sie hören, werden leben.« Wünschte Adolf zu leben? Wollte er nicht ins Gericht kommen? Es waren Frauen und Flüchtlinge in der Kirche und Männer, die schnell in einen Zivilrock geschlüpft waren, um der Gefangenschaft zu entgehen. Es waren auch amerikanische Soldaten in der Kirche, und sie hielten ihre Stahlhelme in den gefalteten Händen, und sie hatten ihre leichten kurzen Gewehre gegen die Kirchenbänke gelehnt. Sie hatten das Leben behalten. Sie sagten, sie seien die Befreier. Sie waren über das Meer gekommen. Sie waren Kreuzritter. Adolf Judejahn hatte in nationalsozialistischer Erziehungsanstalt von den Kreuzzügen gehört; aber seine Erzieher hatten die Kreuzzüge nicht gebilligt. Die Erzieher lehrten die Eroberung der Erde und nicht des Himmels. Für sie lohnte es sich auch nicht, das Heilige Grab zu erobern; doch scheuten sie Gräber nicht. Adolf glaubte seinen Erziehern nicht mehr. Er glaubte den Menschen nicht mehr. Er wollte dem Herrn dienen. Gott Vater Sohn und Heiliger Geist.

Er wollte nicht sterben. Er spürte die Todesnähe. Er fürchtete sich. Judejahn war in das Automobil der ergebenen Untergebenen, der freigelassenen und nicht freigelassenen Knechte gestiegen, es war ein verbeultes Vehikel, fast ein Kriegs- und Kübelwagen, sie waren auf Feldfahrt, auf Spähtour, sie stießen vor. In welcher Richtung stießen sie vor? Die Richtung war gleichgültig. Der Vorstoß war ein Wert an sich. Judejahn hatte »Zum Bahnhof« befohlen. Er wußte nicht, was er auf dem Bahnhof wollte. Aber der Bahnhof war ein Ziel. Er war ein Gelände. Man konnte sich verstecken. Man konnte in Deckung gehen. Man konnte untertauchen, abreisen, wieder verschwinden, wieder gestorben sein und nicht

gestorben sein; Judejahn konnte eine Sage werden wie der
Fliegende Holländer, und Eva würde stolz auf ihn sein. Der
Bahnhof, das Ziel lag in der Nähe. Aber Judejahn, neben
dem Fahrer sitzend, der andere hockte hinter ihm, hockte
in seinem Rücken, Judejahn merkte, daß die Fahrt nicht zum
Bahnhof ging, daß sie schweifend war, weiter, planlos, su-
chend in Bogen fuhren sie, forschten wohl nach Winkeln und
Sackgassen, nach stillen Mordplätzen oder auch nach Lärm
und Verkehrsgewühl, wo ein Schuß nicht zu hören war; die
dachten wirklich, er würde die Zeche bezahlen, blöde Hunde,
sie meinten ihn im Netz zu haben, doch Judejahn kannte
sich aus, so fuhr man in den Femewald, ein Schlag von hinten, ein Schuß von hinten und dann dem Toten die Brieftasche weggenommen und im Mauerschatten die Wagentür
geöffnet und die Leiche in den Kehricht gestoßen, er kannte
sich aus, und Führerbefehl war es am Ende, den Befehlsha-
ber der versagte, den Feigen der kapitulierte, umzulegen,
Befehl an jedermann, besonderer Befehl an diese hier, österreichische SS, des Führers angestammte Garde, aber Judejahn hatte nicht versagt, er hatte nicht kapituliert, und Angst
hatte er nur in Rom, der verfluchten Pfaffenstadt, er hatte
Angst, aber er war nicht feig, und mit ihm war das nicht zu
machen, die wollten mit seinem Geld in den Puff gehen,
aber Judejahn ließ sich nicht auf der Flucht erschießen, er
war der Erfinder der Methode und ließ sich nicht in die
Flucht treiben, er war auf taktischen Umwegen, auf Umge-
hungspfaden, auf Wüstenrouten, folgte Schakallosungen,
aber sein Ziel blieb Deutschland, seine Fata Morgana war
Großdeutschland, nichts konnte ihn beirren, er kotzte sie an.
Der Wagen stand augenblicklich. Das morsche Blech zitterte.
Es tat Judejahn wohl, sie anzukotzen. Sie waren seine Leute,
waren seine Bluthunde, seine Jungens. Er stauchte sie zurecht. Sie erkannten die Stimme ihres Herrn. Sie widerspra-
chen nicht. Sie leugneten nichts. Sie hätten ihm nun die
Stiefel geleckt. Er stieg aus dem Wagen. Er befahl: »Kehrt!«
Sie wendeten den Wagen. Sie brausten ab. Sie fuhren ihren
Weg nach Walhall. Judejahn hätte sie gern zur Meldung
bestellt. Aber wohin hätte er sie bestellen sollen? Zur Mel-

dung in die Hölle? Judejahn glaubte nicht an die Hölle. Er war erwachsen. Er war aufgeklärt. Die Hölle existierte nicht. Sie war ein Kinderschreck. Der Teufel war der schwarze Mann der Pfaffen. So blieb nur die Meldung beim Tod, beim Freund Tod, beim Kamerad Tod sollten sie sich melden, beim Tod, den der kleine Gottlieb fürchtete, und Judejahn hatte getreu nach dem Schullied vom Andreas Hofer, das der kleine Gottlieb gelernt hatte, den Tod so oft ins Tal geschickt — und nicht nur ins Tal.

Hinter ihm war der Tunnel. Er lockte Judejahn. Er lief hinein, er wurde hineingezogen. Wieder ging er durch ein Tor ins Unterirdische. Es war eine Hadespforte. Der Tunnel war gerade und kühl gekachelt, er war eine Kanalisationsröhre des Verkehrs, in der die Omnibusse dröhnten und Neonlichter der Unterwelt Leichenfarben gaben. Hier hatten sie ihn abknallen wollen. Sein Instinkt hatte ihn nicht betrogen; er war im letzten Moment aus dem Kübelwagen gesprungen. Er lief auf dem schmalen Gehsteig längs der Tunnelwand. Es war ihm, als laufe er durch sein Grab. Es war ein langes Grab, ein hygienisches Grab, es hatte was von Küche, Kühlhaus und Pissoir. Man bekam in der Morgue keine Erde zu schlucken. Das Femeopfer hatte Erde geschluckt. Das Opfer war ein junger Mensch gewesen. Auch Judejahn war damals ein junger Mensch. Das Opfer war sein Kamerad. Schnell grub der Feldspaten das Opfer ein. Auch die andern hatten Erde geschluckt. In Polen, in Rußland, in der Ukraine hatten sie Erde geschluckt. Sie mußten einen Graben ausheben. Dann mußten sie sich entkleiden. Nackt standen sie vor dem Graben. Photographien erreichten die höchsten Dienststellen, wurden weitergereicht, wurden beim Frühstück besehen; es gab einen Witz, einen Witz von Titten, Schwänzen und Votzen. Zeugung und Tod, die Todesvermählung, eine uralte Mythe. Ein Rassenprofessor, ein Brauchtumsdozent wurden ausgeschickt, die letzten Erektionen zu studieren. Bilder im *Stürmer*. Der *Stürmer* war ausgebreitet an die Schulmauer geklebt. Achtjährige lasen ihn. Achtjährige schossen. Durchsiebte Leiber füllten den Graben. Der geschundene Mensch der geschändete Mensch der Schandmensch und darüber der

Himmel. Die nach ihnen kamen, deckten die ersten mit Erde zu. Erde war über Judejahn; über dem Tunnel war der Garten des Quirinals. Päpste waren durch den Garten gewandelt. Päpste hatten im Garten gebetet. Ihr Gebet war nicht erhört worden; oder was um Himmels willen hatten sie von Gott verlangt? Zweitausend Jahre christlicher Erleuchtung und am Ende lebte Judejahn! Warum dann die Vertreibung der alten Götter? »Du sollst nicht töten!« Dröhnte es von Tunnelwänden? Der Pontifex maximus im alten Rom hatte das Gebot nicht gekannt. Er sah freundlich den Gladiatorenkämpfen zu. Der Pontifex maximus im neuen Rom war ein Diener des Dekalogs, er ließ das Gebot lehren, er befahl, es zu halten. Und war nun nicht mehr getötet worden, oder hatte der Hirt der Christenheit sich wenigstens vom Töten abgewandt, er wenigstens, er allein, und hatte vor aller Welt bekannt: »Seht, ich bin machtlos, sie töten gegen Gottes Gebot und gegen mein Hirtenwort.«? »Gerechtigkeit für Judejahn«, dröhnten die Tunnelwände. Der kleine Gottlieb hatte in der Schule gelernt, daß auch die Päpste sich dem Tod verbündeten, und es gab eine Zeit, sie war noch nicht so lange her, da beschäftigten die Päpste sogar Henker, Menschen wie Judejahn, und wie viele Feldherren hatten die Päpste geehrt, und wie oft hatten sie die siegreichen Standarten gesegnet! Gerechtigkeit für Judejahn! Auch Könige waren durch den Garten des Quirinals geschritten, den Sonnenuntergang zu genießen. Die Könige waren nicht so imposant wie die Päpste; Judejahn sah sie immer noch als Zerrbilder aus den Witzblättern des Ersten Weltkrieges, der kleine Gottlieb hatte gerade lesen gelernt, klein waren die Könige von Gestalt, der Verrat war ihnen ins Gesicht geschrieben, und in der Hand hielten sie ängstlich den Regenschirm. Hatte nicht auch Chamberlain einen Regenschirm getragen, Chamberlain der Friedensbringer, der dem Führer den Krieg stehlen wollte, eine lächerliche Figur — Könige und ihre Diplomaten, was waren sie anderes als armselige Regenschirmfuchtler gegen die dräuenden Wolken des Verhängnisses? Judejahn war gegen Schirme. Der kleine Gottlieb wollte ein Mann sein; er wollte dem Schullehrer-Vater und Gott-Vater trotzen. Männer stellten sich jedem Wetter, sie spotteten des Himmels Wüten; Männer schritten aufrecht im Kugelregen dem Feind entgegen, Männer gingen durch den Feuersturm — so sah es der kleine Gottlieb, und Gerechtigkeit für Judejahn! Die Scheinwerfer der Automobile waren im Tunnel wie die Lichter großer Raubtiere. Die Raubtiere taten Judejahn nichts. Sie liefen anderen Beuten nach. Die Höllenhunde bissen Judejahn nicht. Sie jagten ein anderes Wild. Judejahn kam durch den Tunnel. Die Unterwelt gab ihn frei. Er erreichte den Ausgang. Das Grab entließ ihn. Der Hades spuckte ihn aus

er stand am Anfang der Via del Lavatore. Sie lag still und verlassen da. Die Nacht war lind. Doch vom Ende der dunklen Straße lockte Gesang.

Ich wollte das Fenster schließen, ich wollte die sonnenausgedörrten windverwundenen hölzernen Läden vor das Fenster klappen, ich wollte zuriegeln, denn nun war Babel zerstört, sie sprachen nicht mehr wie einst in Babel auf der Piazza der Fontana di Trevi, eine Sprache hatte sich durchgesetzt, und ein deutscher Frauenchor stand nun vor der Säulengrotte, stand vor den Göttern und Halbgöttern und Fabelwesen im barocken Gewand, stand vor der Stein gewordenen Mythe aus der alten Zeit, stand vor dem Wasser aus der römischen Wasserleitung, stand im Scheinwerferlicht des Fremdenverkehrs und im Kandelaberschein der Stadtbeleuchtung und sang »Am Brunnen vor dem Tore, da steht ein Lindenbaum«, sang das Lied inmitten von Rom, sang es inmitten der Nacht, keine Linde rauschte, weit und breit wuchs kein Baum, aber sie unten am Wasserbecken, sie blieben sich treu, blieben treu ihrem treuen Gemüt, sie erlebten ihren Lindenbaum, ihren Brunnen, ihr Vor-dem-Tor, eine erhabene Stunde, sie erlebten sie mit Gesang und hatten gespart und waren weit gereist, was konnte ich tun als die Fenster schließen, die hölzernen Läden zuklappen, doch er kam zu mir ans offene Fenster, berührte mich mit seiner Kutte, und wir beugten uns hinaus, und er erzählte mir noch einmal, wie er meine Eltern gesehen hatte, meine Eltern und meinen Bruder Dietrich, durch eine Glastür in ihrem Hotel hatte er sie gesehen, und er sagte mir »deine Eltern sind noch fürchterlicher als meine, sie haben ihr Leben ganz und gar verloren«, und ich, ich sah sie hinter der Glastür ihres Hotels sitzen, und ich war nicht dort gewesen, aber ich sah sie, ich war zu hochmütig, um hinzugehen, sie zu sehen, und was konnte ich tun, ich sagte »komm mir nicht mit Theologie«, aber was konnte ich tun, sie sangen da unten alle Strophen des Lindenbaums, und ein Italiener, der schlafen wollte, schimpfte zu einem Fenster hinaus, und ein Mann, der zum Frauenchor gehörte und den Frauenchor bewunderte, schrie »Fresse, alter Makkaroni«, schrie »Fresse, alter Makkaroni« zum unbekannten Fenster hinauf, was konnte ich tun, und ein Polizeiwagen kam und hielt beim Brunnen, und die Polizisten betrachteten staunend die singenden Frauen, und dann fuhren die Polizisten langsam weiter, verschwanden in einer Straße, was konnten sie tun, und ein Mann kam aus der Via del Lavatore und gesellte sich zu den Frauen und zu dem Mann, der »Fresse, alter Makkaroni« gerufen hatte, und er war froh, sie zu finden, froh, sie getroffen zu haben. Er freute sich. Judejahn war dem Lied nachgegangen, dem deutschen Lied, und andächtig lauschte der mächtig gewesene Mann dem Gesang der deutschen Frauen, ihr Singen war Deutschland, ihr Singen war die Heimat, war »Am Brunnen vor dem Tore«, war der deutsche Lindenbaum, war alles, für das man lebte, kämpfte und starb. Er dachte nicht: und mordete. Judejahn hatte nie gemordet. Er war nur ein braver alter Kämpfer, und dies war Labsal für des braven alten Kämpfers Gemüt, war Musik, die in der Nacht die Seele erneuerte. Judejahn rief »Bravo«, als sie geendet hatten, und er trat näher zu ihnen und machte sich bekannt, wenn auch unter falschem Namen, und da sie in einer Reihe wie eine Truppe beim Appell standen, folgte er seinem Gefühl, hielt eine kleine Ansprache, redete vom erhabenen Gesang, historischer Stunde, deutschen Frauen, denkwürdiger Begegnung im Welschland, schönsten Gruß der Heimat im leider verräterisch gesonnenen Land der deutschen Sehnsucht, und sie verstanden ihn, sie begriffen ihn, und der Mann, der

»Fresse, alter Makkaroni« gerufen hatte, schüttelte Judejahn die Hand und dankte ihm für seine markige Rede, und
beide spürten sie Tränen fließen, und beide drängten sie
männlich die Tränen zurück, denn deutsche Männer weinen nicht und sind voll deutscher Härte, aber weich ist ihr
Gemüt, gedenken sie in der Fremde der Heimat, des Brunnens vor dem Tore, des Lindenbaumes beim Gesang deutscher Frauen
ich dachte:
ich glaube dir nicht, du bist nicht berufen, und du weißt, daß
Gott dich nicht gerufen hat; du warst frei, eine einzige Nacht
lang bist du frei gewesen, eine Nacht im Wald, und dann
ertrugst du die Freiheit nicht, du warst wie ein Hund, der
seinen Herrn verloren hat, und du mußtest dir einen neuen
Herrn suchen; da fand dich der Priester, und du bildetest dir
ein, Gott habe dich gerufen.
Ich sagte ihm aber nicht, was ich dachte. Er störte mich. Er
störte mich mit seinem Familienbericht. Was konnte ich tun?
Ich wollte nichts von ihm wissen. Ich wollte nichts von ihnen
wissen. Ich wollte mein Leben, nur mein kleines Leben,
kein ewiges Leben, ich war nicht anspruchsvoll, kein sündiges
Leben, was war schon ein sündiges Leben, ich wünschte nur
mein egoistisches Leben zu leben, ich wollte nur für mich da
sein und allein mit mir und dem Leben fertig werden, und
er wollte mich bewegen, mit ihm zu gehen, ich sollte mit
ihm, der sich fürchtete, die Sippe suchen, und wie verabscheue ich dieses Wort, und wie absichtlich gebrauche ich es,
um mein Grausen auszudrücken — die Sippe, dieses Gefängnis, in das sie mich sperren wollten, lebenslänglich, doch ich
war ausgebrochen, man hatte mich befreit, ich hatte mich
befreit, ich war wirklich frei, ich wollte nicht zurück! Und
warum suchte Adolf sie? Und warum ging er nicht zu ihnen,
als er sie gefunden hatte, warum kam er zu mir? Wollte er
sie bekehren? Wollte er mich bekehren? Er sagte: »Er ist
mein Vater!« Und ich sagte: »Er ist mein Vater, aber ich
will ihn nicht sehen.« Und er sagte: »Sie ist meine Mutter.«
Und ich sagte: »Sie ist meine Mutter, aber ich will sie nicht
sehen.« Und von Dietrich, dem Bruder, wollte ich schon gar

nichts wissen. Und Judejahn hatte der Teufel geholt, so hatte
ich gehofft, und wenn der Teufel ihm nun Urlaub gegeben
hatte, dann war es des Teufels Sache. Ich wünschte nur, ihm
aus dem Weg zu gehen, dem Onkel Judejahn, dem mächtigen
Parteigeneral, dem Herrn über Leben und Tod, meinem Kinderschreck, dem schwarzen Kasper des braunen Oberschau-
ten.

Doch er sagte: »Wir müssen etwas tun. Wir müssen ihnen
helfen.« Er sagte nicht: »Ich muß sie erlösen.« Dazu fehlte
ihm der Glaube, auch wagte er es mir nicht zu sagen. Und
ich sagte: »Nein.« Und ich sah ihn an. Hager, unsicher,
ärmlich wirkte er in seinem geistlichen Gewand, der hoch-
geschossene Diakon, noch nicht einmal Priester war er. Und
ich spottete: »Wie willst du deinem Vater Judejahn helfen?
Willst du ihn taufen, da du die Sünden nicht vergeben
kannst? Du sagtest mir, daß du die Sünden nicht vergeben
darfst.«

Er zitterte. Ich sah ihn noch immer an. Er war machtlos. Er
tat mir leid. Er glaubte mit Gott im Bunde zu sein, und er
war machtlos.

Da lagen Notenhefte auf der Marmorplatte der Wäsche-
kommode, da lag Notenpapier, und Kürenberg erwartete von
mir die Musik, die bedeutende Männer sich anhören sollten,
um ihre Seele zu erneuern. Die Fliegen umtanzten die unverhüllte Glühbirne. Keusch und unkeusch lag aufgedeckt
das breite Hotelbett, das *letto matrimoniale,* das Ehebett und
Konkubinatsbett unter der Glühbirne mit den Fliegen. Ich
sah einen Mann ein Weib begatten, und mich ekelte, weil
ihre Vereinigung das Leben fortsetzen konnte. Auch ich war
machtlos; und ich wollte nicht einmal Macht haben. Eine
Fliege war im Rest des Weines im Zahnputzglas ertrunken.
Sie war in einem großen Rausch ertrunken, in einem Meer
der Besäufnis; und was war für uns die Luft, was bedeutete
uns Wasser, Erde und Himmel! Hatte Gott die Fliege geleitet? Kein Sperling fällt vom Dach — Ich fragte: »Wo wirst
du schlafen?« Und ich dachte: Soll ich ihm die Hälfte des
Bettes anbieten? Und ich dachte: Ich darf ihm mein Bett
nicht anbieten. Er hatte ein Unterkommen in einer Herberge

für Priester. Er ging. Und ich sah, wie er zur Tür ging, und wieder tat er mir leid, und ich dachte: Er versucht doch, sich von ihnen zu lösen. Und ich fragte ihn, was er morgen tun wolle, und er schien es nicht zu wissen, er zögerte, mir zu antworten, und vielleicht wollte er mir auch nicht antworten, und dann sagte er, er werde in den Petersdom gehen, und ich erbot mich, ihn an der Engelsbrücke zu treffen, vor der Engelsburg, ich hatte kein Verlangen, ihn wiederzusehen, aber ich nannte ihm eine Zeit, und er sagte, er werde dort sein. Jetzt wurde es still in Rom. Der Frauenchor war gegangen, die Wanderer hatten sich entfernt, und irgendwo drehte ein Mann an einem Absperrhahn, und das Wasser der Fontana di Trevi sprudelte nicht mehr über den nach barockem Geschmack aus Stein gemeißelten Olymp der Götter, Halbgötter und Fabelwesen. Das Rauschen des Brunnens fiel aus; es fiel aus der Zeit. Die Stille war zu hören. In der Stille, die ich hörte, vernahm ich nun seinen Schritt, der die Steinstufen der Treppe hinunterstieg, er, ein Priester, ein Diakon, er stieg wie in einem Schacht durch die Zeit. Ich schaute zum Fenster hinunter, ich sah ihn aus dem Haus kommen, ich blickte ihm nach. Wie ein hagerer schwarzer Hund strich er über den stillen und toten Platz und bog um die Ecke der Straße, die zu der Passage an der Piazza Colonna führt. Ich nahm das Glas mit dem Weinrest und der ertrunkenen Fliege, und ich schüttete den Wein und die Fliege in den Ausguß. Machtlos war er
sie strichen um die Passage herum, er schon am Ausgang zum Corso, und er noch bei den Kirchen in der Via S. Maria in Via, und Arbeiter reinigten den Mosaikboden der Passage, sie streuten Sägemehl in den von Menschenfüßen herbeigetragenen Dreck, und sie kehrten mit großen Besen das Sägemehl und den Dreck zusammen, während andere auf die gefegten Steine angerührten Gips schmierten, den sie mit einer Schleifmaschine in die Ritzen und Sprünge des Mosaiks bügelten. Es hörte sich wie das Wetzen langer Messer an. Judejahn fühlte sich durch die schlafende Stadt herausgefordert. Die Stadt spottete seiner. Nicht die Schläfer ärgerten Judejahn, sie mochten in ihren stinkenden Betten,

mochten in den Armen ihrer geilen Frauen liegen, sich schwächen und die Schlachten des Lebens verlieren; ihn empörte die schlafende Stadt in ihrer Gesamtheit, jedes geschlossene Fenster, jede verriegelte Tür, jeder heruntergelassene Rollladen empörte ihn; es ergrimmte ihn, daß die Stadt nicht auf seinen Befehl schlief; dann würden Streifen durch die Straßen gehen, den Stahlhelm auf dem Haupt, die Feldpolizeikette über der Brust, Maschinenpistolen in den Händen, und die Streifen würden darauf achten, daß Judejahns Schlafbefehl eingehalten wurde; aber Rom schlief ohne seine Erlaubnis, es wagte zu träumen, es wagte, sich in Sicherheit zu wiegen. Es war Sabotage, daß Rom schlief, es war Sabotage eines Krieges, der noch lange nicht zu Ende war oder der noch gar nicht recht begonnen hatte und der in jedem Fall Judejahns Krieg war. Wenn er es vermochte, hätte Judejahn die Stadt geweckt; selbst mit den Posaunen von Jericho hätte er Rom wecken mögen, mit den Posaunen, die Mauern einstürzen ließen, den Posaunen des Jüngsten Gerichts, die der kleine Gottlieb in der Schule erst erschrocken bewundert und später aufgeklärt ungläubig verlacht hatte. Judejahn war entmachtet. Es entmutigte ihn. Er ertrug es nicht. In der Wüste hatte er in einem Traum gelebt. Die Kaserne in der Wüste gehorchte ihm; die Kaserne hatte ihm die Illusion der Macht gelassen. Eine Mauer war mit frischen Plakaten beklebt; sie waren feucht und rochen nach Druckerschwärze und Kleister. Wieder hing ein Gebot der Kirche neben einem Aufruf der Kommunisten; rot, aggressiv der Aufruf, weiß und mühsam die Würde wahrend der kirchliche Erlaß. Es waren Kundgebungen einer alten und einer neuen Macht, und beiden Offenbarungen fehlte die unbekümmerte Brutalität, der endgültige Verzicht auf das Denken und Überzeugenwollen, es fehlte der Faustschlag, der absolute Glaube an Gewalt und Befehl, und Judejahn überlegte, ob er sich nicht mit den Roten verbünden sollte, er würde sie auf Vordermann bringen, aber der kleine Gottlieb war dagegen, er haßte die vaterlandslosen Gesellen und glaubte an Deutschland, er glaubte auch an den Besitz, wenn auch an eine neue Verteilung des Besitzes zu Judejahns Gunsten und in rein deutsche Hände, und weil der kleine Gottlieb nicht wollte, konnte Judejahn nicht mit den Kommunisten gehen; er war angetreten, sie totzuschlagen, aber eine schwächliche und korrupte Welt hinderte ihn, es zu tun. An der Piazza Colonna fand er ein Taxi und ließ sich zur Via Veneto fahren, zurück zu dem großen Hotel, zurück zu der Burg, die sein Befehlsstand gewesen war, der Befehlsstand des mächtigen, des großen Judejahn. Und Adolf, der das Messerschleifen nicht hörte und die Plakate an der Mauer nicht sah, Adolf fand die schlafende Stadt still und der unruhigen Seele ihren Frieden gebend, sein Weg war wie ein Gang über einen großen Friedhof mit erhabenen Grabdenkmälern, efeuumwachsenen Kreuzen und alten Kapellen, und es war Adolf recht, daß die Stadt den Frieden eines Friedhofs hatte, und vielleicht war auch er gestorben, es war ihm recht, und ging als Toter durch die tote Stadt und suchte als Toter die Gasse mit der Absteige der reisenden Kleriker, auch sie Tote, tot in ihren toten Betten in ihrer Totenabsteige — sie mußte in der Nähe sein. Da leuchtete auch schon das Licht, eine Ewige Lampe. Und Judejahn ließ das Taxi vorzeitig halten und stieg aus dem Wagen

die Homosexuellen waren gegangen. Judejahn brauchte ihr Girren nicht zu hören. Die schönen Kellner in ihren schönen lila Fräcken stellten die Stühle auf die Tische, schlugen mit leichter Hand leicht gegen die roten Polster der Gesäße, parfümbeladener Staub wirbelte hoch, Lavendel, Portugal und herbe Rasierwasser, und die lächelnde schöne Laura zählte das Geld in der Kasse und zählte die Bons der Kellner, und die Summe der Bons stimmte wieder nicht mit der Summe des Geldes überein, doch Laura lächelte ihr beglückendes Lächeln, das bezaubernde strahlende und von keinem Gedanken getrübte Wunder ihres Lächelns, und der heterosexuelle Besitzer der homosexuellen Bar nahm Lauras Lächeln und die nicht aufgegangene Rechnung beglückt und gnädig entgegen, er war ein guter Mensch und hatte gut verdient, und Judejahn, von Laura, von dem Besitzer, von den Kellnern nicht gesehen, sondierte das Terrain, er hatte die Jagd nicht vergessen, spähte durch einen Spalt in der nun verhangenen

Tür, ein Dieb späht so oder ein Mörder, und er sah Laura, er sah ihr Lächeln, es berührte auch ihn, auch auf ihn wirkte der Zauber, aber das Lächeln quälte ihn auch, Lauras Lider waren zur Nacht blau geschminkt, und groß war so der Blick ihrer Augen, und ihr Gesicht war weiß gepudert, und ihr Mund war kaum bemalt, so wirkte sie sehr blaß, sie wirkte zart und aufgescheucht, aus Nacht gesponnen, in die Nacht gescheucht, und Judejahn drückte gegen die Klinke der Tür, sie gab nach, seine Hand lag groß und schwer auf der Klinke, einer zierlichen Klinke aus Silberbronze, aber Judejahn zog seine Hand zurück, er dachte, man weiß es hier nicht, eine Jüdin ist sie, eine Judenschickse, wer sich in Polen mit einer Judenschickse einließ, der hing, und wieder drückte er die Klinke, und wieder ließ er sie, eine Judensau. Fürchtete er sich? Der Nachtpförtner des Hotels grüßte ihn, grüßte ihn mit der behandschuhten Hand am Mützenschirm, grüßte Judejahn den Kommandierenden, der hier Herr war, wenn auch unter angenommenem Namen. Die Seide der Zimmerwände glitzerte, es war ein Zimmer wie im Puff, der kleine Gottlieb hätte es nicht besser träumen können. Warum hatte er das Mädchen nicht abgefangen? Warum hatte er sie nicht mitgenommen. Er hätte sie gevögelt, und nachher hätte er sie 'rausgeschmissen. Es hätte ihm gutgetan, sie zu vögeln, und es hätte ihm gutgetan, sie 'rauszuschmeißen. Auf dem Damast des Bettes lag der räudige Kater Benito. Er reckte sich, machte einen Buckel und blinzelte. Judejahn kraulte ihm das schüttere Fell. Das Tier stank. Überall stank es. Der Kater blickte ihn spöttisch an: Du hast dich überlebt, du bist machtlos. Ob Judejahn dem Pförtner befehlen konnte, ihm ein Mädchen zu besorgen? Einmal hätte er es gekonnt. Er hätte hundert Mädchen holen lassen können. Er hätte sie umarmen und verurteilen können. Sollte er Eva anrufen? In ihrem bürgerlichen Hotel würde man erschrecken. Man erschrak dort in der Nacht. Man erschrak dort vor dem Tod. Warum sollte Judejahn das bürgerliche Hotel nicht erschrekken? Vielleicht hätte er jetzt in der Nacht mit Eva sprechen können. Er hätte sich mit ihr aussprechen können. Es war gut, durch das Telephon zu sprechen. Den Befehl an das Himmel-

fahrtskommando funkte man, oder man gab ihn durch den
Draht. Man ging nicht persönlich hin. Eva war eine deutsche
Frau, eine Nationalsozialistin, sie mußte ihn verstehen, sie
mußte verstehen, daß Judejahn noch nicht gestorben war,
daß er am Rande des Lebens wanderte. Eva war eine deutsche Frau wie die Frauen, die an dem Brunnen das schöne
deutsche Lied gesungen hatten, aber sie war mehr als diese
Frauen, sie war eine Führerfrau, sie war seine Frau — sie
würde ihn verstehen. Es war dumm von Judejahn gewesen,
daß er sich vor der Begegnung mit Eva gefürchtet hatte.
Was lockte ihn das welsche, vielleicht gar jüdische Mädchen
aus der lila Bar? Das Mädchen war nicht sein Fall. Sie war
nicht deutsch. Aber irgend etwas war an ihrem Wesen, daß
er gerade sie haben wollte. Sie war halt eine Hure. Oder sie
war doch eine Jüdin. Eine magere geile jüdische Hure. Das
war Rassenschande. Er brauchte das Mädchen nicht zu fürchten. Er konnte sie hassen. Das war es, er brauchte eine Frau,
um sie zu hassen, er brauchte für seine Hände, für seinen
Leib einen anderen Leib, ein anderes Leben, das zu hassen
und zu vernichten war, nur wenn man tötete, lebte man —
und wer als ein Barmädchen war jetzt für Judejahns Haß
noch erreichbar? Er war entmachtet. Er war machtlos
und Eva schlief, schlief gerade ausgestreckt, schlief auf dem
schmalen Bett der engen Hotelkammer, schlief unentspannt,
nur der Haarknoten war gelöst, vergilbter und auf dem Feld
gebliebener Weizen, Stroh nicht in die Scheuer gekommen,
erbleicht und ergraut, aber sie schlief fest, traumlos, törichten
offenen Mundes, ein wenig röchelnd, ein wenig nach der
Haut der aufgekochten Milch riechend, die schlafende zür-
nende Norne nächtlichen Nichtdenkens
nächtlichem Nichtdenken anheimgegeben, nur von seinem
Schnarchen bewegt, schlief Dietrich Pfaffrath im weicheren
Bett des Hotels. Der Wein, den er mit seinen Eltern und anderen deutschen Gästen gleichen Standes und gleicher Gesinnung in der Halle getrunken, hatte ihn nicht müde gemacht,
und sein Koffer stand geöffnet vor seinem Lager, denn Dietrich war strebsam und fleißig und bereitete sich selbst auf
der Familienreise und schönen Italienfahrt auf die Große

Juristische Staatsprüfung vor, und er war sicher, sie zu bestehen, und so hatte er noch in den Fachbüchern gelesen, die sein Koffer barg. Auch seine Burschenschaftermütze hatte Dietrich mit auf die Reise genommen, denn vielleicht begegnete man Angehörigen anderer Korporationen und konnte eine Kneipe halten. Die Mütze mit dem bunten Band lag neben den Gesetzesbüchern, und Dietrich war sicher, daß ihm die Burschenschaft und das Gesetz im Leben helfen würden. Dann lagen die Straßenkarten im geöffneten Koffer, denn Dietrich lenkte gern den Wagen des Oberbürgermeisters, seines alten Herrn, und er hatte auf den Karten sorgsam die Orte angekreuzt, die zu erreichen und zu besuchen waren, und ihren Namen hatte er extra auf ein Extrablatt geschrieben und ordentlich die Sehenswürdigkeiten verzeichnet und mit Rotstift die Schlachtfelder, die besichtigt werden sollten, und die genauen Daten der Kämpfe. Doch neben dem Koffer lag, aus dem Bett dort hingeworfen, erst beim Löschen des Lichtes schlecht gezielt geworfen und nicht in den Koffer gefallen, eine Zeitschrift, ein bunt illustriertes Blatt, das er sich an einem Kiosk gekauft hatte, als er sich von keinem beobachtet glaubte, in Rom, wo er sich nicht auskannte und wo niemand ihn kannte, und ein Mädchen stand mit breitgespreizten Beinen auf der Titelseite des Heftes, stand farbig fleischig da mit bis zum Nabel geöffneter Bluse und in weitmaschigen Netzstrümpfen über den prallen fleischig farbigen Schenkeln — sie hatte Dietrich an diesem Abend das Bier ersetzt, diese Schenkel hatten ihn müde gemacht. Machtlos war er gegen den Trieb, aber mächtig trieb es ihn zu den Mächtigen, denen er dienen wollte, um im Haus der Macht zu sitzen, teilzuhaben an der Macht und selber mächtig zu werden

zufrieden schlummerte Friedrich Wilhelm Pfaffrath mit seiner Frau Anna auf der Reise noch einmal im Ehebett, wenn auch nicht in Umarmung vereint; zu Hause hatten sie nun getrennte Betten. Warum sollte er unzufrieden sein? Sein Leben dünkte ihm makellos, und das Leben zeigte sich im ganzen gesehen nicht undankbar gegen die Makellosen. In Deutschland fühlte man wieder deutsch und dachte man wieder deutsch, wenn auch in zwei voneinander getrennten Hälften, und Friedrich Wilhelm Pfaffrath war durch Zustimmung, Sympathie, Anhänglichkeit und demokratische Wahl wieder Oberhaupt seiner Stadt geworden, makellos, nicht durch Machenschaften, Wahlschwindel und Bestechung oder gar von Besatzungsgnaden, sie hatten ihn freiwillig gewählt, und er war es zufrieden, ihr Oberbürgermeister zu sein, wenn er auch Oberpräsident gewesen war und Verwalter großer Parteivermögen, er war zufrieden, er war makellos; doch ein Alptraum beunruhigte unverdient und ungerecht des Makellosen Schlummer: Schwager Judejahn kam in schwarzer Uniform auf schnaubendem Roß an sein Bett geritten, und ein Chor sang »das ist Lützows wilde verwegene Jagd«, und Schwager Judejahn riß Pfaffrath zu sich auf das schnaubende Pferd, hinein in Lützows wilde verwegene Jagd, und sie stürmten gen Himmel, wo Judejahn eine große leuchtende Hakenkreuzfahne entfaltete, und dann ließ er Pfaffrath fallen, stieß ihn hinab, und Pfaffrath fiel fiel fiel — gegen diesen Traum war der mächtige Oberbürgermeister Friedrich Wilhelm Pfaffrath machtlos machtlos

machtlos bin ich. Ich wasche mich. Ich wasche mich mit dem kalten Wasser aus der Leitung des Waschbeckens, und ich denke, das Wasser fließt über die alte römische Wasserleitung, fließt aus den traurigen blauen Bergen zu mir, kommt über das verfallene Gemäuer der alten Aquädukte, wie Piranesi sie zeichnete, in dieses Becken — es ist angenehm, sich mit diesem Wasser zu waschen. Ich gehe barfuß über den kalten Steinboden des Zimmers. Kühl und fest spüre ich den Stein unter der Sohle meines Fußes. Es ist angenehm, so den Stein zu fühlen. Ich lege mich nackt auf das breite Bett. Es ist gut, nackt auf dem breiten Bett zu liegen. Ich decke mich nicht zu. Es ist gut, allein zu liegen. Ich biete meine Blöße an. Nackt und bloß starre ich gegen die nackte und bloße Glühbirne. Die Fliegen summen. Nackt. Bloß. Das Notenpapier liegt weiß auf dem Marmor. Oder es liegt nicht mehr weiß da; die Fliegen haben das Papier beschmutzt. Ich höre keine Musik. Kein Ton ist in mir. Es gibt kein Erquicken. Nichts vermag die dürstende Seele zu erquicken. Es ist kein

Quell da. Augustinus ging in die Wüste. Aber der Quell war damals in der Wüste. Rom schläft. Ich höre den Lärm großer Schlachten. Er ist fern, aber es ist ein schreckliches Toben. Noch ist die Schlacht fern. Sie ist fern, aber sie ist schrecklich. Sie ist fern, aber sie kommt näher. Bald wird der Morgen scheinen. Ich werde den Schritt der Arbeiter in den Straßen hören. Die Schlacht wird näher rücken, und die Arbeiter werden auf die Schlacht zugehen. Sie werden nicht wissen, daß sie zur Schlacht gehen. Wenn man sie fragt, werden sie sagen: »Wir wollen nicht zur Schlacht gehen«; aber sie werden zur Schlacht gehen. Die Arbeiter marschieren immer mit, wenn es zur Schlacht geht. Auch die kleine Kommunistin wird mitgehen. Alle Hochmütigen gehen zur Schlacht. Ich bin nicht hochmütig, oder ich bin auch hochmütig, aber ich bin nicht auf diese Art hochmütig. Ich bin nackt, ich bin bloß, ich bin machtlos. Nackt bloß machtlos.

II

Der Papst betete. Er betete in seiner Kapelle, dem kleinen
Betraum seiner Wohnung im Vatikan, er kniete auf den mit
Purpur belegten Stufen des Altars, ein Bild des Gekreuzigten
blickte auf ihn herab, ein Bild der Mutter Gottes schaute
ihn an, Sankt Petrus lugte aus Wolken herunter, der Papst
betete für die Christen und für die Feinde der Christenheit,
er betete für die Stadt Rom und für die Welt, er betete für
die Priester in aller Welt und betete für die Gottesleugner
in aller Welt, er bat Gott, die Regierungen der Länder nach
seinem Willen zu erleuchten, und er bat Gott, sich auch den
Beherrschern der rebellisch gesonnenen Reiche zu offenbaren,
er erflehte die Fürbitte der Mutter Gottes für Bankiers, Gefangene, Henker, Polizisten, Soldaten, für Atomforscher und
die Kranken und Krüppel von Hiroshima, für Arbeiter und
Kaufleute, für Radrennfahrer und Fußballspieler, kraft seiner Weihen segnete er die Völker und die Rassen, und der
Gekreuzigte blickte schmerzlich auf ihn hinunter, und die
Mutter Gottes schaute ihn lächelnd, aber traurig an, und
Sankt Petrus hatte sich wohl von der Erde in die Wolken
erhoben, aber ein Zweifel blieb, ob er den Himmel erreicht
hatte, denn der Weg in den Himmel fängt bei den Wolken
gerade an, und nichts ist erreicht, wenn man in Wolken
schwebt, die Reise hat noch nicht einmal begonnen, und der
Heilige Vater flehte für die Toten, er flehte für die Märtyrer, für die in Katakomben Begrabenen, für alle in der
Schlacht Gefallenen, für alle im Kerker Gestorbenen, und er
bat auch für seine Ratgeber, für seine spitzfindigen Rechts-
gelehrten, für seine geldkundigen Finanzberater, seine welt-
gewandten Diplomaten, und ein wenig gedachte er der toten
Gladiatoren seiner Stadt, der toten Cäsaren, der toten Tyrannen, der toten Päpste, der toten Condottieri, der toten Künstler, der toten Kurtisanen, er dachte an die Götter von Ostia
antica, an die irrende Seele der alten Götter in den Ruinen,
den Erinnerungsmalen, den verfallenen Mauern, den chri-
stianisierten Tempeln, den entwendeten Kultstätten der al-

ten Heiden, und er sah im Geist die Flugplätze, er sah im Geist den prächtigen Bahnhof von Rom, er sah Scharen von neuen Heiden ankommen zu jeder Stunde, und die neu angekommenen neuen Heiden mischten sich unter die neuen Heiden, die schon in seiner Stadt wohnten, und sie waren gottloser und gottferner als die alten Heiden, deren Götter zu Schatten geworden waren. War auch der Papst ein Schatten? War auch er auf dem Weg zu den Schatten? Einen schmalen, einen unendlich flüchtigen, einen unendlich rührenden Schatten warf der Papst auf den Purpurboden seiner Kapelle. Der Schatten des Papstes dunkelte den Purpur des Teppichs zu Blut. Die Sonne war aufgegangen. Sie leuchtete über Rom. Wer, wenn der Heilige Vater stirbt, wird das *sacrum imperium* erben? Wer werden die Erben des heiligen Reiches sein? In welchen Katakomben beten sie, in welchen Gefängnissen schmachten sie, an welchem Richtblock sterben sie? Niemand weiß es. Die Sonne leuchtete. Ihre Strahlen wärmten, und dennoch war ihr Leuchten kalt. Die Sonne war ein Gott, und sie hatte viele Götter stürzen sehen; wärmend, strahlend und kalt hatte sie die Götter stürzen sehen. Es war der Sonne gleichgültig, wem sie leuchtete. Und die Heiden in der Stadt und die Heiden in der Welt sagten, der Sonnenschein sei ein astrophysikalischer Vorgang, und sie berechneten die Sonnenenergie, untersuchten das Sonnenspektrum und gaben die Sonnenwärme in Thermometergraden an. Auch das war der Sonne gleichgültig. Es war ihr gleichgültig, was die Heiden über sie dachten. Es war ihr so gleichgültig wie die Gebete und Gedanken der Priester. Die Sonne leuchtete über Rom. Sie leuchtete hell.

Ich liebe den Morgen, den Morgen Roms. Früh stehe ich auf; ich schlafe wenig. Ich liebe die Morgenkühle in den engen Gassen im Schatten hoher Häuser. Ich liebe den Wind, wenn er von krummen Dächern in alte Winkel springt; er ist der Morgengruß der sieben Hügel, er trägt den Spott der Götter in die Stadt. Die Sonne neckt die Türme und Kuppeln, sie neckt die mächtige Kuppel von S. Pietro, sie streichelt altes Gemäuer, sie tröstet das Moos in den Dachrinnen, die

Mäuse des Palatins, die gefangene Wölfin des Kapitols, die Vögel, die im Colosseum nisten, die Katzen des Pantheons. In den Kirchen wird die Messe gelesen. Ich brauche nicht weit zu gehen, um die Messe zu hören. Neben der Fontana di Trevi steht eine Kirche, und eine zweite steht an der Ecke der Via del Lavatore, und dann gibt es noch fünf oder sechs andere Gotteshäuser, alle in unmittelbarer Nähe, und ich weiß ihre Namen nicht. Ich gehe gern in die Kirchen. Ich rieche den frommen Geruch aus Weihrauch, schmelzendem Wachs, Staub, Firnis, alten Gewändern, alten Frauen und alter Angst, so groß- und so engherzig. Ich höre den Litaneien zu, *ab omni peccato libera*, dem eintönigen Gemurmel, *a subitanea et improvisa morte*, dem festgelegten und festgefahrenen Wechselgespräch zwischen dem Priester und den alten Frauen, die einen Schleier auf ihr Haupt tun, die sich demütigen, um erhoben zu werden, die auf dem Kirchenboden knien, *te rogamus audi nos*, ich höre das helle Glöcklein des Ministranten. Ich stehe bei der Tür, ein Fremder, beinahe ein Bettler; ich stehe außerhalb der Gemeinde, und das vorbedacht. Ich sehe die Kerzen vor den Bildern der Heiligen brennen, und einmal kaufte ich eine Kerze, steckte sie an, stellte sie in eine leere ungeschmückte noch keinem Heiligen geweihte Nische; ich weihte meine Kerze dem unbekannten Heiligen, so wie die Römer dem unbekannten Gott einen Tempel bauten, denn viel wahrscheinlicher, als daß ein Gott unbekannt geblieben, ist es, daß wir einen Heiligen nicht erkannt haben. Vielleicht lebt der unbekannte Heilige sogar unter uns, vielleicht gehen wir an ihm vorbei, vielleicht ist er der Zeitungsverkäufer in der Passage, der die Schlagzeilen des großen Raubes ausruft, die Betrachtungen über die Kriegsgefahr, vielleicht ist der Heilige der Schutzmann, der in der Via del Tritone den Verkehr stoppt, vielleicht ist er der zu lebenslänglichem Zuchthaus Verurteilte, der nie mehr durch Rom gehen wird, und unwahrscheinlich ist es, daß der Direktor der Banca Commerciale Italiana, die am Corso ihr stolzes Gebäude hat, ein Heiliger sei und noch dazu ein unbekannter, aber die Frommen sagen, bei Gott ist nichts unmöglich, und so mag es denn sein, auch der Bankier ist berufen; doch zu keinem von ihnen wird der Heilige Vater kommen und ihm die Füße waschen, denn der Heilige Vater ahnt ja nicht, daß sie Heilige sind, die in seiner Nähe wohnen, und die Kirche wird nie ihre Namen erfahren, nie wissen, daß sie gelebt haben und daß sie Heilige waren. Aber es ist möglich, daß es überhaupt keine Heiligen mehr gibt, so wie es keine Götter mehr gibt. Ich weiß es nicht. Vielleicht weiß es der Papst. Er wird es mir nicht sagen, wenn er es wissen sollte, und ich werde ihn nicht fragen. Schön sind die Morgenfreuden. Ich ließ mir die Schuhe putzen; sie glänzten wie ein Widerschein der Sonne. Ich ließ mich rasieren; man streichelte meine Haut. Ich ging durch die Passage; der Auftritt meiner Füße auf den Steinboden hallte lustig im Raum. Ich kaufte die Zeitung; sie roch frisch nach der Druckerei und bewertete Geist und Güter der Welt nach den neuesten Kursen. Ich ging in die Espressobar der Passage, stellte mich an die Theke, stellte mich zwischen die Männer, die wohlgewichsten, wohlrasierten, wohlgekämmten, wohlgebürsteten, die saubergehemdeten, steifgeplätteten, streng parfümierten Männer, und ich trank, wie sie, den heißen starken Dampfmaschinenkaffee, ich trank ihn *à la cappuccino* mit Zucker und Rahm gequirlt, hier stand ich gern, hier war ich froh, und auf der sechsten Seite der Zeitung fand ich mein Bild und meinen Namen, und ich freute mich, das Bild des Urhebers der Symphonie, die am Abend gespielt werden sollte, in der italienischen Zeitung zu sehen, wenn ich auch wußte, daß niemand die Photographie betrachten würde, nur ein paar Komponisten würden sie sich genauer ansehen, um den Ausdruck der Dummheit, die Züge der Erfolglosigkeit, der Unbegabung oder des Wahnsinns in meinem Gesicht zu entdecken, und dann würde das Bild Makulatur werden, Einwickelpapier oder von anderer Nützlichkeit, und es war mir recht, es war gut so, ich stimmte zu, denn ich will nicht bleiben, wie ich heute bin, ich will nicht dauern, ich will in ewiger Verwandlung leben, und ich fürchte das Nichtsein. So gehe ich zur letzten Probe zur Santa Cecilia, der Schutzheiligen der Musik. Wird sie mir hold sein? Ich habe ihr keine Kerze geweiht, und ich stelle ihr Klänge vor, die ihr vielleicht mißfallen. Ich gehe zu Kürenberg, dem wissenden Zauberer, zu den hundert Musikern, die meine Noten spielen und die mich einschüchtern, ich treffe wohl Ilse Kürenberg, die nichts zu berühren scheint, die Leben und Tod hinnimmt, wie die Sonne lacht, wie der Regen fällt. Sie ist keine Schutzheilige, ich fühle es, aber vielleicht ist sie die Göttin der Musik oder doch Polyhymnias Stellvertreterin, die Muse des Tages unter der Maske der Flucht, der Verhärtung, der Gleichgültigkeit. In der Via delle Muratte bleibe ich ehrfürchtig vor der Agentur der *Società delle pompe funebri* stehen. Der Tod zieht an; doch wie lächerlich sind die Requisiten, die der Mensch kauft, um sich würdig ins Grab zu legen. Der Agenturleiter, ein schöner dicker Herr mit gelockten, lackschwarzgefärbten Haaren, als gehe es in seinem Beruf darum, alle Vergänglichkeit zu leugnen, schließt die Tür des Ladens auf, und seine Katze, die auf den Särgen, seine Katze, die auf den Bronzekränzen träumte, den gußeisernen Immortellen, die dem Verfall, der Verwesung, dem schmutzigen Zu-Erde-Werden trotzen, seine kleine Katze schritt ihm munter entgegen, und er begrüßte sie liebenswürdig: »Guten Tag, liebe Katze« — fürchtet der Herr die Mäuse, fürchtet er, nachts könnten Mäuse an seinem Totenpomp nagen, am Leichenkleid aus Papier schon den Leichenschmaus halten, die künstlichen Blumen entblättern?

Er saß am unteren Ende der Tafel im Speisesaal der Herberge der reisenden Priester und war in einem bräunlichen schmutzigen Zwielicht, denn das Fenster des Zimmers ging auf einen engen Hof hinaus und war durch Gardinen noch verhängt, so daß Dämmerung herrschte, eine Dämmerung, die man durch ein paar schwache Glühbirnen spärlich erhellte und die dem Tagesschein die bräunlich zwielichte Farbe gaben; sie alle sahen übermüdet wie nach einer schlechten Nachtreise oder einer stürmischen Überfahrt aus, dabei hatten sie im Haus geschlafen oder nicht geschlafen, jedenfalls hatten sie in ihren Betten gelegen, schlafend oder wachend, und schlafend oder wachend waren sie stolz darauf, in Rom, in der Hauptstadt der Christenheit, zu weilen. Einige

waren schon zu frühen Messen gegangen und nun zum
Frühstück zurückgekehrt, das im Preis der Übernachtung
eingeschlossen und ohne Aroma war wie alle Frühstücke in
Seminaren, Krankenhäusern und Erziehungsanstalten, ein
Kaffee wie Spülicht, eine Marmelade ohne Farbe und ohne
Frucht, ein altbackenes krümelndes Brot, und sie würgten es
hinunter und studierten ihre Reisehandbücher und stellten
Adressen zusammen, wo sie hingehen oder vorsprechen wollten, und der Hausvater fragte Adolf, ob er sich an einer
Stadtbesichtigung beteiligen wolle, alle Kultstätten sollten
besucht werden, die Gräber der Märtyrer, die Orte der Offenbarungen, die Wege der Erscheinungen, und der Heilige
Vater wollte die Teilnehmer an der Exkursion empfangen,
doch Adolf dankte, er lehnte ab, er wollte allein sein. Sie
waren Priester, sie hatten die Weihe empfangen, der Bischof
hatte sie aufgerufen, sie hatten sich zur Stelle gemeldet, sie
hatten »Adsum« gerufen, und der Bischof hatte den Archidiakon gefragt: »Weißt du, ob sie würdig sind?«, und der
Archidiakon hatte geantwortet: »Soweit es menschliche Ge-
brechlichkeit erkennen läßt, weiß ich und bezeuge, daß sie
würdig sind der Bürde dieses Amtes.« Und »Deo gratias«
hatte der Bischof gerufen, und sie waren Priester geworden,
waren gesalbt worden, sie hatten Gehorsam versprochen dem
Bischof und seinen Nachfolgern, sie hatten die Absolutionsgewalt erhalten: »Accipe Spiritum Sanctum, quorum remi-
seris peccata, remittuntur eis, et quorum retinueris, retenta
sunt.« Er war noch nicht Priester, er war erst Diakon, er
stand eine Stufe unter ihnen, sie waren seine Oberen, er
sah sie an, wie sie ihr Brot verzehrten, wie sie ihre Pläne
machten für den Tag, ihn nützlich in Rom zu verwenden,
und er fragte sich, ob Gott sie erwählt, ob Gott sie gesandt
hatte, ehrgeizige Raben und schüchterne Vogelscheuchen, und
er zweifelte, denn warum hatte Gott dann nicht mehr getan,
warum wehrten seine Diener sich nicht entschiedener gegen
der Welt unglücklichen Lauf? Adolf war nach einem großen
Unglück zu ihnen gekommen, und da es ihm nun schien,
daß er auch als Priester neues Unglück kaum hindern werde,
ja, daß es nicht einmal sicher war, ob er unbeteiligt bleiben

könne in der anfechtbaren Rechtlichkeit des Pharisäers, fragte er sich, ob er wirklich berufen sei, wenn die andern berufen waren. Er fand keine Antwort, wie er auch keine Antwort auf die Frage fand, ob er seine Mutter aufsuchen, ob er sich seinem Vater stellen sollte; vielleicht liebte er seine Eltern, oder es war Pflicht, sie zu lieben, für einen Priester war es vielleicht besondere Pflicht, sie zu lieben, wie es für einen Priester auch wieder nicht besondere Pflicht war, ein Priester hatte alle Menschen gleichermaßen zu lieben, die Eltern hatten ihn gezeugt, aber Gott verdankte er die Seele, und die Eltern hatten ihn nicht um Gottes willen gezeugt, nicht, um Gott zu dienen, und nicht, um Gottes Gebot zu erfüllen, sie hatten ihn aus Lust gezeugt, weil sie sinnlich gewesen waren, oder sie hatten ihn aus Unachtsamkeit gezeugt oder einfach, weil sie ein Kind haben wollten, oder weil es im Dritten Reich Mode war, Kinder zu bekommen, und weil der Führer Kinder liebte, vielleicht waren auch alle Gründe zusammengekommen, daß er wurde, Wollust, Achtlosigkeit, Wunsch nach Nachkommenschaft und Führergunst, und doch war Gott unsichtbar und ungenannt dabeigewesen, denn keine Zeugung geschieht ohne ein Wunder, und selbst der Betrunkene, der am Wegrand die junge Magd vergewaltigt, zeugt nach Gottes unerforschlichem Ratschluß, aber Adolf der Diakon fragte: »Wozu wozu wozu?« Und in dem Zwielicht der Herberge aus dummer sinnloser Freudlosigkeit und sinnwidriger säuerlicher Frömmigkeit erschien ihm Christus nicht, und er konnte ihn nicht wie Petrus fragen: »Herr, wohin gehst du?«

Sie hatten alles für ein Mittagessen in den Wagen gepackt, Brot, kalten Braten, ein Stück Fasan, Früchte und Wein, sie wollten nach Cassino fahren, nicht zur Abtei, zu den Schlachtfeldern wollten sie reisen, sie hatten sich mit anderen Deutschen verabredet, Teilnehmern an den Kämpfen, die alles erklären würden, aber sie verspäteten sich, denn vorher mußten sie Judejahn aufsuchen, doch wollten sie ihn einladen mitzufahren, die Schlachtfelder würden ihm nicht gleichgültig sein, und so kam man sich wieder näher, wärmte sich an gemeinsamen Idealen, dem nie gebeugten Siegerstolz auch nach verlorener Schlacht, aber Eva, hier die Hauptperson, vereitelte alles, sie weigerte sich, teilzunehmen, teilzunehmen am Wiedersehen, teilzunehmen am Ausflug, sie wünschte in ihrem Zimmer zu bleiben, dem Zimmer zum Hof hin mit Küchengerüchen und Küchenlärm, oder sie wünschte heimzufahren nach Deutschland, auch dort in eine enge Kammer zu gehen, und sie waren wütend und beschworen sie, »warum willst du ihn nicht sehen, was soll er denken«, und sie konnte es ihnen nicht sagen, ihnen, die wieder den Tag genossen und sich abgefunden hatten, sich abgefunden mit allem Zusammenbruch, mit Verrat und Fledderei, sie konnte ihnen nicht erklären, daß ihr und Judejahns Ehebund so eng mit dem Dritten Reich verknüpft war und nur in diesem Glauben bestanden, nur aus diesem Quell sich genährt hatte, daß er nun aufgelöst war, daß der Bund sich von selbst gelöst hatte, als Hitler starb, als das Reich verging und fremde Soldaten auf deutschem Boden der Vorsehung und Zukunftsschau des Führers spotteten. Wer das nicht begriff und wem es nicht unvorstellbar war, daß man anders es sehen und denken mochte, dem war es nicht mitzuteilen, und man schwieg besser und schändete nicht den eigenen Gram. Nicht sie war schuldig, und Judejahn war nicht schuldig, sie hatten beide nicht schuld, an dem was geschehen und nicht wiedergutzumachen war, aber sie teilten zwangsläufig die Schuld eines jeden Überlebenden, Eva hatte diese Schuld getragen, nicht die Schuld am Bau des Weges, der zum Unheil führte, sondern die Schuld der Heilsüberlebung, sie schwand nicht aus ihrem Bewußtsein, und sie fürchtete, daß Judejahn diese Schuld des bloßen Daseins nun mittragen sollte und mittragen mußte, sie wollte es nicht, denn ihn hatte sie noch schuldlos gesehen, einen Helden in Walhall, aber die Teilhaberschaft an der Schuld war jedem Lebenden aufgebürdet, und der Brief, der von Judejahn kam, die Kunde, er lebe, hatte sie erschreckt statt beglückt. Aber wem konnte sie es sagen, wem durfte sie ihr Entsetzen zeigen? Ihr Sohn war ihr Feind. Er war ihr bitterster Feind, wenn das Wort bitter Bitternis enthält, und wäre sie fromm gewesen, hätte sie den Sohn verflucht, aber er war ja der Fromme, und ihr stand als Heidin kein Fluch zu Gebot, die Heidin war arm, sie glaubte nicht an Verwünschungen, nicht an Segensentziehungen, sie glaubte an ein völkisches Leben, und für den wider das völkische Leben Frevelnden gab es allein den Tod. Aber sie konnte ihn ja nicht töten. Sie hatte die Macht nicht mehr. Sie konnte ihn nur vergessen. Das Vergessen dauerte seine Zeit, und am Vergessen war sie, aber nun brachte Judejahn mit seinem Erscheinen alles Vergessene zurück, allen Zusammenbruch, alle Verluste, alle Lossagungen, und sie wollte Judejahn nicht sehen, und sie blieb im Hotel, und es war ihr, als werde sie ausgepeitscht.

Die Pfaffraths dachten im Wagen, den Dietrich zu Judejahns Hotel lenkte: Wir können es ihm nicht sagen, wir müssen es ihm schonend beibringen, sie ist verrückt, und nach allem, was sie durchgemacht hat, ist es kein Wunder, daß sie verrückt wurde, aber wir haben getan, was wir konnten, wir haben uns nichts vorzuwerfen, niemand kann uns etwas vorwerfen, wir haben ihr beigestanden, das wird Judejahn einsehen, wir haben sie hierhergebracht, und jetzt muß Judejahn entscheiden, was geschehen soll. Dietrich dachte: Er wohnt in einem viel besseren Hotel als wir, er muß Geld haben, auf der Ordensburg beneidete ich Adolf, weil sein Vater so viel mehr war als mein Vater, ich möchte wissen, ob er es noch ist, noch mehr ist als mein Vater, wie ist er den Feinden entwischt, wie hat er sich durchgeschlagen, und ist er der Alte, wird er die Macht ergreifen, wird er kämpfen wollen, und darf man sich schon zu ihm bekennen, oder riskiert man noch zuviel? Und Friedrich Wilhelm Pfaffrath sagte: »Vielleicht war es doch noch zu früh, an seine Rückkehr zu denken! Vielleicht sollte er noch ein, zwei Jahre abwarten, bis man klarer sieht. Die Souveränität wird uns gegeben werden, wir werden ein neues Heer bekommen, man darf nicht verkennen, daß die Bonner hier gute Arbeit geleistet haben. Und immerhin müssen wir noch lavieren, aber wenn das Heer erst steht, vielleicht ist dann die Zeit für die wirklich nationalen Kräfte gekommen, das Heft in die Hand zu nehmen und mit den Verrätern abzurechnen.« »Abgerechnet wird«, sagte Dietrich. Sein Gesicht bekam einen verkniffenen Zug, und krampfhaft hielt er das Steuer. Fast überfuhr er einen Herrn mit diplomatisch aufgerolltem Regenschirm, der bei der Porta Pinciana die Straße überquerte und offenbar und offensichtlich zu seiner Gefährdung an die Vernunft glaubte.

Er empfing sie in einem Schlafrock, er hatte sich mit Franzbranntwein abgerieben und ein duftendes Haarwasser auf seine grauen Borsten geschüttet, und er sah wie ein alter erfolgreicher Boxer aus, der für viel Geld noch einmal in den Ring klettert. Der Luxus, der ihn umgab, beirrte sie. Sie standen wie Bittsteller da, wie arme Verwandte, wie sie stets bei ihm gestanden hatten, er merkte es und fühlte sich, es war alles wohlberechnet, und sie sahen die mit Seide bespannten Wände, spürten den dicken Teppich unter ihren Füßen, seine Koffer bestachen sie, und in dem Bett bemerkten sie als Krönung des Reichtums und Zeichen unabhängigen Herrentums einen großen räudigen Kater. »Das ist Benito«, stellte Judejahn den Kater vor, und er freute sich, wie sie sich wunderten und sich insgeheim entsetzten. Friedrich Wilhelm Pfaffrath grauste vor dem räudigen Tier, doch ließ er es sich nicht anmerken; es war ihm, als hätten sich die schwarzen Rosse seines Traumes von Lützows wilder verwegener Jagd in einen räudigen Kater verwandelt. Judejahn fragte nicht nach Eva. Er durchschaute Pfaffraths. Er kniff die Lider zusammen und bekam kleine listige böse Schweinsaugen, er senkte das Haupt im breiten Nacken, wie ein Eber, und der Gegner im Ring mochte sich vor dem alten Schläger vorsehen. Eva war nun die arme Verwandte, und Pfaffraths waren die Wohltäter; das konnte nicht länger geduldet werden. Judejahn beschloß, für Eva zu sorgen. Er würde Geld auftreiben, sie sollte sich ein Haus kaufen, sie sollte unabhängig werden. Als Pfaffraths anfingen, von Eva zu sprechen, winkte Judejahn ab. Er würde für alles sorgen; er machte eine große, er machte eine diktatorische Geste. Er äußerte nicht den Wunsch, Eva zu sehen. Er verstand sie. Er begriff, warum sie nicht gekommen war, und er billigte es. Sie konnten sich nicht sehen, sie konnten sich nicht in die Augen sehen, und sie konnten sich nicht vor Pfaffraths sehen, vor diesen Spießern, die nichts begriffen und verstanden hatten,

471

aber vielleicht konnte Judejahn Eva heimlich sehen, wie eine
heimliche traurige Geliebte, die zu sehen man sich fürchtet.
Da gab er sich eine Blöße, deckte sich nicht ab, er fragte nach
Adolf, und Dietrich fuhr es 'raus, Adolf sei Pfaffe geworden,
und es war wie ein Hieb auf die Halsschlagader, Judejahn
taumelte, sein Gesicht verzerrte sich, er wurde blaß, und dann
rötete sich die Haut, Stirn und Wangen flammten, die Adern
schwollen an, er wirkte apoplektisch, faßte sich an den Hals,
wie einer der erstickt, und dann brach es aus ihm heraus, eine
Flut von Schimpfworten, ein Strom Unflat, er überschwemmte sie mit Auswurf, brüllte sie an, sie die nachlaufenden, sich
anpassenden, gewinngierigen Pfaffraths, die nun zitternd
sich nicht zu rühren wagten, wie zahme Schweine vor einem
wilden Eber, er gab ihnen die Schuld, ihnen die Schuld am
Verrat, am Untergang, an gebrochener Treue, an Fahnen-
flucht und Kapitulation, an Anbiederung an den Feind, sie
waren Hosenscheißer, Speichelsammler, Kollaborateure, Zu-
Kreuz-Kriecher und Arsch-Lecker, lahme Hunde, die wohl
vor der Hölle greinten und vor dem Priester winselten, sie
waren wohl in Rom, um dem Papst die Füße zu küssen, um
Absolution zu erhalten, aber die Geschichte würde sie verurteilen, Deutschland sie verdammen, Germanien sie aussto-
ßen, sie seien wert, als Volk zugrunde zu gehen, der Führer
hatte auch dies schon erkannt, der Führer war einem feigen
Volk erschienen, einem morschen Stamm, das war seine Tra-
gik, und sie hörten sich's an, der Oberbürgermeister hörte
sich's an, Frau Anna, Dietrich, sie hingen an seinen Lippen,
stumm, sie bebten, aber sie hingen an seinen Lippen, es war
wie in alten Tagen, der große Judejahn sprach, der große
Bonze grollte, und sie unterwarfen sich, ja sie fühlten ein
Wohlempfinden, eine Lust im Mark, ein wollüstiges Schneiden im Bauch und in den Genitalien, sie beteten an. Er brach
ab. Er war erschöpft; früher wäre er nicht erschöpft gewesen;
früher stärkten ihn solche Ausbrüche. Schweiß klebte in seinen Borstenhaaren, Schweiß näßte den seidenen Pyjama unter dem Schlafrock; noch immer war sein Gesicht rot wie der
Kamm eines Puters. Aber er war hart im Nehmen, er ging
nicht zu Boden, und bald hatte er sich wieder gefangen,

klatschte sich auf die Schenkel, lachte, was für ein Witz es sei, was für ein prächtiger Witz, und er hätte noch mehr Pfaffen in den Himmel schicken müssen, da er ihnen nun einen in die Kirche geliefert habe, und dann ging er und schenkte sich einen Kognak ein, kippte ihn hinunter, er bot auch ihnen Kognak an, doch nur Friedrich Wilhelm Pfaffrath trank ein Glas, während Dietrich sich entschuldigte, weil er den Wagen lenken solle, eine Enthaltsamkeit, über die Judejahn nur verächtlich lachen konnte. »Was haben wir für Kinder«, rief er, es schien ihm etwas einzufallen, etwas Amüsantes, und er ging zum Bett und entriß Benitos Krallen die italienische Zeitung, die das Hotel mit dem Frühstück geliefert hatte. Judejahn hatte sie durchgeblättert, ohne sie zu verstehen, er hatte die Bilder besehen, die Unterschriften unter den Bildern gelesen und so seinen Neffen Siegfried entdeckt, an den er sich kaum erinnern konnte, aber es mußte wohl sein Neffe sein, Siegfried Pfaffrath, und nun hielt er Friedrich Wilhelm Pfaffrath das Bild hin, empört und hohnvoll, und weil er den Text zu dem Bild mißverstanden hatte, meinte er, daß des Schwagers Sohn ein Geiger sei, was freilich, er mußte es zugeben, nicht so übel wie ein Pfaffe war, aber doch übel genug, abgerutscht und gegen die Tradition der Sippe gehandelt, gegen die Herkunft und gegen die Erziehung in der Ordensschule, und so hatte Judejahn seine kleine Rache. Pfaffrath nahm die Zeitung, er war verwirrt durch den plötzlichen Angriff und sagte, Siegfried sei nicht Geiger, er sei Komponist, und dann ärgerte er sich, weil er das gesagt hatte, denn für Judejahn war es gleichgültig, ob einer in einem Kaffeehaus fiedelte oder Konzerte schrieb, es blieb eine unmännliche Beschäftigung, eine anrüchige Lebensart, Pfaffrath verstand Judejahn, und doch berührte es ihn anders, das Bild seines Sohnes in der römischen Zeitung zu sehen, vielleicht erinnerte er sich seines Bücherschrankes, der Goetheausgabe und der Wagnerbiographie, er war stolz auf Siegfried, stolz auf seine Vaterschaft, und er reichte das Blatt Anna, die gackerte wie die Hühnermutter, wenn das Entenkind in seine Welt springt, in den Teich hüpft, in das Wasser geht und schwimmt, und Dietrich beugte sich über

ihren Arm, sah den Bruder und murmelte »tolle Sache«,
was Erstaunen, Bewunderung, aber auch Abscheu ausdrük-
ken konnte. So blieb Judejahn mit dem frommen Sprößling
blamiert, während Pfaffraths durch den fiedelnden oder kom-
ponierenden Sohn vielleicht sogar geehrt waren, obwohl man
ja nicht wußte, von welcher Gesinnung Siegfried war, mit
welchen Lastern behaftet, in welchem Schmutz er leben mochte, in unvölkischer und jüdischer Gesellschaft, und welcher
Bestechung er die Publizität in der Zeitung verdankte. Judejahn ging in seinem Schlafrock durch sein Zimmer, wie ein
Boxer, der gegen eine Ungerechtigkeit des Kampfgerichts
protestiert, erregt durch den Ring schreitet. Mit heftigen
Worten lehnte er es ab, mit ihnen nach Cassino zu fahren.
Was rührten ihn Schlachtfelder, höhnte er, die still und
kampflos lagen, wo der Boden das Blut aufgesogen hatte,
wo die Leichen begraben waren, wo wieder Pflanzen wuchsen, wo Esel weideten und Touristen lächerlich auf der Esel-
wiese herumkrochen. Und was war das Schlachtfeld von
Cassino gegen das Schlachtfeld von Berlin! In Berlin war
eine Schlacht geschlagen, die nie geendet hatte und nie enden
würde, die immer weiterging, die im Geist weitergeschlagen
wurde, und gern hätte er gesagt, in den Lüften geschlagen,
aber Judejahn hatte die Mär von der Katalaunischen Schlacht
vergessen, die der kleine Gottlieb in der Schule lernte, er
erinnerte sich, daß in den Lüften gekämpft wurde, aber er
dachte nicht an die Geister, die gab es nicht, nicht an die
Toten, die gab es, aber sie kämpften nicht mehr, sie waren
tot, und so waren es wohl Flieger, und es war natürlich, daß
Flieger in der Luft kämpften, und sie würden weiter in der
Luft kämpfen, und schließlich würden sie mit neuen Waffen
kämpfen, mit der Gewalt der Atome, weil sie Berlin nicht
erobert hatten. »Glaubst du an Krieg?« fragte Pfaffrath
Judejahn. Und Judejahn sagte, er glaube immer an Krieg,
woran solle man sonst glauben. Auch Pfaffrath glaubte an
neuen Krieg, er mußte kommen, das erforderte die Gerechtigkeit, aber Pfaffrath hielt die Zeit noch nicht für reif, er
hielt den Krieg noch nicht für nützlich für Deutschland, er
errechnete noch zu unsichere Chancen, aber er wagte das

Judejahn nicht zu sagen, denn er fürchtete, daß der Schwager
ihn für feig halten mochte. »Wirst du dann zurückkehren?«
fragte er ihn, und Judejahn sagte, er sei immer im Krieg und
immer für Deutschland. Und dann erniedrigte er sich, indem
er ihnen ein Theater vorspielte; er telephonierte mit der
diplomatischen Vertretung des Landes, das ihn bezahlte, und
bestellte in einem Gemisch aus französischen, englischen und
arabischen Sprachbrocken den Gesandtschaftswagen, und er
tat so, als ob er tyrannische Befehle erteile und über Krieg
oder Frieden vorerst im Nahen Osten entscheide. Friedrich
Wilhelm Pfaffrath und Frau Anna merkten die Hochstape-
lei des kleinen Gottlieb nicht und waren wieder gefangen
von des Schwagers Größe, aber Dietrich Pfaffrath verkniff
seinen Mund, und er entwirrte das Sprachgemisch nicht, aber
plötzlich hatte er das Gefühl, daß die große Zeit des Onkels
für immer vorbei sei und daß Judejahn nun ein Abenteurer
von unsicherer Existenz und dunkelem Geld war, »Vorsicht«
mahnte eine Stimme in Dietrich, Judejahn konnte der Karriere schaden, und doch wäre Dietrich gern hinter Judejahn
marschiert, an aussichtsreicher und postennaher Stelle natürlich, wenn Judejahn eine Fahne entfaltet und zu nationaler Sammlung gerufen hätte. Noch aber waren im Bund
Stellen zu besetzen, und Dietrich würde sie nach bestandener
Prüfung erlangen. Erst wenn Dietrich arbeitslos wird, erst
wenn er kein Automobil zum Spielen bekommt, erst wenn
er zum akademischen Proletariat geworfen wird, erst in einer
Wirtschaftskrise wird Dietrich blind hinter einer falschen
Fahne marschieren, wird er bedenkenlos in jeden falschen
Krieg ziehen.

Siegfried kam zu spät zur Probe; er kam absichtlich zu spät,
er fürchtete sich, er fürchtete seine Musik, er fürchtete Kürenberg, er war zu Fuß gegangen, er war mit einem falschen
Autobus in falsche Richtung gefahren, er war einem Kind
nachgegangen, er hatte geträumt, und seine Schritte waren
gehemmt, und seine Schuhe waren wie mit Blei gesohlt, als
er sich dem Konzerthaus näherte, und nun stand er zögernd
im Foyer vor der Kleiderablage, ein paar Regenmäntel bau-

melten wie Erhängte an traurigen Haken, ein paar Schirme
lehnten wie Besoffene an der Wand, eine Reinmachefrau
aß eine Semmel, und aus der Semmel hing eklig das in der
Wärme zerlaufende Fett des Schinkens, und eklig hingen die
Brüste der Frau ungehalten in der verschwitzten weitgeöffneten Bluse, und Siegfried dachte an den Schoß des Weibes
und daß sie Kinder hatte, und es ekelte ihn vor dem feuchten
und warmen Schoß, vor den feuchten und warmen Kindern,
dem feuchten und warmen Leben, und unheimlich und eklig
dünkte ihm die Lebensgier, zu der wir verdammt sind, die
Fortpflanzungssucht, die noch die Ärmsten betört, dieser
Schein von Ewigkeit, der keine Ewigkeit ist, die Pandora-
büchse von Not, Angst und Krieg, und er hörte die Posaunen, seine Posaunen, und sie drohten ihm, und er hörte die
Harfen, seine Harfen, und sie schienen zu zittern, und er
vernahm die Geigen, seine Geigen, und es war ihm, als
schrien sie, und seine Musik war ihm fremd, fremd, fremd.
Und außerdem war sie furchterregend. Er ging im Gang auf
und ab. Die Spiegel des Ganges zeigten ihm seine Gestalt,
und er fand sich häßlich. Er dachte: Ich sehe wie ein Gespenst aus, aber nicht wie das Gespenst der Musik. Er bemühte sich nicht, seinen Schritt zu dämpfen. Er ging ziemlich laut über den harten Linoleumbelag des Ganges, fast
war es, als wolle er die Probe stören, als wolle er in den Saal
stürzen und rufen: »Hört auf! Hört auf!«
Da kam Ilse Kürenberg auf ihn zu. Sie trug ein kornblu-
menblaues Tropical-Kostüm, und wieder sah sie jung aus,
war von fester Gestalt, aber fettfrei, und sie war ihm sympathisch, weil sie kinderlos war. Er dachte: Sie hat nicht geboren, sie hat sowenig geboren, wie die Statuen in den römischen Gärten geboren haben, und vielleicht ist sie doch die
Göttin der Musik, die Muse Polyhymnia, erfahren und jung-
fräulich. Aber er täuschte sich. Ilse Kürenberg schien heute
die Göttin der Betriebsamkeit unbekannten Namens zu sein,
denn mit ihr kam ein Herr gegangen, der wie ein großer
gefangener und überaus melancholischer Vogel aussah, und
sie stellte ihn Siegfried als den Leiter der Musikabteilung
eines bedeutenden Senders vor, oder sie stellte Siegfried dem

Vogel vor, weil der Vogel in so bedeutender Stellung war, und Ilse Kürenberg und der Vogel sprachen Französisch, sie sprachen es fließend, schnell und mit Wohlklang, vielleicht war der Vogel Franzose, und Ilse Kürenberg hatte die Sprache gelernt, vielleicht hatte der alte Aufhäuser seiner Tochter eine französische Erzieherin gegeben, vielleicht hatte Ilse Kürenberg in der Emigration Französisch gelernt, vielleicht traf beides zu, aber Siegfried schämte sich wieder, ungebildet dazustehen, die Ordensburg hatte für nichts gesorgt, sein Vater hatte für kein Französisch gesorgt, Friedrich Wilhelm Pfaffrath hielt nichts von Frankreich, nichts von französischer Wohlrede, vielleicht hielt er etwas von Französinnen, aber dies nur als Kriegsbeute, und nun stotterte Siegfried, suchte nach Vokabeln und verstand nicht, was der Vogel von ihm wollte, aber er wollte etwas, denn Ilse Kürenberg nickte und forderte Siegfried zu einer Zustimmung auf, und er stimmte zu, und er wußte nicht, wem er zustimmte, und am liebsten wäre er fortgelaufen, hätte die Göttin der Musik und den eine Musikabteilung leitenden Vogel stehengelassen — mochten sie sich fressen oder miteinander schlafen. Aber da hörte Siegfried den Schlußakkord seiner Musik, wie ein Zusammenbruch aller Hoffnung hörte er sich an, wie eine Woge, die über ein Schiff schlägt, und dann waren nur noch Planken da und etwas Geplätscher. Kürenberg trat in den Gang. Er schwitzte und wischte sich die Stirn. Seltsamerweise benutzte er ein großes rotes Tuch, um sich den Schweiß von der Stirn zu wischen, und er sah so nicht wie ein Dirigent, er sah wie ein Bauer aus, der nach getaner Arbeit vom Felde kommt. Ein paar Leute folgten ihm, Journalisten, Kritiker mit Notizbüchern in der Hand, ein Photograph, der sofort sein Blitzlicht über der Gruppe leuchten ließ. Kürenberg sah, daß Siegfried niedergeschlagen war, und er drückte ihm die Hand und sagte: »Mut! Mut! Mut!« Aber Siegfried dachte: Mut? Ich bin nicht mutlos. Aber ich brauche keinen Mut. Vielleicht brauche ich Glauben. Ich glaube zwar; aber ich glaube, daß alles sinnlos ist. Oder nicht alles ist vielleicht sinnlos, aber daß ich hier bin, ist sinnlos, daß ich mit diesen Menschen rede, ist sinnlos, daß wir hier photographiert wer-

den, ist sinnlos, der künstliche Blitz ist sinnlos, meine Musik
ist sinnlos, aber sie brauchte nicht sinnlos zu sein, wenn ich
nur etwas Glauben hätte. Aber woran soll ich glauben? An
mich? Es wäre wohl vernünftig, an mich zu glauben, aber
ich kann nicht an mich glauben, auch wenn ich es manchmal
versuche, ich schäme mich dann, und doch muß man an sich
glauben, aber man muß es, ohne sich zu schämen, tun. Glaubt
Kürenberg an sich? Ich weiß es nicht. Ich vermute, er glaubt
an seine Arbeit, und an seine Arbeit darf er auch glauben,
aber wenn seine Arbeit nun meiner Musik gilt, an die ich
nicht glaube, darf er dann noch an seine Arbeit glauben?
Es war nett, daß er eben wie ein Bauer aussah, der von der
Feldarbeit kommt. Aber auf welchem Felde arbeitet er? In
welchem Acker? Und wer wird die Frucht ernten?
Kürenberg stellte Siegfried vor. Die Kritiker sprachen zu ihm.
Sie sprachen in vielen Sprachen zu ihm. Er verstand sie nicht.
Er verstand sie in vielen Sprachen nicht. Er war bei ihnen,
und er war nicht bei ihnen. Er war schon weit weg.

Schon nahe der Peterskirche, auf die Kirche zu schreitend,
schon ihrem Anblick hingegeben, angesichts der so seltsam
enttäuschenden, hier klein gedrungen wirkenden Kuppel, vor
dem Prospekt der pompösen Fassade, vor dem Aufbau der
stämmigen Säulen, vor der Kulisse der Kolonnaden, noch
geleitet von den Pylonen der Via della Conciliazione, der auf
den Großdom hinführenden Straßen, deren Häuser zur Rechten wie zur Linken einnehmenden Versicherungspalästen
gleichen, Verwaltungsgebäuden bedeutender Kapitalgesell-
schaften, Kontoren florierender Truste mit kühlen wohlge-
mauerten Fronten, die zu dieser Stunde schattenlos und langweilig wie veröffentlichte Bilanzen im Sonnenlicht lagen, an
teure Mieten denken ließen und an den Heiland, der die
Wechsler aus dem Tempel trieb, angesichts dieses berühmten, erhabenen und hochheiligen und, wie könnte es anders
sein, sehr weltlichen Bildes, vor der sakralen altehrwürdigen
und geschäftig begangenen Bühne, die alle Pilger mit from-
mem Schauer betreten, alle Gesellschaftsreisenden als Pflicht-
fach beflissen absolvieren, wurde Adolf von großer Bangigkeit

befallen. Würde er vor dem Heiligtum genügen, würde er
bestehen, würde es seinen Glauben stärken? Ein Omnibus
hatte ihn und andere Besucher hier ausgeworfen wie eine
Kiepe voll Geflügel, das man auf die Weide läßt, und schon
scharrten sie und rüsteten sich, Bildung und bleibendes Erlebnis aufzupicken, kein Korn des Staunenswerten sollte ihnen
entgehen, schon schnappten sie die Verschlüsse ihrer photo-
graphischen Apparate hoch, schon raschelte Stullenpapier,
wurde Mitgebrachtes ausgepackt, den Hunger zu stillen, zu
dem die Sterne im Baedeker anregen, während andere sich
flink in die Andenkengeschäfte stürzten, die Cartolerien, die
unter der Hand verliehenen kleinen Pfründen gleichen, die
Ausgeflogenen, aus dem Käfig der Heimat, aus dem Pferch
der Gewohnheit Geflogenen sandten Grüße aus Sankt Peter
nach Hause, bevor sie die Stätte überhaupt betreten hatten,
und Adolf stimmte es traurig, er weilte verloren wie ein
Splitter im Strom der Menge, man stieß ihn, einen kleinen
Priester, oder fragte ihn, den man für zuständig hielt, sinnlos um sinnlose Auskunft, und dummerweise nahm er die
Pylonen der Straße wahr und erinnerte sich an andere Weg-
marken, nicht an solcherart mit eigentlich billigen Fabrikla-
ternen gekrönte, sondern an Schmuckpfeiler mit Flammen
und Rauch, an glühende Feuerhäupter, an eine Gasse bren-
nender Säulen, durch die er als bevorrechtigtes Kind, als Sohn
seines Vaters stolz gefahren war, an Nürnberg erinnerte ihn
die Via della Conciliazione, an das Parteitaggelände leider,
nur jenes Aufmarschfeld war dem Knaben prächtiger erschienen als dieser Weg zur Erzkirche, von dem er Pracht nicht
erwartete, Pracht nicht wünschte, der aber doch wiederum
prächtig sein wollte und mit der allgemein verworfenen und
verachteten Nürnberger Pracht sich maß und ihr unterlag,
die freilich nach Pylonenfeuer Häuserbrand, Städtebrand und
Länderbrand gebracht hatte. Gewiß, Hütten waren hier am
Wege, so ist die Welt, nicht zu erwarten gewesen; entblößte
Armut war an diesem Platz, so ist die Welt, nicht zu dulden
gewesen; Bettelmönche, die um Brot und um des Herrgotts
willen blecherne Schüsseln hinhalten, sind wohl ausgestor-
ben, so ist die Welt; aber diese Neubauten, diese Häuser, die

von kluger Bodennutzung und gelungener Spekulation sprachen, waren sie nicht allzudeutlich ein Triumph dieser Welt
und ein spätes Siegesmal Simons des Zauberers, der mit Petrus in dieser Stadt gerungen hatte?

Eine Ellipse, eine ovale Kurve ist der Platz, und Adolf dachte,
ob hier der Circus des Nero gewesen war, ob um den Obelisken in der Mitte des Platzes die vierbespannten Wagen gefahren waren, die man heute noch gern und zur Erregung der
Sinne in Filmen sieht, ob hier das Kreuz gestanden, an dem
Petrus das Haupt nach unten gehangen und über Nero und
Neros Leier und alle Sänger und alle Kaiser, die nach ihm
kamen, seinen tragischen Sieg errungen hatte. Vom Dach der
Kolonnaden winkten Berninis Heilige mit großen pathetischen
Gesten wie erregte Zuschauer in das Oval hinunter, aber
niemand wurde heute sichtbar gekreuzigt, keine Tierhatz
tobte, kein Netzkämpfer erschlug den Schwertfechter, kein
Rosselenker umkreiste die Bahn, nur die Autobusse der Reisebüros überrundeten einander in hartem Konkurrenzkampf,
Rom und der Vatikan und der Heilige Vater und das Apo-
stelgrab wurden für wenig Geld in wenigen Stunden gebo-
ten und als Zugabe noch die Blaue Grotte von Capri, Tibe-
rius' Schloß, Botticellis Frühling in Florenz, die Gondelfahrt
in Venedig und der Schiefe Turm in Pisa. Andere kamen zu
Fuß und schritten in Gruppen über den Platz, Mädchenpen-
sionate, kleine bebende Brüste in blauen Schulblusen, Pfadfinder mit Fähnchen, bloßen Knien, breiten verwegenen Hü-
ten, Cowboyhalstüchern und aller Knabenlüsternheit, die Kon-
gregationen grau, alt und schwarz, zwischen den Barschen und
Schleien einmal ein Hecht, der an seine Karriere dachte,
Pfarrgemeinden unter der Hut ihres Hirten, der einmal sein
Dorf verlassen wollte, englische Frauenvereine, amerikanische
Damenklubs, überdrüssig der Bridgenachmittage, deutsche
Besucherorganisationen, vom Reiseleiter angetrieben, schnell,
hieß es, nur schnell, so viel war noch zu sehen, und das Mittagessen war schon in Cassino bestellt, schnell nur schnell,
aber die Kinder weilen noch, sie halten die wachen, die er-
wartungsgierigen Pulse unter das kühl strömende Wasser der
beiden Brunnen, doch die Mütter eilen mit neuer Frucht

über die Stufen zur Kirche, die Täuflinge in weiße Spitzen gekleidet auf schwankendem Arm.

»Weide meine Lämmer, weide meine Schafe«, also sah Christus sie unverständig, hilflos und verletzbar, und Jesus wollte die Schutzlosen schützen lassen, und Petrus, im Circus gekreuzigt, den Kopf nach unten, und am Hang des Vaticanus genannten Hügels begraben, sollte Kephas der Fels sein, das unerschütterliche Fundament, das »die Pforten der Hölle nicht überwältigen werden«, er lag begraben am Hügel Vaticanus, aber gern gibt sich der Wolf als Schäfer aus, kleidet der Räuber sich als Hirte; Könige, Tyrannen, Diktatoren, Präsidenten weiden ihre Lämmer, scheren ihre Schafe, schlachten ihre Herde zu eigenem Nutzen, und die Prediger der Vernunft, die dann auftauchten und riefen »ihr seid keine Lämmer, ihr seid frei, ihr seid keine Schafe, ihr seid Menschen, brecht aus der Herde, verlaßt den Hirten«, in welche Angst, in welche Wüste trieben sie die Herde, die sich nach dem heimlichen Geruch des Stalles sehnt und vielleicht auch nach dem Blutdunst des Schlachthofes. Adolf schritt durch die Pforte des Doms. Seine Erziehung schritt mit ihm. Diese Erziehung war nicht vollendet, sie war jäh abgebrochen worden, und zudem verleugnete er sie. Aber nun war sie doch wieder bei ihm und begleitete ihn. Wenn er allein war, wenn er mit einem sprach, mit den Mitdiakonen, den gebildeten Lehrern der Priesterseminare, mit seinem Beichtvater, dann war Adolf von der Vergangenheit der Ordensburg gelöst, frei von ihren Parolen, aber wenn er sich unter der Menge bewegte, wenn Massen ihn umdrängten, ihn verwirrten und ihn erbitterten, dann rührten sie die Listen der nationalsozialistischen Erzieher in ihm auf, die Lehre von der Massennützung, von der Massenverachtung, der Massenlenkung, auch die Bonzen hatten ihre Schafe geweidet, mit großem Erfolg, und die Lämmer waren ihnen gierig zugeströmt. Adolf verlangte es ehrlich, die Händel der Welt, das tobsüchtige Walten der Geschichte zu mißachten, ein Kübel von Blut blieb übrig, warmes ekelerregendes Blut von Ermordeten, aber immer wieder, wenn Welt und Geschichte ihm nahe kamen, sich in sein Denken drängten, zweifelte er, ob er sich mit dem Anziehen des Priesterkleides wirklich von all diesem Mord getrennt habe, ob er nicht wieder und trotz aller frommen Übungen in einer Organisation steckte, die mit allem Mordgesindel unwillentlich, aber zwangsläufig grotesk und tragisch verbunden blieb. Lag das Heil in der Absage, im Fliehen, im Alleinsein, war der Eremit die einzig mögliche Gestalt der Bewährung? Aber der einsame Mensch, er schien Adolf sehr schwach zu sein, denn Adolf brauchte eine Stütze, weil er sich vor sich selber fürchtete; er brauchte Gemeinschaft, aber er zweifelte an ihrem Wert. Säulenpracht Säulenpracht Säulenpracht, Bramante, Raffael, Michelangelo, wer dachte ihrer hier nicht, aber die Säulen ihres Baues waren glänzend und kalt, der Stuck war prächtig und kalt, das Ornament des Bodens war bewundernswert und kalt, Karl der Große ritt, ein kalter Mann, auf einem kalten Pferd, und Adolf schritt weiter ins Mittelschiff, und dort war die Porphyrplatte, auf welcher der Kaiser gekrönt wurde, Gußgestein, Kristalle von Quarz, Feldspat und Glimmer, kalt kalt kalt, und die Kaiser wurden gesalbt und nahmen die Salbung als Freibrief, als Freibeuterbrief und zogen aus, ihre Macht zu mehren, in gräßlichen Schlachten zu siegen, von geraubtem Gold und kalt war ihr Thron, und zerstampft war das Gras nach der Schlacht, und zerhauen und starr lagen die Krieger. Warum ließ die Kirche sich mit Kaisern und Generalen ein? Warum übersah man sie nicht in Purpur und in Fräcken, in lamettabehängten Uniformen und schlichten Diktatorenjoppen, warum erkannte man sie nicht, die sich für schmutzige Händel, für Freßlust und Fickgier, für Gold und Landbesitz und gemeiner Herrschsucht mit Gott verbündeten und das Kreuz mißbrauchen wollten? Kapellen waren zu allen Seiten, und an den Altären hantierten geschäftige Geistliche. Sie lasen Messen, sie sprachen Gebete, sie waren in Andacht versunken, fromme Männer von reinem Wandel, aber sie waren zugleich auch Angestellte oder Beamte, die ihren Dienst verrichteten, ihr Pensum erledigten, und kam einem dieser schlechte alle Verzauberung aufhebende Gedanke, dann wurden die Altäre zu Verkaufstischen in einem weitläufigen Warenhaus. Links und rechts standen

Beichtstühle, kleine Burgen aus festem Holz, und Beichtväter
saßen wie Schalterbeamte einer großen Bank in den geweihten Schreinen — in allen Sprachen mochte der Gläubige seine
Sünden bekennen, in allen Sprachen würde ihm verziehen
werden. Auch die Beichtstühle schienen Adolf in kalter Luft
zu stehen; sie dünkten ihm kalt wie die Marmorplatten der
Geldwechsler.
Adolf fühlte sich einsam in der weiten prächtigen Erhabenheit, die ihm gar nicht so erhaben vorkommen wollte, es sei
denn im hochmütigen Sinn des Wortes, er fühlte sich von
Gott und von seinem Glauben an Gott verlassen, er fühlte
sich von Zweifeln bedrängt, vielleicht vom Teufel versucht,
der vielleicht gar kein Teufel war, denn wie hätte ein Teufel
in das Haus Gottes, ein Teufel in die Burg Petri, ein Teufel
in die vielfach geweihte Stätte gelangen können, und allein
die brennenden Öllampen über dem Sarkophag des Apostels
verliehen dem kalten Raum ein wenig Wärme, doch die
Kolossalstatue eines Anbetenden verschattete wieder das
milde besinnliche Licht der Öllampen und ließ an das Grabmal eines Kommerzienrats denken. Erst der Anblick der gepriesenen Pietà gab Adolf Glauben und Atem zurück, sie
war Befreiung für den Versinkenden in krausen Gedanken,
krausem Leid, krauser Erschütterung, und er deutete sie als
Barmherzigkeit, als gewaltige, alles umschlingende Liebe,
Adolf wollte lieben, auch wenn er sich zur Liebe zwingen
mußte, er wollte jedem Menschen freundlich und liebend
begegnen, selbst den Eltern wollte er freundlich und liebend
begegnen, selbst dem eigenen Vater, den zu lieben am
schwersten ist. Hier vor der zu Recht gepriesenen Pietà betete
Adolf, er bat um Liebeskraft; kein weiteres Gebet sprach er
in der Hauptkirche der Christenheit, und dann verließ er,
hochgeschossen, hager und ärmlich, ein kleiner verwirrter,
von allzuviel Pracht erschlagener Diakon, den Petersdom,
dessen Luft und Anblick er nicht ertrug.

Ich wußte die Stunde nicht mehr, zu der ich mit Adolf verabredet war. War es am Mittag, war es am Nachmittag? Ich
wußte es nicht. Ich hatte es vergessen. Vielleicht wollte ich

mich nicht erinnern. Ich wollte Adolf nicht sehen, und doch ging ich zum verabredeten Ort, schon war ich gefangen; ich ärgerte mich, weil ich in der Schlinge saß. Adolf störte meine Freiheit, er störte mein unmittelbares Empfinden des Lebens, störte mein unaufhörliches Staunen. Er ließ an alle Bedrückung der Jugend denken, er rief die Vergangenheit herbei, die Familie, den Frühsport und den völkischen Unterricht in der Nationalpolitischen Erziehungsanstalt, und wenn Adolf sich auch gleich mir losgesagt hatte von jenen Tagen und Parolen, wenn er sich von der Familie getrennt hatte und in einem geistlichen Seminar sein eigenes Leben lebte, so haftete die Familie ihm doch an, ewig wie ein nicht zu beseitigender Geruch selbst noch im Priesterkleid, ewig wie ein Schweiß auf der Haut, den kein Bad wegbringt und der auch mir anhaftet, der Judejahn-Pfaffrath-Klingspor-Mief, die Schwestern Klingspor waren unsere Mütter, und das bedeutete ein Jahrhundert nationaler Dummheit, soldatischen Drills, deutschbürgerlicher Begrenzung, die leider größenwahnsinnig und tobsüchtig wurde, wenn sie endlich aus ihrem zu engen Bett brach. Aus Schwäche erschien ich hier zur Begegnung. Adolf rührte mich in seinem Priesterkleid. Es schien mir eine Verkleidung aus Angst zu sein. Jemand, der fliehen will und auf der Flucht unerkannt bleiben möchte, verkleidet sich so. Wohin aber floh er? Genügte ihm, wie mir, das Davonlaufen, und hatte auch er sich damit abgefunden, ewig auf der Flucht zu sein, ewig auf einem Weg, von dem man wußte, daß er woher kam, aber nirgends wohin führte? Ich fand mein Vergnügen am Weg, oder ich bilde es mir ein, aber Adolf meisterte das neue Leben nicht, die Freiheit von der Familie, die Freiheit von knechtender Überlieferung, so schien es mir, und ich war, gegen den Egoismus, den ich mir predigte, und manchmal schien mir die Selbstsucht die einzige Möglichkeit zur Bewahrung zu sein, wobei allerdings wieder fraglich blieb, ob man sich bewahren sollte, ich war gegen allen Erhaltungstrieb geneigt, Adolf beizustehen, ihm zu helfen — aber konnte ich das? Meisterte ich das freie Leben? Und dann dachte ich: Wenn Adolf und ich das Leben nicht meistern, dann sollten wir uns gegen die verbinden, die skrupellos sind und nach dem Grad ihrer Beschränktheit herrschen wollen, gegen die echten Pfaffraths, die echten Judejahns, die echten Klingspors, vielleicht könnten wir Deutschland ändern? Aber während ich das dachte, schien es mir schon nicht mehr möglich zu sein, Deutschland zu ändern, man konnte nur sich ändern, und jeder mußte das für sich selbst tun, ganz allein, und ich wünschte Adolf zum Teufel.

Ich ging über die Engelsbrücke zur Engelsburg, und die Engel auf ihren Postamenten, die Engel mit ihren Marmorflügeln sahen wie zu schwer geratene Möwen aus, die Blei im Leib tragen oder bleierne Gedanken und sich nie mehr in die Luft erheben werden. Ich konnte mir die Engel der Brücke nicht am Himmel denken. Nie würden sie über Rom schweben, nie mein Fenster aufstoßen, nie an mein Bett treten, nie mich mit ihrem Flügelschlag beglücken, nie mir des Paradieses ungeheures Licht entzünden. Der Tiber floß trübe, schwärzlich, brackig durch die alten Steinbögen, er strömte unter mir nach Ostia und zum Meer, viele Erschlagene waren mit ihm geströmt, er war ein alter erfahrener Fluß, und es lockte mich nicht, in seiner Flut zu baden, die wie das stinkende Waschwasser einer alten nymphomanen Vettel war — es lockte mich doch, vielleicht würde auch ich einmal erschlagen werden!

Adolf wartete nicht an der Pforte der Engelsburg. Ich freute mich. Ich war zu früh gekommen. Jetzt wußte ich es: Ich war um eine Stunde zu früh gekommen, und ich freute mich, daß ich eine Stunde zu früh gekommen war, ich stand gänzlich beziehungslos vor diesem Tor der Engelsburg, es war geschenkte Zeit, es war Freiheit!

Ein Fremdenführer saß auf einem Schemel in der Sonne. Er las den *Avanti*. Vielleicht träumte er von einer gerechten Welt. Er hatte seine amtliche Schirmmütze in den Nacken geschoben. Sein Gesicht war gut genährt; er sah ernst und dumm aus. Seine Schuhe waren alt, aber sie waren glänzend gebürstet. Zuweilen spuckte er zwischen seine glänzend gebürsteten Schuhe.

Eine Pferdedroschke wartete. Man wußte nicht, ob sie bestellt oder frei war, oder ob sie nur um des Wartens willen wartete. Der Kutscher schlief auf dem staubigen Polster des Fonds. Sein offener Mund gähnte zum Himmel. Ein Insekt umsummte ihn. Für das Insekt mußte der Mund des Kutschers der Eingang zur Hölle sein. Der Mund des Kutschers war Drohung und Verlockung. Das Pferd trug ein Fliegennetz über Stirn und Ohren. Es blickte mit dem leeren enttäuschten Ausdruck eines alten Moraltheologen auf das Pflaster. Wenn der Fremdenführer zwischen seine Schuhe spuckte, schüttelte das Pferd mißbilligend den Kopf.

Auch ein großes schwarzes Automobil stand vor der Engelsburg. Ein rechtes Höllenfahrzeug. Vielleicht hatte der Teufel in der alten Papstwohnung noch alte Geschäfte. Mir kam der Wagen bekannt vor. Ich mußte ihn schon einmal gesehen haben. Aber wer hatte nicht schon des Teufels Kalesche gesehen? Der Chauffeur stand in soldatischer Livree, stand in militärischer Haltung neben seinem Fahrzeug. Er hatte knarrende Ledergamaschen, ausgebuchtete Breeches und eine taillierte Jacke an. Sein Gesicht war kantig und braungebrannt. Sein Auge blickte kalt und zugleich mißtrauisch. Es war das Auge eines Soldaten und eines Wächters. Der Chauffeur war mir unheimlich. Ich mochte ihn nicht.

Ich ging zum Tiberufer. Ich lehnte mich über die Brüstung und sah unten auf dem Fluß in malerisch trügendem Glanz das Badeschiff liegen. Das Schiff wiegte sich auf dem trägen Wasser und sah wie die Arche Noah aus. Es war eine schöne und schmutzige Arche Noah. Allerlei Getier, kreischende junge Enten und Gänse, junge Katzen, junge Hunde verschiedenster Rassen und Mischungen wälzten sich verträglich an Deck. Auf dem mit dürrem Gras, mit Exkrementen und glitzernden verbogenen Blechstücken bedeckten Flußrain, zu dem von der Brücke eine steile Treppe hinunterführte, wurde ein Knabe von zwei Jünglingen verfolgt und rauh zu Boden geworfen. Der Knabe und die beiden Jünglinge trugen knappe dreieckige und auffallend grellrote Badehosen. Der Knabe war schön. Die beiden Burschen aber hatten eine fleckige und kranke Haut; sie hatten ordinäre und böse Gesichter. Ich kannte ihre Art. Sie waren mir widerwärtig. Sie waren Prostituierte und Erpresser, sie waren feige, mörderisch

und gemein. Aber ich war einsam. Ich wollte einsam sein,
aber manchmal sehnte ich mich nach Nähe, nach Berührung,
nach einem Herden- und Stallgeruch, nach einer Welt leib-
licher Gemeinsamkeit, die ich verloren und von der ich mich
losgesagt hatte, einem Zwang, aus dem ich mich befreit
glaubte, die Jungenswelt der Ordensburg, den Geruch der
großen Schlafsäle, die nackten Knabenkörper in spartani-
scher Erziehung im Frühnebel des Waldlaufs über den frostigen Boden gejagt, und weiter die Welt der Männerbünde,
die Horte, Lager und Heime der nationalen Bewegungen,
auch die Kameradschaft der Soldaten schloß diese Welt ein,
ich hatte mich von alldem losgesagt, ich war einsam, ich
wollte einsam sein, und Kürenberg lobte mir die Einsamkeit
des schöpferischen Menschen, aber mit diesen Burschen ver-
banden mich Herkunft und Erziehung in unterweltlicher
Weise, und sie waren Erscheinungen eines schlechten Gewis-
sens, von dem ich mich noch befreien mußte. Als nun einer
der Burschen zu mir aufblickte und mich auf der hohen
Uferbrüstung bemerkte, griff er die Spitze seines Badehosen-
dreiecks an und lockte mich mit einer obszönen Geste, die
Treppe zum Uferrain und zum Badeschiff hinunterzukom-
men. Der Bursche hatte prankengleiche Fäuste und schwellende Muskeln, die aber keine wirkliche Kraft, die eher Entartung und Erschlaffung verrieten. Er war mir sehr widerlich. Auch der andere Bursche war mir widerlich. Aber der
schöne Knabe lag zwischen ihnen, rauh angepackt, nicht von
Adlerfängen, von scheußlichen unreinen Geiern, Zeus-Jupiter
war tot, auch Ganymed war wohl tot, ich verfluchte mich, ich
stieg zu den Toten hinab
hinab ins Verlies war er gestiegen, einen Wehrgang hinunter,
tief und tiefer wand sich der düstere, nur von spärlichem
Lampenschein erhellte Weg in den Leib der Papstburg, und
dann kamen niedere Gewölbe, kam Grabesluft, man mußte
gebückt gehen, abgeschirmte Falltüren zeigten noch finsterere
Löcher, bodenlose Abgründe schreckten, Mordgruben, Todes-
brunnen, Ketten fielen aus der Mauer, Kettenringe für die
Füße, Fangeisen für die Arme, geschmiedete Stachelschnal-
len für den Leib, allerlei Martergerät hing von der Decke,

Streckzüge, Knochenbrecher, Werkzeug, die Haut zu schin-
den, Steinbetten daneben, auf denen die Gefesselten verfault
waren und Fäulnis und Gerippe den Schattenriß des Verur-
teilten oder Vergessenen selbst in den harten fühllosen Granit
gezeichnet hatten, und oben waren die Festgemächer, die
traulichen Wohnungen, die geschmückten Kapellen, lebte der
wache Sinn für die Kunst, waren schöne und fromme Bilder,
geschnitzte Betschemel, die silbernen Leuchter Cellinis, in der
Bibliothek freute man sich an Büchern, nahm Weisheit auf,
erbaute sich, hörte vielleicht Musik, atmete den Abendwind,
und ganz oben schwebte der Engel über der Burg, der Erz-
engel Michael sah die Sonne, erblickte die glitzernde Pracht
der Sterne und schaute das berühmte Panorama der Ewigen
Stadt und steckte sein Flammenschwert in die Scheide
Adolf hatte den tiefsten Kerker erreicht. Eine Art Amphore
senkte sich in den Urfels, und da mochte der Gefangene drin
stehen, aufrecht, den Kopf noch über dem Boden, doch der
Unrat, den er unter sich ließ, stieg langsam den Leib hinauf,
er mauerte den Leib ein, den als sündig verschrienen der
Unflat stieg bis zum Hals, und wer hier bei schwelender
Fackel des Menschen Haupt gesehen hatte, ein Haupt nur
noch, durch die Kloake vom Leib befreit, dem brach wohl der
Schrei von den Lippen »*Ecce homo* — Sieh, welch ein Mensch«,
und der Kerkerknecht mochte niederknien und das Wunder
der Christwerdung begreifen, das im untersten Kerker an
dem Ausgestoßenen geschehen war. Adolf kniete an der
Grube nieder und betete. Er betete inbrünstiger, als er in der
Peterskirche gebetet hatte; er betete für die Seelen der unbekannten Gefangenen. Seine Soutane berührte den Staub, der
Stein drückte seine Knie. Er glaubte. Die Welt brauchte Erlösung. Er glaubte. Der Mensch mußte wieder erlöst werden.
Er erhob sich und fühlte sich seltsam gestärkt. Er wollte wieder emporsteigen, wollte das Licht sehen, das man erst nach
dem Dunkeln hell sieht, da hörte er Schritte, feste Schritte
wie von einem, der sich nicht fürchtet, den nichts bedrückt
und der munter durch sein Haus geht, doch sein Haus ist ein
Kerker, und Adolf, von Scheu befallen, als schäme er sich, an
diesem Ort zu weilen, wollte durch eine Nische entweichen,

aber der Weg war dort versperrt, und so stand Adolf versteckt, doch konnte er durch eine Scharte in der Nischenwand den so sicher auftretenden Besucher des untersten Kerkers sehen

der Bademeister war wie ein Faun, feistbäuchig, faltenhäutig, listig, ich nahm Ganymed mit in die Zelle, ich löste das rote Dreieck von seinem Geschlecht, ich sah den Knaben an, er war schön, und Glück und Traurigkeit erfüllten mich beim Anblick seiner Schönheit

sie waren beim Kloster Cassino angekommen und hielten ein fröhliches Picknick auf dem Schlachtfeld. Der Wein kreiste, und die Damen fürchteten, einen Schwips zu bekommen, aber die Herren sagten, daß sie damals noch viel mehr Wein getrunken hätten, die besten Fässer aus den Kellern, und einer erinnerte sich noch sehr gut an alles, er war Regimentsadjutant gewesen, er hatte die Lage übersehen, er übersah sie wieder, dort war die Abtei, hier lagen sie, und da war der Feind. Es war alles in allem ein fairer Krieg gewesen. Der Krieg hatte die alte Abtei zerstört, aber sie war in einem fairen Krieg zerstört worden. Alle hatten fair gekämpft, selbst der Feind, und die Toten waren fair gestorben. Dietrich Pfaffrath hing an des Erzählers Mund. Die neuen weißen Mauern des Klosters leuchteten hell vom Berg. Wo waren die Trümmer der Schlacht? Gerüste kündeten den Aufbau, und es war schön und erhebend, in idyllischer Landschaft von einem fairen Krieg zu hören, nachdem man Mars so geschmäht hatte. Friedrich Wilhelm Pfaffrath, angeregt durch die Unterhaltung, sprach dann von Verdun. Er berichtete vom Grabenkrieg. Der Grabenkrieg war weniger fair gewesen, vielleicht weil man noch nicht so sportlich gesonnen war, aber anständig war der Krieg auch geführt worden, anständig und gerecht. Anständig und gerechterweise hatte man den Feind gehaßt, anständig und gerechterweise hatte man auf den Feind geschossen, und wenn man nun zurückdachte und sich erinnerte — es war ja nicht nur gestorben worden, es gab auch heitere Episoden zu erzählen, lustige Anekdoten aus dem großen Morden. Sie holten noch Speisen und Flaschen aus ihrem Wagen. Sie aßen von einem weißen Tisch-

489

tuch, das Frau Anna, eine aufmerksame Gastgeberin, mitgebracht hatte. Sie tranken fröhlich einander zu, die alten und
die jungen Krieger, und die Frauen tranken auch, die Sonne
schien, und ein Esel stand abseits, schlug mit dem Schweif
nach den Fliegen und wieherte »iaah, ihr habt doch gesiegt!«
Und Dietrich saß hochgemut und hochgereckt da, das Kreuz
durchgebogen, und er war entschlossen, sich keinem Ruf des
Vaterlandes zu versagen, wie kein aufrechter Mann sich ihm
je versagen wird; doch könnte es sein, daß Dietrich dann
amtlich unabkömmlich sein würde, er war nicht feig, aber er
war ehrgeizig und dachte an seine Laufbahn
ich sah den Knaben an, glücklich und traurig. Ich wagte kein
Wort ihm zu sagen. Ich wagte nicht, ihn zu berühren. Ich
wagte nicht, sein Haar zu streicheln. Wehmut erfüllte mich,
Wehmut aus Glück und Trauer und glücklich traurige Einsamkeit. Doch der übelste der Burschen trat in die Zelle, Wasser tropfte herab, er stank nach dem stinkenden Wasser des
Tibers, wie auch das ganze Badeschiff nach diesem Wasser
stank, das unter den Bohlen faulte und gluckste wie tausend
gierige Münder, Flecken sprenkelten die Haut des verkom-
menen Jünglings, Pickel blühten rot und eitrig im schlaffen
Felde des früh verdorbenen Gesichts, die Augen waren trübe,
sie lauerten, sie blickten tückisch und hart, und sein Haar war
strähnig von dem stinkenden Wasser. Ich verabscheute ihn.
Er war nackt, und ich verabscheute ihn. Ich haßte mich. Mein
Knabe schlüpfte zur Tür hinaus. Ich haßte mich. Der Ekel
war mit mir allein in der Zelle. Ich haßte mich und preßte
mich an seinen geschändeten Leib, ich legte meinen Arm um
seinen nassen Nacken, ich drückte meinen Mund auf seinen
gemeinen käuflichen Mund. Es war Lust und Vergangenheit,
die ich empfand, es war Erinnerung und Schmerz, und ich
haßte mich
durch die Scharte in der Wand sah Adolf Judejahn in den
untersten Kerker treten. Er erkannte ihn. Er erkannte seinen
Vater. Er erschrak, er wollte zu ihm stürzen, und dann war
er wie gelähmt, erstarrt und doch ein genauer Beobachter
Judejahn war durch die Engelsburg gegangen, er hatte Waffen und Rüstungen und Kriegsgerät gesehen, und der kleine

Gottlieb hatte den Schauder der Geschichte empfunden, aber Judejahn war eigentlich gelangweilt durch die Säle geschritten, nichts Neues gab es aus alter Zeit zu sehen, er kannte das, er war nicht überrascht, er fühlte sich in seinem Handwerk bestätigt und ging wirklich selbstsicher und gelangweilt wie einer, der nach langer Abwesenheit sein altes Haus besichtigt, in die Verliese hinunter. Im untersten Kerker trat er gelassen an den Schacht im Fels, an das Grab des lebendigen Leibes. Kriege und Kerker, Gefangenschaft und Tod, immer hatte es sie gegeben, Petrus war am Marterkreuz gestorben, und seine Amtswalter hatten den Martertod ihren Feinden bestellt, so würde es bleiben, und so war es gut. Es war menschlich. Wer sprach von Unmenschlichkeit? Judejahn lauschte eine Weile, und da ringsum alles still blieb, kein Schritt zu hören war, folgte er einem Bedürfnis und verrichtete seine Notdurft in das Loch für den ärmsten Gefangenen

Adolf sah wie Ham seines Vaters Noah Blöße, doch wie Sem und Japhet bedeckte er sein Gesicht mit den Händen

das Gesicht mit den Händen bedeckte Eva, seine Mutter, sie wollte das Stück blauen Himmel, sie wollte die heitere römische Sonne nicht sehen. Sie stand, die schwarzgekleidete Frau, das nach Rom verschlagene Gespenst aus Nord- und Nebelland, die Rachesinnende, die auf schreckliche Vergeltung Brütende, die wahre Wahrerin des Mythus des 20. Jahrhunderts, die Trauernde um den Führer, die an das Dritte Reich und seine Auferstehung ewig Glaubende, sie stand am Fenster, und vor ihr lag der Hof des von Deutschen bevorzugten Hotels und im Hof ein Berg geleerter Flaschen. In ihrer Hast, noch rechtzeitig zum Picknick nach Cassino zu kommen, hatten Pfaffraths Eva nicht mehr über das Treffen mit Judejahn unterrichtet. Kein Gruß war zu ihr gelangt. Sie war allein. Im Hof sangen die Küchenjungen und die Küchenmaiden Negerlieder, die Eva nicht verstand und deren Rhythmus sie quälte. Auf dem Gang vor Evas Tür sagte ein Zimmermädchen zum Etagenkellner: »Das alte Weib geht nie aus, warum ist es nach Rom gekommen?« Der Kellner wußte es auch nicht, warum das alte Weib nach Rom gekommen war. Er

rief dem Mädchen eine Obszönität zu. Das Mädchen kreischte
und sah entzückt dem weißen Rücken des weißgekleideten
Kellners nach. Dann klopfte das Mädchen gegen Evas Tür,
trat ein und begann mißgelaunt den Boden zu kehren. Eva
stand vor dem Besen, vor dem Kehricht; sie wußte nicht,
wohin. Das Mädchen öffnete das Fenster, und die Negerlieder
klangen lauter; die Negerlieder klangen wilder, die Negerlieder drangen in das Zimmer, sie drangen in die Ecke, in
der Eva standhielt

Adolf weinte

Ich stieg herauf vom Fluß, die zerschrammte Treppe, ich war
froh, ich kam aus dem Wasser, ich kam vom alten freundlichen träg und trüb strömenden Tiber; am Ufer war die Zeit
stehengeblieben. Der Kutscher schlief, sein Mund stand offen,
das Insekt summte vor der Höllenpforte, das Pferd blickte
bitter und tiefsinnig zu Boden, der Fremdenführer las den
Avanti und spuckte noch immer zwischen seine glänzend gebürsteten Schuhe. Nur der große schwarze Wagen mit der
arabischen Nummer war weggefahren. Ich freute mich, daß
er weggefahren war; ich brauchte den soldatischen Chauffeur
nicht mehr zu sehen, nicht im Blick seiner kalten wachsamen
Augen zu stehen. Der Teufel mochte sein Geschäft in der
Papstburg erledigt haben; noch immer konnten die Engel auf
der Engelsbrücke nicht fliegen, aber mir schienen sie nicht
mehr plump und gedankenschwer, mir schienen sie licht und
schwebend zu sei. Das trübe Wasser des alten götterbefreun-
deten Flusses, in dem ich nun doch gebadet hatte, die feuchte,
umschlingende Umarmung des mythischen Elements hatten
mich euphorisch erquickt.

Er trat aus der Pforte der Burg, und die Sonne schien ihn zu
blenden, denn er sah mich nicht. Er war blaß, und einen
Moment glaubte ich, meine eigene Blässe in seinem Gesicht
zu erkennen. Adolf war nicht mein Spiegelbild, aber vielleicht war er es doch, ein blinder Spiegel, in dem man sich
fremd und ähnlich findet. Als er mich wahrnahm, kam er
heftig auf mich zu. Sein zorniger Schritt schien sein Priesterkleid zerreißen zu wollen. Stoff und Staub wirbelten hinter
ihm, und seine Schuhe, derbe bäuerische Schuhe, wirkten

fremd und ärmlich auf dem römischen Pflaster. Er rief: »Ich
habe ihn gesehen.« Man konnte glauben, dem Priester sei
der Leibhaftige erschienen. Er deutete auf das Tor. »Hier
war er«, rief er. Ich verstand ihn; er hatte Judejahn gesehen,
seinen schrecklichen Vater. Hatte er ihn auch gesprochen?
Ich fragte. Sein Gesicht flammte. Er schämte sich. Also hatte
er ihn nicht gesprochen, hatte sich versteckt, und ich dachte:
Er fürchtet sich vor seinem Vater, er versteckt sich, ein Analy-
tiker würde sagen, vor Gott Vaters Antlitz, dem alten jüdischen Rachegott, er ist nicht frei. Adolf war mir gleichgültig,
er war mir lästig, er blieb für mich ein Glied der Sippe, von
der ich nichts wissen wollte, aber seine Verwirrung rührte
mich, seine Bemühung, sein Suchen nach einem Weg; aber
sein Weg führte nicht in die Freiheit, ich hätte Adolf gern
geholfen, ich hätte ihn gern in die Freiheit geführt. Aber
wollte er frei sein? Ich lenkte unseren Schritt auf die Brücke.
Er war bedrückt, und ich stürmte gegen seine Bedrückung
und rief: »Ist Rom nicht schön!« Ich deutete auf den Fluß
und seine Ufer, als gehörten sie mir. Ich rief: »Schau den
Tiber an, ist er nicht schön, alt und wohltuend? Ich habe im
Tiber gebadet, faß mein Haar an, es ist naß vom guten Wasser des Tibers!« Mein Haar hing in Strähnen. Er sah es erst
jetzt. »Sieh die Engel hier«, rief ich, »und male dir aus, sie
schwingen sich auf, ihre schweren Marmorflügel flattern, sie
fliegen zum Kapitol und tanzen mit den alten Göttern. Hörst
du es nicht, Pan spielt das Saxophon, und Orpheus singt zum
Banjo kleine Dschungellieder!« Wirklich, ich fand auf einmal
die plumpen Engel schön; wirklich, ich sah sie fliegen, ich sah
sie Boogie-Woogie tanzen; ich begrüßte sie, auch die Engel
waren Freunde, ich freute mich, ich war frei. Der Himmel
leuchtete, ein hohe blaue Kuppel. Ich war es, der den Himmel
mit Engeln und Göttern bevölkerte; der Himmel war von
Engeln und Göttern freundlich bewohnt, weil ich es
wollte, weil mir es Spaß machte, weil ich es mir vorstellte; ich
ließ die himmlische Jazzband auf dem Hügel des Kapitols
musizieren, ich träumte die Musik, ich träumte die Tänze; der
Himmel mochte, die Flieger berichten es, in der Höhe besehen schwarz sein und nur ein dünner abweisender Schleier

vor dem eisigen Nichts, das unsere törichte Erde umgibt — ich freute mich meiner Träume, denn ich war frei, war frei zu träumen, ich durfte träumen, ich hatte es mir erlaubt. Ich hätte Adolf gern in den Tiber geworfen, ich wollte ihn zur Freude taufen, aber da er mir nichts entgegnete, stumm neben mir her ging, die Brückensteine hämmernd mit seinen derben Diakonschuhen, und nur zuweilen mich anguckte, seltsam fest, fragend, bohrend, fordernd, und da ich irgend etwas für ihn tun wollte, lud ich ihn zu einem Eis ein.

Er trank nur Milch, entkeimte, sorgsam erhitzte, genauestens auf Euterwärme gebrachte Kindermilch. Eine Kinderschwester betreute ihn, rückte die Kissen im Zimmerrollstuhl zurecht, prüfte mißtrauisch den Geschmack der Milch und roch in ihrem weißblau gestreiften Schwesternkleid selber nach Milch, nach Säugung, nach sterilisierten Windeln und hygienischem Puder, während er mit pergamentfarbenen Händen das Glas vorsichtig zum pergamentenen Gesicht führte, behutsam die messerschnittschmalen Lippen mit dem milden Rahm netzte. Die Sonne schien, aber das Zimmer war abgedunkelt, und starke elektrische Öfen verbreiteten eine schier unerträgliche Hitze, die zusammen mit dem faden Milchgeruch jeden Besucher benommen machte. Er nannte sich Austerlitz, und vielleicht hieß er wirklich Austerlitz, aber man konnte sich kaum denken, daß er überhaupt einen echten Namen hatte; kein Mensch wußte, welche Schmiede er besaß oder welche Aktienmehrheit oder welches Werk er vertrat, vielleicht besaß er alle Waffenschmieden, alle Mehrheiten oder vertrat sie zumindest alle; wo seine Lager waren, blieb immer sein Geheimnis, wie er expedierte, war seine Sache, aber die Gewehre kamen an, und die Geschütze landeten pünktlich im Hafen. Austerlitz war korrekt und vertrauenswürdig, und seine Beziehungen zu allen Regierungen und zu allen Umstürzlern in aller Welt waren wie sein Kredit sagenhaft. Gleich Judejahn trug auch Austerlitz eine blaue Brille, so daß sie sich beide albern geheimnisvoll und lemurenhaft blau anfunkeln konnten. Sie sahen wie düstere Homunkuli aus. Die Kinderschwester hatte Judejahn einen

Wagen mit kräftigen alkoholischen Getränken, mit Eis und Mixbechern zugeschoben, und er hörte erfreut, nur durch die Hitze und den Milchdunst gequält, die ihn zu stärkerem Trinken veranlaßten, was die Großen für die Kleinen abfallen ließen. Manch wohlerhaltenes Mordinstrument war zu überraschend günstigen Preisen zu haben, und es sah aus, als gäbe es ungenannt bleibende Mäzene, stille Wohltäter der Menschheit oder diskrete Freunde des Todes, die sich's was kosten ließen, kleinere tapfere Völker, Länder von geringerem Vermögen mit Waffen zu versorgen, damit auch in abseitigeren Verhältnissen die Kriegsgefahr nicht erlösche. Man hielt den Krieg am Schwelen. Vielleicht sprang der Funke einmal über und entflammte neu die Welt. Investitionen lohnten sich, der Tod war ein sicherer Schuldner. Judejahn wählte mit Bedacht und Kennerschaft, was man in der Wüste brauchen konnte. Seine Vollmacht wurde anerkannt. Aber vom Whisky angefeuert, mit dem er die Hitze bekämpfte, die Hitze und die Milchschwaden, die seinen Atem bedrängten und ihm Brechreiz machten, ärgerte er sich, daß er wieder nur für seinen Semiten- und Mohrenhaufen kaufen durfte, für seine gedrillten Kerle im Wüstenfort, und er sehnte sich nach der Heimat, nach dem deutschen Wald, nach weiteren Verhältnissen und größeren Aufgaben, die es ihm auch erlauben würden, bei Austerlitz noch weit größere Bestellungen aufzugeben. Austerlitz, einen kleinen Milchbart auf der Pergamenthaut über dem Strich der Oberlippe, war über die Bewegungen auf dem wichtigen deutschen Markt natürlich wohl unterrichtet. Sollte er Judejahn die Kurse zeigen? Judejahn war ein alter Kunde. Aber Austerlitz konnte warten. Die Möglichkeiten reiften, und da er Judejahn für einen Mann der zweiten Linie hielt, der zur Stunde noch nicht am Zug war, von dem man auch noch nicht wußte, wann und wo er wieder zum großen Zug kommen würde, sagte er ihm nicht alles, was er wußte. Doch erwähnte er einen General von Teufelshammer als zu den Getreuen gehörig und wieder am Werk und nannte den kleinen Doktor, der schon beim großen Doktor Zuträger gewesen war und nun mit idealistischen Augen die Doktorrolle der nationalen

Politik spielen wollte. Judejahn kannte sie, er sah sie vor
sich, den General mit dem Primusgesicht, der runden Brille,
den abstehenden Ohren und dem kleinen wie zum Bellen
geöffneten Mündchen, er sah ihn noch vor dem Führer tanzen, ganz durchgebogen, ganz Musterschüler und stramm
bereit, bis zum Tod des ältesten Volkssturmmannes die Front
zu halten, und den anderen kannte er auch, den kleinen
Doktor, der bereit gewesen war, die Front bis zum Tod des
jüngsten Hitlerjungen zu halten, er kannte ihn aus seinem
Amtszimmer, er kam manchmal mit Botschaften vom großen
Doktor zu ihm, so ein Klugscheißer mit einem Rattenmund,
dem Mund einer lächelnden Ratte, Judejahn hatte ihn nicht
gemocht, nicht weil er an eine Ratte erinnerte, sondern weil
er studiert hatte und für einen ehrgeizigen Intellektuellen
galt — sieh an, die hatten sich verbündet, oder spielten sich's
zu, und ob sie es in seinem Sinn taten und für ihn das Reich
vorbereiteten, war fraglich, er war vielleicht schon zu lange
tot, er mußte doch hinfahren, er mußte in Deutschland erscheinen, um im deutschen Spiel zu bleiben, er mußte diesen
Schulbuben und Musterknaben auf die Finger sehen, und
das hieß, daß er sich's doch von Pfaffrath richten lassen
wollte, die Urteilsannullierung, die förmliche oder die still-
schweigende Freisprechung, die Geschworenen brauchte Judejahn nicht mehr zu fürchten, die hatten Verständnis für
ihn und dachten an ihre Zukunft, aber es wurmte Judejahn,
daß er sich vorläufig an Pfaffrath halten, daß er Pfaffrath
freundlich behandeln mußte. Er schlug mit der Faust zwischen die Gläser. Es klang, als zerschellten die Retorten, aus
denen die Homunkuli gezeugt waren. Die Kinderschwester
kam erschreckt gelaufen, aber Austerlitz winkte beruhigend
ab. Er zeigte Judejahn noch, aus kleinem Wildlederbeutel
geholt, das Modell einer neuen schallgedämpften Pistole,
Judejahn — schon der kleine Gottlieb hatte mit begehrlichen
Augen vor den Schaufenstern der Waffenhandlungen gestanden — verliebte sich gleich in den handlichen praktischen
Todgeber und konnte sich nicht mehr von ihm trennen.
Austerlitz, gesetzeskundig, versicherte Judejahn, daß es gegen die italienischen Verordnungen sei, Schußwaffen zu ver-

496

kaufen, zu kaufen und zu tragen, doch überließ er Judejahn die Pistole als Muster für einen vielleicht größeren Wüstenbedarf. »Und wo«, fragte Austerlitz mit leiser Stimme, kindisch lächelnd und am faden Milchnäpfchen sabbernd, »wo sei keine Wüste, kein Dschungel?« Er fragte nicht, wo kein Tod sei.

Der Eisladen hatte Tische und Stühle in den Hof des Hauses gestellt; man weilte dort gut, genoß den Schatten, war abseits vom Lärm der Straße, und Siegfried und Adolf saßen, wie zu unterrichtendem Gespräch zusammengekommen, in einer nach altrömischer Weise geschmückten Loggia; Säulenstümpfe, Efeuranken, zerkratzte Masken traulicher Laren umgaben sie, ein kleiner Brunnen plätscherte ein lustiges Lied, eine Palme war freundlich zu sehen, und die Gipsköpfe von Göttern, Dichtern und Philosophen, die schartigen Häupter von Satyrn, Staatsmännern, Cäsaren, die lieblichen von Lustknaben und Nymphen schauten ihnen mit verbeulten Nasen, abgeschlagenen Ohren, blinden Augen zu, wie sie ihr sizilianisch zu Granit gefrorenes Eis spachtelten. Adolf, dem bedrückten Diakon, der erst nur unwillig Siegfried gefolgt war, löschte das Eis den Brand heiß empfundener Scham, es mundete ihm plötzlich, und er schluckte mit gesunder Gier die auf der Zunge prickelnde und aromatisch zerschmelzende künstliche Winterfrucht, während Siegfried nun nachdenklich war, nur spachtelte und bröckelte und die Speise in seiner Schale zu einer rötlich milchigen Sauce zerrinnen ließ. Adolf, von Gaumenlust erfrischt und in dieser Laube alles natürlicher empfindend, harmloser und leichter zu lösen, wandte sich an Siegfried und fragte, warum sie denn ihre Eltern nicht sehen wollten. Adolf schlug vor, zu den Eltern zu gehen, vor sie hinzutreten und ihnen zu sagen, so sei man nun, anders wohl, als die Eltern es gewünscht hätten, aber man könne auch das Leben, das man führe, rechtfertigen. Siegfried rief: »Du bist wohl wahnsinnig! Ich will mein Leben ja nicht rechtfertigen! Wie käme ich dazu, mich vor den Eltern zu rechtfertigen? Ich denke gar nicht daran!« Adolf meinte darauf, man habe sich immer zu rechtfertigen, immer des Lebens wegen, vor Gott und vor den Menschen, und warum nicht auch vor den Eltern. »Hältst du deinen Vater für einen Gott oder gar für einen Menschen?« fragte Siegfried. Er war boshaft. Und Adolf erregte sich. »Das sind doch Phrasen«, rief er, »du bist in Phrasen befangen wie all die anderen, denen du dich weit überlegen wähnst, weil du deinen Phrasen einen negativen, einen zynischen, gegen alles frondierenden Sinn gibst, der mir sinnlos vorkommt oder mir zeigt, wie verzweifelt du bist!« Siegfried: »Lernst du's im Seminar, die Verzweiflung dem anderen vorzustellen als psychologische Vorbereitung einer möglichen Konversion?« Adolf: »Ich spreche nicht vom Seminar. Ich spreche von dir.« Siegfried: »Mich laß in Ruhe. Ich lebe, wie ich will. Ich brauche niemand.« Adolf: »Gut, du willst für dich leben. Du meinst, deinen Weg gefunden zu haben. Das genügt dir. Aber warum bist du dann so unversöhnlich? Mit dem gleichen Recht könnten auch unsere Eltern sagen, sie hätten ihr Leben gelebt, seien ihren Weg gegangen, es hätte ihnen Spaß gemacht.« Siegfried: »Das werden sie auch sagen.« Adolf: »Aber du billigst ihr Leben doch nicht?« Siegfried: »Nein, weil sie andere durch ihre Auffassungen und mit ihren Auffassungen gequält haben, weil sie mir eine militärische Erziehung aufbrummten, weil sie einen Krieg anfingen, weil sie Leid brachten, weil sie unendlich zerstörten, weil sie aus unserer Heimat ein Land der Intoleranz, der Dummheit, des Größenwahns, des Zuchthauses, des Richtblocks und des Galgens machten. Weil sie Menschen getötet haben oder behaglich in ihren Häusern blieben, obwohl sie wußten, daß Menschen getötet wurden.« Adolf: »Und glaubst du, das kann nicht wiederkommen?« Siegfried: »Und ob ich das glaube! In Tag- und Nachtträumen sehe ich die Bräunlinge und die nationale Dummheit marschieren. Und darum will ich mein Leben leben, solange der nationalistische Gott noch entkräftet ist und mich nicht hindern kann. Es ist meine einzige Chance.« Adolf: »Und warum versuchst du nicht, eine dir so verhängnisvoll erscheinende Entwicklung zu bekämpfen?« Siegfried: »Wie soll ich sie bekämpfen?« Adolf: »Versuche die Menschen zu ändern!« Siegfried: »Sie sind nicht zu ändern.« Adolf: »Du mußt es versuchen!« Siegfried: »Versuche du es doch! Deine Kirche versucht es seit zweitausend Jahren.« Adolf schwieg. Wußte er nicht weiter? Sah er ein, daß es keine Hoffnung gab? Aber dann hob er an: »Und deine Musik? Willst du mit deiner Musik nicht die Welt ändern?« Siegfried sagte: »Nein. Du bist ein Phantast.« Aber Adolf blieb hartnäckig und fragte beharrlich: »Warum machst du Musik, warum komponierst du?« Siegfried: »Ich weiß es nicht«

wußte ich es nicht? Er hatte recht: aus Angst, aus Verzweiflung, aus bösen Gesichten, aus schrecklichen Träumen schrieb ich Musik, ich rätselte herum, ich stellte Fragen, eine Antwort wußte ich nicht, eine Antwort hatte ich nicht, eine Antwort konnte ich nicht geben; es gab keine Antwort. Die Musik war ein geheimnisvoller Bau, zu dem es keinen Zugang mehr gab oder nur noch eine enge Pforte, die wenige durchließ. Wer in dem Bau saß, konnte sich den Draußengebliebenen nicht mehr verständlich machen, und doch war auch für diese der geheimnisvolle nach magischer Formel errichtete unsichtbare Bau wichtig. Die Musik war nicht dazu da, die Menschen zu ändern, aber sie stand in Korrespondenz mit der gleichfalls geheimnisvollen Macht der Zeit, und so konnte sie vielleicht mit der Zeit zu großen Veränderungen beitragen, aber was ist in der Zeit ein Jahrhundert, was ein Jahrtausend, wir messen die Zeit aus dem Standort unseres flüchtigen Lebens, aber wir wissen nicht, was die Zeit ist. Vielleicht ist sie freundlich, ist gütiger, als wir meinen, vielleicht ist sie auch eine Gorgo, deren fürchterliches Gesicht wir noch immer nicht ganz erkannt haben. Aber von Zeit und Musik abgesehen, Adolf bewegte mich, denn war es nicht auch mein Gedanke, daß wir, die Söhne, die wir andere Lebensweisen wünschten, auch für sie kämpfen sollten; trotz allem Anschein der Aussichtslosigkeit? Ich wollte Adolf die Hand reichen. Doch

Siegfried sagte: »Wir werden gegen Dietrich unterliegen. Mein Bruder Dietrich siegt immer über uns. Und du wirst auch als Priester unterliegen. Du wirst unterliegen und dich mit Dietrich als dem Vertreter der Ordnung, des Staates und

der festen Hand auf Verderb verbünden, — oder du wirst eben
untergehen. Im übrigen glaube ich dir gar nichts! Ich glaube
dir nicht, daß du an dein Dogma glaubst, und ich glaube dir
nicht, daß du an den Menschen glaubst. Du bist zu Gott gelaufen, du bist zu ihm übergelaufen, weil du einen Herrn
brauchtest, und du wirst einer der enttäuschten und verbitterten Priester werden, die nicht glauben. Du wirst äußerlich
ein tadelloser Priester sein. Aber du wirst leiden.« Adolf
sagte: »Ich weiß es nicht.«
Ich war häßlich, häßlich wie Kaliban. Es war kein Spiegel da,
kein magischer Spiegel; er hätte mir Kalibans Gesicht gezeigt
»von Nattern ganz umwunden«. Ich sah Adolfs abgetragene
durchgescheuerte Kutte. Ich sah, obwohl ich sie nicht sah,
seine derben bäuerischen Stiefel unter dem Tisch. Warum
quälte ich ihn? Warum entmutigte ich ihn? Weil ich selber
entmutigt bin, oder weil mein Entmutigtsein mir das Außen-
seiterdasein sichert, die Panflöte am Sumpf? Suche ich wirklich ein Vaterland, oder berufe ich mich nur auf die Menschheit als auf einen Nebel, in den ich verschwinden kann? Ich
liebe Rom, weil ich ein Ausländer in Rom bin, und vielleicht
möchte ich immer ein Ausländer sein, ein bewegter Zuschauer. Aber andere brauchen ihr Zuhause, und wenn es ein
Vaterland gäbe ohne Geschrei, ohne Fahnen, ohne Aufmärsche, ohne betonte Staatsgewalt, eine gute Verkehrsordnung
nur unter Freien, eine freundliche Nachbarschaft, eine kluge
Verwaltung, ein Land ohne Zwang, ohne Hochmut gegen
den Fremden und den Nächsten, wäre es nicht auch meine
Heimat? Ich werde sie nicht finden. Ich glaube nicht dran.
Ich schenkte Adolf meine Karte für das Konzert. Ich sagte
ihm, er im Priesterrock könne hingehen, aber ich könne nicht
hingehen, ich hätte keinen Frack. Ich sagte: »Aber du wirst
wohl nicht hingehen mögen.« Er sagte: »Doch.« Er sagte:
»Ich werde hingehen.«

Laura, die bezaubernd Lächelnde, ging zu ihrer Kasse, und
da sie nicht rechnen konnte, hatte sie sich auch einmal in der
Zeit verrechnet. Die Bar war noch geschlossen; ihr Besitzer
war noch nicht erschienen, er hatte den Schlüssel noch nicht

ins Schloß des Geschäftes gesteckt, und auch die schönen
Kellner waren noch nicht da, sie hatten ihre lila Fräcke noch
nicht angezogen, sie saßen alle bei ihren Familien, halfen
ihren Frauen im Haushalt, spielten mit den Kindern, und
müd und unlustig schickten sie sich langsam an, in den
Dienst zu gehen, zu den Homosexuellen, von denen sie lebten. Laura stand vor der Tür, blickte sich um, lächelte in die
Via Veneto und lächelte zum großen schwarzen Wagen, der
lautlos vorfuhr, als glitte er mit unsichtbaren Kufen über
unsichtbares Eis, sie lächelte dem Fahrer zu, der 'raussprang,
tailliert, geschient, blank wie ein Blitz, der den Schlag auf-
riß, blankblitzende Hacken zusammenschlug, und Laura
schenkte ihr Lächeln Judejahn, den sie erkannte als nicht-
schwulen Blauen-Brillen-Mann, der schon einmal dem Lokal
die Ehre gegeben hatte, aus Unkenntnis seiner Sonderart und
zu stiller Stunde. Judejahn hatte nach Laura schauen wollen,
und da er sie nun unvermutet auf der Straße sah, vor der
verschlossenen Tür, da begriff er, was geschehen war, daß sie
sich verrechnet hatte in der Zeit, und er sagte auf englisch,
daß es wohl noch nicht an der Zeit sei, die Tür noch versperrt,
tat, als bedauerte er es, sprach vom Whisky, der ihn gelockt
hätte, und Laura lächelte, schickte Strahlen durch das Blau
seiner Brille, wärmte das Herz, beglückte die Sinne, und das
Lächeln umschloß auch den großen Wagen, wie allen Frauen
war ihr die Stärke des Motors, das kräftige pantherleise Gleiten des Fahrzeuges ein Sexualsymbol, das leicht dem Besitzer
des Wagens schmeichelt und dem man sich weiblich unter-
wirft, nicht weil der Besitzer, wie zu vermuten, ein reicher
Kerl ist, ein guter Freier, sondern aus Sklavinneninstinkt,
weil er ein Mächtiger ist, Herr über die Pferdekräfte, die
mächtig pulsend seines Lebens Wagen voranziehen, und dieser verfügte auch noch über einen Fahrer, der vor des Herrn
Majestät erstarrte. Was war zu tun? Judejahn wollte vor-
schlagen, die Konditorei im Nebenhaus zu besuchen, er hatte
Hunger, und Austerlitz' widerliches Milchnäpfchen hatte ihm
Appetit auf Rahmschnitten gemacht, und er dachte sich Lauras große Augen, ihr Traum- und Wollustlächeln über Kom-
potte und Törtchen schwebend in einer Zuckeratmosphäre,

die er mit Kognak würzen wollte, aber als er Laura einlud, verhedderte er sich im stockenden stotternden Englisch, der kleine Gottlieb hatte seine Aufgaben nicht gelernt, und da er ihr Lächeln dem Wagen gelten sah, forderte er sie zu einer Spazierfahrt auf, und sie ließ sich vom Strammstehenden den Schlag aufhalten, stieg ein, und, so sind die Frauen, das Lächeln stieg in einen Käfig.

Sie glitten langsam dahin, unsichtbare Kufen auf unsichtbarem Eis, drunten schillerte die Unterwelt, tobten die Kobolde, wirrten die bösen Wichtel, knirschten die Höllenschergen, waren erwartungsvoll, schürten unsichtbare Feuer, badeten in Flammen, rieben sich geil ihr Glied, und der Wagen fuhr durch die Porta Pinciana, sie rollten in den Park der Villa Borghese, und das gefangene Lächeln verschwendete sich im gepolsterten Gehäuse, wohlig trug es einen durch grüne Alleen, sie lehnte sich zurück, und ihr Begleiter mit der blauen Brille mochte ihr König Faruk sein, ihr Pipeline-Magnat, er hatte große Hände, er war nicht schwul, und er sah ihre Taille, er sah ihren Hals, das, was zu umfassen war, er haßte dies Leben, er haßte diese Art Frauen, als Kriegsbeute ließ er sie gelten, im Puff noch, man zahlte, man zog sich aus, oder man zog sich nicht mal aus, man ließ Gier ab, schnappte Weibdunst ein, duftwasserüberspritzt, doch blieb man sich der Fleischlichkeit des Vorgangs bewußt, und nachher kam Seifenlauge oder vorsichtshalber der Sanitätsgefreite mit der prophylaktischen Spritze, während dies hier die freie Kurtisane war, mit ihrem Lächeln auf Weibesgleichberechtigung und Menschenrechte weisend, pfui Teufel Menschenrecht, das kannte man, er langte in seine Hose, dies konnte zur Unterwerfung führen, zu jämmerlicher Manneserweichung, so wurden Kriegspläne verraten, Reiche zerstört, der kleine Gottlieb wußte Bescheid, Judejahn fühlte in seiner Hose eine weichrauhe, eine sanftfeste Geschwulst, wie eine Maus glitt sie in seine Hand und war das Wildlederbeutelchen mit Austerlitz' schallgedämpften Pistole. Sie glitten an einem Wasser vorbei, sie kamen zu einem Tempel, der vor dem Wasser stand. Wohnte die Liebesgöttin hier? War sie im Park zu Haus? Der Himmel bezog sich, die Bäume bekamen die blaue Farbe des Todestals, ein Blau, das Judejahn schon auf dem Flug nach Rom erschreckt hatte, wie treu war der deutsche Wald gewesen, lautlos wie der Wagen, in dem man fuhr, schritt der Marschstiefel über den Waldesgrund aus Moos und Tannennadeln vom Julbaum, und der Kamerad schritt voran im Schwarzen Reichswehr-Gebüsch, Verrat Verrat Verrat krächzten die Raben, man hielt die Pistole umklammert, der Kamerad fiel in den Waldesgrund, Verrat Verrat Verrat riefen die Raben hoch in den Wipfeln der knorrigen Eichen, und in der Heide blüht ein Blümelein und schwarzbraun ist mein Mägdelein, Heimweh Heimweh Heimweh, sie war nicht schwarzbraun, die neben ihm saß, schwarz wie Ebenholz, welsch, vielleicht eine Jüdin, sie war bestimmt eine Jüdin, eine Aussaugerin, eine Blutverderberin, die lachte, jetzt auch mit dem Mund, rot wie Blut, lachte sie über ihn, rot wie Blut, weiß wie Schnee, war ihr Gesicht weiß wie Schnee, noch nicht, noch nicht ganz, beinahe weiß wie Schnee, den es zu Hause gab im deutschen Wald, Leichen waren schneeweiß, dieser Park war blau, dieses Blau des welschen Parkes, das Blau italienischen Strauchwerks, das todesüppige Blau der römischen Bäume von zerrender Schwermut wurde ihm unerträglich. Er kutschierte in des Teufels Hohlweg. Abrupt befahl er dem soldatisch aufrecht sitzenden, sich kaum bewegenden Chauffeur, zurück zur Via Veneto zu fahren, zurück zur Abfahrt, zurück zur Herkunft, vielleicht zu Eva zurück. Die Tür der Bar war nun geöffnet, die schönen Kellner bewegten sich schon in den schönen lila Fräcken um die verwaiste Kasse herum, Judejahn wollte Laura aus dem Wagen treiben, der Chauffeur riß den Schlag auf, stand mustergültig stramm, aber Laura zögerte noch, lächelte, schmal die Taille, lang das Hälschen, lächelte, schwarz wie Ebenholz, rot wie Blut, weiß wie Schnee, lächelte ihr bezauberndes Lächeln, diesmal erwartungsvoll, und er verabredete sich mit ihr für den Abend. Laura schritt lächelnd zur Kasse, schon im Gehen den Zorn des Besitzers beschwichtigend. Das arme Kind konnte nicht rechnen, und das seltsame Wesen des neuen Freundes versprach ihr viel.

Schwarzgewandet, Schemen auf einer Schattenbühne, die Sonne fiel grell durch das Fenster, standen sie sich bleich gegenüber, er in seiner schwarzen Priestertracht und sie im schwarzen Trauerkleid, und bleich war er, weil es ihn bange erregt hatte, in ihr Zimmer zu treten, und bleich war sie, weil sein Anblick sie erschreckte. Es quälte sie, ihn zu sehen, ihn zu sehen in der gehaßten Uniform einer Macht, die nach ihrer Überzeugung im schändlichen Bündnis mit jüdischer Unterwelt, überseeischen Plutokraten und bolschewistischen Bestien dazu beigetragen hatte, den erhabenen Traum vom Reich, von arischer Weltbeglückung und germanischem Herrentum zu stören, vielleicht für immer zu vernichten. Sie war es nun gewohnt, daß Verrat ihr entgegentrat und frech sein Haupt nicht senkte. Deutsche Frauen zeigten sich schamlos am Arm von Negern, und Landesverräter waren Minister. Sie war es nun gewohnt. Sie war die Schwäche, die Selbstsucht selbst in den Worten deutschgesinnter Menschen gewohnt, die sich mit allem abfanden, wohl heimlich ausspuckten, doch vom Wandel der Dinge profitierten. Aber der Sohn? Der Sohn im Lager der Verräter, der Sohn im weibischen Rock, reichsfeindlicher römischer Pfaffen, er im Bunde mit dem internationalsten Klüngel, vaterlandslos wie die Juden? Es war nicht nur eine Wunde, die bitter schmerzte, ein Brand im Herzen, dies war Anklage und Vorwurf, die gegen sie sich richteten. Woher kam der schlechte Same? Ihr Sippenbuch war sorgsam geführt, an arischer Abstammung war nicht zu zweifeln. Und doch hatte sie Adolf vor Abfall nicht bewahrt. Sie hatte ihn in die Nationalpolitische Erziehungsanstalt gegeben, und sie hatte ihn vor Abfall nicht bewahrt. Die Schule war zersprengt worden, und er war abgefallen, er war in der Stunde der Bewährung zum Verräter an seiner Eltern Werk geworden. Verräter richtete man. Man hängte sie an Bäumen auf oder an Laternen. Man tat ein Prangerschild an ihre Brust. Mußte sie Adolf nicht hinausweisen? Es gab keine Gemeinschaft mehr zwischen ihr und ihm, und doch war er ihr Sohn, Fleisch von ihrem Fleisch, fremd ihr nun in der Heuchlertracht, er hatte sich ans Kreuz gekettet, an die ungermanische Lehre aus Judenland, das Kreuz hing an seinem

Kleid, hing an der Kette, die ihn fesselte, er kam in Feindes-
gestalt, er war so gar nicht der Sproß, den sie sich wünschte,
der Fortführer des Ahnenerbes und nun sein Rächer, aber
er war ihr Sohn, sie hatte ihn früh aus dem Haus gegeben,
um ihn zum Mann reifen zu lassen, er war ein Weib geworden, sie fühlte Schwäche, sie wies dem Verräter nicht die Tür.
Sie fragte abweisend: »Was willst du?« Und er, dem das Herz
hoch schlug und dem Erregung die Rede preßte, er stammelte
»dich besuchen«, als wäre einfach ein Stuhl zu nehmen, sich
zu setzen, ein wenig zu plaudern, und jeder würde den anderen gelten lassen in seiner Art und in seinem Wirken, aber sie
war nicht gesonnen, ihm diesen Stuhl anzubieten, ihm das
Mutterstündchen zu gewähren, sie wandte sich wieder ihrem
Fenster zu, starrte wieder in den Hof hinunter, wieder auf
den Berg leerer Flaschen, die nun in der Sonne funkelten,
trunkene Grüße ihr hinaufwinkten, und wieder hörte sie die
Negerlieder des Küchenpersonals, fremd und ärgerlich. »Vater ist in Rom«, sagte Adolf. »Dann laß dich nicht von ihm
sehen«, murmelte sie, »er mochte die Pfaffen nicht.« »Ich
habe ihn gesehen«, sagte er. Und ungeschickt sagte er: »Im
Kerker.« Das war ein Wort, das sie aus ihrer Erstarrung riß.
Es war Erlösung, es war Erhörung, es war Freisprechung, das
Wort kündete Heldentum und heroisches Beispiel. Judejahn
war im Kerker, man hatte ihn verhaftet, das alte Schandurteil
galt, es würde vollstreckt werden, Judejahn kam nach Walhall, und ihre Ehe war wieder gut. »Wo ist er?« rief sie. Und
als er sagte, er wisse es nicht, da packte sie ihn, zerrte an seinem ihr verhaßten Kleid »sprich, sprich doch«, und er erzählte ihr die Begegnung in den Verliesen, verschwieg ihr
aber Judejahns Verrichtung am Felsloch des untersten Gefangenen, und sie, die ihn erst nicht verstand, wovon sprach
er, von welchem Kerker, von welcher Burg, einer Papstburg,
der Papst hatte Judejahn gefangen, in welche Höhlen tauchte
Judejahn, ging hinein und kam heraus, ein freier Mann, ein
feiner Herr, ein ungeschorener Besucher, und als sie begriff,
ungefähr begriff, was im Kerker gewesen war, da fühlte sie
sich genarrt, sie, die in ihrem Zimmer saß und um Helden
trauerte, und sie lachte, die nordische Erynnie, und schalt sie

Memmen, beide, den Sohn und den Gatten, Kerkerbesucher, die im Kerker miteinander Versteck spielten, man besuchte Kerker nicht, man verurteilte zum Kerker, man tötete im Kerker oder wurde im Kerker getötet, aber es war nicht an der Zeit, die Kerkersehenswürdigkeiten der Stadt zu besichtigen, einer Stadt, die Judejahn hätte zerstören können. »Auch deinen Papst hätte er hängen können, und seine Burg hätte er sprengen müssen«, schrie sie ihn an, der zitternd vor ihr stand. »Er hätte den Papst hängen können, aber er war zu dumm dazu oder zu feig, vielleicht trieb auch er schon Verrat, und der Führer wußte von nichts, der Führer wurde von allen betrogen, man verhehlte dem Führer, daß man den Papst hängen müßte.« Sie war eine Furie. Sollte er niederknien und beten? Sollte er für sie beten, daß ihr die schlimmen Worte vergeben würden? Er sagte »beruhige dich doch, Mutter«, und er empfand, wie läppisch dieser Satz vor ihren Vorwürfen und ihrer Maßlosigkeit war. Eine Weile dachte er, sie sei vom Teufel besessen, aber Adolf war nicht glaubensstark genug, um an die wirkliche Existenz eines Teufels zu glauben, es gibt ihn nicht, sagte er sich, und seine Mutter war nicht vom Teufel besessen, aber von einer teuflischen Idee. Wie konnte er die Idee beschwören, wie konnte er diese Besessenheit bannen? Er wußte es nicht. Er war hilflos. Er dachte: Siegfried hatte recht, es gibt keine Verständigung. Er wollte gehen, er mußte nun wohl gehen, aber sie tat ihm leid. Er fühlte, daß sie litt. Er spürte, daß sie in ihren Ideen brannte und die Hölle in sich trug. Es brauchte keines Teufels. Sie war ihr eigener Teufel, sie quälte Seele und Leib. Er wollte für sie beten, ohne im Augenblick den rechten Glauben zu haben.

Judejahn kam. Er füllte das Zimmer. Er füllte mit seiner gedrungenen Bullengestalt das Zimmer aus. Das kleine Zimmer wurde noch winziger. Es schrumpfte zusammen. Es war, als drängten die Mauern zueinander, als sinke die Decke gegen den Boden. Judejahn ging zu Eva. Er umfaßte sie. Er sagte: »Du trauerst?« Sie sagte »ich trauere«. Und sie dachte: Er ist gekommen, er ist gekommen, doch er ist nicht aus Walhall gekommen. Er sagte: »Ich weiß.« Er führte sie zum Bett.

Sie ließ sich auf das Bett fallen, und er setzte sich neben sie. Er sah das Zimmer, das kleine Zimmer zum Hof, er hörte das Negerlied aus der Küche, er sah den Vulkanfiberkoffer, solide und billig, und er dachte an die Lederschränke, die sie besessen hatten. Er sagte: »Die Juden sind schuld.« Und sie antwortete: »Die Juden.« Er sah seinen Sohn in der Priestertracht in der grellen Sonne stehen, schwärzlich, staubig, ärmlich, er hatte die Kette des Kreuzes um die Hände gewunden, er hielt das Kreuz ihnen entgegen, er war bleich, und er schien nun doch zu beten. Judejahn sagte: »Es war Verrat.« Und sie erwiderte: »Verrat.« »Juden«, sagte er, »internationale Juden.« Und sie wiederholte: »Juden, internationale Juden.« Und Adolf sah sie sitzen, wie Laokoon und seine Söhne am griechischen Strand von der Schlange umwickelt; die haßgeifernden giftzüngelnden Riesenschlangen ihres Wahnsinns verschlangen die Eltern ganz. Er betete. Er sprach die Bitten des Vaterunsers. Und sie fragte Judejahn: »Wirst du weiterkämpfen?« Und er sagte: »Ich werd's ihnen besorgen. Ich werd's ihnen allen besorgen.« Sie blickte ihn an, und ihre verschwimmenden blauen Augen sahen mehr, als sie sehen konnten; ihre Augen kamen aus dem Nebel und durchdrangen nun den Nebel des Seins. Sie glaubte Judejahn kein Wort. Er kam nicht aus Walhall. Aber Eva sah doch den Tod hinter ihm stehen. Der Tod erschreckte sie nicht. Der Tod würde alles richten. Er würde den Helden nach Walhall geleiten. Judejahn sah in ihr Nebelgesicht, und er dachte: Sie ist sehr alt geworden, ich ahnte es. Und dann dachte er: Sie ist mein Kamerad; mein einziger Kamerad ist sie doch geblieben. Er fühlte ihre Hand sich in seiner Hand erwärmen. Er sagte: »Ich werde nach Deutschland kommen. Ich spreche mit Pfaffrath. Ich werd's den Verrätern besorgen. Ich bin noch der alte Judejahn!« Er war noch der alte, er war noch der große Judejahn. Er war wirklich groß in dem kleinen Zimmer. Er war so groß wie der Schatten des kleinen Gottlieb. Und Judejahn befahl. Er befahl ihr, sofort abzureisen. Sie solle nach Hause fahren. Er holte Geld aus seiner großen Brieftasche, Geld für den Schlafwagen. Er gab ihr das Geld. Geld für ein Haus würde er schicken. Und dann

nahm er noch einmal große schmutzige italienische Geldscheine, aufgeblähte Kriegsfolgeziffern, und drückte sie Adolf
in die gefalteten Hände. Das machte Judejahn nun Spaß.
Er sagte: »Kauf dir was zu essen. Oder besauf dich. Oder geh
mit einem Mädchen aus, wenn du noch ein Mann bist.«
Adolf fühlte schwer das Geld in der Hand, aber er wagte
nicht, es zurückzuweisen. Er hielt die Scheine mit der Gebets-
kette und dem Kreuz zusammengefaltet. Judejahn packte
die wenigen Sachen seiner Frau zusammen und warf sie in
den unschönen billigen Koffer aus Kunststoff. Sie rührte sich
nicht. Sie ließ ihn handeln. Es freute sie, daß er befahl, es
freute sie, daß er handelte, doch ihre Augen glaubten ihm
nicht, die sahen den Tod hinter ihm stehen, sie sahen, daß
er schon lange auf dem Weg nach Walhall war, auf dem
Weg zur Heldenrunde. Es war gleichgültig, was er hier noch
tat und bestimmte; sie fügte sich, gleichgültig, und an seinem
Arm verließ sie das Zimmer, entfernte sich von dem Negersong in dem Hof, entfernte sich von dem Sohn, dem fremden
nur feindlich sein könnenden Wesen. Juden Verrat Pfaffen.
Judejahn hatte den Sohn mit Geld abgefunden, mit schmutzigen Scheinen und aufgeblähten Zahlen; er schaute Adolf
nicht an, als er die Mutter aus dem Zimmer führte.
Und in der Halle des von Deutschen bevorzugten Hauses trafen sie Pfaffraths, die braungebrannten Ausflügler, die ani-
miert von den Schlachtfeldern kamen, gestärkt, gehoben und
laut. Friedrich Wilhelm Pfaffrath war erstaunt und beunruhigt, Judejahn im Hotel zu begegnen und Eva an seinem
Arm zu sehen. »Ich bringe meine Frau zur Bahn«, sagte
Judejahn. »Ihr Zimmer gefiel mir nicht. Wir sprechen uns
nachher noch.« Und dann freute es Judejahn, des Schwagers
verblüfftes betroffenes Gesicht zu fixieren. Dieses Gesicht ani-
mierte Judejahn zu Scherzen, und er rief: »Geht ihr ins Konzert? Der Siegfried fiedelt doch heute!«
Aber wie zur Vergeltung des Spottes folgte ihm Adolf, ein
schwarzer Schatten, durch die Halle. Er war eine hagere Erscheinung von Ernst und Trauer. Was hätten sie ihm sagen
können? Verlegen schauten sie weg. Er störte ihren Tag.
Seine schwarze Gestalt war ein Menetekel in Belsazars Saal.

Doch Dietrich eilte nach kurzer Überlegung dem Vetter nach, erreichte ihn und sagte: »Tag Adolf. Vielleicht wirst du Kardinal. Man muß sich gut mit dir stellen.«

Ich hatte keinen Frack, aber ich hätte mir einen Frack kaufen können, oder ich hätte mir einen Frack leihen müssen, es gab wohl in Rom Leute, die davon lebten, daß sie Fräcke verliehen, aber ich wollte mir keinen Frack kaufen und auch keinen leihen; ich sah nicht ein, daß man einen Frack haben mußte, um Musik zu hören.
Ich zog ein weißes Hemd an. Der Trevi-Brunnen rauschte. Ich wusch mich nicht; ich wollte etwas Tibergeruch mit in das weiße Hemd nehmen. Der Trevi-Brunnen rauschte. Ich zog einen dunklen Anzug an. Es war kein römischer Anzug. Er hatte nicht den weichen Schnitt der italienischen Schneider. Der Trevi-Brunnen rauschte. Mein Anzug war ein deutscher Anzug. Ich war ein deutscher Komponist. Ich war ein deutscher Komponist in Rom. Der Opernbrunnen rauschte. Wasser fiel in das Becken. Geld fiel in das Becken. Die Götter und die Fabelwesen bedankten sich nicht. Die Fremden strichen den Brunnen aus ihrem Verzeichnis der Sehenswürdigkeiten; sie hatten den Brunnen besichtigt, sie hatten das Wasser und die Götter photographiert, der Brunnen war geerntet, er war im Gedächtnis eingeweckt, er war eine Reiseerinnerung. Mir war er ein Traum. Die Knaben fischten nach dem Geld, das die Fremden ins Wasser geworfen hatten. Die Knaben waren schön; sie hatten ihre kurzen Hosen über ihren schlanken Beinen hochgekrempelt. Ich hätte mich gern in meinem weißen Hemd und in meinem schwarzen Anzug und mit etwas Tibergeruch auf den Brunnenrand gesetzt. Ich hätte gern den Knaben zugesehen; ich hätte gern beobachtet, wie schön und wie geldgierig die Knaben waren.
Es war eine große bewegte Auffahrt vor dem Konzerthaus. Die Flöte des Schutzmanns trillerte. Seine Handschuhe waren wie elegante weiße Vögel. Spitzenprinzessinnen kamen, Schleiermatronen, Diamantfrisuren, Grafen der Reklame und Grafen des Außenamtes, berühmte Heiratsschwindler, Botschafter, ergraut im Überbringen schlechter Botschaften,

Schneewittchens Mutter, Aschenbrödels Schwestern fuhren
vor, sie traten als Schönheitsköniginnen auf, und die Photographen beleuchteten sie mit Blitzen, tänzelnde Modemeister
schoben auf ehrgeizigen Mannequins ihre neuen geschäftli-
chen Träume ins Licht, bekannte Leinwandgesichter gähnten
wohlhabende Backfische an, und alle gaben der Musik die
Ehre, sie waren die Gesellschaft, man konnte sie nicht voneinander unterscheiden, sie trugen ein Einheitsgesicht. Die
Kritiker verbargen sich hinter Charaktermasken, und die
Verleger strahlten vor lauter Wohlwollen wie der volle Mond.
Manager stellten ihr empfindsames krankes Herz zur Schau.
Ein Lastwagen mit roten Fahnen rumpelte vorüber. Flugblätter flogen wie ein Schwarm neidischer grauer Sperlinge
über die weißen Handschuhe des Schutzmannes. Die Dschungelfestung war gefallen. Wen berührte es? Die Börse reagierte fest. Aga Khan war nicht erschienen. Er wartete in seiner
Villa am Meer auf Hokusais Woge. Doch Aufsichtsräte waren ein Dutzend gekommen, man kannte und begrüßte sich,
die Damen wollten Göttinnen sein. Ich hatte keinen Hut,
sonst hätte ich ihn gezogen; es waren meine Ernährer und
Förderer, die sich hier versammelten, selbst die Industrie war
vertreten, beraten von berühmten Philosophen des Pessimis-
mus, hatte sie einen Musikpreis gestiftet, und nach dem In-
dustriepreis würde der Gewerkschaftspreis kommen, der
Fordstiftung würde die Marxstiftung folgen und das Mäze-
nat immer anonymer werden, Mozart war Kammerdiener
erlauchter Herrschaften gewesen, wessen Kammerdiener war
ich, der ich frei sein wollte, und wo blieben Augustinus'
große Männer, die nach vollbrachter Arbeit sich der Musik
hingeben, um ihre Seele wiederherzustellen? Ich sah keine
Seelen. Vielleicht waren die Kleider zu teuer.
Vielleicht war ich verbittert, weil ich mir keinen Frack gekauft hatte. Wen sollte meine Musik erfreuen? Sollte sie
überhaupt erfreuen? Sie sollte beunruhigen. Sie würde keinen hier beunruhigen.
Am Anfang zur Galerie standen keine Photographen. Junge
Männer, junge Mädchen, sonderbarerweise auch ganz alte
Leute gingen durch dieses Tor. Der Künstler glaubt gern, die

Jugend sei mit ihm im Bunde, und er meint, die Zukunft für sich zu haben, wenn die Galerie klatscht. Würden sie klatschen? Sprach ich zu ihnen, zu den hochmütigen armen Mädchen? Sie sahen mich nicht an. Und die armen jungen Männer? Sie waren wohl Studenten, zukünftige Atomzauberer, immer in der Gefahr, entführt zu werden und zerrissen zerrieben zwischen Ost und West, aber vielleicht waren sie nur zukünftige Wirtschaftsprüfer oder Zahnärzte — ich sehnte mich wohl doch nach Augustinus' bedeutenden Zuhörern. Ein paar Geistliche kamen, ein paar junge Arbeiter. Würde ich sie beunruhigen? Ich hätte gern diese jungen Leute, die jungen Forscher, die Studenten, die Arbeiter, die Geistlichen, die jungen Mädchen, als meine Kameradschaft empfunden; aber das Wort Kamerad war mir in früher Jugend aufgedrängt und verekelt worden. Ich dachte auch, als ich sie sah, Studenten und Arbeiter, »Proletarier und Intellektuelle vereinigt euch«, aber ich glaubte nicht daran, ich glaubte nicht an eine neue Welt aus dieser Vereinigung, Hitler, Judejahn, meine Sippschaft und der Dienst im Heer hatten mir den Glauben an jede Vereinigung genommen. So grüßte ich die wenigen Alten, die unter der Jugend zum Olymp emporstiegen; sie waren einsam, und vielleicht war mein Konzert für die Einsamen gedacht.

Im Dirigentenzimmer wartete Kürenberg auf mich. Er war wahrhaft von der Antike geformt. Sein Frack saß wie auf einer Marmorbüste, und über dem Weiß aus Hemdbrust, Kragen und Schleife blickte sein Kopf augusteisch. Er war weise. Er stellte sich nicht töricht vor das Haus und betrachtete sein Publikum. Er war überlegen. Was kümmerten ihn Wahn und Eitelkeit? Die Gesellschaft hatte für ihn eine Funktion, sie hatte das Märchenschloß der Musik zu unterhalten, den magischen Tempel der Töne karyatidengleich zu stützen, und es war belanglos, aus welcher Einbildung sie es taten. Ilse Kürenberg trug ein einfaches schwarzes Kleid. Auch ihr Kleid saß wie auf Marmor genäht. Es lag wie eine enge schwarze Haut auf einer wohlerhaltenen Marmorbüste. Kürenberg wollte mich in die Loge schicken. Er sah, daß ich ohne Frack erschienen war, und es mußte ihn ärgern. Er stand über der Konvention, und er fand nun, daß ich, indem ich den Frack verschmähte und mich dem Gebräuchlichen nicht unterwarf, Kleidung und Konvention eine Bedeutung verlieh, die ihnen nicht zukamen. Er hatte recht. Ich war wütend auf mich. Man soll die Spielregeln achten und Anstoß und Schwierigkeiten meiden. Es klingelte in den Garderoben, und das Orchester begab sich schon auf das Podium, hundert berühmte Musiker stimmten ihre Instrumente, und hin und wieder vernahm ich ein paar Töne meiner Symphonie; die Töne klangen wie der Ruf eines verirrten Vogels in einem fremden Wald. Ich sollte Ilse Kürenberg in die Loge begleiten, und ich sagte, daß ich meinen Platz einem Priester geschenkt hatte. Ich sagte nicht, daß der Priester mein Vetter war, und erst jetzt fiel mir ein, daß Adolf Judejahn nun in Rom neben Ilse Aufhäuser aus unserer Stadt in einer Loge sitzen würde. Ihr Vater war umgebracht worden, nachdem man sein Warenhaus verbrannt hatte. Adolfs Vater hatte viel dazu beigetragen; er hatte zum Brand des Warenhauses beigetragen, und er hatte dazu beigetragen, daß der alte Aufhäuser umkam. Mein Vater konnte sich einbilden, zu Mord und Brand nicht beigetragen zu haben. Er hatte nur zugesehen. Mein Vater war es, der damals in einer Loge saß. Er hatte aus seiner Loge den Akteuren zugejubelt. Aber es entsetzte mich nicht, daß Adolf Judejahn und Ilse Kürenberg nun auf demselben Sofa sitzen sollten. Warum sollten sie nicht nebeneinander sitzen? Da die Tragödie geschehen war, mußte das Satyrspiel folgen.

Judejahn hatte Eva nach Deutschland geschickt, er hatte sie erstklassig gebettet, das Hotelzimmer war ein Käfig gewesen, das Abteil war ein noch engerer rollender Käfig, in dem sie gefangen stand, die nordische Erinnye, schwarzgewandet, bleichhaarig, voll erhabener Trauer und des Gatten Heimgang nach Walhall nun gewiß. Aber auf dem großen römischen Bahnhof, auf dem Bahnsteig der Station Termini, die nach den nahen Thermen des Diokletian heißt, zerrannen im Neonschein des technischen Geländes für eine Weile die Nebel, klärte sich das Nebelantlitz, das Zweite und Spöken-

kiekergesicht, das Werwolfauge, das Judejahn schon als Toten sah, und sie erblickte ihn aus dem Abteil des Zuges, der
zu den Alpen fahren sollte, nordwärts heimwärts, erblickte
ihn und erkannte ihn, wie er sich der Wirklichkeit darbot
hier in dem gleißenden Neonlicht, ein stämmiger ergrauter
Mann mit einer blauen Brille, und sie rief: »Nimm endlich
die schreckliche Brille ab, steig ein, steig ein in den Zug und
fahr mit!« Und er wandte kläglich ein, sein Paß gelte nicht
für Deutschland, und sein falscher Name würde offenbar
werden, und sie sagte heftig: »Du brauchst keinen falschen
Namen, du brauchst keine Brille, du benötigst keinen Paß.
Die Grenzer werden sagen ›sind Herr General wieder da? wir
freuen uns, daß Herr General wieder hier sind‹, und sie
werden vor dir strammstehen und werden dich reisen
lassen, wohin du willst, und sie werden stolz sein, mit dir
gesprochen zu haben, und zu Hause wird man dich mit Böllerschüssen empfangen, und du wirst unantastbar sein.« Eva
sah seine Heimkehr. Sie sah, dies war die einzige Möglichkeit für ihn heimzukehren, und er verstand sie, er wußte,
sie hatte recht, dies war die Heimkehr, dies war Deutschland
»Herr General sind wieder da, wir freuen uns, Herr General«, so war es, die Grenzer würden es rufen, aber Judejahn
zögerte, irgend etwas hielt ihn in diesem Rom, in dieser
Stadt impotenter Pfaffen, war es Laura, war es Furcht, nein,
Furcht war es nicht, Judejahn kannte ja keine Furcht, aber
auch Laura war es natürlich nicht, die ihn zurückhielt, es
war etwas anderes, vielleicht war es die Wüste, die Kaserne
am Wüstenrand, dort befahl er, und wenn sie ihn in Deutschland mit Böllerschüssen empfingen, Schüsse verhallten, selbst
scharfe Munition verknallte schnell, und dann kam der Alltag, was würde er dann sein, ein Judejahn ohne Gewalt, ein
alter Gottlieb an der Vereinsbank der Mißvergnügten und
Gestrigen, Judejahn fürchtete die Zeit, er fürchtete sein Alter, er sah den Sieg nicht mehr — und so sagte er Eva, daß
Pfaffrath es richten würde, Pfaffrath würde die Heimkehr
günstig vorbereiten, und um Eva verschloß sich der Klarblick,
kam wieder Nebel und Nebelgesicht, sie wußte nun, Judejahn glaubte nicht mehr, er glaubte nicht mehr an die Gren-

zer, er glaubte nicht mehr an die Böller, er glaubte nicht an
Deutschland, und das Zweitgesicht bemächtigte sich Evas, die
Spökenkiekerschau, und auf lahmem Gaul trieb ein schäbiger Tod den Helden nach Walhall, während ihr Zug sie
nordwärts zu den Alpen trug.

Judejahn fuhr nach schmerzlich mißverständlichem Abschied
in das von Deutschen bevorzugte Hotel des Schwagers, damit
Pfaffrath ihm die Heimkehr richte, doch dort vernahm er,
daß die Herrschaften ins Konzert gefahren seien; und wirklich, von Dietrich angetrieben, der, von dem Bild in der Zeitung beunruhigt, des Bruders Situation erforschen wollte,
und auch von eigener Neugier bewogen, von einem Misch-
gefühl aus Unbehagen, Zweifel und Stolz, hatten sie sich
durch den Portier Plätze in den hinteren Reihen besorgen
lassen und diese auch ohne Schwierigkeit erreicht. Judejahn,
der sich so unverrichteterdinge zu seinem Palasthotel fahren
ließ, überlegte unterwegs, daß er erst nach Stunden mit Laura verabredet sei und daß es ihm wohl Spaß machen könne,
Schwager Pfaffraths Sohn fiedeln zu sehen. Das lächerlich anrüchige Ereignis mochte ihm über die langweilige Zeit bis
zu seinem Rendezvous hinweghelfen und würde überdies,
wenn er es gesehen hatte, Zeuge der Familienentartung gewesen war, seine Position gegen den Schwager stärken. Also
bestellte auch Judejahn durch seinen Portier eine Karte für
das Konzert, und weil der Anruf aus dem vornehmen Hotel
kam, wurde ihm ein Platz in der ersten Reihe reserviert.
Doch da er keinen Frack anhatte, wollte man ihn hindern,
den Sitz einzunehmen. Judejahn, der das Italienisch des
Saalschließers nicht verstand, wohl aber begriff, daß man sich
ihm in den Weg stellen wollte, drängte, sich nach erlegtem
und überraschend hohem Eintritt im Recht fühlend, wuchtig
den schmächtigen Kontrolleur zur Seite. Was wollte der Kerl,
eine elende Lakaienseele? Judejahn warf ihm einen Geld-
schein zu, schritt in den Saal und nahm breit seinen Platz ein.
Hier erst bemerkte er, daß er sich unter lauter Leuten in
Gesellschaftskleidung befand, und einen Moment meinte er,
sich unter die Musiker gesetzt zu haben, unter die Spaß-
macher, die ihn unterhalten sollten und deren Berufstracht

der Frack war. Da aber das Orchester auf dem Podium die Instrumente stimmte, war die Annahme, versehentlich unter den Künstlern zu sitzen, nicht zu halten, und Judejahn wunderte sich über die Vornehmheit der Veranstaltung. Dem kleinen Gottlieb imponierte es; er fühlte sich eingeschüchtert. Aber Judejahn ließ sich nicht einschüchtern, er drückte sich noch breiter in den Sessel und sah sich herausfordernd im Saal um. Wie schon einmal zur Korsostunde auf der Via Veneto hatte er das Gefühl, unter verschlagenen Juden und heimatlosen Schiebern zu sitzen. Er dachte: Pack und Laffen. Er erkannte die neue Gesellschaft, die neue Gesellschaft des italienischen Verrätervolkes, die Schicht, die nach dem schmählichen Treubruch an Mussolini zur Macht gekommen war. Und vor diesen Leuten, die ins Zuchthaus gehörten, ins Konzentrationslager und in die Gaskammer, würde Siegfried Pfaffrath fiedeln! Judejahn suchte den Neffen auf dem Podium, aber er entdeckte ihn nicht. Vielleicht trat Siegfried erst später auf, die ersten Fiedler kamen immer zu spät; sie waren eine anmaßende weibische Bande; was hier fehlte was Disziplin. Judejahn erkannte es gleich. Im Grunde ließ er nur Militärmusik gelten. Warum spielten sie nicht einen flotten Marsch, statt das Publikum mit ihrer Stimmerei anzuöden? Er sah sich weiter um, und da entdeckte er in der einzigen Loge des Saales seinen Sohn Adolf, und neben Adolf saß eine Frau, die Judejahn beeindruckte. Hatte Adolf dieser Frau das Geld gegeben, das er ihm in die betenden Hände gesteckt hatte? War sie seine Geliebte? Oder wurde er von ihr ausgehalten? Er hatte diese Liebhaberrolle dem Pfaffen nicht zugetraut. Es verwirrte ihn.

Es verwirrte auch Dietrich, Adolf in der Loge zu sehen. Wie kam er zu diesem Platz? Hatte die Kirche ihm den Platz angewiesen? Wollte sie Adolf seines Namens wegen herausstellen? Als großen Überläufer, als wichtigen Bekehrten? Hatte sie Besonderes mit ihm vor? Am Ende war Adolf klug und würde wirklich Bischof werden — bis auf weiteres ein mächtiger Mann. Wie sollte man sich zu ihm stellen? Und wer war die Frau bei ihm in der Loge? Dietrich konnte sie von seinem Sitz aus nicht deutlich genug sehen. Auch die

Eltern konnten sie nicht deutlich genug sehen. Gehörte sie zu Adolf? Und wo war Siegfried? Hätte er Auskunft geben können? Lauter verwirrende Fragen.

Verwirrende Fragen. Ilse Kürenberg hatte, als sie sich setzte, dem Priester in ihrer Loge freundlich zugenickt, und danach beunruhigte sie sein Gesicht, es war ein Alptraumgesicht, sie wußte nicht warum, aber es war ein Gesicht aus schrecklichen Träumen. Sie dachte: Er sieht wie ein Geißler aus, wie ein Flagellant. Sie sah ihn sich peitschen. Sie dachte: Peitscht er auch andere, peitscht er die Ketzer? Aber das konnte doch wohl nicht so sein, und auch die Juden würde der Priester nicht peitschen. Und dann dachte sie: Vielleicht ist er ein Mystiker. Und dann: Er ist ein katholischer Geistlicher, aber er sieht wie der rebellierende Luther aus.

Doch als die Musik einsetzte, wußte sie, daß er wirklich ein Mystiker war, ein deutscher Priester und ein deutscher Mystiker, denn auch in Siegfrieds Symphonie war trotz aller Modernität ein mystisches Drängen, eine mystische Weltempfindung, von Kürenberg lateinisch gebändigt, aber Ilse Kürenberg ergründete jetzt, warum ihr die Urkomposition bei aller Klarheit der Wiedergabe unsympathisch blieb. Es war zu viel Tod in diesen Klängen, und ein Tod ohne den heiteren Todesreigen auf antiken Sarkophagen. Zuweilen bemühte sich die Musik um diese Sinnenfreude der alten Grabmale, aber dann hatte Siegfried falsche Noten geschrieben, hatte sich in den Tönen vergriffen, sie wurden trotz Kürenbergs kühler Konduktion grell und maßlos, die Musik verkrampfte sich, sie schrie, das war Todesangst, das war nordischer Totentanz, eine Pestprozession, und schließlich verschmolzen die Passagen zu einer Nebelwand. Es war kompositorisch nicht einmal mißlungen, es war in seiner Art begabt, Ilse Kürenberg hatte ein feines Gehör, die Musik erregte sie, aber es war Nebelunheimlichkeit darin, die perverse Hingabe an den Tod, die ihr widerstrebte, ihr gräßlich war und sie widerwillig erregte.

Wie langweilig war doch die Musik! War es überhaupt Musik, oder stimmten sie noch immer und nun unter der Leitung des Kapellmeisters die Instrumente? Und war es schon das richtige Stück? Siegfried trat nicht auf. Hatte er abgesagt? Judejahn fühlte sich enttäuscht. Er war um einen Spaß gebracht. Hunger grimmte in seinem Magen, Durst trocknete die Zunge, aber der kleine Gottlieb traute sich nicht, aufzustehen und zu gehen. Er war gelähmt. Die Geräusche des Orchesters paralysierten ihn. Judejahn konnte bei diesen Klängen nicht denken, er konnte nicht überlegen, wer die Frau bei Adolf war, er konnte nicht klären, ob er mit Laura schlafen möchte oder lieber mit dieser Frau in der Loge. Sie entsetzten sich. Sie waren enttäuscht. Die Musik war anders als alle Musik, die sie kannten. Sie entfernte sich von aller Vorstellung, die Pfaffraths von Musik hatten. Sie entfernte sich sogar von der Vorstellung, die sich Pfaffraths von der Musik ihres Sohnes gemacht hatten. Aber hatten sie sich überhaupt etwas vorgestellt? Und wenn sie sich etwas vorgestellt hatten, was hatten sie erwartet? Beethovens zu oft abgestaubte Totenmaske über dem Zwölf-Röhren-Apparat in der Musikecke des Wohnzimmers oder Wagners bedeutenden Barettträger und sichtbar vom Genius geküßt? Das Ehepaar Pfaffrath vermißte den Edelklang, den hohen erhabenen Ton oder die eingängige Harmonie, sie suchten den wohligen Fluß der Melodie, sie horchten vergebens nach dem ihnen, wie sie meinten, verständlichen Sphärengesang aus höherer Region, in der sie zwar nicht Wohnrecht hatten und auch gar nicht beheimatet sein wollten, die sie sich aber wie einen optimistischen Himmel, eine rosa Kuppel über dem grauen Erdkreis dachten, unten auf der Erde hatte man nüchtern vernünftig und, wenn es sein mußte, hart und Rechnung tragend allem menschlich-unmenschlich Gemeinen zu leben, doch um so erhabener hatte der rosa Überbau über dem Menschlich-Allzumenschlichen zu schweben, Pfaffraths glaubten an den Konditortempel der Kunst, aus süßer Masse allegorisch ideal geformt, er war ihnen, so meinten und heuchelten sie noch vor sich selbst, Bedürfnis, das sie gern »Begeisterung für alles Schöne« nannten, und Musik war ein Aufruf zu gebildetem Schöngefühl und zufriedenem Dösen, doch Siegfrieds Töne machten sie frösteln, sie empfanden Unbehagen, es war, als wehe Eishauch sie an, und dann

517

klang es gar wie Verhöhnung ihrer deutschbürgerlichen Sitte,
sie meinten Jazz-Rhythmen zu erkennen, einen Urwald ihrer
Einbildung, einen Negerkral voll Entblößung und Gier, und
dieser Dschungel entarteten Getöses wurde wieder abgelöst
von einfach langweiligen Stellen, von wahrhaft eintönigen
Partien disharmonischer Notenreihen. Gefiel dieser Miß-
klang? Nahm man ihn hin? Furchtsam wie Mäuse sahen
sie sich um und fürchteten Skandal und Aufruhr, ein Schmä-
hen ihres zu Hause, wie sie überzeugt sein konnten, so angesehenen Namens. Aber noch saß in ihrer Nähe jedermann
gesittet da, die Leute machten das übliche Konzertgesicht
nachdenklichen Musikgenusses, und einige mimten sogar Versunkenheit. Dietrich glaubte eine Rechnung in der Musik
seines Bruders zu entdecken, einen Taschenspielertrick oder
eine mathematische Gleichung, hinter deren Geheimnis er
aber nicht kam; diese Musik war dem Komponisten nicht
zugeflogen, wie die schönen und großen Klänge Beethoven
und Wagner wohl zugeflogen waren, diese Musik war gemacht, sie war ein raffinierter Schwindel, es war Überlegung in den Dissonanzen, und das beunruhigte Dietrich —
vielleicht war Siegfried kein Narr, vielleicht war er gefährlich und am Beginn einer großen Laufbahn. Dietrich flüsterte den Eltern zu: »Er ist ein Neutöner!« Das war schmähend
gemeint, doch sollte man es auch so verstehen, wie objektiv
Dietrich doch sei, wie sachlich urteilend und wie unterrichtet
auch auf diesem Gebiet. Doch veranlaßte die Bemerkung irgendeinen perversen Ausländer in merkwürdig körperengem
Smoking und mit provozierendem Ziegenbart unter dem
Kinn zu einem strafenden »Pst!«.
Adolf gefiel die Musik des Vetters nicht. Sie stimmte ihn
traurig, ja, sie quälte ihn; aber er versuchte, sie zu verstehen.
Er versuchte, Siegfried zu begreifen. Was wollte Siegfried
mit dieser Symphonie sagen? Was drückte er aus? Adolf
meinte, Gegensätzliches, wohltuenden Schmerz, lustige Verzweiflung, mutige Angst, süße Bitternis, Flucht und Verurteilung der Flucht, traurige Scherze, kranke Liebe und eine
mit üppigen Blumentöpfen bestellte Wüste, das geschmückte
Sandfeld der Ironie. War diese Musik Gott feindlich? Sie war

518

es wohl nicht. Es war auch Erinnerung an eine Zeit vor aller Schuld in den Klängen, an die Schönheit und den Frieden des Paradieses und Trauer um den in die Welt gesetzten Tod, es war viel Verlangen nach Freundlichkeit in den Noten, kein Lied an die Freude zwar, kein Panegyrikus, aber doch Sehnsucht nach Freude und Schöpfungslob. Manchmal glaubte Adolf, sich selbst in den Tönen zu erkennen. Es war ihm, als würde ihm in einem zerbrochenen Spiegel die Kindheit reflektiert. Auch die Ordensburg war in der Musik, die Sportwiese, der Wald, die Sonnenaufundontergänge und die Träume in den Schlafsälen. Aber dann wieder stießen Zynismus, Unglaube, eine Verzweiflung, mit der narzißtisch kokettiert wurde, und anarchisches Treiben Adolf von den Klängen ab. Die Kirche würde diese Musik nicht billigen; sie wäre auf dem Konzil zu Trient nicht als vorbildlich anerkannt worden. Durfte Adolf, der Diakon, die Musik seines Vetters billigen? Er billigte sie nicht. Mußte er sie verdammen? Er verdammte sie nicht. Es war nicht Gott, der aus diesen Klängen sprach, es war ein Ringender, und so war es am Ende vielleicht doch Gott in einem seiner unbegreiflichen Selbstgespräche, die Christi Kirche verwirren.

Sie pfiffen, ich hörte sie pfeifen, ich hatte mich zur Tür der Galerie geschlichen, ich verharrte im äußersten Hintergrund, ein Bettler am Kirchentor, ein Bettler bei meiner Musik, sie pfiffen, es überraschte mich nicht, sie pfiffen auf allerlei Schlüsseln und nach Gassenjungenweise, die Finger breit in den Mund gesteckt, sie pfiffen, meine Studenten, meine Arbeiter, meine jungen gefährdeten Atomforscher, meine hochmütigen armen Mädchen, ich hatte es erwartet, die jungen Priester pfiffen nicht, aber ich meine, sie hätten auch pfeifen sollen. Ich hatte von reiner Schöpfung geträumt, aber ich war verführt worden, in die Erdkämpfe einzugreifen. Ich weiß nicht, ob reine Schöpfung möglich ist, die unbefleckte Empfängnis aus dem reinen Nichts, ich träume von ihr, und vielleicht ist es Hochmut und Wahn und die Vermessenheit des Ikarus, und meine Flügel sind schon vor dem Flug gebrochen. Ikarus muß arrogant sein. Es ist die Arroganz der

Physiker in den Laboratorien, ihre phantasielose Klugheit zertrümmert die natürliche Welt, und Kürenberg will mich zu jeder Sprengung anregen, weil sein Hirn die schönen Formeln begeistern, weil er die erhabenen Gesetze erfaßt, nach denen die Zertrümmerung geschieht. Ich begreife die Gesetze nicht und kann die Formeln nicht lesen. Wahrscheinlich bin ich dumm. Wie könnte ich etwas errechnen, und wem sollte ich die Rechnung präsentieren? Ich hoffe immer noch, ohne zu rechnen zur Summe zu kommen, auf einem unbegreiflichen Weg, der Kürenberg wohl zuwider wäre und den er unsauber und töricht fände. Sie pfiffen, aber unten im Saal klatschten sie nun, sie riefen mich, und die schrillen Pfiffe der Galerie schienen sie im Parkett nur zu nachdrücklicherem Beifall anzuregen. Jetzt wäre der Augenblick gekommen, mich im Frack zu zeigen. Ich hätte mich zeigen müssen. Kürenberg reichte immer wieder dem ersten Geiger dankend die Hand, deutete auf das Orchester, wies in die Kulisse, aus der ich nicht erschien, und tat sonst allerlei, um den Applaus von sich abzulenken, ihn zu besänftigen, ohne ihn zu unterbinden, und mit großen Gesten bedauerte er das unbegreifliche Fernbleiben des Tonsetzers. Eines der armen hochmütigen Mädchen neben mir sagte: »Ich könnte ihm in die Fresse spucken.« Sie meinte, sie möchte mir in das Gesicht spucken, mir, dem Komponisten. Ich verstand sie; sie sprach englisch. Und was wollten die unten mit mir tun, die Herren im Frack, die Damen in den teuren Kleidern, die Kritiker, die Verleger, die Manager, was hatten sie mit mir vor, wollten sie mich bekränzen, oder wollten auch sie mich anspucken?

Am lautesten aber klatschte in seltsame Problematik versetzt Judejahn. Seine schweren Hände arbeiteten wie Dampfhämmer. Viel lieber hätte er gebrüllt, geschimpft und alle, die im Saal und auf dem Podium waren, strammstehen oder verhaften lassen. Er hätte Siegfried an den Sockel der Palestrinabüste gestellt; er hätte gern Siegfried und den Kapellmeister dreißig Kniebeugen machen lassen. Aber der kleine Gottlieb traute sich nicht, allein in der Frackgesellschaft, traute sich Judejahn nicht, zu brüllen, zu schimpfen, das Strammstehen und die dreißig Kniebeugen zu befehlen, und als die Galerie zu pfeifen begann, da fand er dies ein ungehöriges Benehmen gegen die Herrschaften im Parkett, gegen die Reichen, gegen die im Licht Sitzenden, die er verachtete und von alters her beneidete und deren empörende Kunstansicht und Lebensauffassung er nun mit dem Dampfhammerschlag seiner Handflächen unterstützte.

So sah ihn Adolf; er sah seinen Vater aus seiner Loge, er sah ihn erregt und klatschend, während er selber nicht wußte, ob er Zustimmung äußern sollte, die er nicht ganz empfand, und ob er in geistlicher Tracht überhaupt Beifall bekunden durfte bei einer so extremen und fragwürdigen Musik. Die Dame, die neben Adolf saß, hielt die Hände ruhig im Schoß; vielleicht würde die Dame es als Herausforderung empfinden, wenn der Priester neben ihr zu den Claqueren überging. Doch würde Adolf sich den mit Geräuschen Dankenden angeschlossen haben, wenn Siegfried sich auf dem Podium gezeigt hätte, denn Siegfried war Dank zu sagen, weil er Gottes Unruhe offenbart hatte, und es sprach sehr für Siegfried, daß er sich nun nicht ins Rampenlicht stellte und den Beifall einheimste. Wie kam es aber, daß Judejahn das Konzert besucht hatte, wie kam es, daß er dieser Musik zustimmte? Hatte Judejahn die Sprache dieser Klänge verstanden? Hatten die Töne ihn bewegt, hatten sie ihn erfreut? Verstanden sich Siegfried und Judejahn plötzlich in der Welt der Musik? Adolf ahnte nichts von der Existenz des kleinen Gottlieb in seinem Vater, und so konnte er Judejahns Verhalten nicht enträtseln und nur mißdeuten.

Sie konnten den Beifall sich nicht erklären, sie hörten die Pfiffe der Galerie, die den Applaus im Saal nur noch anstachelten, sie vernahmen fremdländische Rufe, die den Namen Pfaffrath seltsam konsonantenreich aussprachen, es mußte eine entartete, erschreckend verdorbene und blind in den eigenen Untergang taumelnde Gesellschaft sein, die nun ihres Sohnes Musik feierte, aber dieser nahe bevorstehende Untergang der römischen Oberschicht beunruhigte Pfaffraths nicht, er stärkte im Gegenteil ihre Überheblichkeit, denn in dem Glauben, gute Deutsche zu sein, erbgesund und nicht

ansprechbar für vernegerte Klänge, meinten sie im Fall des
Morschen in Europa einen Vorteil für die eigene Nation zu
sehen, die bald wieder hegemonisch sein würde, und so, die
Binde der nationalen Torheit vor den Augen töricht getröstet,
die Qual dieses Musikhörens und die Furcht vor einem Skandal um den geachteten Familiennamen vorläufig gebannt
sehend, rührten nun auch Pfaffraths die Hände, um den
Sohn und Bruder zu feiern. Dietrich begriff nicht, warum
Siegfried, den man rief, sich nicht zeigte. Und wie alles, was
er nicht verstand, beunruhigte es ihn. Was steckte hinter diesem Verstecken? War es Feigheit oder war es schon Hochmut? Dietrich wollte es ergründen, und er schlug vor, Siegfried in den Künstlerräumen aufzusuchen.
Ich war langsam die Treppe von der Galerie hinunterge-
gangen. Ich wußte, Kürenberg würde mir nun böse sein. Er
würde mir böse sein, weil ich die Konvention, die den Kunst-
betrieb erhielt, wieder mißachtet und mich vor dem Publikum
nicht verneigt hatte. Auch ohne den Frack zu tragen, hätte
ich mich auf das Podium stellen müssen. Aber ich mochte mich
nicht zeigen. Mir war der Beifall zuwider. Ich gab nichts auf
die Stimmung des Saales. Ich fühlte mich dem pfeifenden
Olymp verbunden; doch auch die dort saßen, waren keine
Götter.
Kürenberg hockte erschöpft in einem roten Plüschsessel. Die
Blitze der Photographen umzuckten ihn. Er machte mir keine
Vorwürfe. Er gratulierte mir. Und ich dankte und gratulierte
ihm und sagte, es sei sein Erfolg, und es war auch sein Erfolg,
und er wehrte meinen Dank ab, und irgend etwas stimmte
da nicht, wie wir uns wechselseitig gegen des anderen Schmeichelei stemmten, und doch war es sein Sieg, er hatte mit
meiner Musik brilliert, aber ihm genügte das Bewußtsein,
mit neuen Zusammenstellungen der beschränkten Tönezahl
experimentiert zu haben, er hatte eine von Milliarden Möglichkeiten vorgeführt und die Musik als sich immer weiter
entwickelnde und weiter unter uns lebende Kraft gezeigt,
und nun galt es, neue Versuche zu wagen zu neuen Tonfolgen
vorzustoßen. Er hatte recht. Warum dachte ich nicht an
neue Kompositionen? War ich ausgebrannt? Ich weiß es

nicht. Ich war traurig. Ich wäre gern zu meinem Brunnen gegangen, zu meiner Fontana di Trevi; ich hätte gern auf dem Brunnenrand gesessen und den eilenden törichten Touristen und den geldgierigen schönen Knaben zugesehen.

Ilse Kürenberg kam, und auch sie gratulierte mir. Aber ihre Hand, die sie mir reichte, war kalt. Ich sah in Ilse Kürenberg wieder die nüchterne skeptische Muse der Musik unserer Tage, und ich hatte die Stimme der Muse nicht gewonnen. Ich wollte ihr dafür danken, daß ich ihre Stimme nicht gewonnen hatte, aber ich wußte nicht, was für Worte ich ihr sagen sollte, damit sie auch verstehen würde, wie ich es meinte. Doch während ich noch die Worte suchte, meine Empfindung auszudrücken, sah ich eine solche Ablehnung in ihrem Gesicht, daß es mich erschreckte. Dann aber erkannte ich, daß sie nicht mich mit diesem Entsetzen ansah, sondern daß sie hinter mich blickte, und als ich mich umdrehte, um ihren Schrecken zu begreifen, sah ich meine Eltern auf mich zukommen, sah ich meinen Bruder Dietrich auf mich zukommen, und hinter ihnen stand und lähmte mich das Schreckbild meiner Jugend, der von den Toten zurückgekommene Onkel Judejahn, der mich angrinste, als wolle er sagen, er sei nun wiederauferstanden und ich müsse mich mit ihm abfinden, die alte Macht sei wieder da, und an der Tür wartete Adolf verstörten Gesichtes. Es war ein Pfaffrath-Judejahnscher Familientag, der sich hier versammelte, und mir war, als sähe ich die Gorgonen. Ich schämte mich. Ich schämte mich meiner Familie, und ich schämte mich auch, weil ich mich meiner Familie schämte, und es war mir wie einem Hund zumute, den die Hundefänger mit ihren Netzen umstellt haben. Meine Freiheit war bedroht. Mein Vater und meine Mutter gratulierten mir, und sie bedrohten meine Freiheit. Sie sprachen mit mir, aber ich verstand nicht, was sie sagten; ich wußte nur, daß meine Freiheit bedroht war. Mein Bruder Dietrich meinte, ich hätte es nun wohl geschafft, und er zeigte einen verkniffenen Mund. Auch er bedrohte meine Freiheit. Und dann sah ich, wie mein Vater Kürenberg anredete und ihn wie einen guten alten Bekannten begrüßte. Er erinnerte Kürenberg an das Theater unserer Stadt;

er sprach von dem Theaterorchester, von den Abonnements-
Konzerten und von der guten Zeit von neunzehnhundertdreiunddreißig.

Ilse Kürenberg kannte sie nicht, und doch kannte sie diese
Leute, und es war ihr, als bräche eine Mauer auf, hinter der
man Gespenster eingemauert hatte. Sie hatte sie nie wieder
sehen wollen; sie wollte sich an die Gespenster nicht erinnern,
und nun waren die Gespenster da, waren durch die Mauer
gebrochen, Feuerkobolde eines brennenden Hauses, die Mord-
lemuren eines alten Vaters. Sie ahnte, daß dies Siegfrieds
Familie war, Leute aus ihrer Stadt, die sie vergessen hatte,
Nazis aus ihrem Heimatort, an den sie nicht denken wollte.
Und sie ahnte auch, wer Judejahn war, der Mann im Hintergrund, der Mann der Endlösung, der sie mit entkleidenden
Blicken ansah. Sie dachte: Ich will nicht so träumen. Und sie
dachte: Das ist diese Symphonie, die mir unsympathisch war,
das ist der Priester an der Tür, ein germanischer Mystiker,
vielleicht ein Heiliger, aber wehe mir, wenn er kein Heiliger
ist, oder wehe mir, wenn er abtrünnig wird. Und sie dachte:
Der mit Kürenberg spricht, das ist Siegfrieds Vater, der Oberbürgermeister unserer Stadt, er war Oberpräsident der Provinz, als wir ihn um Verschonung baten, und er sagte, er
sei Oberpräsident, aber er sei nicht zuständig. Sie dachte:
Er hat vielleicht seine Hemden in meines Vaters Kaufhaus
gekauft, er hat das erste Spielzeug für seine Kinder bei meinem Vater gekauft, und als das Kaufhaus meines Vaters
brannte und Hemden und Spielzeug der Straße zufielen, hat
er es gutgeheißen, und als man meinen Vater ermordete, hat
er es in die Akten aufgenommen und gutgeheißen. Und
Friedrich Wilhelm Pfaffrath, an den Ilse Kürenberg als an
einen Helfer und Förderer der Brandstiftung und des Mor-
des dachte, freute sich, mit Kürenberg, der höflich sachliche
Antwort gab, über seine Gemeinde sprechen zu können, und
er machte dem Dirigenten das Angebot eines rühmlichen
Gastspiels im alten, zwar noch zerstörten, aber bald wieder-
hergestellten Theater, und er fühlte sich beleidigt und dachte,
so sind sie, winselnd oder hochnäsig, als die geborene Aufhäuser, ohne Pfaffrath zu beachten, Kürenberg bat, nun mit

ihr fortzugehen. Der Dirigent schaute sich nach Siegfried um, den er zu einem späten Imbiß einladen wollte, aber Siegfried war aus dem Zimmer verschwunden.

Sie wateten durch Papier; das Papier lag auf der Piazza del Popolo, es lag vor den Kirchen Santa Maria dei Miracoli, Santa Maria del Popolo, Santa Maria di Montesanto, die drei Marien bewachten den Platz, das Papier lag um den ägyptischen Obelisken, den Augustus der Sonne und Sixtus V. den himmlischen Heerscharen geweiht hatte, die himmlischen Heerscharen bewachten den Platz, das Papier lag vor dem Tor, durch das Goethe nach Rom gekommen war, auch Goethe war ein Heiliger des Platzes, das Papier lag im Bogenlampenschein wie Winter im Mondlicht. Es hatte auf der Piazza del Popolo eine Kundgebung stattgefunden, und die Flugblätter, die den Menschen einen neuen Frühling versprachen, dem ein nie gekannter Sommer folgen sollte, die vielberufene Goldene Zeit, die Flugblätter waren wie die Herbstblätter der Bäume zu Boden gefallen, und die kühnen Parolen kommenden Glücks hatten sich in Dreck verwandelt, in eine schmutzige Erddecke, die schmutzigem Schnee glich, einem grauweißen Winterkleid.
Das Papier raschelte unter dem Wehen seines Priesterrocks, und ich sagte ihm, daß wir über ein Feld der Verheißungen gingen. Ich sagte ihm, daß die Eschatologien mir vorkämen wie ein Bündel Heu, das an einer Stange einem Esel vorgehalten wird, damit er den Wagen weiterzieht. »Aber die Menschheit braucht die Ausrichtung auf ein Fernes und Höheres«, sagte Adolf, »denke an die Kraft, die der anziehende Himmel im Mittelalter den Menschen gab.« »Ja«, sagte ich, »der Esel zog den Wagen. Er meinte, das Gefährt himmelwärts zu ziehen, und bald würde das Paradies kommen, ohne Eselslast, mit ewig grüner Weide und den Raubtieren als freundlichen Spielgefährten. Aber allmählich merkte der Esel, daß der Himmel nicht näher kam, er wurde müde, und das Heu der Religion lockte ihn nicht mehr, tapfer voranzuschreiten. Und damit der Wagen nicht stehenbleibe, hat man den Hunger des Esels auf ein irdisches Paradies

gelenkt, auf einen Sozialpark, in dem alle Esel die gleichen
Rechte haben werden, in dem die Peitsche abgeschafft, die
Last geringer, die Versorgung besser wird, aber auch der Weg
zu diesem Garten Eden ist lang, das Ziel rückt nicht näher,
und der Esel wird wieder bockig. Zum Glück hat man ihm
immer Scheuklappen angelegt, damit er nicht merkt, daß es
nie voran, sondern immer im Kreis geht, daß er keinen Wagen, sondern ein Karussell bewegt, und vielleicht sind wir
eine Belustigung auf einem Festplatz der Götter, und die
Götter haben nach ihrem Fest vergessen, das Karussell abzu-
bauen, und der Esel dreht es noch immer, nur die Götter
erinnern sich nicht mehr an uns.« Er sagte: »Dann lebst du
in einer sinnlosen Welt.« Ich sagte: »Ja. Aber muß denn
alles einen Sinn haben?« Er sagte: »Wenn ich wie du däch-
te, würde ich mich umbringen.« Ich rief: »Wozu? Ich werde
früh genug tot sein, und sei sicher, ich halte nicht viel von
der Bewegung des Lebens, aber mich graust vor dem Nichtsein des Todes. Warum sollte ich mich umbringen? Ja, wenn
ich, wie du, den Selbstmord für eine Sünde hielte, dann gäbe
es ein Nachher! Die wirkliche Versuchung, dieser Welt zu
entfliehen, ist der Glaube an ein Jenseits. Wenn ich nicht
an den Himmel und nicht an die Hölle glaube, dann muß ich
versuchen, hier etwas Glück, hier etwas Freude zu finden,
hier muß ich Schönheit und Lust suchen. Es gibt keinen anderen Ort für mich, keine andere Zeit. Hier und heute ist
meine einzige Möglichkeit. Und die Versuchung, mich umzu-
bringen, ist dann nur eine Falle, die man mir hingestellt hat.
Aber wer hat sie mir hingestellt? Wenn die Falle da ist, ist
auch der Fallensteller nah. Da beginnt der Zweifel. Der Zweifel des Ungläubigen an seinem Unglauben ist mindestens so
schrecklich wie der Zweifel des Gläubigen. Und wir zweifeln
alle. Sage nicht, daß du nicht zweifelst. Du lügst. Im Käfig
der unseren Sinnen erreichbaren drei Dimensionen kann es
nur Zweifler geben. Wer fühlt nicht, daß eine Wand da ist,
ich nenne dieses Etwas oder dieses Nichts eine Wand, es ist
ein unzulänglicher Ausdruck für etwas, das uns von einer
uns nicht zugänglichen Region trennt, die ganz nahe sein
mag, neben uns, vielleicht gar in uns, und würden wir eine

Pforte zu diesem Bereich finden, einen Spalt in der Wand, sähen wir uns und unser Leben anders. Vielleicht wäre es schrecklich. Vielleicht könnten wir es nicht ertragen. Es ist die Sage, daß man zu Stein wird, wenn man die Wahrheit sieht. Ich möchte das entschleierte Bild sehen, selbst wenn ich zur Säule erstarre. Aber vielleicht wäre auch dies noch nicht die Wahrheit, und hinter dem Bild, das mich erstarren ließ, kämen andere Bilder, andere Schleier, noch unbegreiflichere, noch unzugänglichere, vielleicht noch furchtbarere, und ich wäre ein Stein geworden und hätte doch nichts gesehen. Etwas ist für uns unsichtbar neben der Welt und dem Leben. Aber was ist es?« »Du suchst Gott nicht in seinem Haus, du suchst ihn in Sackgassen«, sagte Adolf. »Wenn er ist, wohnt Gott auch in Sackgassen«, sagte ich.

Wir gingen neben der alten Stadtmauer her durch die Viale del Muro Torot. Auf dem Pincio wehte Wind, und aus dem Garten der Villa Medici drang süßer Duft. Macht hatte diese Gärten geschaffen, Macht die Villen, Macht die Paläste, Macht die Stadt gebaut, Macht die Mauer errichtet, Macht hatte die Schätze herbeigeholt, Macht die Kunst angeregt, die Stadt war schön, ich war glücklich, an ihrer alten Mauer entlangzugehen, aber die Macht war für die Mitlebenden stets schrecklich, war Machtmißbrauch, war Gewalt, war Unterdrückung, war Krieg, war Brandstiftung und Meuchelmord, Rom war auf Erschlagenen aufgebaut, selbst die Kirchen standen auf blutbesudelter Erde, kein Tempel, keine Basilika, kein Dom war ohne vergossenes Blut zu denken. Aber Rom ist herrlich, die Tempel sind herrlich; wir bewundern die Hinterlassenschaft der Macht, wir lieben sie, wenn die Machthaber tot sind.

Es gehörte sich nicht. Er war verschwunden. Er hatte sich nicht von ihnen verabschiedet. Er war gegangen, ohne ein Wort zu sagen, und sie waren doch gekommen und hatten ihm gratuliert, obwohl seine Musik von schlechter Gesinnung sprach und sie befremdet hatte; sie hatten ihm dennoch gratuliert, gratuliert, daß er in Rom ein Publikum gefunden hatte, ein nicht ernst zu nehmendes zwar von Spreu im Welt-

wind, von heimatlosen Modenarren, in keiner Kultur ver-
wurzelt, aber sie hatten ihm dennoch gratuliert und hatten
ihm auch vergeben wollen, vergeben wollen, daß er nach seiner Gefangenschaft in England sich ihnen entzogen hatte,
daß er aus der Sippe ausgebrochen war und offenbar mit den
Feinden lebte. Es war unrecht von ihm gewesen zu gehen,
und Adolf war mit ihm gegangen, die abtrünnigen Söhne
waren wieder davongelaufen, und Kürenberg hatte kurz gegrüßt und war mit seiner Jüdin, der Aufhäusertochter, fortgegangen, und dann hatten sich auch die Journalisten entfernt, die Photographen mit ihren Blitzen, das Gewimmel
von Leuten, merkwürdig gekleidet und sonderbar zweifel-
haften Gehabens, das ganze Gesocks, wie Friedrich Wilhelm
Pfaffrath jiddisch-antisemitisch jargonierte, und auf einmal
standen sie allein im Künstlerzimmer des römischen Kon-
zertbaus, Pfaffrath mit seiner Frau und seinem strebsamen
Sohn Dietrich und Schwager Judejahn, sie standen allein
unter roten Plüschsesseln und vor Wänden, an denen goldene
Kränze hingen, verblichene Schleifen erloschenen italienischen Ruhmes und Bilder toter Tonkünstler mit neckisch
gezwirbelten Bärten, auch schmückte die Mauer eine a fresco
gemalte Frau, eine üppige Gestalt in Kalkfarben, die Harmonie, wie sie das Getöse der Winde bändigt. Sie standen
seltsam beziehungslos in diesem Raum, der nun gespenstisch
wirkte oder sie zu Gespenstern machte. Hatte das Leben sie
aufgegeben, weil die Jugend sich ihnen entzog und nur
Dietrich verkniffenen Mundes bei ihnen ausharrte, ein Bur-
schenschaftler noch in der Aktivitas, doch schon im Vorsatz
ein Staatsbeamter, der nicht dem Staat dienen, sondern ihn
beherrschen wollte?
Judejahn hatte Ilse Kürenberg, die Frau aus der Loge, die
Frau, die neben Adolf gesessen und seine Neugier erregt
hatte, obszön angestarrt. Er hatte sich die sexuelle Gemeinschaft ausgemalt, in der sie mit seinem Sohn lebte, unzüch-
tig unter dem Pfaffenrock. Nun, als sie gegangen war, fragte
er Pfaffrath, ob er sie kenne, und als er vernahm, sie sei die
Tochter des alten Aufhäuser, des Warenhausjuden, den man
liquidiert hatte, da bedauerte er, daß sie ihm entkommen

war; seinen Händen, seinen Stiefeln, seiner Pistole war sie
entwischt, man hatte die Grenzen zu spät gesperrt, man
war wie immer zu großmütig gewesen, man hatte die Bazillen sich in Europa ausbreiten lassen, und das deutsche
Europa war an ihnen gestorben, eine Jüdin hatte neben
Adolf gesessen, eine deutsche Jüdin schlief mit seinem Sohn,
der ein römischer Priester war, es erregte Judejahn, es erregte ihn, wie den Leser der Gerichtszeitung der Blutschande-
prozeß entrüstet und aufregt; Judejahn bedauerte nicht, getötet zu haben, er hatte zu wenig getötet, das blieb seine
Schuld, aber der Wirbel, den man nachher um sein bißchen
Töten gemacht hatte, beschäftigte ihn doch, schmeichelte und
ärgerte ihn, wie ein anrüchiger Ruhm eben schmeichelt und
ärgert, und band Judejahn dergestalt an seine Opfer, daß
der Gedanke an die mißlungene Endlösung der Judenfrage,
der Gedanke an die von ihm befohlenen Massenerschießun-
gen, die Erinnerung an die Photographien nackter Frauen
vor dem Leichengraben nun perverse Vorstellungen in ihm
weckten, es war Sünde, sich mit Jüdinnen zu vermischen, es
war Artur Dinters vom kleinen Gottlieb verschlungene *Sünde
wider das Blut,* aber der Gedanke an die Sünde reizte die
Hoden, regte die Samenzellen an, doch die Verbindung blieb
unerlaubt, es sei denn, dies war ein Traum in einem roten
Nebel, der ihm dann vor die Augen trat, war keine klare
Überlegung, war ein Wachschlafgedanke, man zerschlug
nach vollzogenem Samenopfer, nach den befreienden, Dumpfes lösenden Stößen des Lusthasses die Muschel aus beschnit-
tener Zeugung, das unreine Gefäß unbegreiflicher Verführung und kabalistischer Magie, welches das kostbare Gen des
Ariers erlistet hatte.
Judejahn dachte an Laura. Auch sie konnte eine Jüdin sein,
er wußte es nicht genau, er war mit ihr zur Nacht verabredet, doch lieber hätte er Ilse Kürenberg-Aufhäuser in der
Nacht getroffen, er malte sich die Begegnung in einer einsamen Straße aus, auf einem Trümmerfeld vor einem dunklen Graben, bei vollem Mond, und Schweiß stand auf seiner
Stirn. Pfaffraths hatten sich in die roten Plüschsessel gesetzt.
Die Fahrt nach dem Schlachtfeld von Cassino, ein erhebendes

Erlebnis, Siegfrieds Konzert, ein niederdrückendes und verwirrendes Geschehen, hatten sie ermüdet. Es saß sich gut in
den altmodischen Stühlen, auch Judejahn setzte sich breit in
die Polster, und vor der Harmonie mit ihren Winden, vor
den toten italienischen Musikern, den verblichenen Ruhmes-
schleifen und goldenen Kränzen saßen sie wie im Salon ihrer
Eltern, wie im Weihnachtszimmer des Pfarrhauses, wie in
der guten Stube, aus der sie sich entfernt hatten, um in
Schützengräben, in Feld- und Waldlagern, Befehlsständen
und Wolfsschluchten, an Riesenschreibtischen und an pompösen Tafeln Macht zu erstreben, Macht zu üben und Macht
vorzustellen. Und Judejahn sprach nun, wie er sich die Heimkehr dachte, die Heimkehr nach Deutschland, und sie hörten
ihm aufmerksam zu, aber doch angestrengt und mit dem
Schlaf kämpfend. Judejahn wollte nach der Souveränitäts-
verleihung in Deutschland erscheinen, und Pfaffrath nickte,
dann habe es keine Gefahr mehr, keine deutsche Behörde
würde ein Nürnberger Urteil vollstrecken, und kein deutsches
Gericht würde Judejahn verdammen, und Judejahn sprach
von neuer Kampfzeit und neuer Bewegung und von der
Sammlung der Schar der Getreuen, und Pfaffrath, der Korrekte, erinnerte daran, daß Judejahn dann auch für geleistete
Staatsdienste und erfüllten Generalsrang Pension fordern
könne, ein Recht, das zu verfechten, ein möglicher Prozeß,
der zu gewinnen sei, es gehe hier um Treu und Glauben und
verbrieften Anspruch ans Vaterland, und der Staatsform, die
man bekämpfen wollte, durfte sowieso nichts geschenkt werden.
So durch schöne Aussichten angeregt, lud Judejahn sie noch
zu einem Umtrunk ein. Pfaffraths waren müde. Sie wären
am liebsten in den altmodischen Sesseln eingenickt, den Stühlen aus der guten Stube, und Friedrich Wilhelm Pfaffrath
war es, als säße sein Vater, der Pastor, bei ihnen und erzählte, wie oft, von Gravelotte und von Bismarck und vom
alten Kaiser und von der Reichsgründung in Versailles, dem
bedeutungsvollen tückischen Ort. Aber durften sie Judejahn,
der schon wieder den großen Mann spielte, widersprechen?
Sie folgten ihm, und er stellte sich breitbeinig vor das Kon-

zerthaus und pfiff. Er schrillte ein Signal, einen Takt der Wüstenhymne in die Nacht, sein schwarzer Wagen glitt heran, der Chauffeur, soldatisch straff und wie durch eine Teufelsdroge unermüdlich, sprang vom Volant und öffnete den Schlag. Aber Pfaffraths hatten ja ihren eigenen Wagen, das Oberbürgermeisterfahrzeug, hier abgestellt, und man beschloß, daß sie Judejahn folgen sollten. So fuhr Judejahn wie in alten Tagen des Glanzes durchs nächtliche Rom, zwar trillerten Sirenen nicht, zwar brauste kein Wach- und Schutzwagen voran, die Eskorte fehlte, aber Gefolgschaft war schon wieder hinter ihm. Er hatte ein Phantom belebt, das Phantom nationaler Größe, das Phantom rassischer Erhebung, das Phantom der Schmachvergeltung, und wieder behexte er sie. Wohin ging die Fahrt? Wohin? In die Nacht. In die Versuchung und wie jede Fahrt auf ein Ende zu. Er entschloß sich, den Kurs zur Via Veneto zu befehlen. Warum sollte er die Verwandten nicht in der Bar der lilabefrackten Kellner delektieren? Der Glanz des Lichtes und der Glanz der vielen Spiegel würde sie beeindrucken, der kleine Gottlieb wußte es, und Judejahn konnte derweilen, ohne daß sie es zu merken brauchten, sich schon auf Lauras schmale, von seinen Händen leicht zu umschließende Taille, sich schon auf der lächelnden Kassenschönheit zierliches, zu umhalsendes Hälschen freuen.

Siegfried hatte Adolf nach langem Stadtweg, Nacht-, Garten- und Mauergang, nach pfadlosen Pfadgesprächen, Sternenmelancholien und vergeblichen Annäherungen an das Unsichtbare in die Bar geführt. Er mochte diese Lokale nicht, ihn belustigten die Urninge, ihr weibisches Getue, ihr falsches Vogelgekreisch auf hohen Barhockern, ihre pfauengleiche Eitelkeit, ihre Lügen, ihre Eifersüchteleien, ihre endlosen verwickelten Affären, Siegfried war Päderast, er war keine Tante, die Zuneigung erwachsener Männer war ihm unangenehm, er liebte die herbe bittere Schönheit der Knaben, und seine Bewunderung galt etwas dreckigen von wilden Spielen zerschrammten Straßenjungen. Sie waren unerreichbar und unverletzlich, und deshalb enttäuschten sie nicht, sie waren ein Anblicksbegehren und eine Phantasieliebe, eine geistig ästhetische Hingabe an die Schönheit, ein aufregendes Gefühl voll Lust und Traurigkeit; doch Umarmungen wie die auf dem Badeschiff waren Geschehnisse blinder Torheit, waren freudlose Höllenfahrten, ein wahnsinniger Versuch, das Unberührbare zu berühren, die Tollheit, den Gott im Schmutz zu fassen, wofür Siegfried mit einer flüchtigen, schnell wieder vergehenden Euphorie beschenkt wurde. Zuweilen befreundete sich Siegfried mit Mädchen, die seinen Jungen ähnlich sahen, hierin kam ihm der Geschmack der Zeit entgegen, es gab viele liebliche Mädchen, die in langen Seiden- oder Leinenhosen busenlos und mit zerzausten Bubenhaaren durch die Welt strolchten, aber in ihren engen langen Hosen trugen sie das Organ der Mutterschaft, werkte ständig die biologische Alchimie, und Siegfried wollte sich nicht fortpflanzen. Der Gedanke, ein Leben zu verursachen, das unabsehbaren Begegnungen, Zufällen, Aktionen und Reaktionen ausgesetzt sein und durch Tat, Gedanke oder weitere Vermehrung seinerseits wieder noch in alle Zukunft wirken konnte, die Vorstellung, Vater eines Kindes zu sein, diese Herausforderung der Welt, entsetzte ihn wahrhaft und verdarb ihm den Umgang mit Mädchen, selbst dann, wenn sie Verhütungsmittel anwandten, die an sich schon peinlich eklig waren und peinlich eklig auf das zu Verhütende hinwiesen. Körperliche Zeugung schien Siegfried ein Verbrechen zu sein, was nicht für jedermann so war. Leichtsinn und Undenken entschuldigten, aber für ihn wäre es ein Verbrechen gewesen. Der Same befleckte die Schönheit, und die Geburt war dem Tod zu ähnlich; vielleicht war sie ein Tod, wie auch die fleischliche Lust, die Verschmelzung im feucht Organischen mit Schweiß und Stöhnen, in Todesnähe lag und Erschöpfung sich mit Erschöpfung berührte, ja schließlich ein und dasselbe war, der warme Urschleim des Anfangs. Adolf erschrak etwas vor der Eleganz des Lokals, dessen wahres Gesicht ihm aber verborgen blieb, er scheute vor den Kerzenleuchtern, den blitzenden Spiegeln, den lila Fräcken der schönen Kellner zurück, natürlich konnte er sich nicht in seinem geistlichen Gewand an die Bar setzen, und er meinte auch, es schicke sich kaum für ihn, hier an der Straße zu hocken, auf einem der farbenfrohen Promenadenstühle, und so setzten sie sich an einen Tisch in der Nähe der Kasse, und Adolf Judejahn sah Laura lächeln.

Ich mag sie nicht, aber es amüsierte mich wieder, sie zu sehen, Papageien auf ihrer Stange, meine falschen Brüder, ich sah ihre hysterische Lustigkeit, ihre angeborene Bosheit, ihre echte Trauer, ich sah ihr gebranntes Haar, ihre kokottenhaften Anzüge, ihre klirrenden Armbänder, und der amerikanische Dichter, der ein Romstipendium hat und das ganze Jahr an einem Sonett feilt, das dann in der Zeitschrift einer kleinen Universität gedruckt wird, kam in spitzen Schuhen, einer Röhrenhose und mit einer Directoirefrisur schlängelnder Stirnlöckchen und sprach mit mir über das Konzert, das er besucht hatte, er sprach gescheite unzutreffende Ansichten aus, war aber ehrlich bewegt von meiner Musik, und ich merkte, wie er Adolf ansah und wie es ihn neugierig machte, daß ich mit einem Priester hier war, aber ich lud den Dichter nicht ein, sich zu uns zu setzen, ich stand mit ihm im Gespräch, und schließlich verabredeten wir uns für einen Bardrink, und ich sah, wie das sehr schöne Kassenmädchen Adolf zulächelte, bis er sie und ihr Lächeln wie eine Erscheinung anstarrte. Auch mir gefiel sie, ihr Lächeln war gleichsam körperlos, es war ein Strahlen aus geheimnisvollem Grund, sie war liebreizend, sie wurde Laura gerufen, ich kannte sie flüchtig, ich hatte mit ihr gesprochen, aber ich war nicht der Rechte für sie, Laura zählte mich zu den Schwulen, und die waren ihr, weil sie jeden Abend unter ihnen weilte, brüderlich vertraut geworden und erregten sie nicht. Ich hatte Adolf keiner Verführung aussetzen wollen, ich hatte ihn in ein Männerlokal gebracht, und an Laura hatte ich nicht gedacht, aber nun überlegte ich, ob ich ihn mit dem Kassenmädchen bekannt machen sollte, er war jung, ich hatte über sein Zölibat nicht gegrübelt, ich glaube nicht mal, daß er darunter litt, und wenn er sein Gelübde hielt und keusch lebte, dann war es mir nur recht, und ich dachte mir lieber, daß er sein Gelübde hielt, als daß er es nicht hielt, aber ich fand es auch bedeutungslos, wenn er es brechen und sich

mit einem Mädchen einlassen würde, und Laura war sehr
schön, es mußte schön sein, mit Laura zu schlafen, ich gönnte
es Adolf, Gott würde nichts dagegen haben, die Kirche brauchte es nicht zu erfahren, und wenn sie es erfahren sollte,
würde sie es vergeben, aber Adolf kamen vielleicht Skrupel,
und so ließ er es wohl besser, zumal es fraglich war, ob Laura
zustimmen würde und ob sie Zeit hatte, mit ihm zu gehen,
aber er sah sie so gebannt an, daß ich dachte, ob ihm zu helfen sei, meine Uraufführung war nicht gefeiert worden, und
ich hätte gern etwas Freundliches getan.
Sie sah den Priester in das Lokal kommen, und da sie eine
fromme Katholikin war, verletzte es sie, daß nun auch die
Priester schwul seien, Laura nahm zwar an, daß es homo-
sexuelle Geistliche gab, aber es ärgerte sie, daß dieser nun in
ihre Bar kam, was entblößend und bestimmt nicht recht war,
wenn auch Schamloses im Lokal nicht vorfiel, aber dann
sah sie Adolf sitzen, sie sah, wie er sie anstarrte, und, sie
hatte nun den Blick dafür, sie sah, daß er nicht schwul war,
und sie sah auch, daß er unschuldig war, daß er nicht schwul
und unschuldig in diese Bar gekommen war und nicht schwul
und unschuldig nun vor ihr saß und sie anstarrte, und etwas
war in seinem Gesicht, das sie an ein anderes Gesicht erinnerte, an das Gesicht eines ebenfalls nichthomosexuellen
Mannes, aber sie wußte nicht, an welchen Mann, und das
andere Gesicht war auch nicht unschuldig gewesen, sie lächelte, sie lächelte ihr schönstes Lächeln, und sie dachte: Ja, ja,
ich würde es tun, es ist eine Sünde, aber es ist keine große
Sünde, ich könnte es tun und die Sünde beichten. Und Laura
sah sich selber als ein Geschenk, und es freute sie, daß sie
etwas zu verschenken hatte, man konnte auch einem Priester
etwas schenken, ein sehr schönes Geschenk, und Laura wußte, daß dieses Geschenk Freude bereiten würde.
Adolf hatte mir von dem Geld erzählt, das sein Vater ihm
gegeben hatte. Er hatte mir im Park davon erzählt, und er
hatte das Geld auf den Weg werfen wollen, weil er hoffte,
es werde ein Armer das Geld finden, und ich hatte ihn gehin-
dert, das Geld wegzuwerfen, und hatte ihm gesagt, daß die
Scheine nur ein Reicher finden würde, ein Geizhals oder ein

Wucherer. Und Adolf hatte mir dann gesagt, daß Judejahn ihm das Geld gegeben habe, damit er sich ein Mädchen kaufe. Und ich sagte jetzt zu ihm: »Das Mädchen an der Kasse wirst du für das Geld nicht haben können. Du wirst dir nur ein billiges Mädchen kaufen können und keine von der Via Veneto.« Er sagte, ich sei gemein, und ich sagte, ich sei nicht gemein, und er wurde rot, und dann fragte er mich, ob ich denn die Liebe nur als Unzucht kenne, und ich sagte: »Nein.« Ich sagte: »Ich kenne keine Unzucht.« Und er verstand mich nicht, und dann nannte er mir, das hatte er im Seminar gelernt, griechische Wörter für die verschiedenen Bedeutungen der Liebe — ich kannte seine griechischen Wörter, auch ich bildete mir ein, Phaidros zu suchen. Er mochte es probieren, er mochte vom bittersüßen Trank kosten, ich ging zu Laura und löste einen Bon für die Bar, und dabei fragte ich sie, ob wir sie heimbegleiten könnten, und sie lächelte, als sei ihr ein Engel erschienen.

Sie konnte nicht rechnen. Sie verrechnete sich in Zahlen, Zeiten und Verpflichtungen, in den harten, sparsamen und oft grausamen Gegebenheiten des Lebens. Judejahn hatte Pfaffraths zu den Straßenstühlen geführt; so konnte er im Lokal unbemerkt nach seiner Verabredung sehen. Laura erblickte ihn, den Mann mit der blauen Brille, und weiter schien er ihr ein verheißungsvoller Fremder, eine vielversprechende Bekanntschaft zu sein, aber heute wollte sie sich dem jungen Priester schenken, heute nacht wollte sie Gutes tun, sie wollte sich dem jungen Priester hingeben, der so unschuldig und so traurig war, und am Morgen wollte sie es ihrem Beichtvater erzählen, daß sie sich dem jungen fremden Priester geschenkt habe, und als Judejahn sie fragend anblickte, schüttelte sie verneinend den Kopf. Er trat zur Kasse und stierte sie an. Was war los? Was fiel der Hure ein, Judejahn zu narren? Leider fehlten ihm die Worte, sie fehlten ihm in jeder Sprache, und Laura lächelte, sie fand es schmeichelhaft, daß der Blaubebrillte nun wütend war, und überhaupt schlief sie gern am Tage mit Männern und nicht in der Nacht, wo sie von den Zahlen müde war und wirklich schlafen wollte, und so sagte sie ihm, er könne sie am Mor-

gen treffen, wenn er möge, und sie schrieb das Rendezvous
auf einen Kassenzettel, um zehn Uhr vor dem CIT-Büro auf
dem Bahnhof, da wollte sie sein, und er begriff nicht, was
diese Laune bedeutete, vielleicht hatte einer der schmutzigen
reichen Juden ihn überboten, er hätte sie gern angebrüllt,
aber der kleine Gottlieb traute sich in diesem Lokal nicht zu
brüllen, und Judejahn steckte den Zettel mit Lauras Anga-
ben ein und verlangte dann einen Bon für die Bar, einen
Bon für einen Kognak Napoléon, draußen tranken sie Wein,
aber er wollte schnell an der Bar einen großen Napoléon
kippen.
Er drängte sich zwischen die Hocker, er stieß mich an, ich saß
an der Bar und redete mit dem amerikanischen Dichter, wir
sprachen noch einmal über das Konzert, das in ihm nach-
wirkte und ihn weiterhin erregte, und er erzählte mir von
Homer und Vergil und daß er in dem Sonett, an dem er arbeite, Vergil und Homer zitieren würde und daß nun nach
dem Anhören meiner Symphonie Homer und Vergil ihm
als Gestalten seiner eigenen Einsamkeit erschienen, die er
immer wieder fliehen wolle, was ihn dann auf hohe Bar-
hocker und in Geschwätz führte, und ich drehte mich um und
sah Judejahn sich zwischen die Hocker drängen. Ich war
überrascht, und er schien auch überrascht zu sein, wir starrten uns an, und dann hätte ich mich abwenden müssen, aber
ich fand es komisch, Judejahn in der homosexuellen Bar,
in der Sphäre meiner Verdammnis zu sehen, es reizte mich,
ihn zu ärgern, und ich sagte: »Bist du schwul geworden,
Onkel Judejahn?« Sein Gesicht verzerrte sich, und er schaute sich um, und es schien ihm erst jetzt klarzuwerden, daß
dies ein schwules Lokal war, und er zischte mir zu: »Ich
ahnte immer schon, daß du ein solches Schwein bist!« Hatte
er es geahnt? Ahnte er auch, warum ich so war? Dachte er
an die Ordensburg, an die Knaben in der Zwangs- und Sol-
datenjacke, die schön waren, wenn sie die Uniform auszo-
gen, die nackt aus kleinen Amtswaltern wieder zu Kindern
wurden, zu Knaben voll Sehnsucht nach Liebe und Zärtlichkeit und den jungen Leib voll Begierde? Judejahn kränkte
mich nicht. Warum tat ich es? Warum tat ich es? Haßte ich

536

ihn? Ich haßte ihn nicht mal. Es war vergangen, ich wollte nicht erinnert werden. Der Judejahn meiner Jugend war furchtbar gewesen. Der Parteimann hatte Furcht eingeflößt. Der General hatte Furcht geweckt. Jetzt hielt ich ihn für eine Vogelscheuche. Warum ließ ich ihn nicht? Ich war doch frei! Aber er hatte mich zum Landser gemacht, und ich kannte Landserausdrücke, und es lockte mich sehr, ihm zu sagen, daß er eine durchwachsene Sau sei, aber ich war nun boshaft, die Familie machte mich böse, ich war boshaft auf Pfaffrathsche Art, ich haßte mich, und ich war boshaft auf invertierte Weise, ich haßte mich, und ich sagte ihm: »Adolf ist auch da!« Und er folgte meinem Blick, und wir sahen Adolf allein an seinem Tisch, auffallend in seinem Priesterkleid, allein unter den ringsrum schwirrenden und gackernden Schwulen, und wir sahen, wie er Laura anguckte, und ich sagte zu Judejahn: »Er legt sein Geld an, das du ihm für ein Mädchen gegeben hast.« Und dann sah ich, daß Judejahn das Gesicht eines Apoplektikers hatte, eine blaurote Verquollenheit, und ich dachte: Trifft dich der Schlag? Und ich dachte: Aber bitte nicht hier. Und ich dachte: Es wäre komisch, wenn Judejahn in der lila Bar der Schlag träfe. War es ein Triumph? Es war kein Triumph. Ich fühlte mich schal. Es war mir gleichgültig, ob Judejahn der Schlag traf, oder ob ihn nicht der Schlag traf. Seine Hand, die dem Barkeeper einen Bon hinreichte, zitterte. Ich dachte: Er ist ein alter Narr. Und ich fühlte: Er ist ein Gespenst. Aber beinahe spürte ich so etwas wie Mitleid mit Judejahn. Es war seltsam. Vielleicht war ich sentimental.

Er kippte den Kognak hinunter, ein Strom von Feuer floß ins Eingeweide, breitete mit kleinen Nebenflüssen im Leib sich aus, Wut Wut Wut und Schmerz waren in ihm, nur der kleine Gottlieb mit seiner Hochachtung vor reichen Umgebungen, selbst wenn es Dreckpaläste verkommener Unzucht waren, stand einem Ausbruch der Wut im Wege. Daß Siegfried ihn frech anredete, war schlimm genug. Noch hätte sich Judejahn fähig gefühlt, dem Waschlappen in die unvölkisch intellektuell gewordene Fresse zu schlagen. Aber ein neuer Feind war gegen ihn aufgestanden, ein Feind, der sich

eingeschlichen hatte, ein Feind, dessen Nahen er zur Zeit der
Machtfülle nicht gehört hatte und der auch in der Wüsten-
kaserne noch nicht zu erkennen war, denn auch dort war
Machtfülle gewesen, wenn auch in kleinerem Bezirk, er hatte
befohlen, er hatte kommandiert, er hatte nicht konkurriert,
aber nun war der Feind plötzlich da, zeigte sich, holte aus —
das Alter! Judejahn entrüstete sich nicht, daß sein Sohn unter Homosexuellen saß. Er kam auch nicht auf den Gedanken,
amüsiert zu sein, weil sein Sohn, der Diakon, unter den
Schwulen saß. Er sah nur, daß sein Sohn, dieser Heuchler,
ihm die Hure wegschnappte, und es erbitterte Judejahn nicht
so sehr das Bettvergnügen, das ihm entging, er war verwundert, verwundert und fassungslos, daß er hinter diesem
Schwächling im weibischen Pfaffenrock, den er so sehr mißachtet hatte, daß er ihn nicht einmal richtig gehaßt und sich
seiner nur geschämt hatte wie einer Entstellung, einer komischen Beule, die einen lächerlich macht, zurückgestellt und
der Junge ihm vorgezogen wurde. Judejahn stierte immer
wieder hin zu dem seltsam einsamen Tisch, an dem Adolf
allein und in Lauras schönem Lächeln saß. Judejahn war
es, als sähe er eine üble und gefährliche Fata Morgana, einen
Wüstenspuk, unfaßbar, unangreifbar, grausam, grotesk und
tödlich. Da saß aber wirklich der Erzfeind, er war kein Spuk,
und er war doch ein Spuk, der Erzbetrüger, der sich, um den
törichten Vater zu täuschen, als Pfaffe verkleidet hatte. Die
Jugend stand gegen Judejahn auf, die blöde Jugend hatte
ihn verraten. Die eine Jugend war gefallen, die hatte Judejahn im Krieg verschlungen, die war in Ordnung, die hatte
ihn nicht getäuscht, die konnte ihn nicht mehr täuschen und
verraten, die lag im Grab. Aber die neue Jugend hatte ihn
verraten und verriet ihn immer weiter, und nun bestahl sie
ihn, brachte ihn um die Siegeschancen, raubte ihm das Weib,
das zu allen Zeiten dem Eroberer zufiel, dem Überwältiger,
und dessen Besitz ein wollüstiges Symbol des Sieges, ein warmes Fühlen der Macht und der Unterjochung war. War Judejahn gar der alte Bock, dem der junge Hirsch das Reh ab-
kämpfte und der sich im Gebüsch zu verkriechen und zu ver-
enden hatte? So weit war es noch nicht. Es war Täuschung,

alles war Pfaffenlist. Judejahn war noch lange nicht der alte Bock, dem das Gehörn abfiel und der sich verkroch. Er war der bessere Mann. Seine Taten sprachen für ihn; aber wie konnte er Laura seine Taten mitteilen, seine Siege, seine Vernichtungskampagnen? Die ganze Welt hatte Judejahns Walten gekannt; niemand schien sich erinnern zu wollen. Kam es nun nur auf Wortgewandtheit an, auf die feilen Zungen der Feigen, während die Taten des Tapferen schon vergessen waren, schon ein Nichts waren im Loch der Vergangenheit, wo selbst Blutströme verrannen und Entsetzen modernd zerfiel? Was konnte Judejahn tun? Er konnte das Lokal räumen lassen. Es war Unsinn, er konnte das Lokal nicht räumen lassen. Er konnte nicht einmal zur Kasse gehen und sich einen neuen Kognak-Bon lösen. Er fühlte sich schwindlig, und er fürchtete die Lächerlichkeit, die lächerliche Szene einer Begegnung mit seinem Pfaffensohn. Judejahn hielt sich an der Messingstange der Bartheke fest, als müsse er sich anklammern, um nicht in das Lokal zu fallen, um nicht zu sterben oder blindlings dreinzuschlagen in ach wie hoffnungsloser Lage — eingekesselt.

Ich sah, wie seine Hand sich um die Messingstange krampfte, ich sah, wie er sich nach einem zweiten Glas sehnte und wie er sich nicht traute, die Stange loszulassen, und ich sagte dem Barkeeper, er solle Judejahn einen Kognak geben, und der Barmann schenkte den Kognak ein, weil er mich für einen Schwulen hielt und mir vertraute, daß ich den Bon nachlösen würde. Judejahn nahm das Glas. Wußte er, daß es von mir kam? Er kippte es hinunter mit einem Wippen seines Arsches, als ob er an der Stange Kniebeugen machen wolle. Sein Blick hatte einen Moment lang etwas Glasiges. Aber dann verengten sich seine Lider wieder zu tückischen Schweinsaugen. Die tückischen Schweinsaugen sahen mich an. Sie blickten durch das Lokal. Sie sahen Adolf an, sie ruhten auf Laura, und eigentlich wunderte ich mich, daß er so erregt war. Warum war es so schrecklich für ihn, Adolf hier zu sehen? War er ein Vater, der seinen Sohn behüten wollte? Ich glaubte es nicht. Judejahn wollte niemand behüten. Und da er den Priesterrock seines Sohnes haßte, hätte es ihm doch spaßig scheinen müssen, diesen gehaßten Rock in so verdrehter Umgebung zu sehen. Jetzt ging er von der Bar weg, er ging durch das Lokal. Er drückte sich an Adolf und an der Kasse vorbei, und ich paßte auf, um eingreifen zu können, wenn er Adolf anschreien würde. Judejahn ging an Adolf vorbei, ohne ihn zu beachten, und Adolf schien ihn nicht zu sehen, wie er auch mich nicht vermißte, er saß im Lächeln Lauras wie unter einer großen Sonne, der herrlichen Sonne eines unschuldigen Paradieses.

Sie saßen draußen vor der Bar, die Nacht strömte an ihnen vorbei, das elegante Rom, das reiche Rom, das Rom der großen Besitzer und das Rom der großspurigen Ausländer, die Via Veneto paradierte vorbei an den Stuhlreihen der Cafés, der Bars, der Hotels und der teuren Dancings, und Lichter glühten überall, und die Kastanien blühten und rauschten, und Sterne glitzerten über dieser großen Weltstätte. Zuerst hatten sie alles bewundert, auch die Kellner im lila Frack, doch dann strich das Anrüchige durchs Gestühl, die Gezirpestimmen, die klingelnden Armbänder, der Duft aus gewelltem Haar und fraulich gepflegte Hände, die sich um fremde willige Hüften legten. Friedrich Wilhelm Pfaffrath war entrüstet. Er wagte nicht auszusprechen, was er vermutete, und auf keinen Fall, fand er, hätte Judejahn Frau Anna hierherführen dürfen. Auch Dietrich war empört, aber Entrüstung und Empörung über Anrüchigkeit und Sittenverfall taten andererseits auch wohl, sie stärkten das Rückgrat, sie ließen stolz das Haupt heben, die Wohlanständigkeit saß unter welschem Sybaritentum, und die Goten würden siegen. Dietrich quälten Neugier und Begierde. Die Neugier fragte, was Judejahn bewogen haben mochte, dieses Lokal aufzusuchen. Schwul war er nicht. Aber vielleicht hatte er hier geheime Verbindungsleute, unterweltliche Zuträger, denn Spione und Nachrichtenhändler kamen oft aus verdorbenem Kreis; man bediente sich ihrer, und wenn man zur Macht gekommen war, legte man die nützlich gewesenen verachteten Helfer um. Die Begierde verlangte nach den Mädchen, die vorübergingen. Auf hohen Absätzen trippelten sie in engen, die Schenkel zur Schau stellenden Röcken vorbei, sie waren gepflegt und aufgezäumt wie Zirkuspferde, teure Reittiere, vielverheißende Könnerinnen, Dietrich malte sich's aus, aber er konnte rechnen, und er rechnete, daß es teuer käme, es würde mehr kosten, als er allenfalls anlegen wollte, und so haßte er denn die Mädchen, er fand sie schamlos aufreizend und ihre Promenade auf nächtlicher Straße skandalös, und er dachte mit Gier und Verbitterung an die Zeitschrift in seinem Koffer, an das Bilderblatt mit den Entblößungen, das zu Entspannung und Schlaf führte. Endlich kam Judejahn aus dem Innern des seltsamen Vogelhauses zurück. Er mußte sich geärgert haben, er atmete schwer, die Adern der Stirn und der Hand waren hervorgetreten, und die Hand zitterte, als er nach dem Rest des Weines griff. Und dann beleidigte er sie, er beschimpfte sie, weil Deutschland noch nicht erwacht war, weil die Jugend noch nicht marschierte, weil die Jugend frech war vor höheren Rängen und zuchtlos verkam. Wie konnten sie sich wehren? Sie hatten sich nie gegen Judejahn wehren können. Friedrich Wilhelm Pfaffrath war schmählich wehrlos gegen jeden Schreier, wenn er nur das Nationale genügend betonte, denn das Nationale war ein Abgott, ein Moloch, dem man Verstand und Leben und schließlich selbst noch den Besitz opferte. Die römischen Kastanien rauschten im lauen Abend. Ob wieder Fahnen rauschen würden? Friedrich Wilhelm Pfaffrath wünschte es sehr, Fahnen waren erhabene Symbole, waren der sichtbare Aufbruch der Nation, aber jetzt, vielleicht wurde er alt, als er Judejahns Schimpfreden an sich und an die Nation hörte, packte ihn ein befremdendes leichtes Grauen vor Judejahns Fahnen, die wieder rauschen sollten, und ihm war, als ob die milden römischen Kastanienbäume wie alte Damen kicherten. Er dachte an seine Mutter, an die Pastorsfrau, die der Nationalsozialismus nicht begeistert hatte. Vielleicht schaute sie nun aus dem Sternenhimmel auf ihn herab. Sie hatte fest an ein solches Herabschauen geglaubt. Pfaffrath lehnte die Möglichkeit verständig ab. Dennoch — wenn seine Mutter herabschaute, wenn sie ihn fand und ihn sah, würde sie Mitleid haben? Judejahn beschuldigte Pfaffrath der Feigheit und der Untreue. In diesem verzauberten

Moment der Nacht, müde, erschöpft, erhebender und seltsamer Eindrücke voll, nahm Pfaffrath den Tadel an. Er war feige, er war untreu gewesen, aber es war eine andere Feigheit, eine andere Untreue, als die vom tobenden Schwager gemeinte. Pfaffrath schien es nun, als sei er in jungen Jahren vom Weg abgekommen, als habe es einen anderen Pfad für ihn und für Deutschland gegeben als die Heerstraße, die Pfaffrath gegangen war; eine andere deutsche Möglichkeit, an die er nie geglaubt hatte, lag nun wie eine durch das Gaukelspiel der Erinnerung verklärte Jugendlandschaft vor ihm, doch ihr, dieser anderen Möglichkeit, war er untreu gewesen, und das andere Deutschland war für immer versäumt worden. Die Kastanien erzählten sich von seiner Feigheit, seiner Untreue, seinem Versagen, mehr noch zu Haus die alten Linden, aber für die Menschen verrauscht die Schuldstimme der Nacht mit dem nächtlichen Beben der Bäume, und nach erquickendem Schlaf wird Pfaffrath sich wieder makellos fühlen, ein aufrechter deutscher Mann und Oberbürgermeister, frei von jeder Schuld, frei von Schuld an den Ahnen, frei von Schuld an den Kindern und frei von Schuld an der eigenen Seele. Aber jetzt, in der Verwandlung der Nachtstunde fragte er sich noch, ob Siegfried mit seiner Symphonie vielleicht die bessere Heimat gesucht und ob er in seinem Pfaffraths Ohr mißklingenden Tönen vielleicht Zwiesprache mit seiner jungen Seele gehalten hatte.

Ich störte ihn in seiner Versunkenheit, ich störte ihn in seiner Hingabe an Lauras Lächeln. Wieder rührte mich Adolf. Ich legte meine Hand auf seinen Arm, meine Hand auf sein schwarzes Kleid, aber er zog seinen Arm zurück und sagte: »Du verstehst nicht, was es ist.« Ich sagte: »Doch, du hast einen Schmerz entdeckt.« Er fragte: »Weißt du wirklich, was es ist?« Ich sagte: »Ja.« Ich hatte ihm ein Glas Wermut bestellt, und er hatte den Wermut, und er fragte: »Müssen wir jetzt gehen?« Ich sagte: »Sie heißt Laura. Wir werden mit ihr fortgehen.« Er sah mich an, und es zuckte um seinen Mund, und er sagte: »Du verstehst mich nicht.« Ich sagte: »Doch, ich verstehe dich.« Und ich dachte: Er glaubt, er kann sich mit dem Ansehen begnügen, und er hat recht, das

Ansehen ist das Glück, und wenn er standhaft bleibt und nicht mit ihr ins Bett geht, wird er etwas gewonnen haben. Ich dachte: Er wird etwas gewonnen haben, aber er wird meinen, er habe alles verloren. Ich dachte: Was wäre aus ihm geworden, wenn mit den Nazis nicht auch ihre Ordensburgen zusammengebrochen wären? Ich dachte: Würde er dann Laura überhaupt sehen? Ich dachte: Er ist auf einen schweren Weg geraten. Ich wußte nicht, ob er den Weg weitergehen würde. Weiter, und wohin? Viele Passionspfade gibt es, ein verwirrendes Straßennetz.

Er beobachtete sie aus dem Hinterhalt seines Wagens. Sie kamen aus der Bar. Sie gingen die Via Veneto hinunter, gingen unter ihren langsam erlöschenden Lichtern, gingen unter den rauschenden Bäumen, das Mädchen ging in ihrer Mitte. Judejahns Wagen folgte ihnen nach, ein schwarzer Schatten, der langsam heranglitt, einmal sie erreichte und dann wieder zurückblieb. Sie gingen an Judejahns großem Hotel vorüber, und hinter der amerikanischen Botschaft wandten sie sich nach links, der Via Venti Settembre zu. Judejahn gab die Verfolgung auf. Er hatte Gewißheit haben wollen. Er hatte Gewißheit — sein Sohn hatte ihn bei einer Hure ausgestochen. Sein Sohn schlief mit einer römisch-jüdischen Hure. Seine Entrüstung war lächerlich. Dies entging ihm nicht ganz. Er dachte: Nun wenn schon. Es war ihm nur recht, wenn Adolf mit einem Mädchen schlief; vielleicht würde er ein Mann werden. Aber er war geschlagen worden, er, der große Judejahn war geschlagen worden, war zurückgestoßen worden, sein Befehl hatte nichts gegolten, die Welt war in Rebellion! Das war es, was eine Flut sinnloser Beschimpfungen in ihm aufwühlte. Daß sein Sohn als Priester mit einem Mädchen schlief, berührte ihn nicht. Hierfür fehlte ihm der Sinn. Er hielt alle Pfaffen für Heuchler und geile Böcke. Er würde sich rächen. Er würde sich an allen Pfaffen rächen, an allen Huren würde er sich rächen. Er ließ sich vor das Hotel fahren. Er ging auf sein luxuriöses Zimmer. Der kleine Gottlieb durfte mit dem Zimmer zufrieden sein. Der Kater Benito empfing Judejahn mit Schreien. Er hatte Hunger.

Judejahn war wütend, weil das Tier nichts zu essen bekommen hatte. Er streichelte den Kater, kraulte sein räudiges Fell, sagte: »Armer Benito!« Er klingelte nach dem Kellner, er schimpfte den Kellner aus, er bestellte rohes Hackfleisch für den Kater, und für sich bestellte er Champagner. Es mußte Champagner sein. Der kleine Gottlieb hatte im Kasino immer Champagner getrunken. Der kleine Gottlieb hatte als Sieger Champagner getrunken. Er hatte in Paris, in Rom, in Warschau Champagner getrunken. In Moskau hatte er keinen Champagner getrunken.

Sie gingen stumm durch die Nacht. Keiner berührte den andern. Die hohen Häuser waren stumm. Sie waren freundlich. Das Pflaster lag wohlwollend unter ihrem Schritt. Sie hörten die Glocken von San Bernardo schlagen; auch Santa Maria della Vittoria und Santa Susanna kündeten mit hellem Schlag die Stunde. Sie zählten aber die Zeit nicht. Auf der Piazza della Esedra gingen sie durch den Halbkreis der Arkaden. Die Schaufenster der Geschäfte lagen hinter Gittern. Die Kaufleute waren mißtrauisch, fürchteten die Nacht und die Räuber. Die Auslagen waren erleuchtet. Sie zeigten Schätze. Laura begehrte sie nicht; sie begehrte nichts von allen Schätzen, die mit hohen Preisen ausgezeichnet hinter den verriegelten Gittern lagen. Ihr Lächeln war ein Wohlschein in der Nacht, es erfüllte die Nacht und es erfüllte Rom. Laura lächelte für die Stadt und für den Erdkreis, urbi et orbi, und Rom und die Nacht und die Erde waren verklärt. Sie überquerten den Platz, und Laura tauchte ihre Finger in das Wasser des Brunnens, tauchte sie in die kleine Fontana delle Naiadi, und wie mit Weihwasser benetzte sie, eine fromme Katholikin, mit dem Wasser der Naiadi das Haupt ihres stummen Diakons. Danach traten sie in den Schatten eines alten Gemäuers, wo Nachtvögel hausen mochten. Sie standen vor Santa Maria degli Angeli bei den Thermen des Diokletian. Siegfried lauschte nach dem Eulenschrei. Ihm war, als müsse hier das Käuzchen rufen. Er fand, daß kompositorisch hier das Kiwitt-Kiwitt des Todesvogels hingehöre, aber er vernahm nur den Schrei der Lokomotiven vom nahen Bahnhof, voll Wehmut und voll Angst vor so viel

Ferne. Wie fern waren sie einander, die hier zu dritt die Nacht erlebten. Siegfried sah Adolf und Laura an. Aber sah er sie? Projizierte er nicht nur sich auf die Gestalten seiner Gefährten? Sie waren Gedanken von ihm, und er freute sich, daß er sie dachte. Es waren freundliche Gedanken. Und sie, sahen sie sich? Im Winkel des alten Thermengemäuers war es dunkel, doch vor Santa Maria degli Angeli schimmerte ein Ewiges Licht, und sie versuchten in diesem Licht ihre Seelen zu erkennen.

Ich verließ sie, was sollte ich bei ihnen? Ich hatte sie zusammengeführt, und was sollte ich nun bei ihnen? Ich schlenderte zum Bahnhof hinüber. Ich trat ins Neonlicht. Mochte Adolf vor Santa Maria degli Angeli beten. »*Ut mentes nostras ad coelestia desideria erigas;* daß du unsere Herzen zu himmlischen Begierden erhebest.« Hatte ich Adolf in Versuchung geführt? Ich hatte Adolf nicht in Versuchung geführt. Es gab keine Versuchung. In den Thermen, im Museo Nazionale Romano, waren die Bilder der alten Götter eingeschlossen. Sie waren gut bewacht. Hatte ich Freude gegeben? Ich konnte nicht Freude bereiten. Es gab nur Täuschung, Irrlichter des Augenblicks. Ich ging zu den Bahnsteigen. Ein Zug stand bereit. Die Wagen der dritten Klasse waren überfüllt. In der ersten Klasse saß ein magerer Mann. Würde ich der Mann in der ersten Klasse sein? Vielleicht war er ein schlechter Mensch. Würde ich es sein? Ich wollte nicht in der überfüllten dritten Klasse reisen. Florenz-Brenner-München. Lockte mich die Route? Sie lockte mich nicht. Ich ging ins Albergo di giorno, das wie in einer neonerleuchteten Felsgrotte unter dem Bahnhof liegt. Die Nymphen der Grotte manikürten den Herrn die Hände. Ich liebe die römischen Frisiersalons. Ich liebe die Römer. Zu jeder Stunde denken sie an ihre Schönheit. Männer wurden hier frisiert, rasiert, onduliert, maniküert, massiert, mit Salben beschmiert, mit Duftwasser übergossen; sie saßen ernst unter Frisierschleiern und blitzenden Trockenhauben, Fön strich durch ihre Haare. Ich hatte nichts zu tun. Ich bat um eine Kompresse. Ich bat um eine Kompresse, weil ich mich langweilte. Man deckte mein Gesicht mit einem dampfend heißen Tuch zu, und mir

kamen heiße Träume. Ich war Petronius, der Dichter, und ich sprach im öffentlichen Bad mit Weisen und mit Knaben, wir lagen auf Marmorstufen in der Dampfkammer und sprachen über die Unsterblichkeit der Seele, am Boden war ein Mosaik, kunstvoll und bunt, Zeus der Adler Zeus der Schwan, Zeus der Stier Zeus der goldene Regen — aber das Mosaik hatte ein Sklave gesetzt. Man deckte ein in Eiswasser getauchtes Tuch auf mein Gesicht, ich war Petronius, der Dichter, ich genoß das Gespräch weiser Männer und die Schönheit der Knaben, und ich wußte, es gibt keine Unsterblichkeit und die Schönheit verfault, und ich wußte, daß Nero grübelte, und ich wußte, wo das Messer an die Ader zu setzen war — die letzte Marmorstufe war kalt. Ich verließ die Grotte, ich war nicht schön, ich ging in irgendeinen Wartesaal und trank einen Grappa, weil Hemingway Grappa empfohlen hatte, und wieder schmeckte er mir wie ein deutscher Fusel aus der Zeit vor der Währungsreform. Ich kaufte am großen Zeitungsstand eine Zeitung. Die Dschungelfestung war gefallen. In Genf reiste man ab. Meine kleine Kommunistin mit dem roten Halstuch schritt hochmütig durch Rom. Sie reiste nicht ab. Warum sollte sie abreisen? Sie war ja zu Hause. Die Überschrift der Zeitung lautete: Was nun?
Kürenberg hatte viel telephoniert, er hatte mit den Kritikern und mit den Kunstbehörden telephoniert, er hatte mit den Managern gesprochen und mit den Veranstaltern des Kongresses und mit den Preiseinsetzern und Preisverteilern, es war Politik im Spiel und viel Diplomatie, und jeder Funktionär tat geheimnisvoll und wichtig, aber Kürenberg hatte sich durchgesetzt, Siegfried sollte den Musikpreis kriegen, nicht den ganzen Preis, aber den halben sollte er bekommen; aus diplomatischen Gründen mußte der Preis geteilt werden. Kürenberg sagte Ilse, daß Siegfried den Preis bekäme, und Ilse Kürenberg, die im Badezimmer das Wasser in die Wanne laufen ließ, war es gleichgültig, ob Siegfried den Preis bekam; es ärgerte sie nicht, aber es freute sich auch nicht. Sie dachte: Bin ich angesteckt, bin ich angesteckt von der Gemeinheit, angesteckt von dieser Simplizität des in Gruppen Denkens, angesteckt von der Gruppenfeindschaft, von dem

brutalen Unsinn der Sippenhaftung, wie sie es nannten, bin ich gegen Siegfried und gegen seine Musik, weil er zu dieser Familie gehört? Er ist nicht glücklich mit ihnen. Ich weiß, er hat sich von ihnen getrennt. Aber warum sehe ich die andern, wenn ich ihn sehe? Sie dachte: Ich will keine Rache, ich habe sie nie gewollt, Rache ist etwas Schmutziges, aber ich will nicht erinnert werden, ich kann es nicht ertragen, erinnert zu werden, und Siegfried, er kann nicht dafür, er erinnert mich; er erinnert mich, und ich sehe die Mörder. Die Wanne war vollgelaufen, aber das Wasser war nun zu heiß. Ilse Kürenberg löschte das Licht im Badezimmer. Sie öffnete das Fenster. Sie war nackt. Sie ging gern nackt durch die Wohnung. Sie stellte sich nackt an das offene Fenster. Der Wind berührte sie. Der Wind legte sich wie eine Form um ihren festen wohlerhaltenen Körper. Ihr fester Körper stand fest auf dem festen Boden. Sie hatte standgehalten. Sie hatte dem Sturm widerstanden. Der Wind würde sie nicht davontragen. Aber etwas in ihr sehnte sich danach, davongetragen zu werden.

Der Champagner war ausgetrunken, der Rausch war nicht gekommen, die Siege waren verschüttet. In Judejahn war ein dumpfes Brausen, es war eine Art Ohrensausen, das durch seinen ganzen Körper ging; entschieden war sein Blutdruck zu hoch, er trat ans Fenster und blickte über Rom. Einmal hatte er Rom beinahe beherrscht. Er hatte sogar den Mann beherrscht, der hier herrschte. Mussolini hatte vor Judejahn Angst gehabt. Jetzt hatte Rom Judejahn einen räudigen Kater geschenkt. Eine Hure war Judejahn davongelaufen. Er konnte sie nicht erschießen lassen. Eine Hure war ihm mit seinem Sohn davongelaufen, der ein römischer Priester war. Judejahn konnte auch keinen Priester mehr erschießen lassen. Er war machtlos. Würde er kämpfen, um wieder zur Macht zu kommen? Der Weg war lang. Zum zweitenmal war der Weg zu lang. Jetzt gestand er es sich ein. Der Weg war zu lang. Judejahn sah das Ziel nicht mehr. Das Ziel verschwamm. Ein roter Nebel legte sich vor das Ziel. Eine Hure war Judejahn entkommen, aber eine nackte Jüdin drängte sich vor seinen Blick; die Jüdin gehörte vor den Leichengraben, aber noch triumphierte sie und verhöhnte Judejahn; sie erhob sich nackt über Rom. Er sah sie in den Wolken.

Nachdem sie im Winkel antiken Mauerwerks lange beisammengestanden, oft die Uhr von Santa Maria degli Angeli die Stunde geschlagen, die Lokomotiven geschrien, nun wohl auch das Käuzchen gerufen hatte, doch sie vernahmen nichts, klang Siegfrieds Musik in Adolf unerwartet wider, und er berührte Lauras Gesicht, er versuchte, das Lächeln zu greifen, einen hohen Ton, die Menschlichkeit, eine süße Lust, und dann erschrak er und lief in die Nacht, die nun lächellos war und lange währen sollte.

Die Engel waren nicht gekommen. Die Engel von der Engelsbrücke waren der Einladung der alten Götter nicht gefolgt. Sie tanzten nicht mit den alten Göttern auf dem Kapitolinischen Hügel. Ich hätte es gern gesehen, wenn Strawinsky hier zwischen geborstenen Säulenresten am schwarzen Flügel gesessen wäre. Am schwarzen Konzertflügel hätte der Meister im Kreis der weißen etwas schmutzigen Marmorflügel der Brückenengel und unter dem großen reinen Flügelhauch der Götter, die Luft und Licht waren, seine *Passacaglia* spielen müssen; aber die Engel waren ausgeblieben, die Götter hatten sich versteckt, Wolken drohten am Himmel, und Strawinsky sagte nur: *»Je salue le monde confraternel.» Der* Musik-Kongreß wurde auf dem Kapitol empfangen. Ich hatte das Gefühl, daß wir komisch aussahen in unseren Anzügen, und die Götter, hinter ihren Trümmern versteckt, die Faune im Gebüsch, die Nymphen im wuchernden Unkraut lachten wohl sehr. Nicht sie waren altmodisch, wir waren es. Wir waren albern und alt, und selbst die Jungen unter uns waren albern und alt. Kürenberg blinzelte mir zu. Er wollte wohl sagen: »Nimm es nicht so ernst, aber nimm es ernst genug.« Er war dafür, daß man die Manager schaffen ließ, damit man mit der Muse der Musik zuweilen in ein teures Restaurant gehen konnte. Der Bürgermeister von Rom verteilte die Preise. Er war ein Kollege meines Vaters, und er gab mir einen halben Preis. Er gab mir den halben Preis für die Symphonie, und ich war überrascht, daß er mir den halben Preis gab, und ich dachte, das hat Kürenberg erreicht, und ich war Kürenberg dankbar, und ich dachte, mein Vater würde einen ganzen Tag stolz auf mich sein, weil der Bürgermeister mir den halben Preis verliehen hatte, aber mein Vater würde nie begreifen, warum der Bürgermeister mich auszeichnete. Mir war das Geld des Preises willkommen. Ich würde nach Afrika reisen. In Afrika würde ich eine neue Symphonie schreiben. Vielleicht würde ich sie im nächsten Jahr in Rom den Engeln vorspielen; die schwarze Symphonie des schwarzen Erdteils würde ich den weißen Engeln von Rom auf dem alten Götterhügel vorspielen. Ich weiß, Europa ist schwärzer. Aber ich will nach Afrika reisen, ich will die Wüste sehen. Mein Vater wird es nicht begreifen, daß man nach Afrika fährt, um die Wüste zu sehen und aus der Wüste Musik zu empfangen. Mein Vater ahnt nicht, daß ich der sehr devote Komponist der römischen Engel bin. Das Konzil hat Palestrinas Musik gebilligt, der Kongreß hat meine Musik anerkannt.

Die Reveille weckte ihn nicht, das Maunzen des Katers schreckte ihn auf, Judejahns Kopf brummte, das Wüstenfort war weit, Afrika war weit, Deutschland war noch weiter, er erwachte mit einem schmerzenden Schädel in Rom, mit schlaffen Gliedern, mit Wut, weil er überhaupt aufwachte, mit einem Parfümgeschmack im Mund, der vom Champagner kam und von den verlorenen Siegen, mit Saurem vermischt war, mit Stechendem, mit Zellverfall, und hinter der Stirn schwankte das Bild des Raumes, und Fuß und Schenkel bebten, aber das Mannesglied war erregt, aufgeladen, blutvoll, es brannte in unbefriedigter Gereiztheit. Er duschte, schrubbte sich ab, er dachte im Kasinojargon, jetzt ein Gepäckmarsch, jetzt durchs Feld robben, aber er schwitzte unter der Dusche, er bekam die Haut nicht trockengerieben, immer wieder strömte Schweiß, glimmerte in kleinen Perlen, Judejahn japste nach Luft, und die Luft von Rom war zu weich. Nach alter Trinksitte war es gut, weiterzutrinken, empfahl es sich, sofort am Morgen wieder denselben Saft zu nehmen, den man am Abend genossen hatte und dessen Gift man im Körper spürte. Judejahn bestellte eine halbe Flasche Champagner, den Champagner der Siege. Er bestellte ihn mit sehr viel Eis. Er warf Eisstücke in den Trinkkelch. Das Eis klirrte gegen das Glas. Judejahns Hand zitterte. Er leerte den Kelch in einem Zug. Jetzt sah er klar. Nebel schwanden. Er war mit Laura verabredet. Das war wichtig. Mochte sie mit Adolf geschlafen haben. Er brauchte sie, die eine Jüdin war und die keine Jüdin war, er brauchte sie, um sich von peinlichen Visionen zu befreien. Er bestellte den schwarzen Gesandtschaftswagen, aber nach einer Weile kam ein Anruf des soldatischen Chauffeurs, der mit strammer Stimme, in der kein Gefühlston schwang, eine Reparatur des Wagens meldete, die erst am Abend fertig sein würde. Judejahn hatte die Stimme des Todes gehört. Er erkannte sie nicht. Er schimpfte.

Auch in der alten Kirche Santa Maria degli Angeli, im Gotteshaus unter der Thermenmauer, konnte man in vielen Sprachen beichten, und Adolf Judejahn kniete im Beichtstuhl des Deutsch sprechenden Priesters, und er erzählte dem Deutsch verstehenden Priester, was sich in der Nacht vor dem Tor dieser Kirche zwischen ihm und Laura begeben hatte, und da nichts geschehen war, was die Kirche bei einem Diakon ernstlich erzürnt hätte, wurde Adolf ermahnt, sich fortan nicht der Versuchung auszusetzen, und er erhielt die Absolution. Er sah durch das Gitter des Beichtstuhls das Gesicht seines Beichtvaters. Das Gesicht des Beichtvaters war müde. Adolf hätte gern gesagt: »Vater, ich bin unglücklich.« Aber das Gesicht des Priesters war müde und abweisend. Er hatte so viele Beichten entgegengenommen. So viele Reisende kamen an und beichteten in Rom, was sie zu Hause ihren Beichtvätern nicht anvertrauen wollten. Sie schämten sich vor den Beichtvätern, die sie kannten. In Rom waren sie fremd und schämten sich nicht, und deshalb war das Gesicht des Priesters so müde. Und Adolf dachte: Werde ich einst auch so müde im Beichtstuhl sitzen, und wird auch mein Gesicht so abweisend sein? Er dachte: Wo wird mein Beichtstuhl stehen? In einem Dorf? In einer alten Dorfkirche unter Bäumen? Oder bin ich nicht berufen, bin ich verworfen, verworfen von Anfang an? Adolf hatte Judejahns Geld in eine Opferlade schieben wollen, aber vor dem Schlitz des Opfer-

stocks besann er sich anders. Es war nicht im Sinn des geistlichen Amtes, wie er nun handelte. Er vertraute der Armenpflege der Kirche nicht. Die Armenpflege der Kirche war
säuerlich, sie war säuerlich wie jede Armenpflege und roch
nach Bettelsuppen; das Geld zerrann in Bettelsuppen. Adolf
wollte mit dem Geld Freude bereiten. Er drückte die schmutzigen Scheine seines Vaters in die runzlige Hand einer alten
Frau, die vor der Kirchentür um Almosen bat.

Judejahn wartete. Er wartete in der Halle des Bahnhofs vor
dem CIT-Büro, aber Laura war nicht gekommen. Versetzte
sie ihn auch am Morgen? Lag sie noch mit Adolf in gemeiner
Verschlingung? Wut war ungesund. Judejahn machte noch
immer der Atem zu schaffen. Zuweilen kam wieder der Nebel, ein giftiger Nebel aus rotem Gas. Vielleicht würde ein
solcher Nebel im nächsten großen Krieg um die Erde wehen.
Judejahn ging zu einem der Reiseproviantwagen und ließ sich
einen Kognak geben. Er stand vor dem Reiseproviantwagen
wie vor einem Verpflegungswagen im Feld. Er kippte den
Kognak. Der rote Nebel lichtete sich. Judejahn blickte zu
CIT hinüber, aber noch immer war Laura nicht da. Judejahn
ging am Zeitungsstand vorüber. Er sah die Illustrierte *Oggi*
am Zeitungsstand hängen, und auf dem Titelbild von *Oggi*
war Mussolini zu sehen. Der alte Freund sah angegriffen
aus, und Judejahn dachte: Auch ich sehe heute angegriffen
aus. Hinter Mussolini stand ein Mann mit einer SS-Mütze.
Er stand wie ein Aufpasser hinter Mussolini. Er stand wie
ein Henker hinter ihm. Man konnte auf der Mütze deutlich
den Totenkopf erkennen. Wer war der Mann? Judejahn
dachte: Es muß einer von meinen Offizieren sein. Der SS-
Mann senkte auf dem Bild den Blick, und Judejahn konnte
das Gesicht nicht erkennen. Wahrscheinlich war der Mann tot.
Die meisten seiner Männer waren tot. Auch Mussolini war
tot. Er war scheußlich gestorben. Auch Judejahn hatte man
einmal einen scheußlichen Tod zugedacht. Aber Judejahn
lebte, er war ihnen entkommen. Er lebte, und die Zeit war
für ihn, und da war auch Laura. Da war ihr Lächeln, und
einen Moment dachte Judejahn, laß sie laufen, aber dann
dachte er wieder, sie ist eine Jüdin, und wieder erregte es

ihn. Und Laura sah den vielversprechenden Fremden, und sie dachte: Was wird er mir schenken? Jetzt beachtete sie die Auslagen der Schaufenster. Ein Mädchen brauchte Schmuck, ein Mädchen brauchte Kleider, auch ein Mädchen, das nicht rechnen kann, braucht dünne Strümpfe, und sie war es gewohnt, daß sie gelegentlich etwas bekam; gelegentlich machte sie kleine Fischzüge, in aller Unschuld und am liebsten am Vormittag, sie hatte keinen festen Freund, und nach den Schwulen am Abend war es schön, am Vormittag mit einem richtigen Mann im Bett zu liegen, man brauchte das für die Gesundheit, und später beichtete man's in aller Unschuld, und auch die Alten waren nicht schlecht, sie waren nicht schön, aber sie waren nicht schlecht, es war für den Vormittag genug, was sie konnten. und außerdem schenkten sie mehr als die Jungen, die selber was haben wollten, und Adolf hatte sie enttäuscht, der junge fremde Priester hatte sie doch enttäuscht, sie war so froh gewesen mit ihm in der Nacht, aber der Priester war weggelaufen, er hatte die Sünde gescheut, und Laura hatte geweint, und jetzt hielt sie sich an die Alten; die Alten scheuten die Sünde nicht und liefen nicht weg. Die Verständigung mit Judejahn war schwer, aber sie machte ihm begreiflich, daß sie in ein Hotel in der Nähe des Bahnhofs gehen würden.

Kürenberg hatte mich in das schöne Restaurant an der Piazza Navona eingeladen. Er wollte meinen Preis mit mir feiern. Er entschuldigte seine Frau, weil sie nicht mit uns frühstükken würde, und ich verstand, daß Ilse Kürenberg nicht mit mir feiern wollte, und ich begriff es. Das Restaurant war zu dieser Stunde noch leer, und Kürenberg bestellte allerlei Seetiere, die wie kleine Ungeheuer auf unseren Tellern lagen, und zu den Ungeheuern tranken wir einen trockenen Chablis. Es war unser Abschied. Kürenberg mußte nach Australien fliegen. Er sollte in Australien während der Saison den *Ring* dirigieren. Er saß vor mir, brach die Schalen der monströsen Seetiere, sog ihre wohlschmeckenden Kanäle aus, und morgen würde er mit seiner Frau in der Luft sitzen und ein Luftdinner haben, und übermorgen würde er in Australien speisen und seltsame Tiere des Stillen Ozeans probieren. Die

Welt ist klein. Kürenberg war mein Freund, er war mein einziger wirklicher Freund, aber ich verehrte ihn zu sehr, um wirklich freundschaftlich mit ihm umgehen zu können, und so war ich still, wenn ich mit ihm zusammen war, und er hielt mich vielleicht für undankbar. Ich erzählte ihm, daß ich mit meinem Preisgeld nach Afrika fahren möchte, und ich erzählte ihm von meiner schwarzen Symphonie. Kürenberg billigte meinen Plan. Er empfahl mir, nach Mogador zu gehen. Der Name Mogador klang gut. Er klang schwarz genug. Mogador war eine alte maurische Festung. Aber da die Mauren nicht mehr mächtig sind, konnte ich gut und gern in ihrer alten Festung wohnen.

Sie hatte noch gedacht, ob er die blaue Brille im Bett abnehmen würde, und nun hatte er sie abgenommen, es hatte sie amüsiert, aber dann erschrak sie vor seinen Augen, sie waren blutunterlaufen, und sie bebte zurück vor seinem tükkisch gierigen Blick, vor der gesenkten Stierstirn, die auf sie zukam, und er fragte »hast du Angst?«, und sie verstand ihn nicht und lächelte, aber es war kein volles Lächeln mehr, und er warf sie auf das Bett. Sie hatte ihm diese Leidenschaft nicht zugetraut, die Männer, mit denen sie für die Geschenke schlief, die ein Mädchen so dringend braucht, waren sonst nicht so erregt, es waren ruhige Sachen, die sich im Bett abspielten, aber dieser warf sich wie eine Bestie über sie, er spreizte ihre Glieder, zerrte an ihrer Haut, und dann nahm er sie roh, ging roh mit ihr um, wo sie doch schmal und zart war, er war schwer, er lag schwer auf ihrem Leib, der so leicht und so gut zu umfassen war, und sie dachte an die Schwulen, dachte an die Schwulen in der Bar, an ihre weichen Bewegungen, an ihre duftenden Locken, an ihre bunten Hemden und ihre klirrenden Armbänder, und sie dachte, vielleicht ist es gut, schwul zu sein, vielleicht sollte auch ich schwul sein, dies ist widerlich, er stinkt nach Schweiß, und er stinkt wie ein Bock, wie ein dreckiger gemeiner Ziegenbock im Stall stinkt er, sie war als Kind einmal auf dem Land gewesen, sie war in Kalabrien auf dem Land gewesen, sie hatte sich gefürchtet und hatte sich nach Rom gesehnt, nach ihrer herrlichen Stadt, und das Haus in Kalabrien hatte ge-

stunken, und sie hatte zusehen müssen, wie die Ziegen zum
Bock geführt wurden, und auf der Holzstiege hatte sich ein
Junge vor ihr entblößt, und sie hatte den Jungen anfassen
müssen, sie haßte das Land, und manchmal träumte sie von
dem Bock, und dann wollte sie den Jungen anfassen, aber
der Junge hatte Hörner und stieß sie, und die Hörner brachen
ab, im Traum brachen die Hörner ab wie faule Zähne, da
rief sie »du tust mir weh«, aber Judejahn verstand sie nicht,
da sie auf italienisch rief, und es war auch gleichgültig, ob
er sie verstand, denn es tat weh, aber es tat schön weh, ja,
sie wollte jetzt diese Hingabe, der Alte befriedigte sie, der
verheißungsvolle Fremde offenbarte sich in ungeahnter Weise, sie drängte sich nun an ihn, steigerte seine Erregung,
Bäche von Schweiß rannen von ihm dem Bock über ihren
Leib, flossen über ihre Brust, sammelten sich in der kleinen
Mulde ihres Bauches, brannten ein wenig, aber brannten
nicht schlimm, und der Mann war böse, er flüsterte »du bist
eine Jüdin, du bist eine Jüdin«, und sie verstand ihn nicht,
aber ihr Unterbewußtsein verstand ihn, als die deutschen
Soldaten in Rom waren, hatte das Wort eine Bedeutung
gehabt, und sie fragte »ebreo?«, und er flüsterte »Hebräer«,
und legte die Hände um ihren Hals, und sie rief »no e poi
no, cattólico«, und das Wort cattólico schien ihn auch zu ent-
flammen in Wut und Begierde, und am Ende war es gleich,
Wut oder Begierde, sie schwamm hinweg, und er erschöpfte
sich, röchelte und warf sich ermattet, erschlagen, wie tot zur
Seite. Sie dachte: Es ist seine Schuld, warum gab er so an, die
Alten geben sonst nicht so an? Aber sie lächelte schon wieder,
und sie streichelte das verschwitzte Haar seiner Brust, weil er
sich so angestrengt hatte; sie war ihm dankbar, weil er sich
so angestrengt hatte; sie war ihm dankbar, weil er sie befriedigt und ihr Lust geschenkt hatte. Sie streichelte ihn noch
eine Weile. Sie fühlte sein Herz schlagen; es war ein tapferes
Herz, weil es sich für ihre Mädchenlust so ausgegeben hatte.
Sie stand auf und ging zum Waschtisch, um sich zu waschen.
Judejahn hörte das Wasser plätschern und richtete sich auf.
Wieder war der rote Nebel um ihn. Er sah Laura nackt im
roten Nebel stehen, und das schwarze Becken des Waschti-

sches war der schwarze Erdgraben, in den die Erschossenen fielen. Man mußte die Jüdin liquidieren. Man hatte den Führer verraten. Man hatte nicht genug liquidiert. Er taumelte in seine Kleider. Sie fragte: »Willst du dich nicht waschen?« Aber er hörte sie nicht. Er hätte sie auch nicht verstanden. In seiner Hosentasche lag Austerlitz' schallgedämpfte Pistole. Gleich würde die Pistole alles entscheiden. Gleich würde gesäubert werden. Die Pistole würde wieder Ordnung schaffen. Er brauchte nur noch ein wenig Luft, er keuchte und zitterte zu sehr. Er schwankte zum Fenster, riß es auf und beugte sich in die tiefe Straße, die voll von dichtem rotem Nebel war. Die Straße war eng, und auf ihrem Grund fuhren die Automobile, kreischten, ratterten, machten einen Höllenlärm und sahen wie kriechende Ungeheuer unter dem roten Nebel aus. Aber eine Lichtung bot sich nun in den Schwaden, gerade vor seinem Blick, eine Furt im Nebel, und da stand am bis zum Boden reichenden geöffneten französischen Fenster des gegenüberliegenden großen Hotels Ilse Kürenberg, das Aufhäusermädchen, die Judentochter, die Entkommene, die Frau aus der Loge, das Weib, das er nackt in der Nacht über Rom in den Wolken gesehen hatte, Ilse Kürenberg stand da in einem weißen Frisiermantel, ein wenig vom Fenster entfernt, aber er sah sie nackend, nackend wie in der Nacht, nackend wie die Frauen vor dem Leichengraben, und Judejahn schoß das Magazin von Austerlitz' Pistole leer, er schoß die Grabensalve, diesmal schoß er eigenhändig, diesmal befahl er nicht nur, Befehle galten nicht mehr, man mußte selber schießen, und erst beim letzten Schuß fiel Ilse Kürenberg um, und des Führers Befehl war vollstreckt. Laura schrie, aber sie schrie nur einmal auf, und dann kam ein Schwall italienischer Wörter aus ihrem Mund, verplätscherte mit dem Waschwasser im roten Nebel. Judejahn fand die Tür, und Laura weinte ins Bett hinein, weinte in die noch schweißwarmen Kissen hinein, sie begriff nicht, was vorgefallen war, aber Entsetzliches war geschehen, der Mann hatte geschossen, er hatte zum Fenster hinausgeschossen — und er hatte ihr kein Geschenk gegeben. Sie war noch immer nackt, und sie deckte das Kopfkissen nun

über ihren Kopf, weil ihr Gesicht nicht mehr lächelte und weil
sie das Weinen ersticken wollte. So war sie auf dem zerwühl-
ten Bett anzusehen wie der kopflose schöne Leib der kopflosen Aphrodite Anadyomene.

Er hatte sie nicht nackt gesehen, und so erinnerte dieser nack-
te Leib Adolf nicht an Laura, er dachte auch nicht an ihren
Leib, er dachte an Lauras Lächeln, als er im Museum der
Diokletianischen Thermen vor der kopflosen Aphrodite Anadyomene verweilte, die kopflose Aphrodite hielt noch zwei
Zopfenden in ihren erhobenen Händen, als ob sie ihren Kopf
an den Zöpfen hätte halten wollen, und Adolf dachte, wie ihr
Gesicht gewesen sei und ob sie wie Laura gelächelt habe.
Sie verwirrten ihn. Ringsum die kalten Leiber aus Marmor
verwirrten ihn. Es war Siegfrieds Welt, die sich hier behauptete. Eine Welt schöner Körper. Da war die Venus von Cirene. Sie war makellos. Jeder mußte sehen, daß sie makellos
war. Ein fester wohlerhaltener Leib, aber kalt kalt kalt. Und
dann die Faune und Hermaphroditen und all ihre Leibes-
betonung. Sie verfaulten nicht. Sie wurden nicht zu Erde.
Sie waren nicht von der Hölle bedroht. Selbst das Haupt der
schlafenden Eumenide sprach nicht von Schrecken. Es erzählte von Schlaf. Es erzählte von Schönheit und Schlaf; auch
die Unterwelt war freundlich gewesen, die Hölle war anders.
Sie hatten sie nicht gekannt. Und war es recht, mit Schrek-
ken zu drohen, um die Seele zu retten, und war die Seele
verloren, wenn man die Schönheit erkannte? Adolf setzte
sich in den Garten unter die steinernen Zeugen der alten
Welt. Er war ausgeschlossen aus ihrer Gesellschaft, sein Gelübde schloß ihn aus, sein Glaube schloß ihn aus, für immer.
Er weinte. Die alten Statuen sahen ihm mit tränenlosen
Augen zu.

Er taumelte über den Platz. Bei jedem Schritt hatte er das
Gefühl, ins Bodenlose zu sinken, wegzugleiten, wegzuglei-
ten für immer, er mußte in die Luft greifen, um sich an der
Luft zu halten. Er wußte, was geschehen war, und er wußte
nicht, was geschehen war. Er hatte geschossen. Er hatte zur
Endlösung beigetragen. Er hatte einen Führerbefehl erfüllt.
Das war gut. Und nun mußte er sich verstecken. Es war noch

556

nicht der Endsieg. Er mußte sich wieder verstecken, er mußte wieder in die Wüste fahren, nur der rote Nebel war hinderlich. Es war schwer, in diesem roten Nebel ein Versteck zu finden. Da war Gemäuer. Da waren Ruinen. In Berlin hatte er sich in Ruinen verkrochen. In Rom mußte man Eintritt zahlen, wenn man sich in Ruinen verkriechen wollte. Judejahn zahlte den Eintritt für das Thermenmuseum. Er ging durch Gänge, ging eine Treppe hoch. Lauter Nackte standen im roten Nebel. Es war wohl ein Puff. Oder es war eine Gaskammer. Das erklärte auch den roten Nebel. Er war in einer großen Gaskammer mit nackten Menschen, die liquidiert werden sollten, aber dann mußte er hier nun 'rausgehen. Er sollte ja nicht liquidiert werden. Er war ja nicht nackend. Er war der Kommandeur. Die Höllenhunde hatten das Gas zu früh angedreht. Es war eine bodenlose Schweinerei. Er mußte durchgreifen. Die Disziplin mußte gewahrt werden. Mit allen Mitteln mußte die Disziplin gewahrt werden. Galgen waren zu errichten. Judejahn kam in ein Zimmer, das war der Befehlsstand. Die Nebel lichteten sich. Es waren alte Spiegel da. Die Spiegel waren blind. Er sah in blinde Spiegel. War er das? Er erkannte sich nicht. Da war ein blaurotes Gesicht. Das Gesicht war angeschwollen. Es sah wie das Gesicht eines Boxers aus, der viele Schläge erhalten hat. Die blaue Brille hatte er verloren. Er brauchte die blaue Brille nicht mehr. Aber da kam er vor einen klareren Spiegel, da erkannte er sich, das war er, er stand vor dem Mosaikbild des Athleten, es war sein Gesicht, es war sein Nacken, es waren seine Schultern, es war ein Spiegelbild aus seiner besten Zeit, das ihn ansah, er hatte in der Arena gestanden, er hatte mit dem kurzen Schwert gekämpft, er hatte viele umgelegt. Und da war auch Benito. Er sah das Mosaik der Katze mit dem Vogel. Auch Benito hatte viele gefressen. Die Welt war gar nicht so schlecht. Man hatte viele umgelegt, viele gefressen. Man konnte zufrieden sein. Judejahn taumelte in den Garten. Nackte Weiber, nackte Judenweiber versteckten sich hinter den Hecken. Es würde ihnen nichts nützen. Judejahn liquidierte auch durch Hecken. Hier mußte er durch — und dann schlug er hin.

Adolf hatte ihn kommen sehen, er hatte ihn mit Angst und
Entsetzen kommen sehen, und dann sah er, wie er hinschlug,
wie gefällt schlug er hin, und Adolf rannte nun zu ihm, und
der schwere Körper seines Vaters lag leblos da. War er tot?
Sein Gesicht war blaurot. Ein Museumswärter kam, und er
rief noch einen zweiten Wärter herbei, und sie trugen Judejahn zu dritt in den Schuppen, in dem die Gipser die antiken
Plastiken flicken, und sie legten ihn auf den Boden vor das
Relief eines Sarkophags. Das Relief stellte einen Triumph-
zug dar, und hochmütige Römer hatten gedemütigte germanische Krieger an ihre Pferde gefesselt. Die römischen Gipser standen in ihren weißen Mänteln um Judejahn herum.
Ein Gipser sagte: »Er ist tot.« Und ein anderer Gipser sagte:
»Er ist nicht tot. Auch mein Schwiegervater war nicht gleich
tot.« Der Wärter ging, um mit der Sanitätswache des Bahnhofs zu telephonieren. Der Vater war noch nicht tot, und da
fiel Adolf das Wichtigste ein — es gab die Hölle es gab die
Hölle es gab die Hölle. Und nun war keine Sekunde zu verlieren, er rannte durch den Garten, rannte durch das Tor,
er rannte in die Kirche Santa Maria degli Angeli. Der Deutsch
sprechende Priester war noch da. Er las im Brevier. Kein
Beichtkind kniete im Stuhl. Adolf stammelte, daß er das
Sterbesakrament für seinen Vater erbitte, und der Priester
begriff und eilte; er holte das heilige Öl und nahm Adolf
zum Ministranten, und sie eilten so schnell es schicklich war,
und die Billettkontrolleure ließen sie passieren, und die Wärter nahmen ihre Mützen ab, und die Gipser traten ehrfürchtig zur Seite. Judejahn lag leblos, aber er war nicht tot.
Schweiß und Ausscheidungen liefen seiner Auflösung voran.
Er purgierte, er reinigte sich. Das Purgatorium ist das Fege-
feuer. Hatte er es schon erreicht? Judejahn lag in tiefem
Koma. Niemand weiß, was in ihm vorging; ob er nach Walhall ritt, ob Teufel ihn holten, oder ob seine Seele aufjauchz-
te, weil die Rettung nun nah war. Der Priester kniete nieder. Er schritt zur Letzten Ölung und zur bedingungsweisen
Lossprechung, bestimmt für den Fall der Bewußtlosigkeit.
Der Priester berührte mit dem vom Bischof geweihten Öl
Judejahns Augen, seine Ohren, seine Nase, den Mund und

die Handflächen. Der Priester betete. Er betete: »Durch diese heilige Salbung und seine gütige Barmherzigkeit verzeihe
dir der Herr, was du durch Sehen, Hören, Riechen, Schmekken, Berühren gesündigt hast.« Judejahn rührte sich nicht.
Berührte es ihn nicht, was der Priester sprach? Judejahn
rührte sich nie mehr. Er lag da und rührte sich nie mehr, und
der römische Priester empfahl ihn der Gnade Gottes, und
sein Sohn betete für den Vater in römischer Priestertracht –
zwei Sendboten des Feindes.
Die Sanitäter kamen, und der Arzt schloß ihm die Augen.
Die Sanitäter waren feldgrau gekleidet, und sie trugen Judejahn wie von einem Schlachtfeld.

Die Zeitungen meldeten noch am Abend Judejahns Tod, der
durch die Umstände eine Weltnachricht geworden war, die
aber niemand erschütterte.

die Handflächen. Der Priester betete. Er betete: »Durch diese heilige Salbung und seine gütige Barmherzigkeit verzeihe dir der Herr, was du durch Sehen, Hören, Riechen, Schmekken, Berühren gesündigt hast.« Judejahn rührte sich nicht. Berührte es ihn nicht, was der Priester sprach? Judejahn rührte sich nie mehr. Er lag da und rührte sich nie mehr, und der römische Priester empfahl ihn der Gnade Gottes, und sein Sohn betete für den Vater in römischer Priestertracht — zwei Sendboten des Feindes.

Die Sanitäter kamen, und der Arzt schloß ihm die Augen. Die Sanitäter waren feldgrau gekleidet, und sie trugen Judejahn wie von einem Schlachtfeld.

Die Zeitungen meldeten noch am Abend Judejahns Tod, der durch die Umstände eine Weltnachricht geworden war, die aber niemand erschütterte.